Pronunciation	Meaning
Elohim	God, Mighty Creator
El Roi	The God Who Sees Me
El Shadday	God Almighty
El Olam	The Everlasting God, The Eternal God
Yahweh Yireh	The Lord will Provide
Yahweh	Lord
Adonai	Lord, Master
Yahweh Rophe	The Lord Who Heals
Yahweh Nissi	The Lord My Banner
Esh Oklah, El Kanna	Consuming Fire, Jealous God
Qedosh Ysirael	Holy One of Israel
Yahweh Shalom	The Lord is Peace
Yahweh Tsebaoth	The Lord of Hosts
Yahweh Tsuri	The Lord is My Rock

HOLMAN
BIBLE
HANDBOOK

HOLMAN BIBLE HANDBOOK

GENERAL EDITOR
DAVID S. DOCKERY

EDITORIAL TEAM
TRENT C. BUTLER
CHRISTOPHER L. CHURCH
LINDA L. SCOTT
MARSHA A. ELLIS SMITH
JAMES EMERY WHITE

HOLMAN BIBLE PUBLISHERS NASHVILLE, TENNESSEE

4691-17

ISBN: 1-55819-332-4

Printed in the United States of America
1 2 3 4 5 6 97 96 95 94 93 92

EDITORS' FOREWORD

Certainly it is important to read and study God's written Word and to share in the benefits and blessings of Bible study. The purposes of studying the Bible are many, but primarily such study involves learning more about God and His self-revelation to us so that the Holy Spirit can change our lives. The *Holman Bible Handbook* exists to enable people—laypersons, students, pastors, young and old alike—to study the holy Scriptures with greater understanding. Not every portion of Scripture is easy to understand. We recognize that we are separated from the original setting of the writing by many years, as well as by language and culture. Our handbook seeks to help readers bridge that gap by sharing information and insights into the biblical writings and their time.

Many tools such as commentaries, dictionaries, encyclopedias, and atlases already exist to provide insight into the Bible and its world. This new volume does not attempt to duplicate all of the information from these tools. It is not a commentary, an encyclopedia, an atlas, or a dictionary. Yet it contains aspects of each. Like a commentary, the handbook expounds the meaning of every major section of the Bible. Like an encyclopedia, the handbook surveys matters relating to the nature of Scripture, theology, church history, and world missions. Like an atlas, the handbook provides maps and information concerning the cultural and geographical backgrounds of the Bible. Like a dictionary, the handbook defines, identifies, and clarifies numerous topics in over one hundred feature articles.

The material in the handbook has been researched and written by a vast array of gifted scholars. It has, however, been communicated in a warm, easy-to-read style with laypeople, Sunday School teachers, and beginning Bible students primarily in mind. Each contributor has attempted to provide an overview of the material under consideration in the various sections. Behind each article is an awareness of and interaction with contemporary biblical scholarship. Yet the volume reflects a clear evangelical approach to biblical and theological studies. The handbook emphasizes the type of information and insight that is directly relevant for the reader who seeks to deepen his or her understanding of what the Bible is saying.

The layout of the book includes five major sections. Part one discusses matters related to the general characteristics and inspiration of the Bible. Part two concentrates on the Bible and its setting. Articles in this section focus on the historical backgrounds, geography, and archaeology of the Bible. Part three deals with concerns of the Bible in the church such as how the Bible has been translated, read, interpreted, and applied. Part four is the heart of the handbook. The entire Bible is expounded section by section. Introductory matters, as well as themes and theological teachings, are also discussed. Important topics receive special attention in numerous feature articles. The concluding section, part five, relates the Bible to the contemporary Christian community, its beliefs, its history, and its mission. A special feature of the book making it useful for group study is the inclusion of teaching charts, questions for reflection and suggestions for additional reading at the end of several of the articles.

The *Holman Bible Handbook* is intended to be a companion to the *Holman Bible Dictionary*. This project, like its predecessor, is made possible by the contributions of numerous gifted and godly people. We are greatly indebted to each of them. A list of contributors is included along with a list of the production staff. We trust that the efforts of all of these people will bring glory to our Lord, as the people of God are instructed in what the Word of God has to say. Also, we pray that the understanding and response of the readers will be enhanced by the Holy Spirit's illuminating ministry in their lives, as in the days of Nehemiah when the people of God celebrated with great joy because they understood the words that had been made know to them (Neh 8:12).

Soli Deo Gloria
The Editors

CONTENTS

Part I The Bible

Part II The Bible in Its World

Part III The Bible in the Church

Part IV The Bible and Its Message

Part V The Bible and Christian Faith

Feature Articles

Maps

CONTRIBUTORS

Elizabeth R. Achtemeier, Ph.D.
Adjunct Professor of Old Testament
Union Theological Seminary
Richmond, VA
Types of Old Testament Literature

Daniel L. Akin, Ph.D.
Assistant Professor of Church History
Southeastern Baptist Theological Seminary
Wake Forest, NC
Order of the Gospels; Accounts of the Resurrection

Robert L. Alden, Ph.D.
Professor of Old Testament
Denver Seminary
Denver, CO
Evil and Suffering

David Allen, Ph.D.
Pastor, Audelia Road Baptist Church
Dallas, TX
New Testament Use of the Old Testament; Old and New Covenant

Raymond Bailey, Ph.D.
Professor of Preaching
Southern Baptist Theological Seminary
Louisville, KY
Teaching and Preaching the Bible

Lynn Bauman, Ph.D.
Provost
Anglican School of Theology
Dallas, TX
How to Understand the Bible; Reading Scripture

Robert D. Bergen, Ph.D.
Professor of Christian Studies
Hannibal-LaGrange College
Hannibal, MO
Cities of the Conquest; Neighbors of Israel; The Cycles of the Judges

David Alan Black, D.Theol.
Scholar-in-Residence, Lockman Foundation
La Habra, CA
The Unity and Variety of the Bible

James Blevins, Ph.D.
Professor of New Testament
Southern Baptist Theological Seminary
Louisville, KY
Hymns and Creeds in the New Testament

Craig L. Blomberg, Ph.D.
Associate Professor of New Testament
Denver Seminary
Denver, CO
The Gospel of Matthew; The New Testament and Criticism; Forms of New Testament Literature

Darrell L. Bock, Ph.D.
Associate Professor of New Testament
Dallas Theological Seminary
Dallas, TX
The Gospel of Luke

Gerald L. Borchert, Ph.D.
Professor of New Testament
Southern Baptist Theological Seminary
Louisville, KY
Assurance, Warning, and Perseverance

Geoffrey W. Bromiley, Ph.D.
Senior Professor of Historical Theology
Fuller Theological Seminary
Pasadena, CA
History of English Bible Translations

James A. Brooks, D.Phil.
Professor of New Testament
Bethel Theological Seminary
St. Paul, MN
Differences in Bible Manuscripts

Trent C. Butler, Ph.D.
Manager, Broadman/Holman
Nashville, TN
Marriage and Family in Israel; Death, Resurrection, and Afterlife in the Old Testament; Messianic Prophecies; False Prophets; Babylon; Syria; Persia; Symbolic Actions by the Prophets; Old Testament Apocalyptic

Robert B. Chisholm, Th.D.
Associate Professor of Old Testament
Dallas Theological Seminary
Dallas, TX
The Major Prophets

Christopher L. Church, Ph.D.
Editor, Broadman/Holman
Nashville, TN
The Gospel of Mark

E. Ray Clendenen, Ph.D.
Editor, Broadman/Holman
Nashville, TN
Life in Bible Times; Biblical Chronology; The Sacrificial System; The Exile; Assyria

R. Alan Culpepper, Ph.D.
Professor of Religion, Baylor University
Waco, TX
Between the Testaments

George B. Davis, Jr., M.A.
Asst. Pastor, Springdale Church
Louisville, KY
New Testament Signs and Miracles; Life of Christ

Raymond Dillard, Ph.D.
Professor of Old Testament
Westminster Theological Seminary
Philadelphia, PA
History Writing in Bible Times; The Temple; David as King and Messiah; The Chronology of the Kings of Israel

David S. Dockery, Ph.D.
Dean, School of Theology
Southern Baptist Theological Seminary
Louisville, KY
Christian Faith and the Christian Community; History of Biblical Interpretation; The Pauline Letters; The Lord's Supper

Lewis A. Drummond, Ph.D.
Billy Graham Professor of Evangelism
Beeson Divinity School
Birmingham, AL
Disciple; Belief in the New Testament

David G. Dunbar, Ph.D.
President, Biblical Theological Seminary
Hatfield, PA
The Canonicity of the Bible

Walter A. Elwell, Ph.D.
Dean of the Graduate School
Wheaton College
Wheaton, IL
The Kingdom of God in the Gospels; Titles of Christ in the Gospels

Millard J. Erickson, Ph.D.
Research Professor of Theology
Southwestern Baptist Theological Seminary
Fort Worth, TX
The Inspiration and Authority of the Bible

Donald L. Fowler, Th.D.
Professor of Old Testament
Grace Theological Seminary
Winona Lake, IN
Birds and Beasts; Calendars; Geography and Topography of the Ancient Near East; Money; Plants of the Bible; Times and Seasons; Weights and Measures

David E. Garland, Ph.D.
Professor of New Testament
Southern Baptist Theological Seminary
Louisville, Kentucky
Beatitudes

Duane A. Garrett, Ph.D.
Professor of Old Testament
Canadian Southern Baptist Seminary
Cochrane, Alberta, Canada
The Poetic and Wisdom Books

Timothy George, Th.D.
Dean
Beeson Divinity School
Birmingham, AL
Christian Faith in History

Ron Glass, Ph.D.
Associate Professor of Bible Exposition
Talbot School of Theology
La Mirada, CA
Election in the Old Testament

Stanley J. Grenz, D.Theol.
Professor of Theology
Carey Hall/Regent College
Vancouver, British Columbia, Canada
Church and State; The Value of Human Life

William L. Hendricks, Ph.D.
Professor of Christian Theology
Southern Baptist Theological Seminary
Louisville, KY
Spiritual Gifts

David J. Hesselgrave, Ph.D.
Professor of World Missions
Trinity Evangelical Divinity School
Deerfield, IL
Christian Faith, World Religions, and Christian Missions

Harold W. Hoehner, Ph.D.
Professor of New Testament
Dallas Theological Seminary
Dallas, TX
New Testament Apocrypha; Trial of Jesus

David Howard, Ph.D.
Associate Professor of Old Testament
Trinity Evangelical Divinity School
Deerfield, IL
Egypt; Moses

F. B. Huey, Jr., Ph.D.
Professor of Old Testament
Southwestern Baptist Theological Seminary
Fort Worth, TX
The Flood ; Old Testament Numbers; Patriarchs

Fisher Humphreys, Th.D.
Professor of Divinity
Beeson Divinity School
Birmingham, AL

The Name, Contents, and Characteristics of the Bible

Walter C. Kaiser, Jr., Ph.D.
Professor of Old Testament
Trinity Evangelical Divinity School
Deerfield, IL
Covenants, Dates of the Exodus; Pattern of Faith in Abraham; Routes of the Exodus

Dan G. Kent, Ph.D.
Professor of Old Testament
Southwestern Baptist Theological Seminary
Fort Worth, TX
Israel's Festivals and Feasts; Near Eastern Treaties; Tabernacle

John J. Kiwiet, Th.D.
Senior Professor of Theology
Southwestern Baptist Theological Seminary
Fort Worth, TX
The Uniqueness of the Bible

George L. Klein, Ph.D.
Professor of Old Testament
Criswell College
Dallas, TX
Ancient Civilizations; Christ in the Psalms; Creation and Flood Stories; Hebrew and Aramaic Languages; Near Eastern Religions; Vengeance and Vindication

Thomas D. Lea, Th.D.
Professor of New Testament
Southwestern Baptist Theological Seminary
Fort Worth, TX
The General Letters

Tremper Longman III, Ph.D.
Associate Professor of Old Testament
Westminster Theological Seminary
Philadelphia, PA
Critical Methods and the Old Testament

A. Boyd Luter, Jr., Th.D.
Associate Professor of Bible Exposition
Talbot School of Theology
La Mirada, CA
Apocalyptic Literature; Galatians

W. Harold Mare, Ph.D.
Professor of New Testament
Covenant Theological Seminary
St. Louis, MO
Biblical Archaeology

D. Michael Martin, Ph.D.
Associate Professor of New Testament
Golden Gate Baptist Theological Seminary
Mill Valley, CA
Christian Unity; The Return of Christ

Kenneth A. Mathews, Ph.D.
Associate Professor of Divinity
Beeson Divinity School
Birmingham, AL
The Historical Books

Richard R. Melick, Jr., Ph.D.
Professor of New Testament
Mid-America Baptist Theological Seminary
Memphis, TN
Opponents of Paul

Eugene H. Merrill, Ph.D.
Professor of Old Testament
Dallas Theological Seminary
Dallas, TX
The Pentateuch

E. O. Mims, D.Min.
Executive Vice-President
Baptist Sunday School Board
Nashville, TN
The Gospel

R. Albert Mohler, Jr., Ph.D.
Editor, *The Christian Index*
Atlanta, GA
Introduction to *The Christian Faith and the Christian Community*

Darold H. Morgan, Ph.D.
President Emeritus, Annuity Board of the SBC
Dallas, TX
The Parables of Jesus; The Prayers of Jesus

Carey C. Newman, Ph.D.
Assistant Professor of Religion
Palm Beach Atlantic College
Palm Beach, FL
Glory; Suffering

Robert Stan Norman, M.Div.
Pastor, First Baptist Church
Haslett, TX
Justification by Faith

Harry L. Poe, Ph.D.
Associate Professor of Evangelism
Bethel Theological Seminary
St. Paul, MN
Apostolic Preaching; The Holy Spirit and Acts

John B. Polhill, Ph.D.
Professor of New Testament
Southern Baptist Theological Seminary
Louisville, KY
The Birth of the Church; Greco-Roman Cities; The New Testament and History; Roman Provinces

Kurt A. Richardson, D.Theol.
Assistant Professor of Historical Theology
Southeastern Baptist Theological Seminary
Wake Forest, NC

Adoption; Election in the New Testament

Richard Rigsby, Ph.D.
Associate Professor of Old Testament
Talbot School of Theology
La Mirada, CA
Atonement

L. Joseph Rosas III, Ph.D.
Pastor, Union Avenue Baptist Church
Memphis, TN
Christianity and Its Contemporary Rivals; The Old Testament View of Faith

Charles J. Scalise, Ph.D.
Assistant Professor of Church History
Southern Baptist Theological Seminary
Louisville, KY
Jesus Christ and the Bible

J. Julius Scott, Ph.D.
Professor of New Testament
Wheaton College
Wheaton, IL
Slavery in the First Century; Backgrounds of the New Testament

Mark A. Seifrid, Ph.D.
Assistant Professor of New Testament
Southern Baptist Theological Seminary
Louisville, KY
Salvation in Paul's Thought

Steven Sheeley, Ph.D.
Associate Professor of Religion
Shorter College
Rome, GA
The Acts of the Apostles

Robert B. Sloan, D.Theol.
George Truett Professor of Religion
Baylor University
Waco, TX
Apostasy; The Revelation

David P. Smith, Ph.D. (cand.)
Instructor in New Testament
Southern Baptist Theological Seminary
Louisville, KY
Baptism

Marsha A. Ellis Smith, Ph.D.
Design Editor, Broadman/Holman
Nashville, TN
Compiler of archaeological visuals, charts, and maps

Harold S. Songer, Ph.D.
Vice-President for Academic Affairs
Southern Baptist Theological Seminary
Louisville, KY
The Herodian Family; Jerusalem in New Testament Times; Pilate; Religious Background of the New Testament

Klyne Snodgrass, Ph.D.
Dean of the Faculty
North Park Seminary
Chicago, IL
Gnosticism; The Law in the New Testament

Aida Besancon Spencer, Ph.D.
Associate Professor of New Testament
Gordon-Conwell Seminary
South Hamilton, MA
Virgin Birth

Bill Stancil, Ph.D.
Associate Professor of Theology
Midwestern Baptist Theological Seminary
Kansas City, MO
Models of Church Government; The Bible for Christian Worship

Willem VanGemeren, Ph.D.
Professor of Old Testament
Trinity Evangelical Divinity School
Deerfield, IL
Names of God; Near Eastern Prophecy; The Character of the Prophets

Charles R. Wade, Ph.D.
Pastor, First Baptist Church
Arlington, TX
Ascension of Christ

Bruce K. Waltke, Ph.D.
Professor of Old Testament
Regent College
Vancouver, British Columbia
Themes of Proverbs

John D. W. Watts, Th.D.
Senior Professor of Old Testament
Southern Baptist Theological Seminary
Louisville, KY
The Minor Prophets

C. Richard Wells, Ph.D.
Associate Professor of Divinity
Beeson Divinity School
Birmingham, AL
The Bible for Christian Living; The Bible for the Family and Society

James Emery White, Ph.D.
Consultant for Preaching and Worship
Baptist Sunday School Board
Nashville, TN
The Gospel of John

PRODUCTION STAFF

EDITORIAL TEAM

David S. Dockery, General Editor
Trent C. Butler   Christopher L. Church
Linda L. Scott   Marsha A. Ellis Smith
James Emery White

ADMINISTRATION

President	James T. Draper, Jr.
Director	Thomas L. Clark
Project Manager	Trent C. Butler

SUPPORT STAFF

Karen Bell   Cindy Kephart
Donna Easlick   Kim Overcash
Tracie Gregory   Diane Stem
Janis Whipple

GRAPHICS

Designer	Bill Green
Jacket Design	Jim Bateman
Graphics Director	W. Don Rogers
Graphics Manager	Jack Jewell

ARTISTS

Ed Maksimowicz   Stephen Smith
Tom Seale   Emma Jane Vidrine

TYPESETTING/FORMATS

Carla Dickerson   Sue Kestner

PRODUCTION

Procurement Director	James Shull
Procurement Manager	James Nash
Procurement Buyer	Bob Morrison
Procurement Assistant	Danny Halpin
Printers	Arcata Graphics Company Kingsport, Tennessee

PART I

THE BIBLE

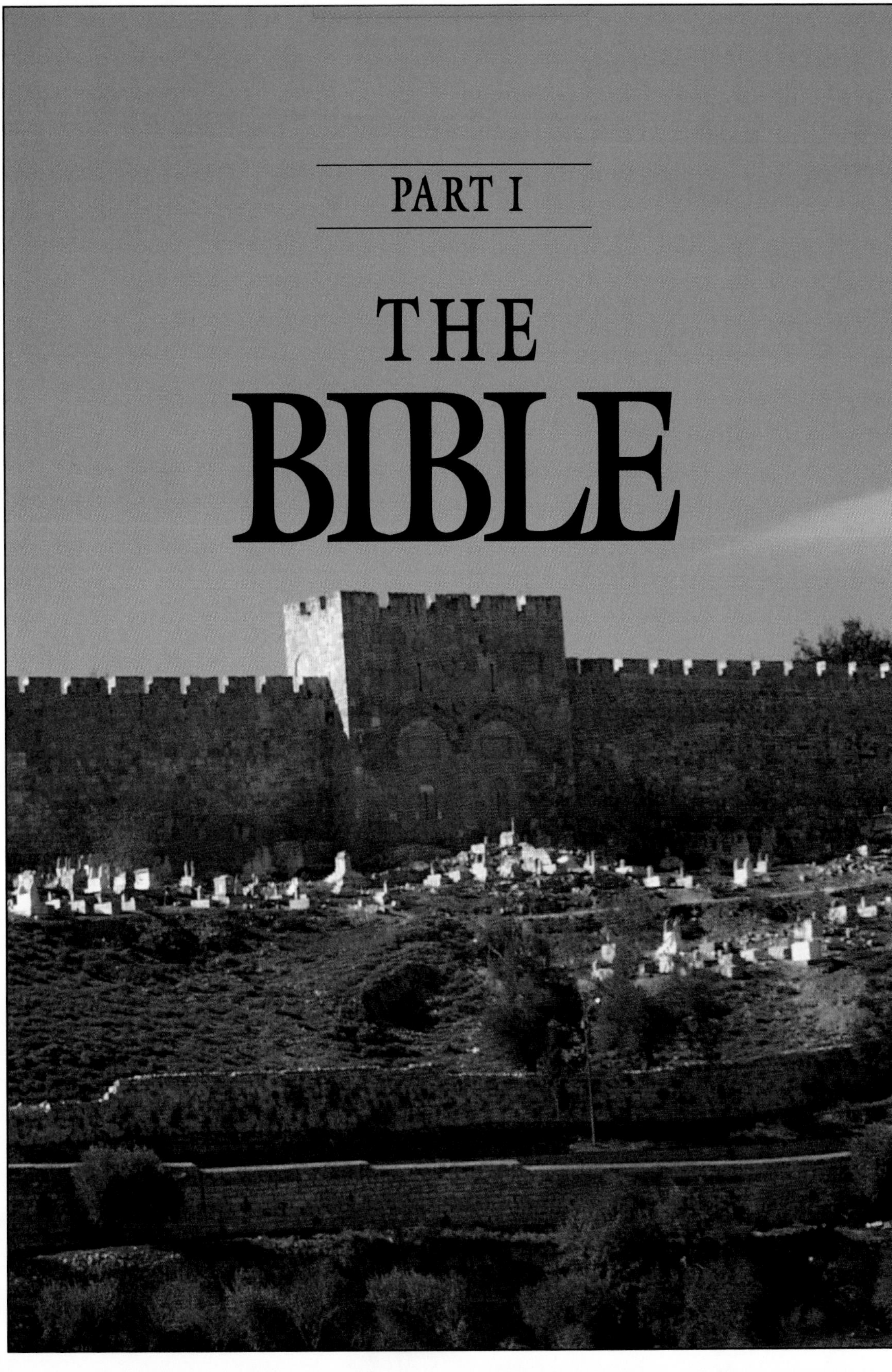

THE NAME, CONTENTS, AND CHARACTERISTICS OF THE BIBLE

English-speaking Christians use three major titles to refer to their holy book. We call it the Bible (or the Holy Bible), the Scriptures (or Holy Scripture), and the Word (or the Word of God). We refer to its two major parts as the Old Testament and the New Testament. We will look at the origin and meaning of each of these terms.

The Name of the Bible

The English word *Bible* is from a Greek word, *biblia*, which means *books* or *scrolls.* Paul used the word *biblia* when he wrote to Timothy and asked him to bring the books (2 Tim 4:13), by which he probably meant some scrolls containing the Hebrew Scriptures (the Old Testament). Although the Greek word is plural, we today think of the English word *Bible* as singular. But our Bible actually is a collection of sixty-six books, so it is appropriate to use as a title for it a word that originally meant *books.* We often refer to the "Holy Bible" because we regard the Bible as a sacred book.

The word *Scripture* is from a Latin word, *scriptura,* which means *writing.* In 2 Timothy 3:15, Paul referred to the "Holy Scriptures" Timothy had known since he was a child.

Word is a translation of the Hebrew word *dabar* and of the Greek word *logos*. These are usually used in the Bible to refer to something that is spoken rather than something that is written. Occasionally what is written is called the "word," as in Psalm 119:105. But in English we customarily use the term *word* to refer both to that which is spoken and that which is written. So Christians naturally refer to the written text of the Bible as "the Word of God." We use the singular rather than the plural probably because the phrase is usually found in the singular in the Bible itself.

Within the Christian community we use the phrases Holy Bible, Holy Scripture, and the Word of God interchangeably. When we are speaking to someone who is not a Christian, however, the phrase "the Word of God" may not be either clear or convincing. Therefore we may find it more effective simply to refer to "The Bible." For example, in listing books in print, it is much more effective to list Bibles in print under the heading of "The Bible" rather than under the heading "The Word of God."

You may wonder why one Book can have three different titles. We are able to use these three different phrases as titles for our holy Book because the Book itself does not indicate what title we should use. There is therefore the possibility that someone will decide to use some other title for the Bible. In fact, in recent years the Bible has been published with titles such as *The Book* and *Good News for Modern Man.*

What the Jewish people call the Hebrew Scriptures, Christians usually refer to as the Old Testament. And we distinguish it from the other, later part of the Bible, the New Testament. The origin of the phrases Old Testament and New Testament is interesting because it is deeply embedded in the history of God's people.

A major theological theme in the life of the nation of Israel was God's covenant with Israel. God made a covenant with Israel that is summarized in the words "I will be your God, and you will be my people" (Lev 26:12). God first made the covenant with Abraham and his descendants. Over the centuries He reaffirmed it to Moses, David, and others. When the holy city, Jerusalem, was conquered by its enemies, many people in Israel felt that God must have canceled His covenant with Israel. But the prophet Jeremiah reassured the people that in the future God would make a new covenant with the house of Israel, a covenant written on their hearts rather than on stone as the Ten Commandments had been (see Jer 31:31-34).

Jesus Christ spoke of His blood as the blood of the new covenant (see 1 Cor 11:25). So it was natural for the early Christians to refer to what God had done before Christ as being under the old covenant and to what He had done in Christ and since Christ as being under the new covenant. From this it was an easy move for Christians to refer to the parts of the Bible that were written before Christ came as the old covenant and to the parts written after Christ came as the new covenant.

The Hebrew word for covenant (*berith*) and the Greek word for covenant (*diatheke*) were both translated into Latin as *testamentum,* from which we have the English *testament.* The Hebrew Bible therefore is the Old Testament, and the texts written by the early Christians are the New Testament.

Christians traditionally think of the Old Testament as promise and of the New Testament as the fulfillment of promise.

The Contents of the Bible

The two major parts of the Bible are the Old Testament and the New Testament. The Old Testament consists of thirty-nine books that were written before Jesus Christ was born. The New Testament consists of twenty-seven books that were written by the early followers of Jesus Christ.

Most of the Old Testament was written in Hebrew. A few chapters were written in a related language, Aramaic. The Old Testament is the Holy Scriptures of the Jewish people, who customarily divide it into three large sections which they call the Law, the Prophets, and the Writings. Christians frequently speak of the Bible as containing books of the law, of history, of wisdom, and of prophecy.

The New Testament was written in Greek. Jesus and His first followers apparently spoke Aramaic, and a few Aramaic words are scattered throughout the New Testament, such as *Abba* (Mark 14:36), *talitha koum* (Mark 5:41), *Maranatha* (1 Cor 16:22, KJV), and *Golgotha* (Matt 27:33). But Greek was a more widely used language than Aramaic, and it was the language employed by the writers of the books of the New Testament. These books are often placed in four groups: the Gospels, the Acts, the Epistles, and the Revelation.

Although we have spoken of sixty-six books of the Bible, many of these texts were not written to be "books" in the modern sense, that is, as fairly long texts written for publication and for distribution to the public. Among other things, several of them are too short to be called books in this sense; 2 John, for example, has only thirteen verses. Many were written as letters (the Epistles) rather than as books for publication. But they have been collected (see the articles on the inspiration, authority, and canonicity of the Bible) and now are published, so referring to them as the "books" of the Bible is appropriate.

In addition to the divisions already mentioned, the Bible contains several kinds of literature, sometimes called "literary genres." Included are histories, parables, songs, proverbs, genealogies, laws, gospels, letters, apocalypses, ethical teachings, narratives, hymns, doctrines, thank-you notes, prophecies, confessions of faith, and sermons, among others.

The Characteristics of the Bible

The Bible is characterized by variety and unity. We have referred to its three diverse original languages and to the diverse books and kinds of literature. In addition, it was written over more than a thousand years by several dozen people living in different societies and in different geographical locations. The purposes of these authors also

NAMES OF THE BIBLE		
βιβλία	γραφή	λόγος τοῦ θεοῦ
biblia	*graphe*	*logos tou theou*
Bible	Scripture	Word of God

were diverse. For example, those who composed and collected the psalms intended to provide a book of hymns for public worship of the Lord, and John intended to help his readers put their faith in Christ (see John 20:31).

We can easily experience the variety of the Bible simply by reading a few verses from each of several different books. For example, we might read verses from Genesis 1; Exodus 2; Leviticus 20; 1 Kings 4; Job 3; Psalm 23; Proverbs 15; Ecclesiastes 1; Isaiah 40; Ezekiel 37; Matthew 5; John 1; Acts 2; Romans 8; 1 Corinthians 13; Philippians 2; 1 Timothy 3; Hebrews 9; James 1; 1 John 1; and Revelation 5. It is not difficult to see that the Bible contains a great deal of variety.

But the Bible is also a unified Book, although not all readers have observed this. What unifies it is that it presents to the reader a message about God. It tells us that the God who is the Creator of the universe is working to create a people to be His own. The Bible contains diverse presentations about God, but through all the diversity the same wonderful God is seen to be carrying out the same great purpose.

The Bible also may be characterized as both historical and contemporary. It is a Book that is embedded in ancient cultures, languages, and traditions. Yet it is also a Book with power to touch contemporary readers. Imagine, for example, that a Christian has died. His family and friends have gathered for a funeral service to worship God, to remember their loved one, and to seek comfort. The minister stands and reads aloud to them, and they listen to his words as God's people have listened for thousands of years. He reads: "The Lord is my shepherd. . . . Yea, though I walk through the valley of the shadow of death, I will fear no evil. . . . I will dwell in the house of the Lord forever" (Ps 23:1,4,6, KJV). Can you imagine that anyone would complain: "Those words are too old. They come from an ancient book. We don't need them today"? On the contrary, these words written three thousand years ago in another language are as beautiful and as powerful and as true and as indispensable today as any words known to human beings. They are the most relevant words a contemporary person can hear when a loved one has died.

The Bible is both a simple Book and a profound Book. Children may begin early to learn the Bible and to love it, and millions of children do. But some of the world's finest scholars have spent their lifetimes studying the Bible and can still confess they have only scratched the surface of this great Book. The Bible is the most studied Book in the world, as well as the most published, and it is almost certainly the most loved Book in the world.

The Bible is both a human Book and a divine Book. Christians do not attempt to conceal the humanity of the Bible. We know that it was written by men, not dropped out of heaven on golden plates. But we also believe that the men who wrote the Bible did so under the inspiration of God (2 Tim 3:16), guided by the Spirit of God (2 Pet 1:21). The Word of God is given to us in, with, and under the words of these human authors.

The Bible is the unique, indispensable resource Book for the Christian and the church. It is light for our paths (see Ps 119:105). To read it aloud is like tasting honey in one's mouth (Ps 119:103). It is a weapon in the fight for a strong faith (Eph 6:17). The life of the Christian is formed by the Bible, which is read, taught, preached, sung, believed, and loved in the church. The Bible provides Christians with a world view. It provides them with a set of moral values. It is an occasion for their experiences with God. It binds them together as a family of God. It tells them the meaning of their lives. Every Christian can say with the psalmist: "Oh, how I love your law! I meditate on it all the day" (Ps 119:97).

THE INSPIRATION AND AUTHORITY OF THE BIBLE

To understand the nature of biblical authority, we must first understand why it is needed. This takes us back into the nature of humans and their relationship to God.

The Need for Biblical Authority

In creating men and women, God had something different in mind than He did for the other creatures. The latter are spoken of as having been created "according to their kinds" (Gen 1:25). Humans, however, are described as being made in the image and likeness of God (1:26-27). Although we are not told just what this image consisted of, we do note that God intended that humans would serve Him by having dominion over the rest of the creation (1:26,28). In addition, it apparently was customary for God to come and have fellowship with the man and the woman (3:8-9).

All creatures are in some sense related to God, for all in one way or another obey Him. They do this, however, in differing ways, corresponding to their respective natures. Thus inanimate objects, such as planets, obey mechanically by following certain natural laws. Animals do so instinctively, such as fish that return to spawn each year in the place where they were spawned. These are unconscious acts of obedience, carrying out God's will by simply following the nature given them in creation.

Only humans are able to obey God voluntarily, by consciously fulfilling His commands as well as loving and worshiping Him. This, however, requires knowledge of God, His nature, and His will if we are to fulfill what the Westminster Confession of Faith identified as the "end" of man: "to glorify God and enjoy Him forever."

Problems exist here, however. For one, humans are limited, and God is unlimited. It is therefore impossible for us to discover God. We are unable to ascend to His level to investigate Him. Consequently, for humans to know, love, worship, and obey God, it would be necessary for God to take the initiative to make Himself known. God's disclosure, or unveiling, of Himself is known as revelation. It is the first step in the process of human knowledge of God. It is referred to technically in theology as "revelation."

A second problem exists for human knowledge of God, namely, the problem of sin. When sin entered the human race, it introduced a "blinding" effect (2 Cor 4:4). This meant that humans became unable to recognize and understand correctly that which could be known of God (Rom 1:19). Like a cloud obscuring the sky, sin makes the truth of God obscure to sinful humans. This compound problem cries out for God's initiative if He is to be known.

General Revelation

There are two major types of revelation, general and special revelation. General revelation is general both in its availability to all persons at all times and its less specific content. It consists of God's self-manifestation through nature, history, and in the human personality.

The nature psalms are noted for their discourse upon these self-disclosures of God in His creation. The psalmist said, "The heavens declare the glory of God; the skies proclaim the work of his hands" (Ps 19:1). Paul similarly said that the visible creation has since the beginning made manifest certain qualities of God (Rom 1:19-20). In fact, he said that these things were "made . . . plain." In contemplating the majesty of the heavenly bodies or the intricacy of the systems of a mammal, one is exposed to the truth of God's power, wisdom, and orderliness. Since the creation is there for everyone to see, it is general, or to all persons.

Paul also pointed to another realm of general revelation: the human personality, with its moral sensitivity. He said that when Gentiles, who of course did not have the law God had revealed to the people of Israel, do what the law requires, "they show that the requirements of the law are written on their hearts" (Rom 2:15). Here is an element of God's truth that apparently all humans possess.

Signs of God's truth also are in history. Although subject to varying interpretations by different people, God's handiwork can be discerned in the patterns of history. One of the most remarkable of these is the survival of the

Jewish people. Even persons who do not know God's promise to Abraham must find the history of his descendants remarkable. Scarcely any group of people from that ancient a time have been subjected to the determined opposition and persecution that has been directed against the Jews. Yet they have survived and prospered, whereas most other groups from the same period of early history have vanished.

One question sometimes raised regarding the general revelation is whether it is possible for a person to be related redemptively to God on the basis of the general revelation alone. Another way of putting it is whether persons can be saved without having the gospel preached to them in the full and formal sense, that is, without knowing the name of Jesus.

Paul apparently allowed for some possibility of this type in the Book of Romans. There he argued that those who had the testimony of the creation are without excuse. In other words, they should have been able to know God (Rom 1:20). He also spoke of their consciences bearing witness and accusing or excusing them. Thus it seems at least theoretically possible that people could know from the general revelation that there is a God, that He is powerful and holy and expects this same holiness from humans.

On the basis of this revelation, people could conclude that they are sinners and cast themselves upon the mercy of God. Such people would seem to possess at least the form of the gospel and could be forgiven and justified, not on the basis of their own righteousness but rather on Christ's redemptive work. The situation of such people would not be greatly different from that of the Old Testament believers, who actually placed their faith in Jesus Christ and were redeemed by His death and resurrection even though they did not know His identity or the details of His life and work.

In practice, however, few persons actually obtain salvation in this fashion. In the same Book of Romans, Paul declared that everyone who calls upon the name of the Lord will be saved (10:13). He then went on to argue for the necessity of these people knowing of the one on whom they are to believe, of hearing, and thus of someone preaching of this Christ (10:14-17). The insufficiency of the general revelation in most cases is apparent from this concern of Paul's.

Special Revelation

At best, therefore, these sources ordinarily give us only vague or general information about God, such as His existence, power, and faithfulness. Much more is needed for the complete knowledge of Him necessary for fellowship. Sin's entrance disturbed the natural knowledge of God through the general revelation and also broke the relationship with Him. Therefore a more complete knowledge is necessary. We refer to this as special revelation.

The Forms of Special Revelation

God acted in several ways to make Himself known more completely to human beings. One mode of this self-manifestation is what we might refer to as divine speech. God "spoke" in various ways to prophets and apostles. Sometimes this was in the form of a vision, such as that of Isaiah in Isaiah 6. On occasion God spoke through a dream, as in the case of Daniel. Sometimes He spoke through audible speech. At other times He communicated by placing thoughts in the mind of the person so that the person's ideas were actually God's thoughts. All of these methods were God's communication of information to human beings.

A second mode of special revelation is through God's acts. While His speech is an act of God in the broadest sense, we are thinking here of acts in the narrower or proper sense of historical events. These were God's actions within history, which, although observable to anyone present, occurred at a specific time and place and did not recur. Thus they were special or restricted to a particular group at a particular time and place. Many examples can be given. The exodus, with the Passover and the crossing of the Red Sea, the fall of the walls of Jericho, and David's victory over Goliath were conspicuous instances of these divine actions. Here were God's demonstrations of His nature.

The third and most complete mode of God's special revelation is the incarnation of Jesus Christ. The other forms were either God telling us about Himself or acting influentially within history. The incarnation was God coming fully and personally into the human sphere and making Himself accessible to human perception. Jesus could say to those about Him, "Anyone who has seen me has seen the Father" (John 14:9). John could write of that "which we have heard, which we have seen with our eyes, which we have looked at and our hands have touched" (1 John 1:1). These statements were true because Jesus was not simply a messenger sent with a message about God. He was God Himself in human form. Without ceasing to be God, He added humanity to His deity. His love was divine love; His holiness was divine holiness. Here we have the other two modes of divine self-manifestation combined, for Jesus was both God's speech and God's action.

The incarnation helps us understand what God is like.

With the other modes of divine revelation, we may wonder whether we really have understood God. We know that God surpasses us, especially in moral qualities. Is God's love, however, so far above ours as to be essentially different from human love? Is His knowledge so superior to ours that we cannot really fathom Him? The answer to the question of the nature of divine love and holiness is to point to Jesus. God's love is like the love Jesus displayed, for Jesus was God loving.

The Nature of Special Revelation

One issue that has been raised especially in the twentieth century pertains to the nature of revelation, or what God reveals and how He reveals. Some theologians have maintained that God does not reveal information about Himself but, rather, reveals *Himself.* Revelation, according to this conception, is an encounter with a Person rather than the communication of truths from God. Thus the statements found in the Bible do not constitute divinely revealed truths but are rather the fallible statements of humans trying to express what happened to them as God encountered them. The words spoken by Jesus were not objectively God's Word. For those, however, to whom God presented Himself through those words, they could be said to be the Word of God during that encounter. Similarly, when we meet God in a person-to-person encounter as the Word is being read or preached, we can say that this is revelation. When that immediate presence ceases, however, what we have are merely the words of Isaiah, Luke, or Paul.

Such a view presents several problems. For one, Jesus, Paul, and others in the New Testament quoted the Scriptures of their day (what Christians today call the Old Testament) as if these very words were God's message. Further, Jesus treated His words as having validity and authority apart from whether His hearers understood and agreed ("He who has ears, let him hear," Matt 11:15). He treated Himself and His actions as being objectively the presence of God ("Anyone who has seen me has seen the Father," John 14:9).

A further problem occurs when we ask how God reveals Himself. Orthodox Christianity's usual answer about what God reveals is that He reveals Himself, but He does it at least in part by revealing information about Himself. This is true of human relationships as well. If it were not, we could not be sure whom we had encountered, whether God or another human being. If in a dark room we bump into ("encounter") someone, how do we know whom we have encountered or what that person is like? We know by observing the person or by having the person tell us something about himself or herself. Either case is self-revelation by the person. But our knowledge of the person comes through sense perception. Certainly no one claims to have sensory perception of God. A nonpropositional encounter with a person who cannot be experienced through sense perception is a meaningless concept. Unless God reveals something about Himself, how do we know that we have encountered God rather than Brahma, our father-image, our superego, or something else of the type?

Another problem pertains to theology. How do we derive from a nonpropositional or noninformational encounter with God the propositions of theology purporting to speak of God? All theologians, including theologians who stress revelation as nonpropostional, claim to make true statements. Two such leading theologians, Karl Barth and Emil Brunner, had vigorous theological disputes over such issues as the empty tomb, the virgin birth, and the image of God. But how do we decide which of these sets of propositions more correctly describes God? How, for example, do we distinguish an encounter with a triune God from an encounter with a god who is not triune? Those who reject propositional revelation never adequately answer this question, perhaps because it is unanswerable on its terms. The best response maintains that the issue is not personal versus propositional revelation but both/and.

Inspiration

The concept of revelation, however, is only part of the answer to the problem of the knowledge of God. For if all persons are to have an opportunity to know God, there must be a way for this special or localized or particular revelation to become available to all persons. If this were not the case, then with the passing of the person or group to which the revelation originally came, the revelation would also be lost and become ineffective. This could be counteracted either by repetition of the process of revelation to each person or by somehow preserving the revelation once given. God has employed this latter method, which we refer to as inspiration.

By inspiration we mean the Holy Spirit's activity of directing and guiding the writers of Scripture so that what they wrote was actually the Word of God or was just what God wanted recorded. In other words, it preserved or recorded what God had revealed so that the resulting document carried the same authority and effect as if God Himself were speaking directly.

The need for this written record is apparent. While in theory the revelation might have been preserved by oral retelling, such a process has certain defects. Anyone who has played the game where each person whispers a story to the next person in the chain, attempting to repeat it as accurately as possible, knows the changes that can result in such serial retelling. Rumors are even more extreme forms of this phenomenon. An accurate and reliable source of truth requires preservation in written form.

Biblical Teachings about Inspiration

What indication do we have that such an influence was actually present upon the biblical writers? Here we have two kinds of considerations. First is the testimony of the writers themselves and others regarding such an occurrence. Second is the way in which New Testament persons, including authors of New Testament books and Jesus Himself, conceive of the Old Testament as God's genuine message.

We note first the claims of the Old Testament writers that the Lord was expressing Himself through their message. Jeremiah prefaced his remarks by saying, "These are the words the Lord spoke concerning Israel and Judah" (Jer 30:4). Isaiah wrote, "The Lord spoke to me" (Isa 8:11). This same theme is repeated throughout the writings of both the Major and Minor Prophets.

The two most prominent New Testament passages generally cited as evidence of the New Testament writers' view of the Scripture of their day are 2 Timothy 3:16 and 2 Peter 1:20-21. In the former passage Paul said, "All Scripture is God-breathed and is useful for teaching, rebuking, correcting and training in righteousness." In the latter Peter wrote: "Above all, you must understand that no prophecy of Scripture came about by the prophet's own interpretation. For prophecy never had its origin in the will of man, but men spoke from God as they were carried along by the Holy Spirit." Both of these affirm that God, through His Holy Spirit, was behind the production of the Bible.

Other passages of the New Testament also express the writer's or speaker's conviction that the Scriptures being consulted were the very word of God. In Acts 1:16 Peter referred to that which the Holy Spirit spoke by the mouth of David and then quoted from Psalms 69:25 and 109:8 regarding the fate of Judas. Not only are David's words authoritative, but they are so because God actually spoke by the mouth of David.

Jesus Himself regarded the Old Testament in this authoritative fashion. He responded to each of Satan's three temptations with words of Scripture. In His disputes with the Pharisees, He regularly appealed to the Old Testament. There were two sacred objects in Israel in Jesus' day: the temple and the Scripture. It is significant that while Jesus did not hesitate to correct His dialogue partners' erroneous conception of the former, He never disputed with them about the latter. He held the same high view of its authority that they espoused. He spoke of how Scripture could not be broken (John 10:35), how not a jot or a tittle would pass away from the law (Matt 5:18).

Theories of Inspiration

There are several different views of the nature of inspiration, or theories of inspiration, as they are sometimes termed.

1. *The intuition theory.* According to the intuition theory, inspiration is an ability of insight or the capability of intuiting spiritual truth. The prophets and apostles who wrote Scripture were, in this view, more gifted religiously, just as some persons are more gifted than others with regard to music and art.

2. *The illumination theory.* The illumination theory sees the work of the Holy Spirit in inspiring servants of God to write the Scripture as being a heightening or stimulation of the natural abilities of the writer rather than the communication of any truth not already possessed.

3. *The dynamic theory.* The dynamic theory emphasizes the role of the Holy Spirit in guiding the writer's thoughts, but not the choice of words.

4. *The verbal theory.* The verbal theory holds that divine inspiration even guaranteed that the writer would use just the words that God desired him to use but without actually dictating the language.

5. *The dictation theory.* According to the dictation theory, God actually prescribed the words to the writer, much as one dictates a letter to a stenographer.

Which of these theories are we to choose? We note that at times the New Testament rests an argument on the exact form of the word or the singular versus the plural in an Old Testament passage that is quoted (Matt 22:32; Gal 3:16). At other times, however, a certain amount of freedom is permitted in quoting from the Old Testament. The former type of instance suggests that even the word or form of the word is significant, that it was just what God intended. In the latter case the New Testament writer was often making an application of the truth of the passage other than that which the original writer intended. That does not, however, preclude the idea that every word in the original passage was just what God intended the writer to pen.

A distinction that may be of help here is that between detail and focus. A picture may either have much or little detail and yet be sharply focused. So sometimes the biblical message is rather general (numbers rounded to the nearest thousand, for example). At other times it is quite specific (a number given to the exact digit, for example). But either way, it is just what God wanted conveyed to

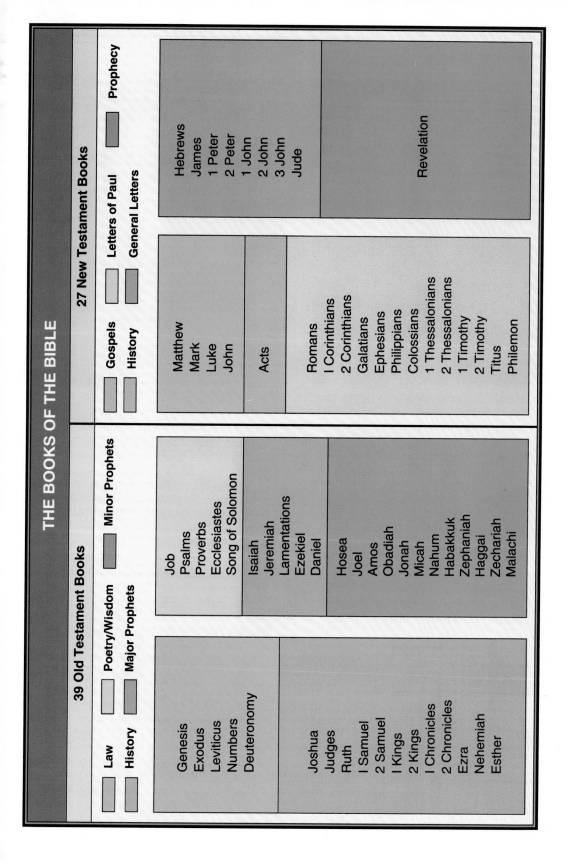

THE BOOKS OF THE BIBLE

39 Old Testament Books

Law · Poetry/Wisdom · Minor Prophets · History · Major Prophets

Law
Genesis
Exodus
Leviticus
Numbers
Deuteronomy

History
Joshua
Judges
Ruth
I Samuel
2 Samuel
I Kings
2 Kings
I Chronicles
2 Chronicles
Ezra
Nehemiah
Esther

Poetry/Wisdom
Job
Psalms
Proverbs
Ecclesiastes
Song of Solomon

Major Prophets
Isaiah
Jeremiah
Lamentations
Ezekiel
Daniel

Minor Prophets
Hosea
Joel
Amos
Obadiah
Jonah
Micah
Nahum
Habakkuk
Zephaniah
Haggai
Zechariah
Malachi

27 New Testament Books

Gospels · Letters of Paul · Prophecy · History · General Letters

Gospels
Matthew
Mark
Luke
John

History
Acts

Letters of Paul
Romans
I Corinthians
2 Corinthians
Galatians
Ephesians
Philippians
Colossians
1 Thessalonians
2 Thessalonians
1 Timothy
2 Timothy
Titus
Philemon

General Letters
Hebrews
James
1 Peter
2 Peter
1 John
2 John
3 John
Jude

Prophecy
Revelation

The apostle John, author of the Gospel that bears his name.

us. Thus the view that accounts for the largest amount of biblical data with the least difficulty is the verbal view (but not dictation).

It might appear that we have argued in a circle: quoting the Bible to establish its own inspiration and then using the fact of inspiration to establish the truth of this claim. While this might seem on superficial analysis to be bootstrap theology, in actuality we are not dealing with a circle but with a spiral. The Bible's own claims do not establish the fact of inspiration. They simply supply us with the hypothesis, which is to be evaluated on the basis of other evidence. The historical accuracy of the Bible, the amazing fulfillment of predictive prophecy, and other evidences give credibility to this claim.

Inerrancy

This leads us to another issue, that of inerrancy. This issue has stirred a considerable amount of controversy within the church in recent years. What is the real issue being debated under this designation? One layperson's question put the issue in the simplest terms: "If the Bible teaches it, can I believe it?"

Some have claimed that inerrancy is a concept that has arisen relatively recently in the church. As such, they would say, it is irrelevant to the tradition of orthodoxy in the Christian church and is an unessential article of faith. Yet although the modern, precise way of stating the concept is of quite recent origin, we find expressions of belief in the Bible's total freedom from error in the writings of Augustine, Luther, Calvin, and others. It is notable that different doctrines of Christian theology were carefully worked out and stated at different stages of the history of the Christian church. Thus the doctrines of the Trinity and the humanity and deity of Christ were carefully spelled out in the fourth and fifth centuries A.D. The atonement was the focus in the eleventh and twelfth centuries, and the nature of salvation and of the church dominated the thought of the sixteenth century.

The understanding of the person and work of the Holy Spirit, certain aspects of eschatology, and the nature of biblical authority have received much greater attention and definition in the twentieth century than in earlier centuries. Yet just as with these other doctrines, this does not mean that the belief was not previously held. It was simply implicit rather than explicit.

Another objection is that inerrancy is a negative term. It tells us what the Bible is not, namely, that it does not contain any errors, rather than what the Bible is. It is true that this can be the case. The Bible's positive characteristic is that it is the truth or teaches the truth. A positive way of putting both of these aspects would be to say that all that the Bible affirms is true. While the form of the word *inerrancy* is negative, its meaning need not be.

Some also allege that the word *inerrancy* is not found in the Bible and certainly is not taught in the Bible. It is true that the term does not appear in Scripture and that the Bible does not explicitly teach the idea. We should note, however, that just as with doctrines such as the Trinity, so the concept of inerrancy is implied by the view of the Bible found within the Bible. The Bible's authority extends to such minute elements of the text that Jesus can rest His argument on the possessive suffix of a noun (Matt 22:44). And Paul's argument can depend upon the singular rather than the plural of a noun (Gal 3:16). Jesus can say that not one jot or tittle shall pass from the law until all is fulfilled (Matt 5:18). That being the case, it is inconceivable that the Bible should err. A God who is omniscient would not make a mistake, and a God who is truthful would not mislead. If the Bible is this thoroughly an expression of His will, then it is inconceivable that it should contain anything untrue.

The doctrine of inerrancy guarantees the dependability of the Bible. One problem is frequently disregarded by Christians who do not hold to the inerrancy of the Bible. Many of the Bible's teachings pertain to doctrines which are not capable of empirical proof. If it is in error in those areas where we can check its content, on what basis do we hold that it is correct on those matters where we cannot check it independently? Faith then becomes mere credulity. Inerrancy means that we can trust all that the Bible affirms.

If, however, the understanding of inspiration requires us to hold that the Bible is inerrant, it does not tell us what that inerrancy must be. Does it mean that every statement must be true specifically? Does a statement that 7,000 soldiers were involved in a battle mean that there could not have been 6,999 or 7,001? Some have seemed to feel that this was required. Yet the degree of detail may vary from one passage to another. That can be determined in a given case only by an examination of the passage involved. Inerrancy does not mean that biblical statements may not involve approximations or rounded numbers, that popular ways of speaking may not be involved, or that scientific matters may not be described as they appear to the eye.

Illumination

There is one other aspect to this doctrine of Scripture, however. For even if the Bible is the revealed truth of God and has been preserved for us by divine inspiration so that it is just what God wanted us to know, that is just the objective truth of Scripture. It is still necessary that persons understand and believe the Bible if it is to have any real value for them.

Jesus spoke of how the Holy Spirit would convince persons of sin, righteousness, and judgment (John 16:8-11). He said that this same Spirit would teach His disciples all things and remind them of everything He had said (John 14:26). He would testify about Jesus to them (John 15:26) and would guide them into all truth (John 16:13). Here is the basis for the doctrine of illumination: the Holy Spirit does not impart truth not already possessed but gives understanding and conviction of the truth of the teachings already given. We now possess these teachings preserved in the Scripture.

Some people have limited the application of Jesus' promises to just the immediate circle of disciples to whom He gave them on this occasion. In this same discourse, however, Jesus made other promises, such as His future coming to take His believers to Himself (John 14:1-4). These promises clearly are for all believers in all periods.

This means that in addition to the external or objective word of Scripture, believers have the internal or subjective testimony of the Holy Spirit. Here is the answer to the charge that an infallible or inerrant Bible is of no value without an infallible interpreter. We have that interpreter, not a human authority but a divine authority. The full principle of authority is not simply the Bible apart from the Spirit, for that can be a lifeless set of words and concepts. Similarly, we do not rely upon the Holy Spirit independently of the Bible. We are not looking for new truths to be revealed. The combination of the external Word of Scripture and the internal testimony of the Holy Spirit is fully adequate.

This does not mean that we do not utilize our human ability to seek fuller understanding of the Bible. Studying the languages in which the Bible was written and the culture of that day will contribute to our grasp of the Bible's meaning. Yet this ability to learn is indeed a gift God has given us. Through our intelligence and study God enables us to discover truth about Him.

The sequence then is complete. God has made Himself known to us through the process known as revelation. He has preserved this truth through inspiration, so that the Bible contains His message, just as He intended it. With the illumining work of the Holy Spirit, we are able to understand this perfect message. Since it is what God wants us to know and do, it therefore possesses authority. It has the right to prescribe our belief and practice because God possesses this right.

In the final analysis, however, our real doctrine of the Scripture is demonstrated not merely by what we say about it but what we do with it. For if this is indeed God's own message to us, our proper response is to act upon it. We have it not merely to inform but to direct us. Our lives will therefore be characterized by the kind of godly living God expects of us.

THE CANONICITY OF THE BIBLE

The Bible is a collection of writings possessing infallible authority for the faith and life of the church. But what writings make up the Bible? How and by whom were they collected? Can we be sure that none were included by mistake or that none were inadvertently omitted? These and related questions constitute the problem of the canon.

The word *canon* derives ultimately from a Semitic word meaning *reed,* which yielded the figurative sense of a *measuring rod* or *ruler*. From this derived the general sense of a *norm* or *standard* and then finally a *list* or a *table.* When used of the Bible, *canon* refers to the list of writings recognized by the Christian church to be the unique rule of faith and life.

It is important to be clear about the canonical process. It is sometimes presented as an evolutionary development through which certain religious writings received increasing acceptance and were ultimately accorded the unique status of inclusion in the canon. In this understanding canonicity is seen as a status *conferred* on the biblical materials.

It is better to see canonization as the human response to the divine authority inherent in the biblical writings from the beginning. When the people of God defined the canon by gathering, preserving, and listing the various books, they confessed that these particular writings were the Word of God. To say this slightly differently: the ultimate basis of canonicity is not the decision of the church (or the synagogue) but the divine inspiration of Scripture.

Old Testament Canon

The details of the process by which the Old Testament writings were recognized as authoritative and distinguished from other Jewish works are largely hidden from view. Accounts purporting to give specific details of the process derive from a later period and have limited value. For example, 2 Esdras (=4 Ezra) 14:44 (about A.D. 100) tells how Ezra the scribe, grieving over the loss of the biblical books during the Babylonian captivity, was directed by God to choose five men as secretaries to whom he dictated ninety-four books in forty days. The first twenty-four were to be circulated generally among the people and apparently corresponded to the entire Old Testament. The remaining seventy were reserved only "to the wise among your people."

The miraculous elements of the recovery of Scripture by Ezra are not present in later Jewish literature. But the association of Ezra with the collection and arrangement of the books is traditional for both Jewish and Christian accounts. Although the fifth century B.C. is almost certainly too early for the collection and ordering of all the Old Testament books, the story does indicate two important aspects of the history of the Old Testament canon.

1. Later Judaism believed that God had given them His Word in twenty-four books. In the Talmudic passage Baba Bathra 14b-15a, the books are listed in the following form: the five books of Moses; eight books of the Prophets (Joshua, Judges, Samuel, Kings, Jeremiah, Ezekiel, Isaiah, and the twelve Minor Prophets); eleven Writings (Ruth, Psalms, Job, Proverbs, Ecclesiastes, Song of Songs, Lamentations, Daniel, Esther, Ezra, and Chronicles).

Jesus and the apostles likely shared the same view of the Old Testament as the Jewish rabbis. Jesus' reference to "the Law of Moses, the Prophets and the Psalms" (Luke 24:44) probably indicates a threefold division of the Old Testament canon with "Psalms" as a general designation for the entire third section. More specific are the implications of Matthew 23:34-35. Jesus spoke of "all the righteous blood that had been shed on earth, from the blood of righteous Abel to the blood of Zechariah son of Berekiah" (Matt 23:35). Abel represents the first righteous man in history to suffer persecution from the wicked, but why the mention of Zechariah? Probably the reference is to Zechariah, son of Jehoiada (2 Chr 24:20,22). Since Zechariah was not *chronologically* the last martyr named in the Old Testament, he probably was mentioned here because Chronicles was, by New Testament times, understood to be the last book in the Hebrew Bible. Thus, Jesus' statement would mean the blood of all the martyrs mentioned in the Old Testament.

Other witnesses, such as the Jewish historian Josephus

THE HEBREW CANON OF THE OLD TESTAMENT		
CLASSIFICATION OF THE BOOKS	**HEBREW NAMES FOR THE BOOKS**	**ENGLISH NAMES FOR THE BOOKS**
THE LAW (Torah)	In the beginning These are the names And He called In the wilderness These are the words	Genesis Exodus Leviticus Numbers Deuteronomy
FORMER PROPHETS	Joshua Judges 1 Samuel 2 Samuel 1 Kings 2 Kings	Joshua Judges 1 Samuel 2 Samuel 1 Kings 2 Kings
LATTER PROPHETS	Isaiah Jeremiah Ezekiel The Book of the Twelve (which includes) Hosea Joel Amos Obadiah Jonah Micah Nahum Habakkuk Zephaniah Haggai Zechariah Malachi	Isaiah Jeremiah Ezekiel Hosea Joel Amos Obadiah Jonah Micah Nahum Habakkuk Zephaniah Haggai Zechariah Malachi
THE WRITINGS (HAGIOGRAPHA)	Praises Job Proverbs Ruth Song of Songs The Preacher How! Esther Daniel Ezra / Nehemiah 1 The words of the days 2 The words of the days	Psalms Job Proverbs Ruth Song of Solomon Ecclesiastes Lamentations Esther Daniel Ezra Nehemiah 1 Chronicles 2 Chronicles

(about A.D. 37–100), give a total of twenty-two books. This is due merely to a different grouping of the same materials, probably counting Judges-Ruth and Jeremiah-Lamentations as single books. It has been argued that the members of the Dead Sea community at Qumran held canonical views that differed significantly from later rabbinic Judaism. Actually the Qumran covenanters left no explicit discussions on the subject, and the inferences drawn from their writings are uncertain.

2. The account in 2 Esdras also suggests that the production and gathering of the biblical books was long since complete. This is a most important point. It supports the

idea that when people drew up lists they were not conferring authority but only recognizing authority that already existed. This understanding of the canonical process is generally rejected by liberal critics of the Old Testament. The prevailing historical-critical opinion finds the first evidence of canonical activity in the discovery of the "Book of the Law" during the reign of Josiah (621 B.C.)—identified as the Book of Deuteronomy or a portion of it. The final stages in the formation of the Pentateuch are thought to have taken place during the fifth century, with canonization following about 400 B.C. Subsequently the Prophets achieved canonical status about 200 B.C., while the Writings only were canonized during the course of rabbinic discussions at Jamnia in the closing decade of the first Christian century.

The evidence for this late dating is weak. The supposed role of the Council of Jamnia has been severely attacked by recent scholarship. The historical evidence is better interpreted in support of a pre-Christian closing of the Old Testament canon, although an exact date is impossible to determine. About 100 B.C. seems to be the latest that can be accepted on the basis of the data. One commentator argues that the closing of the canon was the work of Judas Maccabaeus about 165 B.C. Another commentator has suggested a date of about 300 B.C. for the fixation of the essential parts of the Old Testament even though discussions of certain books continued into the Christian era.

The Apocrypha

While all the major traditions of the Christian church accept the authority of the Hebrew canon, disagreement exists over a group of writings called the "Apocryphya." These writings are regarded as part of the Old Testament by various groups of Christians. For the Roman Catholic church the apocryphal (or deuterocanonical) books include Tobit, Judith, The Wisdom of Solomon, Ecclesiasticus, Baruch, The Letter of Jeremiah, 1 and 2 Maccabees, and certain additions to Esther and Daniel. The Orthodox Church accepts the canonicity of the same books but adds 1 Esdras and 3 Maccabees. However, most Orthodox scholars, while affirming that the deuterocanonical books are genuine parts of Scripture, place them on a lower level of authority than the first-order canonical books.

These materials were all composed between 200 B.C. and A.D. 100. Although they were not included in the Hebrew Old Testament, all were included in the Greek translation of the Old Testament called the Septuagint. As a result many Christians read these works and in the course of time came to regard them as part of the Old Testament even though some scholars, such as Jerome (about 342–420), recognized that the apocryphal books belonged to a different category.

During the sixteenth century the Protestant reformers disputed the canonical status of the Apocrypha and returned to the narrower Hebrew collection. The disputed books continued to be read and valued by many Protestants, but they were not believed to have the authority of Scripture.

Support for the traditional Protestant position is both historical and theological. *Theologically* it is argued that the proper Christian view of the Old Testament must be built on the understanding of Jesus and the apostles. Whatever canonical limits they recognized, we must recognize. *Historically* it is affirmed that Jesus and the apostles accepted only the more restricted twenty-two- (or twenty-four-) book canon of later rabbinic Judaism.

Fresh debate about the Apocrypha has arisen in recent years, especially with the publication of A. C. Sundberg's *The Old Testament of the Early Church* (1964). The author argued that in Judaism prior to A.D. 90 (the Council of Jamnia) only the first two sections of the canon, "the Law" and "the Prophets," were closed. The third section of the canon, "the Writings," was still open. The Jews of Palestine and Alexandria freely employed a wide range of religious literature without definite boundaries. Hence, the Protestant rejection of the canonicity of the Apocrypha can no longer be justified by an appeal to the practice of Jesus.

However, Sundberg's date for the closing of the Old Testament canon is too late. As discussed earlier, a date between 300 B.C. and 100 B.C. is much more likely. Moreover, much of Sundberg's evidence for the shape of the Hebrew canon in New Testament times is based on the variations of the earliest (fourth and fifth century) Septuagint manuscripts from one another and from the ordering and numbering of the rabbinic source. But the Septuagint manuscripts were produced by Christians and are, therefore, questionable sources from which to derive conclusions about the Hebrew canon three or four centuries earlier. In short, there is no pressing reason to revise the traditional Protestant estimate of the Apocrypha: these writings contain much that is useful and spiritually satisfying, but they are not to be regarded as Scripture.

The New Testament

Although the New Testament documents functioned authoritatively from the beginning, their collection and distinction from other literature of the time was also a gradual process spanning several centuries. It was a natural process arising from the circumstances and outlook of the earliest period of the church. We note four contributing

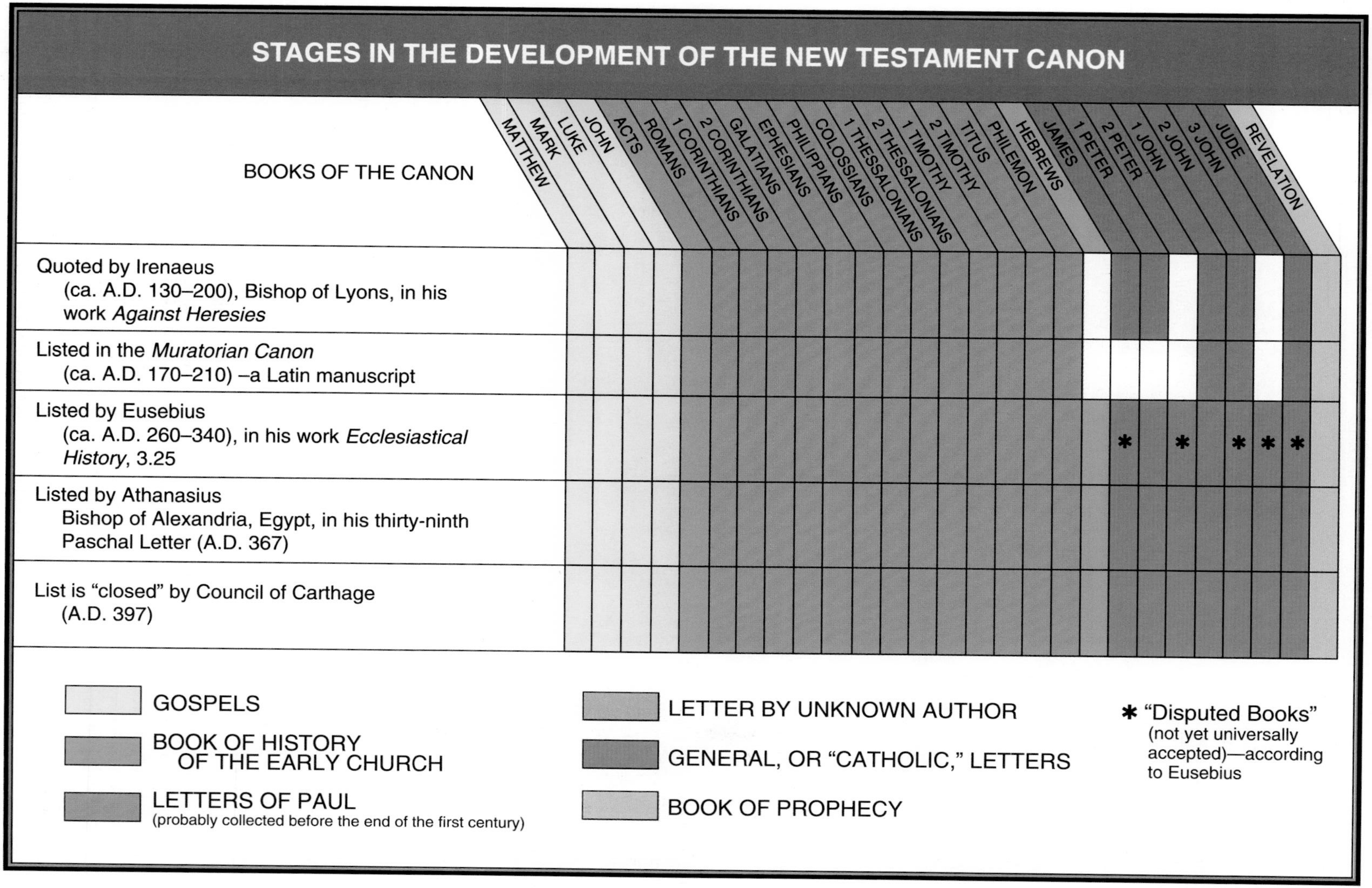
STAGES IN THE DEVELOPMENT OF THE NEW TESTAMENT CANON
BOOKS OF THE CANON
MATTHEW
MARK
LUKE
JOHN
ACTS
ROMANS
1 CORINTHIANS
2 CORINTHIANS
GALATIANS
EPHESIANS
PHILIPPIANS
COLOSSIANS
1 THESSALONIANS
2 THESSALONIANS
1 TIMOTHY
2 TIMOTHY
TITUS
PHILEMON
HEBREWS
JAMES
1 PETER
2 PETER
1 JOHN
2 JOHN
3 JOHN
JUDE
REVELATION
Quoted by Irenaeus (ca. A.D. 130–200), Bishop of Lyons, in his work *Against Heresies*
Listed in the *Muratorian Canon* (ca. A.D. 170–210) –a Latin manuscript
Listed by Eusebius (ca. A.D. 260–340), in his work *Ecclesiastical History*, 3.25
Listed by Athanasius Bishop of Alexandria, Egypt, in his thirty-ninth Paschal Letter (A.D. 367)
List is “closed” by Council of Carthage (A.D. 397)
GOSPELS
BOOK OF HISTORY OF THE EARLY CHURCH
LETTERS OF PAUL
(probably collected before the end of the first century)
LETTER BY UNKNOWN AUTHOR
GENERAL, OR “CATHOLIC,” LETTERS
BOOK OF PROPHECY
* “Disputed Books”
(not yet universally accepted)—according to Eusebius

Jerome, who translated the Old and New Testaments into the Latin language of the common people.

factors:

1. From Jesus Himself the church had learned the importance of the Old Testament. The apostles knew that Jesus had not come to abolish the Law or the Prophets but to fulfill them (Matt 5:17). Therefore they knew that "everything that was written in the past was written to teach us, so that through endurance and the encouragement of the Scriptures we might have hope" (Rom 15:4). Thus the church had a notion of canon from the very beginning. This may not have led Christians to *expect* an addition to the Old Testament, but it would certainly have meant that such an expansion would be easily understood and accepted.

2. The fundamental authority for the early church were the words of Jesus and the revelatory events of His life, death, and resurrection: "In the past God spoke to our forefathers through the prophets at many times and in various ways, but in these last days he has spoken to us by his Son" (Heb 1:1-2). This conviction ensured that the words of or about Jesus would be accorded the highest esteem, whether in oral or written form. This conviction also became the driving force behind the formation of the New Testament.

3. The apostles were chosen by Christ Himself to be His witnesses (Acts 10:39-42; compare 1 Cor 15:5-7). They were to speak for Him, and those who heard them heard Christ: "He who listens to you listens to me" (Luke 10:16). The apostolic witness could be oral or written, but both carried the same authority (2 Thess 2:15). While the New Testament authors made no explicit claims to have been writing Scripture, they did expect at least some of their writings to be circulated among the churches and read in the presence of the congregation (1 Thess 5:27; Col 4:16; 1 Cor 14:37; Rev 1:3,11). This practice was similar to the reading of the Old Testament in the synagogue. The letters of Paul were soon placed on

COMPARISON OF LISTS OF THE OLD TESTAMENT BOOKS

RABBINIC CANON 24 BOOKS	SEPTUAGINT 53 BOOKS	ROMAN CATHOLIC OLD TESTAMENT 46 BOOKS
The Law	***Law***	***Law***
Genesis	Genesis	Genesis
Exodus	Exodus	Exodus
Leviticus	Leviticus	Leviticus
Numbers	Numbers	Numbers
Deuteronomy	Deuteronomy	Deuteronomy
The Prophets	***History***	***History***
The Former Prophets		
Joshua	Joshua	Joshua
Judges	Judges	Judges
1-2 Samuel	Ruth	Ruth
1-2 Kings	1 Kingdoms (1 Samuel)	1 Samuel (1 Kingdoms)
The Latter Prophets	2 Kingdoms (2 Samuel)	2 Samuel (2 Kingdoms)
Isaiah	3 Kingdoms (1 Kings)	1 Kings (3 Kingdoms)
Jeremiah	4 Kingdoms (2 Kings)	2 Kings (4 Kingdoms)
Ezekiel	1 Paralipomena (1 Chronicles)	1 Chronicles (1 Paralipomena)
The Twelve	2 Paralipomena (2 Chronicles)	2 Chronicles (2 Paralipomena)
Hosea	1 Esdras (Apocryphal Ezra)	Ezra (1 Esdras)
Joel	2 Esdras (Ezra-Nehemiah)	Nehemiah (2 Esdras)
Amos	Esther (with Apocryphal additions)	Tobit
Obadiah	Judith	Judith
Jonah	Tobit	Esther
Micah	1 Maccabees	1 Maccabees
Nahum	2 Maccabees	2 Maccabees
Habakkuk	3 Maccabees	
Zephaniah	4 Maccabees	***Poetry***
Haggai		Job
Zechariah	***Poetry***	Psalms
Malachi	Psalms	Proverbs
	Odes (including the prayer of Manasseh)	Ecclesiastes
The Writings	Proverbs	Song of Songs
Poetry	Ecclesiastes	Wisdom of Solomon
Psalms	Song of Songs	Ecclesiasticus (The Wisdom of Jesus the son of Sirach)
Proverbs	Job	
Job	Wisdom (of Solomon)	
Rolls—"the Festival Scrolls"	Sirach (Ecclesiasticus or The Wisdom of Jesus the son of Sirach)	***Prophecy***
Song of Songs		Isaiah
Ruth	Psalms of Solomon	Jeremiah
Lamentations		Lamentations
Ecclesiastes	***Prophecy***	Baruch (including the Letter of Jeremiah)
Esther	The Twelve Prophets	
Others (History)	Hosea	Ezekiel
Daniel	Amos	Daniel
Ezra-Nehemiah	Micah	Hosea
1–2 Chronicles	Joel	Joel
	Obadiah	Amos
	Jonah	Obadiah
	Nahum	Jonah
	Habakkuk	Micah
	Zephaniah	Nahum
	Haggai	Habakkuk
	Zechariah	Zephaniah
	Malachi	Haggai
	Isaiah	Zechariah
	Jeremiah	Malachi
	Baruch	
	Lamentations	***Appendix***
	Letter of Jeremiah	The Prayer of Manasseh
	Ezekiel	The two apocryphal books of Esdras
	Daniel (with apocryphal additions, including the Prayer of Azariah and the Song of the Three Children, Susanna, and Bel and the Dragon)	

The Canonical Books of the Old Testament *

- Books of Law
- Books of History
- Books of Poetry and Wisdom
- Books of the Major Prophets
- Books of the Minor Prophets

* Grouped according to the Christian canon

a par with the Old Testament—"the other Scriptures" (2 Pet 3:16).

4. The definition of the canon was also encouraged by the need to preserve the apostolic teaching from distortion by false teachers. Jesus had warned of the coming of false prophets (Matt 7:15; 24:11,24; Mark 13:22). His followers reiterated this to their own congregations (2 Cor 11:13; 2 Pet 2:1; 1 John 2:26-27; 4:1-6; 2 John 7; Rev 2:2,20). Particularly did the rise of Gnostic teachers in the late first and early second centuries stimulate the church to distinguish authentic writings of the apostles (or "apostolic men" like Luke) from heretical productions.

Among the Apostolic Fathers (about A.D. 96–150) there is no formulated doctrine of Scripture or canon. The common assumption is that the apostolic traditions (whether oral or written) stand alongside the Old Testament as a parallel authority. There are many references to New Testament writings, but only in a few instances are these formally cited as quotations from *Scripture* (Polycarp, *Phil* 12.1; *Barn* 4.14; *2 Clem* 2.4). Ignatius of Antioch (about 107) may have known a collection of the Pauline Letters.

As already noted, heretical movements provided a great stimulus to the consolidation of the canon. Gnostic groups produced a welter of literature, some known to us from ancient sources and some known only through the discovery in 1945 of an ancient Coptic Gnostic library at Nag Hammadi in Egypt. The appearance of documents like *The Gospel of Truth*, *The Gospel of Thomas*, or *The Apocalypse of Paul* forced the church to distinguish those writings that were truly apostolic from those that were not.

In the middle of the second century Marcion of Sinope proposed the first canonical list. His canon rejected the Old Testament in its entirety and accepted ten Pauline Epistles and an edited version of Luke.

The decisive response to Marcion and the Gnostics came from Irenaeus, bishop of Lyons (about 178–200), in his work *Against All Heresies*. Since there are four principal winds and four points of the compass, he argued, there are four and only four Gospels. Irenaeus is perhaps the first of the Apostolic Fathers to cite the Book of Acts explicitly. He definitely cited 1 Peter, 1 and 2 John, Revelation, and all of the Pauline Letters with the exception of Philemon; and there are probably allusions to James and Hebrews. In short, Irenaeus's corpus of authoritative literature closely resembled the shape of the present canon.

A similar picture is given by the Muratorian Canon, which probably originated in Rome about A.D. 200 or earlier. It recognizes the canonicity of all our present twenty-seven books except Hebrews, James, 1 and 2 Peter, and 3 John. In addition it accepts the Apocalypse of Peter and (strangely) the Wisdom of Solomon.

Little further movement occurs in succeeding years. The majority of the books of the New Testament are clearly recognized and accepted; questions remain about a few. A century or more later Eusebius of Caesarea (about 260–about 340) describes the canon under a threefold classification: (1) the recognized books—the four Gospels, Acts, the Pauline Epistles (including Hebrews), 1 Peter, 1 John, and (perhaps) Revelation; (2) the disputed books: those generally accepted—James, Jude, 2 and 3 John—and those that are not genuine—*The Acts of Paul*, *The Shepherd of Hermas*, *The Apocalypse of Peter*, *The Epistle of Barnabas*, *The Teachings of the Apostles*, and (perhaps) Revelation; (3) heretical writings; pseudogospels or acts of some apostle.

In the latter part of the fourth and the beginning of the fifth centuries the majority of the church came to a consensus on the content of the New Testament. The first witness to specify the present twenty-seven books of the New Testament as alone canonical was Athanasias's Easter letter of A.D. 367. At the close of the century the Third Council of Carthage (A.D. 397) prescribed the same list. This was confirmed again at Carthage in 419.

During the fifth century the present canon became the general consensus of the church. The exceptions are the native (as distinct from the Greek-speaking) Syrian church, which acknowledges only twenty-two books (omitting 2 Peter, 2 and 3 John, Jude, and Revelation). The Ethiopian church accepts the usual twenty-seven but includes another eight books that deal primarily with church order. However, when particular groups of Christians who are in communication with the church at large have studied the question of the extent of the canon, there has been remarkable agreement.

That the canon is closed flows from a confidence that God in His providence not only inspired the authors of Scripture to write exactly those things He wished to communicate to the church but also superintended their preservation and collection.

Sources for Additional Study

Beckwith, Roger. *The Old Testament Canon of the New Testament Church*. Grand Rapids: Eerdmans, 1985.

Bruce, F. F. *The Canon of Scripture*. Downers Grove: InterVarsity, 1988.

Metzger, Bruce M. *The Canon of the New Testament*. Oxford: University Press, 1987.

THE UNIQUENESS OF THE BIBLE

The Bible, the written Word of God, has uniquely informed Western culture, which now has become a dominant force in the global development of politics, economics, and social relations. From a religious perspective the Bible has been of major significance. The three great monotheistic religions—Judaism, Islam, and Christianity—trace their roots to the Old Testament. The Bible could have this pervasive role since it deals not just with the beginnings of one race but rather with the creation of all humankind. Its message deals with events in time as well as issues for eternity; it addresses the enormous cosmic forces as well as oppressed human beings. It is therefore unique in its universality, its impact on history, and in its communication.

Unique in Its Universality

A Cosmic Universality. When we describe the embrace of the Scriptures by circles indicating the realms of its revelation, we would first of all draw the widest possible circle. This is the cosmic realm mentioned in Psalm 19:1: "The heavens declare the glory of God; the skies proclaim the work of his hands." The first chapter of the Scriptures majestically unfolds God's creative power in the universe as well as on earth among the creatures "that move along the ground" (Gen 1:24-25). God evoked the light, separated the waters, and created the vegetation and the animal world. God then placed humans in the center of all these potentialities and made them the stewards of all these gifts.

The Bible has invited men and women to praise their Creator for His abundance in nature. The Book of Psalms includes numerous hymns about God's glory in the universe and on earth. Psalm 148 encourages each created being to join the chorus of praise. The sun and moon, the clouds and the stormy winds, the wild animals and all the cattle, young men and old men all are invited to worship the God of the universe.

A Social Universality. Because the Word originates from the God of heaven and earth, it addresses all members of the human society. It challenges men and women; it guides the wise as well as the illiterate; it is the light for our paths (Ps 119:105). This all-inclusiveness has inspired the writers of the various books of the Bible to mention unique women and children alongside the great pioneers of our faith. Miriam, the sister of Moses, led the people in thanksgiving and dance after the deliverance from Pharaoh's men (Exod 15:19-21). A whole book is dedicated to Ruth, who became the grandmother of David because of her obedience to the God of Naomi, her mother-in-law. Also children have a crucial part in the history of salvation (for example, see 1 Sam 2–3).

We also could refer to Joseph, who was sold as a slave by his brothers (Gen 37:12-36), or to Moses, who was educated by an Egyptian princess and yet became a leader of Israel (Exod 2–3). We could mention the beautiful story of David defeating the Gentile giant Goliath (1 Sam 17:41-58). The Bible includes slaves and prostitutes in its records. When the decisive battle for the entry into the holy land was to be waged, it was the prostitute Rahab who provided a refuge to the Israelites' spies. She too filled a crucial role in God's redemptive plan (see Josh 2).

As in the past, the Bible today appeals to people of all races, to men and women, to rich and poor, to adults and children, to the healthy as well as to the sick and suffering. The apostle Paul was one of the first Christian leaders to proclaim this universality when he stated: "There is neither Jew nor Greek, slave nor free, male nor female, for you are all one in Christ Jesus (Gal 3:28). Thus the Bible expresses not only God's concern for the cosmic realm but even more for the various members of the human society.

A Complete Universality. The cosmic and social embrace of the Bible provides the backdrop for a complete and holistic claim upon individuals. God's revelation through the Bible deals with all aspects of life. It therefore is unique among religious books merely filled with sacred incantations or secret formulas or descriptions of the special experiences of the founder. The Bible deals with all of life, religious as well as secular.

Among the enumerations of the Ten Commandments we find, for example, the religious command to keep one day holy. But it also contains the injunction to complete all our work during the preceding six days (Exod 20:8-9; Deut 5:12-13). Our relationship to God is not merely an act of the soul but of the total person. Jesus endorsed the great daily prayer of Israel, saying: "Love the Lord your God with all your heart and with all your soul and with all your mind" (Matt 22:37; see Deut 6:5).

Since the early days of the church, the Bible has challenged an array of scholars, rulers, craftsmen, mothers, and professional women and men to practice their skills in the name of Christ. Because of this universal appeal to all kinds of people using such great variety of talent and skill, the Bible has been the most widely read book in world history. Translated into two thousand languages, it has influenced music, art, architecture, literature, the calendar, and numerous other aspects of life. The Bible shares this universality with our Creator, "for in him we live and move and have our being" (Acts 17:28).

Unique in Its Historical Impact

God's Initiative. The Bible is the only book describing a world history having a definite beginning and conclusion in God's revelatory act. History is the pathway from the first garden of Eden to the glorious city of the New Jerusalem. This winding path guides its pioneers through wastelands and oases. God is experienced by His revelation in the history of humankind as well as in the lives of individual persons. God takes the initiative in human affairs. What is unique in history is that in each incident God's initiative or election clearly keeps the course of history going. Abraham was a Gentile; David was merely a shepherd boy when he was anointed (1 Sam 16:11-13); Amos was a rancher without any special inclinations for the ministry; and Saul was resisting the cause of Christ. Yet all these were used in spite of themselves. That is why this same Saul, later Paul, would emphasize the gospel of grace, which is God's saving act in spite of human effort. In a similar manner God's action was experienced by Augustine in his conversion in 386 and by Martin Luther in 1512 during his "tower experience." At that moment Romans 1:17 became for Luther "the gate of Paradise" because it states that "in the gospel a righteousness from God is revealed, a righteousness that is by faith from the first to the last."

God's Power. The Bible is unique in its impact on history because it contains the message of God's power in history. We preach from the Bible because we see the old story being repeated in our day. Still the most unlikely people are used by God in the advancement of His kingdom. The story of Corrie ten Boom is an example of a traditional Christian woman being drawn into the turbulent events of World War II. In her book *The Hiding Place* she describes how the simple reciting of the Scriptures in the many languages of the prisoners united these martyrs in their stand against Nazism. The history of God's kingdom is carried on by His power, progressing in spite of our own predispositions and plans.

Because of this divine action, the Bible does not need to protect its heroes. It rather is extremely honest about God's elect persons. Abraham lied about the identity of his wife, Sarah, by calling her his sister. He did this for fear that King Abimelech might kill him in order to take Sarah as his wife (Gen 20). David, the man after God's heart, caused a scandal by taking Bathsheba, the beautiful wife of one of his generals (2 Sam 11). The king of peace and wisdom, Solomon, established a harem of a thousand wives and concubines (1 Kings 11:3). Thus the story of human failure continued into the New Testament. One of the followers of Jesus was instrumental in the capture of his Master (Matt 26:47-50). The days of great revival in the early church were overshadowed by the deceit of Ananias and Sapphira (Acts 5:1-11), which caused their sudden death. The history of the church indicates continuing scandals in various forms. The crusades, the inquisition, the religious wars were as many evidences of human failure and of God's victory.

God's Victory. The Bible, then, is a message of general, historical, and special revelation. This message is called the gospel, the message of good tidings, because it announces events that happen in spite of human failure. It is a message that applies to every reader still today. When John Bunyan learned to read the Scriptures, he became a different person; he became a participant in God's history and called himself a pilgrim to the City of God. Millions have been blessed by reading his *Pilgrim's Progress*, which reveals his intensive and extensive study of the Bible. Also Dwight L. Moody discovered the will of God by reading the Bible. He established numerous Bible schools and Bible churches not only on this continent but around the world. Since the Bible shares its uniqueness with Christ, it similarly is a stone precious to those who believe but a stumbling block to the unbelievers (see Rom 9:32-33; 1 Pet 2:8).

Unique in Its Communication

Understanding by Illumination. The Bible records history, but it is more than a history book. It portrays nature and the universe, yet it is not a handbook on natural history. It deals with the deepest feelings of humans, yet it is more than a manual on counseling. The Bible is different from any book because its revelation depends on an existing relationship, an "internal testimony" by the Holy Spirit. In Romans 8:15 the apostle Paul said: "You received the Spirit of sonship. And by him we cry, 'Abba, Father.' "

The inspired text needs an illumined mind to understand the Word. In this respect the Bible is unique in comparison with other books; it is God's unique medium of communication. A Bible study group is therefore different from a book club; for the study of the Bible should be approached in a spirit of devotion or worship. This study is enabled by the illumination of the Holy Spirit.

The illumination of the Holy Spirit means that each reborn Christian can understand the will of God by reading the Scriptures and by participating in worship services with fellow believers. It was for this reason that the Reformers actively engaged in the translation of the Bible into the common language of the people so all men and

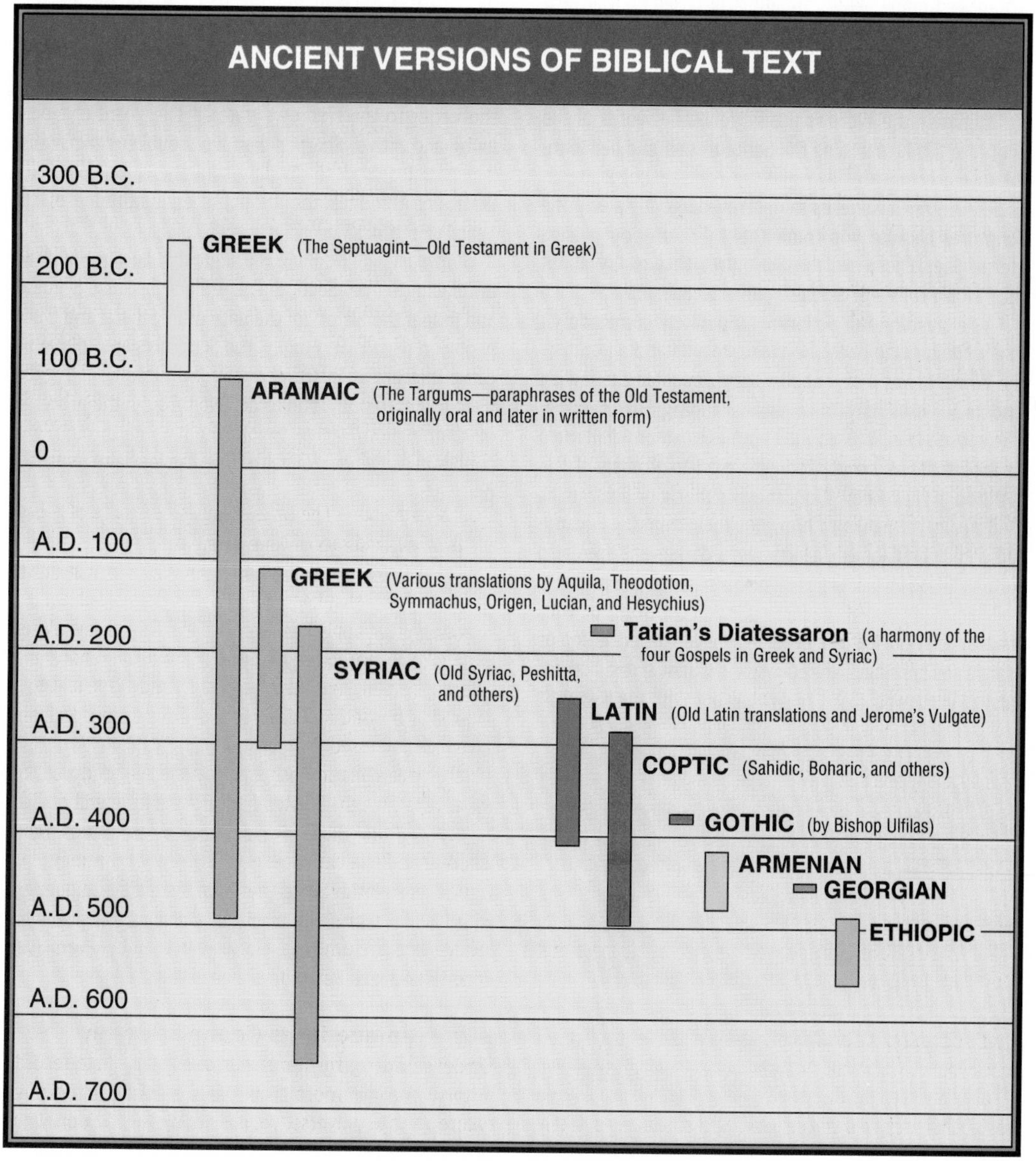

women would to be able to read the Word for themselves. The *Luther Bible* became as beloved by its readers as the *King James Version* in England and the United States. The *Geneva Bible* had a special Calvinist appeal and so the Dutch *Statenbijbel,* which means that also in the process of translation the various Protestant denominations felt free to be led by the Holy Spirit.

Understanding by Faith. The focus of all Christian action ultimately is faith in Christ. One of the great devotional classics was called *The Imitation of Christ,* by Thomas á Kempis. This "imitation" is based on Matthew 16, where Christ encouraged His disciples to take up their crosses and follow Him. Thomas á Kempis admonished us to cling to Christ, to keep Him as our Friend.

Ultimately the Word is the same as the words of the Scripture. Thus searching the Scriptures should be identical to searching the Living Word, or the Logos, mentioned in John 1:1. Jesus said: "You diligently study the Scriptures because you think that by them you possess eternal life. These are the Scriptures that testify about me" (John 6:39-40; see also John 20:30).

Understanding the Scriptures ultimately comes down to a willingness to obey the Word, to a "standing under" the Word. It was their unbelief that prevented the Jewish leaders in Jesus' day from understanding His message. The apostle Paul accused the Gentiles of an unwillingness to accept the Word of God. We read in Romans 1:21: "Although they knew God, they neither glorified him as God nor gave thanks to him, but their thinking became futile and their foolish hearts were darkened" (see also Rom 2:14-15).

The uniqueness of the Bible is that it confronts us with the will of God for our lives. We have to decide for or against the message we receive. As Christ stated according to Matthew 12:30: "He who is not with me is against me, and he who does not gather with me scatters."

The Bible therefore speaks in parables, uses typology, and launches its predictions in the hidden language of apocalyptics. Jesus referred in this connection to Isaiah 6:9: "You will be ever hearing but never understanding; you will be ever seeing but never perceiving" (Matt 13:14). James equally compared the Word to a mirror that reflects our "input" of faith (Jas 1:23). The evangelist John portrayed the Word as water (John 4:14), as bread (6:51), or as meat (6:55) because it is meant to still the thirst or hunger of those who seek it. The Word may have to use force in making us aware of the need of searching faith. The prophet Jeremiah, therefore, compared the Word with a fire torch or with a hammer that can break a rock in pieces (Jer 23:29). As the author of the Letter to the Hebrews states: "The Word of God is living and active. Sharper than any double-edged sword, it penetrates even to dividing soul and spirit, joints and marrow; it judges the thoughts and attitudes of the heart" (Heb 4:12).

Summary. The Bible is unique first because of its all-embracing scope. Second, it is unique because it guides and judges the history of the nations in general and God's people in particular. Finally, the Scriptures are unique because they are an instrument of communication, begging us to listen, to obey, and to believe through the processes of illumination, active involvement, and through our confident surrender of faith. We can exclaim with the psalmist:

> How sweet are your words to my taste,
> sweeter than honey to my mouth!
> I gain understanding from your precepts;
> therefore I hate every wrong path.
> Your word is a lamp to my feet
> and a light for my path.
>
> Psalm 119:104-05

THE UNITY AND VARIETY OF THE BIBLE

Sixty-six writings, two Testaments, one Bible. Such is what we find when we study God's Word. Despite all the diversity in the Bible, it is impossible to ignore the essential unity found within its pages. This unity is not the result of church dogma. It goes far deeper than that. The unity of the Bible rests on its divine Author. This unity is unique among ancient writings and is of utmost importance for biblical interpretation.

Several features of this unity and its importance are evident. Perhaps the most important feature is that the story of the Bible hangs together as a consistent whole. Written long before the birth of Jesus, the Old Testament points to Jesus' death and resurrection as the Savior of the world. Written decades after the ascension of Jesus, the New Testament records the consummation of the messianic anticipations of the Old Testament. In Jesus were fulfilled the deepest hopes of all God's people, whether they lived before Christ or after Him. In this sense one may say that the unity of the Bible finds its center in Jesus Himself, predicted in the Old Testament, manifested in flesh in the New Testament.

Within this essential unity of the Bible is diversity on a grand scale. A portion of the Old Testament is superseded in the New. The author of Hebrews, for example, spoke of a qualitative difference between the message of the Old Testament prophets and the revelation brought by God's Son (Heb 1:1-4). But this element of discontinuity between the Testaments does not rule out a strong line of continuity. The thread that gives unity to the Bible is the divine element, the fact that the same God spoke to both Israel and the church. Hence the same divine inspiration that marks the Old Testament prophets marks the New Testament apostles. This is an essential doctrine of Christianity (see "The Inspiration and Authority of the Bible").

The unity between the Testaments is therefore a unity of development. In the human personality there is growth and development. Yet despite the obvious marks of aging, senior citizens are the same persons they were at twenty. Likewise, the Bible is a unity within a process. In the Old Testament, for example, we find only the seeds of the doctrine of the Trinity rather than the full and explicit Trinitarianism of the New Testament (where Jesus and the Holy Spirit are revealed as God). Typically, what is foreshadowed in the Old Testament is more fully revealed in the New. This suffices to illustrate the kind of unity to be found in the Bible. It is a unity within diversity. Though we are focusing here on the unity, we do well to keep the diversity constantly in mind. The task of the Bible student is to do justice to the unity of Scripture without ignoring the elements of diversity. Neither element should be sacrificed to the other.

Approaches to the Problem of the Unity of the Bible

How the problem of the unity of the Bible has been understood in the history of the church needs to be considered. The problem particularly involves the relationship between the two Testaments. Solutions to this problem have taken various forms.

The Early Church and the Middle Ages

The question of the relationship between the Testaments was frequently posed in the early church. Adopting the New Testament as the basis of its faith, the early church faced the problem of how far the Old Testament was to be considered relevant.

Initially, both Testaments were accepted as Scripture. Old Testament texts were cited side by side with New Testament ones. In the second century, however, Marcion of Sinope challenged this view of unity. Influenced by the dualism of Gnosticism, Marcion preached a radical discontinuity between the Old and New Testaments (see the article on "Gnosticism"). For Marcion the god of Israel was not the Father of Jesus, nor was the law the gospel. Consistent with his theory, Marcion eliminated the Old Testament from his Bible, along with unacceptable (that is, Jewish) parts of the New Testament.

The church was quick to condemn Marcion as a heretic. Justin Martyr (ca. 100–165), for example, rejected Marcion's dualism and defended the unity of the Testa-

Martin Luther preaching while in refuge at the Wartburg Castle.

ments. Both Irenaeus (ca. 130–200) and Tertullian (ca. 160–220) considered Christ to be the link between the Testaments. Finally, Origen (ca. 185–254) defended the Old Testament against Marcion. Thus orthodoxy won the day, and the Old Testament was preserved as part of Christian Scripture.

Scholars in the Middle Ages generally understood the Bible as a unity. They frequently drew upon allegory to illumine the Old Testament. The New Testament was considered superior to, though continuous with, the Old Testament, much like the relationship of a tree to a seed. Both Testaments, however, gave a clear witness to Christ.

From the Reformation to the Modern Period

The authority and interpretation of the Bible became central issues of the Protestant Reformation. Not surprisingly, therefore, the question of the relationship between the two Testaments was reopened.

Martin Luther (1483–1546) accepted the unity of the Bible. But for him the diversity of Scripture was paramount. The Old Testament is to be praised as the ground and proof of the New Testament. But the New Testament alone is uniquely the book of grace and salvation; the Old Testament functions mainly to point men and women to the New Testament and to Christ.

In contrast to Luther, John Calvin (1509–1564) stressed the unity of the Bible, devoting a large portion of his *Institutes of the Christian Religion* to a discussion of the many similarities between the Testaments. The differences do not detract from the essential unity of the Bible.

In reaction to the Reformers, the Roman Catholic Counter-Reformation convened the Council of Trent (1546). The Council recognized the unity of the Bible but mandated that all biblical interpretation had to conform to the teaching of the Roman Church. The implications of this for the understanding of the relationship between the Testaments was that there was no allowance for further investigation of the problem.

In a sense the Council of Trent illustrated the growing tension between the champions of orthodoxy and more progressive thinkers. The Reformation brought new problems for the interpretation of the relationship between the Testaments. Although Calvin's view of the unity of the Bible was widely followed, an increasing number of theologians began to challenge traditional ways of interpreting the Bible.

In the seventeenth century rationalists such as Hobbes (1588–1679) and Spinoza (1632–1677) sought a more humanistic approach to the Bible. One consequence of this "humanizing" of Scripture was a readiness to reject less acceptable parts of the Old Testament. Lessing (1729–1781) and Kant (1724–1804) continued this trend in the eighteenth century. In the nineteenth century the famous German scholar Friedrich Schleiermacher (1768–1834) relegated the Old Testament to the status of an appendix to the New Testament. He asserted that the Old Testament Scriptures do not have the inspiration of the New. Schleiermacher's views came close to the wholesale rejection of the Old Testament espoused by Marcion.

As the twentieth century dawned, one basic approach to the relationship between the Testaments became widely accepted. This approach asserted the "progressive" nature of revelation. The Old Testament is needed but only in its relationship to the New. Hence the Old Testament is valid only in so far as it is fulfilled in Christ. The Old records an incomplete, progressive revelation; but the New is final and complete. Moreover, since the Old Testament is the record of a developing religion, it is to be interpreted historically.

In summary, at the beginning of the twentieth century scholars generally came to view the use of the Old Testament in relationship to the New Testament in three main ways. First, the Old Testament is the historical basis of the New. Second, an understanding of the language and theology of the Old Testament is essential to New Testament interpretation. Finally, the Old Testament witnesses to Christ. In short, the Old Testament has permanent value in that it prepares for the perfect revelation in Christ.

The Twentieth Century

Many scholars during the early years of the twentieth century accepted the progressive revelation approach described earlier. Yet dissenting voices were also to be heard.

The Fundamentalists of the early part of the twentieth century rejected critical scholarship but generally held to the concept of progressive revelation. The Roman Church reacted even more strongly to historical criticism, yet it too continued to view the Old Testament as the historical preparation for the New.

The work of two well-known German scholars introduced a radical devaluation of the Old Testament. Friedrich Delitzch and Adolph von Harnack resurrected the view of Marcion that the Old Testament should be excluded from the Christian Bible. In so doing they were taking the idea of progressive revelation to its logical, if also extreme, conclusion. Shortly thereafter the Nazis and the "German Christians" sought to eliminate every trace of Judaism from Christianity. The Nazi "Bible" excluded the Old Testament and any portions of the New Testament "stained" by Jewish elements. Scholars such as Karl Barth and Emil Brunner vigorously reacted to this Neo-Marcionism but to no avail.

In the aftermath of World War II, open attack upon the Old Testament all but disappeared. But more subtle ways of disposing of the Old Testament developed. Today many Christians, including Evangelicals, consider the Old and New Testaments to belong to two different religions. Scholars still vigorously debate the significance of the Old Testament for the Christian faith. It can at least be said, however, that the existence of a theological relationship between the two Testaments of the Christian Bible is an assured result of evangelical scholarship.

The Old Testament View of the New Testament

The Old Testament has much to say about its relationship to the New. Although the Old Testament was very much concerned with the past, it had a forward-looking aspect as well.

First, a significant aspect of Old Testament faith was its expectation of God's activity in the future. This is seen in such passages as Genesis 12:1-3; Numbers 24; Deuteronomy 24; 2 Samuel 7; and Psalms 2; 45; 68; 110. This view of the future is essentially optimistic, anticipating material and political as well as spiritual blessing. It presupposes that God was active in the history of Israel and that He will act in the future as He has acted in the past.

Second, within this framework of future expectation there developed a prophetic expectation that God would intervene in the future in an entirely new way. This development is sometimes referred to as "prophetic eschatology." The term *eschatology* refers to a radical change to be brought about by God in the future.

The prophets of Israel introduced both a new pessimism (God would radically judge the nation) and a new optimism (God would provide a new creation and a new salvation). This prophetic eschatology had four major features. (1) The *time* of God's intervention in human history will be "the day of the Lord" (Isa 13:6,9; Zeph 1:7,14), "the day of vengeance" (Isa 34:8; Jer 46:10), or simply "that day" (Ezek 29:21). (2) The *person* God will send to meet the nation's political and spiritual needs will be the Messiah, perceived as the Son of David (2 Sam 7; Isa 9:11) and the Servant of the Lord (Isa 42; 49; 50; 53). (3) The *place* where this renewal will occur will be the land of Israel (Isa 62:4; Jer 30:3; Ezek 20:45), and especially the holy city (Isa 60–66; Ezek 40–48; Mic 4:1-2). (4) Finally, the *people* involved will be the nation of Israel, once exiled but now restored and enjoying a new covenant made by God (Isa 7:3; Jer 23:3; 30–33; Ezek 16:16).

In summary, in the Old Testament period there arose an expectation that God would intervene in Israel's history to bring about a radical renewal. In the writings of the prophets, both judgment and salvation are portrayed with unparalleled clarity. The hard realities of life caused many to look beyond the present age to a new age to be inaugurated by God.

The New Testament View of the Old Testament

If the Old Testament anticipates the New, the New Testament clearly looks back to the Old. The New Testament writers firmly believed that the Messiah had come, that the day of the Lord had arrived, and that the people of God were about to be renewed.

This conviction of the New Testament writers is nicely summarized in Luke 24:44: "Everything must be fulfilled that is written about me in the Law of Moses, the Prophets and the Psalms." The result of this pronouncement of Jesus was that the historical and theological basis for the New Testament became the writings of the Old Testament.

The New Testament apostles, all of whom were Jews, understood that the Old Testament in itself was incomplete. Yet the Old Testament looked forward to its own completion by an act of God outside its limits. This new act would be similar to, yet radically different from, earlier acts of God described in the Old Testament. It would, however, be performed by the same God who acted in Israel's history and whose deeds were recorded in their Scriptures. Hence in the messianic predictions of the Old Testament, as well as in the more general "types" of His own person and work, Jesus saw His life and ministry foreshadowed.

The New Testament apostles, following the example of their Lord, presupposed the Old Testament as the basis of their newfound faith. Likewise, the early church recognized both the Old and New Testaments as equally Christian Scripture. These early believers did not deny that there are differences between the two Testaments. Instead, they affirmed that in terms of revelation the two Testaments are one. Both are united in their history and theology. The concern of both is with the people of God. And most important of all, the distinctive claim of the New Testament that Jesus is the Messiah is based on the Law and the Prophets. The unity of the Bible may therefore be summarized as follows: the Old and New Testaments are equally Scripture in that both point to Christ, the center of Christian faith.

Thematic Unity

Evidence of the unity of the Bible is to be found in its teachings on various themes. Several of these are presented here.

The Doctrine of God

When we examine the Bible as a whole, we find a remarkable degree of unity about its doctrine of God. For example, the belief in monotheism (there is only one God) is characteristic of the whole Bible. The worship of one God was established in Israel (Exod 20:3; Deut 5:7). This teaching is carried over into the New Testament. For the apostles, monotheism in no way menaced the New Testament teaching on the deity of Christ. Jesus could be "with God" yet also "God" (John 1:1). In the Godhead there is a unity of essence but a distinction of Persons. But there is still only one God, manifested in Father, Son, and Holy Spirit. Hence the New Testament denies both unitarianism (only the Father is God) and tritheism (there are three Gods).

If the Bible teaches that there is only one God, it also teaches that He is a God of love and forgiveness. God is a saving God. The unity of the Bible is to a large degree the attestation of that fact. From beginning to end the Bible asserts God's saving purpose. The sin of humankind is the starting point of this activity. A backsliding and rebellious Israel could not defeat God's purpose but carried it on to surer completion.

This plan of salvation finds its conclusion and fulfillment in the person and work of Jesus Christ. It is this aspect of Scripture—this story of salvation—that makes the Bible distinct from all other "bibles" of pagan religions. These reveal no order or plan. They embody no historical revelation of God working out His saving purposes. The Bible, by contrast, is a unity because it is the record of a progressive revelation of the will of God for humankind's salvation. The Bible is, in short, a "gospel" in the fullest sense of the word.

The New Covenant

The Bible, as we have seen, is concerned essentially with the story of salvation. Prophesied in the Old Testament, this salvation was achieved by Christ at the cross. The covenant that was sealed in His blood is something "new." Yet this New Covenant corresponds to the Old Covenant. Once again, there is both continuity and discontinuity. Jesus claimed that He fulfilled much of the Old Testament (Matt 5:17-20).

Paradoxically, however, this supersession finds its roots in the Old Testament (compare Heb 8 with Jer 31). Thus in the very supersession of the Old, the bond between the Old and the New is clearly to be found. The New carries the principles of the Old further, but it does not contradict the law. Hence in the establishment of the new covenant through the blood of Christ, we have the fulfillment of something that was promised in the Old Testament.

The Death of Christ

In the cross of Christ, then, we have the fullest expression of the love and justice of God. And in the teaching of the Old Testament we have the clearest foreshadowing of this event. The death of Christ is inseparably linked with the concept of Old Testament sacrifice. Hence the New Testament thinks of the death of Jesus in terms of the Passover lamb (John 1:29).

The death of Christ was the climax and crown of the Old Testament sacrificial system. The author of Hebrews insists that the shedding of blood was necessary for redemption (Heb 9:22). Likewise, Paul recorded that the death of Christ was an offering and a sacrifice unto God (Eph 5:2).

These interpretations of the cross are directly linked to the Old Testament Passover ritual. When the sacrifice was rightly provided, it was the power of God to forgive sin. In the same manner, Christ became the sin offering on our behalf in order that we might be made righteous (2 Cor 5:21). Only the Old Testament provides the background for the understanding of the death of Christ as it is set forth in the New Testament. This is one of the strongest marks of the unity of the Bible.

Conclusion

The doctrine of the unity and variety of the Bible has now been outlined. We can see many reasons to accept the Bible as a literary, historical, and theological whole.

We have not denied the existence of marked differences between the Testaments. Yet tensions between monotheism and trinitarianism, between old creation and new creation, between Old Covenant and New Covenant do not overturn the essential oneness of Scripture. The Old Testament concept of God is consistent with faith in Christ. God is the only Creator and the Author of both Covenants. The same God who called Israel into existence has called the church into being.

The theological problem of the relationship between the Testaments is solved in the person of Jesus Himself. He is the center of all biblical revelation. In Him we find not merely the difference between the Testaments but the glue that holds them together. It is therefore unnecessary and irreverent to assert the priority of one Testament over the other. The New Testament is not merely an interpretative supplement to the Old. Nor is the Old Testament merely the preface to the New. Both Testaments are bound together by divine Providence into one Bible.

The implications of the unity of the Bible should be obvious. The tendency among Evangelical Christians, who acknowledge Scripture as authoritative, is to plead for a return to *New* Testament Christianity. The Old and New Testaments are often thought of as belonging to two different religions. Moreover, new Bible translations almost always begin with the New Testament, and some never reach the Old. On a more basic level, there is an increasing tendency to ignore the Old Testament in preaching. These practices are clearly misguided in light of the unity of the two Testaments. New Testament believers need to do more to acknowledge this unity so that the Old Testament may be given its rightful place in the Christian Bible.

Sources for Additional Study

Baker, D. L. *Two Testaments, One Bible*. Downers Grove: InterVarsity, 1976.

Bruce, F. F. *The Canon of Scripture*. Downers Grove: InterVarsity, 1988.

Fuller, Daniel. *The Unity of the Bible*. Grand Rapids: Zondervan, 1991.

Sloan, Robert B. "Unity in Diversity" in *New Testament Criticism and Interpretation*, edited by D. A. Black and D. S. Dockery. Grand Rapids: Zondervan, 1991.

Jesus Christ and the Bible

The criterion by which the Bible is to be interpreted is Jesus Christ. This declaration offers a doctrinal guideline specifying the relationship between Jesus Christ and the Bible.

Like most important doctrinal statements, this declaration raises new questions as it attempts to resolve old ones. The obvious question that now emerges is, *How* does Jesus Christ serve as the criterion by which Christians should interpret the Bible? We will seek to offer some answers to this basic but challenging question.

Organization

The subject of Jesus Christ and the Bible may be divided into two parts. We will call the first part the *historical question.* This part deals with the issue of how Jesus used the Bible during His ministry. Since none of the New Testament was written until after our Lord's death and resurrection, the historical question becomes, How did Jesus use the Old Testament in His ministry?

The second part of the subject of Jesus Christ and the Bible may be labeled the *hermeneutical question.* Hermeneutics refers to the theory of the interpretation of texts. So biblical hermeneutics is thinking about the process of how one interprets the Scriptures. If Jesus Christ is "the criterion by which the Bible is to be interpreted," then there is a special relationship between Jesus Christ and the way Christians should interpret the entire Bible. We will analyze this special relationship in the latter part of this article.

The Historical Question

Canonization of the Old Testament

The process by which first Jews and later Christians came to recognize the books of the Hebrew Bible and Greek Septuagint as canonical (that is, as Holy Scripture) is a long and complex one. The finalization of the Old Testament canon—the list and arrangement of books first in the Hebrew Bible and then in its translation and expansion in the Greek Septuagint—was not complete in Jesus' day. Most of the Law and Prophets were complete, although many of the Writings (for example, the Psalms) were probably not in their final form (that is, the form in which we have them in the Old Testament today). The Bible Jesus knew and used was written in the form of scrolls made of animal skins, not in the book form (technically called a codex) in which we now read the Old Testament.

Historical Study and Theological Interpretation

Christian scholars are divided over the question of how many of the Old Testament Scriptures cited in the Gospels are sayings of Jesus and how many are biblical citations of the early church. These divisions usually reveal more about a particular scholar's hermeneutical and theological assumptions than they do about the obscure question of who really is responsible for the first citation of a specific Old Testament passage. In these disputes scholars are trying to "get behind" the text of Scripture and reconstruct what happened to produce the final form of the text we have in the Bible.

In terms of theological interpretation it would seem wise to take the final form of the Bible as we know it today and use that text as the norm against which all historical reconstruction and all later interpretations are to be tested. This approach sees scholars' debates about "what really happened when" as an important stage in biblical interpretation but not as the ultimate goal of interpretation. Critical-historical study uncovers the "archaeology of the text," the underlying factors leading to its formation. The history of interpretation analyzes levels of meaning of the text—the changing understanding and application of the Scripture throughout the centuries. The ultimate goal of theological interpretation is the discerning of the meaning(s) of the text as Holy Scripture to us today.

This complex relationship between critical-historical study and the theological interpretation of Scripture may be clarified by thinking of the analogy of growing a flower garden. To grow a garden one needs to use a variety of tools to break up and prepare the soil. The initial seed, hidden in the ground, must then be carefully protected and nurtured day after day if eventually it is going to blossom into a beautiful flower.

Similarly, in order to understand the meaning of Scripture, the critical tools of historical study enable us to break up and prepare the text. The Word of God, hidden in the text, has been carefully protected and nurtured in the interpretation of Jewish and Christian communities for generation after generation. The end result is the flowering of God's Word, as the Scriptures speak to the people of God today. Theological interpretation of Scripture should enable the Christian minister to show people the flowers that bloom from the prayerful and critical study of the biblical text.

Jesus and the Old Testament

Some evangelical scholars maintain that Jesus was familiar with most of our Old Testament and treated it all equally as history. This view, however, claims less than the biblical evidence shows. Jesus' creative use of the Old Testament was not limited to a flat reading of historical facts but involved a divinely inspired reinterpretation and application of the Scriptures as God's Word to each new situation.

Jesus as Creative Interpreter

Instead of a narrow historical-facts-only approach, many conservative Christian scholars would tend to see Jesus as the "creative mind" behind the entire process of the early church's interpretation of the Old Testament, both in the New Testament and throughout the early centuries of church history.

C. H. Dodd (*According to the Scriptures* [New York: Scribner's, 1953], 109-11) describes this view:

> At the earliest period of church history to which we can gain access, we find in being the rudiments of an original, coherent and flexible method of biblical exegesis which was already beginning to yield results . . . This is a piece of genuinely creative thinking. Who was responsible for it? The early church, we are accustomed to say, and perhaps we can safely say no more. But creative thinking is rarely done by committees . . . the New Testament itself avers that it was Jesus Christ Himself who first directed the minds of His followers to certain parts of their Scriptures as those in which they might find illumination upon the meaning of His mission and destiny . . . To account for the beginning of this most original and fruitful process of rethinking the Old Testament we found need to postulate a creative mind. The Gospels offer us one. Are we compelled to reject the offer?

Jesus' Interpretive Methods

The New Testament portrays Jesus as using a variety of creative, interpretive approaches to the Old Testament. Many of these approaches are similar to those of other Jewish rabbis who interpreted the Hebrew Scriptures. For example, the Jewish authors of the Qumran (Dead Sea) scrolls used a method of interpretation called *pesher* exegesis. The *pesher* is a compact oracle in which *this* passage in the Scriptures is *that* event the Qumran community could see in their own history. From the beginning announcement of His ministry (Luke 4:16-21) and throughout the Gospels, we can see Jesus interpreting His ministry and the events of His day in a similar manner.

The most familiar rabbinic method of interpretation is *midrash,* which seeks to make the Hebrew Bible relevant to contemporary society by citing a host of rabbinical legal opinions, applications, and commentary. Although Jesus did not seek to produce a verse-by-verse legal commentary on Scripture, He shared the rabbis' concern for applying Scripture to the situations of His time. That concern is particularly reflected in the fulfillment of Scripture described in the Gospel of Matthew (1:22; 2:15,17,23; 8:17; 12:17; 13:35; 21:4; 26:54,56; 27:9).

Jesus and the Targums

In addition, Jesus' creative biblical interpretation seems to have made use of early traditions related to the Targums—Aramaic paraphrases of the books of the Hebrew Bible. The Targums were developed for use in worship in the synagogues and so were perhaps closer to the religious faith of the common people of Palestine than the more scholarly rabbinical interpretations of early Judaism.

The Targums were compiled several generations after the time of Jesus. Jesus was not bound to the letter of the biblical text but was free to follow the contemporary interpretation and application of the Old Testament to the culture of His day.

Jesus' Use of Typology

A final major method of biblical interpretation used by our Lord is typology. Essentially this method consists of seeing a pattern (type) in one person or event that is connected to a later person or event (antitype).

Scholars have long debated the nature of the connection involved in typology and how one distinguishes it from the "parallelomania" of allegory, which can manufacture a connection between anything in the Old Testament and anything in the New Testament. The key seems to be in showing some sort of *historical* connection between the type and antitype. This historical connection prevents the loss of hermeneutical control found in some of the wildly fantastic interpretations of later allegory. For instance, Origen claimed to find the "soul of Christ" in

NEW TESTAMENT REFERENCES TO JESUS CHRIST	
HIS RELATION TO THE OLD TESTAMENT	"It is written . . ." (Matt 4:4). "Do not think that I have come to abolish the Law or the Prophets; I have not come to abolish them but to fulfill them" (Matt 5:17). "Beginning with Moses and all the Prophets, he explained to them what was said in all the Scriptures concerning himself" (Luke 24:27). "These are the Scriptures that testify about me" (John 5:39). "If you believed Moses, you would believe me, for he wrote about me" (John 5:46). "Scripture cannot be broken" (John 10:35).
HIS DEITY	"In the beginning was the Word, and the Word was with God, and the Word was God" (John 1:1). "My Lord and my God!" (John 20:28). "Christ, who is God over all" (Rom 9:5). "Jesus Christ is Lord" (Phil 2:11). "By him all things were created" (Col 1:16).
HIS HUMANITY	"The Word became flesh and made his dwelling among us" (John 1:14). "She gave birth to her firstborn, a son. She wrapped him in cloths and placed him in a manger, because there was no room for them in the inn" (Luke 2:7). "The child grew and became strong" (Luke 2:40). "As they sailed, he fell asleep" (Luke 8:23). "Jesus, tired as he was from the journey, sat down by the well" (John 4:6). "We have one who has been tempted in every way, just as we are–yet without sin" (Heb 4:15).

the "fatty parts" of the sacrificial calf of Leviticus!

R. T. France has surveyed the great variety of typological interpretations attributed to Jesus in the Gospels. France shows that this great diversity of interpretation points away from Jesus' use of any uniform method of typology and toward a variety of ways of expressing a historical and "theological conviction working itself out in practice" (*Jesus and the Old Testament*, 77). This conviction sees a correspondence between the people, institutions, and events of the Old Testament and the historical person of Jesus and the events surrounding His ministry.

The Hermeneutical Question

Looking at Jesus' interpretive methods—particularly His use of typology—soon brings us face-to-face with the question of *our own* interpretive approaches. How do we understand and use the whole Bible as the authority and guide for our Christian faith and practice? This leads to the hermeneutical question of Jesus Christ and the Bible: If Jesus Christ is "the criterion by which the Bible is to be interpreted," then what is the special relationship between Jesus Christ and the way Christians should interpret the Scriptures?

Christocentric Interpretation

The most simple and direct answer to the hermeneutical question is offered by Christocentric interpretation—biblical interpretation that puts Christ at the center of our understanding of Scripture. We must move beyond our fallible historical efforts to recover and our feeble attempts to reproduce Jesus' creative methods of biblical interpretation. For Jesus Christ is not merely a *model* for our biblical interpretation. He is the main *theme* and ultimate *goal* of our study of Scripture. All of our study of the Bible originates from our faith in Christ and refers back to our faith in Christ as the final test for the conclusions.

We must be careful to distinguish this thoughtful, prayerful, and historically informed Christocentric interpretation from a wild and uncontrolled pious imagination. Such pious imagination seeks to find the person of Jesus everywhere in the Bible—even in the "fatty parts" of the sacrificial calf of Leviticus. Instead, thoughtful Christocentric interpretation first seeks to understand a passage of Scripture in its own historical horizon and development and then *evaluates* interpretive conclusions by the criterion of Jesus Christ.

A Biblical Example

A simple example of this Christocentric approach may be found in the struggle for an adequate Christian interpretation of the conclusion of Psalm 137. The psalm says: "O Daughter of Babylon, doomed to destruction, happy is he who repays you for what you have done to us—he who seizes your infants and dashes them against the rocks" (Ps 137:8-9).

Compare this passage with Jesus' command in the Sermon on the Mount: "You have heard that it was said, 'Love your neighbor and hate your enemy.' But I tell you: Love your enemies and pray for those who persecute you" (Matt 5:43-44). If Jesus Christ is to be the criterion by which the Bible is to be interpreted, clearly the literal meaning of the psalm must be subordinated to the command of our Lord. Smashing the children of one's enemy against the rock stands in direct opposition and contradiction to loving one's enemy. The psalm must be evaluated by the criterion of Jesus Christ.

Perhaps we may try to spiritualize the psalm to deal with this opposition. Like the Christian monks who prayed it every day, we might take the "infants" to refer to our own sinful thoughts, which must be smashed against the rocks. In any case, the interpretation of this difficult passage must be evaluated and brought into conformity with the criterion of Jesus Christ.

Classical Reformation Approaches

Although the Reformation preceded the rise of modern historical-critical study of the Bible, there is much we can learn about the relationship of Jesus Christ and the Bible from the Reformers' enduring biblical interpretation. The Reformation cry of *sola Scriptura!*—Scripture alone!—was accompanied by some major advances in biblical hermeneutics.

Martin Luther, through his rediscovery of Paul's teaching of justification by faith, elevated our saving relationship to Jesus Christ to the central place in biblical interpretation. The Word of God in Scripture is what drives us to Christ. For Luther the fundamental hermeneutical rule is that Scripture is its own interpreter. The critical perspective for Luther's salvation-centered interpretation was his discovery of a gracious God. This discovery occurs in the experience of salvation through justification by faith. Whatever in the Bible does not seem to fit with this pattern (for example, the "right strawy epistle" of James) is relegated to secondary status in the canon. So Luther developed a "canon-within-the-canon" hermeneutical approach.

Through his emphasis on the sovereignty of God and our election to salvation in Jesus Christ, John Calvin moved away from Luther's canon-within-the-canon approach. For Calvin it was not our experience of justification but God's election of us "before the creation of the world" (Eph 1:4) that is the point of reference in our saving relationship to Jesus Christ. Therefore the whole of Scripture becomes a stage upon which the divine drama of salvation is enacted. The careful interpreter will find Jesus Christ present throughout the Old as well as within the New Testament.

A Theological Example

Calvin's Christocentric interpretation is clearly revealed in this sample passage concerning Jewish rites in the Old Testament. It is taken from his famous *Institutes of the Christian Religion* (book 4, chap. 14, p. 21):

> For the Jews, circumcision was the symbol by which they were admonished that whatever comes forth from man's seed, that is the whole nature of mankind, is corrupt and needs pruning. Moreover, circumcision was a token and reminder to confirm them in the promise given to Abraham of the blessed seed in which all nations of the earth were to be blessed [Gen 22:18], from whom they were also to await their own blessing. *Now that saving seed* (as we are taught by Paul) *was Christ* [Gal 3:16], in whom alone they trusted that they were to recover what they had lost in Adam. Accordngly, circumcision was the same thing to them as in Paul's teaching it was to Abraham, namely, a sign of the righteousness of faith [Rom 4:11]; that is, a seal by which they are assured that their faith, with which they awaited that seed, is accounted to them as righteousness by God . . . Baptisms and purifications disclose to them their own uncleanness, foulness, and pollution, with which they were defiled in their own nature; but these rites promised another cleansing by which all their filth would be removed and washed away [Heb 9:10-14]. *And this cleansing was Christ.* Washed by his blood [1 John 1:7; Rev 1:5], we bring his purity before our sight to cover our defilements.

Calvin's Christocentric theory of interpretation enabled him to move across the Bible in one unbroken stride from Genesis to Revelation in this sample passage. Paul's interpretation of Christ in Galatians is the pivot upon which Calvin's discovery of Christ in the Jewish rite of circumcision turns. For Calvin, however, Christ was

Jesus teaching from a boat

not only found in the rite of circumcision but in all the Jewish rites of purification. Christian scholars today would have historical difficulties with Calvin's all-too-easy identification of Jesus Christ hidden throughout the Old Testament. Nevertheless, the capacity of a Christocentric approach to discover theological unity within the historical diversity of the Bible contributes greatly toward our response to the hermeneutical question of the relationship between Jesus Christ and the Bible.

A Canonical Approach

Since the time of the Reformation a host of Christian scholars have offered a great variety of responses to the hermeneutical question. Among the most valuable recent responses is a canonical approach to the question.

Canonical hermeneutics offers a helpful contemporary way of centering biblical interpretation around Jesus Christ. The canonical approach focuses on the ways in which past communities of faith *theologically* shaped and interpreted the texts of the Bible as Holy Scripture (canon). The canonical shape of the Bible provides the context for theological interpretation. For Christian communities biblical interpretation proceeds from the faith assumption of the lordship of Jesus Christ. Theological interpretation of Scripture thus becomes "faith seeking understanding." Jesus Christ, the incarnate Word of God, is the One to whom the written Word of God bears witness. Therefore, the "old, old story of Jesus" becomes in itself the criterion for understanding and interpreting God's Word for us today.

Sources for Additional Study

Calvin, John. *Institutes of the Christian Religion.* Edited by John T. McNeill. Translated by Ford Lewis Battles. Philadelphia: Westminster, 1960.

Childs, Brevard S. *Introduction to the Old Testament as Scripture.* Philadelphia: Fortress, 1979.

———. *The New Testament as Canon: An Introduction.* Philadelphia: Fortress, 1985.

France, R. T. *Jesus and the Old Testament: His Application of Old Testament Passages to Himself and His Mission.* Downers Grove: InterVarsity, 1971.

Lampe, G. W. H. and K. J. Woolcombe. *Essays on Typology.* London: SCM, 1957.

Longenecker, R. N. "Can We Reproduce the Exegesis of the New Testament?" *Tyndale Bulletin* 21 (1970): 3-38.

Wenham, John W. *Christ and the Bible.* Downers Grove: InterVarsity, 1973.

PART II

THE BIBLE IN ITS WORLD

ANCIENT CIVILIZATIONS

A discussion of world civilizations must be guided by two important observations. First, numerous cultures will be omitted from our study because they were not important for biblical history, our primary interest here. Some cultures were too far removed geographically from the land of the Bible to play a discernible role in the biblical account. Other cultures existed long before or long after the story of the Bible and are not pertinent to our discussion.

Second, we will restrict our discussion to that of civilization as it can be historically treated. Few people believe that humanity began at the end of the fourth millennium B.C., but that is the absolute earliest "history" can be said to exist. History can only be studied when texts exist for the historian to analyze. Before the end of the fourth millennium, no written texts existed. Archaeologists and anthropologists have unearthed a great deal of evidence that "prehistoric" humanity was alive, prospering, and surprisingly adept at managing the environment. Moreover, scientists can derive much information from the ruins of ancient dwellings. But without texts these scholars can never reconstruct the history of the people who dwelt there. The best the anthropologist could do would be to draw certain conclusions about the site's material culture. With these restrictions in mind, we turn to several of the most influential cultures in the ancient world.

The Sumerian King List (second millennium B.C.) gives a chronological list of the Sumerian kings before and after the flood.

Sumer

History Begins at Sumer was the appropriate title of a famous work authored by S. N. Kramer some years ago, since Sumer was the womb of civilization. Nestled deep in Mesopotamia, Sumer lay near where the Tigris and Euphrates Rivers drained into the Persian Gulf, present-day Iraq. We know from their language that the Sumerians were not related to the other Semitic peoples who populated Mesopotamia for millennia. These people dominated Mesopotamia culturally from before 3000 B.C. until at least 2000 B.C. Indeed, the origin and demise of the Sumerian people are part of ancient history's greatest mysteries.

With no exaggeration one can say that the influence of the Sumerians is still felt today. The Sumerians were the first culture whose written texts have been discovered, and they were also some of the most sophisticated people we might meet. A peace-loving people, the Sumerians developed extensive trade throughout the known world and became one of the world's greatest economic powers. However, the Sumerians are not admired today primarily for their economic accomplishments. They are appreciated because of the intellectual legacy they left. They developed a lengthy and well-organized educational system. But their most important contribution was the invention of writing. These innovative people developed a writing system using a reed and soft clay, making wedged-shaped symbolic impressions called *cuneiform*.

The Sumerian system of writing was soon adopted by

other Semitic peoples (most importantly the Assyrians), who used it to enhance their own cultures. It is difficult to overemphasize the role writing played in the advancement of humanity.

A deeply religious people, the Sumerians built numerous temples to their many gods, often in the form of ziggurats, or man-made mountains, on which their deities could reside. Other major areas of interest known to us are in the fields of medicine, geography, and law. Sumerian government was ordered in the form of a city-state led by a king. The Sumerians were even interested in agriculture, with a "farmer's almanac" that has been discovered telling young farmers how best to get a good crop.

Another leading Sumerian contribution was in the area of literature. The Sumerians were highly appreciative of beautiful literature; widely divergent types have been discovered. One of the most significant for our interests is that of wisdom. The Sumerians loved proverbial literature, not unlike that found in the Book of Proverbs. Other types of wisdom are more like narrative, with one lament being named by modern scholars "Job." We should note also that Ur, Abraham's home according to Genesis 11:28, was in Sumer.

Old Babylon

Old Babylon is not to be confused with the Babylon in the sixth and seventh centuries B.C., which was a renaissance of Old Babylonian culture. As the name indicates, it was a Semitic civilization. This empire developed directly from the Sumerian people, although they were not related ethnically. In fact, the Babylonians owed most of what they knew and possessed to the great Sumerian people.

The connection can be clearly demonstrated today in several areas. For one, the Babylonians adopted cuneiform and modified it to meet the need of their language. The important law codes from earlier days evolved into the imposing Code of Hammurabi, the single most important king from this period. This collection of laws shows some similarities to biblical law, but the spirit of the laws is different. Hammurabi generally dealt more severely with property crimes, whereas the Bible treats crimes against God and humanity much more seriously than did the Hammurabi laws.

The Old Babylonian culture also depended upon Sumer for its literature and religion. The well-known religious epics dealing with the creation of the world, *Enuma Elish* (see "Creation and Flood Stories") and the flood account (the *Gilgamesh Epic*) are both known to have become prominent in Old Babylonian times. They both depend on earlier forms. Even the types of deities worshiped, the most important of which was the sun god, were imported from Sumer.

Tablet XI of the Gilgamesh Epic tablets found at Nineveh which contains a Babylonian version of the great flood.

Egypt

Of all the civilizations in the ancient world, perhaps no culture achieved more spectacular results in material terms than did Egypt. The imposing pyramids and stately sphinx are examples. In fact, Egypt's main contributions were in terms of its material culture.

Located in northernmost Africa, Egypt came to exist as a result of the mighty Nile, a river four thousand miles long that brought life to the desert. So important was the Nile to Egypt that it was worshiped as a life-giving deity whose annual flooding irrigated the land and whose silt replenished the soil without the need of fertilization. The localization of the Egyptian people (who were not Semites) around the river was so extreme and the surrounding desert was so harsh that Egypt remained rather isolated culturally.

The most important period in Egypt's history was the Old Kingdom (2700–2200 B.C.), known also as the Pyramid Age. In this era the pharaoh was worshiped unquestionably as god incarnate. This blind allegiance gave the pharaoh sufficient power to spend the majority of the national economy for a lifetime on a tomb for himself, a pyramid. Obviously this course of events could not go on indefinitely because any people would eventually begin to doubt such beliefs and because no economy could sustain such a tremendous drain.

Egyptian society is known for its general contributions in several areas. Certainly pride of place should go to architecture since the aesthetics and construction techniques are admired to this day. The Egyptians produced some art, but most was fashioned to adorn the pharaoh's tomb. While not as prolific literarily as other cultures, the

The sphinx and pyramids of Giza, Egypt, are testimony to the architectural expertise of the ancient Egyptians. They are seen here spotlighted in the dark of the Egyptian night.

Egyptians did produce some notable pieces of literature. For instance, the Egyptians were deeply concerned with defending the character qualities of individuals, most notably deceased ones, in the funerary texts. The Egyptians also admired wisdom literature, among the most important of which was the Wisdom of Amenemope, which is similar to the text of Proverbs 22–24.

Assyria

Semitic cultures continued, although in an unimpressive fashion, from the time of Old Babylon until the beginnings of the Assyrian Empire. In 859 B.C. Shalmaneser III began a ruthless policy of divide and conquer that would last for about two centuries. The court annals of such kings as Tiglath-Pileser III (744–727 B.C.) and Shalmaneser V (727–722 B.C.), who defeated and exiled Israel, are full of boasts about the quantity of heads in piles, the number of pregnant women ripped open, and the quantity of little ones who had been "dashed against the rocks." No wonder the mere mention of Assyria brought fear to all in their day.

Babylon

Neo-Babylon prevailed from 626–539 B.C. This Semitic civilization built upon the political power structure left by the Assyrians and expanded upon it with a lessened degree of violence. The Babylonians were much more intellectual than were the Assyrians. They were deeply interested in the study of the heavenly bodies. They also pursued the sciences and mathematics, developing a numerical system based on the number six, unlike our decimal system, which is based on ten. The Babylonian King Nebuchadnezzar is infamous for crushing Jerusalem and imposing a severe exile on all of Judah's leaders.

Persia

The Persians reigned from 539 B.C., when Cyrus the Great conquered the Babylonians, until 330 B.C., when the Greeks defeated them. These people were non-Semitic and are best remembered for overseeing a far-flung empire with a minimum of harsh treatment for the subservient peoples. A good example of this is Cyrus's decree allowing the exiles to return to Israel after the end of the Babylonian captivity. These people are also known for their development of astrology.

Greece

One of civilization's most surprising events was the emergence of Greece to become an intellectual giant. Greece is located on a rocky, barren peninsula in the Aegean Sea; therefore geography alone served to isolate the Greeks from most of the world in their earliest history. Their beginnings are unknown, but the period from 1100–800 B.C. is regarded as their Dark Ages.

One major contribution the Greeks made was governmental, the city-state. The extreme isolation imposed by the rugged geography fostered an amazing cultural development. Two of Greece's most important city-states were Athens, which was noted for its intellectual life, and Sparta, known for its rigorous, militarism.

Another striking development was philosophical. The Greek outlook on life was one of the first to be regarded as logical and empirical in the modern sense. The Greek was supremely concerned with that which was "the good" in life. The unexamined life was not worth living. Literature was also highly developed, so much so that the standards of literature developed by the Greeks themselves are utilized today. Moreover, Greek philosophy and literature were so imposing that the Romans adopted them wholesale upon their domination of the Greeks. Politically speaking, the Greek intellectual achievements had so pervasive an influence largely because Philip of Macedon (359–336 B.C.) and his son Alexander the Great (336–323 B.C.) conquered the known world and resolved to Hellenize these areas completely.

Rome

In broad terms the Roman Empire spanned the period from the eighth century B.C. to the fifth century A.D., representing what was perhaps the single most influential culture in history. Rome was founded, according to legend, in 753 B.C. on the Tiber River. Its true history began around 500 B.C., when the Etruscans, an imperfectly known, intelligent people, were expelled. A republic was established with a senate appointed to govern, a practice that would prevail through most of the Empire's history. In the ensuing centuries Rome consolidated its power over numerous foes, the most influential of which were the Phoenicians. For most of the third century Rome fought with the Phoenicians, with the second century seeing major conflicts with the Macedonians and Syrians.

As the second century B.C. came to a close, the Roman republic came to a close. It was followed by a dictatorial form of government led by a series of caesars. One

The Parthenon, dedicated to the goddess Athena, has dominated the Acropolis in Athens, Greece, since the fifth century B.C.

of the most important of these caesars was Augustus, who oversaw one of the longest periods of peace in Roman history, from 27 B.C. to A.D. 14. During this period of relative tranquility, Christ was born. Some of the following caesars such as Nero (A.D. 54–68) and Domitian (A.D. 81–96) were known for their tumultuous reigns, not to mention their persecution of Christians.

As the Empire began to age, corruption increasingly became a major part of Roman life. This led to a greater role for the military until the state was controlled by the army. Probably the most important leader in the latter part of the Empire was Constantine (A.D. 306–337), who is best known for his adoption of Christianity.

The legacy of the Romans is so great that it is difficult to calculate. Such diverse areas as architecture, literature, science, medicine, agriculture, and law were so great that their culture influenced our own more than any other ancient culture. Both our government and language also owe a great debt to Rome.

Sources for Additional Study

Hallo, William W. and William Kelly Simpson. *The Ancient Near East: A History.* New York: Harcourt, Brace, Jovanovich, 1971.

Starr, Chester G. *A History of the Ancient World.* New York: Oxford University Press, 1983.

The Cambridge Ancient History. 12 Vols. New York: Cambridge University Press, 1971.

Ancient Near Eastern Religions

Speaking definitively about the origin of religion in the ancient Near East is impossible since scant written records remain from this time. Moreover, it is impossible to speak descriptively of any religion that left no written account of its beliefs and practices. Students of the history of religions cannot accurately reconstruct the beliefs of a group when all that is left for examination is a drawing on a cave wall or a piece of pottery that appears to have had a cultic use. Every religion dating prior to 2500–3000 B.C. was too early to leave such texts and must remain the subject of conjecture.

In this study our focus will be upon ancient Near Eastern religions and not upon the religion of ancient Israel. The faith of Israel is accurately attested in the Old Testament. We will examine the faiths of Mesopotamia, Egypt, and religions of the regions that coexisted with Israel in and around the land of Palestine.

Mesopotamia

In Mesopotamia, as in every other land, religion was always closely allied with culture. In Mesopotamia this was particularly true in that cultural conventions, political activity, economic interchange, and religious practices were inseparable. These diverse areas of Mesopotamian life converged at the local temple.

No structure in any Mesopotamian city ranked higher in importance than did the temple. Not even the royal palace received the prominence enjoyed by the local house of the gods. Located centrally within each major city, the Mesopotamian temple, known as a ziggurat, was seen as a stair-stepped sacred mountain worshipers could ascend in order to be nearer the gods. These towering structures were architecturally feasible due to the development of sun-dried bricks. For a biblical illustration of this process, see Genesis 11:1-9.

Under the control of both priests and king, temple activity was responsible for recording historical data that is our primary basis today for reconstructing secular and religious aspects of Mesopotamian society. In addition to economic and political texts found in these ancient temples, most of the literary texts from this period stem from the temple. Scribal schools were traditionally allied with the temple, which was concerned with promoting the difficult skill of cuneiform writing for the general economic/political and religious welfare of the temple.

Throughout Mesopotamian history religious beliefs were characterized by polytheism, the belief in and worship of multiple deities. At times religion bordered on henotheism, the worship of a single deity without denying the existence of other deities. However, there never developed a true monotheism, the exclusive belief in and worship of only one god, as occurred in Israel.

When we examine Mesopotamian religious texts, we are struck by the overwhelming complexity and diversity of religious belief. It is somewhat of an oversimplification to speak of the Mesopotamian pantheon of gods as though the relationship between the various deities were well organized. In fact, most of the time multiple gods' "responsibilities" were poorly defined and overlapped with other gods, so that it is difficult to reconstruct ancient beliefs. One of the clearer guides to determining relationships was genealogical, since the gods were seen as descending from the greater gods. Moreover, their religion included vast numbers of "demons," lesser deities whose primary responsibility seemed to have been that of plaguing humanity.

Mesopotamian religion concerned itself little with the afterlife. The primary concern was to achieve a pleasant life in this world by manipulating the deities. Ancient worshipers attempted to continue the favor of good deities and to placate the whims of the demons through a series of sacrifices and magical incantations.

Ancient Mesopotamian deities were associated almost exclusively with the physical realm. Although described in anthropological terms, these gods represented major aspects of the world in which the Mesopotamians lived. For example, An was the chief god, the sky god from whom all ultimately derived. Next was Enlil, the god who embodied the forces of nature, which sometimes aided and at other times opposed the progress of humanity. The earth goddess was Ninhursag, and the god of waters who gave fertility to the earth was Enki. Subordinate to these deities were the host of gods mentioned earlier.

In time other deities became prominent as Assyrian

and Babylonian history unfolded. As this occurred, major cities became sacred to these important gods. For instance, Ur became sacred to the moon god Nanna; Larsa, to the sun god Utu (Shamash); Uruk, to the heaven god An; and Inanna (Ishtar), to the goddess of heaven.

For the Mesopotamian, then, there was no single supreme god whose authority governed other deities and the world. Consequently, a kind of capriciousness developed around religion. In order for the pious to be safe from harm, no single deity could be appeased in order to assure security. This was because no one god had ultimate authority and because the lines of responsibility were not clearly drawn. Thus the worshiper was obliged to appease as many gods as possible in hopes of securing protection and prosperity. Moreover, some deities had a reputation in religious mythology for being particularly fickle and inclined to turn against the humans they had previously helped. These deities/demons were particularly worrisome to the ancient Mesopotamians and received great attention in worship in order to assure continued favor.

The major deities were associated with the physical world. In fact, it was inconceivable for the Mesopotamian mind to view a god as distinct from the physical world itself. With this backdrop in view, the Genesis 1 narrative appears in stark contrast to Mesopotamian theology. The notion of a deity being separate from and antecedent to the physical world as presented in the biblical account was inconceivable in the pagan world. The emphasis on God as Creator in Genesis 1 should be seen as a defense against the animistic tendencies of Mesopotamian religion.

Egypt

The Greek historian Herodotus stated that the Egyptians were the most religious people of all. But it is even more difficult to reconstruct Egyptian religion than Mesopotamian because of the relative lack of Egyptian religious texts. The texts that survive do not reflect a systematic presentation of beliefs. Rather, they are primarily pyramid texts that describe in general terms the beliefs of the people at the time the pyramid was constructed. Basically, these texts portray the one for whom the pyramid was built as a pious follower of the deities and as one who did not do a series of things that represented sin in Egyptian society.

As did the Mesopotamians, the Egyptians worshiped their physical realm as the embodiment of deity. Naturally, the two most prominent features of the Egyptian world, the sun and the Nile, were preeminent. In addition to the sun god Re were other solar deities, Aten and Horus. The earth and sky were deified as Geb and Nut, respectively. Two other important deities were Apis, the sacred bull, and Hathor, the cow goddess, which together may have been the precursor of the Israelite preoccupation with fashioning idols in the form of bulls (Exod 32:4; 1 Kgs 12:28). And one of the most important deities in earliest Egyptian history was the pharaoh himself, who was viewed as god incarnate.

The reason for building the pyramids was to construct

This ziggurat (Mesopotamian temple-tower), dedicated to Nannar, the moon god and located at ancient Ur of the Chaldeans (in modern Iraq), rose high above the other buildings of the city.

a dwelling for the deceased king in the afterlife. Osiris, the god of reconstruction, was believed to grant immortality to the privileged. It was this preoccupation with the next life that drove these kings to spend most of the national economy on such an abode. This preoccupation with the afterlife was unparalleled in ancient Near Eastern religion. In later periods of Egyptian history, the pharaoh was no longer viewed as divine, other deities fell into disfavor, and Egyptian religion took on a much more "this worldly" emphasis. One example of this would be the interest in wisdom texts as a means to achieving successful life in the here and now.

One fundamental difference exists between the Mesopotamian and Egyptian mind-sets. Religious memorials of the Egyptian culture remain today, while Mesopotamian ones do not. This twist of historical fate is representative of the different perspectives of the respective cultures. Egyptian society, particularly in its early days, was quite self-assured, confident that humanity's achievements would last for all time. On the other hand, the works of the Mesopotamians were never expected to last because they were always cognizant of their mortality. Thus, for Mesopotamians, the significance of humanity lay beyond themselves, a belief shared with the Hebrew mentality.

Palestinian Idolatrous Religions

While the Old Testament mentions several pagan gods, such as Dagon and Molech, our attention will focus upon Baal and Asherah. While sometimes treated separately, these two deities represent fertility religions, with Baal being the male and Asherah the female deity.

That ancient Near Eastern religion focused primarily upon fertility was no coincidence. Infertility of crops meant hunger, if not starvation, while the infertility of animals and people meant economic loss. The lack of socioeconomic security in ancient life meant that the people were never further than one failed crop away from potential starvation.

Baal (*master*) is mentioned in numerous biblical references as well as abundant material found at Ras Shamra (ancient Ugarit, about 1400 B.C.), which reflected expressions of praise to Baal from his devotees. The numerous expressions in the Bible such as Baal-peor (Num 25:3) indicate the locale where a particular baal-god was worshiped. The normal title given to Baal was "Rider of the Clouds," which reveals his status as a storm god. The abundant examples of Baal statues found to date portray Baal with a thunderbolt in his right hand, preparing to hurl it to the ground. He was known also for giving rain to the earth, thus fertilizing it.

The classic Old Testament passage dealing with Baalism is Elijah's confrontation with the prophets of Baal on Mount Carmel (1 Kings 18). This powerfully controversial text demonstrated the superiority of Yahweh in accomplishing the deeds normally ascribed to Baal himself. In the Elijah-Elisha narratives taken together, several crucial features of Baalism are disputed, such as the fire motif (1 Kgs 18–19; 2 Kgs 1–2; 6); rain (1 Kgs 17–18; 2 Kgs 3; 7); giver of oil and grain (1 Kgs 17; 19); giver of children (2 Kgs 14); healer (2 Kgs 4–5); and the resurrection motif (1 Kgs 17; 2 Kgs 4; 8).

The Asherah was the female consort to Baal whose specific role in their religion is not precisely described. At a minimum she seems to have been partially responsible for the gift of fertility, a type of mother goddess.

All of the religions of the Ancient Near East stand in sharp contrast to the monotheism of the Old Testament. Indeed the message of the Old Testament moves its readers to recognize that the Lord is our God, the Lord is One (see Deut 6:4-5). He alone is our Creator, our Redeemer, the Source of all life, and the object or our adoration and worship.

In the photo to the left is a bronze statue of a god (probably Baal) overlaid with gold leaf and found at Megiddo. The cylinder seal above from Bethel depicts a god and a goddess—Ashtoreth (or Ashtart) daughter of Asherah—each holding a spear.

Sources for Additional Study

Albright, William Foxwell. *From the Stone Age to Christianity*. 2nd ed. Garden City: Doubleday, 1957.

Frankfort, Henri, et al. *The Intellectual Adventure of Ancient Man*. Chicago: University Press, 1946.

Wong, David W. F. "Israel's Faith: A Pagan Legacy?" *Themelios* 11 (1975): 18-23.

LIFE IN BIBLE TIMES

Five main sources exist for our information about daily life in Bible times: the Bible, other texts contemporary with the Bible, archaeology, Jewish tradition, and modern Arabic culture. We must proceed carefully, however, with these sources.

Biblical laws, for example, may not always have been followed; and references to customs in historical, poetic, and prophetic texts are often enigmatic. Efforts to fill in details of culture completely missing from the Bible with practices evidenced from Babylonian, Syrian, Canaanite, or late Jewish texts or from modern Arabic culture must be tentative at best. Some facets of Arabic culture continue probably much as they were thousands of years ago. Determining which facets these are, however, is not easy.

Another difficulty in describing biblical culture is that the main story of the Bible covers a period of about two thousand years, during which customs changed (although not nearly as much as during the two thousand years since). Customs also varied socioeconomically and regionally, especially between town and country. Working classes, for example, could not afford all the proprieties the aristocrats considered essential. Furthermore, in New Testament times response to Greek influence had resulted in distinctions between "Hellenistic" and "Palestinian" Jews. Bearing these cautions in mind, however, we can survey what is known about typical Israelite customs in Canaan during the biblical period.

Family Relationships

The Family

Though terminology varied and overlapped, strictly speaking (see Josh 7:16-18) an individual Israelite was first a member of a family or household, then a clan, then a tribe, and then the people or nation of Israel.

The typical Israelite family consisted of a male head; his wife (or wives); their sons and their wives and children; and any unwed, widowed, or divorced daughters. At least some families had one or more slaves who were regarded almost as family members, especially if they had been born in the household (Gen 14:14). When a son married, his immediate family usually became members of the household of his father, moving into either the same house or an adjoining house (or nearby tent among nomads). Jacob's family of tent dwellers numbered about two hundred, plus probably several hundred slaves. The father was the master of the entire family, controlling all property, and sons almost always followed their father's occupation.

Polygamy

We find six biblical examples of polygamy in pre-Mosaic times, four during the period of the judges and nine among kings of Israel. The wealthy in New Testament times also practiced polygamy, and the Mishnah and Talmud sanctioned it. One commentator points out, however, that after the mention of Elkanah (1 Sam 1:1-2), the Books of Samuel and Kings contain no references to polygamy among "commoners." Monogamy was divinely approved (see Gen 2:18-25; Prov 5:15-21; Luke 16:18; 1 Cor 7:1-2), and it was by far the most common form of marriage in Israel, although a second wife or concubine (a slave-wife with no property and fewer rights than a regular wife) was sometimes acquired in cases where the first was barren.

Wedding Customs

The typical Israelite marriage was arranged by the fathers between distant relatives and probably occurred when the boy was almost twenty and the girl in early to mid-teens. It was arranged without the young persons' consent, although they could make their wishes known (Judg 14:2; 1 Sam 18:20). In New Testament times girls over twelve and a half had the right of refusal.

Negotiations included the amount of the *mohar*, a compensation presented to the bride's parents to overcome their loss in housekeeping chores and to seal the engagement. A portion of the *mohar* may have been kept for the girl, at least in later times, in case of some emergency or her husband's death, since she inherited none of his property if there were sons.

Also involved in the negotiations was an amount the wife should receive in case the husband divorced her. During the period of engagement, which often lasted about a year, the boy was not supposed to look on the girl's face until the wedding (Gen 24:65). At the time of the wedding, the bride's parents as well as the groom gave her presents (compare Ezek 16:10-13), which would remain her personal property. The wedding itself involved a feast, typically for seven days, inaugurated by the veiled bride being ceremoniously escorted with music and dancing from her parents' house to the marriage tent (Gen 24:67; Num 25:8; Ps 19:5). After the marriage was consummated, the "token of virginity," a blood-stained garment, was publicly presented to the bride's parents for safekeeping (Deut 22:13-21). Also involved in the marriage was a covenant (Mal 2:14; Prov 2:17; Ezek 16:8) which, like the act of divorce (Deut 24:1-3; Jer 3:8), was put in writing, at least after the exile. The covenant among fifth century B.C. Jews in Egypt consisted of the bridegroom's declaration that "she is my wife, and I am her husband, from this day forever."

Women

Women in Israel were considered to be socially, legally, and religiously inferior to men. Although he could not sell her, the husband had absolute authority over his wife and was called her *baal*, "master" (as a verb meaning either *rule over* or *marry*). He also was called her "lord," just as he was of his children, slaves, and other property.

A wife in New Testament times could divorce her husband only if he demanded vows unworthy of her, had leprosy or polypus, or was a dung collector, copper smelter, or tanner by trade. First-century husbands, on the other hand, generally were allowed to divorce their wives for any reason whatever. In Jesus' day, at least in Jerusalem, women left the house only if it could not be avoided and then only if their faces were covered. They could not speak to strangers on the street, especially to teachers. Exceptions to the face covering were made on feast days, and rules were not as strict in the country as in the city.

According to the Talmud, a husband was obligated to support his wife, redeem her from captivity if necessary, and provide her with medicine when she was sick and an appropriate funeral when she died. The wife, on the oth-

Weights and Measures

The vast majority of references to weights and measures in the Bible are found in the OT. A wide variety of values exists for these categories. In part this can be explained because both sexigesimal (counting by sixes) and decimal systems were used. Furthermore, Mesopotamian, Egyptian, and Canaanite systems were in evidence concurrently. Thus the same Hebrew word can have several incremental values.

Weights

Stones with a flat base were the most common device for weights, although examples shaped like animals and made of metal have been found. In some weight systems a mina is fifty shekels.

In Ezekiel's time, perhaps under Mesopotamian influence, the mina had come to be composed of sixty shekels (Ezek 45:12). The actual mathematical value of these words varied. There were, for example, at least two kinds of talents (heavy and light) and three shekels (see Gen 23:16; Exod 30:13; 2 Sam 14:26). Precise values cannot yet be assigned to these words. There are also other, more obscure weights such as the *nsp* (not mentioned in the OT), *pim* (1 Sam 13:21), *hms* (not attested), *peres* (Dan 5:25,28), and the *kesita* (Gen 33:19).

This painting from the tomb of Rekhmire at Thebes dating to the Eighteenth Dynasty depicts the weighing of gold and silver rings on scales. The scribe to the right is recording the weight of the rings as they are measured.

er hand, was expected to help her husband in the fields and with the flocks as well as to grind flour; make bread and cook meals; make and wash clothes; nurse the children; make her husband's bed; and wash his face, hands, and feet. Some of these chores could be delegated to servants, of course, if there were any. The Talmud remarks that if the wife brought four servants into the marriage she could sit on a *cathedra* all day if she wanted to. Anything a wife found belonged to her husband. Furthermore, she had to reckon with the possibility that if he found her contentious or barren he could either take a second wife (or concubine) or divorce her (either possibility depending upon his finances), in which case he kept the sons.

Women were bound by the biblical prohibitions but were exempted from requirement to attend the three major Jewish feasts in Jerusalem: Passover, Pentecost, and Tabernacles. They usually were kept from the study of the Torah. According to one rabbi, "If any man gives his daughter a knowledge of the Law, it is as though he taught her lechery." Women were also forbidden by some to teach children, give the benediction after a meal, or to testify, due to their frivolous and foolish nature (Josephus, *Antiquities,* 4.219). Becoming a mother, however, and diligence in the exercise of her duties earned for her respect and special consideration. A woman's lower status did not keep her from being regarded with great affection (Prov 31:10-31). According to Roland de Vaux, within the family Israelite husbands loved their wives, listened to them, and treated them as equals.

Children

Children were a treasure and a source of great happiness in Israelite society. Childbirth often occurred while a woman sat on two separated stones and usually involved the aid of a professional midwife (Exod 1:15-16). Infants were immediately washed, rubbed with salt, wrapped in strips of cloth so that they could not move and thus injure their limbs (Job 38:8-11; Ezek 16:2-5), and named (in New Testament times the naming often occurred at cir-

Linear Measures

Linear measurements are taken from the average length of human limbs. The best known of these is the cubit, which roughly spans from the elbow to the finger tip. Once again the issue is complicated because there were two cubits in OT times—short and long. The former was the more common. The exact values of many linear measurements are unknown.

Distance. The various ways of reckoning distances were apparently less precise than for weights. Perhaps the primary marker was the *zemed,* which was the area that a pair of oxen could plough in a day. As inaccurate as this seems, the same method was used in Mesopotamia and the Mediterranean and persisted into Mishnaic and Talmudic eras. An even less precise method was equated with the quantity of seed necessary to plant an area (Lev 27:16, for example). This system also was used in Mesopotamia and continued in Palestine into postbiblical times. By NT times Roman measurements had stabilized these mathematically.

Volume. Exact identification of measures of capacity is still not possible. The basic unit of measure was a *homer* (donkey load), while its liquid counterpart was the *kor.*

Exaggerating the importance of an orderly society throughout the entire ancient Near Eeastern world would be difficult. Justice was the responsibility of the king. Thus in the earliest law code (Ur Nammu, about 2050 B.C.) the king boasted he regulated weights and scales and established justice. This was also a common theme in Egypt as seen in Amenemope (approximately New Kingdom period): "Do not make the scale uneven or render the weights false or reduce the parts of the grain measure."

Amazingly, the prophets (Amos 8:5; Hos 12:7; Mic 6:11) spoke to the same issue. Moses gave careful legislation about dishonest scales (Lev 19:35-36; Deut 25:13-16) and borderlines such as the landmark (Deut 19:14; 27:17). The intricate measurements of the tabernacle and the temple are testimony of God's interest in exactness. The theological importance of these things is best seen in Proverbs 16:11, which speaks about the anointed king's responsibilities: "Honest scales and balances are from the LORD; all the weights in the bag are of his making."□

The photo above is of a Babylonian mina—a weight of measure equal to sixty shekels—from the time of Nebuchadnezzar II.

TABLE OF WEIGHTS AND MEASURES

WEIGHT

Biblical Unit	Language	Biblical Measure	U.S. Equivalent	Metric Equivalent	Various Translations
Gerah	Hebrew	1/20 shekel	1/50 ounce	.6 gram	gerah; oboli
Bekah	Hebrew	1/2 shekel or 10 gerahs	1/5 ounce	5.7 grams	bekah; half a shekel; quarter ounce; fifty cents
Pim	Hebrew	2/3 shekel	1/3 ounce	7.6 grams	2/3 of a shekel; quarter
Shekel	Hebrew	2 bekahs	2/5 ounce	11.5 grams	shekel; piece; dollar; fifty dollars
Litra (Pound)	Greco-Roman	30 shekels	12 ounces	.4 kilogram	pound; pounds
Mina	Hebrew/Greek	50 shekels	1 1/4 pounds	.6 kilogram	mina; pound
Talent	Hebrew/Greek	3000 shekels or 60 minas	75 pounds/ 88 pounds	34 kilograms/ 40 kilograms	talents/talent; 100 pounds

LENGTH

Biblical Unit	Language	Biblical Measure	U.S. Equivalent	Metric Equivalent	Various Translations
Handbreadth	Hebrew	1/6 cubit or 1/3 span	3 inches	8 centimeters	handbreadth; three inches; four inches
Span	Hebrew	1/2 cubit or 3 handbreadths	9 inches	23 centimeters	span
Cubit/Pechys	Hebrew/Greek	2 spans	18 inches	.5 meter	cubit(s); yard; half a yard; foot
Fathom	Greco-Roman	4 cubits	2 yards	2 meters	fathom; six feet
Kalamos	Greco-Roman	6 cubits	3 yards	3 meters	rod; reed; measuring rod
Stadion	Greco-Roman	1/8 milion or 400 cubits	1/8 mile	185 meters	miles; furlongs; race
Milion	Greco-Roman	8 stadia	1,620 yards	1.5 kilometer	mile

DRY MEASURE

Biblical Unit	Language	Biblical Measure	U.S. Equivalent	Metric Equivalent	Various Translations
Xestēs	Greco-Roman	1/2 cab	1 1/6 pints	.5 liter	pots; pitchers; kettles; copper pots; copper bowls; vessels of bronze
Cab	Hebrew	1/18 ephah	1 quart	1 liter	cab; kab
Choinix	Greco-Roman	1/18 ephah	1 quart	1 liter	measure; quart
Omer	Hebrew	1/10 ephah	2 quarts	2 liters	omer; tenth of a deal; tenth of an ephah; six pints
Seah/Saton	Hebrew/Greek	1/3 ephah	7 quarts	7.3 liters	measures; pecks; large amounts
Modios	Greco-Roman	4 omers	1 peck or 1/4 bushel	9 liters	bushel; bowl; peck-measure corn-measure; meal-tub
Ephah [Bath]	Hebrew	10 omers	3/5 bushel	22 liters	bushel; peck; deal; part; measure; six pints; seven pints
Lethek	Hebrew	5 ephahs	3 bushels	110 liters	half homer; half sack
Cor [Homer]/Koros	Hebrew/Greek	10 ephahs	6 bushels or 200 quarts/ 14.9 bushels or 500 quarts	220 liters/ 525 liters	cor; homer; sack; measures; bushels/sacks; measures; bushels; containers

LIQUID MEASURE

Biblical Unit	Language	Biblical Measure	U.S. Equivalent	Metric Equivalent	Various Translations
Log	Hebrew	1/72 bath	1/3 quart	.3 liter	log; pint; cotulus
Xestēs	Greco-Roman	1/8 hin	1 1/6 pints	.5 liter	pots; pitchers; kettles; copper pots; copper bowls; vessels of bronze
Hin	Hebrew	1/6 bath	1 gallon or 4 quarts	4 liters	hin; pints
Bath/Batos [Ephah]	Hebrew/Greek	6 hins	6 gallons	22 liters	gallon(s); barrels; liquid measure/ gallons; barrels; measures
Metretes	Greco-Roman	10 hins	10 gallons	39 liters	firkins; gallons
Cor [Homer]/Koros	Hebrew/Greek	10 baths	60 gallons	220 liters	cor; homer; sack; measures; bushels/sacks; measures; bushels; containers

cumcision on the eighth day). Mothers generally nursed their children longer than is normal in Western cultures—three years according to one intertestamental text.

Children spent their earliest years in the care of their mother, singing and dancing in the town square (Zech 8:5) and playing with clay figures (discovered by archaeologists). Most girls continued to learn from their mothers at home (Ezek 16:44) the necessary household skills, as well as any professional skills she might have, such as midwifery, weaving, cooking, ointment mixing (1 Sam 8:13), mourning (Jer 9:17), singing (2 Sam 19:35; Eccl 2:8), sorcery (1 Sam 28:7), or perhaps prophecy (Exod 15:20; Judg 5; Ezek 13:17-23)—a skill that would have demanded a better than average education.

Education

Fathers were primarily responsible for most of the education of their sons (compare Prov 1:8; 6:20; 31:1) in the traditions of Israel (Deut 6:7,20-25) and in ethical and practical affairs. They made liberal use of physical punishment (Prov 13:24; 22:15). Although literacy was widespread even during the Monarchy (more than in surrounding countries where the writing systems were much more complicated), education was mostly conducted through memorization and recitation. Its primary content was the history, literature, and laws of Israel, besides training in necessary skills. Young princes were educated by professional tutors in matters of government and war as well as religion.

Formal education of the masses did not begin until the first century B.C., but there were schools, probably from the nation's beginning, to teach aspiring scribes the art of document preparation, since writing skills were less common than reading even in NT times. These schools required time and money, however, which only upper classes could have afforded. Teachers were called "father" and their pupils "sons," as reflected in the Book of Proverbs. Some type of formal education also was available for priests, probably connected with the temple. Many of the prophets were educated either in the royal court schools, the scribal schools, or the school for priests.

In first-century B.C. synagogues, for boys about six to twelve, the Pharisees seem to have begun mandatory elementary schools called *bet sefer*, the "house of the book" (which taught the reading of the Torah) and *bet talmud*, the "house of learning" (which taught Mishnah or oral law). Adult education in the Torah had been conducted at first by itinerant priests and Levites (Deut 31:9-13; 2 Chr 17:7-9; Neh 8:7-9; Mic 3:11; Mal 2:6-7). During the late Persian period the Scriptures were read and explained in the square on market days (Monday and Thursday), a system eventually organized into a three-year cycle through the Torah. After the exile scribes, many of whom were Levites, had begun to replace priests as teachers. The most famous were Shammai, Hillel, and his grandson Gamaliel, under whom Paul studied. Some of these teachers started schools, called *bet midrash*, "house of study," for promising boys who had completed elementary school.

Family Life

Dwellings

Typical tents in Israel were made of woven brown or black goat's hair. Probably like Bedouin tents today, they were supported by three center poles about seven feet tall and three slightly shorter ones on either side. They were often divided by a linen cloth into a back "bedroom" and a front "living room," with a campfire at the entrance. The floor was dirt, but residents and guests always left their shoes outside. The eating "table" (Ps 73:5) consisted of a goatskin spread on the ground, and the bed was simply a straw mat.

Houses changed relatively little through Israel's history. Houses of the poorest people consisted of one room about ten feet square and a courtyard, sometimes shared with other houses. They were made of sun-dried mud brick, bonded with mud mortar, and plastered on the inside. The lower courses of the walls were usually made either of kiln-dried mud brick or uncut stone filled with rubble. In New Testament times walls on the first floor were often made from finely cut stones. The roof, perhaps supported by a single pillar in the center of the room, consisted of crossbeams and poles, then branches and clay, rolled smooth after a heavy rain. Tiled roofs also appeared late in the biblical period. Reached by a staircase or ladder on the outside of the house, many household chores were done on the roof during the day. In the evening it was used for eating, hospitality, relaxing, and sleeping in the summer. The main source of ventilation and outside light in the house was the doorway. Doors were made of cloth or wood, hinged with leather, and could often be locked or bolted (Judg 3:25; 2 Sam 13:17; Isa 22:22). There were also a few high narrow windows that were simply slits in the wall that could be covered with lattice or shutters. Glass windows were available in New Testament times but only for the very wealthy.

Animals were often kept inside the house, so many houses had a platform inside, about eighteen inches high, for eating and sleeping. Floors were usually clay or limestone plaster but could be paved with flagstone (with gaps large enough for losing a coin; see Luke 15:8-10). Many houses had several rooms arranged around two or three sides of an enclosed courtyard. Some of the rooms were often separated from the courtyard only by pillars. Families that engaged in a trade such as tent-making or carpentry would do their work in the courtyard of their home. Nicer houses had bedrooms on a second floor, the first floor being used only for work, storage, and animals in the winter and perhaps at night. The wealthy in the New Testament period even had bathrooms.

Hospitality

Throughout the Mediterranean hospitality was not merely a courtesy but a necessity and a reciprocal understanding in a society without dependable hotels for travelers. Inns do not appear in the Bible until the New Testament (with the possible exceptions of Josh 2:1 and Jer 41:17), and then they had questionable reputations. Hospitality was even considered a sacred duty and privilege, so that a traveler had a right to expect food, shelter, and protection (Gen 19:1-11; Judg 19:16-30). The Old Testament law commanded it (Lev 19:33-34), and failure to offer it was considered a disgrace and a crime (Deut 23:3-4; Judg 19:12-15; 1 Sam 25:2-42).

One's willingness to care for strangers was considered a test of his character (Job 31:32; 1 Tim 3:2; 5:10; compare 1 Pet 4:8-10). The Talmud lists it with studying the Torah as one of the five acts that brings eternal reward and declares that "the entertainment of travelers was as great a matter as the reception of the *Shekinah*." A Jewish interpretive note on Psalm 109:31 interprets that whenever a man stands in need at your door, the Lord stands with him (compare Heb 13:2). Some villages provided accommodations for travelers, and some houses had guest rooms on an upper floor for this purpose (1 Kgs 17:19; 2 Kgs 4:10; Luke 22:11).

Food and Drink

The evening meal was the big meal of the day, typically consisting of bread and whatever fruits and vegetables were in season. On special occasions these were accompanied by meat or fish, the latter being more common in the Galilean region. Fruits available at various times were melons, figs, pomegranates, and grapes (also dried and pressed into cakes; compare Hos 3:1). Vegetables included lentils, beans, cucumbers, leeks, onions, and garlic. Boiling with herbs was the most common method of cooking, though meat could also be roasted. Stews often included almonds and pistachio nuts.

Seasonings available were mint, dill, cummin, rue, and mustard, which when combined with onions and garlic would make a very spicy dish. Salt obtained from the

An Egyptian stone statue of a woman baking bread in an oven made of stones (dating from the time of the Fifth Dynasty in Egypt).

Dead Sea or the Mediterranean was also important for seasoning as well as for preserving. For sweetening the Jews could use syrup made from cooking grapes or dates. This is probably what is meant by "honey" in the Bible (except in Judg 14:8-9 and 1 Sam 14:26-27, which refer to wild honey), since the Jews did not keep bees.

For meat, hunted animals such as deer or partridge were available; but sheep, goat, or beef were more common as food in later times. Chickens were known in the Roman period, though eggs were considered to be children's food. As a rule food was eaten with the hands out of a common pottery dish; utensils were only used in the preparation of food.

Bread making was very important (compare Deut 24:6) and often involved the whole family (Jer 7:18). Families would bake enough bread for a week prior to the Sabbath and keep it in a basket. Wheat or barley flour was mixed with olive oil, salt, yeast (fermented dough from the previous baking), and water and formed into flat, round loaves. (Olive oil was one of the most valuable commodities in the ancient world, an essential cosmetic, medicine, fuel, and food.) The oven was located in the courtyard and was either a huge overturned clay "bowl" under which a fire was built and the bread "fried" on top or a huge clay pot with a hole in the bottom where the fire was built. When the oven was hot, the fire was raked out, and the bread was stuck to the inside or laid on stones at the bottom to cook. Cooking fire was commonly fueled by grass and dried dung mixed with straw.

There were few professional millers in Old Testament times, and even later the women usually ground their own grain on millstones called "saddle querns." It was a concave rectangular stone eighteen to thirty inches long by ten to fifteen inches wide against which the grain would be ground with a cylindrical upper millstone held in the hands (Judg 9:23). Rotary querns about eighteen to twenty inches in diameter also began to be used during the Monarchy. The grain would be poured in through a hole in the top stone, and the flour would come out the sides. Finer flour could be obtained with a mortar and pestle (Num 11:8). Grain was stored in large ceramic jars or in stone-lined pits sunk into the floor of the house.

Since nothing was more precious than water, homes usually had their own cisterns for drinking water unless

Money

Precoinage. For thousands of years simple barter served adequately the economic needs of humankind. The most common item for measuring wealth was cattle. Indeed, the Latin word for money (*pecunia*) is derived from the word for cattle. Of course, there was a wide variety of other items ranging from perishable goods to metals. Interestingly, an early biblical reference to wealth was in Genesis 13:2, where Abraham is said to have been "very wealthy in livestock and in silver and gold."

From early times there were attempts to standardize commodity values. For metals this resulted in uniformity of shapes and weights. Thus, Abraham gave "a gold nose ring weighing a beka and two gold bracelets weighing ten shekels" (Gen 24:22). Ultimately, metal ingots came to be stamped, rendering them of reliable quality. This may have been the forerunner of coinage.

Early Coinage. Most historians credit the Lydians with the invention of coinage. Herodotus wrote that it was Croesus who first minted coins, but at least one coin of his father Alyattes (617–560 B.C.) has been found. Interestingly, Sennacherib (705–681 B.C.), king of Assyria, claimed: "I caused a mold of clay to be set up and bronze to be poured into it to make [as in making] pieces of half a shekel."

Apparently, Darius I (521–486 B.C.), king of Persia, was the first to introduce coinage to his empire. Hence, the name for the coin was "daric." Early mention of coinage in the OT may be found in Ezra 2:69 and perhaps Haggai 1:6. A half dozen

A coin from the time of Mattathias Antigonus, last of the Hasmoneans (40-37 B.C.). The obverse shows the table of the tabernacle; the reverse, the menorah.

coins from Palestine called *Yehud* (Judean) in the Persian period have been found.

Maccabean Coins (115–37 B.C.). By this time period, the right of a state to mint coins was tremendously important for the prestige of the king and his country. The first Maccabean ruler to strike coins was John Hyrcanus I (135–104 B.C.). Apparently, high priests also minted coins, thus suggesting that the power of the kings was not absolute. A coin lacking quality was indicative of a gradual weakening of the throne.

Herodian Coins. Antipator, father of King Herod and Hyrcanus's chief minister, was represented by the letter *A* placed on a coin inscribed "Yehohanan the High Priest and the Council of the Jews." The coins of his son Herod the Great clearly show that Judah had become a Roman client-state. For the most part the various Herodian coinage reflect Greco-Roman inclinations rather than Jewish.

Roman Procurators. Valerius Gratus (A.D. 15–26) issued the largest number of coins, while his successor, Pontius Pilate (A.D. 26–36), clearly issued coins for Judah with heathen symbols on them.

NT Coins. Coins in Palestine had one of three possible origins: Imperial Roman coinage, provincial coinage (minted at Antioch and Tyre), and Jewish coinage. Coinage was minted in gold, silver, or copper. The only Jewish coin mentioned in the NT was the bronze *lepton,* the famous widow's mite—the least valuable coin in the NT.

Among Greek coinage there was the *drachme, didrachmon* (2 *drachm*), the coin Jews paid for their half-shekel temple tax in Matthew 17:24, and the *stater* or *tetradrachmon* (Matt 17:27). The most common Roman coin was the *denarius,* which was the equivalent of a day's wages (Matt 20:2-3).

The smallest Roman coin was the *quadrans* (Mark 12:42), which was twice the size of the *lepton*. The copper *as* was one-quarter of the bronze *sestertius,* which was one-sixteenth the silver *denarius* (see Matt 10:29; Luke 12:6).

The issue of money presents a challenge to the believer. We must earn it (2 Thess 3:6-10), and an unwillingness to provide for one's family is to deny the faith (1 Tim 5:8). The love of money, however, is the enemy of the faith (1 Tim 6:10). "You cannot serve both God and Money" (Matt 6:24). □

there was a large community spring or well nearby. Cisterns were usually dug bottle shaped in the ground and lined with lime plaster. They were filled from drains that collected rain water from the roof and other run-off points. Public cisterns during the Roman period were sometimes filled by aqueducts. Even wine was usually mixed with water before drinking.

The many stages of wine production provided several types of drink from grapes—from sweet grape juice to a cheap vinegar and water drink. Grapes were pressed and fermented in vats, then stored in a cool place in skins or large ceramic jars. Other intoxicating drinks could also be made from pomegranates and from dates (perhaps the "strong drink" referred to in the Bible). Milk was mostly from goats and was drunk or eaten as a yogurtlike substance or as cheese.

Clothing and Cosmetics

There was comparatively little variety in clothing in ancient Israel. The most common materials were wool and linen. The basic outfit of a soldier or worker was a skirt ("girdle," KJV) reaching to midthigh and held up by a woolen belt or girdle, which could also hold weapons and valuables. The girdle itself could be woven in several colors and therefore would be valuable enough to serve as a reward for service (2 Sam 18:11). Men otherwise wore a pullover knee- or ankle-length tunic (Hebrew *kutonet*, Greek *chiton*, unfortunately called a "coat" in the KJV), which hung from one shoulder or was short-sleeved. It might be undecorated or have a woven, colored border at the neck and could also be girdled at the waist. This is sometimes described as an "undergarment" since it was worn under the cloak, but what we call underwear was apparently unknown except for priests (Exod 28:42).

The cloak (Hebrew *meil, simlah,* or *kesut;* Greek *himation*), worn over the tunic in the day and used as a covering at night (Exod 22:26), was open in front with short, loose sleeves. It was typically of wool, although that of the shepherd was often animal skin or camel's hair, apparently also the mark of a prophet (Zech 13:4; 2 Kgs 1:8; Matt 3:4). A cloak usually had a colored band at the border of the neck and also the front and sleeves. What usually made festive garments distinct from daily ones was the amount of this embroidery. Tassels or fringes were prescribed to be worn on the "corners" of the cloak (Deut 22:12; Num 15:38-40). These were tufts of bread sewn on. Their length was unspecified, and since they came to represent one's devotion to the Torah, Jewish leaders in Jesus' day made a show of them (Matt 23:5). Since clothing was handmade, it was greatly valued and sometimes used as articles of exchange or plunder (Judg 5:30; 14:12; Prov 31:24).

Men were usually bareheaded with perhaps a strip of cloth around the head, or they wore a skullcap or turban. Their hair could be moderately long or short, and they usually wore beards but shaved their upper lip.

Women's garments were quite similar to the men's, except they did not wear the short skirt and probably had distinctive embroidery, girdles, and head wear (Deut 22:5). In Israel clothing was designed modestly to hide rather than to accentuate the body. It does not appear from the Old Testament that women generally were required to cover their faces in public. Rebekah, riding with Isaac's servant, only covered hers when she saw her betrothed approaching (Gen 24:65). An eighth-century Assyrian relief shows Israelite women in long scarves or capes reaching from their foreheads to the hems of the tunics in the back. This may be like the veil mentioned in the Old Testament that could be drawn up to cover the face.

Archaeologists have discovered an abundance of anklets; bracelets; necklaces; rings for ears, noses, and fingers; and beads that were available to Israelite women, although Isaiah disdains women who wore them ostentatiously (3:16-24). Jewelry was made of gold, silver, copper, bone, ivory, or colored stones (Exod 28:17-20; Ezek 28:13; Rev 21:19-21).

An abundance of cosmetic utensils has also been discovered. With these utensils women could reduce various minerals to powder, mix them with water or oil, then apply them to their faces. With a wooden or bronze spatula or the finger, women could apply black galena to their eyebrows and eyelashes and green malachite or turquoise to their lower eyelids. Then with a brush they could paint their lips and cheeks with red ochre. Surrounding nations, and probably some of the Israelites as well, also used yellow ochre face powder and red dye for hands, feet, nails, and hair. Mirrors were available as early as the time of Moses, though, in spite of the *King James Version* of Exodus 38:8; Job 37:18; Isaiah 3:23, they were made not of glass but of polished metal such as bronze, silver, or gold. Perfumed ointments were used in medicine and religion as well as for cosmetics. It was obtained by heating various kinds of flowers in oils or fats (Exod 30:22-25) and was kept in small pottery or ivory flasks from which it could be poured onto the hair and body after a bath or onto the clothing or the bed (Ps 45:8; Prov 7:17).

Burial and Mourning

Evidence for customs of death, burial, and mourning is fragmentary, often weighted toward practices among the wealthy and sometimes difficult to date. But it is clear that news of death always met with immediate and unreserved outward expressions of grief, as did other sorrows. These expressions would include the tearing of either the outer or inner garments (Gen 37:34; Job 1:20; 2:12; 2 Sam 1:11), and wailing with cries such as, "Alas, my brother!" (1 Kgs 13:30; Jer 22:18; Mark 5:38).

Mourners would typically sit barefoot on the ground with their hands on their heads (Mic 1:8; 2 Sam 12:20; 13:19; 15:30; Ezek 24:17) and smear their heads or bodies with dust or ashes (Josh 7:6; Jer 6:26; Lam 2:10; Ezek 27:30; Esth 4:1; 2 Macc 3:47). They might even cut their hair, beard, or skin (Jer 16:6; 41:5; Mic 1:16), though disfiguring the body in this way was forbidden as pagan (Lev 19:27-28; 21:5; Deut 14:1).

The mourning process was continued by refraining from washing and other normal activities (2 Sam 14:2) and by wearing a garment of sackcloth (Isa 22:12; Jer 48:37; Matt 11:21), a dark material made from camel or goat hair (Rev 6:12) and used for making grain bags (Gen 42:25; Josh 9:4). It might be worn instead of or perhaps under other garments tied around the waist outside the tunic (Gen 37:34; 2 Sam 3:31; Jonah 3:6), or in some cases sat or lain upon (2 Sam 21:10; 1 Kgs 21:27). Fasting was also involved, usually only during the day (2 Sam 1:12; 3:35), typically for seven days (Gen 50:10; 1 Sam 31:13).

Since a house that had been in contact with a corpse was unclean, food could not be prepared there. A corpse was referred to by the rabbis as the "father of fathers of uncleanness." It was necessary, therefore, for friends and relatives to bring food (Jer 16:7) until the household could be cleansed (Num 19:11-16).

The absence of embalming practices in Israel, the curse associated with lack of burial (Deut 21:23), and the extreme uncleanness of the dead (the only object that could defile something for seven days—Num 19:11-18; 31:19-24) made hasty burial a necessity. Cremation was practiced only as a means of degradation (Lev 20:14; 21:9; Josh 7:15; Isa 30:33; Amos 2:1), as was the refusal to bury (1 Kgs 14:11; Jer 16:4). Although a corpse might be left briefly in a home awaiting the funeral procession (Matt 9:23-24; Mark 5:35-43; Acts 9:37), burial almost always occurred the same day as death. Whereas the Canaanite cult of the dead had frequently involved burials under their houses, the practice in Israel was to bury outside the city. (Verses indicating burial *in* a town [1 Sam 25:1; 28:3] probably mean *in the vicinity of.*) In spite of prophetic criticism (Ezek 43:7-9), kings were usually buried in Jerusalem (1 Kgs 2:10; 11:43; 14:31; wicked king Manasseh and his son were even buried in their own house, 2 Kgs 21:18; 2 Chr 33:20; 2 Kgs 21:26). But the Kidron Valley east of Jerusalem was the regular burial site (2 Kgs 23:6; Judg 16:31; 2 Kgs 13:21; 23:16).

After death the body would be washed and anointed (Acts 9:37; Mark 16:1—the anointing of Jesus seems to have required two stages, first by Joseph and Nicodemus, then by the women). The mouth was bound, and the body was wrapped or clothed in simple attire (John 11:44; 19:39-40; Matt 27:59). Coffins were not used until the New Testament era (2 Kgs 13:21; Luke 7:14) and then only for transporting the body on a funeral couch or bier (2 Sam 3:31) to the burial site.

Besides family and friends, the funeral procession would include professional mourners (Jer 9:17-18; Amos 5:16), flute players (Matt 9:23), and anyone who happened to see it pass by (Luke 7:12). At the grave incense would be burned for purification and honor (2 Chr 16:4; 21:19), and words of lament would be spoken (2 Sam 1:17-27; 2 Chr 35:25). Burial was usually either in a cave or an excavated tomb used for all the members of a family or clan (Gen 50:13; Judg 8:32; 2 Sam 2:32; John 11:38). The body was laid on a shelf of rock carved out along the wall, sometimes requiring the bones from a previous burial to be pushed aside or deposited in a pit inside the tomb or (from about the third century B.C. to the third century A.D.) in a stone chest called an ossuary. Those who could not afford a family tomb were buried in a simple grave.

Sources for Additional Study

Miller, Madeleine S. and J. Lane. *Harper's Encyclopedia of Bible Life.* San Francisco: Harper & Row, 1978.

Safrai, S. and M. Stern, eds. *The Jewish People in the First Century.* Philadelphia: Fortress, 1974.

Thompson, J. A. *Handbook of Life in Bible Times.* Downers Grove: InterVarsity, 1986.

Vaux, Roland de. *Ancient Israel.* New York: McGraw-Hill, 1961.

BIBLICAL CHRONOLOGY

Some have tried to claim infallibility for the theology of the Bible, while treating the historical aspects as capable of error. But the Bible cannot be the final authority of the church if it is true only in some areas yet false in others, especially in its history. Biblical faith is a faith in God's acts in history.

Furthermore, biblical interpretation is dependent not only on the grammatical-lexical details of the text, but also on the historical situation of that text, insofar as it can be known. And in order to establish that historical situation as broadly (geographically) and as deeply (culturally) as possible, we must establish biblical chronology. The interpreter of the Book of Malachi, for example, wants to know as much as possible about what people were doing, saying, and thinking at that time in Persia, Egypt, Babylon, and elsewhere. The author of the book assumed a certain amount of that knowledge on the part of his readers. The modern interpreter therefore needs a basic understanding of how the events of the Bible fit the events of the biblical world. As E. A. Thiele has written, "Chronology is the backbone of history."

Principles of Chronology

Historical chronology involves measuring the distance in time of an event from the present. Since ancient peoples did not use our chronological system, however, this involves converting the chronological references in our ancient sources to our Julian system. According to Suetonius, the poet Horace was born on the sixth day before the Ides of December during the consulate of Lucius Cotta and Lucius Torquatus, which is December 8, 65 B.C. Conversion, however, necessitates understanding both systems.

The Julian system, invented by Julius Caesar, is based on a 365-day year arbitrarily divided into twelve months of twenty-eight to thirty-one days. Since a solar year is actually 365 days, five hours, forty-eight minutes, and almost forty-six seconds (about 365¼ days), a "bisextile" day (now Feb. 29) was added every four years. Since this moved the calendar year ahead of the solar year by forty-four minutes every four years, however, Pope Gregory XIII found it necessary to omit ten days from October in 1582, hence the "Gregorian" calendar. Considering these factors, historians can count backward into antiquity with the Julian calendar, being careful to remember that the eras change from A.D. 1 to 1 B.C. So there are only three years, not four, between 2 B.C. and A.D. 2.

Except for the Egyptians and the Romans, the ancients had a "lunisolar" year; that is, they used the moon as well as the sun for their calendar. As the moon rotates counterclockwise around the earth (every 29.26–29.8 days), it is between the earth and the sun from one to three days during which it cannot be seen. The reappearance of the right crescent moon at twilight, often announced by the priest, was used by most peoples to mark the beginning of a new month (hence the Hebrew word *hodesh* meaning both *month* and *new moon*).

Since twelve lunar rotations are only 354 days, it was necessary to adjust the lunar cycle to the solar to account for the eleven days. Otherwise December would eventually occur in the summer. Since the Babylonians wanted to keep the barley harvest in the month Nisan for religious and tax purposes, they followed a practice later used by the Greeks and others of adding whenever necessary an "intercalary" month. Eventually this addition became regular so that seven intercalary months were added every nineteen years (about one every three years). This system was adopted by the Assyrians around 1100 B.C. and imposed by the Babylonians on their empire, including the Jews. After Persia conquered Babylon in 539 B.C., they adopted the same system and made it official throughout their empire.

This system presented a problem to the Jews because their religious festivals and calendar were closely and inextricably bound to the lunar (Num 10:10; 28:11) and agricultural cycles. According to Leviticus 23:4-14, for example, Passover was to be on the fourteenth day of the first month, at which time they were to offer the firstfruits of the barley harvest. The precalculated Babylonian calendar did not maintain this close connection; therefore a distinction began, probably in the sixth century, between the religious and the civil calendar. In the religious calendar (which was continued at least until the fourth century A.D.) months and days were added whenever necessary.

Some have argued that before the Babylonian period

The Gezer Calendar dating from the tenth century B.C. records an agricultural calendar in old Hebrew script (see p. 56).

the Jews followed what is called a "Jubilees" calendar in which a year consisted of fifty-two weeks, hence 364 days. The New Year, as well as Unleavened Bread (Lev 23:6) and Tabernacles (Lev 23:34), began on Wednesday, the day on which God created the sun and moon (Gen 1:14). One function of the "jubilee year" (Lev 25) might have been to add forty-nine days to the calendar every forty-nine years, a "little year," realigning the calendar with the seasons.

Roman control of Palestine did not greatly alter their chronological system. Since Rome did not impose their Julian calendar on the provinces, the Babylonian system continued in use (complete with Babylonian names for the months) for the civil year, though some sectarians refused to use it. The Roman presence is evident, however, in the use of Roman regnal years (that is, the number of years a ruler has been in office, used as a method of naming a year) as in Luke 3:1.

The oldest and simplest method of dating was to relate one event to another such as a flood, war, or the administration of a king or government official. This method is called relative chronology. If it is to have meaning for the historian, the event must then be related to an absolute chronology. That is, it must be placed (with varying degrees of exactness) on a time scale of equal units connected to the present—the Julian calendar.

Most of our sources for the ancient Near East, Greece, and Rome date an event according to an "eponymous year," a year named for an official such as the Roman consul (as with the birth of Horace referred to earlier). Lists were made of these years in antiquity, often including certain events that occurred in a particular year. If historians can relate one of those events to the Julian calendar, then they can synchronize the whole "eponym list" with an absolute chronology. By this means we have a firm Assyrian chronology, since we have eponym lists from 891 to 648 B.C. which contain a reference to a solar eclipse that occurred when Bur-Sagale was governor of Guzana. Astronomers have dated that eclipse to June 15, 763 B.C.

Old Testament Chronology

The Old Testament historical books are full of relative chronological references. One of the most important is 1 Kings 6:1:

> In the four hundred and eightieth year after the Israelites had come out of Egypt, in the fourth year of Solomon's reign over Israel, in the month of Ziv, the second month, he began to build the temple of the LORD.

If dates can be established for the reign of Solomon, this verse provides a means to date the exodus, from which other verses can yield dates for the patriarchs. Solomon's reign can be dated, through not directly.

The primary tool by which absolute dates are provided for ancient Israel is Assyrian chronology because two Israelite kings, Jehu and Ahab, are referred to on Assyrian tablets. By them we know that King Ahab (1 Kgs 16–22) fought Shalmaneser III at the Battle of Qarqar and died in 853 B.C. Furthermore, King Jehu (2 Kgs 9–10) in the first year of his reign paid tribute to the same Assyrian king in 841 B.C. Since the Books of Kings give the names and length of reign of all the kings of Judah and Israel (see 1 Kgs 2:11; 11:42; 14:20; 15:25,33; 16:8,23,29), the years of Solomon's reign were 970 to 930 B.C.; and David's, 1010 to 970 B.C. The date of the exodus, then, assuming a literal interpretation of 1 Kings 6:1, is 1446 B.C. The dates of the Patriarchs are established as follows:

Jacob's migration to Egypt
1446 + 430 (Exod 12:40) = 1876 B.C.
Birth of Jacob
1876 + 130 (Gen 47:9) = 2006 B.C.
Birth of Isaac
2006 + 60 (Gen 25:26) = 2066 B.C.
Birth of Abram
2066 + 100 (Gen 21:5) = 2166 B.C.

Because the genealogical lists in Genesis are believed by most to be intentionally incomplete ("open"), attempts are usually not made to establish historical dates prior to Abraham.

Such an exact chronology is made problematic, however, especially for the Patriarchal Age, by several factors. One is the claim of some that many of the numerical references (especially the number forty and its multiples) should be understood figuratively. Some will even discount them altogether.

Another difficulty is the inconsistency of certain biblical references in Kings and Chronicles. Jerome wrote:

> Reread all the books of the Old and New Testaments and you will find such confusion of years and numbers between the two kingdoms of Judah and Israel that getting stuck in such questions fits more a man who has too much free time than a man who is eager to study.

For example, Ahab's second son, Jehoram, succeeded his first son, Ahaziah, as king of Israel in the second year of *Jehoram* (same name!), king of Judah, son of Jehoshaphat (2 Kgs 1:17). But 2 Kings 3:1 says that Jehoram became king of Israel in *Jehoshaphat's* eighteenth year as king (2 Kgs 8:16). Furthermore, 1 Kings 22:42 says that Jehoshaphat ruled twenty-five years. Based on the assumption

TIMES AND SEASONS

The title of this article suggests a different view of time than ours. With few expectations the biblical view of time is neither abstract nor cyclic. For the Hebrews the idea of time was related inextricably with God's actions and the response of humans. The fact that the date of the exodus can be identified in only one biblical passage (1 Kgs 6:1) is surprising to us. Yet the exodus was a focal point of past, present, and future time. It was perpetually memorialized in the Passover (Deut 16:1; Exod 13:3). Though Scripture gives instructions for celebrating Passover, it does not tell us the date of the exodus.

Old Testament

The Hebrews saw time as the arena for God's acts. Consequently, the primary word for time was "day"—the fifth most common substantive in the OT. Fittingly, Genesis closes each of the first six acts of creation and then introduces the seventh day when God rested.

"Days" that God had acted were to be memorialized through ritual celebration. Though ritual is regularly scorned by modern Christians, celebrations are inseparably related to the events in Hebrew thinking. Thus our Lord, His disciples, and even Paul observed the appointed holy days (for Paul note especially Acts 20:6,16; 21:17-20).

Time for the Hebrews was regarded both as an opportunity and responsibility for persons. Proper response to time resulted in a rebuilt temple (Hag 1:1) and a people saved from extermination (Esth 4:14).

Seasons

Ecclesiastes 3 is the closest the Hebrews came to the cyclic thinking so common in the ancient Near East. The Gezar calendar (see "Calendar") shows indisputably that one way of viewing time was seasonal. The primary difference in their view was that there was an order and goal for time. Israel's God had created the seasons and knew the course of time (Dan 2:20-23). Time, therefore, is to be thought of primarily in theological terms.

New Testament

The focal point for time in the OT was related to either the Day of the Lord or to the national future. The NT, however, focuses time against the coming of Christ. The Baptist's message was "the time has come" (Mark 1:15). John's confusion (Matt 11:2-3), however, was not clarified even when Jesus announced at the end of His life, "My appointed time is near" (Matt 26:18). Even after Christ's resurrection the disciples failed to understand His teachings about time: "Lord, are you at this time going to restore the kingdom to Israel?" (Acts 1:6).

Paul's teaching in 2 Corinthians 6:2 reflects the NT's unique view of time: "I tell you, now is the time of God's favor, now is the day of salvation." It is precisely this Christological emphasis that delineates the Jewish and Christian traditions. The New Testament idea of time and Christ can thus be summarized: The future (present salvation) is available now, and in the present we are in the latter days. Jesus appears to have been the hinge between the two eras—the past (Israel and the OT) and the future (days are coming).

Eternity

The idea of eternity may be understood in two ways. One view is derived from the Greek philosopher Plato. He taught that there is a fundamental difference between time in our world and time in eternity. The other view teaches that eternity is an unending continuation of time. Whatever the debate, God is Master of time in all forms (2 Pet 3:8). □

THE JEWISH CALENDAR

Year		Month	English Months (nearly)	Festivals	Seasons and Productions
Sacred 1	Civil 7	Nison/Abib 30 days	April	1 New Moon 14 The Passover 15-21 Unleavened Bread	Spring rains (Deut 11:14) Floods (Josh 3:15) Barley ripe
2	8	Iyyar/Ziv 29 days	May	1 New Moon 14 Second Passover (for those unable to keep first)	**Harvest** Barley Harvest (Ruth 1:22) Wheat Harvest Summer begins No rain from April to Sept. (1 Sam 12:17)
3	9	Sivan 30 days	June	1 New Moon 6 Pentecost	
4	10	Tammuz 29 days	July	1 New Moon 17 Fast for the taking of Jerusalem	**Hot Season** Heat increases
5	11	Ab 30 days	August	1 New Moon 9 Fast for the destruction of Temple	The streams dry up Heat intense Vintage (Lev 26:5)
6	12	Elul 29 days	September	1 New Moon	Heat intense (2 Kgs 4:19) Grape harvest (Num 13:23)

7	1	Tishri/Ethanim 30 days	October	1 New Year, Day of Blowing of Trumpet Day of Judgment and Memorial (Num 29:1) 10 Day of Atonement (Lev 16) 15 Booths 21 (Lev 23:24) 22 Solemn Assembly	**Seed time** Former or early rains begin (Joel 2:23) Plowing and sowing begin
8	2	Marchesran/Bul 29 days	November	1 New Moon	Rain continues Wheat and barley sown
9	3	Chislev 30 days	December	1 New Moon 25 Dedication (John 10:22,29)	**Winter** Winter begins Snow on mountains
10	4	Tebeth 29 days	January	1 New Moon 10 Fast for the siege of Jerusalem	Coldest month Hail and snow (Josh 10:11)
11	5	Shebat 30 days	February	1 New Moon	Weather gradually warmer
12	6	Adar 29 days	March	1 New Moon 13 Fast of Esther 14-15 Purim	Thunder and hail frequent Almond tree blossoms
13	Leap year	Veadar/Adar Sheni	March/April	1 New Moon 13 Fast of Esther 14-15 Purim	Intercalary Month

Note 1 The Jewish year is strictly lunar, being 12 lunations with an average 29-1/2 days making 354 days in the year.

The Jewish sacred year begins with the new moon of spring, which comes between our March 22 and April 25 in cycles of 19 years.

We can understand it best if we imagine our New Year's Day, which now comes on January 1 without regard to the moon, varying each year with Easter, the time of the Passover, or the time of the full moon which, as a new moon, had introduced the New Year two weeks before.

Note 2 Hence the Jewish calendar contains a 13th month, Veadar or Adar Sheni, introduced 7 times in every 19 years, to render the average length of the year nearly correct and to keep the seasons in the proper months.

Note 3 The Jewish day begins at sunset of the previous day.

that the chronological references in the Bible are essentially correct and consistent if properly understood, E. A. Thiele produced a consistent chronology of Israel. In order to solve problems like the one just mentioned and others, he based his system on the suppositions that co-regencies (a king and his successor ruling at the same time) and rival reigns (two kings claiming the throne at the same time) occurred in both Israel and Judah and that regnal years were counted differently in the two nations. He argued that a co-regency of Jehoshaphat and his son Jehoram explains the difficulty mentioned earlier. This co-regency began in 853 B.C., Jehoshaphat's sixteenth year, when he went to war against Aram with Ahab (1 Kgs 22:2-37), leaving the kingdom securely in the hands of his son Jehoram.

Most scholars have accepted Thiele's system of dating. Hayes and Hooker, however, have offered an alternate system based on supposed editorial changes to the biblical text. Their solution to the problem discussed earlier involves the claim that there was only one Jehoram (the son of Jehoshaphat) and that he occupied both thrones for over ten years. Fortunately, the two systems of Thiele and of Hayes and Hooker usually vary by only a few years. Thiele dates the death of Solomon, for example, in 931 or 930 B.C.; whereas Hayes and Hooker have it in 926 B.C.

New Testament Chronology

In A.D. 525 John I, Bishop of Rome, commissioned a Scythian monk to prepare a standard calendar for the

Calendars

One of the most surprising aspects of the OT is that while it explicitly orders its cultic system according to the phases of the moon (lunisolar), it never speaks to the issue of the calendar. In Exodus 12:2 God commanded, "This month is to be for you the first month, the first month of your year."

Of course, reckoning time solely on the phases of the moon is impossible. The solar year represents the actual seasonal cycle. The earth circles the sun in 365 1/5 days. The problem with the lunar calendar is that it is approximately eleven days shorter than the solar year. With the exceptions of the Egyptians and Romans, all ancient peoples followed a lunar calendar. The Hebrews seem to have adopted the West Semitic lunar calendar (1 Kgs 4:7).

The Calendar

Four Canaanite names for the months appear in the OT: Abib, first month; Ziv, second month; Etanim, seventh month; Bul, eighth month. The postexilic names were Babylonian and are listed in ascending order: Nisan, Iyyar, Sivan, Tammuz, Ab, Elul, Tishri, Marchesvan, Chislev, Tebeth, Shebat, Adar. Nisan, mid-March to mid-April, coincides with the grain harvest. Thus the Feast of Unleavened Bread (Lev 23:6) and Firstfruits (Lev 23:10f.) occur in this month.

The centrality of the moon to this discussion may be seen in that Hebrew word *Yerah* means both *moon* and *month.* The same is true for the Hebrew word *Hodesh,* which means *new moon* and *month.* Both the Greek word *men* and English *month* point to the word *moon.* The apparent source of lunation is probably ancient Sumer, for which there is evidence as early as 2500 B.C. that a lunar calendar was being used.

Other Calendars

In 1908 a tablet that was dated from the tenth century B.C. was found at Gezer. While attempts to translate the tablet have differed, one common discovery was that the tablet was a record of an agricultural calendar separating a year into eight periods beginning with September and ending with October.

Some biblical evidence suggests that several changes in calendars had occurred. While the calendar used will probably remain unknown, 1 Kings 12:32-33 might suggest that Jereboam's innovations included a different calendar. The Talmud's interpretation of 2 Chronicles 30:2,13-15 might also support this idea. The possibility that a change may have occurred during Josiah's reform has also been suggested.

NT Issues

By NT times a number of competing calendars were being used. The calendar was a major point of conflict between the Pharisees and Sadducees since that would determine the dates for the actual holy days. The Samaritans seem to have followed Jereboam's, for theirs differed (and still does) from the others. Interestingly, the pseudepigraphic works, the Ethiopian Book of Enoch and Jubilees, both advocated strongly a solar calendar of 364 days. The publication of the temple scroll from Qumran has led scholars to agree that the sect there supported the 364-day solar calendar. The calendar appears to have been the sect's outstanding characteristic. Clearly the choice of a calendar had major theological implications for the followers of Moses. □

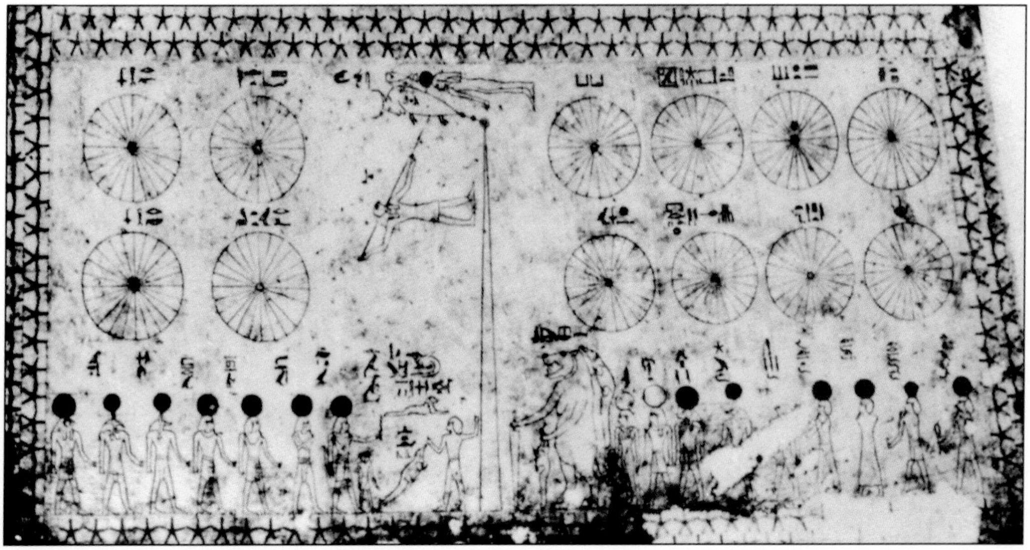

Astronomical drawings from the ceiling of the tomb of Senmut at Deir el-Bahri in Egypt (Eighteenth Dynasty). The circles represent the months of the civil year.

Western church based on the birth of Christ. He determined that birth to have been on December 25, 753 years after the agreed date for the founding of Rome, making the following January 1, A.D. 1. We know today that he was wrong. According to evidence from Josephus, Herod the Great, who was still very much alive when Jesus was born, died between March 12/13 and April 11, 4 B.C. Jesus was probably born not long before that, perhaps in late 5 B.C. or early 4 B.C.

The year of Jesus' crucifixion has been dated by various scholars at A.D. 21, 27, 28, 29, 30, 32, and 33. Although A.D. 30 is probably the majority opinion, Harold Hoehner presents a good argument for A.D. 33. According to Luke 3:1, John the Baptist began his ministry in the fifteenth year of Tiberias, which (if not counted from his co-regency with Augustus) was A.D. 28/29. Since the Gospel of John mentions three Passovers (2:13; 6:4; 11:55), tradition has held that Jesus' ministry lasted a little more than three years (although some have argued for a ministry of as little as three or four months). According to John 2:20, the first of those Passovers occurred forty-six years after Herod completed the temple building, which was in 18/17 B.C. Jesus' first Passover, then, was in A.D. 30, and he was crucified in A.D. 33.

Paul's conversion (Acts 9) is usually dated in A.D. 33 or 34, although Hoehner favors A.D. 35. The rest of Paul's life is dated as follows:

First Missionary Journey
Acts 13–14 A.D. 47/8–48/9
Second Missionary Journey
Acts 15–18 A.D. 49/50–51/2
Third Missionary Journey
Acts 18–21 A.D. 52/3–56/7
Arrest in Jerusalem
Acts 21 A.D. 56/7
Roman Imprisonment
Acts 28 A.D. 60–62
Death
A.D. 64–68?

Sources for Additional Study

Bickerman, E. J. *Chronology of the Ancient World.* Ithaca, N.Y.: Cornell University Press, 1965.

Finegan, Jack. *Handbook of Biblical Chronology.* Princeton, N.J.: Princeton University Press, 1964.

Hayes, John H. and Paul K. Hooker. *A New Chronology for the Kings of Israel and Judah.* Atlanta: John Knox, 1988.

Hoehner, Harold W. *Chronological Aspects of the Life of Christ.* Grand Rapids: Zondervan, 1977.

Thiele, Edwin A. *The Mysterious Numbers of the Hebrew Kings.* Revised. Grand Rapids: Zondervan, 1983.

Pentateuch

BIBLICAL HISTORY

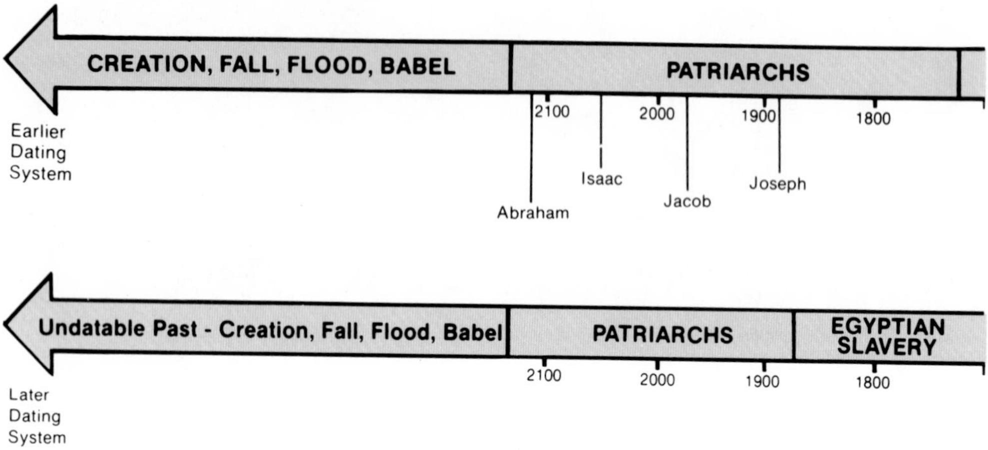

ANCIENT HISTORY

WORLD HISTORY

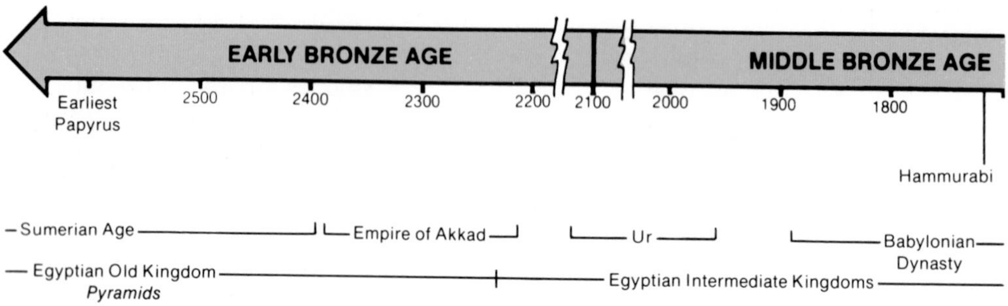

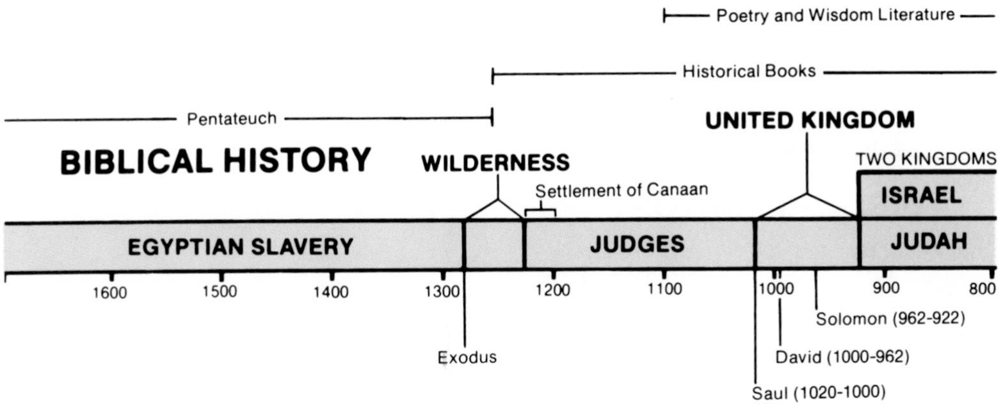
Poetry and Wisdom Literature
Historical Books
Pentateuch
UNITED KINGDOM
BIBLICAL HISTORY
WILDERNESS
TWO KINGDOMS
Settlement of Canaan
ISRAEL
EGYPTIAN SLAVERY
JUDGES
JUDAH
1600
1500
1400
1300
1200
1100
1000
900
800
Solomon (962-922)
Exodus
David (1000-962)
Saul (1020-1000)

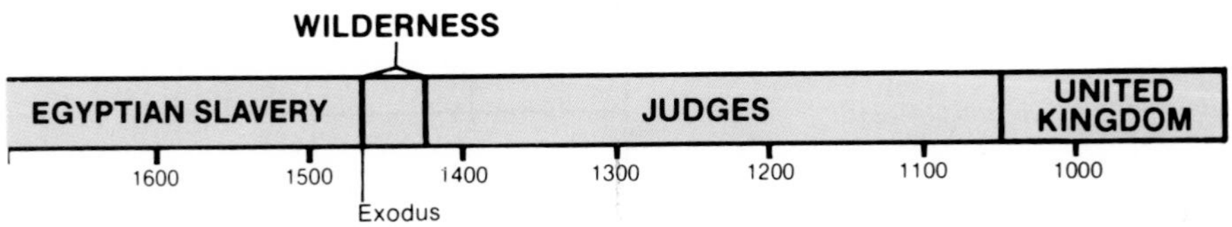
WILDERNESS
EGYPTIAN SLAVERY
JUDGES
UNITED KINGDOM
1600
1500
1400
1300
1200
1100
1000
Exodus

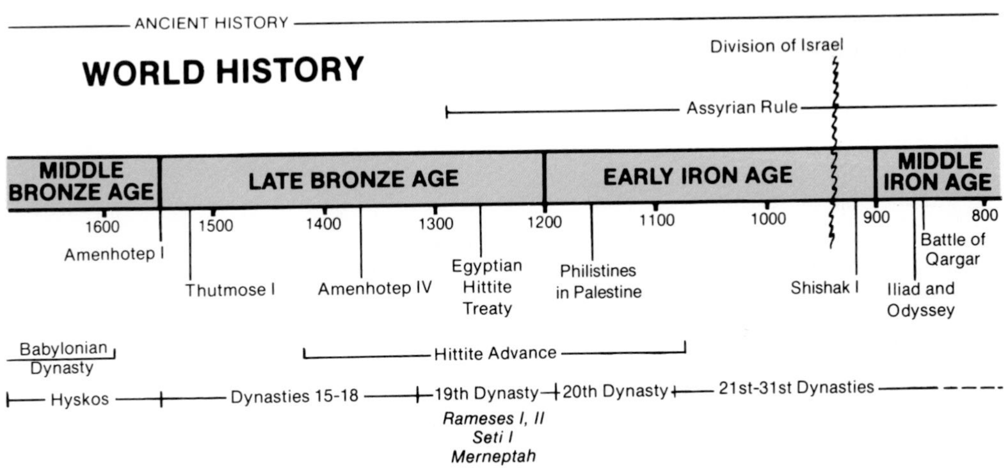
ANCIENT HISTORY
WORLD HISTORY
Division of Israel
Assyrian Rule
MIDDLE BRONZE AGE
LATE BRONZE AGE
EARLY IRON AGE
MIDDLE IRON AGE
1600
1500
1400
1300
1200
1100
1000
900
800
Amenhotep I
Thutmose I
Amenhotep IV
Egyptian Hittite Treaty
Philistines in Palestine
Shishak I
Battle of Qargar
Iliad and Odyssey
Babylonian Dynasty
Hittite Advance
Hyskos
Dynasties 15-18
19th Dynasty
20th Dynasty
21st-31st Dynasties
Rameses I, II
Seti I
Merneptah

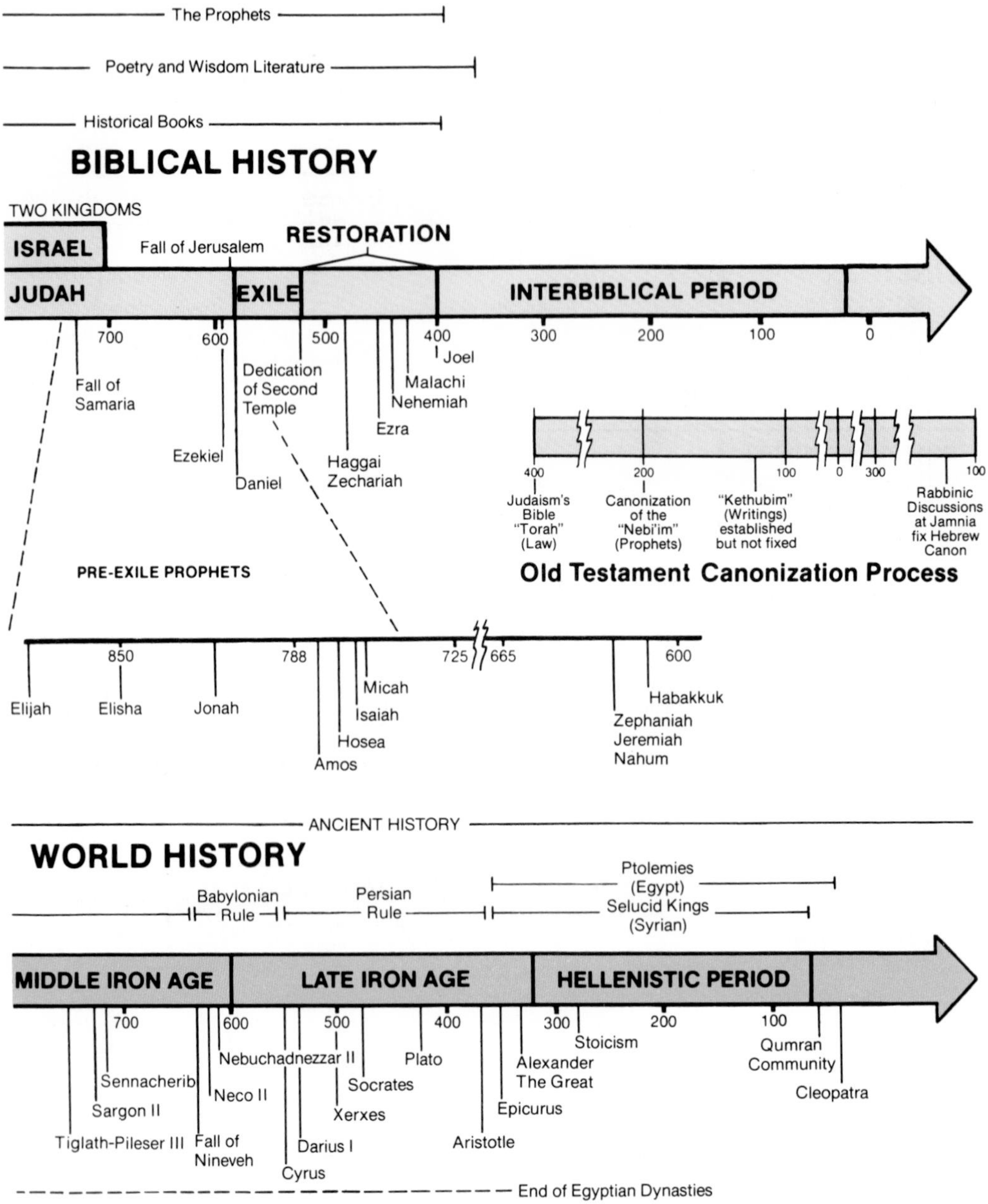
The Prophets
Poetry and Wisdom Literature
Historical Books
BIBLICAL HISTORY
TWO KINGDOMS
ISRAEL
JUDAH
Fall of Jerusalem
RESTORATION
EXILE
INTERBIBLICAL PERIOD
700
600
500
400
300
200
100
0
Joel
Fall of Samaria
Dedication of Second Temple
Malachi
Nehemiah
Ezra
Ezekiel
Haggai
Zechariah
Daniel
400
200
100
0
300
100
Judaism's Bible "Torah" (Law)
Canonization of the "Nebi'im" (Prophets)
"Kethubim" (Writings) established but not fixed
Rabbinic Discussions at Jamnia fix Hebrew Canon
Old Testament Canonization Process
PRE-EXILE PROPHETS
850
788
725
665
600
Elijah
Elisha
Jonah
Micah
Isaiah
Hosea
Amos
Habakkuk
Zephaniah
Jeremiah
Nahum
ANCIENT HISTORY
WORLD HISTORY
Ptolemies (Egypt)
Babylonian Rule
Persian Rule
Selucid Kings (Syrian)
MIDDLE IRON AGE
LATE IRON AGE
HELLENISTIC PERIOD
700
600
500
400
300
200
100
Nebuchadnezzar II
Plato
Stoicism
Qumran Community
Sennacherib
Alexander The Great
Socrates
Neco II
Sargon II
Epicurus
Cleopatra
Xerxes
Tiglath-Pileser III
Fall of Nineveh
Darius I
Aristotle
Cyrus
End of Egyptian Dynasties

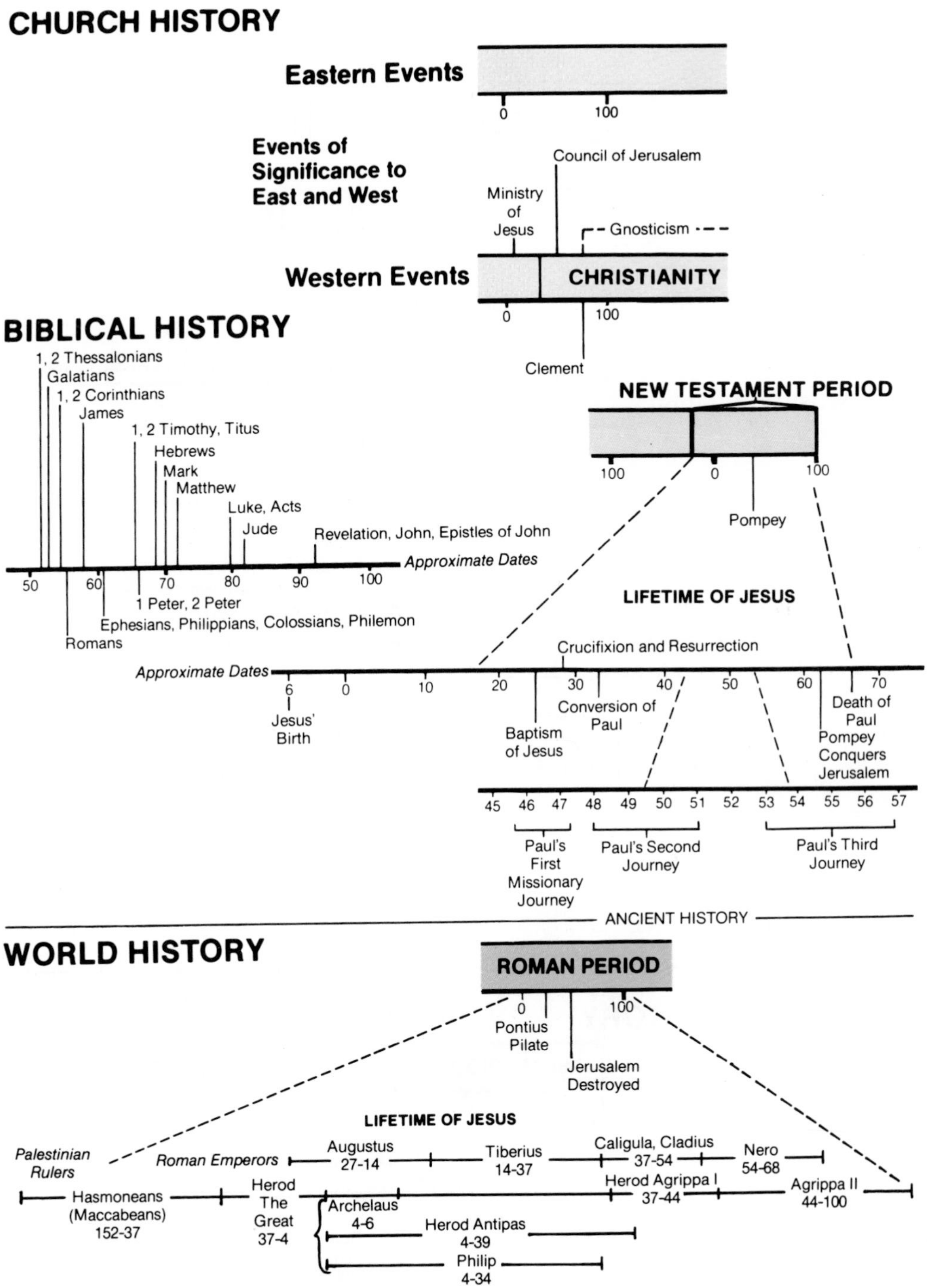
CHURCH HISTORY
Eastern Events
0
100
Events of Significance to East and West
Council of Jerusalem
Ministry of Jesus
Gnosticism
Western Events
CHRISTIANITY
0
100
Clement
BIBLICAL HISTORY
1, 2 Thessalonians
Galatians
1, 2 Corinthians
James
1, 2 Timothy, Titus
Hebrews
Mark
Matthew
Luke, Acts
Jude
Revelation, John, Epistles of John
Approximate Dates
50
60
70
80
90
100
1 Peter, 2 Peter
Ephesians, Philippians, Colossians, Philemon
Romans
NEW TESTAMENT PERIOD
100
0
100
Pompey
LIFETIME OF JESUS
Crucifixion and Resurrection
Approximate Dates
6
0
10
20
30
40
50
60
70
Jesus' Birth
Baptism of Jesus
Conversion of Paul
Death of Paul
Pompey Conquers Jerusalem
45
46
47
48
49
50
51
52
53
54
55
56
57
Paul's First Missionary Journey
Paul's Second Journey
Paul's Third Journey
ANCIENT HISTORY
WORLD HISTORY
ROMAN PERIOD
0
100
Pontius Pilate
Jerusalem Destroyed
LIFETIME OF JESUS
Palestinian Rulers
Roman Emperors
Augustus 27-14
Tiberius 14-37
Caligula, Cladius 37-54
Nero 54-68
Hasmoneans (Maccabeans) 152-37
Herod The Great 37-4
Archelaus 4-6
Herod Antipas 4-39
Philip 4-34
Herod Agrippa I 37-44
Agrippa II 44-100

CHURCH HISTORY

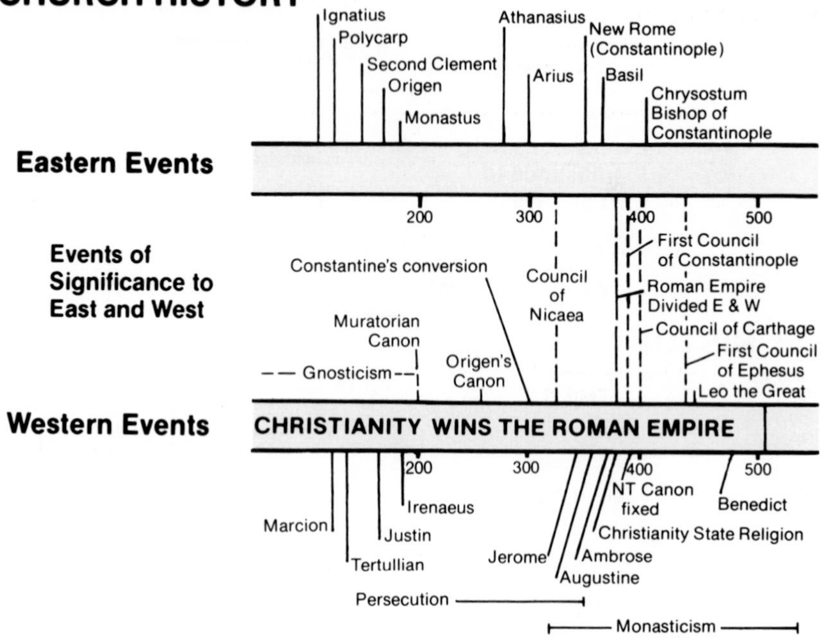
Ignatius
Polycarp
Second Clement
Origen
Monastus
Athanasius
Arius
New Rome (Constantinople)
Basil
Chrysostum Bishop of Constantinople
Eastern Events
200
300
400
500
Events of Significance to East and West
Constantine's conversion
Council of Nicaea
First Council of Constantinople
Roman Empire Divided E & W
Council of Carthage
First Council of Ephesus
Leo the Great
Muratorian Canon
Gnosticism
Origen's Canon
Western Events
CHRISTIANITY WINS THE ROMAN EMPIRE
200
300
400
500
Marcion
Tertullian
Justin
Irenaeus
Jerome
Augustine
Ambrose
Christianity State Religion
NT Canon fixed
Benedict
Persecution
Monasticism

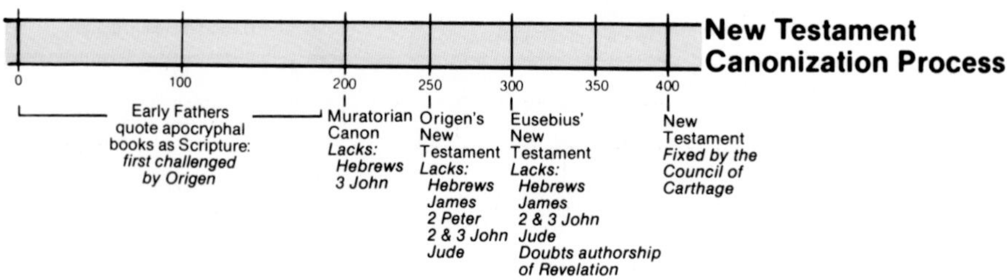
New Testament Canonization Process
0
100
200
250
300
350
400
Early Fathers quote apocryphal books as Scripture: first challenged by Origen
Muratorian Canon Lacks: Hebrews 3 John
Origen's New Testament Lacks: Hebrews James 2 Peter 2 & 3 John Jude
Eusebius' New Testament Lacks: Hebrews James 2 & 3 John Jude Doubts authorship of Revelation
New Testament Fixed by the Council of Carthage

ANCIENT HISTORY —— MEDIEVAL HISTORY

WORLD HISTORY

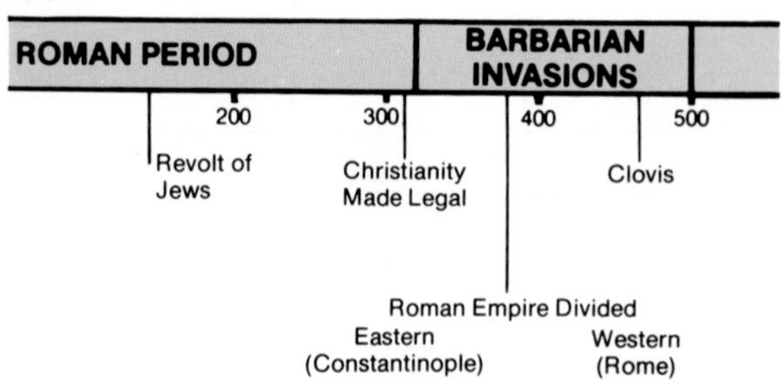
ROMAN PERIOD
BARBARIAN INVASIONS
200
300
400
500
Revolt of Jews
Christianity Made Legal
Clovis
Roman Empire Divided
Eastern (Constantinople)
Western (Rome)

CHURCH HISTORY

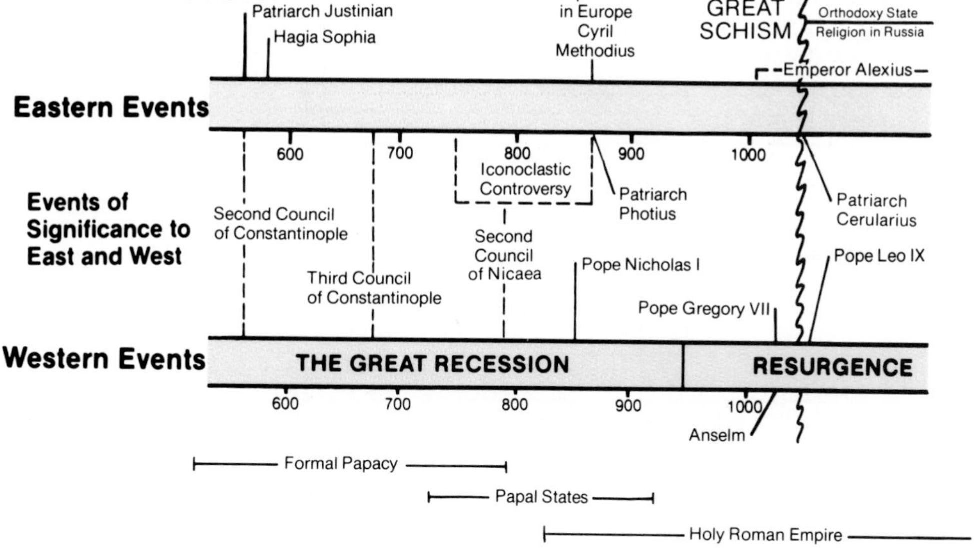

Patriarch Justinian
Hagia Sophia
Missionary Expansion in Europe Cyril Methodius
Imperial Byzantium
GREAT SCHISM
Orthodoxy State Religion in Russia
Emperor Alexius
Eastern Events
600
700
800
900
1000
Iconoclastic Controversy
Events of Significance to East and West
Second Council of Constantinople
Patriarch Photius
Patriarch Cerularius
Second Council of Nicaea
Pope Leo IX
Pope Nicholas I
Third Council of Constantinople
Pope Gregory VII
Western Events
THE GREAT RECESSION
RESURGENCE
600
700
800
900
1000
Anselm
Formal Papacy
Papal States
Holy Roman Empire

Doctrines Addressed by the Early Church Councils

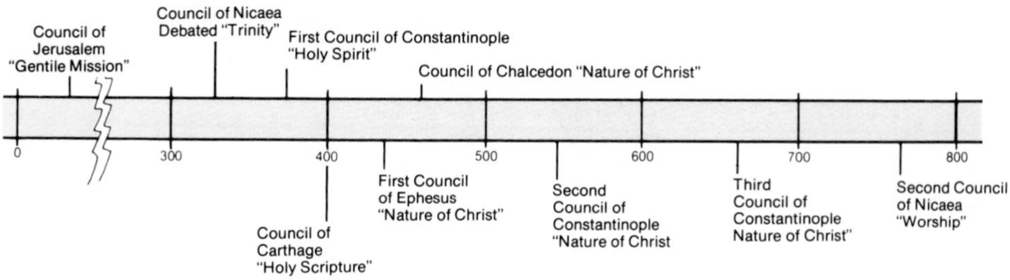

Council of Jerusalem "Gentile Mission"
Council of Nicaea Debated "Trinity"
First Council of Constantinople "Holy Spirit"
Council of Chalcedon "Nature of Christ"
0
300
400
500
600
700
800
First Council of Ephesus "Nature of Christ"
Second Council of Constantinople "Nature of Christ
Third Council of Constantinople Nature of Christ"
Second Council of Nicaea "Worship"
Council of Carthage "Holy Scripture"

MEDIEVAL HISTORY

WORLD HISTORY

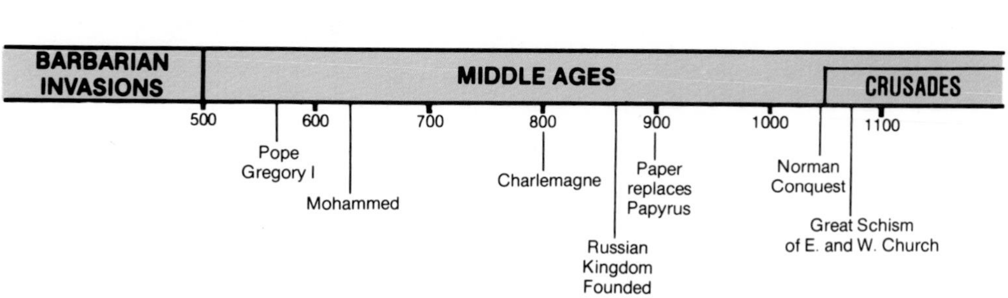

BARBARIAN INVASIONS
MIDDLE AGES
CRUSADES
500
600
700
800
900
1000
1100
Pope Gregory I
Mohammed
Charlemagne
Paper replaces Papyrus
Norman Conquest
Great Schism of E. and W. Church
Russian Kingdom Founded

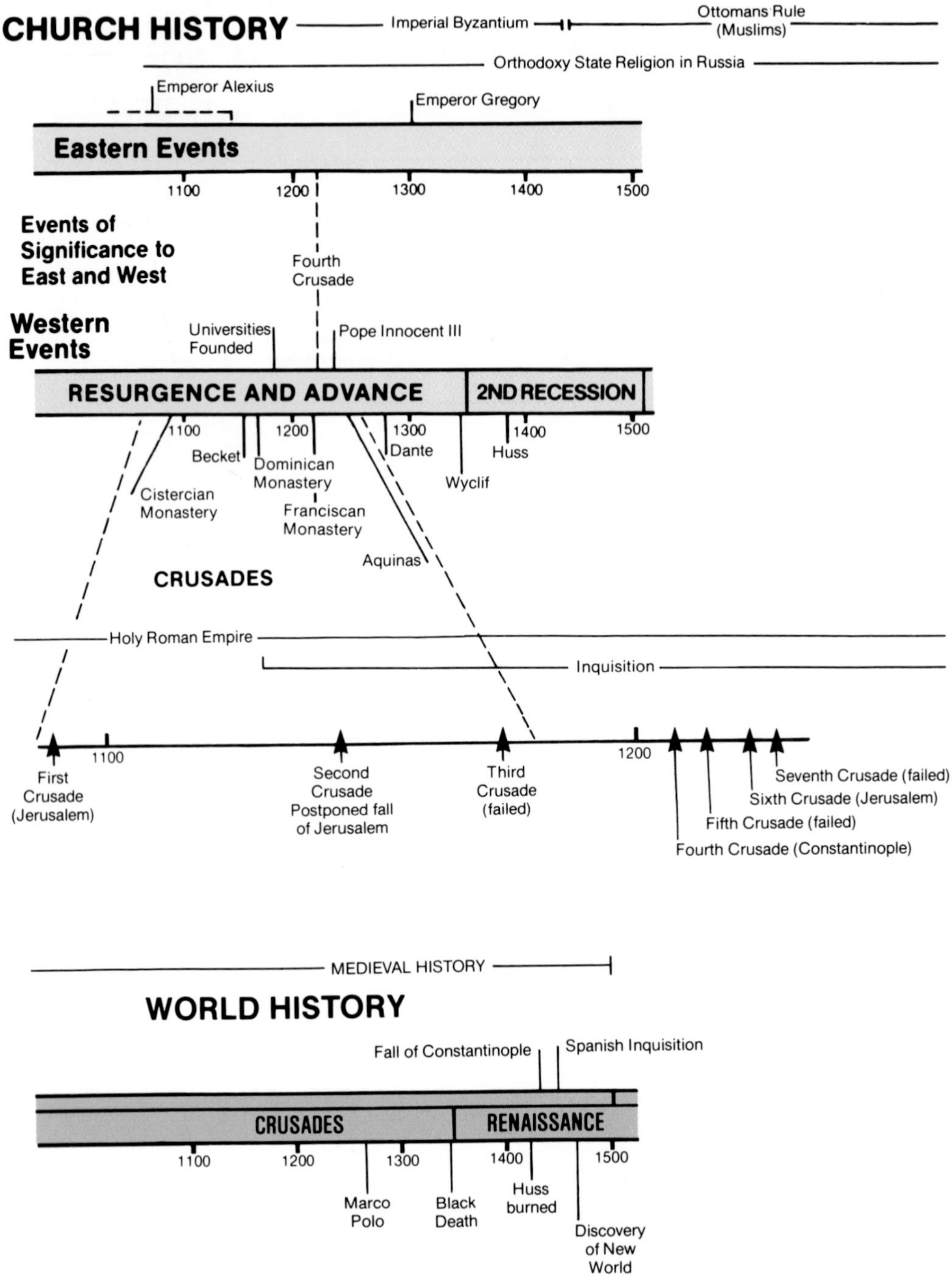
CHURCH HISTORY
Imperial Byzantium
Ottomans Rule (Muslims)
Orthodoxy State Religion in Russia
Emperor Alexius
Emperor Gregory
Eastern Events
1100
1200
1300
1400
1500
Events of Significance to East and West
Fourth Crusade
Western Events
Universities Founded
Pope Innocent III
RESURGENCE AND ADVANCE
2ND RECESSION
Becket
Dominican Monastery
Dante
Huss
Wyclif
Cistercian Monastery
Franciscan Monastery
Aquinas
CRUSADES
Holy Roman Empire
Inquisition
First Crusade (Jerusalem)
Second Crusade Postponed fall of Jerusalem
Third Crusade (failed)
Seventh Crusade (failed)
Sixth Crusade (Jerusalem)
Fifth Crusade (failed)
Fourth Crusade (Constantinople)
MEDIEVAL HISTORY
WORLD HISTORY
Fall of Constantinople
Spanish Inquisition
CRUSADES
RENAISSANCE
Marco Polo
Black Death
Huss burned
Discovery of New World

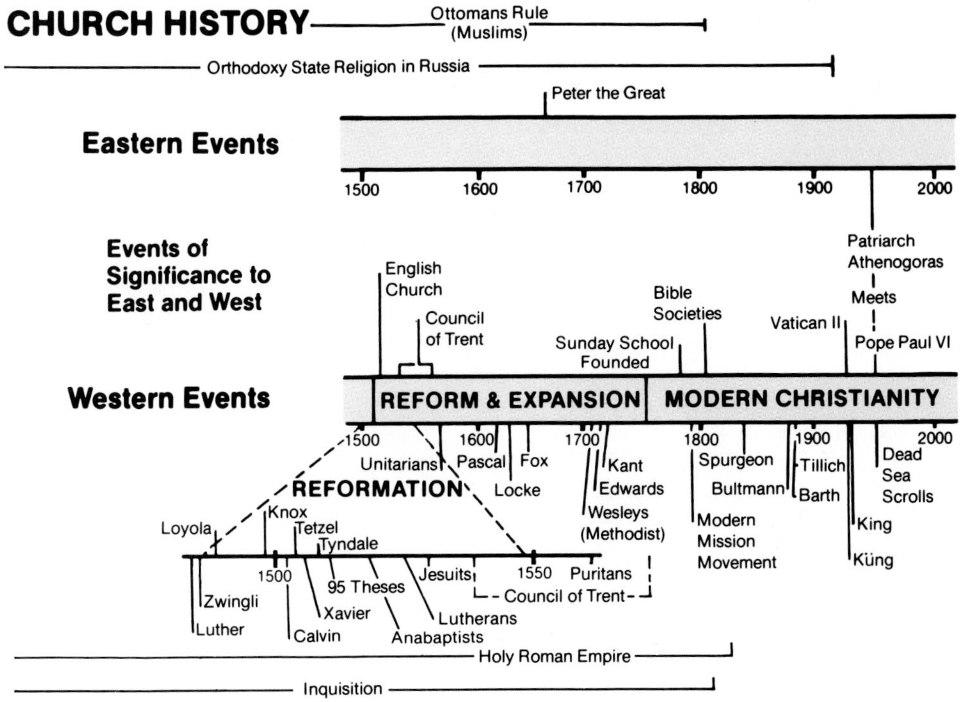
CHURCH HISTORY
Ottomans Rule (Muslims)
Orthodoxy State Religion in Russia
Peter the Great
Eastern Events
1500
1600
1700
1800
1900
2000
Events of Significance to East and West
Patriarch Athenogoras
Meets
Pope Paul VI
English Church
Council of Trent
Bible Societies
Sunday School Founded
Vatican II
Western Events
REFORM & EXPANSION
MODERN CHRISTIANITY
Unitarians
Pascal
Fox
Locke
Kant
Edwards
Wesleys (Methodist)
Spurgeon
Bultmann
Tillich
Barth
Dead Sea Scrolls
Modern Mission Movement
King
Küng
REFORMATION
Loyola
Knox
Tetzel
Tyndale
Zwingli
Luther
95 Theses
Xavier
Calvin
Jesuits
Anabaptists
Lutherans
1550
Puritans
Council of Trent
Holy Roman Empire
Inquisition

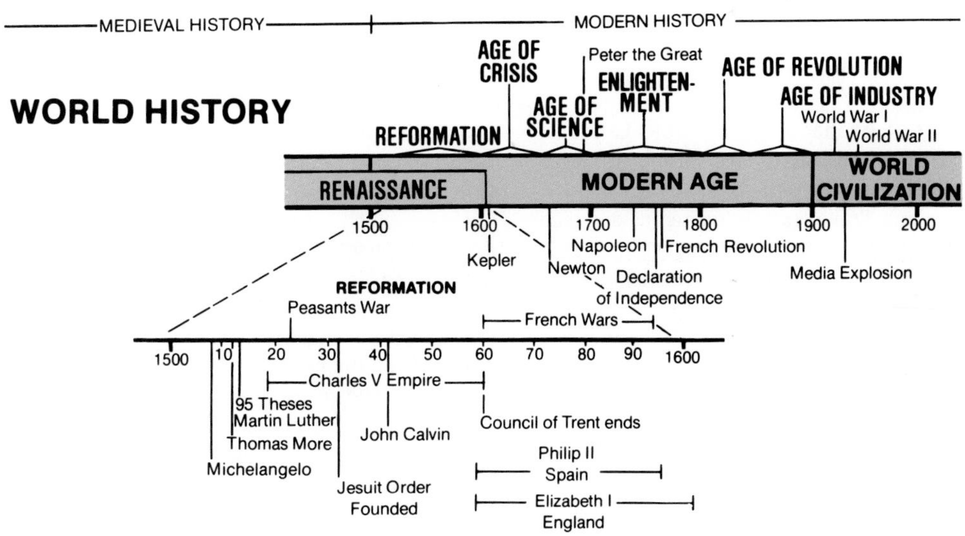
MEDIEVAL HISTORY
MODERN HISTORY
WORLD HISTORY
AGE OF CRISIS
Peter the Great
ENLIGHTEN-MENT
AGE OF REVOLUTION
AGE OF SCIENCE
AGE OF INDUSTRY
World War I
World War II
REFORMATION
RENAISSANCE
MODERN AGE
WORLD CIVILIZATION
1500
1600
1700
1800
1900
2000
Kepler
Newton
Napoleon
French Revolution
Declaration of Independence
Media Explosion
REFORMATION
Peasants War
French Wars
10
20
30
40
50
60
70
80
90
Charles V Empire
95 Theses
Martin Luther
Thomas More
Michelangelo
John Calvin
Jesuit Order Founded
Council of Trent ends
Philip II Spain
Elizabeth I England

BIBLICAL ARCHAEOLOGY

Archaeology is the study of ancient cultures as found in the material remains left in the ancient sites where people have lived.

Biblical archaeology is the systematic study of the material/physical remains of ancient persons in the lands where biblical history has taken place. Such places include Palestine (present-day Israel), Transjordan (modern Jordan), Egypt, Syria, Lebanon, Turkey (ancient Asia Minor), Greece, and Italy. A biblical archaeologist seeks to correlate archaeological findings with biblical narratives.

Types of Archaeological Materials

The objects of archaeological investigation of ancient cultural remains include mounds (tells); caves; man-made tombs and graves; human and animal skeletal remains; pottery remains and other artifacts of metal, stone, and glass. They include inscriptions/texts found on stone, parchment, papyri, and baked clay; coins; building remains; religious and legal items, such as altars, religious equipment, fertility figurines and other cult objects; testimonial monumental stones; the sequence of soil layers (laid down by humans); microscopic material in soil deposits indicating human and animal diet; water supplies; defense devices; agricultural production; road systems; bridges; and commercial structures. Archaeologists also study modern patterns of living and working that reflect the life-style of the people there in ancient times.

History of Archaeology in Bible Lands

Archaeological investigation in the Bible lands began early and in a simple fashion.

Pilgrims and Travelers. In the second and third centuries local and pilgrim Christians were interested in the holy lands. They thought about the biblical events and the material remains pointing to those events. For example, they were interested in the early indication that Jesus was born in a cave (Justin Martyr, Jerome), that He was crucified at the place of the skull and buried in a new tomb of Joseph of Arimathea. They wanted to know about the Pool of Siloam, the place where Jesus sent the blind man He healed, and other sites.

The Explorers. About 1800 a German named Seetzen first scientifically investigated Transjordan and discovered Caesarea Philippi. (There Jesus had asked His disciples, "Who do you say I am?" [Matt 16:15].) They discovered Amman (Rabboth Ammon, where at David's command Uriah the Hittite died in battle, 2 Sam 11:15) and Jerash (Gerasa, where Jesus healed the Gerasene demoniac, Mark 5:1). The Swiss explorer Burckhardt rediscovered Petra.

Topographers and Surveyors. In 1838 an American named Edward Robinson went to Palestine and identified for the first time in the modern period many of the biblical places. In the mid-1800s the Frenchman de Saulcy was the first modern excavator of a Palestinian site. The Englishman Charles Warren was sent to excavate Jerusalem. He dated the Herodian masonry of the great retaining wall of the ancient temple platform. The Frenchman Charles Clermont-Ganneau in the 1870s recovered the famous Mesha inscription stone (2 Kgs 3:4) and found the famous stone inscription prohibiting the admission of the Gentiles into the temple court on pain of death (see Acts 21:28-29).

Beginning of Pottery Analysis. In the 1890s the Englishman Sir Flinders Petrie, first working in Egypt and then in Palestine, developed a system of dating the biblical periods and events by observing and recording the differences in pottery forms, texture, and painting. As pottery sherds were found in the various layers of soil at the ancient sites, Petrie discovered differences that showed up in the same sequential order in various sites.

Stratigraphic Recording. In the twentieth century the Britisher Kathleen Kenyon and others developed the technique of observing and drawing the distinctive soil layers and other features exposed in the perpendicular walls of the squares of a site. They related these results to the pottery and other items found there in sequential order. By this method different and successive cultural patterns were distinguished.

Interdisciplinary Team. Recognizing the complex task of interpreting the cultural material unearthed, archaeologists began bringing together experts from a number of scientific disciplines. They formed teams of experts such as surveyors/architects, photographers, geologists, and osteologists.

Volunteer archaeological field workers at a site in central Israel meticulously scrape away the soil of their area in order to discover the history of the site's various layers.

The Chronological Scope of Biblical Archaeology

To understand the chronological setting and cultural background of the Bible events, it is necessary to relate them to the standard chart of Palestinian chronological periods (see chart).

Scope of Researchers

The countries involved in archaeology in Bible lands include the United States, Canada, England, France, Germany, Denmark, Spain, Italy, Greece, Turkey, Egypt, Israel, Jordan, and Syria.

The persons involved are usually professors and their students from colleges, universities, and seminaries and also national departments of antiquities in many of the foreign countries.

Survey of Recent Results

Sites with a Long History. Examples of sites with a long archaeological history are: (1) Jerusalem, with a history extending from Neolithic times to modern period; (2) Abila, of the Decapolis (Matt 4:25; Mark 5:20; 7:31), with an archaeological history from Neolithic times down through Late Islamic and Turkish times; and (3) Pella, also of the Decapolis, with habitation from Chalcolithic to Islamic times.

Sampling of Recent Findings

Ebla, Tell Mardikh in northern Syria. Although Ebla (about 2300–2600 B.C.), is not mentioned in the Bible, it may be that the Ebla tablets mention Jerusalem. In the 1970s Italian excavators found about fifteen to twenty thousand tablets and fragments in the Royal Archives section of ancient Ebla by the Italian excavators. Excavation continues at Ebla, now known to have been a city of international importance in the third millennium.

Tell Daba/Rameses, in the Eastern Nile Delta. Tell Daba probably is biblical Rameses (Exod 1:11) in the Eastern Nile Delta region. Excavations there are important in relating Egyptian chronology to ancient Israelite chronology, especially in the Middle and Late Bronze Ages, and can have a bearing on the dates of Israel's exodus and conquest of Canaan.

Jericho/Ai/Heshbon. Each of these sites has been excavated within the past four to five decades. The results of the excavations relate to the problem of the date of Israel's conquest of Canaan, whether the older traditional time of about 1400 B.C. or later, about 1290 or 1250 to 1225 B.C. or even later. The pottery and other artifactual evidence and building remains have given rise to differences of opinion about an early or late date of the exodus. Some scholars have proposed that the traditional identification of et-Tell as Ai (Josh 7–8) is incorrect, and search is underway in the nearby area to find the Ai of the Late Bronze period.

At Heshbon (Num 21:25) the excavations have uncovered material that only takes the site archaeologically back to 1200 B.C. Therefore it is argued that the earlier Late Bronze Heshbon of the conquest, thoroughly destroyed by the Israelites, is to be located at nearby Tell Jalul, a site within view of Heshbon and just east of Madaba. Jalul does have Late Bronze sherds on its surface and needs to be excavated to test this hypothesis. At Jericho (Josh 6), because the mudbrick walls have largely been washed away, excavators have felt that the city does not fit a date for the conquest at 1400 B.C. However, some scholars have argued that a reevaluation of the pottery of Jericho, which has been published recently, points to a Late Bronze Jericho of the conquest after all.

Arad. Arad is west of the Dead Sea and at the northern edge of the Negev. Excavated in the 1960s and 1970s, Arad was one of the cities conquered by Joshua (Josh 12:14; compare Num 21:1; 33:40). It is of particular interest because archaeologists found there an Iron Age temple. (It probably served as a border sanctuary in the time of the monarchy; the cult objects found point to a fairly pure worship of Yahweh.) Arad's temple was similar in plan to Solomon's temple, with altar, holy place, and holy of holies. Evidence at the site shows habitation back to the Chalcolithic and Early Bronze Ages.

Beersheba. At the northern edge of the Negev, Tell Beersheba is located about five miles east of the modern city. Beersheba was important in the lives of Abraham (Gen 21:14,31-33; 22:19), Isaac (Gen 26:23,33), and Jacob (Gen 28:10; 46:1,5). It was known as one of the boundaries of Israel (Judg 20:1; 1 Sam 3:20; 1 Kgs 4:25; 1 Chr 21:2).

In the area of Tell Beersheba, Chalcolithic remains have been found, but habitation on the mound itself dates from the twelfth to the seventh centuries B.C. Excavation at the tell began in 1969 and continued into the 1970s. Remains were found of an Iron Age temple, probably a border sanctuary in the time of the monarchy, but the cult objects show a strong pagan influence, mainly Egyptian. Amos 5:5 and 8:14 condemn the pagan worship there. Also found were a crater (bowl) with the Hebrew word for "holiness" inscribed on it and a horned altar (Exod 29:12), similar to the ones found at Megiddo and Dan.

Dan. Located in northern Galilee near the foot of Mount Hermon, Dan (Gen 14:14) was formerly known as Laish (Judg 18:29). After the conquest it became the northern border of Israel (Dan to Beersheba, Judg 20:1; 2 Sam 3:10; 2 Chr 30:5) and was also famous for the golden calf Jeroboam I set up there (1 Kgs 12:29,30; 2 Kgs 1:29). Excavation, which has continued there from 1966 on, has shown human habitation in the Early, Middle, Late Bronze, and Iron Ages. Important finds at the site include a high place (1 Sam 9:19; 1 Kgs 12:31), a horned altar (similar to the one found at Tell Beersheba), an eighteenth century B.C. Middle Bronze gateway cominscription in Greek and Aramaic on a limestone plaque that mentions worship of "the god of Dan." (Compare Amos 8:14, which also speaks of the god of Dan.) Also recently found were an eighth century B.C. altar and three incense shovels, part of the ancient sacrificial system, as existed there in the time of Amos (Amos 8:14).

Deir Alla/Succoth, the Jordan Valley. Deir Alla, generally identified with Succoth, was inhabited in the Chalcolithic, Late Bronze, and Iron I and II periods. Deir Alla is near where the burnished bronze objects for Solomon's temple were cast (1 Kgs 7:46). Painted religious texts found there in the eighth century B.C. preserve the religious tradition of centuries past in the mention of "Balaam, son of Beor, who was a seer of the gods" (compare Num 22:5).

Gezer. Located in the Shephelah, northwest of Jerusalem, Gezer (Josh 10:33; 16:3,10; 1 Kgs 9:16) shows habitation from the Chalcolithic to Roman times. It has

ARCHAEOLOGICAL METHODOLOGY

PRELIMINARY PROCESS

Site Selection and Identification: locating an excavation site.

Fund Raising: obtaining financial assistance from individuals and institutions.

Staff and volunteer selection: assembling a competent staff (usually composed of college, university, and seminary professors who have archaeological expertise) and volunteers (students and others with an interest in archaeology) who will go to the site for six to eight weeks during the summer months and "dig" at their own expense.

Field Survey: collecting and studying ancient remains (metal, glass, and pottery) that lie on the surface of the ground at the site in order to determine their age and thus the periods when people lived on the site.

PROCEDURE AT THE SITE

Using a surveyor's instrument, the architect begins by laying out units or squares (sixteen feet by sixteen feet each). A unit or square is dug by using a small pick to penetrate the soil one or two inches at a time. The soil is then scraped back with a small trowel, insuring that each distinctive layer of soil, ash, and floor is recognized as a separate living unit.

As each layer (or locus) is reached, it is recorded accurately on the locus sheet in the field book. All of the artifacts are collected and placed in tag-identified buckets for processing. (When the artifacts are brought from the excavation, they are cleaned and chemically treated where necessary to conserve their structure and preserve them for future study and display.) All features such as walls and column pieces are analyzed, described on the field locus sheet, and drawn to scale. The photographer takes photos of the work as it progresses and takes final photos at the end. (Video camcorders are now beginning to be utilized in this process.)

The square supervisors must make a scale drawing of each of the four perpendicular sides (or balks) of the square. This gives a perpendicular profile, layer by layer (called a stratigraphic profile) of the cultural and chronological changes that have taken place at that point.

Computer technology is often utilized today in archaeological field work to store pottery and artifact data and to aid in the various analytical studies, and computer graphics are often used in drawing architectural features of the site.

TECHNICAL ANALYSIS

NUMISMATIC ANALYSIS

The presence of coins at a site can aid in the dating of the particular stratas in which they are found. The layer or stratum cannot be dated to an earlier time than the date of the coin found in it. Coins were first used in Asia Minor by the Lydians about 650 B.C.

OSTEOLOGICAL ANALYSIS

All human skeletal remains found in the site's tombs or living quarters are excavated; conserved; identified; and analyzed for age, sex, diet, and pathological abnormalities. This is the job of either an anthropologist or an M.D. Some excavations also hire zoologists to do the same analysis of animal remains.

ETHNOARCHAEOLOGICAL ANALYSIS

People currently living around the site are studied, and comparisons are drawn between the results of this study and the cultural information obtained from the excavated ancient layers/strata of the site.

SOIL ANALYSIS

Systematic samplings of soil deposits from living areas and the cemetery of the site are analyzed to help determine the concentration of human beings and animals at the site and to identify the type of diet consumed by both humans and animals. They are screened to separate the carbonized seeds and other particles and are sometimes chemically treated to determine the alkaline and acid content of the soil, which also gives clues about the concentration of humans or animals.

CERAMIC ANALYSIS

After pottery is soaked, washed, and dried in the sun, it is "read" (that is, critical judgments are made about the chronological time period in which the vessel was made and was in use). All whole or sufficiently whole vessels are saved, as well as those pieces (called "sherds") that have distinctively characteristic rims, bases, handles, clay texture, surface decoration, or painting. These pieces are registered, drawn, and photographed for further study.

SPECIALIZED ANALYTICAL PROCEDURES

(related to the study of artifacts, bone, charcoal, and stone)

Dendrochronology: dating based upon the growth rings in the wood of trees.

Radiocarbon (Carbon–14) Dating: dating based upon the level of carbon–14 residue in the specimen.

Potassium–Argon Dating: dating of a mineral based upon the level of original potassium that has decayed.

Thermoluminescence Dating: dating of pottery based upon the radioactive energy stored in the pottery from the day it was fired in the kiln.

Fission Track Dating: dating by using an electron microscope to track the fossil fission concentration in natural and man-made glass and other material.

Archaeomagnetic Dating: dating by measuring the earth's magnetic field intensity locked up in the baked clay objects at the time they cooled after being baked in a kiln or oven.

Flourine Dating: relative dating of bone by measuring the flourine which has been absorbed by the bone from the earth surrounding it and comparing this level with the level found in other bones in the same area. (Not used for absolute dating.)

Radiometric Assay: relative dating of bone or other artifact based upon the amount of uranium it contains. (Not used for absolute dating.)

Collagen Content: relative dating of bone by the amount of collagen remaining in it (which involves measuring the nitrogen content of the bone).

Pollen Analysis (also called Palynology): the analysis of pollen grains in relation to the soil and the environment from which they were extracted (acidity level of the soil, arid climate of the region, and so forth).

Other techniques, including thermal neutron analysis of metals, neutron activation analysis, and X-ray fluorescence spectroscopy, might also be employed depending upon cost and applicability.

been clearly identified by several nearby boundary stones reading, "The boundary of Gezer." Excavation first occurred at Gezer early in the twentieth century and then in the 1930s, 1960s, and 1970s. Important finds include a 1600 B.C. south gate and large tower; an important "high place" also of about 1600 B.C., consisting of ten monoliths (large standing stones; the Solomonic gate similar to the ones built at Megiddo and Hazor (compare 1 Kgs 9:15); and also an agricultural calendar written in an old Hebrew script.

Hazor. North of the Sea of Galilee, Hazor was first excavated in 1928 and at various intervals in succeeding decades. It has yielded evidence showing that this city was important in the Middle, Late Bronze, and Iron Ages. Excavation has shown that Hazor continued in its strength until it was fully destroyed in the thirteenth century B.C. It was conquered by Joshua (Josh 11:10-13), later fortified by Solomon (1 Kgs 9:15), later taken by the Assyrians (2 Kgs 15:29), and taken still later by the Babylonians (Jer 49:28-30).

Three Canaanite temple sites have been found in the lower city, one of which from Late Bronze II A and B has a porch, a holy place, and a holy of holies, similar in design to Solomon's temple (1 Kgs 6) and to the one at Arad. A number of standing stones (stele) and statuettes from the Late Bronze Canaanite temple were also found. The Hazor upper city yielded a Late Bronze palace structure. The city of Solomon's time, with a gate system similar to those at Gezer and Megiddo (1 Kgs 9:15) did not cover the whole tell. However, in Ahab's time (874–853 B.C.) the city had strong fortifications and was much larger. Also discovered was an elaborate underground Iron Age water system, similar to the ones discovered in Jerusalem (2 Kgs 20:20), Megiddo, Gezer, and in recent days at Abila of the Decapolis, to the southeast of Hazor in Transjordan.

Lachish (modern Tell ed-Duweir). Lachish (Josh 10:3,31) is in the Shephelah, west of Hebron. It was fortified by Rehoboam (2 Chr 11:9), captured by the Assyrian Sennacherib (2 Kgs 18-19), taken again by the Babylonians (Jer 34:7), and occupied later after the exile (Neh 11:30). Like Gezer to the north, it was one of the fortress cities guarding the passes up into the hill country. Lachish was first excavated in the 1930s and then again in the 1970s and 1980s. The city's human history goes back to 8000 B.C. and on into the Chalcolithic and Early Bronze Ages when the people lived in nearby caves. Then they moved to the tell. The Egyptians exercised strong influence on the site in the Middle and Late Bronze periods. Important archaeological finds here include a Canaanite temple of the Late Bronze period and a palace of the Israelite period (Iron Age). Also found were numerous Egyptian seals, scarabs and tax records, a number of Hebrew seals, weights, inscribed jar handles, and a group of eighteen ostraca (pottery sherds with notes written on them). The ostraca are written in Hebrew and date to just before Lachish's fall to Nebuchadnezzar in 587/6 B.C.

Meggido, Tell el-Mutesellim. Meggido is on a southeast edge of Mount Carmel, guarding the pass to the Mediterranean Sea coast. Megiddo was first excavated in the first decade of the twentieth century and then in the 1920s, 1930s, and again in the 1960s. The finds included a cuneiform tablet (a clay tablet inscribed with wedge-shaped characters) containing part of an early heathen creation poem (the *Gilgemish Epic*) and a number of imports from Egypt and the Aegean area, including carved ivories. Also found was a large Canaanite temple (about 1800 B.C.) with a *bamah,* or high place (1 Kgs 11:7). Megiddo was defeated by Israelites under Joshua (Josh 12:21) and finally defeated about 1150 B.C. by Egyptians or Philistines. A rather poor but new Philistine/Canaanite city then grew up.

Megiddo was considerably renovated in Solomon's time (1 Kgs 9:15). The six-chambered Solomonic gate, similar to the ones in Hazor and Gezer, has been found. The stables (or possibly storehouses) attributed by earlier excavators to Solomon's time have been reinvestigated and found to be of the time of the Omri Dynasty (1 Kgs 16:23-24), probably of the time of Ahab.

The Megiddo water tunnel system seems to belong to this same period. A number of ceramic heathen cult figures were also found in the various Israelite levels of Megiddo, indicating the influence foreign religious practices had among the people. Archaeological research has shown that in the Assyrian period (compare 2 Kgs 15:19) Megiddo was made into an administrative center based on the Assyrian plan.

Sarepta. Sarepta is a Phoenician town belonging to Sidon Sarafand, Lebanon, the biblical Zarephath. The results of the 1969 to 1974 excavations at Sarepta dealing with the Late Bronze and Iron Ages (1600 to 600 B.C.) were published in 1988. Zarephath is mentioned in 1 Kings 17:8-28 as the place to which Elijah the prophet went to meet the widow who was to supply him with food. It is also mentioned in Obadiah 20 and in Luke 4:26, where Jesus mentioned the story of this miraculous provision.

Jerusalem, Old Testament. This jewel of Palestine, Zion, the city of God, was inhabited as far back as prehistoric times. Excavation there has been undertaken from 1870 on. The most recent excavations have concentrated on the City of David on the southeast spur of

ARCHAEOLOGICAL PERIODS OF PALESTINE

Archaeological Period	Approximate Dates *	Biblical Events
PALEOLITHIC (Old Stone Age)	Before 10,000 B.C.	Gen 1–11
MESOLITHIC (Middle Stone Age)	10,000–8000 B.C.	Gen 1–11
NEOLITHIC (New Stone Age)	8000–4500 B.C.	Gen 1–11
Pre-Pottery Neolithic	8000–6000 B.C.	
Pottery Neolithic	6000–4500 B.C.	
CHALCOLITHIC (Bronze/Stone Age)	4500–3150 B.C.	Gen 1–11
BRONZE (or CANAANITE)	3150–1200 B.C.	
Early Bronze	3150–2200 B.C.	Gen 1–11
I	3150–2850 B.C.	
II	2850–2650 B.C.	
III	2650–2350 B.C.	
IV	2350–2200 B.C.	
Middle Bronze	2200–1550 B.C.	
I	2200–1950 B.C.	Abraham
IIA	1950–1750 B.C.	Jacob enters Egypt
IIB	1750–1550 B.C.	
Late Bronze	1550–1200 B.C.	The exodus and conquest
I	1550–1400 B.C.	
IIA	1400–1300 B.C.	
IIB	1300–1200 B.C.	
IRON (or ISRAELITE)	1200–586 B.C.	
Iron I (or Early Iron)	1200–1000 B.C.	
IA	1200–1150 B.C.	
IB	1150–1000 B.C.	David becomes king
Iron II (or Middle Iron)	1000–800 B.C.	
IIA	1000–900 B.C.	
IIB	900–800 B.C.	
Iron III (or Iron IIC)	800–586 B.C.	Israel and Judah fall (722 and 586 B.C.)
PERSIAN (or BABYLONIAN/PERSIAN, or Late Iron)	586–332 B.C.	Babylonian captivity (586–539 B.C.)
HELLENISTIC	332–37 B.C.	
I	332–152 B.C.	
II (or Hasmonean/Maccabean)	152–37 B.C.	
ROMAN	37 B.C.–A.D. 324	
I (or Early Roman, or Herodian)	37 B.C.–A.D. 70	Jesus Christ
II (or Middle Roman)	A.D. 70–180	
III (or Late Roman)	A.D. 180–324	
BYZANTINE (Early Church Age of Roman Empire)	A.D. 324–640	
Early Byzantine	A.D. 324–491	
Late Byzantine	A.D. 491–640	

* Dates vary, but they give the reader some idea about the definition of the various archaeological time periods as they are utilized in current archaeological writings.

the site, just south of the temple platform on which Solomon's temple was built. Excavations at the City of David (first mentioned as such in 2 Sam 5:7,9; 6:10) have uncovered extensive remains. They include the rock shaft David's men climbed up to capture the city, Hezekiah's tunnel (2 Kgs 20:20), and the ruins of the rock terraces on which David's palace (2 Sam 5:9-11) and Israelite houses were built.

On the western hill of Jerusalem, excavations have revealed remains of ancient Iron Age tombs and a massive broad wall which in the monarchy period was part of the defense when the city was extended to the western hill. Search for Solomon's temple on the sacred temple platform has not been possible, but parallels to the description of the temple in 1 Kings 6 have been found in the archaeological remains of similar sanctuaries of the time in Palestine and Mesopotamia: structures with a porch, a holy place, and a holy of holies.

Qumran and the Dead Sea Scrolls. Khirbet Qumran is the modern name for this important site on the northwest shore of the Dead Sea. It contained a settlement of ancient Jewish Essenes who lived there in the second and first centuries B.C. The earthquake of 31 B.C. caused them to scatter. They came back about 4 B.C. and stayed on until A.D. 68, when they hid their writings in the caves in and around the site and fled before the Roman army.

Actually there was a settlement at Qumran as early as the eighth century B.C. Many of the scrolls or parts of scrolls of these Jewish ascetics were found in 1947 and the following years by local Bedouin shepherds and by archaeologists. The small settlement of buildings excavated in the 1950s included a scroll room, dining and meeting rooms, cisterns, pottery kiln and storage area, and cemetery. In the scroll room benches and tables and two ink wells were found.

The Qumran Dead Sea Scrolls literature (dating between about 200 B.C. and A.D. 100) found in a number of caves in and around the site consisted of:

- copies or parts of copies of all the canonical Old Testament books (except Esther);
- commentaries on the Scriptures;
- materials from the intertestamental apocryphal and pseudepigraphical books;
- manuscripts on the rules of the sect and their beliefs (such as their belief in two messiahs, one secular and one religious, and their hope for the immanent judgment of God on the wicked);
- writings on other subjects, such as the Temple Scroll and the hidden treasure described in the Copper Scroll.

Although some similarities exist between some beliefs of the Essenes and Christianity (because they both relied on the OT), the differences between the two are greater.

Bethlehem. This town of David (1 Sam 16:1) where Jesus was born (Luke 2:4,11) is six miles south of Jerusalem. It is famous for the Church of the Nativity, which is built over the cave referred to in ancient tradition as early as the second century and later (Justin Martyr, Origen, and Jerome) as the birthplace of Jesus. The area was inhabited in the Bronze and Iron Ages. The first biblical reference to Bethlehem is in Genesis 35:19. The first church was built there in the earlier part of the fourth century by Constantine, and in the end of that century Jerome lived for some time in the labyrinth of caves under the church. The church was rebuilt by the emperor Justinian in the sixth century. Archaeological investigation and study began in 1934 and has continued. Today, besides the cave that is constantly used by churches and pilgrims, lovely geometric mosaic pavements of the Constantinian period are to be seen. Also near the traditional tomb of Rachel, a high level aqueduct (about A.D. 135) was found containing Roman inscriptions.

Beth Shan/Scythopolis. This site, located at the eastern end of the Valley of Jezreel near the Jordan River, was inhabited almost continuously from Chalcolithic to modern times. It was important in Old Testament times as the place where the bodies of Saul and Jonathan were fastened to the city's wall (1 Sam 31:10-12). The Old Testament city was located on the high mound, and in the 1920s and 1930s excavation there uncovered Late Bronze and Iron Age temples and an important stele of the Egyptian pharaoh Seti I. In the Hellenistic, Roman, and Byzantine periods the city, now called Scythopolis, or Nysa Scythopolis, was situated below the high mound. Here are to be seen the ruins of the Roman theater. Since 1950 excavation has revealed synagogues, burial sites, and a Roman villa. Excavations in the late 1980s have produced a broad complex of Roman/Byzantine civic buildings, including colonnaded streets, bath complexes, music hall, amphitheater, and fountain.

Caesarea Maritima (by the Sea). This Caesarea by the Sea (Acts 23:31–26:32) is to be distinguished from Caesarea Philippi located near the foot of Mount Hermon (Matt 16:13-20). Caesarea Maritima is on the Mediterranean Sea about twenty miles south of Mount Carmel. The Herodian part of the city covered 164 acres. In Paul's time of imprisonment here (Acts 23:35–27:1) many monumental buildings were to be seen.

Excavations have continued at the site over the last several decades. They have exposed a Roman theater; a series of vaulted warehouses along the ocean front; evidence of Herod's elaborate harbor (including his massive breakwaters), the harbor from which Paul sailed; a large first-century B.C. merchant ship, 165 feet long (Acts 27:1,2); and the first- and second-century A.D. high aqueduct. A stone inscription referring to Pilate, one of the few such references outside of the Bible (Matt 27:2) was found in 1961 at the theater. It reads: "Pontius Pilate, the Praefect of Judea [who] has dedicated to the people of Caesarea a temple in honor of Tiberius." Also found were evidence of the Cardo Maximus north-south main street (dating probably from both the Roman/Herodian and Byzantine times), city sewers running under the street system, and a second-century A.D. hippodrome. Additional finds were ruins of a fourth-century A.D. synagogue, several churches, and the other remains of Byzantine, Crusader times.

Capernaum. This site, Kefar Nahum (the Village of Nahum), located on the northwestern shore of the Sea of Galilee, is prominently mentioned in the New Testament (Matt 4:13; 8:5; 11:23; 17:24) and is also mentioned in Josephus and in Talmudic literature, which mentions that in the second century A.D. a Judeo-Christian community resided at Capernaum. Excavation began in 1856 and has continued at other times since, especially from 1968 on. Prominent is the second-fourth century A.D. synagogue of white limestone, consisting of a colonnaded hall with three doors on the south side toward Jerusalem, galleries above, and a colonnaded service (or community or school) room on the east.

Recent excavations have shown that below the present structure there was an earlier synagogue of black basalt stone with walls almost four feet thick. Pottery found in situ (in place) in and under the basalt floor shows this synagogue to be of the first century A.D. or earlier. (Underneath the floor was found pottery of the third and second centuries B.C.) This earlier synagogue is the one in which Jesus no doubt preached (Mark 1:21), the synagogue built for the Jews by the centurion (Luke 7:1-5).

To the south of the synagogue is an insula (block) of early private homes. South of that is an octagonal fifth-century church structure that has preserved in it earlier ruins of a private home of the first century B.C. containing domestic type pottery. This house was plastered in the second half of the first century A.D. with graffiti on its walls, including mention of Jesus as "Lord," "Christ," and also forms of the cross.

The pottery of this period consisted of just storejars and lamps, suggesting the structure was now used as a public building, a house church, commemorating Christ.

This scale model of ancient Jerusalem at the Holyland Hotel in Jerusalem is based largely on data gleaned from archaeological research and is modified as necessary when new data becomes available. (Herod's Palace is in the foreground.)

The limestone cliffs of the Qumran area showing the caves in which the Dead Sea Scrolls were discovered beginning in 1947. The discovery of these scrolls and the information they have provided constitute a major contribution of archaeology to biblical studies.

The excavators have popularly called this church complex "St. Peter's House." All around the site have been found sculptured stones depicting the ark of the covenant, floral and geometric designs, and also parts of Roman grain mills and olive presses.

Gennesaret, Sea of Galilee. In 1986 on the western shore of the Sea of Galilee in the vicinity of ancient Gennesaret, near modern Kibbitz Gennosar, were found the remains of a small boat with a rounded stern. It possibly could have held as many as fifteen persons, including a crew of five (Mark 1:19-20); thus it was large enough to have held Jesus and His disciples. The type of construction of the boat, carbon 14 dating, and pottery found at the site point to the period of time from the first century B.C. to the first century A.D. as the time of the boat's use.

Jericho, New Testament. New Testament Jericho, also known today as Tulul Abu el-Alaiq, is located at the lower end of Wadi Kelt about two kilometers south of Old Testament Jericho (Tell es-Sultan). (The old Roman road from Jericho to Jerusalem ran up this wadi; see Luke 10:30.) It was at New Testament Jericho that Herod the Great built winter residences, including a palace, theater, hippodrome, amphitheater, bath complex, gardens, and ponds. Excavations have revealed five aqueducts to bring water for these installations. Also high quality paintings were found. In between this New Testament Jericho (Luke 18:35) and the Old Testament Jericho ruins (Matt 20:29), Jesus met the blind man. Excavation took place here in 1909 and 1911, but more extensive work was done in 1950-51, in the 1970s, and later in the mid-80s.

Jerusalem, New Testament. After the conquest of Palestine by the Roman General Pompey in 63 B.C., Jerusalem entered into a new era, that of Herodian Jerusalem. Scattered blocks of the surrounding colonnades of the magnificent Second Temple (Matt 24:2) have been found in the debris outside the temple platform at the bottom of the Herodian foundation wall. The monumental stairway leading to the southern entrance of the temple area has been uncovered. Excavation has shown that the first and second walls of Jerusalem, mentioned by Josephus as existing in the early part of the first century A.D., ran in such a way as to leave outside the city walls (Heb 13:12) both Gordon's Calvary and the Church of the Holy Sepulchre. However, the evidence of an ancient quarry and the early Jewish type tombs at the Church of the Holy Sepulchre and the early reliable Christian tradition about this place point to the location of this church as the place of the crucifixion and burial of Jesus.

Excavations at Bethesda (John 5:1-15) have uncovered remains of the two pools and remains of the colonnaded porches where the miracle of healing took place. Near the temple platform a stairway, known as Robinson's Arch and giving access into the temple area at its southwestern corner, has been uncovered. And a column with an inscription honoring the emperors Vespasian and Titus, and the commander of the Tenth Roman Legion, has been found. Portions of Hadrian's second-century triple Damascus gateway have been excavated, including part of the plaza inside, in the center of which a central column stood, no doubt displaying a statue of the emperor. Also the excavators have partially uncovered remains of the north-south Roman/Byzantine main street, the Cardo Maximus. Work also has been done on remains of a number of churches built in the Byzantine period.

The Madaba Mosaic Map, dated to about A.D. 575 (and which is part of the floor of a Greek Orthodox church in Madaba, Jordan), confirms the locations and designs of many of these churches. Some examples are the Church of the Holy Sepulchre, the Nea Church, the Church near the Pool of Siloam, and the Mother of All Churches.

Tombs and cemeteries have been excavated. The tombs in the Kidron Valley, past which Jesus no doubt walked on his way to Gethsemane (John 18:1), and tombs on the Mount of Olives (such as tombs at the Dominus Flevit) have been excavated. Recently from an area tomb came an important find: a heel bone of a Jewish man crucified in the early first century A.D. that was pierced by a large nail (Luke 24:40; John 20:25,27), thus pointing to an aspect of Roman crucifixion. Excavations have continued in Jerusalem over the decades.

Transjordan

Abila of the Decapolis. Abila, one of the Decapolis cities Jesus probably visited (Mark 7:31), is located about eighteen miles east of the southern end of the Sea of Galilee. The site has a long archaeological history, going back as early as the Neolithic period. Excavation has continued there since 1980. Besides Bronze and Iron Age materials, Hellenistic, Roman, and considerable Byzantine finds have been uncovered, including three churches. Islamic materials have also been found.

Gerasa/Jerash. Modern Jerash, ancient Gerasa, about thirty-five miles southeast of the Sea of Galilee, gives its name to the region of the Gerasenes mentioned in Mark 5:1; Luke 8:26-39, where Jesus went with His disciples and met the demoniac(s), whom He healed. Gerasa may have controlled territory along the Sea of Galilee. Thus it gave its name to the village of Khersa, near the cliff where the pigs ran into the sea. Jerash contains many ruins, mainly of the Roman-Byzantine periods, including two theaters, temples of Zeus and Artemis, a forum, a hippodrome, a north-south, east-west street system with a central square, ancient baths, and a number of churches. Excavation began in the 1930s and has continued to the present. In the 1980s a number of international excavation teams combined their efforts toward restoring Gerasa/Jerash.

Pella of the Decapolis. The archaeology of this city, located on the eastern side of the Jordan River about eight miles southeast of Beth Shan/Scythopolis, goes back as far as Chalcolithic times. It was this city to which Christians fled in A.D. 66 at the impending destruction of Jerusalem. Here there are extensive remains from the Early Bronze to the Hellenistic periods. Included in the Roman and Byzantine period finds is a civic center including an odeon (music hall) and churches. Excavation has gone on at Pella from the late 1960s.

Petra, Southern Jordan. Petra, the rose red city of sandstone, was the capital of the Nabatean kingdom east of the Jordan River system. It was ruled by Aretas IV in the time of the apostle Paul (2 Cor 11:32). Some have identified Petra, meaning *rock* in Greek, with Old Testament Sela (Judg 1:36; 2 Kgs 14:7; Isa 16:1), the Hebrew for *rock*. The site goes back to the Iron Age, the time of the Edomites, and continues on into the Persian, Hellenistic, and Early Roman times of the Nabatean kingdom. To be seen are high places of worship, spectacular tomb facades, fortress ruins, temples, a Roman theater, and a monumental gate and street. Excavations have continued here in recent decades.

Asia Minor and Greece

Ephesus, Asia Minor. Ephesus (Acts 18:19-20; Eph 1–6; Rev 1:11; 2:1), on the western coast of Asia Minor, goes back in history to at least the tenth century B.C. First excavated in 1869, when the ancient Temple of Artemis was discovered, Ephesus has continued to be excavated in various periods of the twentieth century to the present. One of its flowering periods was in the time of the New Testament and the early church. Besides ruins of the Temple of Artemis, important archaeological finds include remains of the ancient theater where Paul was denounced and the goddess Artemis defended (Acts 19:28-41). Finds also include the harbor gymnasium and baths, the marble road, market squares (agoras), the town hall (where the city clerk probably worked, Acts 19:35), and temples of Serapis (a pagan deity), Emperor Domitian (A.D. 98–117), and Emperor Hadrian (A.D.

As archaeological excavation provides data, structures can be restored to much of their original magnificence. An example of this is seen in the above photo taken during the restoration of the Celsus Library at Ephesus.

117–138). In the 1980s extensive restoration work continued on the second century A.D. Celsus library as well as on the wealthy Roman villas lining the hill to the south of Curetes Street and extending from the library up toward the state marketplace.

Pergamum (modern Bergama), Asia Minor. The letter to the church at Pergamum (Rev 1:11; 2:12) refers to the church at this spectacular site. It consists of an upper and middle city of Hellenistic times located on the acropolis hill, a hospital center (founded about 400 B.C.), and a site of the Roman Imperial period in the plain below. The site is located in western Asia Minor about sixty-five miles north of Smyrna (modern Izmir). Its history goes back to at least the fifth century B.C. In the time of Eumenes II (197–159 B.C.) many beautiful buildings were constructed, and a library of 200,000 volumes was amassed.

In the Roman period Pergamum continued to be prominent. Among the important buildings at Pergamum are the Altar of Zeus (Rev 2:13 speaks of the place "where Satan has his throne," which may particularly refer to this structure) now in an East Berlin museum; the ancient Hellenistic theater; and the hospital complex of the pagan god of healing, Asclepius. Currently on the acropolis the second century A.D. Temple of Trajan is being reconstructed. Excavation was begun at Pergamum in 1878 and has continued intermittently to the present.

Sardis, Asia Minor. The letter to the church at Sardis (Rev 3:1-6) refers to the church in this famous Lydian city located about fifty miles northeast of Ephesus. The history of Sardis goes back to at least 3000 B.C. It became prominent as a Lydian city under Kings Gyges (680–665 B.C.) and Croesus (560–547 B.C.) about the time when coinage was invented. Important archaeological remains include the ruins of the Temple and Altar of Artemis, a Jewish synagogue (largely restored), a large gymnasium complex with palaestra (exercise room), and large baths. Excavations at Sardis began early in the twentieth century and have continued, particularly since 1958.

Philippi, Northern Greece. The Letter to the Philippians refers to the church of this city in northern Greece. Philippi was founded in the fourth century B.C. by people who called it "Springs" (*Krenides* in Greek). A short time later Philip II of Macedon (father of Alexander the Great) took the city and renamed it Philippi. In Roman times the city was given the privileged status of "colony" and was noted by Luke as a "leading city of that district of Macedonia" (Acts 16:12). Among the many ruins is the Via Egnatia, the main highway that ran

A view of the site of Sepphoris prior to recent extensive excavation. This town near Nazareth probably was known well by Jesus.

through Philippi, connecting the East to the West. When Paul was there, he met with a group (Acts 16:13) by the river, which no doubt carried the water from the spring *Krenides,* the name of the earlier town.

Athens, Greece. The history of Athens, whose high classical period was in the fifth century B.C., goes back to Neolithic times. Paul visited Athens on his second missionary journey (Acts 17:15-34) and saw many ancient temples and civic structures there. Other ancient authors, such as Pausanias, mention altars to unknown gods among the many altars in the city. Similarly, Paul spoke of an altar "TO AN UNKNOWN GOD" (Acts 17:23) that he had seen in the marketplace. Excavation has been carried on in Athens for many years.

Corinth, Greece. Corinth, whose history goes back at least to the Neolithic period, became prominent in the Classical period and was also important in the Roman period. In 46 B.C. Julius Caesar made it a Roman colony. When Paul visited Corinth on his second missionary journey (Acts 18:1-18), he saw the famous sixth-century-B.C. Temple of Apollo and stood before the bema, the platform (seat) from which Gallio, proconsul of Achaia, heard Paul's defense (Acts 18:12-17). Paul also may have seen the Hebrew synagogue there, whose name, inscribed on a lintel block, is partially preserved today. He also could have seen the inscription in the paved street indicating it was laid by one Erastus, probably the man Paul mentioned in Romans 16:23.

The reference to the "mirror" in 1 Corinthians 13:12 may allude to the excellence of the bronze metal produced at Corinth and used in finely polished bronze mirrors. Paul's reference to his being "an expert builder" (1 Cor 3:10) may be an allusion to the city's major construction activities in the times of Tiberius (A.D. 14–37) and Claudius (A.D. 41–54). Paul may have had in mind the athletic games at nearby Isthmia when he used the imagery of the runner and boxer (1 Cor 9:24-27). His reference to "jars of clay" (2 Cor 4:7) may have been calling to mind the excellent pottery products, including lamps, made at Corinth. The reference to "eating in an idol's temple" (1 Cor 8:10) may have vividly brought to the Corinthian mind the dining rooms in the Temple of Demeter at Corinth, where sacrificial meals were eaten. Extensive excavations at the site have continued over recent decades.

Archaeology enables us to understand the historical and cultural setting from which the biblical message came and thus helps us better understand that message for our day.

Sources for Additional Study

Mare, W. Harold. *The Archaeology of the Jerusalem Area.* Grand Rapids: Eerdmans, 1987.

Schoville, Keith N. *Biblical Archaeology in Focus.* Grand Rapids: Eerdmans, 1978.

View of the covered water conduit that connected the various cisterns and pools of the community at Qumran discovered during excavation of the site.

Geography and Topography of the Ancient Near East

The term *Fertile Crescent* is often used to describe the lands of the Bible. The name is derived from the topographical phenomena of a fertile band of ground of varying boundaries that stretches in a giant arc over the great desert, which fills the core of the crescent. At the far southwestern curve of the crescent is the country called Palestine.

Palestine

This small land is famous far beyond its geopolitical status in the ancient world. Ironically, it has received its name from Aegean peoples known as Philistines from which *Palestine* is derived. Within those boundaries is a land that is holy to Christians, Jews, and Moslems. There perhaps is no place on earth that better combines rich history with topographical diversity. A careful study of this land and its neighbors is essential for understanding certain portions of the Bible.

The Four Zones. The Palestinian area may be understood to have four major topographical zones running north and south. Moving from west to east, they are the coastal strip, the central hill country, the Jordan Rift, and the hills of the Transjordan (the modern country of Jordan). These regions, with variations, are characteristic of Syro-Palestine (the modern countries of Syria, Lebanon, Israel, the Gaza Strip, and Jordan).

The Coastal Plain. The southern boundary is the River Besor, while the northern is the "ladder of Tyre"—a distance of about a hundred and twenty miles. The average width south of Mount Carmel in the north is ten miles, and in the south it reaches twenty-four miles near Gaza. This semitropical region (sometimes called the Via Maris) provided an ancient highway for armies going north or south. In Old Testament times it was the residence of the Canaanites and Philistines. Until New Testament times it was never heavily populated with Jews.

The Hill Country. This mountainous area may be divided into three regions: the mountains of Samaria in the north, the plain of Benjamin in the center, and the hill country of Judah in the south. The mountains of Samaria vary in height from roughly 1,300 to 3,300 feet. Generally speaking, however, travel is not hard south and north. Wadis of varying sizes course east and west from the central range. This land was allotted to the tribes of Ephraim and Manasseh in the conquest and later came to be the heartland of the Northern Kingdom in the Divided Monarchy.

The center area of Benjamin is about ten by ten miles of plateau just north of Jerusalem and the hill country of Judah. The Judean hills vary in height from 2,600 feet near Bethlehem to 3,300 feet near Hebron. South of that the hills diminish rapidly. Benjamin is separated from Judah by the Wadi Sorek, which runs westerly. The area to the east is the desert of Judah (Arabah).

The heart of much of Old Testament history is centralized in the area named after the tribe of Judah. It lies south of Benjamin and is bounded by the wilderness to the east (adjacent to the Dead Sea), Philistia to the west, and the Negev in the south. A region called the Shephelah (Hebrew for *lowland*) runs north/south between the central hill country and the coastal plain. This area is characterized by wadis running westerly intersected with hills. The hill country is approximately thirty miles long and fifteen miles wide and is not easily approached from the west. Historically, armies attacking from the west have taken the "road going up to Beth Horon" (Josh 10:10). Judah and its capital, Jerusalem, were accessible to invasion from the north or south.

The Jordan Rift. This great valley runs for about 165 miles from Dan in the north to the southern tip of the Dead Sea (Salt Sea in the OT). Its larger setting is found in the great fault that stretches from northern Syria through Phoenicia (Lebanon) and Israel and continuing on as the Red Sea. From the southern tip of Lake Galilee to the northern shore of the Dead Sea is a distance of sixty-five miles. The valley averages about ten miles in

A NASA photo showing most of the area of Israel and some of the area to the east of the Jordan River. The Dead Sea is in the center of the photo, the Mediterranean coastline upper left, Sea of Galilee upper center, and the Negev lower center left.

width. As the Jordan River exits Lake Galilee, it descends into a spacious plain where the Jezreel Valley to the west converges with the Jordan Valley. Once south of Mount Gilboa the valley constricts rapidly. Once south of Wadia Faria in the east central mountains, the valley again widens to as much as twelve miles. Lush vegetation grows along the banks of the Jordan and its flood plain while the rest of the valley is desert.

Huleh. This northernmost lake was about four miles long and three miles wide in biblical times. Today it has been drained for the most part and the valley turned into fertile farmland. Both Huleh and the Jordan River receive their water from the rain in the mountains to the north and especially Mount Hermon in the northeast. In Old Testament times the marshy ground made it inaccessible, allowing the small six-hundred-man army of Danites to conquer the secluded city of Laish (Judg 18).

Galilee. This beautiful lake is also known by its Hebrew name, Sea of Chinnereth (in New Testament times it was called Tiberias and Gennesaret). At its extremities the lake is thirteen miles long and eight miles wide. The lake is as much as 165 feet deep. For the most part it is surrounded by mountains. There is, however, some flat ground, particularly in the northwest, where a stunning view of the plain can be seen from Mount Arbel on the northwest side.

The Jordan River. The Jordan River (in Hebrew it means *descender*) is quite serpentine in its southerly descent. It takes more than three times the distance of a straight line from Galilee to reach the Dead Sea. In ten places the river actually flows north. While its headwaters are north to Huleh, it receives substantial water from the various tributaries on the west and east ranges. Today most of the Jordan's water is used for irrigation purposes. It was never used for navigation in ancient times; rather, it served to mark the boundaries of the Transjordan from Cis-Jordan by creating a dense jungle within its flood plain.

Salt Sea. The Jordan in antiquity flowed into the Salt Sea, which is fifty miles long and eleven miles at its wid-

A relief of Ashurbanipal of Assyria (seventh century B.C.) depicting two Assyrian warriors astride a camel—one urging the camel on and the other shooting an arrow at the enemy.

est point. In the north it is as much as 1,300 feet deep, while the southern half is as shallow as thirty-three feet. Today there is an eight-mile plain of ground that has separated the sea into two sections. Since 90 percent of its water came from the Jordan, it is drying fast. The sea itself is about six times saltier than other seas, so no animal or plant life exists.

Wadi-el-Arabah. The area south of the Salt Sea is

Birds and Beasts

For the student of the Bible, the subject of the fauna of the Holy Land is both a fascinating and foreboding endeavor. Variations in climate and geographical proximity to three continents ensure a richness in animal life out of proportion to Israel's small area. The OT has nearly 180 words for animal names, while the NT has over fifty. Indeed, animal life is prominent for both practical and theological matters.

Difficulties

The systematic study of animal nomenclature in the Bible has only been in existence for the last several centuries. Hebrew words tend to refer to animals in groups of species rather than use the more specific terminology necessary for modern categorization. Consequently, exact identification of many OT animals, especially the unclean, is impossible.

Perhaps the most difficult problem for the average Bible reader is that the English versions represent diverse translations for the most difficult names. This is especially true for the *Authorized Version,* which, when in doubt, tended to render those names with European substitutes. Consequently, an English reader should consult modern books on the fauna of Palestine.

Discussion

Mammalia. Mammals were important for practical (food, clothing) and theological (sacrifices) reasons.

Domestic mammals, in particular, dominated. The donkey was of major importance for

A bearded hunter in this Assyrian relief (eighth century B.C.) carries a gazelle on his shoulders and a rabbit in his hand. Two birds can be seen in the upper background.

transportation and agriculture, while horses were introduced later and were used primarily in warfare. Cattle, sheep, and goats were most dominant. Goats have brought great ecological damage to the terrain because they uproot the vegetation rather than just graze on it.

Large, wild mammals also were well represented, including jackal, fox, bear, hyena, leopard, and especially lions. Lions would range forth from the Negev, Syrian Desert, and Lebanon Mountains. They would prey upon both flocks and wildlife. A favorite prey must have been one of the three deer species—red, fallow, and roe. The land also sported gazelle, orex, and ritually unclean antelope and wild boar.

Invertebrates. This largest group of animals does not merit equal time with mammals. In the OT just under thirty names are mentioned with 20 percent of these names being either locusts or grasshoppers. Not surprisingly, most were destructive.

Aves. While more than 350 birds can be identified in Israel, only about thirty-seven are mentioned in the Bible. While the Pentateuch mentions the clean mammals, it only lists the unclean birds (twenty in Lev 11 and an additional one in Deut 14). Twelve names for the owl are also given in the Pentateuch. Birds such as the dove, goose, partridge, and quail were important food sources.

Reptilia. With few exceptions, reptilia is the least-known class of animals. The crocodile and Palestinian viper were both mentioned, although the viper played a greater role.

Pisces. Even though not one fish is mentioned by name in the OT, it was an important food item. The importance of fish is evidenced by the mention of more than a dozen terms of fishing implements used at that time.

Conclusion

A student of the Bible must remember that the Bible mentions animals selectively. That is, to be mentioned the animal must touch the ordinary (or sometimes the extraordinary) course of life, especially in the religious sphere. □

The dog, faithful companion from the beginning of history, was known in the Middle East from the Stone Age. Above is a relief from Nineveh showing a hunting dog straining at his master's leash (seventh century B.C.).

called Wadi-el-Arabah, biblical Edom. The distance from the Salt Sea to the Straits of Tiran is 217 miles. The terrain leading to the ancient port city of the Gulf of Aqabah, named Ezion Geber, is arid and inhospitable.

The Eastern Mountains. These mountain regions are also clarified by wadis. The area immediately to the east of Galilee is called Bashan and was a fertile and prosperous land (Jer 50:19). Its southern boundary was marked off by the important Yarmuk. The territory between the Yarmuk and the Arnon is Gilead. Its terrain is more difficult than Bashan with less moisture and poorer soil. The area between the Arnon and the Zered in the south is Moab (roughly an area of thirty square miles). North-south travel is difficult because of these two wadis. The area south of the Zered was Edom, a mountainous and arid land. The great Arabian desert begins south of Edom.

Varia. A few topographical varia interdict these four zones. The east-west interruption is in the northern third of the country. It is a valley that runs southeasterly from the Mediterranean Sea to the Jordan River, including the Plain of Acco and the Megiddo and Jezreel Valleys. This spacious, fertile valley has received various names from local topographic factors. This valley is about fifty miles wide from the Mediterranean to the Jordan. Today it is the breadbasket of the country. In the past the river Kishon kept the westerly half marshy.

Another interruption in the north-south zone structure is the Carmel Mountain range that runs southeasterly contiguous to the great valley mentioned above. It is shaped somewhat like a fish hook, with Mount Carmel being the "eye" of the hook as it sits on the Mediterranean Sea completely interrupting traffic along the coast. Mount Gilboa in the east is shaped like the "business" end of the hook as it curls out into the plain. This range varies in height (Mount Carmel is 1,791 feet, and Mount Gilboa is 1,758 feet), but travelers through one of its three main passages going north or south found it easier to travel through one of its three main passages This was especially true for armies.

The last interruption in the topographical zones is the area called the Negev, which means *south.* This region is topographically complex. Between the Judean hills and the mountainous part of the Negev is a plain that rises gradually toward the east. The soil (called loess) is fertile, but there is insufficient moisture for farming. This flat ground gradually gives way to mountains (as high as 1,650 feet) that are part of the central hill zone though much smaller in height and width.

Rain. Moisture-bearing clouds are seasonal (Sept. through May) and in the winter may bring snow to the hill country. The major source of moisture in the summer months was the famous dew, which was seen as from the Lord (Gen 27:28). Between the rainfall and the dew, there was sufficient moisture in normal years. Since Palestine straddles the southern edge of the rain line, droughts are common (1 Kgs 17–18).

Climate. There is amazing climatic variation that can best be understood as the direct product of the elevation of the land. Thus in the winter the Judean hills may be covered with snow while it may be seventy-five degrees only twelve miles to the east. With the exception of winters on the hill country and summers in the Rift, the land is comfortable and the climate moderate.

Phoenicia

With some variations the same zones in Palestine can be found in Phoenicia. The coastal plain is much more irregular and at times is completely interdicted by mountains. The so-called ladder of Tyre effectively separates Palestine from Phoenicia. Inland the same central mountain zone continues except it is much higher (as high as 6,550 feet) with steep wadis. In antiquity this central mountain range was not a viable transportation route. As in Palestine there is a great valley between its central mountains, the Lebanon and Anti-Lebanon, called the Beqa (literally, *the Valley*), which is seventy-five miles long and five to eight miles wide. It is not actually a part of the Rift in Palestine. It has an elevation of over 3,000 feet and plentiful rainfall.

North of the Beqa is the Anti-Lebanon, which stretches about a hundred miles. Going east, this range decreases irregularly but eventually into the arid plateau like that east of the Jordan Rift. Damascus is on the eastern side of Mount Hermon and was situated astride the ancient trade route from Egypt to the Euphrates River, a journey of about 620 miles. This, of course, made the Arameans of Damascus a double economic challenge for Israel. Damascus was also situated for close relations with the great port city of Tyre on the Mediterranean.

Mesopotamia

"Mesopotamia" is a Greek term that means *the land between the rivers.* Ironically the rivers were the originators of the fascinating history that developed at the opposite end of their headwaters. The Tigris originates in the mountains to the north in Armenia and to the east in the mountains called the Zagros. The Euphrates draws its water from the rainfall on the mountains of eastern Asia Minor. Over the millennia they have deposited rich silt on the basin which, from Charchemish on the Euphrates to the Persian Gulf, stretches for 750 miles. While the climate varies from north to south, neither extremity receives much more than eight inches of annual rainfall. Irrigation, therefore, was the mother of civilization in this great alluvial plain.

The remarkable people known as Sumerians gave the area its first civilization in the fourth and third millennia in southern Mesopotamia. During the second millennium power had shifted to the central portion of the flood plain under the leadership of Babylon. In the first millennia the power base had again shifted to the northern part of the basin represented by the great power Assyria. Perhaps the most important factor in this migration of power from Sumer to Assyria was the problem of salinization of the soil. Mineral deposits left by the annual floods and especially mineral residue from irrigation resulted in the complete ruin of the ground. Nevertheless, Mesopotamian powers color the pages of every period of biblical history.

The Desert Between

This great fertile crescent arches over a formidable desert core through which few trade routes coursed. On the whole, it was too dangerous and inconvenient to serve as the primary means of trade. This great desert results from the prevailing winds coming from the northwest and the coastal mountains extracting the moisture, thus leaving a nearly uninhabited core area.

The Mountains to the North

The mountains of Asia Minor stretch for over a thousand miles east and west. They are actually part of the mountain chain that extends from the Alps in Europe to the Balkans, Asia Minor, Persia, and India. Asia Minor is commonly called Anatolia, from a Greek word meaning *sunrise, east.* Its topography is complex, hence it was rarely politically united.

The Pontus mountains are over the northern part of Anatolia, reaching about two thousand feet in the west to around ten thousand feet in the east. The Taurus mountains in the south are up the Pontus on the east and the west. With peaks of ten thousand feet, travel and trade in Anatolia was easiest on an east/west axis through the

A NASA photo showing the topography of the Bible lands. Nile River, lower left; Mount Sinai, above center crossmark; Gulf of Aqaba, center right; Israeli coastline, top center crossmark; and Dead Sea, lower right of top center crossmark.

central Anatolian plateau. With its copper and iron deposits and strategic location astride four major trade routes, it was an economically important part of the ancient world.

The Lands to the East

The most ancient of these lands was Elam, which was separated from Sumer by the Zagros range. The river Karun watered the low plain that supported the population. Southeast of Elam was the homeland of the Persians. It occupied the area of the southern Zagros and the plateau to the east. Media was to the north of Elam and Parthia to the east of Media. Taken together, these nations make up the modern country of Iran. The area is surrounded by mountains. The Elburz range on the north has peaks over eighteen thousand feet. In the core is the massive plateau of around thirty-three hundred feet in height. Much of this area receives less than four inches of rain annually.

Egypt

In many ways Egypt's geography is the most peculiar of ancient toponomy. With the trackless Sahara to the west, the formidable desert to the east, the river cataracts on the south, and the Mediterranean Sea and Sinai Desert on the north, Egypt was uniquely isolated. Egyptian lifestyle and thought forms were correspondingly unique.

Life is made possible almost solely due to the Nile. This great river flows gently northward from Aswan to Cairo over six hundred miles. In the months of July to November, the river would flood, leaving a new layer of rich silt. Some flood water was retained in reservoirs and channeled out as needed during the growing season. The regularity of this flood made farming here less risky than for the rest of the ancient world. Later, Egypt would become the granary for the Greeks and Romans.

Although blessed with abundant food and secure borders, the Egyptians lacked other important commodities essential for their national well-being. For the Egyptians to be a great power, they needed the copper from the Sinai to the east, the gold from Nubia to the south, and the timber of the Syro-Phoenician coast. Without control of these, Egypt could not remain a superpower. Thus the Assyrian field commander taunted Hezekiah over his alliance with Egypt: "You are depending on Egypt, that splintered reed of a staff, which pierces a man's hands and wounds him if he leans on it!" (Isa 36:6).

Greece

To understand the land called Greece, it is necessary to think of mountains surrounded by the sea. A central chain of mountains called the Pindus, with peaks as high as ninety-eight hundred feet, effectively divides the land east and west. As spurs descend east and west from the center, regions are formed. In the northwest the region is known as Epirus, while in the southwest it is Aetolia.

East of the Pindus in the north is Macedonia with Mount Olympus dominating its southern border. Ancient Thrace lies to the east of Macedonia. South of Macedonia lies the region named Thessaly, which boasts the widest plain in all of Greece. The lowest region is south of the Pindus and is called the Peloponesus.

With such limited ground available for farming (80 percent is mountainous), the sea provided solutions. It was a source for food, trade, and immigration since Greece has long been unable to support its population from its soil. With the exception of higher elevations, the climate is mild. The regions on the west side of the Pindus get considerably more rain than the east. These topographic features seem to have kept Greece in the past

PLANTS OF THE BIBLE

Plants are living organisms that possess cellulose cell walls and synthesize food from carbon monoxide. Palestine has a wide variety of climates and elevations that support a rich and varied plant life. These include trees, shrubs, herbs, vegetables, flowers, fruits, or ornamental forms of life characterized by roots, a stem, and leaves or foliage equivalent.

"To plant" identifies the action of placing either seeds or small samples of plants into the soil so they can grow. Biblical usage includes both the noun and the verb forms. This brief survey offers a representative overview of the various usages in both the OT and NT.

The Bible pictures plants, like all other forms of life, as good gifts from God. As such they are to be grown or processed, cherished, enjoyed, employed, and shared for the good of all of God's people (Gen 1:29-30; 2:8). Planting is seasonal activity (Eccl 3:2), but plants need sustained care to be productive (Isa 5:1-4). The Mosaic law did not allow early exploitation of fruit-bearing trees (Lev 19:23). The Israelites were forbidden to plant a tree as the religious symbol of the Canaanite fertility goddess Asherah (Deut 16:21).

Some plants are particular instruments of divine blessing.

High value was placed on the fruit of the fig tree by the biblical writers (see Isa 28:4; Jer 24:2; 1 Sam 25:18; 30:12). Pictured in the above photo are figs ripening in the sun.

Trees growing by water (Ps 1:3; Jer 17:8) and rich vineyards (2 Kgs 19:29; Amos 9:14) exemplify these special messengers of blessing. On the other hand, some forms of judgment are portrayed as deprivation of the normal benefits from plant life. The prophet Isaiah was particularly fond of such descriptions (Isa 17:10-11): "You have forgotten God your Savior; you have not remembered the Rock, your fortress. / Therefore, though you set out the finest plants and plant imported vines, / though on the day you set them out, you make them grow, and on the morning when you plant them, you bring them to bud, / yet the harvest will be as nothing in the day of disease and incurable pain."

The biblical writers used plants as symbols of theological or ethical teachings. Overgrown, deserted, and barren sites often were employed as metaphorical expressions of God's anger or judgment (Amos 4:9; 5:11). Plants can symbolize strength (Ps 144:12) or weakness (2 Kgs 19:26). They can picture God's nourishment (Ps 104:14) or His destruction (Isa 40:24). They can portray the persistence of life (Job 14:7-9) or its unstable and temporal character (Job 8:12; Eccl 2:4).

Jesus and the apostles used various descriptions of plants. Jesus described God's proper action, saying: "Every plant that my Heavenly Father has not planted will be pulled up by the roots" (Matt 15:13). Similarly, Jesus adopted a metaphor for life that examines human conduct (Matt 23:33-41). Paul indicated that planting is one stage in the growth of a church (1 Cor 3:6-8), whose life is a gift of God.

(For a detailed listing of the various kinds of plants in the Bible, see the article on "Plants" in the *Holman Bible Dictionary*, edited by T. Butler [Nashville: Holman, 1991], 1116-19.) □

Cedars signified royal wealth and strength in the Old Testament (see 1 Kgs 10:27; Ps 92:12). Shown above is one of the "cedars of Lebanon."

from political unification.

The Bible frequently mentions the nations of its world. In certain ways God's blessings and curses on Israel were directly related to Israel's relationship with those nations. This tiny land called Israel is the land bridge of three continents. For nearly all of its history it has been the vassal of some great neighboring power. Its terrain permanently decreed that it could never bear populations competitive with those far larger nations such as Egypt, Assyria, Babylon, and Persia. Without modern weapons the new state of Israel could not have survived either. The lesson for ancient Israel was clear—Israel's relationship with God would determine its borders. Thus God would warn them before they were in the land, "When the LORD your God brings you into the land . . . do not forget the LORD" (Deut 6:10-12).

Even the climate reinforces this idea of dependency. The precipitation line ran through the center of the country. The weather would be another means for God's blessings or curses. It was a "land flowing with milk and honey" (Exod 33:3). The loss of land was, therefore, the means by which God revealed Israel's lack of obedience. There was a sacredness to the land: "The land must not be sold permanently because the land is mine" (Lev 25:23). Understanding the land of Israel and the lands around it will greatly help in understanding the Bible and its message.

Sources for Additional Study

Aharoni, Y. *The Land of the Bible: A Historical Geography.* Philadelphia: Westminster, 1980.

Daniel-Rops, Henri. *Daily Life in the Time of Jesus.* Ann Arbor: Servant, 1981.

PART III

THE BIBLE IN THE CHURCH

How to Understand the Bible

The sacred Scriptures of the Old and New Testaments have been the subject of uninterrupted study for thousands of years by multitudes of Bible students. The Bible has been central to all Christians regardless of their denominational affiliations. Along with Jews and Muslims, who are also part of our common Semitic culture and heritage, Christians have traditionally been called "people of the Book." This means that at the center of the spiritual life of Christians is a precious written document that contains a treasury of sacred wisdom and the core of its revelation. In addition, Christians hold that the Scriptures contain all things necessary for salvation. To study the Bible as a sacred text, therefore, is part of the duty of the followers of Jesus Christ. For not only do the Scriptures reveal who Jesus Christ is, but in them also is found the way to eternal life.

Some say the Bible is a dark and mysterious book, difficult to read, impossible to understand, and that one must take care in reaching out to it because it is obviously obscure and does not yield its secrets easily. Others treat the Bible in an opposite way, as an old and beloved friend, easily approached and more easily read. Often people with this view imagine that reading and understanding the Bible is much like picking up the Sunday newspaper and reading it through. They would claim that if you can read, you should have no trouble with the Bible.

Problems exist, of course, with either position. The difficulty with the first position that the Bible is inaccessible and mysterious is that it assumes the Bible was never really written for ordinary people, only for religious experts or the spiritually elite. Parts of the Bible do address different groups of people, the Jewish people, for example, or Christians in a particular city. These portions, however, are normally expressed to ordinary Jews and Christians with the common concerns of average human beings who have religious and spiritual interests. The Bible is not meant to be a book only for the experts or for a special, chosen few.

The difficulty with the second position, however, is that the Bible is not just a "simple" book. The Bible is really a library of books that have been written by many different authors. All sorts of literary styles are used, and the Bible contains, in fact, almost all the kinds of literature ever written. Furthermore, the Bible comes to us from a history and culture different from our own. This makes the Bible both very interesting and yet more complex than reading the newspaper from our own familiar hometown. Also the Bible was written for purposes other than merely passing along information, which is the major purpose of a newspaper. The Bible has many purposes, only one of which is to give us factual information. Its main task is to help change or transform the spiritual nature of human beings.

The study of Holy Scripture is a necessary obligation for any educated Christian and also a sacred responsibility for those who take their faith seriously. Many questions arise about how to approach the study of the Bible. Some questions that need to be answered before we can begin a meaningful study of Scripture are: How do students of the Bible approach the study of sacred Scripture? With what attitudes should we come? What tools and preparation should we bring? What methods can be used to enrich that study? What results are we to expect from such a study? These questions are to be answered in this survey on the subject of Bible study.

Approach

A serious Bible study should be approached first with the knowledge that the Bible invites our inquiry and that it is possible to learn deeply from it if we take the opportunity to do so. As in any other serious endeavor, it will take time and patience to build a good, working knowledge of the Bible. And like any other important and complex subject of study we undertake, we must be prepared to invest ourselves in the work, giving it both concentrated time and energy.

The Bible as an object of study cannot be mastered quickly. Understanding the Bible is not only a matter of learning the many facts and details of biblical history. We must also live with the truth of Scripture in order to know it. For example, when we say, "I know how to ride a bike," we do not mean that we understand all the laws of physics concerning motion, balance, velocity, and the aspects of momentum and wheel rotation. In fact, we may know none of these. We mean something far more important, which is sometimes difficult to put into words. We in fact are saying that we *know by experience* the art of bicycle riding. We in fact know how to ride a bicycle because we have actually tried it, and the knowledge of bicycle riding is now "inside" us or a part of us in a way that the knowledge of certain other facts is not. The Bible is exactly like that. You cannot really say you "know" the Bible until you have lived out its truth in experience to see how it actually works in real experience. The practice of the truth of Scripture is perhaps the most important concept of all to understand before we ever do formal Bible study.

Attitude

Like any other subject we have decided to learn, how well we do will depend on the kinds of attitudes with which we begin. For example, if our minds are already made up on what the Bible says or means and we are basically closed to new understanding, there is no real reason to study the Bible further. Openness in learning, as opposed to being closed minded, is the first key to studying the Scriptures. This is an attitude that says, "I am teachable because I do not know everything but want to learn more."

The second attitude is characterized by a hunger and thirst for truth. No one who does not possess a strong desire to learn the truth of Scripture in the way we have just described will pursue it for very long. A real longing to know truth is accompanied, of course, by a willingness to let the Holy Spirit teach us through our own efforts as well as through the work of others. This means, of course, that we will have to learn how to listen both with our minds and with our hearts to the Spirit of God who dwells in all those who have come to know and follow Christ.

Two other vital attitudes are more difficult to explain. One is the necessity of ambiguity when it is called for. Ambiguity is the willingness to let issues remain indefinite or undecided until we have more information or better understanding. We will not jump to conclusions too quickly, remembering that growth is a progressive thing. We should expect, therefore, that the truth of Scripture will be made known to us gradually, and we should not assume we will know everything at once. Knowing the truth of Scripture is like the way we came to know many other complicated subjects in school; one grade or level builds upon another. You cannot know, for example, the complex theorems of geometry if you have not first studied basic math. The same is true spiritually. Certain complex ideas follow more basic truths, and many of them must be learned in progression or only after we have developed in our spiritual maturity. We therefore should have the attitude that allows for the progressive unfolding of truth.

Tools and Preparation

Besides the obvious fact that students of Scripture must begin with a basic ability to read English literature, other essential tools are needed. In order to study the Bible, it would be good to have two or three readable translations of the Bible available and perhaps one paraphrased edition. There are many good translations in English today, and reading them side by side helps to explain difficult passages much more easily. Various publishing houses in fact print the Bible in parallel versions so the versions can be compared easily. Study Bibles, such as the *Disciple's Study Bible,* can be very helpful tools.

Next, a student should purchase a complete Bible concordance, which is an index of the English words used by one of the major translations. With a concordance words and phrases that are used over and over can be looked up, and different usages of the same word can be compared to see how they are used in different contexts to help clarify the many meanings a word may have or the different ways it can be used.

Many guides and commentaries have been written on the Bible. Some guides, like the present volume you are using now, give considerable background material for Bible study. Commentaries on the meaning of the text and the background of the book are available for every book of the Bible and can be quite helpful. A good religious book store will carry different types of commentaries, some for beginners and some for advanced Bible students. If you are studying just one book of the Bible, it is helpful to use several commentaries such as *The New American Commentary* to help you better understand that book.

For the advanced Bible student it is possible to learn to use what are called lexical aids and advanced critical commentaries. These are books that help the student to understand the original languages of the Bible and the historical, literary, and theological issues that concern scholars of Scripture study today. Even though you may not have a knowledge of the ancient Greek and Hebrew languages, which are the original languages of most of the Bible, you can still use these books if only to learn the alphabet of each language.

To start you will need an interlinear text of the Bible (one line in English and the next in the original Greek or Hebrew). You will also need a dictionary like *The Holman Bible Dictionary* to help you look up the definitions of words and trace their original meanings. Finally, students of Scripture need to be part of a worshiping and studying community of committed people. It is very important to be able to share your study and discovery with others and receive help from others as well. To study alone is more difficult than to be a part of a group of people who also love the Scriptures, who worship and pray together, and who share what they learn comfortably together.

Methods

Two basic methods of Bible study are topical study and exegetical study. Topical study means that you take a topic or theme and follow it through the entire Bible, seeing all the ways it is used or discussed by the writers of the Scripture. You might, for example, take the topic of the relationship between God and humanity and see how it develops throughout the Bible. There are of course innumerable ideas and topics to be studied. It is good, usually, to begin with a practical topic that both interests you and relates to the way you live now. The subject of "priestly dress" as described in the Old and New Testaments might be interesting for some, but it does not relate to where most people live today.

To do a topical study you would need both a Bible and its concordance. Some study Bibles have topical indexes at the back that list different topics and the basic references. Using that as a guide, the student would need to begin a list of references and put them perhaps in chronological order, beginning with the oldest books in the Bible and moving toward the ones written last. Note that the order of books in the Bible is a traditional order and not necessarily chronological. It would be good to find out about biblical chronology as a first part of your study.

Another important area for topical study is to notice how different kinds of biblical literature (poetry versus letters or epistles, for example) use themes and words differently. Do not assume that all writers will mean the same thing by a similar topic or word. This should be part of your study. Next, after listing each reference and usage so that you understand it, then you might want to group the topic into categories that seem to say separate things about the same topic. You might want to write out a summary statement for each grouping and then summarize the whole topic, so that in your own words you feel you do understand that theme. Finally, you might also want to check to see what has been written on that same theme by other Christian authors. Compare your findings with theirs, helping you to expand your own understanding.

Exegetical study is different from topical study because typically it takes a particular book or passage in one of the books of the Bible and studies it in depth by looking at many different levels in and around that particular text. Exegetical study also examines various topics and themes, but usually only in relationship to what is addressed in a particular book or passage, and tries to understand these in the larger framework of that particular book or in the context of other books written by the same author. This form of study is somewhat more complex, but it usually yields interesting results.

To better understand what exegetical study is and how it is done, it is important to know about the levels of meanings that surround a book or passage in the Bible. Meanings are always understood "in context." You have perhaps joined a conversation in the middle of a topic. Though you knew all the words used, still you did not understand what was being said because you did not know what the actual context or background for the conversation was. Only after a while did you understand the context, that the words actually made sense. This is true often in Bible study. What a passage means is usually made clear when it is put in context.

This concept explains why many times in exegetical study a student of the Bible will begin with the largest context around the Scripture first and later move to the meaning of a particular passage. Others, however, prefer to start with the words of a passage themselves and then continue outward until as much of the context is understood as possible. Exegetical study could either begin on the "inside" of a particular passage and work out or on the "outside" and work in. Either way is possible. But picture a circle with five smaller circles inside it. To understand the Scriptures it is important to pass through all the circles.

If we start on the "inside," the first circle is the meaning of the words of Scripture in their immediate context. This first step in study involves understanding the definitions and shades of the meaning of words used in that book or by that author. It also entails understanding how those words are employed in particular sentences. Defining words, seeing how they are used in sentences, and then understanding the sentences themselves as they are placed in groups of larger ideas is the first important part of exegetical study. These ideas are then seen in the whole context of the complete message of the book. This is the first circle, and its focus is the literary meaning of the text. But it also examines the symbols and stories and ideas of that book as they are woven together to form one whole piece. Students would do well to make a list of all the important meanings of words and sentences; usages of idioms, symbols, and ideas; and then outline how they fit together in the whole book. Also it would be important to list what you do not yet understand.

We move from the first circle to the second in order that the first meaning of the immediate text is put within wider context of the life and circumstances of the author of the book, what the author was "about." The questions we would want to ask are: Who was this person, what did he intend to say, and why did he wish to say it? Answering these questions is often much more difficult than it seems. First, we can never get back into the mind of the author. Yet through the study of other parts of an author's work, the events that became the context for writing a particular text, and by knowing something of the person of the author and the reasons he had for writing the book, it is possible to understand partially the immediate context for the larger meaning.

We are then ready to move to the third circle and look at the larger historical and cultural setting and the influences that prevailed to help create this literary work. Knowing another culture even in our own day is often difficult for us. When that culture existed in the past, understanding it becomes even more complex. Yet serious study of the cultural and historical context can make much of the thought and events of that time available to us and provide a historical context whereby we might better understand the meaning of a particular text of Scripture. For example, what was Semitic or Hebrew culture like in contrast to Greek culture or the Roman world? How did the cultural and religious thought of Persia influence the later writing of the Old Testament? These are the sorts of questions that can be asked in circle three.

For the Christian, however, human culture cannot be examined in isolation from an understanding of the unfolding of the divine drama. Our human story must also be seen against the backdrop of the sweep of the purpose of God within our human story. As part of a long spiritual tradition we inherit a certain understanding of the themes and motifs of our sacred past which we can use to begin to determine the goal of the revelation of God. This area of study, the fourth circle, weaves the themes of the whole Bible together to form a tapestry of thought that guides all our study. This tapestry is often called biblical theology since it attempts to understand in one piece all of the themes of the Bible as one whole story.

An understanding of Scripture arrives in our day through the living tradition of faith as the church has come to understand itself on its long historical journey. The traditions, teachings, doctrines, and history of the church therefore contribute greatly to our contemporary understanding of Scripture. We do not understand Scripture without that context. The apostle Peter expresses the profound insight that no Scripture is of any "private interpretation" (2 Pet 1:20-21). One way of understanding what he means is to see that none of us finds meaning in a vacuum. Each person is part of an "interpretive community" that sees things in its own unique fashion and shares those perceptions with its members. What we understand, therefore, and the meanings we perceive are part of a heritage that is passed down to us through history and tradition. The community of Christian faith, therefore, is a living organism with a tradition that shapes and is shaped by the meaning of the Scriptures and forms the fifth circle.

A final circle of meaning around the Bible by which we seek to understand and interpret for ourselves is perhaps the largest circle of all. It is the area of our contemporary world where our own current needs as individuals and as Christian communities are expressed and exposed to the wisdom of the Scriptures. We need to ask ourselves: What is happening in our own world, culture, and society that calls upon the truth of Scripture? What is the need of the community of faithful Christians worldwide that elicits out of the ancient writings new understandings applicable to our own time? What, finally, do we need to understand and do that will help us become better followers of Jesus Christ? Ultimately, we are the immediate context through which the power and significance of Holy Scripture meets and interacts with the present moment. We are filters through which its meaning is passed. Who am I? What have I become in my own spiritual development? Where have I journeyed spiritually? What am I currently able to understand that will help define the meanings Scripture can express to me?

Results

Each individual Christian is an active participant in the process of understanding the meaning of the Bible. As a member of the Christian community, each student is placed within all these layers of meaning and can use them as lenses through which to explore the truth of God. The meaning of Scripture is not, therefore, a static thing. It is extremely dynamic. What is happening to each of us personally and to our world invites the truth of the Word of God to act in new ways, and we are challenged by it to change into new creatures, to be transformed. We should expect the study of the Bible to help revolutionize our understanding, our behavior, our awareness of the world and ourselves, and to bring us into closer relationship with God Himself.

READING SCRIPTURE

Today we are told that more Bibles are sold than any other book on the market. The implication is that the Bible is read more than any other piece of literature, at least in Christian society and perhaps in the entire world. One wonders, of course, whether there is an exact correlation between Bibles sold and Bibles read? Regardless of the answer, however, the fact remains that the Bible has stood at the center of the Western spiritual tradition, and it is the basic foundation of both its literature and its faith. It is the ultimate authority for the church's teaching and has been the text that informs and enriches the lives of Christian people everywhere and in every age. Therefore it is critical that all Christians have a basic knowledge of Scripture, which can come only from personal reading and the effort to understand it.

The Bible as Library

It would be easy to imagine that since the Bible is the book that is central to Christian faith, the most obvious thing to do would be to simply find a translation easily understood and start at the beginning of the Bible, as you would do with any normal book, and proceed straight through reading the text until you reach the end. The Bible, however, is not a "normal" book. As has been said elsewhere in this guide, the word Bible means, literally, in the Greek language *library* (*Biblos*).

The Bible is in fact a library of many books written by a wide variety of authors at separate times for different purposes and in many diverse styles. You would never go into a library and treat all the books alike. Neither would you read all of the books in the library starting with the one nearest the entrance and proceed straight through every text until you exhausted all there was to read. As in any library, you would want to start selectively. First you would probably browse, get familiar with the whole library. Later you would find out about all the different categories of books in the library and then start to read from the standpoint of your own personal needs or interests. Eventually you would want to learn how to utilize the whole library.

This is indeed what this project of the *Holman Bible Handbook* is about, acquainting you with the library of the Bible. Again, understanding the library is not all you would need to know if you are to read the Holy Scripture. There are in fact many different ways of reading. We read for pleasure differently from reading for study or analysis. When we pick up the daily newspaper, for example, we read the comic pages differently from the business or advertisement section, and these are read differently from the editorial page. Each of us utilizes many separate skills in reading. The same should be true for reading the Bible. There are various ways of reading Scripture, and each has its own specific purpose.

Two of the primary ways of reading the Bible are for study (the gaining of basic knowledge concerning the facts of Scripture) and for worship, personal devotion, or spiritual growth. These are not necessarily opposite ways of reading, but they do entail different skills. The skills needed for Bible study are complex and are discussed in a separate section of this text. In this article the focus is on general Bible reading and more particularly on the reading of Scripture for personal, spiritual sustenance and insight. Again, even here there are multiple approaches to reading the Scriptures that require special consideration. Throughout the church's life, Christians have developed certain helpful disciplines and methods that enrich the way they have read Scripture. These methods have been passed on to us as our present heritage.

Systematic Reading

Normally we feed ourselves day by day in order to sustain normal human life and growth and also for enjoyment. The regular and systematic intake of food is considered to be essential for human living. The same principle holds true for the spiritual life. Throughout history Christians have maintained that the regular and systematic intake or reading of Scripture was of great spiritual benefit.

Systematic daily reading was first used by Jewish believers and was developed during the time of their exile when, in synagogue worship, readings from different portions were appointed for each day. The first Christians, of course, were Jews. So this tradition continued on into the life of the early church and has been maintained down through the centuries up until the present time. Today many Christians follow what is called the "common lectionary," which is a two-year cycle of daily readings through the entire Bible and a three-year cycle of weekly readings appointed for Sunday worship. Others adopt readings in accordance with the weekly Sunday School lesson or other devotional guides. Systematic reading in this way has proved to be of great benefit in maintaining balanced, long-term Bible reading.

Reading in Context

One practice adopted by some Christians involves selecting readings within the context of the "Church Year Calendar." In this calendar the church observes the entire life of Christ and remembers His work on earth by dividing the year into seven sections or seasons of differing lengths, much in the same way that a week is divided into seven days. Each of these seven seasons or sections emphasizes a different aspect of the life of Jesus Christ and God's revelation and work through Him.

Normally the readings from the common lectionary are selected to reflect upon the particular significance of each season observed in this yearly cycle and the meaning for the body of Christ, the church, in the world and also each individual member of it.

Prayerful Reading for Spiritual Growth

Christians in every century have stressed that the reading of Scripture should be done carefully and deliberately. In that way its spiritual strength can be assimilated and digested into one's entire being through prayerful reflection. The reading of the Bible as spiritual food cannot be done as one would read a newspaper in the morning, skimming over it for interesting tidbits of information. The following approaches can give guidance for reading Scripture for our spiritual development and growth.

1. Oral Reading. Read each portion of Scripture aloud, allowing yourself to hear the Scripture as though it were the very first time and in a new way. Such reading should be done slowly and deliberately so that it can be truly heard with the whole of one's being.

2. Active Reflection. Explore the many meanings of the readings perhaps through its story and narrative forms or through the multiple symbols and metaphors used by the authors. Allow these to offer fresh insight and understanding concerning the spiritual truth that is available to you as spiritual food.

3. Careful Application. Enter into a personal and vigorous dialogue with the reading, permitting its truth to offer you new understanding and its insights to challenge and confront you in ways that demand your acceptance and obedience.

4. Prayerful Listening. Sit silently and attentively in the presence of God and permit the Holy Spirit to quietly illumine your mind and begin His inner work of transformation. Listen prayerfully as He teaches and instructs you, seeking for His guidance upon the path of your life.

Each aspect of general Bible reading as it has been outlined above constitutes means by which the Scriptures can become a source of spiritual sustenance. Systematic reading in a larger context that follows the steps outlined above will inevitably strengthen the Christian life. The methods shared in this article are part of our Christian heritage, made available to us through the patient labor of our fellow Christian brothers and sisters through the centuries. We should accept with thanks their gift to us.

52-WEEK BIBLE READING PLAN

Guides the reader through the Old Testament once and the New Testament twice in one year.

1 — Genesis 1-26
2 — Genesis 27-50
3 — Matthew
4 — Mark
5 — Exodus 1-21
6 — Exodus 22-40
7 — Luke
8 — John
9 — Leviticus
10 — Acts
11 — Numbers 1-18
12 — Numbers 19-36
13 — Romans; Galatians
14 — 1, 2 Corinthians
15 — Deuteronomy 1-17
16 — Deuteronomy 18-34
17 — Ephesians; Philippians; Colossians; 1, 2 Thessalonians; 1, 2 Timothy; Titus; Philemon
18 — Hebrews; James; 1, 2 Peter
19 — Joshua
20 — 1, 2, 3 John; Jude; Revelation
21 — Judges; Ruth
22 — Job 1-31
23 — Job 32-42; Ecclesiastes; Song of Solomon
24 — 1 Samuel
25 — 2 Samuel
26 — Psalms 1-50
27 — 1 Kings
28 — 2 Kings
29 — Psalms 51-100
30 — 1 Chronicles
31 — 2 Chronicles
32 — Psalms 101-150
33 — Ezra; Nehemiah; Esther
34 — Proverbs
35 — Matthew
36 — Isaiah 1-35
37 — Isaiah 36-66
38 — Mark
39 — Luke
40 — Jeremiah 1-29
41 — Jeremiah 30-52; Lamentations
42 — John
43 — Acts
44 — Ezekiel 1-24
45 — Ezekiel 25-48
46 — Romans; Galatians
47 — 1, 2 Corinthians
48 — Daniel; Hosea; Joel; Amos
49 — Ephesians; Philippians; Colossians; 1, 2 Thessalonians; 1, 2 Timothy; Titus; Philemon
50 — Obadiah; Jonah; Micah; Nahum; Habakkuk; Zephaniah; Haggai; Zechariah; Malachi
51 — Hebrews; James; 1, 2 Peter
52 — 1, 2, 3 John; Jude; Revelation

TEACHING AND PREACHING THE BIBLE

Teaching or preaching the Bible may be thought of as three-sided conversation. The teacher speaks to the student about the Bible but with a view to leading the student to personally engage the text. The teacher begins preparation by conversing with the text but on behalf of those who will share the learning situation. The teaching moment should bring together people who have dialogued with the Scriptures and who will now dialogue with one another and together reengage the text.

Preparation

Preparation for teaching or preaching begins with an attempt to discover the possible meanings of the text for the present time and for the particular audience for whom the lesson or sermon is being prepared. The best teaching occurs when a presentation has been prepared for a particular audience and a particular time. When meanings have been discovered, then a plan must be devised for translating those meanings into a form that can be understood by the audience. Implicit in the discovery of the meanings in a text for a particular time and people are applications to life experience. The teacher must ask what gift is in the text and what demand accompanies the gift.

Biblical Interpretation

The process of investigating the meaning of a biblical text is called exegesis. The passage must be analyzed in its literary context and in its cultural context to determine what God is saying to us through the words. The theological context of the whole Bible should also inform the message of a passage. One of the chief obstacles to hearing what a passage of Scripture is saying is a preconceived idea of the message. Because of sermons and lessons heard over the years and interpretations of others read in nonbiblical sources, people sometimes make up their minds about a passage before careful objective analysis. The good teacher must deal with his or her preconceived ideas and with those likely to exist among the audience to be addressed.

A serious student of the Bible seeks to let the Scriptures speak without the bias of various interpreters no matter how well intentioned they may have been. A popular text sometimes is assigned standard meaning that has been passed down uncritically from preacher to preacher. That standard interpretation may be correct or incorrect. Often these interpretations are valid but are too limited, and when they are accepted too quickly, the full impact of the passage is not discovered.

A single source, human or written, may result in too limited an understanding of a passage. Bible translations can also be misleading. Hebrew and Greek words often contain several possible meanings, and the English word chosen or the verb tense used may shape the meaning of the text. Teachers and preachers should have available several translations and compare how passages have been rendered. Commentaries and other forms of helps should be used carefully. Older commentaries and dictionaries may not reflect recent discoveries of texts and archaeological findings that shed light on ancient customs and

George Whitefield, outstanding preacher of the Great Awakening in America (1740–1743), was known for his compelling yet unadorned preaching style.

beliefs. Teachers must always resist personal bias and the inclination to make the text say what they want it to say. The goal is to let the Scripture speak and not to use it to make a personal statement.

Free from preconceived notions about the meaning of a text, the teacher is ready to let the text speak. Begin by reading a passage completely through in your favorite English translation. Seek to experience the message in your own spiritual pilgrimage. Ask yourself what it means to you. Go back and read it in the context of the entire book and the writer's purpose as you understand it. Ask yourself why the author has included this material at all and why it has been placed in this particular location in this specific book of the Bible and in the Bible as a whole.

Asking the Right Questions

The teacher will examine the text in the framework of the history of God's revelation and in the particular cultural context in which the event occurred. A simple way to approach a story or event is to use the questions any good reporter would ask. The well-known writer Rudyard Kipling wrote that he kept six honest men who served him well and taught him all he knew. They were:

What? and Why?
When? and How?
Where? and Who?

These questions serve the teacher or preacher well in the discovery process and can serve well in the teaching or preaching event. The answers can be stated in a positive manner to form the structure of the lesson or sermon.

A text that is often misinterpreted is Philippians 4:13, "I can do everything through him who gives me strength." This verse is often employed to urge people to become super-Christians in the accomplishment of Herculean tasks. I have heard preachers suggest that this passage means that Christians should be able to achieve any goal and live above the strife of other mortals. If the exegete uses the reporters questions wisely, this error will likely be avoided. *What?* Paul wrote to his friends and supporters who were concerned about how he was doing in prison and about the recent serious illness of Epaphroditus. *Why?* He wrote to assure them that he had not been overwhelmed by difficulties and that one could survive perilous conditions through faith. *When?* He wrote while still in prison with the possibility of execution before him. *How?* Faith removes fear and sustains one in dire circumstances. *Where?* The *where* has been answered and is important in interpreting the passage. The fact Paul was in prison indicated he could not escape persecution and injustice because he was a Christian. Indeed, his proclamation of the gospel led to his imprisonment. *Who?* The *who* includes Paul, Epaphroditus, and all others who might suffer for the sake of the gospel.

The Philippian passage dealt with an actual historical situation, but some biblical passages are not descriptions of events. One of the things a teacher needs to do is to determine what kind of literature the passage is. Is it poetry or prose? Some translations will indicate this by the form used. Ask yourself if, on surface reading, the material seems to be literal or symbolic. Some passages state that they are not to be taken literally (for example, Isa 5; Ezek 1). If the passage is poetry, some imagination is called for. A literal interpretation doesn't make sense of language that is clearly figurative (see Matt 5:29-30; 7:15-20). Writers sometimes use contradictory figures of speech (Isa 34:8; 66:24).

The biblical writers were often inspired to use different literary forms to reduce divine truths to a form comprehensible by human intellect. Jesus Himself relied heavily on parables, brief stories about everyday life situations, to explain the kingdom of God and to make clear the choices open to those He taught.

The basic questions of the journalist can be applied with profit to all kinds of literature. Look at the unit and ask: Who said what to whom? Where? Why? Is the principal spokesman Jesus, one of the apostles, or an adversary? The story of the exodus will be heard differently by those who identify with Pharaoh and those who identify with the Hebrews.

The characters cannot always be divided into the good guys and the bad guys. And when they can be, it is not always easy for contemporary readers to decide whose side they are on. God's friends have often created as many problems for Him as His enemies; consider Abraham, Jacob, and David. Moses as God's representative had more difficulty with the Hebrews than he did with the Egyptians. He also lost his temper and suffered the wrath of God.

The prophets' words were sometimes addressed to Israel and sometimes to Israel's enemies. Much of the advice addressed to Job by his "friends" was consistent with accepted biblical theology and is sometimes treated positively by preachers speaking to contemporary audiences. Why was it rejected in the context of the drama of Job? The time, place, and cultural circumstances often alter the message. Recall the importance of knowing the circumstances under which Paul wrote to the Philippians in order to interpret correctly 4:13. This kind of analysis calls for commentaries, biblical dictionaries, and biblical background studies to provide required information.

Setting and audience analysis is especially helpful in the study of the Gospels. The troubling passage that records Jesus' apparent rebuke of His family (see Matt 12:46-50; Mark 3:31-35; Luke 8:19-21) takes on a different complexion when the question of audience is addressed. Most scholars stress the effort of Jesus' family to get Him to come home and stop His public ministry. One may see here a willingness of the Lord to practice His own principles and to "hate" even mother, brothers, and sisters for the sake of the gospel. But we possibly also could see His words as making His family more inclusive. That is, rather than rejecting His nuclear family, He extended family to include "whoever does the will of my Father in heaven" (Matt 12:50). Either or both lessons appear to be reasonable interpretations.

Knowing the Audience

Effective teaching or preaching requires a continuing consciousness of the audience throughout the preparation process. Some groups will best hear God's truth for them from the perspective of the Egyptians; others will best hear from the vantage point of the oppressed Israelites. A good teacher will make clear the difference between the good-sounding advice of the friends and the troubling truth of Job's struggles. Some congregations are suffering with Job; others are more like the friends. The interpretation should be adapted to the particular audience.

Christian teaching and preaching is never transference of information for its own sake. It is always directed toward human transformation. It is imperative then that the application of truth of the texts be made clear. The truth must be translated into a form recognizable in the present age. Such translation requires relating the unknown, the foreign, the old to the known, the familiar, the new. A conscious effort must be made to translate language not just from Hebrew or Greek to English but from everyday life in biblical time to everyday life in our time.

Jesus provides an excellent model for the contemporary teacher or preacher. He used familiar images to convey divine truth. Jesus used images common to first-century Israel and comparisons with experiences and events familiar to His audience. Those images will be understood by today's audiences only when they are explained with images common to contemporary experience.

As contemporary teachers move from the meaning of the text to the communication of that text to a particular group of people, they must look for images the people will recognize. The vineyard may have to become an assembly line. The steward becomes a union steward or foreman. The building of more grain storage bins might be compared to the corporate workaholic and the accumulation of more stock. The Jewish attitude toward Samaritans can best be understood in terms of the oppression of Blacks, Hispanics, and other minorities. Middle-class Americans can be contrasted with the tension between choosing the good and the better and the difference between being religious and being Christian, as illustrated by Jesus' conflict with the Pharisees and scribes.

Any preaching or teaching situation requires that the speaker get and maintain the attention of the audience. The next step is to demonstrate how the material will benefit the listeners.

The teacher or preacher seeks to remove all obstacles to a clear and fresh hearing of Holy Scripture. Available resources such as commentaries and Bible dictionaries are used to set the text in historical, literary, and cultural context. When the original meaning of a text is grasped as much as is humanly possible, then that meaning must be examined in light of contemporary culture and the particular audience with whom it is to be shared.

Since the 1950s, evangelist Billy Graham has preached the simple Bible-centered gospel message of salvation around the world and touched the lives of millions with the love of Christ.

THE HISTORY OF BIBLICAL INTERPRETATION

From the beginning of the church a dual heritage developed: (1) one that maintains that Scripture's meaning is found only in its primary, historical sense and (2) another that considers Scripture's ultimate meaning to rest in its plenary, or full, sense. From these distinctives several models and combinations of models developed for interpreting Scripture in the early church.

The Early Church

The apostolic fathers in the second century found the true understanding of the apostles. The rise of false teachings (particular Gnosticism) and challenges to accepted orthodoxy created confusion in interpretation. To demonstrate the unity of Scripture and its message, theological frameworks were implemented by such scholars as Irenaeus (about A.D. 140–202) and Tertullian (about A.D. 155–225). These frameworks served as guides for faith in the church.

Continuing the Christological emphasis of the first century, the rule of faith outlined the theological beliefs that found their focus in the incarnate Lord. Sometimes, however, the interpretation of Scripture through this theological grid forced the biblical text into a preconceived set of theological convictions. This approach resulted in a safeguard for the church's message but reduced the possibility of creativity among the individual interpreters. It also tended to divorce the biblical text from its literary or historical context.

Creative biblical interpretation reached new levels with the rise of the school of Alexandria in the third century. The innovation of allegorical interpretation developed in this context. Allegorical interpretation assumes that the Bible intends to say something more than what its literal wording suggests. It seeks to draw out the deeper, mystical sense beyond the words themselves. The two great representatives of the Alexandrian school were Clement (about 150–215) and Origen (A.D. 185–254).

The literal sense, however, was not the primary meaning of Scripture for the Alexandrians. Origen particularly thought it absurd that a God-inspired Bible could not be interpreted spiritually. From this supposition followed Origen's threefold hermeneutical approach. He maintained that the Bible had three different yet complementary meanings: (1) a literal or a physical sense, (2) an allegorical or a spiritual sense, and (3) a tropological or a moral sense. Yet at places the Alexandrians ignored the literal sense and found numerous spiritual meanings in a single passage, thus creating an entire scale of allegorical interpretation. Alexandrian interpretation was primarily practical. The work of these allegorical interpreters cannot be understood until this is realized.

The successors of Origen were challenged by the school of Antioch, which emphasized a literal and historical interpretation. The great Antiochene interpreters included John Chrysostom (about A.D. 347–407) and Theodore of Mopsuestia (about A.D. 350–428). They conceived of biblical inspiration as a divinely given quickening of the writers' awareness and understanding, in which their individuality was not impaired and their intellectual activity remained under conscious control. The Antiochenes focused on the biblical writers' aims, motivations, usages, and methods. They believed the literal-historical sense of Scripture was primary and moral applications were made from it. The mature exegesis of Theodore and Chrysostom, while literal, was not a crude or wooden literalism that failed to recognize figures of speech in the biblical text. In continuity with the previous practices of Jesus and the early church, the Antiochenes read Scripture Christologically through the application of typological interpretation.

As the church moved into the fifth century, an eclectic and multifaceted approach to interpretation developed, which sometimes emphasized the literal and historical and sometimes the allegorical but always the theological. Augustine (A.D. 354–430) and Jerome (about A.D. 341–420) established the directions for this period. The biblical text was interpreted in its larger context, understood as the biblical canon. The biblical canon established parameters for validating both typological and allegorical interpretations so that the historical meaning remained primary, even though the deeper spiritual meaning was not ignored. Neither the allegorical practices of Alexandria nor the historical emphases of Antioch dominated. A balance emerged, influenced by pastoral and theological concerns. The Bible was viewed from the standpoint of faith, producing interpretations that emphasized the edification of the church, the love of neighbor, and primarily a knowledge of and love for God.

The Medieval and Reformation Period

From the time of Augustine the church, following the lead of John Cassian (died about 433), subscribed to a theory of the fourfold sense of Scripture: (1) The literal sense of Scripture could, and usually did, nurture the virtues of faith, hope, and love. When it did not, the interpreter could appeal to three additional virtues, each sense corresponding to one of the virtues. (2) The allegorical sense referred to the church and its faith, what it was to believe. (3) The tropological or moral sense referred to individuals and what they should do, corresponding to love. (4) The anagogical sense pointed to the church's expectation, corresponding to hope. For example, the city of Jerusalem, in all its appearances in Scripture, was understood literally as a Jewish city, allegorically as the church of Jesus Christ, tropologically as the souls of men and women, and anagogically as the heavenly city. The fourfold sense characterized interpretation in the Middle Ages.

Martin Luther (1483–1546), the great reformer, began by using the allegorical method but later claimed to have abandoned it. It was Erasmus (1466–1536), more than Luther, who rediscovered the priority of the literal sense. John Calvin (1509–1564), the most consistent interpreter of the Reformation, developed the emphasis on the grammatical-historical method as the foundation for developing the spiritual message from the Bible. Luther's stress on a fuller sense located in the Christological meaning of Scripture linked the reformers with Jesus, the apostles, and the early church.

It is commonly believed that the followers of the reformers shrank from the freedom in interpretation employed by Luther and Calvin. While this is an overstatement and an oversimplification, it is true they conducted their exposition along new theological boundaries. This new form resulted in an authoritative and dogmatic interpretation. Almost simultaneously, enlightenment thought began to develop. This movement rejected both authoritative and dogmatic approaches, resulting in two reactions: (1) a newfound pietism associated with Philipp Jakob Spener (1635–1705) and August Herman Franke (1663–1727) and (2) a historical-critical method that stressed the importance of the historical over the theological interpretation of the Bible. The modern era has generally continued in one of three directions: the Reformation, pietistic, or historical-critical approach.

The Modern Era

The modern era has seen the rise and development of a variety of critical approaches to Scripture (see the articles "The Old Testament and Criticism" and "The New Testament and Criticism"). Existential interpretation has been widely cultivated in the twentieth century, especially under the influence of Rudolf Bultmann (1884–1976). This approach emphasized that interpreters should project themselves into the author's experience so as to relive it. The "New Hermeneutic" developed from the existential approach. They regarded the task of interpretation as the creation of a "language event" in which the authentic language of the Bible encounters contemporary readers, challenging them to decision and faith.

In addition to existentialist hermeneutics, recent concerns have included linguistic, literary, structuralist, and sociological approaches. These approaches tend to de-emphasize the historical background of a text and its original life setting. More fruitful approaches are the "redemptive-history" hermeneutic and the canonical hermeneutic. The former views the biblical text in light of God's saving activity that finds its climax in Christ. The latter interprets the biblical text in light of the entire biblical canon. Canonical hermeneutics must be careful not to reduce the distinction emphases within the canon in the interests of superficial harmonizations. How the interpreter can do full justice both to the biblical unity and diversity remains a major focus of contemporary biblical interpreters.

Even though there is much diversity in contemporary approaches to biblical interpretation, the goal of discovering God's message through the illumination of the Holy Spirit remains the ultimate aim and purpose for all interpreters.

Augustine of Hippo (A.D. 354–430)

HISTORY OF ENGLISH BIBLE TRANSLATIONS

All English translations were called forth by practical needs. The movement to translate the Bible into the language of the people found little support before the time of the Reformation. Yet there were several movements worthy of mention. In this article we will survey some of those early movements and then look at the more recent translations, of which there are many.

Anglo-Saxon Versions

The first English Bibles were not in English at all, nor were they strictly translations. Under Roman occupation the British churches probably had used Latin. With the barbarian invasions a need for the new vernacular arose as evangelization began in the sixth century. The initial works in the late seventh century focused on poetic paraphrases, first on the creation story and then on other parts of the Pentateuch and perhaps some of the New Testament.

True Anglo-Saxon translations began with Aldhelm's rendering of the Psalms about A.D. 700. A touching picture from A.D. 725 is that of the aged Bede translating John's Gospel on his deathbed.

Middle Ages

The English Bible made little progress during the early Norman years after 1066. The Normans, of French lineage, did not speak the native tongue, and Anglo-Saxon was itself developing into early English, though very slowly as a literary language. A monk named Orin made a fresh start in the late twelfth century with a poetic version of the Gospels and Acts. Poetic renderings of Genesis, Exodus, and the Psalter followed in the thirteenth century and two prose versions of the Psalms in the fourteenth, one of them the popular Rolle version. The fourteenth century also saw some further work on the New Testament.

These renderings had aimed only at a limited readership, but finally the late fourteenth century produced a more ambitious project. The reformer John Wycliffe, stressing the function of Scripture, had a vision of rendering the whole Bible for more widespread use. The first Wycliffe Bible came out in 1380–84, and the initial *j.* in some portions has inspired the theory that Wycliffe himself did much of the work. The first edition is so close to the Latin that it was perhaps meant for lay preachers rather than directly for the people, many of whom could neither read nor afford copies. A revised edition by John Purvey (possibly the mysterious j.?) proved to be more radical. It came out in 1396. In the preface Purvey stated that he had sought a purer text, was focusing on the sense and not just the words, and aimed to put the original in the speech of the people.

Reformation

Tyndale. The Wycliffe Bible was an important step forward, but fierce opposition, the labor and expense of production, and rapid linguistic change reduced its impact. By the early sixteenth century a fresh need had arisen. This time, in spite of unremitting traditionalist resistance, such factors as the invention of printing, Renaissance biblical studies, new Reformation emphases, able and dedicated translators, and enthusiastic church and middle-class patronage ensured the success of the enterprise.

William Tyndale was the pioneer and catalyst. Stirred by the call of Erasmus for Bible translations and shocked by the ignorance of Scripture in his native Gloucestershire, even among higher clergy, he sought official sponsorship. When rebuffed, he engaged in a clandestine work of translation and publication abroad, first at Cologne, then at Worms and Antwerp. His New Testament came out in 1526. At once a battle started in which the bishops blundered by buying up copies, thus encouraging pirated editions and providing Tyndale with funds for the improved edition of 1534.

Before his betrayal and execution (1536) Tyndale also translated the Pentateuch and probably prepared materials for Joshua to Second Chronicles. In his work he used Purvey, Luther, and the Vulgate, but he also showed originality in his handling of Greek and Hebrew. Above all he added to accuracy an idiomatic freshness and force that would have a beneficial influence on future renderings.

William Tyndale printing his translation of the Bible into English at Cologne.

Great Bible. Tyndale could not finish the Old Testament, but some of the gaps were later filled in with the addition of the Psalms, Isaiah, and Jeremiah (1530, 1531, 1534). Coverdale, protected by Archbishop Cranmer, then did a quick translation of the whole Bible from secondary sources (1535); for this he secured a royal license. The way thus opened up for a project dear to Cranmer, the setting up of an official copy of the English Bible in every parish church.

Injunctions to this effect were passed in 1536 and 1537 but with no approved text. In 1537, however, Matthew's Bible came to Cranmer's notice. In reality this was the work of John Rogers, Tyndale's assistant. It consisted of all Tyndale supplemented by Coverdale. With the political help of Thomas Cromwell, Cranmer—to his great delight—secured the consent of King Henry to this version. When a large edition was prepared, revised by Coverdale, it came out as the Great Bible (1539), the "book of the whole Bible, of the largest volume, in English" that all parishes were ordered to purchase.

For a further revision in 1540, often called Cranmer's Bible, the archbishop wrote a preface commending the Bible as the book in which we learn what to think, what to do, and what not to do. New editions came out under Edward VI in 1549 and 1553, and the Prayer Books of 1549 and 1552 included English Psalms and readings.

Geneva, Bishops', and Rheims Bible. Reaction under Queen Mary, a strict Catholic, temporarily blocked Bible translation in England. But the Great Bible survived, and English exiles in Geneva continued the work. Whittingham in 1557 issued a revision of Tyndale's New Testament that introduced to English Bibles the verse divisions first used in a 1551 Greek edition. A revised Old Testament completed the Geneva Bible in 1560. The preface defended the new version on two grounds: first, the need to check by the originals the non-Tyndale portions and second, the access to richer scholarly resources at Geneva. The version included the Apocrypha but specifically denied its canonical authority. Under Queen Elizabeth the Geneva Bible experienced no restrictions and became popular with the growth of Geneva-oriented Puritanism. A Scottish edition (1579) seems to have been the first Bible published in Scotland. Printing of the Geneva Bible ceased only when the Authorized Version ousted it in 1644.

Meanwhile the opponents of Puritanism were not idle.

In 1561 Archbishop Parker initiated a revision of the Great Bible that would update the scholarship, provide notes, and improve the style. In 1571 an official church of England Convocation gave approval to this revision, which came to be called the Bishops' Bible. After further polishing of the New Testament, it became the official translation for public worship in the Church of England, except for the continued use of Coverdale's Psalms. Although it sold well, this version failed to arouse the same enthusiasm as the Geneva Bible, which appealed to the Puritan segment noted for its high regard for Holy Scripture.

Authorized Version (AV, KJV). The accession of James I to the English throne in 1603 made possible an important new step. At the Hampton Court Conference, held to discuss Puritan issues, little agreement resulted. The king, who had tried his hand at Bible translation, did welcome a proposal by the Puritan leader John Reynolds for a commonly revised and accepted rendering of Scripture. To implement the proposal, the finest Anglican and Puritan scholars were enlisted in six panels, three for the Old Testament, two for the New, and one for the Apocrypha. Individual scholars prepared drafts which the panels then discussed, consulting the other panels and submitting the approved drafts to a group of two representatives from each panel for final scrutiny.

The aim, as the preface would state, was revision. Hence the translators began with existing versions, consulted other renderings and commentaries, and used the Hebrew and Greek texts as their ultimate court of reference. They resisted change for the sake of change, followed popular usage in names, retained traditional terms like church and baptism, eliminated notes apart from alternative readings, and added simple chapter headings. The preface modestly admitted imperfection and stressed the need for continuous revision, especially where meanings were uncertain.

The panels worked diligently, and the first edition of this definitive translation appeared in 1611. Probably because of the king's sponsorship and the phrase "appointed to be read in churches," it came to be called the *King James Version* (KJV) or the *Authorized Version* (AV), though not in fact authorized by king, convocation, or parliament.

Like all new versions, the KJV had to contend with prior loyalties, but gradually it established itself in a series of new editions. As time passed, publishers updated archaic spellings, and the Scots appended the metrical Psalter. The body of the work, however, met with little challenge in English-speaking lands. It commended itself for its accuracy on the basis of available texts but above all for the literary qualities of directness, force, and simplicity, which it inherited from Tyndale and Coverdale. Later translators have found emulating these popular qualities difficult.

Modern Period

Post-Reformation. Further work on the English Bible took three different courses: paraphrase, scholarly research, and stylistic modernizing. The seventeenth century saw correction of obvious errors, new work on individual sections, and an attempt by the Long Parliament to start a new version.

Paraphrases, however, held the field. One of the more popular was Richard Baxter's New Testament published in 1685. Paraphrases, which actually seek to interpret the text in a popular fashion for the reader, remained fashionable up to the early eighteenth century. At that time a rekindled academic interest led scholars like A. Mace and W. Whiston to write fresh NT renderings on the basis of new textual findings.

Others focused on linguistic updating. J. Worsley tried to put the New Testament in "the present idiom" (1770). E. Harwood offered an odd version in "elegant" speech (1768), and John Wesley did a revision of the NT for the "unlettered" (1768). Corporately, the Friends published their own Bible in 1764, and R. Challoner put out a revision of Rheims-Douay (1749/50) that simplified the language and reduced the notes. This would influence all further editions, and it received approval for American use in 1810.

Nineteenth Century. In the nineteenth century advancing biblical studies and increasing use soon brought a demand for revision to reflect scholarly conclusions and linguistic development. Opposition was strong, but in 1870 B. Lightfoot argued forcefully for the revision, though with adherence to AV style and the noting of changes in the margin. Old Testament and New Testament committees were appointed, and eight years of work produced the *Revised Version* (RV) of 1881. Timidity marked most of the alterations, which included the use of paragraphs, inner self-consistency, and elimination of archaisms. Nevertheless, the RV provoked controversy, for example, by its rendering of 2 Timothy 3:16. In general it was a solid, scholarly production but hardly exciting enough to establish itself for liturgical and devotional use.

The American revision was more successful. British scholars had sought American cooperation, and an American committee began work in 1872. It favored a different approach, however, and finally decided on a different translation. The NT came out in 1897; and the whole

Bible, the *American Standard Version* (ASV), in 1901. This version not only differed from the RV in detail but achieved a higher literary quality that earned it many appreciative readers.

Other nineteenth century contributions meriting notice include the Unitarian Bible (1840–1860), R. Young's *Literal Translation* (1862), a word for word rendering, J. N. Darby's *Bible for Plymouth Brethren* (1887), and J. Rotheram's *Emphasized Bible* (1872–1902).

Twentieth Century

If the nineteenth century focused chiefly on scholarship, the twentieth showed special interest in modernizing. Already in 1901 an anonymous *Twentieth Century New Testament* appeared, and in 1903 F. Fenton published his *Holy Bible in Modern English.* Also in 1903 R. F. Weymouth's *New Testament in Modern Speech* caused real excitement with its more radical use of contemporary idioms. J. Moffatt followed this with his *New Translation of the New Testament* (1913), which commanded wide sales with its clear and felicitous renderings but also provoked criticism at specific points. Moffatt's Old Testament (1924) proved less successful.

Along similar lines E. J. Goodspeed's *American Translation,* first of the New Testament (1923) and then of the Old Testament (1935) and Apocrypha (1939), combined a fresh look at the originals with enhanced readability. Tending more toward paraphrase J. B. Phillips did especially helpful work in his *Letters to Young Churches* (1947), *Gospels* (1952), and *Young Church in Action* (1955). Discarding existing versions and working directly from the Greek, Phillips gave the content as it might have been expressed in twentieth-century English.

In 1956-59 K. W. Wuest published an Expanded Version that tried to catch the nuances of each verse by what is often verbose expansion. The *Amplified Version* (1958) offered the alternative meanings of Greek words but without indicating the most appropriate sense in context. The International Council of Religious Education resolved in 1937 to undertake a revision that would use scholarly findings and aim at modern, liturgically suitable English. A committee that included Moffatt and Goodspeed started work, assisted by an advisory board, and the result was the *Revised Standard Version* (RSV) of 1952 (Apocrypha 1957). Though it profited from textual and linguistic research, the RSV was consciously a revision. It sought greater accuracy and updated words and idioms but stayed as close as possible to the AV in rhythm, style, and wording.

British churches, however, decided on a new translation rather than a revision (1947). A joint committee undertook the project and produced the New Testament in 1961 and the full *New English Bible* (NEB) in 1970. Unlike the RSV, the translators of the NEB made radical changes in vocabulary, syntax, and word order, concentrating on the meaning rather than the words yet also avoiding paraphrase. The NEB undoubtedly recaptured something of the vigor of the original but can hardly claim literary excellence.

Evangelicals did their own updating of the KJV in the *Berkeley Bible* (1959), the *New American Standard Bible* (NASB, 1963), and finally the *New International Version* (NIV, 1973-8). The NASB attempts to offer a literal, word-for-word equivalent. The NIV translators felt the need to express the meaning of the original in the language of their times. The *New Revised Standard Version* (1990) and the *Revised New English Version* (1990) are further attempts to employ idiomatic English to communicate for contemporary readers the range of meaning of words in the original Greek and Hebrew.

Finally, the late twentieth century brought fresh attempts at popular versions. In 1976 the Bible Societies brought out the *Good News Bible,* complete with line drawings, explanations of technical terms, identifications, and index and setting vigor and relevance above exactness with the aim of helping young believers and seekers. The Evangelical layman K. Taylor produced an alternative in his *Living Bible Paraphrased* (1972), which he wrote primarily for children, beginners, and outsiders and which enjoyed phenomenal popularity in spite of some obvious weaknesses in what is admittedly a paraphrase.

Surprisingly amid the profusion of modern renderings the KJV, either in its traditional form or with slight modernizations (*New King James Version,* 1979-82), still holds its own in sales and maintains a loyal following. All revisions face the problem that a successful version achieves a familiarity and venerability that hamper the acceptance of needed alternatives. At root is the inherent difficulty of combining accuracy, clarity, dignity, and relevance in a version serving liturgical, devotional, instructional, and academic purposes.

Yet the task of providing the best possible English Bible remains. No version is perfect, and new work must be done as new materials become available and language changes. The Bible is no ordinary book. It is God's written Word bearing authoritative witness to the incarnate Word. It must not be obscured by inaccuracies or outdated English terms. If it is to do its proper work in the power of the Holy Spirit, then no definitive rendering can ever conclude the history of English Bible translation. As of making books in general, so of making English versions of the Book of books there can be no end.

THE BIBLE IN ENGLISH

(Some translations are omitted due to space constraints)

OLD ENGLISH TRANSLATION (A.D. 300–1100)

A.D. 300s—First Christians arrived in Britain
A.D. 400s—Angles, Saxons, and Jutes arrive in Britain
A.D. 500–700—Evangelization of Angles, Saxons, and Jutes
A.D. 700–100—Only parts of the Bible translated into "Old English"

MIDDLE ENGLISH TRANSLATION (1100–1500)

1066—Norman Invasion brings French influence into language development and creates "Middle English"

Important persons:

John Wycliffe—died 1384. Wanted to take gospel to the commoners. Began translating from Latin into English in 1380. Was assisted by:

Nicholas of Hereford—whose translation followed the Latin Vulgate very closely

AND

John Purvey—whose revision of Nicholas's translation used more idiomatic expressions.

Important events at the end of this period:

The Renaissance—a revival of learning occurred which prompted a renewed interest in the original Hebrew and Greek. A new challenge to authority also emerged.

The invention of the printing press (1453)—made printed material accessible to the masses rather than to a few.

The Protestant Reformation (beginning in 1517)—Martin Luther and those who followed had a tremendous desire to get the Bible into the hands of the common people.

MODERN ENGLISH TRANSLATION (1500–1900)

1525/6	William Tyndale translated New Testament into English from Greek. Was translating Old Testament at the time of his death as a martyr in 1536.
1535	Miles Coverdale completed and published first complete Bible in English from Tyndale's work, Greek and Hebrew, and other sources.
1537	**Matthew's Bible**. A complete English Bible from Tyndale's and Coverdale's work by John Rogers. Received royal sanction of King Henry VIII.
1539	**The Great Bible**. A revision by Coverdale of Matthew's Bible. Was placed in every church in England at the order of King Henry.
1560	**The Geneva Bible**. Produced by Protestant scholars in Geneva from the original languages and from Tyndale's work. (Sometimes called "Breeches Bible" because in Gen 3:7 Adam and Eve made "breeches" for themselves from fig leaves.)
1568	**The Bishop's Bible**. A revision of the Great Bible. Was authorized by the Church of England as their official translation.
1582 and 1609-10	**Rheims/Douai Translation**. Roman Catholic translation from the Latin Vulgate of the Old and New Testaments so named because of where they were translated: the Old Testament at Douai in 1609-10 preceded by the translation of the New Testament at Rheims in 1582.
1611	**The King James Version (or Authorized Version)**. Commissioned by King James I of England and translated by a number of Bible scholars. A revision of the 1602 edition of the Bishops' Bible with the aid of the Hebrew and Greek texts and a dependence upon the work of William Tyndale.
1885	**The Revised Version**. A revision of the Authorized Version incorporating more recently discovered manuscripts and more modern language usage. By a group of British scholars and some American scholars.

TWENTIETH-CENTURY ENGLISH TRANSLATIONS (1900–)

1901	**The American Standard Version**. An American revision of the Authorized Version growing out of American scholars' participation in the Revised Version.
1903	**The New Testament in Modern Speech**. R. T. Weymouth's attempt to render Greek grammatical constructions carefully.
1924	**A New Translation of the Bible**. An idiomatic, colloquial, and sometimes Scottish translation by James Moffatt.
1927	**Centenary Translation of the New Testament**. Helen B. Montgomery's missionary heart produced a translation in the language of everyday life.
1937	**Williams New Testament**. By Charles B. Williams. A Baptist professor's attempt to translate into English the nuances of the Greek verbs.
1938	**The Bible: An American Translation**. E. J. Goodspeed and J. M. Powis Smith produced the first modern American translation with the Apocrypha.
1952	**The Revised Standard Version**. Revision of the American Standard Version and the King James Version by an international translation committee seeking to maintain literary awesomeness for worship.
1955	**The Holy Bible**. Translated by Ronald Knox, a Roman Catholic, from the Latin Vulgate.
1958	**The New Testament in Modern English**. A free translation by J. B. Phillips originally done for his youth club.
1965	**The Amplified Bible**. A version by the Lockman Foundation suggesting various wordings throughout the text.
1966	**The Jerusalem Bible**. Originally translated into French by Roman Catholic scholars from the original languages.
1969	**The New Berkeley (Modern Language) Bible**. A revision of the Berkeley Version of 1959 by Gerrit Verkuyl with attached notes.
1970	**The New English Bible**. A translation with literary quality but some idiosyncratic language. Translated by representatives of Britain's major churches and Bible societies and based on the most recent textual evidence.
1970	**The New American Bible**. A new translation by Roman Catholic scholars (the Bishops' Committee of the Confraternity of Christian Doctrine) from the original languages.
1971	**The New American Standard Bible**. A revision by the Lockman Foundation of the American Standard Version of 1901 with the goal of maintaining literal translation.
1971	**The Living Bible**. A conservative American paraphrase by Kenneth N. Taylor originally for his children (begun in 1962).
1976	**The Good News Bible (Today's English Version)**. A translation by the American Bible Society into "vernacular" English.
1979	**The New International Version**. A readable translation by evangelical scholars incorporating the most recent textual evidence.
1982	**The New King James Version**. A modernization of the King James Version of 1611. Based on the original language texts available to the King James Version translators.
1987	**The New Century Version**. A translation committee's update of the International Children's Bible.
1989	**The New Revised Standard Version**. A translation committee's update of the Revised Standard Version.
1989	**The Revised English Bible**. A British committee's update of the New English Bible maintaining literary quality but avoiding idiosyncratic language.
1991	**The Contemporary English Version (New Testament)**. A simplified text originally conceived for children and produced by the American Bible Society.

DIFFERENCES IN BIBLE MANUSCRIPTS

Prior to the invention of printing about 1450, all books had to be written and copied by hand. A handwritten work is called a manuscript. Not one of the original manuscripts of the books of either the Old or the New Testament has survived, and all of the copies differ from one another in some places. The differences are referred to as variant readings.

That there are differences in the ancient manuscripts is not surprising. The laborious process of copying by hand inevitably led to accidental errors. Some words were omitted, some were added, some were substituted, and some were rearranged. Scribes (copyists) would sometimes misread the text they were copying; sometimes they would misunderstand a text that was being read to them. Sometimes they would forget between the moment of reading or hearing and writing down, and sometimes they would unconsciously substitute a more familiar synonym.

In addition to accidental errors, apparently some scribes deliberately deviated from the text they were copying. In most instances they did so with a good motive. They thought they were correcting a previous error. No doubt sometimes they did correct an error, but in many instances they produced another variant reading. In a few instances scribes apparently made a deliberate change for a theological reason, to make the text either more or less orthodox than it was.

The amount of variation in surviving Hebrew manuscripts of the Old Testament is relatively small. This is because of the careful work of medieval Jewish scholars known as the Masoretes. Most of these manuscripts, however, are medieval—removed from the originals by more than a thousand years. Notable exceptions are manuscripts of comparatively small portions of the Old Testament which were found at Qumran and which were written about the beginning of the Christian era, that is, some of the Dead Sea Scrolls.

The amount of variation in Greek manuscripts of the New Testament is comparatively large, in part because during the early centuries when the church was poor and persecuted, the copying had to be done by amateur scribes. Only during medieval times did the manuscripts of the New Testament achieve a high degree of uniformity. A few manuscripts containing substantial portions of the New Testament go back to about the year 200, only 100 to 150 years after the originals. One manuscript containing all and one containing most of the New Testament are dated about 350. Unfortunately most of the surviving copies are from the medieval period.

Because of the large number of variant readings in the ancient biblical manuscripts, translating from Hebrew or Greek into English some other modern language is no "simple" matter. First, scholars must make decisions about the original text. The scholarly discipline that makes such decisions is called textual criticism. Textual criticism is not only legitimate, but it is absolutely necessary. It must precede translation, interpretation, and theology. Only highly trained scholars can perform such a task, but they have the obligation to explain their principles to laypersons, who then have the right to evaluate the principles and individual decisions. Laypersons should realize, however, that conscientious textual critics, no matter what their theological positions are, do not want to take anything away from or add anything to the Bible. Their one motive is to restore the original text.

In addition to Hebrew and Greek manuscripts, scholars also employ the ancient versions (translations) in attempting to restore the original text. These translations are older than most of the existing Hebrew or Greek manuscripts. In order to be used in textual criticism, they must be retranslated into Hebrew or Greek, something that is not always possible to do accurately. New Testament textual critics also have another source of information, quotations from the New Testament in the works of ancient Christian writers who are earlier than most surviving Greek manuscripts.

What principles are employed in textual criticism? Most New Testament textual critics give equal weight to external and internal evidence. External evidence is that of the textual witnesses themselves. Preference is given to the variant reading having the earliest attestation, the attestation that is most widespread geographically, and the attestation of the most reliable text-types.

A text-type is a group of Greek manuscripts, versions,

and early quotations that have much in common. The type usually considered to be the most reliable is the Alexandrian, which flourished in Alexandria, Egypt, between about 180 and 700. Its early date is one reason for preferring it; that its readings are often supported by internal evidence is another. Most twentieth-century translations have preferred it, including the *Revised Standard Version, New English Bible, Good News Bible, New American Standard Bible, New International Version*—the last two avowedly "conservative" versions.

Another type recognized by most but not all scholars is the Western. Its members do not have as much in common with one another as do those of the Alexandrian and Byzantine types, but it goes back to the midsecond century. Only a few have claimed that it approximates the original, and no translation of the entire New Testament is based upon it. Some scholars also recognize a Caesarean type, but no one claims that it is nearest to the original, and no English version reflects it.

The other type is the Byzantine, so called because it flourished in the Byzantine Empire during the Middle Ages. Its earliest representatives are mid to late fourth century. It is only natural that more copies would have been made during the later Christian centuries than during the earlier and that a larger percentage of the later manuscripts would have survived. As a result about 90 percent of the surviving Greek manuscripts are of this type. These late manuscripts have more in common with one another than the representatives of any other text-type. The Byzantine type of text was the only one in widespread use in western Europe in the sixteenth century and therefore was the one captured in print in 1516 when the first Greek New Testament was published by Erasmus. His third edition of 1522 became the basis of the "received text" that dominated until shown to be inferior to the satisfaction of most scholars by B. F. Westcott and F. J. A. Hort in 1881. It is the type that lies behind the *King James Version* of 1611 and the *New King James Version* of 1979. Some defend it dogmatically with such arguments as the text of the majority of manuscripts must be the original, the text of the Greek church must be the original, the text used by the Reformers must be the original, and the text employed by the *King James Version* must be the original. Only a few defend it with rational arguments such as mathematical probability indicating that it could never have become the majority text unless it was the original. Nevertheless, most contemporary scholars prefer the Alexandrian readings, especially when they also have some Western support.

Internal evidence consists of what scribes probably did while copying and what the author probably wrote. With reference to the former, preference is given to the shorter reading where deliberate change seems to have taken place. Scribes seem to have been much more reluctant to leave anything out of the Word of God than to add something to it in trying to correct what they thought was an error. Where accidental omission appears to have taken place due to skipping from one word to another with a similar ending or beginning, the longer reading is preferred.

The first page of the Book of Joshua from Aharon ben Asher's Keter Hatorah—an important manuscript dating from the end of the ninth or beginning of the tenth century A.D.

A second criterion of internal evidence is that preference is given to the reading that is different from the parallel passage. This is a major factor in the Synoptic Gospels, that is, Matthew, Mark, and Luke, which have so much in common. Scribes tended to eliminate seeming contradictions. Then preference is given to the more difficult reading, especially if upon further consideration the difficulty can be resolved. Scribes attempted to eliminate difficulties.

Finally, preference is given to the reading, that, if assumed to be the original, best explains the origin of the other(s). In connection with what the author probably wrote, consideration is given to such things as his grammar, vocabulary, style, and theology. This is the most tenuous of all the criteria, but a few textual critics make most of their decisions on this basis alone. They have not produced, however, either a Greek text or a translation of the entire New Testament.

Rarely do all of the previously mentioned critics support the same reading. When the evidence is divided, the textual critic must decide which criteria are the most weighty in the particular textual problem. This is not subjective if they give a rational explanation that will commend itself to most competent, unbiased scholars and informed laypersons.

The remainder of the article will deal with examples of famous variant readings in the Gospels. In Matthew 6:13 the earliest and best representatives of the Alexandrian text and several Western witnesses conclude the Lord's Prayer with "Deliver us from evil" (compare RSV, NEB, GNB, NASB, NIV). The majority of medieval witnesses plus some fair to good witnesses add "For yours is the kingdom and the power and the glory forever. Amen" (KJV, NKJV). Date and text-type favor the former; geographical distribution, the latter. The former is the shorter reading and is different from the parallel in 1 Chronicles 29:11-13. It ends abruptly and is therefore more difficult. If the latter were the original, there is no reason, either accidental or deliberate, why it would have been omitted. Therefore the shorter reading is almost certainly the original.

In Matthew 27:16 a few Greek manuscripts of medium value, a few versions of medium value, and one important Christian writer have "Jesus Barabbas" (NEB, GNB), whereas all the other textual witnesses have "Barabbas" alone (KJV, NKJV, RSV, NASB, NIV). The external evidence overwhelmingly favors the latter, but every item of internal evidence favors the former. The decisive consideration is the criterion of the more difficult reading. Pious scribes were no doubt horrified by the association of the precious name *Jesus* with that of the criminal Barabbas—not realizing that Jesus was a common name in first-century Palestine. "Jesus Barabbas" is therefore possibly the original.

The earliest known complete scroll of the Book of Isaiah found among the library of the Qumran community (the Dead Sea Scrolls).

In Mark 1:2 the Byzantine witnesses have "in the prophets" (KJV, NKJV), whereas most others read "in Isaiah the prophet" (RSV, NEB, GNB, NASB, NIV). External evidence heavily favors the latter, as does also the more difficult reading and the reading *that* best explains the other. The quotation is in fact a composite of Isaiah 3; Exodus 23:20; and Malachi 3:1. And in order to eliminate any thought of inaccuracy, scribes almost certainly changed "in Isaiah the prophet" to "in the prophets."

Mark's Gospel ends in four different ways in the ancient textual tradition: (1) with 16:8 (supported by the earliest and best Alexandrians, one Western witness, and a few others); (2) with 16:20 (called the long ending and supported by the majority of medieval manuscripts plus some fair and good witnesses—some of which, however, mark vv. 9-20 as suspect); (3) with what is known as the short ending (one important Latin manuscript; see RSV, NEB, GNB, NASB notes); and (4) with the short ending plus the long ending (fair attestation). The issue is obviously between the first and second. Early date favors the first; and geographical distribution, the second. Textual relationships are about evenly divided. Number one has the best Alexandrian witnesses but only one Western witness. Number two has the later Alexandrians but most of the Western. Number one is the shorter reading and differs from the other Gospels because it has no resurrection appearances. Having no resurrection appearances makes it the most difficult reading and the one that best explains the origin of the others.

The decisive consideration is that the grammar and vocabulary of both the long and short endings are definitely non-Markan. Nothing after verse 8 therefore is original. The KJV and NKJV certainly accept the authenticity of the long ending. The other translations cited in this article print it in the text but mark it in some way as to indicate that they do not believe that it was part of the original.

In Luke 2:14 the earliest Alexandrians and most of the Westerns have "among men of good will" (literal translation, compare RSV, NEB, NASB, GNB, NIV), whereas the later Alexandrians and most of the Byzantines have "good will toward men" (KJV, NKJV). There is only one letter difference in the Greek, and the change could have been accidental in either direction. The change may have been deliberate, however, and the first is the more difficult and therefore best explains the origin of the other.

Luke 22:17-20 exists in six different forms: (1) verses 17-20 (KJV, NKJV, RSV 2nd ed., NASB, GNB, NIV); (2) verses 17-19a—omitting verses 19b and 20 (RSV 1st ed., NEB); (3) verses 19a,17, and 18—omitting verses 19b and 20; (4) verses 19,17,18—omitting verse 20); (5) verses 19-20—omitting verses 17-18; and (6) verses 19-20a,17,20b,18.

The first is supported by virtually all of the Alexandrian and Byzantine witnesses and some Western ones and therefore by every criterion of external evidence. The second has only Western attestation. Each of the others is found in only one or two manuscripts of medium quality and merits no serious consideration. The first is difficult because it seems to have two cups during the institution of the Lord's Supper. The second seems to be an attempt to deal with the difficulty of the first by omitting the first cup, but in doing so it created a difficulty of its own, namely reversing the usual order of first bread and then cup. There is little doubt that the first is the original. The difficulty can be resolved by realizing that the first cup was connected with the Passover meal rather than the Lord's Supper.

The external and internal evidence is evenly divided between the inclusion (KJV, NKJV, NEB, NASB, GNB, NIV) or omission (RSV) of Luke 22:43-44, and a few witnesses even place the passage after Matthew 26:39. A decision is difficult, but the fact that the account is found at two different places may indicate that it was not part of the original of either Luke or Matthew but that it was a true story that circulated in the oral tradition, refused to die, and eventually worked itself into two of the Gospels.

Similar is the problem of whether to include or omit Luke 23:34. The external evidence is evenly divided, but the inclusion is different from what is in the other Gospels, was the more difficult for medieval scribes who were obsessed with the necessity of doing penance before forgiveness was possible, and alone can explain the origin of the other reading.

In John 1:18 the earliest and best Alexandrian witnesses and a few others read "the unique God" (NASB, NIV), while most of the Western and Byzantine ones have "the unique Son" (KJV, NKJV, RSV, NEB, GNB). ("Unique" or "only" is a better translation than "only begotten.") Obviously the reference is to Jesus, and there is some difficulty in calling him "God." This, plus the fact that "unique God" is different from John 3:16,18 and 1 John 4:9, plus its stronger external attestation, points toward "unique God" being the original.

John 5:4 is omitted by the earliest Alexandrian witnesses, some Western witnesses, a few others, and by the RSV, NEB, GNB, NIV. (The NASB prints it in brackets, indicating a later insertion.) Geographical distribution favors the inclusion, but the other criteria favor the omission. The large amount of internal variation and the large number of non-Johannine terms weigh against the inclusion. It appears to have originated as a scribal explanation of what was involved in the bubbling up of the waters in verse 7.

The famous account of the woman taken in adultery is omitted by most of the Alexandrian witnesses, about half of the Westerns, some other witnesses of medium quality, and even by a few Byzantine witnesses. It is found between John 7:52 and 8:12 by a few good and medium quality witnesses and most of the Byzantine ones (although some mark it as suspect). It is found after John 21:21 by some medium quality manuscripts, after Luke 21:38 by some medium quality manuscripts, after Luke 24:53 by one inferior manuscript, after John 7:36 by one inferior quality manuscript, and after John 7:44 by some manuscripts of a late version. The language of the passage is unquestionably non-Johannine, and the large amount of internal variation and the various placements make authenticity most unlikely. Most scholars think that the passage contains a true story that circulated orally and refused to die and eventually crept into the written Gospels at various places. The passage is printed without reservations in the KJV and NKJV, relegated to the margin by the NEB, and printed in the text but marked as not authentic by the RSV, NASB, GNB, and NIV.

Textual criticism is not an exact science. It deals in the realm of probability, not certainty. No type of text is a heretical text. No Christian doctrine is dependent upon the adoption of a particular variant reading or a particular type of text. God has blessed the use of both the Byzantine type (in the KJV and NKJV) and the Alexandrian type (in the RSV, NEB, NASB, NIV, and GNB). Nevertheless, conscientious Christians should want to use a translation that is based upon the most accurate Hebrew and Greek texts. Since the Bible is inspired, and since inspiration extends even to the words of the Bible, good stewardship requires that a diligent attempt be made to determine what those words are (see the article "The Inspiration and Authority of the Bible").

PART IV

THE BIBLE AND ITS MESSAGE

THE PENTATEUCH

The term *Pentateuch* is the title most commonly employed to describe the first five books of the Bible. It derives from the Greek *pente* (*five*) and *teuchos* (*scroll*) and thus describes the number of these writings, not their contents.

Pentateuch is a satisfactory way of identifying these books. By virtue of nearly two thousand years of usage, it is deeply ingrained in Christian tradition. However, a more accurate and informative term is *Torah* (Hebrew *torah*). This name is based upon the verb *yarah, to teach. Torah* is, therefore, *teaching.* Careful attention to this will lead to an appreciation both of the contents of the Pentateuch and of its fundamental purpose: the instruction of God's people concerning Himself, themselves, and His purposes for them.

The enormous amount of legal material in the Pentateuch (half of Exodus, most of Leviticus, much of Numbers, and virtually all of Deuteronomy) has led to the common designation *Law* or *Books of the Law*. This way of viewing the Pentateuch does enjoy the sanction of ancient Jewish and even New Testament usage and is not without justification. However, recent scholarship has shown conclusively that the Pentateuch is essentially an instruction (hence *torah*) manual whose purpose was to guide the covenant people Israel in the way of pilgrimage before their God. For example, Genesis, though containing few laws, still instructs God's people through its narratives of primeval history and the patriarchs. The law was the "constitution and bylaws" of the chosen nation. *Torah* is therefore the title best suited to describe the full contents and purpose of this earliest part of the Bible.

Until the Enlightenment in the 1700s, there was a consensus within Jewish and Christian tradition that the witness of the Pentateuch revealed Moses as its author. Both the Old (Deut 1:5; 4:44; 31:9; 33:4; Josh 8:31-34; 1 Kgs 2:3; 2 Kgs 14:6; 23:25; 2 Chr 23:18; Ezra 3:2; Neh 8:1; Mal 4:4) and New Testaments (Luke 2:22; 24:44; John 1:17; 7:19; Acts 13:39; 28:23; 1 Cor 9:9; Heb 10:28) support the tradition of Mosaic authorship. Some pre-Enlightenment interpreters raised incidental questions about chronological discrepancies. For example, they noted reference to kings of Israel in Genesis 36:31, Moses' reference to himself as "a very humble man, more humble than anyone else on the face of the earth" (Num 12:3), and his authoring the account of his own death (Deut 34:5-12). These, however, can be explained as either the result of divine revelation of the future or more likely as examples of later additions to the text. Those accepting Moses as a historic person whose life and experience are evidenced by Scripture (Exod 2:10-11; Heb 11:23-24) must admit the genuine possibility of his authorship of those writings that traditionally bear his name.

Many scholars affirm Moses' significant contributions to the formation of the Pentateuch but hold that the *final* form of these books evidences some editing after the time of Moses. Such critics in no way deny the divine inspiration of the Pentateuch or the reliability of its history. Rather, they affirm that after the death of Moses, God continued to move people of faith to elaborate those truths Moses taught earlier. Evidence for such retelling of accounts after Moses' death includes the account of his death in Deuteronomy 34, especially 34:10-12, which appears to reflect a long history of experience with prophets who failed to measure up to Moses. Further evidences are historical notes that appear to reflect a time after Israel's conquest of the Canaanites' land (Gen 12:6; 13:7) and place names that have apparently been updated to those used after Moses' death (compare Gen 14:14 with Josh 19:47 and Judg 18:29).

Some radical critics have denied the possibility of God's supernatural involvement in history and questioned the trustworthiness of the history found in the Pentateuch (see "Criticism and the Old Testament"). Yet any adequate view of the Pentateuch must recognize Moses' real contribution and the historical reliability of its traditions (see the discussion of the Pentateuch as history that follows).

Deuteronomy, the last book of the Pentateuch, was composed by Moses in the Plains of Moab (Deut 1:1-5; 4:44-46; 29:1) just before his death (Deut 31:2,9,24). The first four books probably share this time and place of origin. Genesis, Exodus, and Leviticus, however, could have been penned as early as the convocation at Mount Sinai, thirty-eight years earlier. This setting in Moab is particularly appropriate because God had already informed Moses that he would not live to cross the Jordan and participate in the conquest and settlement of Canaan (Num 20:10-13; 27:12-14). It was thus urgent that he bequeath to his people the legacy of divine revelation—the Pentateuch—that the Lord had entrusted to him. The inspired prophet had to address any questions they had about their origins, purpose, and destiny then and there. The date of the final form of the Pentateuch as it came from Moses' hand is about 1400 B.C., forty years after the exodus from Egypt. (See "Biblical Chronology" in "The Bible in Its World.")

The description of the Pentateuch as *torah,* "instruction," immediately reveals its purpose: to educate the people of Israel about their identity, their history, their role among the nations of the earth, and their future. The Pentateuch contains information about such things as creation, the cosmos, and the distribution and dispersion of the peoples and nations. However, this information finds its relevance primarily in relation to Israel, the people to whom Moses addressed himself at Moab.

Biblical literature's true and ultimate purpose cannot be separated from its theological message. The Pentateuch sought to inform God's people of their identity and focus. Though both themes emerge regularly in Exodus and Deuteronomy especially, the focal text where Israel's identity and focus are found is Exodus 19:4-6. Here, on the eve of the Sinai covenant encounter, the Lord spoke to Israel.

> You yourselves have seen what I did to Egypt, and how I carried you on eagles' wings and brought you to myself. Now if you obey me fully and keep my covenant, then out of all nations you will be my treasured possession. Although the whole earth is mine, you will be for me a kingdom of priests and a holy nation.

Here then is what it meant to be Israel and to serve the Lord as Israel. This core text of the Pentateuch presents the central theme to which all the other themes and teachings relate and in light of which they and the whole Pentateuch find their meaning. In this magnificent affirmation the Lord proclaimed that He had brought Israel to Himself. The text immediately presupposes the exodus deliverance, the redemptive act in which God overthrew Egypt ("you yourselves have seen what I did to Egypt") through miraculous intervention ("how I carried you on eagles' wings"). It furthermore declares that the sovereign God of all nations was offering to only one nation—Israel—a covenant that would allow them the privilege of serving all the peoples of earth as "a kingdom of priests and a holy nation."

This pivotal text looks both backwards and forwards. Reference to the exodus would naturally draw attention to Israel's past. Israel had come out of Egypt, a land of bondage, where it had sojourned for 430 years (Exod 12:40). The reason for the long stay there had been a famine that forced the patriarchs to flee Canaan for relief. Another reason, however, was that Jacob

Samaritan priests with their sacred copy of the Samaritan Pentateuch (Genesis–Deuteronomy), the only section of the Old Testament that Samaritans accept as canonical.

and his sons had begun to lose their identity as the family of promise by intermingling with and becoming tainted by the Canaanites and their ungodly ways. The sordid affairs of Judah (Gen 38) illustrate this leaning most clearly.

Moses thus had to reach back into the times of the nation's ancestors to account for the Egyptian sojourn and the exodus event itself. Beyond this he needed to explain who the patriarchs were and why God called them. The answer lay in the ancient patriarchal covenant. One man, Abraham, was called out of Sumerian paganism to found a nation that would be a blessing to all nations who recognized its peculiar nature and calling (Gen 12:1-3). Israel was that nation, that offspring of Abraham, that now was ready to undertake the role long ago revealed to the founding father.

The purpose for the call of Abraham and the covenant promise entrusted to him are carefully spelled out as well. Humankind, which God had created to be in His image and to rule over all His creation (Gen 1:26-28), had violated that sacred trust and had plunged the whole universe into chaotic ruin and rebellion. What was required was a people called out of that lostness to exhibit godly obedience before the world, to function as mediators and a redemptive priesthood, and to provide the matrix from which the incarnate God could enter the world and achieve His saving and sovereign purposes of re-creation. That people, again, was Israel. They surely understood their calling, but it likely had never been fully spelled out until Moses did so there on the edge of conquest.

The form this rehearsal of Israel's significance took was, of course, the Book of Genesis. Whether or not the account of these grand events had ever existed in written form cannot be known for sure, though there are strong hints of such in the Book of Genesis itself (2:4; 5:1; 6:9; 10:1; 11:10; 11:27; 25:12; 25:19; 36:1). Moses, who was about to pass from the scene, shaped the story as we now have it. He wanted to provide Israel with a historical and theological basis for their status as a peculiar people (that is, God's "treasured possession").

The remainder of the Pentateuch is, for the most part, a historical narration of events contemporary with Moses and his generation. Embedded in it are the Sinaitic covenant text (Exod 20:1–23:33), instructions for the creation of a tabernacle (Exod 25:1–27:21; 30:1-38; 35:4–39:43; Num 7:1–

A view of the Near East (courtesy of NASA) from the northeastern part of the African continent across Saudi Arabia to the Persian Gulf, the Arabian Sea, and the modern countries of Iraq and Iran.

8:4), selection and setting apart of a priesthood (Exod 28:1–29:46), a system of sacrifices and other cultic regulations (most of Leviticus), law and ritual appropriate to the people in the desert (Num 5:1-4; 9:15-32), and the covenant renewal text (most of Deuteronomy). All of these nonnarrative sections and the narratives themselves relate to the theme of Israel as a community of priests. The Pentateuch then tells where Israel came from and why. It tells how they entered into covenant with the Lord following their redemption from Egypt, what claims this covenant laid upon them, and how they were to conduct themselves as the servant people of a holy and sovereign God. (See "Covenants" and "Near Eastern Treaties.")

Interpreters take one of three broad approaches to the Pentateuch as a source for history. (1) Many interpreters read the Pentateuch as a straightforward recounting of events. (2) Radical critics disregard the Pentateuch as a source for history. For example, Julius Wellhausen and his source-critical school saw the narratives—especially those of Genesis—as

Critical Methods and the Old Testament

The use of critical methods to study the OT began with the work of Jean Astruc, physician to the French King Louis XV. In 1753 Astruc developed a method he felt successfully separated the different sources standing behind Genesis. He used his discovery as a defense of Mosaic authorship of the book.

In later years, however, the results of the application of critical methods often were used as evidence against an orthodox view of Scripture. Thus, in the minds of many, *criticism* means *judgmental.* Some people often recoil against the use of critical methods on the grounds that it is improper or even blasphemous to stand as judge over the Scriptures.

However, the intended meaning of the adjective *critical* is not *judgmental* but *analytical.* The various branches of critical method, though sometimes used in a negative or destructive manner, may provide insights into God's message for us today.

We will examine the four principal critical methods in the order in which they came into use.

Jewish rabbis in debate before an opened scroll of the Torah (Genesis–Deuteronomy).

Source Criticism

Source criticism attempts to uncover the documents used to compose a biblical book. No one doubts that some biblical authors used sources. Perhaps the best known example is the author(s) of Chronicles, who used Samuel and Kings as a source. The Book of Kings often mentions other sources such as the "book of the annals of Solomon" (1 Kgs 11:14).

Source criticism originated and developed with a focus on the Pentateuch, the first five books of the OT. Scholars developed criteria by which the original sources of the Pentateuch could be separated from one another. Julius Wellhausen, a German scholar, who published his major work in the 1880s, represents this type of source criticism.

Wellhausen felt that he could distinguish five sources which he named the Yahwist (J), Elohist (E), Deuteronomist (D), and Priestly (P) sources. He argued

reflecting the first millennium era in which they were allegedly composed rather than the times of Moses and the patriarchs (second millennium). The form critic Hermann Gunkel coupled this historical skepticism with a dismissal of the supernatural. He viewed the first eleven chapters of Genesis as largely myth and legend and the patriarchal stories as folktale and epic. The most radical critics regarded only the core of the Mosaic traditions, the exodus event itself, as reliable history. Even that event had to be rid of all its miraculous overtones before it could be accepted as history in the strict sense. The rest of the Moses stories were regarded as embellishments of actual events or stories thought up to justify later religious belief and practice. (See "Critical Methods and the Old Testament.") (3) Others see the Pentateuch primarily as a theological interpretation of real persons and events. For these interpreters the narratives were written from the perspective of a later time. Such scholars differ widely over the possibility and value of recovering the "bare facts" behind the biblical *interpretation* of

that these sources were produced by different, sometimes conflicting, schools of thought at different time periods. According to this scheme the books of the Pentateuch were not completed until late in OT history, hundreds of years after Moses.

Wellhausen's approach received a hostile reception from biblical scholars holding a traditional view of the Bible. The trend of the past decade has been away from a classic source-critical approach to a renewed appreciation for the literary integrity and wholeness of the text (even in light of the obvious use of some sources).

The use of sources demonstrates that the Hebrew people treasured the accounts of how God worked in their history. The writer(s) of Chronicles demonstrated how God's people drew from such sources to meet the challenges of a new time in much the same way as Christian theologians and pastors have turned to the NT for God's word for their day.

Form Criticism

Interest in types of literature (genre) was reawakened in the early 1900s primarily through the work the German scholar Hermann Gunkel. Gunkel felt that source criticism was unprofitable and supplemented it with study of the form (literary category) of the text. He applied his method mainly to the Psalms and Genesis. Others, notably Gunkel's student, Hugo Gressmann, and the Scandinavian scholar Sigmund Mowinckel, carried his ideas even further.

Simply put, Gunkel's approach focused on identifying the type of text he was studying. In the Psalms, for instance, two main types were hymns and laments. Laments expressed a sorrowful, often repentant mood and were characterized by language used in mourning ("woe," "alas"). Gunkel was confident that, like a detective, he could work backward from a written text through countless retellings to the original oral material. Gunkel also felt that each type of literature had been determined by being retold in a particular setting or situation in the life of the community.

Gunkel's confidence that he could get behind a literary text to the original oral saying was unwarranted. Some of his genre categories ("legend," "saga") also discounted the historicity of the Bible.

Form criticism has yielded great benefits to Penteteuchal scholarship. To see that the genealogies of Genesis have a particular function based on their form (that is, to represent connections between covenant promises and to highlight specific links) is exegetically and theologically useful. Likewise, to know that the covenant texts associated with Abraham and the patriarchs are, by form, in the pattern of royal land-grant treaties gives the Abrahamic covenant a rich theological dimen-

what happened.

Many scholars take the findings of scientific biblical archaeology as confirmation that the Pentateuch is most at home precisely in the second millennium setting in which the OT located it. Thus the discovery of ancient Sumerian and Babylonian creation and flood stories at the library of Ashurbanipal at Nineveh and at other places has lent credence to their antiquity in Israelite tradition. Documents by the thousands from Ebla, Mari, Alalakh, and Nuzi confirm for some interpreters that the life-style, customs, and habits of the biblical patriarchs are most at home in the Middle Bronze Age (about 2000–1550 B.C.) where biblical chronology places them. The now well-understood environment of New Kingdom Egypt and Amarna Canaan (about 1570–1300 B.C.) likewise demonstrates that the account of Israel's history assigned to the time of Moses is compatible with that period. In short, the historicity of the Pentateuch is affirmed by much that has been and is being understood about its setting in the ancient world. Though this

sion. The book of the covenant (Exod 20:1–23:33) and the Book of Deuteronomy are patterned after classic Hittite sovereign-vassal treaty texts. Form criticism, judiciously employed, has self-evident value. (See "Types of Old Testament Literature.")

Redaction Criticism

Form criticism tended to fragment a text by examining isolated passages. Redaction criticism corrects the dangerous side effects of a form-critical analysis.

Form criticism focuses on how a single passage was shaped by the process of repeated telling before being written down. Redaction criticism focuses on the final written form of a biblical book. Form criticism focuses on what is typical of a *type* of literature (hymns, miracle stories). Redaction criticism focuses on what is distinctive to a specific *work* of literature (Genesis, Deuteronomy). It asks what theological concerns motivated the biblical redactor (editor) to bring together isolated, traditional materials.

Such an approach is most helpful when there are two parallel sources. A comparison between accounts of Solomon's life in Kings and Chronicles allows the reader to see the different (not contradictory) theological concerns of the two books.

Redaction criticism, though, becomes much more speculative when applied to books without parallels.

Literary Approach

There has been a steady movement away from approaches that isolate Scripture texts and look at them outside of their present literary contexts. The resurgence of a literary approach to biblical texts is a further step in this direction.

A literary approach recognizes that the OT texts are mostly poems and stories and applies the methods and categories of contemporary literary analysis to discover the conventions of Hebrew literature.

Poetry has long been subjected to this kind of analysis, and literary devices such as parallelism and imagery have been analyzed and debated. Only recently, however, has narrative been treated like story. Since each culture and time period have different conventions of story telling, scholars have concentrated on what goes into a Hebrew narrative.

Literary study and other analytical methods are *tools* for understanding the Scripture. Their usefulness, like that of any tool, depends finally on the worker who uses them. Occasionally such study obscures rather than illuminates the text. In some hands it becomes a tool for negating the historical value of the text. In other hands literary and other analytical methods have produced many helpful insights. □

A scroll of the Pentateuch, or Torah (Genesis–Deuteronomy), being held in its wooden case at a celebration in Jerusalem.

may not (and indeed cannot) prove the historicity of individual details, especially personal and private episodes and miraculous intervention, evidence suggests the Pentateuch recounts genuine historical events centered around actual historical persons.

The fundamental importance and relevance of the Pentateuch lies in its theology, not in its historicity or even its literary form and content. What truth is God communicating about Himself and His purposes? What meaning *did* that communication have for OT Israel and the NT church (biblical theology)? What meaning *does* it have for contemporary Christian theology?

Such questions are obviously related to the matter of the Pentateuch's theme and purpose, matters dealt with previously. The historical, social, and religious setting of the Mosaic writings points to their purpose as that of instructing Israel about its past, its present, and its future. The nation had been redeemed by the great exodus event as a result of Yahweh's free choice of Israel in fulfillment of the promises to the patriarchs. Israel had to understand the context of those promises and their necessary fulfillment in light of the exodus salvation and the subsequent Sinai covenant. Israel now stood as covenant heir and servant people charged with mediating the saving purposes of Yahweh to the whole earth.

The great theme of the Pentateuch, then, is the theme of reconciliation and restoration. God's creation, having been affected by human disobedience, stood in need of restoration. Humanity, having been alienated from God, stood in need of forgiveness. God's saving plan began with a solemn pledge to bless the world through Abraham and his offspring (Israel). The pledge found expression in a covenant granting Abraham descendants and land and designating Abraham as God's instrument of redemption. Centuries later that covenant with Abraham incorporated within it a covenant of another kind. The Sinai covenant—a sovereign-vassal treaty—offered to Israel the role of redemptive mediation if Israel submitted to God's rule. Israel's acceptance of that servant role produced the whole apparatus of law, religious ritual, and priesthood. These institutions enabled the nation to live out its servant task as a holy people and by that holiness to attract lost humanity to the only true and living God. In brief, that is the theology of the Pentateuch.

The Christian is also part of a "kingdom of priests" (Exod 19:6; 1 Pet 2:5,9; Rev 1:6) with privileges and responsibilities corresponding to those of Old Testament Israel. The church and each and every believer stand within the stream of God's gracious covenant promises. Believers have been made "children of God" (John 1:12), delivered from bondage to sin by an exodus of personal redemption, established on the pilgrim way to the land of promise, and provided with every means through the new covenant of serving as the instruments of God's reconciling grace. The theology of the Pentateuch is important for Christians because it models God's timeless purposes for creation and redemption.

GENESIS

The Book of Genesis takes its name from the Greek version of the Old Testament (the Septuagint), which called it *Genesis,* meaning *beginning.* This is an accurate translation of *bereshit,* the first word in the Hebrew book. The title is most appropriate to the book's contents, for it concerns the divine origin of all things, whether matter or energy, living or inanimate. It implies that apart from God everything can be traced back to a beginning point when God's purposes and works came into being. *Bereshit* indicates that God brought forth the "heavens and the earth" as the first act of creation (Gen 1:1).

Jewish and Christian tradition has nearly unanimously attributed the authorship of Genesis to Moses (see "The Pentateuch"). Genesis is the only book of the Pentateuch that does not mention Moses' name or indicate something about its authorship. This omission may well be because the latest events of the book predate Moses by several centuries. Also biblical books seldom designate their authors. Yet the remainder of the Pentateuch builds upon Genesis, without which the constant allusions to the patriarchs and other persons and events would make no sense. The summary of the conclusion of Genesis (Gen 46:8-27) in Exodus 1:1-7 serves as a bridge between the patriarchs and the exodus deliverance and highlights the continuity of the Pentateuch's story.

Theme

The name *Genesis* describes what is at least a major theme of the book—beginnings. It recounts the beginnings of the heavens and earth, of all created things within them, of God's covenant relationship with humankind, of sin, of redemption, of nations, and of God's chosen people Israel.

Beginnings, however, is not a completely satisfying summary theme because it fails to answer the fundamental historical and theological question—why? To know *what* God did—He created all things "in the beginning"—is important. But to know *why* God acted in creation and for redemption is to grasp the very essence of divine revelation.

The theme of Genesis centers around the first utterance of God to man and woman recorded in the Sacred Text, namely Genesis 1:26-28:

> Then God said, "Let us make man in our image, in our likeness, and let them rule over the fish of the sea and the birds of the air, over the livestock, over all the earth, and over all the creatures that move along the ground." So God created man in his own image, in the image of God he created him; male and female he created them. God blessed them and said to them, "Be fruitful and increase in number; fill the earth and subdue it. Rule over the fish of the sea and the birds of the air and over every living creature that moves on the ground."

Here God clarifies that He created man and woman to bless them and so that they could exercise dominion on His behalf over all creation. Human disobedience threatened God's purpose for humanity in creation. God responded by calling Abraham, through whom God's blessing would ultimately triumph. Admittedly, this interpretation of the theme derives not only, if at all, from Genesis but from a total biblical theology (see "The Pentateuch"). Because it is a matter of theology, it will be more productive to consider it later under that heading.

Literary Forms

The three major sections of Genesis are characterized by distinct literary types. The primeval events (Gen 1–11) are cast in a poetic narrative form to aid in oral transmission. The accounts of the first three patriarchs (Gen 12–36; 38) are reports about ancestors that were retained in family records. The Joseph narrative (Gen 37; 39–50) is a short story containing tension and resolution. Within each of these major literary types, however, are other minor types such as genealogies (5:3-32; 11:10-32), narratives in which God appears (17–18; 32:22-30), words from God (25:23), blessings (1:28; 9:1; 27:27-29), and tribal sayings (49:3-27). Genesis presents history in every sense of the term. Genesis, however, presents history in the form of narrative that embraces a host of literary types to communicate its theological message clearly and effectively. (See "Types of Old Testament Literature.")

I. God's Creation Goal: Dominion, Blessing, and Relationship (1:1–2:25)
II. Sin, Its Consequences, and God's Saving Grace (3:1–10:32)
III. Abraham: The Obedience of Faith (12:1–22:19)
IV. Isaac: The Link with God's Promises to Abraham (22:20–25:18)
V. Jacob's Struggle for the Promises (25:19–36:43)
VI. Deliverance through Joseph (37:1–50:26)

Purpose and Theology

The purpose of Genesis was to give the nation Israel an explanation of its existence on the threshold of the conquest of Canaan (see Themes). Moses had at hand written and oral traditions about Israel's past and records concerning the other great themes of Genesis. He was, however, the first to organize these, select from them those that were appropriate to the divine redemptive purposes, and compose them as they stand. His task as inspired, prophetic author was to clarify to his people how and why God had brought them into being. He also wanted them to know what their mission was as a covenant, priestly nation and how their present situation fulfilled ancient promises.

Close attention to the themes that link Genesis and the remainder of the Pentateuch clarify these purposes. God had revealed to Abraham that he would be granted the land of Canaan (Gen 12:1,5,7; 13:15), that his descendants would leave that land for a time (15:13), but that they would be delivered from the land of their oppression to return to the land of promise (15:16). This land would be theirs forever (17:8) as an arena within and from which they would be a means of blessing all nations of the earth (12:2-3; 27:29). Joseph understood this and saw in his own sojourn in Egypt the divine preservation of his people (45:7-8). God had sent him there to save them from physical and spiritual extinction (50:20). The time would come, he said, when God would remember His promise to Abraham, Isaac, and Jacob and would return them to Canaan (50:24).

The link with Exodus is clear in the call of Moses to lead his people from Egypt to the land of promise (Exod 3:6-10,16-17; 6:2-8). Their charter as a covenant nation—a "kingdom of priests and a holy nation" (Exod 19:6)—recalls God's promise to bless the nations through Abraham (Gen 12:3; 22:18). The covenant renewal at the Plains of Moab repeats those same themes. The Lord was about to lead His people into Canaan to possess it as their inheritance (Deut 4:1; 5:33; 7:1,12-16; 8:1-10; 9:5; 11:8-12,24-25). There they would serve Him as a redemptive agent, a catalyst around which the nations would be reconciled to God (Deut 4:5-8; 28:10).

The theological message of Genesis, however, goes beyond the narrow concerns of Israel alone. Genesis does indeed provide Israel's reason for being, but it does more. It explains the human condition that called forth a covenant people. That is, it unfolds the great creative and redemptive purposes of God that found focus in Israel as an agency of re-creation and salvation.

God's original and eternal purposes are outlined in Genesis 1:26-28. God created man and woman *as* His image to bless them and so that they could exercise dominion over all creation on His behalf. The key themes of biblical theology and of Genesis are, therefore, God's blessing and human dominion under God's reign.

The fall of humankind into sin subverted God's goal of blessing and dominion. A process of redemption from that fallenness and of recovery of the original covenant mandate of God had to be effected. That took the form of the choice of Abraham through whose offspring (Israel and ultimately the Messiah) the divine creation purposes might come to pass. That man and nation, joined by eternal covenant to Yahweh, were charged with the task of serving Him as the model of a dominion people and the vehicle through which a saving relationship could be established between Him and the alienated world of nations.

Of course, Israel failed to be the servant people, a failure already anticipated in the Torah (Lev 26:14-39; Deut 28:15-68). God's goals cannot, however, be frustrated. So from the nation arose a remnant, a remnant finally compressed to only one descendant of Abraham—Jesus the Christ—who accomplished in His life and death the redemptive and reigning purposes of God. The church now exists as His body to serve as Israel was chosen and redeemed to serve. God's Old Testament people served as the model of the kingdom of the Lord and the agency through which His reconciling work on earth can be achieved through His New Testament people.

The theology of Genesis then is wrapped up in the kingdom purposes of God who, despite human failures, cannot be hindered in His ultimate objective of displaying His glory through His creation and dominion.

GOD'S CREATION GOAL: DOMINION, BLESSING, AND RELATIONSHIP (GEN 1:1–2:25)

Primeval history describes the accounts of the creation, the fall, the flood, the tower of Babel, and the distribution

Creation and Flood Stories

In giving us the Scriptures, God used human writers who were at home in the world of the ancient Near East. The biblical writers addressed many of the same questions that were of interest to neighboring peoples: How did the world come to be? What is the special place of humankind in the world? What is God [or the gods] like? How does He [they] continue to relate to the world?

The biblical writers made use of some *ways of speaking* shared by numerous ancient Near Eastern accounts of creation and the flood. The *faith* and *message* of the biblical writers is, however, quite distinct from that of other ancient Near Eastern writers.

The biblical writers believed in one God. Their neighbors believed in many gods. The biblical writers viewed God as Creator and the world as His work. Their neighbors believed their gods were involved in creation but were not separate from the creation. Rather, their gods were personifications of elements of the created order.

The biblical writers knew God to be a moral God, who punishes sin but responds in grace to save His creation. Israel's neighbors believed in immoral gods, concerned with their own pleasure rather than the good of humanity.

Creation Stories

Isolated elements in the biblical creation account are paralleled by elements of ancient Egyptian accounts. For example, in a creation story from Memphis the god Ptah creates by his word and rests following creation. Egyptian creation accounts, unlike their biblical counterparts, are polytheistic. That is, they describe not only the creation of the world but the creation of the numerous lesser gods who personify nature. The mythological origin of these lesser gods varies. In one account they are body parts of the chief god Atum; in others they are Atum's breath, spittle, or tears; in still others they are products of sexual acts.

The primary Mesopotamian creation story, the Enuma Elish, is an epic intended to praise the god Marduk and is not essentially a creation story. In this epic the god Marduk battled the sea goddess Tiamat. Marduk prevailed, dividing Tiamat's body in half, with part becoming the sky and the other the earth. Subsequently, the rest of creation was made and ordered.

While one can say that both the biblical and other ancient Near Eastern accounts view the world as created, the differences far outweigh this similarity. The number and immoral behavior of the Egyptian and Mesopotamian gods stands in marked contrast to that of the Holy One of Israel. The Egyptian and Mesopotamian epics are profoundly mythological, whereas the biblical story is not. The biblical story is also unique in presenting God as preexistent and distinct from the created order.

Finally, the conception of humanity is fundamentally distinct. The Egyptian and Mesopotamian myths see humanity as an afterthought; human beings are mere by-products of a god's congestion or serve only to relieve the gods of daily drudgery. But the biblical story portrays humanity as creation's climax—the image of God. It is unlikely, then, that the biblical accounts are a simple reworking of earlier Near Eastern creation stories.

Flood Stories

The most important and complete Mesopotamian flood story is found in the eleventh tablet of the Gilgamesh Epic, a moving account of Gilgamesh and his friend Enkidu's futile search for eternal life. This Mesopotamian flood account does not diverge nearly so widely from the biblical one as did the respective creation stories. In fact, the similarities are too striking to be coincidental.

In both stories God or the gods initiated the flood out of displeasure with humanity but informed the main character of the impending flood and admonished him to construct a massive boat covered with asphalt according to predetermined dimensions. In both stories the hero and his family were delivered from a deluge of lengthy duration, and the hero sent out a bird to see if the floodwaters had abated. In both stories the hero sacrificed and worshiped God or the gods after the deluge, and the hero was praised for his faithfulness.

On the other hand, the most fundamental difference between the two stories lies in the demeanor of God and the Mesopotamian gods. In the Bible, God is morally outraged by humanity's perversity. The gods in the Gilgamesh Epic are sophomoric, perturbed, and sleepless at humanity's noisiness. In Genesis, God's gracious will is to save those in the ark. The hero in the Gilgamesh epic discovered the coming flood despite the will of most of the gods. In the end the hero of the Gilgamesh epic became a god, quite unlike Noah's experience in Genesis 9.

Many of the details of the stories such as the dimensions of the ark and the length of the flood are also quite different. These differences are significant enough to make it highly unlikely that there was a literary connection between the two texts. However, the similarities argue for some association. Since the flood was a historical event, it is plausible that the memory of the event was preserved by the survivors and their descendants. □

of the human race. It embraces all those facets of human experience that led up to and necessitated the call of Abraham to covenant service to the Lord.

The two accounts of creation (1:1–2:3 and 2:4-25) are designed respectively to demonstrate the all-wise and all-powerful sovereignty of God (first account) and His special creation of humanity to rule for Him over all other created things (second account). Though the creation stories are fundamentally theological and not scientific, nothing in them is contradicted by modern scientific understanding. Genesis insists that all the forms of life were created "after their kind" (1:11-12,21,24-25); that is, they did not evolve across species lines. Most importantly, the man and the woman were created as "the image of God" (1:26). In other words, humanity was created to represent God on the earth and to rule over all things in His name (1:26-28). God's desire was to bless humanity and to enjoy relationship with them.

SIN, ITS CONSEQUENCES, AND GOD'S SAVING GRACE (GEN 3:1–10:32)

The privilege of dominion also carried responsibility and limitation. Being placed in the garden to "work it and watch over it" represented human responsibility (2:15). The tree in the midst of the garden from which humans should not eat represented those areas of dominion reserved to Yahweh alone. The man and woman, however, disobeyed God and ate of the tree. They "died" with respect to their covenant privileges (2:17) and suffered the indictment and judgment of their Sovereign (3:14-19,22-24). This entailed suffering and sorrow and eventual physical death. God had created man and woman to enjoy fellowship with Himself and with each other. Their disobedience alienated them from God and each other.

Adam and Eve being driven out of the Garden of Eden

The pattern of sin and its consequences set in the garden is replayed throughout Genesis in the accounts of Cain, the generation of the flood, and the men of Sodom. The fall means that we humans are predisposed to sin. Though God punishes sin, sin does not thwart God's ultimate, gracious purpose for His human creation. Embedded in the curse was the gleam of a promise that the offspring of the woman would someday lead the human race to triumph (3:15).

The consequences of sin became clear in the second generation when Cain, the oldest son, killed Abel his brother (4:8). Just as his parents had been expelled from the presence of God in the garden (3:23), so now Cain was expelled from human society to undertake a nomadic life in the east (4:16). Embedded in the curse was the gleam of grace, the "mark on Cain" (4:15), symbolizing God's protection.

4:17–5:32
The Blessing of Dominion and the Curse of Sin

Cain's genealogy illustrates the tension between God's blessing and spreading sin. Through the achievements of Cain's descendants, humanity began to experience the blessing of dominion over creation. Progress in the arts and technology was, however, matched by progress in sin as illustrated in Lamech's boastful song of murder (4:23-24).

Meanwhile, God's redemptive, creation mandate continued through another son of Adam and Eve—Seth (4:25-26). His genealogy (5:1-32) led straight to Noah, to whom the original creation promises were reaffirmed (6:18; 9:1-7).

6:1–9:29
Deliverance through God's Grace and Noah's Obedience

With the passing of time it became increasingly clear that humanity was unwilling and unable to live out the responsibilities of stewardship. Humans again violated their proper place within God's order by overstepping the limits God had placed on them. As a result of the improper intermingling of the "sons of God" (understood as either the angels or the rulers on the earth) and "the daughters of men" (6:1-4), God again saw the need to reassert His lordship (6:3) and make a fresh beginning that could give the human race another chance at obedience.

The consequence of sin was the great flood (6:5-8), a catastrophe so enormous that all life and institutions perished from the earth (7:22-23). God's grace was still active in preserving a remnant on the ark. In response to the worship of His people, God promised never again to destroy the earth so long as history ran its course (8:20-22). God's pledge to Noah reaffirmed the creation promises of blessing and dominion (9:1-19). Though differing in detail from the original statement of Genesis 1:26-28, the central mandate is identical. The new humanity springing from Noah and his sons was called on to exercise dominion over all the earth as the image of God. The sign of the permanence of that arrangement was the rainbow (9:12).

Once more, as though to underline the effects of the fall on human faithfulness, Noah fell victim to his environment. Adam had sinned by partaking of a forbidden fruit; Noah sinned by perverting the use of a permitted fruit. Both cases illustrate that unaided humans can never rise to the level of God-ordained responsibility.

When Noah learned of the abuse he had suffered at the hand of his son Ham, he cursed the offspring of Ham—the Canaanites. He blessed those of his other two sons (9:24-27). This set in motion the relationships among the threefold division of the human race that would forever after determine the course of history. God

THE FLOOD

The cataclysmic deluge described in Genesis 6–9 as God's judgment on the earth is mentioned elsewhere in the OT (Gen 10:1,32 11:10; Pss 29:10; 104:6-9; Isa 54:9) and in the NT (Matt 24:38-39; Luke 17:26-27; Heb 11:7; 1 Pet 3:20; 2 Pet 2:5; 3:3-7). That more verses are devoted to the flood than to the creation (Gen 1–2) or the fall (Gen 3) suggests the significance of the account.

The Old Testament Account

Because of the great wickedness of humanity (Gen 6:5,11), God resolved to destroy all living beings (6:13) with the exception of righteous Noah and his family (6:9,18). God instructed Noah to make an ark of cypress wood (6:14; "gopher wood," KJV). He told Noah to take his family and seven [pairs] of every clean species and two of every unclean species of animals, birds, and creeping things, along with provisions for the duration of the flood (6:18-21; 7:1-3). The rains lasted forty days and nights, covered "all the high mountains under the whole heaven" (7:19), and destroyed every living creature on land (7:21-23). When Noah and his family emerged from the ark after a year and ten days, he built an altar and offered sacrifices to God (8:14-20). God blessed Noah and his family (9:1) and made a covenant that He would never again destroy the earth by flood (8:21; 9:11). God gave the rainbow as a visible sign of that covenant (9:12-17).

Date and Extent of the Flood

It is impossible to determine the exact date of the flood, since no archaeological or geological materials have been found that would enable its accurate dating. Estimates have placed it between 13,000 and 3000 B.C.

The extent of the flood has been debated. Arguments for a universal flood include: (1) the wording of Genesis 6–9, which is best interpreted as a universal flood (compare 7:19-23); (2) the widespread flood traditions among many, widely scattered peoples that are best explained if all peoples are descended from Noah; (3) the unusual source of water (Gen 7:11); (4) the length of the flood, whereas a local flood would have subsided in a few days; (5) the false assumption that all life resided in a limited geographical area; and (6) God's limitless ability to act within history.

Arguments against a universal flood have persuaded some scholars to accept a limited flood. Some arguments are: (1) the amount of water needed to cover the highest mountain, which would be eight times as much as there is on earth; (2) the practical problems of housing and feeding so many animals for a year; (3) the destruction of all plant life submerged in salt water for over a year; (4) the view that destruction of the human race required only a flood covering the part of the earth inhabited at that time; and (5) the lack of geological evidence for a worldwide cataclysm. While all of our questions cannot be answered, the biblical data points in the direction of a universal flood.

Theological Significance

(1) The flood demonstrates God's hatred of sin and the certainty of His judgment on it. (2) God's giving people 120 years to repent before judgment came demonstrates His patience in dealing with sin. (3) The sparing of one family demonstrates God's saving grace. (4) The flood reveals God's rule over nature and over humanity. □

FAMILY OF ABRAHAM

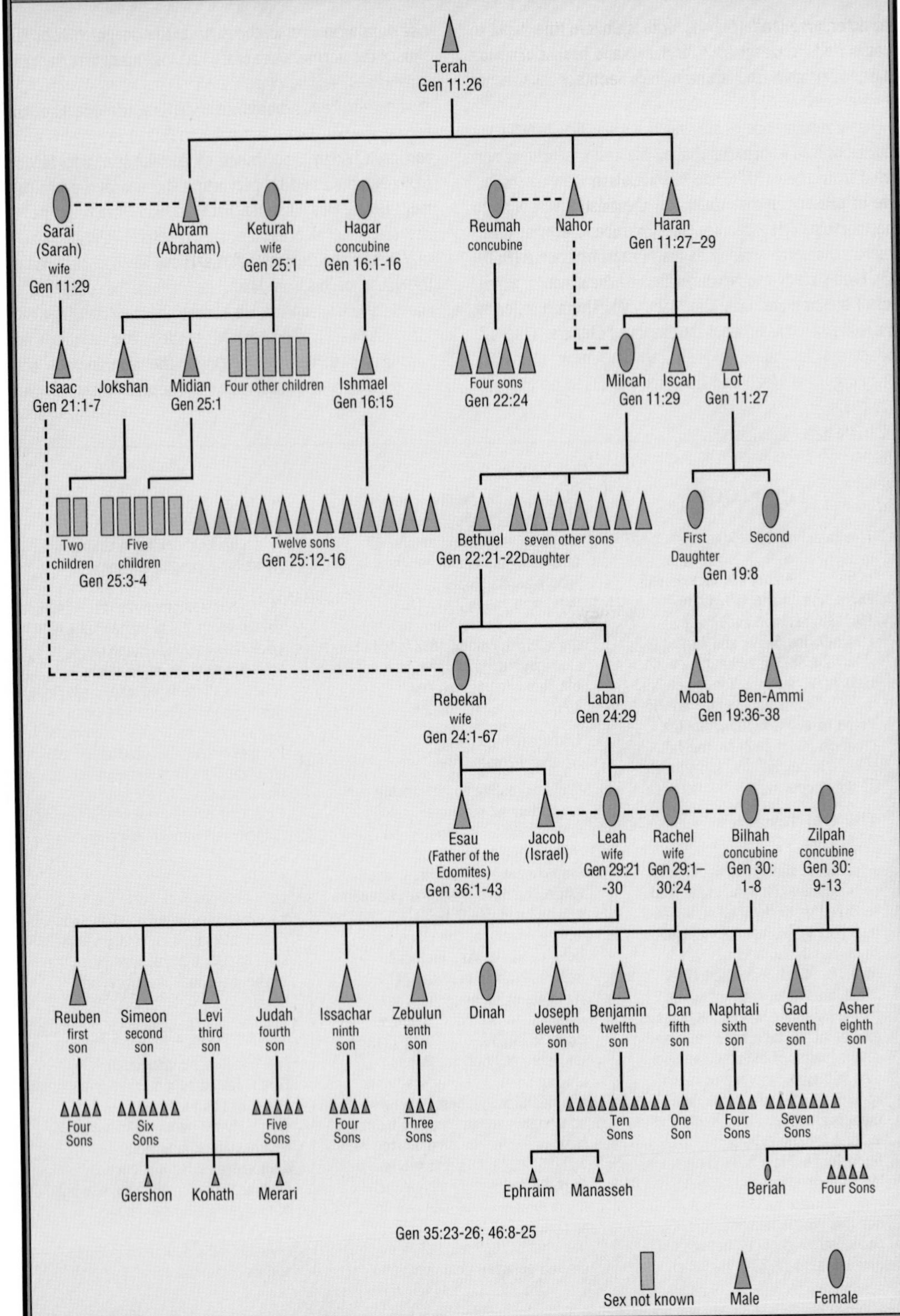

would enlarge Japheth (the Gentiles), but in time Japheth would find refuge in the preserving and protecting tents of Shem (Israel). The Shemites (or Semites) thus would be the channel of redemptive grace.

10:1-32
Reaffirmation of God's Blessing

The "table of nations" (Gen 10) demonstrates the fulfillment of God's command to be fruitful and fill the earth. The climactic position of the Shemites focuses attention on Eber (10:21,24-25), for whom the Hebrews (Hebrew *ibri*) were named. This ancestor of Abraham anticipates the Jewish patriarchs who are the focus of the second half of Genesis.

11:1-32
Confusion at Babel

The story of the tower of Babel (11:1-9) separates the genealogy of the descent from Noah to Eber and Peleg and the genealogy that connects Noah to Abraham (11:10-32). In the days of Peleg, son of Eber, the earth was "divided" (10:25). Through Abraham and the Abrahamic covenant it someday would be reunited. The Babel narrative thus illustrates the false and defiant sense of humanistic solidarity that sought to evade the creation mandate to fill the earth under God's dominion. The scattering of the nations accomplished that purpose but did not effect compliance to the will of God that made true servanthood a reality. That is why a new covenant, one with redemptive aspects, had to be implemented.

ABRAHAM: THE OBEDIENCE OF FAITH (GEN 12:1–22:19)

The story of the patriarchs is centered and grounded in the covenant to which the Lord called Abraham. The history of the human race from the fall to Abraham's own day was sufficient to show that the great kingdom purposes of God could not be achieved until humanity could be redeemed and restored to covenant-keeping capacity. The promise had been given that the offspring of the woman would someday prevail over anti-God forces. Now that offspring promise was to find fulfillment in one man and his descendants, chief among whom was to be the Messiah who would effect salvation and dominion.

LIFE OF ABRAHAM

EVENT	OLD TESTAMENT PASSAGE	NEW TESTAMENT REFERENCE
The birth of Abram	Gen 11:26	
God's call of Abram	Gen 12:1-3	Heb 11:8
The entry into Canaan	Gen 12:4-9	
Abram in Egypt	Gen 12:10-20	
Lot separates from Abram	Gen 13:1-18	
Abram rescues Lot	Gen 14:1-17	
Abram pays tithes to Melchizedek	Gen 14:18-24	Heb 7:1-10
God's covenant with Abraham	Gen 15:1-21	Rom 4:1-25 Gal 3:6-25 Heb 6:13-20
The birth of Ishmael	Gen 16:1-16	
Abraham promised a son by Sarah	Gen 17:1-27	Rom 4:18-25 Heb 11:11-12
Abraham intercedes for Sodom	Gen 18:16-33	
Lot saved and Sodom destroyed	Gen 19:1-38	
The birth of Isaac	Gen 21:1-7	
Hagar and Ishmael sent away	Gen 21:8-21	Gal 4:21-31
Abraham challenged to offer Isaac as sacrifice	Gen 22:1-19	Heb 11:17-19 Jas 2:20-24
The death of Sarah	Gen 23:1-20	
The death of Abraham	Gen 25:1-11	

12:1-9
God's Promises: Descendants, Blessing, Land
Abraham was called from Sumerian paganism to faith in the living God. God granted him an unconditional set of promises—descendants and blessing. God promised to lead him to Canaan, the earthly scene for the working out of God's promises (12:1-3). On Abraham's arrival in Canaan, he received God's promise of land (12:4-9).

12:10-20
The Promises Threatened
No sooner were God's promises given than their fulfillment was "threatened." Faced with famine, Abraham deserted the promised land and placed Sarah—the link with the promise of descendants—in a potentially compromising position as a member of Pharaoh's harem (12:10-20).

13:1-18
Realizing the Promise of Land
Abraham anticipated the history of his descendants by dwelling briefly in Canaan, sojourning in Egypt (12:10-20), and coming out with riches and honor as Israel did later in the exodus (Exod 11:1-3; 12:35-36). Then, in his own "conquest" and occupation, Abraham divided the land between himself and Lot (Gen 13:6-13). The territories through which he had previously traveled as a nomad now became his in permanent habitation (13:14-18).

14:1-24
Possessing the Land, Blessing Neighbors
Abraham's dominion over his inheritance was not to be uncontested. The invasion and subjugation of the cities of the plain by the kings of the east (14:1-12) represented resistance to Abraham's claim to the land. Abraham, acting on behalf of El Elyon, the Almighty God (14:20,22), overcame this threat. In rescuing Lot's people (14:16), Abraham was fulfilling his God-given charge to be a blessing to other nations.

15:1-21
The Promise of Descendants and Land
Though he had inherited the land by promise, Abraham did not yet have the promised offspring, even after ten years in the land (compare Gen 16:3). The Lord reaffirmed His promise (15:4), enlarging it to include innumerable offspring (15:5). That host of descendants,

COVENANTS

A covenant is a compact or agreement made between two parties binding them mutually to some agreed upon obligations and benefits. Much of the history of salvation can be traced by noting both the presence and the contents of biblical covenants. Covenants may be either bilateral ("two-sided"), where both parties are obligated, or unilateral ("one-sided"), where only one party is bound by the agreement.

Genesis 15:9-21 offers the best illustration of the unilateral type of covenant. The verb "to make" a covenant is literally "to cut" a covenant. Thus when one made a covenant, several animals were brought, cut in half, and arranged opposite each other. The person or parties making the covenant would then walk through the aisle formed by the carcasses and say in effect, "May it happen to me as it has happened to these slain animals if I do not keep all the provisions of this covenant." (Compare Jer 34:18-20.)

In a bilateral covenant both parties would take the oath. If one defaulted, the other was released from any further obligations. But in the case of Genesis 15:9-21, the "smoking fire pot with a blazing torch" pictures God as the *only* One who walked between the pieces and thus obligated Himself alone to bring all the blessings and benefits of the Abrahamic covenant. God's blessings were apart from any works of obedience on the part of Abraham or any of the patriarchs who followed him who also enjoyed the benefits of this covenant.

The Sinai covenant offers the best illustration of a bilateral covenant. The people of Israel agreed to accept the terms of relationship God offered (Exod 19:5-6; 24:3). In their preaching, the later prophets often placed Israel on trial for failure to fulfill their covenant commitments (Jer 11:10; Ezek 16:59; Hos 8:1). In times of spiritual revival, the people of Israel would reaffirm their commitment to the covenant (Deut 5:2-3; Josh 24; 2 Kgs 23:3; 2 Chron 15:12).

Scripture presents a fairly large number of covenants. Many were instituted by the one true living God. The primary divine covenants include those made with Noah (Gen 9:9-17), Abraham (Gen 15:18; 17:2), Moses (Exod 19:5-6), David (2 Sam 23:5; compare 7:12-16), and the new covenant of Jeremiah 31:31-34.

The *content* of covenants is more important than their *form*. The content of all these divine covenants exhibits a unity, continuity, and building theme. The form changes since there are different "signs" of the covenant

Yahweh promised, would go to a land of sojourn, just as Abraham had done. They eventually would return with the riches to fill the land of promise (15:12-21).

16:1-16
Human Effort to Realize God's Promise

Sarah, Abraham's wife, was past the age of childbearing. Thus she and her husband, following the custom of the time, decided that the offspring promise could find fulfillment only if they took matters into their own hands. Sarah presented her slave girl to Abraham as a surrogate mother. In due time a son, Ishmael, was born (16:15-16). This attempt to short-circuit the ways and means of the Lord was to no avail.

17:1–18:15
Reaffirmation of God's Promise of an Heir

Once more the Lord affirmed His covenant intentions. Abraham would be the father of nations (17:1-8), but the nations would be born of Sarah, not Hagar (17:16). As a token of His steadfast loyalty to His covenant pledge, the Lord established the rite of circumcision (17:9-14).

Soon the Lord appeared as the angel of the Lord, revealing to Abraham and Sarah that she would give birth to the promised offspring within the year (18:10).

18:16–19:38
A Blessing on Neighboring Nations

God reminded Abraham that he was the chosen means of blessing the nations (18:18). As an illustration of what that meant, Yahweh revealed to Abraham that He was going to destroy Sodom and Gomorrah, cities whose sinfulness was beyond remedy. Abraham was aware that this implied the death of his own nephew Lot, who lived in Sodom. Abraham exercised his ministry of mediation by pleading with the Lord to spare the righteous and thus the cities in which they lived. Though not even ten righteous ones could be found and the cities therefore were overwhelmed in judgment, Abraham's role as the one in whom the nations could find blessing is clearly seen (18:22; 19:29).

20:1-18
A Threat to the Promise of an Heir

Abraham's encounter with Abimelech of Gerar (Gen 20) also testifies to Abraham's role as mediator. He had lied to Abimelech concerning Sarah, maintaining that she was only his sister. Abimelech took Sarah into his own

(for example, a rainbow in Noah's case, circumcision in Abraham's case), types of covenants, and "people" addressed in the covenant. If we keep our eyes on their content, we will note how the everlasting plan of God, both for our redemption and our successful living, was unfolded.

One three-part formula acts as a summation of God's covenant relationship: I shall be your God, you shall be my people, and I shall dwell in the midst of you. The repetition of elements of this formula as part of many of these covenants supplied one of their unifying themes: God would be in the midst of His people and they would be His special possession. (Compare Gen 17:7; Exod 6:6-7; 19:4-5.)

In spite of their structural and thematic unity, the major OT covenants exhibit a diversity of focus as history progresses. God's covenant with Noah focused on preservation. The Abrahamic covenant focused on land and descendants. The Mosaic covenant emphasized obedience to the law of God, and the Davidic covenant focused on preservation of David's dynasty. The new covenant of Jeremiah 31 focused on God's forgiveness of His people, on whose hearts He would write His law. The covenants with Abraham and David and Jeremiah's new covenant anticipated redemption through the promised Messiah.

To clarify the relationship between the old covenant (usually equated with the Mosaic covenant) and the new covenant is difficult. Paul apparently set the promise of the Abrahamic type covenants over against the law of the Mosaic type. But Paul's contrast was in no way absolute or unqualified. Paul affirmed that the law-covenant did not annul the covenant of promise (Gal 3:17) and that the promise-covenant did not annul the covenant of law (Rom 3:31).

At the apex of all the covenants is the new covenant found in Jeremiah 31:31-34. The phrase *new covenant* is found six times in the NT (1 Cor 11:25; 2 Cor 3:6; Heb 8:8; 9:15; 12:24; and possibly in Luke 22:20). The idea is also present in Romans 11:27 and Galatians 4:21-31. Since much of the content of the new covenant repeats the previous covenants' promises, it may be best to represent this covenant as a "renewed covenant." It fulfills the promises of the older covenants, but it is better by virtue of its clearer view of Christ, its richer experience of the Holy Spirit, and the greater liberty it grants to believers. □

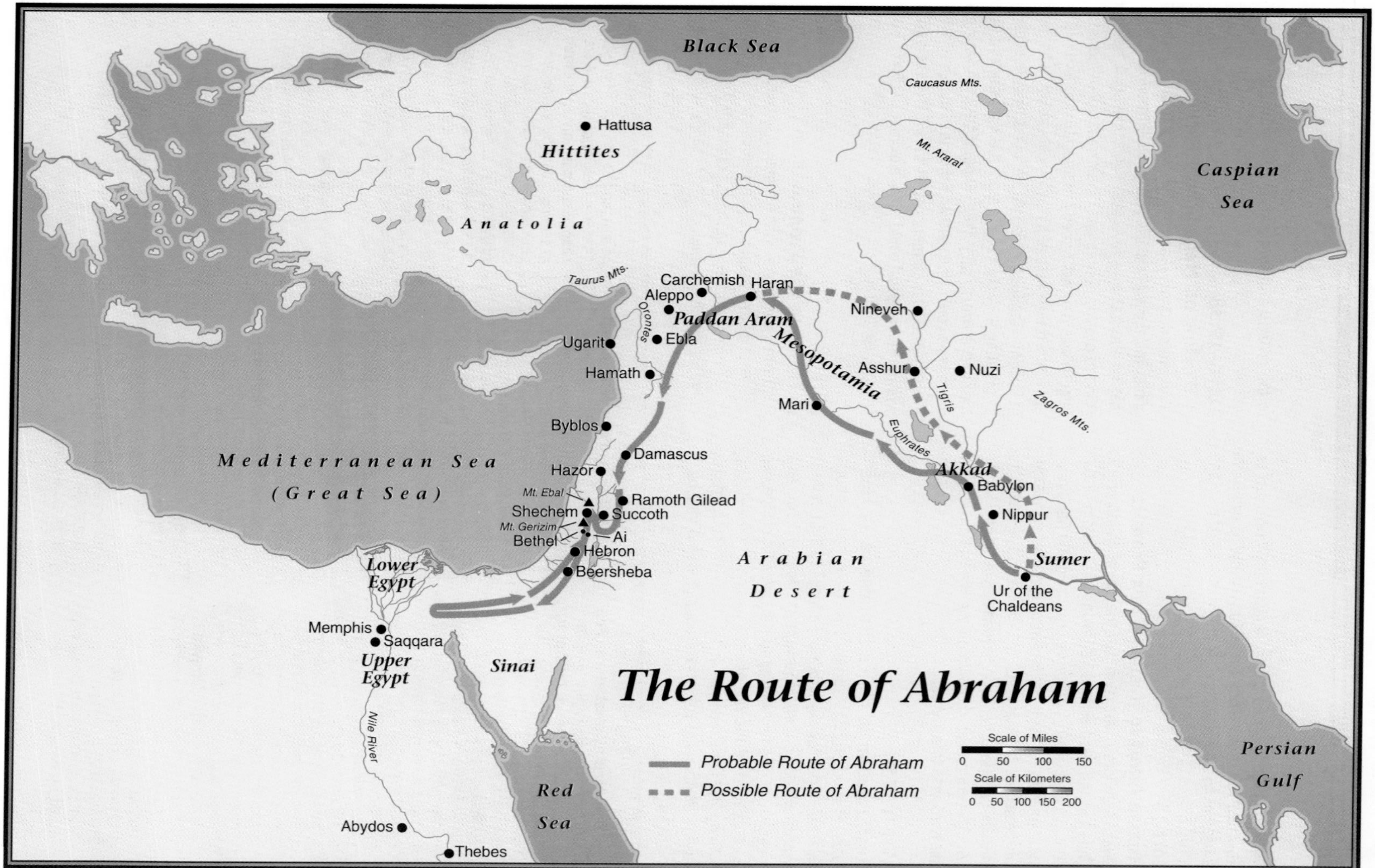
The Route of Abraham
Black Sea
Caspian Sea
Persian Gulf
Red Sea
Mediterranean Sea (Great Sea)
Caucasus Mts.
Mt. Ararat
Hattusa
Hittites
Anatolia
Taurus Mts.
Carchemish
Haran
Aleppo
Paddan Aram
Orontes
Ebla
Ugarit
Hamath
Mesopotamia
Nineveh
Asshur
Nuzi
Tigris
Zagros Mts.
Mari
Euphrates
Byblos
Damascus
Hazor
Akkad
Babylon
Nippur
Mt. Ebal
Shechem
Ramoth Gilead
Succoth
Mt. Gerizim
Bethel
Ai
Hebron
Beersheba
Arabian Desert
Sumer
Ur of the Chaldeans
Lower Egypt
Memphis
Saqqara
Upper Egypt
Sinai
Nile River
Abydos
Thebes
Probable Route of Abraham
Possible Route of Abraham
Scale of Miles
0 50 100 150
Scale of Kilometers
0 50 100 150 200

harem, putting God's promise of offspring through Sarah in jeopardy. Before matters could proceed further, the Lord revealed to Abimelech that Abraham was a prophet (20:7), one whose prayers were effective. Then the plague that Yahweh had brought upon Abimelech because of his dealings with Sarah was removed in response to Abraham's intercession (20:17). Once more Abraham's function as dispenser of blessing and cursing is evident.

21:1-34
Fulfillment of the Promise of an Heir

At last Isaac, the covenant son, was born (21:1-7). Through Ishmael, God honored His promise that not only the Hebrews but "many nations" would call Abraham "Father" (21:8-21; compare 25:12-18).

22:1-19
Abraham's Obedience and Blessing

Within a few years the Lord tested Abraham (22:1) by commanding him to offer his covenant son as a burnt offering. The intent was to teach Abraham that covenant blessing requires total covenant commitment and obedience. The narrative also stresses that covenant obedience brings fresh bestowal of covenant blessing (22:16-18). Abraham's willingness to surrender his son guaranteed all the more the fulfillment of God's promises to him.

ISAAC: THE LINK WITH GOD'S PROMISES TO ABRAHAM (GEN 22:20–25:18; 26:1-33)

Isaac fulfilled a *passive* linking role quite unlike the other patriarchs, who took an *active* role in the outworkings of God's promises. Already Abraham had waited for Isaac's birth; Abraham stood ready to offer Isaac as a sacrifice. Following the death and burial of Sarah (23:1-20), Abraham made arrangements for Isaac to take a wife from among his own kinfolk of Aramea (24:1-67; compare 22:20-24). Abraham thus worked to insure that the promise of offspring would continue into the next generation. This done, Abraham died (25:7-8) and was buried

Pattern of Faith in Abraham

The greatest text on faith in the Bible may well be Genesis 15:6—"Abram believed the LORD, and he credited it to him as righteousness." In that simple formula the pattern for faith was set for all ages, peoples, and persuasions.

God continues to offer salvation on the same basis, that is, by grace through faith—plus nothing. That is the clear teaching of both the OT and NT.

But questions are sometimes raised about who or what was the *object* of faith in the Old Testament. Some have answered that Genesis 15:6 simply says that Abram became a general believer in the one true God and abandoned the worship of other gods. Such a conclusion, however, does not take the context of Genesis 15:6 seriously.

Why did the narrator of Genesis wait until Genesis 15 to inform us about Abraham's faith? According to Hebrews 11:8-9, Abraham left the city of Ur of the Chaldees in southern Mesopotamia "by faith" twenty-five years earlier than the events of Genesis 15. The answer rests in the fact that during the twenty-five years covered by Genesis 12–14 the promise of the land took precedence. When the issue of the promise of a son and offspring was raised in Genesis 15, Abraham was one hundred years old, and his wife Sarah was ninety. God refused to allow Abraham to adopt his servant Eliezer of Damascus as his legal son. God would still give to Abraham and Sarah their own natural son as promised.

In this very context the issue of what it means to believe God was raised. What, then, was the object of Abraham's faith? It was simply and solely belief in the Promised One who was to come through the offspring of Abraham. Abraham's faith had the same *object* as ours must, the promised Christ.

Is Abraham's faith any different from the justifying faith of the NT believer? No. In principle it remains the same. This is not to say, of course, that Abraham possessed as full an understanding of our Savior and His atoning work as we do. Yet the similarity and pattern still exist. Both the OT and the NT believer had to put their trust in the same person, Christ, the Offspring promised to the woman (Gen 3:15), to Abraham (Gen 15:5), and to us (Gal 3:16,29).

Some have argued that Abraham's belief is only an illustration that favors from God are not earned but come only through faith; it is not an example of saving faith. But this interpretation will not hold up under the accounting figure ("he credited it to him for righteousness") or the use Paul made of this verse in Romans 4:1-16. The discussion of Abraham's faith was delayed from Genesis 12 until Genesis 15 so that the strongest connection between belief in Christ, the promised Offspring, and Abraham's justification apart from any works might be made. Every time Abraham decided to extricate himself by his own works in Genesis 12–22, he only dug himself in deeper trouble. Only God's gracious gifts were effective in granting him relief; so it was with his salvation and ours. □

with his wife by his sons Ishmael and Isaac. Isaac rarely occupied the center stage. In the following years Isaac, who had been the object of his father's actions, became an object in his son Jacob's struggle for the promises (27:1-40).

A rare scene focusing on Isaac pictures him as the link through whom God's promises to receive land and to be a source of blessing for the nations were fulfilled. The Lord sent Isaac to live among the Philistines of Gerar as Abraham had done (26:1-6). There Isaac unwillingly blessed the nations by digging wells which the Philistines appropriated to their own use. Isaac and his clan proved to be such a source of nourishment to their neighbors that Abimelech their king made a covenant with Isaac, recognizing his claim in the promised land.

JACOB'S STRUGGLE FOR THE PROMISES (GEN 25:19-34; 27:1–36:43)

Isaac served as a passive link with God's promises to Abraham. In contrast, Isaac's younger son, Jacob, fought throughout his life for the very best that God had promised to give.

25:19-26
The Beginning of the Struggle

Just as the barrenness of Sarah called for Abraham to trust God for offspring, that same deficiency in Rebekah called for earnest prayer from her husband Isaac (25:21). Faithful to His promise to Abraham, Yahweh responded and gave not one but two sons, Esau and Jacob. Jacob's grasping Esau's heel in an effort to be the firstborn (25:26)

PATRIARCHS

The term *patriarch* comes from a Greek word meaning *the head of a tribe or family.* The term usually refers to the Israelite forefathers Abraham (Heb 7:4), Isaac, and Jacob. It is used more loosely of Jacob's twelve sons (Acts 7:8-9) and David (Acts 2:29).

Date and Historicity

The time of the patriarchs has been estimated between 2200 and 1300 B.C. Available evidence suggests a time early in the second millennium B.C. Some doubt the patriarchs were historical characters, seeing them as legendary figures who explain the names of the tribes of Israel. Yet no evidence has been discovered to refute the existence of the patriarchs.

Names

Many of the personal names in the patriarchal narratives appear in early second millennium B.C. texts written by other Near Eastern peoples. Texts from Ugarit and Assyria combine the name *Jacob* with the names of local gods (Jacob-el, Jacob-baal). The OT understands Abram to mean *exalted father;* and Abraham, *father of many* (Gen 17:5). Isaac, from the Hebrew *to laugh,* brought joy to his parents by his birth (Gen 21:6). Jacob likely comes from the word *grasp the heel.* The patriarchs were Arameans (Deut 26:5), Semitic peoples of northwestern Mesopotamia.

History

The patriarchal narratives are found in Genesis 12–50. Genesis 11:31 describes Abraham's migration with his family from Ur of the Chaldeans to Haran in northern Mesopotamia, where God made a covenant with him (12:1-3). The covenant promised innumerable descendants and a land known today as Israel. Abraham lived a typical seminomadic life. He dwelt in tents and moved from place to place, seeking pasture for his flocks. Even before the death of his father, Terah, Abraham journeyed with his family and possessions to Canaan, where he settled at Shechem (12:4-6). He later relocated near Bethel (12:8). During a famine, he lived for a time in Egypt (12:10-20). After returning from Egypt, he and Lot agreed to separate and settle in different areas. Lot chose the Jordan Valley near Sodom, and Abraham settled in Hebron (13:2-18).

God promised Abraham an heir when he was seventy-five and Sarah, his wife, was ten years younger. The child, Isaac, was born twenty-five years later (Gen 12:2; 17:1,17,21; 21:5). Little information is given about Isaac except the choosing of his wife, Rebekah (Gen 24), and the blessing Jacob received from him by disguising himself as Esau (Gen 27). Jacob's twelve sons, the ancestors of the twelve tribes of Israel, were born to Jacob's wives, Leah and Rachel (Gen 29; 30; 35:16-19). The aged Jacob's blessings on his sons singled out Judah as the one from whom a ruler would emerge (49:8-12).

Patriarchal Religion

Abraham probably was a worshiper of the Mesopotamian moon god Sin before God made a covenant with him. Joshua 24:2,14 affirms that the patriarchal ancestors worshiped pagan gods in Mesopotamia. Some argue that the patriarchs worshiped one god without denying the existence of other gods. While they became worshipers of the *only* living God, their descendants reverted to polytheism, worshiping the many gods of the Canaanite fertility cults (Exod 32; Num 25:1-3; Josh 24:14; Ezek 6:13; 20:8). The prophets constantly condemned the people for their worship of their neighbors' gods. □

introduces the major theme of the Jacob stories—Jacob's struggle for the promised blessings.

25:27-34
The Struggle for the Birthright

Contrary to the norms of succession and inheritance, the Lord gave to Jacob the rights of the firstborn, though on the human level Jacob manipulated his brother in order to receive them (25:27-34). Esau, as the older son of Isaac, should have inherited the birthright, the claim to family leadership. He forfeited that, however, in a moment of self-indulgence (25:27-34).

26:34–28:9
The Struggle for the Blessing

Esau still retained his position as heir of the covenant promises in succession to Abraham and Isaac. But when it was apparent through his marriages to Hittite women that he was unworthy of covenant privilege (26:34-35), his mother, Rebekah, set about to replace him with his brother Jacob.

When the day came for Isaac to designate Esau as the recipient of God's promised blessing, Jacob appeared in his place. Blind Isaac, deceived by the substitution, granted his irrevocable blessing (27:27-29). In the ancient world the speaking of a blessing, like the signing of a contract in our day, gave the words binding force. Jacob thus controlled both the birthright and the blessing. Though the means of their acquisition was anything but honorable, the Lord had foretold Jacob's triumph on the occasion of the birth of the twins (25:23).

Enraged by this turn of events, Esau plotted to kill his brother. Rebekah urged Jacob to flee for his life to Paddan-Aram, her homeland, so that he might also acquire a wife from among their kin.

28:10-22
God's Faithfulness to the Promises

God's watchcare became apparent at Bethel, where Jacob encountered Yahweh in a dream (28:10-12). He revealed Himself to Jacob as the God of his fathers, the one who would continue the covenant promises through him (28:13-14).

29:1–31:55
The Struggle Continues

Thus encouraged, Jacob went on to Haran, where he struggled with his uncle Laban for the right to marry his daughters Leah and Rachel (29:1-30). God's promise of many offspring began to be realized as Jacob fathered eleven sons and a daughter in his wives' struggle for children (29:31–30:24). In his struggle against scheming uncle Laban, Jacob became prosperous beyond his wildest expectations (30:25-43). By stealing the household gods, Rachel joined Jacob in the struggle against Laban (31:17-35). With Laban intent on revenge, only God's intervention in a dream brought a peaceful end to the struggle with Jacob (31:36-55).

Jacob wrestling with the angel

32:1–33:17
The Return to the Promised Land

Finally, after twenty years Jacob returned to his homeland. On the way he learned that Esau was coming to meet him (32:3-8). Fearing that his own efforts to safeguard himself from Esau's revenge were inadequate, Jacob entreated the Lord to deliver him (32:9-21). The Lord again appeared to Jacob, this time as a human foe, and wrestled with the patriarch through the night (32:22-32). Impressed with his persistent struggle, the "man" blessed Jacob with a change of name (*Jacob* to *Israel, prince of God*). The deceiver (Hebrew *ya akob*) had become a nobleman, one fit to rule through the authority of the sovereign God. The subsequent encounter with Esau proved to be peaceful (33:1-17). Indeed, Jacob saw in Esau's forgiveness a reflection of God's face.

33:18–34:31
The Threat of Assimilation

Jacob moved on into Canaan, coming first to Shechem, the first stopping place of his grandfather Abraham (33:18-20; see 12:6). Having secured property there, Jacob built an altar.

The rape of Dinah graphically illustrates the loose morals of the native Canaanites (34:1-7). Shechem's proposal of marriage illustrates the threat of intermarriage (34:8-24). The slaughter of the men of Shechem (34:25-31) anticipates Israel's conquest of the land under Joshua.

35:1–36:43
Reaffirming the Promises

Jacob traveled on to Bethel, again in the footsteps of Abraham (35:1-7; see 12:8). There, as he had before, Jacob saw the Lord in a vision and received yet another promise of the divine presence and blessing (35:9-12). He would father nations and kings and would inherit the land of his fathers. The list of his immediate descendants (35:23-26) attests to the onset of promise fulfillment. Even Esau, who had to settle for a secondary blessing (27:39-40), gave rise to a mighty people (Gen 36).

Joseph identifying himself to his brothers

DELIVERANCE THROUGH JOSEPH (GEN 37:1–50:26)

Israel's role as the people of promise was being jeopardized by their acceptance of the loose moral standards of the native Canaanites. The incest between Reuben and his father's servant-wife (35:22) hints at that moral compromise. Judah's marriage to the Canaanite Shua and his later affair with his own daughter-in-law, Tamar, makes the danger clear. To preserve His people, Yahweh removed them from that sinful environment to Egypt, where they could mature into the covenant nation that He was preparing them to be.

This explains the Joseph story. His brothers sold him to Egypt to be rid of their brother the dreamer. God, however, used their act of hate as an opportunity to save Israel from both physical famine and spiritual extinction. The rise of Joseph to a position of authority in Egypt in fulfillment of his God-given dreams illustrates the Lord's blessing upon His people. Joseph's wisdom in administering the agricultural affairs of Egypt again fulfilled God's promise that "I will bless him who blesses you." What appeared to be a series of blunders and injustices in Joseph's early experiences proved to be God at work in unseen ways to demonstrate His sovereign, kingdom work among the nations.

No one was more aware of this than Joseph, at least in later years. After he had revealed himself to his brothers, he said, "God sent me ahead of you to preserve for you a remnant on earth and to save your lives by a great deliverance" (45:7). Years later after Jacob's death, when Joseph's brothers feared his revenge, he reminded them that they had intended to harm him, "but God intended it for good to accomplish . . . the saving of many lives" (50:20). Human tragedy had become the occasion of divine triumph. Joseph's dying wish—to be buried in the land of promise—looks past the future tragedy of Israel's experience of slavery and anticipates God's triumph in the exodus (50:22-26).

Contemporary Significance

One obvious contribution of the Book of Genesis to the modern world is its explanation of the origins of things that could be understood in no other way. That is, it has scientific and historical value even if that is not its primary purpose.

More fundamentally, Genesis deals with the essence

of what it means to be human beings created as the image of God. Who are we? Why are we? What are we to do? Failure to appreciate God's purpose for humanity has resulted in chaotic, purposeless thought and action. Ultimately, life without true knowledge of human nature as the image of God and human function as stewards of God's creation is life without a sense of meaning. When one lives out life in light of Genesis, life is seen as being in touch and in tune with the God of the universe. God's rule becomes a reality as human beings conform to His goals for His creation. Genesis outlines the Creator's intentions.

As sinners we are unable to realize God's purpose for our lives through our own efforts. Only God's intervention brings promise to our lives. Our salvation is God's work.

Ethical Value

The awful effect of sin is one of the striking themes of Genesis. Sin frustrated the purposes of God for the human race. Sin had to be addressed before those purposes could be realized. Genesis teaches the heinousness and seriousness of sin and its tragic repercussions.

In addition to the story of "the fall," narrative after narrative in Genesis shows people how to live victoriously in the face of anti-God elements at work in this fallen world and describes what happens when they fail to do so. Cain, through lack of faith, dishonored God and then killed his brother. Lamech, in boasting pride, revealed the absurdities of humanistic views of life. The intermingling of angelic and human societies shows the inevitable result of breaking the bonds of God-ordained positions in life. The pride of the Babel tower builders demonstrates the arrogance of people who seek to make a name for themselves rather than to honor the name of the Lord.

The models of faith and obedience—Abel, Enoch, Noah, Abraham, and Joseph—are instructive as well. Their commitment to righteousness and the integrity of life-style speak eloquently of what it means to be a kingdom citizen, faithfully at work discharging the high and holy elements of that call.

Questions for Reflection

1. How does the meaning of the name *Genesis* relate to the contents of the book?
2. Why did God create humankind?
3. What does Genesis teach about the consequences of sin? Does human sin thwart God's ultimate purpose for humanity?
4. What were God's goals in calling Abraham?
5. What events seemed to threaten the fulfillment of God's promises to Abraham? How did God overcome these obstacles?
6. What was Isaac's role in the story of Genesis?
7. Why can the story of Jacob be called "the struggle for God's promises"?
8. How does the story of Joseph inspire hope at times when God seems to have forgotten you?
9. How did Joseph help realize God's promises
   (a) to make Abraham a blessing to the nations?
   (b) to make Abraham the father of a multitude?
10. How do Christians participate in realizing God's promises to Abraham?

Sources for Additional Study

Butler, Trent C. "Genesis." *Holman Bible Dictionary.* Nashville: Holman, 1991.

Coats, George W. *Genesis, with an Introduction to Narrative Literature. Forms of Old Testament Literature,* vol. 1. Ed. R. Knierim and G. Tucker. Grand Rapids: Eerdmans, 1983.

Francisco, Clyde T. "Genesis." *The Broadman Bible Commentary,* vol. 1, rev. Nashville: Broadman, 1973.

Garrett, Duane. *Rethinking Genesis.* Grand Rapids: Baker, 1991.

Kidner, Derek. *Genesis: An Introduction and Commentary.* London: Tyndale, 1967.

Kikawada, I. M., and Arthur Quinn, *Before Abraham Was.* Nashville: Abingdon, 1985.

Leupold, H. C. *Exposition of Genesis.* 2 vols. Grand Rapids: Baker, 1942.

Ross, Allen P. *Creation and Blessing.* Grand Rapids: Baker, 1988.

EXODUS

Exodus, meaning *way out,* was the title the early Greek translation, the Septuagint, gave to the second book of the Torah (compare Exod 19:1).

Some interpreters understand statements within Exodus (17:14; 24:4; 34:27) to mean that Moses is the author of the final form of the book. Other scholars take such statements to mean that Moses wrote only specific portions of Exodus, such as the account of the defeat of the Amalekites (17:8-13), the "Book of the Covenant" (chaps. 21–23), and the instructions in Exodus 34:10-26. Only the most radical critics have denied Moses any link with the materials in Exodus. (See "Literary Forms"; also see the feature article "Critical Methods and the Old Testament.")

Interpreters who accept the traditional authorship of Exodus hold that Moses put it in its present form as early as the sojourn at Sinai (about 1444 B.C.) or as late as the encampment on the plains of Moab just before his death (about 1406 B.C.). Except for Exodus 1:1–2:10, Moses was eyewitness to virtually all the incidents of the book. The early section could certainly have come to him by means of either written or oral sources. The remainder of the book gives every evidence of having been composed as a journal, recorded as the various episodes themselves transpired. *Author* then designates Moses as the final editor of a collection of memoirs. Other interpreters view the Book of Exodus as the product of the inspired reflection of many generations of God's people who worked to discern the meaning of the exodus event for worship and practice.

Theme

Deciding on a single theme that unifies all the varied materials of Exodus is difficult. One approach views the Sinai meeting where the redeemed nation encountered Yahweh and agreed to enter into covenant with Him as the theological center. The persecution of Israel in Egypt; the birth of Moses, his exile to Midian, and his return to Egypt as Israel's leader; the plagues upon Egypt; and the mighty exodus event itself—these all lead up to the climax of covenant commitment. Likewise, everything after that—the establishment of methods of worship, priesthood, and tabernacle—flow from the covenant and allow it to be put into practice.

A second approach views the presence of Yahweh with and in the midst of Israel as central. Yahweh's saving presence with Israel results in its deliverance from Egyptian slavery (Exod 1–15). Yahweh's continuing presence with Israel calls for obedience to covenant commitments and for worship (Exod 16–40).

A third approach views the lordship of Yahweh as the central theological theme. In Exodus God is revealed as Lord of history (1:1–7:7), Lord of nature (7:8–18:27), Lord of the covenant people Israel (19:1–24:14), and Lord of worship (25:1–40:38).

Literary Forms

Exodus includes various literary types and genres including poetry, covenant texts, and legal materials. It is not possible here to examine the entire book and identify the rich variety of literary expression, so a few passages will have to suffice.

One of the great poems of the OT is "The Song of the Sea" (Exod 15:1-18,21). This piece celebrates Israel's exodus deliverance from Egypt through the Red Sea (15:1a). The poem mixes the traits of a hymn of praise, a coronation song, a litany, and a victory psalm. Its mixed form suggests that it is multipurposed.

The presence in the song of certain themes and terms characteristic of Mesopotamian and Canaanite myths neither suggests that the song is only a myth nor even patterned after a myth. It is merely employing the vivid images and style of mythical poetry in order to communicate the awesome majesty of Yahweh and His dominion over His foes. On the other hand, the parallels between it and Ugaritic epic poetry of the Late Bronze Age (about 1500–1200) lend credence to its great antiquity and Mosaic composition.

Even greater benefit has come from the discovery that parts of Exodus, specifically 20:1–23:33, resemble in both form and content certain covenant texts and law codes from the ancient Near East. Scholars have observed striking parallels between ancient Hittite texts and covenant and law texts of the OT. One result is that these Exodus passages at least are now thought by many scholars to be much earlier than some had generally held.

According to some scholars Exodus 20–23 follows the pattern of a sovereign-vassal treaty in which a great king such as the Hittite king initiated a contract with a defeated or less powerful king. Such a treaty made certain demands on the weaker king (now a vassal or agent of the Hittites) and pledged certain commitments on the part of the Hittite king. Hittite treaty texts invariably contain certain clauses in a generally unalterable order.

The covenant text of Exodus 20–23, like Hittite treaties, contains both basic and specific stipulations. The Ten Commandments (20:1-17) make up the so-called "basic stipulation" section of the covenant text. They lay down fundamental principles of behavior without reference to motive or results.

The second main section, Exodus 21:1–23:19, is otherwise described as the "specific stipulations." Its purpose is to elaborate on the principles established in the Ten Commandments and to address particular concerns faced by the community. The first subdivision of this portion (21:1–22:17) consists of case law. There the statutes read, "If one does thus and so . . . then here is the penalty." The second subdivision (22:18–23:19) is mainly moral absolutes—"Thou shalt not" or "If you do thus and so . . . you shall not do thus and so." (See the feature article on Near Eastern treaties.)

The important theological insight gained by recognizing that Exodus 20–23 is covenant in nature and not just law does not finally depend on comparison with ancient Near Eastern treaties. Exodus "sandwiches" legal material (Exod 20–23) between narratives that anticipate (Exod 19) and relate Israel's commitment to the covenant (Exod 24). This "sandwich" structure suggests the legal portions find their rightful place in the context of the covenant. In other words, Exodus is not an "abstract" legal treatise. Rather, Exodus is law born in the "concrete" situation of Yahweh's covenant commitment to the nation Israel, whom He has freed from Egyptian slavery.

Literary Structure

Discovering the literary structure of Exodus is a difficult task. Some interpreters discern a geographic outline.

- Israel in Egypt (1:1–13:16)
- Israel in the Wilderness (13:17–18:27)
- Israel at Sinai (19:1–40:38).

Others focus on content in outlining Exodus:

- Deliverance from Egypt and Journey to Sinai (1:1-18:27)
- Covenant at Sinai (19:1-24:18)
- Instructions for Tabernacle and Worship (25:1-31:18)
- Breach and Renewal of Covenant (32:1–34:35)
- Building the Tabernacle (35:1-40:38)

Still other interpreters focus on a central theological theme. For example, Exodus can be divided into two parts focusing on the *physical* (1:1–15:27) and *spiritual* birth (16:1–40:38) of the nation Israel. The outline that follows takes the presence of Yahweh as the central theme of Exodus.

I. God's Saving Presence: Liberation from Egyptian Slavery (1:1–13:16)
II. God's Guiding, Providing Presence: The Journey to Sinai (13:17–18:27)
III. God's Demanding Presence: Sinai Covenant (19:1–24:18)
IV God's Worshipful Presence: Rules for the Tabernacle and Priests (25:1–31:18)
V. God's Disciplining, Forgiving Presence with a Disobedient People (32:1–34:35)
VI. God's Abiding Presence with an Obedient, Worshiping Community (35:1–40:38)

Purpose and Theology

The Book of Exodus is the story of two covenant partners—God and Israel. Exodus sets forth in narrative form how Israel became the people of Yahweh and lays out the covenant terms by which the nation was to live as God's people.

Exodus defines the character of the faithful, mighty, saving, holy God who established a covenant with Israel. God's character is revealed both through God's name and God's acts. The most important of God's names is the covenant name Yahweh. Yahweh designates God as the "I AM" who is there for His people and acts on their behalf. (See the feature article "Names of God" and the commentary on Exod 3.) Another important name, "the God of Abraham, the God of Isaac and the God of Jacob" (3:6,15-16), pictures God as the One who is true to His promises to the patriarchs.

Exodus also reveals God's character through His acts. God preserved Israel from famine by sending Joseph to Egypt (1:1-7). Pharaohs come and go (1:8); God, however, remains the same and preserves His people through the oppression of slavery (1:8–2:10). Israel's God rescues and saves (6:6; 14:30), guides and provides (15:13,25; 16:4,8), disciplines and forgives (32:1–34:35).

Exodus also defines the character of God's people. Lines of connection to Genesis, especially to the narratives of the patriarchs, demonstrate that the purposes of the Lord for Israel rested on the promises to the fathers. Exodus also looks to the future, to the land of promise, for the land was indispensable to Israel's full nationhood. Exodus stands then at a crossroads between the promises of the past and their culmination in the future.

A theological high point in Exodus appears in 19:4-6, which outlines Israel's true nature and role within God's plan. Yahweh had judged the Egyptians, had delivered His own people "on eagles' wings," and had brought them to Himself at Sinai. There the Lord offered Israel a covenant. If it was accepted and lived out, the covenant would result in Israel's being God's "treasured possession," a chosen "kingdom of priests," and a "holy nation." The people accepted these terms and pledged, "We will do everything the LORD has said" (19:8).

For Israel to be a kingdom of priests implied that God's people functioned as mediators and intercessors, for that is at the heart of the priestly function. Israel was to bridge the gap between a holy God and an alienated world. In other words, Israel was made a servant people, a servant of Yahweh, whose task was to be the channel of reconciliation. This mission was already anticipated in the Abrahamic covenant where Abraham's offspring (Israel) was destined to become the means whereby all the nations of the earth would be blessed (Gen 12:1-3; 22:18; 26:4).

Israel's call to covenant was founded not on its merit but on God's free choice: "I carried you on eagles' wings and brought you to myself" (Exod 19:4). The covenant then did not make Israel the people of Yahweh. They were the people of Yahweh by descent from Abraham, Isaac, and Jacob, the recipients of God's promises. Even the exodus, therefore, did not create the people of God. It rescued Yahweh's enslaved people, forged them into a nation, and brought them to the historical and theological position where they could willingly accept (or reject) the responsibility of becoming God's instrument for blessing all nations (compare Ps 114:1-2).

In other words, the offer of covenant entailed function only. It did not make Israel Yahweh's people, for that relationship had long since been established and recognized (compare Exod 3:7; 4:22-23; 5:1). What the Sinai covenant did was to define the task of the people of Yahweh.

In conclusion, the theology of Exodus is rooted in servanthood. It centers in the truth that a chosen people, delivered from bondage to a hostile power by the power of Yahweh, were brought to a point of decision. What would they do with God's offer to make them the servant people long before promised to Abraham? Their willing acceptance of this generous offer then obligated them to its conditions, conditions spelled out in the Book of the Covenant (Exod 20:1–23:33) and the remainder of the Book of Exodus.

Moses breaking the tablets of the law

GOD'S SAVING PRESENCE: LIBERATION FROM EGYPTIAN SLAVERY (EXOD 1:1–13:16)

1:1-22
God's Presence with His Oppressed People

The Exodus story begins by recalling the Genesis account of the descent of Jacob and his sons to Egypt and their sojourn there until after Joseph's death (Gen 46–50). The Genesis link reminds readers that God sent Israel into Egypt to deliver them from famine. Their prosperity and success in their new land show that Israel was the recipient of God's blessings on creation and to Abraham (Exod 1:1-7).

Egyptian hospitality did not long outlive Joseph, however, and within a generation or two before Moses' birth had changed to bitter hostility and oppression. Israel was put under forced labor and eventually subjected to the slaughter of their male newborns (1:8-22). Even in the years of oppression God was with Israel and caused them to prosper (1:12,20). The Lord had revealed to Abraham that his offspring would suffer oppression but that their bondage would be lifted by a great redemptive act. The Egyptians would be judged and the slave people set free to return to their own land (Gen 15:13-16). Israel's experience of slavery was not a disaster that proved its God to be irrelevant; it was but part of the redemptive plan of the Lord of history. In contrast to the Lord of history stand the pharaohs who came and went (1:8; 2:23) and trembled with fear (1:9-10).

2:1-22
God's Presence with Young Moses

God's saving presence is clear in the early life of Moses, the human agent of God's deliverance. Moses' Levite parents saved him from a cruel death by hiding him in a basket in the Nile (2:1-10). Rescued by Pharaoh's daughter, Moses was reared by his mother, who introduced him to the God of Israel. Though Moses later enjoyed the privileges of the Egyptian royal court, he never forgot his Israelite heritage. When he saw a fellow Hebrew being abused, he came to his rescue, slaying the offending Egyptian official in the process (2:11-14). This rash, though heroic, act forced Moses into exile in Midian. There Moses came to the rescue of the daughters of Reuel (Jethro), a Midianite priest. Moses married Zipporah, one of the shepherd daughters (2:15-22).

2:23–4:17
God Reveals His Presence to Moses

The death of the former king of Egypt paved the way for

NAMES OF GOD

NAME	REFERENCE	MEANING	NIV EQUIVALENT
HEBREW NAMES			
Adonai	Ps 2:4	Lord, Master	Lord
El -Berith	Judg 9:46	God of the Covenant	El -Berith
El Elyon	Gen 14:18-20	Most High God/ Exalted One	God Most High
El Olam	Gen 21:33	The Eternal God	The Eternal God
El Shaddai	Gen 17:1-2	All Powerful God	God Almighty
Qedosh Yisra'el	Isa 1:4	The Holy One of Israel	The Holy One of Israel
Shapat	Gen 18:25	Judge/Ruler	Judge
Yahweh-jereh	Gen 22:14	Yahweh Provides	The LORD Will Provide
Yahweh-seba'ot	1 Sam 1:3	Yahweh of Armies	LORD Almighty
Yahweh-shalom	Judg 6:24	Yahweh Is Peace	The LORD Is Peace
Yahweh-tsidkenu	Jer 23:6	Yahweh Our Righteousness	The LORD Our Righteousness
ARAMAIC NAMES			
Attiq yomin	Dan 7:9	Ancient of Days	Ancient of Days
Illaya	Dan 7:25	Most High	Most High

Moses to return to lead his people to freedom (2:23-25). But first the ever-living God had to reveal Himself to Moses in a convincing display of His power and purposes. God did this at Mount Horeb (Sinai) in the burning bush that was not consumed (3:1-12). In this marvelous appearance the Lord identified Himself as the God of the ancestors of Israel, the One who was aware of His people's suffering and was coming now to fulfill His pledge of deliverance and land. Though he knew of the God of his fathers and of the ancient covenant promises, Moses needed to know precisely how his God would identify Himself to His people. The answer was as Yahweh, the "I AM," who by that name would redeem them and live among them (3:13-22). (See the feature article "Names of God.")

Moses felt inadequate for the task God gave him. What was crucial was not Moses' "Who am I?" but God's "I will be with you" (3:11-12). Moses doubted that the people would accept his leadership or believe his report about the burning bush experience. Therefore Yahweh gave Moses some tangible evidence of His presence and blessing, turning Moses' shepherd's staff into a serpent and causing his hand to become leprous (4:1-9). Still not confident of success, Moses argued that he was not articulate. To still his objections once more, Yahweh promised to make his brother Aaron his spokesman. Indeed, God had already sent Aaron on his way (4:10-17).

4:18–13:16
God's Presence with Moses in Egypt

Moses at last yielded to God and made his way back to Egypt with this message for Pharaoh: "Israel is my firstborn son . . . Let my son go, so he may worship me" (4:22-23). Along the way Yahweh met Moses and threatened to kill him because he who was about to lead the circumcised people of Israel had failed to circumcise even his own son. Only the quick intervention of Zipporah saved him, for she hastily circumcised her son in obedience to the covenant requirements (4:18-26).

MOSES

Moses was the great leader, lawgiver, prophet, and judge of Israel. God raised up Moses to lead the nation out of Egyptian bondage into the land promised centuries earlier to Abraham. Moses also was to be the mediator of God's law to His people. His story is told in the Books of Exodus, Numbers, and Deuteronomy; and he is perhaps the most significant human in the OT.

Moses' life was providentially spared as an infant. He spent his first forty years in the courts of the Pharaoh's daughter, where he undoubtedly learned many administrative, literary, and legal skills that would serve him in good stead in his years as Israel's leader and lawgiver.

Moses probably lived early in the New Kingdom era (about 1550–1200 B.C.). This time was the cultural and military peak of Egypt's three-thousand-year history. Moses lived within one hundred years of King Tutankhamen (about 1347–1338 B.C.), the boy-king whose undisturbed tomb was discovered in 1922. The magnificent objects found in that tomb are typical of the art, wealth, and workmanship amid which the young Moses lived and which was later represented in much of the artistry of the tabernacle.

As an adult, Moses was forced to flee to the Midianite wilderness in the Sinai desert. There he met his wife and spent the next forty years. There he learned practical skills that would help him in leading Israel through the wilderness. During this time, he received God's call at Mount Sinai to lead Israel out of Egypt. He also received the revelation of God's covenant name, *Yahweh.* Moses was a reluctant leader, but he obeyed. He confronted the Pharaoh repeatedly until he let Israel go.

Moses' tenure as Israel's leader lasted another forty years. They were years filled with God's impressive miracles through Moses, such as the parting of the Red (Hebrew "Reed") Sea, repeated provision of food and water, and deliverance from enemies. The high point was the year spent at Mount Sinai in the southern Sinai Peninsula during which Moses communed closely with his God and received the Ten Commandments and the rest of the law to deliver to Israel.

Moses was barred from entering the promised land of Canaan because of his sin at Meribah, so he was able only to view it before he died.

Despite this, the universal testimony of the Scriptures is that Moses held an unrivaled place in all of Israel's history. Theologically, the exodus out of Egypt that he helped to effect and the law that he delivered to Israel are twin towers to which the Scriptures refer again and again as key factors in God's dealings with humanity. Personally, we are instructed by Moses' humility and by his life of submission to God's will. His example of obedient faith and his roles as deliverer, lawgiver, author, prophet, and even judge all place him in the first rank of Israel's heroes. □

Names of God

The names the OT uses for God speak of His rule (God, Lord), His perfections (the Holy One of Israel), and His involvement in human affairs (I Am or I Cause to Happen).

Elohim

Elohim, the usual designation for God, is the Creator, the God of all gods, the transcendent One (Gen 1:1–2:3).

El

El was known to the Canaanites as the chief of their many gods. The Hebrews freely spoke of their God by the name *El.*

El is generally used in compound names. Examples are *El Elyon* (*God Most High,* Gen 14:18-22) and *El Shaddai* (*God Almighty*, Gen 17:1). *El* is frequently compounded with a noun or verb to form personal or place names such as Elimelech (*My God is king*), Eliezer (*God of help*), and Elijah (*My God is Yahweh*).

El also occurs in some of Scripture's oldest confessional phrases. Examples are "jealous God" (Exod 20:5), "God brought them out of Egypt" (Num 24:8), "great and awesome God" (Deut 7:21; Neh 1:5), "great and powerful God" (Jer 32:18). *El* is common in Job (forty-eight times) and in Psalms (sixty-nine times).

Adonai

Adonai (*Lord*) is a special form of the common word *adon,* meaning *lord. Adonai* is used only in reference to the one true God, never to refer to humans or other gods. It signifies the exalted being of God, who alone is Lord of lords (Deut 10:17). He is "the Sovereign" of Israel (Exod 34:23). *Adonai* also occurs in compounds such as Adonijah (*Yahweh is my Lord,* 1 Kgs 1:8).

Yahweh

Yahweh, meaning *I Am,* is a shortened form of God's response to Moses' request for the name of the patriarchs' God (Exod 3:13-14). The full name identifies God as the Living God (*I Am Who I Am*) or as the God who acts in creation and redemptive history (*I Cause to Be What Is*). Out of extreme reverence for Yahweh's name (Exod 20:7), the Jews read Adonai (or Elohim) wherever the Hebrew text had YHWH. English Bibles likewise represent the four consonants YHWH by "LORD" or "GOD" in large and small caps.

Yahweh revealed His name in the context of redemption of Israel from Egyptian slavery. With the name came the assurance that Yahweh would fulfill all His promises (Exod 3:15; 6:2-8). The Lord's name is the concrete confirmation that God who "is" will "make things happen" and fulfill His promises.

Yahweh's name is thus associated with God's faithfulness, by which He binds Himself to His covenant promises. In the familiar words of Psalm 23:1, the Hebrew reads, "Yahweh is my shepherd." A reader of the English Bible can enter more deeply into the spirit of closeness and personal fellowship that existed between Yahweh and His ancient covenant people by substituting the name Yahweh for "the LORD." In Jesus' use of "I am" (*ego eimi*), He claimed to be Yahweh in the flesh (John 8:58).

Shortened forms of Yahweh occur in phrases (Hallelujah, *praise Yahweh*) and in names (Jonathan, *Yahweh gives,* and Adonijah, *Yahweh is Lord*).

Other Names

In their adversity God's covenant people called on Him by the familial name "our Father" (Isa 63:16; 64:8). Jesus invites all who come to God through Him to call God "our Father" or "Abba" (Mark 14:36; Rom 8:15; Gal 4:6).

Other designations for God include "the Rock" (1 Sam 2:2; 2 Sam 22:47), "the Holy One of Israel" (Isa 1:4; 5:19; 43:3), "the LORD of Hosts" (Sabaoth, "Almighty," Ps 24:10; Zech 1:3-4), Shepherd (Isa 40:11; Jer 31:10; John 10:11-14), and King (Pss 5:2; 24:7,10).□

At the edge of the desert Moses met Aaron. Together they entered Egypt to confront the elders of Israel. After Moses had related all that God had said and done, the elders and the people heard with faith and bowed themselves before the Lord (4:27-31).

Pharaoh's question, "Who is the LORD, that I should obey him and let Israel go?" (5:2), sets the stage for the conflict that dominates the scene through Exodus 15. Before the drama of redemption was over, Pharaoh would "know the LORD" and would yield to His powerful saving presence. But for now Pharaoh intensified the Israelites' sufferings (5:1-21). This led a bitter Moses to accuse Yahweh (5:22–6:1).

Yahweh renewed His pledge to be with Israel in deliverance, a pledge grounded securely in His very covenant name Yahweh (6:2-9). God commanded Moses to go back to Pharaoh with the promise that the Egyptian monarch would know that there was a higher authority. Moses would seem like God Himself to Pharaoh, and Aaron would be his prophet. By His mighty acts of judgment, God would make Himself known to the Egyptians (6:28–7:7).

Again and again Moses and Aaron commanded Pharaoh to let God's people leave Egypt to worship. Despite the signs, wonders, and plagues that revealed the mighty presence of the Lord, the king of Egypt would not relent.

In round one of the conflict, the rod of Aaron became a serpent that swallowed those of the Egyptian magicians (7:8-13). Three plagues followed. The Nile was turned to blood (7:14-25), the land was filled with frogs (8:1-15), and Egypt was plagued by gnats (8:16-19). Pharaoh's own magicians could duplicate the first two feats, so he was not impressed. Pharaoh did however request that Moses and Aaron pray "to the LORD to take the frogs away" (8:8). Pharaoh was becoming acquainted with Yahweh, the God of Israel. The plague of gnats, the final plague of round one, exceeded the magical powers of the Egyptian magicians and led them to confess, "This is the finger of God" (8:19).

In round two of the conflict, the plague of flies (8:20-32) demonstrated that Yahweh was present in Egypt (8:22). In this plague, the grievous disease of the cattle (9:1-7), and the boils (9:8-12), God distinguished between the Egyptians who suffered God's judgment and the Israelites who experienced God's protection (8:23; 9:7,11).

Round three of the conflict likewise consists of three

The famous sphinx of Chephren (or Khafre) located with the three great pyramids at Giza, Egypt (near modern Cairo).

EGYPT

Ancient Egyptian history spanned an unbroken period of almost three thousand years, down to the time of the Roman conquest in 31 B.C. It spanned some thirty dynasties, each consisting of several generations of kings. Modern Egyptian people and culture trace direct influences from the ancient periods.

Egypt's history was played out on a long, narrow strip of fertile land following the Nile River, winding more than sixteen hundred miles through Egypt. The Upper Nile (southern part) flows in a narrow valley never more than about twelve miles wide. The Lower Nile (northern part) widens north of Memphis and Cairo into the Nile Delta, emptying into the Mediterranean Sea. The Nile flooded annually, providing irrigation for growing crops in the otherwise arid desert.

The time of the Old Kingdom (the Third through the Sixth Dynasties, about 2700–2200 B.C.) represented an early peak of prosperity and cultural achievement. The Great Pyramids were built during this time.

A second peak was reached during the Middle Kingdom (especially the Eleventh and Twelfth Dynasties, about 2000–1800 B.C.). During this time, Egypt expanded into Syria-Palestine and produced a golden age of classical literature, especially short stories. Following a period of domination by foreign (mostly Semitic) rulers called the "Hyksos" (about 1675–1550 B.C.), the New Kingdom arose. It represented the zenith of Egyptian culture and political power (especially the Eighteenth and Nineteenth Dynasties, about 1550–1200 B.C.).

At this time Egypt controlled territory stretching a thousand miles from the Euphrates River in the north to the fifth set of rapids on the Nile in the south. Egypt's greatest temples and its short-lived but much-celebrated experiment with monotheism under Pharaoh Amenophis IV (Akhenaten) come from this period. Much of its great literature also comes from this cosmopolitan age. Following this, a long period of decline and relative isolation set in. Egypt still ventured forth but was overshadowed by other powers, especially from Mesopotamia.

Israel had scattered contacts with Egypt throughout its history. The most significant contacts were early, the several hundred years between Abraham's and Moses' times (about 2100–1400 B.C.). (Most dates here are approximate, since dating schemes for Egypt vary widely—often by two or more centuries—as do those for early Israel. Synchronizing these for both nations poses even more difficulties.)

In patriarchal times Abraham spent time in Egypt due to a famine in Canaan (Gen 12:10-20). Joseph was sold into slavery by his brothers, ending up in Egypt. He rose to prominence there, possibly during the late Middle Kingdom, and helped Egypt and surrounding lands prepare for another famine (Gen 37–50). Many of the customs seen in the Joseph story reflect known Egyptian practices from the period in question.

Following the glory years under Joseph, Israel was subjected to Egyptian slavery for many years until God raised up Moses and delivered Israel (Exod 1–15). The great event of the exodus (about 1446 B.C.) is not mentioned in Egyptian records. This oversight is not surprising, since ancient Near Eastern chronicles tended to record political successes, not failures.

Egypt's religion was polytheistic. Its major national gods were Ra, the sun god; Osiris, the god of the dead; and Isis, Osiris's wife. Elaborate ritual systems built up around the cults of the dead associated with Osiris. Egyptians also worshiped numerous lesser gods, many of them associated with specific locales and households. In addition, Pharaoh was considered to be divine, in contrast to beliefs about kings in most of the ancient Near East. □

plagues. Before sending hail (9:13-35), the Lord asserted that He alone is the Lord of history. Yahweh had raised up Pharaoh for the express purpose of demonstrating His mighty power and proclaiming His holy name (9:16). Indeed, some of the officials of Pharaoh "feared the word of the LORD" (9:20), and Pharaoh confessed his sin (9:27). Moses' prayer to end the hail demonstrated "that the earth is the LORD's" (9:29). Pharaoh, however, again hardened his heart. Plagues of locusts (10:1-20) and thick darkness (10:21-29) followed to no avail.

The fourth and deciding round of the conflict consisted of but one final plague—the death of the firstborn of every family in Egypt. At last Pharaoh permitted Israel to leave Egypt with their flocks and herds (12:31-32). The structure of Exodus 11–13 underscores the abiding theological significance of this final plague. Here narrative language relating once-for-all saving events (11:1-10; 12:29-42; 13:17-22) alternates with instructional language applicable to the ongoing worship of Israel (12:1-28,43–13:16). The Passover celebration, the consecration of the firstborn, and the feast of unleavened bread serve as continuing reminders of what God did to redeem His people. The firstborn of all the families of Israel belonged to the Lord because He had spared them when He had decimated the families of Egypt (13:11-16).

GOD'S GUIDING, PROVIDING PRESENCE: JOURNEY TO SINAI (EXOD 13:17–18:27)

Exodus 1:1–13:16, which focuses on God's powerful, saving presence, builds steadily to its dramatic conclusion—the death of the firstborn of Egypt and Israel's exodus. Exodus 13:17–18:27 likewise focuses on God's presence, which here guides, guards, and protects.

By means of the pillars of cloud and fire, the Lord guided Israel from Succoth to the wilderness of Etham, just

DATES OF THE EXODUS

The Book of Exodus does not give specific data that definitely links the biblical events with specific events or persons in Egypt. We are only told of "a new king" (Exod 1:8) "who did not know about Joseph," an anonymous "Pharaoh" (Exod 1:11,19,22; 2:15), and a "king of Egypt" (Exod 1:15; 2:23).

This much we do know: *Pharaoh,* meaning *great house* and designating the monarch's residence, was used as a title for the king himself for the first time in the Eighteenth Egyptian Dynasty. Also, the Pharaoh of the oppression died (Exod 2:23) and was not the Pharaoh of the exodus (Exod 4:19).

The two main views identify the Pharaoh of the exodus as a Pharaoh of (1) the Eighteenth Dynasty (1580–1321 B.C.) or (2) of the Nineteenth Dynasty (1321–1205 B.C.). The first is called the "early date," and the latter is called the "late date."

The early date of the fifteenth century has two main arguments in its favor. (1) The summarizing statement in 1 Kings 6:1 that there were 480 years from the exodus until the fourth year of Solomon (967 B.C.) yields a date of 1447 B.C. for the exodus (967 + 480 = 1447). (2) The supporting figure from Judges 11:26 comments that three hundred years had elapsed since Israel entered Canaan until the commencement of Judge Jephthah's rule (Jephthah is commonly placed around 1100 B.C. (1100 + 300 = 1400).

Both of these texts would set the exodus at 1446 B.C. and the conquest forty years later at 1410–1400 B.C. They would also make Thutmose III the pharaoh of the oppression (1490–1436 B.C., as dated by Albright, Wright, and Pritchard, or 1504-1450 B.C. as dated by the revised *Cambridge Ancient History*). In this case, Amenhotep II would be the pharaoh of the exodus

Lately, many have pointed to one Greek manuscript that has 440 years instead of 480 or to the fact that 480 is a round number involving twelve generations of forty years each. The first variation is too insignificant to count. The second argument of round numbers fails because the priestly line in 1 Chronicles 6:33-37 actually yields eighteen generations, not the stylized twelve that many have assumed. Moreover, the numbers recorded in Judges do support the total given in Judges 11:26 (see chart).

It is important to note that the oppression by the Ammonites (Judg 10:8–12:14) and the oppression by the Philistines (Judg 13:1–16:31) occurred simultaneously, one on the east side of the Jordan and the other on the west. Thus the forty-seven years of the Ammonite oppression does not continue the chronology since it fits into the narrative of the Philistine oppression featured in the first Book of Samuel.

Even when the additional fifteen to twenty years for Israel's conquest and settling of land are allowed, we still come up with 480 years from the exodus to Solomon's fourth year (see chart).

Over against the early or fifteenth century date for the exodus stands the late or thirteenth century date. Most biblical scholars and archaeologists conclude that the Israelites entered Canaan around 1230–1220 B.C., ⇨

THE TEN PLAGUES OF EGYPT

PLAGUE	SCRIPTURE
1. WATER TO BLOOD—The waters of the Nile turned to blood.	Exod 7:14-25
2. FROGS—Frogs infested the land of Egypt.	Exod 8:1-15
3. GNATS (Mosquitoes)—Small stinging insects infested the land of Egypt.	Exod 8:16-19
4. FLIES—Swarms of flies, possibly a biting variety, infested the land of Egypt.	Exod 8:20-32
5. PLAGUE ON THE CATTLE—A serious disease, possibly anthrax, infested the cattle belonging to Egyptians.	Exod 9:1-7
6. BOILS—A skin disease infected the Egyptians.	Exod 9:8-12
7. HAIL—A storm that destroyed the grain fields of Egypt but spared the land of Goshen inhabited by the Israelites.	Exod 9:13-35
8. LOCUSTS—An infestation of locusts stripped the land of Egypt of plant life.	Exod 10:1-20
9. DARKNESS—A deep darkness covered the land of Egypt for three days.	Exod 10:21-29
10. DEATH OF THE FIRSTBORN—The firstborn of every Egyptian family died.	Exod 11:1–12:30

toward the end of the late Bronze Age (generally accepted date is 1550–1200 B.C.).

Four arguments are usually advanced to support this theory.

1. The two store-cities built by the Israelites in Egypt—Pithom and Rameses (Exod 1:11)—were built just before the exodus. Rameses is equated with Pi-Ramesse built by Pharaoh Ramses II, who ruled from 1240–1224 B.C. This would place the exodus in the thirteenth century.

2. The Transjordan, where Israel was said to have encountered several nations, was thought to be uninhabited from 1800–1300 B.C.

3. Archaeological evidence shows many destruction levels in the cities of Canaan west of the Jordan in the second half of the thirteenth century. Though the Scriptures record that Israel burned the cities of Jericho and Ai (Josh 6:24; 8:19-21), archaeologists have been unable to confirm that these sites were occupied in the Late Bronze Age, the era of the conquest.

4. The final argument for the late date notes that the capital of Egypt was moved north to Pi-Ramesse in the Nineteenth Dynasty (thirteenth century). The Eighteenth Dynasty of the fifteenth century had its capital in the south at Thebes.

Opponents of the late date have replies for the four previous arguments.

1. Exodus 1:7-14 seems to place the building of these cities as one of the first tasks Israel accomplished during its four centuries of bondage. Rameses is probably to be identified with Qantir. The use of the name Rameses may simply be a case of a modernization of a name much as modern historians might say that Julius Caesar crossed "the English Channel." Note that Genesis 47:11 referred to the area where Jacob's family settled in Egypt as "the district of Rameses." This certainly is a case of updating terms. Exodus 1:11 offers no definitive proof for a late date; archaeology offers no proof for equating Pi-Ramesse with biblical Rameses.

2. The conclusion that the Transjordan was unoccupied at the early date of the exodus was based solely on surface observation of these territories fifty years ago. Since that time excavations at Dibon have demonstrated thirteenth-century occupation. A tomb excavated in Heshbon has yielded a number of artifacts dating from 1600 B.C.

3. The alleged Israelite burning levels in such sites as Lachish, Bethel, and Debir were probably caused by later thirteenth century incursions by the Egyptians, but certainly by the invasion of the Sea Peoples in 1200 B.C.

4. Important inscriptions are now coming to light that indicate that the Eighteenth Dynasty did have a keen building interest in the delta region of Goshen where the Israelites resided. Some texts imply that these Eighteenth Dynasty pharaohs had a secondary or temporary residence in the delta region.

5. The strongest evidence for the early date continues to be 1 Kings 6:1 and Judges 11:26. Many, but not all, conservatives tend to favor the early date. Some archaeological evidence supports this date while other evidence tends to question this conclusion or is itself subject to interpretation and in need of further confirmation. □

Near Eastern Treaties

Ancient Near Eastern treaties are important because they shed light on pacts and treaties in the OT. They are especially important because they provide some background understanding of one of the most important of all biblical terms, *covenant.* (See "Covenants.")

Historical Discoveries

We knew almost nothing about ancient Near Eastern treaties until archaeological research began in the nineteenth century. Since then numerous examples of such pacts (covenants) have been discovered, made available to Bible scholars, and studied at length.

The most important of these were Hittite treaties from their ancient capital of Boghazkoy (in modern Turkey). These date from the late Bronze Age and early Iron Age (about 1400–1200 B.C.), in the early biblical period.

Treaty Forms

Hittite and other treaties took one of two forms: parity or suzerainty. A parity treaty was between equals. A suzerainty treaty was between a sovereign (suzerain) and a vassal (subject). It was drawn up by the superior power and imposed on the inferior. This latter type is the more important for biblical studies.

Both types of treaties contain certain clauses including a title identifying the chief partner, a historical prologue to show how past benefits from the chief partner should inspire the vassal to a grateful response, and a list of stipulations (obligations, laws). They also contain provision for the preservation of the document (usually by deposit in the vassal's chief shrine), the witnesses to the covenant (usually the gods of both parties), the blessings and curses that will result from keeping or breaking it, a prescribed regular public reading of it, and an oath ratifying the covenant in a solemn ceremony.

Even in the case of a suzerainty treaty, which was in effect imposed by the sovereign on the vassal, the superior power also bound himself by certain obligations to his vassal.

Application to Biblical Studies

The biblical covenant form shows remarkable resemblance to the Hittite treaty form. Scholars have found similarity of approach and even of outline between the Hittite form and the book of the covenant (the covenant code) of Exodus 20–23, the entire Book of Deuteronomy, and Joshua 24. Deuteronomy is almost entirely covenantal in its form and content, as are other parts of the OT. (Some suggest analyzing the entire Bible according to this pattern.)

Moses seems to have been making use of the treaty format that was already in common use in the world of his day as he expressed the covenant relationship between the Lord and His people.

The slaughter of an animal at the ratification of a treaty implies that the one who violated the treaty could expect a similar fate as a consequence. There was probably also a sense of the binding together of the two contracting parties through the animal sacrifice and perhaps through the sprinkling of its blood on the participants or their representatives.

The covenants of Scripture were not isolated or unrelated to what was going on in the world of that day. The Lord chose to make use of a common, well-known covenant approach. As they did with so many other things, the biblical writers took over patterns they already found in the world around them and redeemed ("baptized") them to the glory of God.

The Lord chose to reveal Himself to His people not in a vacuum but in a definite cultural setting. This is why it is so important to know the world of that day, its circumstances, its customs, and its patterns of thought as we try to better understand Scripture. □

west of the Red (or Reed) Sea (13:17-22). There they appeared to be boxed in by the sea to the east, the deserts to the north and south, and the advancing Egyptian armies to the west. Once more the Lord hardened the heart of Pharaoh so that through his defeat Egypt would know that Yahweh is God (14:1-18). For a tense night the presence of the Lord guarded Israel from the armies of Egypt (14:19-20). Then Yahweh, in the most marvelous redemptive act of Old Testament times, opened up the sea so His people could go safely through while their enemies perished (14:21-31). For generations thereafter Israel commemorated its salvation by singing the triumphant songs of Moses and Miriam, hymns that praised Yahweh as the Sovereign and Savior (Exod 15:1-21).

The journey from the Red Sea to Sinai was filled with miracles of provision of water (15:22-37), quails (16:1-20), manna (16:21-36), and water once more (17:1-7). All this occurred despite Israel's complaining insubordination. Hostile and savage desert tribes likewise fell before God's people as He led them triumphantly onward (17:8-16). When heavy administrative burdens threatened to overwhelm Moses, his father-in-law, Jethro, instructed Moses about how the task could be better distributed (18:1-27).

GOD'S DEMANDING PRESENCE:

THE TEN COMMANDMENTS

COMMANDMENT	PASSAGE	RELATED OLD TESTAMENT PASSAGES	RELATED NEW TESTAMENT PASSAGES	JESUS' TEACHINGS
You shall have no other gods before me	Exod 20:3; Deut 5:7	Exod 20:23; 34:14; Deut 6:4,13-14; 2 Kgs 17:35; Ps 81:9; Jer 25:6; 35:15	Acts 5:29	Matt 4:10; 6:33; 22:37-40
You shall not make for yourself an idol	Exod 20:4-6; Deut 5:8-10	Exod 32:8; 34:17; Lev 19:4; 26:1; Deut 4:15-20; 7:25; 32:21; Ps 115:4-7; Isa 44:12-20	Acts 17:29-31; 1 Cor 8:4-6, 10-14; Col 3:5; 1 John 5:21	Matt 6:24; Luke 16:13
You shall not misuse the name of the Lord	Exod 20:7; Deut 5:11	Exod 22:28; Lev 18:21; 19:12; 22:2; 24:16; Ezek 39:7	John 5:12	Matt 5:33-37; 6:9; 23:16-22
Remember the Sabbath day by keeping it holy	Exod 20:8-11; Deut 5:12-15	Gen 2:3; Exod 16:23-30; 31:13-16; 35:2-3; Lev 19:30; Isa 56:2; Jer 17:21-27	Heb 10:25	Matt 12:1-13; Mark 2:23-27; 3:1-6; Luke 6:1-11
Honor your father and your mother	Exod 20:12; Deut 5:16	Exod 21:17; Lev 19:3; Deut 21:18-21; 27:16; Prov 6:20	Eph 6:1-3; Col 3:20	Matt 15:4-6; 19:19; Mark 7:9-13; Luke 18:20
You shall not murder	Exod 20:13; Deut 5:17	Gen 9:6; Lev 24:17; Num 35:33; Exod 3:3	Rom 13:9-10; Jas 5:21	Matt 5:21-24; 19:18; Mark 10:19; Luke 18:20
You shall not commit adultery	Exod 20:14; Deut 5:18	Lev 18:20; 20:10; Deut 22:22; Num 5:12-31; Prov 6:29,32	Rom 13:9-10; 1 Cor 6:9; Heb 13:4; Jas 2:11	Matt 5:27-30; 19:18; Mark 10:19; Luke 18:20
You shall not steal	Exod 20:15; Deut 5:19	Lev 19:11,13; Exek 18:7	Rom 13:9-10; Eph 4:28	Matt 19:18; Mark 10:19; Luke 18:20
You shall not give false testimony	Exod 20:16; Deut 5:20	Exod 23:1, 7; Lev 19:11; Pss 15:2; 101:5; Prov 10:18; Jer 9:3-5; Zech 8:16	Eph 4:25,31; Col 3:9; Titus 3:2	Matt 5:37; 19:18; Mark 10:19; Luke 18:20
You shall not covet	Exod 20:17; Deut 5:21	Deut 7:25; Job 31:24-28; Ps 62:10	Rom 7:7; 13:9; Eph 5:3-5; Heb 13:5; Jas 4:1-2	Luke 12:15-34

SINAI COVENANT (EXOD 19:1–24:18)

Again and again in the account of the plagues, Moses delivered God's message to Pharaoh: "Let my people go, so that they may worship [or serve] me." At last the moment of worship and service arrived which the exodus deliverance had made possible. At Sinai Israel was to commit itself to God in covenant. Yahweh based His call to covenant commitment on His mighty acts of deliverance (19:4). Only through obedience to God's covenant could Israel fill its role as "a kingdom of priests and a holy nation" (19:5-6).

Unanimously they agreed to its terms, so Moses prepared to ascend Mount Sinai to solemnize the arrangement (19:7-15). As Moses was about to go up, Yahweh came down, visiting the mountain with the thunder and lightning of His glorious presence. Moses warned the people to respect the holy (and potentially dangerous) presence of God on the mountain (19:16-25).

As suggested already, the Sinaitic (or Mosaic) covenant is in the form of a sovereign-vassal treaty text well attested from the ancient Near East. The treaty established the relationship between the King (God) and His servants (Israel). (See the article "Near Eastern Treaties.") Its first section is a preamble introducing the Covenant Maker, the Lord Himself (20:2a). Next a historical prologue outlines the past relationship of the partners and justifies the present covenant (20:2b). Then follows the division known as the general stipulations, in this case the Decalogue, or Ten Commandments (20:3-17). After a brief narrative interlude (20:18-22), the Book of the Covenant (20:23–23:33) gives the specific stipulations of the treaty.

Contracting parties often sealed their agreement with oaths and a ceremony that included a fellowship meal. The Sinaitic covenant also had its sacrifice, sealing of the oath by blood (24:1-8), and covenant meal (24:9-11). The covenant or treaty texts also had to be prepared in duplicate and preserved in a safe place for regular, periodic reading. Moses therefore brought down from the mountain the tablets of stone to be stored in the ark of the covenant (24:12-18; 25:16).

GOD'S WORSHIPFUL PRESENCE: RULES FOR THE TABERNACLE AND PRIESTS (EXOD 25:1–31:18)

Once Yahweh and His people Israel had concluded the covenant, arrangements had to be undertaken for the Great King to live and reign among them. Therefore elaborate instructions follow for the building of a tabernacle (or worship tent) and its furnishings (25:1–27:21; 30:1–31:18) and for the clothing and consecration of the priests (28:1–29:46). The priests, of course, functioned as the covenant mediators. They offered sacrifices on the nation's behalf and presented other forms of tribute to the Great God and King.

GOD'S DISCIPLINING, FORGIVING PRESENCE WITH A DISOBEDIENT PEOPLE (EXOD 32:1–34:35)

The covenant fellowship almost immediately fell on hard times, however. Even before Moses could descend from the mountain with the tables of stone and other covenant texts, the people, with Aaron's consent, violated the covenant terms by casting an idol of gold and bowing down to it. This act of apostasy brought God's judgment and even a threat of annihilation (32:1-29). (See the feature article "Apostasy.") Only Moses' intercession prevented the annulment of the covenant with the larger community (32:30-35).

The Lord was attentive to Moses' cry and did not utterly destroy the idolaters immediately (32:33-34). God did renew His promise to bring His people into the land of promise. Yahweh, however, declared that He could not go with Israel lest He destroy the stubborn, rebellious people (33:1-6). Two narratives stressing God's intimacy with Moses (33:7-11,18-23) only highlight the Holy One's separation from Israel more. God's people would never make it to the land of promise without God's presence. Twice Moses interceded with God on behalf of rebellious Israel (33:15-17; 34:9). Yahweh twice revealed Himself to Moses as a God of mercy and compassion (33:19; 34:6-7). God's mercy and compassion—not Israel's faithfulness—formed the basis for renewal of the broken covenant (34:1-28). Descending from the mountain with the tablets of the covenant, Moses appeared before his people, his face aglow with the reflection of the glory of God (34:29-35).

GOD'S ABIDING PRESENCE WITH AN OBEDIENT, WORSHIPING COMMUNITY (EXOD 35:1–40:38)

Exodus concludes with Israel's response to God's offer of forgiveness. Without delay the work of tabernacle construction was underway (35:1–40:33). When it was finally completed, all according to the explicit instruction of the Lord and through the wisdom of His Spirit, the building was filled with the awesome glory of God (40:34-38). By cloud and fire God revealed His presence among the people of Israel whether the tabernacle was at rest or in transit to its final earthly dwelling place in Canaan.

A view of the rugged mountainous terrain of the Sinai area taken from the top of Jebel Musa (the traditional Mount Sinai).

Contemporary Significance

The exodus deliverance is to the Old Testament what the death and resurrection of Christ are to the New Testament—the central, definitive act in which God intervenes to save His people. The Old Testament illustrates how God's acts of redemption call for a response from God's people. The proclamation of God's saving acts in the exodus was the central function of Israel's worship (compare Pss 78:11-55; 105:23-45; 106:7-33; 136:10-16). Christian worship focuses on God's saving act in Christ. (Compare the hymns in Phil 2:6-11 and Rev 5:12.) God's saving intervention in the exodus formed the basis both for the prophetic call to obedience (Hos 13:4) and the announcement of judgment on covenant breakers (Amos 2:10; 3:1-2; Hos 11:1-5; 12:9; Jer 2:5-9). Today God's saving act in Christ forms the basis for the call to live a Christlike life (Rom 6:1-14). God's saving acts in the past gave Israel hope that God would intervene to save in the future (Isa 11:16; Mic 7:15). Likewise, God's saving act in Christ is the basis for the Christian's hope (Rom 8:28-39).

The exodus deliverance, the Sinaitic covenant, the wilderness experience, and the promise of a land provide models of the Christian life. The believer, having already and unconditionally been adopted into the family of God, undertakes his or her own "exodus" from bondage to sin and evil to servanthood under the new covenant. Christians live out their kingdom pilgrimage in the wilderness of this world system, as it were, pressing toward and in anticipation of the eternal land of promise to come.

Ethical Value

God saved and made covenant with His ancient people Israel and demanded of them a life-style in keeping with that holy calling. He demands that same adherence to His unchanging standards of all who call themselves His people. The Ten Commandments are an expression of the very character of a holy, faithful, glorious, saving God. Even the "statutes" and "judgments" designed specifically for Old Testament Israel exemplify standards of holiness and integrity that are part and parcel of God's expectations for His people of all ages.

One can also learn a great deal about practical living and relationships by examining carefully the narrative sections. One must be impressed with the faith of godly parents who, in the face of persecution and peril, placed their son in the hands of Yahweh to wait to see how He would spare him. From his birth, then, Moses enjoyed the benefits of a wholesome spiritual environment in the home.

Clearly Moses himself inspires one to a life of dependence and yet dogged determination. Despite his slowness in responding to the call of the Lord in the wilderness, he went on in faith to challenge the political and military structures of the greatest nation on the earth. By the power of his God he overcame the insurmountable and witnessed miraculous intervention over and over again.

Many other examples could be cited, but these are enough to show that Exodus is timeless in its moral and ethical as well as theological relevance.

Questions for Reflection

1. What do you think is the central theme of Exodus?

2. What is a covenant? Why is the Sinai covenant important?

3. How is God's presence made known in Exodus? How does God demonstrate His lordship?

4. What does Exodus teach about the character of God? What is the significance of God's name (Yahweh)? What is the significance of God's mighty acts?

5. How is Exodus 20–23 similar to ancient treaties?

6. How does the history of God's dealings with Israel serve as a basis for the demands of the law?

7. What does Exodus teach about the character and responsibilities of God's people Israel? What are the implications for the church?

Sources for Additional Study

Cates, Robert L. *Exodus. Layman's Bible Book Commentary,* vol. 2. Nashville: Broadman, 1979.

Cole, R. Alan. *Exodus.* Downers Grove: InterVarsity, 1973.

Honeycutt, Roy Lee, Jr. "Exodus." *The Broadman Bible Commentary,* vol. 1, rev. Nashville: Broadman, 1973.

Youngblood, Ronald. *Exodus.* Chicago: Moody, 1983.

LEVITICUS

The name *Leviticus* comes from the ancient Greek translation, the Septuagint, which titled the composition *Leueitikon*, that is, *[The Book of the] Levites.* The Levites are not, however, the major characters of this book. The title rather points to the book as useful to the Levites in their ministry as worship leaders and teachers of morals.

The last verse of Leviticus sets the book in its scriptural context: "These are the commands the LORD gave Moses on Mount Sinai for the Israelites" (27:34). An expanded translation makes that context clearer: "These are the commands [covenant obligations] the LORD [Yahweh, the covenant God] gave Moses [the covenant mediator] on Mount Sinai [the covenant place] for Israel [the covenant people]."

First, Leviticus cannot be understood apart from God's purpose for His covenant people. In the account of Moses' struggle with Pharaoh in Exod 4–12, God repeatedly called for the freedom of Israel to worship Him (4:23; 7:16; 8:1; 9:1; 10:3; 12:31). In a real sense the exodus deliverance was incomplete until Israel began the worship of God at Sinai (Exod 3:12), thus fulfilling God's goal for the exodus. Israel was set free from Egyptian slavery and brought into a new, covenant relationship with God precisely so that they might be free to worship.

Second, Leviticus cannot be understood apart from God's desire to be with His covenant people. But because a Holy God cannot condone sin, Israel's experiment in idolatry with the golden calf (Exod 32) presented God with a dilemma. Twice God warned the Israelites: "You are a stiff-necked people. If I were to go with you even for a moment, I might destroy you" (Exod 33:5; also see 33:3). How could a holy God continue to go with a disobedient and rebellious people? Exodus 34–40 and the Book of Leviticus answer that question.

Theme

The overall burden of the Book of Leviticus was to communicate the awesome holiness of Israel's God and to outline the means by which the people could have access to Him. This is in line with the great central covenant theme of the Pentateuch, a theme that describes the relationship between the Lord and Israel as one of Great King and vassal (servant) people. Just as a servant had to follow proper protocol to approach the king, so Israel had to recognize its own unworthiness to enter the sacred precincts of God's dwelling place. The gulf between the people and their God could be bridged only by their confession of their unworthiness and their heartfelt adherence to the rites and ceremonies prescribed by Him as a precondition to fellowship.

Literary Forms

With the exception of a few narrative passages (Lev 8–10) and a blessing and curse section (Lev 26), Leviticus consists of legal material, particularly of a cultic (or ceremonial) nature. Much of this legal material is highly structured in an almost poetic form (Lev 1–7 and to a lesser extent Lev 11–15). The final part of Leviticus (chaps. 17–26) is a looser collection of legal material known as the "Holiness Code," an appropriate term given the prevailing notion of holiness there.

The legal form of most of Leviticus (prescriptions and statutes) suggests that it is part of a covenant text. In fact, it deals with the covenant requirements that regulate the means by which the nation and individual Israelites could enter into and maintain a proper relationship with the Lord God. In this sense Leviticus, like much of Exodus, is a body of covenant stipulations designed to help close the gap between God's holiness and humanity's sin.

I. The Need for Sacrifice (1:1–7:38)
II. The Need for Priestly Mediators (8:1–10:20)
III. The Need for Separation between the Clean and the Unclean (11:1–15:33)
IV. The Need for a Day of Atonement (16:1-34)
V. The Need for Holy Living (17:1–25:55)
VI. The Blessing and Curse (26:1-46)
VII. Offerings of Dedication (27:1-34)

Purpose and Theology

Israel was "a holy nation," that is, a nation set apart to be God's special people. As such, Israel was called on to accomplish a special mission for God on the earth by virtue of His saving act. (Compare Lev 22:32-33: "I am the LORD, who makes you holy and who brought you out of Egypt to be your God.") Having accepted this covenant role at Sinai, Israel became God's vassal, the mediator of His saving grace to all the nations of the earth. (See "Purpose and Theology" in the Exodus commentary.) Israel's inability to abide by the requirements of God's covenant, however, threatened its status as "a holy nation."

To be a holy nation Israel had to have a means whereby that holiness—or separatedness—could be maintained. Israel needed a set of guidelines stipulating every aspect of that relationship between the nation and its God. God's people had to learn the relationship of holiness as a position and holiness as a condition. As a position holiness means the setting apart of a person, object, or institution for the use of a god. It has no necessary ethical or moral corollary; Israel's pagan neighbors set apart "holy" prostitutes for the service of their gods. Israel set apart a holy place (the tabernacle), rituals (the sacrifices), persons (the priests), and times (the Sabbath, the feasts, the Sabbatical and Jubilee Years). Whatever has not been designated as holy is common or profane. As a condition holiness comes to embody moral purity and righteousness. God's own personal holiness entails not only His remoteness and uniqueness but also His moral perfection. Persons and things that He sanctifies and declares holy must also exhibit moral uprightness. The Holiness Code of Leviticus 17–25 stresses holiness as a moral condition.

Leviticus outlines how Israel could offer God appropriate homage to cultivate and maintain the relationship brought about by mutual commitment to covenant. Because Israel was unable to live up to its covenant commitments, they could not approach the holy God. Only God could provide a system to purify the sinful people and their worship place so that they could appear before and serve the Holy One. These sacrifices rendered a person righteous who by faith accepted the atoning benefits of the sacrifices. God also provided a system of offerings for a person to express proper understanding of and thanksgiving for the benefits of His grace. The holy people also had to be taught about and continually reminded of the strict lines that separate the holy from the profane by seeing examples of these differences in everyday life.

A thing was holy or unholy only as the sovereign God declared it to be such in line with His own inscrutable criteria and His own inherent holiness. In His sovereignty God listed unclean animals, separating them from the clean ones. He described certain diseases and certain fungi and other phenomena as unclean. Those who came in contact with the unclean became unclean as well. Even bodily secretions were unclean, their appearance being sufficient to mark the individual so affected as unholy.

The apparently arbitrary nature of the categories of clean and unclean makes it clear that holiness is essentially a matter of divine discretion. The sovereign God made these distinctions for educational purposes. Israel as a people separated from all other peoples had to learn from everyday and commonplace examples that God sits in sovereign judgment over all things. They had to learn that He alone reserves judgment about whether or not a person, object, or condition conforms to His definition of holiness. Only in this way could Israel understand what its own holiness was all about and how that holiness was essential if it were to live out the purposes for which it was elected and redeemed.

If Israel was called on to be holy, it was all the more necessary for the priests, who in a sense were the "mediators of the mediators," to be holy before God. The nation with its individuals had access to the Lord but in a limited way. Only through the priests was perfect access achieved. Clearly the priests had to measure up to unusual standards of holiness. Leviticus therefore addresses the matter of the consecration and instruction of the priests as well.

Finally, the sovereign God ordained not only principles of access by which His servant people might approach Him, but He also designated special times and places. Thus Leviticus, like Exodus, instructs the covenant community to meet the Lord as a community at the tabernacle, the central sanctuary that He invested with His glory as a visible sign of His habitation among them. He could not be approached randomly or whimsically. No king holds audience at the discretion of his subject. Rather, the king establishes regular times of assembly with his people when he receives their tribute and addresses their concerns. Likewise, the Lord revealed a calendar of ritual, a schedule according to which the community as such could (and should) appear before Him to praise Him and to seek His face on their behalf. Sabbaths, new moons, and festival days were therefore set aside for the regular encounter of the servant nation with its sovereign God. Times and places were not irrelevant, as Leviticus makes clear. In a covenant context they attested to the rule of the Lord among His people and to their need to come where and when He decreed for them to do so.

The Sacrificial System

A great deal can be learned about what a society values from what it expresses in rituals. The study of OT ritual, far from being boring and unintelligible, can unlock the fundamentals of biblical theology.

Meaning

To all who enter a relationship with God through faith, God gives commandments that the faithful follow in evidence of their faith (Deut 5:29; Rom 1:5; Heb 3:18-19; John 14:15). When believers express their faith in obedience, they experiences fullness of life (Lev 18:5; Deut 30:15-16; Ezek 20:10-12).

For the OT believer, God's commands were given in the law of Moses. These included instructions on how God was to be approached in rituals of worship and repentance. Ritual that does not arise from hearts committed to God is worthless (Prov 15:8; Isa 1:11-17; Hos 6:6; Amos 5:21-24). Israel tended to neglect justice, mercy, and faithfulness, "the weightier matters of the law" (Matt 23:23; compare Mic 6:6-8) and to be satisfied with ritual. Yet it is not true that authentic worship is found only in spontaneous acts and that formal, ritual acts necessarily represent sham or hypocrisy.

The sacrifices were a secondary though vital part of Israel's religion. Through them Israel expressed their faith and learned the nature of a holy God, sinful humanity, and the necessity of atonement. They also received forgiveness (Lev 1:4; 4:20,26,31,35; 5:10,16) based upon Christ's final sacrifice (Rom 3:25; Heb 9:9-10; 10:1-4).

The Offerings

The most common offering in Israel was the burnt offering (Lev 1). It was presented by the priests every morning and evening and more frequently on holy days. Its main distinction was that the animal was entirely consumed by the altar fire. In response to the faithful offering, God's anger would be turned; and the worshiper would be accepted, freed from punishment by payment of the ransom.

The priest was to eat a portion of the other offerings (joined by the worshiper with the fellowship offering, Lev 3). The sin or purification offering (Lev 4:1–5:13) served to purify the sanctuary so that God could continue to dwell with a sinful people. The guilt or reparation offering (5:14–6:7) accompanied compensation that was required in the case of certain sins. The fellowship or peace offerings (Lev 3) were unique in that these were optional, brought in response to an unexpected blessing (a "thank" offering), a general thankfulness (a "freewill" offering), or a prayed-for deliverance (a "vow" offering).

Finally, the grain offerings (Lev 2) accompanied the daily burnt offerings or were presented independently in thanks at harvest. □

THE NEED FOR SACRIFICE (LEV 1–7)

The first major section of Leviticus (chaps. 1–7) deals with the nature, purpose, and ritual of sacrifice. The summary statement that concludes this section (7:37-38) sets the entire sacrificial system in the context of God's covenant with Israel at Mount Sinai. God freed Israel from Egyptian slavery so that it would be free to worship. Leviticus 1–7 instructed Israel in how properly to worship God. God desires the fellowship of His people. The Israelites' rebellion, however, made continued relations a problem for a holy God. Leviticus 1–7 introduces those sacrifices that made possible renewed fellowship between God and His people. (See "Purpose and Theology.")

As an expression of tribute and devotion to the Lord, sacrifice had to be offered with a willing heart but also according to clearly articulated and well-understood prescriptions. Different kinds of offerings served a variety of purposes. Therefore an elaborate manual of procedure was necessary to show God's people how to approach the Lord God in an appropriate manner.

1:1-17
Burnt Offering

The burnt offering could consist of an animal of the herd (1:3) or flock (1:10) or even of a bird (1:14). "Burnt offering" (Hebrew *olah*) suggests that the victim was totally consumed on the altar; that is, everything was given to the Lord, and nothing remained for either the offerer or the priest. The purpose was to provide atonement for the offerer (1:4). By laying a hand on the head of the animal, the offerer was recognizing the substitutionary role of the victim. The animal was, in effect, paying the price of the offerer's sin. Whether bull, sheep, or dove, the animal's death became a "soothing aroma" (1:9,13,17) before God, a means of effecting a harmonious relationship between a person and God.

2:1-16
Grain Offering

The grain offering appears always to have followed the burnt offering (Num 28:1-8) and consisted of flour and oil (Lev 2:1-2). Though it too provided a "soothing aroma" (2:2,9,12), it was not totally consumed in fire but was shared with the priests (2:3). Thus its purpose was not so much to secure atonement. But as its name (*minhah*, that is, *gift*, *tribute*) and the use of salt (2:13) imply, it attested to the covenant relationship (re)established by atonement. That is, the grain offering was a harvest tribute paid to the sovereign Lord.

3:1-17
Peace Offering

The peace offering could be an animal of the herd (3:1), a lamb (3:7), or a goat (3:12). The purpose was, like the grain offering, not to effect atonement but to celebrate covenant union. It produced a soothing aroma (3:5,16), thereby attesting to God's pleasure with the offerer. So much was this the case that the peace offering actually was viewed as a common meal in which the Lord, the offerer, and the priests "sat down" together to share their respective parts (3:5,11,16; see further 7:15-18,28-34).

4:1–5:13
Sin Offering

Peace or fellowship between a human being and God could not be achieved as long as sin created a barrier between them, so means had to be found to deal with that

SACRIFICIAL SYSTEM

NAME	REFERENCE	ELEMENTS	SIGNIFICANCE
Burnt Offering	Lev 1; 6:8-13	Bull, ram, male goat, male dove, or young pigeon without blemish. (Always male animals, but species of animal varied according to individual's economic status.)	Voluntary. Signifies propitiation for sin and complete surrender, devotion, and commitment to God.
Grain Offering Also called Meal, or Tribute, Offering	Lev 2; 6:14-23	Flour, bread, or grain made with olive oil and salt (always unleavened); or incense.	Voluntary. Signifies thanksgiving for firstfruits.
Fellowship Offering Also called Peace Offering: includes (1) Thank Offering, (2) Vow Offering, and (3) Freewill Offering	Lev 3; 7:11-36	Any animal without blemish. (Species of animal varied according to individual's economic status.)	Voluntary. Symbolizes fellowship with God. (1) Signifies thankfulness for a specific blessing; (2) offers a ritual expression of a vow; and (3) symbolizes general thankfulness (to be brought to one of three required religious services).
Sin Offering	Lev 4:1–5:13; 6:24-30; 12:6-8	Male or female animal without blemish—as follows: bull for high priest and congregation; male goat for king; female goat or lamb for common person; dove or pigeon for slightly poor; tenth of an ephah of flour for the very poor.	Mandatory. Made by one who had sinned unintentionally or was unclean in order to attain purification.
Guilt Offering	Lev 5:14–6:7; 7:1-6; 14:12-18	Ram or lamb without blemish	Mandatory. Made by a person who had either deprived another of his rights or had desecrated something holy.

problem. Sin could be either unintentional or by choice. The rituals of Leviticus provided atonement only for unintentional sin (4:2,13,22,27). The person who sinned by choice ("sin defiantly," NIV; Hebrew "sin with a high hand") was forever cut off from God's people (Num 15:30; compare Ps 19:13).

The removal of unintentional sin required appropriate sacrifices (Lev 4:1–5:13). These included not only the bull and lamb (here the female, 4:32) but also the goat, dove, or even flour. The nature of the offering depended on the status of the offerer. Thus the sin of the priest required the bull (4:1-12), the blood of which was sprinkled within the holy place of the tabernacle (4:6-7). The purification of the congregation as a whole also demanded a bull whose blood was applied by the priest in the way just described (4:13-21). The inadvertent sin of a ruler was atoned by the sacrifice of a male goat, the blood being applied to the great altar (4:22-26). An ordinary person presented a female goat or lamb or even, if poor, two doves or a mere handful of flour (4:27–5:13). When all of this was done with proper ritual and intent, the sin would be forgiven (4:26,31,35; 5:6,10,13).

5:14–6:7
Trespass Offering

Atonement for either sins of inadvertence (4:1-35) or sins of omission (5:1-13) had to be followed by appropriate compensation to the one sinned against (5:14-19). The trespass offering was always a ram without blemish (5:15). If the offerer had withheld anything from the sanctuary, perhaps a promised offering, a 20 percent penalty had to be added to the offering (5:16). If the sin involved the loss or destruction of another's property, the guilty party had to offer a perfect ram and again make restitution of 120 percent (6:1-7). Reparation was expected; for though forgiveness comes by grace, sin always produces damaging consequences, particularly in terms of loss to fellow human beings.

6:8–7:38
Priests and Offerings

Leviticus 6:8–7:36 is a brief "handbook for priests" to instruct these worship leaders in the proper ritual for sacrifices and offerings. Its order of contents conforms largely to that of the sacrifices just outlined.

The law of the burnt offering (6:8-13) required that the fire of the altar be kept burning day and night. The continual fire points to the continuing need for sacrifice to atone for the people's sins. The law of the grain offering (6:14-23) and sin offerings (6:24-30) repeat the earlier instruction (chaps. 2; 4) but from the priests' perspective. The priestly role in the guilt offering (7:1-10) and peace offerings (7:11-36) specifies in greater detail what portion of the offerings was the priests' share.

Leviticus 7:37-38 summarizes the entire system of sacrifices and sets that system in the context of the Mosaic covenant at Mount Sinai. (See the introduction.)

THE NEED FOR PRIESTLY MEDIATORS (LEV 8–10)

Moses' role as mediator on behalf of rebellious Israel (Exod 32:30-32; 33:12-17; 34:8-9) points to the need for God-ordained mediators to continue his ministry of intercession throughout Israel's history. Exodus 28–29 specifies that these mediators will be the priests. The second major part of Leviticus—chapters 8–10—describes the establishment of the priesthood in answer to this need.

8:1-36
Consecration of Priests

Moses called for all the congregation to assemble at the front of the tabernacle where they would witness the consecration of Aaron and his sons to the priesthood (8:1-5). Their adornment by the clothing and other trappings gave them identity and symbolically spoke of the meaning and function of their office (9:6-9; see Exod 28). They were then anointed (Lev 8:10-13). And on their behalf Moses offered up a sin offering (8:14-17), a burnt offering (8:18-21), and an offering of consecration that symbolized the total commitment of Aaron and his sons to the priestly ministry (8:22-30). Then, as with all peace offerings, they ate of the ram of consecration during a seven-day period of purification (8:31-36).

9:1-24
Function of Priests

Once Aaron and his sons had been duly set apart, they could and did offer sacrifice, a matter that occupies Leviticus 9. The purpose of these first sacrifices was to effect oneness between God and His people (9:1-7). The great variety of offerings, for both priests and people, attests to the significance of this particular day. The day was to mark the appearance of the Lord among them (9:4,24), an appearance that required their total commitment and purity (9:8-24).

10:1-20
Failure of Priests

That the ritual of priestly function and sacrifice must be performed precisely according to divine prescription is highlighted in Leviticus 10. Failure to do so met with most severe judgment. Two of Aaron's sons, Nadab and

Abihu, offered "unauthorized fire" before the Lord on the altar of incense (10:1). The "unauthorized fire" may have been fire like that used in foreign worship. What is clear is that violation of God's demand to be glorified (10:3) invited His swift retribution. Aaron and his two surviving sons had to remain in the tabernacle to complete the offerings described in chapter 9. Their failure to eat of these parts of the animals to which they were entitled brought Moses' displeasure (10:16). Upon hearing Aaron's explanation—that he was afraid of further offending the Lord (10:19)—Moses understood and relented.

THE NEED FOR SEPARATION BETWEEN CLEAN AND UNCLEAN (LEV 11–15)

God had called Israel to be a people separated for service (Exod 19:5-6). Israel was, however, constantly tempted to conform to the standards of its neighbors in Egypt and Canaan (Lev 18:3). The laws of clean and unclean witness the "separateness" of Israel and remind God's people that there can be no compromise of His standards. The Lord had charged Aaron directly to distinguish between the holy and the profane (10:10). Leviticus 11–15 provides examples.

11:1-47
Clean and Unclean Animals

The first of these examples was in the area of animal life, for not all were fit for human consumption. Though hygienic principles may be indirectly involved, the major lesson to be learned here was that because God is holy His people must also be holy (11:44,47). Their holiness or separateness was to be illustrated by their distinctive eating habits.

12:1-8
Uncleanness after Childbirth

The second example of the distinction between ritual cleanness and impurity is seen in the uncleanness associated with childbirth (chap. 12). Comparison with the similar legislation in chapter 15 clarifies that impurity stems from bodily discharges associated with birth and not the act or fact of birth itself. Why discharges or emissions are unclean is not so clear. Many scholars have proposed that the loss of bodily fluids, especially blood, may signify the onset of death itself, the ultimate uncleanness.

13:1–14:57
Uncleanness of Disease

Leviticus 13–14 deals with the manifestations of "infectious skin disease" and "mildew" on the body, clothing, or even houses of the afflicted, considering it as a sign of uncleanness (13:8,11,15). Of all the diseases of the Bible none is deemed more serious or loathsome than those often (though imprecisely) called leprosy. The many symptoms and prescriptions for cure listed in 13:1-46 indicate a variety of different afflictions. Their cleansing after healing had occurred required the offering of appropriate sacrifices (14:1-32). Similarly, clothing contaminated by such diseases also had to be treated either by washing or, if that failed, by burning (13:47-59). Houses polluted by disease would manifest it by mildew, a condition that had to be remedied by repairing the affected parts of the house or even tearing it down (14:33-53).

15:1-33
Unclean Emissions

The final kind of uncleanness dealt with in Leviticus concerns abnormal male emissions by disease (15:1-15), the release of semen (15:16-18), and menstrual flow (15:19-24) and other kinds of female discharge of blood (15:25-30). These all were not inherently unclean. But they symbolize impurity and must therefore be cleansed by appropriate ritual and sacrifice in order that the holiness of God's people might be asserted and maintained (15:31-33).

THE NEED FOR A DAY OF ATONEMENT (LEV 16)

The greatest act of purification—one involving the entire nation—was that achieved on the Day of Atonement. On this day the high priest first offered up sacrifice for himself (16:1-14). He then slaughtered one goat as a sin offering for all the people (16:15-19) and expelled another goat (the scapegoat) from the camp as a symbol of the removal of sin from the community (16:20-22). Following a whole burnt offering (16:24), the camp was purified of the blood and animal remains by ceremonies of bathing and burning outside the camp (16:27-28). The writer of Hebrews developed images from the Day of Atonement to stress the superiority of Christ's priesthood (Heb 8:6; 9:7,11-26). Hebrews 13:11-12 uses the picture of the bull and goat burned outside the camp as an illustration of Christ's suffering outside the Jerusalem city walls. According to one interpretation of 2 Corinthians 5:21, Paul alluded to the ritual of the Day of Atonement by speaking of Christ as a sin offering.

THE NEED FOR HOLY LIVING (LEV 17–25)

The longest section of Leviticus (chaps. 17–25) is sometimes called the "Holiness Code" because it contains an exhaustive list of miscellaneous regulations pertaining to the acquisition and maintenance of holiness in Israel. The previous sections of Leviticus have been concerned primarily with holiness as "position." In chapters 17–25 (especially chap. 19) the focus shifts to holiness as moral condition. These miscellaneous laws may be categorized under eight major headings.

17:1-16
Sacrifice and Blood

Because blood was tantamount to life itself and was the God-ordained means of effecting atonement (17:11), no animal could be slaughtered outside the tabernacle (17:1-7). In the ancient Near East there was no such thing as ordinary slaughter for meat. For Israel to slaughter meat outside the tabernacle precincts was to shed blood to alien territory and perhaps to alien gods. The Christians of Corinth faced a similar problem regarding meat slaughtered in a pagan context (1 Cor 8; 10:14-33).

As a metaphor for life, blood was sacrosanct and could not be eaten (Lev 17:10-13). This pertained not only to animals offered in sacrifice but to wild game and other edible animals as well (17:14-16).

18:1-30
Sexual Relationships

Strict standards of holiness also had to be observed in the area of sexual relationships. Contrary to the practices of the pagan world (18:1-5,24-30), the people of the Lord had to marry among their own society but not incestuously. Thus a man could not marry his mother (18:7), stepmother (18:8), sister or half-sister (18:9), granddaughter (18:10), stepsister (18:11), blood aunt (18:12-13), uncle's wife (18:14), daughter-in-law (18:15), sister-in-law (18:16), or stepdaughter or step-granddaughter (18:17). Likewise, adultery (18:20), child sacrifice (18:21), homosexuality (18:22), and bestiality (18:23) were strictly prohibited.

19:1-37
Interpersonal Relationships

The holiness of God (19:1-2) meant that the Israelites had to display holiness in their interpersonal relationships. The frequent echoes of the Ten Commandments (worship the one God, honor parents, keep the Sabbath, 19:3; the prohibitions against stealing, lying, and false swearing, 19:11-12) serve as reminders that a life-style of holiness was a condition of God's covenant with Israel. Again and again God's people were reminded that moral behavior is not optional for those who call Yahweh Lord (19:3-4,10,12,14,16,18,25,28,30-32,34,36-37). The conduct required of God's people went beyond ritual matters to include providing for the poor (19:9-10), caring for the disadvantaged (19:13-14), practicing justice (19:15-16), loving one's neighbor (19:17-18), respecting the aged (19:32), caring for foreigners (19:33-34), and

Israel's Festivals and Feasts

For the early Hebrews, public worship perhaps centered not in the more familiar sacrificial offerings but in the great annual feasts. These festivals formed an integral part of OT life and are vital to the understanding of much in the NT.

All of the annual Jewish religious observances, except the Day of Atonement, were joyous occasions. They were feasts, festivals, and fiestas.

The Sabbath (Lev 23:3)

The Sabbath was the most important religious festival for the Hebrews because it came every week. The Sabbath commemorates not only God's rest following creation (Exod 20:11) but God's freeing Israel from Egyptian slavery (Deut 5:15).

Passover (Lev 23:4-5)

The name "Passover" indicates deliverance from the tenth plague in Egypt, the death of the firstborn. The observance falls in the spring, at the beginning of the barley harvest. It commemorated the exodus from Egypt. Along with Pentecost and Tabernacles, Passover was one of three annual pilgrimage festivals (see Deut 16:16).

Unleavened Bread (Lev 23:6-8)

This seven-day observance immediately following Passover recalls the Israelites' hasty departure from Egypt. Together the two festivals made up an eight-day celebration something like our Christmas through New Year's Day does.

Firstfruits (Lev 23:9-14)

Firstfruits involved the offering of the first sheaf of grain that was harvested. This symbolized that the entire crop belonged to the Lord and that it all was a gift from His hand.

Weeks (Lev 23:15-21)

This feast came seven weeks after the Feast of Unleavened Bread. It was a grain (wheat) harvest festival. The people read the Book of Ruth and recited the Psalms. The NT calls this festival "Pentecost" from the Greek word for *fifty*.

Trumpets (Lev 23:23-25)

The beginning of the civil year ▷

dealing fairly in business and trade (19:35-36). The memory of God's mighty acts in delivering Israel from Egyptian slavery was to motivate God's people to lives of compassion and justice (19:34-35). An appreciation of the holiness of God and the memory of what God has done for our deliverance—not from Egyptian slavery but from sin through Christ's death—continue to motivate Christians to holy living. It is thus not surprising that New Testament writers often echo the ethical teaching of Leviticus 19 (for example, Matt 22:39; Rom 13:9; Gal 5:14; Jas 2:8).

20:1-27
Capital Offenses

The laws concerning capital offenses have to be understood against the backdrop of paganism. Capital crimes tended to obliterate the differences between God's holy people and the world at large. Thus the worship of Molech, the god of the Ammonites, was punishable by death (20:2-5). So were other heathen religious practices (20:6), cursing of one's parents (20:9), and incest and other sexual deviations (20:10-21). Again, Israel was a separated people whose life-style was to reflect that separation for service to a holy God (20:22-26).

21:1–22:33
Worship and Holiness

Obviously holiness had to pervade Israel's religious life, so detailed injunctions regulated the priesthood (chap. 21) and the eating of sacrificial offerings (chap. 22). The ordinary priests (21:1-9) and the high priest (21:10-15) had to follow strict guidelines in regard to mourning rites and marriage. They had to adhere to strict criteria of physical perfection to qualify for service (21:16-24). This requirement suggests that inward holiness must have outward, physical expression.

The priests had to be ceremonially clean before partaking of sacrifices (22:1-9). Then they and their families could enjoy their meal together as they took the portions to which they were entitled (22:10-16). All animals devoted in sacrifice had to be perfect specimens, for to offer Yahweh anything but the best would profane His holy name (22:32; compare Mal 1:6-8).

23:1-44
Holy Days

For the ancient Israelite holy living entailed the proper observance of holy days (chap. 23). These include the Sabbath (23:1-3), Passover and Unleavened Bread (23:4-8), Firstfruits (23:9-14), and the Feast of Weeks (or Pentecost, 23:15-22). The fall festivals also were observed, which consisted of the Feast of Trumpets or New Year's Day (23:23-25), the Day of Atonement or Yom Kippur (23:26-32), and the Feast of Tabernacles or Booths (23:33-36), a reminder of Israel's wilderness experience (23:39-43). (See the feature article "Israel's Festivals and Feasts.")

was marked by this New Year's Day feast. It was a day of rest, of sacred assembly commemorated with trumpet blasts, and of offerings made to the Lord.

Day of Atonement (Lev 23:26-32)

This observance, in many ways the most important annual activity, was a solemn fast. This was the one day of the year the high priest entered the holy of holies in the tabernacle or temple. At this time the scapegoat was sent into the wilderness, signifying the sending away of the people's sins (see Lev 16).

Tabernacles or Booths (Lev 23:33-43)

This fruit harvest festival in the fall was the most joyous occasion of the year. It lasted for seven days. Some say it was a time for the renewal of the covenant.

Sabbatical Year (Lev 25:1-7,20-22)

Every seventh year the land was to be given a year of rest. Fields were to lie fallow. Vineyards were not to be pruned.

Jubilee Year (Lev 25:8-17,23-55)

Each fiftieth year was also special. Property was to be returned to the family that originally owned it. Hebrew slaves and their families were to be released. Once again the land was to be given rest.

Purim (Esth 9:20-28)

This feast, not mentioned in the Mosaic law, is described in the Book of Esther. It was established by Mordecai to commemorate the deliverance from the threats of Haman. It was a time of feasting, gladness, and the giving of gifts to the needy.

Hanukkah

This feast was established just before NT times. It celebrated the recovery and cleansing of the Jerusalem temple by Judas Maccabaeus in December of 164 B.C. John 10:22 calls Hanukkah the "Feast of Dedication." It is also called the Festival of Lights. □

JEWISH FEASTS AND FESTIVALS

NAME	MONTH: DATE	REFERENCE	SIGNIFICANCE
Passover	Nisan (Mar./Apr.): 14-21	Exod 12:2-20; Lev 23:5	Commemorates God's deliverence of Israel out of Egypt.
Feast of Unleavened Bread	Nisan (Mar./Apr.): 15-21	Lev 23:6-8	Commemorates God's deliverence of Israel out of Egypt. Includes a Day of Firstfruits for the barley harvest.
Feast of Weeks, or Harvest (Pentecost)	Sivan (May/June): 6 (seven weeks after Passover)	Exod 23:16; 34:22; Lev 23:15-21	Commemorates the giving of the law at Mount Sinai. Includes a Day of Firstfruits for the wheat harvest.
Feast of Trumpets (Rosh Hashanah)	Tishri (Sept./Oct.): 1	Lev 23:23-25 Num 29:1-6	Day of the blowing of the trumpets to signal the beginning of the civil new year.
Day of Atonement (Yom Kippur)	Tishri (Sept./Oct.): 10	Lev 23:26-33; Exod 30:10	On this day the high priest makes atonement for the nation's sin. Also a day of fasting.
Feast of Booths, or Tabernacles (Sukkot)	Tishri (Sept./Oct.): 15-21	Lev 23:33-43; Num 29:12-39; Deut 16:13	Commemorates the forty years of wilderness wandering.
Feast of Dedication, or Festival of Lights (Hanukkah)	Kislev (Nov./Dec.): 25-30; and Tebeth (Dec./Jan.): 1-2	John 10:22	Commemorates the purification of the temple by Judas Maccabaeus in 164 B.C.
Feast of Purim, or Esther	Adar (Feb./Mar.): 14	Esth 9	Commemorates the deliverance of the Jewish people in the days of Esther.

24:1-23
Consecration and Desecration

God provided proper protocol in the administering of the affairs of the tabernacle (24:1-9). But He demanded punishment for violation of divine holiness, a point clearly made in the narrative about the blasphemer (24:10-16). This incident gave rise to related cases that directly or indirectly impinged upon the character of God and the requirements mandated to a people who claimed allegiance to Him (24:17-23).

25:1-55
Sabbatical and Jubilee Years

The proper observance of Sabbatical and Jubilee years was to testify to Israel's status as a holy people (25:1-55). The land, like the people, had to have rest; so every seventh year was set aside as a year when nothing would be planted (25:1-7). Then after seven such cycles, the fiftieth year too would be set apart for the rejuvenation of the land, the forgiveness of mortgages on it, and the like (25:8-22). The redemption of property was to remind the people that the land was Yahweh's and was actually leased out by Him to them (25:23-38). Likewise, those who had been forced to indenture themselves were to be released on the Year of Jubilee. It was most unfit that Israel, itself a slave people released from bondage by Yahweh, should tolerate bondage within its own borders. A holy people had to be a free people (25:39-55).

THE BLESSING AND CURSE (LEV 26)

The essentially covenantal nature of Leviticus is made crystal clear in the summary statement of 27:34, which sets the whole book in the context of the Sinai covenant. The lists of blessings and curses that comprise Leviticus 26 reinforce this view of Leviticus as a covenantal text. Such lists are well known from other ancient Near Eastern texts where they impress upon the covenant recipient the seriousness of the covenant commitment. To be obedient resulted in great blessing, but to fail to obey brought judgment.

Thus a general exhortation (26:1-2) introduces blessings (26:3-13) and curses (26:14-45) that follow obedience and disobedience to the covenant terms. The sting of the curses, however, is eased by a declaration of grace. The Lord affirmed that even though His people would sin and suffer exile, repentance was possible. Then God, in line with His ancient covenant promises, would restore them to Himself and to the land (26:40-45).

OFFERINGS OF DEDICATION (LEV 27)

Leviticus closes with regulations concerning offerings of dedication (chap. 27). Placed here, these laws perhaps suggest appropriate ways to respond to the life-style choice posed by the blessing and curse. They form a fitting conclusion to Leviticus, for the dedication of oneself and possessions to the service of God is at the heart of holiness. These laws consist of personal vows of service to the Lord (27:2-8), votive gifts of clean and unclean animals (27:9-13), and gifts of one's house (27:14-15) or lands (27:16-25). These could all be redeemed or reclaimed for "secular" use by payment of the appropriate redemption price to the priest. The firstborn and tithe could not be dedicated to the Lord because they were already His possession (27:26-27,30-33). Whatever was irrevocably devoted to God could not be sold or reclaimed for private use but had to be destroyed as an offering to God (27:28-29).

Contemporary Significance

The Book of Leviticus, without doubt, is one of the most neglected of the Old Testament precisely because modern Christians fail to see what relevance it has to contemporary life. When one realizes, however, that its principal themes or ideals—the holiness of God, His covenant with His people, and the resultant demands for holy living—are timeless and irrevocable, the pertinence of the book becomes immediately evident. God chose Israel to be His servant people and to represent Him and His saving purposes on the earth. This same God in Jesus Christ has redeemed a people in this day to serve a corresponding function. The sacrifices, rituals, ceremonies, and holy days may have lost their legal status for the church. But the principles of holiness they embodied and demonstrated are principles that must characterize the people of the Lord of every generation if they are to serve Him effectively as salt and light.

Ethical Value

The rituals of Leviticus found their fulfillment in Christ's sacrifice and are thus not binding rules for Christian worship. (See the commentary on Heb 9–10.) In contrast, an appreciation of the holiness of God and the memory of what God has done for our deliverance—not from Egyptian slavery but from sin through Christ's death—continue to motivate Christians to holy living. It is thus not surprising that New Testament writers often echo the ethical teaching of texts such as Leviticus 19 (Matt 22:39; Rom 13:9; Gal 5:14; Jas 2:8). The detailed and complicated legislation of Leviticus is grounded squarely on the great covenant principles of the Ten Commandments. These laws find their ultimate meaning in the recognition that the God who freed Israel from Egyptian slavery (and

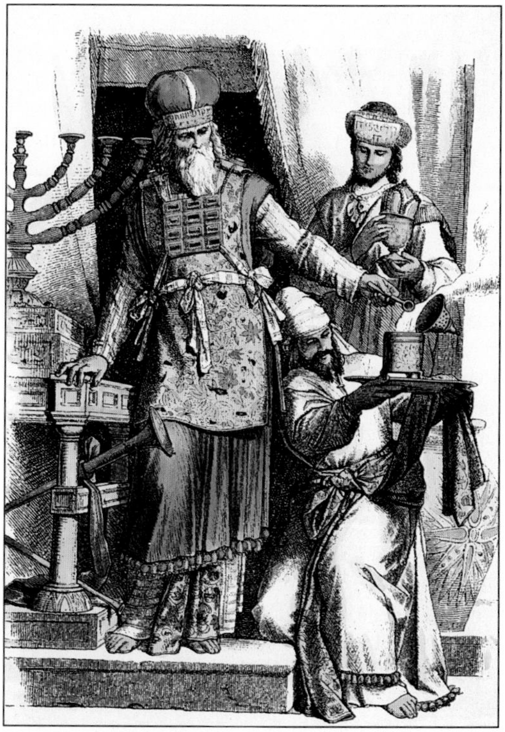

High priest performing his duties

freed us) is absolutely holy. True hope and happiness are found only in responding rightly to that God through holy lives of dedicated service. Again and again, Leviticus pleads that these things must be done because "I am Yahweh." That is, human behavior is successful to the extent that it acknowledges the Redeemer's claim to our lives and strives to mirror the holiness of God. No higher motivation for personal and community integrity can be found than in the governing theme of Leviticus: "I am the LORD who brought you up out of Egypt to be your God; therefore be holy, because I am holy" (Lev 11:45).

Questions for Reflection

1. Why is the context of Leviticus (27:34) important for understanding its message?
2. How do the instructions for worship relate to God's purpose for the exodus?
3. What was Israel's role as God's people, and why was holiness necessary in fulfilling this role?
4. Why were sacrifices and priests necessary?
5. What were the major types of sacrifices, and what were their purposes?
6. Why is Leviticus 17–25 known as the "Holiness Code"? What does God's demand for holiness teach about His moral character?
7. What do we mean by holiness as "position" and as "condition"?
8. How do the commands to distinguish the ritually clean from the unclean reflect God's lordship?

Sources for Additional Study

Clements, Ronald E. "Leviticus." *The Broadman Bible Commentary*, vol. 2. Nashville: Broadman, 1970.

Harrison, R. K. *Leviticus: An Introduction and Commentary. The Tyndale Old Testament Commentaries.* Downers Grove: InterVarsity, 1980.

Schultz, Samuel J. *Leviticus*. Chicago: Moody, 1983.

Wenham, Gordon J. *The Book of Leviticus. The New International Commentary on the Old Testament.* Grand Rapids: Eerdmans, 1979.

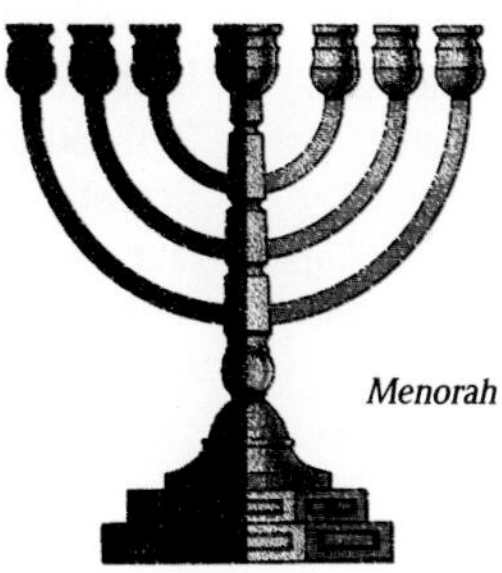

Menorah (Jewish seven-branched candlestick)

NUMBERS

The Hebrew name of this book (*bemidbar*) means *in the desert* and is thus a most appropriate way of describing its contents as a treatise whose entire setting is in the Sinai, Negev, and Transjordanian wilderness. The English title "Numbers" translates *Arithmoi,* the title used by the ancient Greek translation, the Septuagint. The term obviously reflects the census of the tribes of Israel at the beginning of the book and the other lists and totals.

The last verse of Numbers summarizes the whole by saying, "These are the commands and regulations the LORD gave through Moses to the Israelites on the plains of Moab by the Jordan across from Jericho" (36:13). Moses had led the Israelites from Mount Sinai to the borders of the promised land. The concluding verse suggests that Numbers instructs Israel in the preconditions of their possession and enjoyment of the promised land. (See "The Pentateuch" for a discussion of Mosaic authorship and the "Dates of the Exodus" for matters of chronology.)

Theme

The Book of Numbers is more than a mere travelogue tracing Israel's journey from Mount Sinai to the plains of Moab. The narratives and laws in Numbers give the conditions of Israel's possession and enjoyment of the promised land. These conditions included an unflinching desire to possess the land God promised, respect for God-ordained leaders, and concern for maintaining the holiness of the covenant community and of the land of promise. Frequent warnings of the danger of rebellion and the certainty of God's judgment on sin likewise prodded Israel ahead to the goal of possession of the land.

Numbers documents that when God's people were faithful to the covenant conditions, their travels and lives went well. When they were disobedient, however, they paid the price in defeat, delay, and death in the wilderness. The book thus teaches subsequent generations that covenant conformity brings blessing but covenant rejection brings tragedy and sorrow.

Numbers also documents the effective organization of the tribes into a discernible religious and political community in preparation for their conquest and occupation of Canaan. This explains the extraordinary interest in the numbering of the tribes, their arrangement for travel and encampment, and the centralizing of the tabernacle and priesthood as the focal point of Israel's life as a covenant people. This also explains the introduction of new legislation, especially of a cultic or ceremonial nature. The commandments and statutes appropriate for the forthcoming settlement in Canaan could not in every case be relevant to the people in a nomadic, transient stage of their lives. Numbers anticipates the possession of the promised land and therefore provides special instruction for those times and conditions.

Literary Forms

The great bulk of Numbers describes a nearly forty-year period of Israel's history in a story or almost "diary" form. Moses apparently kept a log book in which he noted significant events that could and did constitute his personal memoirs (compare 33:2). Numbers, then, is history but narrative history of an individualistic type.

In addition to narrative materials, Numbers contains census lists (1:5-46; 3:14-39; 4:34-49; 26:5-51), an organization manual for encampment and march (2:1-31), and regulations for the priesthood and Levitical orders (3:40–4:33; 8:5-26; 18:1-32). It also contains laws of sacrifice and ritual (5:1–7:89; 9:1–10:10; 15:1-41; 19:1-22; 28:1–30:16), instructions about the conquest and division of the land (32:33-42; 34:1–35:34), and laws regulating inheritance (36:1-12). Numbers even contains poetry: a portion of "The Book of the Wars of Yahweh" (21:14-15), the "Song of the Well" (21:17-18), the "Song of Heshbon" (21:27-30), and the various prophetic oracles of Balaam (23:7-10,18-24; 24:3-9,15-24).

This rich diversity of forms is one of the major characteristics of biblical history writing. The story of God's redemptive purposes for Israel and all the world is told in narrative punctuated and illuminated by command, exhortation, illustration, proverb, and song. Numbers is thus not mere history but *torah*, instruction in holy living. Though the types of literature in Numbers are diverse, the goal of the possession of God's promised land is a constant unifying factor.

I. **Organizing Israel to Take the Promised Land (1:1–10:10)**
II. **Rejecting God's Promise of Land (10:11–14:45)**
III. **Wandering outside the Promised Land: The Journey on the Plains of Moab (15:1–22:1)**
IV. **Encountering Obstacles to God's Promise of Land (22:2–25:18)**
V. **Preparing for Conquest Again (26:1–36:13)**

Purpose and Theology

The diverse materials in Numbers point toward a common goal—the possession of the land God promised the patriarchs. Numbers opens with a census that reveals God had blessed Israel with the strength necessary for the conquest of the promised land (1:1–2:34). Organization for worship (3:1–4:49), instructions for preserving the purity of God's people (5:1–6:27), and the building of the tabernacle (7:1–8:26) all made possible God's dwelling with this people (9:15)—a necessary condition for reaching the land. Though God equipped His people for conquest (10:11-36), their hearts repeatedly longed for Egypt (11:1-35; 14:2-4; 20:2-5; 21:4-5). They rejected Moses, the leader God had appointed to lead them to the land (12:1-15). Ultimately, Israel rejected God's gift of the land (12:16–14:45). Having spurned God's gift, Israel was condemned to wander in the desert (15:1–22:1). Again and again Israel rebelled against God's chosen leaders and suffered judgment (16:1-50). Even Moses failed to trust in the power of God's word (20:1-29) and was excluded from the land of promise.

God, however, is true to His promises. God overcame obstacles to Israel's possession of the land—the external threat of Balaam's curses (22:2–24:25) and the internal threat of Israel's idolatry and immorality (25:1-18). After the death of the rebellious generation, God again blessed Israel with a force capable of conquering the land (chap. 26). God rewarded the daughters of Zelophehad who, unlike the previous generation, earnestly desired their share in the land (27:1-11; 35:50–36:13). God's provision of Joshua as Moses' successor prepared for the successful conquest of the land.

Even the legal texts in Numbers anticipated life in the promised land. These texts regulated its worship (chap. 15) and maintained its purity (chaps. 19; 35). The Book of Exodus tells how the Israelites placed themselves under God's sovereignty—with all the responsibilities and privileges that entailed—by accepting the terms of the Sinaitic covenant. They became a holy nation (their status) and a kingdom of priests (their function). Numbers tells of Israel's successes and failures in living out the covenant as they made their way to the land of promise. The wilderness became a proving ground, an arena in which Israel had opportunity to display their commitment to the God who had called and commissioned them. It was historically their first opportunity to move beyond the place of covenant reception and enter the sphere of covenant implementation.

Israel's inability or, at least, refusal to exhibit its role as obedient mediator became clear again and again. They rebelled at Taberah and Kibroth Hattaavah (11:3,34). They challenged Moses' authority as covenant representative (chap. 12). They rejected the spies' report that encouraged conquest of the land of Canaan (14:1-10). They rejected the priestly role of Aaron (chap. 16). They committed idolatry and immorality of Baal Peor (chap. 25). Each case of rebellion was met by divine displeasure and punishment. The constancy of the Lord, His faithfulness to His covenant pledge, however, remained unaltered. Indeed, the ancient Abrahamic promise that those who blessed Israel would be blessed and those who cursed Israel would be cursed remained intact (24:9). Even more remarkable, since it came from the lips of the pagan seer Balaam, was the great messianic revelation that "a star will come out of Jacob; a scepter will rise out of Israel" (24:17), a word that confirmed the function of Israel as the source of redemptive and reigning blessing for the whole world (compare Gen 49:10).

ORGANIZING ISRAEL TO TAKE THE PROMISED LAND (NUM 1:1–10:10)

The covenant with Israel had been concluded at Sinai. And its social, political, and religious stipulations had been outlined (Exod 20–40; Lev). Then the Lord commanded His people to leave the holy mountain and to make their way to the land of promise.

1:1–2:34
Organizing the Tribes for War

The census of the men of military age (1:3) revealed a fighting force of 603,550 (1:46), excluding the Levites. God had fulfilled His promise to Abraham of numerous descendants. With such an army Israel was well equipped to take the promised land. To facilitate moving and en-

Old Testament Numbers

In the Hebrew text of the OT numbers are written out as words, never represented by symbols or abbreviations. The numbers most frequently found in the OT are one, two, ten, and seven (in that order).

Hebrew also used separate words for fractions, such as one-tenth (Exod 16:36), two-tenths (Lev 23:13), one-third (2 Sam 18:2), and one-half (Exod 25:10).

During the Intertestamental Period a system of numerical equivalents for the letters of the Hebrew alphabet was developed. Thus *'alep* represented one, *bet* represented two, and so forth, following the order of the alphabet. Numerals beyond ten were formed by a combination of letters. This system is commonly used to denote chapter and verse divisions in printed texts of the Hebrew Bible today.

Numbers are most frequently found in the OT in the enumeration of age or a census. Much attention has been given to the great ages of certain persons who lived before the flood. Examples are Methuselah, 969 years; Adam, 930 years; Seth, 912 years (Gen 5:5-27). Bible interpreters understand these large numbers in various ways. (1) Some explain the numbers as based on a different reckoning of time. (2) Others take the numbers as a reference to an entire family rather than one individual. (3) Others see the large numbers as evidence that sin or disease had not yet sufficiently infected the human race to shorten the life span, or due to cosmological conditions that were different, making longevity commonplace. (4) Others believe that these ages had symbolic significance, whose meaning is unknown. (5) Others accept the ages as historical fact without explanation.

The large numbers found in census and enumeration lists (for example, Num 1:21-46; 1 Kgs 4:26) have been explained as textual errors or as symbolical numbers. (For example, the large number of people involved in the exodus from Egypt in Exod 12:37 has been explained as symbolically suggesting power, importance, and victory of the Israelites.) Others insist the numbers should always be taken literally since apparent problems can be explained by careful analysis.

Numbers are sometimes used literally (for example, Asa ruled forty-one years, 1 Kgs 15:10). Other numbers are approximations (1 Kgs 20:29; 2 Chr 17:14-18). Sometimes numbers represent an indefinite number (Judg 5:30; 2 Kgs 9:32; Isa 17:6).

Numbers are sometimes used in the OT for rhetorical or poetic effect. For example, numbers may express a striking contrast between God's limited judgment and great mercy (Exod 20:5-6) or between military strength and weakness (Lev 26:8; 1 Sam 18:7).

A further example is a sequence of two consecutive small numbers, which should be interpreted as an indefinite number or perhaps a large number (Amos 1:3,6,9,11,13; Prov 30:15,18,21,29).

Much attention has been given to discovering symbolic and mystical significance in biblical numbers. For example, "one" represents unity; "four" is the world; "seven" represents completeness. But the Bible itself neither affirms nor denies hidden meanings, which are often determined by the ingenuity of the one interpreting them.

A system called *gematria* developed in late Judaism that found hidden meaning in numbers. By giving numerical value to the letters of a word or phrase, hidden meanings were discovered. For example, 603,550 (Num 1:46) means *the sum of all the children of Israel* (Num 1:2). By gematria the enigmatic "Shiloh comes" (Gen 49:10) has the numerical value of 358, the numerical value of the word "messiah." Correct interpretation of a passage will often depend on a proper understanding of how the numerals are being used. □

camping such a vast force, explicit instructions as to tribal, clan, and family organization became mandatory.

The Israelite camp was organized with God's dwelling, the tabernacle, at its center (2:17). The Levites and priests camped nearest to the tabernacle, the priests guarding the entrance on the east side (3:38). The "lay tribes" camped somewhat farther away, with Judah occupying the position of leadership, again to the east (2:9). Such organization lays stress on preserving the purity of the tabernacle. The Levites were responsible for the movement and care of the tabernacle and so remained outside the military census (1:47-54).

3:1–4:49
Organizing the Levites for Worship

The Levites had been set apart for Yahweh's special service as a substitute for Israel's firstborn sons (3:12-13; compare 4:34-49). Moses organized them according to Levi's three sons—Gershon, Kohath, and Merari (3:14-20). The Gershonites were responsible for the curtains, drapes, and coverings of the tabernacle (3:21-26; 4:21-28); the Kohathites, for its furnishings (3:27-32; 4:1-20); and the Merarites, for its supporting structure (3:33-37; 4:29-33).

5:1–6:27
Preserving the Purity of God's People

The sanctity of the tabernacle—a point made clear by the detailed regulation concerning its handling (chaps. 3–4)—gave rise to a consideration of various ordinances having to do with holiness and separation (5:1–6:27). Thus Moses addressed ritual uncleanness (5:1-4), sin and restitution (5:5-10), and tests to be administered to a woman whose husband accused her of adultery (5:11-31). Since the Nazirite was a classic example of one who set himself apart for divine service, Moses set forth lengthy guidelines concerning the Nazirite vow (6:1-21).

The blessing Moses taught Aaron and the priests captures the very essence of what it means for Israel to be the people of Yahweh—a source of blessing that makes God's gracious presence known (6:24-27).

7:1–8:26; 9:15
Providing God a Dwelling in the Camp

The tribal leaders of the respective twelve tribes brought their own gifts of tribute to the Lord at the tabernacle, thereby recognizing His sovereignty over all political as well as religious affairs (7:1-88). Day by day the tribes came in succession, bringing silver and gold vessels and a great number of sacrificial animals. More important than even these lavish gifts, however, was Israel's giving of itself to the Lord. They separated and dedicated the Levites to Yahweh as His own special treasure (8:5-19). This

TABERNACLE

The tabernacle was a portable shrine. It served the Hebrew people as their center of worship during the years of desert wanderings, conquest of Canaan, settlement in the land, and early monarchy. The English word *tabernacle* comes from the Latin Vulgate. It means *tent* or *wooden hut.* The Hebrew term translated "tabernacle" means *to dwell.* Thus the tabernacle represented the Lord's presence with His sojourning people.

Importance

Exodus 25–31 told the people how to make the tabernacle. Exodus 35–40 reports that they made it just that way. Thirteen chapters out of forty, over a third of the Book of Exodus, concern the making of the tabernacle. (Of course, many details of furnishings, ritual, and priestly activity were included, in addition to the actual construction.)

Plan

The tabernacle was a rather small prefabricated tent made of a wooden frame and elaborate curtains. It sat in an outer court that measured 150 by 75 feet. The court was formed by a fence of posts and curtains.

The tent faced east and measured forty-five by fifteen feet. The first chamber, the holy place, was thirty by fifteen feet. The holy of holies (the holiest of all) was a cube and measured fifteen feet in every direction.

Furniture

Six items of furniture were associated with the tabernacle. In front of the tent, nearest the outer fence, sat the huge brazen altar on which the priests offered the sacrifices. Behind it was the large laver or basin for ceremonial washing.

Inside the holy place, at the north wall, stood the table of showbread (bread of the presence). Some think it was an acknowledgment of the Lord's bounty in providing food for His people. On the south side of the holy place stood the seven-branched lampstand (not candlestick).

At the curtain separating the two sections of the tabernacle stood a second, smaller altar, the altar of incense.

Inside the holy of holies the ark of the covenant rested. It was a chest overlaid with gold. Its lid was a slab of solid gold called the mercy seat (RSV; the atonement cover, NIV). Over it the cherubim stood (or knelt, depending on the interpretation). The atonement cover was the *X*-marks-the-spot where the Lord was enthroned and where He came down to meet His people.

Meaning

In Exodus 25:8 God instructed Moses, "Then have them make a sanctuary for me, and I will dwell among them." Some commentators find Christian significance in every detail of the tabernacle construction. This approach should not be overdone, lest we miss the main point: the Lord's presence. The NT applies this image of God's presence in the tabernacle to Jesus' presence with His first disciples: "The Word became flesh and made his dwelling among us" (John 1:14).

The Book of Hebrews often applies the image of the priest serving in the tabernacle to Christ's saving work (Heb 6:19-20; 8:2; 9:24; 10:19-20). Because Christ died for us and lives to intercede for us, Christians have access to the presence of God. In the OT only priests could enter the tabernacle building. Lay worshipers had to remain outside the outer fence unless they were allowed to bring their sacrifices as far as the altar just inside. The tabernacle helps us to appreciate the free access Christ provides for us to the Father (Heb 10:19-20). (See "The Sacrificial System" and "The Temple.") □

had already been commanded (3:5-10), but now it actually took place (8:20-26).

9:1–10:10 Celebrating the Passover and Breaking Camp

Appropriately Israel's move from Sinai to Canaan followed celebration of the Passover, the same festival that preceded the exodus from Egypt (9:1-14). Likewise, just as that first exodus was marked by the appearance of the glory of God, who led them by fire and cloud, so the wilderness journey followed His leadership in the same form (9:15-23). The movement and settlement of Israel was determined by the movement and settlement of Yahweh as represented in the symbols of His glorious presence. The signal for that movement and for other occasions in which the Lord would lead His people would be the blowing of silver trumpets, an audible witness to His presence among them (10:1-10).

REJECTING GOD'S PROMISE OF LAND (NUM 10:11–14:45)

A little more than a year after the exodus (10:11) and after nearly a year at Sinai (Exod 19:1), Israel pressed on to the land of promise, mobilized for conquest. Taking their cue from the movement of the cloud of glory, the camp set out in the manner previously commanded. Preceding the whole camp was the ark of God, the symbol of His guiding and protecting presence (Num 10:33-36).

11:1-35 Longing for Egypt

No sooner had the journey commenced, however, than the people began to complain and murmur. The result

Routes of the Exodus

Four principal routes for the exodus have been suggested.

1. A shorter, northeastern route going through Philistine territory along the "way of the sea."

2. A middle route heading across the Negeb to Beersheba (the Way of Shur), the probable route the patriarchs traveled to Egypt.

3. The Way of Seir that led from the Gulf of Suez via Eilat to the mountain of Seir in Edom, present-day southern Jordan, a route Moslem pilgrims travel on the *hajj* to Mecca.

4. "The way to the hill country of the Amorites" (Deut 1:19), a route leading to the southernmost extremities of the Sinai peninsula.

Israel was specifically warned not to take the northernmost route through the land of the Philistines (Exod 13:17). The Egyptians frequently used this route. In the reign of Seti I (1313–1301 B.C.) it was known as the Way of Horus, but Scripture labels it the Way of the Philistines or the Way of the Sea.

The second route, called the Way of Shur, passed between the lakes where the Egyptians had constructed a fortification line named "Shur Mitzrayim" (*Wall of Egypt*). Israel would not have wanted to encounter Egyptian soldiers in such fortifications. Besides, Mount Sinai cannot be equated with Jebel Helal as champions of this view argue.

The Way of Seir or the Way of the Celebrants is a more modern route and does not appear to play a part in the biblical narrative.

If we accept a southern location for Mount Sinai, then the fourth option is the proper one for the exodus route.

The staging point for Israel's journey was Rameses (Exod 12:37; Num 33:3,5), one of the store-cities in the eastern Nile Delta. This site is best identified with Qantir on the eastern arm of the Nile River Delta. Later the Israelites would arrive in Kadesh Barnea (Num 33:36; Deut 1:19) where they would spend "many days" (Deut 1:46).

Kadesh Barnea is almost unanimously identified with Ain el-Qudeirat, where two ancient and important desert routes merged in northeastern Sinai, next to the most important spring in the northern Sinai peninsula. These two sites form the beginning and the end of the wilderness trek.

After leaving Rameses, Israel came to Succoth (Exod 12:37; Num 33:5). They went on to Etham "on the edge of the wilderness" (Num 33:6; probably a region known as Atuma, a desert beginning at Lake Timsah and extending west and south). Then they turned back to the west and then south to get around the bulging upper part of the large Bitter Lake, camping at Migdol (Num 33:7). A possible location for Migdol (*tower*) is a Migdol near Succoth or the ruins of a square tower on a height known as Jebel Abu Hasan overlooking the southern part of the small Bitter Lake.

The exact place where Israel crossed the Red (Hebrew "Reed") Sea is unknown. But that crossing is best placed at the southern end of the Bitter Lakes or even better in the northern tip of the Gulf of Suez itself.

The wilderness itinerary begins in Exodus 12:37, continues in 13:20; 14:2, and resumes after the crossing in Exodus 15:22-27.

The first stops Israel made are generally agreed upon identifications. The Wilderness of Shur ranges on Egypt's northeastern frontier eastward into the northwestern quarter of the Sinai pen-

was judgment by fire, a visitation of God halted only by Moses' urgent intercession (11:1-3). The major complaint seems to have been dissatisfaction with the manna God had miraculously provided (Exod 16:13-20) and a longing for the delicacies of Egypt (Num 11:4-9). So intense was the agitation that Moses seemed crushed under the load of leadership. Graciously, therefore, the Lord provided him with seventy Spirit-filled leaders who could assist him in these matters (11:10-30). He followed this with the provision of low-flying quail, which the people consumed with such gluttonous lust that the Lord once more inflicted them with His judgment (11:31-35).

12:1-15
Rejecting God's Prophet

The selection of seventy elders of Israel to assist Moses infuriated his own sister Miriam and brother Aaron. They sensed in this a decrease in their own prestige and leadership. Miriam, a prophetess, had played a leading role in the exodus (compare Exod 15:20-21); whereas, Aaron, of course, was the great high priest. Under the pretense of criticizing Moses for having married outside the covenant people (Num 12:1), they registered their true feelings by challenging his prophetic authority (12:2). The result was Yahweh's severe chastening of them and His reminder that Moses, the covenant mediator, was unique among all of God's servants: God spoke to Moses openly and not in visions and dreams (12:5-8). The sign of that special relationship was in Moses' very ability to restore his stricken sister to ritual cleanliness (12:9-15).

13:1–14:15
Rejecting God's Gift of Land

Somewhere in the northern Negev, close to Canaan, the

insula. Israel's first stop is traditionally placed by local Arabs at Ain Musa, the "Springs of Moses." This site is sixteen to eighteen hours north of the first site mentioned in Scripture, Marah. Ain Musa is about ten miles south of the northern end of the Red Sea and about one half mile inland from the eastern shore of the Red Sea.

The journey from Ain Musa to Marah is about forty miles. Bounded by the blue waters of the Gulf of Suez on their right and the mountain chain of El Ruhat off to their left at some distance, Israel had to contend with rocky desert at first. Nine more miles and they came to the glaring sands of the desert plain called Ati. Then the sand dunes turned into a hilly country rolling out to the coast.

Marah is usually identified with Ain Hawarah, a site several miles inland from the Gulf. It is a place still notorious for its brackish, salty, bitter, and unpleasant tasting water. Arabs still consider it the worst water in all the region!

Numbers 33:5-11 lists seven places of encampment, but only one three-day journey. Israel no doubt stayed at several of these places for a number of days or they camped at a number of places not mentioned, or places with no distinct names. From Elim they came to the Wilderness of Sin. This wilderness is either along the coastal plain, el Markha, or inland Debbet er Ramleh. This area forms a crescent between the famous ancient Egyptian copper and turquoise mining center at Serabit el Khadim and the et Tih Plateau.

Israel rested at Dophkah (Num 33:12), meaning *smeltery,* a probable allusion to the copper and turquoise mining center of Serabit el Khadim of the Eighteenth and Twentieth Dynasties of Egypt.

Rephidim is best identified with Wadi Refayid in southwest Sinai. Here Israel was attacked by the Amalekites.

Finally Israel reached Sinai. Several mountains have been associated with Sinai: Gebel Musa, Ras es-safsafeh, Gebel Serbal, and a mountain near al-Hrob. The al-Hrob location is the least likely since it is a volcanic mountain to the east of the Gulf of Aqabah. Gebel Serbal does not have a wilderness at its base, so the choice must be made between Gebel Musa (7,363 feet elevation at the southern end of er-Rah) or Ras es-safsafeh (6,540 feet high at the northern edge of the plain). Most prefer to identify Mount Sinai with Gebel Musa because of its important granite formations and, more importantly, because of its relation to the plain. (Exod 20:18, "They stayed at a distance.")

The route from Sinai to Kadesh Barnea is described in Deuteronomy 1:19 as "that great and terrible wilderness." According to Deuteronomy 1:2, this journey would have led Israel up a series of valleys between the main Sinai plateau and the coastal chain of mountains of Ezion Geber on the north end of the Gulf of Aqabah. The journey covered only eleven days. None of the stops listed in Numbers 33:17-35 can be identified with any degree of certainty except Hazeroth with Ain Khadra, a spring some eighteen hours from Sinai. The two terms used to describe this general area are the Wilderness of Paran and the Wilderness of Zin. The first is just outside of Sinai, and the latter is the region in which Kadesh was located.

From Kadesh Barnea, Israel eventually made its way to the plains of Moab and poised for finally entering the land. □

Lord commanded Moses to send out spies who could ascertain the strengths and weaknesses of its inhabitants and prescribe a course of action in regard to conquest (12:16–13:2). The twelve, including Joshua and Caleb, traveled the length of Canaan (13:17-25) and returned with a divided report. The land was rich and fertile, they said, but the majority argued it could not be taken because of the superior might of its citizens (13:26-29). Caleb's affirmations of the Lord's presence and power notwithstanding, the people listened to the majority report and refused to press forward (13:30–14:3). The people rejected God's gift of the promised land.

Once more Moses' leadership was at stake. In fact, the people demanded that he step down in favor of someone who would guide them back to Egypt (14:4-10). His striking response to them—and to the Lord who tested him by threatening to destroy them—is remarkable. If Israel failed to enter Canaan, he said, the whole world would view Yahweh as unreliable (14:11-19). He had to pardon His people for His own name's sake if not for theirs.

Moved by this intercession, the Lord relented but announced to Moses and the people that they would not live to see the land of promise. Instead, they would die in the wilderness, leaving the promises of God to be enjoyed by their children (14:26-35). Only Joshua and Caleb, who had trusted God for victory and conquest, would see for themselves the land of milk and honey (14:36-38).

Having refused the opportunity to enter Canaan with the Lord, the people now perversely determined to do so without Him. Leaving the ark in the camp, they pushed north, only to be confronted and defeated by the Amalekites and Canaanites of the southern hill country (14:39-45). Thus began their forty years of aimless wandering in the wilderness.

WANDERING OUTSIDE THE PROMISED LAND (NUM 15:1–22:1)

With striking irony the Lord, who had just sentenced the people of Israel to death in the wilderness, outlined immediately the principles of sacrifice and service to be followed by their descendants in the land of Canaan (15:1-41). These generally agree with the procedures of Leviticus 1–7, though there are certain amendments appropriate to a settled rather than nomadic life. Particular attention is focused on the sin offerings, for sin would always be a problem even in the land of promise.

As though to illustrate this fact, the brief narrative of a Sabbath breaker appears after the instruction concerning willful sin (15:32-36). His death by stoning underlined the seriousness of such sin and gave rise to the reemphasis on Israel's need to remember who they were and what the Lord required of them (15:37-41).

16:1-50
Rejecting God's Priest

A second illustration of the continuing problem of sin follows in the story of the rebellion of Korah against Aaron's priestly authority (16:1–17:13). Korah was a Levite, but not a priest. He resented this exclusion and challenged the claim of Aaron and his sons to hold sole rights as mediators before God. Moses, therefore, arranged for Korah and his followers to appear at the sanctuary, where they and Aaron would offer incense before the Lord. He whose offering was accepted would stand vindicated (16:4-17).

When the moment of truth came, the Lord appeared in His glory, threatening to destroy not only Korah and his collaborators but the entire congregation. Only the intercession of Moses and Aaron prevented this (16:20-24). Korah, with his friends and family, was swallowed up in a great crevice in the earth (16:25-35). Thus the rebellion of competing priests was put down.

God's judgment did not end the murmuring of the people. Again the Lord threatened them with annihilation. Only the faithful mediation of Moses saved them once more, though several thousand of them died of plague (16:41-50).

17:1-13
Vindicating God's Priest

The congregation again challenged God's choice of leaders. When Aaron's rod (the symbol of the tribe of Levi) budded and bloomed, it was clear that the priestly line lay in him and his family and nowhere else (17:1-13).

18:1–19:22
Priests, Levites, and Purity

Once this crisis was over, it was necessary once more to spell out the duties and privileges of the priests and Levites (18:1-32). This led naturally to a discussion of other cultic matters, especially purification (19:1-22). This required such things as the slaughter of a red heifer as a sin offering and was applicable to uncleanness incurred by touching a dead body (19:11-13) and a tent made unclean by someone dying therein (19:14-19).

20:1-13
Failing to Trust God's Word

The narrative of the journey continues with the account of Israel's arrival at Kadesh Barnea, the center of Israel's

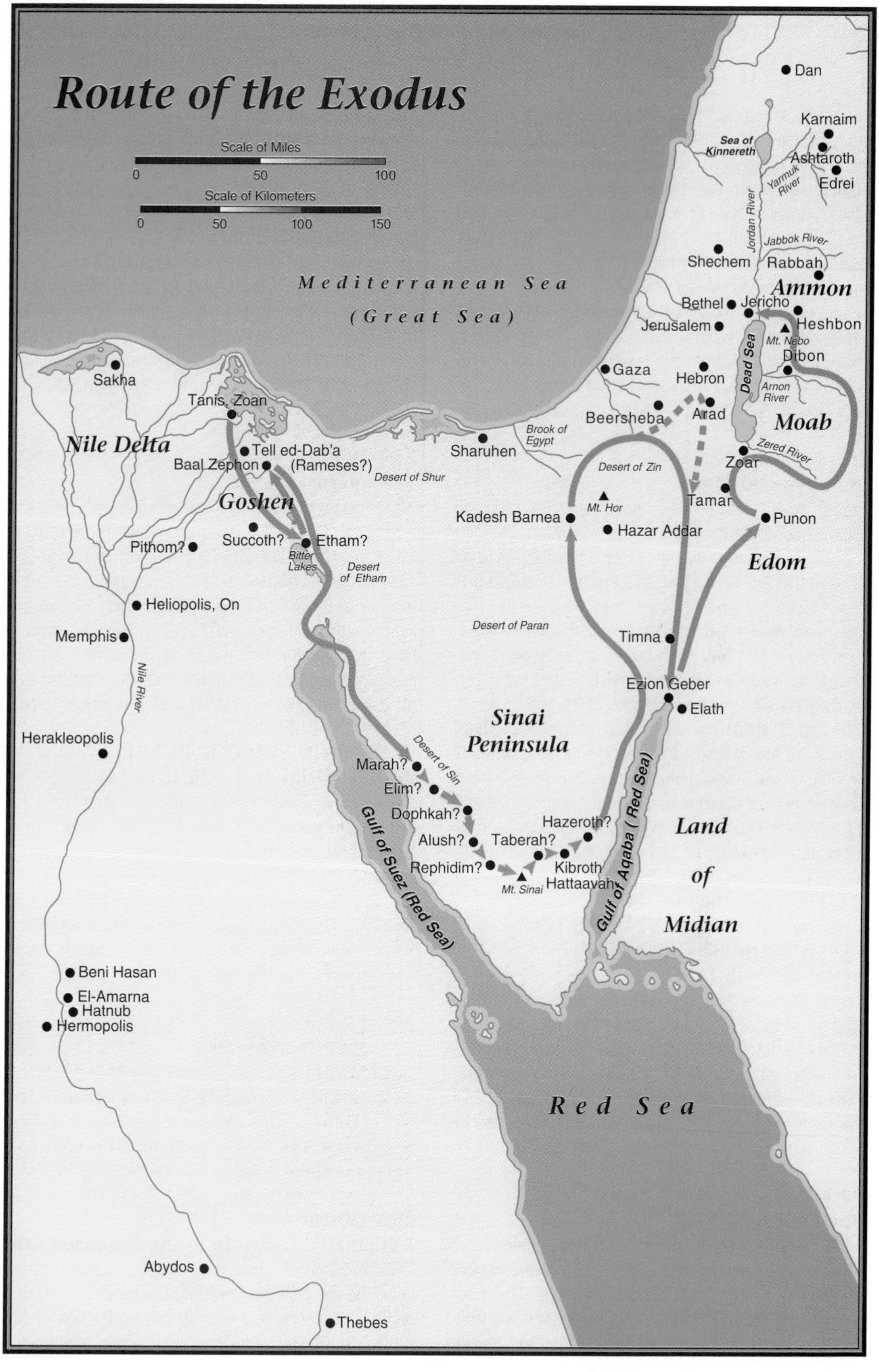
Route of the Exodus
Scale of Miles
0
50
100
Scale of Kilometers
0
50
100
150
Mediterranean Sea
(Great Sea)
Dan
Karnaim
Sea of Kinnereth
Ashtaroth
Edrei
Yarmuk River
Jordan River
Jabbok River
Shechem
Rabbah
Ammon
Bethel
Jericho
Jerusalem
Heshbon
Mt. Nebo
Dead Sea
Dibon
Gaza
Hebron
Arnon River
Sakha
Tanis, Zoan
Beersheba
Arad
Moab
Nile Delta
Tell ed-Dab'a
(Rameses?)
Baal Zephon
Sharuhen
Brook of Egypt
Zered River
Zoar
Desert of Shur
Desert of Zin
Goshen
Tamar
Mt. Hor
Kadesh Barnea
Hazar Addar
Punon
Succoth?
Etham?
Pithom?
Bitter Lakes
Desert of Etham
Edom
Heliopolis, On
Memphis
Desert of Paran
Timna
Nile River
Ezion Geber
Elath
Sinai Peninsula
Herakleopolis
Desert of Sin
Marah?
Elim?
Dophkah?
Hazeroth?
Alush?
Taberah?
Rephidim?
Kibroth Hattaavah
Mt. Sinai
Gulf of Suez (Red Sea)
Gulf of Aqaba (Red Sea)
Land of Midian
Beni Hasan
El-Amarna
Hatnub
Hermopolis
Red Sea
Abydos
Thebes

desert wanderings for thirty-eight years. In and near Kadesh, Miriam and Aaron died (20:1,28), underscoring the serious consequences of the rebellion of the first wilderness generation. There once again the people rebelled against Moses because of the lack of water (20:1-9). This time, burning with rage, Moses struck the rock rather than speaking as the Lord had instructed him. Numbers later describes Moses' sin as a failure to respect God's holiness (27:14). Moses' rash act resulted in a blessing for Israel—abundant water—but a curse for Moses—rebuke and exclusion from the promised land (20:10-13). According to Psalm 106:32, Moses suffered for the people's sin: "Trouble came to Moses because of them."

20:14–22:1
Journeying to Moab

Faithful to his commission, nonetheless, Moses made plans to continue the journey on to Canaan. He first sought permission from the king of Edom to pass through that land on the King's Highway—a petition that was refused (20:14-21). Moses then engaged the Canaanites of Arad in a skirmish that ended in a solid Israelite victory (21:1-3). Encouraged, Israel pressed on. Though persisting in rebellion from time to time (21:4-9), they eventually reached Moab (21:10-20). Their arrival caused great concern to Israel's enemies. Sihon, king of the Amorites, tried to stem the advance of God's people but was unsuccessful (21:21-32). Og of Bashan likewise suffered defeat at Israel's hands. Thus Moses and his followers found themselves at last on the plains of Moab, directly east of the land which the Lord had promised to give them (21:33–22:1).

ENCOUNTERING OBSTACLES TO GOD'S PROMISE OF LAND (NUM 22:2–25:18)

The defeat of the Amorites and Bashanites suggested the way was clear for Israel's conquest of the promised land. Before entering the land, Israel would, however, face obstacles to God's promise of land. The first obstacle was external—the threat of curse from Balaam (22:2–24:25); the second, internal—the threat of compromise to the sexual standards of the Moabites (25:1-18).

22:2–24:25
The External Threat

Balak, the king of Moab, concluded that his nation would be next to fall to Israel. He therefore engaged the services of Balaam, a famous Mesopotamian seer. The Lord warned him not to collaborate with Balak, for it was fruitless to attempt to curse a people whom God had blessed (22:2-20). Balaam went on to Moab, hoping to satisfy the request of Balak but having learned that he could say only what the God of Israel would permit (22:21-55).

Once at Moab, Balaam commenced a series of curses that were converted by the Lord into magnificent blessings for His people (22:36–24:25). He first predicted the innumerable host of Israel, then the faithfulness of the Lord to His people, their prosperity and success, and the rise of an Israelite ruler who would subdue Israel's neighbors. Thus Balak's diabolical plan to curse Israel resulted in just the opposite—a magnificent outpouring of God's blessing upon His people and, through them, upon the whole world.

25:1-18
The Internal Threat

What Balaam could not do, however, Israel's own base inner impulses could and did do. While in the plains of Moab, they came upon the licentious cult of Baal at Peor and soon were attracted to its allurements (25:1-5). Only the zeal of Phinehas, son of the high priest Eleazar, prevented wholesale apostasy (25:6-13). With his spear in hand, he slew the ringleaders of the affair. Thus he brought atonement (25:13), but not before thousands of his fellow Israelites perished in a plague sent by God.

PREPARING FOR CONQUEST AGAIN (NUM 26:1—36:13)

Having now cleared the way for the crossing of the Jordan and the conquest of Canaan, the Lord gave instructions concerning those matters. He first ordered a new census of the tribes (26:1-65) and outlined some principles of land inheritance in families where there were no sons (27:1-11). The earnest desire of the daughters of Zelophehad to share in God's gift of land contrasts sharply with the earlier generation's spurning of the gift.

27:1-23
A Successor to Moses

God revealed His will concerning a successor to Moses, someone who would become covenant mediator in the land of Canaan, which Moses could not enter. This successor was Joshua, the faithful servant of the Lord, upon whom the honor of Moses was bestowed (27:12-23).

28:1–30:16
Anticipating Worship in the Promised Land

The conditions of settled life dictated adjustment in religious life and practice. Therefore the Lord revealed new regulations regarding sacrifices and holy days (28:1–29:40) and reiterated, with some refinements,

ANCIENT NUMBER SYSTEMS

AMERICAN	SUMERIAN	EARLY EGYPTIAN (HIEROGLYPHIC)	LATER EGYPTIAN (HIERATIC)	CANAANITE (and PHOENICIAN)	POST-EXILIC HEBREW	EARLY GREEK	LATER GREEK (IONIC)	ANCIENT ROMAN (LATIN)
1	𒁹 (or ∨)	𓏺	ǀ	/	א	I	A	I
2	𒁹𒁹 (or ∨∨)	𓏻	ϥ	//	ב	II	B	II
3	𒁹𒁹𒁹 (or ∨∨∨)	𓏼	ɰ	///	ג	III	Γ	III
4	𒁹𒁹𒁹𒁹 (or ∨∨∨∨)	𓏽	ɰǀ	////	ד	IIII	Δ	IIII (or IV)
5	𒐊 (or ∨∨∨∨∨)	𓏾	"/	// ///	ה	Γ	E	V
6	𒐋 (or ∨∨∨∨∨∨)	𓏿	"ɿ	/// ///	ו	ΓI	F	VI
7	𒐌 (or ∨∨∨∨∨∨∨)	𓐀	ɀ	/ /// ///	ז	ΓII	Z	VII
8	𒐍 (or ∨∨∨∨∨∨∨∨)	𓐁	ꝛ	// /// ///	ח	ΓIII	H	VIII
9	𒐎 (or ∨∨∨∨∨∨∨∨∨)	𓐂	ʕ	/// /// ///	ט	ΓIIII	Θ	VIIII (or IX)
10	𒌋 (or <)	𓎆	ʌ	𐤗	י	Δ	I	X
20	𒌋𒌋 (or <<)	𓎇	ʌ́	𐤘	כ	ΔΔ	K	XX
50			˥		נ		N	L
100		𓍢	⌐		ק	H	P	C
200		𓍢𓍢			ר	HH	Σ	CC
1,000		𓆼	ƀ			X	͵A	M

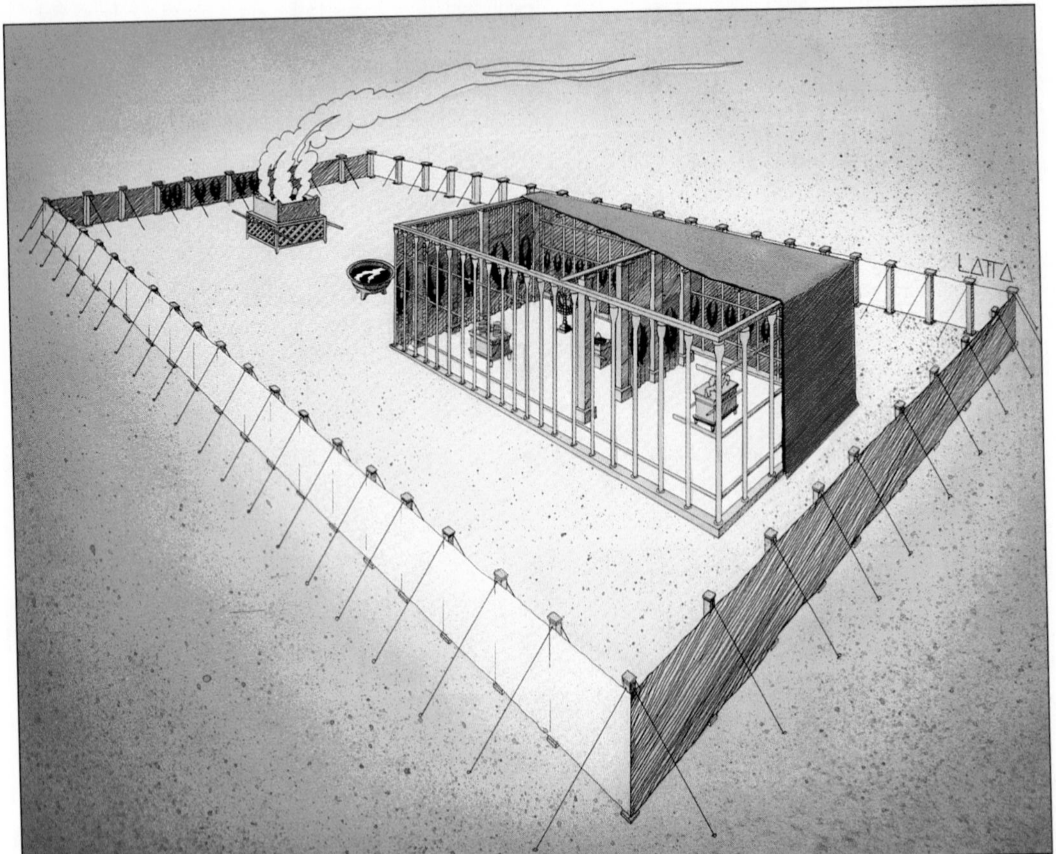

Reconstruction of the Israelite tabernacle and its court. The court was formed by curtains attached to erect poles. Before the tent was placed the altar of burnt offerings and the laver. The tabernacle was always erected to face the east.

laws pertaining to the making and terminating of vows (30:1-16).

31:1-54
Keeping Israel Pure

There was also the unfinished matter of the Midianites. They had drawn Israel into the degrading debauchery of Baal Peor (25:16-17) and therefore had to suffer God's awful judgment. Twelve thousand men of Israel were tapped for the assignment. Having slain Balaam and all the kings and men of Midian, they returned in triumph to the camp (31:1-12). Since the rebellion at Baal Peor involved sexual immorality, Moses demanded that those Midianite women who were not virgins also be slain (31:13-54).

32:1-42
Turning Back Again

Canaan proper was the land promised to the patriarchs. Yet some of the Israelites, namely, Reuben, Gad, and half the tribe of Manasseh, pleaded with Moses that they be allowed to take their inheritance in the Transjordan, right where they were (32:1-19). These tribes, like the previous generation, seemed ready to reject the land God had promised to give. Moses reluctantly granted their request but only on condition that they help their kindred in the conquest of Canaan and that they forever after be faithful to the Lord (32:20-42).

33:1–36:13
Remembering the Journey, Anticipating the Conquest

The recital of Israel's itinerary since Egypt (33:1-49) serves as a reminder of God's care through the wilderness years. Moses' final instructions about conquest (33:50-56) and the tribal allocations (34:1-29) anticipate the fulfillment of God's promise of land recorded in the Book of Joshua. Instructions concerning the Levitical cit-

PRIESTS IN THE OLD TESTAMENT
(Listed alphabetically)

NAME	REFERENCE	IDENTIFICATION
Aaron	Exod 28–29	Older brother of Moses; first high priest of Israel
Abiathar	1 Sam 22:20-23; 2 Sam 20:25	Son of Ahimelech who escaped the slayings at Nob
Abihu	See Nadab and Abihu	
Ahimelech	1 Sam 21–22	Led a priestly community at Nob; killed by Saul for befriending David
Amariah	2 Chr 19:11	High priest during the reign of Jehoshaphat
Amaziah	Amos 7:10-17	Evil priest of Bethel; confronted Amos the prophet
Azariah	2 Chr 26:16-20	High priest who stood against Uzziah when the ruler began to act as a prophet
Eleazar and Ithamar	Lev 10:6; Num 20:26	Godly sons of Aaron; Eleazar—Israel's second high priest
Eli	1 Sam 1–4	Descendant of Ithamar; raised Samuel at Shiloh
Eliashib	Neh 3:1; 13:4-5	High priest during the time of Nehemiah
Elishama and Jehoram	2 Chr 17:7-9	Teaching priests during the reign of Jehoshaphat
Ezra	Ezra 7–10; Neh 8	Scribe, teacher, and priest during the rebuilding of Jerusalem after the Babylonian captivity
Hilkiah	2 Kgs 22–23	High priest during the reign of Josiah
Hophni and Phinehas	1 Sam 2:12-36	Evil sons of Eli
Ithamar	See Eleazar and Ithamar	
Jahaziel	2 Chr 20:14-17	Levite who assured Jehoshaphat of deliverance from an enemy
Jehoiada	2 Kgs 11–12	High priest who saved Joash from Queen Athaliah's purge
Jehoram	See Eliashama and Jehoram	
Joshua	Hag 1:1,12; Zech 3	First high priest after the Babylonian captivity
Nadab and Abihu	Lev 10:1-2	Evil sons of Aaron
Pashhur	Jer 20:1-6	False priest who persecuted the prophet Jeremiah
Phinehas	(1) Num 25:7-13 (2) See Hophni and Phinehas	(1) Son of Eleazar; Israel's third high priest whose zeal for pure worship stopped a plague
Shelemiah	Neh 13:13	Priest during the time of Nehemiah; was in charge of administrating storehouses
Uriah	2 Kgs 16:10-16	Priest who built pagan altar for evil King Ahaz
Zadok	2 Sam 15; 1 Kgs 1	High priest during the reign of David and Solomon

ies and cities of refuge (35:1-8) were to safeguard the promised land from pollution caused by shedding innocent blood (35:9-34). The final narrative in Numbers highlights the desire of the daughters of Zelophehad to share in the inheritance in the land. God rewarded their desire for His promises by providing laws of inheritance for families that had no male heirs (36:1-12). All was now ready for the final statement of covenant embodied in the Book of Deuteronomy and for the conquest of Canaan related in the Book of Joshua.

Contemporary Significance

God desired the very best for the ancient Israelites—to give them a beautiful land as their home. God likewise desires the best for people today. People, however, are free to choose—either to accept God's gifts of love or else to spurn God's promises. The Israelites who left Egypt rejected God's gift of land and suffered death in the wilderness. Likewise those today who reject God's free gift of salvation in Christ do so at their own peril.

The story of the pilgrimage of Israel from Sinai, the place of initial commitment to God, to the plains of Moab, where Israel stood ready to realize all God's promises, sheds light on the Christian experience. Clearly Israel, like today's believers, experienced times of abysmal failure. Israel's frequent murmuring against Moses (and God) illustrates how God's people then and now are not satisfied with what should be our highest pleasure—to experience God's care and guidance in our lives. Israel's longing for good times in Egypt illustrates that the pleasures of sin remain attractive even to those whom God has redeemed. Then and now rebellion against God has dire consequences. Judgment is not, however, God's final word: those who cling tenaciously to God's promises find themselves rewarded.

Ethical Value

Israel's response to the leadership of Moses and Aaron and to the covenant requirements in general dictated the degree of success or failure that characterized their wilderness sojourn. The principle is crystal clear: whenever there was unqualified obedience, there was unmitigated success. Whenever there was obstinate rebellion, there was failure. The demand for commitment to God is no less real and necessary today.

The strong ethical message that comes through loud and clear in Numbers is that God has a plan that leads to blessing. But that plan is built around principles and practices of behavior that cannot be compromised or negotiated. God desires to bless His own, but that blessing is predicated upon submission to God's rule. Success in life depends not only on doing the will of God but on doing it in the manner He prescribes.

Questions for Reflection

1. What were God's conditions for Israel's possession and enjoyment of the promised land?
2. What does Numbers teach
   a. about the dangers of disobedience?
   b. about God's sovereign grace?
3. What is the significance of the location of the tabernacle in the center of the camp?
4. What were the consequences of Israel's rejecting
   a. its God-appointed leaders?
   b. God's gift of the land?
5. What obstacles (external and internal) did Israel face on route to the promised land?
6. Why was Moses not permitted to enter the promised land?
7. How do the daughters of Zelophehad serve as models of faith for Israel?

Sources for Additional Study

Honeycutt, Roy L. Jr., *Leviticus, Numbers, Deuteronomy*. Nashville: Broadman, 1979.

Jensen, Irving L. *Numbers: Journey to God's Rest-Land.* Chicago: Moody, 1964.

Wenham, Gordon J. *Numbers: An Introduction and Commentary*. Downers Grove: InterVarsity, 1981.

DEUTERONOMY

The name *Deuteronomy* (from the Greek for *second law)* arose from the Septuagint's translation of the Hebrew phrase meaning *a copy of this law* (Deut 17:18). Deuteronomy is not a second law but an amplification of the first given at Sinai. The Greek (and hence English) title is thus somewhat misleading. The Hebrew title "these are the words" (from the first two words of the the book) is appropriate for these last words of Moses to Israel. (For discussion of Mosaic authorship and date see "The Pentateuch.")

In recent decades scholars have drawn attention to striking parallels between the Book of Deuteronomy and both Hittite (1400–1200 B.C.) and later Assyrian (850–650 B.C.) treaties. Though many analysts are convinced that Deuteronomy has been influenced by the ancient Near Eastern treaty tradition, it is more than a treaty or covenant text. (See "Near Eastern Treaties.") It is a covenant statement embedded in the farewell address of Moses to Israel (Deut 1:1-3; 34:1-8).

Israel had completed nearly forty years of wilderness wandering and was about to enter and occupy the land of Canaan. The old, rebellious generation had died. The new generation had to hear and respond to the covenant that God had made with their parents at Sinai. Moses repeated the history of God's faithfulness and exhorted the new generation to be obedient to the covenant mandates. He repeated the covenant terms but with amendments and qualifications appropriate to the new situation of conquest and settlement that lay ahead. In addition, Moses provided for future generations to renew their allegiance to the God of the covenant. Thus Deuteronomy is a "farewell" sermon centered on the covenant, an address that takes its fundamental shape from the pattern of Late Bronze Age covenant documents.

Theme

The overarching theme of Deuteronomy is covenant relationships. What would it mean for Israel to be the people of God in the context of conquest and settlement? What privileges and responsibilities did that status as chosen people entail for that generation of Israel and for future generations of God's people?

At the initial revelation of the covenant (Exod 19:4-6), the Lord stated that He had delivered His people from Egypt "on eagles' wings" and had made them His own special people, "a kingdom of priests and a holy nation." Their calling was to be a servant people who would mediate the saving grace of God to all the nations of the earth. Deuteronomy continues that theme by emphasizing the divine election of Israel (Deut 7:6-11; 10:12-15). This role of chosen people was to be lived out within the framework of clearly defined guidelines. These covenant stipulations governed every aspect of the political, social, and religious life of God's people.

Literary Forms

There is a widespread consensus that Deuteronomy is modeled after well-known ancient Near Eastern (specifically Hittite and/or Assyrian) treaty forms. Though the ancient treaty tradition provides the general structure and outline of the book, Deuteronomy adds exhortations, poetry, and other elaborations appropriate to its larger character as a farewell sermon of Moses.

Study of sovereign-vassal treaties made by the great king of the Hittites with conquered or dependent rulers reveal certain common components, which Deuteronomy embodies in the same general order. Following Peter Craigie (*The Book of Deuteronomy,* 24, 67-68), the following standard elements of Hittite covenant texts and their corresponding place in Deuteronomy may be set forth.

1. The Preamble (1:1-5) provides the setting in which the text is presented to the vassal by the Great King.

2. The Historical Prologue (1:6–4:49) rehearses the past relationships between the contracting parties.

3. The General Stipulations (5:1–11:32) are the basic principles of relationship. These reveal the purposes of the Great King and alert the vassal to the guidelines for implementing those purposes.

4. The Specific Stipulations (12:1–26:15) further define the general stipulations by particular cases. In specific situations the vassal would not always be able to deduce the proper application of the general principle without further guidance. Thus the Great King had not only to lay down generalized expectations but to anticipate peculiar or unique circumstances.

5. The Blessings and Curses (27:1–28:68) outline the consequences of faithfulness and disobedience to the covenant. Faithful obedience to the terms of the covenant, that is, to the stipulations laid down in Deuteronomy, would ensure that the vassal would be appropriately rewarded. Conversely, disobedience would bring swift and sure retribution at the hands of the Great King.

6. The Witnesses to the Treaty (30:19; 31:19; 32:1-43) testify to its worth and to the commitments made by the contracting parties. Even the Great King acknowledges the need to stand by the promise He has solemnly sworn.

The elements of the ancient Near Eastern treaties can be seen not only in the larger structure of Deuteronomy but also in the organization of smaller units of the book. For example, Deuteronomy 5 contains (1) an introduction of the Great King ("I am the LORD your God," 5:6); (2) a historical prologue ("who brought you out of Egypt, out of the land of slavery," 5:6); (3) covenant stipulations (5:7-21); (4) blessings and curses ("punishing the children . . . of those who hate me, but showing love to a thousand generations of those who love me and keep my commandments," 5:9-10); and (5) the recording of the covenant (5:22).

I. The Covenant Setting (1:1-5)
II. Learning from the History of God's People (1:6–4:40)
III. Basic Covenant Principles (4:44–6:25)
IV. Auxiliary Covenant Principles (7:1–11:32)
V. Aids and Threats to the Worship of the One God (12:1–16:17)
VI. The Distinctiveness of God's People (16:18–26:19)
VII. The Curses and Blessings of the Covenant (27:1–28:69)
VIII. Renewal of Commitment to the Covenant (29:1–30:20)
IX. The Future of the Covenant (31:1-29)
X. Moses' Song of God's Faithfulness and Israel's Unfaithfulness (31:30–32:43)
XI. The Conclusion of Moses' Ministry (32:44–34:12)

Purpose and Theology

The Book of Deuteronomy first restates the covenant between Yahweh and Israel for the generation assembled in the plains of Moab prior to the conquest of Canaan under Joshua. Most of the generation that had heard and accepted the covenant at Sinai thirty-eight years earlier had died (Deut 2:14; compare Num 14:34). Their sons and daughters now needed to hear the covenant for themselves and to affirm their loyalty to it (Deut 4:1-2; 5:1-5). Provision for future affirmation of the covenant suggests that each generation of God's people has to make the history of God's saving acts its own (26:5-9) and commit itself afresh to the covenant (26:16-19; compare 5:3-4).

Second, Deuteronomy's mix of exhortation and covenant prescription suggests that the book was to record for posterity Moses' words of admonition, encouragement, and warning. Those about to enter the land of promise had to learn from the past, he maintained, if they were to fulfill the purposes for which the Lord had created them (Deut 8:11-20).

The theology of Deuteronomy cannot be separated from its theme and form. As a document influenced by the form of covenant texts, it becomes the vehicle by which the sovereign God expresses His saving and redemptive purposes to His servant nation, His kingdom of priests whom He elected and delivered from bondage in response to the ancient patriarchal promises.

The truth that the God who delivered Israel from Egyptian slavery is the only true God is central to Deuteronomy's presentation of the covenant. Because there is but one God, He demands the total loyalty of His people (6:5; 10:12-13). Because there is but one God, He is to be worshiped in the one place of His choosing (12:5,11; 14:23).

THE COVENANT SETTING (DEUT 1:1-5)

The beginning of Deuteronomy finds Moses addressing the assembly of Israel in Moab, just east of the Jordan River. Forty years had transpired since the exodus, the long trek from Sinai had been completed, the enemies in the Transjordan had been defeated, and everything was in readiness for the conquest of Canaan. Moses therefore delivered a farewell address of covenant instruction and pastoral exhortation.

LEARNING FROM THE HISTORY OF GOD'S PEOPLE (DEUT 1:6–4:40)

Hittite treaties included a summation of past relations between the great king and his vassal. Moses likewise recited the highlights of God's dealings with His people since the giving of the covenant at Sinai nearly forty years before (Deut 1:6–3:29). Following this résumé of Israel's failures and successes on route to the promised land, Moses exhorted God's people to treasure God's commands, to avoid idolatry, and to marvel at God's saving acts (Deut 4:1-40).

1:6–3:29
Failures and Successes on Route to the Promised Land

The Lord had commanded Israel to leave Sinai and to press toward the land of promise (1:6-8). The way had been hard, taxing Moses almost to the limit (1:9-18). But eventually they had arrived at Kadesh Barnea on the borders of the promised land (1:19-25). There the people rebelled, refusing to enter the land (1:26-33). The Lord thus condemned them to wander in the wilderness until they died (1:34-40). After futile attempts to invade Canaan without God's aid (1:41-46), the tribes pressed north, bypassing Edom (2:1-8a) and eventually arriving at Moab (2:8b-25). From there they sought permission to pass through Amorite territory but were soundly rebuffed by both Sihon, king of the Amorites, and Og, king of Basham. These two the Lord delivered into Israel's hands (2:26-37; 3:1-11), thereby allowing Israel to come into possession of the entire Transjordan region (3:12-17). From there Moses had requested that he be allowed to lead his people into Canaan. The Lord, however, denied the request because at Meribah Moses had not trusted God or respected His holiness (3:18-29; 33:51; compare Num 20:12).

4:1-40
Treasure God's Commands; Avoid Idolatry; Marvel at God's Saving Acts

Following this sketch of history, Moses reminded his people of their special privileges as recipients of Yahweh's covenant grace (4:1-8). He urged them to remember what God had done in the past in making Himself known to them (4:9-14). The invisible God who acts in history cannot be represented in lifeless stone or wood or in His creation (4:15-24). Idolatry would lead to His punishment of destruction and exile (4:25-31). Israel's motive for serving and worshiping Yahweh exclusively lies in Yahweh's unique intervention on Israel's behalf, freeing them from slavery and making a covenant with them (4:32-40).

4:41-43
Establishing Cities of Refuge

In a brief narrative interlude Moses set aside three Transjordan cities as places of refuge in the event of manslaughter (4:41-43; compare 19:2-13). Such cities were intended to free the promised land from the stain of innocent blood.

BASIC COVENANT PRINCIPLES (DEUT 4:44–6:25)

A brief introduction sets the covenant in the context of the exodus from Egypt (4:45) and the successful conquest of the territory across the Jordan (4:46-49).

5:1-21
The Heart of the Covenant: The Ten Commandments

After exhorting the present generation of Israelites to identify with their parents at Sinai (5:1-5), Moses listed the Ten Commandments, the very heart of the Sinai covenant (5:6-21). The Ten Commandments share the basic form of ancient Near Eastern treaties.

The Great King is identified ("I am the LORD your God"), and the history of His dealings with His servant people is outlined ("who brought you out of Egypt, out of the land of slavery," 5:6). The first command ("You shall have no other gods before me," 5:7) is *the* basic covenant principle. The following commands detail what Israel's exclusive devotion to God entails for Israel's relations with God (5:8-15) and interpersonal relations (5:16-21). The form of these commands is virtually identical to that in Exodus 20:2-17. Here, however, remembering the Sabbath commemorates the saving deliverance from Egypt (Deut 5:15) rather than creation (Exod 20:11).

5:22-33
Moses' Role as Covenant Mediator

The following flashback to the Sinai revelation emphasizes Moses' role as covenant mediator to fearful Israel (5:22-33). Moses challenged the new generation "to do what the LORD your God has commanded you" (5:32-33) as a condition for prosperous life in the land of promise.

6:1-25
The Most Basic Principle: Complete and Exclusive Love for God

The fundamental nature of the relationship between Yahweh and Israel consists of the recognition that God is one (6:4-5) and that His people, if they are to enjoy the benefits of His promises to the patriarchs, must give Him undivided allegiance and unswerving obedience (6:1-25).

AUXILIARY COVENANT PRINCIPLES (DEUT 7:1–11:32)

The basic requirement of complete and exclusive love for God (6:5; 10:12) is worked out in various ways in 7:1–11:32.

LAW CODES AND COVENANTS (2nd Millennium B.C.)

LAW CODE		COVENANT *
Title	Identifies superior partner.	Title
Prologue	Shows how the superior partner has cared for the subordinate one in the past, thereby inspiring gratitude and obedience within the subordinate partner.	Prologue
Laws	Lists the laws given by the superior partner which are to be obeyed by the subordinate partner	Stipulations/Laws
Blessings and Curses	Provides for the preservation of the text in the temple of the subordinate partner.	Depositions Reading
	Witnessed and guaranteed by the gods of both partners.	Witnesses
	Pronounces curses on those who disobey and blessings on those who obey.	Blessings and Curses
	Ratified by an oath and a ceremony, and sanctions are pronounced against any person who breaks the covenantal relationship.	Oath Ceremony Sanctions

* Covenants also follow the pattern of an ancient Near Eastern treaty. See the discussion in the introduction to the Book of Deuteronomy.

7:1-26
The Total Destruction of the Canaanites

Because Israel was to serve only God in the land of promise, they were to destroy completely the native inhabitants of Canaan who served other gods. They were also to refuse any entangling alliance with them (7:1-26).

8:1–9:6
Yahweh as the Source of Blessing in Canaan

Israel was to acknowledge that Yahweh—not the fertility gods of Canaan—is the source of all blessings in the land (8:1-20). Israel was also to acknowledge that blessing is a product of God's grace, not their righteousness (9:1-6).

9:7–10:11
Moses' Role as Covenant Mediator and Intercessor

Moses' role as covenant mediator and intercessor for disobedient Israel is again highlighted. The incidents of the golden calf (9:7-21), the wilderness murmurings (9:22), and the rejection of God's gift of land (9:22-24) illustrate Israel's persistent rebellion. Moses' appeal to the patriarchal promises and to God's honor (9:25-29) resulted in a renewal of the covenant (10:1-11).

10:12-22
Love for Yahweh and Love for the Disadvantaged

The oneness and exclusivity of Yahweh demand that He be loved by His people with a love that is synonymous with covenant fidelity. But love for God cannot be divorced from love for others, especially for the disadvantaged. Thus the center and substance of the covenant relationship is not legalism but love (10:12-22).

11:1-32
Obedience as Evidence of Love for God

Love must be manifest, and in covenant terms that means obedience. Israel had already seen what disobedience could bring (11:1-7). Now they had to understand afresh that the bounties of God's goodness (11:8-12) were theirs only as they loved Him and kept His commandments (11:13-25). Now, and when they later entered the land, Israel would have opportunity to pledge its faithfulness to the Lord (11:26-32).

AIDS AND THREATS TO THE WORSHIP OF THE ONE GOD (DEUT 12:1–16:17)

Having expounded the broad principles of covenant relationship and responsibility (Deut 5:1–11:32), Moses turned to more specific examples of their application.

12:1-28
The Central Sanctuary

The native Canaanites worshiped many gods at numerous local shrines. As an aid to the worship of the one true God, there was to be only one sanctuary where Israel's community worship was to be carried out (12:1-14). This could not be at the whim of the people but where Yahweh would cause His name to dwell (12:11). Before the building of the Jerusalem temple this central sanctuary was the site of the tabernacle and ark of the covenant.

12:29–13:19
Pagan Gods and False Prophets

Israel was to worship not only in the place of God's choice but in the manner of God's choice. God's people were prohibited from adopting the worship practices of the native Canaanites (12:31). When animal blood was shed, either for offering or human consumption of meat, the blood could not be eaten because it symbolized life itself and therefore was sacred (12:15-28). God's people were not to consume blood as the native Canaanites did. God's people were further prohibited from adopting other Canaanite worship practices such as human sacrifice and cultic prostitution (12:29-31).

Canaanite religion depended on soothsayers and enchanters as channels of revelation and power. Since such practices entailed dealing with gods other than Yahweh, it was obviously forbidden for the people of Israel. Any prophet who counseled God's people to defect from Him, even if he came from within Israel itself, was to be put to death (13:1-18).

14:1-21
The Distinctive Concern for Clean and Unclean Animals

Further differences between Israel and the unbelieving nations around them lay in their perception and use of the animal world. Israel was to demonstrate its calling and character as a holy people by conforming to the Lord's definitions of clean and unclean by eating only those animals that were not forbidden (14:1-21).

14:22-29
Offerings of Thankful Hearts

A further expression of reverence of the sovereign God of Israel was the people's generous offer of tribute to Him in the form of tithes of all their increase (14:22-29). This could be in produce or, if the central sanctuary were too far way, in money. Every third year that tithe was to be used to meet the needs of the Levites, God's specially chosen servants, as well as needs of the poor (14:28-29).

15:1-18
The Distinctive Concern for the Poor and Oppressed

Israel also acknowledged God as its sole Lord by its distinctive concern for the poor and the oppressed. Every seventh year was a year of release in which poor Israelites were freed of all financial encumbrances that had befallen them as a result of their indenturing themselves to their fellow countrymen (15:1-18).

15:19–16:17
Offerings and Festivals of the Central Sanctuary

Deuteronomy 15:19–16:7, like 12:1-28, emphasizes Israel's worship of the one, living God at the central sanctuary. Because the Lord had spared the firstborn of every house of Israel from the tenth plague (Exod 13:11-16), faithful Israelites were to offer up the firstborn of their herds and flocks annually as an expression of devotion (Deut 15:19-23). This was done as part of the Passover celebration and the Feast of Unleavened Bread that followed immediately thereafter (16:1-8). Other occasions for the community of faith to offer tribute to the Great King were the Feast of Weeks (or Pentecost), seven weeks after Passover (16:9-12), and the Feast of Tabernacles in the seventh month of the year (16:13-17).

THE DISTINCTIVENESS OF GOD'S PEOPLE (DEUT 16:18–26:19)

16:18–18:22
Kingdom Officials Who Love Justice and Are Faithful to God's Word

The implementation of the demands of the covenant on the part of the community required political and religious officials who, under God, could ensure stability and obedience. The first group consisted of "judges and officials" (Deut 16:18–17:13). Their task was to apply fair administration of justice (16:18-20) without resorting to pagan means (16:21–17:1). In the interest of justice, Deuteronomy 17:2-7 provides guidelines for admissible evidence. Matters too difficult for resolution at the local level were to be decided by a high court of priests and judges at a central sanctuary, with punishment appropriate to the crime (17:8-13).

Eventually the nation would develop a monarchial government (17:14-20). The king was to be a native Israelite chosen by the Lord Himself (17:14-15). He was to adopt a humble and dependent life-style contrary to that of neighboring kings. This would preclude the amassing of horses as a sign of military might and the multiplication of wives as a sign of entangling international political alliances (17:16-17). Finally, he was to trust in the Lord and seek to live by the principles outlined in the very book of the covenant, the Book of Deuteronomy (17:18-20).

The religious officials of Israel included the priests and Levites. Their responsibilities as leaders in Canaan also receive brief attention in 18:1-8. Since the Lord was their inheritance, they had no land or properties but were to live off the offerings and gifts of God's people.

The prophets also were important in shaping the course of Israel's life as God's people (18:9-22). All peoples, including the Canaanites, had their prophets. These practitioners of sorcery and incantation were so evil before God, however, that they and their demonic techniques were to be repudiated totally (18:9-14). In their place God would raise up an order of prophets in the tradition of Moses, spokesmen who would speak the true word of the Lord (18:15-19). This is therefore a collective reference to the prophets who would follow. As such, it received its ultimate fulfillment in Jesus (see John 1:21,25,45; 5:46; 6:14; 7:40; Acts 3:22-26; 7:37).

Any among this group of prophets who defected from this high and holy calling by prophesying falsely had to die. The fundamental test of their integrity would be whether or not their predictive word came to pass (18:20-22).

19:1-21
The Distinctive Civil Law of God's People

Though Israel was by definition a religious community, it was nevertheless a community composed of individual citizens who were to live together in peace and order. There was, in other words, a social and civil dimension to life as a covenant people. This dictated the need for civil legislation, for rules of behavior in a social setting (Deut 19:1–22:4).

The first of these dealt with the issue of homicide (19:1-13). The Sixth Commandment had already addressed this in principle (Deut 5:17), but not all homicide was murder. Killings were to be considered on a case-by-case basis. If the killing was purely accidental (19:4-6), the perpetrator could flee to a designated city of refuge until his case could be judged (19:1-3,7-10; compare Num 35:9-34). If, however, the deed was intentional or there was malice aforethought, the killer was to be apprehended and slain by the avenger of the aggrieved party (19:11-13).

The second civil statute concerned the removal of boundary markers (19:14). Land was at the very heart of covenant inheritance, so for one to cheat his neighbor by moving property lines was to infringe on God's gift to him. Central to equitable civil law was the innocence of the accused unless proven guilty. One was not to be condemned on the testimony of one witness only; there were to be at least two for corroboration (19:15-19). False witnesses were to suffer the consequences of their perjury to the degree the accused party would have obtained if he had been found guilty and punished (19:20-21), showing that care must be taken to provide justice.

20:1–21:14
The Conduct of Holy War

As a nation about to engage the Canaanite nations in wars of conquest, Israel was given guidelines for this undertaking. God's people were to trust that God was with them and that He would achieve the victory (20:1-4). This allowed for many kinds of exemptions from military service. The sheer numbers of troops would not determine the outcome but only faithfulness to the Lord's commands (20:5-9).

In wars against distant nations, terms of peace were to be offered first. If they were accepted, the populace would be spared but would be reduced to the service of Israel and its God (20:10-15). If, however, the cities were devoted to the Lord as part of Israel's inheritance in Canaan, they were to be annihilated lest their peoples draw Israel away into apostasy (20:16-18).

From time to time homicides would occur without witnesses. Israel's sense of corporate solidarity was such that the citizens of the village nearest the corpse were held liable. They were to offer up a heifer as an atonement for the whole community to absolve it thus of guilt (21:1-9).

As a result of war, prisoners would frequently come under Israelite control. Females in such cases could become the wives of their captors after a period of adjustment. If the arrangement proved unsatisfactory, they were to be freed (21:10-14).

21:15–22:4
More Distinctives of the Civil Law of God's People

Though the Lord nowhere sanctions multiple marriages, He did provide guidelines for making the best of a bad situation. A preferred wife was to have no advantage over a less-loved wife in the allocation of inheritance rights to their respective sons (21:15-17).

Rebellious sons who were unmanageable to their parents could be prosecuted by them and even executed by the civil authorities (21:18-21). In any capital case, however, the dead corpse was not to lie exposed after sundown but was to be buried that very day (21:22-23; cf. John 19:31).

The final example of civil law has to do with lost property (22:1-4). Any Israelite who found anything belonging to a fellow citizen either had to return it to him or wait for him to come and claim it. If it were an animal that had fallen by the wayside, brotherliness mandated that the beast be lifted up and restored.

22:5–23:18
The Distinctive Purity of God's People

As the Mosaic covenant testifies over and over again, Israel was a holy people and was to live a holy life before the world. Like Leviticus (compare Lev 17–25), Deuteronomy also has its "holiness code," its set of guidelines by which Israel was to achieve and maintain its purity (Deut 22:5–23:18). Though the reason for the inclusion of some of these laws may escape the modern reader, in their own time and circumstances they undoubtedly contributed to Israel's understanding of what it meant to be a people peculiar to the Lord and unique among the peoples of the earth.

Transvestism was condemned because it spoke of unnatural mixing of clothing (22:5). Rules about the protection of young birds (22:6-7), the building of roof railings (22:8), sowing mixed seed, plowing with mixed teams, wearing clothing of mixed material (22:9-11), and wearing garments with tassels (22:12) either positively or negatively speak of Israel's role as a people distinct from the heathen around them.

Purity or impurity frequently expresses itself in sexual relationships. Thus a man who married a woman who, in his opinion, turned out not to have been a virgin might demand that she prove her purity. If she could, he stood condemned; but if she could not, she was to be stoned to death (22:13-21). Adulterers, both male and female, were to die (22:22) as were engaged girls who had undertaken sexual relations willingly (22:23-24). An assailant who raped an engaged woman was to pay with his life (22:25-27). One who raped a maiden who was not betrothed had to marry her, pay her father a generous bride price, and never divorce her (22:28-29). Finally, one was not to engage his father's wife (that is, his stepmother) in sexual relations (22:30).

The holiness of God's people also revealed itself in the rejection from its assembly of those who had been emasculated (23:1), born out of wedlock (23:2), or who were of Ammonite or Moabite descent (23:3-6). This was because these latter refused hospitality to Israel in the wilderness. The Edomites, Israel's kindred people, and the Egyptians, Israel's hosts in times of famine, could however eventually enter the covenant privileges (23:7-8).

Both male and female cult prostitutes were strictly forbidden in Israel. Their ungodly gain could not serve as offering to the Lord (23:17-18). An escaped slave was welcome, however, and in fact was not to be forced to return to his master (23:15-16).

Finally, purification pertained to matters of bodily cleanliness, especially in the context of holy war (23:9-14). Soldiers contaminated by bodily secretions were to purify themselves. They were also to bury their excrement. The reason was that the Lord walked in the midst of the camp. Physical impurity was an affront to a holy God and pointed to spiritual impurity as well.

23:19–25:19
The Distinctive Interpersonal Relationships of God's People

Attention to the laws of purity gives rise to an association with precepts governing interpersonal relationships in general (Deut 23:19–25:19). There are areas of societal life which, though not cultic in nature, have moral and ethical implications important to covenant life and faith. Such matters as loans to fellow Israelites and foreigners (23:19-20), vows to the Lord (23:21-23), and the right to help oneself to a neighbor's grapes and grain while passing through his land (23:24-25) illustrate the principle that one's fair dealings with both God and others are on the same level.

Similarly, the covenant addresses the problems of divorce (24:1-4) and the newlywed (24:5); loan security (24:6,10-13); kidnapping (24:7); contagious skin diseases (24:8-9); the charitable care of the poor, weak, and disenfranchised (24:14-15,17-22); and the principle of responsibility for one's own sin and of liability to punishment (24:16).

Justice demanded that the guilty suffer appropriate punishment (25:1-3), that a brother of a deceased and childless Israelite raise up offspring in his name by marrying his widow (25:5-10), that a woman not dishonor a man sexually (25:11-12), and that weights and measures be according to standard (25:13-16). Justice even extended to the animal world, for the ox was allowed to eat of the grain it was threshing for its owner (25:4; compare 1 Cor 9:9). At the other extreme, God's justice demanded that the enemies of His chosen people experience judgment at their hands. Thus Amalek, who had attacked the elderly and defenseless of Israel in the wilderness journey (compare Exod 17:8-16), was one day to be destroyed from the earth (Deut 25:17-19).

26:1-15
Reaffirmation of the Covenant in Worship

The specific stipulations section of Deuteronomy concludes with the laws of covenant celebration and confirmation (26:1-15). When Israel finally entered the land of Canaan, they were to acknowledge the Lord's faithful provision. They were to do this by offering their firstfruits to Him while reciting the history of His beneficent covenant dealings with them from the ancient days of the patriarchs to the present (26:1-11). This ceremony appears to have been a part of the celebration of the Feast of Weeks (or Pentecost or Harvest; compare Exod 23:16; Lev 23:15-21). Following the offering of the first of the grain harvest to the Lord, Israelite farmers were to provide the Levites and other dependent citizens the tithe of their produce (Deut 26:12-15). In this manner tribute to God and support of the needy merged into one glorious act of worship.

26:16-19
Exhortation and Narrative Interlude

Having outlined the long body of stipulations, Moses commanded the people to obey them, not just perfunctorily but with all their heart and soul (26:16). The very essence of the covenant was the pledge they had made to be God's people and the Lord's reciprocal promise to be their God. It was the will of God that Israel continue to be His special people, a holy communion called to be an expression of praise and honor of the Lord.

THE CURSES AND BLESSINGS OF THE COVENANT (DEUT 27:1–28:69)

An element of many ancient treaties was the description of the rewards for faithful compliance to its terms and the punishments befitting disobedience to it. The curses and blessings of Deuteronomy 27–28 show the influence of this treaty form.

27:1-10
The Gathering at Shechem

The ceremony of blessing and cursing, to take place once Canaan had been occupied, was to occur in the vicinity of Shechem, the site of early patriarchal encounters with God (27:4; compare Gen 12:6; 35:4; Deut 11:26-29). There Israel was to erect great plastered monuments containing the covenant text and an altar of stone upon which appropriate offerings of covenant renewal could be sacrificed (27:1-8).

27:11-26
The Curses That Follow Disobedience of Specific Stipulations

As God's people (27:9-10), Israel would stand half on Mount Ebal and half on Mount Gerizim to affirm their covenant commitment (27:11-14). As a great responsive chorus, tribal representatives would stand on Mount Gerizim to shout "amen" at the listing of the blessings while others, on Mount Ebal, would do so when the curses were sounded.

The first list of curses (27:15-26) deals with representative covenant violations without specifying the form the curses might take.

28:1-14
The Blessings That Follow Obedience of General Stipulations

The blessing section (28:1-14) promises prosperity in physical and material ways and reaffirms God's intention to make Israel an exalted and holy people.

28:15-68
The Curses That Follow Disobedience of General Stipulations

The second list of curses threatens loss of prosperity (28:15-19), disease and pestilence (28:20-24), defeat and deportation with all that would entail (28:25-35), and a reversal of roles between Israel and the nations (28:36-46). Rather than being exalted among them, Israel would become their servant. All of this would result in indescribable misery and hopelessness (28:47-57). In effect, covenant violation would undo the exodus and deliver the nation back into the throes of bondage (28:58-68).

RENEWAL OF COMMITMENT TO THE COVENANT (DEUT 29:1–30:20)

29:1-9
Remembering God's Saving Acts

Moses rehearsed God's dealings with Israel in the exodus and wilderness (29:2-9). He exhorted them to pledge themselves to covenant fidelity as the new generation chosen by the Lord to represent Him on the earth (29:10-21). Their commitment was to be personal and genuine. If not, the time of judgment would come in which the nations would question whether or not Israel was in fact the people of the Lord (29:22-29).

29:10–30:10
Anticipating Israel's Rebellion, God's Judgment, and Grace on the Repentant

Moses anticipated not only Israel's rebellion and God's judgment (29:10-29) but also God's grace toward the repentant. God would visit His people in their day of calamity and exile and would cause them once more to reflect on their covenant privileges.

God then would exercise His grace and restore them to full covenant partnership with its blessings (30:1-10).

30:11-20
Choosing to Follow God and Live or to Rebel and Die

Israel's pledge to faithful adherence to the terms of covenant could bring immediate and lasting reward (30:11-16). But disobedience would produce only judgment (30:17-20).

Replica of the Stele of Hammurabi (dating from 1765 B.C.) on which is inscribed the Code of Hammurabi—a Babylonian law code written during the reign of Hammurabi.

THE FUTURE OF THE COVENANT (DEUT 31:1-29)

31:1-8
God as the True Leader of His People

Though the ceremony of covenant renewal is not narrated, it is clear that the new generation of Israelites recommitted themselves to the covenant. (It is implied in 29:10-13.) Moses reaffirmed God's role as the true leader of His people (31:1-8).

31:9-13
God's Word to Be Recorded and Read

God's provision for the future of the covenant included a leader (Joshua) to succeed Moses as covenant mediator (31:1-8), as well as a law, the covenant text delivered to the priests for safekeeping (31:9-13).

31:14-29
God's Provision for the Future: A Leader, a Song, a Law Book

God provided Joshua as a successor to Moses (31:14,23). God's provision for the future of the covenant also included a song, whose purpose was to remind the nation of the covenant pledges they had made (31:15-23; compare 31:30–32:43). Finally, God provided a record of the law so that future generations could know God's will (30:24-27). The Lord, true to ancient treaty form, invoked heaven and earth as witnesses to the promises that Israel had sworn (31:28-29).

MOSES' SONG OF GOD'S FAITHFULNESS AND ISRAEL'S UNFAITHFULNESS (DEUT 31:30–32:43)

This wonderful hymn of covenant commitment (32:1) extols the God of Israel for His greatness and righteousness (32:2-4) despite the wickedness of His people (32:5-6a). He had created them (32:6b) and had redeemed (32:7-9) and preserved them (32:10-14). They rebelled in turn and followed other gods (32:15-18). This course of action provoked His judgment in the past and would do so in the future (32:19-38). At last, however, God would remember His covenant and bring His people salvation (32:39-43).

THE CONCLUSION OF MOSES' MINISTRY (DEUT 32:44–34:12)

32:44-52
Narrative Interlude: Anticipating Moses' Death

Having sung his song, Moses urged his people to subscribe to its demands as a covenant instrument (32:44-47). Then, in response to the command of the Lord, Moses ascended Mount Nebo to await the day of his death (32:48-52). That so great a leader as Moses was not spared judgment when he failed to trust God and respect His holiness served as a stern warning to Israel to avoid his mistakes.

33:1-29
Moses' Final Act: The Blessing of Israel

Before he left them, Moses offered his fellow Israelites a will and testament similar to that with which Jacob had blessed his sons (compare Gen 49:2-27). After praising the God of deliverance and covenant (Deut 33:2-5), he listed the tribes by name, assigning to each a prophetic blessing (33:6-25). He concluded with praise of Israel's Lord (33:26-28) and a promise that His chosen ones would ultimately triumph over all their foes (33:29).

34:1-12
Narrative Epilogue: The Death of Moses

Having ascended Mount Nebo (or Pisgah), Moses viewed all the land of promise, a land promised to the patriarchs but denied to Moses because of his sin (34:1-4; compare 32:51). He then died and was buried by the Lord in an unknown and unmarked grave (34:5-6). With great lament the people of Israel mourned his passing. Though Joshua possessed the spirit and authority of Moses, neither he nor any man to come could compare with this giant on the earth whom God knew "face to face" (34:10) and who had been the great spokesman for God.

Contemporary Significance

Deuteronomy was addressed specifically to a younger generation of Israelites poised to enter the promised land. However, it conveys timeless principles and theological truths that are appropriate to the modern church and world. That new generation of Israelites serves as a model for God's people in every age. We, like they, are a people with a past in which God has acted for our salvation and has revealed His will for our lives. But it is not enough to have a proud heritage of faith. We, like they, are a people with a present. We too are personally to commit ourselves to God today. Finally, we, like they, are a people with a future dependent on our continuing faithfulness to God.

Deuteronomy's covenant anticipates that new covenant—not written on stone but on human hearts (Jer 31:33-34)—which is finally fulfilled in Christ (Matt 26:28; Mark 14:24; Luke 22:20). The God of Israel redeemed them from bondage and chaos and chose to identify with them in an everlasting covenant bond. In and through His Son Jesus Christ, He has graciously offered the same to all people everywhere.

Ethical Value

Deuteronomy's frequent appeal for Israel to love God (6:5; 10:12; 11:1,13,22; 19:9; 30:6,16,20) shows that the aim of Old Testament law was not legalism but love-inspired service. Indeed when Jesus was questioned about the greatest of the Old Testament laws, he quoted Deuteronomy 6:4-5. Israel's love—like that of the Christian (1 John 4:19)—is grounded in a prior experience of God's redeeming love. Israel's love for God—again like that of the Christian (1 John 3:18; 4:20-21)—is true love only to the extent it is shared with others (Deut 10:19). The Ten Commandments underscore that God demands not just respect from people (5:6-15) but respect for other people (6:16-21). While the Ten Commandments have a timeless quality, they are truly significant only to those committed to the God behind them.

Moses and the law

Questions for Reflection

1. What is the meaning of the name *Deuteronomy?* How appropriate is it for the contents of the book?
2. What are the basic elements of the ancient treaty form? How is Deuteronomy like ancient treaties? How is it different?
3. Why is it important for each generation to commit itself afresh to God's lordship?
4. Explain how the command to love God completely and exclusively is the foundation of the whole law. Can one love God and not love others?
5. Why was it important
   a. for the Israelites to destroy the Canaanite population of the promised land?
   b. to worship God at one central sanctuary?
6. What qualities were to distinguish the leaders of God's people? What qualities were to distinguish God's people from the Canaanites?
7. How does the history of Israel from the conquest through the exile to the restoration of Jerusalem illustrate the blessings and curses of the covenant?
8. How does God provide for the future of His covenant people?

Sources for Additional Study

Craigie, Peter C. *The Book of Deuteronomy. The New International Commentary on the Old Testament.* Grand Rapids: Eerdmans, 1976.

Goldberg, Louis. *Deuteronomy. Bible Study Commentary.* Grand Rapids: Zondervan, 1986.

Kline, Meredith G. *Treaty of the Great King.* Grand Rapids: Eerdmans, 1963.

Rad, Gerhard von. *Deuteronomy.* Philadelphia: Westminster, 1966.

Schultz, Samuel J. *Deuteronomy: The Gospel of Love. Everyman's Bible Commentary.* Chicago: Moody, 1971.

Thompson, J. A. *Deuteronomy: An Introduction and Commentary.* Downers Grove: InterVarsity, 1974.

The Historical Books

The Historical Books in the English Bible are Joshua, Judges, Ruth, 1 and 2 Samuel, 1 and 2 Kings, 1 and 2 Chronicles, Ezra, Nehemiah, and Esther. At first the Books of 1 and 2 Samuel were one book as were Kings, Chronicles, and Ezra-Nehemiah. The Septuagint, the ancient Greek translation, was the first to divide the books. The Latin Vulgate and English versions have continued this practice. (The Hebrew division of these books did not occur until the Middle Ages.) Our English translators, again following the Septuagint, arrange the Historical Books in a loosely chronological order. (See "How We Got Our Bible.") This continuous narrative traces the history of Israel from the conquest of Canaan by Joshua (about 1400 B.C.) to the restoration of the Jews during the Persian period (about 400 B.C.).

The Hebrew canon arranges the Historical Books differently. The Hebrew canon consists of three divisions (Law, Prophets, and Writings). Joshua, Judges (omitting Ruth), 1 and 2 Samuel, and 1 and 2 Kings are in the second division, the Prophets. Within this division they are designated the Former Prophets (the Latter Prophets are Isaiah, Jeremiah, Ezekiel, and the twelve Minor Prophets). First and Second Chronicles, Ezra, and Nehemiah occur in the Writings as the final four books of the Hebrew canon. They, however, have a reverse order: Ezra, Nehemiah, and 1 and 2 Chronicles. The Books of Ruth and Esther also appear in the Writings. They, with the Song of Solomon, Lamentations, and Ecclesiastes, constitute the five *Megilloth* (*scrolls*) read by the Jews at various feasts.

The Former Prophets (Joshua, Judges, Samuel, and Kings) continue the narrative of Genesis through Deuteronomy which tells of Israel's birth and rise as a nation. Deuteronomy concludes with the appointment of Joshua as Moses' successor who eventually led Israel into the land. Joshua through 2 Kings relate the occupation of the land of Canaan, the rise of the Hebrew monarchy, and conclude with the destruction and exile of the nation by the Babylonians.

The heading Former *Prophets* indicates that the rabbis did not read these books as histories (in our modern sense). Although written in narrative form, they were *prophetic.* Like the oracles of the Latter Prophets, these "histories" declared the word of the LORD. They do not give an exhaustive history or a political account (as modern history writing would do). Rather, they interpret Israel's history from the theological perspective of God's covenant with Israel. As prophetic writings, they present God's evaluation and verdict on the history of Israel. They are not merely a history of Israel's religion either. (The Hebrew historians did not differentiate between Israel's political fortunes and its religious life.) The narrative in Joshua through 2 Kings shows that Israel's success or failure as a nation was determined by God's intervention in its history. God's kindness or judgment was in

HISTORY WRITING IN BIBLE TIMES

How to define history and history writing has been one of the unending problems of philosophy. In ordinary use *history writing* designates an extended narrative chronicle of the facts that a writer considers important to understanding a period, an individual, a movement, a crisis, or some other event or series of events.

Several principles are very important in understanding history writing. They apply as well to modern, ancient, or biblical history writing.

Selectivity

No work of history records all the facts and details. In the first place, this would be an impossible task; and in the second, such a history would include all sorts of data not germane to the author's intent. Each author selects that information which helps achieve his or her goal for writing. That is, each author is unavoidably selective in the material reported.

The biblical writers were likewise selective. For example, why didn't the writers of Kings and Chronicles include more detail on the architecture of the temple? Much more could have been said about details of its construction. But at some point they chose not to include more information, either because they did not have it or because in light of the overall intent of their narrative they felt a sufficient amount had been included. Another example: some details of the life of David are only known from either Samuel or Chronicles. Neither historian set out to write all that could be known.

Perspective

No writer of history stands outside history. He or she is always a part of particular culture and holds or rejects particular value systems. These attitudes and values affect the writer's selection of data, often even in unconscious ways. They influence the way a writer organizes material and impart to it a certain "slant."

Biblical historians also wrote from the vantage of a particular historical moment and culture. For example, the writer of Chronicles lived in the postexilic period when the northern tribes had long been carried into cap-

response to the spiritual and moral condition of the people with respect to their fidelity to the Mosaic covenant (Exod 20–24). In particular, the Former Prophets—especially 1 and 2 Kings—were influenced by Deuteronomy's understanding of the covenant. This understanding emphasizes covenant loyalty and exclusive worship of God and explains how history is affected by a nation's morality.

The authors of Joshua, Judges, Samuel, and Kings are unknown since the works are anonymous. The six books show independence but also have a relationship. Each book can be read as a literary whole, possessing its peculiar literary arrangement and theological emphasis. They also evidence continuity based on their common subject and, in some cases, their common forms of expression. Each contributes to the consecutively told history of Israel. The books overlap in other respects too. David's reign is related primarily in 2 Samuel but continues into 1 Kings 1–2. The death of Joshua is recounted in both Joshua (24:29-33) and Judges (2:8-10). Deuteronomy's style of language and its basic approach to interpreting history significantly influenced all four works.

The traditional view emphasized the discontinuity of the six books, attributing the four works to different authors. Even the early rabbis,

tivity. He did not give us a history of both kingdoms (like that found in 1 and 2 Kings), but only of the kingdom of Judah, which survived as a political entity in his own day.

Purpose

While *perspective* in this context refers to items influencing the writer in more unconscious and subliminal ways, *purpose* refers to the writer's conscious agenda. Historians often write to demonstrate the validity of a particular thesis. Some examples are the economic causes of the American revolution, the adequacy or inadequacy of a Marxist interpretation of European history, and the impact of the idea of "Manifest Destiny" on the expansion of America. No historian, ancient or modern, escapes these foundational concerns.

The biblical historians also wrote with particular purposes and goals. The compiler or author of the Book of Kings lived during the Babylonian captivity. Those to whom he wrote had witnessed the destruction of Jerusalem and the end of David's dynasty ruling there. But what of God's promises that David would never lack a son sitting on his throne and that God had chosen to dwell in Jerusalem? The writer of Kings recounted the history of the kingdoms to show that God had not failed. The exile did not show that God could not keep His promises, but to the contrary showed that He is indeed in control of history.

The biblical historians were seeking to minister to the needs of the generations to which they wrote. We are not just interested in what they said, but also in why they chose to present it the way they did. Not just the individual narratives are important, but also the thrust and intent of the entire work.

Similar principles apply to historical writings from the other cultures of the biblical period. For example, the annals of the Assyrian kings were summaries of important events in each year of the reigning king. The scribes who wrote them assumed the superiority and right of the Assyrian empire (perspective). They wrote in order to glorify the reigning king (purpose) and would not report any reverses of defeats suffered by him (selectivity). □

however, attributed Judges and 1 and 2 Samuel to the prophet Samuel (with 2 Samuel finished by others). A convincing reconstruction of the history of the writing of these four works has to account both for their differences and distinctives and the apparent continuity of the books.

Some critical scholars believe that Joshua is best understood as the *conclusion* of the Pentateuch rather than the *introduction* to the history of Israel in the land. These scholars use the term *Hexateuch* (*six-book unit*) to highlight the unity of Genesis through Joshua. The remaining books, Judges through 2 Kings, are regarded as a separate composition. The editor of this history combined extensions of the sources that underlie the Hexateuch. (See "The Pentateuch.")

A competing opinion among scholars treats Deuteronomy through 2 Kings as the work of an unnamed editor deeply influenced by the themes of Deuteronomy. This editor wove sources together during the exile (about 550 B.C.). This history was at first unrelated to and independent of the Tetrateuch (Genesis through Numbers). The composition of this history involved lengthy and complex processes of sewing together written sources, authoring new material, and editing the whole into one narrative. Scholars debate the details of date and authorship, some suggesting one author and others proposing several with two or three editions of the work. Its proponents, however, generally accept that the core of Deuteronomy was authored in the mid-seventh century by an author drawing on ancient traditions from the time of Moses. Later an individual or group supporting Josiah's reforms expanded and reworked this core into the bulk of Deuteronomy through 2 Kings. This expanded history was later issued with minor additions to reflect the fall of Jerusalem in about 550 B.C.

In contrast to the traditional rabbinic opinion, these two critical theories emphasize the continuity of the Former Prophets. But in doing so they create a number of problems of their own. Scholars, for example, are not agreed on the process of compilation or on who the nameless editors were (priests, prophets, or sages?). The criteria used by source critics for discovering the underlying literary strands in the Former Prophets are as suspect as those employed for the Pentateuch. Most troubling to these composition theories is their dependence on a seventh-century date for Deuteronomy. Its literary form has, however, been shown to be much older

RULERS OF ISRAEL AND JUDAH

RULERS OF THE UNITED KINGDOM

Saul 1 Sam 9:1–31:13
David 1 Sam 16:1–1 Kgs 2:11
Solomon 1 Kgs 1:1–11:43

RULERS OF THE DIVIDED KINGDOM

RULERS OF ISRAEL		RULERS OF JUDAH	
Jeroboam I	I Kgs 11:26–14:20	Rehoboam	1 Kgs 11:42–14:31
		Abijah (Abijam)	1 Kgs 14:31–15:8
Nadab	1 Kgs 15:25-28	Asa	Kgs 15:8-24
Baasha	1 Kgs 15:27–16:7		
Elah	1 Kgs 16:6-14		
Zimri	1 Kgs 16:9-20		
Omri	1 Kgs 16:15-28		
Ahab	1 Kgs 16:28–22:40	Jehoshaphat	1 Kgs 22:41-50
Ahaziah	1 Kgs 22:40–2 Kgs 1:18	Jehoram	2 Kgs 8:16-24
Jehoram (Joram)	2 Kgs 1:17–9:26	Ahaziah	2 Kgs 8:24–9:29
Jehu	2 Kgs 9:1-10:36	Athaliah	2 Kgs 11:1-20
Jehoahaz	2 Kgs 13:1-9	Joash	2 Kgs 11:1–12:21
Jehoash (Joash)	2 Kgs 13:10–14:16	Amaziah	2 Kgs 14:1-20
Jeroboam II	2 Kgs 14:23-29	Azariah (Uzziah)	2 Kgs14:21; 15:1-7
Zechariah	2 Kgs 14:29–15:12		
Shallum	2 Kgs 15:10-15	Jotham	2 Kgs 15:32-38
Menahem	2 Kgs 15:14-22		
Pekahiah	2 Kgs 15:22-26		
Pekah	2 Kgs 15:25-31	Ahaz (Jehoahaz)	2 Kgs 16:1-20
Hoshea	2 Kgs 15:30–17:6		
		Hezekiah	2 Kgs 18:1–20:21
		Manasseh	2 Kgs 21:1-18
		Amon	2 Kgs 21:19-26
		Josiah	2 Kgs 21:26–23:30
		Jehoahaz II (Shallum)	2 Kgs 23:30-33
		Jehoiakim (Eliakim)	2 Kgs 23:34–24:5
		Jehoiachin (Jeconiah)	2 Kgs 24:6-16; 25:27-30
		Zedekiah (Mattaniah)	2 Kgs 24:17–25:7

than proposed. In fact, it corresponds in general to the political treaties among the Hittites (about 1400–1200 B.C.).

The challenge is to give due both to the continuity and disunity evidenced in the Former Prophets. The four books were likely once independent works, largely in their present form. These underwent a brief period of editorial integration after the destruction of Jerusalem. What they share with Deuteronomy is best attributed to the imposing figure of the prophet Moses. His theology of history, reflected in Deuteronomy, became the theological model by which Israel interpreted its history. The Former Prophets play out what in essence Moses had forewarned concerning God's blessing and cursing (Deut 28).

First and Second Chronicles and Ezra-Nehemiah give a second perspective on Israel's history, complementing the account of Genesis through 2 Kings. First and Second Chronicles parallel this first history from creation to the destruction of Jerusalem. Ezra-Nehemiah continues the account with the return of the exiles from Babylon and the restoration of the religious life of Judah (about 400 B.C.). Since these books were written during and after the exile when there was no monarchy, they focus on the religious life of restored Israel. Temple worship and observance of the law of Moses are particularly emphasized.

Like the Former Prophets, the Books of Chronicles and Ezra-Nehemiah have been ascribed to a single author or compiler. The rabbinic tradition attributed these four books to Ezra the scribe. Some modern scholars who have emphasized the unity of the books in language, content, and perspective follow this position. Others, agreeing in principle with the idea of a single author or compiler, have proposed an unnamed author (the "Chronicler"). The Chronicler drew on sources, including the memoirs of Ezra and Nehemiah and the Books of Samuel and Kings. He completed his "Chronicler's History" no earlier than 400 B.C.

In a variation on this view, two different viewpoints are discerned within the history. First and Second Chronicles plus Ezra 1–6 was an early edition by the Chronicler (about 515 B.C.), in conjunction with the prophetic ministries of Haggai and Zechariah. At this time Israel's hope was for a restored Davidic monarchy (1 Chr 3:17-19; compare Ezra 1:8; 3:8; 5:1-2; 6:14; Hag 2:6-9; 3:23; Zech 3:1–4:14; 6:9-15). The inclusion of Ezra 7–10

QUEENS OF THE OLD TESTAMENT (Listed alphabetically)

NAME	REFERENCE	IDENTIFICATION
Abijah	2 Kgs 18:2	Mother of King Hezekiah of Judah
Athaliah	2 Kgs 11	Evil daughter of Ahab and Jezebel; mother of King Ahaziah of Judah (only woman to rule Judah in her own right)
Azubah	1 Kgs 22:42	Mother of King Jehoshaphat of Judah
Bathsheba	2 Sam 11–12; 1 Kgs 1–2	Wife of Uriah, then wife of David and mother of Solomon
Esther	Esth 2–9	Jewish wife of King Ahasuerus of Persia
Hamutal	2 Kgs 23:31; 24:18	Mother of King Jehoahaz and King Zedekiah of Judah
Hephzibah	2 Kgs 21:1	Mother of King Manasseh of Judah
Jecoliah	2 Kgs 15:2	Mother of King Azariah of Judah
Jedidah	2 Kgs 22:1	Mother of King Josiah of Judah
Jehoaddin	2 Kgs 14:2	Mother of King Amaziah of Judah
Jezebel	1 Kgs 16:31; 18:13,19; 19:1-2; 21:1-25; 2 Kgs 9:30-37	Evil wife of King Ahab of Israel (who promoted Baal worship, persecuted God's prophets, and planned Naboth's murder)
Maacah	1 Kgs 15:10; 2 Chr 15:16	Mother of King Abijah and grandmother of King Asa of Judah
Meshullemeth	2 Kgs 21:19	Mother of King Amon of Judah
Michal	1 Sam 18:20-28; 26:44; 2 Sam 3:13-16; 6:20-23	Daughter of Saul and first wife of David
Naamah	1 Kgs 14:21,31	Mother of King Rehoboam of Judah
Nehushta	2 Kgs 24:8	Mother of King Jehoiachin of Judah
Queen of Sheba	1 Kgs 10:1-13	Foreign queen who visited Solomon
Zebidah	2 Kgs 23:36	Mother of King Jehoiakim of Judah

(Ezra's reforms) and Nehemiah's material came later (about 400 B.C.). At this later time the community shifted its emphasis from the monarchy and the religious role of David to the law of Moses. Some prefer, therefore, to speak of a "Chronistic school" rather than one person.

The similar language and content of Chronicles and Ezra-Nehemiah points to a single work. Both works stress, for instance, the role of the temple and worship customs. Further evidence of linkage is 2 Chronicles 36:1-21, which recounts the pilfering of temple articles, and Ezra 1:7-11, which inventories the restored temple treasuries. Most significant is the *verbatim* agreement of 2 Chronicles' final verses (36:22-23) with the opening paragraph of Ezra (1:1-3a). These verses relate the decree of Cyrus announcing the release of the Jews from captivity. In fact, the last verse of 2 Chronicles ends in the middle of a thought that is completed in the Ezra version (1:3b). This duplication of verses, it is argued, indicates that the books were once bound as a consecutive whole. Evangelical as well as critical scholars hold this view of a single work. Conservative scholarship uniformly holds that the Chronicler used reliable sources and did not materially distort them.

Other scholars, both evangelical and critical, argue that Ezra and Nehemiah were the authors of their own works. Proponents of this position point to significant differences in both language and content between Chronicles and Ezra-Nehemiah. (For instance, Chronicles does not address the subject of mixed marriages.) Finally, the Hebrew arrangement of Ezra-Nehemiah followed by 1 and 2 Chronicles is said to evidence that the two were *not* authored as one piece. The common paragraph shared by the two can best be explained as a much later attempt to bind together what were once separate books.

The arrangement of the Hebrew canon, however, is not a decisive witness for either position. The arrangement is better explained by appeal to the envelope construction created by the repetition of the decree of Cyrus. In this arrangement, like bookends, Ezra begins and 2 Chronicles closes with the decree of Cyrus. This proclamation of freedom embodied the abiding hope that God would yet again gather the Jews dispersed among the nations. By closing the Hebrew canon on this note of freedom, the compiler emphasized this proclamation and therefore encouraged the Jews throughout the Diaspora.

In conclusion, the differences between the books cautions against concluding without more evidence that the works of Chronicles and Ezra-Nehemiah constituted an original Chronicler's history.

Ruth and Esther are included among the five *Megilloth*. These books—Song of Solomon, Ruth, Lamentations, Ecclesiastes, and Esther—are related to the five festivals (and fasts) of the Jewish calendar. Ruth, set at the harvest, is read at the Feast of Weeks (Pentecost), which celebrates the spring gathering (May-June). Esther's story gives the origins of the Feast of Purim and is read on that occasion (14th and 15th of Adar [Feb.–Mar.]). Purim is the only Old Testament feast not legislated by the Mosaic law.

JOSHUA

The Book of Joshua is named after the book's focal character, who as Moses' successor led Israel into the promised land. The English title is derived from the Greek and Latin translations. The Hebrew name *Joshua* (*Yehosua*) means *The LORD is salvation.* The shortened form of Joshua (Hebrew *Yesua*) is *Jesus* in Greek. Traditionally, the Jews assigned the book's authorship to Joshua. However, they recognized the evidence of later contributors too (for example, the report of Joshua's death [24:29]).

The authorship and date are disputed since the book is anonymous. Some interpreters believe the book was completed in the seventh or sixth centuries B.C. after a long process of compilation by unnamed editors as part of a large history influenced by the themes of Deuteronomy. (See "The Historical Books.") Other scholars argue for a view closer to the traditional opinion, dating the book within one generation of the events recorded (fourteenth century B.C.).

The book includes sources that are contemporary with Joshua (for example, 5:1,6; 6:25; 8:32; 18:9; 24:26) and also sources from a later time (for example, "to this day," 4:9; 5:9; 7:26; 10:27; 13:13). The book probably was based on an early core of testimony that was supplemented by an author no later than the tenth century B.C. There are hints that the book came from the early monarchy. (Compare, for example, the "book of Jashar" quoted in 10:13 and 2 Sam 1:18.) The Book of Joshua addresses many of the same problems faced by Israel's kings. Leadership, land dispute, the location and role of the tabernacle, and how to deal with Canaanite populations were problems shared by Saul and David.

Although the book is constituted of different sources, this does not mean that they are inconsistent or contradictory. They have been written and gathered under the supervision of God's Spirit to present a unified message to God's people.

Historical Setting of Joshua's Conquest

Opinions differ on the date of the conquest. The traditional view has set the conquest in the fifth century (1406 B.C.), based on the date of the building of the temple in 966 B.C. This view is derived from the literal computation of 1 Kings 6:1, which places the exodus 480 years before Solomon's fourth year of reign. Other scholars have dated the conquest in the thirteenth century (about 1250 B.C.) because of archaeological evidence from Egypt and Palestine. In the latter view the 480 years of 1 Kings 6:1 is explained as a symbolic number for twelve generations between Solomon and the exodus (see the feature article "Dates of the Exodus").

The dispute cannot be easily resolved since the archaeological record is inconsistent and difficult to interpret. It cannot be decisive by itself, and therefore the question will eventually be decided on the balance of all the evidence.

More important is that varying views exist concerning the nature of the conquest. One school of thought rejects the tradition of a military invasion by Israel. It holds that the "conquest" was a slow infiltration of seminomadic tribes who migrated into Canaan from the desert over hundreds of years. These diverse tribes brought various traditions which together were shaped into a religious heritage adopted as Israel's history. This unsatisfactory opinion does not adequately account for the Bible's testimony of a rapid occupation by Joshua. Also it fails to explain why and how over such a long period of time these diverse tribes became unified.

A second view is that Israel emerged as a result of a social revolution inside Canaan. The people of Canaan rebelled against their kings, rejected Baalism, and adopted the new religion of Yahweh. This view is insufficient by itself since the biblical account does not explain the conquest as a political revolution with religious overtones. Also this interpretation imposes on the biblical traditions a contemporary model of social revolution.

Third, the traditional interpretation of a military invasion has the advantage of the biblical testimony. However, with this invasion the Joshua account also shows that there was some internal conversion to the religion of Yahwism brought by these newcomers. Rahab is an example. Also the four cities of the Hivites (9:17) entered into league with Israel. These examples may reflect a much wider movement within Canaan. Conversion of

Canaanite peoples may explain the need for the covenant renewal ceremony in Joshua 24.

Theme

Under Joshua's leadership the people of God entered into the land of rest promised to their ancestors, because the people were careful not to depart from the "Book of the Law" of Moses (1:8).

I. Claiming the Land in Obedience (1:1–5:15)
II. Conquering the Land by Faith (6:1–12:24)
III. Distributing the Land in Victory (13:1–21:45)
IV. Living in the Land with Devotion (22:1–24:28)
V. Resting in the Land with Promise (24:29–33)

Purpose and Theology

1. The Book of Joshua traces the victory of God's people when they possessed the land of Canaan. The book continues the story of Israel's pilgrimage from Egypt to the promised land, demonstrating to all nations that Yahweh is God and He alone is to be worshiped (2:11; 4:24).

2. The Book of Joshua explains that God acts as the sovereign Lord of history who fulfills His promises to His people. The LORD is depicted as Israel's mighty warrior (5:14) who fights for His people and gives them rest from their enemies (11:20; 23:4).

3. The land is an important motif in the book. The promise of land for the patriarchs finds fulfillment in the conquering tribes who received what their fathers failed to enjoy (1:6; 11:23; 21:43-44). The importance of this theme is indicated by the detailed distribution of the land (13:1–21:45).

4. However, God grants His blessing only to a holy and obedient people (3:5; 4:10). Because the LORD is holy (5:15), He punishes the sin of His people (23:15-16) and restores them only upon their repentance (7:11-13).

5. The word of God given through Moses was the standard by which both God's faithfulness and Israel's fidelity were measured. God keeps His promises (21:45; 23:9). The people were to be careful to live according to the law of Moses (1:7,16-17).

6. The LORD accomplishes His purposes for Israel through a chosen leader. Joshua followed in the footsteps of Moses as God's ordained spokesperson (1:5; 4:14).

7. The book also has a message of hope for later generations of the Hebrew people who had lost the land through dispersion or captivity. Future generations of God's people could take hope that since God had achieved this victory for ancient Israel, He could do it again for them.

8. God's people will enter into a final rest through faith in the Lord Jesus Christ (Heb 4:6-11).

CLAIMING THE LAND IN OBEDIENCE (JOSH 1:1–5:15)

The opening section shows how God enabled Israel to enter the land. The commander was chosen (1:1-18) and the land surveyed (chap 2:1-24). The people crossed the Jordan with the help of the LORD (3:1-17), which was memorialized for future generations (4:1-24). Once in the land, the people renewed their commitment to the LORD and worshiped in celebration (5:1-15).

1:1-18
Commission of Joshua

The LORD commissioned Joshua as Moses' successor (compare Num 27:18; Deut 34:9) to lead Israel into the promised land. God instructed Joshua to be obedient to the law of Moses and to be courageous so that he might succeed (1:1-9).

Joshua commanded the officers of the camp to prepare the people for crossing the Jordan. He reminded the Transjordan tribes of Reuben, Gad, and the half-tribe of Manasseh that they had committed themselves under Moses (compare Num 32) to cross and help their brothers (Josh 1:10-15).

The people agreed and echoed the exhortation of God to Joshua, "Only be strong and courageous!" (1:18; compare 1:6).

2:1-24
Conversion of Rahab

Joshua dispatched two spies to discover the strength of Jericho. The city was strategically located at the pass leading from the Jordan Valley to the central highlands. (See "Cities of the Conquest.") The spies entered the house of the prostitute Rahab, who concealed their presence from the king of Jericho (2:1-7).

The story's events confirmed to the spies that Israel's enemies were weak in spite of their towering walls. Jericho's foolish king was easily tricked by the lowly harlot Rahab, whereas the Hebrew spies were clever when they entered into an oath with her. Also the spies learned that the city's population was terrified of Israel (2:11). Another assurance of Israel's ultimate victory was Rahab's

The Israelites crossing the Jordan River

conversion and admission that the LORD had given the land into their hands (2:8-11).

Rahab showed her faith in God's promises by helping the spies escape. She tied a scarlet thread to her window that signaled her salvation (2:12-24). Rahab's faith in God and her action in behalf of the spies became a model for Christian faith and works (Heb 11:31; Jas 2:25).

3:1-17
Crossing the Jordan

Joshua ordered the people to prepare for crossing by sanctifying themselves. The priests carrying the ark of the covenant led the procession (3:1-13). The ark symbolized the presence of God. It commonly rested in the tabernacle's holy of holies where the glory of God appeared (compare Exod 25:1-22; see the feature article "Tabernacle").

When the Levites who bore the ark entered the river, the waters stopped flowing at Adam (Tell ed-Damiyeh) near Zarethan. The extraordinary nature of the crossing is emphasized by the author, who explains that the river flooded its banks at that time of year. Yet Israel crossed the river bed on "dry" land (3:14-17).

The miraculous crossing magnified Joshua's leadership because it paralleled Moses' leadership at the Red Sea (3:7; 4:14). The crossing also proved that the LORD was alive and would drive out Israel's enemies (3:10).

4:1-24
The Memorial Stones

The Israelites erected a monument to commemorate their crossing. It was built of twelve stones, representing the twelve tribes of Israel. The stones were taken from the river where the Levites bearing the ark had stood. When future generations asked, "What do these stones mean?" (4:6,19-23), the monument served to remind them of the miraculous crossing (4:1-8). Because of this miracle Joshua was exalted in the eyes of the people (4:14). Another purpose of the miracle was that all nations might recognize the power of God (4:24).

5:1-15
Spiritual Readiness

The crossing of the river terrorized the Canaanite populace (5:1). Before Israel could proceed, however, the people had to prepare themselves spiritually.

God ordered Joshua to renew their covenant commitment by circumcision (5:2-3), the sign of God's election of Abraham and his descendants (compare Gen 17). Circumcision had been abandoned during Israel's sojourn in the wilderness because of disobedience. This new generation underwent circumcision as a test of their loyalty to the LORD (5:4-8). By following God's directions, Joshua in effect disabled his whole army. Because of their circumcision, God named the place Gilgal, meaning *a roll-*

ing. God explained that He had rolled away the disgrace of Egyptian bondage (5:9).

The people celebrated a new Passover (compare Exod 12; Lev 23:4-5; Num 9:1-14). The Passover festival remembered God's deliverance of Israel when the angel of death plagued the firstborn of Egypt. (See the feature article "Israel's Festivals and Feasts.") For God's people today, Jesus is the Passover Lamb who delivers them from sin and death (1 Cor 5:7).

The people for the first time began to eat food harvested from Canaan (5:11-12). In the wilderness their diet was the manna provided by God. The cessation of manna and their harvest of the land were reminiscent of God's promises that they would possess a land flowing with milk and honey (Exod 3:8).

Also the LORD prepared Joshua spiritually by appearing to him. Joshua did not recognize the LORD until He identified Himself as the commander of the LORD's armies. Like Moses, Joshua stood on holy ground because of the presence of God (compare Exod 3:1-12). He humbled himself by taking off his sandals.

CONQUERING THE LAND BY FAITH (JOSH 6:1–12:24)

Joshua directed three campaigns in Canaan. The central campaign included Jericho, Ai, and Gibeon (Josh 6–9). The southern campaign was against a five-king coalition, which was led by the king of Jerusalem (Josh 10). The northern campaign was against a coalition of city-states led by Hazor (11:1-15). Through these battles the people learned that Yahweh fought for them and secured their victory (23:9-10).

6:1-27
Shouting Jericho Down

The city of Jericho stood in the way of Israel's possession

CITIES OF THE CONQUEST

To lead Israel in the conquest of Canaan, God chose the brilliant general Joshua, His loyal servant. Joshua had previously led Israel to victory against the Amalekites during the exodus (Exod 17:8-13). Joshua's plan of attack was simple: split the promised land in two by cutting into the heart of central Canaan. Then attack the two smaller portions—first the southern section and finally the one in the north.

Central Thrust

Joshua 5:13–10:28 outlines the Israelite army's thrust into central Canaan. The first city the Lord delivered into the hands of Israel was Jericho (modern Tell es-Sultan), the gateway to the promised land. (A tell is an artificial mound built up by centuries of occupation of a site.) Jericho was a walled city built on a hill situated six miles north of the Dead Sea and adjacent to the main ford of the Jordan River. The city's destruction was a necessary first step in any successful invasion of the land. The next major objective was Ai (et-Tell, Bireh, or Beitin), a city with twelve thousand inhabitants located in the hills ten miles west of Jericho (Josh 8).

The residents of nearby Gibeon (al-Jib), in Canaan's central highlands (eight miles northwest of Jerusalem), tricked the Israelites into making a peace treaty with them. The Israelites, however, forced them to perform slave labor (Josh 9).

One other city mentioned in connection with the central campaign was Makkedah (Khirbet el-Kheishum or Khirbet Beit Maqdum), a Canaanite royal city located near Lachish and Eglon (Josh 10:28). (The Arabic term *khirbet* in place names means *ruin*.)

Southern Campaign

Following the stunning successes in the central campaign, Israel made a coordinated attack on key southern cities (Josh 10:29-43). This was a necessary second step, since these cities had most actively resisted the Israelite advance in the central highlands. The first objective was Libnah (Tell es-Safi or Tell Bornat), a city located in a rich farming region twenty-two miles southwest of Jerusalem (10:28-29). After putting that city to the sword, the Israelites conquered Lachish (Tell ed-Duweir), one of the largest and most important cities in southern Canaan (10:31-32). Next the Israelites attacked Eglon (Tell el-Hesi or Tell Nagila) and the historic city of Hebron (el-Khalil), where Abraham had first built an altar to the Lord (10:34-37). The last city mentioned by name in the southern campaign was Debir (Tell Beit-Mirsim[?]) a royal city located twelve miles south of Hebron (10:38-39).

Northern Campaign

The final thrust of Israel's invasion of Palestine centered around a major battle fought northwest of the Sea of Galilee at the Waters of Merom (Josh 11:1-15). Hazor (Tell el-Qedah), an important city in upper Galilee located on a major trade route, led the unsuccessful resistance against Israel. For its efforts, Joshua had the city burned (11:13). Evidence for the burning of the city was discovered in an excavation of the site by Yigael Yadin in the late 1950s.

Joshua 12:7-24 mentions thirty-one other cities whose kings the Israelites defeated during the Canaan conquest. □

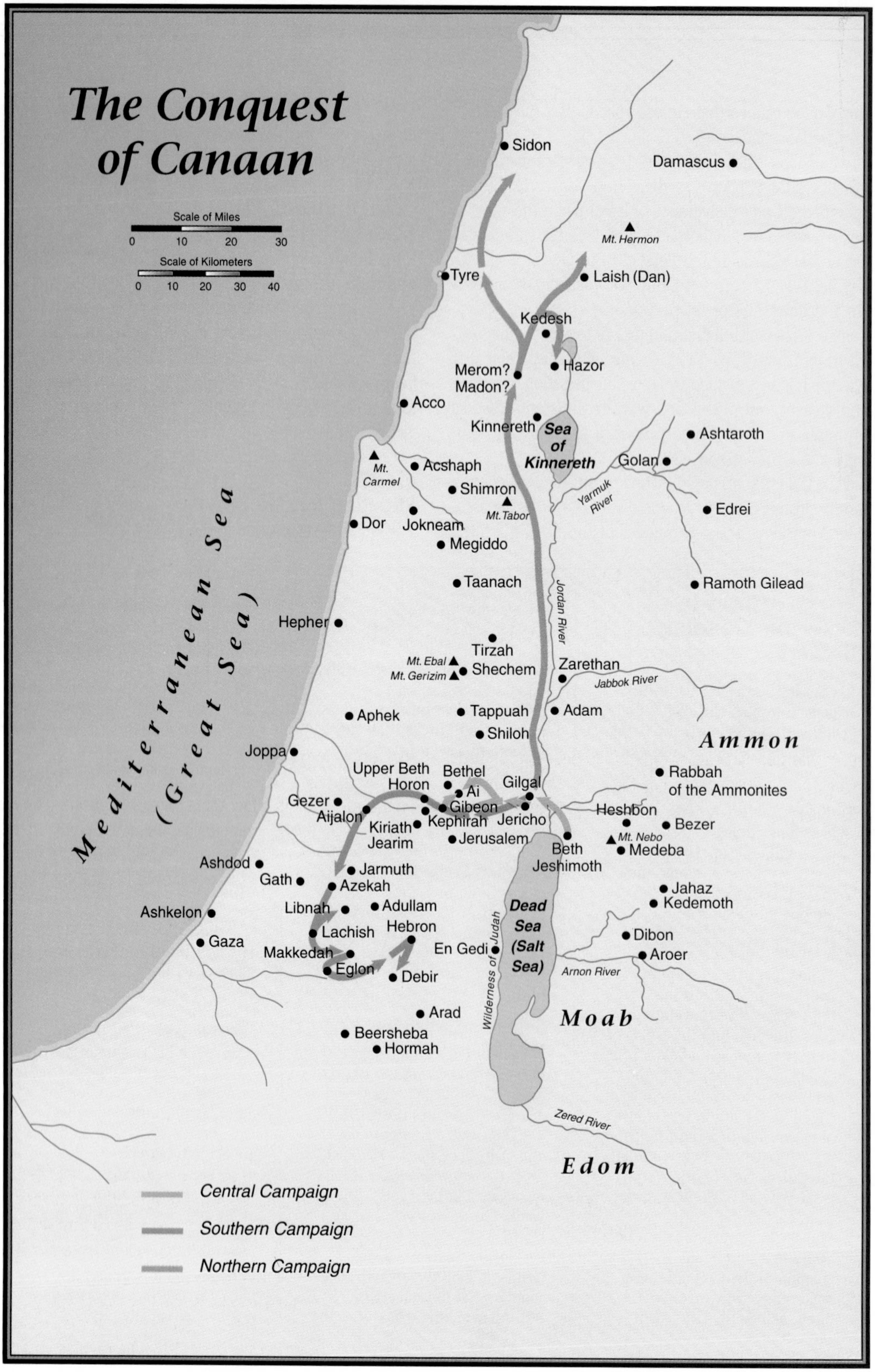

The Conquest of Canaan
Scale of Miles
0 10 20 30
Scale of Kilometers
0 10 20 30 40
Sidon
Damascus
Mt. Hermon
Tyre
Laish (Dan)
Kedesh
Hazor
Merom?
Madon?
Acco
Kinnereth
Sea of Kinnereth
Ashtaroth
Mt. Carmel
Acshaph
Golan
Shimron
Mt. Tabor
Yarmuk River
Edrei
Dor
Jokneam
Megiddo
Taanach
Ramoth Gilead
Jordan River
Hepher
Tirzah
Mt. Ebal
Mt. Gerizim
Shechem
Zarethan
Jabbok River
Aphek
Tappuah
Adam
Shiloh
Ammon
Joppa
Upper Beth Horon
Bethel
Ai
Gilgal
Rabbah of the Ammonites
Gezer
Aijalon
Gibeon
Kephirah
Jericho
Heshbon
Bezer
Kiriath Jearim
Jerusalem
Mt. Nebo
Medeba
Beth Jeshimoth
Ashdod
Jarmuth
Gath
Azekah
Jahaz
Kedemoth
Ashkelon
Libnah
Adullam
Dead Sea (Salt Sea)
Lachish
Hebron
Dibon
Gaza
Makkedah
En Gedi
Wilderness of Judah
Aroer
Eglon
Debir
Arnon River
Arad
Moab
Beersheba
Hormah
Mediterranean Sea (Great Sea)
Zered River
Edom
Central Campaign
Southern Campaign
Northern Campaign

Round Neolithic (New Stone Age) defense (or gate) tower at Old Testament Jericho, from ca. 7000 B.C.

of the land. The city was one of the oldest in the world, but it was not particularly large. (See the feature article "Cities of the Conquest.") The Bible presents Jericho as a formidable city with imposing walls that could not be scaled (6:1).

Joshua and the people marched in silence around the city one time for each of six days. On the seventh day they marched seven times. At the appropriate signal the priests blew their trumpets, and the people gave a mighty shout. The walls collapsed, and the soldiers entered straight into the city (6:2-20).

The organization of the march placed the ark at the center of the parade. The ark indicated that God was in their midst as He was when they crossed the Jordan. No military general could have accepted such a plan, but Joshua was not counting on human ingenuity. The purpose of the strategy was to test their faith and their patience. By faith the walls collapsed (Heb 11:30).

The spies rescued Rahab and her family, but the rest of the population was killed and the city burned. The city and all that was in it were "devoted to the LORD" (6:17). The expression "devoted" (*herem*) meant that the city was banned from Israelite possession because it was solely for the LORD (compare Deut 20:16-18). The ban removed any economic motivation for the Israelites' action. It was a "holy war" because Israel fought at the instructions of the LORD and received no benefits from the city's destruction.

The ban was not always employed by the Israelites, and even when in effect there were exceptions. The exceptions at Jericho were Rahab and some costly metals that were placed in the LORD's treasury (6:24-25). By the grace of God, Rahab was spared from the ban because of her faith (Heb 11:31).

God placed Canaanite cities under the ban so that Israel would not fall victim to the sinful influence of their enemies (Deut 20:18). In this case the ban was eternal, and anyone who rebuilt the city was cursed of God. The truth of God's word was demonstrated in the judgment rendered against Hiel, who lost his two sons for rebuilding the city (1 Kgs 16:34).

7:1-26
Disobedience and Defeat at Ai

The Israelites stood guilty before God because of the sin of Achan, who took from the devoted things at Jericho (7:1-2). The covenant requirement of community responsibility explains why all Israel suffered as a result of Achan's sin. Since they were bound together as one family, the whole group suffered for one man's sin.

The people acted presumptuously by not consulting the LORD before they launched an offensive against Ai.

They met with sudden defeat, and "the hearts of the people melted" with fear (7:3-5; compare 2:9).

Joshua interceded for his people and questioned why God had brought Israel to this tragic end (7:6-9). God chided Joshua, explaining that Israel suffered because of sin, not because the LORD had failed Joshua. The sin of Israel meant that God no longer fought for them (7:10-12). Joshua called all the people together, and by the process of casting lots he discovered that Achan was the culprit (7:13-18).

Achan confessed that he "saw . . . coveted . . . and took" the devoted things and hid them in his tent (7:20-21). This incident illustrates James's warning that wicked desires lead to sin, and sin leads to death (Jas 1:14-15). Achan and his family were stoned, and his possessions were burned (Josh 7:24-25). Because the entire community was responsible for covenant holiness, all of Israel participated in destroying what pertained to the sin. The site of the stoning was named Achor, meaning *trouble.* The name plays on the name of Achan because he had troubled Israel (7:26).

8:1-35
Obedience and Victory at Ai

God instructed Joshua to attack Ai with all his troops. When Israel had attacked before, they did not have the explicit direction of the LORD; and they were presumptuous and haughty (7:3). Now with their sin behind them, Israel chose to obey the LORD (8:1-2).

Unlike Jericho, where God performed a miracle, Israel accomplished the defeat of Ai through Joshua's God-given military strategy. Although they surprised the city by ambush (8:3-23), the success of the war was dependent upon God's blessing. As long as Joshua stretched forth his javelin in petition to God, the victory was Israel's (8:26). This is reminiscent of Moses' uplifted arms when Israel defeated Amalek (Exod 17:8-13).

Israel destroyed the city but was permitted to take the spoil. Since the place was condemned to be a ruin, its name Ai, meaning *ruin,* was appropriate (8:28). Ancient Ai has been identified with the modern site of et-Tell, but this identification is disputed. (See the feature article "Cities of the Conquest.")

Israel had learned through tragedy that their success was solely dependent upon God. Therefore after their victory at Ai they worshiped the LORD with thanksgiving at Shechem (8:30-31). In accordance with Moses' instructions (Deut 27:2-8), they read the covenant from Mount Gerizim and Mount Ebal (8:32-33). These two mounts form a natural amphitheater. The reading of the law by Joshua (8:34-35) reflected the renewed commitment of God's people (compare 2 Kgs 23:2; Neh 8).

9:1-27
Deception of the Gibeonites

Moses gave Israel the rules of warfare (Deut 7:1-2; 20:10-18). He required Israel to destroy the nations nearby in Canaan and spare the nations living afar.

The Gibeonites conspired to trick the Israelites into forming a peace treaty by giving the appearance of traveling from a far country. They wore old clothes, carried mended sacks, and had dry, moldy food (9:3-6). They acted as though they knew only of Israel's early wars under Moses and not their recent victories. They repeatedly flattered Joshua and the elders by referring to themselves as "your servants" (9:7-13). Israel failed by not consulting the LORD before entering the covenant (9:14-15). The people grumbled when they learned that the Gibeonites had deceived them (9:16-21). They probably feared God's wrath as at Ai because they were prohibited from falsely swearing an oath in the LORD's name (Lev 19:12).

When the Gibeonites confessed their trickery (9:22-25), Joshua punished them by conscripting the Gibeonites and their descendants to serve the tabernacle's altar (9:26-27). This oath was observed until the days of Saul, when he ruthlessly broke the treaty (2 Sam 21:1-2).

Although the Israelites failed God, the fear of the Gibeonites was another assurance that Joshua would succeed among the nations.

10:1-43
God Fights for Israel

The Gibeonite deception gave occasion for Israel to fight a coalition of kings in the south (10:1-5). Neighboring Amorite kings led by Jerusalem waged war against Gibeon because of its defection. With the destruction of Jericho, Ai, and now the capitulation of Gibeon and its Hivite cities (9:17; 11:19-20), Jerusalem was threatened on all sides.

The Gibeonites appealed to Joshua for deliverance, and he marched by night from Gilgal to Gibeon. The conflict spread to the countryside as the fleeing Amorites escaped. God intervened miraculously as at Jericho and fought for Israel by hurling hailstones that killed more than even Israel's swords killed (10:6-11).

Since the enemy was in disarray, Joshua wanted to finish the battle before they could regroup the next day. He prayed to the LORD for the sun to delay its descent. Joshua's prayer was also found in another source called the book of Jashar (compare 2 Sam 1:18). The victory was God's more than Israel's: "Surely the LORD was

Overview of the excavations at Tell el-Qedah (ancient Hazor—one of the cities of Joshua's conquest of the land).

fighting for Israel!" (10:14). The author declared that there was no day like it (10:12-15).

The kings of the coalition were captured and executed by Joshua (10:16-28), and the southern cities were destroyed according to the LORD's command (10:29-43). Since Jerusalem is not included in the cities captured, it probably survived. Nonetheless the area was incapacitated by Joshua.

11:1-15
Hamstringing Hazor

A confederation of kings led by Jabin, the dynastic ruler of Hazor, campaigned against Israel. The military strength of the alliance was its numerous chariots. The battle waged at the Waters of Merom near Hazor (11:1-5). (See the feature article "Cities of Conquest.")

Unlike the previous accounts, the author did not give as many details of the battle and was satisfied with giving a theological summary. God required Joshua to hamstring the captured horses and burn their chariots. This prevented Israel from relying on military prowess (11:6-9). Like Jericho and Ai, Hazor was burned in accordance with Moses' instructions (Deut 7:1-2; 20:16-17).

11:16–12:24
Counting the Kings

This summary of captured lands and their slain kings is a tribute to God's faithfulness. The passage emphasizes that Joshua took "the entire land" (11:16,23). This included the lands of the Anakites (11:21), whom the Israelites had initially feared the most (Num 13:28,33; Deut 9:2). God incited Israel's enemies to wage war, and then He destroyed them because of their sin (Josh 11:20). This was the method God used to give the land to Israel as He fulfilled His promise to Moses (11:23).

The list of kings begins with Og and Sihon (12:1-6), whom Moses defeated (compare Num 21:21-35). The kings defeated by Joshua were thirty-one (Josh 12:7-24). This list of kings includes some kings not specifically mentioned in the narrative. This record of Israel's acquisitions showed future generations what faith could accomplish. It also was a rebuke to those who had refused to take the land.

DISTRIBUTING THE LAND IN VICTORY (JOSH 13:1–21:45)

The detailed description of Israel's inheritance may be tedious to modern readers. For the author it proved the

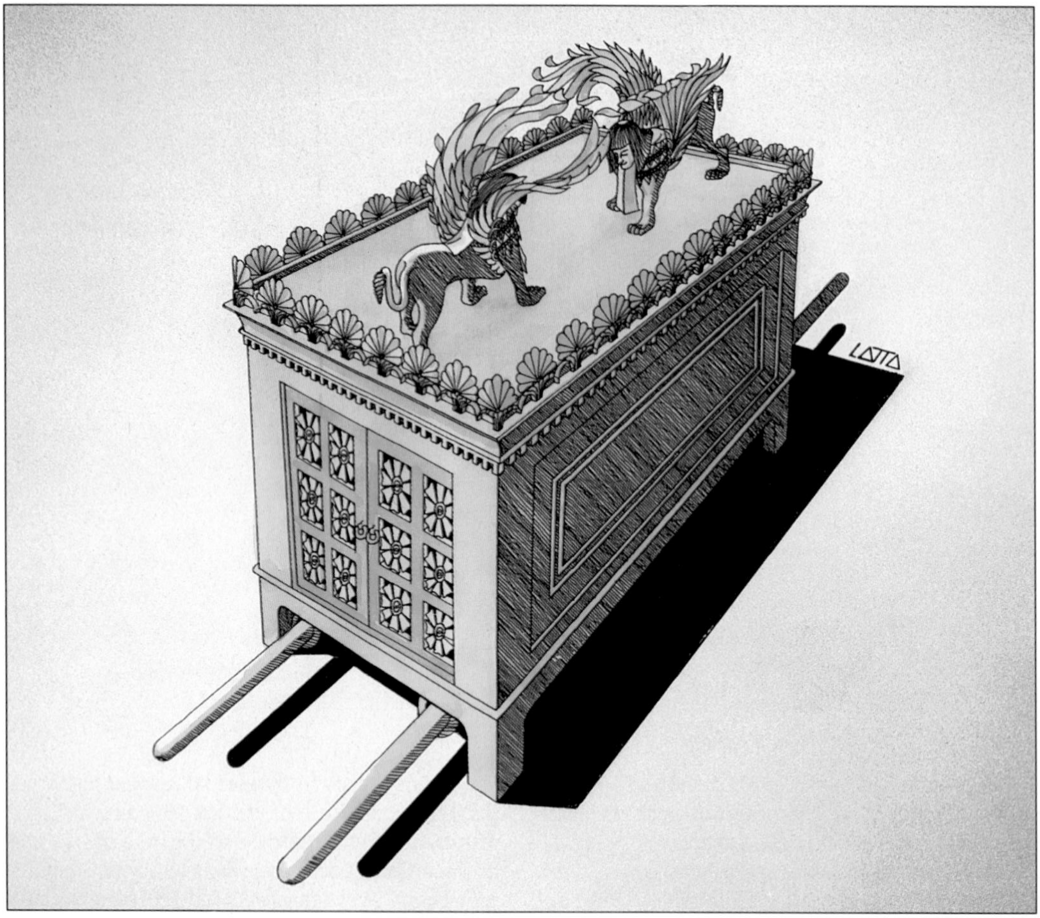

Reconstruction of the ark of the covenant

faithfulness of God's word. The territories given by Moses are listed first (Josh 13) and then the land distributed by Joshua (Josh 14–21).

13:1-7
Nondistributed Lands

Joshua was too old to finish driving out Israel's enemies. However, God promised Joshua that the remaining lands would also become an inheritance for Israel. These territories were the Philistine cities, the Phoenician coast, and the mountain area of Lebanon. During the reigns of David and Solomon, Israel conquered these areas (2 Sam 8:1; 24:6-7; 1 Kgs 9:19).

13:8-33
Transjordan Lands

Joshua allocated the lands across the Jordan that Moses had promised to Gad, Reuben, and the half-tribe of Manasseh. These tribes had initially questioned Joshua's leadership (1:17), but Joshua proved himself by following the example of Moses.

14:1-5
Land West of the Jordan

The remaining tribes, with the exception of Levi (compare 21:1-42), received from Joshua their possessions on the west side of the Jordan. Each allotment was determined by the casting of lots (compare Num 26:55).

14:6-15
Caleb's Courage

Caleb was the first of Judah to claim his land. He recalled how forty-five years earlier he had brought a favorable report at Kadesh Barnea when he urged Israel to possess

Canaan. Caleb's testimony magnified God's faithfulness. Even in his old age Caleb had the courage and vigor to follow the LORD.

15:1-63
Judah's Allotment

Judah was the first tribe to receive its inheritance. It was the largest and most prestigious tribe (compare Gen 49:8-12). Caleb's lot was in Judah. He possessed Hebron by driving out the Anakites. Othniel in behalf of Caleb captured Debir and received Caleb's daughter Acsah in marriage. Acsah, like her father, had a zeal for the promises of God (Josh 15:13-19). Jerusalem was in Judah's territory, but the Israelites could not dispossess the Jebusites (15:63).

16:1–17:18
Ephraim and Manasseh's Allotments

The lands belonging to the two sons of Joseph, Ephraim and Manasseh, were in the central highlands. Ephraim received its allotment before Manasseh because it had the greater blessing of Jacob (Gen 48:17-20). Ephraim failed to drive out the Canaanites from Gezer, although Joshua had killed its king (Josh 12:12). Ephraim chose to use them as forced labor (16:10). The city became a royal possession under Solomon (1 Kgs 9:16).

Joshua distributed land to the families of Manasseh west of the Jordan. He honored all of God's promises (Josh 17:3-4), as shown by his giving land to Zelophehad's daughters (Num 27:1-7). Like Ephraim, Manasseh also chose to coexist with Canaanite cities (17:11-12). Later these areas were subjugated by Israel (17:13; compare 1 Kgs 9:15-22). When Ephraim complained that their lot was too small, Joshua challenged them to increase their territory by driving out the Canaanites (Josh 17:14-18).

18:1-10
Distributing the Land from Shiloh

The people set up the tabernacle at Shiloh, giving evidence that Israel had gained control of the land. However, seven tribes had not made their claim, and Joshua chided them for their reluctance.

18:11–19:48
The Last Tribes

The land was apportioned to Benjamin, Simeon, Zebulun, Issachar, Asher, Naphtali, and Dan. The inheritance of Benjamin was small but strategic (18:11-28); it was a buffer zone between the mighty states of Judah and Ephraim. Its cities of Bethel and Jerusalem were the most influential cities in the worship of Israel. King Saul and the apostle Paul were Benjamites.

The inheritance of Simeon (19:1-9) was absorbed by the tribe of Judah according to Jacob's blessing (Gen 49:7). Simeon may have lost its blessing as a result of Simeon and Levi's murder of Shechem (Gen 34:25).

The final lot fell to the Danites (Josh 19:40-48). Its territory was very small, and the Amorites were too great for them (compare Judg 1:34). Yet even they succeeded in having a portion with Israel by possessing Leshem, which they renamed Dan (compare Judg 18).

19:49-51
Joshua the Builder

The courageous leader Joshua was the last to receive his portion. The people triumphantly gave Joshua his allotment in Ephraim. Joshua was not only a defender of the land but also a builder.

20:1-9
Cities of Refuge

The cities of refuge illustrated God's continued grace toward Israel while living in the land. According to Moses' instruction, six cities were set aside as places of safety for manslayers who unintentionally killed (20:3; compare Num 35:9-34; Deut 4:41-43; 19:1-14).

When the manslayer appealed for refuge at one of the designated cities, the elders protected him from a relative of the deceased who was the avenger. If the elders found the manslayer innocent of murder, he remained in the city until the death of the high priest (Josh 20:6; compare Num 35:25-28). However, if the slayer was found guilty of homicide, the city executed him (compare Exod 21:12-14; Num 35:29-34).

21:1-42
The Levites' Possession

Rather than receiving a tract of land, the service of the LORD was the Levites' special possession (Deut 10:8-9). They received forty-eight cities scattered throughout all Israel (Josh 21:41-42) in accordance with God's promise (Num 35:1-5). This geographical distribution enabled the Levites to influence all the tribes as they taught them God's precepts (Deut 33:10).

21:43-45
Summary of God's Promises

The summary emphasizes the major motif of the book: God fought Israel's battles and fulfilled His promises to their fathers. They rested from their wars and enjoyed the inheritance from the LORD.

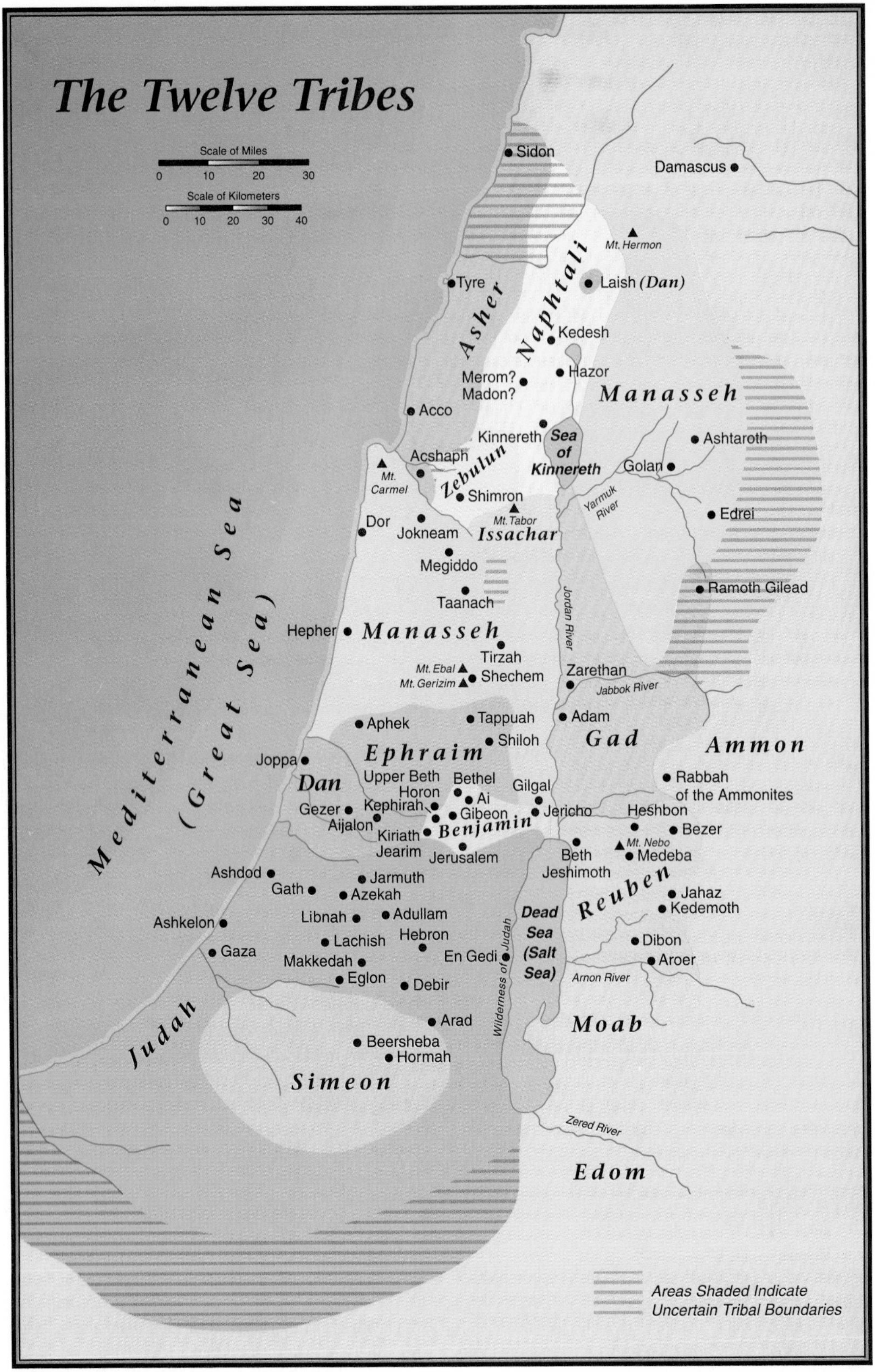

The Twelve Tribes
Scale of Miles
0 10 20 30
Scale of Kilometers
0 10 20 30 40
Sidon
Damascus
Mt. Hermon
Tyre
Asher
Naphtali
Laish (Dan)
Kedesh
Hazor
Merom?
Madon?
Manasseh
Acco
Kinnereth
Sea of Kinnereth
Ashtaroth
Acshaph
Zebulun
Mt. Carmel
Golan
Shimron
Yarmuk River
Mt. Tabor
Edrei
Dor
Jokneam
Issachar
Megiddo
Ramoth Gilead
Taanach
Jordan River
Mediterranean Sea
(Great Sea)
Hepher
Manasseh
Tirzah
Mt. Ebal
Mt. Gerizim
Shechem
Zarethan
Jabbok River
Aphek
Tappuah
Adam
Shiloh
Gad
Ammon
Ephraim
Joppa
Dan
Upper Beth Horon
Bethel
Gilgal
Rabbah of the Ammonites
Gezer
Kephirah
Ai
Aijalon
Gibeon
Jericho
Heshbon
Kiriath Jearim
Benjamin
Bezer
Mt. Nebo
Jerusalem
Beth Jeshimoth
Medeba
Ashdod
Jarmuth
Gath
Azekah
Reuben
Jahaz
Kedemoth
Libnah
Adullam
Dead Sea (Salt Sea)
Ashkelon
Lachish
Hebron
Dibon
Gaza
Makkedah
En Gedi
Aroer
Wilderness of Judah
Eglon
Debir
Arnon River
Arad
Moab
Judah
Beersheba
Hormah
Simeon
Zered River
Edom
Areas Shaded Indicate Uncertain Tribal Boundaries

LIVING IN THE LAND WITH DEVOTION (JOSH 22:1–24:28)

This section shows how Israel preserved itself in the land by carefully observing the word of the LORD (Josh 22). Joshua exhorted them to live in faith (Josh 23), and the people entered into a covenant to serve the LORD (Josh 24). This served as an example of how future generations should live in commitment to one another and to God.

22:1-34
Israel's Unity Preserved

With the land under the control of Israel, Joshua commended and then released the Transjordan tribes to return to their allotted territories (22:1-9).

The Transjordan tribes erected an altar on the west bank as a testimony to their relationship with their brothers, but Israel misunderstood this as an act of idolatry. Israel gathered for war because they feared that the anger of the LORD would be kindled against them as it was at Peor (Num 25) and at Ai (Josh 7:6-12). Israel had learned not to tolerate sin (22:10-20).

A delegation led by Phineas investigated. The Transjordan tribes explained that the altar was built for a witness and not for animal sacrifice (22:21-29). The war was averted, and the altar was named "Witness" (22:30-34). This incident showed how Israel should resolve intertribal disputes.

23:1-16
Farewell Sermon

At the end of his public ministry, Joshua summoned Israel and exhorted them not to ally with the nations remaining in the land. God had fought for Israel; but if they turned from their love of God, then they would be abandoned by the LORD (23:1-13).

Joshua's final words reminded them that God would be as sure to carry out His threats as He had been with His blessings. If they violated the covenant by pursuing other gods, then God would expel them (23:14-16).

24:1–28
Covenant Renewal

Joshua convened the tribes at Shechem to renew their oath of covenant loyalty (compare 8:30-35). The preamble of the covenant identified God and Israel as the parties of the covenant (24:1-2a). The historical prologue rehearsed God's benevolent acts toward Israel (24:2b-13). The covenant stipulated the requirements God expected of His vassals (23:14-24). Joshua challenged them to decide whom they would serve: "As for me and my household, we will serve the LORD" (23:15). The elders consented and ratified the covenant (23:16,24).

Joshua recorded the covenant in the "Book of the Law of God" (24:6). This implies that Joshua was contributing to Holy Scripture (compare 8:31-34; 23:6). Also Joshua placed a memorial stone under a tree as a witness against the people if they failed the LORD (23:27-28).

RESTING IN THE LAND WITH PROMISE (JOSH 24:29-33)

The epilogue ends with three heroes of faith buried in the promised land. Joshua died at at the age of 110 years and received his inheritance as a reward for his courage at Kadesh Barnea (Num 13–14). Under his leadership Israel served the LORD obediently (Josh 24:29-31).

Joseph also believed God would lead His people into the promised land. His bones were buried in Canaan (24:32) as he requested in faith (Gen 50:25-26). Unlike Aaron, who died in the wilderness (Num 20:28), his son Eleazar entered the promised land and was buried there (Josh 24:33).

These three burials were three seals attesting to God's fulfillment of His promises to the fathers.

Theological and Ethical Value

The Book of Joshua portrays Yahweh first as the God who acts in history to fulfill His promise to the patriarchs by giving the land to Israel. That the land is God's gift is made clear by the stopping of the Jordan River (Josh 4) and the falling of the walls of Jericho (Josh 6). God's faithfulness to fulfill His promises in the past (21:43-45) is the ground for confidence that God will continue to be faithful. In time all the promised land would belong to God's people (compare 13:1). In time God's people will enjoy the promised rest (Heb 3–4).

Second, Yahweh is a God with high ethical expectations who punishes sin and rewards faithfulness. Possession of the land of promise was contingent on its inhabitants' conformity to God's moral demands. For their sins the Canaanites suffered a judgment of annihilation and enslavement at the hands of Israel (compare Gen 15:16). When Achan sinned, Israel likewise experienced judgment in the form of defeat (Josh 7:1-26). Future generations of Israelites would learn the cost of disobedience when the Assyrians and Babylonians would exile them from the land of promise. In contrast, Caleb and Joshua serve as models of those whom God rewards for faithfulness (14:1-15; 19:49-51).

Joshua before the people of Israel

Walls of Jericho

Questions for Reflection

1. What are the characteristics of godly leadership?

2. What does the Book of Joshua teach about God and His relationship to nature and human history?

3. What are God's expectations of His people?

4. How should God's people live during times of prosperity?

5. How should God's people deal with problems that threaten their unity?

Sources for Additional Study

Davis, Dale Ralph. *No Falling Words. Expositions of the Book of Joshua.* Grand Rapids: Baker, 1988.

Enns, Paul P. *Joshua.* Grand Rapids: Zondervan, 1981.

Jensen, Irving L. *Joshua: Rest-land Won.* Chicago: Moody, 1986.

JUDGES

The Book of Judges is entitled after the military and civic leaders who were raised up by God to deliver Israel from its oppressors (2:16-19; Ruth 1:1; Acts 13:20). The Hebrew title *Judges* is followed by the ancient versions and the English tradition.

The judges were not trained arbiters of legal cases as the word *judge* means today. They were Spirit-endowed leaders who were chosen by God for specific tasks (compare 3:9-10; 6:34; 11:29; 13:25). As judges they worked to bring about justice for the oppressed people of Israel. To avoid confusion with the modern connotation of *judged,* the NIV has translated "led" in many passages where it is more appropriate in context (4:4; 10:2-3; 12:8-11,13-14; 15:20; 16:31). The verb *led* is used most often by the author to describe the judges' function. The judges also "saved" and "delivered" Israel from their enemies (for example, 3:9,31; 4:14; 10:1; 13:5).

Two of the leaders, Othniel and Ehud, are described as "deliverers" (3:9,15). Only Gideon is not called judge or deliverer, but he is said to have saved Israel (6:14). On one occasion the LORD is described as "Judge" (11:27).

Although the judges were remembered primarily for their military prowess (2:16), they also functioned as civil authorities (compare Deborah, 4:4-5). Some judges were not specifically said to have engaged in warfare (compare Tola and Jair, 10:1-5).

The Book of Judges is an anonymous writing. The Jewish tradition that Samuel wrote the book cannot be substantiated. Some scholars believe, however, that Samuel best fits the evidence of the book. Other interpreters believe the traditions of the judges came from times before Israel had a king but that the book was not completed until the seventh or sixth centuries B.C. (compare 18:30). These interpreters view Judges as part of a large history influenced by the ideas of Deuteronomy. (See "The Historical Books.")

The book probably was compiled during the early monarchy. The recurring expression "in those days Israel had no king" (17:6; 18:1; 19:1; 21:25) indicates that the book was written from a later period when there was a central authority in Israel.

The book's sources were gradually collected at several stages into a unified whole. The stories of the individual judges (3:7–16:31), with their introduction (2:6–3:6), formed the first part of the book. These episodes were placed by the author in an interpretative framework introducing and concluding each judgeship. (For example, compare the opening and closing of the story of Othniel, 3:7,11.)

The appendix of stories about the Danite migration (Judg 17–18) and the rape of the Levite's concubine (Judg 19–21) were added last to illustrate the spiritual depravity of the period. The migration of the Danites actually occurred in the early part of the Judges period. The author, therefore, arranged his book along thematic lines rather than a strictly chronological one (compare 18:1-31 with Josh 19:40-47; also Judg 1:34; 13:25).

The final step was the addition of 1:1–2:5, which served as an appropriate introduction to the book. It described events during the transition from Joshua to the next generation, while containing some flashbacks to the days of conquest.

Some scholars have questioned the literary and theological integrity of the book. However, the book's composite sources are not conflicting accounts. They rather have a thematic unity and a complementary theological perspective.

The era of the judges included the judgeships of Eli and Samuel, which are recorded in 1 Samuel (compare 1 Sam 4:18; 7:15; 8:1-2). The period of the judges extended from Joshua's death to the reign of Saul (about 1050 B.C.). The beginning of this period is debated since it is dependent on the date of the Exodus. (See "Dates of the Exodus.") If the early date is followed, the period was from about 1400–1050 B.C. The late date places the period from about 1250–1050 B.C.

During this period, the tribes of Israel were loosely bound together around the central sanctuary. The tribes were bound by their common commitment to the covenant made with God at Sinai (Exod 20; 24). Their unity, however, was weakened by the inroads of Canaanite religion. When the tribes defected from the covenant, God used foreign oppressors to bring Israel to repentance.

Theme

Although Israel inherited the land of promise, they

repeatedly disregarded their covenant obligations by doing what they "saw fit" (Judg 21:25). Israel's disobedience resulted in their oppression at the hands of neighboring peoples (3:7-8). Such oppression led Israel to cry to the LORD for help (3:9). God responded to Israel's repentance and cries for mercy by sending judges or deliverers (3:9-10). Israel, however, returned to disobedience following the death of the judge (3:11-12). (See the feature article "The Cycle of the Judges.")

I. Spiritual Disobedience in the Land (1:1–3:6)
I. Political Destruction in the Land (3:7–16:31)
III. Moral Depravity in the Land (17:1–21:25)

Purpose and Theology

1. The Book of Judges continues the unfolding story of Israel's life in the land promised to their fathers. Whereas the Book of Joshua describes Israel's faithfulness and success, Judges depicts Israel's covenant apostasy and the resulting oppression at the hands of their neighbors (2:6-7,10-16). The author tells events in the life of early Israel to warn his own generation about the results of disobedience.

2. The book explains why Israel suffered from their enemies (compare 6:13). The fault lay in Israel's sin and not in God's failure to keep His covenant promises. God was longsuffering and merciful as He continued to raise up saviors to deliver His people even though they repeatedly forgot Him and worshiped the gods of Canaan (2:2-3,10-14,20-21). The book further explains that God left the nations among Israel so that He might test Israel's faithfulness (2:22-23; 3:4). Israel was also to learn discipline through warfare (3:1-3).

3. The book also demonstrates that God held Israel to account for its moral and religious behavior. Although they were the elect people of God and the recipients of God's promises, they would not enjoy the blessing of that privileged position if they continued in sin (2:1-15; 9:56-57; 10:11-16).

4. The book shows that the LORD, not the Canaanite deities, is the God of history and salvation. He is the true "Judge" who gave Israel into the hands of their enemies and then by His Spirit empowered deliverers to give them victory over their oppressors. Through miraculous intervention in history and nature, God accomplished His purposes for Israel (2:16-18; 3:9-10,15; 4:15; 6:34; 7:22; 11:29; 14:6,19; 15:14).

5. An important issue facing the author was the leadership of the nation. The Book of Judges illustrates the kind of moral decay that occurred when there was an absence of godly leadership. There was a decline in the spiritual condition of the judges themselves as each cycle describes the judge and his era. Samson, the last judge of the book, was the embodiment of the immorality of the period.

The book shows what happened to Israel when there was no godly king to lead them. In this way the book advocates the institution of kingship. It must, however, be a kingship characterized by piety. Without godly leadership, the people drifted from the objective standard of God's word, and each "did as he saw fit" (17:6; 18:1; 19:1; 21:25).

6. The Book of Judges also shows the power of faith and prayer. The writer to the Hebrews recognized that the judges accomplished their exploits through faith in God (Heb 11:32-33).

SPIRITUAL DISOBEDIENCE IN THE LAND (JUDG 1:1–3:6)

The introductory section explains that Israel failed in the land because of its disobedience, immorality, and intermarriage with the Canaanites.

1:1–2:5
Incomplete Obedience

The Book of Judges begins by showing the proper way Israel should have dispossessed the Canaanites. Judah and Simeon joined forces to defeat the Canaanite despot Adoni-Bezek (1:1-8). A second example of success was Caleb's family, whose courage paved the way for the Judahites to control the hill country. Othniel, Caleb's nephew, captured Debir; and Caleb and drove out the Anakites from Hebron (1:9-15,20; compare Othniel, 3:7-11).

However, the Israelites did not follow Caleb's example. All of the tribes, including Judah and Benjamin, failed to drive out the Canaanites completely. Even the nations they did subdue were placed under forced labor rather then destroyed. Israel chose material wealth over obedience to God (1:16-36).

The LORD came to Israel, appearing as an angel, and condemned them for their disobedience. Because Israel had disobeyed, God left their enemies in the land to be as "thorns" and a "snare" to Israel. Israel "wept" before the LORD for its sins, and the place was called Bokim, meaning *weepers* (2:1-5).

2:6–3:4
Idolatry

The second reason for Israel's failure was its idolatrous worship. This section previews the seven cycles of the judges who are described in the major section of the book that follows (3:7–16:31). The recurring cycle is Israel's sin, its servitude to foreign enemies, its cries of supplication, and the salvation God provided through a divinely appointed deliverer. (See the feature article "The Cycle of the Judges.")

The death of Joshua and his generation explained why Israel began the cycles of sin and apostasy. The new generation did not know the LORD as their covenant God (2:6-10).

The *sin* of Israel was its worship of the Baals and Ashtoreths of the Canaanites. These were the male and female gods of the Canaanite religion (2:11-13). The religion of Canaan was a fertility cult known for its ritual prostitution. Therefore the author spoke of how Israel "prostituted themselves to other gods and worshiped them" (2:17).

The chastening of the LORD was Israel's *servitude* to foreign nations. God responded to their repentance and *supplication* for deliverance by granting *salvation* through appointed judges. However, when the judge died, Israel repeated its idolatry; and the cycle of sin began again (2:14-19).

The LORD left the nations among Israel to punish them and to test Israel's faith (2:20-22). This testing also meant Israel would learn the discipline of warfare (3:1-4). Because of Israel's sin, the promise of rest and peace in the land was not realized (Josh 23:1). Ongoing warfare became the pattern for Israel's existence.

3:5-6
Intermarriage

A third reason for Israel's failure was its intermarriage with the Canaanites. The prohibition of marrying the Canaanites was because Israel "served their gods" and not because of racial differences (compare Deut 7:3-4).

POLITICAL DESTRUCTION IN THE LAND (JUDG 3:7–16:31)

This section describes the seven cycles of Israel's sin and salvation by telling the stories of Israel's judges.

3:7-11
Othniel

Because Israel sought the Baals and Asherahs of Canaan, God used the Mesopotamian King Cushan-Rishathaim to bring Judah to repentance. The name of the king, *Cushan of double-wickedness,* may have been a deliberate epithet given him by his enemies. The Spirit of the LORD came upon Othniel, Caleb's nephew (1:13; Josh 15:18), and he expelled Cushan from the land. The eight-year reign of Cushan was followed by forty years of peace.

Statue of Baal, the Canaanite weather god, dating from the fifteenth to fourteenth century B.C.

3:12-31
Ehud and Shamgar

Eglon of Moab established a provincial capital at the "City of the Palms" (Jericho) and held Israel under tribute for eighteen years. The Benjamite Ehud brought Israel's annual tribute to the king. Because Ehud was left-handed (3:15), his weapon was undetected by the king's bodyguards.

Ehud told the king that he had a secret message from God. The message was the sword of Ehud (3:16-22)! He slayed the king and escaped, rallying the people to defeat the Moabites (3:23-29). Israel subjugated Moab and rested from war for eighty years.

While Eglon oppressed Israel in the east, the Philistines troubled Israel in the west (3:31). Shamgar kept the Philistines at bay by using an oxgoad (compare 5:6). The oxgoad was a farm tool of about eight feet in length that had a metal, chisel-shaped blade at its tip. Shamgar killed six hundred Philistines during his judgeship.

4:1–5:31
Deborah and Barak

Both prose (4:1-24) and poetic descriptions (5:1-31) are given of Deborah and Barak's victory over the Canaanites. The two accounts, though having differences, are best interpreted as supplementary and not necessarily contradictory. An important theme of this cycle is the role women played in the defeat of the Canaanites.

Israel was oppressed by Jabin, the king of Hazor who ruled over a coalition of cities, one of which was ruled by Sisera (4:1-2). The name Jabin was probably a dynastic title (compare Josh 11:1). Although Joshua destroyed Hazor, the city had been rebuilt because of its strategic location.

Because of Sisera's superior chariots, Israel had been oppressed for twenty years. Deborah, a woman recognized for her civil authority (4:4-5), was a prophetess of God. She called on Barak to lead Israel against Sisera. Barak was reluctant to go without Deborah, and for this reason a woman received the honor of the victory rather than Barak (4:8-9,21-22).

With ten thousand soldiers gathered from Naphtali and Zebulun, the LORD routed Sisera's nine hundred chariots at the River Kishon. Sisera fled by foot toward Kadesh (4:10-17). Jael, the wife of Heber who had friendly relations with Jabin, gave him refuge. Sisera fell asleep in the tent of Heber, where Jael killed him by driving a

THE CYCLE OF THE JUDGES

During the period of the judges, Israel was caught in a whirlpool of sin and judgment that threatened to destroy the young nation. The stories of the judges portray a frustratingly predictable cycle of events summarized by four key words: sin, suffering, supplication, and salvation. Both Samuel and Ezra used this dark period of Israel's history to remind the Israelites of their sinful tendencies and God's mercy (1 Sam 12:9-11; Neh 9:26-28).

Sin

The basic cause of Israel's problems in Canaan was spiritual, not agricultural, economic, educational, or military. Israel had turned from a wholehearted obedience to God. They put God's law behind their backs (Neh 9:26), "forgot the LORD their God" (1 Sam 12:9), and "followed and worshiped various gods of the people around them" (Judg 2:12; see also 3:7,12; 4:1; 6:1; 10:6; 13:1). Two of the major foreign deities the Israelites worshiped were Baal, a Canaanite storm and fertility god, and Ashtoreth, a fertility goddess associated with ancient Near Eastern religions.

Suffering

The price of Israel's sin was high—decades of national suffering and oppression. Israel had sinned against God; therefore, God punished Israel. God did not punish Israel impersonally through the forces of nature. Instead, He chose to use the surrounding foreign nations whose gods the Israelites were serving to cause them misery. As the writer of Judges said: "In his anger against Israel, the LORD handed them over to raiders who plundered them. He sold them to their enemies all around, whom they were no longer able to resist" (Judg 12:14). Enemies used by the Lord include groups from northwest Mesopotamia (3:8), Moab (3:12), northern Israel (4:2), Midian (6:1), Philistia (10:7; 13:1), and Ammon (10:7). (See the feature article "Neighbors of Israel.")

Supplication

The Israelites' troubles eventually brought them to their knees before God (Judg 3:9,15; 4:3; 6:7; 10:10,15). Their prayer was: "We have sinned; we have forsaken the LORD and served the Baals and Ashtoreths. But now deliver us from the hands of our enemies" (1 Sam 12:10; see also Judg 10:15). This prayerful request was predictably also accompanied by repentance (Judg 10:16), which involved getting rid of the foreign idols and a return to their worship of the one true God.

Salvation

In response to the Israelites' repentant prayers and actions, God brought deliverance. Just as God used people to bring judgment on Israel, so God used people to bring deliverance. These God-picked liberators—usually termed "Judges"—are most remembered as military leaders who performed heroic individual actions (Judg 3:21; 14:19; 15:8; 15; 16:30) and who mobilized the Israelite tribes against their enemies (Judg 4:14; 7:1-18; 11:6).

Unfortunately, Israel's memory was short. Rather than learning the painful lesson of sin's price, whenever the rescuing judge died they "returned to ways even more corrupt than those of their fathers, following other gods and serving and worshiping them" (Judg 2:19). Thus the painful cycle was begun again. □

RULERS OF OLD TESTAMENT PAGAN NATIONS (Listed Alphabetically)

NAME	REFERENCE	NATIONALITY
Abimelech	(1) Gen 20	Philistine
	(2) Gen 26	Philistine
Achish	1 Sam 21:10-14; 27–29	Philistine
Adoni-Zedek	Josh 10:1-27	Canaanite
Agag	1 Sam 15:8-33	Amalekite
Ahasuerus	See Xerxes I	
Ammon, King of (Unnamed)	Judg 11:12-28	Ammonite
Artaxerxes	Ezra 4:7-23; 7; 8:1; Neh 2:1-8	Persian/Mede
Ashurbanipal (also known as Osnapper)	Ezra 4:10	Assyrian
Baalis	Jer 40:14	Ammonite
Balak	Num 22–24	Moabite
Belshazzar	Dan 5; 7:1	Babylonian
Ben-Hadad I	1 Kgs 20:1-34	Syrian
Ben-Hadad II	2 Kgs 6:24	Syrian
Bera	Gen 14:2-24	Canaanite
Cyrus the Great	2 Chron 36:22-23; Ezra 1; Isa 44:28; 45:1; Dan 1:21; 10:1	Persian/Mede
Darius the Great	Ezra 4–6; Neh 12:22; Hag 1:1; Zech 1:1,17	Persian/Mede
Darius the Mede	Dan 11:1	Persian/Mede
Edom, King of (Unnamed)	Num 20:14-21	Edomite
Eglon	Judg 3:12-30	Moabite
Egypt, Pharaoh of (Unnamed)	(1) Gen 12:18-20	Egyptian
	(2) Gen 41:38-55	Egyptian
	(3) Exod 1:8	Egyptian
	(4) Exod 2:15	Egyptian
	(5) Exod 3:10; 5:1	Egyptian
	(6) 1 Kgs 3:1	Egyptian
Esarhaddon	Ezra 4:2	Assyrian
Evil-Merodach	2 Kgs 25:27-30; Jer 52:31-34	Babylonian
Hanun	2 Sam 10:1-4	Ammonite
Hazael	1 Kgs 19:15; 2 Kgs 8:7-15	Syrian
Hiram	1 Kgs 5:1-18	Tyrian
Hophra	Jer 44:30	Egyptian
Jabin	(1) Josh 11:1-11	Canaanite
	(2) Judg 4:2	Canaanite
Jericho, King of (Unnamed)	Josh 2:2	Canaanite
Merodach-Baladan	2 Kgs 20:12; Isa 39:1	Babylonian
Mesha	2 Kgs 3:4-27	Moabite
Nahash	1 Sam 11:12	Ammonite
Nebuchadnezzar	2 Kgs 24–25; Dan 1–4	Babylonian
Neco	2 Kgs 23:29-30	Egyptian
Nergal-Sherezer	Jer 39:3,13	Babylonian
Osnapper	SEE Ashurbanipal	
Pul	SEE Tiglath-Pileser III	
Rezin	2 Kgs 15:37; 16:5-9	Syrian
Sargon II	Isa 20	Assyrian
Sennacherib	2 Kgs 18–19; Isa 36–37	Assyrian
Shalmaneser V	2 Kgs 17:1-6	Assyrian
Shishak	1 Kgs 14:25-26; 2 Chr 12:2-9	Egyptian
Tiglath-Pileser III	2 Kgs 15:19,29; 16:7-10	Assyrian
Tyre, Prince of (Unnamed)	Ezek 28:1-10	Tyrian
Xerxes I (also known as Ahasuerus)	Ezra 4:6; Esth	Persian/Mede

tent peg through his temple (4:18-21). For Sisera to die at the hand of a woman rather than in battle was a grave disgrace for a professional soldier (4:9,22).

The Song of Deborah is the poetic version of the battle (5:1-31). Deborah praised God for His deliverance of Israel (5:1-5). She described how commerce and village life were disturbed under Canaanite harassment. Israel was disarmed and depended on foreign alliances (5:6-9). The poem honored the tribes who responded to Barak's call and rebuked those who refused (5:13-18).

While the battle began near Harosheth Haggoyim (4:13), the decisive moment was at Megiddo near Taanach (5:19). Traversing the valley of Jezreel, where these cities are located, is the Kishon River. Evidently the Kishon flooded and swept away the chariots of Sisera (5:19-23). From archaeological findings at Megiddo, scholars have concluded that the battle took place about 1125 B.C.

The final stanzas of her poem repeated the theme of Sisera's shameful death at the feet of Jael (5:24-27). The song concludes with a taunt by depicting Sisera's mother awaiting his return. In fact, Sisera lay dead at the feet of a woman (5:28-30).

6:1–8:32
Gideon

The story of Gideon focuses on his struggle to overcome fear. The Midianites along with other eastern peoples had oppressed Israel for seven years (6:1-10). The LORD came to Gideon and challenged him to lead Israel like a "mighty warrior" (6:12).

Gideon passed his first test of faith by tearing down the altar of Baal that belonged to his father (6:25-32). The Spirit of the LORD came upon Gideon, and he prepared for battle against the Midianites (6:33-35). By setting out a fleece of wool, he devised a test to learn that God was with him (6:36-40).

Gideon gathered 32,000 soldiers, but the LORD tested Gideon's courage once again. So that the LORD might receive the credit for the victory (7:2), He reduced Gideon's army to ten thousand. He then chose only the three hundred who lapped "the water with their tongue like a dog" (7:5). These three hundred were selected because they showed that they were more watchful for the enemy.

The LORD reassured fearful Gideon through the dream of a man in the Midianite camp that Gideon would win the battle. The barley loaf in the dream was Israel, and the tent it struck was representative of the nomadic Midianites (7:9-14).

With three companies of one hundred men, Gideon launched a surprise attack; and the Midianite camp fell into panic (7:15-21). In spite of a weak leader, small army, and the foolish weapons of trumpets and torches, Israel won the day because of the power of the LORD (7:22).

The Ephraimites complained to Gideon that they were not called to the battle. He satisfied them by praising their part in the war (8:1-3). No longer afraid of battle, Gideon humbled the cities of Succoth and Peniel, which had refused to gave aid to his fatigued army (8:4-17). By executing the Midianite kings, Zebab and Zalmunna, Gideon avenged his brothers (8:18-21).

The grateful Israelites invited Gideon to rule over them. But Gideon refused and declared, "The LORD will rule over you" (8:23). However, Gideon failed the LORD because he made an ephod that became an object of worship in his hometown, Ophrah (8:24-27). The ephod was the garment of the high priest which contained the lots used to discern the will of God (Exod 28:30; 39:1-26). Here the *means* of discerning God's will became a substitute for God. Gideon succeeded in bringing peace to the land for forty years (8:28), but his obsession with knowing the certainty of God's favor became his downfall.

Gideon's career also was marred by his polygamous life. Abimelech, who was born to Gideon by one of his concubines, became a wicked leader in Israel (8:29-31).

8:33–10:5
Abimelech, Tola, and Jair

The fifth cycle of stories focuses on the treacherous life of Abimelech. It also includes brief comments on the judges Tola and Jair. The people's desire for a king of their own choosing led them to the despot Abimelech, whose career brought continual warfare and insurrection.

Abimelech, born of a Shechemite woman, convinced the citizens of Shechem to make him king and to kill his half-brothers, the seventy sons of Gideon. Only Jotham escaped the slaughter. From Mount Gerizim, which overlooks Shechem, he taunted them by telling the fable of the "Bramble King" (9:7-15). He cursed them and predicted that they too would be killed by the treachery of Abimelech (9:19-20).

After three years the LORD caused dissent between the Shechemites and Abimelech (9:22-23). The ensuing bloodshed and cruel deaths of Gaal and the Shechemites (9:26-49) was God's vengeance for murdering Gideon's sons (9:24).

The rebellion against Abimelech spread to the city of Thebez. Abimelech stormed the city's tower. From the tower a woman dropped a millstone, crushing his skull. To escape the shame of being killed by a woman, he called for his armor bearer to kill him (9:50-54). The careers of Tola and Jair followed Abimelech's debacle. Tola led Israel for twenty-three years.

Jair was probably a contemporary of Tola. He was from Gilead and led Israel for twenty-two years. Since Jair had thirty sons, he probably was a polygamist like Gideon. The prestige of Jair's family is reflected by the donkeys (1 Sam 25:20) and cities his sons possessed (10:3-5).

10:6–12:15
Jephthah and Ibzan, Elon, and Abdon

The sixth cycle concerns the judgeship of Jephthah and includes the minor judges Ibza, Elon, and Abdon. An important feature of Jephthah's story is Israel's fickleness toward Jephthah. They turned to him for deliverance after they had earlier disowned him. This parallels how Israel had treated the LORD. A second theme is Jephthah's hasty judgments.

Because Israel fell into grave idolatry, God raised up the Philistines to trouble Israel in the west and the Ammonites to subdue Israel in the east (10:6-10). The Ammonites had oppressed Israel eighteen years when the LORD heard the cries of the Gileadites (10:11-18).

Jephthah had been exiled by the Gileadites because he was born of a harlot. When the Gileadites were humiliated by the Ammonites, they asked for Jephthah's help and vowed to make him their leader (11:1-11).

Jephthah sent a diplomatic delegation to the Ammonites to argue for Israel's right to their land, but the Ammonites rejected their claims (11:12-28). Then the Spirit of the LORD empowered Jephthah, and he advanced against the Ammonites. To secure the favor of God, he vowed to sacrifice as a burnt offering the first one who came out of his house to greet him upon his return from battle (11:29-31). The LORD gave the victory to Jephthah (11:32-33), but his hasty vow sacrificed his family lineage. His only child, a virgin daughter, was the first to greet him (11:34-40).

Some commentators believe that Jephthah offered her as a human sacrifice. Others believe the sacrifice of Jephthah was her service to the LORD as a perpetual virgin. The text does emphasize her virgin state (11:37,39). The

JUDGES OF THE OLD TESTAMENT

NAME	REFERENCE	IDENTIFICATION
Othniel	Judg 1:12-13; 3:7-11	Conquered a Canaanite city
Ehud	Judg 3:12-30	Killed Eglon, king of Moab, and defeated Moabites
Shamgar	Judg 3:31	Killed 600 Philistines with an oxgoad
Deborah	Judg 4–5	Convinced Barak to lead an army to victory against Sisera's troops
Gideon	Judg 6–8	Led 300 men to victory against 135,000 Midianites
Tola	Judg 10:1-2	Judged for 23 years
Jair	Judg 10:3-5	Judged for 22 years
Jephthah	Judg 11:1–12:7	Defeated the Ammonites after making a promise to the Lord
Ibzan	Judg 12:8-10	Judged for 7 years
Elon	Judg 12:11-12	Judged for 10 years
Abdon	Judg 12:13-15	Judged for 8 years
Samson	Judg 13–16	Killed 1,000 Philistines with a donkey's jawbone; was deceived by Delilah; destroyed a Philistine temple; judged 20 years
Samuel	1 and 2 Sam	Was the last of the judges and the first of the prophets

vow, however, refers to "a burnt offering" (11:31; compare 2 Kgs 3:27). Both Jephthah and his daughter believed that the LORD expected him to keep the vow (11:36). God, however, did not request this "burnt offering." Indeed, the pagan practice of human sacrifice is contrary to God's expressed will (Deut 12:31; 18:10).

As in the days of Gideon (8:1), the Ephraimites were angry that they did not participate in the battle and receive its spoil. Jephthah did not exhibit the patience of Gideon and fought against them. Ephraim fled back across the Jordan, but Jephthah controlled the fords. His armies identified the Ephraimites by a difference in their pronunciation of the word *Sibboleth* instead of *Shibboleth* (Hebrew *ear of corn*). This intertribal war led to the death of 42,000 Ephraimites (12:1-6). Although the career of Jephthah spanned only six years (12:7), his judgeship epitomized the problems of Israel's declining leadership.

Three minor judges—Ibzan of Bethlehem (located in Zebulun, Josh 19:15), Elon of Zebulun, and Abdon of Ephraim—are mentioned. Ibzan led for seven years and was remembered for his influential family (12:8-10). Elon judged for ten years, but little else is known of him (12:11-12). Abdon was also polygamous and had a prestigious family. He ruled for eight years. These judges may not have engaged in any military missions.

13:1–16:31
Samson

The Philistines oppressed Israel for forty years (13:1), which included the twenty-year career of Samson (15:20; 16:31) and the judgeship of Samuel (1 Sam 1–7). The Philistines were a people from the Aegean region who migrated to Canaan in the mid-thirteenth century and settled in the coastal plain. The Philistines pressured Dan and Judah in the west by infiltrating the tribes through trade and intermarriage.

The story of the Danite hero Samson epitomizes the spiritual and political disarray of the nation. There are many contrasts in the story which the author used to highlight the moral impotence of the people. Samson was strong physically but weak morally. Though he made poor decisions and could not control his emotions, God used his mistakes as occasions to demonstrate His sovereign power. Another startling contrast is the sanctity of his Nazirite vow versus the disregard he showed for his Hebrew heritage. The victories of Samson were incomplete, and it was not until David that the Philistines were finally subjugated (2 Sam 5:17-25).

The LORD, who appeared as the angel of the LORD (Exod 3:1-8; Josh 5:13-15), announced to Samson's mother that she would bear a son and rear the child as a Nazirite (Judg 13:2-7). The Nazirite vow included abstinence from any drink derived from the grapevine, abstaining from cutting one's hair, and avoiding contact with a dead body (Num 6:1-21).

The angel of the LORD confirmed the calling of Samson by revealing Himself to his mother and father, Manoah. As with previous judges, the empowerment of the Spirit began to move Samson (13:8-25). The devotion of his mother, who also took the Nazirite vow (13:4), stood in stark contrast to the licentious career that Samson would choose to live.

Against the advice of his parents, Samson wanted to arrange a marriage with a Philistine woman from Timnath. As they journeyed to her home, a lion attacked; the Spirit enabled Samson to kill it (14:1-6). Later, when he returned to marry the woman, he saw that the carcass of the lion had become the home of wild bees. He took honey from the carcass and shared it with his parents (14:8-9). In doing so, he violated his vow by touching the dead lion (compare Num 6:6-12).

Out of this experience Samson made up a riddle at his wedding. He challenged his Philistine guests to solve it for thirty changes of clothing. The riddle was too clever for them, and they forced Samson's new bride to discover the answer for them. The LORD used their treachery, however, to incite Samson against the Philistines. At Ashkelon he killed thirty men to pay his thirty changes of clothing (14:10-20).

Samson killing a lion

When Samson returned to Timnath and learned that his bride had been given to another man, he swore to harm the Philistines more. He burned the wheat harvest of the Philistines by releasing into the fields foxes with lighted torches tied to their tails. The Philistines responded by burning his wife and her father to death, but this only made Samson slay many more (15:1-8a).

The Philistines gathered in Judah near Lehi (Hebrew *jawbone*) to fight Samson, and the Israelites bound Samson to give him over to the Philistines. When he was delivered over, the Spirit came upon Samson again, and with the fresh jawbone of a donkey, he killed one thousand Philistines (15:8b-17). God miraculously provided water for Samson, who was dying of thirst from the battle (15:18-20).

Samson's lust for a prostitute at Gaza led him again into trouble. He was surrounded by the people of the city, but he escaped to Hebron by removing the city gates (16:1-3).

The final betrayal of Samson came from yet another woman, named Delilah. The woman enticed Samson to tell her the secret of his strength. After several tests she learned that the cutting of his hair would break his Nazirite vow. During his sleep, a man cut off Samson's braided hair. Samson fell into the hands of the Philistines, who bound and blinded him. Samson was taken to Gaza,

Neighbors of Israel

Israel did not live out the exciting events of the OT in a vacuum. The stage of history in the ancient Near East was crowded with many national groups. During most of Israel's and Judah's history, their borders connected with those of six different nations.

Phoenicia

Living just north of Israel along the Mediterranean coast, the Semitic Amorites who populated the shoreline were famous merchants and seafarers who established colonies in north Africa, Spain, Asia Minor, and various Mediterranean islands. Israel usually maintained peaceful relations with this country, especially under David and Ahab. But they also fought wars against it. Phoenicia's two major city-states were Sidon and Tyre. Sidon was destroyed in 677 B.C. by the Assyrian king Sennacherib; in 571 B.C. Nebuchadnezzar, the Babylonian king, captured Tyre.

Aram/Syria

Located northeast of Israel, this collection of Semitic city-states—especially Damascus, Zobah, and Hamath—is mentioned frequently in Scripture as an aggressive enemy of Israel and Judah. The Bible records that Saul, David, Solomon, Baasha, Ahab, Joram, Joash, Jehoahaz, and Jehoash all fought battles against Aram. The Arameans' greatest cultural contribution to the world was their alphabet, on which the "square" Hebrew script is based.

Ammon

Situated east of Israel, this Semitic nation traced its roots to Abraham's nephew Lot. Rabbah Ammon (modern Amman, Jordan) served as their capital. Their chief god was Milcom. Israel's relations with Ammon were stormy and included conflicts dating from the period of the judges to the final years of the kingdom of Judah. During David's reign, Ammon was conquered, though soon after Solomon's reign it declared independence. During the sixth century B.C. it was overrun first by Arab invaders, then by the Persians.

Moab

Located east of the Dead Sea, Moab, another Semitic nation, traced its origin to Lot. The chief Moabite god was Chemosh. David's great-grandmother Ruth was a Moabite, but both he and later Israelite kings fought many bloody battles with Moab. A famous archaeological find, the Mesha stele (about 850 B.C.), describes the Moabite king Mesha's war of liberation from Israel, probably during Jehoram's reign. Like Judah, Moab was conquered by Nebuchadnezzar about 587 B.C. and later was dominated by the Persians.

Edom

A Semitic nation southeast of the Dead Sea, Edom traced its roots to Jacob's brother, Esau. Prosperity in this mountainous nation was primarily due to caravan tolls and mining. During the exodus, Edom refused Israel permission to pass through its territory. Though Moses commanded the Israelites not to hate the Edomites, hostilities existed between the two peoples from that time onward. Israel dominated Edom throughout most of the biblical period.

Philistia

Israel's only non-Semitic neighbor, the Philistines came from Caphtor (possibly Crete or some other Aegean land) to settle on the Mediterranean shores west of Judah. Their chief god was Dagon, an agricultural deity. With their superior metal weapons and technology, the comparatively wealthy and sophisticated Philistines were Israel's greatest threat to national security during the early years of the monarchy. They killed Israel's first king (Saul) in battle. David dealt them major defeats, though they presented great problems for Israel over the years. □

The death of Samson

where he was forced to grind grain in the prison like a common animal (16:4-21). But his hair began to grow again. The LORD used this last humiliation of Samson to kill the enemies of Israel (16:22).

At a Philistine festival to honor their god Dagon, the rulers boasted that Dagon had rendered Samson helpless. The crowd in the temple called for blinded Samson to entertain them. Samson prayed for strength to avenge himself. He pulled down the central pillars of the temple and killed all the Philistines and their rulers. Samson killed more in this act of death than all those killed during his life (16:23-31). Ironically, his inability to control his lusts meant that the Nazirite's death was more valuable to Israel than his life.

MORAL DEPRAVITY IN THE LAND (JUDG 17:1–21:25)

The final section of the book gives two parade examples of Israel's moral defection. The first case concerns idolatry by the tribe of Dan (Judg 17–18). The second case is about intertribal warfare that resulted from the rape and murder of a Levite's concubine by the men of Benjamin (Judg 19–21).

The author used these two events to show his own generation the need for a righteous king like David. In the tenth century B.C., Dan became a center for the worship of Baal established by the apostate King Jeroboam (1 Kgs 12:25-33). Also the story of Benjamin cast a poor light on the tribe of Ish-bosheth, Saul's surviving son, who rivaled David for the throne (compare 2 Sam 2:10-11). The opponents of David's dynasty had their roots in the period of the Judges.

Both stories tell of priests who acted corruptly and of tribes who killed for gain. What was needed for an antidote was a righteous ruler like David so that Israel might do what was right in God's eyes (compare 17:6; 18:1; 19:1; 21:25).

17:1–18:31
Micah's Gods and the Danites

The story of Micah shows how Israel adopted the idolatrous religious practices of its neighbors. Micah constructed a private shrine from stolen silver including an ephod and several idols. He conscripted his son to serve as its priest until he hired a wandering Levite from Bethlehem. Micah foolishly believed he had the favor of God because of his personal shrine and priest (17:1-13).

The Danites, meanwhile, dispatched five spies to search for a new tract of land because they were pressed for space by the Amorites (compare 1:34; Josh 19:47). On their way to Laish, they discovered Micah's priest and shrine (18:1-12).

Later the Danites returned with six hundred men and stole Micah's valuable idols. His Levite saw the chance to improve his status by serving a whole tribe. The Danites took the Levite with them to Laish where they dispossessed the people and renamed the city Dan (18:13-29).

Micah's Levite was a direct descendant of Moses (18:30). This showed how low the spiritual leadership of the nation had fallen. Whereas Moses had established proper worship at the tabernacle, his descendants were functioning at rival sanctuaries in the land (compare 18:31).

19:1-30
The Rape of the Levite's Concubine

The second story tells of a Levite whose concubine left him for her father's house at Bethlehem. The Levite convinced her to return, and together they journeyed toward Ephraim. Along the way they looked for lodging and chose Gibeah (the home of the future king, Saul) rather than the Jebusite city of Jerusalem (the residence of the future king, David) because Gibeah was inhabited by Israelites. There they expected treatment as brothers (19:12-14). Ironically, pagan Jerusalem would have proven a safer refuge.

At Gibeah, however, no one offered them hospitality,

except an old man from Ephraim who had migrated to Gibeah. That evening the men of Gibeah came to the old man's house to have sexual relations with the Levite (19:15-22).

The old man was so embarrassed by this breach of hospitality that he offered his virgin daughter and the Levite's concubine. The men refused and pressed against the door, so the Levite pushed his concubine outside. The men ravaged her for their sport and left her for dead. Out of revenge the Levite carved up her body into twelve pieces and sent them to the tribes of Israel (19:23-30). So great an atrocity became a long-remembered symbol of Israel's sin (19:30; compare Hos 9:9; 10:9).

20:1–21:25
War with Benjamin

Covenant law required the tribes to punish anyone guilty among them or they would become the object of God's wrath too. Israel learned this in the days of Joshua at Ai (Josh 7–8). Because Benjamin refused to give up the offenders, all Israel agreed to march against their kindred tribe Benjamin (20:1-17).

The LORD instructed them to attack, but each time the Israelites suffered numerous casualties. This was God's way of punishing Israel for its immorality to bring out repentance and true worship. In the third battle God gave them victory. The whole tribe of Benjamin was destroyed except for six hundred survivors (20:18-48).

The Israelites mourned for their lost tribe Benjamin (21:2-3,6,15), and to revitalize the tribe they had to find wives for the six hundred survivors (21:1,5,17-18). Jabesh-Gilead had not fought in the war; therefore Israel led a punitive expedition against them and took four hundred virgins for Benjamin. The Benjamites stole two hundred more virgins at the festival of Shiloh (21:19-23).

The final verse captured the spirit of the times: "In those days Israel had no king; everyone did as he saw fit" (21:25).

Theological and Ethical Value

The Book of Judges presents Yahweh as the Lord of history. As such, God used foreign peoples to test the Israelites' loyalty to God and to punish their idolatry. Testing and punishment were not, however, God's ultimate goal for Israel. When God's people repented and appealed to God for aid, God did His heart's desire—He raised up deliverers to save His people. Salvation is the goal toward which God was and is directing history.

As Lord of history, God was free to choose whomever He pleased to act as deliverer. From the human point of view God's choices are surprising: an assassin (Ehud), a woman (Deborah), a coward from an insignificant family (Gideon), the rash son of a prostitute (Jephthah), and a womanizer (Samson). Many of these chosen deliverers had obvious moral shortcomings. Still, God used them to save His people. True, Christians are called on to make every effort to be holy (Heb 12:14). But God is sovereign and free to use whomever He chooses to further His saving purposes.

Human sinfulness necessitates governments to enforce morality. In the days of the judges when there was no king, "everyone did as he saw fit" (21:25). Governments have a God-given responsibility to punish wrongdoing (compare Rom 13:3-5). The later history of Israel, however, reveals that just having a king was not the answer to Israel's moral failure. Indeed, Israel's and Judah's kings often led God's people into even greater disobedience. What was most needed was not for God's covenant to be enforced from without but written on the hearts of His people (compare Jer 31:31-34).

Questions for Reflection

1. What are the effects of immorality on society?
2. In what different ways does God respond to sin among His people?
3. How does God's Spirit work in the world and with God's people?
4. What can be learned from Judges about God's forgiveness and longsuffering?
5. What are some examples of godly leadership in the book?

Sources for Additional Study

Cundall, Arthur E., and Leon Morris. *Judges and Ruth.* Downers Grove: InterVarsity, 1968.

Goslinga, C. J. *Joshua, Judges, Ruth.* Grand Rapids: Zondervan, 1986.

Lewis, Arthur H. *Judges/Ruth.* Chicago: Moody, 1979.

RUTH

The Book of Ruth is named for its heroine, whose devotion to God and love for family has endeared her to generations of readers. It tells how God graciously rewarded the faithfulness of the widows Ruth and Naomi by delivering them through their kinsman-redeemer Boaz, who married Ruth and maintained the property of Naomi's family. The story takes place during the time of the judges (about 1150 B.C.). For this reason our English versions and the Greek translation of the Old Testament put the book after the Book of Judges.

In the Hebrew Bible, Ruth appears in the third section of books known as the *Hagiographa* or "Writings." Traditionally, the Jews read Ruth at the Feast of Weeks (Pentecost), which is a harvest celebration.

The authorship of Ruth is unknown. The book is named for its chief character, not necessarily for its author. A late Jewish tradition ascribes the book to the prophet Samuel.

The date of the composition is disputed and has been dated to either the early monarchy (about 950 B.C.) or the postexilic period (about 450 B.C.). Linguistic arguments have not been decisive, since they can be used to date the book either early or late. Also scholars are divided about whether the story fits better with the concerns of the monarchy or the setting of the postexilic period.

The question is complicated by problems concerning the relationship of the story and the genealogy of David, which ends the book (4:18-22). It is unusual for a book to end with a genealogy. Some scholars believe that the story is fictional and originally had no connection with David. In this view an editor during the postexilic period borrowed the genealogy of David from 1 Chronicles 2:4-15 and added it as an appendix to the story.

Recently, however, many biblical scholars have adopted the traditional view of Ruth, accepting it as the historically trustworthy work of one writer from about 950 B.C. They believe that the story presupposes the genealogy. The genealogy in Ruth and Chronicles probably came from a common temple source. These scholars argue that it is unlikely that David would have been linked to a Moabite ancestress unless he was *in fact* her descendant.

Theme

Ruth is a story of faithfulness, both human and divine. Naomi demonstrated faithfulness by returning to the land of promise. Ruth demonstrated her faithfulness by accompanying Naomi to Bethlehem and working the fields to provide for her. Ruth further demonstrated faithfulness to her deceased husband by her desire to marry into his family. Boaz demonstrated his faithfulness by fulfilling his covenant role as near kinsman.

Above all, Ruth is a story of God's faithfulness. God was faithful in preserving a family line, which—in God's time—led to King David and ultimately to Jesus. Ruth's story serves as a reminder that our faithfulness plays a part in the fulfillment of God's promises.

I. Ruth's Choice of Faith (1:1-22)
II. Ruth's Challenge in Faith (2:1-23)
III. Ruth's Claim by Faith (3:1-18)
IV. Ruth's Child because of Faith (4:1-18)

Purpose and Theology

1. The story provides a transition from the patriarchs to the monarchy. The genealogy at the end of the book traces the lineage of Boaz from Perez, the son of Judah, down to King David. For many Israelites the most important word of the book was the last—*David.*

2. The story of Ruth shows how God sovereignly, though almost imperceptively, achieves His purposes through the faithfulness of His people. The book speaks about God indirectly through the prayers and blessings of the story's characters. Although the book reflects a strong belief in God's lordship over history, it equally convinces readers that human decisions and actions play a significant role.

3. The book teaches that God's will is sometimes accomplished by common people with uncommon faith. The Book of Ruth does not have miracles or revelations. It does not mention the institutions of Israel's religion, such as tabernacle and prophecy. It has simple people going about everyday affairs.

4. The theological emphasis of Ruth can be summed up by two key words—*kindness* (*hesed*) and *kinsman-redeemer* (*goel*). The word *kindness* indicates covenant faithfulness and occurs three times in the prayers and commendations spoken by the characters (1:8; 2:20; 3:10). There is an implied contrast between the story's characters, who are righteous, and those of Judges, who "did as he [they] saw fit" (Judg 21:25).

The story teaches that God rewards the faithfulness of His people. God accomplished this by using Boaz as the family's "kinsman-redeemer" (2:20; 3:12-13; 4:1-10). *Kinsman-redeemer* refers to a relative who helped a troubled family member so that the family was not dispossessed of land or left without an heir (Lev 25:25-34; Deut 25:5-10).

5. The story corrected the Jews when they made the worship of God exclusively the prerogative of Israel. Although Ruth was a Moabitess, she was blessed by God.

RUTH'S CHOICE OF FAITH (RUTH 1:1-22)

1:1-5
Ruth's Dilemma

Because of famine the family of Elimelech moved from Bethlehem to Moab. "In the days when the judges ruled" (1:1) describes the hostile and sinful times when the story transpires.

Elimelech was accompanied by Naomi, his wife, and their two sons, Mahlon and Kilion. The story describes them as "Ephrathites." *Ephrath* was another name for Bethlehem (Gen 35:19; 48:7; Ruth 4:11; Mic 5:2).

Elimelech died and left Naomi and her sons behind. The sons married Moabite women, Ruth and Orpah. Then they too died, leaving the Moabite widows and Naomi with the dilemma of facing life without the security of a husband or sons. In the ancient world women had security through their husbands and sons.

Nearby Moab was east of the Dead Sea and south of the Arnon River. The Moabites were descendants of Lot (Gen 19:30-38). They fought the Israelites during the judgeship of Ehud (Judg 3:12-30). The story of Ruth probably took place during a period of peace.

1:6-22
Ruth's Decision

Faced with little hope, the three widows considered the extent of their obligation to the family. Naomi decided to return to her homeland in Bethlehem. She had heard that God "had come to the aid of his people by providing food" (1:6). This is the first hint that God would save the widows. Ruth 1:6 and 4:13, where Ruth conceived a child with the help of God, are the only passages where the story specifically says that God acted on behalf of His people. Just as God had caused the land to grow, God would bless the house of Elimelech through Ruth's womb.

Ruth and Orpah insisted that they return to Bethlehem, but Naomi urged them to seek "rest," that is, homes, in Moab (1:9). She explained that it was impossible for her to marry and have sons who could become their new husbands (1:11-13).

She was referring to the Israelite custom known as levirate marriage. A brother-in-law (Latin *levir*) or other near kinsman married the wife of his deceased brother and had a child in the name of the deceased (Deut 25:5-10). This practice perpetuated land possession within a family and protected the widow.

Orpah stayed in Moab, but Ruth "clung" to Naomi (1:14). The depth of her commitment is poignantly expressed by the Moabitess: "Your people will be my people and your God my God" (1:16).

1:19-22
Ruth's Destiny

When Naomi and Ruth arrived in Bethlehem, the women of the town asked, "Can this be Naomi?" (1:19). Naomi answered that her name was no longer *Naomi* but *Mara* because the Lord had afflicted her (1:20-21).

Her reply involves a play on the meaning of her name. *Naomi* means *pleasantness*, and *Mara* (*mara'*) means *bitterness.* Naomi considered her condition a bitter experience because she left Bethlehem with a full, happy house and had returned empty without children.

They returned to Bethlehem at the time of harvest (1:22). This is another hint that their fortunes would change in Bethlehem. Among the plentiful fields, God *would* again restore fullness to Naomi and Ruth.

RUTH'S CHALLENGE IN FAITH (RUTH 2:1-23)

2:1-3
Ruth's "Chance" Meeting

Boaz was a relative of Elimelech (2:1). He was a man of importance and wealth who was able to act as Ruth's kinsman-redeemer.

According to Mosaic law, the poor could glean the corners of the fields. Ruth looked for work (2:2), and "as it turned out" she came to the field of Boaz (2:3). The Hebrew text says literally "her chance chanced" to work in the fields of Boaz (2:3). This expression intentionally exaggerates the way the human eye saw her actions. The author does this to draw attention to the hidden reality of God's providential intervention. This was not accidental but the work of God veiled from Ruth's eyes.

2:4-18
Ruth's Commendation

Boaz invited Ruth to work exclusively in his fields. Ruth was surprised by Boaz's generosity, particularly since she was a Moabitess, a foreigner. Boaz explained that he had already heard a good report about her commitment to Naomi. He commended Ruth for her faithfulness and prayed that God might bless her (2:11-12).

Boaz acted on his prayer. He rewarded Ruth with roasted grain and instructed his laborers to leave stalks behind for her to glean. At the end of her work, Ruth had enough food for Naomi. As God had used Boaz and Ruth to feed Naomi, God would use them to give Naomi a son.

2:19-23
Ruth's Care

Naomi exulted in the LORD when she learned about Boaz because she knew that he was a kinsman-redeemer (2:20). She urged Ruth to follow Boaz's instructions because he would care for her safety.

RUTH'S CLAIM BY FAITH (RUTH 3:1-18)

3:1-6
Ruth's Obedience

Naomi instructed Ruth to prepare herself properly and approach Boaz during the night at the threshing floor. She obeyed Naomi's instructions carefully (3:5-6). Ironically, Naomi is the one who would find "a home" (Hebrew "rest," 3:1) for Ruth and not a Moabite husband (1:9).

A threshing floor was a stone surface in the fields where the harvest husks were crushed and the grain sifted from the chaff.

3:7-15
Ruth's Trust

Ruth secretly approached Boaz. By lying at his feet, Ruth humbled herself as one of his servants. She trusted God to use Boaz to answer her needs and to protect her. Ruth startled Boaz since women were usually not with the men at night.

She made her request: "Spread the corner of your garment over me, since you are a kinsman-redeemer" (3:9). By this expression Ruth was asking Boaz for marriage (compare Ezek 16:8). The Hebrew word translated "corner" can also be translated "wings." Boaz had prayed that Ruth might have refuge under the "wings" of God (2:12). He was used by God to provide the refuge for which Boaz himself had prayed.

The threshing and winnowing of grain is accomplished today in the Middle East in much the same way as in the days of Ruth and Boaz.

Boaz commended Ruth for her righteous conduct because she chose him instead of a younger man. This was a greater act of loyalty ("kindness," 3:10) than even her initial faithfulness ("kindness") to the family (1:8).

Boaz told Ruth that there was another kinsman who had the first right to redeem her. If he declined, then Boaz promised to marry her. He gave Ruth a bounty of grain as an indication of his commitment.

3:16-18
Ruth's Patience

Ruth reported to Naomi about Boaz's promise, and she gave her the grain from Boaz. This was another sign that God was answering their prayers through the hand of Boaz. Naomi told Ruth that she must be patient until the man carried out his pledge that day.

RUTH'S CHILD BECAUSE OF FAITH (RUTH 4:1-22)

4:1-12
Ruth's Redemption

Just as the widows had weighed their responsibility, the

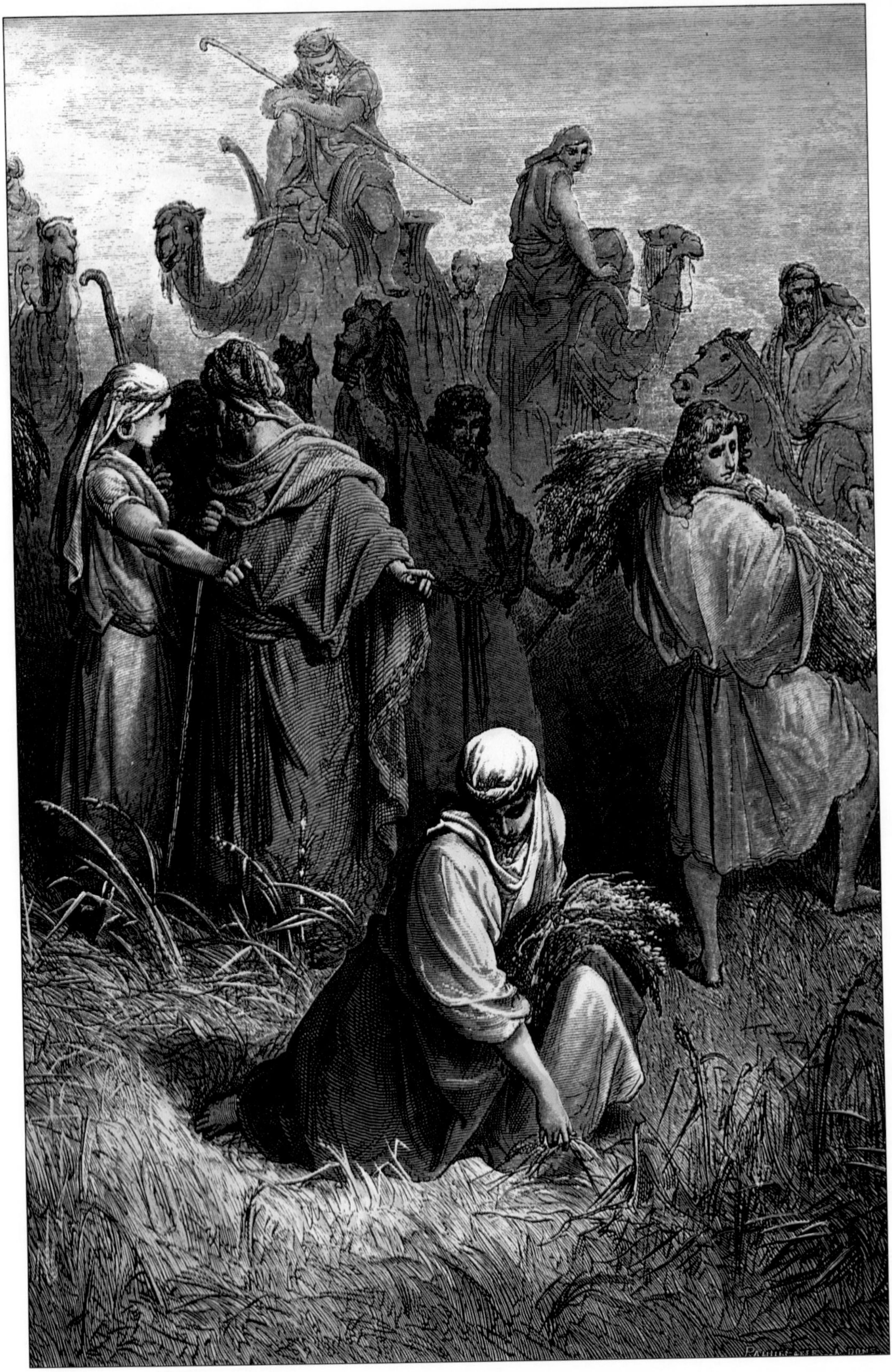

kinsmen of the Elimelech family discussed their roles. Boaz informed an unnamed kinsman that Naomi's fields were his to redeem (4:1-4). The kinsman agreed to buy the fields, but Boaz added that whoever bought the land ought to marry Ruth to "maintain the name of the dead with his property" (4:5). The Mosaic law does not tie the role of purchasing property with the custom of kinsman marriage. Therefore the kinsman could have declined without embarrassment. The kinsman explained that marriage would jeopardize his own inheritance. Boaz happily announced that he would redeem the property and marry Ruth himself.

Both the nearer kinsman and Orpah were not required technically by law to help the family. Ruth and Boaz decided to go beyond the prescription of the law to fulfill the purposes of the covenant. Because of their actions, the redemption of the family could be completed. Through their action, God worked to redeem Israel by making possible the birth of David.

The contract was sealed when the nearer kinsman gave his sandal to Boaz. This symbolized the transfer of his right to redeem (4:7-8).

The elders witnessed it and offered a prayer of blessing. They asked God to give Boaz children as He did the wives of Jacob and the house of Judah through Tamar, who bore Perez (4:11-12). The wives of Jacob bore twelve sons, the progenitors of all Israel; and Tamar bore twin sons to Judah (Gen 38:27-30).

The blessing implied two comparisons. First, Ruth was a Moabitess, whereas Leah and Rachel were the mothers of Israel. The comparison, however, was not offensive to the elders because Ruth had become integrated into the family of faith.

Second, Tamar and Ruth both were without children. Tamar achieved her ends through trickery, but Ruth received her son through righteous obedience. Judah tried to avoid his responsibility to perpetuate his own son's family line. Ruth and Boaz, the descendant of Judah, went beyond the letter of the levirate law and acted righteously before the LORD. Ironically, the righteousness of a Moabitess, a foreigner to Israel's covenant, brought salvation to Judah's family.

4:13-22
Ruth's Rest

God rewarded the couple by giving them the child Obed. The women of the city praised God and recognized that Obed would sustain Naomi and possess Elimelech's property. In this sense Naomi was regarded the mother of the child (4:17).

Ruth was more valuable to Naomi than seven sons (4:15). Naomi had lost two sons. Through Ruth, who continued the house of her husband and provided Israel with its greatest king, Naomi gained far more (4:17). This signals the completed reversal in the life of Naomi. She was no longer empty.

The genealogy linked David with the patriarchs through Perez, the son of Judah. Because of the faithfulness of Ruth and the faithfulness of God, the promises of the patriarchs could be realized through David and his greater Son, Jesus Christ: "A record of the genealogy of Jesus Christ the son of David, the son of Abraham" (Matt 1:1).

Theological and Ethical Significance

The Book of Ruth shows God working behind the scenes in the lives of ordinary people, turning apparent tragedy into joy and peace. The Book of Ruth shows God as concerned not only for the welfare of one family—Naomi and Ruth—but for the welfare of all God's people who would be blessed by David and by David's Son, Jesus Christ. The participation of Ruth, the Moabitess, in the fufillment of God's promises indicates that God's salvation is for people of all nationalities.

By their faithfulness, integrity, and love, the characters of the Book of Ruth mirrored the character of God. They serve as reminders that the lives of godly people are a powerful witness to God's self-sacrificing love.

Questions for Reflection

1. What does the book teach about the loving care of God?
2. How should the people of God respond to the sorrows of life?
3. How should those who are different in race, color, or economic status be treated?
4. How does the book encourage the people of God to be faithful?
5. Why should the people of God pray?

Sources for Additional Study

Atkinson, David. *The Message of Ruth*. Downers Grove: InterVarsity, 1983.
Cundall, Arthur E., and Leon Morris. *Judges and Ruth*. Downers Grove: InterVarsity, 1968.
Enns, Paul P. *Ruth*. Grand Rapids: Zondervan, 1982.

Ruth and Boaz

1 SAMUEL

First and Second Samuel are named for the principle character in the early chapters of the book. Samuel led Israel as its last judge and anointed Israel's first two kings, Saul and David.

First and Second Samuel were originally one book in the Hebrew Bible. The Greek Septuagint and the Latin Vulgate first divided the Hebrew into two books. The Septuagint entitled Samuel and Kings as four consecutive books called "First—Fourth Kingdoms." The Vulgate also had four books but with the title "Kings." In the Hebrew Bible the division into two books was established with the first printing of the Hebrew Bible (A.D. 1488). The English versions followed the Hebrew title "Samuel."

First and Second Samuel are anonymous. According to Jewish tradition, based on 1 Chronicles 29:29, the Books of Samuel were authored by Samuel and completed by the prophets Nathan and Gad. Since 1 Samuel 25:1 records Samuel's death and he seldom appears after the anointing of David (1 Sam 16:1-13), alternative explanations for the compilation of the books of Samuel have been sought.

As the Jewish tradition itself indicates, the Books of Samuel are a composite work of more than one hand. Among the materials used were eyewitness accounts, archival materials, independent narratives, and poetry.

Scholars disagree on how and when the Books of Samuel were written. Some believe the work was completed soon after the time of David (1011–971 B.C.). Other scholars have dated the completed work about 650–550 B.C. as part of a larger history influenced by the central ideas of Deuteronomy. (See "The Historical Books.")

Some commentators have charged that 1 Samuel evidences sources of contradictory theological viewpoints (for example, views on kingship). However, this diversity has been explained on other grounds, such as differences in emphasis or supplementation. The book's variety of sources have been integrated into a unified work with a consistent theme.

Theme

Through the prophetic ministry of Samuel, God established the monarchy of Israel by choosing David, "a man after his own heart," to rule over His people (13:14). The book helps us see that God is Lord over history. His sovereign plans are accomplished in spite of human failure.

I. The Righteous Leadership of Samuel (1:1–7:17)
II. The Rejection of Disobedient Saul (8:1–15:35)
III. The Rise of Faithful David (16:1–31:13)

Purpose and Theology

1. The book tells of the transition in leadership from the period of the judges to the rise of the monarchy. The book continues the story of Israel's wars with the Philistines begun in the Book of Judges (compare Samson, Judg 13–16). Samuel was a transition figure who, as the last judge, inaugurated the first king, Saul (10:1), and initiated the dynasty of King David (16:1,13).

During the judges period, the nation was a theocracy. The LORD was its only king and authority. The tribes had no central authority to govern them and were held together because of their common commitment to the covenant with the LORD. With the establishment of the kingdom, God would express His rule in a new way, through his chosen king.

2. The LORD's choice of godly leadership is focal. Samuel is extolled in contrast to Eli and his sons, Phinehas and Hophni. They were rejected by God because of their evil deeds (2:12-36). Under their leadership the Philistines captured the ark of the covenant at the battle of Aphek (4:1b-11); but under Samuel, Israel defeated the Philistines at Mizpah (7:1-17). Yet Samuel's sons were also unfit (8:1-6). So the LORD permitted the people to have a king (8:6-9,19-20; 9:17). King Saul, however, rejected the prophetic word of Samuel for reasons of political expediency (15:26-29). God, who "looks at the heart" (16:7), chose David as His anointed servant to rule over Israel (16:1-13; 28:16-19).

3. For Israel to prevail over its enemies, God required

covenant faithfulness and moral responsibility from Israel's leadership. The sin of Israel's leaders resulted in death for them and the people. The Philistine's defeat of Israel under Eli's evil sons (4:1-21) and under wicked Saul (31:1-13) is contrasted with Samuel's and David's victories (7:13; 23:1-5; 30:1-31).

4. God's continued grace is another significant theme in the book. In spite of Israel's repeated failures, the LORD raised up new deliverers in Samuel, Saul, and David. God answered the cry of Hannah (1:9-20), called the boy Samuel (3:1-21), granted the request for a king (8:6-9), and spared David for Israel's golden age to come (18:6-11,24-27; 19:9-10; 21:10-15).

5. The book demonstrates that God is Lord over history. His dominion is exercised over the rise and fall of important figures as well as whole nations. The motif of prophecy and its fulfillment shows that the LORD accomplishes His will in spite of human plans. Also the presence and empowerment of the Holy Spirit in the lives of Saul and David evidences God's sovereignty (10:6,10; 11:6; 16:13). When God disapproved Saul, the Spirit departed (16:14).

THE RIGHTEOUS LEADERSHIP OF SAMUEL (1 SAM 1:1–7:17)

In the opening section the godly life of Samuel is distinguished from the failures of the high priest Eli and his sons, Hophni and Phinehas (1 Sam 1–3). Although Samuel and the sons of Eli were reared in the same house, their dedication and destinies were very different. The Philistine wars led to the end of Eli's family (1 Sam 4–6), but Samuel prevailed over the Philistines and led Israel as judge and prophet (1 Sam 7).

1:1–2:10
Samuel's Dedication

Samuel's unusual birth was an early indication of the special dedication Samuel would have to the LORD throughout his life. Barren Hannah, Samuel's mother, prayed for a son. She vowed to rear the child as a Nazirite (1:1-20; compare Num 6:1-21 and Judg 13). Because the LORD answered her prayer, she dedicated Samuel to serve at the tabernacle under Eli's care (1:21-28).

Hannah's prayer in song celebrated the righteousness and sovereignty of God. He defeats the proud and exalts the humble. He will protect His saints and strengthen His anointed king (2:1-10).

2:11-36
Eli's Corruption

The corruption of the tabernacle at Shiloh by Eli's sons is contrasted with the faithful ministry of young Samuel (2:11-26). Whereas Hannah's son "ministered before the LORD" (2:11), the sons of Eli "had no regard for the LORD" (2:12). Eli's servants had contempt for the LORD's offerings, and his sons engaged in temple prostitution. Yet young Samuel, as it would be said of Jesus (Luke 2:52), grew in "favor with the LORD and with men" (2:26).

A man of God prophesied the death of Hophni and Phinehas (2:27-34) and the appointment of a "faithful priest" (2:35). The immediate context suggests that Samuel is meant (1 Sam 3), though Samuel did not exhaust this powerful image. This priest has also been identified as the high priest Zadok (1 Kgs 2:35), or Jesus Christ the priestly Messiah (Heb 5:1-10; 7:1-28).

3:1–4:1a
Samuel's Ministry

Because of the sin at Shiloh's shrine, the "word of the LORD was rare" and "visions" were not seen (3:1). However, the word came to Samuel (3:2-18), and the LORD appeared to him at Shiloh (3:21). Samuel's ministry reached throughout the land, and the people recognized that he was a prophet of the LORD (3:19–4:1a).

4:1b-22
Judgment of "Ichabod"

As in the Book of Judges, God's judgment on sin came in the form of foreign oppression. Here God's judgment fell on the house of Eli through the Philistine's victory over Israel at Ebenezer (compare 7:12). The battle had a major impact on the religious life of Israel because the ark of the covenant was captured. Israel's defeat and the deaths of Eli's sons showed that God would not tolerate their sin.

Hophni and Phinehas ordered the ark brought into the battlefield because they believed it would give them victory (compare Josh 6). The LORD rejected their superstitious actions, and they died in the battle (1 Sam 4:10-11). When Eli heard the news of the captured ark, he fell over backward and died (4:18). The deaths of his family brought the end to Eli's priesthood, fulfilling the prophecy of the man of God (2:27-34). Eli's daughter-in-law named her newborn son "Ichabod" (*no glory*) to remember this tragic day of the ark's loss (4:19-22).

5:1-12
LORD of the Ark

The god of the Philistines was the vegetation deity Dagon. The Philistines believed Dagon had given them victory by defeating the LORD of Israel. The Philistines placed the ark in their temple like a trophy for their vic-

The seacoast resort area of modern Ashkelon—site of an ancient Philistine city.

torious deity. The failure of Dagon, however, to stand before the ark showed that the LORD was greater (5:1-5). God brought a plague of tumors upon the Philistines (5:6-12). Perhaps this disease was bubonic plague related to an infestation of rats (compare 6:4).

6:1–7:1
The Ark and God's Holiness

The Philistines feared the LORD and honored Him by returning the ark on a new cart bearing a guilt offering (6:1-12). The Israelites at Beth Shemesh welcomed the ark, but they too suffered death because some men looked unlawfully into the ark (6:13-19; compare Num 4:20). They learned like the Philistines that the LORD was a holy God (6:20). They sent the ark to the house of Abinadab at Kiriath Jearim (6:21–7:1), where it resided until the days of David (2 Sam 6).

7:2-17
Samuel's "Ebenezer"

Unlike the sons of Eli, who sinned, Samuel was faithful. He turned the people away from their worship of the Canaanite fertility deities, Baal and Ashtoreth (7:1-6). As in the Book of Judges, God responded to His people's repentance by raising up a judge or national deliverer. God honored Samuel's faithfulness by giving him victory over the Philistines (7:7-13a). Samuel commemorated the victory by erecting a stone at the site. He named it "Ebenezer" (*stone of help*), saying, "Thus far has the LORD helped us" (7:12). Samuel spent his life serving the LORD as an itinerant judge, priest and prophet (7:13b-17).

THE REJECTION OF DISOBEDIENT SAUL (1 SAM 8:1–15:35)

Israel's disappointment with the priesthood of Eli and the sin of Samuel's sons led Israel to turn to a new form of leadership. The people, following the example of the nations around them, demanded a king (1 Sam 8). God granted their desires, and Samuel reluctantly appointed a king (1 Sam 9–10). Saul's reign had a promising beginning (1 Sam 11). King Saul, however, proved unlike Samuel because he did not listen to the word of the LORD (1 Sam 13–15). The LORD thus rejected Saul as he had the house of Eli.

8:1-22
God Permits a King

The people requested a king because Samuel's judgeship had begun to fail. He was old; and his sons, like Eli's, were wicked men who perverted justice. Also the people wanted the benefits of a central authority like the other nations had (8:1-5). Although Samuel resisted, God graciously permitted Israel to have a king (8:6-9). Samuel warned the people of the troubles of kingship, but they persisted; so God granted their request (8:10-22).

9:1-27
God Reveals Israel's King

A Benjamite named Saul searched with his servant for the lost donkeys of his father, Kish. Saul's servant knew of Samuel, the prophet of God. They sought him to inquire of God where they might find the donkeys (9:1-14). On the previous day God had informed Samuel that he would meet a man from Benjamin whom he should anoint king over Israel. God reserved the right to choose Israel's king (Deut 17:15). Saul remained with Samuel to attend a sacrificial feast. The next day Samuel detained him to receive a message from God (1 Sam 9:15-27).

10:1-27
Samuel Anoints Shy Saul

The message was that God had chosen Saul to be king over Israel. Samuel anointed him with a flask of oil, indicating the special relationship between God and king (see Deut 17:15). Because of this custom, the king of Israel became known as the "anointed one" (Hebrew *Messiah*). Three signs followed the anointing to confirm to Saul that God had indeed chosen him (1 Sam 10:1-13). Saul sought after lost donkeys, but he discovered a kingdom.

Samuel anointed Saul again but this time publicly at Mizpah. The people found Saul hiding among the baggage, and they hailed him king (10:17-24). They longed for a king to rival the nations; ironically, they were elated with a shy keeper of donkeys.

11:1-15
The Spirit Empowers Saul at Jabesh

The first test for Saul's reign was the attack of the Ammonites upon Jabesh Gilead across the Jordan (11:1-5). As in the days when the judges ruled, the Spirit came upon Saul, and he became angry (11:6). No longer was Saul shy. By exercising his authority as king, he rallied the Israelites (11:7-8). His forces defeated the Ammonites (11:9-11). This confirmed to the people that Saul was an able king (11:12-15).

12:1-25
Samuel's Final Warning

With the installation of Saul, Samuel retired as Israel's civic leader. His final sermon defended his leadership (12:1-5) and reviewed God's favor in the past (12:6-11). He indicted the people's sinful choice of a king because they had set aside the kingship of the LORD (12:12-15). Samuel proved his charge by calling upon God to send a thunderstorm. It came during the dry season of the year (May-June) when a thunderstorm was unexpected (12:16-18). After the people confessed their sin, Samuel reminded them that they had nothing to fear from God if they continued in the LORD. If they failed to obey the LORD, however, they and their king would be swept away (12:19-25).

13:1–14:52
Saul's Foolishness at Gilgal

Saul's son, Jonathan, bravely initiated a war with the Philistines (13:1-4). However, the troops of Israel feared the numerous Philistines gathered at Michmash (13:5-7a).

Saul awaited Samuel for seven days at Gilgal to offer a sacrifice to entreat the LORD's blessing. When Samuel did not come at the appointed time (compare 10:8), Saul's army began to defect. Saul acted foolishly because of impatience. Out of desperation, he disobeyed the prophet Samuel's instructions and offered burnt offerings (13:7b-9). Samuel arrived and rebuked Saul for his disobedience (13:10-15). Because he acted foolishly (13:13), Samuel prophesied that Saul would lose his kingdom. God would choose "a man after his own heart" (13:14). Samuel's rebuke of Saul set the pattern for future relations between the leaders of God's people—prophets and kings. The future history of Israel and Judah illustrates that their kings disobeyed God's prophets to their own peril.

Although Israel had no weapons and were greatly outmanned (13:16-22), Jonathan courageously attacked the Philistines while Saul waited behind in Gibeah (14:1-14). The Philistines fell into disarray because of an earthquake, and Saul called for the ark to consult the LORD's guidance (14:15-18). Yet after he saw the Philistines panic all the more, he abandoned the inquiry and hurried to attack (14:19). In spite of Saul's impulsive actions, God gave them a great victory (14:20-23).

Saul's pride and hasty decision to restrict Israel from eating during the battle jeopardized his armies' strength and his son's life (14:24-34). Saul built an altar and inquired of the LORD, but the LORD did not answer him because of his unbelief (14:35-37). By casting lots, Saul discovered that Jonathan had unknowingly broken Saul's ban of eating (14:38-44). The men of the camp refused Saul's order to execute Jonathan, saving him from Saul's foolish oath (14:45).

Because of his disobedience, Saul never totally defeated the Philistines. In spite of his sin, God graciously gave

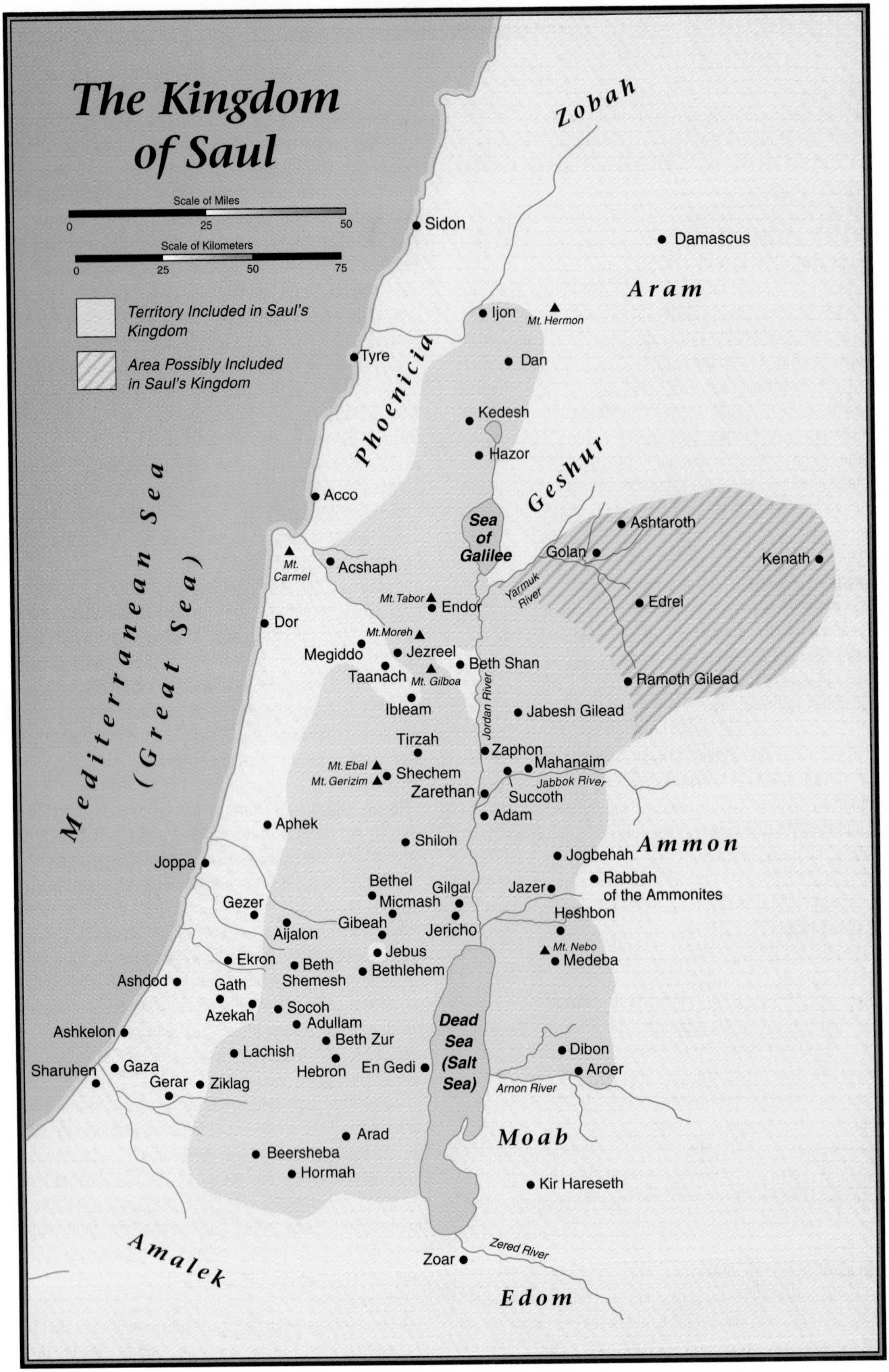
The Kingdom of Saul
Scale of Miles
0
25
50
Scale of Kilometers
0
25
50
75
Territory Included in Saul's Kingdom
Area Possibly Included in Saul's Kingdom
Zobah
Sidon
Damascus
Aram
Ijon
Mt. Hermon
Tyre
Phoenicia
Dan
Kedesh
Hazor
Geshur
Acco
Mediterranean Sea
(Great Sea)
Sea of Galilee
Ashtaroth
Golan
Kenath
Mt. Carmel
Acshaph
Yarmuk River
Mt. Tabor
Endor
Edrei
Dor
Mt.Moreh
Megiddo
Jezreel
Beth Shan
Taanach
Mt. Gilboa
Ramoth Gilead
Jordan River
Ibleam
Jabesh Gilead
Tirzah
Zaphon
Mt. Ebal
Mahanaim
Mt. Gerizim
Shechem
Jabbok River
Zarethan
Succoth
Adam
Aphek
Shiloh
Jogbehah
Ammon
Joppa
Bethel
Rabbah of the Ammonites
Gilgal
Jazer
Gezer
Micmash
Heshbon
Gibeah
Aijalon
Jericho
Jebus
Mt. Nebo
Ekron
Medeba
Beth Shemesh
Bethlehem
Ashdod
Gath
Azekah
Socoh
Adullam
Dead Sea (Salt Sea)
Ashkelon
Beth Zur
Dibon
Lachish
Sharuhen
Gaza
Hebron
En Gedi
Aroer
Gerar
Ziklag
Arnon River
Arad
Moab
Beersheba
Hormah
Kir Hareseth
Amalek
Zered River
Zoar
Edom

him victories and a large family (14:47-52).

15:1-35
God's Rejection of Proud Saul

Saul's pride and desire for economic gain fueled his continued disobedience. Saul went so far as to build a monument for himself (15:12). The LORD "grieved" (15:11,35) that he had made Saul king over Israel. The LORD instructed Saul by the prophet Samuel to put to death the Amalekites and all their possessions because of their past sins (15:1-6; compare the law of holy war, Deut 20:16-18). Saul, however, permitted Agag, the Amalekite king, and the best of the spoil to live. The LORD rejected Saul because of his sin, and Samuel wept for him (15:7-11).

When Samuel confronted Saul with his sins (15:12-19), Saul tried to justify his actions by explaining that he wanted to make a sacrifice of the spoil to the LORD (15:20-21). Saul had failed to learn that God does not accept ritual without obedience (15:22-23). Samuel refused to support Saul any longer because God had torn away his kingdom (15:24-31). Samuel himself executed Agag in accordance with the LORD's command. Samuel, as the prophet of God, never advised Saul again (15:32-34; compare 19:24; 28:11).

THE RISE OF FAITHFUL DAVID (1 SAM 16:1–31:13)

The book's final section focuses on the personalities of Saul and David. Although Saul is king until the end of the book, the story turns to his successor's rise (1 Sam 16–17). David's story is told from the viewpoint of Saul's continued failures. Saul's reign was chaotic, marred by personal problems and the threat of Philistine oppression. While it became clearer that Saul was unfit for leadership, David emerged before the nation as God's champion to defeat the Philistines and rule the land (1 Sam 18–30). In the end Saul would take his own life (1 Sam 31).

16:1-23
God Anoints David

The LORD instructed Samuel to go to the house of Jesse in Bethlehem to anoint Israel's new king. Although frightened that he might be found out by Saul, Samuel went to Bethlehem to offer a sacrifice. There he was joined by the family of Jesse (16:1-5). Samuel looked upon Jesse's seven older sons and was impressed by their appearance. But God rejected them and looked instead for one who had a faithful heart (16:6-10). David, the youngest, was called to the house, and the LORD instructed Samuel to anoint him. David was empowered by the Spirit from that day forward (16:11-13).

Since the LORD rejected Saul as king, He withdrew His Spirit; and Saul received an "evil spirit" (16:14). The identity of this "evil" spirit has been disputed. Some believe that it was a demon. Others argue that it was a troubling spirit causing emotional disturbance (compare Judg 9:23). Some have suggested that the LORD permitted Satan to afflict Saul as punishment for his sin (compare 2 Sam 24:1 with 1 Chr 21:1). What is clear is that this spirit was sent by the LORD (compare 1 Kgs 22:20-23) to show that Saul had been rejected. It caused Saul to experience bouts of rage and despondency (16:15; 18:10-11; 19:9-10; 20:33). Christians do not have to fear that the LORD will remove his Spirit from them, since the Spirit is the believer's permanent possession (Rom 8:9,12-17; Eph 1:13; 4:30).

Saul's attendants sought a musician to soothe troubled Saul (16:15-17). David was selected to enter into the service of the king (16:18-23).

17:1-58
David Defeats Goliath

The Philistines were at war with Saul. Their greatest champion, Goliath (who stood over nine feet tall) taunted the Israelites for their cowardice. In ancient times it was common for champions of opposing armies to face off in a personal duel. No Hebrew had the courage to face Goliath (17:1-11).

Jesse's older sons were in the battle lines, and Jesse sent David to the field with provisions (17:12-20). David heard the defiant words of Goliath and was zealous to defend the name of the LORD by challenging the giant to combat (17:21-47). With the weapons of a lowly shepherd but armed with the power of God, he killed Goliath, and the Philistines scattered in defeat (17:48-54).

The stunning victory caused Saul to inquire of Abner, the captain of Israel's army, about the lineage of David (17:55-58). Since David was already in the service of Saul (16:14-23), the inquiry of Saul and his address to David seem out of place. Some scholars have suggested that the two accounts of David's introduction to Saul come from separate sources. This conclusion is reasonable, but this does not mean that the stories are two garbled accounts of the same event. Since Saul would reward David with his daughter in marriage (17:25), David's lineage became particularly important. Saul, therefore, investigated David's background anew.

18:1-30
Saul's Fear of David

David's success in battle and the people's love for him

made Saul wildly fearful for his kingdom (18:8,12,29). Saul's son Jonathan loved David and entered a covenant of loyalty with him. Whenever David returned from battle, the women of the city exclaimed, "Saul has slain his thousands, and David his tens of thousands" (18:7). Saul in a fit of rage attempted to spear David twice. Saul feared him because he realized that God had turned to David (18:10-16).

Saul plotted to kill David by the hands of the Philistines. He offered his daughter Michal in marriage if David would kill one hundred Philistines. When David and his men killed two hundred, Saul feared David all the more. Saul knew that God favored David (18:17-30).

19:1-24
God's Spirit Saves David

Saul instructed his men to kill David, but Jonathan intervened. Saul, however, could not control his anger, and again he threw a javelin at David (19:1-10). David fled to his house, where Michal warned him that the king's men planned to kill him in the morning. She helped him escape unseen and then deceived her father about David's whereabouts (19:11-17).

David took refuge with Samuel at Ramah. The Spirit of God protected him from the king by mysteriously causing the king and his men to act "crazy" like the prophets (19:18-24).

20:1–42
Jonathan's Selfless Love

David met his friend Jonathan and appealed for his help (20:1-11). Jonathan knew that he would never be king of Israel because the LORD had chosen David to succeed his father. He loved David (18:1; 20:17), and they covenanted together to spare each other's lives (20:12-17). Jonathan agreed to signal David in the field if his father again planned to kill him (20:18-23).

At the Feast of the New Moon, David's absence caused Saul to become enraged, and he charged Jonathan with treachery. He tried to kill his own son, but Jonathan escaped to warn his friend David (20:24-42).

21:1–22:5
David's Deceptions at Nob and Gath

For fear of his life, David took matters into his own hands. At Nob he lied to the priest Ahimelech to save

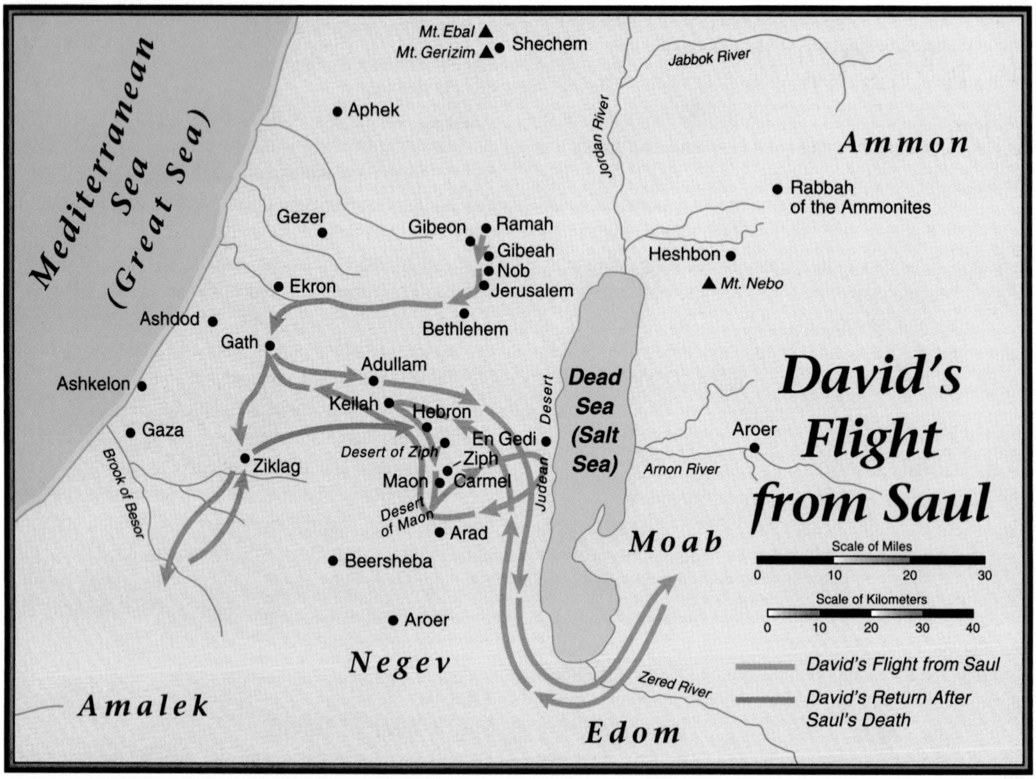

himself by receiving food and Goliath's sword (21:1-9). His deception would cost many innocent lives (compare 22:18-19).

David mistakenly thought he could find refuge as a mercenary soldier in the Philistine city Gath, but Achish the king discovered his identity. David pretended to be a madman to save himself (21:10-15).

22:6-23
Saul Murders the Lord's Priests

David hid in the wilderness of Adullam where he was joined by social outcasts like himself. He arranged for his family's care in Moab, and he hid in the forest of Hereth at the advice of the prophet Gad (22:1-5). David likely turned to Moab because of his ancestral linkage with Ruth, the Moabitess (Ruth 4:18-22), and because of Moab's hatred for Saul (compare 14:47).

Saul learned from Doeg, the Edomite, that David had received comfort from the priest Ahimelech (compare 21:1-9). Saul's paranoia led him to think that Ahimelech had conspired with David against him. The deranged Saul ordered the murder of the priests of the Lord! His guards refused to obey, however, because they would not harm the Lord's servants. Doeg, of Edomite descent, had no regard for the Lord and carried out the king's command. Only Abiathar, the son of Ahimelech, escaped to David's camp. There he found safety under David's protection.

23:1-29
David Depends on the Lord

David's deception of Ahimelech had led to the death of the Lord's priests. From this tragic episode David learned to depend on the Lord's help to escape Saul. David turned to the priest Abiathar, who possessed the sacred ephod, to inquire of the Lord. He followed God's guidance to save the city Keilah from Philistine invaders (23:1-6). By inquiring of the Lord he also escaped Saul at Keilah and fled successfully from place to place in the wilderness of Ziph (23:7-29). The author presents a striking contrast between Saul, who killed the servants of the Lord, and David, who honored them.

24:1-22
David Spares Saul

Saul pursued David into the region of En Gedi. There he went aside into one of the many caves nearby to relieve himself. David and his men were hidden in the back of the same cave. His men urged him to kill the king, but David chose to trust God's providence. However, he quietly cut off the hem of Saul's garment. David later regretted doing it, however, because the hem was symbolic of Saul's position as the Lord's anointed (24:1-7). Once the king left, David called out to him and showed the hem as evidence of his innocent intentions toward the king. Saul openly admitted his sin against David and confessed with his own mouth that the Lord had chosen David to be king (24:8-22).

25:1-44
David Spares Foolish Nabal

The notice of Samuel's death is not incidental to the author (25:1). He shows how the people's love for Samuel's godly leadership continued with David as well.

David kindly protected the flocks of a wealthy herdsman named Nabal (Hebrew *fool;* compare 25:25). As a result, none of his flocks were stolen or lost to wild animals. It was not unreasonable then for David to ask Nabal to respond kindly to him. But Nabal angrily refused, and David threatened to kill him. The shepherds of Nabal, who had benefited from David's protection, entreated Abigail, Nabal's wife, to intercede. Abigail pleaded with David that the Lord's anointed had no need to avenge himself since the Lord would do so. David gratefully agreed and resisted the evil deed. Later, God struck Nabal dead (25:2-38). This event exemplifies the Old Testament understanding of God's sovereignty over all things. Everything happens as part of the outworking of God's will.

This famous incident involving Abigail led the author to list David's wives (25:39-44). He married Abigail from Carmel and Ahinoam from Jezreel. His first wife, Saul's daughter Michal, was given to another man (compare 18:27).

26:1-25
David Spares Saul Again

The Ziphites feared David and urged the king to pursue him in their territories (compare 23:19-24). When David learned of Saul's arrival, he discovered the location of the camp. Abishai joined David in spying out the camp at night. They discovered Saul asleep with Abner resting nearby. Although Abishai interpreted the occasion as the Lord's opportunity for him to kill the king, David rebuked Abishai, pointing out that Saul was the Lord's anointed. Instead, David took a spear that was stuck in the ground at the king's head along with the king's water jug. David left without detection because the Lord had caused Saul to fall into a deep sleep (26:1-12).

David crossed to a distant hill and called out to awaken Abner. He challenged him to consider his lapse in protecting the king. When the king realized that David had taken the spear and jug, he regretted unjustly pursuing

David. He believed that because David had spared the LORD's anointed that the LORD in turn would deliver David. Saul confessed a second time that David would triumph (26:13-25; compare 24:20).

Some scholars hold that this account is a retelling of how David spared Saul's life at En Gedi (1 Sam 24). While there are a number of similarities, David's different responses show that the two stories are distinct incidents. As a result of En Gedi and the encounter with Nabal, David realized that God would care for him. David left Judah for a life among the Philistines in order to avoid further contact with Saul.

27:1-12
David Tricks the Philistines

David feared that any further encounters with Saul would lead to bloodshed. In the service of King Achish of Gath he would escape Saul's attention. David's troops were headquartered at Ziklag, where he raided the enemies of Judah. He duped the Philistine king into thinking that he was attacking the towns of Judah.

The passage does not condone David's deception of Achish; rather, the author includes this to show how God used David even in this situation to aid the covenant people. Also it continued the theme of how David outwitted the foolish Philistines (compare 21:10-15).

28:1-25
Saul Consults the Witch of Endor

The Philistines threatened war in the Jezreel Valley. Out of fear Saul sought a word from the LORD. Ironically, Saul, who had once despised the LORD's will (14:18-19; 15:26), could not discover it now that he desperately needed it (compare 28:16). When God refused to answer Saul through legitimate means, Saul sought a spiritual medium (28:1-7).

By deceiving the witch at Endor, Saul convinced her to bring Samuel from the dead. Much to her surprise the appearance was a genuine one, and by it she discovered Saul's true identity. God intervened in an unprecedented way and actually sent Samuel to prophesy Saul's judgment (compare 15:27-29). Samuel condemned Saul to death because he "did not obey the LORD" (28:18). So great was Saul's despondency that he could not continue. At the urging of Saul's men and the sorceress, he took food to strengthen himself for his travel (28:8-25).

The passage contrasts the true prophetic word of Samuel with Saul's attempt to consult the dead (compare

The Judean desert through which David journeyed during his flight from Saul.

Saul's condemnation in 1 Chr 10:13-14). The prophetic word would be fulfilled, and Saul could not hope to escape it.

29:1-11
God Spares David

This episode precedes the events in chapter 28 since the Philistines were gathered at Aphek (29:1) and then moved to Shunem in the Jezreel Valley (29:11; 28:4). This arrangement serves to heighten without interruption David's success against the LORD's enemies (continued in 1 Sam 30).

The Philistines refused to include David in their battle against Israel. God used the discontent of the Philistines to spare David from fighting against his own people and jeopardizing, in their eyes, his place as the LORD's anointed (29:1-5). Achish apologetically dismissed David to Ziklag (29:6-11).

30:1-31
God Strengthens David

David and his men arrived in Ziklag, where they discovered the city burned and their families captured by raiding Amalekites. So distraught were the men that they threatened to stone David, but the LORD strengthened him (30:6). At the instruction of the LORD by the ephod of Abiathar, David pursued the Amalekites (30:1-8).

During the march, two hundred men remained behind because of exhaustion, but four hundred pressed ahead. With the aid of an Egyptian slave who was left behind by the Amalekites, David's men discovered their camp, overtook them, and retrieved all their possessions (30:9-20). David won the hearts of his men and the elders of Judah by sharing with them—even the two hundred who stayed behind—a portion of the booty taken from the Amalekites (30:21-31).

31:1-13
Saul's Shameful End

The final chapter resumes the account of the Philistine war (1 Sam 28–29). The Israelites were defeated and many killed on Mount Gilboa. The proud king died shamefully by ending his own life. His corpse was publicly abused by the Philistines. Three of Saul's sons were also killed in battle, preparing the way for David to be king (31:1-10).

The people of Jabesh Gilead remembered how Saul had delivered them from the Ammonites (compare 11:1-11). They journeyed all night to Beth Shan, where Saul's body had been impaled. They stole the body away and honorably buried Saul at Jabesh, where they mourned his death (31:11-13).

Theological and Ethical Significance

God desires people "after his own heart" (13:14). Such people mirror God's love and faithfulness. God rejected Eli's sons as worship leaders because of their wickedness. In their place God raised up "a faithful priest" who would do what was in God's heart and mind (2:35). God rejected Saul as king because of his disobedience. God looked at David's heart and chose him to lead God's people (16:7).

God is free to choose leaders for His people (see Deut 17:15). Samuel was not a Levite, but God chose him to minister as a priest (1 Sam 1:1). Saul was from the least significant family of "the smallest tribe in Israel," but God chose him to deliver His people (9:16,21). David was the youngest in his family but God chose him as king (16:11-12).

Christians are to respect those whom God has chosen to lead His people. David showed respect for Saul because he was the Lord's anointed. Christians should also remember that God is the true Leader of His people. No Christian leader can take God's place. God dealt harshly with Eli's sons, who had no respect for God's sacrifices and abused the laypeople who looked to them for religious leadership. God dealt harshly with Saul, who disregarded God's command given through the prophet Samuel. No Christian leader is above God's word.

Questions for Reflection

1. What influence can godly parents have on the lives of their children?
2. By what different means does the LORD accomplish His purposes for His people?
3. What are the consequences of disobedience to the word of the LORD?
4. What are proper ways the people of God may seek the LORD's will?
5. What kind of person does the LORD choose to lead His people?

Sources for Additional Study

Baldwin, Joyce G. *1 & 2 Samuel.* Downers Grove: InterVarsity, 1988.

Laney, J. Carl. *First and Second Samuel.* Chicago: Moody, 1982.

Payne, David F. *I & II Samuel.* Philadelphia: Westminster, 1982.

2 SAMUEL

First and Second Samuel form an uninterrupted narrative in the Hebrew Bible (compare the introduction to 1 Samuel). Second Samuel continues the story of Israel's monarchy, tracing the history of David's reign from its triumphs to its troubles.

Theme

God consolidated the kingdom through the reign of David, who unified the nation, conquered Israel's foes, and received God's covenantal promise of an eternal dynasty and kingdom (7:5-16). Though David sinned, God's grace proved greater than David's sin. Though David suffered consequences of his sin, God continued to watch over him and preserve his rule. Through David, God blessed Israel with its next king (Solomon) and, in time, with Jesus, its Messiah.

I. God Establishes David's Kingdom (1:1–10:19)
II. God Chastens David's Kingdom (11:1–20:26)
III. God Preserves David's Kingdom (21:1–24:25)

Purpose and Theology

1. Second Samuel continues the story of how God established His kingdom through the leadership of Israel's monarchy. In this second portion of Samuel, the anointing of David for rule (1 Sam 16:12-23) was realized. David secured the borders of Israel, subjugated its enemies, and brought prosperity to the fledgling kingdom.

2. The Davidic covenant is the theological centerpiece of the book (chap. 7). God promised David and his heirs an eternal lineage that would rule over an everlasting kingdom (7:12-16). The Davidic king was God's adopted son who ruled in the name of the LORD and enjoyed God's providential care. This covenant promise became the messianic hope of God's people (compare Pss 2; 110). The messianic expectation was a source of great comfort in Israel's darkest days (compare Isa 9:1-7; 11; Amos 9:11-15; Zech 9:9-13). This promise is fulfilled by David's Greater Son, Jesus Christ (Luke 1:31-33).

3. The book also shows how the Davidic covenant affected Israel's national fortunes. The favor of God enabled David to establish Jerusalem as the political and religious center of the nation by bringing the ark into the city and establishing a ruling bureaucracy (2 Sam 6; 8:15-18). David also experienced victories over the powerful Philistines and Arameans (8:1-14; 10). David's house grew in international prestige, paving the way for a mighty dynastic order. However, while the covenant contained promised blessing, it also included God's chastening for sin. The book details the troubling consequences for the nation because of David's sin (chaps. 12–20).

4. Second Samuel teaches that God is faithful and merciful. God remained loyal to His promise although David at times failed the covenant. David and Bathsheba sinned, and their child died in judgment. God, however, gave Bathsheba the child Solomon, whom the LORD loved (12:24-25). God continued to reveal His will to David through the prophets Nathan and Gad and the priests Zadok and Abiathar (12:1-14; 15:24-29; 24:11-14). Also, He was merciful by safeguarding David during the rebellions of Absalom and Sheba (chaps. 18; 20).

5. The narrative of 2 Samuel indicates that God expects faithfulness and righteousness. The Davidic covenant had the provision of punishing David for sin (7:14-15). Nathan the prophet delivered a divine oracle of judgment against David for his sin with Bathsheba (12:1-23). God also judged David for his pride in Israel's military strength (chap. 24). Unlike Saul, who tried to excuse his sin, David confessed his sins before the LORD (12:13; 24:10).

6. Second Samuel depicts Israel's God as the covenant LORD of history (5:19b; 6:21-22; 8:14; 12:11; 23:10b; 24:25).

GOD ESTABLISHES DAVID'S KINGDOM (2 SAM 1:1–10:19)

This section of the book traces the triumphs of David's reign, first over the tribe of Judah (chaps. 1–4) and then over all Israel (chaps. 5–6). The high point of David's career was the covenant the LORD made with David and his descendants (chap. 7). Because of God's blessing, David successfully expanded his kingdom by defeating Israel's enemies (chaps. 8–10).

1:1-27
David's Lament

God gave the throne to David; David did not steal the kingdom from Saul. David proved this by dealing swiftly with Saul's alleged killer and publicly lamenting his personal loss of Saul and Jonathan.

An Amalekite came to David at Ziklag and related how he had killed Saul on Mount Gilboa (1:1-12). Most likely the Amalekite was fabricating his story in order to receive a reward (compare 1 Sam 31:3-6; 2 Sam 18:22). The Amalekite was greeted with David's strongest rebuke. David, who had more cause than anyone to kill the king, had refused to raise his hand against the LORD's anointed (1 Sam 24:6; 26:23). But this pagan slave did not respect the LORD's anointed. David's men executed the Amalekite for his alleged deed (1:13-16).

David lamented the deaths of Saul and Jonathan (1:17-27). His sorrowful refrain "How the mighty have fallen!" (1:19,25,27) expressed tribute to these great men whom David loved and missed.

2:1-32
David Anointed at Hebron

David showed his dependence on the LORD by inquiring what he should do about Saul's kingdom. The LORD instructed David to go to Hebron. There the elders of Judah anointed him king (2:1-4a). His first act as king was the gracious commendation of the men of Jabesh Gilead who had bravely rescued the body of Saul (2:4b-7; compare 1 Sam 31:8-13).

David was appointed by God. In contrast, Abner installed the surviving son of Saul, Ish-Bosheth, as David's rival. Ish-Bosheth, meaning *man of shame,* was changed from the original Esh-Baal (*man of Baal;* compare 1 Chr 8:33; 9:39). Ish-Bosheth reigned from Mahanaim in Transjordan during David's rule in Hebron (2:8-11).

With the outbreak of war, Abner confronted Joab, David's general, in battle at Gibeon. Abner was pursued by Joab's brother, Asahel. Abner warned him to stop, but he continued; and Abner was forced to kill him (2:12-32).

3:1-39
God Strengthens David

David's house increased while Ish-Bosheth's foothold weakened (3:1). David possessed many sons, a sign in antiquity of strength and blessing (3:2-5).

As a result of his dispute with Ish-Bosheth, Abner defected to David's side. Abner had sexual relations with a concubine in the royal harem. Ish-Bosheth interpreted this as a threat to his throne (compare 16:21-22; 1 Kgs 2:22). Abner was so incensed at this charge that he secretly met with David in Hebron. Abner vowed to bring all Israel under David's rule (3:6-12). David agreed on the condition that Abner return his wife Michal, whom Saul had given to another man (1 Sam 18:20-27). Abner left under a covenant of peace (3:13-21). When Joab returned to Hebron from battle, he was told of Abner's arrangement with David. Because of his blood feud with Abner (2:23-24), Joab plotted the assassination of Abner without David's knowledge (3:22-30).

David was so distraught at Abner's murder that he took special steps to disassociate himself from the guilt of Joab's wicked deed. He declared a national day of mourning and personally abstained from food. The people concluded from this that David was innocent; his stature increased in their eyes (3:31-39).

4:1-12
David Avenges Saul's House

The defection of Abner discouraged Ish-Bosheth's already-dwindling support. Two of his captains, Baanah and Recab, murdered and decapitated the king during his midday's rest. With the death of Ish-Bosheth, David had no serious rival. Mephibosheth, the only surviving son of Jonathan, suffered from a crippling disability and was not a threat (4:1-7; compare chap. 9).

Ish-Bosheth's assassins presented the king's head to David as the LORD's vengeance upon the house of Saul. Although Ish-Bosheth's death advanced David's kingdom, he abhorred their treason and executed the murderers (4:8-12).

5:1-25
David Reigns from Jerusalem

After Ish-Bosheth's death the northern tribes joined Judah in making David their king (5:1-2). All Israel anointed him at Hebron "before the LORD" (5:3). David reigned for forty years (5:4) from 1011–971 B.C.

David marched on Jerusalem to dispossess the Jebusites from their mountain fortress upon Zion. The citadel of Jerusalem became known as the City of David because it became his personal royal possession. The move from Hebron to Jerusalem gave David a military and political advantage. The site was strategically located, easy to defend, and had no strong political association with the northern or southern tribes (5:6-9; compare 1 Chr 12:23-40). The respect Hiram, king of Tyre, showed David's emerging kingdom assured him that the LORD was

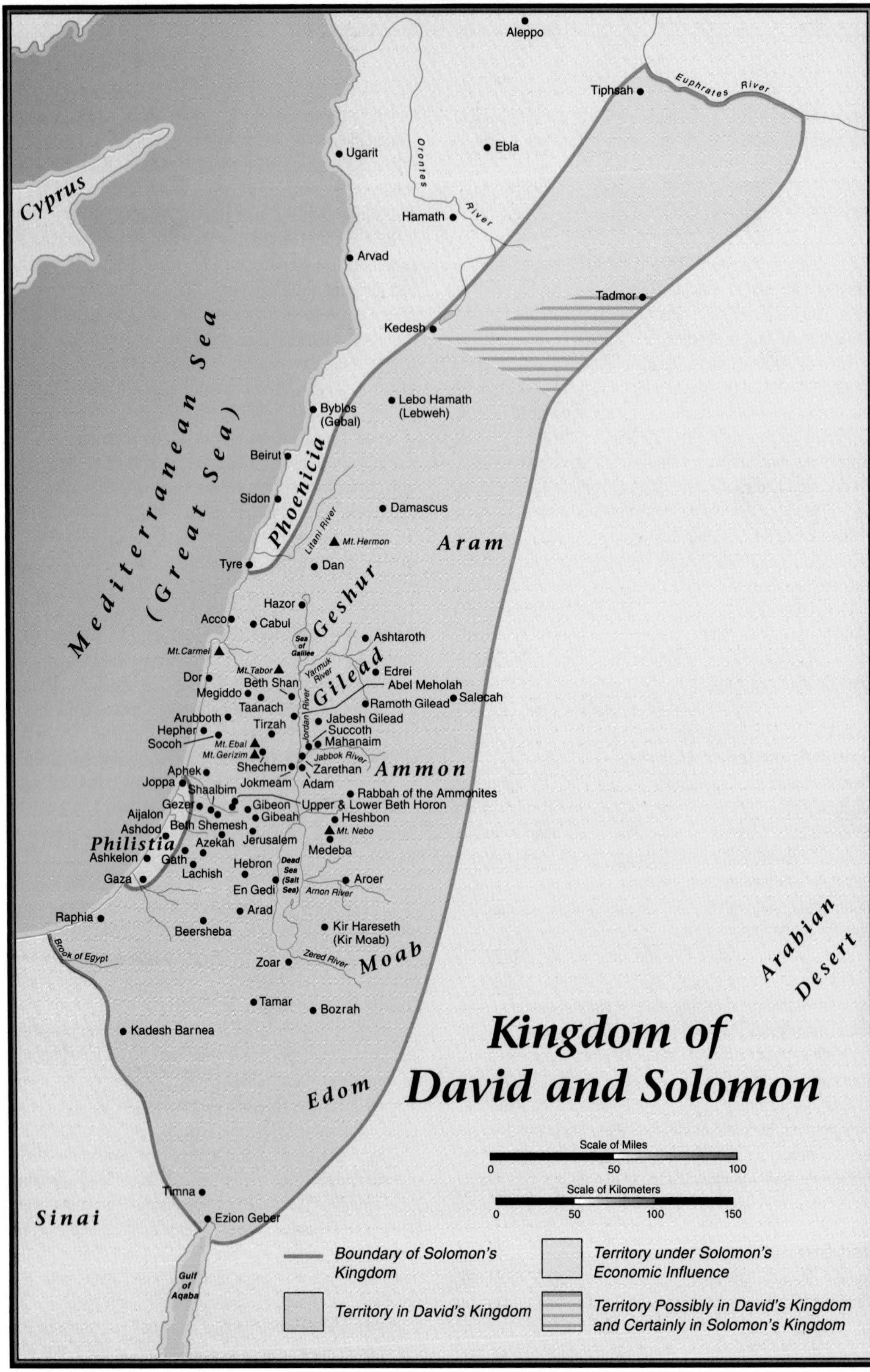

Kingdom of David and Solomon
Aleppo
Tiphsah
Euphrates River
Ugarit
Ebla
Orontes River
Cyprus
Hamath
Arvad
Tadmor
Kedesh
Mediterranean Sea (Great Sea)
Byblos (Gebal)
Lebo Hamath (Lebweh)
Beirut
Phoenicia
Sidon
Damascus
Litani River
Mt. Hermon
Aram
Tyre
Dan
Geshur
Hazor
Acco
Cabul
Sea of Galilee
Ashtaroth
Mt. Carmel
Mt. Tabor
Yarmuk River
Gilead
Edrei
Dor
Beth Shan
Abel Meholah
Megiddo
Salecah
Taanach
Ramoth Gilead
Arubboth
Jordan River
Jabesh Gilead
Hepher
Tirzah
Succoth
Socoh
Mt. Ebal
Mahanaim
Mt. Gerizim
Jabbok River
Aphek
Shechem
Zarethan
Ammon
Joppa
Jokmeam
Adam
Shaalbim
Rabbah of the Ammonites
Gezer
Gibeon
Upper & Lower Beth Horon
Aijalon
Gibeah
Heshbon
Ashdod
Beth Shemesh
Mt. Nebo
Jerusalem
Philistia
Azekah
Medeba
Ashkelon
Gath
Hebron
Dead Sea (Salt Sea)
Lachish
Aroer
Gaza
En Gedi
Arnon River
Arad
Raphia
Kir Hareseth (Kir Moab)
Beersheba
Brook of Egypt
Zered River
Zoar
Moab
Arabian Desert
Tamar
Bozrah
Kadesh Barnea
Edom
Timna
Sinai
Ezion Geber
Gulf of Aqaba
Scale of Miles
0
50
100
Scale of Kilometers
0
50
100
150
Boundary of Solomon's Kingdom
Territory under Solomon's Economic Influence
Territory in David's Kingdom
Territory Possibly in David's Kingdom and Certainly in Solomon's Kingdom

establishing his throne (5:10-12).

The triumphs of David are no better illustrated than in his victories over Israel's archenemies, the Philistines. Unlike Saul, who failed against the Philistines, David succeeded because he was careful to follow the word of the LORD (5:17-25).

6:1-23
The Ark of God

David wanted to bring the ark of the covenant to Jerusalem from the house of Abinadab, its home base after its capture by the Philistines (1 Sam 7:1-2). With the ark in Jerusalem, the religious and political life of the nation could be unified around David.

The ark was called the "Name," a reverential reference to the holy name of the LORD. The presence of the ark symbolized the presence of God (2 Sam 6:1-2). Because of its close association with God, the Israelites were instructed that only the Levites (sons of Kohath) should carry it and that it was not to be touched (compare Exod 25:12-15; Num 4:15; 7:9; Deut 10:8). The sons of Abinadab, Uzzah and Ahio, set the ark on a new cart, as the Philistines had done (1 Sam 6:7), and guided it. Uzzah steadied the ark with his hand when it shifted on the cart. God struck him dead at the site of the ark because he showed disrespect for the holy things of God (2 Sam 6:3-7; compare 1 Chr 15:13).

Because of this unusual demonstration of God's holiness and wrath, David learned to fear the LORD. He showed special homage by sacrificing a burnt offering after the ark had been carried six paces. The ark entered the city without incident only when the priests carried it properly. When David brought the ark into Jerusalem, he celebrated with dance and dressed humbly before the LORD (2 Sam 6:8-23).

7:1-29
The LORD's Covenant with David

God's covenant with David followed his humble display before the LORD and the Jerusalem crowds. After securing his kingdom, David showed his concern for the reputation of the LORD, who dwelt in the wilderness tabernacle and not in an impressive temple structure (7:1-3).

The LORD, however, would build a "house" for David—not a building but a dynasty. The prophet Nathan instructed David in the LORD's covenant (7:4-17). The Davidic covenant consisted of three eternal promises: a dynastic lineage, a kingdom, and a throne (7:13). The LORD would be as a father to David's son, the LORD's representative in the earth (7:14). If David's descendants sinned, the LORD warned of chastening. But He promised never to annul His covenant (7:15-16).

This covenant gave rise to the messianic hope in the Old Testament. Although David's descendants failed, the people clung to the hope of a Greater David. The angel Gabriel echoed the words of David's covenant when he announced the birth of Israel's King, Jesus the Savior (Luke 1:32-33)

David responded with praise, recognizing God's greatness and the blessedness of His favor (2 Sam 7:18-24). He petitioned the LORD to keep His promise forever so that the LORD might be magnified by all nations (7:25-29).

8:1-18
David's Victory

God's promises for David's kingdom were first realized through the military and administrative successes of his rule. David subjugated the Philistines in the west, the Moabites in the east, Zobah and Damascus in the north, and the Edomites in the south (8:1-14). Indeed, "The LORD gave David victory wherever he went" (8:14).

The expanding bureaucracy included the mercenary soldiers of the Kerethites (Crete) and Perethites (Philistines?) under the command of Benaiah (compare 15:18; 20:7,23). Abiathar was joined by Zadok as priest. Civil advisers included a recorder and a secretary (8:15-18).

9:1-13
David's Kindness to Mephibosheth

David was not only an effective warrior and administrator, but he also was a beneficent ruler. He desired to honor the pledge he had made to Jonathan and his family (1 Sam 20:14-15). He inquired and learned from Ziba, a servant in Saul's household, about Mephibosheth, who was Jonathan's only surviving son. Mephibosheth was crippled and lived in obscurity (9:1-4). When he was brought before David, the king calmed his fears and returned Saul's property to him. Mephibosheth lived in Jerusalem and ate at the king's table (9:5-13).

10:1-19
David Defeats the Ammonites and Arameans

David also desired to be generous to the son of his deceased ally King Nahash and sent a delegation to express his sympathies (10:1-2a). But David's delegation was charged with espionage and was humiliated by Nahash's son, Hanun. The Ammonites hired Aramean mercenaries and prepared for David's advance. The armies of Joab and Abishai prevailed by outmaneuvering them (10:2b-14). But the Arameans under Hadadezer gathered more troops from beyond the Euphrates. David subjugated them, expanding his realm to the east (10:15-19).

View of Jerusalem from the southwest during the time of David (1000–962 B.C.), showing the tabernacle pitched atop the threshing floor of Araunah (or Ornan) the Jebusite (upper right). David's palace (center, right) overlooked the tabernacle. The Citadel fortress (center) and City of David (left, center) can also be seen. The Typopoeon Valley (top, center) and the Kidron Valley (lower right) flanked each side of the city perched high on the escarpment of Zion.

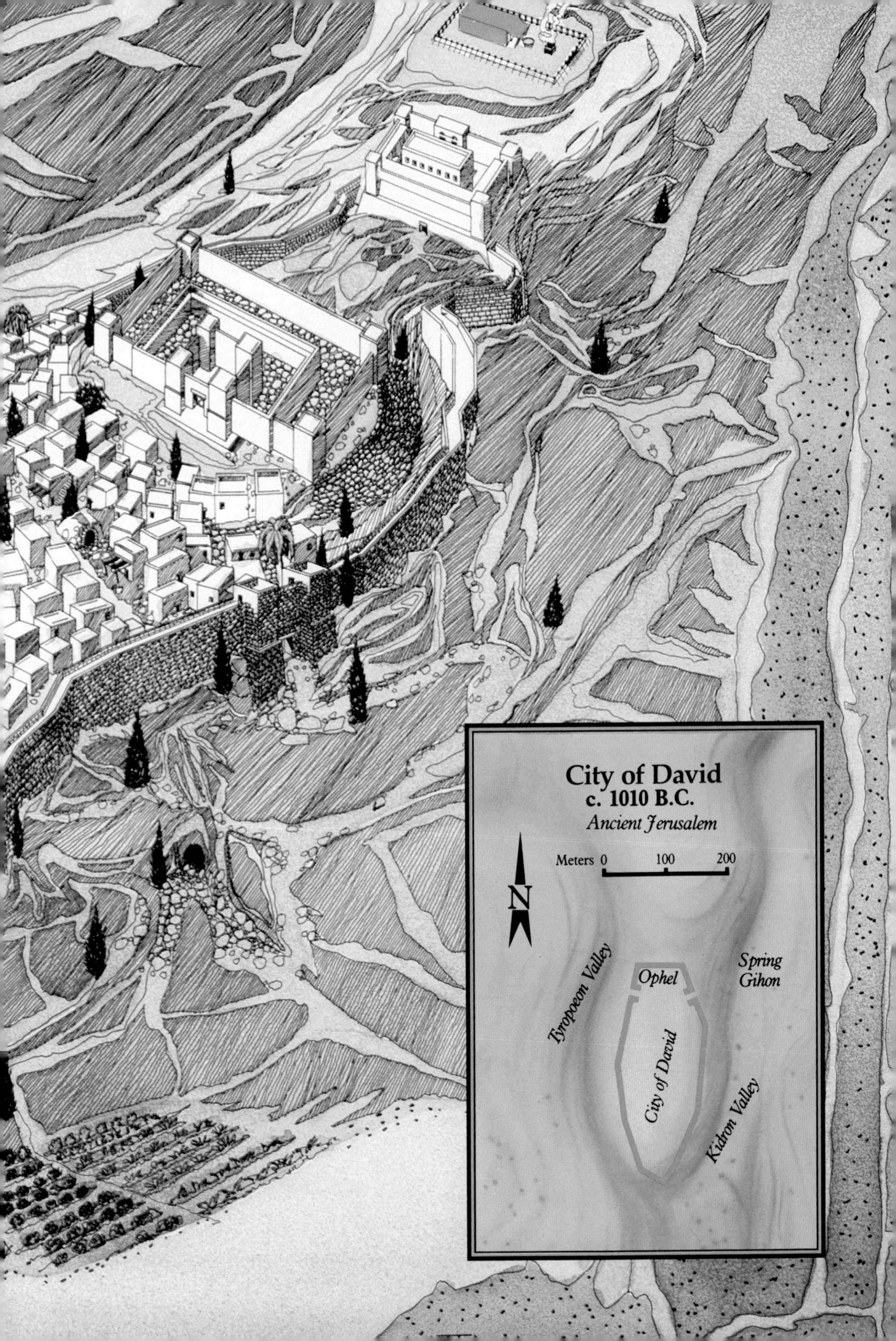
City of David
c. 1010 B.C.
Ancient Jerusalem
Meters 0 100 200
N
Tyropoeon Valley
Ophel
Spring Gihon
City of David
Kidron Valley

THE FAMILY OF DAVID

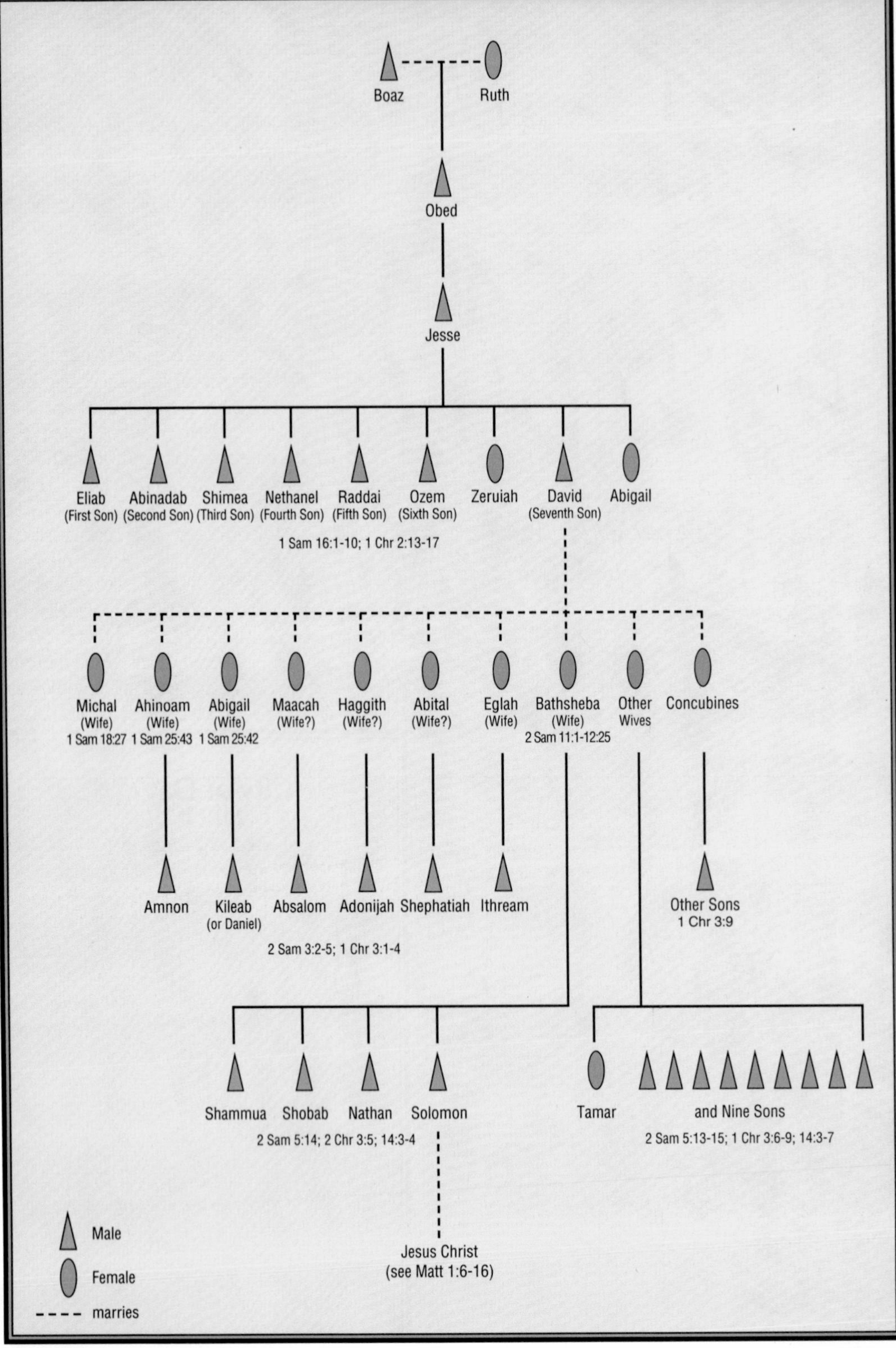
Boaz
Ruth
Obed
Jesse
Eliab (First Son)
Abinadab (Second Son)
Shimea (Third Son)
Nethanel (Fourth Son)
Raddai (Fifth Son)
Ozem (Sixth Son)
Zeruiah
David (Seventh Son)
Abigail
1 Sam 16:1-10; 1 Chr 2:13-17
Michal (Wife) 1 Sam 18:27
Ahinoam (Wife) 1 Sam 25:43
Abigail (Wife) 1 Sam 25:42
Maacah (Wife?)
Haggith (Wife?)
Abital (Wife?)
Eglah (Wife)
Bathsheba (Wife) 2 Sam 11:1-12:25
Other Wives
Concubines
Amnon
Kileab (or Daniel)
Absalom
Adonijah
Shephatiah
Ithream
2 Sam 3:2-5; 1 Chr 3:1-4
Other Sons 1 Chr 3:9
Shammua
Shobab
Nathan
Solomon
2 Sam 5:14; 2 Chr 3:5; 14:3-4
Tamar
and Nine Sons
2 Sam 5:13-15; 1 Chr 3:6-9; 14:3-7
Jesus Christ (see Matt 1:6-16)
Male
Female
marries

The author also recorded this rout of the Arameans in the summary of David's victories in 8:3-8. These two battles, which the author describes in more detail (10:6-14 and 10:15-19), took place before David's final victory over the Arameans (8:3-8).

GOD CHASTENS DAVID'S KINGDOM (2 SAM 11:1–20:26)

The sin of David and Bathsheba (chaps. 11–12) changes the tenor of the story from David's triumphs to his troubles. The following events (chaps. 13–20) tell the consequences of their sin as David's kingdom was rocked by moral and political problems.

11:1-27
David's Sin

Israel's war with Ammon was the background for David's sin against God. The author implied that David should have been at war, rather than remaining behind (11:1). Perhaps his earlier successes gave him a sense of false security. The author's description of David's temptation is reminiscent of Achan's sin (Josh 7): he saw her, inquired about her, and then he took her (2 Sam 11:2-5).

When Bathsheba learned of her pregnancy, David attempted to cover up his sin. He sent for her husband, Uriah the Hittite, who was in the field of battle. Uriah refused to go home to his wife, even at David's insistence. Uriah did not want to enjoy his wife and home when the ark and armies of God were on the battlefield (11:6-13).

In desperation David plotted with the aid of Joab to murder Uriah by exposing him to the Ammonites in battle. The plot succeeded, and David took Bathsheba as his wife (11:14-27). The sin, however, did not go unnoticed, for "the thing David had done displeased the LORD" (11:27).

12:1-31
Nathan's Oracle against David

About one year later, God sent Nathan to confront David. Nathan told a parable of a poor man's only ewe lamb taken away by a rich man for his selfish pleasure. David, who as king was responsible for justice in the land, burned with anger against the culprit. Unwittingly, David condemned himself. Nathan accused the king, "You are the man!" (12:7). Nathan declared God's judgment. Because he murdered Uriah by the sword, his household would likewise experience the sword. Since he took the wife of another man, David's wives would be taken. And though David sinned in secret, he would be publicly humiliated before all Israel (12:1-12; compare 15:16; 16:21-22). These curses were fulfilled by the deaths of three of David's sons (Amnon, Absalom, and Adonijah) and the strife David's reign experienced toward the end

DAVID AS KING AND MESSIAH

Messiah is a Hebrew term meaning *anointed one*. The NT term *Christ* represents a translation of this Hebrew word into Greek.

In the OT the king of Israel was often called "the LORD's anointed" or some equivalent such as "my anointed" or "his anointed" (1 Sam 2:10; 16:6). The act of anointing symbolically conferred God's Spirit on the king and designated him as God's representative (1 Sam 24:6,10).

The ideals for kingship in Israel are perhaps most clearly seen in Psalms. Israel's king was to be a righteous and universal ruler (Pss 2:8-12; 45:4-7). His rule was to be everlasting (Pss 21:4; 45:6). He was to befriend the poor and resist their oppressors (Ps 72:2-4,12-14). He was to be honored as God's Son (Ps 2:7) and to lead the nation to victory over its foes (21:8-12; 89:22-23). Though no human king could fully measure up to these ideals, they were closely associated with David. David became the standard by which later kings were measured (1 Kgs 3:3,14; 2 Kgs 14:3).

When Israel's prophets spoke of a future ideal King, this Anointed One (*messiah*) was described in terms of the Davidic ideal. David was used as a model, a pointer or type, of what this future King would be like. Like David, the Messiah would be a king of Israel, born in Bethlehem (Mic 5:2), who would rule in righteousness (Isa 11:1-16). But the coming King would be more than David. He would have universal rule (Mic 5:4). He would be "God with us" (Immanuel—Isa 7:14; Matt 1:23), the Prince of peace and mighty God (Isa 9:6-7). He would be called "Branch" and "The LORD Our Righteousness" (Jer 23:5; 33:15-16). This Anointed One is the Servant of the Lord (Isa 42:1-4; 49:1-6; 50:4-9; 52:13–53:12). From his vantage during the exile, when no son of David sat on a throne in Jerusalem, Ezekiel could still hope for a new Shepherd like David (Ezek 34:23-24; compare 1 Sam 17:34-35). □

of his life.

To David's credit, however, he did not shirk his guilt as Saul did when Samuel accused him (compare 1 Sam 15). David confessed his guilt openly and lamented his spiritual impurity (compare Ps 51). The judgment of God began with the child of David and Bathsheba. David prayed and fasted earnestly for the child's life. David had felt the heavy hand of God's judgment, but he also knew God's mercies. For that reason he prayed, believing God might deliver the child. Though the child was not spared, David believed that he would see the child again (12:13-23). In the midst of His chastening, God also was merciful to David and Bathsheba. God gave them another child, Solomon, whom the LORD named Jedidiah ("beloved of the LORD"). From their union came the king who would build the LORD's temple and rule Israel during its golden age. Evidence of God's continued forgiveness was Israel's victory over the Ammonites—this time led by David himself (12:24-31).

Players of a tambourine, hand-cymbals, and eight-stringed and five-stringed harps shown on a seventh-century relief.

13:1-39
Absalom Murders Amnon

Although God forgave David, the consequences of his sin were immediately seen in his household. Just as David had lusted for Bathsheba, Amnon, the king's eldest son, desired his half-sister Tamar. He lured Tamar into his private quarters and raped her. However, his guilt was too great for his conscience, and he despised her afterwards. He dismissed her, and she took refuge in the house of Absalom, her brother (13:1-20).

David, like Eli and Samuel, had no control over his sons. Absalom harbored his hatred for Amnon for two years until an occasion arose to kill him. Absalom held a festival attended by Amnon. At the command, Absalom's servants murdered Amnon. Absalom fled to Geshur where he took refuge with his maternal grandfather, Talmi, the king of Geshur (3:3). David wept for his son Amnon, who was special to the king as his eldest and successor to the throne. Yet he longed to see Absalom for the three years they were estranged (13:21-39).

14:1-33
Absalom Returns to David

Perhaps out of concern for the state of the kingdom, Joab wanted David's potential successor returned to the royal house. Similar to Nathan's ruse (chap. 12), Joab sent to the king a woman of Tekoa who pretended to be a woman in mourning. She sought the king's mercy on her only surviving son, who had murdered his brother. When David ruled that the son should be spared, the woman challenged David to reconsider his banishment of his own son Absalom. David agreed and dispatched Joab to retrieve him. David, however, refused to see Absalom's face upon his return to Jerusalem.

15:1-37
Absalom's Coup

Four years later the crown prince mounted an insurrection against the king by taking the king's place in the eyes of the people. Ironically, David's kingdom almost collapsed as a result of his own mishandling of his subjects rather than external threats. Absalom began to play the role of king. He had a private standing guard and functioned as final arbiter of judicial cases. Absalom stole away the hearts of the people, and he attempted to steal the kingdom from David. At Hebron, where his father had been declared king, Absalom's coconspirators acclaimed him king. Among their ranks was David's political advisor, Ahithophel (15:1-12).

Joined by a small but loyal contingency of Kerethites and Pelethites (8:18), David fled across the Kidron Valley toward the desert. He left behind his royal harem. Ittai the Gittite and his six hundred mercenary soldiers (Philistines from Gath) went with David. David sent Zadok and Abiathar back to Jerusalem with the ark of the LORD. David knew that the ark belonged in the house of God. He believed that if God so desired he would return one day to see the holy place of the LORD. The two priests, as prophetic seers, could aid David by learning of Absalom's plans and inquiring of the LORD in his behalf. Also, David countered the wisdom of Ahithophel by ordering Hushai the Arkite to remain in Absalom's service in order to confound the coup's strategy (15:13-37).

16:1-23
David's Anguish in Flight

The dark shadow of Saul again was cast over David as he fled his kingdom. Ziba, Saul's servant and manager of Mephibosheth's estate, maliciously defamed Mephibosheth to better himself (compare 19:24-28). David granted the lands of Saul to Ziba (16:1-4). Shimei, a member of Saul's family, cursed David, calling him a "man of blood" (16:7). This charge probably reflected the enmity many harbored against David. It may refer to David's turning members of Saul's family over to the Gibeonites for execution (chap. 21). Shimei attributed David's pain to the LORD's retribution. David perceived that Shimei's curse, though not altogether just, was part of God's chastening for his sin. David repelled Abishai's ambition to kill Saul's kinsman. David believed that God's vengeance or mercies alone would decide his and Shimei's fates (16:5-14).

Meanwhile, Hushai arrived in Jerusalem to win Absalom's favor. Absalom, not yet ready to trust Hushai, turned to Ahithophel for advice. He counseled Absalom to announce his takeover by the symbolic gesture of publicly sleeping with David's concubines (compare 1 Kgs 2:17-25). Absalom's incestuous act thus fulfilled Nathan's prophecy (12:11). The narrator compared the political adeptness of Ahithophel to the word of God revealed to the prophets (16:15-23).

17:1-29
God Frustrates Ahithophel's Advice

Hushai's task was a formidable one (16:23). Ahithophel advised Absalom to attack David while his troops were in disarray (17:1-4). This time Absalom heard the second opinion of Hushai, who argued that such a tactic would fail because of David's wily experience in warfare (17:5-13). Absalom postponed his attack, which meant that David had the opportunity to withdraw. The LORD "determined to frustrate the good advice of Ahithophel" and thereby doomed Absalom (17:14; compare 15:34). The outcome of the war was decided before the first blow was struck.

Absalom's strategy was relayed to David's camp at the river fords through Jonathan and Ahimaaz, the sons of Zadok and Abiathar (compare 15:35-36). Meanwhile, the wicked Ahithophel took his own life because he knew that Hushai's plan meant the end of Absalom's kingdom (15:15-23).

David in exile set up his provisional base in Mahanaim across the Jordan (compare 2:8). Absalom established his military command by giving Amasa, Joab's relative, charge of the army. While Absalom organized for battle, David's friends—Shobi, Makir, and Barzilli—refreshed his fatigued army (17:24-29).

18:1-33
Absalom's Death

The story of Absalom's death focuses on David as father rather than as king. David himself remained behind the battle lines at the advice of his troops. He dispatched his commanders, instructing them to care for Absalom's life. Absalom, on the other hand, entered into the battle as it raged in the forests of Ephraim and beyond. The terrain was so precarious that more died from its pits and thickets than the sword. Absalom himself was its victim. He was caught by the head (compare 14:26) in a tree and was suspended in midair. Though reminded of David's instructions to spare Absalom, Joab killed the helpless prince (18:1-17). The tragedy and disgrace of how Absalom died was even sadder because he had no heir (18:18). His three sons had apparently also died (compare 14:27).

The story's detailed description of the two messengers and David's hopes dashed by their news accentuates the anguish of David the father (18:19-33). David's sin had spelled disaster for his family and crippled his own soul: "O my son Absalom! My son, my son Absalom. If only I had died instead of you—O Absalom, my son!" (18:33).

19:1-43
King David Returns

Joab continued to place the state of the nation above the feelings of the king. The aftermath of the war required a stronger show of Davidic leadership. Joab rebuked David for mourning the death of his enemies instead of greeting his triumphant soldiers. David took his place at the gate to receive his troops (19:1-8).

The tribes of Israel urged their leaders to reinstall David as their king. The men of Judah were initially reluctant. David replaced Joab with Amasa in a gesture of reconciliation. No doubt, Joab's demotion was also due to his killing of Absalom. The king also extended his generosity by sparing Shimei's life, hearing out the explanation of Mephibosheth, and sharing Saul's inheritance with Ziba in spite of his treachery. Furthermore, he welcomed to his court the son of his loyal advisor Barzillai (19:9-40).

The undercurrent of strife between Israel and Judah became apparent when the men of Israel were left out of the welcoming party that ushered David home. They interpreted this as exclusion from David's kingdom (19:41-

David mourning the death of Absalom

43). The succession of northern tribes from Jerusalem occurred in the reign of David's grandson, Rehoboam (compare 1 Kgs 12:16-20).

20:1-26
Sheba's Revolt

The conclusion of this section concerning David's troubles appropriately ends with yet another rebellion. Sheba, a Benjamite, led an insurrection against David. The tribe of Benjamin, the kin of King Saul, had a long-standing feud with David as evidenced already by Shimei (16:7). Now fueled by animosity against Judah, Sheba seized the opportunity to rally the men of Israel to support his coup (20:1-3).

Amasa's slowness to attend to the rebellion forced David to appoint Abishai and Joab to deal with Sheba. When Amasa finally joined Joab's campaign, Joab greeted him with a treacherous kiss and then thrust his sword into Amasa's belly (20:4-13). Meanwhile, Sheba took refuge in Abel Beth Maacah, where the Judahites besieged the city. The people of Israel must have been skeptical of Sheba's chances for success. A woman of the city convinced its citizens to offer the head of Sheba to Joab, thereby averting the city's massacre and ending the schism (20:14-22).

The author concluded this section with a brief report on David's bureaucracy. This final listing of David's officials is similar to 8:15-18 with two important differences. There is no mention of slave labor in David's earlier administration, and also David's sons are absent (20:23-25).

GOD PRESERVES DAVID'S KINGDOM (2 SAM 21:1–24:25)

The last section of the book is an appendix to David's career as the LORD's anointed. Here the emphasis falls on David's praise for God's sovereign mercies (chap. 22) and the mighty warriors the LORD used in the service of the king (chap. 23). The stories of famine, war, and pestilence resulting from Israel's sin were fitting reminders that no king was above the word of the LORD (chaps. 21; 24).

21:1-22
God Avenges the Gibeonites

A three-year famine caused David to inquire how Israel had offended the LORD. It was common in the Old Testament to attribute such catastrophies to the LORD's intervention. King Saul had breached Israel's long-standing covenant with the Gibeonites (compare Josh 9:25-27). Although 1 Samuel does not narrate Saul's murder of these Amorites (who resided in his homeland of Benjamin), such an act was consistent with Saul's policies (compare 1 Sam 22:16-19). David turned over seven descendants of Saul's house (sparing Mephibosheth) to the Gibeonites for execution to avenge their loss (21:1-9). David buried Saul's kin honorably with his and Jonathan's bones (21:10-14). The execution of Saul's kinsmen may have been the reason Shimei claimed David was guilty of bloodshed (compare 16:7-8).

The catalog of wars against the Philistines is a commentary on the continued troubles in the reign of David but also a tribute to God's abiding favor as Israel prevailed over their foes (21:15-22).

22:1-51
David's Thanksgiving Hymn

The core of the appendix is David's tribute to the LORD (chap. 22). This song was also included in the Book of Psalms (Ps 18). The occasion for David's thanksgiving was his deliverance from King Saul (2 Sam 22:1).

David recalled his cry for deliverance (22:2-7). He described the LORD's intervention in words reminiscent of His appearance at Mount Sinai (22:8-16; compare Exod 19; Ps 68:7-18; Hab 3). The LORD, awesome in might, came to his personal rescue (2 Sam 22:17-20) because David was upright and faithful (22:21-28). God was his Lamp, Rock, and Shield of Salvation (22:29-37), giving David complete victory over all his enemies (22:38-46).

The song concludes with a doxology (22:47-51).

23:1-39
Oracle of David and the Mighty Men

Although other words from David are recorded in the Old Testament books that follow (1 Kgs 2:1-9; 1 Chr 23:27), this oracle was David's last formal reflection on the enduring state of his royal house under the covenant care of the LORD. The term "oracle" (23:1) commonly introduces prophetic address (Num 23:7; Isa 14:28; Mal 1:1). David declared by the Spirit (2 Sam 23:2) that God had chosen him from all Israel and made an everlasting covenant with his lineage. Those who opposed him would be cast aside as thorns for the fire (23:3-7). This messianic description is fully realized in Jesus Christ, who as David's son establishes the rule of God in the earth.

The catalog of mighty men and their exploits was another tribute to God's enablement of David. Among David's armies were two elite groups of champions who served as the king's bodyguard and special fighting force (compare 21:15-22; 1 Chr 11:10-47). The first group consisted of the "Three" whose exploits against the Philistines were renown (23:8-17; compare the cave of Adullam, 1 Sam 22). Abishai and Benaiah were singled out, although they were not as great as the "Three," because they held high honor in the annals of David's wars (23:18-23). The second group, the "Thirty," is also listed, giving a total count of thirty-seven heroes (including Joab, 22:24-39).

24:1-25
God Punishes Proud David

The final episode of the appendix concerns the plague the LORD brought against Israel because of David's sin. It parallels the beginning story of the appendix where Israel suffered famine because of Saul's sin (21:1-14). The specific reason for God's anger at Israel is unstated. The LORD, however, used David's census to chasten the people by plague (24:1). In the parallel passage (1 Chr 21:1) the author explained that the immediate cause for David's sin was the work of Satan.

David's taking of the census was an indication of his pride and self-reliance (24:2-9). In the law the taking of a census required an atonement price to avert plague (Exod 30:11-16). God instructed the prophet Gad to announce His judgment on Israel. God presented David a choice of three punishments—famine, plague, or war. These three sanctions were the curses God threatened to bring upon Israel for breaking the covenant (Deut 28). David wisely placed himself at the mercy of God and not the temperament of man. The LORD punished Israel by a devastating plague. David confessed that he was guilty for misleading the sheep of Israel (24:10-17).

To make atonement for Israel, the prophet Gad instructed David to build an altar at the threshing floor of Araunah. There David had seen the avenging angel carry out the deadly plague (24:18-20). He would later choose this site for the building of the temple (1 Chr 22:1).

Araunah offered to give the floor to the king, but David knew that acceptable atonement required a price. He built the altar, offered sacrifices, and prayed in behalf of his people. The LORD acknowledged David's intercession, and the plague ceased (24:21-25).

Ethical and Theological Significance

David's story, like Romans 7:7-25, speaks to the Christian's experience of sin. David was a man after God's own heart (1 Sam 13:14). Like Paul, he could have said, "In my inner being I delight in God's law" (Rom 7:22). But like Paul, David saw "another law at work in the members of [his] body, . . . making [him] a prisoner of the law of sin" (7:23). David coveted Uriah's wife, and "sin sprang to life" (7:9). With Uriah's murder, David's sin became "utterly sinful" (7:13).

Nathan's parable roused David's moral outrage at his sin (2 Sam 12). Today Scripture functions like Nathan's tale to help us see what we are really like. David saw and experienced heartbreak over his sin.

David suffered short- and long-term consequences of his sin. His sin did not, however, thwart God's ultimate, saving purpose for and through him. "In all things God works for the good of those who love him" (Rom 8:28). God worked through the lives of David and Bathsheba to give Israel its next king (Solomon) and, in time, its Messiah (Matt 1:6). God continues to work through the lives of repentant sinners. "Thanks be to God—through Jesus Christ our Lord!" (Rom 7:25).

Questions for Reflection

1. What does 2 Samuel teach about war and peace?
2. How does personal sin affect family and friends?
3. What responsibilities does a Christian have in civic and business leadership?
4. What character traits made David a great man of God?

Sources for Additional Study

Baldwin, Joyce G. *1 & 2 Samuel.* Downers Grove: InterVarsity, 1988.

Laney, J. Carl. *First and Second Samuel.* Chicago: Moody, 1982.

1 KINGS

The title *Kings* reflects the content of 1 and 2 Kings, which trace the history of God's covenant people under Israel's kings.

Like the Books of Samuel, 1 and 2 Kings were one book in the Hebrew tradition. The division of the book first occurred in the Greek version, which translated Samuel and Kings as four consecutive books entitled *First–Fourth Kingdoms.* Jerome's Vulgate followed the Greek tradition of four books but with the title *Kings.* The English title *Kings* was derived from the Latin Vulgate. The English version followed the Greek and Latin practice of four books but with the Hebrew titles *Samuel* and *Kings.* The division of Kings was not commonly practiced in Hebrew until the first printed edition in 1488.

The Books of Kings are anonymous. Jewish tradition assigns their authorship to Jeremiah. Rabbinic custom attributed unnamed works to famous religious leaders of the era. Many critical scholars believe 1 and 2 Kings are the last books of a consecutive history from Deuteronomy through Kings. This account is called the "Deuteronomistic History" because many of the major themes of the Book of Deuteronomy recur in the larger history. Other scholars who reject this reconstruction believe that the authorship of Kings is independent of Deuteronomy (see "The Historical Books").

Most commentators agree that much of Kings was written before the destruction of Jerusalem (586 B.C.), although how much is disputed. There is agreement on the date for the completion of the work. The last historical reference in Kings is 562 B.C., the first full year of Babylon's Evil-Merodach's reign (2 Kgs 25:27). The completion of the book must be after this date but before the return of the exiles to Judah in 539 B.C. since 1 and 2 Kings do not mention this event. The book is dated at about 550 B.C., during the exile.

The author used a variety of sources, many of them early, in the writing of Kings. The sources ranged from royal and temple records to stories about the prophets. Excerpts from three royal annals are specifically cited: "the book of the annals of Solomon" (1 Kgs 11:41; compare also 11:27), "the book of the annals of the kings of Israel" (for example, 1 Kgs 14:19), and "the book of the kings of Judah" (for example, 1 Kgs 14:29). The author, however, was not merely an editor but a composer whose work was based on these sources.

The structure of Kings is built upon a fixed framework having introductory and concluding formulas about each king's reign. The structure deviates from this framework with the inclusion of the Elijah and Elisha narrative cycles. The "deviation" points to the force of the prophets as shapers of the history of God's people.

Chronology of the Kings

Interpreters have a problem understanding how the chroniclers calculated the dates for the reigns of the kings. The reigns are dated by comparing the date a ruler began to reign with the number of years his counterpart in the other kingdom had reigned at that time. The length of the reign is provided for each king. However, there are problems reconciling the various dates. Additionally, Judah and Israel may have followed calendars beginning the new year at different times. Finally, there may have been differences in how the rulers counted the beginning of their reigns. Some began counting with their coronation, while others began counting only after their first year of reign. Therefore scholars have attempted reconstructions, including overlapping reigns of a father and son, to help explain the dates.

There is no consensus among scholars on all the dates of the kings. The differences are not so remarkable so as to impede our understanding of the historical background of the period. The dates followed here are those suggested by E. R. Thiele (*The Mysterious Numbers of the Hebrew Kings* [Grand Rapids: Eerdmans, 1965]).

Theme

God established Solomon as David's successor over Israel; but Solomon sinned, and God "humbled David's descendants" (11:39) by dividing the nation into two kingdoms. The ten tribes of the Northern Kingdom retained the name *Israel.* The Southern Kingdom took the name of its dominant tribe, *Judah.*

I. Solomon's Ruthless Succession (1:1–2:46)
II. Solomon's Riches and Spiritual Ruin (3:1–11:43)
III. Judah and Israel Divided under Apostasy (12:1–16:34)
IV. God's Prophets Elijah and Micaiah (17:1–22:53)

Purpose and Theology

1. First and Second Kings trace the history of Israel's monarchy during four tumultuous centuries from the reign of Solomon (971 B.C.) to Jehoiachin's imprisonment in Babylon (562 B.C.). They tell of Solomon's reign, including the building of the temple (1 Kgs 1–11), the era of the Divided Kingdom to the fall of Samaria (1 Kgs 12–2 Kgs 17), and the last years of Judah down to the Babylonian exile (2 Kgs 18–25).

2. This history of 1 and 2 Kings is not merely a political history of the monarchy. It is a prophetic interpretation of how each king affected the spiritual decline of Israel and Judah. The kings who had a greater religious impact receive more attention. For example, Omri was one of the most significant kings in the history of the ancient Near East, but his reign is only mentioned in a few verses (1 Kgs 16:23-28). Much more is said about his son Ahab. The destruction of Israel and Judah was due to the idolatry advocated by their kings. By reciting this history from a theological perspective, the author both warned against idolatry and encouraged renewed commitment (8:33-34; 11:6,9-13; 13:34; 14:14-16; 18:39; 19:18).

3. First and Second Kings explain how history is governed by God's moral law. The theological perspective of Kings is the same as Deuteronomy's. Faithfulness to God's word is rewarded with blessing, but disobedience reaps God's judgment. This principle is demonstrated in the life of the two kingdoms whose rise and fall were dependent upon their obedience to the covenant of the LORD. The kings were evaluated on the basis of their fidelity to the LORD.

All the kings of the Northern Kingdom were condemned because of their idolatrous worship. In this they followed the ways of Israel's first king, Jeroboam, who introduced calf worship at Dan and Bethel (for example, 15:25-26,33-34). The kings of the Southern Kingdom, Judah, were approved if they followed after their father David (for example, 15:13). Only Hezekiah and Josiah met with full approval because they removed the high places and reformed the defiled worship of the temple (2 Kgs 18:1-8; 22:1-2; 23:24-25).

4. The people of God are held responsible for their actions. The kings of David's descent experienced the same chastening for their sins as the evil kings of Israel (1 Kgs 11:9; 14:22). Even a prophet, the "man of God," suffered death for his unfaithfulness (13:26).

5. God is portrayed as the sovereign LORD of history. The prophets were God's spokespersons who announced the rise and fall of kings and kingdoms because God controls their destinies (1 Kgs 11:29-32; 13:1-4; 16:1-7; 20:13,28; 22:13-28).

6. God is faithful. Although Judah's kings sinned, the LORD upheld His promise to David (2 Sam 7:16) by preserving his kingdom and retaining his descendants on the throne (1 Kgs 11:31-36; 15:3-5; 2 Kgs 25:27-30). The LORD was faithful to His prophets who heralded His message in the face of danger (1 Kgs 19:3-4,18; 22:24-28).

SOLOMON'S RUTHLESS SUCCESSION (1 KGS 1:1–2:46)

This section completes the succession story of David begun in 2 Samuel 9–20. It depicts the ruthless struggle for power between Adonijah and Solomon as David neared his death. Only God's providential grace preserved the throne intact.

1:1-53
Solomon Becomes King

In his old age David needed the warmth and nursing of a servant girl named Abishag (1:1-4). The imminent death of the king explained the struggle that ensued between David's strongest allies. Adonijah, who was David's oldest living son (2 Sam 3:4), led a conspiracy to make himself king. He was joined by Joab and the priest Abiathar at En Rogel, where they celebrated his impending enthronement. However, Nathan the prophet, Zadok the priest, Benaiah the captain of the king's bodyguard, and Solomon his brother were excluded (1 Kgs 1:5-10).

Nathan knew that this meant banishment or death if Adonijah succeeded. Nathan encouraged Bathsheba to ask the king to fulfill his prior commitment to make Solomon king (1:11-27). Perhaps David had interpreted the special naming of Solomon (Jedidiah) by God as indicative of the LORD's choice (compare 2 Sam 12:24-25 and Deut 17:15).

David ordered the anointing of Solomon at the spring Gihon. When Adonijah heard the people shout, "Long live King Solomon," he fled for safety in the tabernacle, where he grasped the horns of the altar. The "horns" were the four projectiles at the corners of the altar where the blood of the sacrifice was smeared. Solomon spared Adonijah but placed him under house arrest (1 Kgs 1:28-53).

2:1-46
Solomon's Kingdom Established

David's deathbed instructions warned Solomon that only obedience to the LORD would secure his kingdom. He advised Solomon to execute Joab for murdering Abner and Amasa (see 2 Sam 3:22-27; 20:4-10) and to deal swiftly with Shimei for his treachery (see 2 Sam 16:5-14). David died after his forty-year rule (1011–971 B.C.), but the kingdom was secure in the hands of his successor (1 Kgs 2:1-12).

The enemies of David and Solomon received their retribution. Adonijah was executed because he asked for the hand of Abishag, a member of the royal harem. Solomon interpreted this request as tantamount to staking another claim to the throne (2:13-25). Zadok replaced Abiathar as chief priest because the latter had sided with Adonijah (2:26-27). This banishment of Abiathar fulfilled God's judgment on his ancestor Eli's house (1 Sam 2:27-36). Benaiah executed Joab and replaced him as captain of Solomon's armies (2:28-35). Shimei also was executed because he disregarded the limitations of his house arrest (1 Kgs 2:36-46a). The narrator aptly stated the conclusion of this struggle: "The kingdom was now firmly established in Solomon's hands" (2:46).

SOLOMON'S RICHES AND SPIRITUAL RUIN (1 KGS 3:1–11:43)

The second section of the book concerns Solomon's reign. It focuses on the wisdom he received from the LORD (chaps. 3–4). He was able to assemble an impressive administration and to undertake numerous building projects, in particular the Jerusalem temple (chaps. 5–8). He became an important international figure through wealth, trade, and politics (chaps. 9–10). These accomplishments were God's blessing because of His covenant with David. But the author also tells how Solomon's apostasy (chap. 11) caused Israel to lose all he had achieved.

3:1-28
God's Gift of Wisdom

Solomon married Pharaoh's daughter (3:1), which evidences Solomon's significance in the international community (7:8; 9:24). Solomon loved the LORD and obeyed Him as his father had, but he also practiced sacrifice at local shrines. This custom would become a snare when he turned to idolatrous worship at such high places (3:2-3; compare Deut 12:11-14).

The judgment and wisdom of King Solomon

Solomon requested in a dream the wisdom needed to serve the people of God. God granted him wisdom and more (1 Kgs 3:4-15). An example of his wisdom was his ability to settle a dispute between two prostitutes. The people realized that his wisdom came from God (3:16-28).

4:1-34
Solomon's Wisdom in Administration and Learning

The list of officials, twelve administrative districts, and the necessary provisions for this bureaucracy show how God blessed Solomon in his administrative skills (4:1-28). This change in the tribal boundaries to twelve districts with their heavy taxation angered the northern tribes (compare 12:1-17).

God gave Solomon great learning. The extent of his learning exceeded even the famous sages of Egypt and the East. He was gifted in the arts and also possessed unusual knowledge in the life sciences (4:29-34).

5:1-18
Preparations for the Temple

Like his father, Solomon was zealous for the reputation

of the LORD. He allied himself with Hiram, king of Tyre in Phoenicia, and acquired from him building materials for the temple. When Hiram witnessed Solomon's wisdom, he praised the God of Israel (5:1-12). Solomon's laborers were drafted from among the Israelites (5:13-18). Samuel had warned Israel of such conscription under a king (1 Sam 8:11-12,16).

6:1-38
Construction of the Temple

The importance of this event in the life of Israel is indicated by the careful dating of the event and the elaborate description of the temple's architectural plan. The date is the fourth year of Solomon's reign (966 B.C.). (See "Dates of the Exodus.") An architectural parallel to the Jerusalem temple's design is a Phoenician temple from about 850 B.C. recovered at Tell Ta'inat in Northern Syria. The Phoenician craftsmen, who were specialists, were employed for the temple (1 Kgs 7:13-14; 2 Chr 2:7,12-13). Between the description of the temple's external features (1 Kgs 6:2-10) and its luxuriant furnishings (6:14-36) the author emphasized the LORD's promise to bless Solomon (6:11-13). The construction required seven and a half years (6:37-38). (See "The Temple.")

7:1-51
Solomon's Houses and the Temple Furnishings

The palace complex took almost twice as long to build as the temple. The proximity of Solomon's house to the LORD's house reflected the close relationship between God and king (compare Ps 2:7). Included with his own

THE TEMPLE

The story of redemption is one of God's overcoming the breach sin caused in His relationship with humanity. The sanctuaries God instructed Israel to build reiterated God's intention to be Immanuel, God in their midst (Isa 7:14; Matt 1:23). But contact between a holy God and sinful people was restricted and mediated by priests. Each of Israel's sanctuaries had zones of increasing sanctity. The outer areas were open to all, while the inner court and the temple building were restricted to priests. The most holy place within the temple was restricted to the high priest who entered there only on the Day of Atonement each year.

In the course of Israel's history God instructed Israel to build three sanctuaries. The first was the tabernacle, a portable shrine that fit Israel's nomadic existence during the wilderness period (Exod 25–40). Once Israel settled the promised land, the tabernacle continued to serve as the central shrine (Deut 12).

That the tabernacle remained a portable shrine is clear from the sites associated with it: Shiloh (1 Sam 1–4), Kiriath-Jearim (1 Sam 7:1), Gibeon (1 Chr 21:29), and Jerusalem (1 Chr 23:25-26).

Solomon built the temple in Jerusalem on land David acquired in connection with his disastrous census (1 Chr 21:1–22:1; 1 Chr 28:1-19; 2 Chr 3:1). The architectural details are described in 1 Kings 6–7 and 2 Chronicles 3–4. This temple was destroyed by the Babylonians in 586 B.C.

When Israel returned from the Babylonian captivity, a second temple was constructed in Jerusalem on the site of the first. This work was completed in 516 B.C. (2 Chr 36:22-23; Ezra 1:1-6:18).

The temple of NT times was actually a third structure. By Jesus' ministry, this temple had been under construction for forty-six years (John 2:20). It was completed just before the destruction of Jerusalem by the Romans in A.D. 70.

In addition to these sanctuaries, during the Babylonian captivity God gave Ezekiel an extensive vision of a new Jerusalem, including a temple (Ezek 40–48). Just as during the wilderness period, the tribes were arrayed around the sanctuary, portraying once again that God was in their midst (Ezek 48; Num 2; 9:15–10:36).

God indicated His acceptance of the tabernacle, the first temple, and the temple in Ezekiel's vision by the appearance of the pillar of fire and cloud—the Shekinah glory—to take up residence above the most holy place in those structures (Exod 40:34-38; 1 Kgs 8:10-13; 2 Chr 5:13–6:2; 7:1-3; Ezek 43:1-12). This pillar was a visible manifestation of God's presence, once again saying to Israel that God was with them, in their midst. Though prophets did say that God's glory would appear there (Hag 2:1-9; Zech 2:5,10-13), the OT does not narrate the appearance of the pillar of fire and cloud at the second temple.

The NT views Jesus as the fulfillment of the temple's true meaning: God with us (John 2:19-22; Heb 10:19-22; Rev 21:22). God takes residence in the church as His temple; believers enjoy the indwelling presence of God's Spirit (1 Cor 3:16-17; 2 Cor 6:16; Eph 2:21-22; 1 Pet 2:4-5). The goal of redemption history is in large measure overcoming that breach between God and humanity introduced in the fall. When that relationship is fully restored, in God's new city no temple will be needed (Rev 21:1-3,22). □

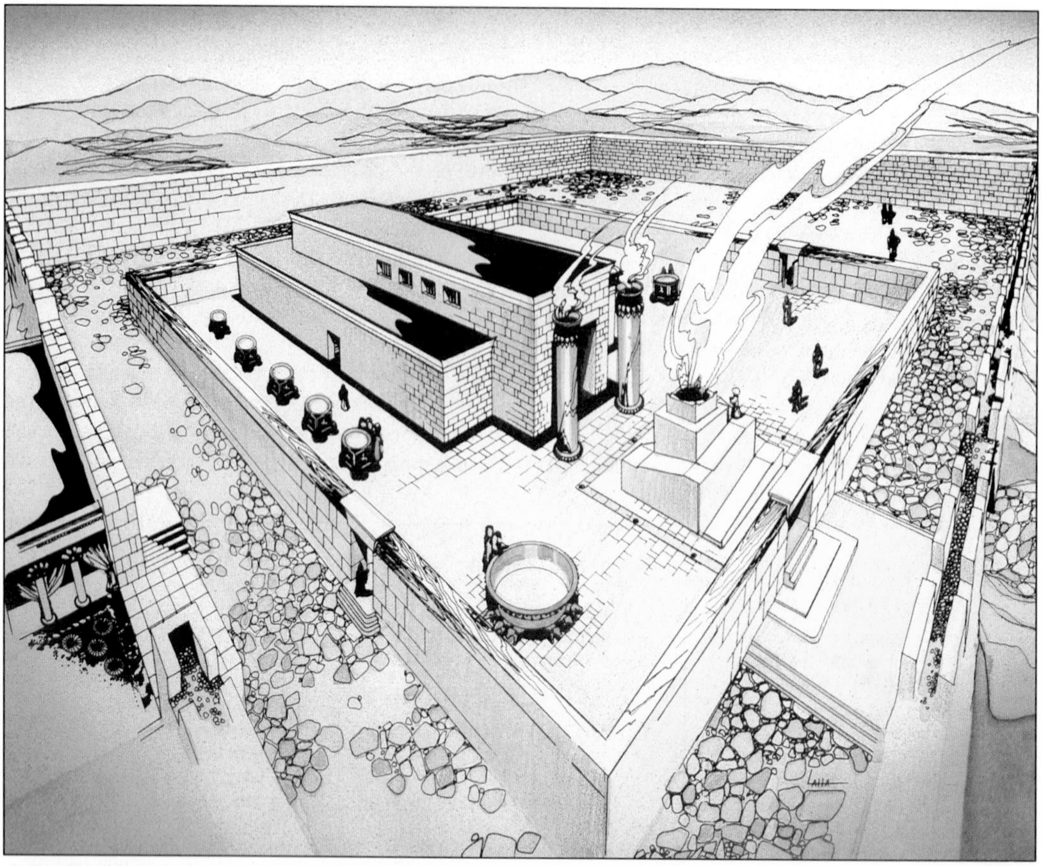

Reconstruction of Solomon's Temple (957–587 B.C.) at Jerusalem and its courts. Shown are the ten lavers (five on each side of the temple), the Molten Sea (lower center), and the Altar of Burnt Offerings (center). Solomon's palace (left) stood immediately west of the temple court, overlooking the temple.

palace and the palace of Pharaoh's daughter was the costly Palace of the Forest of Lebanon with its elaborate halls (1 Kgs 7:1-12).

The author was more interested in the construction of the temple and returned to describe its furnishings. Huram of Tyre, whose mother was a Hebrew, made the bronze furniture (compare Bezalel, Exod 31:3; 35:31). The bronze work consisted of the two pillars (named Jakin and Boaz) their capitals and designs, ten lavers, and the molten sea (1 Kgs 7:13-47). The gold work included the altar, table of bread, lampstands, basins, and door sockets (7:48-50). (See the feature article "The Temple.") Solomon placed in the temple the gifts and spoils of war dedicated by David (2 Sam 8:10-12).

8:1-66
Dedication of the Temple

This event was the highlight of Solomon's career just as the bringing of the ark into Jerusalem was David's (2 Sam 6). Solomon was accomplishing what the LORD promised to David's descendants. After the ark was set under the cherubim in the holy of holies, the whole house was filled with a cloud. The glory of the LORD was so great that it prohibited entry into the temple (compare Exod 40:34-35). This meant that the presence of the LORD was in the temple. The ark was moved in the wilderness from place to place, but the temple provided a permanent dwelling for the ark (1 Kgs 8:1-21).

Solomon showed in his prayer that he did not conceive of the LORD as bound to a sacred place like the deities of the Canaanites (8:22-53). The temple could not house the God of heaven. The "Name" of the LORD transcends a mere physical structure (8:22-30).

Solomon anticipated Israel's captivity. He prayed that God would hear the repentant prayers of His people and bring them back to their inheritance (8:31-53; compare

Deut 28:15-68). Solomon exhorted the people to walk faithfully before the LORD (1 Kgs 8:54-61). The dedicatory service concluded with a fourteen-day feast of worship and celebration (8:62-66).

9:1-9
The LORD Appears Again

In response to Solomon's prayer, the LORD appeared as He had at Gibeon (3:4-15). The LORD exhorted Solomon to be obedient and warned that disobedience would result in exile and a rejection of the temple (9:1-9). Second Kings describes how this happened to the two kingdoms of the divided monarchy (chaps. 17; 25).

9:10-28
Solomon's Commercial Policies

Solomon's acquisition of wealth further demonstrated the fulfillment of God's promise to David. He acquired gold from King Hiram in exchange for twenty cities (9:10-14). Solomon's extensive building projects, including fortifying Jerusalem and other royal cities, required him to conscript slave labor and to install Israelites as overseers (9:15-24).

10:1-29
The Queen of Sheba Praises the LORD

Just as Hiram of Phoenicia praised God (5:7), the Queen of Sheba extolled the LORD because of Solomon's international fame (10:1,9). Sheba has been traditionally associated with South Arabia, which controlled the sea lanes between India and the East. God used Solomon's prestige to bring glory to Himself throughout the world.

Solomon's possession of gold, the extent of his shipping enterprises, and his military armament made him the most powerful king among the nations. He controlled the merchandising of horses from Kue (Cilicia) and of chariots from Egypt. The author attributed all of Solomon's splendor to the divine wisdom God gave him (10:14-29).

11:1-43
Solomon's Apostasy and Antagonists

Deuteronomy warned of forgetting God in prosperity (Deut 6:10-12; 8:7-20). The troubles of Solomon's reign can be traced to the misuse of God's blessing. His success in international trade encouraged him to marry foreign wives for diplomatic reasons. He loved the LORD, but he also "loved many foreign women" (1 Kgs 11:1).

This love for foreign women grew greater than his love for the LORD's commandments. The wives caused him to pursue idolatrous worship. The hills of Jerusalem were dotted with high places sacred to the Phoenician fertility goddess Ashtoreth (compare Deut 16:21; Judg 3:7; 1 Sam 7:3-4), the god Molech of the Ammonites (Lev 18:21), and Chemosh of Moab (Judg 11:24).

The author concluded that "Solomon did evil in the eyes of the LORD" and did not obey "as David his father had done" (1 Kgs 11:6). Although David sinned against the LORD, his reign was not evil because he never fell into the contemptuous practice of idolatry. This practice brought God's judgment, which entailed Israel's division into two kingdoms (11:1-13). Solomon's wisdom and possessions were not subjected to the LORD. Therefore the LORD raised up three antagonists: Hadad the Edomite (11:14-22), Rezon of Aram/Syria (11:23-25), and Jeroboam of the tribe Ephraim. Ahijah, the LORD's prophet, incited Jeroboam to lead the ten northern tribes to secede from Jerusalem (11:26-40).

Solomon died after forty years of rule (971–931 B.C.). Rehoboam succeeded his father and reaped the whirlwind of God's judgment.

JUDAH AND ISRAEL DIVIDED UNDER APOSTASY (12:1–16:34)

The book describes the period of antagonism between the two kingdoms of Israel and Judah. Jeroboam's revolt fulfilled God's judgment on Solomon's kingdom (chap. 12). Jeroboam's dynasty was condemned and usurped for its evil idolatry (chaps. 13–14). Israel suffered the bloodshed of war and political coups (chaps. 15–16). In all, nine dynasties ruled Israel in its two hundred years (931–722 B.C.). The kingdom of Judah enjoyed the stability of only one dynastic house since the LORD preserved the throne of David. Yet its kings also committed the idolatrous sins of their northern counterparts. The kings of Judah continually experienced war, and only righteous Asa had a long, prosperous rule (chaps. 14–15)

12:1-33
Jeroboam's Golden Calves

This chapter treats the watershed event in 1 Kings. King Rehoboam's refusal to rescind the oppressive forced labor and tax measures of his father, Solomon, split the kingdom. The ten tribes of Israel under Jeroboam seceded from Jerusalem, fulfilling the prophecy of Ahijah (12:15; compare 11:29-39). Rehoboam attempted to reclaim his kingdom, but the prophetic word from Shemaiah (12:22) prohibited him (12:1-24). Rehoboam's greatly reduced kingdom became known as Judah. Rehoboam's name means *one who enlarges the people*, but ironically he divided the people.

The above reconstruction of a Phoenician ship is based on information from eighth-century B.C. reliefs. The ships of Solomon's fleet were of similar construction. (See 1 Kgs 9.)

King Jeroboam built his military command at Shechem, an important religious and political site in Israel's history (compare 12:1; Josh 24). He knew that his political fortunes were tied to the religious life of the nation. He set up two golden calves at Dan and Bethel (compare Hos 8:4-6; 10:5; Amos 7:8-13). He encouraged local high places and authorized a non-Levitical priesthood. He initiated an annual feast at Bethel in the eighth month to rival the Feast of Tabernacles traditionally celebrated in the seventh month (1 Kgs 12:25-33; compare Leviticus 23:33-43). Jeroboam cried out, "Here are your gods, O Israel, who brought you out of Egypt" (1 Kgs 12:28). These gods were patterned after the sacred bull of Egypt (compare Exod 32:4) and the calf worshiped by the Canaanites. Yet Jeroboam tied the worship of these calves to the LORD's deliverance of Israel from Egypt. If Jeroboam intended to continue the worship of the LORD, the calves were meant only as pedestals for Israel's invisible God. From the sacred writer's viewpoint these calves were signs of pagan idolatry.

13:1-34
The Man of God and the True Word

An unnamed prophet of the LORD delivered a message of judgment against Jeroboam's royal shrine at Bethel. He predicted that Josiah would destroy the Bethel worship site. This occurred in 621 B.C. when King Josiah of Judah initiated extensive religious reforms (2 Kgs 23:15-17). When Jeroboam saw that he could not harm the prophet, he enticed him to stay. But the LORD had forbidden the prophet to eat or drink in the Northern Kingdom (1 Kgs 13:1-10).

As the man of God left Bethel, an old prophet hoping to fellowship with him met the prophet and, using deceit, persuaded him to stay. The man of God foolishly agreed to dine with him. After the man of God left his host, a lion on the road killed him. When the old prophet discovered the body, he exclaimed, "It is the man of God who defied the word of the LORD" (13:26). Ironically, the death of the man of God proved that his predictions about Bethel would "certainly come true" (13:32).

Jeroboam's sinful altar was the reason for his downfall and ultimately the demise of Israel (13:33-34; compare 14:16; 15:29; 2 Kgs 17).

14:1-20
Denouncing Jeroboam

Jeroboam's wife, disguised as another woman, visited

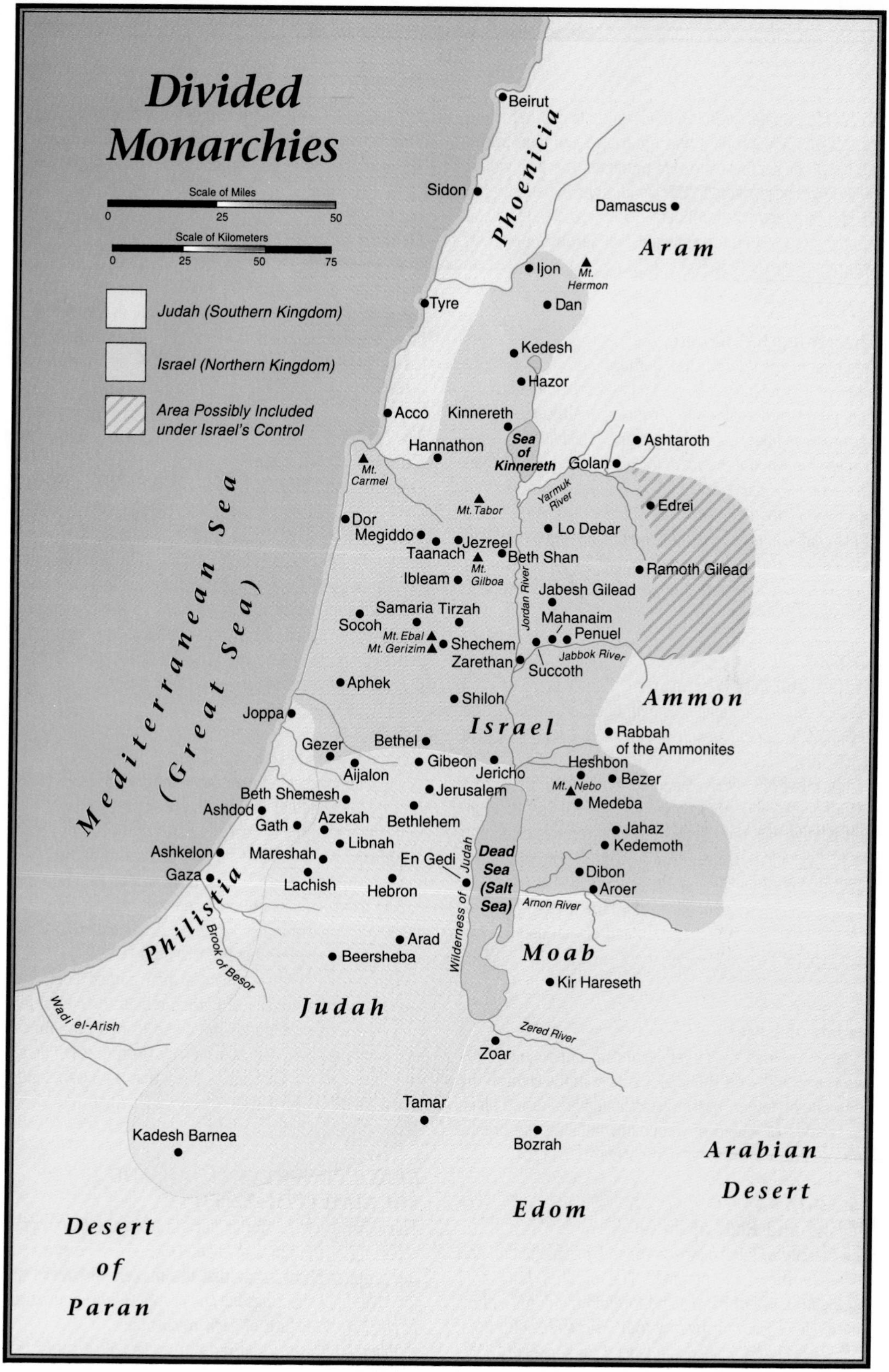

Divided Monarchies
Scale of Miles
0 25 50
Scale of Kilometers
0 25 50 75
Judah (Southern Kingdom)
Israel (Northern Kingdom)
Area Possibly Included under Israel's Control
Beirut
Phoenicia
Sidon
Damascus
Aram
Ijon
Mt. Hermon
Tyre
Dan
Kedesh
Hazor
Acco
Kinnereth
Sea of Kinnereth
Hannathon
Ashtaroth
Golan
Mt. Carmel
Yarmuk River
Mt. Tabor
Edrei
Dor
Megiddo
Jezreel
Taanach
Lo Debar
Beth Shan
Mt. Gilboa
Ibleam
Jordan River
Ramoth Gilead
Jabesh Gilead
Samaria
Tirzah
Socoh
Mahanaim
Penuel
Mt. Ebal
Mt. Gerizim
Shechem
Zarethan
Succoth
Jabbok River
Aphek
Shiloh
Ammon
Mediterranean Sea
(Great Sea)
Joppa
Israel
Rabbah of the Ammonites
Gezer
Bethel
Gibeon
Jericho
Heshbon
Aijalon
Mt. Nebo
Bezer
Beth Shemesh
Jerusalem
Medeba
Ashdod
Azekah
Bethlehem
Gath
Jahaz
Libnah
Kedemoth
Ashkelon
Mareshah
En Gedi
Dead Sea (Salt Sea)
Dibon
Gaza
Lachish
Hebron
Wilderness of Judah
Aroer
Arnon River
Philistia
Brook of Besor
Arad
Beersheba
Moab
Kir Hareseth
Wadi el-Arish
Judah
Zered River
Zoar
Tamar
Kadesh Barnea
Bozrah
Arabian Desert
Edom
Desert of Paran

Ahijah the prophet at Shiloh to learn the fate of her ailing son Abijam. The prophet was not fooled and denounced the house of her husband. He predicted the boy would die and the LORD would raise up another dynasty to cut off the progeny of Jeroboam (compare 15:29). The prophet also foretold the exile of Israel. Jeroboam reigned twenty-two years (930–909 B.C.).

14:21-31
Chastening Rehoboam

Rehoboam squandered his heritage through spiritual apostasy. His reign was as wicked as Jeroboam's with its high places and male cult prostitutes. Although Judah was preserved because of the promise to David, the LORD in anger punished Rehoboam for his wickedness. He was afflicted by Shishak (Shoshenq), who was the founder of Egypt's Twenty-second Dynasty (945–924). An account of his wars is inscribed on the wall of the temple at Karnak. Rehoboam paid him handsomely from the gold accumulated by Solomon. Rehoboam reigned for seventeen years (930–913 B.C.).

15:1-24
Abijah and Asa of Judah

Abijah's three-year reign was evil, but God sustained his throne as a "lamp" in Jerusalem for the sake of David (15:1-8).

Asa, however, received a good report from the sacred historian. His reign of forty-one years (910–869 B.C.) included reforms, though he did not remove the high places (15:9-15). During Asa's reign, Baasha of Israel built a fortress near Jerusalem at Ramah. Asa entered a treaty with Ben-Hadad, king of Aram (Syria), who attacked Israel. Baasha left Ramah and dismantled the fortress (15:16-24).

15:25-32
Nadab of Israel

Nadab succeeded his father Jeroboam but reigned only two years (909–908 B.C.). He did evil in the sight of the LORD like his father. Baasha assassinated Nadab and killed the whole household of Jeroboam, fulfilling the prediction of Ahijah (15:25-32; compare 14:10-11,14).

15:33–16:14
Baasha and Elah of Israel

The dynasty of Baasha was founded by assassination and ended in the same manner. The prophet Jehu condemned the evil of Baasha and foretold the demise of his house. He reigned for twenty-four years (908–886 B.C.; 15:33–16:7) and was succeeded by his son Elah (886–885 B.C.). In a drunken stupor he was assassinated by Zimri, a court official. Zimri executed the whole family of Baasha just as Jehu had prophesied (16:8-14).

16:15-20
Zimri's Seven Days

Zimri's reign, the Third "Dynasty," had the distinction of being the shortest in the history of Israel. He ruled for seven days before he committed suicide in the flames of his palace. His demise was plotted by General Omri, who led an expedition against Zimri for his murder of King Elah.

16:21-28
The House of Omri

Omri defeated Tibni, a rival to the throne, and founded the Fourth Dynasty in Israel. His reign was only twelve years (885–874 B.C.). His fame was so great that a hundred years after his death the nation Israel was still called the "house of Omri." Omri had close ties with the Phoenicians, even marrying his son Ahab to the Tyrian princess Jezebel. Omri moved the capital of Israel from Tirzah to Samaria. There the kings of Israel ruled until its destruction by the Assyrians in 722 B.C.

16:29-34
Ahab and Jezebel of Israel

Ahab and Jezebel reigned for twenty-two years (874–853 B.C.). Together they attempted to make Israel a pagan nation devoted to Baal and Asherah, the deities of the Sidonians. Ahab erected an idol of Baal in Samaria and built an image of the Canaanite goddess Asherah. The sacred historian was unimpressed with Ahab's many political accomplishments. Twice he evaluated Ahab's rule as more evil than all his predecessors (16:29-33).

During the reign of Ahab, a man named Hiel, who was from the sinful city of Bethel, rebuilt the city of Jericho. His sons died under the curse Joshua pronounced upon anyone who restored the city (Josh 6:26). The author included this account to show that the LORD's judgment on sin is certain (1 Kgs 16:34). Ahab too would suffer for his sins.

GOD'S PROPHETS ELIJAH AND MICAIAH (17:1–22:53)

The Elijah cycle of stories departs from the stereotyped reporting of the kings in chapters 12–16. The stories of the prophet Elisha show that the makers of Israel's history were not the kings but the prophets who dramatically shaped the future of each royal house.

Elijah's ministry occurred during Israel's greatest religious crisis under Ahab (chaps. 17–19) and Ahaziah (1 Kgs 22:51–2 Kgs 1:18). Ahab's reign declined because of wars with Aram and his theft of Naboth's vineyard (chaps. 20–22).

17:1-24
God's Trouble for Ahab

Elijah the Tishbite is introduced in the book suddenly as an envoy from the LORD. He proclaimed to Ahab a great drought which would end only when Elijah gave the word (compare Jas 5:17-18). The drought was a refutation of Ahab's Baalism because Baal was reputed to be the god of rain and vegetation (1 Kgs 17:1-6). This showed that the LORD was the true Lord of nature.

During the three-year drought, Elijah dwelt with a widow and her son in Zarephath of Phoenicia, the native land of Jezebel, where Baal was worshiped. The drought had spread to Phoenicia, and the LORD used the prophet

THE CHRONOLOGY OF THE KINGS OF ISRAEL

Chronology is the backbone of history. Yet precisely in this area we encounter one of the most difficult aspects of biblical study. The chronological notices found in the Bible concerning the period of the divided kingdoms contain information which at first glance appears self-contradictory and impossible to reconcile. These seeming discrepancies have been used as prime evidence for errors in the Bible or for mistakes in the copying of our present Hebrew text.

Examples of chronological difficulties are not hard to find. We read that Ahaziah became king of Judah both in the eleventh year and twelfth year of Joram (2 Kgs 8:25). We are told that Joram became king of Israel in the second year of Jehoram of Judah (2 Kgs 1:17), in the eighteenth year of Jehoshaphat, Jehoram's father (2 Kgs 3:1). And we are told that Jehoram of Judah began his reign in the fifth year of Joram of Israel (2 Kgs 8:16). We read that Nebuchadnezzar became king in the fourth year of Jehoiakim (Jer 25:1) and that he was already king in the third year (Dan 1:1).

These difficulties were considerably eased when scholars learned the principles on which ancient scribes based this data. Different procedures for computing the first year of reign were followed in Egypt and in Mesopotamia. In Mesopotamia even if a king came to the throne in the first month of the year, that year would be called "the year of the beginning of kingship" (the "accession year"). What would then actually be his second year of rule was counted as "year one." In Egypt even if a pharaoh came to the throne in the last month of the year, that was called "year one," and the second month of his rule would begin "year two." The administrations in Israel and Judah had each adopted one of these systems. They also differed regarding which month began the new year, whether Tishri or Nisan. Thus, what a scribe in one nation might call the eleventh year of Joram would be called the twelfth year by a scribe in the other kingdom.

There is also the possibility of coregencies or overlapping reigns. For example, when Uzziah was ill with leprosy, his son Jotham ruled in his place until Uzziah died and he became the sole ruler (2 Chr 26:21-23). But how did Jotham calculate his reign? The kings of Israel and Judah counted their years of rule from the beginning of their coregencies, and Jotham would probably have been in about his eleventh year of reign when he began his first year of sole rule.

Taking account of how coregencies were calculated helps to reduce the impossibly large figure if the lengths of reigns are simply added up. When these and other principles are taken into account, the result is a complex but essentially harmonious set of data in the Hebrew Bible concerning the kings of Israel and Judah. Far from being the primary evidence for mistakes in copying the Hebrew Bible during the centuries, these chronological notices become the showcase for its reliable transmission. However, not all individual pieces of information are as easily accommodated, and some difficulties remain. The various Greek translations of the OT appear to have relied on a different set of data from that contained in the Hebrew Bible.

Two documents in the extrabiblical literature are of fundamental importance for our understanding of the chronology of the ancient Near East. These are the records of an Egyptian astronomer named Ptolemy (A.D. 70–161) and the Assyrian eponym list. Ptolemy recorded the lengths of reign for the kings of Babylon from 747 B.C. to the second century A.D. He included a series of astronomical observations from which we can calculate the dates of the reigns he mentioned. The Assyrian eponym list gives officials, one for each year from about 900 to 650 B.C. It overlapped with Ptolemy's list for a century and also included important astronomical observations by which it could be anchored to an absolute chronology. The synchronisms between the Bible and the surrounding kingdoms can thus be tied to a firm chronology in the first millennium. □

to provide food to this family. When the woman's son became ill and stopped breathing, Elijah prayed three times, and the LORD answered by raising up the boy. Because God did these miracles in Phoenicia, this showed that the LORD was the God of all nations and that Baal did not exist (17:7-24).

18:1-46
Choosing the Real King

For three years Ahab and his servant Obadiah desperately sought the elusive Elijah. Elijah unexpectedly met Obadiah in the road and promised Obadiah that he would see the king. When Ahab met the prophet, he called Elijah the "troubler of Israel" (18:17). Yet it was Ahab who caused Israel's distress. Elijah proposed a contest with the prophets of Baal and Asherah at Mount Carmel.

The contest was for the benefit of the people to learn who truly ruled Israel—the Baals of Ahab and Jezebel or the LORD God of their fathers. The contest consisted of preparing a sacrifice and praying for the deity to prove his existence by answering with fire from heaven. Baal was reputed to be the god of storm and therefore should at least have been able to bring down fire (lightning).

The prophets of Baal prayed all morning, but there was no answer. Elijah ridiculed their pagan theology. Then in ecstatic frenzy they frantically slashed themselves to draw their god's attention (compare Lev 19:28; Deut 14:1), but there was no answer. At the evening hour of sacrifice, it was Elijah's turn. He rebuilt the altar of the LORD and called upon God, identifying Him as the "God of Abraham, Isaac and *Israel* " (1 Kgs 18:36). Fire fell and the people exclaimed, "The LORD—he is God!" (18:39). The people executed the evil prophets (18:20-40).

God also sent a great rainstorm to end the drought. The storm rained upon Ahab as he hurried to Jezreel. The hand of the LORD empowered Elijah to run ahead of Ahab's chariot to the city (18:41-46).

19:1-21
Elijah Hides at Horeb

Elijah's victory, however, turned into fear and depression. Surprisingly, Jezebel was not intimidated by Ahab's report of Elijah's deeds. She vowed to kill the prophet, who ran again but this time away from Jezebel to the desert. In despair the prophet prayed to die (compare Num 11:11-15; Job 6:8-9; Jonah 4:8). The angel of the LORD strengthened him with food, and he journeyed forty days and nights to a cave at Mount Horeb (1 Kgs 19:1-9a). It was upon the same Mount Horeb, another name for Mount Sinai, that the LORD had revealed Himself to Moses (compare Exod 3; 19).

Elijah complained that the Israelites had abandoned God and that he was the last prophet of the LORD. But Elijah was mistaken. God brought in succession a great wind, an earthquake, and a fire to ravage the mountain. But the prophet did not hear God in these events. Instead, Elijah heard the LORD in a small whisper. By this the prophet learned that sometimes God works in quiet ways (19:9b-14).

There were in fact seven thousand who had not worshiped Baal. God sent Elijah to anoint three men who would ultimately destroy Ahab's house—Hazael of Aram, Jehu of Israel, and the prophet Elisha (19:15-18). The call of Elisha was the beginning of a large school of prophets (19:19-21; compare 2 Kgs 6:1-2).

20:1-43
God Gives Ahab Victory

The Aramean king, Ben-Hadad, forged a coalition of thirty-two kings that besieged Samaria and held it hostage (20:1-12). Ahab, at the bidding of an unnamed prophet, secretly attacked the drunken Arameans, and the LORD granted Ahab's weaker armies a surprising victory. By this God demonstrated to Ahab that He was the true LORD of Israel (20:13). The next year the Arameans, believing that the LORD was a god only of the hills, attacked the city of Aphek located in a valley. God again granted victory to show that He ruled over hill and valley (20:28). In spite of God's grace, evil Ahab violated the rules of holy war and spared the life of Ben-Hadad (20:13-34). The LORD sent another prophet to the king to condemn Ahab for his neglect of the LORD's word. Ahab confirmed the truth of the message by announcing his own judgment (20:35-43).

21:1-29
Ahab's Theft of Naboth's Vineyard

The evil plot against Naboth brought God's wrath against Ahab, including the deaths of Jezebel and his son Joram (1 Kgs 22:37-38; 2 Kgs 9:24-26,30-37). Because of the law of Moses, Naboth refused the king's request to acquire his vineyard. The law taught that God was the owner of Canaan and that the people, as its tenants, could not dispose of their land (Lev 25:23; Num 27:1-11; 36:1-12). Ahab, perhaps respecting the law of God more highly than Jezebel, only sulked about the refusal whereas Jezebel took steps to steal the land. She sent letters to powerful leaders of Jezreel to entrap Naboth with false charges of sedition and blasphemy. He was executed for these crimes, and his land was gobbled up by Jezebel and Ahab (1 Kgs 21:1-16).

Yet their murder of Naboth did not go unnoticed.

Elijah delivered God's denunciation in the very vineyard Jezebel conspired to get. Although Ahab was the passive player in this evil deed, he was held responsible for failing to stop his wicked wife. The prophet predicted that in the place the dogs licked the blood of Naboth, Ahab's blood also would be the delight of the city's stray dogs. Jezebel also would be a delicacy for the ravenous hounds of Jezreel (21:17-24).

Ahab repented when he heard the word of the LORD. Though he was the most wicked man of Israel, God took mercy on him and prolonged his life (21:25-29). This postponement did not mean, however, that God had changed His opinion on the character of Ahab's reign (compare 22:37-38).

22:1-53
Micaiah's Prophecy and Ahab's Death

A monument of the Assyrian king Shalmaneser III tells how he fought the united armies of Ahab and Ben-Hadad at Qarqar on the Orontes River in 853 B.C. (compare 20:34). The result was probably a stalemate. When the Assyrians retreated, Ben-Hadad renewed his hostilities by capturing Ramoth Gilead near the border of Israel (compare 2 Kgs 10:32-33). Jehoshaphat, the king of Judah, joined Ahab to fight the Arameans. Jehoshaphat was not satisfied with the prophets at Ahab's court and insisted on hearing from the prophet of the LORD. Micaiah, brought from Ahab's prison, predicted that Ahab would be killed in defeat. Ahab ridiculed his prophecy. But Micaiah told him how in a vision he had seen God send a deceiving spirit to mislead Ahab's counselors (22:1-28).

This vision does not mean that Micaiah believed God was a liar. This vision was a pictorial way to explain that God had permitted the false prophets to mislead Ahab to effect His divine judgment.

Ahab went into the battle disguised, but God found him through a bowman's arrow! Ahab's bloody chariot was washed in Samaria, and his blood was licked by dogs just as the word of the LORD had said (22:29-40; compare 21:19).

Jehoshaphat's twenty-five-year reign continued the religious reforms of his father Asa (22:41-50). Meanwhile, Ahaziah followed his father Ahab by worshiping Baal. His two-year reign was shortened by the judgment of God (22:51-53; compare 2 Kgs 1:1-18).

Theological and Ethical Significance

First Kings, like Deuteronomy, warns against forgetting God in times of economic prosperity. Having known material abundance, many today have left God out of their lives as the ancient Israelites did. Having abandoned faith, many have compromised their values to those of pagan society. The collapse of Israelite society warns of the consequences of sin.

First Kings reveals the power of the word of God in shaping history. The courage of those, like Elijah, whose hearts were captive to the word of God challenges today's Christians to let their presence be felt. After the prophet Micaiah had seen Yahweh's throne room, he was not impressed by King Ahab's threats. Those of us who have experienced the height and depth and breadth of God's love in Christ Jesus should be bold to speak God's word of judgment and grace to our world.

The history of Israel and Judah is the story of a people's failure to fulfill God's purpose for them. God, however, is faithful in spite of human failure. Though we are called to obedience, our hope lies in God's grace. We see this grace most clearly Jesus Christ, "who as to his human nature was a descendant of David" (Rom 1:3).

Questions for Reflection

1. How does prayer affect the lives of God's people?
2. How is wisdom more valuable than wealth?
3. How should God's people use their prosperity?
4. In what ways does God use wicked instruments to achieve His purposes?

Sources for Additional Study

McNeeley, Richard I. *First and Second Kings.* Chicago: Moody, 1978.

Millard, Alan. *1 Kings - 2 Chronicles.* Ft. Washington, Pa: Christian Literature Crusade. London: Scripture Union, 1985.

Vos, Howard F. *1, 2 Kings.* Grand Rapids: Zondervan, 1989.

2 KINGS

First and Second Kings form one narrative which recounts the history of Israel's monarchy (compare the introduction to "1 Kings" for a fuller discussion).

Theme

God destroyed the kingdoms of Israel and Judah because their kings led the people to do evil by disobeying the covenant of the LORD (22:13).

I. God's Prophet Elisha (1:1–8:29)
II. Decline and Destruction of Israel (9:1–17:41)
III. Survival and Final Days of Judah (18:1–25:30)

Purpose and Theology

1. Second Kings continues the recital of Israel's demise. One objective of Kings is to show how God was justified in destroying His people. Israel was given over to the Assyrians because it persisted in the idolatrous worship promoted by Jeroboam (17:21-22). Judah suffered the judgment of God because of the sins of Manasseh, whose reign epitomized the evil of Judah's kings. King Josiah's revival of orthodox worship was not sufficient to turn away God's appointed wrath (21:10-15; 23:25-27)

2. The basis of God's judgment was the Mosaic covenant as described in Deuteronomy. The kings fell far short of the divine ideal (Deut 12). Because Israel broke the law of Moses by worshiping at the pagan high places, God set in motion the curses of the covenant (2 Kgs 10:21; 17:7-13; compare Deut 28). The recurring theme of divine retribution peaks in the latter half of 2 Kings. (For example, 5:26-27; 9:25-37; 13:2-3; 17:7,25; 19:27-28; 20:16-18; 21:12.)

3. The author showed that the Lord is at work in the history of Israel. God's activity is seen in His warnings delivered by the prophets and His judgment carried out "according to the word of the LORD" (for example, 1:17; 10:17; compare 9:25-26,36-37; 10:10; 14:25; 15:12; 17:18-23). His sovereignty is demonstrated by His assigning victory or defeat to nations and by His establishment of kings or deposing of kings. (For example, 5:1; 7:6; 10:32; 13:5; 14:27; 15:37 and 8:13; 9:6.) Through Israel's history, the Lord is proven to be the one true God (5:15; 19:19).

5. Another evidence of God's intervention is Elijah's numerous miracles. Although it was a dark hour in the life of the nation, Elijah's ministry demonstrated that God was still mighty among His people (for example, 2:13-14; 4:34-35; 5:1-18; 13:20-21).

6. Finally, the grace of God is an important theological lesson of the book (13:22-23; 14:26-27). God spared Judah from Assyria and Hezekiah from a fatal illness in response to his prayers for deliverance (19:14-34; 20:1-11). A glimmer of hope concludes this gloomy book of destruction (25:27-30). David's descendant Jehoiachin was alive in Babylon, and there was hope that God would restore Israel and its king. The book was directed to those living in the Babylonian exile. It was their duty to heed the warnings of the book and repent in preparation for the return to their homeland.

GOD'S PROPHET ELISHA (2 KGS 1:1–8:29)

The introductory section continues the story of the prophets, Elijah and Elisha, who delivered the word of the LORD during this decadent period in the life of the nation. Elijah's ministry closed with his ascent to heaven. But his successor, Elisha, picked up his mantle and performed a double portion of God's wondrous acts (chaps. 1–2). Through the prophetic ministry of Elisha, the LORD guided Israel to victories over their enemies, the Moabites and Arameans (chaps. 3; 6–7). God showed through Elisha that He also is the LORD of all nations who shapes their destinies (chaps. 5; 8). While the LORD met the specific needs of His faithful people (chap. 4), He judged the servant Gehazi for his greed (5:19-27).

1:1-18
Ahaziah Consults Baal-Zebub

The reign of Ahaziah (853–852 B.C.) was introduced in 1 Kings 22:51-53. When Ahaziah suffered an accident in his palace, he sent messengers to consult the Phoenician god Baal-Zebub to learn if he would recover. But Elijah interrupted the travel of Ahaziah's messengers and announced that the king would die because he sought Baal-Zebub rather than the LORD (2 Kgs 1:1-4). Time and again 2 Kings emphasizes that dependence on other gods is a way that leads to death. After three attempts by Ahaziah's delegations, Elijah went personally to the bed of the king to repeat his message. The king died just as the LORD had said through His prophet (1:15-18).

The name Baal-Zebub (*lord of the flies*) was an intentional play on the original name Baal-Zebul, meaning *lord of the lofty abode* or *princely lord.* Beelzebub, the New Testament form of the name Baal-Zebub, became a symbol of Satan by the time of Christ (Matt 10:25; 12:24-27).

2:1-25
Elijah's Ride to Heaven

The final days of Elijah prepared the way for Elisha to follow in his footsteps. Elisha accompanied Elijah from town to town awaiting the arrival of the whirlwind of God that would usher the great prophet into heaven. Elisha swore that he would not leave Elijah's side until he received a "double portion" of Elijah's spirit (2:1-10). As the firstborn, a son received a double portion of a father's inheritance (compare Deut 21:17). When the chariot of fire came for the prophet, Elisha exclaimed: "My father! My father! The chariots and horsemen of Israel!" (2:12). Elijah had at one time prayed to die under a broom tree (1 Kgs 19:3-4), but God took him in a whirlwind to heaven. He and Enoch (Gen 54:24) were the only two men in Scripture to be translated to heaven.

The fallen cloak of Elijah was symbolic of Elisha's spiritual inheritance (2 Kgs 2:13). With the cloak he duplicated Elijah's miracle of crossing the Jordan River on dry ground. This proved that Elisha had received his ministry (2:11-18).

The company of prophets doubted Elisha's credentials. Elisha demonstrated his authority by healing, that is, purifying, the polluted waters of Jericho. Also he invoked a divine curse upon his detractors, who mocked Elisha by urging him to ascend into heaven like Elijah. Two ravenous bears killed the wicked young men (2:19-25).

The Moabite Stone (ninth century B.C.) contains ancient Moabite script memorializing the military campaigns of Mesha, king of Moab.

3:1-27
Joram of Israel

During the reign of Joram (852–841 B.C.), Mesha, king of Moab, rebelled against Israel. Joram recruited King Jehoshaphat of Judah (compare 1 Kgs 22) and the king of Edom to help subjugate Mesha. The absence of water because of dry stream beds hindered their campaign. Elisha, for the sake of David's descendant Jehoshaphat, agreed to consult the LORD in behalf of Joram (3:1-15a).

The LORD instructed them to dig trenches which He flooded with water. When the Moabites saw the water, it appeared red like blood to them, and they mistakenly believed that the three kings had fought among themselves. The reddish appearance has been explained as the water's reflection of a colored red stone known in that area bordering Edom and Moab. The Moabites attacked prematurely and were defeated. When Mesha saw the battle was lost, he offered his firstborn son as a sacrifice to appease the anger of the Moabite deity Chemosh (compare 2 Kgs 16:3; 21:6). Human sacrifice was prohibited by the LORD, who called upon the Israelites to give their firstborn to God as *living* sacrifices, devoted to His service (Exod 22:29-30; 34:20; Deut 18:10). The armies of Israel withdrew out of fear (3:15b-27).

The Moabite stone found at Dhiban, Jordan in 1868 contains an inscription by Mesha, who offered a different interpretation of his wars with Israel. He admitted his subjugation to Ahab but boasted that Chemosh had given him victory over Israel.

4:1-44
God Remembers His Faithful Servants

A prophet's widow had no means to pay her creditors

except selling her sons into slavery. Elisha multiplied the small amount of oil she possessed, and it was sold to pay her debts (4:1-7).

In Elisha's itinerate ministry, he stayed in the house of a wealthy Shunnamite woman whenever he traveled in Jezreel. Because of her ministry to the prophet, the LORD gave the woman and her aged husband a son (4:8-17). Later when the boy took ill and died, God answered the prayer of Elisha and restored him to life (4:18-37; compare Elijah, 1 Kgs 17:17-24).

The LORD met the needs of his prophets through Elisha's ministry of miracles. Elisha purified a pot of poisonous stew by throwing flour into it. The LORD fed one hundred of the prophets from only twenty loaves of bread (4:38-44; compare Matt 14:13-21; 15:32-38; John 6:5-13).

5:1-27
Healing of Naaman's Leprosy

Naaman, the second in command to the king of Aram (Syria), suffered from the dreaded disease of leprosy. A captured Israelite girl told Naaman's wife about Elisha, the LORD's prophet, who could invoke the LORD to heal the general. When Naaman arrived at Elisha's house bearing great sums of money, a messenger instructed Naaman to bathe seven times in the River Jordan. Because of his pride he went away angry, refusing to wash in the muddy waters. His servants convinced him to do so, and the LORD healed him. Naaman declared, "There is no God in all the world except in Israel" (5:15). Naaman converted to the LORD and regretted that in carrying out his official duties he would have to accompany his king into the temple of their pagan god Rimmon (5:1-19a).

Although Elisha had refused a gift from Naaman, the prophet's servant Gehazi secretly detained Naaman to ask for money. But Elisha knew of Gehazi's greed and condemned him to Naaman's leprous disease (5:19b-27).

6:1-33
The Axhead and the Blinded Arameans

Among the miraculous stories about Elisha is his retrieval of a lost axhead. The prophets experienced the blessing of the LORD, and their increasing number required new housing. A prophet's axhead was lost in the Jordan where he was cutting down trees. Elijah threw a stick into the river, whereupon the axhead came to the surface (6:1-7).

The Arameans led two campaigns against the king of Israel (6:8-23; 6:24–7:20). In the first raid the LORD enabled Elisha to tell the king of Israel the precise movements of the Aramean armies so that Israel might escape entrapment. The Aramean armies attempted to kill the prophet, but the LORD's horses and chariots of fire encircled Elisha and his servant. The LORD answered Elisha's prayer and struck them blind. After God restored their sight, Elisha released them for home so that they might warn their king (6:8-23).

Later the Arameans under Ben-Hadad ordered a full-scale invasion of Samaria. The siege caused famine in the city, and the king of Israel blamed the prophet Elisha for their misery. He probably interpreted this as a punishment from the LORD. The king sent a messenger to kill the prophet (6:24-33).

7:1-20
The LORD Delivers Samaria

When the king's messenger approached the prophet, Elisha prophesied that within a day they would be delivered. The messenger ridiculed the prophet's words and later paid for it with his life (7:1-2,19-20).

That night the LORD created the rumbling noise of an approaching army, and the Arameans left their camp, thinking that mercenary troops had come to Samaria's aid. On the next day lepers discovered the abandoned camp with its provisions. The whole city rushed through the gateway, trampling to death the messenger who had mocked the prophet's message (7:3-20).

8:1-15
The Shunnamite Woman and the Anointing of Hazael

The LORD brought a great famine against Israel, and Elisha advised the Shunnamite woman, whose son was brought back to life (4:8-37), to reside in Philistia. After the seven-year famine, her lands were restored to her by the king because he heard of her story from Gehazi, the servant of Elisha (8:1-6).

Elisha went to Damascus to anoint Hazael, Ben-Hadad's military commander, to be king over Aram. Elisha wept because he knew Hazael would oppress the LORD's people. Ben-Hadad was ill, and Hazael, incited by the word of the LORD, assassinated the king (8:7-15).

8:16-29
Jehoram and Ahaziah of Judah

Jehoram's reign included a coregency with his father Jehoshaphat (853–841 B.C.). Jehoshaphat foolishly married Jehoram to Athaliah, the daughter of Ahab. Jehoram behaved like the wicked kings of Israel, but God spared his reign because he was of the house of David (8:16-24; compare 2 Sam 7:13-16).

Ahaziah's rule (841 B.C.) was wicked like his father's because he was influenced by his in-laws, the family of Ahab. This ultimately spelled disaster for the house of Judah since his reign was followed by that of his evil queen mother, Athaliah, Ahab's daughter. During Ahaziah's reign, King Joram of Israel was wounded by the Arameans at Ramoth Gilead. Ahaziah visited his uncle Joram at Jezreel, where he was recuperating (8:25-29).

DECLINE AND DESTRUCTION OF ISRAEL (2 KGS 9:1–17:41)

The second section describes the deterioration and eventual collapse of the northern state of Israel under the weight of its religious paganism and political infighting. Jehu's dynasty rid Israel of its Baalism, postponing God's wrath. But the slide to destruction came quickly afterwards with the rise and fall of four dynasties within the short span of thirty years. The climax of the account is the final chapter of the section, which explains why Israel did not survive (17:7-41). By disregarding the covenant, Israel chose death (Deut 30:19-20).

Meanwhile, the descendants of David escaped annihilation only by the grace of God. The alliances of Jehoshaphat with Israelite kings (compare 1 Kgs 22; 2 Kgs 3; 2 Chr 20:35-37), sealed by intermarriage (2 Kgs 8:18; 2 Chr 18:1), threatened the very existence of the Davidic line when Athaliah became queen mother. The salvation of Judah by Joash and the success of Amaziah's reign were the only two periods of stability in the otherwise tottering kingdom to the south.

9:1-37
Jehu Purges the House of Ahab

Jehu, King Joram's commander, defended Ramoth Gilead against the Arameans. Elisha delegated one of the prophets to anoint Jehu king of Israel. The Lord commanded Jehu to avenge the blood of His prophets by killing the ruling descendants of Ahab and Jezebel (9:1-13).

Jehu drove his chariot furiously from Ramoth to Jezreel. When the two kings Joram and Ahaziah saw him approach, they met him in the field that had belonged to Naboth. When the kings recognized his intentions, they fled for their lives. Jehu killed Joram and tossed his body on Naboth's land, fulfilling God's judgment on Ahab's house (compare 1 Kgs 21:21-22,29). Ahaziah also was fatally wounded (2 Kgs 9:14-29).

Jezebel mocked Jehu from her Jezreel residence by likening him to the murderous Zimri (1 Kgs 16:9-10). Jehu called for the palace guards to toss her from the window. Where her body splattered, horses trampled her and ravenous dogs chewed her body (2 Kgs 9:30-37). Her death fulfilled God's vengeance for the murder of Naboth (1 Kgs 21:23).

10:1-36
Jehu's Bloody Coup

Jehu threatened Samaria's officials, and they appeased him by decapitating Ahab's seventy sons. Jehu did this in accordance with the Lord's command (2 Kgs 9:7-10), but Jehu's coup went beyond the specific directives of the Lord. He slaughtered forty-two relatives of King Ahaziah of Judah, seizing the opportunity to weaken his rival's throne. The bloodbath was remembered for almost one hundred years (compare Hos 4:1-2). He also killed all the relatives and associates of Ahab (2 Kgs 10:12-17).

Jehu continued his purge by exterminating the worshipers of Baal and burning their temple. Yet Jehu sinned like his fathers because he did not remove the golden calves at Dan and Bethel. God nevertheless preserved the house of Jehu for four more generations lasting almost one hundred years (10:18-31).

During his reign (841–814 B.C.), Jehu's kingdom lost the Transjordan to Hazael of Aram (10:18-36). To avert further loss, Jehu made an alliance with the Assyrians. The black stone monument Assyria's king Shalmaneser III erected tells how Jehu became an Assyrian vassal (841 B.C). The stone depicts Jehu kneeling before the king and bearing gifts.

11:1-21
Athaliah and Joash of Judah

With the death of her son Ahaziah, Athaliah seized the throne and killed the royal descendants of David. But God, upholding His promise to David, preserved Joash the son of Ahaziah. Jehosheba, the half-sister of Ahaziah and wife of the high priest Jehoiada (2 Chr 22:11), hid the boy in the temple for the six years of Athaliah's reign. In conspiracy with the temple guards, army, and mercenary Carites (compare the Kerethites of 2 Sam 20:23), Jehoiada proclaimed Joash king in the temple (11:1-12).

Athaliah was taken and executed by the guards. Jehoiada renewed the covenant of the Lord, and the people removed the idols associated with the Baal worship Athaliah had promoted. Joash was enthroned at the age of seven (11:13-21).

12:1-21
Joash's Religious Reform

The forty-year reign of Joash (835–796 B.C.) was righteous in the sight of the Lord because of the religious reforms he introduced in Judah. When the priests failed to raise the funds to repair the neglected temple, Jehoiada collected monies in a chest located in the temple (12:1-16). Joash's rule was marred, however, when he sent the holy articles of God to the Aramean king, Hazael, as payment of tribute. The people God had redeemed from Egyptian slavery were to remain politically free so that they would be free to serve God. Political unrest led governmental officials to assassinate Joash (12:17-21).

13:1-25
Jehoahaz and Jehoash of Israel

Jehoahaz (814–798 B.C.) succeeded his father, Jehu, but led Israel to worship the Asherah pole, a representation of the Canaanite fertility goddess. The LORD used the Arameans to reduce Israel's army (13:1-9).

Jehoahaz's son Jehoash ruled for sixteen years (798–782 B.C.) and was remembered for his oppression of King Amaziah of Judah (13:10-13; compare 14:1-14). During his reign Elisha was dying from an illness, and Jehoash came to his bedside and wept. Elisha instructed him to strike the floor with his arrow. After he struck the floor three times, Elisha predicted that the LORD would give him three victories over the Arameans (13:14-19). The LORD granted those victories over the Aramean king, Ben-Hadad, who succeeded his father Hazael (13:22-25).

God honored both the life and death of the great prophet Elisha. A dead man was brought back to life when his body was placed in the tomb with Elisha's bones (13:20-21).

14:1-29
Amaziah of Judah

Amaziah (796–767 B.C.) pleased the LORD during his reign as his father Joash had done. He executed his father's assassins (compare 12:20-21) and defeated the rebellious Edomites. His arrogance, however, brought him defeat by Jehoash of Israel. Jehoash broke down the walls of Jerusalem, raided the temple treasuries, and took hostages (14:1-16). Ironically, like his father's, Amaziah's rule ended by a conspiracy of assassins in Lachish (14:17-22).

14:23-29
Jeroboam II of Israel

The kingship of Jeroboam gave Israel one of its greatest periods of political stability and territorial growth (793–753 B.C.). The prophet Jonah advocated the expansionistic policies of Jeroboam. The LORD gave Israel a respite from their woes through Jeroboam, but Jeroboam too followed in the wicked ways of his namesake. The prophet Amos condemned the greed and immoral decadence of Israel during Jeroboam's reign. (See "Amos.")

15:1-7
Azariah of Judah

Azariah's coregency and reign totaled fifty-two years (792–740 B.C.). Azariah, also named Uzziah, was contemporary with Jeroboam II, giving Israel and Judah their

A panel from the Black Obelisk of Shalmaneser III (dating from the ninth century B.C.) depicts Jehu paying tribute and bowing before Shalmaneser (see 2 Kgs 10).

greatest periods of prosperity. The LORD struck Azariah with leprosy because he offered incense in the temple (compare 2 Chr 26:16-20). He shared his rule with his son Jotham.

15:8-31
Zechariah, Shallum, Menahem, Pekahiah, and Pekah of Israel

After Jeroboam's death his kingdom deteriorated rapidly. Zechariah ruled for six months and was killed by Shallum (15:8-12). This ended Jehu's dynasty in the fifth generation as the Lord had foretold (10:30). Shallum ruled only one month before he was assassinated in the ruthless coup of Menahem from Tirzah (15:13-16).

Menahem held his crown for ten years (752–742 B.C.). He paid tribute to the Assyrian monarch, Tiglath-Pileser III (745–727 B.C.), called by his Babylonian throne name "Pul" in the Bible. The annals of Tiglath record the heavy taxation Menahem endured.

Pekahiah inherited his father's policies of appeasement toward Assyria. After a two-year reign (742–740 B.C.), the commander of Israel's armies, Pekah, engineered an anti-Assyrian coup, murdering the king (15:23-26). (The name *Pekah* is a shortened form of the name *Pekahiah*.) His reign was twenty years (752–732 B.C.). (See the "Chronology of the Kings of Israel.") Perhaps during this period Pekah ruled from Gilead independently of the Samarian regime until the death of Pekahiah. Eventually the anti-Assyrian policy of Pekah failed when Tiglath annexed portions of Israel and deported its citizens. Hoshea usurped the throne with the backing of Assyria (15:27-31; compare 17:1-6).

15:32-38
Jotham of Judah

Jotham, who coreigned with his father, Azariah (15:5), ruled for sixteen years (750–732 B.C.). His reign pleased the LORD, except that he left the high places for sacrifice. Pekah of Israel and Rezin of Aram collaborated to threaten Jotham at the end of his rule. The prophets Hosea, Isaiah, and Micah were his contemporaries.

16:1-20
Ahaz of Judah

Ahaz (735–715 B.C.) was one of the most wicked of kings in Judah's history. He committed the horrible atrocity of human sacrifice and promoted the practice of sacrifice at the high places (16:1-4; compare 2 Chr 28). Ahaz inherited the political problems of his father. The coalition of Rezin and Pekah marched against Jerusalem to force Judah to join in their war against the encroaching armies of Assyria. But Ahaz, against the counsel of the prophet Isaiah (compare Isa 7:1-17), sought the aid of Tiglath-Pileser and bought his intervention with the temple and royal treasuries. Assyria's war resulted in the capture of Damascus (732 B.C.), the humiliation of Samaria (15:29), and the vassalage of Ahaz to Tiglath (16:5-9).

To comply as a dutiful vassal, Ahaz replaced the bronze altar of the LORD in the temple with a replica of the Assyrian altar Tiglath erected in Damascus. He also removed other features of the temple which were offensive to the Assyrian monarch (16:10-20).

17:1-41
Hoshea and the Fall of Samaria

Hoshea's (732–722 B.C.) pro-Assyrian policies (15:30) had saved Samaria, but it was at the high cost of vassalage to Tiglath and his son Shalmaneser V (727–722 B.C.). Hoshea tested Shalmaneser's strength and recruited the aid of So, king of Egypt. Hoshea was imprisoned, and Samaria endured a three-year siege led by Shalmaneser and completed by his brother Sargon II (722–705 B.C.). Samaria's destruction in 722 B.C. sounded the end of the northern state of Israel (17:1-6).

A black granite head of Tirhakah of Egypt showing the covering probably worn under a metal helmet (see 2 Kgs 19:9).

THE LOST TRIBES

The story of the "Lost Tribes" is the tragic conclusion of the history of the Northern Kingdom of Israel. Samaria, its capital, fell to the Assyrians in 721 B.C. following a three-year siege (2 Kgs 17:5-6). Assyrian policy called for resettling conquered peoples far from their homes and replacing them with conquered peoples from other parts of the empire. Such policy sought to pacify potential rebels by absorbing exiled minorities into the general population. According to Assyrian records 27,290 inhabitants of Samaria were deported. The Assyrians resettled Israelites in northeastern (Halah) and northwestern (Gozan) Mesopotamia and in Media, the eastern frontier of their empire (2 Kgs 17:10). Israelites were still in Assyria in ca. 560 B.C. when the account in 2 Kings concludes (2 Kgs 17:23; 25:27).

The territory of the old Northern Kingdom, now called Samaria rather than Israel, was resettled by conquered peoples from central (Babylon, Cuthah) and northwestern (Avva, Hamath, Sepharvaim?) Mesopotamia (2 Kgs 17:24). These foreigners intermarried with the remnant of Israelites remaining in the land. The Assyrians eventually allowed an exiled priest to return to Samaria to instruct the new population in what the Lord, "the god of the land," required (2 Kgs 17:28). But the new population, like their predecessors, mixed the worship of the Lord with that of their native gods (2 Kgs 17:29-33,41).

Some residents of Samaritan cities continued to identify strongly with the God of Israel. In 582 B.C. pilgrims from Samaritan cities (Shechem, Shiloh, Samaria) were massacred while on route to offer grain and incense at the ruins of the Jerusalem temple (Jer 41:4-9). When Zerubbabal returned to Jerusalem from Babylonian exile (ca 538 B.C.), the Samaritans offered to assist in rebuilding the temple (Ezra 4:1-3). The exile had, however, impressed the Judeans of the dangers of religious compromise. The Jews thus refused to allow the mixed population of Samaria to participate in rebuilding the Jerusalem temple.

The descendants of the old Northern Kingdom—called Israel, Ephraim, and the house of Joseph—shared in the promises to the patriarchs. The OT prophets thus hoped for their return to the land of promise and the worship of Yahweh (Isa 11:12-16; Jer 31:4-9; Zech 10:6-10). The NT mentions that one individual who traced her descent to one of the northern tribes (Anna from the tribe of Asher, Luke 2:36) was a regular participant in worship at the Jerusalem temple. □

While secular history gives political and military causes for a nation's demise, the inspired historian gave religious reasons for the fall of Samaria. The lengthy commentary on Israel's sins exonerated God but also warned Judah not to imitate their northern kin.

Israel sinned against the LORD and disregarded the warnings of the covenant made with their fathers. They made the golden calves of Jeroboam, erected the Asherah pole, committed human sacrifices, worshiped the stars, and practiced sorcery. The LORD removed Israel from the land because they sinned like the Canaanites whom the LORD had removed before them (17:7-23).

Through a policy of resettlement, the Assyrians subjugated the conquered nations of their empire. The nations transplanted in Samaria worshiped the LORD in name but also worshiped their own national deities (17:24-41). Their mixed worship alienated them from the Jews (Ezra 4:1-3; John 4:4-9,39-40).

SURVIVAL AND FINAL DAYS OF JUDAH (2 KGS 18:1–25:30)

The final section of Kings traces the survival of Judah after Samaria's collapse. From the perspective of the biblical writer, the reigns of Hezekiah (chaps. 18–20) and Josiah (chaps. 22–23) brought sweeping moral and religious reforms which prolonged Judah's existence for another hundred years. However, this period also saw Judah's most wicked king, Manasseh (chap. 21). Because of Manasseh's heinous sins, Jerusalem fell under God's final judgment of expulsion (chaps. 24–25).

18:1-37
Hezekiah of Judah

The account of Hezekiah's career is also recorded in 2 Chronicles 29–32 and Isaiah 36–39. The three sources do not always give a sequential chronology of the events in his reign since the authors gave a thematic presentation of his career.

Hezekiah, unlike his father, Ahaz, trusted the LORD throughout his reign (715–686 B.C.) and introduced radical reforms by removing the high places, destroying idolatrous symbols, and centralizing worship in Jerusalem. Although he inherited vassal status from Ahaz, Hezekiah rebelled against Sargon (compare Isa 20:1) and his successor Sennacherib. The sacred historian gave Hezekiah the highest commendation (2 Kgs 18:5).

The account of Sennacherib's invasion is also told in Isaiah 36–37. When Sennacherib became king (705–681

The tunnel built by King Hezekiah (see 2 Kgs 20:20) is shown in the above photograph. The building of the tunnel (which brought water from Gihon Spring outside Jerusalem underground into the city to the Pool of Siloam) is described in the Siloam Inscription (shown at right) inscribed in Hebrew on the tunnel wall.

B.C.), Hezekiah with the encouragement of Egypt rebelled against Assyria. Sennacherib responded (701 B.C.) by surrounding Jerusalem (18:13). The Assyrian's annals report that he had Hezekiah caught "like a bird in a cage." Hezekiah paid a handsome tribute (18:13-16), but it did not appease Sennacherib for long.

Sennacherib sent a delegation from his headquarters in Lachish to negotiate a surrender. The Assyrians ridiculed Hezekiah's dependence on Egypt and his hope in the Lord. They addressed Hezekiah's representatives in Hebrew, refusing to speak in the Aramaic language of diplomacy so that the people of Jerusalem would understand their threats (18:17-37).

19:1-37
God Delivers Jerusalem

When Hezekiah heard the report of the Assyrians' threats, he consulted Isaiah for a word from the Lord. Through the prophet the Lord promised to deliver Hezekiah by a rumor that would distract the Assyrians. Meanwhile, Sennacherib's attention had turned to the fortress of Libnah and the approach of an Egyptian army led by Tirhakah. Sennacherib sent a letter, threatening Hezekiah a second time not to ally himself with the Egyptians (19:1-13).

Hezekiah took the letter before the LORD and prayed for God's deliverance, knowing that the LORD alone could save him. Isaiah announced the LORD's response, prophesying the salvation of Jerusalem and end of Sennacherib's reign. That night the LORD slaughtered the armies of Assyria, forcing Sennacherib's retreat to Nineveh. Several years later, as the LORD had foretold (19:7), Sennacherib's sons assassinated him in an effort to save their crumbling kingdom (19:14-37).

20:1-21
God Heals Hezekiah

Hezekiah became deathly ill, and the Lord sent Isaiah to

This relief depicts the deportation of the inhabitants of Lachish after its defeat to Sennacherib (see 2 Kgs 18).

tell the king to prepare to die. But Hezekiah prayed earnestly, and the LORD through the prophet Isaiah promised to prolong Hezekiah's life for fifteen years. The LORD encouraged the king by a sign, causing the shadow of the king's sundial to move backward ten steps (20:1-11). The thanksgiving hymn of Hezekiah is preserved in Isaiah 38:9-20.

Merodach-Baladan, the king of Babylon (721–710 B.C.), sent a delegation to congratulate Hezekiah for his recovery. Merodach-Baladan is known from ancient annals as Marduk-apla-iddina II, a chieftain of southern Chaldea who led a successful rebellion against Sargon. Although recounted in Kings after Sennacherib's invasion (chap. 19), his visit actually occurred before.

Merodach-Baladan sent envoys to learn of Judah's strength and lure Hezekiah into an alliance. Isaiah condemned Hezekiah for his sinful pride in openly displaying his treasuries. The prophet continued with a divine oracle in which he prophesied that Judah's treasures and people would be carried away to Babylon (20:12-21; compare 25:21b).

21:1-26
Manasseh and Amon of Judah

Remarkably, Hezekiah bore a son (Manasseh) who would undo all that he had achieved in turning Judah back to God (21:1-18). During his fifty-five year reign (697–642 B.C.), the longest in Judah's history, Manasseh committed every pagan atrocity. The historian remarked that Judah "did more evil than the nations the LORD had destroyed before the Israelites" (21:9) and blamed Manasseh for the eventual fall of Jerusalem (21:12-15; 22:16-17; 24:3-4). Although Manasseh experienced a short imprisonment in Assyria (2 Chr 33:10-13), Assyrian records show that he was loyal for most of his reign.

Such wickedness yielded the fruit of more violence. Amon (642–640 B.C.), the son of Manasseh, was assassinated by palace officials after only two years on the throne (2 Kgs 21:19-26).

22:1-20
Josiah and the Book of the Law

Josiah (640–609 B.C.) began to reign at age eight after the assassination of his father. In his eighteenth year of reign (621 B.C.), Josiah initiated repairs on the temple Manasseh and Amon had neglected. The high priest Hilkiah recovered the book of the law among the rubble of the temple (22:1-10).

When the book was read before the king, he feared the LORD's wrath and sent a delegation to the prophetess Huldah to inquire of the Lord concerning Judah's fate. She prophesied that the LORD would destroy Judah for its idolatry but that Josiah would not witness it because he had repented (22:11-20). Scholars generally agree that this "book" was Deuteronomy or some part of it.

23:1-30
Josiah's Reforms and Tragic Death

Josiah renewed the covenant with the Lord and celebrated the Passover in an unprecedented way. He removed all evidence of pagan worship and centralized worship in Jerusalem. As the prophet had predicted (1 Kgs 13:32), Josiah tore down the shrine at Bethel, which Jeroboam had erected three centuries earlier. The biblical writer gave Josiah the highest commendation of all the kings: "Neither before nor after Josiah was there a king like him who turned to the LORD as he did" (23:25). Jerusalem enjoyed a national revival under Josiah. However, it came to a crashing halt when the king was killed at Megiddo by Pharaoh Neco. Josiah had attempted to block Neco's efforts to aid the faltering Assyrians in their last stand against Nebuchadnezzar's Babylonian armies.

23:31-37
Jehoahaz and Jehoiakim of Judah

Necho deposed Jehoahaz, Josiah's son, after only three months and imprisoned him in Egypt. He set up in his place another son of Josiah, the puppet king Jehoiakim, also called Eliakim (609–598 B.C.).

24:1-20
Jehoiachin and Zedekiah of Judah

The balance of power turned to the Babylonians in 605 B.C. when Nebuchadnezzar defeated the combined armies of Egypt and Assyria at Carchemish in North Syria (24:7). After three years of vassalage to Nebuchadnezzar (605–602 B.C.), Jehoiakim attempted an insurrection that failed. Jehoiakim resisted the word of the LORD by burning Jeremiah's scroll that foretold Judah's subjuga-

The Exile

Having just become a vassal of Babylon in 605 B.C., Judah rebelled and suffered the punitive actions of King Nebuchadnezzar in 597. Besides looting Jerusalem, the Babylonians deported to Babylon King Jehoiachin, his family, and thousands of officials and leading citizens. They then installed Zedekiah as puppet king (2 Kgs 24:1-17).

Rebellion broke out again in Judah in 589. A Babylonian army came, destroyed a number of cities in southern Judah, and took Jerusalem in 587/586 after a lengthy and severe siege. The puppet king Zedekiah was deported to Babylon, where he soon died. His sons and many of the Jewish officials were executed, Jerusalem and the Jewish temple were looted and destroyed, and another group of citizens was deported (2 Kgs 24:18–25:21; Jer 37:1–39:10; 52:1-30).

No longer a monarchy, Judah became a province of the Babylonian empire, administered from a new capital at Mizpah by a Jewish governor, Gedaliah. The assassination of Gedaliah and his Babylonian guards resulted in another deportation in 582. A number of Jews fled to Egypt, and Judah may have become part of the province of Samaria (Jer 39:11–44:30).

Literary and archaeological evidence shows that Judah was severely devastated and depopulated in the sixth century (compare Lam 2:2,5,11-12,20-22; 4:9-20; 5:1-18). Thousands of men had been deported. Second Kings 24:14-16 gives the number as eighteen thousand men (excluding their families) for 597 B.C. alone. According to Ezra-Nehemiah the number returning over some period of time was 42,360 (Ezra 2:64), yet we know that many remained in Babylon. In addition to those deported, thousands had died either in battle or of starvation and disease. Many were executed, and many had fled. Except for the Negev and along the northern frontier, virtually all the fortified towns in Judah had been destroyed. One archaeological estimate is that of a population of 220,000 to 300,000 in preexilic Judah, only about 150,000 remained after the exile. Others have claimed the number was much less.

Refugees drifted back gradually (compare Jer 40:11-12), but the conditions in Judah were very poor. During the exile, the Edomites, having been driven from their homeland by Arabs, began taking over southern Judah. Those returning from Babylon at the end of the sixth century held little but Jerusalem and its suburbs. The temple site was still considered holy and was visited by pilgrims who continued to make sacrifice throughout the exile (Jer 41:4-5).

Those captured in battle were probably taken to Babylon as slaves. Most of the other exiles were reduced to poverty. Nevertheless, for most Jews in Babylon, after their recovery from the emotional and physical distress of being uprooted (compare Pss 74; 137), conditions were good (Jer 29:4-7; Ezek 8:1; Ezra 2:65-69). Only the king and his family captured in 597 B.C. were confined. The rest were free to settle in communities and to engage in normal agriculture or trade. They likely experienced economic well-being and limited autonomy. Not surprisingly, considering conditions in Judah and Babylon, later Jewish leaders had difficulty getting large numbers to return with them to Judah. □

This ninth- or eighth-century B.C. relief from Carchemish (site of Pharaoh Necho's defeat to Nebuchadnezzar in 605 B.C.) shows two warriors probably of the king's bodyguard.

tion to Babylon (Jer 36:29). The historian attributed Judah's continued subservience to the wickedness of Manasseh, whose reign grieved the LORD (2 Kgs 24:1-7).

Jehoiachin, Jehoiakim's son, was eighteen when he ascended the throne at his father's death (598 B.C.). He too rebelled, and Nebuchadnezzar besieged Jerusalem. He deposed the young king after only three months (compare Jer 52:31-34). At that time the temple and palace were stripped (compare 2 Kgs 20:17), and the king's household as well as the city's leading citizens were exiled (compare Jer 22:24-30). Nebuchadnezzar installed Mattaniah, Jehoiachin's uncle, as king and renamed him "Zedekiah" (2 Kgs 24:8-17).

25:1-30
The Destruction of Jerusalem

Zedekiah (597–586 B.C.), in spite of Jeremiah's warnings (compare Jer 37–39; 52), led a final rebellion against the Babylonians in 588 B.C. After a lengthy siege and resulting famine, the city fell in July 586 B.C. Zedekiah fled but was captured and taken to Nebuchadnezzar's headquarters in Riblah. There Zedekiah witnessed the execution of his sons before he was blinded and led to Babylon for imprisonment (2 Kgs 25:1-7). Nebuzaradan, the Babylonian commander, raided the city, confiscated the temple furniture, and burned Jerusalem to the ground (25:8-21). Gedaliah was appointed governor but was assassinated in an anti-Babylonian coup. For fear of Babylonian reprisals, many of the Jews fled to Egypt (25:22-26).

The final paragraph of the book indicates how the sacred historian responded to the catastrophe. He saw in the improved conditions of King Jehoiachin's imprisonment a message of hope. Babylon's ruler, Evil-Merodach (561–560 B.C.), released Jehoiachin from prison and placed him under house arrest, where he drew a royal stipend from the Babylonian treasury (25:27-30). Although Jerusalem was no more, Israel still had its king. If God so pleased, Judah could be restored to its land.

Ethical and Theological Significance

Again and again 2 Kings warns against the dangers of compromise. Those who compromise their witness for selfish gain risk God's judgment. Gehazi's attempt to profit financially from Elisha's healing ministry is a stern warning to Christians that the gospel is not a "mask to cover up greed" (1 Thess 2:5).

In 2 Kings dependence on other gods led to death for both individuals and nations. If our security rests on our own wealth or military might, we are trusting in a house built on sand (compare Matt 7:26). The failures of the kings of Israel and Judah remind Christians to fix their trust on God alone.

The kings of Israel and Judah often sought to preserve national security at the expense of their distinctive religious convictions. The people God freed from Egyptian slavery should have avoided political situations that compromised their freedom to worship their God. Baptists have championed a free church in a free state as the best setting for Christians to exercise their discipleship.

The tragic end of the nations of Israel and Judah demonstrates the awful consequences of sin. However, no catastrophe is so great that God cannot work through it to give hope to His people.

Questions for Reflection

1. What can be learned from 2 Kings about the holiness of God?
2. How should God's people live in a society that is wicked?
3. How can God's people have hope in the midst of social and political unrest?
4. What is spiritual revival? How does God respond to repentance and prayers for revival?
5. In what ways does God use wicked people or nations to achieve His purposes?

Sources for Additional Study

McNeeley, Richard I. *First and Second Kings*. Chicago: Moody, 1978.

Millard, Alan. *1 Kings - 2 Chronicles*. Ft. Washington, Pa: Christian Literature Crusade, 1985.

Vos, Howard F. *1, 2 Kings*. Grand Rapids: Zondervan, 1989.

1 CHRONICLES

Like the Books of Samuel and Kings, 1 and 2 Chronicles were originally one book. The Hebrew title means *the chronological events of the period*. The Greek version, which divided Chronicles into two books, entitled them "The Things Left Out" or "Omitted." This title reflects the misunderstanding that Chronicles was written to supplement the events left out of Samuel and Kings. The English name is derived from the Latin Vulgate's title, "The Chronicle of the Whole Sacred History."

The Books of Chronicles are not to be confused with the "annals of the kings of Judah" and "annals of the kings of Israel," which were official royal accounts used in writing 1 and 2 Kings (for example, 1 Kgs 14:19; 15:7).

The Greek and English traditions have the Books of Chronicles in the collection of historical books, with Chronicles followed by Ezra and Nehemiah. In the Hebrew collection, however, Chronicles is the last book in the canon. There it is grouped with the Writings and is preceded by Ezra-Nehemiah.

The author is unknown. Tradition assigned the book to Ezra (compare 2 Chr 36:22-23 with Ezra 1:1-2). The author probably was a Levite or someone closely associated with the temple since Chronicles focuses on worship in Jerusalem. Many scholars believed that an individual or school, called the "Chronicler," produced Chronicles and Ezra-Nehemiah as one continuous history. Others have rejected this idea of a "Chronicler's History," arguing that all ancient traditions separated the books and that they have a different viewpoint (see "The Historical Books" and "Ezra"). For this latter group, the term "Chronicler" is limited to the author of 1 and 2 Chronicles.

The date of Chronicles is about 400 B.C. Chronicles uses sources from an earlier period, particularly the canonical works of Genesis, Samuel, and Kings. Other sources named are "the annotations on the book of the kings" (2 Chr 24:27); "the book of the kings of Israel and Judah" (27:7; 35:27), which also contained oracles by Isaiah (32:32); "the annals of the kings of Israel" (20:34; 33:18); "the records of the seers" (33:19); and Isaiah's prophetic works (26:22).

Differences with Samuel and Kings

While Chronicles shows a dependence on the books of Samuel and Kings, there are remarkable differences in content and theological perspective.

1. Chronicles was not written to supplement these former works, nor was it simply a rewriting. These books offer a fresh interpretation of Israel's monarchy. Samuel and Kings addressed the exilic community and explained why Israel's monarchy failed. Chronicles addressed the restored community and explained that God still had a purpose for Israel. Chronicles was written from a priestly perspective, whereas Samuel and Kings were written from a prophetic perspective.

2. Chronicles attempts a comprehensive history, beginning with Adam, but Samuel and Kings are limited to the time of the monarchy. In the Book of Kings, Judah still awaits release from captivity, but Chronicles ends with the decree of Cyrus anticipating Judah's return.

3. Chronicles features David and the kings of Judah and avoids commenting on the Northern Kingdom. Even the reign of Saul is treated as a preamble to David's accession. Chronicles tells the positive contributions of David and Solomon and omits unflattering events in their reigns.

4. The palace is center stage in Samuel and Kings, but the temple is central in Chronicles. For the Chronicler the lasting contribution of the kings was religious. Samuel and Kings condemn sin and urge repentance, but Chronicles encourages the faithful to make a new start.

Theme

God promised David an eternal throne, choosing David to found the true center of worship in Jerusalem and appointing Solomon to build His temple (28:4-7).

I. Genealogies: God's Redemptive Plan (1:1–9:44)
II. God's Redemptive Plan through David (10:1–20:8)
III. God's Redemptive Plan of Worship (21:1–29:30)

Purpose and Theology

1. First and Second Chronicles give the history of Israel from its ancestral roots in Adam to the period of restoration after the Babylonian exile. An important function of the genealogies that begin Chronicles is to provide continuity in God's plan for Israel. The retelling of Israel's history was to encourage the Jewish community by emphasizing God's selection of Israel and His promises to them. Chronicles shows that the enduring purpose of Israel was the worship of God. Israel could take heart because, although it had no king, the temple remained.

2. The dominant motif is the temple and its service. Chronicles focuses on the institution of worship, especially music, and the role of the Levites. The book gives attention to David's preparations for the building of the temple almost to the exclusion of other accomplishments (1 Chr 6:48-49; 22:1–26:32; 28:1–29:9).

3. First Chronicles exhorts Israel to be faithful so that the redemptive plan promised to David might be fulfilled through them (17:7-15; 28:4-7). God's reward for faithfulness is emphasized, particularly in response to prayer (4:9-10; 5:20-22; 16:8-36; 17:16-27; 29:10-19). The Chronicler explained that unfaithfulness was the reason for the failure of Israel's kings and the exile (5:25-26; 9:1b; 10:13-14).

4. Since God is holy, His people were to worship properly as Moses had commanded and as David ordained. As a consequence of God's holiness, anyone who profaned the sanctity of worship or transgressed the law experienced His wrath (13:10-12; 15:11-15; 21:1-8; 27:23-24; 28:7). David sang of God's holiness when he invoked all creation to worship Him (16:10,29,35; 17:20; 29:11,16).

Tiglath Pileser III (or Pul) is depicted on this relief found at Calah on the Tigris River (see 1 Chr 5:6,26).

5. The LORD is also sovereign in world affairs, in particular the rise and success of David's kingdom (1:1–9:44; 17:7-15; 28:4-7; 29:25). Three times the Chronicler returned to the giving of the Davidic covenant (17:1-27; 22:6-13; 28:1-10). Chronicles tends to speak of God's direct involvement (14:2,10,15; 18:6,13) whereas Samuel and Kings include intermediate causes. The plans for the Jerusalem temple are attributed to God's direct revelation and not the creation of David (28:12).

6. Leadership is a significant teaching for the author, who sought to encourage Israel in a day when it had no king. The messianic expectation was still alive for the author, who therefore idealized David's role (17:7-15; 28:5; 29:23). The Chronicler emphasized the spiritual leadership of the nation, particularly the Levites and officials (15:2-27; 23:2–26:32; 29:1-9).

GENEALOGIES: GOD'S REDEMPTIVE PLAN (1 CHR 1:1–9:44)

The genealogies are not a sterile recitation of names. They are a significant statement of Israel's place in the whole sweep of God's plan for the world. The Chronicler found the proper appreciation of universal history in the founding of Israel, the appointment of David, and the building of the temple, where God resided in the world (a foretaste of the true Temple, Jesus Christ, who resided in the world as a man; see John 1–2).

1:1–3:24
The Promise from Adam to David

The genealogies from Adam to Abraham (1:1-27), from Jacob (Israel) to David (2:1-17), and from David to his postexilic descendants (3:1-24) show the continuity of God's redemptive plan. The divine plan, which began before creation, began to develop in the realm of history in the garden with Adam (Gen 3:15) and continued through Abraham who would bring blessing to the world (12:1-3). This promise of blessing would be realized in the lineage of David (2 Sam 7). The genealogy of David is traced by the Chronicler beyond the exile (1 Chr 3:17-24), indicating that the promise had not been abandoned. The purposes of God always outweigh the circumstances of Israel's political misfortunes.

4:1–5:26
Judah, Simeon, Reuben, Gad, and Half of Manasseh

More descendants of Judah are listed (4:1-23). Among

The Moslem Dome of the Rock mosque built on the site of Solomon's Temple in Jerusalem.

them is Jabez, who is a model of the faith (4:9-10). Simeon's descendants are listed next (4:24-43) since this tribe was assimilated into Judah's territory (Josh 19:1-9). The families beyond the Jordan are listed, with Reuben honored as the firstborn (1 Chr 5:1-26).

6:1-81
Levi

The lineage of the high priest is carefully traced (6:1-15,50-53) and distinguished from the other Levitical families (6:16-30) since only Aaron's sons were permitted to offer sacrifice at the temple (6:49). The Levites served as temple musicians and carried out other temple duties (6:31-48,54-81).

7:1-40
Issachar, Benjamin, Naphtali, Half of Manasseh, Ephraim, and Asher

The remaining tribes are listed, but Dan and Zebulon are absent since the Chronicler wanted to retain the traditional number of twelve tribes.

8:1–9:44
The Family of Saul

The narration repeats that Saul was from the Benjamites who lived in Gibeon and not the Benjamites of Jerusalem (8:28-29,33; 9:35-44). The Chronicler reaffirmed that the LORD had chosen David and Jerusalem, not Saul of Gibeon. Those among the tribes who returned from the exile and resided in Jerusalem were cataloged by genealogies (9:1-34).

GOD'S REDEMPTIVE PLAN THROUGH DAVID (1 CHR 10:1–20:28)

The episode of Saul's death provides the background for David's kingdom (chap. 10). David's rule was glorious (chaps. 11–12), and the pinnacle of his reign was the bringing of the ark into Jerusalem (chaps. 13–16). God honored David's desire to build a temple by granting him an eternal throne (chap. 17). David prospered all the more because of God's blessing and dedicated to the LORD the spoils of his victories (chaps. 18–20).

10:1-14
Saul's Unfaithfulness

Saul's final defeat and suicide are told (compare 1 Sam 31). The Chronicler concluded that Saul's death was God's judgment on unfaithfulness (1 Chr 10:13-14; compare 1 Sam 13; 15; 28).

11:1-47
God Prospers David

David became king according to God's promise (1 Chr 11:1-3; 2 Sam 5:1-3). He conquered the stubborn Jebusites in Jerusalem and became increasingly powerful because the LORD was with him (1 Chr 11:4-9; 2 Sam 5:6-12). The evidence of David's strength was the awesome deeds his corp of mighty men accomplished (1 Chr 11:10-47; 2 Sam 23:8-39).

12:1-40
The Army of God

Those who joined David at Ziklag (1 Sam 27:2-6) were numerous and from many tribes throughout Israel (1 Chr 12:1-21). His army was like the army of God (12:22). All the tribes rejoiced at David's coronation as king over all Israel (12:23-40).

13:1-14
God's Holiness and the Ark

Saul did not inquire of the LORD during his reign, but David with all Israel's consent attempted to return the ark of God from Abinadab's house at Kiriath Jearim (13:1-6; 2 Sam 6:2-11).

Although the people were zealous for the LORD, they sinned by transporting the ark improperly on a cart (1 Chr 15:13). According to Moses' instructions, the Levites were to carry it by poles without touching it. The penalty for disobedience was death (Exod 25:14; Num 3:31; 4:15). Uzzah steadied the ark when it slipped from the cart. The LORD struck him dead. When David witnessed this, he feared the LORD as never before. The ark was left in the care of Obed-Edom, and the LORD blessed his household because of the ark (1 Chr 13:7-14).

14:1-17
God Establishes David

All the nations began to fear David (14:17). Hiram, king of Tyre, sent building materials for David's palace. David knew that the LORD had established his reign and a growing family (14:1-7; 2 Sam 5:11-16). The LORD led David's armies into battle and delivered up the Philistines (1 Chr 14:8-16; 2 Sam 5:17-25).

15:1-29
The Ark Rests in the City of David

Jerusalem was called the "City of David" because David captured it as a royal possession (11:4-9). He attempted again to return the ark and was successful because he carefully followed the LORD's word (Exod 25:14; Num 4:5-6,15). The priests and Levites consecrated themselves in preparation to carry the ark (1 Chr 15:1-15).

David, an accomplished musician himself (compare 1 Sam 16:18,23), prepared the people for worship by establishing a complete orchestra and appointing three Levitical choirs under the direction of Heman, Asaph, and Ethan (Jeduthun; compare the superscriptions of Pss 50; 73–83; 88–89). When the ark was brought to Jerusalem, David ordered sacrifices offered to God. David's, wife Michal, Saul's daughter, disdained David's free worship (1 Chr 15:16-19; 2 Sam 6:12-23).

These small bronze cymbals (from the time of the Divided Kingdom) were strapped to players' fingers (1 Chr 15:19).

16:1-43
David's Prayer

After David worshiped with sacrifice (1 Chr 16:1-3), he called for the Levites to offer thanksgiving, prayer, and praise (16:4-6).

David presented a thanksgiving hymn. The Chronicler compiled excerpts from well-known psalms to convey the meaning of David's hymn for the Chronicler's community (1 Chr 16:8-22; Ps 105:1-15; 1 Chr 16:23-33; Ps 96; 1 Chr 16:34-36; Ps 106:1,47-48). David called the righteous to worship (16:7-13), extolled the LORD's grace from the days of Abraham (16:14-22), and concluded by invoking all creation to worship the Creator (16:23-36).

David provided for the daily sacrifice by appointing Asaph to minister at the ark in Jerusalem and Zadok to serve the tabernacle at Gibeon (16:37-43).

17:1-27
God's Promises to David

After David had brought the ark to Jerusalem, he decided to build a "house" (temple) for the LORD. By divine oracle the prophet Nathan learned that God would instead build David a dynastic "house." God promised David a kingdom, a throne and an eternal dynastic house. David's son would build the LORD's house and would rule as God's son over the LORD's kingdom (17:1-14). The

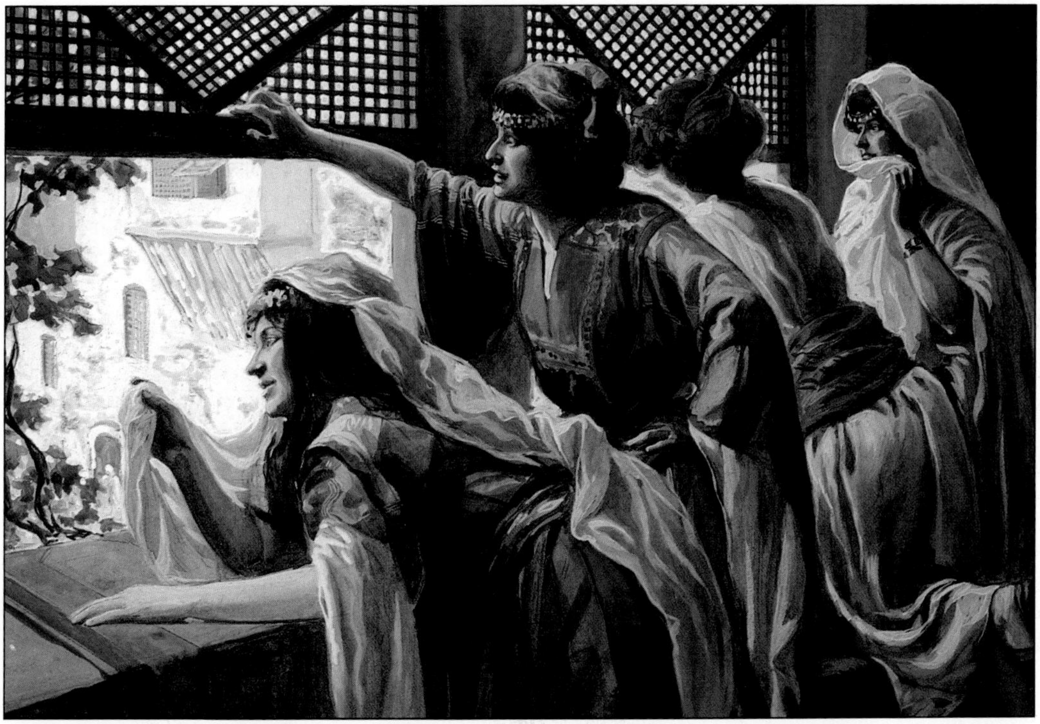

David's wife, Michal (Saul's daughter), and her attendants watching with disdain as David dances before the ark of the covenant (1 Chr 15:29).

Chronicler explained elsewhere that God prohibited David from building the temple because David's career was known for war and bloodshed (22:8; 28:3).

When Nathan reported the oracle, David prayed, admitting his unworthiness and marveling at the magnitude of God's greatness and grace (17:15-27). The ultimate fulfillment of God's pledge is realized in David's Greater Son, Jesus Christ (compare Luke 1:32-33).

18:1-17
David's Continued Conquests

The sincerity of God's promise to David was evidenced by the immediate victories the LORD granted over the Philistines, Arameans, and Edomites. David responded with thanksgiving by giving the spoils of battle to the LORD (18:1-13). The Chronicler concluded: "The LORD gave David victory everywhere he went" (18:6,13). As a result of his new triumphs and expanding kingdom, David increased his governing bureaucracy (18:14-17; 2 Sam 8:15-18).

19:1-19
David Defeats the Ammonites

The LORD remained faithful to David by enabling his victory over a coalition of Ammonites and Arameans. David sent a delegation of envoys to befriend Hanun, who succeeded his father, Nahash, as king of the Ammonites. But Hanun spurned David's offer of peace (1 Chr 19:1-5). A major battle ensued, and David's troops outmaneuvered the enemy (19:6-19; 2 Sam 10:1-19).

20:1-8
Wars with Rabbah and Philistia

Joab, David's military commander, routed the Ammonites by capturing their capital city Rabbah (1 Chr 29:1-3; 2 Sam 12:26-31). David's champions subjugated the Philistine giants (1 Chr 20:4-8; 2 Sam 21:15-22). Typical of the Chronicler, he omitted the embarrassing incident of David's sin with Bathsheba (2 Sam 11) and left out the account of Absalom's rebellion (2 Sam 13–19). Chronicles passes over these accounts because they do not serve its purpose. The Chronicler overlooked moral defeats and highlighted David's victories to draw attention to God's sovereignty in David's life. God succeeded in using David to fulfill His purposes for him. David's greatest accomplishments were not political but spiritual—moving the ark to Jerusalem and preparing for the construction of the temple.

GOD'S REDEMPTIVE PLAN OF WORSHIP (1 CHR 21:1–29:30)

The final section features the preparations David made for the building of the temple. For the Chronicler this was the most important contribution of the king and predominated his account of David's reign. The temple site was divinely chosen (chaps. 21–22). David organized the Levites and priests for the temple work (chaps. 23–26), organized the the army (chap. 27), and held a national convocation. There the people contributed gifts, and David appointed Solomon king and Zadok priest.

21:1-30
Atonement for David's Evil

While the Chronicler was careful to extol David's virtues, he included the sin of David's census because it explained the choice of the temple site. David took a census of his military troops, presumably because of his pride (21:1-7; compare Exod 30:11-16).

The parallel in 2 Samuel ascribes David's temptation to God (2 Sam 24:1), but the Chronicler attributed it to Satan (1 Chr 21:1). The reason for this difference is the theological purpose of each writing. The Old Testament ascribes all things to the sovereignty of God, indicating His control over all creation (Isa 45:7). The Chronicler, however, emphasized the holiness of God and therefore featured Satan as the direct cause for David's sin. Elsewhere in the Old Testament, the Satan (*the accuser*) acts under God's direction (Job 1:6; Zech 3:1).

Although David confessed his sin, he suffered the consequences of his evil deed. God sent an angel to chasten Jerusalem by a plague. To atone for his sins, David built an altar of sacrifice at the site of Araunah's threshing floor. David bought the place, though Araunah volunteered it, because David knew that true atonement always requires payment (1 Chr 21:25-26). God consumed the offering with fire from heaven, and the plague ceased (21:27-30).

22:1-19
David's Charge to Solomon

In Kings David's charge included the elimination of his enemies (1 Kgs 1–2). The Chronicler, whose interest was in David's role as a spiritual leader, omitted this and told only of Solomon's appointment to build the temple.

David established Araunah's threshing floor as the future temple site. He gathered materials and workmen in preparation for the building because Solomon was inexperienced (22:1-5). He charged Solomon to build the edifice, explaining that he was disqualified because of his reputation as a warrior. Peaceful Solomon would be permitted to build the temple. David illustrated his point by making a word play on the name of Solomon (*shelomoh*), which is similar in sound to "peace" (*shalom*). David finally instructed Solomon to be faithful so that he might have success. David assembled numerous materials and workers to assure Solomon's achievement.

David commanded his officials to help in the task and to serve the LORD with full devotion. He believed that for this purpose God had granted them victory over their enemies (22:17-19).

23:1-32
Organizing the Levites

The Chronicler was not concerned with the political details of Solomon's accession (compare 1 Kgs 1–2). He presented the transition as peaceful and orderly (23:1).

The appointment and work of the Levites was divinely ordained through Moses (Num 3:1–4:49). David organized the Levites into three groups by families—Gershonites (1 Chr 23:7-11), Kohathites (23:12-20) and Merarites (23:21-23). The Levites were assigned to assist the priests' work in the service of the temple (23:24-32).

24:1-31
Organizing the Priests

Aaron's descendants had the exclusive assignment of ministering before the ark (23:13-14; 24:19; Num 18:1-7). The descendants of Eleazar and Ithamar were divided into twenty-four orders, which served at the temple in rotation (24:1-19; compare Luke 1:5,8-9). The order of service for the remaining Levites was determined by the casting of lots in the same manner for as the priests (1 Chr 24:20-31).

25:1-31
Music for the LORD

David established three musical guilds under his supervision (25:6). Asaph, Heman, and Jeduthun (Ethan) were Levites David appointed for the musical accompaniment of temple worship (25:1-8; compare 15:16-22). The guilds were drawn from all age groups and those with differing musical skills. They were divided into twenty-four courses like the priests (25:9-31).

26:1-32
Serving the LORD's House

Levites from the families of Korah and Merari were entrusted with the security of the temple as gatekeepers (26:1-19). They were chosen because of their exceptional ability (26:8). The gatekeepers were stationed day and night to protect the temple (26:14-19). The Levites also

MUSICAL INSTRUMENTS OF THE OLD TESTAMENT

TYPE	NAME	SCRIPTURE REFERENCES	LANGUAGE OF ORIGIN	NIV TRANSLATION
PERCUSSION	Bagpipe	Dan 3:5,7,10,15	Aramaic: *sumponeyah*	pipes
	Bells	(1) Exod 28:33-34; 39:25-26 (2) Zech 14:20	(1) Hebrew: *paamon* (2) Hebrew: *metsilloth*	(1) bells (2) bells of the horses
	Cymbals	(1) 2 Sam 6:5; Ps 150:5 (2) 1 Chr 13:8;15:16,19; 2 Chr 5:12-13; Ezra 3:10; Neh 12:27	(1) Hebrew: *tseltselim* (2) Hebrew: *metsiltayim*	(1) cymbals (2) cymbals
	Sistrum	2 Sam 6:5	Hebrew: *menaanim*	sistrums
	Tambourine	Gen 31:27; Exod 15:20; Judg 11:34; 1 Sam 10:5; 18:6; 2 Sam 6:5; 1 Chr 13:8; Job 21:12; Pss 81:2; 149:3; Isa 5:12; Jer 31:4	Hebrew: *toph*	tambourine
STRING	Harp	(1) 1 Sam 10:5; Neh 12:27; Isa 5:12; 14:11; Amos 5:23; 6:5 (2) Dan 3:5,7,10,15	(1) Hebrew: *nebel* (2) Aramaic: *pesanterin*	(1) lyres, harp(s) (2) harp
	Harplike Instrument	Dan 3:5,7,10,15	Aramaic: *sabbeka*	lyre
	Lyre	(1) Gen 4:21; 1 Sam 10:5; 2 Sam 6:5; Neh 12:27 (2) Dan 3:5,7,10,15	(1) Hebrew: *kinnor* (2) Aramaic: *qitharos, qathros*	(1) harp (2) zither
	Zither	Pss 33:2; 92:3; 144:9	Hebrew: *nebel asor*	ten-stringed lyre
WIND	Double Pipe	1 Sam 10:5; 1 Kgs 1:40; Isa 5:12; Jer 48:36	Hebrew: *chalil*	flutes
	Horn, Cornet	Dan 3:5,7,10,15	Aramaic: *qeren*	horn
	Pipe, Reed	Dan 3:5,7,10,15	Aramaic: *mashroqitha*	flute
	Ram's Horn	(1) Josh 6:4-20; Judg 7:16-22; 2 Sam 15:10; Pss 47:5; 150:3; Amos 2:2 (2) Exod 19:13	(1) Hebrew: *shophar* (2) Aramaic: *yobel*	(1) rams' horns, trumpets (2) ram's horn
	Trumpet	(1) Num 10:2-10; 1 Chr 15:24,28; 2 Chr 15:14; 23:13; Ps 98:6; Hos 5:8 (2) Ezek 7:14	(1) Hebrew: *chatsotsrah* (2) Hebrew: *taqoa*	(1) trumpet (2) trumpet
	Vertical Flute	Gen 4:21; Job 21:12; 30:3; Ps 150:4	Hebrew: *uggab*	flute

provided caretakers for the treasuries (26:20-28). The temple's treasuries included gifts dedicated by David, Samuel, and Saul (26:26-28). The Levites collected taxes for the king (25:29-32).

27:1-34
Organizing the Army and Administrators

The twelve army divisions (27:1-15) and the officers of Israel's tribes (27:16-24) are listed. Population figures were not kept because of God's wrath (27:16-24; compare 21:1-7). Administrators over civil matters are named, followed by the members of the royal cabinet.

28:1-21
Providential Plans

David assembled Israel to witness his final charge to Solomon. David was precluded from building the temple, but God providentially prepared Solomon to accomplish that task. David repeated the provisions of God's covenant and commissioned Solomon to build the temple (28:1-10; see also 17:1-27; 22:1-19).

David delivered the plans for the temple to Solomon that he had written under the LORD's guidance. Just as the LORD revealed the tabernacle plan to Moses (Exod 25:1–30:38), the Spirit instructed David's mind.

The plans included the structure of the temple, the treasuries, storehouses, and the holy furniture (1 Chr 28:11-19). The specific document written by David is not preserved in Scripture, but the substance of it probably is found in Chronicles where the temple and its worship are described (1 Chr 22:1–26:32; 2 Chr 3:1–4:22). David assured Solomon that the LORD would help him and that the men and materials were prepared (28:20-21).

29:1-30
Worship through Giving

David exhorted the assembly to follow his example of stewardship. The people rejoiced when they saw their leaders give willingly and liberally (29:1-9). David led Israel in worship, praising God for His greatness and acknowledging that the gifts came from the LORD Himself (29:10-20). The congregation recognized Solomon as their king and Zadok as their priest and pledged their allegiance. The LORD exalted Solomon in the eyes of Israel (29:21-25).

David died after forty years of service to the LORD. The Chronicler concluded by referring the reader to the records of Samuel, Nathan, and Gad, which give a comprehensive account of David's reign (29:26-29).

Theological and Ethical Significance

The Persian period, in which Chronicles was compiled, was a time of half-fulfilled hopes. The Jews had been allowed to return from Babylonian exile but without a king. They had been allowed to rebuild the temple, but the "second temple" paled in comparison with the first. The Chronicler reaffirmed for that generation (and ours) that despite the ambiguities of history God is in control and involved in the lives of His people. First Chronicles overlooks the moral defeats and highlights the victories of David to draw attention to God's sovereignty in his life. God succeeded in using David to fulfill His purposes for him. Chronicles challenges today's Christians to trace the high points of God's working in their own lives. Our hope is that the One who began a good work in us will complete it (Phil 1:6).

First Chronicles illustrates a responsible use of Scripture. The Chronicler's use of the Pentateuch and Prophets to shed new light on his major sources—the Books of Samuel and Kings—demonstrates that Scripture is the best guide to the interpretation of Scripture. The need to interpret "the old, old story" of Samuel and Kings for a new, postexilic generation led to the writing of 1 and 2 Chronicles. Each generation is faced with the task of confronting their world with the truth of Scripture in a way that speaks to the distinctive needs of its age.

First Chronicles recognizes that the greatest accomplishment of David's dynasty was spiritual—the organization and support of temple worship. Worship continues to be the center of Christian life. Worship empowers believers for lives of Christian service.

Questions for Reflection

1. How can a person's family roots lead to salvation?
2. What does 1 Chronicles teach about the nature and practice of worship, particularly the use of music?
3. What does God expect of those who lead congregational worship?
4. What can God's people depend on in times of discouragement?
5. What does 1 Chronicles teach about stewardship?

Sources for Additional Study

McConville, J. G. *I & II Chronicles.* Philadelphia: Westminster, 1984.

Sailhamer, John. *First and Second Chronicles.* Chicago: Moody, 1983.

Wilcock, Michael. *The Message of Chronicles.* Downers Grove: InterVarsity, 1987.

2 CHRONICLES

First and Second Chronicles are one continuous narrative (compare the discussion of 1 Chronicles). Second Chronicles describes the construction of the Solomonic temple and the religious life of the nation under Judah's kings.

Theme

God dwells in His holy temple and is faithful to His promise to redeem Israel (7:12).

I. Solomon's Reign and God's Temple (1:1–9:31)
II. Spiritual Lessons from Judah's Kings (10:1–36:13)
III. God's Temple and Cyrus's Decree (36:14-23)

Purpose and Theology

1. Second Chronicles continues the story of God's redemptive plan for Israel presented in 1 Chronicles. The break between the books is a convenient one because the first half ends with David's preparations for the temple and the second describes the building and history of the temple under Judah's kings. Second Chronicles covers four and a half centuries, from Solomon's reign (about 971 B.C.) to Cyrus's edict (539 B.C.).

2. Second Chronicles narrates Israel's past from the standpoint of its religious history. The building of the temple is the central concern (chaps. 2–7). The history of the monarchy is told from the perspective of how temple worship fared under Judah's kings. For example, the reign of Hezekiah is given greater attention because of his special temple reforms (chaps. 29–32). As in 1 Chronicles, the role of temple personnel, music, and festivals is featured (2 Chr 5:4-14; 11:13-17; 17:8-9; 20:21; 23:2–24:16; 29:4–30:27; 31:2-19; 34:9-30; 35:1-19). The Chronicler explained in his concluding sermon that the temple's destruction occurred because of Judah's sinful leadership and not God's negligence (36:14-19). However, the book ends on a note of promise with Cyrus's edict to rebuild the temple (36:22-23). Although the restored community lived under Persian dominance, the temple's rebuilding indicated God's presence as in Solomon's days.

3. A recurring theme in Chronicles is faithfulness to God's covenant. In 2 Chronicles the kings of Judah are judged on the basis of their fidelity to Moses' commandments (6:16; 7:17-18). Those kings who were faithful prospered in their reigns, such as the reformers Asa (14:4), Jotham (27:6), Hezekiah (31:20-21), and Josiah (34:31-33; 35:26). The kings that were unfaithful to the law of Moses met with disaster. Jehoram experienced disease and defeat (21:12-20), Joash was assassinated (24:24-25), Uzziah suffered leprosy (26:16-21), Ahaz was humiliated (28:19,22), and Manasseh was imprisoned (33:7-11). The presence of a Davidic king by itself did not guarantee God's favor on Israel. Obedience was the LORD's requirement.

4. Second Chronicles emphasizes God's faithfulness, particularly His forgiveness and promises of restoration (6:21,25,38-39; 7:14; 30:9). The LORD accepted the repentant prayers of Rehoboam (12:5-8), Hezekiah (31:25-26), and Manasseh (33:12-13). God also was faithful to His promises to David, although Judah's kings acted wickedly (21:7).

5. An important theme in 2 Chronicles is God's holiness shown by His anger against the wicked. In particular the kings who committed idolatry merited the God's anger (12:5,12; 21:12-19; 25:14-15; 33:6). Kings Jehoshaphat (19:10), Hezekiah (29:8-10; 30:8), and Josiah (34:21,23-28) understood this principle and implored Israel to obey God's law to avert His anger. Even those kings who won approval, such as Joash (24:17-25) and Hezekiah (32:25), experienced God's anger when they sinned. The Chronicler attributed Jerusalem's fall to God's wrath (36:16).

6. The theme of God's sovereignty in human affairs continues in 2 Chronicles. Cyrus's edict is the parade example of how God intervened to change the course of Israel's fortunes (36:22-23). In its recorded sermons and prayers 2 Chronicles reflects God's intervention (6:5-6; 7:17-22; 9:8; 13:5-12; 20:6-7; 32:6-8; 34:24,28). The LORD established kings (17:5; 20:15; 26:5), aroused enemies (21:16; 28:5; 33:11; 36:17), and afflicted or deliv-

ered kings (13:15; 21:18; 32:21-22).

SOLOMON'S REIGN AND GOD'S TEMPLE (2 CHR 1:1–9:31)

The introductory section is occupied with the temple and Solomon's role in its construction (chaps. 1–7). The splendor of Solomon's kingdom was evidence for the Chronicler that Solomon as David's son was the recipient of God's covenant promises (chaps. 8–9).

1:1-17
God Establishes Solomon

The Chronicler omitted Solomon's early struggle for control (1 Kgs 1–2). In his view the highlight of Solomon's career was the temple construction. The LORD elevated Solomon in the eyes of the people. Solomon worshiped the LORD at the tabernacle and sacrificial altar at Gibeon (2 Chr 1:2-6). The LORD granted to Solomon his request for wisdom but also rewarded him with the promise of riches and power (1:7-12). The Chronicler demonstrated the truth of God's promise by listing Solomon's wealth and military power (1:13-17).

2:1-18
Solomon's Letter to Hiram

Solomon contracted with Hiram, king of Tyre, for building materials and skilled workmen (2:1-10). In his letter to Hiram, Solomon indicated Israel's God was not a deity who could be housed in a temple. Still the LORD was worthy of the very best talent and materials (2:5-6). Hiram replied by confessing to the greatness of Solomon's God. He agreed to send a craftsman of Hebrew extraction named Huram-Abi and all the materials requested (2:11-16). Solomon conscripted the aliens in his kingdom to form a large labor force (2:17-18).

3:1-17
Solomon Builds the Temple

The the temple site was Araunah's threshing floor, where David offered atonement for Israel (1 Chr 21:28–22:1). The Chronicler identified the site as Mount Moriah, where Abraham offered sacrifice (2 Chr 3:1; compare Gen 22:2,14). The author emphasized the temple's role as the place of sacrifice where the LORD could be worshiped (3:1-2). More detail is given to the holy of holies than the temple's design because it was the place of meeting with God (3:3-17).

4:1-22
The Temple Furniture

The bronze altar, molten sea, basins, lampstands, tables, and courtyards are described (4:1-11a; see the feature article "The Temple"). The Chronicler listed the bronze work exquisitely made by Huram-Abi (4:11b-18) and the items of gold Solomon gave (4:19-22).

5:1-14
The Glory of the Ark

Solomon brought the things David dedicated into the sanctuary (5:1). Then he assembled all Israel to accompany the ark into the temple. Typical of the Chronicler's interest, he elaborated on the role of the Levites and the the three musical guilds (5:2-13a). The evidence of God's presence was the glorious cloud that filled the house (5:13b-14).

6:1-42
Faithfulness of God

Solomon extolled God's faithfulness and applied the Davidic covenant to himself, indicating that he had successfully built the promised house of God (6:1-11).

In the presence of all Israel, Solomon humbled himself by kneeling in prayer (6:12-13). His dedicatory prayer centered on God's faithfulness to David and pleaded with God to hear the prayers and supplications that would be offered in the temple. He appealed to God to forgive and restore His people when they offered up prayers of repentance (6:14-39; 1 Kgs 8:12-52). Solomon concluded his prayer with a final hymn of exultation (2 Chr 6:40-42).

7:1-22
Dedication of the Temple

The LORD answered Solomon's prayer by fire from heaven (compare Elijah, 1 Kgs 18:38-39). The LORD's glory filled the place so as to prohibit the priests from entering (2 Chr 7:1-2). The dedicatory service lasted seven days, followed by the seven-day Feast of Tabernacles. The dedication included sacrifice and Levitical music. Worship gladdened the hearts of the people.

The LORD appeared to Solomon a second time as He had at Gibeon. The LORD's message encouraged the people by expressing God's readiness to hear their prayers of repentance (2 Chr 7:13-16). The LORD exhorted Solomon to walk in the ways of his father David (7:17-22; compare 1 Kgs 9:1-9). This message was a reminder in the author's time that the LORD continued to hear Judah's prayers offered in the temple.

8:1-18
God Expands Solomon's Kingdom

The Chronicler showed that the LORD blessed Solomon

(compare 2 Chr 7:18) by describing his many accomplishments. Solomon had extensive building projects, developed international relations with Egypt and Phoenicia, and created a navy for trade (compare 1 Kgs 9:10-28). Typical of the Chronicler, he highlighted Solomon's religious advances. Solomon was careful not to profane God's holy things, and he followed David's instructions (2 Chr 8:11,14-16).

9:1-31
Solomon's Fame and Wealth

The Queen of Sheba (Arabia) visited Solomon and was overwhelmed by his kingdom. She praised the LORD for His love of Israel (9:1-12; 1 Kgs 10:1-13). Solomon's wealth was fulfillment of God's promises to the king (2 Chr 1:12). The writer included the details of Solomon's wealth and his special throne, indicating that no king possessed as many riches (9:13-28; 1 Kgs 10:14-29).

The Chronicler identified particular prophetic writings as additional sources for Solomon's reign (2 Chr 9:29-31; 1 Kgs 11:41-43). The Book of Kings includes Solomon's foreign marriages and the idolatry that caused Israel to deteriorate (1 Kgs 11:1-40). Chronicles omits this because the compiler wanted to limit his account to the positive contributions of Solomon to fulfilling God's redemption through David's seed.

SPIRITUAL LESSONS FROM JUDAH'S KINGS (2 CHR 10:1–36:13)

The second section of the book reviews the spiritual life of the nation under the kings of Judah during the divided monarchy. After the revolt of the northern tribes is recounted (chap. 10), the narrative alternates between periods of spiritual decay and religious reforms. Special consideration is given to the reformers Asa and Jehoshaphat (chaps. 14–20), Joash (chap. 24), Hezekiah (chaps. 29–32), and Josiah (chaps. 34–35). The final period of degeneracy is the last days of Judah's kings (36:1-13).

10:1-19
Rehoboam's Selfishness

Rehoboam (930–913 B.C.) succeeded his father, Solomon, and was confronted at his coronation by the rebel Jeroboam. Jeroboam appealed to Rehoboam to lighten the burden of taxation his father had levied (10:1-4; compare 1 Kgs 11:26-40). Rehoboam followed the poor advice of his young counselors by threatening to increase the levy (2 Chr 10:5-15). The northern tribes rebelled, ousting the king and his officials (10:16-19). This fulfilled Ahijah's prophecy of God's judgment against Solomon's house (1 Kgs 11:29-33). The Chronicler omitted Jeroboam's coronation, because he did not consider Jeroboam or the later kings of the Northern Kingdom legitimate heirs to Israel's throne.

11:1-23
Rehoboam's Strength

Rehoboam wanted to wage war against Jeroboam, but God hindered him (2 Chr 11:1-4; 1 Kgs 12:21-24). Rehoboam then turned his attention to fortifying Judah's cities (2 Chr 11:5-12). Oppressed by Jeroboam, Levites and priests fled to Judah, where they strengthened Rehoboam's kingdom (11:13-17). The strength of Rehoboam's kingdom was also evidenced by the increasing size of his family (11:18-23).

12:1-16
Shishak's Invasion and God's Wrath

Shishak, king of Egypt, invaded Judah and threatened the city of Jerusalem (12:1-4; 1 Kgs 14:25-28). Shishak, whose Egyptian name was Shoshenq I (945–924 B.C.), ruled from Tanis (biblical Zoan). He was Pharaoh when Jeroboam went to Egypt to escape Solomon (1 Kgs 11:40). The Egyptian account of his invasion is recorded on the walls in the temple at Karnak (Thebes). There Shishak listed 150 cities captured in Israel and Judah. The prophet Shemaiah interpreted this invasion as God's wrath because of Judah's sin (12:5-8). Rehoboam paid a heavy ransom, including the temple treasuries and Solomon's vast wealth. Because Rehoboam and the people humbled themselves, the LORD saved Jerusalem from total destruction (12:9-12). Rehoboam's reign was remembered for its years of warfare with Jeroboam (12:13-16).

13:1–14:1
Abijah's Sermon on Apostasy

The author of Kings condemned the reign of Abijah (Abijam; 913–910 B.C.; 1 Kgs 15:1-8), but the Chronicler depicted his reign in a more positive light. Using Iddo's account (2 Chr 13:22), he included Abijah's sermon delivered before a battle against Jeroboam (13:1-3). Abijah charged Jeroboam with apostasy, arguing that God had made a permanent bond ("covenant of salt," compare Num 18:19) with David's descendants (2 Chr 13:5). He defended Jerusalem's worship because it was conducted by priests descended from Aaron as the LORD required (13:4-12). The LORD "routed Jeroboam" (13:15), giving Judah a great victory because they trusted in the LORD.

14:2-15
Asa Relies on the LORD

Asa (910–869 B.C.) enjoyed the blessing of God because

he removed the symbols of paganism (14:1-8; 1 Kgs 15:11-12). The Cushite (Ethiopian) Zerah attacked Judah from the south, but Asa appealed to the LORD and won an impressive victory at Mareshah (2 Chr 14:9-15).

15:1-19
Asa's Religious Reform

The prophet Azariah called for repentance, instigating Asa's religious reforms (15:1-7). Asa removed idols and repaired the LORD's altar. He led Judah to renew its covenant with the LORD not to follow after other gods (15:8-15). Asa also removed the queen mother, Maacah, who had erected an Asherah pole (15:16; compare 1 Kgs 15:13). The LORD gave Judah peace and prosperity (2 Chr 15:17-19).

16:1-14
Asa's Wars and Disease

Baasha, king of Israel (908–886 B.C.) built a fortress at Ramah near Jerusalem. In desperation Asa bribed Ben-Hadad of Aram (Syria) to attack Baasha's territory (16:1-6; 1 Kgs 15:17-22). The prophet Hanani condemned Asa because he relied on Aram rather than the LORD. Asa imprisoned Hanani and oppressed the people (2 Chr 16:7-10). God chastened Judah with continued warfare, and Asa experienced a debilitating foot disease. Asa's funeral was an elaborate spectacle (16:11-14; compare 1 Kgs 15:23-24).

17:1-19
Righteous Jehoshaphat

Jehoshaphat's reign (872–869 B.C.) was remembered for his devotion to the LORD. He sent Levites throughout the territory of Judah to instruct the people in the Book of the Law (17:1-9) The LORD rewarded the king with peace and international respect. His fighting forces grew in strength (17:10-19).

18:1-34
Micaiah Prophesies Ahab's Death

A fuller account of Ahab's reign (874–853 B.C.) is found in Kings. The story of Ahab's death is the only account in the lives of the northern kings the Chronicler used.

Jehoshaphat had allied himself with Ahab through marriage, giving his son Jehoram to Ahab's daughter Athaliah (2 Kgs 8:18,25-26). He was persuaded to join Israel in a campaign against the Arameans at Ramoth Gilead. In contrast to Ahab, Jehoshaphat insisted on hearing from a prophet of the LORD. Ahab reluctantly called for Micaiah, whom he had imprisoned (2 Chr 18:1-11; 1 Kgs 22:1-9).

The false prophet Zedekiah had predicted a victory for Israel, but Micaiah condemned his prophecy, attributing it to a lying spirit. As Ahab returned him to prison, Micaiah predicted Ahab's death (2 Chr 18:12-27; 1 Kgs 22:10-28). Ahab disguised himself as he entered the battle, and Jehoshaphat alone wore his royal regalia. When the enemy mistook Jehoshaphat for Ahab, they pursued him, but the LORD spared Jehoshaphat. Ahab was "at random" mortally wounded by a bowman (2 Chr 18:28-34; 1 Kgs 22:29-36).

19:1-11
Jehoshaphat Repents

The prophet Jehu scolded Jehoshaphat for his alliance with Ahab. He declared God's impending wrath but reminded him that early in his reign he had acted righteously (2 Chr 19:1-3; compare 17:3). The king repented and personally led a revival among the people. He appointed judges who feared the LORD. These included Levites and priests, who taught Judah to love the LORD and fear His wrath (19:4-11).

20:1-37
God Fights for Jehoshaphat

A coalition of Ammonites, Moabites, and others marched against Judah. Jehoshaphat prayed, calling upon God to deliver Judah based on His promises to Abraham (20:1-12). Jahaziel, a Levite, prophesied that the battle was the LORD's, and the Levites worshiped the LORD with a psalm and music (20:13-21). As they worshiped, the LORD responded to their prayers of deliverance by causing the enemy to turn upon one another. The place became known as the Valley of Beracah (*blessing*). The nations recognized that Israel's God had given them the victory, and they feared Jehoshaphat so that Judah remained at peace (20:22-30).

Although Jehoshaphat acted righteously by removing pagan objects of worship, he failed the LORD later in his reign when he became an ally with Ahaziah, Ahab's son (853–852 B.C.). Together they built a navy, but it never set sail from port. The LORD destroyed it as the prophet Eliezer predicted (20:31-37; 1 Kgs 22:41-50).

21:1-20
Jehoram the Murderer

Upon succeeding his father as king, Jehoram murdered his brothers. He was married to Ahab's daughter, Athaliah, and was wicked like his in-laws, the kings of Israel. The LORD used several enemies to trouble his reign (2 Chr 21:1-11; 2 Kgs 8:16-24). The prophet Elijah sent a letter of doom to the king, predicting defeat and disease for the king. The LORD incited the Philistines and Arabs to attack Judah (2 Chr 21:12-17). This is the only account from the life of Elijah that the Chronicler included in his history. Kings does not record this incident.

God inflicted the king with a horrible disease which led to his death. The Chronicler added that no one regretted the king's passing (21:18-20).

22:1-12
Jehu Kills Ahaziah

Jehoram's son, Ahaziah (841 B.C.), was wicked like his father. His mother was Athaliah, the daughter of Ahab. Ahaziah visited his uncle, King Joram of Israel at Jezreel, where he was recuperating from a wound received in battle against the Arameans at Ramoth. God used this evil relationship to end Ahaziah's life (22:1-6). Jehu (841–814 B.C.), a commander in Joram's armies, was commissioned by the LORD's prophet to purge Israel of Baalism and take the throne of Ahab and his son Joram (2 Kgs 9:1–10:36). Jehu executed Ahab's family and also killed Ahaziah and his relatives (2 Chr 22:7-9; 2 Kgs 9:21-29).

Athaliah (841–835 B.C.) seized her opportunity to rule Judah by executing the legitimate heirs to the throne. However, the LORD preserved young Joash, the true heir to David's throne. Jehosheba, the wife of the priest Jehoiada and sister of King Ahaziah, hid him in the temple for six years (2 Chr 22:10-12; 2 Kgs 11:1-3).

23:1-21
Joash Becomes King

A conspiracy led by the priest Jehoiada plotted to enthrone Joash. The Chronicler emphasized the heroism of the priests and omitted the role of the foreign Carites (2 Kgs 11:4). The Levites and priests assembled the people, and they covenanted to make Joash king. Jehoiada ordered the priests to guard the king at all times since they alone were qualified to be in the holy temple precincts. Together they enthroned the king (2 Chr 23:1-11).

The priests captured Athaliah and executed both her and Mattan, the high priest of Baal (23:12-21). The writer was particularly concerned about the holiness of the temple in his telling of the story (23:14,19). The Levites reinstituted the worship of the LORD in the temple as David had provided (23:18).

24:1-27
Joash Restores the Temple

Joash (835–796 B.C.) launched a major restoration project of the temple, which had been neglected during Athaliah's rule. He requested the Levites to gather annual monies due the temple from the people (Exod 30:12-16), but they were slow in fulfilling the charge. So Joash provided a chest in the temple itself where the people brought their tax so that the restoration was carried out (2 Chr 24:1-14; 2 Kgs 12:1-16). The Chronicler mentioned the priest's failure but softened the tone of the account in Kings.

When the priest Jehoiada died, apostasy resurged under Joash's authority. Joash refused to listen to God's prophets. Zechariah, son of Jehoiada, condemned the people for their religious infidelity and was stoned to death in the king's presence. As he died, the priest swore God's vengeance on Joash. The Chronicler explained the tragic end of Joash's rule as God's judgment on Judah's wickedness (24:24). Judah was defeated by invading Arameans, and Joash was murdered in his bed (24:23-27; 2 Kgs 12:17-21).

Joash's career illustrated the Chronicler's major theme: God's blessing on David's house but also God's anger when the kings acted wickedly. Zechariah's murder is the last one mentioned in the Hebrew Bible since Chronicles ends the Hebrew arrangement (compare Luke 11:51).

25:1-28
Amaziah's Idolatry

Amaziah (797–767 B.C.) began his career by avenging his father's assassins. They were placed under trial in accordance with the law (2 Chr 25:1-4; 2 Kgs 14:1-6).

The Edomites rebelled against the young king, and he gathered a vast army of mercenaries, including a thousand hired from Israel. But an unnamed prophet convinced him to release the Israelites and depend on the LORD alone for victory (2 Chr 25:5-12; 2 Kgs 14:7). Judah crushed the Edomites, but the disgruntled Israelites plundered Judah's cities as they marched home. Amaziah angered the LORD because he returned with Edomite gods whom he worshiped. The LORD's prophet condemned the king for his resistance to the LORD's word (2 Chr 25:13-16). Fresh from his victory over Edom, Amaziah challenged the stronger Jehoash of Israel (798–782 B.C.). The result of the conflict was the destruction of Jerusalem's defenses and Amaziah's capture. The Chronicler attributed Amaziah's defeat and his subsequent murder to his sin of idolatry (2 Chr 25:17-28; 2 Kgs 14:8-20).

26:1-23
Uzziah the Leper

Uzziah (Azariah) succeeded his father at the age of sixteen. Zechariah tutored Uzziah in the things of God. God blessed Uzziah in all he did; his fifty-two-year reign (792–767 B.C.; coregency, 767–740) was one of the longest and most prosperous among the kings of Judah (2 Chr

ASSYRIAN RULERS

RULER	DATES OF RULE	SCRIPTURE REFERENCE
Ashur-uballit I	1354–1318 B.C.	
Adad-nirari I	1318–1264 B.C.	
Shalmaneser I (Shulman-asharid)	1264–1234 B.C.	
Tukulti-Ninurta I	1234–1197 B.C.	
Ashur-dan I	1179–1133 B.C.	
Tiglath-pileșer I (Tukulti-apil-Ešarra)	1115–1076 B.C.	
Ashur-rabi II	1012–972 B.C.	
Ashur-resh-ishi II	972–967 B.C.	
Tiglath-pileser II	967–935 B.C.	
Ashur-dan II	935–912 B.C.	
Adad-nirari II	912–889 B.C.	
Tukulti-Ninurta II	889–884 B.C.	
Ashurnasirpal II (Ashur-nasir-apli II)	884–858 B.C.	
Shalmaneser III (Shalman-Ashar-id II)	858–824 B.C.	
Shamsi-Adad V	824–810 B.C.	
Adad-nirari III	810–782 B.C.	
Shalmaneser IV	782–773 B.C.	
Ashur-dan III	773–754 B.C.	
Ashur-nirari V	754–745 B.C.	
Tiglath-pileșer III (Tukulti-apil-Ešarra III, or Tiglath-pilneser, or Pul(u))	745–727 B.C.	2 Kgs 15:19,29; 16:7-10
Shalmaneser V (Ululai)	727–722 B.C.	2 Kgs 17:1-6
Sargon II	721–705 B.C.	
Sennacherib (Sin-abho-eriba)	704–681 B.C.	2 Kgs 18–19
Esarhaddon	681–669 B.C.	
Ashurbanipal	669–633 B.C.	
Ashur-etil-ilani	633–622 B.C.	
Sin-shur-ishkun	621–612 B.C.	
Ashur-uballit	612–608 B.C.	

26:1-5; 2 Kgs 14:21–15:1-3). The king subjugated many peoples, built a huge army, and pioneered military weaponry. Because of his success he became proud and, though not a priest, attempted to officiate at the altar. God struck the king with leprosy, and his son Jotham carried on in his place (2 Chr 26:6-23; 2 Kgs 15:5-7).

27:1-9
Jotham's Success and Favor

Jotham (750–732 B.C.) was righteous like his father, but

BABYLONIAN RULERS

RULER	DATES OF RULE	SCRIPTURE REFERENCE
Merodach-Baladan II (Marduk-apal-iddin)	721–689 B.C.	2 Kgs 20:12; Isa 39:1
Nabopolassar	625–605 B.C.	
Nebuchadnezzar II (Nebuchadrezzar II)	605–562 B.C.	2 Kgs 24–25; Dan 1–4
Evil-Merodach (Amel-Marduk)	562–560 B.C.	2 Kgs 25:27-30; Jer 52:31-34
Nergal-Sharezer (Nergal-shar-usur, or Neriglissar)	560–556 B.C.	Jer 39:3,13
Labashi-Marduk	556 B.C.	
Nabonidus (Nabu-na'id)	556–539 B.C.	
Belshazzar (Bel-shar-usur)	Co-regent with Nabonidus 556–539 B.C.	Dan 5; 7:1

he did not act presumptuously by entering the temple proper in his reign. His conquest of the Ammonites was attributed to the favor God showed toward him (2 Chr 27:1-9; 2 Kgs 15:32-38).

28:1-27
The Wicked Reign of Ahaz

Chronicles, based on the report of 2 Kings 16:1-20, emphasized the wickedness of King Ahaz's reign (735–715 B.C.). Ahaz was remembered for his practice of human sacrifice and Baal worship (2 Chr 28:1-4). The writer interpreted Judah's war with Israel and Aram (Syro-Ephraimite war) in 732 B.C. as God's judgment upon Ahaz (28:5-8; compare Isa 7). The Chronicler commended the victorious Northern Kingdom for obeying the prophet Oded and releasing the captured Judahites (28:5-15).

The LORD punished Judah further by pressuring it with the raiding armies of the mercenary Edomites and Philistines. Ahaz appealed to the Assyrian king Tiglath-Pileser III (745–727 B.C.), who promptly obliged by marching west, destroying Damascus and conquering Samaria (732 B.C.). Ahaz failed at buying his independence with temple and royal treasuries. He became a vassal of the Assyrian king and bowed to the gods of Assyria. Second Kings 16:10-14 reports that Ahaz reproduced in the Jerusalem temple Tiglath's pagan altar which he had seen at Damascus. Ahaz eventually closed the temple and erected numerous idols in the land. Whereas the Chronicler tried to introduce something positive about each king of Judah, for vicious Ahaz there was nothing good to report.

29:1-36
Hezekiah's Restoration

Hezekiah's reign (715–686 B.C.) is given inordinate attention because of the prominence he gave to temple music and worship. Much of the Chronicler's account (chaps. 29–31) is not paralleled in Kings.

The neglect of the temple under Ahaz (28:24) prompted Hezekiah to order the Levites to consecrate themselves and begin repair of the sanctuary. After sixteen days the Levites completed the task and opened the temple once again (29:1-17). After the Levites had cleansed the articles of worship, the king led the congregation in worship through offerings. The musical guilds functioned again as David had intended and performed the psalms of David and Asaph (29:18-30). After the people had atoned for their sins, they offered burnt and thank offerings so numerous that the Levites were requested to assist the overburdened priests. The sight and sounds of the temple brought great joy to the congregation (29:31-36).

30:1-27
Celebration of the Passover

The king planned a great convocation in Jerusalem to celebrate the Passover. He invited their estranged kin in the North who had survived the collapse of Samaria in 722 B.C. under Assyrian might. Because the temple was not yet prepared and many remained ceremonially impure, the Passover was held in the second month rather than the first as the law commanded (compare Exod 12; Num 9:10-11). Letters were dispatched throughout the land exhorting the northern remnants to repent of their former ways and join Judah in worship (30:1-12).

The Chronicler, always concerned for the propriety of worship, reported the unusual circumstances attending this celebration which the LORD graciously permitted. Hezekiah's prayer of repentance on behalf of the people was accepted by God (30:13-20). So devoted was the worship of the people that they extended the Feast of Unleavened Bread a second week. The Chronicler compared the joy of Jerusalem on that occasion to the days of King Solomon (30:21-27). The Chronicler extolled Hezekiah's Passover in the same way the author of Kings praised Josiah's (2 Kgs 23:21-23; compare also 2 Chr 35:18).

31:1-21
Gifts for the LORD's Work

The revival spurred the people on to remove the symbols of any illicit worship (31:1). Hezekiah reorganized the priests and Levites to serve the temple. At this spiritual outpouring the people happily brought their tithes and offerings as the law commanded. So vast were the offerings that there was an overabundance distributed among the priests (31:2-19). The LORD prospered Hezekiah for his faithfulness (31:20-21; 2 Kgs 18:5-7).

A relief from Nineveh (dating to Sennacherib's reign) depicts Assyrian soldiers using large shields and bow and arrow.

32:1-33
God Destroys Sennacherib

The Chronicler, concerned with Hezekiah's religious contributions, shortened the record of Hezekiah's political career in 2 Kings 18:13–19:37 (compare Isa 36:2–37:38).

The LORD delivered Jerusalem in 701 B.C. from the Assyrian armies of Sennacherib (705–681 B.C.) because of Hezekiah's faithfulness. Hezekiah made preparations for war (32:1-5). The king encouraged the people to remain faithful because the LORD was more powerful than the Assyrians or their gods (32:6-8). An Assyrian delegation addressed the people of Jerusalem in their native Hebrew. They threatened the city by ridiculing Hezekiah's dependence on the LORD (32:9-19). The Chronicler was offended by the Assyrian derision of Israel's God when they likened the LORD to an idol, "the work of men's hands" (32:19). An account of Sennacherib's invasion is recorded on his palace walls in Nineveh in which he boasted that he had Hezekiah caged like a bird.

Yet Hezekiah, supported by Isaiah the prophet, resisted their threats, praying for God's intervention. The LORD honored their prayers and sent an angel of destruction among the Assyrians. Sennecherib retreated to Nineveh, where he was later murdered by his own sons. The people greatly rejoiced at the deliverance and worshiped the LORD anew (32:20-23).

When Hezekiah became ill unto death, the LORD answered the king's prayers for mercy by giving a sign. However, the king became proud, and the LORD convicted him of his sins. His repentance averted the LORD's wrath (32:24-26). The final years of Hezekiah were blessed of God, and he prospered in all that he attempted (32:27-33; 2 Kgs 20:1-21; Isa 37:21–38:8).

33:1-25
Manasseh's Repentance

The Chronicler detailed the despicable acts of this king who indulged in every evil act of idolatry, sorcery, and astrology (33:1-9). The writer of Kings blamed Manasseh's reign for the LORD's destruction of Jerusalem and the deportation to Babylon (2 Kgs 21:10-15).

The Chronicler's account of Manasseh's reign (697–687 B.C.) departs from the narrative of 2 Kings 21:1-18 by including the unusual story of Manasseh's imprisonment in Assyria. During this exile, he repented and God answered by returning him to Jerusalem (33:10-13).

Many scholars have questioned the authenticity of the Chronicler's account. However, its omission in Kings can be attributed to that author's purpose of presenting a case for the apostasy of Judah. Chronicles, on the other hand, demonstrates how God forgives and restores the humble (compare 7:14). The Chronicler cited an independent witness to corroborate his story (33:18).

Upon his return Manasseh repaired the temple and renewed proper worship (33:14-17). The reference to his repentant prayer (33:18) gave rise to speculation about its contents in the apocryphal book "The Prayer of Manasseh" (ca. 200–100 B.C.).

His successor was Amon (642–640 B.C.) for whom the Chronicler had no words of commendation (33:21-25; 2 Kgs 21:19-24).

The famous "Lion of Babylon" at the site of the ancient city of Babylon in the modern country of Iraq.

34:1-33
Josiah and the Book of the Law

Josiah reigned for thrity-one years (640–609 B.C.) and walked in the way of the LORD as David had done (34:1-2,33; 2 Kgs 22:1-2). For the author of Kings, Josiah's significance was second only to David's. Therefore more attention is devoted to his reign in Kings than in Chronicles (1 Kgs 13:2; 2 Kgs 22:1–23:30).

Chronicles (34:3-7) indicates that religious reform began in Josiah's eighth year (632 B.C.), a full decade before the discovery of the Book of the Law (622 B.C.). The purge of idolatry and high places extended to northern towns as well as Judah, indicating that Josiah's rule was expanding into the old Northern Kingdom without Assyria's interference.

The Levites received money from the rulers and common people to refurbish the temple (34:8-13). As the Levites worked, the high priest Hilkiah found a copy of the Book of the Law (also called "Book of the Covenant," 33:30). From Josiah's response most scholars have concluded that it was a portion of Deuteronomy. Upon hearing the book read, Josiah was remorseful and feared the LORD's wrath. The prophetess Huldah declared that the LORD would destroy Judah but preserve Josiah's reign because of his humble contrition. Josiah led the people in a covenant renewal ceremony (34:14-33).

35:1-27
Josiah's Passover

Celebration of Passover and the week of Unleavened Bread followed the reforms of Hezekiah (chap. 30) and Josiah. Chronicles, because of its interest in cultic matters, elaborated on the few verses given to it in 2 Kings 23:21-23.

The celebration occurred in the appropriate month, unlike Hezekiah's Passover renewal (2 Chr 30:15). To worship the LORD properly the Levites and priests consecrated themselves and then prepared the sacrifices in behalf of the people (35:1-9). The Levites functioned in their proper order in accordance with the Book of Moses. Typical of the Chronicler, he also included the role of the musical guilds David appointed. The celebration exceeded that of any previous Passover since the days of Samuel. Josiah's reforms culminated with the Passover observed in the same year as the finding of the Book of the Law (35:10-19).

The Chronicler also clarified the events of Josiah's death at the battle of Megiddo, where Pharaoh Neco defeated him (35:20-24; 2 Kgs 23:26-30). Neco was marching through Jezreel to assist the Assyrians, who were pinned down by the Babylonians at Carchemish (North Syria). Ironically, Josiah, whose reign was remembered for its righteousness, died because he failed to adhere to the LORD's command (2 Chr 35:22). The prophet Jeremiah (not mentioned in Kings) lamented in song the death of the monarch (35:25-27).

36:1-13
Judah's Last Days

The Chronicler gave a brief account of Judah's last kings (compare 2 Kgs 23:30–25:21; Jer 52:4-27), focused on the temple and its ministries (2 Chr 36:14-19).

Jehoahaz (609 B.C.), whom Necho installed, was deposed after only three months and replaced by a second son of Josiah, Jehoiakim (2 Chr 36:1-4). Nebuchadnezzar was victorious at Carchemish and subjugated the petty kingdom of Judah. Jehoiakim's evil reign (609–598 B.C.) ended in deportation by Nebuchadnezzar, who invaded rebellious Jerusalem and plundered the temple (36:5-8). King Jehoiachin (598–597 B.C.) was quickly supplanted with the puppet king Zedekiah (597–586 B.C.), whose rebellion led to Jerusalem's final demise in 586 B.C. (36:9-13).

GOD'S TEMPLE AND CYRUS'S DECREE (2 CHR 36:14-23)

The Chronicler's final remarks are a sermon blaming the failure of the priests and leaders to obey the LORD's commands for the temple's and city's destruction (36:14-19). Writing almost two centuries after Kings, the Chronicler (36:20-21) included in his story the return of the exiles, adding that Jeremiah predicted this (Jer 25:11; 29:10). The Chronicler commented that the land had its sabbath rest as the law required (compare Lev 26), for the seventy years from the ruin of the temple (586 B.C.) to its rebuilding (516 B.C.).

With the ousting of the Babylonians, the Persian emperor Cyrus inaugurated a new policy toward the exiles. Cyrus's edict, published in the famous Cyrus Cylinder (539 B.C.), was quoted by the Chronicler in its Hebrew version. Cyrus permitted the conquered peoples of Babylon to return to their homelands and revive their religious traditions. For the Jews he ordered the rebuilding of the Jerusalem temple (36:22-23).

A scene of battle is depicted on this relief from the palace of Sennacherib at the site of ancient Nineveh.

Although it appeared that God's promises to David were abandoned, the Chronicler showed through his review of history that God remains faithful and can change history to accomplish His purposes. The story of Israel's fortunes was not finished. These last two verses were repeated in Ezra 1:1-3a to indicate that the story of God's redemptive work through the temple continued in the accounts of Ezra and Nehemiah.

Ethical and Theological Significance

Second Chronicles speaks of the importance of worship and obedience. The Chronicler evaluated the kings of Judah not on their secular accomplishments but on the basis of their faithfulness to God, especially as evidenced in their support of temple worship. The Chronicler's verdict on these kings reminds today's Christians that our lives will someday be judged as well. As we live our lives, we should keep God's goals in mind and strive for His commendation, "Well done, good and faithful servant" (Matt 25:21).

Sin is serious. The sin of God's people led to the destruction of Jerusalem, the temple, and to the exile. Though God punishes sin, judgment is not God's final word. God "is good; his love for Israel endures forever" (Ezra 3:11). Second Chronicles ends with the exiles' being given freedom to go home and rebuild the temple. Our God is a God of second chances, who through Jesus offers sinners new freedom, a chance to come home to His family, and opportunities for service.

Questions for Reflection

1. Why are special days of religious celebration important to the spiritual life of a religious community?
2. What does Chronicles teach about spiritual renewal among God's people?
3. In what ways does God chasten His people?
4. How does God reward the faithfulness of His people?
5. What difference does a nation's morality make in its life and destiny?

Sources for Additional Study

McConville, J. G. *I & II Chronicles.* Philadelphia: Westminster, 1984.

Merrill, Eugene H. *1, 2 Chronicles.* Grand Rapids: Zondervan, 1988.

Sailhamer, John. *First and Second Chronicles.* Chicago: Moody, 1983.

EZRA

The Book of Ezra is named for the book's principle character. This scribe revived the law of Moses as the basis for Jewish religious and social life during the period of restoration following the Babylonian exile.

In the Hebrew Bible, Ezra-Nehemiah is one book. It occurs in the third and final section (called the "Writings") and precedes Chronicles, which is the last book of the Hebrew Bible. The English Old Testament follows the Latin in separating Ezra-Nehemiah into two books. The English Old Testament with the Greek and Latin places Ezra in its proper chronological sequence, following 1 and 2 Chronicles, as the tenth of the historical books.

There is a continuing debate about the relationship of Chronicles and Ezra-Nehemiah. The last verses of 2 Chronicles (36:22-23) are the same as Ezra 1:1-3a. In fact, Chronicles ends in the middle of a sentence that only occurs in full in Ezra. This overlapping may indicate that the books were intended to be read together.

Many scholars think that Chronicles and Ezra-Nehemiah formed a single historical work, called the "Chronicler's History," authored by an anonymous individual or school of historians. Other scholars, both evangelical and critical, believe that Ezra and Nehemiah have independent authorship from Chronicles. There are significant dissimilarities in language and viewpoint. (See "The Historical Books.")

In Jewish tradition Ezra the scribe is the author of Chronicles and Ezra-Nehemiah. (See the introduction to "1 Chronicles.") While the attribution of all these books to Ezra cannot be demonstrated it is clear that at least he contributed personal memoirs to the book that bears his name and probably had a significant role in the compilation of Ezra-Nehemiah. The Book of Ezra dates in the later half of the fifth century B.C.

Sources for the Book of Ezra included Ezra's firsthand account (probably 7:11–9:15), empirical documents and correspondence written in Aramaic (4:8–6:18; 7:12-26), and registers of Jewish immigrants (2:1-70; 8:1-14).

Chronology of Ezra and Nehemiah

The date of writing is dependent on the chronology of Ezra's return to Jerusalem. The traditional opinion has Ezra's ministry in the seventh year (458 B.C.) and Nehemiah's ministry in the twentieth year (445 B.C.) of Artaxerxes I (Ezra 7:8; Neh 2:1). Problems exist with the traditional opinion. For example, the high priest in Nehemiah's time was Eliashib (Neh 3:1,20-21; 13:28), but Ezra ministered during the priesthood of Jehohana, the son of Eliashib (Ezra 10:6).

Because of such problems, alternative opinions have been suggested. Another view dates Ezra's expedition in the seventh year of Artaxerxes II (398 B.C.) after the time of Nehemiah. A third alternative dates Ezra in 428 B.C. by emending Ezra 7:8 to read the "thirty-seventh year" rather than the seventh year of Artaxerxes.

Although the traditional view has difficulties, its arguments are more compelling. For example, scholars have suggested that there was more than one Eliashib and Jehohanan and that Nehemiah and Ezra speak of different ones. Therefore, following the fifth century date for Ezra's ministry, the composition of Ezra-Nehemiah was about 400 B.C. or soon thereafter. If Ezra-Nehemiah were written as part of the Chronicler's History, it was written after 400 B.C. since the genealogies of Chronicles exceed this date (compare 1 Chr 3:19-24; see the "The Historical Books").

The restoration period commenced with the defeat of Babylon by the Persian monarch Cyrus, who ordered the release of the Jews in 538 B.C. The chronology of the period can be summarized by the expeditions that returned from the captivity.

1. Under the Jewish prince Sheshbazzar (538 B.C.) the first group returned. Later the new governor Zerubbabel and high priest Jeshua completed the temple (515 B.C.) with the help of the prophets Zechariah and Haggai (Ezra 1–6).

2. During the reign of Artaxerses I (464–424) Ezra led a second party and initiated religious reforms (Ezra 7–10). This expedition was fifty-eight years after the completion of the temple (458 B.C.).

3. Nehemiah, appointed governor by Artaxerxes I, led the third party and rebuilt Jerusalem's walls. Nehemiah's first term was twelve years (445–433 B.C.; Neh 1:1–13:6), and the second term was soon thereafter (430 B.C.?; Neh 13:6-31).

Theme

God used pagan kings and godly leaders to restore His people by reinstituting temple worship and reviving the law of Moses.

I. Zerubbabel and Rebuilding the Temple (1:1–6:22)
II. Ezra and Reform under the Law (7:1–10:44)

Purpose and Theology

1. The Book of Ezra tells the history of the Jews' return from Babylon. It continues the story that Chronicles left unfinished. The first half of the book (chaps. 1–6) concerns the expedition ordered by King Cyrus (538 B.C.) to rebuild the temple under Sheshbazzar of Judah. The book continues the theme of temple and priesthood begun in Chronicles (Ezra 3:1-6,10-11; 6:16-22). The importance of the Levites and priests to the community is evidenced by the careful cataloging of those who returned (2:36-54,61-62). The Levites supervised the rebuilding of the temple and were reorganized in time to officiate at the first Passover celebration (3:8-9; 6:16-20)

Priests and Levites were a major concern of Ezra's administration (chaps. 7–10). Ezra was careful to include them among those returning from exile (7:7,13,24; 8:15-20,24-34). Their sinful intermarriage with Gentiles provoked Ezra's reforms (9:1-2). They were placed under oath (10:5), and the guilty were noted (10:18-24).

2. Ezra's theological focus is how God accomplishes His will through different human agents. God restored His people by moving the pagan ruler Cyrus to release Judah (1:1-2) and by inciting the Jewish people to volunteer (1:5). The Cyrus Cylinder inscription gives the Persian account of Cyprus's decree. It explains that the Babylonian god Marduk called him to release the exiles to return to their homelands. The Hebrew version of this decree applied to the Jews (2 Chr 36:22-23; Ezra 1:1-4). Biblical writers interpreted the decree as the act of God (Isa 45:1-3) in fulfillment of Jeremiah's prophecy (Jer 25:11-12; 29:10). Cyrus and Darius even supplied necessary provisions for the temple (Ezra 1:7-11; 6:8-10). The Gentiles were perceived as coworkers in the building of the Jewish temple (6:22).

The LORD also was responsible for the success of Ezra's expedition. Ezra was called and protected by the LORD's "gracious hand" (7:9; 8:18,22). God used the Persian government to enable Ezra to accomplish his task (7:27-28).

God accomplished His purposes through special spokesmen as well. The prophets Zechariah and Haggai delivered the message of God, which motivated the people to complete the temple (5:1-2; 6:14). Together pagan kings, godly leaders, common people, and prophets were the LORD's hands and feet to do His bidding.

3. The book reflects the optimism of a restored Davidic throne, keeping the messianic hope alive. Sheshbazzar and Zerubbabel, who returned from exile to lead Judah, were descendants of Judah's king Jehoiachin, who had been taken captive to Babylon. (Compare 1:8; 1 Chr. 3:18-19 [Sheshbazzar = Shenazzar?]; and 2 Chr 36:9-10). The prophecies of Zechariah and Haggai during this period depicted the messianic age by idealizing Zerubbabel and Jeshua as the new David and high priest Zadok (Ezra 3:8; 5:1-2; 6:14; Zech 3:1-4:14; 6:9-15; Hag 2:6-9; 3:23).

4. The second half of the book (chaps. 7–10) concerns Ezra's ministry, which began fifty-eight years (458 B.C.) after the completion of the temple (515 B.C.). In the latter half of the book the emphasis shifts to the law of Moses. Ezra was commissioned to teach and establish the customs of Jewish law (7:11,14,25-26). Ezra was a learned scribe devoted to the law (7:6,10-12). He led the people in a spiritual awakening that resulted in a covenant renewal (10:3).

5. The book also expresses the responsibility for human sin. The people of Ezra's day had sinned by intermarrying with the Gentile populace (9:1-2; 10:1-44). Ezra's intercession (9:6-15) and the people's weeping confession (10:1-2) led to a renewal of covenant commitment to the LORD (10:3). The community felt the responsibility of those who had sinned and collectively dealt with the guilty, including their leaders (10:16-24).

6. Antagonism toward those building the temple was commonplace and official avenues were used to stop the work (4:1-24; 5:3-6:12). However, the author showed that God's help enabled them to finish the work under His watchful eye in spite of opposition (5:5).

7. The people of God as the remnant of Israel is important to the theology of the restoration period. They are the remnant that escaped the wrath of God (9:8,15). Therefore their company, though small in number (chap. 2), was significant because they were "all Israel" (8:25) who were regathered as the "holy race" (9:2).

ZERUBBABEL AND REBUILDING THE TEMPLE (EZRA 1:1–6:22)

The first section centers on the building of the temple. The LORD inspired Cyrus to permit the return of the Jews to worship their God (chap. 1). Those who volunteered

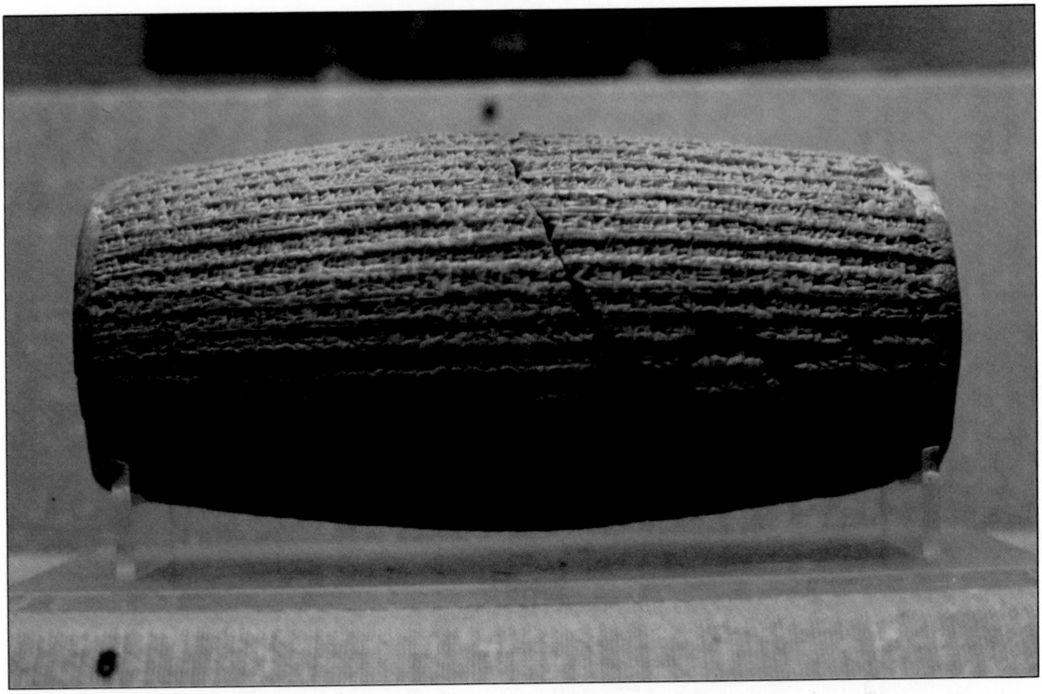

The Cyrus Cylinder, dating from the first year of Cyrus the Great's rule over Babylon, details his famous edict permitting the Jewish people to return to their homeland.

for the first expedition are listed (chap. 2). The foundation of the temple was laid, and the people worshiped God (chap. 3). But opposition from their enemies stopped the work (chap. 4). The LORD stirred up the people by the prophets Zechariah and Haggai to complete the work in spite of inquiries from the Persian governor (chap. 5). King Darius authorized and funded the project, which was completed with great celebration (chap. 6).

1:1-11
The Decree of Cyrus

In the first year of Cyrus's reign over Babylon (539–530 B.C.), the Persian monarch permitted the Jews to return and rebuild their temple for the purpose of worshiping the LORD (1:1-4). This was attributed to the inspiration of the LORD both by Cyrus (1:2) and by the biblical writer (1:1; compare 2 Chr 29:22-23), who interpreted it as the fulfillment of Jeremiah's prophecy (Jer 25:11-12; 29:10; compare Isa 44:28–45:3). The prophet Isaiah identified Cyrus as the anointed servant of the LORD (45:1-3). The Cyrus Cylinder reports how the king tolerated the religions of many nations by restoring the images of their deities and rebuilding their sanctuaries. Cyrus's sympathy was politically motivated to encourage the loyalty of his new subjects upon their release.

The LORD also stirred up some of the exiles of Judah to return. Cyrus returned the temple vessels stolen by Nebuchadnezzar (2 Kgs 25:13-15; 2 Chr 36:18). Sheshbazzar, identified as the "prince of Judah" (1:8), received the inventory of temple articles and led the exiles to Jerusalem (1:5-11). Sheshbazzar may be the same as Shenazzar, a son of Jehoiachin (1 Chr 3:18). If this identification is correct, the equation of Sheshbazzar with Zerubbabel on the basis of comparison of Ezra 5:14,16 with Zechariah 4:9 is questionable. Zerubbabel was the son of Shealtiel (3:8) or Pedaiah (1 Chr 3:19), making him the nephew of Sheshbazzar. Zerubbabel was the grandson of King Jehoiachin (1 Chr 3:19) and succeeded Sheshbazzar as governor of Judah (Hag 1:1).

2:1-70
Register of the Remnant

The author included the register of the remnant to honor those who trusted in the LORD and to show that the prophecy of Israel's return from exile was fulfilled. The registry includes the leaders (2:1-2a), general populace (2:2b-35), temple personnel (2:36-54), descendants of Solomon's servants (2:55-58), and those of uncertain genealogical claims (2:59-63). The listing is only representative since the total number (2:64-67) exceeds those counted. The revised list is repeated with revisions in Nehemiah 7:6-73.

3:1-13
Worship and Rebuilding

The first concern of the community was the worship of the LORD. Sacrifice had not been offered for fifty years since Jerusalem's fall (586 B.C.). The seventh month (Tishri) was the most holy month of the calendar when the Feasts of Trumpets, Atonement, and Tabernacles were celebrated (Lev 23). Zerubbabel and Jeshua, the high priest, supervised the reconstruction of the altar and the offering of sacrifice. The Feast of Tabernacles was the first holy day celebrated (Ezra 3:1-6).

In the second year of the return (536 B.C.), materials were imported from Lebanon. The temple foundation was laid under the supervision of priests and Levites appointed by Zerubbabel and Jeshua (3:7-11). The Levites led in praise through song and musical accompaniment. The response was a mixture of joy by the young and weeping by the old because they had seen the glory of Solomon's temple (3:12-13). Zechariah reminded the people not to despise a small work done for the LORD (Zech 4:9-10). Haggai declared that the glory of this temple would exceed that of the former temple (Hag 2:9).

4:1-24
Opposition to the LORD's Work

The residents of Samaria offered to assist the exiles because they claimed to worship the God of the Jews. Zerubbabel spurned their help because their religion was a mixed cult that included elements of paganism as a result

PERSIAN RULERS

PERSIAN RULER	DATES OF RULE	SCRIPTURE REFERENCE
CYRUS	539–530 B.C.	2 Chr 36:22-23; Ezra 1; Isa 44:28; 45:1; Dan 1:21; 10:1
CAMBYSES	530–522 B.C.	
DARIUS I HYSTASPES	522–486 B.C.	Ezra 4–6; Neh 12:22; Hag 1:1; Zech 1:1,7
XERXES I (AHASUERUS)	486–465 B.C.	Ezra 4:16 Esth
ARTAXERXES I LONGIMANUS	464–423 B.C.	Ezra 4:7-23; 7; 8:1; Neh 2:1-8 (Probably ruler during the time of the prophet Malachi.)
DARIUS II NOTHUS	423–404 B.C.	
ARTAXERXES II MNEMON	404–359 B.C.	
ARTAXERXES III OCHUS	359–338 B.C.	
ARSES	338–335 B.C.	
DARIUS III CODOMANUS	335–331 B.C.	

of the Assyrian policies of intermingling foreign populations (compare 2 Kgs 17:24-41). The Assyrian kings from the time of Esarhaddon (681–669 B.C.) had exiled foreigners to the northern provinces of Israel (Ezra 4:1-3). The Samaritans impeded the work by harassing the builders (4:4) and hiring counselors (4:5). The work stopped for sixteen years (536–520 B.C.) until the reign of Darius (5:24).

In a parenthetical summary (4:6-23), illustrations of such ongoing opposition are taken from letters available to the author. The documents come from a later period during the reigns of Xerxes I (486–465 B.C.) and Artaxerxes I (464–424 B.C.). These letters, along with the other materials in Ezra 4:8–6:18, are written in Aramaic, the official language of the court.

A letter from the time of Xerxes (Hebrew "Ahasuerus"; Esth 1:1) is only mentioned (4:6). But the second, from the period of Artaxerxes, is quoted at length (4:7-16). The authors of the second letter identified themselves (4:10) as descendants of those deported by Ashurbanipal (Hebrew "Osnapper"; 668–627 B.C.). They recalled Jerusalem's history of insurrection and charged the Jews with sedition (4:12-16). Artaxerxes ordered the work stopped (4:17-23).

5:1-17
God's Authority to Build

The prophets Haggai and Zechariah urged and helped the community to renew its labor (Ezra 5:1-2; Hag 1:1-4,14; 2:1-4; Zech 4:9; 6:15). Haggai criticized the people for living in fine homes while the temple lay in ruins (Hag 1:3-6). Zechariah unveiled the glorious future that awaited the temple in the days of the messiah (the "Branch"; Zech 3:8; 6:12-15). Tattenai, governor of the provincial areas west of the Euphrates, questioned their authority to build. But their authority came from God, and it was He who watched over them (Ezra 5:3-5).

Tattenai sent a letter to King Darius (522–486 B.C.) in which he reviewed the history of the Jewish city and the exiles. Tattenai requested a search in the royal archives for Cyrus's authorization for rebuilding, which the Jews claimed (5:6-17).

6:1-22
Darius and the Finished Work

A search conducted first at Babylon and then Ecbatana (Media) recovered the decree in its official Aramaic version (6:1-5; compare 1:1-4). Darius ordered the governor not to stop them but to pay for their expenses out of the royal treasury and to carry out sanctions against anyone who opposed their work (6:6-12). What had jeopardized the work proved under God's care to expedite its completion.

The speedy response of Tattenai enabled the completion of the temple four years later in 515 B.C. (compare 6:15 with 4:24). By providential plan, Jewish elders, Hebrew prophets, and pagan kings all contributed to complete the task (6:13-15). The dedicatory service was celebrated with joy and sacrifices. The Levites and priests were organized into their orders as Moses (Num 3; 18) and David (1 Chr 24) had ordained (Ezra 6:16-18). Out of the four surviving orders (2:36-39), twenty-four were formed (compare Luke 1:5).

The text reverts to Hebrew at Ezra 6:19 because it describes the reenactment of the Passover (6:19-22). It was the first Passover commemorated in the temple since the fall of Jerusalem. The exiles were careful to worship the LORD in ritual pureness. They rejoiced that the LORD had changed the heart of the Assyrian king for their good. "Assyria" is named rather than Persia (6:22) because Persia ruled the former region of Assyria and it was Assyria which had begun the captivity of God's people.

EZRA AND REFORM UNDER THE LAW (EZRA 7:1–10:44)

This last section concerns Ezra's memoirs, and it warns the restored community not to follow the sins of their fathers. Ezra, a trained scholar in the law, was commissioned by Artaxerxes to return to Jerusalem and teach the statutes of Jewish religious life (chaps. 7–8). Ezra initiated religious reforms that led to repentance and a covenant commitment (chaps. 9–10).

7:1-28
God's Hand on Ezra

Ezra's credentials to fulfill God's calling were his priestly genealogy (7:1-5; compare 2:62), his knowledge of the law (7:6-9), and his commitment to the law as a practitioner and teacher (7:10). God's "gracious hand" of favor was upon Ezra's life (7:9). King Artaxerxes recognized Ezra's qualifications (7:11) and issued a decree written in Aramaic (7:12-26). The decree said Ezra should lead a company of volunteers to supervise proper religious life in Jerusalem and establish a judicial system in accordance with the law of their God. Ezra praised God for the benevolence of the king and took courage from this sign of God's hand on him (7:27-28).

8:1-36
Spiritual Preparations

His companions on the journey are listed by family heads (8:1-14). Ezra specially recruited Levites to assist him in teaching the law in Jerusalem. Ezra attributed his success to the LORD (8:15-20). As spiritual leaders the Levites had to meet the qualification of proper genealogical heritage as the law required (8:20b). Ezra showed his dependence on God by prayer and fasting in preparation for his journey. He recognized that God had answered his petitions (8:21-23).

Ezra's company, bearing an enormous treasure, arrived successfully without incident. Ezra acknowledged that God's protective hand had spared him from the threat of enemies (8:24-32). The treasure was deposited, and the exiles offered sacrifice for all Israel. The provincial governors were notified of Ezra's new administration (8:33-36).

9:1-15
Ezra's Prayer of Confession

When Ezra arrived in Jerusalem, the city leaders confronted him with the problem of intermarriage. Echoing the days of Moses, the sins of the people were likened to those of the Gentiles who had ensnared Israel in the past (9:1-2; Exod 34:11-12; Deut 7:1-6). The purpose of this segregation was not to create a pure race but to avoid marriages that would lead to spiritual unfaithfulness (compare Judg 3:5-6).

Ezra's distress over the people's sins moved him to pray for God's forgiveness (9:3-5). He recalled the sins of their ancestors who suffered exile for their guilt (9:6-7). He offered thanksgiving that the LORD had spared them as a remnant (9:8-9). Yet he feared that they had repeated their ancestors' sins and neglected their prophets' warnings. He confessed the inadequacy of the people and invoked the continued mercy of God (9:10-15).

10:1-44
Repentance of the Guilty

Ezra's prayer and example of contrition contributed to the people's conviction for their sins. They recommended a covenant renewal and urged Ezra to reform the community (10:1-4). Ezra called for a convocation of all the tribes under threat of confiscation of property and excommunication (compare 7:26). Ezra chastened them and ordered them to separate from their pagan wives (10:5-11). Divorce was not God's will for His people (compare Mal 2:16; Matt 19:4-6), but it was permitted in this situation in order to preserve the spiritual life of the nation (compare Deut 24:1-3). The practice was so widespread that it took three months for a tribunal to hear the cases (10:12-17).

A listing of the guilty ends the book (10:18-44). The religious leaders are listed first. No group escaped the sin nor the punishment. This somber conclusion contrasts with the register of those honored for their faith (Ezra 2). The conclusion indicates that the exiles still had further strides to make in doing God's work.

Theological and Ethical Significance

Before the exile the national and religious hopes of God's people went hand in hand. After the return from Babylon, temple worship was restored, and the people recommitted themselves to the law of Moses. But a Davidic king no longer ruled over an independant Judah; Judah was a province of the Persian Empire and was ruled by an agent of the Persian king. The Jews survived because they found their identity as God's people not in nationalistic dreams but in renewed commitment to God's Word. Christians should be careful not to limit God to the national interest of any one people.

The Book of Ezra stresses Scripture as the governing principle for the life of God's people. Confronted with the demands of God's Word, we, like those of Ezra's generation, fail to measure up to God's standards. Our repentance, however, must move beyond remorse for moral failure to the reality of changed lives. Ezra's demand for the divorce of foreign wives demonstrates that the demands of true repentance and obedience to God's Word are sometimes painful.

Questions for Reflection

1. What should be the Christian's attitude toward civil authority?
2. How should the people of God and their leaders labor together to do the Lord's work more effectively?
3. What priority should God's people give to worship and praise?
4. How is Ezra an example for Christians to follow today?
5. What motivates God's people to act courageously in perilous situations?

Sources for Additional Study

Kidner, Derek. *Ezra and Nehemiah.* Downers Grove: InterVarsity, 1979.

Laney, J. Carl. *Ezra and Nehemiah.* Chicago: Moody, 1982.

McConville, J. G. *Ezra, Nehemiah, and Esther.* Philadelphia: Westminster, 1985.

NEHEMIAH

The Book of Nehemiah is named for its principal character. In the postexilic period Nehemiah refortified Jerusalem, established civil authority, and began religious reforms.

Ezra and Nehemiah were one book in the Hebrew Bible until the fifteenth century A.D. The English versions follow the tradition of the Greek church fathers and Latin Old Testament by separating them. In the Septuagint, the pre-Christian Greek version of the Old Testament, Ezra and Nehemiah form one book.

The English arrangement of Old Testament books follows the Greek tradition by placing Nehemiah in the proper chronological sequence. Here Nehemiah follows Chronicles and Ezra as the eleventh historical book. In the Hebrew Bible, Nehemiah appears in the third and final section known as the Writings. There Ezra-Nehemiah precedes Chronicles, which ends the Hebrew Bible.

Some scholars believe that Ezra-Nehemiah was formerly the second half of a larger history known as the "Chronicler's History." This history consisted of 1 and 2 Chronicles and Ezra-Nehemiah. This reconstruction has been rejected by many scholars, both evangelical and critical, and continues to be disputed (see introduction to "The Historical Books" and "Ezra"). The Jewish Talmud names Ezra as the author of Chronicles and names Ezra and Nehemiah as joint authors of Ezra-Nehemiah. In any event, the identity of the compiler, who would have used a number of written sources, such as Nehemiah's first-person account, cannot be known. Ezra-Nehemiah dates to the latter half of the fifth century B.C., no earlier than 430 B.C.

The majority of the book is Nehemiah's first-person memoirs (1:1–7:73; 12:27–13:31). Ezra's ministry is reported in the third person (Neh 8:1–12:30). Among the sources used were genealogical records (Neh 7:6-73 and Ezra 2; Neh 12:1-26, especially v. 23), a covenant document (9:38–10:39), and a residency list (11:4-36).

The date of completion for Ezra-Nehemiah is no later than 400 B.C. If considered part of the Chronicler's History, its date may be soon thereafter (see the introduction to "The Historical Books"). Some scholars have dated Nehemiah (and thus the Chronicler's History too) no earlier than the time of Alexander the Great (about 331 B.C.) on the basis of the high priest "Jaddua" named in Nehemiah 12:11,22. The Jewish historian Josephus reported that Jaddua was high priest when Alexander entered Jerusalem. However, the balance of evidence indicates that the Jaddua Josephus named probably is a descendant of the biblical Jaddua.

The chronology of Nehemiah's ministry in Jerusalem includes two periods of administration. His first tenure covered twelve years (445–433 B.C.; Neh 2:1). He returned for a second term about 430 B.C. (13:6). For a chronology of the period and the relationship of the two reformers Ezra and Nehemiah, see the introduction to "Ezra."

Theme

God encircled His people with protection by the walls Nehemiah rebuilt and by the law Ezra reestablished.

I. Rebuilding the Walls (1:1–7:73)
II. Reading the Law (8:1–10:39)
III. Reforming the People (11:1–13:31)

Purpose and Theology

Nehemiah continues the story of the restored community. Whereas The Book of Ezra focuses on the religious restoration of Jerusalem, the Book of Nehemiah describes its political restoration. Nehemiah's rebuilding of Jerusalem's wall restored political integrity and muted the threats of intimidation by neighboring adversaries (chaps. 1–7). However, the book does not neglect the Jews' religious status. The political and religious spheres are inextricably bound together. Therefore another "wall" of protection was the knowledge and observance of God's law. Ezra and Nehemiah together regulated the exiles' social and religious life on the basis of the law of Moses (chaps. 5; 8–13).

2. The book continues the theme of worship, which is pervasive in Chronicles and Ezra. The author drew attention to the Levites and priests, who were the first to begin work on the wall (3:1,17,22,28) and were promi-

nently listed among those who repopulated the city (11:10-23; 12:1-26,29). They functioned in their expected roles as teachers and temple officials (8:7-8; 9:4; 12:27-36,45-46). The Levites were leaders of Israel's covenant renewal (9:38; 10:9-13,28) and won the community's approval for their service (12:44,47). Yet they did not escape the need for reformation since their sins were exposed (13:4-11,28,30).

3. God is the "God of heaven," who as Creator of the universe is awesome and great (1:5; 2:4,20; 4:14; 9:6,32). The LORD's sovereignty is seen most clearly in His appointment and protection of Nehemiah, accomplished through the mighty kings of Persia (2:8,18). He was the guarantor of Nehemiah's success (2:20), which even his enemies admitted was divinely accomplished (6:16). God frustrated the plots of the Jews' enemies and was the source for the rallying cry, "Our God will fight for us!" (4:15,20).

But God is not just awesome in might. He is also depicted as a God of covenant steadfastness who dealt faithfully with Israel on the basis of its election (1:5-7; 9:7-37). He is holy and demands a righteous people, a sanctified priesthood, and a hallowed place of worship (12:30; 13:9,23-28,30).

4. Prayer is the fulcrum that engages God to act in Israel's behalf. Nehemiah's prayers sprinkle the narrative with invocations for divine blessing (5:19; 6:9b; 13:14, 22b,31b) or curses upon wicked opposition (4:4-5; 6:14; 13:29). Prayer matched with levelheaded pragmatism marked Nehemiah's ways (2:4-5; 4:9). Confession of Israel's past sin reflected the community's sense of continuity with past guilt and the continuing need for God's merciful intervention (1:4-11; 9:5b-37).

5. Scripture engendered the returned exiles' recommitment to the LORD. The law of Moses, in particular, was the plumb line by which they measured the success of their spiritual rebuilding. The law was read, interpreted, and applied to regulate the community's life (8:1-18; 9:3). The law convicted (8:9; 9:2-3), incited worship (8:11-18), and generated reform (13:1-3,17-22a,23-27).

6. The cooperative work of the remnant was evident in the priests and Levites, rulers, artisans, merchants, and their sons and daughters, who labored side by side to refortify the walls (3:1-32). Their diligence was paralleled by their wits (4:6,16-18). Intimidation was deflected by the community's persistence (4:14; 6:13,19), and their

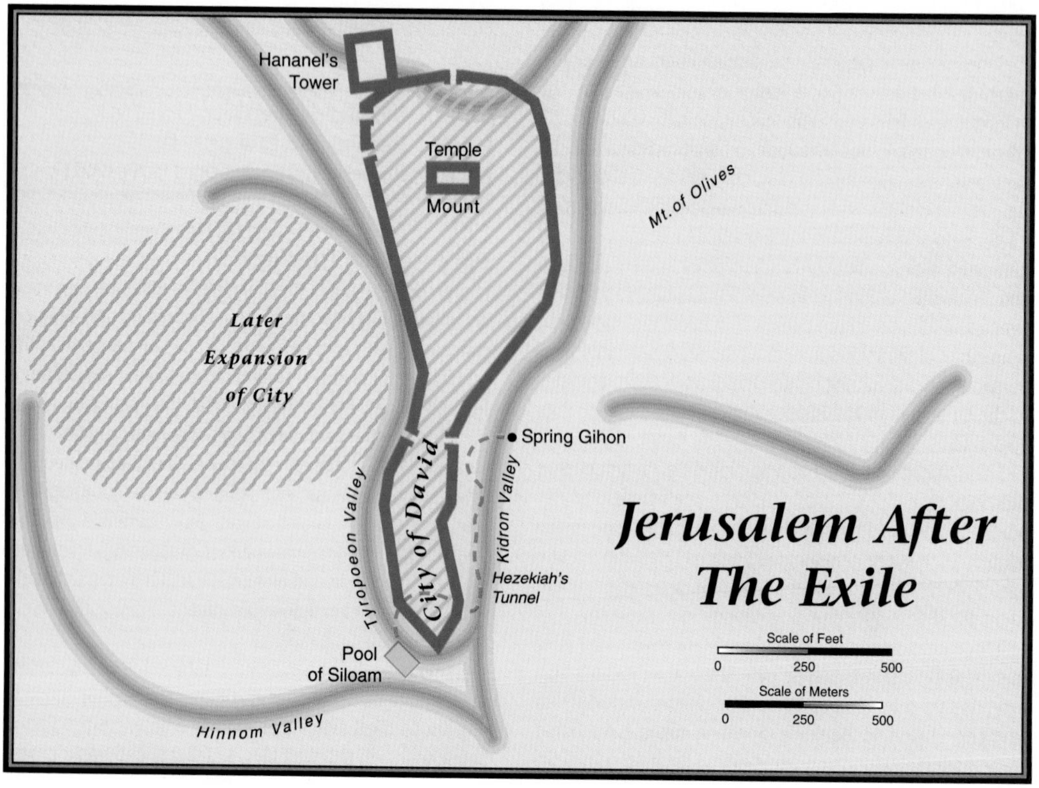

adversaries became fearful of what they said the Jews could not do (4:1-3; 6:16).

7. The book's report on the community's stewardship ties together the themes of community, Scripture, and worship. The Jerusalem walls, even in Nehemiah's day, did not overshadow the temple: "We will not neglect the house of God" (10:39). Thus, the returned exiles swore to fulfill their obligations of service to the house of God through tithes and votive gifts in accordance with the law of Moses (10:32-39; 12:44). The sanctity and perpetuation of temple life were the agenda of Nehemiah's second term as governor (13:4-13,30).

REBUILDING THE WALLS (NEH 1:1–7:73)

The book opens with Nehemiah's memoirs, which tell the governor's role in refortifying Jerusalem (chaps. 1–3). He reported the opposition he encountered from the Samaritans and showed how God had enabled him to succeed (chaps. 4–6). At God's prompting, Nehemiah took steps to repopulate the city by reviewing those who had first returned (chap. 7).

1:1-11
Nehemiah's Prayer

Nehemiah received a delegation of Jews led by Hanani in modern southwestern Iran, the winter palace of the Persian kings (Esth 1:2,5; Dan 8:2). The visit was made in the month of Kislev (Nov.-Dec.) in the twentieth year (445 B.C.) of Artaxerxes I (464–424 B.C.; Neh 1:1-3). When Nehemiah heard Jerusalem was unprotected, he sought God's help through fasting and prayer (1:4-11a). His appeal was based on God's covenant with Israel as given in Deuteronomy. There the LORD threatened the unfaithful but also promised to assist the repentant (compare Deut 28:14; 30:1-4; 9:29). As the king's cupbearer, Nehemiah ended his petition by anticipating an audience with Artaxerxes ("this man," 1:11). Nehemiah's burden for Jerusalem required his personal involvement. The "cupbearer" was a personal butler who functioned as the king's wine taster (1:11).

2:1-20
Nehemiah's Preparations

After four months of prayer and preparation, Nehemiah was ready to answer the king's inquiries about his sad demeanor. Nehemiah feared the king's response, but with God's help he courageously petitioned the king for the authority to rebuild Jerusalem's defenses (2:2-8). The LORD favored the cupbearer so that the king granted his petition by giving him letters of authority and royal protection (2:9). Sanballat's and Tobiah's displeasure (2:10)

Lion's (Stephen's) Gate, one of the entrances into the old city of Jerusalem, probably is built near the ancient Sheep Gate.

was an early omen of trouble (2:19; 4:1-2; 6:1-7). Sanballat is named in the Elephantine papyri (407 B.C.) as "governor of Samaria." The Elephantine papyri are Aramaic documents of the fifth century B.C. recovered from a Jewish military colony stationed at modern Aswan at the southern border of Egypt.

Upon arriving in Jerusalem, Nehemiah quietly reviewed the condition of the city in preparing to meet with the Jewish leaders (2:11-16). The people accepted the challenge of rebuilding the walls. Sanballat and Tobiah, joined by Geshem the Arab, scoffed at them, accusing them of sedition (2:17-19). The same tactic had been effective against Zerubbabel (Ezra 4:4). Nehemiah answered by asserting that the true authority for his actions came from God (Neh 2:20).

3:1-32
Restoring the Gates and Walls

The high priest Eliashib (12:10,22; 13:4) led the work by reconstructing the Sheep Gate (3:1-2). The Fish Gate and wall followed (3:3-5). Workers on the Jeshanah ("Old")

The Wailing Wall has been revered by Jewish people for centuries as the only remaining wall of the ancient temple area in Jerusalem.

Gate and wall included rulers, perfume makers, and women (3:6-12). The Valley Gate and Dung Gate, leading to the city's dumpsite, were next (3:13-14). The restorers of the Fountain Gate and wall included nobility and Levites (3:15-25). Temple servants worked at the Water Gate and wall (3:26-27), and the priests repaired the Horse Gate (3:28). The residents near the East Gate and wall repaired it (3:29-30). Among those laboring at and nearby the Inspection Gate were a goldsmith and merchants (3:31-32). People of all occupations participated, including whole families. Despite opposition, they cooperated in their common goal to do the LORD's work.

4:1-23
Opposition to God's Work

Sanballat's conspiracy included taunts and threats (4:1-3). Nehemiah prayed for God's intervention (4:4-5), and the people labored "with all their heart" (4:6). The opposition broadened and intensified, but the people responded again with prayer (4:7-9). Rumors weakened their resistance, but Nehemiah organized a civil defense (4:10-23). He exhorted the Jews to remember their "great and awesome" God (4:14), who stood able to confound their enemy (4:15) and fight their battles (4:20).

5:1-19
Economic Oppression

Internal dissent threatened the building project as much as the threat of war. The absence of food caused the poorer Jews to mortgage their homes and even sell their children into servitude in order to pay indebtedness. They complained that their oppressive creditors were fellow Jews (5:1-5). Nehemiah convened a hearing and charged the creditors with exacting usury (compare Deut 23:19-20). He considered their actions a reproach in the eyes of their Gentile enemies since the community was already struggling to buy back enslaved Jews from the Gentiles. Nehemiah acknowledged he had made loans but not unfairly. The guilty agreed to return the confiscated possessions (Neh 5:6-13).

This incident led Nehemiah to defend his conduct during the twelve years of his term as governor. Unlike his predecessors, he did not govern out of greed but placed the building of the wall above his personal interests. By sharing his wealth with many on a daily basis, he set an example for the people (5:14-19).

6:1-19
Final Intimidation

With the work near completion, out of desperation Nehemiah's enemies entreated him four times to meet them at Ono, a site located between Judah and Samaria at the southern end of the Plain of Sharon. He refused on the grounds that the LORD's work was more important (6:1-4). Sanballat, frustrated by Nehemiah's refusals, stepped up his intimidation by charging him with sedition. Nehemiah responded with prayer as he had in the past (6:5-9). Sanballat hired Shemaiah and the prophetess Noadiah to give false counsel as though it were from the LORD. Shemaiah advised Nehemiah to take refuge in the temple because he might be assassinated that night. Nehemiah, however, saw the plot for what it was. He did not want such an act of cowardice to discredit him before the people. Again Nehemiah prayed for God's justice (6:10-14).

The wall was completed after only fifty-two days because of the LORD's help. Ironically, the nations became intimidated by the success of the Jews, realizing that they had accomplished an impossible task. Nevertheless, Tobiah convinced some of the Jews to act treacherously by pressuring Nehemiah. Tobiah had close ties with Eliashib the high priest (compare 13:4) and also had financial dealings among the Jews (6:15-19).

7:1-73
Protecting Jerusalem

Nehemiah charged Hanani with the security of the city because he was able and pious. The city was now secure for new residents (7:1-4; compare 11:1-36). God impressed upon Nehemiah the need to keep genealogical records (7:5). Therefore Nehemiah began by reciting the first record of the exiles under Zerubbabel's tenure (7:6-73; compare Ezra 2:1-70).

READING THE LAW (NEH 8:1–10:39)

The account of Ezra's ministry is told in the third person. Ezra's proclamation of the law began on the first day of the seventh month (8:2) and continued probably each morning for one week. His reading of the law encouraged the exiles to rejoice and to celebrate the Feast of Tabernacles in the proper way (chap. 8). By hearing the law, the people came under conviction, and collectively the nation recalled the evil of Israel's past (chap. 9). The result was a covenant renewal in which they pledged themselves to the law (chap. 10).

8:1-18
Ezra Reads the Law

The last half of 7:73 introduces chapter 8. The seventh month was the most important month of the ceremonial calendar (compare Lev 23). On the first day of the month (compare Num 29:1), the people assembled and called for Ezra to read the law. The purpose of the reading was so they could understand the law (8:1-4). The people stood in reverence when the law was read; and their response included praise, tears, and joy. The Levites interpreted the law for those who did not understand its meaning (8:5-12).

After hearing the law, the elders urged Ezra to call for a general assembly of all the Jews to observe the Feast of Booths (Tabernacles). Tabernacles was traditionally celebrated for seven days at the time of harvest ingathering (Exod 34:22). It commemorated God's provision during the wilderness when Israel lived in temporary shelters or booths (compare Lev 23:33-43). For these exiles, this festival was particularly meaningful because they had experienced the second "Exodus" from Babylon. The booths, made of tree branches, were constructed in the city. Not since Joshua's time had the feast been celebrated in this way. The law was carefully followed. The Jews set aside the eighth day (Lev 23:36) for special assembly (Neh 8:13-18).

9:1-38
Israel Confesses Its Sin

On the twenty-fourth of the month, two days after the feast, the exiles fasted while dressed in the clothing of contrition. They prepared for confession by sanctification, reading the law of Moses, and worship (9:1-3).

The Levites led a prayer of confession, calling the pilgrims to arise (9:4-5a). They praised God as great and gracious. From Abraham's call to Moses' experience at Sinai, God protected and provided for Israel (9:5b-15). In contrast to the longsuffering of God, Israel was stiffnecked and rebellious throughout its history. Still, the LORD remained merciful (9:16-31). The prayer concluded with supplications. They admitted that God had justly chastened them by Gentile oppression, but now they prayed that God might see their economic distress and rescue them from oppression (9:32-37). Their prayer of confession concluded with the nation entering an oath of commitment to obey the law of Moses (9:38).

10:1-39
Signing of the Covenant

The chapter lists those who signed the oath, beginning with the governor. Also priests, Levites and rulers are noted (10:1-27). The features of the covenant included (1) submission to the Law, (2) separation from foreign marriages, (3) Sabbath observance as the sign of the Mosaic covenant, and (4) service to God through tithes and offerings. They agreed to fulfill what the Law required of them. They would pay the temple tax (Exod 30:11-16) contribute wood for the continual burnt offerings (Lev 6:12). They would dedicate their firstfruits and firstborn (Exod 23:19a; Num 18:17-19) and pay tithes for the Levites and priests (Lev 27:30-33; Num 18:21-32; Deut 12:5-18; 14:22-29).

REFORMING THE PEOPLE (NEH 11:1–13:31)

The concluding section completes the themes already begun in chapters 1–10. The repopulation theme begun in chapter 7 continues with the catalog of new residents in Jerusalem to show a continuity with their ancestral faith and their hope in a new Israel (11:1–12:26). The dedication ceremonies of the walls (12:27-47) reminds the reader of the opposition the Jews endured yet the success they enjoyed because of God's good favor. Finally, the variety of reforms introduced by Nehemiah enforced the features of the covenant undertaken by the community (13:1-31).

11:1-36
Settling the Cities

The exiles organized their society by lot and by volunteers who migrated to the Holy City (11:1-2). While descendants of all of Israel's tribes returned to Judah, Jerusalem would be comprised particularly of those whose ancestors had populated the city in the days of David's kingdom—Judah, Benjamin, and Levi (11:3-36).

12:1-47
Dedicating the Walls

Nehemiah's memoirs are taken up with the continuing

THE RETURN FROM EXILE

PHASE	DATE	SCRIPTURE REFERENCE	JEWISH LEADER	PERSIAN RULER	EXTENT OF THE RETURN	EVENTS OF THE RETURN
FIRST	538 B.C.	Ezra 1–6	Zerubbabel Jeshua	Cyrus	(1) Anyone who wanted to return could go. (2) The temple in Jerusalem was to be rebuilt. (3) Royal treasury provided funding of the temple rebuilding. (4) Gold and silver worship articles taken from temple by Nebuchadnezzar were returned.	(1) Burnt offerings were made. (2) The Feast of Tabernacles was celebrated. (3) The rebuilding of the temple was begun. (4) Persian ruler ordered rebuilding to be ceased. (5) Darius, King of Persia, ordered rebuilding to be resumed in 520 B.C. (6) Temple was completed and dedicated in 516 B.C.
SECOND	458 B.C.	Ezra 7–10	Ezra	Artaxerxes Longimanus	(1) Anyone who wanted to return could go. (2) Royal treasury provided funding. (3) Jewish civil magistrates and judges were allowed.	Men of Israel intermarried with foreign women.
THIRD	444 B.C.	Nehemiah 1–13	Nehemiah	Artaxerxes Longimanus	Rebuilding of Jerusalem was allowed.	(1) Rebuilding of wall of Jerusalem was opposed by Sanballat the Horonite, Tobiah the Ammonite, and Geshem the Arab. (2) Rebuilding of wall was completed in 52 days. (3) Walls were dedicated. (4) Ezra read the Book of the Law to the people. (5) Nehemiah initiated reforms.

account of the walls. The elaborate festivities planned (12:27-29) included Levitical singers and orchestra. The people, aware of their standing before God, cleansed themselves to prepare for the celebration (12:30). Ezra and Nehemiah led the two processionals. After marching around the city on its wall, the two parades convened at the temple to offer God thanksgiving (12:31-43). Provisions for the Levites and priests were restored and the choirs David had ordered were reestablished (12:44-47).

13:1-31
Renewing the People

Another line of defense constructed by Nehemiah was the community's spiritual life. The basis for the reforms Nehemiah enforced was the Mosaic law. He attempted to reflect the Mosaic ideal that Ezra's reading of the law had set before the people (chaps. 8–10). The people segregated themselves from foreign influences that would jeopardize their spiritual commitment (13:1-30; compare Deut 23:3-5).

However, Eliashib the high priest (Neh 3:1,20; 12:22; Ezra 10:6) had already compromised the holiness of God's temple. He cleared the storerooms for the Ammonite Tobiah (Neh 6:18) to occupy. Nehemiah explained that he was in Persia when Tobiah occupied the temple. Upon his return, he immediately expelled Tobiah and cleansed and restored the storerooms for service (13:4-9). He reinstated the Levitical offerings, which had ceased during his absence, and charged the people with breaking their oath (13:10-14; 10:39; compare Mal 2:8-12). He took further steps against merchants who violated the Sabbath by selling goods to the Jews. He charged the Jews with repeating their fathers' sins and threatened the merchants' lives (13:15-22).

Nehemiah's final action addressed the continued problem of intermarriage (compare Ezra 9:1–10:44). To Nehemiah, the different languages he heard spoken by Judah's children indicated that the Jews were losing their distinctive identity as God's people (13:23-24). The problem was the foreigners' religion, not their ethnicity. He argued that the Jews were reviving the sins of Solomon, whose unfaithfulness caused Israel to sin and suffer the God's judgment. Nehemiah took drastic action because of the severe threat. He physically chastened those married to foreigners and forced them to abstain from such marriages (13:25-27). So sordid was the situation that even Sanballat's daughter (2:10,19) had married into the priestly line (13:28).

Nehemiah concluded his reforms by caring for the needs of the priesthood (13:30). Nehemiah was conscious that he was carrying out God's mandates and not his own. With each reform he prayed for God's blessing on his faithful service (13:14,22b,29,31).

Theological and Ethical Significance

The Book of Nehemiah illustrates how much a layperson committed to a life of prayer, God's Word, and active obedience can do. Nehemiah serves as a reminder that Christians are needed in leadership positions not only within the church but also in civil government. Those attempting to mold society on the principles of Scripture will doubtless experience opposition like Nehemiah did. Prayer, Nehemiah's most potent weapon, continues to serve Christians in their struggle to do God's will in spite of opposition.

Nehemiah's call for divorce of foreign wives is not an endorsement of divorce or racism but a desperate command for a desperate time. (Compare Mal 2:10-16; 2 Cor 6:14–7:1.) The survival of the Jews as a people committed to God demanded *exclusion* of Gentiles *for a time.* The survival of the church demands *inclusion* of *all* who will hear the gospel and commit their lives to Christ.

Questions for Reflection

1. How should the people of God work together to achieve the Lord's purpose?

2. What does the life of Nehemiah teach about the layperson's devotion to God?

3. What is the role of Scripture in the life of the church?

4. How should Christians respond to opposition to God's kingdom?

5. What does the Bible teach about interracial marriage? about marriage to unbelievers?

Sources for Additional Study

Kidner, Derek. *Ezra and Nehemiah.* Downers Grove: InterVarsity, 1979.

McConville, J. G. *Ezra, Nehemiah, and Esther.* Philadelphia: Westminster, 1985.

Vos, Howard F. *Ezra, Nehemiah, and Esther.* Grand Rapids: Eerdmans, 1987.

ESTHER

The Book of Esther is named after its heroine. Esther used her prominent position as queen of Persia to save the Jewish people from destruction. "Esther" is probably derived from the Persian word *stara,* meaning *star.* Some scholars have related it to "Ishtar," the Akkadian goddess associated with the planet Venus. Esther's Hebrew name was "Haddassah," meaning *myrtle* (Esth 2:7).

In the Greek and English versions, Esther is the last book in the collection of Historical Books. In the Hebrew arrangement of the Old Testament, the book is one of the five *Megilloth* (*rolls* or *scrolls*) occurring in the third and final section (the *Kethubhim* or *Writings*) of the Hebrew Bible. The book's plot includes the origins of the Jewish festival of Purim. Esther is traditionally read upon that annual celebration (Adar 14 and 15).

The Greek translation has five additions to the Hebrew (and English) text. These additions to Esther supplement the narrative and make the book more religious in tone (see below). Jerome's Latin Vulgate removed the additions and placed them at the end of the book. Luther also separated the additions by placing them with the Apocryphal books.

The author of the book cannot be known. The author probably used sources available from the period. The story mentions the use of royal archives (2:23; 6:1; 10:2). And Mordecai, a key figure in the story, is said to have recorded some events (9:20,23,29-32). Some interpreters have speculated that the author was a Persian Jew.

The date of writing is difficult to determine. The setting of the story is the fifth century B.C. in the reign of the Persian king Ahasuerus (1:1), who is commonly identified with Xerxes I (485–464 B.C.). Scholars have suggested dates of authorship ranging from as early as the fifth century B.C. to as late as the Maccabean period (second to first centuries B.C.). A date of about 400 B.C. coincides well with the linguistic evidence and the author's excellent knowledge of Persian life.

Question of History and Literary Genre

The reliability of the Book of Esther as a historical witness has been challenged. In more recent years many scholars have recognized that it has a historical nucleus. Some of these same scholars believe that the literary genre of Esther is historical novel or historical romance. The Book of Esther, as the argument goes, has the properties of legend and fiction. Internal oddities include Mordecai's age (at least 124 years old if he indeed were deported by Nebuchadnezzar; compare 2:6; 3:7) and other questionable exaggerations (for example, 1:4; 2:12; 5:14; 9:16). It is argued that the story's protagonists and the incidents related cannot be corroborated outside the Bible. Furthermore, the Greek historian Herodotus (*History* VII, 114) identified Xerxes' queen as Amestris, not Vashti or Esther.

However, scholars who esteem the book as a reliable historical witness have answered that it shows an accurate and detailed knowledge of Persian life, law, and custom. Archaeological information about the architecture of the palace and about Xerxes' reign harmonizes well with the story's depictions. The occasion of the banquet in the third year (1:3) corresponds to the remarks of the Greek historian Herodotus (*History*, VII.8) that Xerxes convened his leading men in that year to plan a campaign against Greece. Also the name of a court official, *Marduka* (Mordecai?), has been attested in Persian tablets from this time. While it is not possible to identify with certainty this figure as Mordecai, the name gives the story a ring of authenticity.

As for the incongruities, evangelicals answer with alternative explanations. For example, the Hebrew text can be interpreted to mean that Mordecai's ancestor Kish was deported by Nebuchadnezzar (2:6). As for Amestris, some have attempted to equate the names of Esther and Amestris on a linguistic basis, but this has been questioned. Others have accounted for the discrepancy by suggesting that Xerxes had more than one queen or that Amestris was queen during the four years between the removal of Vashti and the wedding of Esther (1:3; 2:16).

If it can be shown that the author intended the book to be read as a literary fiction, it should be interpreted accordingly as one would a parable or allegory without doubting its inspiration. However, if the author intended it as historically verifiable, interpreters should treat it as a reliable account of the Persian Jews. The author indicates that the book should be read as historical when he invites his readers to verify this account by consulting Persian annals where the story's events (and more) can be found (10:2). This is the same kind of invitation found among the histories of Kings and Chronicles. Unless there is compelling evidence otherwise, the trustworthiness of the account should be the interpreter's guide.

Esther without "God"

Esther is the only book in the Hebrew Bible that does not mention God's name. Also absent is any reference to the law, Jewish sacrifice, prayer, or revelation. It is the only book of the Old Testament absent from the Dead Sea Scrolls. Opinion about the book's religious value has varied. Luther considered it worthless. The famous Jewish scholar Maimonides (twelfth century A.D.) set it beside the Torah in importance. The book's canonical status has been disputed by Jews and Christians (see "The Canonicity of the Bible").

One explanation for the book's "secular" nature is that a Jewish author took the story almost verbatim from an official Persian record that omitted God's name. Others have suggested that the author was more concerned about the Jewish people as a nation than their religious practices. However, official records (for example, the Cyrus Cylinder and Moabite Stone) are known to have invoked or referred to deities without reservation. There is no reason the name of Israel's God would have been offensive to Persian religion. Old Testament literature does not make the modern dichotomy between secular concerns and religious ones when describing historical events.

A better explanation is that the absence of religious language best suited the author's theological purposes. The author expressed his theology through the vehicle of story, arranging the events and dialogue to accentuate that theology. He omitted Israel's religious distinctives because he wanted to veil God's presence. The author believed in God's sovereignty but that God's intervention is expressed through human instrumentation.

The author did not directly speak of God's participation; rather, he only hinted at God's presence. He did this through the characters who recognized divine intervention in their lives (4:15-16b). The mention of fasting and the wearing of sackcloth and ashes (4:1-3; 4:16; 9:31) imply that the Jews worshiped since prayer commonly occurred with fasting in the Old Testament. The author perceived that God effectively orchestrated the salvation of the Jews, but he did not want God's actions to be obvious.

Another way the story shows God's hand is by reversing the expected outcome of the events. Human intrigue, manipulation, and simple coincidence are the overt explanations for the dramatic changes in the story's conclusion while covertly God is at work. The story's structure further enhances the author's theme of reversals. By omitting reference to religious activities, the author commented on the spiritual status of the Jews living in the Diaspora. These Jews were the ones who did not volunteer to return to Jerusalem as part of the "remnant" through whom God would work again (Ezra 1:4; 9:8-9). Though their faith was fragile, God remained faithful to His covenant by preserving them.

Theme

God worked behind the scenes to save the Jews from destruction by exalting Esther as queen of Persia and turning the tables on their enemies (4:14; 9:1).

I. Vashti's Demotion (1:1-22)
II. The King's Decree to Destroy the Jews (2:1–3:15)
III. Haman Threatens Mordecai (4:1–5:14)
IV. Mordecai Defeats Haman (6:1–7:10)
V. The King's Decree on the Jews' Behalf (8:1–9:32)
VI. The Promotion of Mordecai (10:1-3)

Purpose and Theology

1. The book's primary theological purpose is God's subtle providence in the life of His people. While Ezra-Nehemiah tells how the exiles fared in Jerusalem, the story of Esther answers what happened to those who stayed behind. The author showed through unexpected reversals in his characters' lives how God superintended the deliverance of the Jews. The theme of reversal is best illustrated by the careers of Haman and Mordecai (7:10–8:2) and by the Jews' triumph instead of extermination (9:1).

2. The book also explains the origins of the festival of Purim (Hebrew *lots*) the Jews celebrated annually on the fourteenth and fifteenth of Adar (3:7; 9:26). While the casting of lots appeared to seal their doom (3:7), the lots became their reason for celebration (9:23-26). The Fast of Esther in Jewish tradition precedes Purim to commemorate the fasting that precipitated their victory.

3. The idea of wealth and power is pervasive in the story with its focus on the Persian court (1:1-9; 3:1-2; 10:1). However, the power of Esther (5:1-3; 7:7) and Mordecai (6:11; 9:4; 10:2), acquired because of their loyalty to the king, triumphed over their Persian enemies.

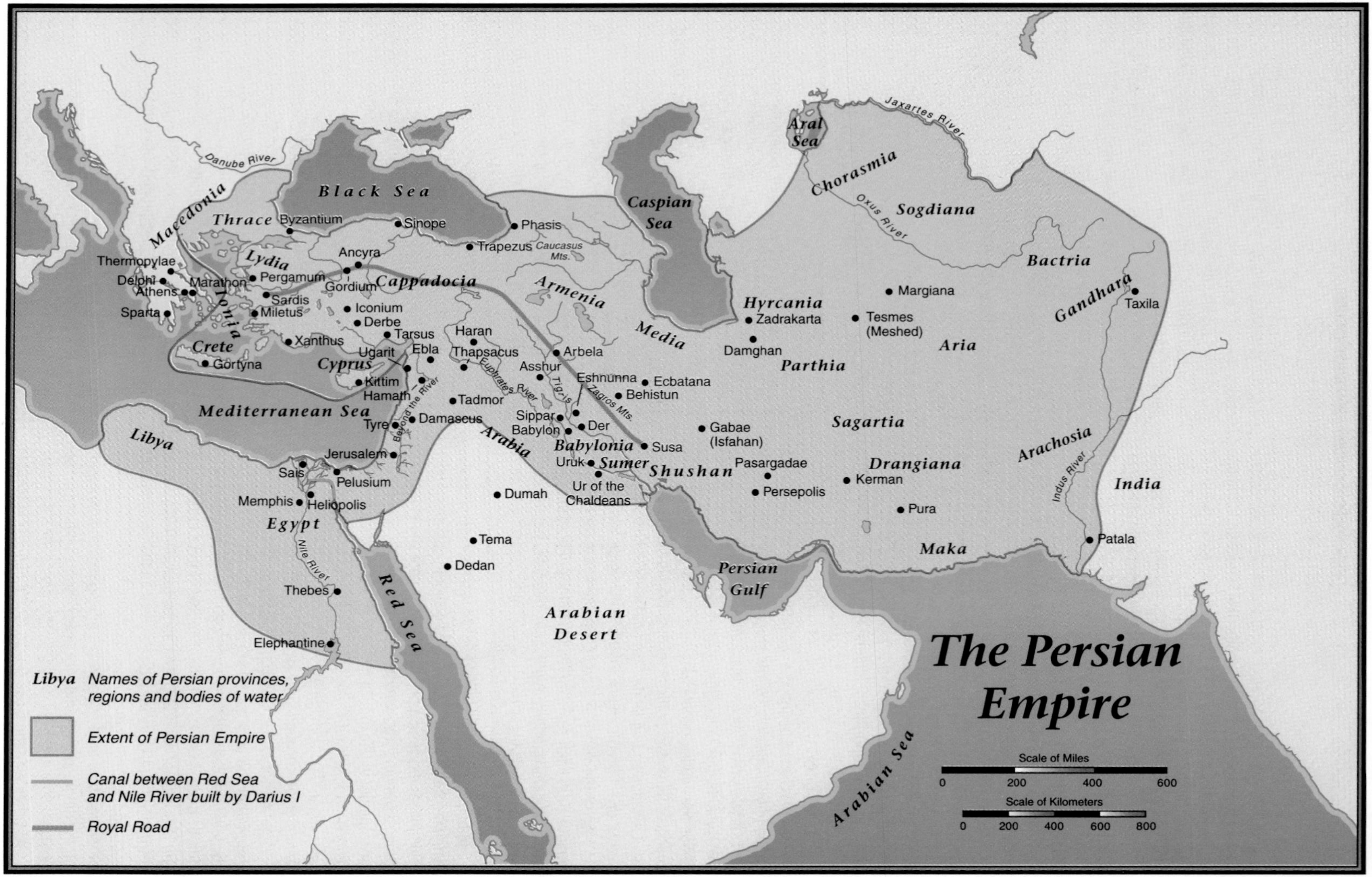
The Persian Empire
Libya Names of Persian provinces, regions and bodies of water
Extent of Persian Empire
Canal between Red Sea and Nile River built by Darius I
Royal Road
Scale of Miles
0 200 400 600
Scale of Kilometers
0 200 400 600 800
Black Sea
Caspian Sea
Aral Sea
Mediterranean Sea
Red Sea
Persian Gulf
Arabian Sea
Danube River
Jaxartes River
Oxus River
Euphrates River
Tigris
Nile River
Indus River
Beyond the River
Caucasus Mts.
Zagros Mts.
Macedonia
Thrace
Lydia
Ionia
Crete
Cyprus
Cappadocia
Armenia
Media
Hyrcania
Parthia
Chorasmia
Sogdiana
Bactria
Gandhara
Aria
Sagartia
Drangiana
Arachosia
India
Maka
Shushan
Sumer
Babylonia
Arabia
Egypt
Libya
Arabian Desert
Thermopylae
Delphi
Athens
Marathon
Sparta
Byzantium
Pergamum
Sardis
Miletus
Gortyna
Xanthus
Ancyra
Gordium
Sinope
Trapezus
Phasis
Iconium
Derbe
Tarsus
Ugarit
Ebla
Kittim
Hamath
Haran
Thapsacus
Tadmor
Damascus
Tyre
Jerusalem
Sais
Pelusium
Memphis
Heliopolis
Thebes
Elephantine
Dumah
Tema
Dedan
Arbela
Asshur
Eshnunna
Ecbatana
Behistun
Sippar
Babylon
Der
Susa
Uruk
Ur of the Chaldeans
Gabae (Isfahan)
Pasargadae
Persepolis
Zadrakarta
Damghan
Tesmes (Meshed)
Margiana
Kerman
Pura
Taxila
Patala

Whereas the Jews were helpless before their Gentile lords, in the end the magistrates feared and honored the Jews (8:17; 9:2).

The moral is that power should be used for righteous purposes and not for self-gratification. Moredecai, for instance, recognized that Esther's power was a gift to be used for her people's deliverance (4:14). Abusive power became Haman's noose (5:11-14; 7:10), whereas Mordecai used authority to help his people (8:7-8; 10:3).

Finally, the book is a parody on Gentile domination. Mighty Xerxes, draped in royal splendor, is depicted as a weak, easily manipulated monarch who was ill-informed about the events of his own kingdom. The prerogative of Gentile authority—the irrevocable law of the Medes and Persians—entrapped the king and ultimately brought down Gentile authority (epitomized in Haman). True power is found in the virtues of loyalty, honesty, and fasting in worship of God.

4. God rewards loyalty. Vashti's disloyalty is contrasted with Esther's loyalty to the king and her people. Another contrast is the bumbling Haman, who hanged for his conspiracy (7:3-10), while Mordecai was honored for saving the king from assassins (2:21-23). Mordecai, in particular, exemplifies loyalty to the Jewish tradition. He functioned as Esther's Jewish conscience (4:12-14), and as a "Jew" (3:3) he refused to pay homage to Haman the "Agagite" (3:1-2; 5:9). Mordecai attempted to hide their Jewish extraction, but he learned in the end that the revelation of Esther as a Jewess gave them the upper hand (2:10,20). The story shows that those of the Diaspora could be faithful to their heritage while living as honorable citizens of a Gentile state.

5. Another recurring theme is the contrast between festival and fasting. The story begins with Xerxes' elaborate seven-day feast which ultimately resulted in Esther's appointment as queen. Later, Esther's two feasts resulted in the death of the Jews' archenemy Haman. Finally, Mordecai established the Feast of Purim, enjoyed by Jews and Gentiles for generations to come (8:15,17; 9:17,19,26-28).

The foil for this feasting is Jewish fasting which was the author's way of expressing this people's commitment to their religious heritage (4:1-3,16). Fasting preceded feasting in the case of Esther's approach to the king (4:16), and thus fasting was also commemorated as part of their Purim (9:31). Their fasting, the outward expression of their trust in God, precipitated their victory and celebration.

6. Finally, the story addresses the problem of social and religious bigotry. Haman's anti-Semitism was frightfully expressed when he swore he would not rest until he rid himself of "that Jew Mordecai" (5:13). The Jews are warned by this story not to escape their heritage. In fact, their spiritual heritage preserved them as a people.

A gold cup from Persia decorated with winged lions and dating from the sixth to fifth century B.C.

VASHTI'S DEMOTION (ESTH 1:1-22)

The Persian King Khshayarsha was known as Ahasuerus in Hebrew and Xerxes in Greek. He is commonly identified with Xerxes I (485–464 B.C.), who is remembered for his devastating naval loss to the Greeks at Salamis in 481. The Greek historian Herodotus described his kingdom as consisting of twenty provinces and extending from India to Ethiopia.

The king convened a royal reception in his third year (483 B.C.) at Susa of Elam (modern SW Iran), which was the winter resort of the Persian kings (Esth 1:1-3; Neh 1:1; Dan 8:2). Archaeological work has uncovered the elaborate royal palace of the city.

The assembly Xerxes called lasted for 180 days, during which he displayed the splendor of his wealth. It culminated in a seven-day feast of luxurious dining and drunkenness. The opulence of the Persian court is described to indicate the vast resources and power of the king (1:4-9).

In a drunken stupor, the king called for Queen Vashti to "display her beauty" before his guests (1:10-11). Her refusal, probably out of decency, threatened the king's reputation. At Memucan's advice, the king deposed her (1:10-22). Xerxes' action is a parody on Persian might, for the powerful king could not even command his own wife.

THE KING'S DECREE TO DESTROY THE JEWS (ESTH 2:1–3:15)

The second section of the story concerns the exaltation of

A colossal Persian column capital from Susa (the winter capital of the Persian kings) decorated with two stylized bulls.

Esther (chap. 2) and the evil plot by Haman to exterminate the Jews (chap. 3). The role of Mordecai as Esther's cousin and Haman's hated enemy links the two episodes.

2:1-23
Queen Esther's Rise

Xerxes, at his attendants' advice, ordered a search for Vashti's successor (2:1-4). The narrator revealed Esther's nationality by first identifying Mordecai's lineage as a Benjamite of the family of Kish. Mordecai was Esther's foster parent and elder cousin. Esther ("Hadassah," her Hebrew name) was among those brought to the king's palace because of her exceptional beauty (2:5-9). At Mordecai's advice she concealed her nationality, a factor that figured in her advantage over the enemy Haman.

One year of purification was required for an audience with the king. Esther was received by the king four years after the deposition of Vashti (479 B.C.; 2:16; 1:3). She won his approval and became queen (2:10-18). The western expedition against the Greeks by Xerxes' Persian ships ended in disaster at Salamis in 481 B.C. His selection of Esther occurred after this debacle.

Mordecai, who may have been in the king's service as a gatekeeper (2:19), discovered a plot to kill Xerxes (perhaps because of disaffection over his losses at Salamis). The two culprits were hanged on gallows, and Mordecai's heroism was recorded (2:21-23). From this incident Mordecai learned of Esther's new power at court. The concealment of her identity and the record of Mordecai's deed would lead to Haman's eventual undoing (6:1-2; 7:3-6). The traitors' gallows anticipated Haman's own death for the same crime of treachery (7:10).

3:1-15
Haman's Murderous Plan

The theme of power is continued by the introduction of Haman as second in position to the king. This incident took place about five years after the installation of Queen Esther (2:16; 3:7). Haman is identified as an "Agagite," perhaps a descendant of the Amalekite king, Agag, who was defeated but spared by King Saul (3:1; 1 Sam 15). Israel and Amalek were enemies from Moses' time (Exod 17:8-16). For the author, the contention between Haman and Mordecai, a descendant of Kish (as was Saul), typified the enmity between Israel and the Gentiles. This Agagite, however, would not be spared.

While others bowed to Haman, Mordecai refused to worship him because of his Jewish faith (3:2-4)—as Daniel had declined to worship Darius (Dan 6). Haman masterminded a plot to exterminate all the Jews. The divinely appointed day and month was determined by the casting of the *pur*, meaning *lot* (Akkadian). The king was persuaded to permit the mass murder by official decree and sealed by the king's own signet ring (Esth 3:7-11; compare 8:2,8). Couriers raced throughout the empire to deliver the decree that on the thirteenth day of Adar, some eleven months later, the Jews were to be destroyed (3:12-14). The common people of Susa were shocked by the cold-blooded decree in contrast to the conspirators, who meanwhile confidently celebrated (3:15).

HAMAN THREATENS MORDECAI (ESTH 4:1–5:14)

Esther's position enabled her to save the Jews if she were willing to risk her own standing (chap. 4). After recounting Esther's vow of devotion, the author told how Esther took the lead and devised her own scheme to outmaneuver Haman. Ironically, Haman unwittingly devised his own end (chap. 5).

4:1-17
Mordecai's Plea to Esther

When Mordecai learned of the murderous plot, he and all

the Jews joined in mourning, fasting, and the wearing of sackcloth and ashes (4:1-3). This spontaneous act of grief evidenced the solidarity of the Jews. The custom of sackcloth and ashes included prayers of confession and worship (1 Kgs 21:27-29; Neh 9:1-3; Dan 9:3). Esther learned of the decree from her messenger Hathach, who relayed Mordecai's plea for her help (4:4-9). But Esther explained that she could not approach the king because Persian law meted out death to anyone entering uninvited. Mordecai answered by warning her that as a Jewess her own life was in jeopardy and that God could save His people by another means if she failed. He believed that her exaltation in the palace had a holy purpose (4:10-14). Esther's trust in God was the turning point. She requested a communal fast by all the Jews as they petitioned God (Ezra 8:21-23; compare Acts 13:3; 14:23). She replied to Mordecai with courage and confidence in God's will: "If I perish, I perish" (Esth 4:15; compare Dan 3:16-18).

5:1-14
Esther's Banquet and Haman's Folly

The prayers of God's people were answered because Xerxes received Esther without incident. She invited the king and Haman to a banquet whereupon she would make her request known (5:1-5a). Once the guests had enjoyed their fill, Esther wisely delayed her request for another day of feasting—no doubt to heighten the king's interest in the petition (5:5b-8).

Haman left in a happy mood (5:9-10a), but it was tempered by his fury for "the Jew Mordecai" (5:13). Haman boasted of his authority, (5:10b-13) but these boasts would later turn into tears of humiliation (6:12-13a; 7:7-8a). Haman's friends and family (5:14) would be repaid with their own lives on the very gallows they had recommended for Mordecai (7:10; 9:14).

MORDECAI DEFEATS HAMAN (ESTH 6:1–7:10)

This section features the key reversal in Haman's and Mordecai's fates. Mordecai was honored by the king, much to Haman's humiliation (chap. 6). The final indignity of foolish Haman was his pathetic effort to save himself from the gallows (chap. 7).

6:1-14
Mordecai Honored by Haman

The unstated reason for the king's insomnia was God's providence. To pass the sleepless night, servants brought the royal annals where Mordecai's deed of saving the king was read (6:1-2; compare 2:19-23). Haman was consulted, but ironically his egotism caused him unintentionally to honor Mordecai (6:3-10). The depiction of Mordecai dressed in royalty and being led on horseback by Haman anticipates their inverted roles to come (6:11). Even his friends and wife voiced the theological proposition of the book: Mordecai is invincible because he is a Jew (6:12-14).

7:1-10
Haman's Hanging

Not only did Mordecai get the best of Haman, but Esther outsmarted him. On the following day, Esther assembled her guests for the second banquet, during which she revealed her entreaty (7:1-4; cf. 5:7-8). The fivefold repetition of "Queen Esther" in this chapter (7:1-3,5,7) echoed Mordecai's plea that she had come to power for this moment (4:14). Alluding to Haman's bribe (3:9), she described herself and the Jews as "sold for destruction" (7:4). She identified Haman as the adversary (7:5-6a).

Haman, true to his character as a blundering dunce, begged for the queen's mercy, thus breaking protocol with the king's harem. He magnified his folly by stumbling to her couch, creating the appearance of improprieties and thereby sealing his doom with the irate king (7:6b-8a). The gallows, whose references tower over much of the narrative (2:23; 5:14; 7:9-10; 8:7; 9:13,25), afforded the Jews their vindication by the hanging of Haman (7:8b-10).

THE KING'S DECREE ON THE JEWS' BEHALF (ESTH 8:1–9:32)

This royal decree Mordecai wrote answered Haman's evil decree (compare 3:8-11). This parallelism continues the theme of reversal, the decree enabling the Jews to take the offensive against their enemies (chap. 8). The thirteenth of Adar, the day planned for the Jews' destruction, was exchanged for the two-day celebration of Purim because of the Jews' conquest (chap. 9).

8:1-17
Mordecai's Plan of Defense

Rather than Jewish property falling into Haman's hands (3:13b), Haman's property and authority were given to Esther and Mordecai (8:1-2). But Haman's villainous plot remained, and Esther successfully pleaded for the king's assistance to avert the disaster (8:3-6). The decree Mordecai wrote gave the Jews the right to defend themselves (8:7-14).

Mordecai took Haman's place as second to the king (8:15). Whereas the city of Susa was disturbed at Haman's decree (3:15), Mordecai's edict gladdened their hearts and converted some to the Jewish faith (8:15-17).

9:1-32
The Jews' Feast of Victory

The dates of the edict and the subsequent victory of the Jews were repeated by the author because they established the traditional calendar for the Feast of Purim (9:1,17-18,21). On the thirteenth day of Adar (Feb.–Mar.), the appointed day of Haman's plot (3:13), the Jews defeated their enemies. The nations feared the Jews, and local magistrates were favorably influenced by Mordecai's position in Xerxes' court. The king granted a second day of vengeance (the fourteenth of Adar). In Susa eight hundred were killed, and Haman's ten sons were hanged. Among all the provinces, the Jews killed seventy-five thousand (9:2-17).

This explained why Purim was celebrated in the city on the thirteenth and fourteenth and in the provinces on the fourteenth and fifteenth of Adar (9:18-19). The author reiterated that the Jews, however, did not loot their enemies (9:10,15). The motivation for the purging was not economic but an avenging of crimes committed against the Jews. Mordecai gave the official decree establishing Purim (9:20-28). The feast was named Purim because of the *pur* ("lot") cast by Haman (9:26). The purpose of the feast was a memorial to Haman's wicked plot, which returned "onto his own head" (9:25). To promote the feast Esther added her authority to a joint letter distributed with Mordecai (9:29-32).

MORDECAI'S PROMOTION (ESTH 10:1-3)

The story concludes in the way it began by describing the power and influence of Xerxes' kingdom. The author refers the reader to the official records of the empire where a full account of the kingdom and the role played by Mordecai could be examined (10:1-2; compare 1 Kgs 14:19; 15:7). Mordecai contributed to the prosperity of the empire and cared for the Jews' welfare (10:3). The greatness of Mordecai vindicated the Jews as a people. Their heritage was not a threat to the Gentiles, but rather through Mordecai and the Jews the empire enjoyed peace.

Theological and Ethical Significance

Our modern experience of God is more like that of the Book of Esther than that of many Old Testament books. In Esther, God worked behind the scenes to bring about deliverance for His people. God did not bring deliverance through spectacular plagues or a miracle at the sea as in the exodus. Rather, God worked through a courageous old man who refused to abandon his principles and a courageous woman who valued the lives of her people more than her own life. The Book of Esther calls us to look at the lives of people committed to God if we want to know what God is doing to bring about deliverance in our own world.

The outlook for Mordecai and the Jews looked bleak through much of Esther. Today we may feel that God has abandoned us or that it is not profitable to be on the Lord's side. The last chapters of Esther brought about God's reversal of circumstances. We should live our lives with a view to how our story is going to end. Someday every knee will bow "and every tongue confess that Jesus is Lord" (Phil 2:10-11). What occasioned fasting and anxious prayer will be forgotten in heaven's feasting (compare Rom 8:18).

As Christians our power and influence should be used for righteous purposes and not for self-gratification. Power is a gift from God to be used for the benefit of His people and His creation. Christian citizenship demands involvement in the affairs of the state. Anti-Semitism and other forms of racial and religious bigotry easily lead to dangerous abuses of power. Today's Christians, like Esther, must be courageous in opposing such abuses.

Questions for Reflection

1. What is the proper relationship between religion and politics?
2. What does the story of Esther teach about evil and suffering?
3. What godly traits does Mordecai exemplify?
4. What is the purpose of fasting?
5. What does this story teach about the care of God for His people?

Sources for Additional Study

Baldwin, Joyce G. *Esther*. Downers Grove: InterVarsity, 1984.

McConville, J. G. *Ezra, Nehemiah, and Esther*. Philadelphia: Westminster, 1985.

Vos, Howard F. *Ezra, Nehemiah, and Esther*. Grand Rapids: Eerdmans, 1987.

The Poetic and Wisdom Books

The Bible is not a manual of religious teachings like the *Baptist Faith and Message* or the *Thirty-Nine Articles* of the Anglican Church. It is the Word of God as it has come to us through the experiences of the people of God. It expresses all the emotions of the life of faith, and it deals with many areas of experience that might seem mundane and unspiritual.

This is nowhere more true than in its poetic and wisdom literature. The Psalms express every emotion the believer encounters in life, be it praise and love for God, anger at those who practice violence and deceit, personal grief and confusion, or appreciation for God's truth. Proverbs not only examines moral issues, but it also helps us deal with the ordinary matters of life, such as indebtedness and work habits. Song of Songs celebrates the joy of love between man and woman. Job and Ecclesiastes make us face our most profound questions and thereby bring us to a more genuine faith in God. In sum, all these books deal with real life.

Traditionally, we speak of Psalms and Song of Songs as being the books of biblical poetry and Job, Proverbs, and Ecclesiastes as biblical wisdom. These books will be the focus of this section. Other Old Testament books, however, share many of the features of poetic and wisdom books. Lamentations is essentially a collection of psalms of lament. Psalms are also found in the prophets (for example, Jonah 2; Hab 3). Ruth, Esther, and Daniel have much more in common with wisdom literature than the casual reader might realize. In the apocrypha Ecclesiasticus and the Wisdom of

Solomon imitate the wisdom features of their biblical counterparts. Even the New Testament has a few psalms and proverbs (Luke 1:46-55,68-79; Acts 20:35; 1 Cor 15:33).

The five books of Job, Psalms, Proverbs, Ecclesiastes, and Song of Songs still give us the best examples of how biblical hymns, songs, proverbs, and reflections are to be read. This in turn allows us to see how wisdom and poetry have affected the rest of the Bible.

What gave rise to the wide variety of songs, proverbs, and theological reflection we see in this literature? The Old Testament was not written in a cultural or literary vacuum. Many of the motifs and features of Egyptian, Canaanite, and Mesopotamian literature are also found in the Old Testament, especially in the poetic and wisdom passages. Some of the most common are the following:

Parallelism is a device in which one line of poetry is followed by a second that in some way reiterates or reinforces the first. Several types of parallelism are found. In *synonymous parallelism* the second line says the same thing in the same word order as the first line. Only the vocabulary differs. For example: "A false witness will not go unpunished / and he who pours out lies will not go free" (Prov 19:5). See also Psalm 114:8: "Who turned the rock into a pool, / the hard rock into springs of water." In *antithetic parallelism* the second line often reinforces the first by stating the same thought from a negative perspective. For example, "The LORD is king forever and ever; / the nations will perish from his land" (Ps 10:16). Also: "A gentle answer turns away wrath, / but a harsh word stirs up anger" (Prov 15:1). With *synthetic parallelism* the second line is not actually parallel to the first, but it reinforces the idea expressed by adding a reason or explanation. For example: "Train a child in the way he should go, / and when he is old he will not turn from it" (Prov 22:6); "Stay away from the foolish man, / for you will not find knowledge on his lips" (Prov 14:7).

In ***Chiasm*** the second line reinforces the first by reversing the sequence of words or phrases. For example, Proverbs 2:4 in the Hebrew order reads:

"If you look for it [A] as for silver [B]

and as for hidden treasure [B'] search for it [A']" (author's translation).

The word order of the second line [B'-A'] is the reverse of the first [A-B]. Parallelism and chiasm also occur on a much larger scale. Entire chapters or

BIBLICAL PRAYERS				
Type of Prayer	**Meaning**	**Old Testament Example**	**New Testament Example**	**Jesus' Teaching**
Confession	Acknowledging sin and helplessness and seeking God's mercy	Ps 51	Luke 18:13	Luke 15:11-24 Luke 18:10-24
Praise	Adoring God for who He is	1 Chr 29:10-13	Luke 1:46-55	Matt 6:9
Thanksgiving	Expressing grati-tude to God for what He has done	Ps 105:1-7	1 Thess 5:16-18	Luke 17:11-19
Petition	Making personal request of God	Gen 24:12-14	Acts 1:24-26	Matt 7:7-12
Intercession	Making request of God on behalf of another	Exod 32:11-13, 31-32	Phil 1:9-11	John 17:9,20-21
Commitment	Expressing loyalty to God and His work	1 Kgs 8:56-61	Acts 4:24-30	Matt 6:10 Luke 6:46-49
Forgiveness	Seeking mercy for personal sin or the sin of others	Dan 9:4-19	Acts 7:60	Matt 6:12 Luke 6:27-36
Confidence	Affirming God's all-sufficiency and the believer's security in His love	Ps 23	Luke 2:29-32	Matt 6:5-15; 7:11
Benediction	A request for God's blessing	Num 6:24-26	Jude 24	Luke 11:15-13

even entire books can be constructed in parallel or chiastic fashion, in which entire blocks of text parallel one another.

Other literary patterns are also found. ***Numeric proverbs*** enumerate a number of items or occurrences that share a common characteristic. For example: "There are six things the Lord hates, / seven that are detestable to him: /haughty eyes, / a lying tongue" (Prov 6:16-19).

In an ***acrostic poem*** each line or section begins with a successive letter of the Hebrew alphabet. The first begins with *aleph,* the second with *beth,* the third with *gimel,* and so on. The twenty-two stanzas of Psalm 119, the Bible's largest acrostic, have eight verses for each consecutive Hebrew letter.

Rhetorical Devices are also found. The language of biblical poetry and wisdom is meant to make it entertaining and easy to remember. The Hebrew text contains rhyme, alliteration (repetition of initial sounds), and even puns. Simile, a comparison using *like* or *as*, also occurs frequently (Ps 131:2; Prov 25:25). One can also find sarcastic humor (Prov 11:22; 19:24) as well as paradox, a statement contrary to common sense that is nevertheless true (Prov 25:15).

Biblical poetry and wisdom are at the same time both great literature and the eternal Word of God. It intrigues and delights us even as it rebukes and instructs. For the reader who gives due attention to these songs and lessons, "They will be a garland to grace your head and a chain to adorn your neck" (Prov 1:9).

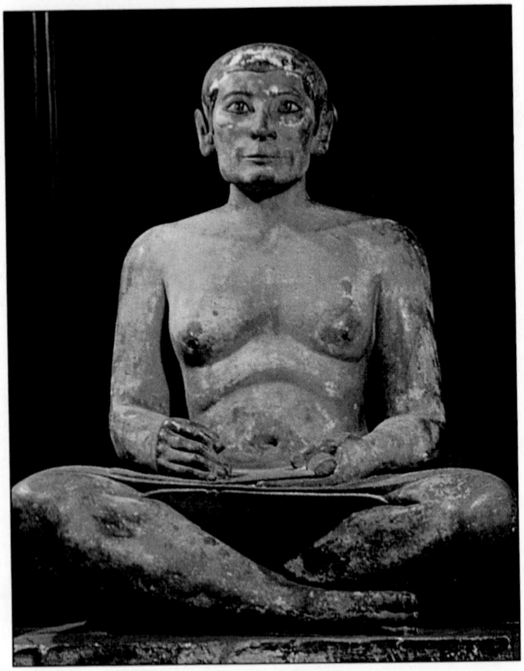

Statue of an Egyptian scribe discovered at Saqqara (about 2500–2300 B.C.). Wisdom literature was an important aspect of Egyptian culture.

JOB

The Book of Job tells of a righteous man (Job) whom God, at Satan's insistence, afflicted as a test of his fidelity and integrity. Three friends (Eliphaz, Bildad, and Zophar) came to comfort him but were horrified at his anger at God. They tried without success to persuade him to repent of some sin. Job concluded this dialogue with a monologue in which he lamented his fate but continued to protest his innocence.

A fifth speaker, Elihu, tried to make sense of the situation and to point out Job's error. Finally God confronted Job, who could then only prostrate himself and repent. God restored Job's fortunes and declared him to be more righteous than his friends.

What can all this mean? Many say Job answers the question of why the righteous suffer. But in order to understand the meaning of the book, we should first look at its background.

Literary Background and Parallels

Outside the Bible. The ancient sages wrote a great deal about human suffering. The Mesopotamian myth of Atrahasus tells of human affliction by the apparently blind wrath of the gods. Canaanite literature from Ugarit describes the trials of King Keret who, like Job, lost seven sons. In a Babylonian hymn to Marduk, a sufferer bewails his losses with as much pathos as Job. An even older Sumerian work models the complaints one ought to raise to one's god when calamity strikes. The Egyptian *Protests of the Eloquent Peasant* challenges social injustice and has a structure somewhat like Job's.

The ancient literature of lamentation certainly influenced Job, particularly in the way Job expressed his complaints. But no true parallel to Job exists outside the Bible. The Book of Job does more than grieve over human pain. Job's travail poses questions never considered in any other ancient literature. Its literary structure, moreover, has no true parallel.

Inside the Bible. Job is in many ways like other writings in the Bible and yet is in a class by itself. Some of the types of biblical material found in Job follow:

Laments. Job repeatedly bewailed what had befallen him, as in 3:1-26; 6:2-7; 10:1-12. Compare Psalms 22:1-18; 102:1-11; Lamentations 3:1-20.

Hymns of Praise. Job often praised God for His power and righteousness, as in 5:9-16 and 26:5-14. Compare Psalms 94 and 97.

Proverbs. Pithy statements of wisdom and metaphor appear in Job 5:2 and 6:5-6. Compare these respectively to Proverbs 14:30 and Isaiah 1:3. Also note the wisdom sayings in Job 28:28 and Proverbs 1:7.

Prophetic Speech. The friends sometimes claimed to have had prophetic experiences, and they preached as the prophets did. See Job 4:12-14; 11:13-20; 32:8.

Wisdom Poems. Job has several lengthy poems on the value of wisdom and right behavior. Compare Job 28 to Proverbs 30:2-4 and Job 8:11-22 to Psalm 1.

Numeric Sayings. Compare Job 5:19 to Proverbs 30:21.

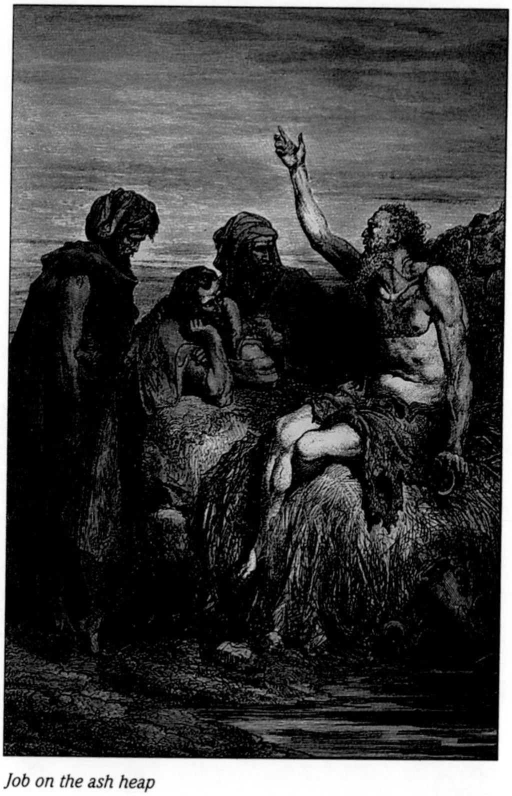

Job on the ash heap

Reflective Questioning. Job sometimes bluntly challenges conventional wisdom. Compare Job 21:17-19 to Ecclesiastes 9:2-3.

Apocalyptic. Job has some features in common with books like Daniel and Revelation. The earthly struggle is part of a heavenly conflict between God and Satan (Job 1–2). Human foes tempt the believer to abandon his perseverance (Job's wife and three friends). But faithful endurance leads to triumph and blessings (Job 42).

The Book of Job draws on many types of literature to set forth its message, but it does not belong to any one of these categories. It must be interpreted as unique both in literary type and message. Job is not a conventional book.

Date and Authorship

No one knows when or by whom Job was written. Some have suggested it was written in the Babylonian exile, but the book does not allude to that or any event from Israel's history. It does often allude to other biblical passages, especially Genesis 1–3 and certain psalms of David (compare Job 7:17-21 to Ps 8). This implies it was written after David. A good possibility is that the book appeared in the reign of Solomon or Hezekiah, both of whom encouraged the study of wisdom literature.

I. Prologue (1:1–2:13)
II. Dialogue with Three Friends (3:1–31:40)
III. Elihu's Speeches (32:1–37:24)
IV. God's Speeches (38:1–42:6)
V. Epilogue: Job Restored (42:7-17)

Unity and Integrity

Some scholars assert that portions of the book are later additions—that is, that they were not written by the original author and are not true to his intentions. The prologue, epilogue, and Elihu speeches are often so regarded. Many allege the writer of the Elihu speeches was a pious Israelite who was offended at much of what Job had to say and felt a need to correct it. But the book makes no sense if the prologue and epilogue are deleted. The Elihu speeches are essential to the plan of the book.

Evil and Suffering

Ever since Adam and Eve disobeyed in Eden, the ground has been cursed (Gen 3:17-18). Weeds and thorns, literal and otherwise, have plagued humanity. Evil has been rampant, and people have suffered. The diversity of evil and suffering can be seen best in seven categories.

1. Judgment. Some people suffer punishment because of their own disobedience or hostility toward God. Cain suffered for the murder of his brother Abel (Gen 4:13-14). God repaid Adoni-Bezek for his inhumane treatment of conquered kings (Judg 1:7). Solomon executed Joab for killing two innocent men (1 Kgs 2:32). Such retribution warns others to avoid violence.

2. Discipline. The purpose of discipline is correction and repentance. When Nathan the prophet announced God's judgment on David for his adultery with Bathsheba and murder of Uriah (2 Sam 11–12), David repented (Ps 51).

3. Training. Here what believers suffer is in no way connected to their failures. It is undeserved. God sends such suffering for their own growth and maturity. Sometimes it comes through the agency of Satan or wicked people. Job 1–2 indicates that "blameless" Job was really in this category. He was unknowingly and unwillingly the subject of a test.

4. Persecution. By persecution Satan or the enemies of God strive to destroy God's people or their faith. Saul's pursuit of David (1 Sam 23) and Haman's attempt to annihilate the Jews (Esth 3:5-6) are OT examples. Persecution involves suffering for one's faithfulness to God. Daniel and his three friends suffered under these circumstances (Dan 3; 6).

5. Purposeful Suffering. Sometimes suffering finds meaning in God's wider purposes. Joseph understood that what his brothers intended for his harm God intended for good, that his family might be saved from the famine (Gen 50:20). The Servant of Isaiah 53 suffers in place of God's people. His suffering results in their forgiveness, peace, and healing (53:5).

6. Natural consequences. Some suffering is the natural consequence of foolishness or stupidity. Whoever builds a house upon the sand finds the winds and the water will wash it away (Matt 7:26-27). Proverbs is filled with advice to avoid the natural consequences of sinful life-styles.

7. Catastrophe. Sometimes earthquakes, hurricanes, volcanoes, plane wrecks, and plagues produce enormous suffering. Death indiscriminately comes to the good and the bad. In specific ways this suffering is undeserved. The victims of the collapse of the Siloam tower or the Galilean victims of Pilate's death squad were no worse than their neighbors (Luke 13:1-4). Such suffering underscores how uncertain life is and challenges us to repentance while there is yet time. □

We cannot interpret Job by omitting difficult or unusual chapters.

Central Problem

The Book of Job confuses modern readers. Often said to be about the problem of why the righteous suffer, it never really solves that problem. To be sure, some readers believe that the prologue resolves the problem: suffering is a test of humanity in a cosmic trial before God and Satan. This concept is present in Job and has validity.

But this hardly explains the whole book. If this is the message of Job, then the dispute between Job and his friends, the very heart of the book, is pointless. Also, although God never said that Satan was the reason for Job's pain, Job was satisfied by God's answer. This implies that the prologue is not the whole answer.

Job actually says remarkably little to explain the problem of pain. Instead, the speakers hurled lengthy and highly poetic speeches at one another in which they alternatively insisted or denied that the wicked suffer retribution for their deeds. Unlike modern Christian theologians, they scarcely considered other explanations for pain and evil. Even God, in His lengthy speeches, said not a word to explain why Job had suffered. The Christian who reads Job for an explanation of the trials and suffering of life may leave more bewildered than comforted.

The fault, however, is not with Job but with us. Although suffering is an important factor in the book, the central question is not why the righteous suffer but why a person should serve God. Or, to put it in the terms of the one who first posed the question, Satan, "Does Job fear God for nothing?" (1:9).

And why should a person fear God? For Job's friends the answer was simple: because that is the safe thing to do. Wickedness invites the fury of an angry God, but righteousness brings prosperity. This reasoning, moreover, dominates not only the friends but also Job himself at the beginning (1:5). He was one of them. But the undeserved pain of his own life and the condemnation by his friends, like the successive blows of a whip, drove him to face questions he had never faced.

That reality, which he finally proclaimed in chapter 21, was that in his experience the wicked were not often brought to calamity for their sin: "They spend their years in prosperity and go down to the grave in peace" (21:13). In exasperation Job cried out, "Who is the Almighty, that we should serve him?" (21:15) even as he called on his friends to cover their mouths in horror (21:5). Not only his world but theirs had collapsed.

Where is the answer to Satan's challenge and Job's anguished outcry? It is found, of course, in the text of the book itself. In the following comments, we will travel through the book and seek that answer.

PROLOGUE (Job 1:1–2:13)

The prologue is a tightly woven narrative that blends both chiasm (a pattern repeating ideas in inverted order) and parallelism (a pattern repeating ideas in sequence), as follows:

A Background of the Story (1:1-5)
B Dialogue in Heaven (1:6-12)
C Affliction of Job (1:13-19)
D Job's Response (1:20-22)
B' Dialogue in Heaven (2:1-6)
C' Affliction of Job (2:7-8)
D' Job's Response (2:9-10)
A' Background of the Dialogue (2:11-13)

In 1:1 Job is declared to have been altogether upright and blameless. At the very outset, therefore, the possibility that his sufferings might be punishment or discipline is thrown out of court. The text does not even allow the possibility that they were preventative disciplines given in order that he would not be tempted to stray. Job was careful about that danger even for his children (1:5). This declaration of Job's innocence prevents the reader from escaping the dilemma of the book by the assumption that Job must have been guilty of something. He was not.

Satan (meaning *adversary* or *accuser*) appeared before God in 1:6 and challenged the validity of Job's piety. Some claim that Satan here was merely a loyal angel whose task was that of chief prosecutor, but this misreads the text. His hostility to God was transparent (1:11; 2:4-5), as was his malice (1:13-19). He was evil. Nevertheless, he posed the central question of the book: "Does Job fear God for nothing?" (1:9).

Job lost all his wealth and children in the first affliction (1:13-19) and his health in the second (2:7-8). Satan's proverb "skin for skin" means that Job valued nothing so much as his own skin, since only skin can equal it. Still, Job did not lose his faith or integrity, even after his wife lost hers. His friends visited him to comfort him, but they sat in horror for a week before anyone could speak (2:11-13).

DIALOGUE WITH THREE FRIENDS (JOB 3:1–31:40)

3:1-26
Job's Opening Soliloquy

The day of birth is to the individual what creation is to the whole world. Job cursed the day of his birth and, in doing so, reversed the language of Genesis 1. He called for darkness to overwhelm the day in contrast to the "Let there be light" of Genesis 1:3. He called for the stars and sun to be blotted out (Job 3:9; contrast Gen 1:14-19). Job even invoked the name of Leviathan, a monster symbolic of destruction and chaos (Job 3:8; see comments on chap. 41). Job desired creation to revert to chaos (Gen 1:2). For him the order and structure of the universe had already been turned upside down, and life no longer made sense.

4:1–5:27
Eliphaz's First Response

Eliphaz tried to persuade Job that the world's moral order was still stable. God rewards the righteous and punishes the wicked. Eliphaz claimed that both experience (4:7-8) and a private revelation (4:12-17) supported his case. He asserted that humans are such lowly and foolish creatures that their lives are naturally full of trouble (4:18–5:7). Still, he urged Job to call upon God, who would hear and help (5:8-27). Ironically, this happened, though not in the way Eliphaz supposed.

Job 3:14 discusses places kings and counselors built for themselves. This could refer to the pyramids of ancient Egypt.

6:1–7:21
Job Responded and Prayed

Job argued that Eliphaz's doctrine, however orthodox and tidy it might be, failed utterly to answer the hard facts of his experience (6:2-30). Animals only bellow when they are hungry (6:5). Likewise Job hungered for some answers. He cried out for wisdom to deal with the calamities and questions that had filled his life. But he would not accept cheap and phony answers, such as Eliphaz had just given. They were as inspired as unsalted egg white (6:6-7). Job lamented his agonies and identified with the sufferings of people everywhere, especially slaves and day-laborers (7:1-6).

Job prayed for mercy in 7:7-16. Wondering how he could possibly have been bad enough to merit this treatment from God, he reversed the meaning of Psalm 8. Instead of asking, "What is man?" that God would take notice and exalt him (Ps 8:4-8), he asked, "What is man?" that he deserves such intense scrutiny and punishment (Job 7:17-21). Job again alluded to Leviathan, here portrayed as a sea monster. Was Job such a threat that he needed to be caged like a wild animal (7:12)?

8:1-22
Bildad's First Response

Eliphaz did not directly accuse Job of having done something to deserve all that had befallen him. Bildad moved closer to doing this first in claiming that Job's children did deserve their fate (8:4) and second in promising that Job would be restored if he was upright (8:6). The "if" naturally implies that he may not be.

Bildad continued Eliphaz's argument that the moral order of the world was not threatened by what had happened to Job (8:3). He claimed the accumulated wisdom of generations supported his point (8:8-10). He developed the familiar simile of the two plants in which the one that thrives represents the righteous and the one that withers represents the wicked (8:11-19; see Ps 1 and Jer 17:5-8).

9:1–10:22
Job Responded and Prayed Again

In this section Job first responded to his friends (chap. 9) and then offered a prayer of complaint to God (chap. 10). But his response was directed more to Eliphaz than Bildad. Job's opening, "How can a mortal be righteous before God?" (9:2) virtually quoted Eliphaz (4:17).

As Job developed the idea, he turned Eliphaz's meaning upside down. Eliphaz claimed that human folly being what it is, no one has grounds for challenging God's right to punish as He wills. Job replied that God's power and

The Old Testament View of Faith

The OT assumes the existence of God, opening with the bold declaration, "In the beginning God" (Gen 1:1). No attempt is made to "prove" God's existence. Only a fool would deny God's reality (Ps 53:1).

God is the One to whom the world and every living being owe their existence and upon whom all depend for survival and redemption (Gen 1:1-2; Exod 3; 20:2-3; Deut 4:39; Isa 43:10-11). As Augustine observed, "We should cease to be if God were to take His eyes off of us."

The Hebrew term for faith is based upon the root *aman*, which denotes *firmness* or *trustworthiness.* This usage points both to God's trustworthiness and human faithfulness as a response to God.

Faith is a moral quality (faithfulness), and its focus is on trust rather than mere belief. The fear of the Lord (*reverence of, respect for*) is the beginning of knowledge (Prov 1:7). Humanity's status before God is that of a creature related to the Creator.

God's faithfulness to His promise to Abraham (Gen 12:1-3) is foundational to the covenant between Yahweh and Israel. Abraham's willingness to believe God's promises is the model for future generations of the faithful.

Faith (faithfulness) is understood primarily in the light of God's covenant. Early in Israel's history, the covenant requirements were interpreted primarily as ritual holiness. The prophets increased emphasis on ethical holiness.

The OT concept of faith has a strong corporate side. The language of election, God choosing Israel (Deut 7:6-7), pictures God as taking the initiative in bringing the nation out of Egypt. The covenant indicates that God is faithful and that Israel has an obligation to respond in kind. The Book of Deuteronomy emphasizes that Israel is to keep the commandments (Deut 6:17; 7:11), to heed the law (4:1; 7:12), and to hold fast to Yahweh (4:4; 10:20). The faith community is to seek the Lord (4:29-30), to repent when there is unfaithfulness (30:2-10), and to obey God's voice (4:30). The nation is to love God "with all your heart" (6:5), to fear God (6:2,13; 10:20), and to remember God (7:18-19; 8:2-3,18-20; 9:7).

Israel's failure to keep the covenant illustrates not only a lack of faith but unfaithfulness. The latter prophets often used the language of marital infidelity (compare Hosea) and fornication to describe Israel's moral and spiritual lapses from faithfulness. Hosea would lament, "There is no faithfulness" (Hos 4:1).

Faith in the OT also has individual expressions. Habakkuk said, "The righteous will live by his faith" (Hab 2:4). In its historical context, this passage refers both to the trustworthiness of God in keeping Divine promises and the faithfulness of the individual in response to God. The idea of moral firmness, then, is the OT emphasis that is picked up in the NT concept of the faith. □

lofty position being what it is, no one, no matter how innocent, has a chance to question God's wrath or make an appeal. Even if he were clean, God would push him into the mud (9:30-31). God's omnipotence and sovereignty, normally objects of praise, had become objects of terror to Job (9:2-32).

Job's despair led him to call for an arbitrator between himself and God (9:33-35). The distance between humanity and God was too great for Job to bridge. He did not develop this idea here but took it up later.

In his prayer Job appealed for mercy on two grounds. First, God had no experience of human mortality and frailty (10:4-7; compare Heb 2:14-18). God ought to understand that it is not easy being human.

Second, Job pointed out that he was God's creature and wondered if God's only purpose in creation was to destroy what He had made (Job 10:8-22). Job's prayer recalled Moses' intercession for Israel (Exod 32:12). Job again alluded to the creation narrative (compare Job 10:9 to Gen 2:7). Job had been knit together by God (Job 10:11; compare Ps 139:13). But in Genesis 1:31 God saw that all He had made was very good (Hebrew *tob*). Now Job asked, "Is it good [*tob*] to You that You persecute, that You disdain, the work of Your hands?" (10:3, author's translation).

11:1-20
Zophar's First Response

Zophar, in an angry retort, was the first to accuse Job of having committed some sin by which he deserved his fate (11:14). To be sure, he did not yet make a specific accusation. He was only sure Job must have done *something.*

Zophar's rejoinder turned on the fact that Job, a mere mortal, could not possibly have understood God's ways. He used four dimensions—height, depth, length, and width—to show how far God's ways were beyond Job's (11:8-9; compare Eph 3:18, which uses similar language

Papyrus plants growing in the Huleh Valley in Egypt. Bildad referred to papyrus in his argument to Job (see Job 8:11).

to encourage Christians to pursue deeper wisdom rather than to prove that it is beyond their reach).

Zophar wished God would rebuke Job (Job 11:5). He was sure God could point out Job's sins (11:11). Still, like his two friends, Zophar encouraged Job to turn to God, who would hear his prayer and restore what Job had lost (11:13-20).

To the reader, Zophar's speech is laced with irony. God's wisdom is indeed far deeper than Job's, and God would speak to him to that effect. Afterwards God would restore Job's fortunes, as Zophar predicted. But how different it would all be from what Zophar expected. For it was not Job but the three friends whom God would accuse (42:8).

The proverb in 11:12 should probably be translated, "A stupid man will get sense when a wild donkey [perhaps *zebra*] is born tame." This metaphor of human stubbornness means that some fools are all but beyond hope (compare Jer 13:23). It was a thinly veiled reproach against Job, who had described himself as a braying wild donkey (Job 6:5). But in 39:5-8 God said it was He who gave the wild donkey his freedom. What to Zophar was a worthless animal was of far more value to Job and God.

12:1–14:22
Job Opened the Second Cycle

The major divisions of this lengthy discourse are as follows: (1) The Shallowness of the Wisdom of the Three Friends (12:2–13:19) and (2) Job's Third Prayer (13:20–14:22).

Job's assault on the advice of his friends is in two parts. First, he proved that he could cite the wisdom of the former generations as well as anyone (12:2–13:2). Second, he said his argument was really with God and appealed for the friends at least to be quiet if they could not say anything better than what they had already said (13:3-19).

After the initial outburst of anger (12:2-6), chapter 12 recites traditional teaching (indeed, much of it could have been said by any one of the friends). The natural world (12:7-8) and the teachings of the aged (12:12) are both guides into wisdom. God's power is irresistible and sovereign: all of life is in His hands, and He brings down the haughty and the proud (12:13-25). Job was in effect saying to his friends: "I know all this. You have told me nothing." But in Job's mouth even orthodoxy appears dark and threatening. God's power appeared almost arbitrary and destabilizing. It negated all human attempts at wisdom (12:17,20).

For Job his friends' hackneyed and conventional arguments were meaningless (13:3-19). They were worthless physicians who always prescribed the wrong medicine (13:4). Job even claimed that God could not be satisfied with their hollow defense of divine justice and correctly predicted that God would not be pleased with their refusal to look at the facts of this case objectively (13:7-10). It would have been better by far if they had just let Job take up his case with God, for it was He with whom Job had a complaint (13:3,13-16). Job knew that God, although He had become like an enemy to him, was still his only hope.

Job's third prayer, like the second, appealed to God to cease tormenting him (13:20-27). In the second prayer, however, Job pleaded on the grounds that he was God's creation (10:8-12). Here he emphasized more his mortality and weakness (14:5-12). This led him to consider the doctrine of resurrection and to wonder if it would be best for him to die and thus rest until the day when the dead rise (14:13-17). Even so, he was tortured by his pain and the brevity of life and concluded this prayer in bleak discouragement (14:18-22).

Some assume that the Book of Job cannot possibly

have a true concept of resurrection, but that assumption is groundless. Job 14:14-15 begins with a *question*, not a confession of faith. Job's sufferings forced him to think about God's ways on a deeper level than ever before. Here the idea of resurrection entered the discussion and gave Job reason to hope (the friends never considered the idea of resurrection).

The term the NIV translates "renewal" (14:14) may be rendered "transformation." Job here combined the pleas of his two prayers—Job was both mortal and God's creation. The resurrection would both answer his need for immortality and make the creation understandable. God did not make people just to watch them die off. But Job had only begun to deal with this question.

15:1-35
Eliphaz's Second Response

Eliphaz now directly accused Job of sin (15:5) and threw Job's own words back into his face (15:5-6; compare 9:20). He was alarmed that Job's attitude might undermine piety (15:4) and once again claimed that Job needed to recognize his limitations and return to traditional wisdom (15:9-10).

He repeated the argument that since all people are sinful God is justified in punishing whenever He chooses (15:14-16). Another poem on the fate of the wicked (15:17-35) was no doubt meant to convict Job and persuade him to repent of whatever sin he had committed.

Does the Book of Job deny the universal sinfulness of humanity? Texts like 15:14-16 give an orthodox if somewhat harsh statement of universal depravity. On the other hand, this text is put in the mouth of Eliphaz, who would be shown to be in the wrong. The characterization of Job as "blameless" (1:1) also seems to contradict universal depravity.

Nevertheless, the book does not claim that some people are sinless. The prologue does not say Job had never committed any sin. It only stresses that he was righteous and that his suffering had nothing to do with any past or potential guilt on his part. Job confessed to having sinned in life (14:16-17) although he was certain he had not deserved what had befallen him.

The book does not imply that everything the three friends said was wrong. Most of what they asserted fully agrees with the rest of the Bible (compare 15:17-35 with Prov 6:12-15). But they misapplied the biblical teachings. The doctrine of universal sin made them cynical about people (and even about God, although they did not realize it). And the doctrine of retribution made them judgmental. The book does not deny that all have sinned, but it forces the reader to think in terms other than a simple equation of guilt and punishment.

This lion hunt is part of a set of hunting reliefs found at Nineveh from the reign of Ashurbanipal of Assyria. Job likened himself to a hunted lion (Job 10:16).

16:1–17:16
Job Lamented and Prayed

Job vented his frustration over his pain, his confusion about what God had done to him, and his anger at the empty words of his "comforters." But the careful chiasm (a pattern repeating ideas in inverted order) shows that there is more here than an emotional outburst, and a confession of hope stands at the very center of the whole (16:18-21).

That confession returns to the theme of the heavenly Arbitrator or Intercessor. Job was now certain of the reality of the Intercessor. He had previously only wished that such an Intercessor existed (9:33-34). Job had already far surpassed his friends in the understanding of God's ways, and his sufferings would drive him deeper still.

18:1-21
Bildad's Second Response

Bildad angrily replied (18:2-3) and gave Job another fairly conventional poem on the fate of the wicked (18:5-21). Most significant is the point in 18:20 that men from east and west would be appalled at the fall of the wicked. Surely no one was more famous than Job (1:3), and Bildad here took up Job's own words (17:8). Bildad's slightly concealed meaning was that Job had not only sinned but was one of the proverbial wicked. Job's friends were progressing in bitterness toward him.

19:1-29
Job Lamented and Hoped

Job again bemoaned his fate and called attention to how those who formerly loved him had abandoned him. He first spoke of God's antagonism to him (19:6-12) and then of the contempt he had received from relatives, friends, and subordinates (19:13-20). He pleaded for pity from his friends (19:21-22) and warned them that they too might face judgment for their hostility (19:28-29).

In the middle of this cry for love, Job made his most profound confession of hope (19:25-27). The somewhat obscure Hebrew may be translated: "I know that my redeemer lives and that the final One will arise against the dust. After they have done away with my skin, from my flesh I shall have a vision of God. I will have this vision for myself; my eyes will see that He is no stranger. My heart yearns within me!"

The term "the final One" refers to the divine Redeemer (the Hebrew word is translated "the last" in Isa 44:6 and 48:12). "Done away with" translates a word elsewhere used of cutting away underbrush (Isa 10:34). Job assumed his tormented body (19:17-22) would soon die and be thrown out like garbage. The phrase "have a vision" ("see") translates a Hebrew word often used of seeing God or a vision (Exod 24:11; Isa 1:1).

Job's yearning for an Intercessor and hope for a resurrection came together here, in the middle of deep dejection, in a triumphant assertion of faith. Job's "Redeemer" would arise against the dust. In other words, He would conquer human mortality. Job was therefore sure that he too would rise from the dead and in his body behold God. At the same time, we note that Job's problems were not over. He still did not understand why God treated him as an enemy.

It is pointless to deny that Job looked for a resurrection and a Redeemer. The book, through the sufferings of its hero, points to the two universal human needs: the need for a Deliverer and the need for release from mortality. No one is competent to stand before God, and everyone longs to escape death (in that sense the three friends were correct in their estimate of human sin and divine power). These needs, poignantly portrayed in Job, are dramatically fulfilled in the New Testament.

20:1-29
Zophar's Second Response

As Zophar rehashed the fate of the wicked, it is clearer still that Job was the subject. Job had said his Redeemer would arise against the dust (19:25); Zophar said Job's vigor would lie dead in the dust (19:11). He accentuated the unrepentant attitude (19:12-19) and fleeting wealth (19:20-23) of the wicked, which was exactly how the friends regarded Job.

21:1-34
Job's Response

All at once Job challenged his friends' tedious sermons on the fate of the wicked. How often, he demanded, had they ever really seen it like this? Far more often the reverse was true: the wicked prospered. Rather than parrot traditional doctrine, the friends should have been dumbfounded (21:5). Job's case had undermined the precepts by which they lived. The question remained, Why should we serve God? (21:15).

22:1-30
Eliphaz's Third Response

Eliphaz now hit Job with a frontal assault. He directly accused Job of being a great sinner and particularly charged him with greed and oppression (22:5-9). But the attack began and ended on ironic notes, although Eliphaz did not know it. He sarcastically asked Job if God had rebuked him for his piety, when in fact that was the precise reason for Job's misfortune. He also promised that if

Job would repent, he would be able to intercede for sinners (22:29-30). And Job would intercede—for Eliphaz.

The friends had nothing more to say. They repeatedly made their point on the lot of sinners. Their accusations against Job could hardly become any more brutal. Job now began to turn from them.

23:1–24:25
Job Looked for Justice

Job mourned here first for himself (23:2-17) and then for all the oppressed and suffering (24:1-12). Behind this was a plea for God to vindicate the righteous and punish sinners (24:1). The book gives its deepest expressions of struggle in chapter 24. Job voiced the sorrow and bewilderment of believers of every generation. He had not abandoned the faith, however, and returned to traditional expressions of God's justice in 24:18-24.

25:1-6
Bildad's Third Response

Bildad began a third discourse in which he returned to the idea of God's holiness against human lowliness. His very short speech appears to have been cut off. Job likely interrupted him.

Because Bildad's third speech was so short and Zophar had none at all, many scholars suppose that 26:5-14 concludes Bildad's speech and 27:13-23 is Zophar's missing third speech.

This approach is unnecessary. The friends really had nothing more to say, and Job had no intention of listening to them anymore. Having interrupted Bildad, Job in effect gave Bildad's and Zophar's speeches for them. He did this for two reasons. First, Job somewhat sarcastically showed that he knew their theology better than they. Second, Job suggested that he agreed with them in principle but was dumbfounded by what had happened to him. He knew he was innocent.

26:1–27:23
Job's Last Address to the Friends

Job interrupted Bildad with bitter sarcasm (26:2-4). He described the power of God (26:5-14) and the end of the ungodly (27:13-23), but he defiantly maintained that he deserved nothing of what had happened to him (27:2-6). He had nothing more to say to them.

28:1-28
A Hymn to Wisdom

This poem may be regarded as Job's own words or the author's own transition. It differs from its context and does not begin with the phrase "And Job said." The text does not, however, suggest that these were not Job's words. Either way the interpretation of the chapter is only slightly altered.

A glass vase dating from 500–300 B.C. which may have held cosmetics. Job 28:17 states that wisdom is much more valuable than gold or glass (NIV "crystal").

The poem contrasts human technical skill in mining out precious metals and gems (28:1-11) with the inaccessibility of wisdom (28:12-27). The human condition is indeed pitiful. Although adept at tunneling into the deepest recesses of the earth for treasure, humans are neither willing nor able to penetrate the mysteries of life itself.

The poem concludes with what may be called the heart of biblical wisdom, "The fear of the Lord—that is wisdom" (28:28). For Job this became far more than a cliche. The former, calm assurance that he understood life had been shattered. The old order of his life was in ruins. He now had to look to God and not to his own wisdom about God.

29:1–31:40
Job's Final Discourse

This discourse is in three parts: (1) Job's former glory (29:2-25), (2) Job's present humiliation (30:1-40), and

(3) a negative confession (31:1-40).

Job remembered his former glory especially as a time when he was respected and loved by one and all. He now looked upon his former belief that all was secure (29:18-20) as mistaken, although in fact those words would come true (42:12-16).

Chapter 29 begins and ends with the term "light." In chapter 3 Job cursed the light, but here he remembered when he blessed God's light (29:3) and others blessed the light of his own face (29:24; compare Exod 34:29-35 and Num 6:25-26).

From a position of highest renown, Job had fallen to complete infamy. He once enjoyed universal respect. Now even the sons of the dregs of society mocked him (Job 30:1-15). His physical pain was more than he could endure, and he awaited death (29:16-19,27-31). He voiced another prayer of complaint to God in 19:20-23.

Ancient Egyptian literature preserved examples of the "negative confession," a text in which a deceased person's spirit, facing divine judgment, claimed not to have committed sins described in a detailed list. Job 31 is similar to these. Here Job claimed he was not lustful or adulterous (31:1,9-12), a swindler (31:5-8), or an unjust employer (31:13-15,38-40). He was not uncharitable (31:16-23), greedy or idolatrous (31:24-28), or vindictive and cunning (31:29-34). This negative confession, coming as it does at the end of his speeches, implies that Job believed death was near and wanted to end his life with a protest of innocence. He had nothing more to say.

An example of a "mirror of cast bronze" (Job 37:18) was found in a tomb at Thebes in Egypt. The reflecting area is of bronze, and the handle is wood overlaid with gold.

ELIHU'S SPEECH (JOB 32:1–37:24)

Elihu, who is mentioned neither before nor after these six chapters, suddenly appeared and made a particularly wordy speech (32:18). Some consider his words to be the high point of the book and claim he resolved the dilemma, but this interpretation is hard to justify.

First, Elihu was overconfident of his own wisdom (32:9,17,21-22; 33:1-5,33; and especially 36:4: "Be assured that my words are not false; one perfect in knowledge is with you"). For all his bravado, however, Elihu said nothing that had not already been said: God inflicts pain on people to prevent them from falling into sin (33:12-22); God is the wise and all-powerful Ruler of the world (34:10-33; 36:27–37:24), and the wicked will be destroyed but the repentant will prosper (36:5-21). What Elihu said was not wrong, but everything he proclaimed had already been explored in great detail.

He also wrongly assumed Job was being punished for something (34:37). Finally, and most significantly, Elihu was ignored by everyone else in the book. Surely this would not be the case if he were the fount of wisdom he claimed to be.

Some scholars consider the Elihu speeches to be a later insertion by a pious Israelite who was distraught at Job's remarks and sought to correct them. This view also must be rejected. A pious scribe would certainly not put his words into the mouth of such an arrogant young man as Elihu. His speech does provide a transition to God's reply to Job (compare 37:1-2 with 38:1). More importantly, the Elihu speeches perform a special function for the reader.

As we progress through the Book of Job, we feel the same distress Elihu voiced. We are sure there is something wrong with Job's comments but are aware that the three friends failed to answer him (32:2-3). We try to find an alternative answer. Perhaps, we think, God afflicted Job to keep him from falling into sin. We thrash about for a solution much as Elihu did and repeat old arguments without knowing it. And if we are not careful, we fall into the same vain certainty. We think we are wiser than Job and his friends put together.

Job and his friends were each wrong in his own way, but so are we. We need to hear the voice of God.

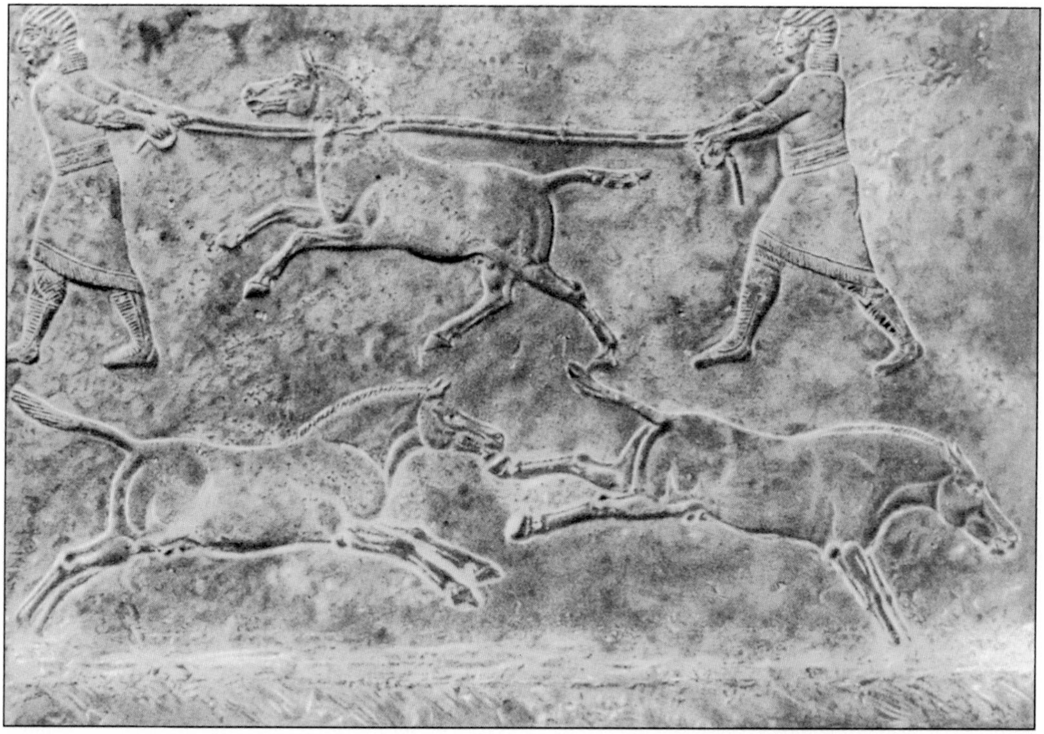

This Assyrian relief of a wild donkey hunt depicts two hunters struggling with one of the donkeys they have roped.

GOD'S SPEECHES (JOB 38:1–42:6)

The divine speech falls in two parts divided by Job's first response (40:3-5). The first (38:2–40:2) portrays God's dominion over creation, and the second (40:7–41:34) focuses on behemoth and leviathan.

Many interpreters are frankly confused if not disappointed by God's speech. Instead of giving a profound explanation of Job's sufferings, God gave him something of a lesson in natural history. What is the reason for this? Again we must recall that the central question of the book is not why the righteous suffer but whether Job served God for nothing (1:9-11). Both Job and his friends had assumed that life and prosperity were the benefits from service to God.

The meaning of God's reply now begins to appear. Nowhere does He say that Job's affliction was a punishment for sin or even, as Elihu suggested, a way of keeping Job from falling into sin. God did accuse Job of having attributed injustice to God (40:8), which Job certainly had. And Job's repentance (42:1-6) shows that he came to realize that God had not been unfair. What did God say that so thoroughly convinced Job of his error?

God's words focused entirely on His work in creation (and on the fact that Job was not there). In chapter 3 Job had wanted to bring creation crashing down, but God, in terms that often recall Genesis 1, challenged Job to rethink what he had said.

In Job 38:4-38 God repeatedly spoke of the creation of the earth, the morning, and the stars (Gen 1:1,14-19); the separation of light from darkness and of sea from land (Gen 1:3,9-10); and the formation of clouds (Gen 1:6-8). God then called attention to the wild animals such as lions, goats, eagles, and ostriches (Gen 1:20,24). He emphasized the powerful and wild forces of nature.

In addition, God showed that He has placed all these forces in an order and controls every one. He keeps the sea in its place (Job 38:8), separates day and night (38:12,19), feeds the lions, and provides all the animals with what they need to survive (38:39–40:30). The powers that otherwise would destroy one another and fall into chaos are kept in an ordered balance.

God told Job he had to show he could crush the proud and the wicked if he wanted to be on equal footing with God (40:7-14). Then He turned to the creatures called behemoth and leviathan. The former, behemoth, may have been the elephant or hippopotamus. A powerful creature who dwelt among the lotuses and poplars (40:15-24), he was only the prologue to a much more awesome creature, leviathan (41:1-34).

Leviathan is sometimes interpreted as the crocodile but, even allowing for poetic license, this makes God guilty of considerable exaggeration. For leviathan is invulnerable to human weapons (41:7,26-29), his eyes and nose flash with light (41:18), and fire pours out of his mouth (41:19-21). He is covered with armor (41:15-18) and is lord of all creatures (41:34). This is more like a terrible dragon than a crocodile.

The Bible and other ancient literature speak of leviathan as a terrible, supernatural creature. Ugaritic texts speak of a serpent with seven heads called "lotan," and Psalm 74:14 says God crushed the heads of leviathan. Isaiah 27:1 calls leviathan a serpent and a sea monster. And in Job, God repeatedly pointed out Job's inability to subdue this monster (41:1-8). What was this beast?

Readers are often confused that although Satan is the prominent adversary of Job 1–2, he seems to disappear after that. Also we note that although the book often speaks of creation and the fall, it has until now said nothing about the agent of the fall, the serpent. A likely solution is that Satan has not been forgotten but has reappeared at the end as the serpent leviathan.

Job had challenged the justice of God, and God had responded that only He, and not Job, is able to control and destroy the chaotic and evil powers. Just as God uses all the natural powers in His creative purpose, even so He allows evil to thrive for a season but always governs it by His providence to bring about the final destruction of the evil one. Therefore it was not for Job to challenge God's moral governance of the world. God knows what He is doing.

Against this address from God, Job's complete repentance is not surprising. It is important to see, however, that he repented of having challenged God's justice in his speeches (42:3). He did not do as his friends wanted and confess that he had done something to deserve his sufferings.

EPILOGUE: JOB RESTORED (JOB 42:7-17)

Job's vindication was complete. God told the friends that they had not spoken what was right, "as my servant Job has." Job's words, however rash, were far better than the hollow defense the friends gave of their religion of rewards and punishments. Job's intercession for them (42:8-9) and the restoration of his former glory (42:10-17) not only show that his suffering was not punishment but that he was right to refuse to make a meaningless confession of sins he did not commit.

Theological Significance

What is the answer to Satan's challenge? Did Job fear God for nothing? The answer, remarkably, is no. Job did not serve God for nothing. Job learned that the real benefit of his piety was not his health and wealth and children; *it was God Himself.* God, the Creator and Judge of all, is bringing about the triumph of righteousness. And Job now knew he could trust God to do all things right, even if it cost Job all he had. For he still had God.

Questions for Reflection

1. Why do we assume that we are being punished for sin whenever calamity strikes?

2. In what ways did the strict religion of the three friends make them less than human?

3. Do we sometimes wonder why God waits so long and seems to allow sinners to go unpunished? How does Job help us to solve this problem?

4. What is the difference between serving God for God Himself and serving Him in order to be safe from trouble and hardship? How does Job help us to see the difference?

5. How did Job come to see his need for resurrection and for a Mediator? How did God meet those needs for us?

Sources for Additional Study

Andersen, Francis I. *Job.* Downers Grove: InterVarsity, 1974.

Janzen, J. Gerald. *Job.* Atlanta: John Knox, 1985.

PSALMS

The Book of Psalms or Psalter is the hymnal of Israelite worship and the Bible's book of personal devotions. In it we not only find expression of all the emotions of life but also some of the most profound teaching in the entire Scripture.

Date and Authorship of Psalms

The Psalter was not completed until late in Israelite history (in the postexilic era). But it contains hymns written over a period of hundreds of years. Many *individual* psalms are far older than the whole book.

Evidence of the Superscripts. A primary source of information regarding the date and authorship of individual psalms are the superscripts found above many psalms. According to these, some of the authors include David, the sons of Korah, Asaph, Moses, and Solomon. Other psalms, including some of the "Psalms of Ascent" (Pss 120–134) and "Hallelujah" Psalms (Pss 146–150) are anonymous. These titles, if taken at face value, would date many of the psalms to the early tenth century (psalms of David) and at least one to the fifteenth century (Ps 90).

David playing his harp before King Saul

Meaning and Reliability of the Superscripts. Some scholars, however, question whether the superscripts are meant to ascribe authorship to the psalms. The phrase *ledawid* used frequently in the psalm superscripts could mean *by David,* but it also could mean *for David.* But most scholars would admit that the word means *by David.* There is no reason to think it is some kind of dedication.

A more serious question is whether the superscripts are reliable. Some scholars believe they were added at a late date and are no more than conjectures that have no real historical value. But there are good reasons to believe the superscripts can be trusted. Many of the psalm superscripts refer to incidents in the life of David about which Samuel and Chronicles say nothing. For example, the superscript of Psalm 60 mentions battles with Aram-Naharaim, Aram-Zobah, and Edom. It would be strange if, in the late postexilic period, rabbis invented this. Another example is the superscript of Psalm 7, which speaks of a certain "Cush the Benjamite" (he is mentioned here only in the OT). If the superscripts were late fabrications, one would expect that they would refer more to incidents from David's life mentioned in Samuel.

Many of the psalm titles contain technical musical terms, the meanings of which were already lost by the time the Old Testament was translated into Greek. For example, *lammenasseah,* "for the choir leader," is wrongly translated "to the end" in the Septuagint, the pre-Christian Greek translation of the Old Testament. A number of these terms are still not understood. Obscure or difficult words in the superscripts include: *song titles* ("Do Not Destroy"; "A Dove on Distant Oaks"; "The Doe of the Morning"; "Lilies"; "The Lily/ies of the Covenant"; and "Mahalath"); *musical instruments or techni-*

cal terms ("stringed instruments" and "Sheminith"); *musical guilds or singers* ("Asaph"; "Sons of Korah"; "Heman the Ezrahite"; "Ethan the Ezrahite"); and *types of psalms* ("Songs of Ascent," likely sung by those who were making a pilgrimage to Jerusalem; *maskil*, possibly an instructional or meditative psalm; *miktham*; *shiggayon*).

Ancient terminology and references to old guilds and bygone events all imply that the titles are very old. This supports confidence in their reliability.

Davidic Authorship of Psalms. Many scholars have asserted that David did not write the psalms attributed to him. But there are no historical reasons why David could not have authored those psalms. David had a reputation as a singer and as a devoted servant of the Lord, and nothing in his life is incompatible with his being a psalmist.

One difficulty here is that some of the psalms of David seem to refer to the temple (for example, 27:4), which did not exist in his day. But terms like "House of the Lord," "Holy Place," and "House of God" are regularly used of the tent of meeting and need not be taken as references to Solomon's temple (see Exod 28:43; 29:30; Josh 6:24; Judg 18:31). Certainly David could have written the psalms attributed to him. Other psalms that mention the temple, however, are also ascribed to David (Pss 5; 11; 18; 27; 29; 65; 68; 138). It is perhaps worth noting that New Testament writers ascribe none of these psalms to David.

The Date of the Psalms. Earlier critics dated many of the psalms late in Israel's history, some as late as the Maccabean period. For two reasons, however, this is no longer possible.

First, the Ugaritic songs and hymns show parallels to many of the psalms. The grammar and poetic forms are similar. The Ugaritic tradition of hymn writing is ancient (before twelfth century) and implies that many of the psalms may be ancient too.

Second, a fragmentary, second-century B.C. copy of the biblical collection of psalms was found in the Dead Sea Scrolls. This proves beyond doubt that the psalms

Types of Old Testament Literature

It helps to understand the OT if we know what type of literature we are reading in any particular passage. For example, the meaning of Amos 5:2 is clearer when we know it is a funeral song. Or Psalm 17 loses its seeming self-righteousness when we know it is the lament of one falsely accused of a crime.

Since the turn of the century, biblical scholars have classified and named various types of OT literature. By comparing them with similar forms found in other ancient Near Eastern literature, scholars have delineated their typical traits and attempted to place them in their original situations in Israel's life. This branch of biblical science is called form criticism. (See "Critical Methods and the Old Testament.")

Form criticism says nothing about the historical basis of an OT passage. The names of the forms refer to the literary structures in the stories. There are no complete myths (timeless stories of the gods and their relationships) in the OT. The God of the Bible is one God, who acts in history. Occasionally some of the *language* of ancient Near Eastern myths is borrowed, for example, from the Mesopotamian chaos dragon myth (Ps 74:13-14; Isa 51:9). In such cases that language is always used in a *historical* context.

Most of the OT's forms were first shaped and handed down orally before being written down. (There are some exceptions; for example, the biographical portions of Jeremiah.) Typical structures made the forms easy to remember and pass on by word of mouth. By knowing the typical structure of a form, we are able to see how any biblical author has changed the form and thus given it a particular emphasis. For example, Jeremiah 15:15-18 has the form of an individual lament. Laments are usually followed by an expression of trust and hope (as in Jer 20:7-13). But Jeremiah 15:18 is followed by a challenge from God, thus emphasizing 15:19-21.

The various types of OT literature found are almost too many to list. Among prose types are speeches (2 Kgs 18:28-35), sermons (Jer 7:1-15), prayers (1 Kgs 8:23-53), letters (1 Kgs 21:8-10), and lists. Other prose forms include rules governing worship and sacrifice (Lev 1–7), short stories (Ruth and the Joseph story), fables (Judg 9:8-15), and autobiographies (Neh 1–7).

Other representatives of prose forms are accounts of dreams and visions (Gen 37:5-10), proverbs (1 Sam 10:12), riddles (Judg 14:18), wisdom sayings (Proverbs), and allegories (Ezek 17:22-24). Second Samuel 6–20 and 1 Kings 1–2 are generally acknowledged to be eye-witness histories written by someone in David's court.

There are several collections of laws. The most important are ⇨

were composed well before the second century B.C., since it must have taken a long time for the written psalms to be recognized as Scripture and for the psalter to be organized.

There is no reason, therefore, to date all the psalms late. Generally speaking, they can be dated to three broad periods: (1) *Preexilic.* This would include those psalms that are very much like the Ugaritic songs, the royal psalms, and those that mention the Northern Kingdom. (2) *Exilic.* This would include the dirge songs that lament the fall of Jerusalem and call for vengeance on the Edomites and others. (3) *Early postexilic.* This would include psalms that emphasize the written law, such as Psalm 119.

The Compilation of the Psalms

Psalms divides into five sections or "books": (1) Psalms 1–41; (2) Psalms 42–72; (3) Psalms 73–89; (4) Psalms 90–106; (5) Psalms 107–150.

We have no precise information regarding the dates when the five books of the Psalms were compiled or what the criteria of compilation were. Psalm 72:20 implies that a compilation of David's psalms was made shortly after his death. In Hezekiah's time there were collections of the psalms of David and Asaph, which may account for the bulk of the first three books (2 Chron 29:30). At a later date another scribe may have collected the remaining books of the Psalter. Psalms was put into its final form some time in the postexilic period.

The five books each close with a doxology, and Psalm 150 is a concluding doxology for the entire Psalter. But the numbering of the psalms varies. The Jerusalem Talmud speaks of 147 psalms. The Septuagint divides Psalms 116 and 147 into two psalms each but numbers Psalms 9 and 10 and Psalms 114 and 115 as one psalm each.

Types of Psalms

When studying a psalm, one should ask the following questions: (1) Was it sung by an individual or the

---

the Decalogue or Ten Commandments (Exod 20:1-17; Deut 5:6-21), the Book of the Covenant (Exod 20:22–23:33), the Holiness Code (Lev 17–26), and the Book of Deuteronomy, which is shaped in the form of sermons.

Among poetic types are songs of all kinds: work songs (Num 21:17-18), love songs (Song of Songs), mocking songs (Isa 14:4-21), victory songs (Exod 15:21), funeral songs (Lamentations). Worship songs include the forms found in the Psalter: hymns of praise (Ps 96), thanksgivings (Ps 116), songs of Zion (Ps 48), royal psalms (Pss 2; 110), both individual (Ps 22) and communal (Ps 44) laments, processional hymns (Ps 15), songs of trust (Ps 27), enthronement hymns (Ps 72), and wisdom psalms (Ps 49).

The two most frequent types found in the Psalter are the hymn and the individual lament. These represent the two poles of Israel's worship, praise and lament. The hymn structure is found throughout the Bible. It opens with a call to praise or to bless God (Ps 98:1a). This is followed by the transitional word "for" and a sentence giving the reason for the praise (Ps 98:1b). Or it is followed by sentences beginning with "who" that describe God's person or activity (compare Ps 103:3-5). Then follows the hymn body, giving a further description of God (Ps 98:1c-3). Sometimes there is a conclusion (Ps 104:34-35); sometimes the structure of the hymn is just repeated (Ps 98:4-9). This typical hymn structure may be seen still in use in the NT (for example, Luke 1:46-55). The purpose of a hymn is always to praise God.

The lament also has a typical form. It opens with an invocation of God (Ps 22:1-5) followed by a description of the sufferer's situation (Ps 22:6-8,14-18). There is then petition to God for aid (Ps 22:11,19-21). A lament usually closes with the expression of certainty that God has heard the prayer and will save (Ps 22:22-31). That is, lament turns into praise.

In the prophetic literature we find oracles of judgment on both individuals (Amos 7:14-17) and nation (Isa 8:6-8), oracles of salvation (Jer 35:18-19), and woe oracles (Isa 5:8-10, often put in a series as in Isa 5:11-25). Other prophetic forms include legal procedures (Isa 1:18-20) and prophetic torahs (Isa 1:10-17).

The basic structure of the prophetic oracle of judgment is as follows: introduction (Amos 4:1a,b), a description of Israel's sinful situation (Amos 4:1c,d), the messenger formula that indicates that the oracle comes from God (Amos 4:2a), and the announcement of God's coming action (Amos 4:2b-3). This form was used until the time of Ezekiel, although with variations.

The OT is a marvel of literary variety and form. □

This wall painting from an Egyptian tomb at Thebes depicts the winnowing of corn and shows the process of the grain and chaff being separated. (See Ps 1:4.)

congregation? (2) What was the psalm's purpose (praise, cry for help, thanksgiving, admonition)? (3) Does it mention any special themes, such as the king and the royal house, or Zion? By asking these questions, scholars have identified a number psalm types.

Hymns. In this type of psalm, the whole congregation praises God for His works or attributes (Ps 105). Six subcategories of hymn are: *victory songs,* which praise God for His victories over the nations (Ps 68); *processional hymns,* sung as the worshipers moved into the temple area (Ps 24); *Zion songs,* which praise God and specifically refer to His presence in Zion (Ps 48); *songs of the Lord's reign,* which begin with the words, "The Lord reigns" (Ps 99); *antiphonal hymns,* chanted by either the priests or choir with the congregation responding antiphonally (Ps 136); *hallelujah hymns,* which begin or end with "Praise the Lord!" (Hebrew *hallelu Yah;* Ps 146).

Community complaints. In these psalms the whole nation voiced its complaints over problems it was facing, such as defeat in battle, famine, or drought (Ps 74). A subcategory of this is the *national imprecation,* in which the people cursed their oppressors (Ps 83).

Individual complaints. These psalms are like the community complaint except that they were prayers given by one person instead of the whole nation. The reason for the prayers might be that the individual was sick, hounded by enemies, or in need of confessing personal sin (Ps 13). This type of psalm may include substantial *imprecation* or curses against the psalmist's personal enemies (Ps 5). A subcategory is the *penitential psalm,* in which the speaker is dominated by the sense of his guilt (Ps 51).

Individual songs of thanksgiving. In these psalms an individual praises God for some saving act. Usually it alludes to a time that the individual was sick or in some other kind of trouble (Ps 116).

Royal psalms. These psalms deal with the king and the royal house. Subcategories include: *wedding songs,* sung at the marriage of the king (Ps 45); *coronation songs* (Ps 72); *prayers for victory,* chanted when the king went to war (Ps 20); *votive psalms,* perhaps sung by the king at his coronation as a vow to be faithful and upright (Ps 101).

Torah psalms. These psalms give moral or religious instruction (Pss 1; 127). Subcategories include: *testimony songs,* in which the psalmist used his personal experience of God's salvation to encourage the hearer (Ps 32); *wisdom songs*, in which the psalmist instructed the hearer more in practical wisdom similar to that in

---

On the facing page is a reproduction of the illustrated first page of the Book of Psalms from the Rothschild Manuscript.

[illegible]

האיש אשר לא הלך בעצת רשעים ובדרך חטאים לא ע
עמד ובמושב לצים לא ישב: כי אם בתורת יהוה חפצו וב
ובתורתו יהגה יומם ולילה: והיה כעץ שתול על פלגי מים
אשר פריו יתן בעתו ועלהו לא יבול וכל אשר יעשה יצל
יצליח: לא כן הרשעים כי אם כמץ אשר תדפנו רוח: על
כן לא יקומו רשעים במשפט וחטאים בעדת צדיקים
כי יודע יהוה דרך צדיקים ודרך רשעים תאבד:
למה רגשו גוים ולאמים יהגו ריק: יתיצבו
מלכי ארץ ורוזנים נוסדו יחד על יהוה ועל משיחו: ננתק
ננתקה את מוסרותימו ונשליכה ממנו עבתימו: יושב
בשמים ישחק יהוה ילעג למו: אז ידבר אלימו באפו ובחר
ובחרונו יבהלמו: ואני נסכתי מלכי על ציון הר קדשי: א
אספרה אל חק יהוה אמר אלי בני אתה אני היום ילדתיך:
שאל ממני ואתנה גוים נחלתך ואחזתך אפסי ארץ: ת
תרעם בשבט ברזל ככלי יוצר תנפצם: ועתה מלכים השכ

[illegible]

Proverbs than in the law (Ps 49).

Oracle psalms. These psalms report a decree of God (Ps 82). The content of the oracle is often divine judgment, and the psalm concludes with a prayer for God to carry out His decree. But see also Psalm 87, an oracle of salvation for the Gentiles.

Blessing psalms. In these psalms a priest pronounced a blessing upon the hearer(s) (Ps 128).

Taunt songs. These psalms reproach the godless for their vile behavior and promise that their doom is near (Ps 52).

Songs of trust. In these psalms the psalmist may face difficulty but remains assured of God's help and proclaims his faith and trust (Ps 11).

When interpreting a psalm, it is important first to determine what kind of psalm it is. In this way one can see how the psalmist intended it to be read. (See "Types of OT Literature.")

Psalm 1
A Torah Psalm

To avoid walking, standing, and sitting with the wicked (1:1) is simply to avoid participation in their way of life. "Streams" in 1:3 is best translated as "irrigation canals." The streams of Palestine regularly dried up, but the irrigation canals that came off the great rivers never did.

Psalm 2
A Royal Psalm/Taunt Psalm

The covenant of David underlies this psalm. The Davidic king is the Lord's anointed (Messiah) and receives the whole world as His domain. All the peoples of the earth are warned to submit to Him. The royal house of Judah obviously never ruled the whole world; the fulfillment is in the greater Son of David, Christ. He is God's Messiah, who was crucified by the rulers of this age (2:2; Acts 4:25-26), the Son of God (Ps 2:7; Matt 3:17), and the King with an iron scepter (Ps 2:9; Rev 2:27). The phrase "Kiss the Son" (Ps 2:12) is unusual in that it is in Aramaic, not Hebrew. The Septuagint reads, "Lay hold of instruction." (See "Christ in the Psalms.")

Psalm 3
An Individual Complaint/Prayer for Victory

David's prayer for victory over his enemies is more than a plea for himself. It is also a prayer for his people (3:8), over whom God made him king.

Psalm 4
An Individual Complaint

The psalmist called for God to hear him but then turned to address those who doubted or rejected God. He warned them to abandon idols (4:2), to be warned that God watches over His own (4:3), to meditate in silence and without anger (4:4), and to worship and trust the Lord (4:5). He then proclaimed his confidence in God (4:6-8).

Psalm 5
An Individual Complaint

The righteous are outraged by the behavior of the wicked and wait for God to act. This psalm progresses in five stanzas: (1) an opening call for God to hear (5:1-3), (2) an affirmation of God's hatred of evil (5:4-6), (3) a resolution to serve God and a prayer for help (5:7-8), (4) a prayer for the destruction of the wicked (5:9-10), and (5) a prayer for the protection of the righteous (5:11-12).

Psalm 6
An Individual Complaint

David wrote this psalm when his enemies had him in a desperate situation (6:7). He protested that he would be cut off from Israel's worship if he were killed (6:5). But he concluded in confidence that God would help him (6:8-10).

Psalm 7
An Individual Complaint

At a time of conflict, David was driven to see whether or not he was at fault. His protests of innocence did not stem from pride or refusal to acknowledge guilt but from the insight that he could not expect God to help him if he were as guilty as those who opposed him.

Psalm 8
A Hymn

God is praised as Creator and for having given humanity such a high place in creation. Verse 2 literally reads, "From the mouths of children and babies you have established strength." Matthew 21:16, following the Septuagint, has "praise" instead of "strength." In either case the paradox is that God puts His enemies to shame by infants (see 1 Cor 1:18-25).

Psalm 9
An Individual Song of Thanksgiving

In the Septuagint Psalms 9 and 10 form one psalm. Since the two together form an acrostic, they may well have been originally a single psalm. They were probably separated at an early date to make Psalm 10 an individual complaint psalm. Psalm 9 also has a complaint (9:13), but the overall tone is thanksgiving and certainty of victory.

David saw in his personal victory a type of God's triumph in the last judgment (9:19-20).

Psalm 10
An Individual Complaint

In every age believers are dismayed at the impunity of the violent, the criminal, the vile, and the ungodly. But God remains the hope of the hopeless (10:14-18). He knows our troubles.

Psalm 11
A Song of Trust

The psalmist was aware of the power of evil men but rejected all counsel of despair (11:1-3). He awaited judgment from God (11:4-7). Seated on His throne, God is in control.

Psalm 12
A Community Complaint

Truth is trampled underfoot in a corrupt society, and words are only tools of self-interest (12:4). But the certain word of God, given in an oraclelike response in 12:5, contrasts with the empty words of people (12:6).

Psalm 13
An Individual Complaint

David's trials were such that he wondered how long he could hold on. But trials produce endurance, and the outcome is joy and singing (13:5-6).

Psalm 14
An Oracle Psalm/Taunt Song

God sees the folly and vice of those who live as though He did not exist and declares His anger at those who abuse His people. To treat people as objects of plunder is to be a practical atheist and to invite judgment.

Psalm 15
A Torah Song/Processional Hymn

Only those who are morally qualified may dwell with God. Anyone who would claim to be God's must be free of slander and greed.

Psalm 16
A Song of Trust

Security comes only by trust in the one true God rather than in the many false gods. "Libations of blood" (16:4) could refer to ceremonies involving human sacrifice or ceremonies in which some blood was poured out and the rest was drunk. Peter cited 16:8-11 and interpreted it as a prophecy of the resurrection in Acts 2:25-31.

Psalm 17
An Individual Complaint

David asserted his innocence as a prerequisite to his prayer for deliverance from his enemies. He did not claim sinless perfection in 17:3-5, nor did he deny the universal sinfulness of humanity. But he understood that he could not expect God to save him from his enemies if he cherished deceit or violence in his own life.

Psalm 18
An Individual Song of Thanksgiving

As the superscript says, David gave thanks for the many victories God had given him. In 18:7-15 David described the fury of the Lord in terms reminiscent of the Sinai appearance. Similar language is also found in the ancient Canaanite texts from Ugarit in Syria. David saw his salvation not as personal or private but claimed that God moved heaven and earth—that He set His great power in motion—to save him. God's vindication of David extends to his whole dynasty (18:50) and thus to the Messiah.

Psalm 19
A Torah Psalm

God's revelation through nature and through Scripture each have their place. The natural world gives plain evidence of the glory and power of God (19:1-6; see Rom 1:19-20). The law, however, goes beyond that and instructs and revives the human heart (Ps 19:7-11).

In this relief from Abu Simbel in Egypt, Pharaoh Ramses is "crushing" one enemy while holding one beneath his feet (see Ps 18:37-38).

THE CHARACTERISTICS OF GOD PRESENTED IN THE PSALMS	
CHARACTERISTICS	SELECTED PASSAGES
Anger	5:6; 6:1; 27:9; 30:5; 73:20; 76:7,10; 89:38; 103:8; 106:29,32,40; 108:11; 145:8
Avenger	9:12; 24:5; 26:1; 53:5; 58:6; 59:4; 68:22; 72:4; 86:17; 112:8; 139:14; 148:7
Creator	8:3; 22:9; 24:2; 78:69; 86:9; 93:1; 95:4; 96:5; 119; 73; 91; 121:2; 124:8; 136:5
Deliverer (Savior)	7:1,10; 9:14; 24:5; 27:9; 37:39; 39:8; 71:2; 80:2; 105:37; 119:41,94, 123,146, 173; 132:16
Faithful	40:10; 54:5; 91:4; 92:2; 94:14; 98:3; 100:5; 106:26; 115:1; 119:75; 143:1
Forgiving	25:11; 32:5; 65:3; 78:38; 79:9; 85:2; 86:5; 99:8; 103:3,12; 130:3
Glory	8:1; 24:7; 26:8; 29:1; 63:2; 66:2; 79:8; 89:17; 97:6; 106:20; 113:4; 115:1; 138:5
Good	13:6; 25:7; 27:13; 31:19; 34:8; 73:1; 86:5,17; 100:5; 106:1: 119:65, 68; 125:4; 145:7,9
Gracious	67:1; 86:15; 103:8; 111:4; 112:4; 116:5; 119:58; 145:8
Healer	6:2; 30:2; 103:3; 107:20; 147:3
Holy	16:10; 19:1; 20:6; 22:3; 29:2; 30:4; 68:5,35; 71:22; 77:13; 78:41; 89:7,18,35; 99:3,5,9
Jealous	78:58; 79:5
Judge	7:8,11; 9:4,7-8; 50:4,6; 52:5; 75:2,7; 98:9; 103:9,106:15; 110:6; 120:4
Justice	7:6; 9:8,16; 11:7; 33:5; 36:6; 67:4; 96:10; 99:3; 101:1; 103:6; 140:12
King	5:2; 9:7; 11:4; 44:4; 47:2-9; 66:7; 68:16,24; 74:12; 89:14; 96:10; 97:1; 145:1,115
Living	18:46; 42:2; 84:2

THE CHARACTERISTICS OF GOD PRESENTED IN THE PSALMS	
CHARACTERISTICS	**SELECTED PASSAGES**
Love	6:4; 21:7; 25:6; 47:4; 48:9; 52:8; 60:5; 62:12; 66:20; 98:3; 103:4,8,11,17; 106:1,45; 112:4; 117:1; 119:41,64
Majesty	8:1; 68:34; 76:4; 93:1; 96:6; 104:1; 111:3; 145:5
Mercy	4:1; 5:7; 9:13; 26:11; 30:10; 31:9; 41:4,10; 57:1; 77:9; 78:38; 116:1; 119:132,137
Only God	18:31; 35:10; 73:25; 95:3; 96:4-5; 97:7; 113:5; 135:5
Perfect	18:30; 92:15; 115:3; 135:6
Present	16:11; 22:19; 23:4; 35:22; 38:21; 48:3; 73:23; 75:1; 89:15; 105:4; 110:5; 114:7; 139:7-12
Protector	3:3; 5:11; 7:10; 16:5; 33:20; 66:9; 89:43; 97:10; 115:9; 127:1; 145:20
Provider	67:6; 68:9; 78:23-29; 81:16; 85:12; 107:9,36; 132:15; 136:25; 144:13; 145:15
Redeemer	19:14; 25:22; 55:18; 106:10; 107:2; 119:134,154; 130:8
Refuge, Rock	7:1; 14:6; 19:14; 27:1; 28:1; 42:9; 62:1,8; 73:28; 89:26; 91:2,9; 92:15; 118:8
Repent	7:12; 90:13; 106:45
Righteousness	4:1; 11:7; 22:31; 36:6; 50:6; 65:5; 72:1; 89:14; 96:13; 111:3; 119:40; 129:4
Shepherd	23:1; 28:9; 74:1; 77:20; 78:52; 79:13; 80:1; 95:7; 100:3
Spirit	51:11; 104:30; 106:33; 139:7; 143:10
Universal	24:1; 50:1,12; 59:13; 65:2,5; 66:4; 68:32; 69:34; 86:9; 96:1,7; 99:3; 100:1; 138:4; 150:6
Wisdom	104:24
Wonder Worker	40:5; 46:8; 65:5; 66:3,5; 68:7; 72:18; 73:28; 74:9,13; 78:4; 81:10; 86:8,10; 98:1; 107:8,15; 119:126; 135:8; 136:4,10; 145:4

HUMAN CHARACTERISTICS PRESENTED IN THE PSALMS	
CHARACTERISTICS	**SELECTED PASSAGES**
Afflicted, Poor, Needy	12:5; 14:6; 22:26; 25:16; 34:2,6; 49:2; 68:5,10; 72:2; 74:19; 76:9; 82:3; 113:7; 136:23; 145:14
Anger	37:8; 124:3; 138:7; 139:21
Blessed	1:1; 2:12; 3:8; 5:12; 24:5; 34:8; 41:1; 65:4; 84:4,12; 106:3; 119:1; 129:8; 132:15; 134:3
Confident	3:5; 4:8; 27:1; 30:6; 41:11; 71:5
Covenant	25:10; 50:5,16; 74:20; 78:10,37; 89:3,28,34,39; 103:18; 105:8; 106:45; 111:5,9; 132:12
Death	6:5; 16:10; 23:4; 31:17; 44:22; 49:9-20; 55:4,15,23; 68:20; 78:33,50,57; 82:7; 89:4-8; 103:15; 104:29; 115:17
Enemies	3:1,7; 4:2; 6:10; 8:2; 9:3; 18:37,48; 27:2; 41:2,7; 66:3; 68:1,21; 78:53,61,66; 81:14; 107:2; 108:12; 129:1; 132:18
Faithful, Godly	4:3; 18:25; 26:1; 31:23; 37:28; 73:1; 84:11; 85:10-11; 86:2; 97:10; 101:2; 108:1; 125:4; 131:1; 139:23-24
Fool	14:1; 53:1; 74:18,22; 85:8; 92:6; 94:8; 107:17
Humans	22:6; 33:13; 49:7; 55:13; 56:4; 62:9; 82:5; 89:47; 115:16; 133:1; 139:16; 146:3
Joy	4:7; 16:9; 20:5; 21:1; 27:6; 28:7; 34:2; 47:1; 48:11; 53:6; 63:11; 68:3; 81:1; 90:14; 98:4; 100:1; 107:22; 145:7

HUMAN CHARACTERISTICS PRESENTED IN THE PSALMS	
CHARACTERISTICS	**SELECTED PASSAGES**
King of Israel	2:2,6-8; 20:6; 28:8; 45:1,6; 61:6; 63:11; 78:70; 84:9; 92:10; 119:14,74; 122:5; 144:10
Kings of Earth	33:16; 48:4; 58:1; 68:12; 76:12; 94:20; 102:15; 106:41; 110:5; 119:23,46,161; 138:4; 146:3; 149:8
Loving God	5:11; 18:1; 69:36; 70:4; 91:14; 97:10; 116:1; 119:132; 145:20
Nations	9:5,15,19; 22:27; 44:11; 46:6; 59:5; 67:2; 68:30; 72:17; 78:55; 82:8; 99:1-2; 105:1,13,38; 110:6
Righteous	5:12; 11:5; 14:5; 15:1; 17:1,15; 18:20; 23:3; 33:1; 34:15; 37:6,12,16,21,25,30; 55:22; 58:10; 68:3; 72:2; 92:12; 97:11; 106:31; 125:3; 142:7; 146:8
Sacrifice	4:5
Sin	5:10; 14:3; 18:22; 19:13; 25:7; 36:1-2; 51:1,5,13; 52:2; 58:3; 66:18; 68:21; 89:32; 99:8; 103:10,12; 106:6,13-39,43; 107:11,17
Suffering	22:24; 31:7; 38:3; 41:3; 55:3; 119:50,107,153
Trust	4:5; 9:10; 13:15; 20:7; 21:7; 22:4,9; 28:7; 37:3; 40:3; 52:8; 62:8; 84:12; 112:7; 115:9; 116:10; 125:1
Wicked	5:4; 6:8; 7:9,14; 11:2; 23:4; 26:5; 27:2; 32:10; 52:1,7; 53:1,4; 55:3; 58:3; 59:2; 68:2; 73:3; 82:4; 84:10,22; 94:3,13,16,23; 104:35; 107:34,42; 119:53,95,119,150,155; 147:6
Wisdom	90:12; 107:43; 111:10; 119:98

Walking in this light, the believer is moved to seek divine forgiveness and approval (19:12-14).

Psalm 20
A Prayer for Victory/Blessing Psalm

The king's victory depended not on his cavalry but on his piety and the power of God (20:3,7). All his people would rejoice to see him return in triumph (20:5).

Psalm 21
A Prayer for Victory

Because God had established the Davidic king (21:1-6), the king trusted Him for victory as he went out to meet his foes (21:7). The total victory of the king (21:8-12) anticipates the messianic judgment.

Psalm 22
An Individual Complaint

This psalm follows the pattern of many individual complaint psalms in that it begins with a cry for help and concludes in assurance of deliverance with a promise to fulfill vows. The triumphant conclusion is unusually long (22:22-32). David's situation is a type of the sufferings and resurrection of Christ. The psalm anticipates Christ's outcry from the cross (22:1; Matt 27:46), the mockery He received (Ps 22:7; Luke 23:35), His pain and thirst (Ps 22:14-15; John 19:28), the piercing of His hands and feet (Ps 22:16), and the casting of lots for His clothes (22:18; John 19:23-24). But it also looks forward to His victory and the coming of people from all nations to submit to Him (Ps 22:27-28). (See "Christ in the Psalms.")

Psalm 23
A Song of Trust

The pastoral serenity of the psalm has made it a favorite of generations of readers. Verse 6 contains an implicit promise of eternal life.

Psalm 24
A Processional Hymn

Worshipers may have chanted this hymn as they entered the temple. Verses 3-6 list the qualifications for entering God's congregation. The hymn may have been antiphonal, with the congregation asking the questions (24:3,8,10) and the priest or choir chanting the body of the psalm.

Psalm 25
A Penitential Psalm

Once again David prayed for deliverance, but here he confessed his sinfulness rather than protested his innocence (25:7,11). He desired his forgiveness to take the concrete form of salvation from personal foes (25:19-20). The overall tone of the psalm is of confident assurance in God's mercy. The psalm is acrostic.

Psalm 26
A Song of Trust

Although this psalm is in the form of a "negative confession" (see Job 31), it is not a prideful boast on the psalmist's part (as in Luke 18:11-12). Rather, it teaches the kind of life one must follow to be a part of God's assembly.

Psalm 27
A Song of Trust

True righteousness is above all love for God and the joy of worship (27:4). The one who so loves God is secure even in the tribulations of life because he or she is accepted in the arms of God (27:5,10).

Psalm 28
A Song of Trust

The psalmist prayed for mercy for himself even as he

A beautiful expression of a shepherd is seen in this statue from Mari in ancient Mesopotamia (dating from around 2000 B.C.).

Vengeance and Vindication

Sensitive readers of the Psalms have long been troubled by the harsh expression of vengeance uttered by psalmists, often attributed to David himself. Take for example the statements: "Break the arm of the wicked and evil man: call him to account for his wickedness" (Ps 10:15); "Let the wicked be put to shame and lie silent in the grave" (Ps 31:17); "Break the teeth in their mouths. . . . The righteous will be glad when they are avenged, when they bathe their feet in the blood of the wicked" (Ps 58:6-10). Such unloving statements raise serious ethical questions about the vindictive spirit reflected in these statements. Other prominent curses are found in Psalms 3:7; 5:10; 28:4; 35; 40:14-15; 55; 69; 79; 109; 137; 139:19-22; 140:9-10. Attempts to explain such fierce expressions fall into several categories.

First, some think that these curses only reflect the humanity of the author expressing his deepest desires for vindication when wronged by the wicked. Thus, he was reflecting a lower standard of morality than that found in the NT. This explanation does not adequately account for the fact that the verses in which these curses occur are inspired by the very God who taught the virtue of turning the other cheek.

We must also recognize that 1 Samuel portrays David in a very different light. Although provoked almost beyond imagination, David did not respond vengefully but by tolerance and patience. The occasions on which David refused to kill his mortal enemy Saul provide eloquent testimony to this. Furthermore, Leviticus 19:18 forbids any attempt to exact vengeance against personal enemies, arguing against interpreting these curses as personal vendettas.

Second, another explanation sees the curses as only predictions of the enemy's ruin rather than as expressions of the psalmist's desire that the enemy meet an unhappy end. But Psalm 59 is clearly a prayer to God in which the psalmist asks God to wreak havoc on his enemies.

A plausible understanding of these difficult sayings must take account of the significant role enemies play in the Book of Psalms. Their presence goes far beyond the relatively limited number of psalms that curse the psalmist's enemies. The psalmists were often kings or represented the king in some official capacity. God mandated Israel's king to rule over God's covenant people in order to safeguard them and all God had promised to do through them.

Thus, any threat to God's people was also a threat to the very promise of God. In this unique situation, to oppose the God-anointed king was to oppose God Himself. So the king/psalmist prayed that God would judge those evildoers who intended to hinder the work of God, desiring that God and His work on earth would be vindicated.

Because of the unique position held by the king as God's anointed, he represented God's will in a measure unlike that of anyone today. For this reason believers today must not pray curses, for they are not in a position like that of the king/psalmist in ancient Israel. □

prayed that God would punish evildoers. This came not from selfishness but a profound sense of right and wrong. For those who hate Him to go unpunished would be a perversion of God's justice.

Psalm 29
A Hymn

A terrible storm displays the power of God. The thunder and rain (29:3), lightning (29:7), and wind (29:5,9) all speak of His power. It provokes His people to praise (29:1-2,9).

Psalm 30
An Individual Song of Thanksgiving

God's anger against His children is for only a moment, but His favor is forever (30:5). David confessed, "Thou hast drawn me up" like a bucket from a well (30:1, RSV). David proclaimed the danger of complacency (30:6) and the value of prayer (30:8).

Psalm 31
An Individual Complaint

David professed his confidence in God (31:1-8) and only then voiced his complaint (31:9-13). He mixed his appeal with trust (31:14-18) and concluded in praise (31:19-22) and encouragement for others (31:23-24). Compare 31:5 to Luke 23:46; the sufferings of David typify the sufferings of Christ. David prayed that the wicked might lie silent in the grave so that they could no longer slander him (Ps 31:17-18). (See "Vengeance and Vindication in the Psalms.")

Psalm 32
A Testimony Song

The theme and lesson of the psalm (32:1-2) is followed by a personal testimony to its truth (32:3-5) and further encouragement and exhortation (32:6-11). Paul cited 32:1-2 in Romans 4:7-8. Forgiveness is by God's sovereign mercy, and righteousness comes from faith in Christ rather than by human effort. At the same time, those who genuinely confess live in true obedience rather than mule-headed stubbornness (Ps 32:9).

Psalm 33
A Hymn

After an opening exhortation to praise (33:1-5) the body of the hymn is taken up with the reasons God should be praised (33:6-19). God's power in creation merges into His sovereign control of human history (33:6-11). National security is in the Lord, not in military power (33:12-19). A communal profession of trust and a prayer conclude the psalm (33:20-22).

Psalm 34
A Testimony Song

This psalm is an acrostic. Its primary purpose is to teach the hearer moral lessons about God. The personal testimony is in 34:4-6. The rest of the psalm is made of theological proverbs. The theme is God's continuous care for His own. The psalm does not say that the righteous have no troubles but that God delivers them from their troubles (34:19).

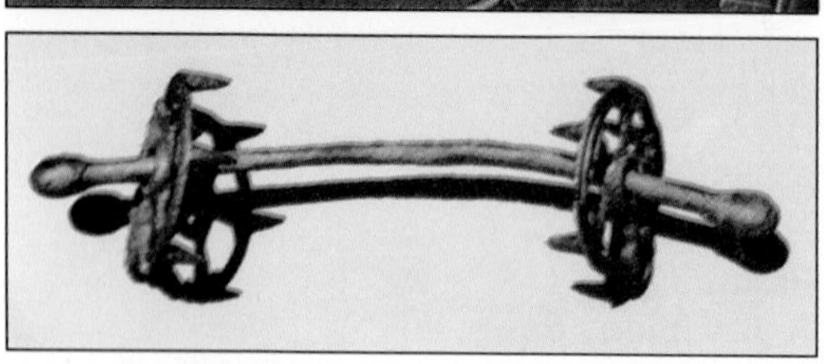

The psalmist warned not to be like a horse or mule, who are controlled "by bit and bridle" (32:9). The upper illustration is an Assyrian relief dating from 900–800 B.C. and discovered at Nineveh. It shows a horse in full harness. The lower photo shows a horse's bit from the Hyksos period (1500s B.C.) and was found at Tell el-Ajjul in Egypt.

Psalm 35
An Individual Complaint

In this prayer David called down curses on his enemies for their treachery and malice. Above all, David condemned false friendship and ingratitude (35:12-16). The angel of the Lord appears in the psalms only here (35:5-6) and in 34:7. (See "Vengeance and Vindication in the Psalms.")

Psalm 36
A Torah Psalm

This psalm is an "oracle" (36:1, a word usually used of prophetic utterances) on the nature of human sin. The wicked continue to love evil even though they too depend on God, the Creator, for life (36:6). But their fate is sure (36:12).

Psalm 37
A Torah Psalm

The righteous should not be dismayed over the apparent prosperity of the wicked, for it is fleeting. This psalm, like many passages in Proverbs, reinforces this truth through descriptions of the kindness of the righteous (37:26,30-31), the fierceness of the wicked (37:14,21), and their respective fates (37:9-10,15,18-20,28-29). In addition, it uses personal observation (37:25,37) and exhortation (37:1-8).

Psalm 38
An Individual Complaint

David confessed his sin (38:3-4,18), described his pain (38:5-10,14), and complained about his false friends and gloating enemies (38:11-12,19-20). The wounds and sickness he mentioned were literal and not symbolic. His isolation and silence were like that of Christ in the passion (38:13; compare Isa 53:7 and Mark 14:61). In his pain he saw that his only help was God (Ps 38:21-22). (See "Christ in the Psalms.")

Psalm 39
An Individual Complaint

The meditative silence of a righteous man pondering the brevity of life gives this psalm a quality of distress like that of Job 7. He had been afflicted by God and longed for restoration. He could never again be secure in his possessions and mortal life, for he now saw how transitory they were.

Psalm 40
An Individual Complaint

This psalm, which begins like an individual song of thanksgiving, becomes a cry for help in 40:9-17. David believed that God would save him again as He had before (40:1-5). Hebrews 10:5-10 cites Psalm 40:6-8 and interprets it as Christ's fulfillment and abolition of the Old Testament sacrificial system. The Hebrew phrase "you have dug ears for me" in 40:6 is difficult. The verb "dug" is often translated "pierced" as in the ritual of Exodus 21:6. But that is unlikely since a different verb is used there and only one ear was pierced. It probably means *you opened my ears* in the sense *you made me obedient* (see Isa 50:5; Jer 6:10). The Septuagint, followed by Hebrews 10:5, has "a body you have prepared for me."

Psalm 41
An Individual Complaint

The malice and hypocritical love of his enemies continues to dominate David's psalms of complaint. As in Psalm 38, he spoke here of his own sin (41:4) and illness (41:8). And again David's isolation in suffering, typical of the righteous, was prophetic of the Messiah's affliction (41:9; see John 13:18). (See "Christ in the Psalms.")

Psalm 42
An Individual Complaint

The exact nature of the psalmist's distress is not given, but it brought him to a state of deep depression (42:3, 5,9-11). Yet he focused not on his trouble but on God and thirsted for God as for water (42:1; Matt 5:6).

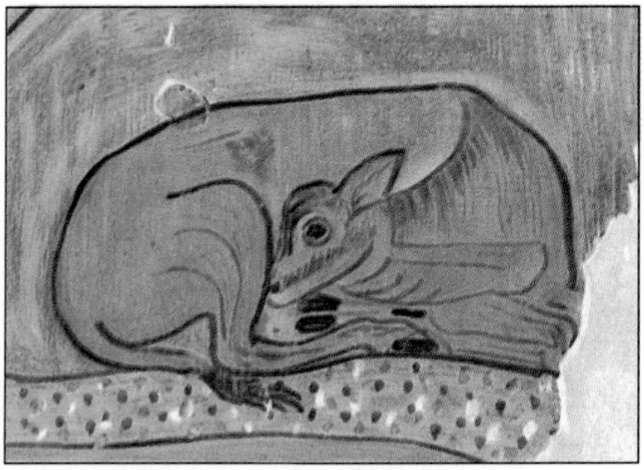

The deer is utilized often in the psalmist's imagery (for example, 42:1). Here in an Egyptian wall painting a newborn deer is seen curled up on the ground just after its birth.

Psalm 43
An Individual Complaint

Psalms 42 and 43 may have originally been a single psalm. The thought and language of the two are very similar (compare 43:5 to 42:5,11), and the Hebrew meter is the same. Also Psalm 43 has no superscript.

Psalm 44
A Community Complaint

God's present abandonment of the nation (44:9-24) contrasts with His former mighty presence among them (44:1-3). With remarkable boldness (44:17-19) the people call on God to fight for them again.

Psalm 45
A Royal Wedding Song

The composition celebrates the wedding of a king of the house of David. Psalm 45:1-9 praises the king, and 45:10-17 instructs and praises the princess-bride. Christians have long seen here an image of Christ and the church (compare 45:6-7 to Heb 1:8).

Psalm 46
A Hymn

The kingdom of God is like a mighty fortress against which the waters, which here as often in Psalms represent chaos and death, have no power (46:1-3). The psalm looks forward to the eternal reign of God in the new earth (46:8-9) but celebrates the present reign of God in this troubled world (46:4-6).

Psalm 47
A Hymn

Someday, the psalm promises, even the Gentile nations will come and worship the God of Abraham (47:9). This has been completely fulfilled in Christ's church.

Psalm 48
A Zion Song

The psalm praises Jerusalem as a type of visible manifestation of the reign of God. The city was glorious and awesome (48:1-3), and God made it secure. There God's people think on His love (48:9).

Psalm 49
A Wisdom Song

This psalm draws on themes used extensively in Ecclesiastes. Among these are the transitory nature of life (49:12; Eccl 3:18-21) and the limitations of learning and wealth (Ps 49:10,12; Eccl 2:15-16; 5:8-17). Psalm 49:15 is a clear promise of the resurrection.

The city of Jerusalem, praised by the psalmist in Psalm 48, viewed from the east. The ancient Temple Mount, now dominated by a Muslim mosque, is in the center of the photo.

Psalm 50
A Zion Song

God here judges the world in a way very similar to the judgment described in Matthew 25:31-46. He accepts the righteous but not because of their sacrificial animals, for which God has no need. He then exhorts them to true piety (50:7-15). The wicked are condemned for theft, adultery, and other sins (50:16-21).

Psalm 51
A Penitential Psalm

This profound plea for forgiveness was written, according to the superscript, after David committed adultery with Bathsheba and murdered her husband. "In sin my mother conceived me" (51:5, KJV) may mean that as David's mother and father were sinners, so was he. Or it may mean that he had been sinful from birth. It does not mean that the act of procreation was itself evil.

Psalm 52
A Taunt Song

The psalmist taunted a godless and cruel individual for his behavior and asserted that his end was near. He did not ask God to avenge his personal loss but claimed that the godless person would be destroyed for lying.

Psalm 53
An Oracle Psalm/Taunt Song

This psalm is almost identical to Psalm 14.

Psalm 54
An Individual Complaint

The treachery of the Ziphites is described in 1 Samuel 23:19-23; 26:1. As in other psalms, David was so certain of God's help that he vowed a thanksgiving offering (54:6).

Psalm 55
An Individual Complaint

This is the strongest statement in the psalter on the cruelty of false friendship. In Psalm 11:1 the psalmist rejected counsel of flight, but here he was so discouraged by betrayal he longed for it (55:6-8).

Psalm 56
An Individual Complaint

On the incident at Gath, see 1 Samuel 21:10-15. In structure this psalm is chiastic. (See the introduction to "Psalms.") Between the initial call for help (56:1-2) and the concluding vow (56:12-13) are two assertions of trust in God (56:3-4,10-11). At the center of the psalm is a call for deliverance from the enemy (56:7-9).

Psalm 57
An Individual Complaint

Praying for help changes the psalmist's attitude from despair to exultant confidence. Surrounded by persons of animal violence (57:4), he could sing out joyfully to God (57:8-9).

Psalm 58
An Individual Complaint

The evil of those who misuse their power for personal gain is here graphically portrayed. They are evil from birth (58:3), incorrigible snakes (58:4-5), and ravenous as lions (58:6). Their deaths will be as little lamented as that of a slug in the sun (58:8). Faith in God is vindicated when they are destroyed (58:11).

Psalm 59
An Individual Complaint

People are instructed when God makes an example of the wicked. This is brought about not by their sudden death but by their gradual and visible demise (59:11-13). In this their true character as wild dogs destined for an ignoble death is clear to all (59:6-8,14-15).

Psalm 60
A Community Complaint

This psalm is a prayer for victory in battle, but it complains of God's apparent abandonment of His people (60:1-3,10). God's election of Israel contrasts with His rejection of its neighbors (60:7-8). Shechem and Succoth (60:6) were on opposite sides of the Jordan and together represent God's (that is, Israel's) ownership of the entire territory.

Psalm 61
A Song of Trust

Many seek sanctuary from the weariness and struggles of life. But that asylum is found only in the Rock that is higher and stronger than any human (61:2). The prayer for the king to have an eternal reign (61:6-7) is fulfilled perfectly in the Son of David, Christ.

Psalm 62
A Song of Trust

Trust in God and Him alone. He is like a fortress (62:2,6) in that He protects against all who are hostile (62:3-4). People will fail (62:9; the Hebrew text reads, "Humans are worthless [as an object of trust]; people are a lie"). Riches are no security (62:10). A numeric saying, familiar in wisdom literature, concludes the psalm (62:11-12; compare Prov 30:21-23).

The psalmist compared himself in 52:8 to an olive tree "flourishing in the house of God." Pictured above is an olive tree growing in the southern coastal region of Israel.

Christ in the Psalms

One of the most controversial questions facing interpreters of the Book of Psalms is how to understand the many references to the "king" or "anointed one" (Hebrew *Messiah*). Do these references speak of a human king of ancient Israel or point ahead to Jesus as the ideal King and Messiah?

The biblical writers wrote of real-life persons and situations. The king played a most prominent role in ancient Israel's national life. Over sixty references in the Psalms highlight the king's prestige. The original readers of the psalms naturally understood that these references spoke of the human king, whose role was so very important in their day-to-day existence. Because the basic meaning of any text is what the author intended the original audience to understand, "king" in the Psalms refers primarily to a human king of ancient Israel.

It may be possible for references to the "king" or "anointed one" to speak of both a human king *and* point ahead to Jesus as the ideal One.

The only clear passage that describes a human king in its OT context who is seen as the ideal messianic King in a subsequent text is Psalm 2. (Hebrews 1:5 treats this psalm as explicitly messianic.) Thus the human king in Psalm 2 functioned as a type, that is, one who had significance in his own historical setting but who also served as a divinely ordained foreshadowing of someone in later biblical revelation.

Generally speaking, references to the king in Psalms speak of the human king in the biblical writer's time. Occasionally, reference to the king was originally understood as a human king but later applied to the ideal Messiah. In one psalm (Ps 110) the king can mean none other than the ideal messianic King of kings.

The superscription of Psalm 110 portrays it as Davidic. Surprisingly, the first verse speaks of David's successor as his lord. In ancient Israel this was inconceivable. David was the greatest king, the standard by which his successors were measured. Early in Israel's history this passage was understood as a prophecy of the coming Messiah. Jesus interpreted Psalm 110:1 in this way in a dispute with the Pharisees (Matt 22:41-45; Mark 12:35-37; Luke 20:41-44). Jesus' riddle—If "David himself calls him 'Lord,' how can he be his son?"—captures the mystery of the incarnation. Jesus is the Son of David but also more than David's son (Rom 1:3-4). □

Psalm 63
A Song of Trust

So profound was his love for God that even in a desert the psalmist longed for Him rather than water (63:1). The worship of God is better than the most delicious food (63:2-5). At night he thought on God rather than sleep (63:6). He stayed close to God in the knowledge that he was safe there (63:7-11).

Psalm 64
An Individual Complaint

No one is capable of foreseeing and protecting himself or herself from all the plots of evildoers. Only God is a sufficient defense. He turns the schemes of the cruel and the criminal back on their own heads (compare 64:3-4 to 64:7-8).

Psalm 65
A Zion Song

This song may have been sung in the temple as part of a thanksgiving for a good harvest (65:9-13). The occasion of its singing may have been the Feast of Unleavened Bread at the beginning of the barley harvest or at Pentecost after the general harvest.

Psalm 66
A Hymn/Testimony Song

After a general praise to God and thanks for His deliverance of Israel in the exodus (66:1-12), the psalmist testified to his personal experience of God's grace (66:13-20). The historical experience of the whole community was repeated in the individual life of the believer.

Psalm 67
A Blessing Psalm

The psalm is built upon the priestly blessing of Numbers 6:24-26.

Psalm 68
A Victory Song/Hymn

The people praised God for His protection of Israel and for the victories they had received. Israel's triumph over its enemies typified God's final triumph in Christ over all the powers. Paul cited 68:18 to that effect (Eph 4:8).

Psalm 69
An Individual Complaint

David typified the suffering of the righteous believer at the hands of the godless, but this concept finds its fullest expression in the travails of Christ (compare 69:9 to John 2:17 and Ps 69:21 to Matt 27:34,48). (See "Christ in the Psalms.")

Psalm 70
An Individual Complaint

Compare Psalm 40:13-17. The brevity of this psalm matches the urgency of its tone (70:1,5). It is a call to God in a desperate moment.

Psalm 71
An Individual Complaint

The psalmist, aware that he was aging and his strength was failing (71:9,18), called on God to walk with him as he entered this period of life. Prior experience told him that God would continue to be faithful (71:20).

Psalm 72
A Coronation Song

The superscript should be translated *For Solomon* since 72:20 implies that the psalm was by David. The song is a prayer for Solomon's coronation. It is based on 2 Samuel 7 and typifies the messianic reign. God's king was to exhibit righteousness, justice, and concern for the poor and oppressed (72:1-4).

Psalm 73
A Wisdom Song

The psalmist wondered how the wicked could impudently flaunt God's ways and thrive (compare Job 21). He wondered if his piety had been for nothing (73:13-14). But he came to understand that God sustained him, not his own will, and that grace would lead him to eternal glory (73:23-24).

Psalm 74
A Community Complaint

The psalm was probably written shortly after the Babylonian exile began. The people mourned the destruction of the temple (74:3-8). Remembering God's triumph over chaos at creation (74:13-17; Gen 1:2), they prayed for God to defeat the enemy that conquered them and to restore the order of the temple.

Psalm 75
An Oracle Psalm

God's determination to judge the earth and punish the wicked is certain. Verse 8 is a familiar prophetic image (see Isa 51:17; Jer 25:15-29; 49:12; 51:7).

Psalm 76
A Hymn

Victory over one of Israel's enemies portrayed here typifies the final victory of God over all earthly powers.

Psalm 77
An Individual Complaint/ Community Complaint

Although voiced by an individual, these laments relate to the whole nation and not one person. Compare 77:16-19 to 74:13-17, which alludes to God's victory over the pre-creation chaos. Here the reference is to the exodus.

Psalm 78
A Torah Psalm

This psalm recites the events of the exodus, as recorded in the law, and ties the continual rebellion of the Israelites to the secession of the Northern Kingdom (Ephraim) from the house of David (78:9-11,67-72).

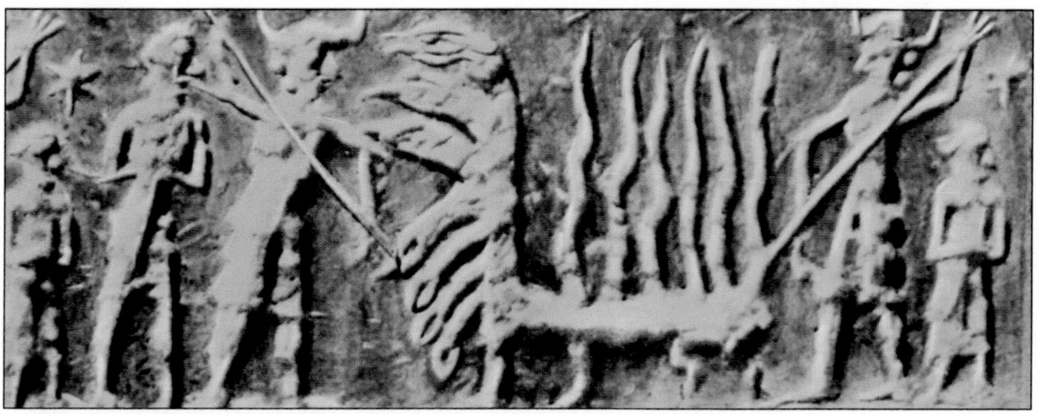

The psalmist wrote that God has "crushed the heads" of leviathan (74:13-14). In the Akkadian cylinder seal above (dating from around 2500 B.C.) two Mesopotamian gods are fighting a monster with seven heads.

The spring of Kadesh (Ain Qudeirat) pictured above flows out of a rock and is thus a good example of the water God provided for the Israelites during the exodus (Ps 78:15-16).

Psalm 79
A Community Complaint

Like Psalm 74, this was apparently written in the Babylonian exile. Unlike the former lament, this psalm emphasizes the plight of the people (79:2-4,10-11) rather than the destruction of the temple.

Psalm 80
A Community Complaint

This psalm again laments the Babylonian captivity and calls on God to remember His former election of Israel. The image of the vine (80:8-11,14-16) reappears in the prophets (Isa 5:1-7; Ezek 15).

Psalm 81
An Oracle Psalm

This psalm begins like a hymn (81:1-2) but moves to a long oracle of exhortation from God (81:6-16). It may have been sung at Passover (81:5) or Tabernacles (81:3; Tabernacles was celebrated from the fifteenth of the month, at full moon).

Psalm 82
An Oracle Psalm

God accuses the "gods" of having misgoverned the world. The identity of these "gods" is hard to determine. Some interpret them as spiritual powers that rule the world and others as human judges. But these alternatives are not mutually exclusive. Probably the human powers are treated as the earthly counterparts to spiritual forces (compare Col 1:16). God has determined to judge the powers and rulers who maintain a world system of oppression and injustice.

Psalm 83
National Curses

The psalmist listed the nations that he desired to see punished (83:5-8). The psalm likely was written sometime between 900 and 600 B.C., when Assyria (83:8) was still a threat.

The psalm is not a mere cry for vengeance. Rather, it is a plea for the righteous God to demonstrate His sovereignty by defending His chosen people.

Psalm 84
A Processional Hymn
The singer celebrates the joy of worship in God's house. The "valley of Baca" (84:6) was apparently along the path the worshipers took to the temple.

Psalm 85
A Community Complaint
The problem the people faced is unclear (85:4-6). They prayed in an optimistic way, sure of God's help; for His love is unfailing.

Psalm 86
An Individual Complaint
The psalmist based this appeal on the kindness (86:5) and universal power (86:8-10) of God.

Psalm 87
An Oracle Psalm
God has determined to bring even the Gentiles into His kingdom. "This one was born in Zion" (87:4,6) means that the Gentile has been adopted into the covenant.

Psalm 88
An Individual Complaint
The sage Heman "the Ezrahite" is perhaps the same as the son of Zerah in 1 Chronicles 2:6 (compare 1 Kgs 4:31). This psalm shows remarkable parallels to Job, especially in the psalmist's personal affliction and abandonment.

Psalm 89
A Community Complaint
Ethan the Ezrahite was possibly the brother of Heman (Ps 88; see 1 Kgs 4:31; 1 Chron 2:6), but the psalm may have been written as late as the exile. It laments that although God made an eternal covenant with the house of David (Ps 89:19-37; see 2 Sam 7), the dynasty now seemed abandoned (Ps 89:38-51).

Psalm 90
A Wisdom Song/Community Complaint
In this psalm the community called on God for mercy (90:7-11), but in the tradition of wisdom literature the song strongly emphasizes the shortness of human life.

Psalm 91
A Wisdom Song/Oracle Psalm
God extends the promise of protection to all who turn to Him. Contrary to Satan's interpretation (Matt 4:6), Psalm 91:11-12 does not allow reckless behavior.

Psalm 92
A Hymn
In 92:10 "you have exalted my horn" means that God had given the singer victory. "Fine oils are poured upon me" means that God had lavished favor upon him. The image of the righteous person as a flourishing tree is common in the Bible (92:12-14; see Ps 1).

Psalm 93
A Song of the Lord's Reign
The permanence of the Lord's reign is the security of all who trust in Him. The pounding of the waves (93:3-4) represents the power of death and destruction, but God's eternal regime controls all things. And as God's rule is eternal, so also are His statutes (93:5).

A seven-stringed harp, a musical instrument used in Old Testament worship. (From an Egyptian tomb painting dating about 2000 B.C.)

The psalmist wrote that the cedars of Lebanon are planted and cared for by the Lord (104:16). A cedar forest in the mountains of Lebanon is shown in the above photo.

Psalm 94
A Community Complaint/Song of Trust
Distress over the crimes of the wicked gives way to confidence in God's justice. The psalm calls for patience and endurance.

Psalm 95
An Oracle Psalm
Because God is sovereign over all, we must submit to His demand for obedience. Hebrews 3:7–4:11 expounds this psalm in detail. (See "Christ in the Psalms.")

Psalm 96
A Hymn
The Lord God of Israel rules over all the earth, and all its peoples must bow to Him. This is the great missionary song of the Bible.

Psalm 97
A Song of the Lord's Reign
The power of the Lord is awesome enough to melt even the mountains (97:5). Israel can rejoice that its God is greater than all idols and so-called gods (97:7-12). For His people, God's fury promotes not terror but joy.

Psalm 98
A Hymn
This psalm is a variant of Psalm 96 and follows the same missionary theme. All the world, not Israel alone, must submit to the Lord.

Psalm 99
A Song of the Lord's Reign
The Lord of heaven and earth has chosen Israel as His people and from them has taken His priests and prophets

(99:2,4,6-8). All the nations, therefore, should acknowledge Him as the sole God and worship at His mountain (99:2-3,5,9).

Psalm 100
A Processional Hymn

The people may have chanted this psalm as they entered the temple or began their worship (100:4).

Psalm 101
A Votive Psalm

In resolving to remain faithful to God, the psalmist especially pledged to keep himself from association with evil men and abide with the righteous. He knew how strong the influence of others could be.

Psalm 102
An Individual Complaint

This psalm may have been written in the exile (102:13-17). The outcry of the psalmist is individual in perspective but concerns not a private problem but the destruction of Zion.

Psalm 103
A Hymn

The people praise God for His compassion and forgiveness of sins. Verses 14-18 imply the eternal life of the believer. We are not by nature immortal, but God does not abandon us to death (103:15-16).

Psalm 104
A Hymn

All creation testifies to the goodness and power of God. This psalm is based on Genesis 1:3-19.

Psalm 105
A Hallelujah Hymn

This psalm recites the history of the Israelites from the patriarchs to the exodus as a reason for praise. Note the positive tone of the song. Contrary to Psalm 106 (which covers the same history) the sins of Israel are not mentioned. These two psalms form a pair. Psalm 105 ends where Psalm 106 begins: "Praise the Lord!"

Psalm 106
A Hallelujah Hymn

This psalm praises God by reciting Israel's history from the exodus to the judges' time. God forgave many rebellions. Israel failed to believe at the Red Sea (106:7-12; Exod 14:10-12). They complained about food in the wilderness (Ps 106:13-15; Num 11). Dathan and Abiram rebelled (Ps 106:16-18; Num 16). Israel worshiped the golden calf (106:19-23; Exod 32). They proved cowards at Kadesh-Barnea (106:24-27; Num 14). Israel joined Moabite women in sexual sin and idolatry (106:28-33; Num 25). Israel complained at Meribah (106:32-33; Num 20:1-13). They accepted Canaanite ways (106:34-39; see Josh 23) and repeated apostasy in the judges' time (106:40-43; Judg 1:16).

Psalm 107
A Hymn

Those who have suffered and then have seen God's salvation all have reason to praise God. This includes homeless aliens (107:4-9); war captives (107:10-16); those punished for their sin with personal illness (107:17-22); and those who have encountered dangers on the sea (107:23-32), famine (107:33-38), and other afflictions (107:39-42).

Psalm 108
A Hymn/Community Complaint

Verses 1-5 are from Psalm 57:7-11, and verses 6-13 are from Psalm 60:5-12.

Psalm 109
An Individual Complaint

The massive curse on the enemy (109:6-20) is founded not on personal vendetta but rather on a sense of justice. (See "Vengeance and Vindication in the Psalms.")

Psalm 110
A Royal Psalm

This prayer for the Davidic king typologically portrays the glory of the ultimate Davidic King, the Messiah. He is a Lord above even His father David (110:1; Matt 22:41-46) and a priest though not of the Levitical line (Ps 110:4; Heb 7:11-28). He is victor over all His enemies (110:2-3,5-6). (See "Christ in the Psalms.")

Psalm 111
A Hallelujah Hymn

This general song of praise in acrostic form ends with the motto of biblical wisdom (111:10; compare Prov 1:7). Here we see the Old Testament proclamation of God's love and grace.

Psalm 112
A Hallelujah Hymn/Wisdom Song

This acrostic psalm develops the praise of the Lord entirely along the lines of wisdom literature. (Compare the fates of the righteous and wicked in Prov 10:3-30).

Psalm 113
A Hallelujah Hymn
Compare this to the Song of Hannah in 1 Samuel 2:1-10.

Psalm 114
A Hallelujah Hymn
The congregation praised God for the exodus and conquest. The seas and mountains represent the apparently unconquerable earthly power opposed to Israel.

Psalm 115
A Hallelujah Hymn/Taunt Song
This psalm mocks idols (and those who worship them) in the spirit of Isaiah 40:18-20 and 44:6-20.

Psalm 116
An Individual Song of Thanksgiving/ Hallelujah Hymn
Compare 116:3 to Jonah 2:5, in another individual song of thanksgiving.

Psalm 117
A Hallelujah Hymn
Opening and concluding exhortations to praise the Lord envelop the reason He ought to be praised: His enduring love.

Psalm 118
An Individual Song of Thanksgiving/ Antiphonal Hymn
An individual sang his thanks to God (118:5-7,10-14,17-21,28) as the congregation responded with praise 118:1-4,8-9,15-16,22-27,29). Jesus took 118:22 as a prophecy of His rejection by the Jewish leaders (Matt 21:42). (See "Christ in the Psalms.")

Psalm 119
A Torah Psalm
This massive psalm is a song in honor of the law. It is in twenty-two eight-verse stanzas, which are organized in acrostic order. Each verse of each unit begins with the same letter. This made the psalm easier to memorize.

Psalm 120
An Individual Complaint
The peace-loving psalmist was distressed at the slanders spoken against him but was certain that God would save him. Meshech was in Anatolia near the Black Sea, but Kedar was in Arabia (120:5). The psalmist did not literally live in these places. The names represent distant barbarian and pagan lands and picture his enemies.

Psalm 121
A Processional Hymn
Pilgrims going to Jerusalem may have sung this prayer for safety in the journey. The dangers along the way—accidents, wild animals, robbers, heat stroke —are implied in 121:3-6. The "sun" and "moon" (121:6) represent all the dangers of day and night. A safe trip is promised in 121:7-8.

Psalm 122
A Processional Hymn
The pilgrims going up to Jerusalem here prayed for the security of the city and the house of David. The city was sacred because God's temple was there (122:9).

Psalm 115 condemns idols. Above is a bronze (overlaid with gold) head of the Egyptian goddess Hathor found at Beth Shan.

Psalm 123
A Community Complaint

The worshipers in the temple prayed on behalf of their nation. The touching metaphor in 123:2 vividly portrays the people's dependence on God.

Psalm 124
A Victory Song

The people gave thanks for having escaped conquest at the hands of their enemies. The two images of a flood and a bird in a trap portray the helplessness they felt.

Psalm 125
A Zion Song

The psalmist rejoiced in the enduring security of Zion and its people but prayed that God would provide just rulers (125:3-5). God's people were secure in Him but groaned because of the evil powers among whom they dwelt.

Psalm 126
A Zion Song

This touching song may have been sung by the returnees from the Babylonian captivity. It is both a hymn of thanksgiving for restoration to Zion (126:1) and a prayer for restored prosperity (126:4).

Psalm 127
A Torah Psalm

This psalm acclaims the value of family life under God. Working to the point of fatigue for the sake of one's family is useless; it is better to trust God and be able to rest in His care and protection (127:1-2). When living in God's care, children are not a nuisance or a burden but a gift.

Psalm 128
A Blessing Psalm

This psalm may have been recited as a blessing upon a groom in a wedding ceremony. ("You" and "your" are masculine singular in Hebrew.) The prayer for sons, long life, and prosperity (128:3,5-6) is natural in such a setting. The vine represents not only the wife's fruitfulness but also her cheerfulness (Judg 9:13) and feminine beauty (Song 7:8).

Psalm 129
National Curses

Israel had suffered mightily under the Egyptians, Philistines, Assyrians, Babylonians, and others; but it had survived. Its enemies were cursed with a prayer that they become as insubstantial and insignificant as dried grass on the housetops (129:6-7).

Psalm 130
An Individual Complaint

The psalmist did not clarify the nature of his troubles or explicitly confess any sin. But he was aware of his sinfulness and need for grace (130:3). The closing (130:7-8) could suggest this was not a private but a national complaint, but many psalms conclude with a prayer for Israel. The repetition of "more than watchmen wait for the morning" in 130:6 heightens the sense of longing.

Psalm 131
A Testimony Song

The psalmist testified to the tranquility of the one trusting God (131:1-2) and exhorted others to trust as well (131:3).

Psalm 132
A Zion Song

As the people prayed for the house of David and the temple, they cited God's promises.

Psalm 133
A Wisdom Song

The image of brotherly unity being like the oil that runs down Aaron's beard is striking. Unity is God's gift and a sacred duty.

Psalm 134
A Hymn

This psalm exhorts the priests of the temple to praise God and blesses them for their service.

An Assyrian relief from Sennacherib's palace at Nineveh showing captives playing their lyres for their captors (see Ps 137:3-4).

Psalm 135
A Hymn/Taunt Song
This psalm praises the God of Israel for creation (137:6-7) and the exodus and conquest (137:8-12). It mocks the foolishness of idol worshipers (137:15-18).

Psalm 136
An Antiphonal Hymn
Apparently the people responded, "His love endures forever" as the temple priests or choir chanted the body of the psalm. The psalm links the theme of creation (136:5-9) to the exodus (136:10-16) and conquest (136:17-22). Israel was God's new creation, as miraculous as the first creation.

Psalm 137
A National Curse
After the beautiful lament of 137:1-6, the reader is jolted by the astonishing ending to the psalm (137:9). This brutal blessing shows the Jews' anguish over what had happened to their nation. Other Jews (Daniel, Esther) learned God was with them in the exile.

Psalm 138
An Individual Song of Thanksgiving
The so-called "gods" of 138:1 may have been supernatural beings who filled God's heavenly court or the term may refer to pagan powers and rulers (138:4).

Psalm 139
A Song of Trust
David praised God for His omniscience and omnipresence. Verses 13-15 draw together the concepts that a person is formed in his or her mother's body and that humans are made from the clay of the earth (Gen 2:7). Thus we, no less than Adam, are God's creation.

Psalm 140
An Individual Complaint
David's enemies were out to trap him and especially used slander as their tool (140:3,11).

Psalm 141
An Individual Complaint
By his willingness to suffer at the hands of the righteous

A view of the beautiful snow-capped peaks of Mount Hermon, a mountain mentioned in several psalms (Ps 42:6; 89:12; 133:3).

(141:5), David showed that he was motivated by integrity and love for God rather than by a selfish desire for personal victory.

Psalm 142
An Individual Complaint

This psalm follows the normal pattern for the Song of Individual Complaint: introductory affirmation of God's goodness (142:1-3a), complaint and appeal (142:3b-7), expectation of deliverance, and promise of praise (142:7b).

Psalm 143
An Individual Complaint

From beginning to end this psalm is an appeal to God. As part of his plea for help the psalmist also asked for instruction (143:10).

Psalm 144
A Prayer for Victory

The martial spirit of this prayer is tempered by the fact that the object of victory is not conquest or military honor but security for the people (144:12-14).

Psalm 145
A Hymn

Verses 3-7 stress the importance of passing from one generation to the next the tradition of what God has done.

Psalm 146
A Hallelujah Hymn

It was the duty of the ancient king to be the protector and advocate of the helpless, but many failed in this and instead became oppressors. But God cares for the oppressed, the hurting, and the abandoned. Compare this to Mary's "Magnificat" (Luke 1:46-55).

Psalm 147
A Hallelujah Hymn

The hymn alternates between praising God as Protector of Israel (147:2-3,12-14,19-20) and as Creator (147:7-11,15-18).

Psalm 148
A Hallelujah Hymn

Heaven (148:1-6) and earth (148:7-12) and all that is in them are exhorted to praise God.

Psalm 149
A Hallelujah Hymn

Exuberant, joyful praise of God's people is the weapon by which they conquer all their enemies. Spiritual conflict requires spiritual weapons (compare Eph 6:10-18).

Psalm 150
A Hallelujah Hymn

The loud, joyful, and exultant tone of this psalm tells us something of the nature of Israel's worship. It could be solemn and grand without tedium or empty pomp. The psalm tells where (150:1), for what (150:2), how (150:3-5), and by whom (150:6) the Lord is to be praised.

Theological Significance

The psalms help today's believers to understand God, themselves, and their relationship to God. The psalms picture God as the Creator, who is worthy of praise and is capable of using His creative might to rescue His people from current distress. The psalms picture God as the just Judge of all the world, who rewards the righteous and opposes the wicked. Prayers that God curse the enemies of the psalmist must be understood in part as affirmations of God's justice and the certainty of His judgment. The psalms picture God as the faithful Friend of the

A clay plaque from Mesopotamia (dating from about 3000 B.C.) showing a musician playing a seven-stringed harp (see Ps 92:2-3).

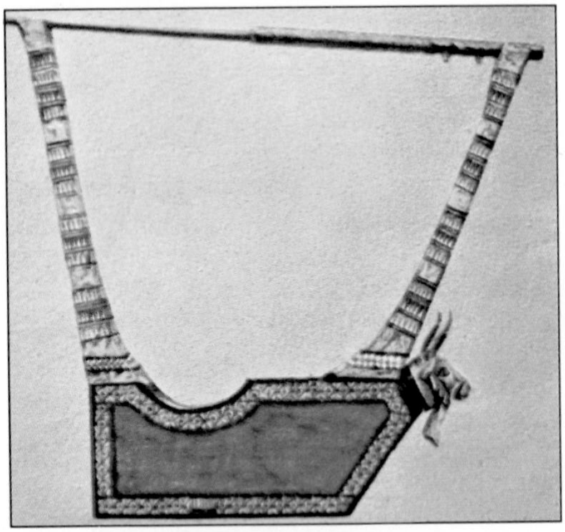

A reconstruction of the harp of Ur (from the First Dynasty of Ur, about 2500 B.C.). It is made of wood overlaid with gold and is shaped like a boat with a bull's head at one end.

oppressed. The psalms offer a refresher course in God's faithfulness throughout Israel's history. The psalms highlight God's promises to David and his descendants, promises that are not finally realized until Christ.

The psalms picture the full range of human emotions: joy, despair, guilt, consolation, love, hate, thankfulness, and dissatisfaction. The psalms thus remind us that all of life is under God's lordship. The psalms likewise illustrate the broad range of human responses to God: praise, confession, pleas for help, thanksgiving. The psalms thus serve as a source book for Christian worship, both public and private.

Questions for Reflection

1. How can we use the Torah psalms and Wisdom psalms for personal growth?
2. In what ways does the Davidic king in Psalms point forward to Christ?
3. How can the hymns in Psalms be used to enhance our corporate worship?
4. Do the psalms of complaint have any place in our prayer life today? If so, how are they to be used?

Sources for Additional Study

Alden, Robert L. *Psalms*. 3 Vols. Chicago: Moody, 1975.

Kidner, Derek. *Psalms*. 2 Vols. Downers Grove: InterVarsity, 1975.

Weiser, Artur. *The Psalms*. Philadelphia: Westminster, 1962.

Wiersbe, Warren W. *Meet Yourself in the Psalms.* Wheaton: Victor, 1983.

A relief discovered at Carchemish of musicians playing a double pipe (middle figure) and cymbals (second figure from right) and dancing (far right figure). (See Ps 150:3-5.)

PROVERBS

In spite of its name, the Book of Proverbs is more than a collection of individual proverbs. Chapters 1–9 contain some lengthy discourses, and the book ends with a poem of praise for the virtuous woman (31:10-31). Nevertheless, a great deal of the book is taken up with the individual sayings and proverbs for which it is best known.

The Nature of Proverbial Literature

Every culture has its own proverbs and traditional wisdom. In fact, the study of wisdom and proverbs was a favorite activity of ancient scribes and teachers. Writings that preserve this ancient wisdom have survived from Egypt, Mesopotamia, and Greece.

In ancient times collections of traditional wisdom were the textbooks for educating young men of aristocratic birth. Proverbs often implies that it was written for young men for a similar purpose. For example, the reader is frequently addressed as "my son" (2:1; 3:1,11; 4:1,10; 5:1; 6:1) and is warned to avoid prostitutes (5:3-6; 6:20-35). Although Proverbs can be profitably read by anyone, its interpretation is easier if we keep in mind the original audience for whom it was written.

Proverbs has other features in common with the wisdom writings of the other nations of the ancient Near East. Like them, it is very practical. It deals with ordinary matters of life more than with great philosophical concepts. Also its structure and organization are in many ways like the other wisdom writings, especially those from Egypt.

But Israelite wisdom is distinct from that of the other nations in its assertion that God is the starting point in the search for true wisdom: "The fear of the Lord is the beginning of knowledge" (Prov 1:7; compare 9:10; Ps 111:10). From beginning to end, Proverbs deals with the practical concerns of an individual who knows God. It teaches the believer how to live. In this sense even when it deals with mundane issues, Proverbs is never "secular."

Forms of Wisdom Teaching

Even a casual reading of Proverbs reveals the many creative ways in which the book teaches its lessons. Proverbs is not only interesting to read, but its teachings are also memorable. Some of the major types of expressions follow:

Proverb. A proverb is a short, carefully constructed ethical observation (13:7) or teaching (14:1).

Admonition. An admonition is a command written either as a short proverb (16:3) or as part of a long discourse (1:10-19).

Numerical Saying. The numerical pattern lists items that have something in common after an introduction like, "There are six things, indeed seven" (see 30:24-31).

Better Saying. A better saying follows the pattern "*A* is better than *B*." See 21:19.

Rhetorical Question. A rhetorical question is a question with an obvious answer that still draws the reader into deeper reflection. See Proverbs 30:4.

Wisdom Poem. Wisdom poems or songs teach a series of moral lessons, as in 31:10-31. These poems are often acrostic.

Example Story. An example story is an anecdote meant to drive home a moral lesson (7:6-27).

Structure of Proverbs

Proverbs is actually a collection of several books:

The Proverbs of Solomon (Prov 1–24). This work includes a title and prologue (1:1-7) and a main text divided into discourses (1:7–9:18), proverbial sayings (10:1–22:16), thirty "sayings of the wise" (22:17–24:22), and additional "sayings of the wise" (24:23-34).

Proverbs of Solomon copied by the men of Hezekiah (Prov 25–29). This collection has no prologue; it is simply an assortment of individual proverbs.

The sayings of Agur (Prov 30). This collection has seven numerical sayings (30:7-9,15a,15b-16,18-19,21-23,24-28,29-31) and several proverbs. Verses 2-9 could be regarded as a prologue.

The sayings of King Lemuel (Prov 31). This two-part book concerns the duties of a king (31:2-9) and the praise of the virtuous woman (31:10-31).

I. The Proverbs of Solomon (1:1–24:34)
II. Solomon's Proverbs as Copied by Hezekiah's Men (25:1–29:27)
III. The Sayings of Agur (30:1-33)
IV. The Sayings of King Lemuel (31:1-31)

The Date and Authorship of Proverbs

The text says that the above four works are respectively by Solomon, by Solomon as edited by Hezekiah's scribes, by Agur, and by Lemuel as learned from his mother. This means that the bulk of Proverbs (1–29) is essentially from Solomon. Even so, many modern scholars believe that these collections came together long after Solomon. Some believe that Proverbs was not written until over five hundred years after Solomon, although others would date the collections to the late monarchy, some three hundred years after Solomon.

But no hard evidence exists that forces us to abandon the Bible's assertion that Solomon wrote most of the book. Some have argued that passages like Proverbs 8 are too advanced in thought to have come from Solomon. Yet other advanced and complex works of wisdom literature that are far older than Solomon's day appear in ancient Near Eastern texts. In addition, we read in the Bible that Solomon's reign was something of a flowering of wisdom in ancient Israel and that Solomon was at the head of its study (1 Kgs 10:1-9). That being the case, it is not strange that the greatest Israelite wisdom literature should come from this period.

Agur and Lemuel may be pen names of someone otherwise familiar to us; more likely Agur and Lemuel were simply sages about whom we have no other information.

Since we do not know the identities of the writers, we cannot know the dates of composition. But there is no reason to date these sections very late. Also, although we cannot be sure when something like the present Book of Proverbs first appeared, the reign of Hezekiah (716–687 B.C.) may be a reasonable surmise (25:1).

The Origin of the Individual Proverbs

To say that Solomon was the principal author of Proverbs is not to imply that he coined every single proverb in his sections. To the contrary, much of his work was as a collector of the "sayings of the wise" (22:17; 24:23). From whom did these proverbs come?

Certainly a primary source of Israelite wisdom was the family, where traditional teachings were handed down for generations. Proverbs frequently addresses its reader as "my son" and urges him to adhere to the teachings of his father and mother (for example, 1:8).

A second source was in the schools where scribes both compiled and composed wisdom literature. Many such scribes are known from Egyptian literature, and the Bible speaks of scribes and wise men in ancient Israel and Judah (Prov 25:1; 1 Chron 27:32; Jer 18:18). These men were not only the intellectual class of their day, but they also were the counselors of the kings (Gen 41:8). Solomon, as king, would have had close contact with such men in order to develop his own studies and writings (1 Kgs 4:31,34).

It is easy to see, therefore, why Proverbs contains such a variety of types of teachings. The more homey and humorous proverbs may have come from the traditional teachings of the Israelite family (see 11:22 and 26:3). The more literary compositions show the influence of court scribes (1:20-33).

"THE PROVERBS OF SOLOMON" (PROV 1:1–24:34)

1:1-7
Title and Prologue

The prologue states the purpose for the work in 1:2-7. For the Israelites wisdom not only promoted a life of discipline and prudence (1:3), but it also enabled persons to unravel clever and mysterious sayings (1:6).

The heart of Israelite wisdom asserts that no one can begin to understand God's ways and life's mysteries apart from God's revelation (1:7). All human attempts at wisdom will ultimately fail.

1:8–9:18
Solomon's Discourses

Discourse 1 (1:8-33). The teacher warns the young man not to abandon the teachings of father and mother for the sake of lawless companions. Those who accept this kind of peer pressure are on their way to death (1:10-19). Wisdom herself calls on all to learn of her. Those who reject the call have no excuse when disaster strikes (1:23-33).

Discourse 2 (2:1-22). The primary benefit of wisdom is the protection she gives. The two main dangers she saves her followers from are the crafty man (2:11-15) and the adulterous woman (2:16-19). This again indicates that the book was originally written for young men.

Discourse 3 (3:1-35). Wisdom is more than a matter of knowing rules of right and wrong; it is a matter of knowing God. The wise trust in the Lord rather than in their own wisdom (3:5-6). They fear and honor Him (3:7-10) and accept His discipline (3:11-12). The Lord, not just their awareness of certain principles, protects them (3:26).

THEMES OF PROVERBS

The Book of Proverbs begins by challenging the young and simple as well as the wise and discerning to seek wisdom through its study (1:1-7). Ancient wisdom recognized the God-given *order* underlying creation (3:19-20; 8:22-30) and human society. For ancient wisdom saw God as a just Judge, who observes human conduct and upholds the moral order of His world by rewarding the righteous and punishing the wicked. The bulk of Proverbs takes up the practical application of wisdom. What to do in specific, day-to-day situations was often not directly addressed by the OT laws and the prophets. These problems included how to relate to spouses (12:4; 31:10-31), parents (23:22), and children (19:18). How was one to relate to kings (16:10-15) and subjects (27:23-27), to friends (18:24) and enemies (25:21-22), to rich and poor (14:20-21)? How was one to respond to poverty and riches (18:11; 30:7-9)? Wisdom literature offered the ancient Israelites God-given counsel on such everyday matters.

God inspired Scripture in different ways. God spoke to Moses face to face. God spoke to the boy Samuel as an audible voice. God inspired wisdom teachers through the world they observed. Solomon (1 Kgs 4:29-32; Prov 1:1; 10:1; 25:1), Agur (30:1), and Lemuel and his mother (31:1) observed and reflected on the order of creation and society.

For example, seeing the sluggard's untended stone walls lying in ruin and his unworked fields bearing inedible vegetation, the inspired wisdom teacher learned a lesson. He learned that poverty will destroy a lazy individual just as surely as a bandit invades and robs. But through wisdom and discipline, the wise can overcome this evil (compare 24:30-34). Although God spoke to the wisdom teachers in a less dramatic fashion than He had to Moses and prophets, those teachers were just as inspired (Prov 2:6). Their words were just as authoritative as the laws or prophecies. The wisdom teachers referred to their proverbs as "teaching" (Hebrew *torah*, also rendered "law"; 1:8; 3:1) and "commands" (2:1; 3:1).

The wisdom teachers viewed life through the lens of Israel's faith, that is through the law and the prophets (29:18).

They recognized a proper respect for God as the foundation of all wisdom. "The fear of the Lord" (1:7) is the essential spiritual quality for those seeking to learn the inspired teacher's wisdom. What the alphabet is to reading, notes are to music, and numerals are to mathematics the fear of the Lord is to wisdom.

The wise, motivated by a healthy fear that God will uphold His revealed moral order, accept God's objective standards of wisdom. Those who accept the teachings of the wise and actively pray and search for wisdom come to understand the fear of the Lord (Prov 2:1-5). With this spiritual attitude God's people find the spiritual strength to master their tongue (21:23) and themselves (16:32; 25:28) and to live in harmony with all creatures and with creation.

The inspired writer was well aware that the righteous may first endure poverty (17:1; 19:1) and even death (1:10-19) before God rewards them. In fact, the righteous person may appear to be knocked out for the full count, but they will rise (24:16). Whereas the Books of Job and Ecclesiastes focus on the morally topsy-turvy world in which the wicked prosper and the righteous suffer, Proverbs looks at the end of the matter. The righteous will ultimately prosper in this life or the next. For the righteous God-fearer, the grave is merely a shadow along the trail (12:28; 14:32). Without this kind of faith it is impossible to please God (3:5; 22:19).

Faith in God's promises and warnings and obedience to His revealed will are contrary to human nature. Folly is bound up in the child's heart (22:15). In fact, sinful humans cannot speak for any extended period without sin (10:19). Like Solomon, persons who stop listening to instruction quickly stray from words of knowledge (19:27). Wisdom is gained through discipline. It is implanted by instruction (22:6; 4:3-4) and pruned with corporal punishment (10:13; 13:24; 23:13-14). Above all, the wise commit themselves in faith to God and pray to Him (15:8,29). □

Discourse 4 (4:1-27). This chapter has all the urgency of a father's appeal to his son. The plea is that the boy learn right from wrong and stay in the right path for all his life. "Wisdom is supreme; therefore get wisdom. Though it cost all you have, get understanding" (4:7). It is as though father and son were in the marketplace and the father was urging the son to spend his money on wisdom rather than on anything else. The price is the son's whole life.

Discourse 5 (5:1-23). Here the father urges his son to avoid every form of promiscuity and be faithful to his own wife. Some may consider the emphasis on the dangers of adultery in these chapters of Proverbs to be excessive. But many go astray and warp their lives precisely here. A primary purpose of wisdom is to teach the reader to avoid self-destruction, and few things are more dangerous and yet so alluring as sexuality. Sexuality itself is not, however, an unhealthy or bad thing. Verses 15-19

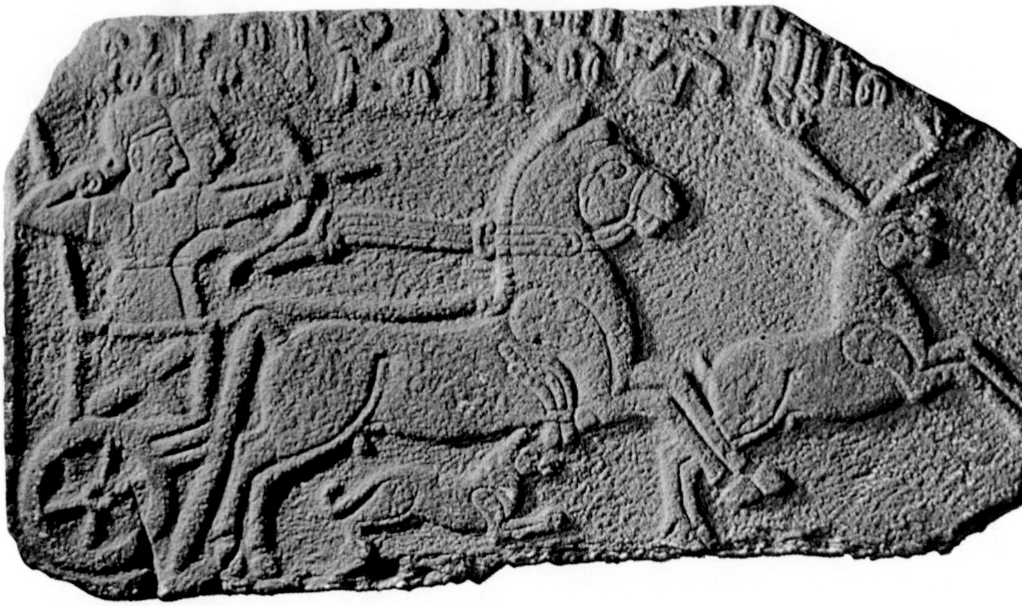

Proverbs 6:5 warns to free oneself from indebtedness like a "gazelle from the hand of the hunter." Above is a Hittite relief from Asia Minor showing a deer fleeing from a hunter in a chariot.

eloquently celebrate the beauty and joy of sexual love in its proper place.

Discourse 6 (6:1-35). No one can live a peaceful life with financial chaos due to excessive debt. Proverbs urges diligence in labor and caution about entering into contracts and indebtedness. Again the book warns the young man to avoid both the devious man (6:12-19) and the wanton woman (6:20-35). The numeric saying in 6:16-19 serves as an easy-to-remember rule of thumb for evaluating character. In the modern day 6:25 applies to pornography as well as to acts of adultery.

Discourse 7 (7:1-27). This chapter offends some readers on the grounds that it seems to attack women. The harlot, a woman, is presented as a deadly, wicked person whom the wise young man will avoid. But no similar warning is issued for the benefit of young girls. Nothing is said about lecherous men. Yet we must remember that the book was written for young men (see "Introduction"). That being the case, we would not expect similar warnings for girls. Verse 6 begins an example story in which the young man is taken in by the harlot and is on his way to destruction. He becomes a bird in a snare or an ox going to slaughter (7:22-23).

Discourse 8 (8:1-36). Wisdom calls out for young men to come to her. She both parallels and contrasts with the harlot, who likewise patrols the streets looking for young men (7:6-27). The difference is that wisdom leads young men to life, but the harlot takes them to the grave (compare 7:27 to 8:35). Wisdom is of more value than gold or jewels (8:10-11,18). More than that, she was present with God at creation (8:22-31). Nevertheless, she should not be interpreted in a mythological sense, as if she were a goddess, or in a Christological sense, as if she were Christ. Lady Wisdom is a personification, not a person (see also 8:12, where wisdom dwells with "prudence"; this too is a personification and not a second person). When the text says wisdom was there when God made heaven and earth, it means that wisdom is not some recent innovation. Principles of right and wrong are not human inventions but are embedded in the very fabric of the created order. Those who reject wisdom, therefore, are going against the very principles God built into the world and are on a path of self-destruction.

Discourse 9 (9:1-18). The lady wisdom (9:1-12) contrasts with the woman folly (9:13-18). Once again we are dealing only with metaphoric personifications. Like vendors calling for customers to come to their shops, wisdom and folly invite the reader to choose which path to take. It is a decision of life and death (9:11,18).

10:1–22:16
Proverbs

Proverbs on labor, prosperity, and wealth (10:1-32). Wealth does have value as security from trouble

(10:15), but riches wrongfully gained will not protect (10:2). Diligent workers enrich themselves (10:4-5), but lazy people irritate everyone (10:26). Above all, integrity and the Lord's blessing provide the most sure security (10:16,22). Several proverbs on the use of the tongue also appear in this chapter (10:18-21,31-32).

Proverbs contrasting the nature and destiny of the righteous and wicked (11:1-31). The righteous follow a clear path in life (11:3,5), are delivered from troubles (11:6), are generous (11:25), and strengthen their communities (11:11). The wicked hoard money but are not saved by it (11:4,18,24,26), are a curse to their families and communities (11:9-13,29), and face certain punishment (11:4,7,23,31).

Proverbs urging discernment in dealings with others (12:1-28). The wise know how to recognize and what to expect of various kinds of people. A good woman will help rather than weaken her husband (12:4), and a good man is kind even to his animals (12:10). The fool is always sure of himself, speaks without thinking (12:15-16,18,23), and is destroyed by his own lies (12:19). But the wise both listen and speak well (12:6,8,14-16,19).

Proverbs on life's realities (13:1-25). Things are not always as they seem (13:7). The wise must learn to look beneath the surface. Verse 23 does not sanction the plundering of the poor by the rich but shows a common tragedy in society.

Important lessons with touches of humor (14:1-35). Oxen require feeding, and no one enjoys cleaning up after them (14:4). But their strength makes farming much easier and leads to a better harvest. Sometimes we have to give up something for a greater gain. Verse 15 shows that gullibility should not be considered a Christian virtue!

Proverbs on teaching and instruction (15:1-33). The wise deal with a problem gently (15:1), lead people rightly (15:2-7), and will themselves listen to a rebuke (15:14,31). Fools only do harm when they speak (15:4,18) and will not themselves listen to any admonition (15:5,10,32).

Proverbs on God's sovereignty over all of life (16:1-33). All our plans depend on God (16:1-4,33). Human government is also to be respected (16:12-15). No one is truly independent in life.

Proverbs on family life and relationships (17:1–19:29). In any family love is more important than riches (17:1). Parents and children are bound to each other by a common identity (17:6), although even a servant, if wise and faithful, can take the place of a disgraceful son (17:2,25). Family conflicts can go on forever (18:19), and bad relatives can ruin life (19:13). Many who would

Parallel rows of seven columns each are found in the temple to the god Amon at Luxor in Egypt. To have seven columns in a colonnade seems to have special significance (see Prov 9:1).

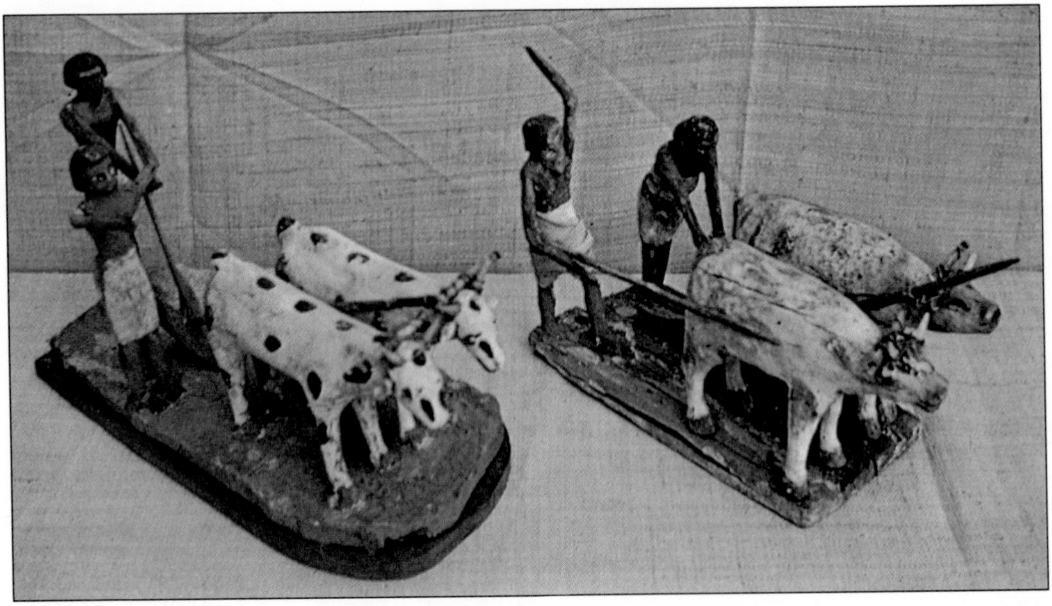

The wooden models above are from the Twelfth Dynasty (about 1991–1786 B.C.) in Egypt. They depict two pairs of oxen being driven to plow. The strength of oxen is attested in Proverbs 14:4.

call themselves friends are merely attracted by money and power (19:4,6); they show their real character in dealing with someone who has neither (19:7). A faithful friend or relative is a protection from trouble (17:17; 18:24), and a good wife is a gift from God (18:22; 19:14).

Warnings against wrong choices (20:1–22:16). The Lord despises fraud (20:10,17,23; 21:6), violence (21:7), a cold heart (21:13), and faithlessness (22:12). Drunkenness, laziness, poor investments, and pleasure seeking all lead to destruction (20:1,16; 21:5,17; 22:13-14). All things are in God's hands (21:30-31), and therefore the fear of God leads to a life worth living (22:4).

22:17–24:22
Thirty Sayings of the Wise

Proverbs 22:17–23:14 contains striking parallels to the Egyptian *Teachings of Amenemope.* The Egyptian wisdom book appears to be older, which indicates that Solomon knew and used it. This is not surprising, since an Egyptian influence is seen throughout Solomon's writings. These "sayings of the wise" contain a number of proverbs on proper etiquette in the presence of the rich and powerful, with the warning that it is foolish to try to ingratiate yourself before such men (23:1-8).

Proverbs 23:15–24:22 resembles the discourses in the prologue. It again addresses the reader as "my son" (23:15,19,26,24:13,21), encourages the pursuit of wisdom (23:19,23; 24:3-7), and warns of the dangers of the immoral woman (23:26-28). This may have been the original conclusion to the Book of Solomon, with 24:23-34 being the equivalent to an addendum or appendix.

24:23-34
Additional Sayings of the Wise

Proverbs 24:23-34 is a further collection of wise sayings. An example story on the danger of laziness appears in 24:30-34.

THE HEZEKIAH COLLECTION (PROV 25:1–29:27)

25:1-15
Royal Etiquette

A proper understanding both of the king's role and of how to behave in his presence was essential for the courtier in ancient Israel. Prudence, discretion, and patience are essential for anyone who would deal with government authorities (compare Eccl 8:2-6).

25:16-27
Interpersonal Relations

The one who too frequently visits at a friend's house risks becoming an unwelcome sight (25:16-17). The one who does not know how to read a friend's mood will soon

Marriage and Family in Israel

Family is an emotional term that raises strong feelings. Such feelings color our understanding of family. We project our experience onto the written words we read. When *family* describes life far from us in geography and times, we must carefully consider the situation of that place and time. It is easy to think that biblical families were just like our families. In some ways they were quite different.

Israel's family structure resulted from its early experiences of nomadic or seminomadic life and then of agricultural life. Such life-styles demanded a strong work force either to herd the animals or tend the crops. Often, then, a family consisted of the oldest male, his wife, son(s), daughter(s)-in-law, and grandchildren. Widowed grandmothers, daughters, aunts, uncles, or other relatives might live in the home. If a family had sufficient wealth, slaves would also live with the family. At times a man had multiple wives, but this was not the usual case.

The oldest male served as the family head and as a community elder. He exercised control and gave protection to the family. The Song of Songs shares the love and mutual respect man and woman had for each other. The Ten Commandments show that both father and mother deserved the child's respect. Divorce laws show God wanted Israel to protect the wife's rights and to offer guidelines in case of divorce (Exod 21:7-11; Deut 21:14; 22:13-19,25-30; 24:1-5). The urban woman especially had much freedom to engage in social and business affairs (Prov 31:10-31).

Birth of children brought great joy to families. Mothers and other women in the family cared for and trained children until puberty. Boys then looked to the father to teach them a trade and adult responsibilities. Fathers taught children the religious tradition of Israel (Exod 10:2; 12:24-28; 13:8,14; Deut 4:9; 6:20-25; 32:7; Josh 4:6-7,21-24; Ps 44:1; Joel 1:3). The eldest son received special training to become family head.

Marriage was the foundation of Israel's life. A woman left her family to become a part of a man's family geographically. But a man also left his family, giving allegiance to wife above father and mother (Gen 2:24-25). Marriage forged an emotional, physical, and spiritual unity.

The normal and prescribed practice was one man and one woman sharing mutual love (Prov 5:15-20; Eccl 9:9). Marriage—like Israel's relationship to Yahweh, their God—was a covenant relationship not to be broken (Mal 2:14-15). Only such a union could produce "godly offspring." Marriage occurred at what we would consider a relatively young age, fourteen or a little later. Normally the father chose a bride for his son, at least in Israel's early days (Gen 38:6; compare Exod 2:21; Josh 15:17; Ruth 3:1-4).

Families apparently negotiated a proper price for the bride called a *mohar* in Hebrew (Gen 34:12; Exod 22:16; 1 Sam 18:25). This apparently repaid the bride's family for the economic loss suffered by losing a valuable family member. At times the future husband could do service for the bride's family rather than pay the *mohar* (Gen 29:15-30; Josh 15:16-17; Judg 1:12-13; 1 Sam 18:17-27). The practice of families exchanging daughters was also known in the Near East. Payment of the *mohar* signaled the beginning of marriage legally, though the actual ceremony and consummation came later (2 Sam 3:14; compare 1 Sam 18:25).

Weddings took place at the bride's home. Bride and groom dressed elegantly (Isa 61:10), the groom having a special head adornment (Song 3:11). The bride wore a veil (Gen 29:25; Song 4:1). Music and rejoicing marked the event (Jer 7:34), as did feasting (Gen 29:22; Judg 14:10). Festivities lasted for a week (Gen 29:27; Judg 14:12). Once begun the marriage continued as a commitment of love and a place for bringing children to know God and His way of life and to learn to become good citizens of Israel, God's people. □

anger him or her (25:20). Sometimes the best way to win a conflict is to surprise an adversary with kindness (25:21-22).

25:28–26:28
Dealing with Difficult People

Troublesome and difficult people are recognized by lack of self-control (25:28), dogmatic self-assurance (26:12), and laziness (26:14-15). They provoke conflict (26:18-20) and are deceitful (26:25). They should never be honored (26:1,8) and cannot be trusted (26:6,10). The apparent self-contradiction in 26:4-5 indicates many proverbs are general statements rather than invariable rules.

27:1-27
Faithfulness in Love

Sometimes true love may be hidden in a rebuke just as hatred may be hidden in a kiss (27:5-6). There is no love where there is no fidelity to one's wife and friends (27:8,10-11). True friends can improve each other's character, but nagging only irritates (27:15-17).

28:1–29:27
Exploitation and the Need for Law

The powerful and wealthy often exploit the poor. Oppressors govern without benefiting the governed (28:3; 29:2,4), know nothing of justice (28:5; 29:7), amass fortunes by exorbitant interest (28:8), and ignore the needs of the poor (28:27). Lawlessness brings down societies and families (28:4,7,24; 29:15), and people groan under oppressive rule (28:12; 29:2). Governments should establish justice through law. But in the end justice comes only from God (29:26).

THE SAYINGS OF AGUR (PROV 30:1-33)

30:1-9
Title and Prologue

We must acknowledge our inability to understand the ways of God before we can accept revelation from God. Compare 30:4 with John 8:23. The prayer of Proverbs 30:7-9 is a clear example of the piety of the wise.

30:10-33
Various Teachings

The numerical saying in 30:18-19 is tied to the proverb in 30:20. An eagle in the sky, a snake on a rock, and a ship on the sea all have in common that they move without leaving any tracks. In the same way, those committing adultery assume they can do so without leaving a trace of what they have done.

THE SAYINGS OF KING LEMUEL (PROV 31:1-31)

31:1-9
Title and Prologue

Although these are the "sayings of King Lemuel," they actually come from his mother (31:1). This is one passage of Scripture, therefore, that we may confidently ascribe to a woman (compare Exod 15:21; Judg 5).

Those in authority should not use their power for self-indulgence and depravity (31:2-7). Instead, they should devote themselves to defending the poor and the powerless (31:8-9).

31:10-31
In Praise of the Virtuous Woman

This poem is an acrostic. Although the object of praise is the virtuous woman, the original audience of the piece

A basalt mortar and pestle discovered in excavations in Israel. Pestles are used to grind material against the mortar. They date back to the Mesolithic (Middle Stone Age) time period and are still in use today. (See Prov 27:22.)

Proverbs 31:19 depicts the virtuous woman as industrious, which in biblical times included spinning wool to make clothes (see Prov 31:19). This stone relief from Susa in Mesopotamia shows a woman holding a spindle in her left hand and winding the thread with her right hand.

was again the young man. The opening question in 31:10 implies that the reader ought to find such a wife for himself. The woman is trustworthy (31:11), industrious (31:13-19), intelligent (31:16,18), and kind (31:20). She adds dignity to the family (31:23,25) and has much foresight and prudence (31:21,26). For all this she is much loved in her family and is the real center of the home (31:27-29). Above all she fears God (31:30). The final verse speaks eloquently against the tendency to regard her role as of inferior significance.

Theological Significance

Proverbs challenges believers, especially the young, to learn the lessons of past generations. It gives the *practical* implications of the confession that God is the Lord of all of life. The truly wise show respect for God and His standards in all life situations. Living faith can never be divorced from lives of faithfulness. Faith must be lived out in the day-to-day world where problems call for practical wisdom. How we relate to others serves as an indicator of our relationship with God.

Questions for Reflection

1. What does Proverbs mean by the "fool"? Is it simply a stupid person or a buffoon; or does the term have a deeper, moral dimension?
2. Granted that Proverbs 7 was originally addressed to boys, how can its message be redirected in contemporary society for the teaching of girls also?
3. Briefly describe the teaching of Proverbs on wealth.
4. Proverbs has a practical message. How does this supplement the more "spiritual" teachings of the Bible?

Sources for Additional Study

Alder, Robert L. *Proverbs.* Grand Rapids: Baker, 1983.
Bullock, C. Hassell. *An Introduction to the Poetic Books of the Old Testament.* Chicago: Moody, 1979.
Draper, James T., Jr. *Proverbs.* Wheaton: Tyndale, 1971.
Kidner, Derek. *Proverbs.* Downers Grove: InterVarsity, 1975.

ECCLESIASTES

Many Christian readers are troubled by Ecclesiastes. From the very beginning, where it declares that everything is meaningless (1:2), it seems unashamedly pessimistic and negative on life. Some wonder why this book is in the Bible. But if we carefully examine its background and message, we discover that Ecclesiastes confronts us and drives us to God in a way that few books do.

Authorship and Date

Ecclesiastes tells us it was written by a son of David who was king in Jerusalem over Israel (1:1,12). This points to Solomon since he alone, after David, ruled both Judah and Israel. But many believe that Solomon (who reigned about 961–922 B.C.) could not have written the book and assert an unknown Jewish scribe composed it between 500 and 250 B.C.

The Language of Ecclesiastes. The Hebrew of Ecclesiastes is quite unusual and sometimes almost obscure. These peculiarities have led many scholars to believe Ecclesiastes was composed late in Old Testament history. But the Hebrew of Ecclesiastes is not characteristically "late" or "early"; it is simply unusual. The language of Ecclesiastes does have much in common with the language of Song of Songs. Several allegedly late Hebrew words in Ecclesiastes also appear in the Song. For this reason many scholars regard Song of Songs as a late book as well. But it is quite possible they have so much in common because they come from the same hand—Solomon's. (For particulars see the introduction to "Song of Songs.")

Internal Evidence. Some argue the text itself hints that Solomon was not the author. For example, in 1:12 the writer states that he "was" king in Jerusalem. The real Solomon, of course, never ceased to be king until the day he died. Some assert that passages like 8:2-3, which exhorts the reader to be tactful in the presence of the king, could not have been written by the king himself.

These arguments are rather weak. If, as it appears, Ecclesiastes was written by an aged man (12:1-7), it is not strange that he would speak of his reign in the past tense. Also it is not clear why a king could not be objective enough to give advice like that found in 8:2-3.

Literary Evidence. Certain passages of Ecclesiastes closely resemble other literature from the ancient Near East. For example, the Egyptian *Song of the Harper* exhorts the reader to enjoy life in terms almost identical to those found in Ecclesiastes 3:22 and 9:7-9. The *Gilgamesh Epic*, a Mesopotamian classic, also has parallels to Ecclesiastes 9:7-9 that are far too precise to be accidental.

It is almost impossible to account for the strong similarities between Ecclesiastes and these other ancient texts if we assume Ecclesiastes was written by an obscure Jewish scribe between 500 and 250 B.C. Literary practices changed greatly by that time. A scribe of that late a period would probably not even have known, much less used, the ancient Mesopotamian and Egyptian literature.

Solomon, however, is known to have had wide contacts with the wisdom and learning of the ancient world of his day (1 Kgs 4:34). He doubtless knew works like the *Song of the Harper* and the *Gilgamesh Epic.* The similarities between Ecclesiastes and those texts are easy to explain if Solomon's authorship is assumed. All in all, therefore, the case for believing Solomon to have written Ecclesiastes is stronger than the case against it.

Message and Purpose

Christian readers, after they have shaken off the initial shock of reading Ecclesiastes, have often described it as a defense of the faith or even an evangelistic work. Ecclesiastes shows that many of the pursuits of life, including wealth, education, and power, do not really fulfill. In that way Ecclesiastes shows that life without God is meaningless and drives the reader to faith.

Many readers have pointed out how much stark skepticism is in Ecclesiastes. If Ecclesiastes is an apologetic work, it is surely unlike any other defense of the faith ever written. But the defensive and evangelistic purpose of Ecclesiastes is clearer if one takes into account its original audience. A careful study of the text demonstrates conclusively that its first readers were not "ordinary" people but the wealthy, the powerful, and those who had access to the royal court. Again and again it deals with the study of wisdom (which the average person did not have time to do), the value of wealth, and the problems involved in being in the king's court. These things did not apply as issues in the lives of most people.

Addressed to the intellectual and political elite of Israel, the book's "pessimism" makes sense. It was speaking to the very people who were most likely to build their lives on success, wealth, power, and an intellectual reputation. Ecclesiastes repeatedly points out the futility of such a way of life and urges the readers to face their need for God. In that sense Ecclesiastes is indeed evangelistic and in fact can be read profitably by anyone.

Ecclesiastes should not be called pessimistic or cynical, but it is brutally realistic. In particular Ecclesiastes makes the reader confront the full and dreadful significance of death. Most people, whether or not they are religious, refuse to face what death really is: a calamity that nullifies the achievements of human life. Ecclesiastes strips away the myths we use to shield ourselves from this stark fact.

In pointing out the dreadfulness of death, Ecclesiastes helps us see how profound is our need for resurrection. More simply, Ecclesiastes drives us to Christ. The New Testament shares this perspective; death is not a friend or even a doorway but a terrible enemy. It will be, however, a conquered enemy (1 Cor 15:26,54-55; Rev 20:14).

Structure

To the modern reader, Ecclesiastes at first appears to have no structure at all. The book does not follow modern standards of setting topics in a hierarchy. But a careful reading shows that Ecclesiastes carefully moves among a group of selected subjects. These include wealth, politics, wisdom, death, and aging. As the book moves to and fro among these and other topics, a complete statement gradually emerges.

I. Introduction (1:1-2)
II. On Time and the World (1:3-11; 3:1-15a; 11:7–12:7)
III. On Wisdom (1:12-18; 2:12-17; 6:10–7:6; 7:11-29)
IV. On Wealth (2:1-11,18-26; 4:4-8; 5:10–6:9; 7:11-14; 10:18-20; 11:1-6)
V. On Politics (3:15b-17; 4:1-3,13-16; 5:8-9; 7:7-10; 8:1–9:6; 9:13–10:20)
VI. On Death (3:18-22; 8:1–9:6)
VII. On Friendship (4:9-12)
VIII. On Religion (5:1-7; 7:15-29)
IX. On Evil (8:1–9:6)
X. On Contentment (9:7-12; 11:7–12:7)
XI. Conclusion (12:8-14)

1:1-2
Introduction

Verse 1 gives the title of the work, and verse 2 gives its theme. The word *vanity* or *meaningless* translates the Hebrew word *hebel*, which originally meant *breath.* From *breath* comes the idea of *that which is insubstantial, transitory, and of fleeting value.* For Ecclesiastes, anything that does not have eternal value has no real value. Everything in this world is fleeting and therefore, in the final analysis, pointless.

1:3-11
On Time and the World

All of nature is in constant motion and yet is going nowhere. This is a parable of human life; it is a long flurry of activity that accomplishes nothing permanent. Not only that, but there is nothing new in this world (1:8-10). "New" does not mean merely *unfamiliar* or *novel* but *something fresh that breaks into the cycle of life and gives meaning and value.* The desperate needs of humanity described here are answered in Christ, in whom we have a new covenant, a new birth, a new commandment, and a new life. Meanwhile, we and this weary creation (Rom 8:19-22) await the glory of the resurrection: new bodies for ourselves in a new heaven and a new earth.

1:12-18
On Wisdom

Education and intellectual pursuits fail to satisfy our deepest needs. The task of the intellectual, the quest to understand life, is itself a hopeless endeavor. The proverb in 1:15 indicates this: "What is twisted cannot be straightened"; that is, no one can solve an insoluble problem. "What is lacking cannot be counted"; that is, no one can add up unknown sums. We cannot understand life because the problem is too complex, and there is too much we do not know. Only the one who is from above (John 8:23) can answer our deepest needs.

2:1-11
On Wealth

Ecclesiastes now considers the matter of whether pleasure and luxury can give meaning to life. Solomon experimented in pleasure with his mind still guiding him—in other words, he did not become corrupted but remained in control of himself. Not only illicit pleasures disappointed him but even morally acceptable activities and things done in moderation left him empty. (On Solomon's buildings, gardens, and vineyards see 1 Kgs 7; 9:1; 10:21; 2 Chron 8:3-6; Song 1:14; 8:11.)

A portion of a wall painting at Thebes in ancient Egypt showing an artificial pond filled with different birds and fish. The entire painting shows palms and pomegranate trees surrounding the pond. (An example of Eccl 2:5-6.)

2:12-17
On Wisdom

In 1:12-18 Solomon had spoken of humanity's inability to solve the riddles of life. The quest for wisdom was hopeless. Now he showed that even what wisdom one gains is of no real value because it does not alter one's destiny. The wise man, no less than the fool, is doomed (2:15). Of course, the wise go through life with better understanding of what lies ahead than do fools, but neither can escape death (2:14). Attempting to achieve immortality through fame and accomplishments is senseless (2:16).

2:18-26
On Wealth

In 2:1-11 Ecclesiastes points out how the spending of wealth on personal pleasure finally becomes irksome. Now the book exposes the folly of a life devoted to earning money. Many people devote themselves to incessant labor under the justification that they are doing it for their children. But this is no excuse for wasting one's own life. The children may well simply squander all that their parents struggled to accumulate (2:18-19). Going through life with contentment is better than forever trying to increase one's bank account.

3:1-15a
On Time and the World

Our existence in this world is a mixture of joy and sorrow, harmony and conflict, and life and death. Each has its own proper moment, and we, as creatures of time, must conform to the temporal limitations that are built into the cycle of life. No permanent state of affairs exists in this world. This is a great source of frustration for people since longing for eternity is planted within us (3:11). We can neither be satisfied with what we are nor understand God's purpose in all this. We can only humbly accept what we are in this world and confess our faith that God's way is right (3:11-14). In light of this text, the meaning of the resurrection of Christ as the victory over death is clear.

3:15b-17
On Politics

The last line of 3:15, usually translated something like, "God calls back the past," is literally, "God seeks the persecuted." It anticipates the brief discussion of oppression in 3:16-17 and means *God will hold the oppressors accountable.* Ecclesiastes voices dismay at the widespread corruption in places of political power, but it asserts that someday God will judge.

3:18-22
On Death

Ecclesiastes states that no one, by comparing the carcass of an animal to a human corpse, can find any evidence that the human, unlike the animal, is immortal. The thought that persons have "no advantage" over the ani-

"A time to mourn and a time to dance" (Eccl 3:4). The dancer shown above left is a Greek statuette dating from around 300 B.C. The middle and right photos show two sides of an Attic vase probably dating from about 475 B.C. It is decorated with figures of fourteen mourners—seven men and seven women. In the middle photo the men's arms are stretched out in front of them. The photo on the right shows the women in mourning beating on their shaven heads.

mals (3:19) astonishes many readers. But it does not mean that we are in all respects like the animals, nor does it contradict the rest of the Bible. It means that humans can no more claim to have the power to beat death than can any other animal. For Christians this should only drive us closer to Christ, who did conquer death in His resurrection. Our confidence is not in some innate power of our own but in the gift from God of eternal life through Jesus Christ (Rom 6:23). Ecclesiastes forces the reader to see the dreadful terror of death and therefore to cling to God for salvation (see Heb 2:14-15).

The NIV translation ("Who knows if the spirit of man rises upward and if the spirit of the animal goes down into the earth?") better renders the thought of 3:31 than the KJV's translation.

4:1-3
On Politics

The assertion that it is better to be dead (and even better never to have been born) than to have to face all the oppression that exists in the world is hyperbole. But this exaggeration shows how profoundly Ecclesiastes opposes the abuse of political power.

4:4-8
On Wealth

Ecclesiastes again shows how futile is the life devoted to the acquisition of wealth. The two proverbs in 4:5-6 are set in opposition to each other in order to provide balance in life. Laziness leads to poverty and self-destruction (4:5). But it is better to be content with what one has than to spend life toiling away for more possessions.

4:9-12
On Friendship

In all the hardships and disappointments of life, few things give more real, lasting satisfaction than true friendship. A friend is a comfort in need and a help in trouble. Verse 11 does not refer to sexual relations but to shared warmth between two traveling companions on a cold desert night. At the same time, it may imply that the best friend for life ought to be one's spouse.

4:13-16
On Politics

Political power and the popularity that accompanies it are short-lived. Those who have long held power tend to become inflexible and thus vulnerable. But the entire struggle, an endless game of "king of the hill," is pointless.

5:1-7
On Religion

Fools assume they know all about God and are able to please Him. True piety and wisdom recognize the limitations of both our understanding of God and our ability to please Him with our deeds. The attitude of awe toward God that Ecclesiastes recommends (5:7) is in reality dependence on God's grace and recognition that the benefits we have from Him are only by His mercy.

5:8-9
On Politics

Corruption of government officials is a universal occurrence and should not surprise anyone. But anarchy is not the answer. Verse 9 should be translated: "In all, this is an advantage to the land: a king, for the sake of cultivated fields." Despite all the problems of government, it is necessary for a well-ordered society and economy.

5:10–6:9
On Wealth

Through a series of proverbs and short reflections, Ecclesiastes warns the reader not to fall into the trap of the quest for wealth. Where riches are concerned, enough is never enough (5:10; 6:7). The laborer has more peace and better sleep than the affluent man (5:12).

6:10–7:6
On Wisdom

Ecclesiastes here summarizes its position on wisdom through a series of proverbs and reflections. We must

Death, Resurrection, and Afterlife in the Old Testament

Death, resurrection, and afterlife in the OT represent a subject that keeps us in the dark. Death represented a departure after which the individual was "no more" (Ps 39:13; Job 14:10). Death was pictured as "the place of no return," "the land of gloom and deep shadow," and "the land of deepest night, of deep shadow and disorder, where even the light is like darkness" (Job 10:20-22). Death is also pictured as a place of sleep and rest apart from the world's troubles (3:13).

To die is to join the vast number of ancestors who have already gone that way (Gen 47:30; 49:29). After death came burial, usually in a family tomb with multiple burials (2 Sam 17:23). For the aged such death was normal, the person being "old and full of days" (Job 42:17 NASB), having completed the normal accomplishments of life. But not all have that normal experience; some die in punishment before they are full of years (Num 16:29-30).

Death brought the family and community together to mourn (1 Sam 25:1). Mourning included tears (Gen 23:2) and led to recovery (38:12) and consolation (2 Sam 13:39). Pagan mourning rites such as slashing one's skin were forbidden to Israel (Deut 14:1). Even touching a corpse was forbidden (Lev 11:31).

Death is more than a physical event. Sin leads to death (Gen 2:17; Ezek 18), but humans can choose life (Deut 30:15-20). The sin and death relationship is an individual one, but those who understand the relationship have responsibility to warn others (Ezek 3:17-21).

What happened to the dead? They went through the "gates of death" (Ps 9:13; Isa 38:10) into the "chambers of death" (Prov 7:27). They became entangled in the "cords of death" (Ps 18:4), awash in the "torrents of destruction (Ps 18:4), and trapped in the "snares of death" (Ps 18:5). Unable to partake of the tree of life, the dead returned to dust (Gen 3:19; compare Ps 90:3). Humans die like animals (Eccl 3:19).

Nations die as well as individuals. Such a nation can live again (Ezek 37). Israel can at least say that God gives hope for new life to those sick unto death (Pss 33:19; 56:13; 116:8). Did Israel have a greater hope for triumph over death than this? The answer rests with the understanding of the Hebrew concept of Sheol and with our understanding of key verses. ⇨

recognize the limits of our wisdom. There is much we will never know (6:10-12). But it is better to go through life with sobriety and understanding than in inane pleasure seeking (7:1-6).

7:7-10
On Politics

Verse 7 is transitional from the previous passage. Bribery can destroy personal integrity and lead to injustice in government. Verse 10 counsels readers not to lose heart or suppose that their generation is the most corrupt that has ever been. When dealing with injustice, be patient and careful.

7:11-14
On Wisdom and Wealth

Ecclesiastes now compares wisdom to wealth and considers wisdom better because it does not disappear in hard times. The wise understand that both prosperity and adversity are from the hand of God and accept both.

7:15-29
On Wisdom and Religion

In this complex section Ecclesiastes discusses the attempt to secure happiness and divine protection through self-discipline and scrupulous observance of religion and morality. Verses 15-18 at first appear to say that a little sinning is acceptable as long as it is not excessive, but this is not the real meaning. Ecclesiastes here addresses those who follow the traditional teaching of wisdom that a disciplined life is prosperous and safe but a life of indulgence is fraught with disaster. Rigorous self-depravation for the sake of religion does not really guarantee a peaceful life. No one can truly please God by his or her righteousness, since all are sinful (7:20). This ought to make us more forgiving of others (7:21-22).

The mystery of human sin and how it impinges on behavior is perplexing (7:23-25), but it does have one clear implication: sin makes domestic life very painful (7:26-29). This text, more than any other, demonstrates our need for God's grace.

On the basis of 7:26-29, some readers think the author was prejudiced against women. In fact, this section reflects on the pain sin has brought upon marriage. It looks back to Genesis 3:16b. There the woman desired to manipulate her husband, but he harshly dominated her. Sin made the home into a battlefield.

Similarly, Ecclesiastes says (again using hyperbole) that a man may find one man in a thousand who can be his true friend, but he will not find a single woman in whom

Sheol is a Hebrew synonym for death (2 Sam 22:6). This has led the NIV translators to translate *Sheol* consistently as *death.* Many interpreters, however, see Sheol as the abode of the dead (see Deut 32:22). All people go to Sheol at death, good or bad (compare Gen 37:35; Num 16:30). Sheol can be compared to a large animal with insatiable appetite (Isa 5:14; compare Prov 30:16). It is excited at the prospect of guests coming (Isa 14:9). In contrast to heaven Sheol is the deepest part of the earth and thus the widest distance from the heavens (Amos 9:2). Sheol shuts people off from God and from worship (Isa 38:18; Ps 6:5) and shuts people off from God's care (Ps 88:3-5). Still, Sheol is no place to escape from God (Amos 9:2; compare Ps 139:8).

Two passages are crucial for understanding Sheol. Ezekiel 32:17-32 describes the wicked activities in Sheol. These people speak (v. 21). Isaiah 14:9-17 describes the fate of the Babylonian king in Sheol. There he was greeted by the dead. There former leaders rose from their thrones. They mocked him, saying he was as weak as they. All pomp was gone.

Was this poetic description of death designed to mock and degrade Babylon without picturing life in Sheol literally? Or does it picture Sheol as a place of shadowy existence with earthly rank and power still recognized but in meaningless form.

Death holds no hope for Israel then. It leads only to Sheol, however existence there is pictured. But God does hold hope for Israel (Hos 13:14). Not only nations can rise. So can individuals. Some OT passages provide language from which the church easily draws hope for resurrection (Job 14:1-22; 19:25-27; Pss 16:7-11; 17:15; 33:18-22; 71:20).

Three OT passages are mountain peaks from which we can view the clear NT hope of resurrection and eternal life. Psalm 49:9-15 promises redemption from Sheol and presence with God. Isaiah 26:19 promises that the earth will give birth to its dead so that the dead will live. Thus the dead can shout for joy. Daniel 12:2 declares resurrection for both the wicked and the faithful, either to eternal contempt or eternal life.

The resurrection of Jesus Christ made totally clear what the OT had begun to point toward. Life after death is a reality, not just a hope. Death in all its ugliness is real. Resurrection through Christ is the beautiful reality that leads from death to everlasting life. □

he can have the same confidence (7:28). This is not because women are innately worse than men—a woman has the same problem finding a man she can trust but may have one woman friend. Humanity's history of domestic strife and faithlessness fully vindicates this passage.

8:1–9:6
On Politics, Death, and God's Justice

The wise know how to behave with discretion and tact toward those in power (8:2-6), but the uncertainty of life makes it difficult to stay on the right path (8:7-8). Many who have power use it ruthlessly for their own gain. That they often seem to go unpunished aggravates the situation (8:9-15). This is, perhaps, the most troubling problem of life (8:16-17). Death levels the differences between the powerful and the powerless, but it aggravates the problem in that the good and bad suffer the same fate. For the reader, however, this should not lead to cynicism. Instead, it should provoke deeper faith that only God knows the end from the beginning and only He can finally set all things right.

9:7-12
On Contentment

This passage builds upon the certainty of death as described in 9:1-6. Life is short and therefore should not be lived in sorrow. Enjoy the good things of life (9:7-9), and do not let ambition for success ruin the time you have (9:11-12). The advice in 9:9, "Enjoy life with your wife," seems to contradict 7:28, but wisdom literature often gives counsel that is paradoxical or apparently contradictory. The reason is that life itself is complicated.

9:13–10:17
On Politics

Prudence and political skill are essential for effective governance of a nation, but they are often neglected or lacking. Ecclesiastes presents this concept here first in a short anecdote (9:13-16) and then in a series of proverbs and reflections (9:17–10:17). Whether the wise man saved his city by military strategy or diplomacy is not clear (9:15). What is clear is that he was soon forgotten because he was not wealthy or from an influential family. But the worst fate that can befall a nation is that it have ignoble or self-indulgent rulers (10:5-7,16-17). Such fools are not even capable of giving a stranger correct directions to the nearest town; they can hardly be trusted in matters of state (10:12-15).

The series of proverbs in 10:8-11 emphasizes the importance of forethought and careful planning. Those who practice cunning often bring about their own demise (v. 8). They dig a pit for someone else and fall into it themselves. Or they are bitten by a snake while breaking into another's home. But even legitimate activities can be dangerous (v. 9). Thorough planning must precede any enterprise (vv. 10-11). In context this means that one must exercise great care in dealing with the intrigues of political life.

10:18-20
On Politics and Wealth

Three transitional proverbs bridge the gap between the political and economic realms. First, diligence is necessary to maintain an economy (10:18), be it the national household or a private home. Second, at least some money is essential in order to enjoy the good things of life (10:19; this verse is not cynical, as it appears to be in many translations). Third, be careful of those who have power, be it political or economic (10:20).

11:1-6
On Wealth

While Ecclesiastes discourages the pursuit of wealth, it favors wise investment and diligent work. Verses 1-2 speak of long-term investment, not charity. To "give portions to seven or eight" is, in modern terminology, *to diversify investments.* While we do have to look out for dangers on the horizon (11:3), we cannot allow ourselves to be so cautious that we do nothing (11:4). Better to recognize that all things are in God's hands (11:5) and proceed with our work with an eye toward all possible contingencies (11:6).

11:7–12:7
On Contentment, Time, and Aging

This section is in two parts: counsel to youth (11:7-10) and a poem on aging and death (12:1-7). To the young Ecclesiastes advises that their brief time of youthful vigor be spent in joy rather than in anxiety. But they are not free to pursue folly and immoral behavior. Awareness of divine judgment and the fleeting nature of youth should always govern their decisions (11:9-10).

The poem in 12:1-7 is also meant as a warning to the young concerning things to come. Its imagery is in some points obscure, but it is nevertheless poignant and moving. Verse 2 may refer to the day of death or to failing eyesight. Verse 3 describes the loss of strength in the arms ("keepers of the house") and legs ("strong men"), the loss of teeth ("grinders"), and encroaching blindness ("those looking through the windows"). Verse 4 alludes to failing hearing that is yet coupled to the sleeplessness whereby one awakes at the slightest sound. Verse 5

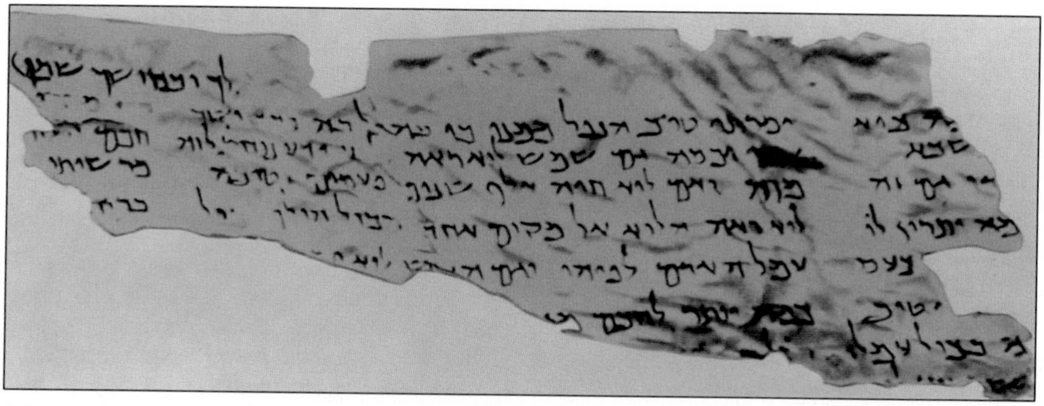

A fragment of the Book of Ecclesiastes found with the Dead Sea Scrolls and dating from about 150 B.C. It contains verses from Ecclesiastes 5–7 and is written in a beautiful Hebrew script.

speaks of the general loss of courage, confidence, and sexual drive. Finally, in 12:6-7 death is portrayed as the shattering of a vessel whereby its contents—life—are spilled out.

12:8-14
Conclusion

The book concludes in four subsections. (1) Verse 8 reaffirms the theme of 1:2. These two verses bracket the beginning and ending of the main body of the work. (2) Verses 9-10 describe Solomon's work. Compare 1 Kings 4:32. (3) Verses 11-12 offer a final word on wisdom. (4) Verses 13-14 conclude with a call to fear God.

True wisdom comes from God, the one Shepherd, and is worthy of acquiring. But one should be wary of endless academic pursuits. Ecclesiastes is not anti-intellectual; still, no one should try to build a meaningful life on the reading and writing of books.

Some readers feel the concluding call to fear God does not follow from all that has gone before, but it is in fact the perfect conclusion. The pursuit of wealth, knowledge, and political power is ultimately unsatisfactory and leads to divine judgment. Life is short and full of mystery. All our attempts to make life meaningful fail. The wise response, therefore, is to cling to God and His grace.

Theological Significance

Ecclesiastes challenges its readers to live in the world as it really is instead of living in a world of false hope. It addresses those who have sought meaning through wealth, education, or political power. For some this search for lasting meaning and value has left them empty. Others have yet to realize the futility of this search.

Ecclesiastes challenges its readers to abandon illusions of self-importance, face death and life squarely, and accept with fear and trembling their dependence on God. Solomon's faith in the justice of God and the goodness of His commands was stronger than his pessimism (8:12-13; 11:9). Even when he did not understand life or God's ways, his response was one of faith. The seeming senselessness of life in the real world drove him to God, the only Giver of permanent worth. Life is God's precious gift. Its fleeting pleasures should be enjoyed, even while pursuing the lasting joy that comes only from God.

Questions for Reflection

1. How does our mortality render "meaningless" much of what we do in life?
2. What are some ways people try to add meaning to their lives? What does Ecclesiastes say about them?
3. How does Ecclesiastes help us to understand the importance of Christ's resurrection and His victory over death?
4. How would you summarize the teaching of Ecclesiastes on political power?

Sources for Additional Study

Eaton, Michael A. *Ecclesiastes.* Downers Grove: InterVarsity, 1983.

Gordis, Robert. *Koheleth: The Man and His World.* New York: Schocken, 1968.

Kaiser, Walter C., Jr. *Ecclesiastes.* Chicago: Moody, 1979.

Wardlaw, Ralph. *Exposition of Ecclesiastes.* 1868; reprint, Minneapolis: Klock and Klock, 1982.

SONG OF SONGS

The full name of this book is "The Song of Songs, which is Solomon's." Often called Song of Solomon or, after the Latin, Canticles, it is best to call it Song of Songs. But we should note that the Hebrew idiom *Song of Songs* actually means *the best song.*

Date and Authorship

The title probably implies that Solomon wrote it, but it could be taken to mean that it was simply part of Solomon's collection and was written perhaps by a court singer. Still, many scholars believe that the Song was written late in Israelite history (500–100 B.C.) and therefore could not possibly have been written by Solomon or his contemporaries (961–922 B.C.). It is important, therefore, to see what evidence there is for dating the book.

Most scholars who regard the Song as a late work do so primarily because some of the vocabulary found in it appears to be incompatible with the earlier date. For example, many argue that the Hebrew word for "orchard" in 4:13, *pardes*, is derived either from the Persian word *pairidesa* or the Greek word *paradeisos* (compare the English *paradise*). It is difficult to see how Hebrew could have borrowed a word from either Persian or Greek as early as Solomon's day.

Some scholars believe that the Song has several Aramaic words. Many Jews spoke this language during the intertestamental and New Testament periods. Finally, the Song frequently uses the Hebrew pronoun *she* (meaning *which, what,* or *who*) instead of the more common *asher* (which has the same meaning). The Hebrew pronoun *she* is relatively rare in the Bible but became common in postbiblical Hebrew. For these reasons, many are convinced that the Song must have been composed very late in Jewish history.

These arguments are not as convincing as they first appear. The word *parades* ("orchard") may come from a Sanskrit root word that is far older than either Persian or Greek. In addition, many words once asserted to be from a late Aramaic background have been found to be more ancient than originally supposed. Also the use of the Hebrew word *she* is not as significant as once was thought. Similar relative pronouns have been found in some ancient Semitic languages, such as Akkadian and Ugaritic. This implies that the use of Hebrew *she* is not an exclusively late phenomenon. In short, the vocabulary of the Song does not prove that it is a late work.

Geographical Evidence

The Song of Songs mentions locations from all over ancient Palestine. These include places both in northern Israel (Sharon, Lebanon, Hermon, and Carmel) and in the southern territory of Judah (Jerusalem and Engedi). The Song also mentions the Transjordan territories of Heshbon and Gilead. This geographic outlook reflects a time when all Israel was unified and even territories in the Transjordan were under Israelite dominion. These conditions never prevailed after the death of Solomon.

Song 6:4 sets the city of Tirzah in parallel with Jerusalem. This implies that at the time of writing, Tirzah was considered the major city of the north and was comparable to Jerusalem in the south. When the kingdom split early in the reign of Rehoboam of Judah (931–913 B.C.), Tirzah immediately became the capital of the Northern Kingdom. But Omri of Israel (reigned 886–874 B.C.) made Samaria the capital of the Northern Kingdom, and from that time forward Tirzah never was prominent again. Song 6:4, therefore, implies that it was written before Omri's time.

Cultural Evidence

The poetic imagery of Song of Songs reflects an age of great prosperity. This also lends support to the belief that it was written in Solomon's day. Only then did Jerusalem possess the spices, perfumes, and luxuries mentioned in the book as well as great quantities of gold, marble, and precious jewels (Song 5:14-15; see 1 Kgs 10:14-22).

Of course, one can argue that these are only similes and do not prove that the writer actually lived in an age when such things were common. But it is doubtful that a poet would use imagery, described in such detail, that was outside his own frame of reference and experience.

Literary Evidence

The poetry we see in Song of Songs is not quite unique in the ancient world. From Egypt, in the period of approximately 1300 to 1100 B.C., come a number of love songs which are remarkably like Song of Songs. Many of the motifs and ideas that appear in the Song are also found in the Egyptian poetry. Outside of this ancient body of literature, however, it is difficult to find any writings comparable to Song of Songs.

What is the reason for this unusual parallel between a book of the Bible and Egyptian poetry? Solomon made an alliance with the Egyptian Pharaoh and married his daughter (1 Kgs 3:1). The court of Solomon and Egypt doubtless had extensive contacts. Solomon also had contact with wise men—and thus their literature—from all over the world (1 Kgs 4:29-34).

Solomon likely would have become familiar with the love poetry that had appeared within the previous three hundred years in Egypt. This would explain how the Song has so much in common with its Egyptian counterparts. Solomon, after all, was cosmopolitan in his learning and tastes.

Difficult to explain, however, is why the Song and the Egyptian love poetry have so much in common if the Song were written some 650 years after Solomon. An obscure Jewish songwriter, working a millennium after this kind of love poetry was produced in Egypt, could not have written by accident a work so much like the Egyptian poetry. Nor is it reasonable to argue that he would have known and deliberately imitated an ancient, foreign, and by then probably forgotten art form.

The poetry of Song of Songs reflects Solomon's age better than any other of Israelite history. It is thus best to assume it was written in that period.

Interpretation

No other book of the Bible (except perhaps Revelation) suffers under so many radically different interpretations as the Song of Songs. The major approaches are as follows:

Allegorical Interpretation. From early times both Christians and Jews have allegorized the Song of Songs. Jews have taken it to picture the love between the Lord and Israel, and Christians have regarded it as a song of the love between Christ and the church. (Traditional Roman Catholic interpreters have often identified the woman with the virgin Mary.) The allegorical approach was standard from the medieval period through the Reformation, but it has few adherents now.

Common allegorical identifications are that the man is Christ and the woman is the church, his kisses (1:2) are the Word of God, the girl's dark skin (1:5) is sin, her breasts (7:7) are the church's nurturing doctrine, her two lips (4:11) are law and gospel, and the "troops with banners" (6:4) is the church as the enemy of Satan. Advocates of this approach claim that the New Testament supports their case, since Ephesians 5:22-33 and other texts describe the church as Christ's bride.

But the New Testament never gives the Song an allegorical interpretation. New Testament passages that do speak of the bride of Christ do not refer to Song of Songs. The material of Song of Songs is grossly inappropriate for worship. It is impossible to imagine a Christian praising Christ in the terms of 1:2,16; or 5:10-16. It is equally bizarre to think of Jesus Christ describing His church in the terms of 7:1-9. This ancient interpretation has rightly been abandoned.

Dramatic Interpretation. For the past two hundred years, many interpreters have argued that the Song is a dramatic story. Some say it is a two-character drama in which Solomon and the girl are the main actors. Others take it as a three-character drama in which Solomon, the girl, and a shepherd boy are the main actors.

In the two-character interpretation, the Song tells the story of the romance between Solomon and the one girl he truly loved. The three-character interpretation is altogether different. It says the story tells how Solomon attempted to seduce a beautiful girl but failed because of her faithfulness to her true love, the shepherd boy.

Neither approach is convincing. A romantic drama of this kind was altogether unknown in the ancient Near East. Also both interpretations are at many points forced and unnatural. Considering the size of Solomon's harem and in light of 1 Kings 11:1-6, it is pointless to follow the two-character theory and assert he had one woman toward whom he was exclusively devoted (see Song 2:2; 7:10).

The three-character theory is equally artificial. According to that approach, for example, chapter 7 describes an attempt by Solomon to seduce the girl and her rebuff of his advances. This would mean that the poetry of 7:1-9a, spoken by the man, was not genuine love but cheap enticement. The girl, moreover, in saying, "Come, my lover, let us go to the countryside" (7:11), was not speaking to the man with her but to an absent lover. This can hardly be the intended meaning.

Wedding Song Interpretation. Some have argued that Song of Songs is a wedding song. Some scholars have studied Near Eastern wedding ceremonies and have pointed out similarities between those rituals and the lyrics of the Song. Even so, it is difficult to read Song of Songs as an order of service for a wedding. But even though the Song is not the text of a wedding ceremony, it indicates that the young lovers were marrying each other.

The writer compares his lover to a beautiful horse adorned with ornaments (see Song 1:9-10). Shown here is part of a relief from Khorsabad from the time of King Sargon II of Assyria depicting two horses with "circlets" (NIV "earrings") attached to their bridles and inlaid with jewels and precious stones.

Love Song Interpretation. The best interpretation is the most simple and obvious. Song of Songs is a love song in three parts—a man, a woman, and a chorus of women. It has no secret allegories or identifications. It tells no story and has no plot. It is a lyrical expression of romantic love between a couple who are in the process of marrying. Its language and imagery, which go from royal pomp and majesty to the rustic, pastoral setting of the meadow, is meant to convey all the grandeur and glory as well as the simplicity and natural beauty of love.

Meaning and Message

One reason for the rise of the allegorical interpretation of the Song is that many felt that a simple love song had no place in the Bible and that, unless it was allegorized, no theological message could be found in it. This concern, however, is misguided. Song of Songs conveys important meaning if left as it is, a love song, and not turned into something it is not.

First, as the Bible is meant to serve as a guide in every aspect of life, so the Song deals with one universal aspect of human life—love, marriage, and sexuality. People need direction and teaching in the matter of how to nurture love for a spouse just as they need guidance in every other matter. The song teaches that this love relationship is to be both physical and verbal. Again and again the two lovers speak of their desire for and joy in each other. For many couples the inability to express love is a profound problem.

Second, although the Song teaches by example and not be decree, its message is clear. The love the couple shared was exclusive and binding (7:10). By implication this ideal portrait excludes extramarital sex as well as all perversions and abuses of sexuality, such as promiscuity and homosexuality.

Third, Song of Songs celebrates love between man and woman as something that is valid and beautiful even in a fallen and sinful world. In this way Song of Songs testifies in a significant way to the grace of God. Although we are sinners, God tells us that the love relationship is a thing to be cherished and enjoyed. If the Bible said nothing in this area beyond prohibitions and warnings, we might suppose that all sexuality is innately evil and is to be suppressed entirely except for procreation. But because the Song is in the Bible, we understand that it is not sexuality but the misuse and abuse of sex that is wrong. In the Song we see that genuine love between man and woman, and the physical affection that follows, is a good and tender thing.

Fourth, the Song of Songs is unlike its ancient Near

Eastern counterparts in one significant respect: it does not turn sexuality into a sacred ritual. In the ancient world fertility cults and religious prostitution abounded. The sexual act was thought to have religious meaning. Not only that, but desperate souls often used incantations and love charms to win the affection of another person. None of this is found in Song of Songs. The romantic love between man and woman is a joy, but it is exclusively a joy of this world.

In this way the Bible avoids the two pitfalls of human religion. It neither condemns sexual love as innately evil and dangerous (as do legalistic cults) nor elevates it to the status of religious act (as do sensual cults and religions).

The Song of Songs, therefore, should be taken as it stands. It is a song of love and an affirmation of the value of the bond between a man and a woman. In this way it adds greatly to our appreciation of God's creation.

SONG OF SONGS

Introduction (Song 1:1). This verse is the title; the song actually begins in 1:2. In Song of Songs the groom, the bride, and the chorus each take turns singing their parts, but they do not follow a consistent sequence. At times it is difficult to tell who is singing a given line of lyrics because the Hebrew text does not delineate the parts. But usually the singer is evident.

Bride (Song 1:2-4a). She calls the groom a king (1:4), but this is not to be taken literally. This is the language of love.

Chorus (Song 1:4b). The bride's friends enhance her appreciation for the groom by joining in his praise.

Bride (Song 1:4c-7). The bride is embarrassed at her dark skin. In contrast to modern standards of beauty, the ancients regarded light skin as most attractive.

Groom (Song 1:8-11). The groom is at the same time a rustic shepherd (1:8) and yet able to give his beloved gold jewelry (1:10-11). Again, however, this is not to be pressed literally. The pastoral images and the mention of fine jewelry heighten the sense of joy in love.

Bride (Song 1:12-14). Semitropical vegetation, including henna, grew at the oasis of En Gedi on the western shore of the Dead Sea.

Groom (Song 1:15). "Eyes are doves" means that they are tranquil in appearance. Her eyes convey feelings of peacefulness.

Bride (Song 1:16). "Our bed is verdant" means it is lush and luxurious, like a tree thick with foliage.

Groom (Song 1:17). It was a luxury to have a house paneled with cedar.

Bride (Song 2:1). The flower mentioned here is not the modern rose of Sharon but probably a crocus, daffodil, or narcissus.

Groom (Song 2:2). Compared to the groom's beloved, all other women are thorns. True love is exclusive and not distracted by others.

Bride (Song 2:3-13). He is "like an apple tree," that is, protective ("shade") and pleasurable ("his fruit").

Groom (Song 2:14-15). Despite the endless variety of interpretations that have been heaped upon 2:15, the "little foxes" probably do not represent anything. The man simply invites the woman to join in a chase. This is the kind of childlike play that young lovers often engage in.

Bride (Song 2:16–3:5). The woman concludes the first section of Song of Songs in 2:16-17 and sings a separate solo in 3:1-5. This section is symbolic of the woman's longing for the groom and is not to be read literally. The proverb that says not to arouse love until it desires (3:5; also 2:7 and 8:4) means that sexual love is to be avoided until the proper time and person arrive.

Chorus (Song 3:6-11). The chorus women call for the Jerusalem girls to come and see Solomon's

An ivory from Calah in Mesopotamia (dating from 900–800 B.C.) in which the lady's long neck is adorned with a wide necklace from which hang small shield-shaped pendants. (See Song 4:4.)

splendor. This does not mean that Solomon is the singer of the groom's part or a "character" in a story. Instead, the figure of Solomon is more a contrasting poetic symbol here. Every young man in love is a "Solomon in all his glory." The arrival of Solomon stands for the arrival of the groom at the wedding ceremony (compare Matt 25:6). This is a song about a couple just married. But young lovers really do not need the trappings of glory, as Solomon did, since they have each other (see 8:11-12).

Groom (Song 4:1-15). The metaphors seem harsh and unnatural to the modern reader because we take them in too literal a sense. What the poet meant was that aspects of the woman's beauty provoke profound emotional responses. Her neck was like the tower of David (4:4) in that both were statuesque and caused feelings of admiration and wonder. He did not mean that her neck was unusually long. Similarly, he described the pleasures she gave him in terms of fruits and spices (4:13-15).

Bride (Song 4:16). This, with 5:1, is the high point of the Song of Songs. Using the metaphor of the garden, she invites her groom to come and enjoy her love.

Groom (Song 5:1a). The man responds. He calls her his bride, which again indicates they are newly married. The poetry is discreet and restrained; it conveys the joy of sexual love without vulgarity.

Chorus (Song 5:1b). The chorus' brief call ("Eat, O friends") breaks the tension of the previous verses and opens the way for a second solo similar to 3:1-5.

Bride (Song 5:2-8). This section is to be read symbolically and not literally. The main point of the text is to describe that the woman experiences pain and not only pleasure in love. The watchmen who beat her represent this.

Chorus (Song 5:9). This verse introduces the bride's next solo, in which she praises her beloved's beauty. There is no rational transition from the previous segment (5:1-8) because, again, it is not meant to be read as a story.

Bride (Song 5:10-16). Her beloved is like Lebanon in that he, like it, is majestic (5:15). He does not literally look like a forest. Here too the comparisons deal more with emotional response than actual similarity of appearance.

Chorus (Song 6:1). The chorus, following her answer to 5:9, now ask where he has gone.

Bride (Song 6:2-3). She answers that he has gone to "his garden" (that is, he has come to her).

Groom (Song 6:4-9). He praises his beloved in terms similar to 4:1-15.

Chorus (Song 6:10). The chorus announces the bride's approach and describes her beauty as like that of the moon and sun. Compare 3:6-11.

The beautiful red flowers of the pomegranate tree are in full bloom in early summer. (See Song 6:11.)

Bride (Song 6:11-12). Verse 12 seems to be saying that her love for the man swept her away. She is about to depart with the groom, as was apparently the custom after a wedding.

Chorus (Song 6:13a). The chorus, representing the bride's friends, long to be with her as they realize they are losing her to her beloved.

Groom (Song 6:13b–7:9a). He answers the chorus in 6:13b and then moves into another song of praise for the bride's beauty.

Bride (Song 7:9b–8:4). Her wish that her lover was her brother seems strange to the modern reader. The point is that she wishes she were free to display her affection openly. In the ancient world this would have been impossible for a woman with any man except a near relative.

Chorus (Song 8:5a). Once again the song of the chorus contains the idea of movement. See 6:13a.

Bride (Song 8:5b-7). In saying that her beloved was born under the apple tree, she is alluding to his romantic character. See 2:3.

Chorus (Song 8:8-9). The chorus desires that their young sister remain chaste until the proper time for love arrives. This may answer the proverb in 8:4.

Bride (Song 8:10-12). The woman says she has reached maturity and found fulfillment (8:10). The thousand shekels Solomon received from his vineyard may be a cryptic reference to Solomon's three hundred concu-

A tomb painting from Egypt of Queen Ahmose-Nefertari in full queenly attire. Notice the elegant sandals on her feet. (See Song 7:1.)

bines and seven hundred wives (1 Kgs 11:3). The love between the groom and the bride is better than Solomon's sexual extravagance.

Groom (Song 8:13). He calls on everyone to rejoice with him.

Bride (Song 8:14). She calls the groom away with her.

Theological Significance

The sexual and emotional aspects of love between a man and a woman are worthy of the Bible's attention. Sexuality and love are fundamental to the human experience. As a book meant to teach readers how to live a happy and good life, the Bible naturally has something to say in this area. The Song of Songs celebrates the joy and passion of married love as God's good gifts. The united love of the man and woman in Song of Songs is a reenactment of the love between the first man and woman. As such it witnesses to the triumph of God's gracious purposes for creation in spite of human sin. Likewise, such faithful love beautifully pictures God's love for and commitment to His people.

Questions for Reflection

1. What are some wrong attitudes toward love and sexuality, and how does Song of Songs correct them?

2. How has God's creation of humanity as male and female made life richer?

3. What can we learn about maintaining a healthy love relationship in courtship and marriage from how the groom and bride express their love for each other?

Sources for Additional Study

Carr, G. Lloyd. *The Song of Solomon. Tyndale Old Testament Commentaries.* Downers Grove: InterVarsity, 1984.

Glickman, S. Craig. *A Song for Lovers.* Downers Grove: InterVarsity, 1976.

THE MAJOR PROPHETS

The Historical Books showed the dominant role the prophets played in directing and interpreting Israel's history. Not surprisingly, then, the final books of the Old Testament preserve prophetic messages. Traditionally the prophetic books are divided into Major and Minor Prophets, basically on the length of the books.

The Books of the Major Prophets include Isaiah, Jeremiah, Lamentations, Ezekiel, and Daniel. That Isaiah, Jeremiah, and Ezekiel should be classified as major prophets should be self-evident. All three were prominent figures in the history of Israel and have left us with large collections of prophetic messages and biographical materials. Isaiah ministered in Judah from about 742 to 700 B.C. His prophecy addresses issues facing his contemporaries as well as the situation of the future exilic generation in Babylon. Jeremiah lived in Judah during its final days prior to the fall of Jerusalem in 586 B.C. After the fall of the city, he was forced to accompany a group of refugees to Egypt. His prophecy, while focusing on contemporary events, also looks forward to a time of restoration for God's people. Ezekiel was an exile in Babylon whose prophetic ministry took place between 593 and 571 B.C. Like his counterparts Isaiah and Jeremiah, he prophesied both judgment and restoration for God's people. (See "The Character of the Prophets.")

In the Hebrew Bible, Lamentations and Daniel are included in the Writings, not the Prophets. However, the English Bible, following the earliest

The Character of the Prophets

God's prophets experienced a call to be His spokespersons (Isa 6; Jer 1:4-10; Amos 7:15). The prophets challenged God's people to lead lives worthy of a people in covenant with God. The prophets' repeated call to "return" (*shub*) to God assumes a *history* of covenant commitments between God and His people. At times the prophetic message builds on God's covenant with the patriarchs (Jer 25:5). At times the warning builds on the exodus deliverance and Mosaic covenant (Jer 11:2-11). At times the prophetic message is hopeful, based on God's covenants with David and the Levites (Jer 33:19-22).

God gave His prophets access to His heavenly council room (1 Kgs 22:19-22), which let them see how God was at work in His world.

At their best God's prophets were courageous, unafraid to deliver their God-inspired message regardless of the danger involved. Often God called the prophets to confront Israel's kings with their sin. Samuel challenged Saul's disobedience (1 Sam 13; 15). Nathan exposed David's adultery and murder (2 Sam 12).

At other times the prophets felt all-too-human emotions. Elijah feared for his life and hid from Jezebel (1 Kgs 19:3). In despair Jeremiah complained that God had deceived him and brought him insults and reproach (Jer 20:7-8).

At their best God's prophets were honest individuals concerned with the truth. Micaiah warned Ahab of the dangers of going to war (1 Kgs 22). Isaiah exposed the foolishness of idol worship (Isa 44:9-20).

At their best God's prophets were moral persons who challenged God's people to high ethical standards. Amos challenged God's people to "let justice roll on like a river, righteousness like a never-failing stream" (Amos 5:24). Micah answered the question "What does the LORD require of you?" with a call "to act justly and to love mercy and to walk humbly with your God" (Mic 6:8).

At their best God's prophets were compassionate and sensitive to the oppressed. Amos announced God's judgment on Israel's people because "they sell the righteous for silver and the needy for a pair of sandals. They trample on the heads of the poor as upon the dust of the ground" (Amos 2:6-7).

Hebrew uses several terms for prophets. "Seer" (*ro'eh*) was an early title for a prophet (1 Sam 9:9). Seers like Samuel were able to see lost objects and future events. The phrase "man of God" designates a traveling preacher through whom God worked mighty acts (for example, Elijah and Elisha). The "prophets" (*nevi'im*) were spokespersons for God much as Aaron was spokesman for Moses (Exod 7:1).

The prophets came from different backgrounds. Isaiah was born and raised in the city and prophesied in Jerusalem. He addressed God's Word to kings, such as Ahaz (Isa 7) and Hezekiah (Isa 36–39). Micah came from the country town of Moresheth-gath in the Philistine territory. He criticized the political, moral, and social corruption of the big cities of Jerusalem and Samaria (Mic 1:5-7; 2:1-11; 3:1-12). His only hope was in the transformation of Zion (4:1-5).

Ideally court prophets served as God's advisers to and/or critics of the king. Some (Nathan, 2 Sam 12; Isaiah, Isa 7; Micaiah, 1 Kgs 22) challenged their kings not to stray from the covenant and to fulfill their God-ordained role as shepherds of God's people. The ideal of Israel as a theocracy—a nation ruled by God through His chosen kings—was realized only to the extent that its rulers heeded the counsel of God's prophets. Court prophets gave religious and political advice, rebuked, declared God's judgment, and kept record of the deeds of the king. Other court prophets were no more than yes men, repeating whatever message their king wished to hear (for example, the lying prophets of 1 Kgs 22).

Some prophets (Nathan, Jonah, Huldah) enjoyed a positive response to their messages. But most, like Elijah and Elisha (1 Kgs 19:1-5; 2 Kgs 7:1-2), experienced alienation and disgrace. The fall of Israel and Judah was due to their insensitivity to and outright disregard of the prophetic word. Too often the people of Israel and of Judah resisted the prophets and had them imprisoned or even killed (Jer 26:20-23; 37:15,18; 38:6-9; Matt 23:37).

The varying treatment of the prophets mirrored the shifting political scene of Judah. Unlike its northern neighbor, Judah was ruled by both godly and wicked kings. Sometimes its kings responded to the prophetic word, even as their ancestor David had. But all too often the kings disregarded—and even despised—the prophetic word. Yet the prophets faithfully and courageously served the Lord. □

Greek translation, places these books with the Major Prophets. Lamentations has traditionally been attributed to Jeremiah and, in lamenting the city's tragic destruction, focuses on an event that occupied a great deal of

Near Eastern Prophecy

Prophecy—like the institutions of kingship, temple, and sacrifice—was not unique to Israel (Num 22–24; 1 Kgs 18:18-40; Jer 27:8-11). Israel's prophets revealed God's word in a variety of ways (Heb 1:1), some roughly parallel to those of Israel's neighbors. What distinguished Israel's prophecy from that of its ancient Near Eastern neighbors was its source: Israel's God, Yahweh. Israel's prophets were spokespersons of Israel's God, who interpreted the promises and demands of His covenants to God's people.

The nations around Israel sought to know the will of the gods (and thus secure peace and prosperity) through *divination*. Divination is the practice of knowing the gods' will for the present and future. It occurs in two forms: *inductive* and *intuitive* divination.

In *inductive* divination a diviner uses *something* to discern the god's will. That something or omen might be a natural event (signs in the sky) or unusual phenomena (the behavior or noise of animals). Or that something might be a ritual involving liquids (Gen 44:5), fire, the shooting of arrows (Ezek 21:21), or the casting of lots (Exod 28:30; 1 Sam 28:6). In Assyria and Babylonia priests specialized in examining the entrails of sacrificial sheep. The position of the internal organs within the animal's body cavity were "read" for signs of future events (Ezek 21:21). The diviner sometimes used a variety of omens to confirm a divine word.

In *intuitive* divination an individual acted as a medium through whom the god spoke. Forms of intuitive divination include dreams (Gen 37:5-11; 41:1-36; Num 12:6; Deut 13:1-5), consultation of the dead by mediums (1 Sam 28), and ecstasy—the loss of control when seized by the spirit of the god (1 Sam 19:23-24; 1 Kgs 18:26-30).

Intuitive divination approaches biblical prophecy but was relatively rare among the nations surrounding Israel. Egyptian prophecy did little more than strengthen the kings' power or affirm social values. The *Prophecy of Nefer-Rohu*, written during the reign of Pharaoh Amen-emhet I (Twelfth Dynasty, 1990–1785 B.C.), claims to be presented to Pharaoh Snefru (Fourth Dynasty, 2650–2500 B.C.). This after-the-fact prophecy "predicts" a coming period of chaos, which a king from the south (Amen-emhet I) ends by defeating Egypt's enemies and establishing justice. The vision of a coming period of peace has similarities with some Hebrew messianic prophecy.

Wen-Amen, an Egyptian official (about 1060 B.C.), reported ecstatic prophecy in the Phoenician port city of Byblos. As priests were sacrificing, a youth was possessed by a god, who threw him to the ground. Following this seizure, the youth delivered the god's message: The god Amon had sent Wen-Amen on mission to Byblos.

The forty-six Mari tablets (about 1800–1600 B.C.) picture intuitive divination as practiced in northwestern Mesopotamia. Prophecy at Mari demonstrates rough parallels with biblical prophecy of one thousand years later. (1) The god took the initiative in giving the prophetic word. The prophet was viewed as the servant of the god: "Dagan sent me"; "Thus spoke Annunitum." (2) The use of "objects" for divination or unintelligible ecstatic speech was rare. (3) The prophet's call was legitimized by signs and wonders. (4) The prophets were openly critical of the court and state religion. (5) The prophets delivered both present and future messages. (6) The prophets delivered oracles against neighboring nations.

Some of Mari's prophets came from a seminomadic background, like that of Israel's patriarchs. They were ecstatics whose messages were transcribed and sent to a king or official. Other prophets were professionals or laypersons closely associated with the king. These court prophets generally spoke words of encouragement or mild rebuke. Such prophets offered Mari's last king false prophecy of victory against Hammurabi of Babylon. Likewise in Jeremiah's day Hananiah offered Judah false assurance of victory against Nebuchadnezzar of Babylon.

About the time of Amos, a court "seer" gave Zakir, king of Hamath in Syria (about 800–700 B.C.), an encouraging message from his god: "Do not fear; I made you king, and I shall stand by you and deliver you."

The intuitive prophets gave isolated oracles. Collections of written prophecies were rare in the ancient Near East. There is some evidence for the collecting of oracles, sorted by inspiring deity, at Nineveh and Arbela (800–600 B.C.). However, no evidence survives to suggest that other ancient Near Eastern peoples sought to preserve so large a collection of prophetic oracles as that found in the Hebrew Scriptures. □

Jeremiah's attention. The Book of Daniel, of course, contains several prophecies of future events, though they are presented in an apocalyptic literary style that differs significantly from traditional prophetic forms.

THE PROPHETS IN HISTORY
(9th—5th century B.C.)

Prophet	Approximate Dates	Location/ Home	Basic Bible Passage	Central Teaching	Key Verse
Elijah	875–850	Tishbe	1 Kgs 17:1–2 Kgs 2:18	Yahweh, not Baal, is God	1 Kgs 18:21
Micaiah	856	Samaria	1 Kgs 22; 2 Chr 18	Proof of prophecy	1 Kgs 22:28
Elisha	855–800	Abel Meholah	1 Kgs 19:15-21; 2 Kgs 2–9; 13	God's miraculous power	2 Kgs 5:15
Jonah	775	Gath Hepher	2 Kgs 14:25; Jonah	God's universal concern	Jonah 4:11
Amos	765	Tekoa	Amos	God's call for justice and righteousness	Amos 5:24
Hosea	750	Israel	Hosea	God's unquenchable love	Hos 11:8-9
Isaiah	740–698	Jerusalem	2 Kgs 19–20; Isaiah	Hope through repentance & suffering	Isa 1:18; 53:4-6
Micah	735–710	Moresheth Gath Jerusalem	Jer 26:18; Micah	Call for humble mercy and justice	Mic 6:8
Oded	733	Samaria	2 Chr 28:9-11	Do not go beyond God's command	2 Chr 28:9
Zephaniah	630	?	Zephaniah	Hope for the humble humble righteous	Zeph 2:3
Nahum	625	Elkosh	Nahum	God's jealousy protects His people	Nah 1:2-3
Habakkuk	625	?	Habakkuk	God calls for faithfulness	Hab 2:4
Jeremiah	626–584	Anathoth/ Jerusalem	2 Chr 36:12; Jeremiah	Faithful prophet points to new covenant	Jer 31:33-34
Huldah (the prophetess)	621	Jerusalem	2 Kgs 22; 2 Chr 34	God's Book is accurate	2 Kgs 22:16
Ezekiel	593–571	Babylon	Ezekiel	Future hope for new community of worship	Ezek 37:12-13
Joel	588 (?)	Jerusalem	Joel	Call to repent and experience God's Spirit	Joel 2:28-29
Obadiah	580	Jerusalem	Obadiah	Doom on Edom to bring God's kingdom	Obad 21
Haggai	520	Jerusalem	Ezra 5:1; 6:14; Haggai	The priority of God's house	Hag 2:8-9
Zechariah	520–514	Jerusalem	Ezra 5:1; 6:14; Zechariah	Faithfulness will lead to God's universal rule	Zech 14:9
Malachi	433	Jerusalem	Malachi	Honor God and wait for His righteousness	Mal 4:2

ISAIAH

According to the book's heading, Isaiah prophesied from about 740 until about 700 B.C., during the reigns of the kings Uzziah, Jotham, Ahaz, and Hezekiah of Judah. Several New Testament passages appear to attribute the entire book to the prophet Isaiah (see, for example, John 12:38-41). However, for various reasons modern critical scholars deny much of the book, including chapters 40–66, to eighth-century Isaiah. Appealing to differences in style, as well as to the exilic and even postexilic perspective of many sections, these scholars contend that the prophet's messages have been supplemented by later anonymous writers (two of whom have been labeled Second and Third Isaiah).

Certainly the perspective of chapters 40–66 is much later than Isaiah's time, as the many references to the situations of the exiles, the naming of Cyrus of Persia, the exhortations to leave Babylon, and the description of ruined and uninhabited Jerusalem indicate. However, this need not mean that the author of the chapters lived in this later period. Isaiah could have projected himself into the future and addressed the exilic situation he knew God's people would eventually experience (compare 39:5-7). Though such a projection into the future would be unique among the writing prophets, at least on the scale proposed for Isaiah, it would be consistent with one of the major theological themes of the book's later chapters, namely, God's ability to predict events long before He actually brings them to pass.

Historical Background

Isaiah lived in momentous times for Israel and Judah. Both nations had experienced prosperity during the first half of the eighth century B.C. But not long after the midpoint of the century, the Assyrians appeared on the horizon like a dark, ominous storm cloud. In an effort to resist the Assyrians, the Northern Kingdom formed a coalition with the Arameans (Syrians). When Judah refused to join the effort, Israel and Aram attacked.

Some of the early chapters of the book reflect this background (compare chaps. 7–8). The Assyrians defeated Aram and Israel, reducing the latter to a puppet state. The morally corrupt Northern Kingdom was moving headlong toward final judgment. In 722 B.C. the Assyrians conquered Samaria and made Israel an Assyrian province. Following in the footsteps of the Northern Kingdom, Judah also rebelled against God's commandments.

Isaiah warned his countrymen to change, and the reign of Hezekiah saw a revival of sorts. Hezekiah also resisted the Assyrians. In 701 B.C. the Assyrian ruler Sennacherib marched against Judah and besieged Jerusalem. Isaiah encouraged the king to trust in the Lord, who miraculously delivered the city from the Assyrian hordes. However, Isaiah also foresaw the eventual exile of Judah and addressed the situation of that future generation.

Theme

The theme of Isaiah's prophecy may be summarized as follows: God's ideal for His covenant people Israel will indeed be realized but only after His judgment purifies the covenant community of those who rebel against His authority. God is the "Holy One of Israel," who sovereignly controls the destiny of nations but who also demands loyalty from His people.

Literary Form

The book contains a multitude of individual literary types, often woven together in a highly artistic and rhetorically effective manner. Among the more common forms are the judgment speech (where the prophet accuses the nation of wrongdoing and announces its coming doom), the exhortation to repentance, the salvation announcement (which promises God's intervention for His suffering people), and the salvation oracle (in which the Lord encourages His people not to fear). Other forms include the disputation speech (where God responds to an accusation or complaint by His people) and the trial speech (where God argues His case with Israel or with the pagan nations). The book contains prophetic messages, mostly in poetic form characterized by parallelism of thought and vivid imagery, and biographical material about Isaiah.

Most of the judgment messages appear in chapters 1–39. The majority of the salvation speeches occur in chapters 40–66. Still it is overly simplistic to say that the

Isaiah the prophet

theme of chapters 1–39 is judgment and that of chapters 40–66 salvation. In each of the major sections of chapters 1–39, the message moves from judgment to salvation.

I. **Judgment and Restoration of God's People (1:1–12:6)**
II. **Universal Judgment and God's Kingdom Established (13:1–39:8)**
III. **Hope and Restoration for God's Exiled People (40:1–66:24)**

Purpose and Theology

As a messenger of Israel's and Judah's covenant Lord, Isaiah warned that God's people were about to be judged for breaking their covenant with Him. Though their punishment would be severe, God would ultimately judge the nations as well and reestablish His people in their land.

In the development of this major theme of salvation through purifying judgment, several contributing themes emerge. Isaiah has much to say about Zion (Jerusalem), God's dwelling place. He prophesied and witnessed the city's miraculous deliverance from the Assyrians. The event foreshadowed and became a guarantee of Jerusalem's eventual vindication and glorification before the nations. However, a time would come when Jerusalem would have to endure extreme hardship and its people suffer the humiliation of exile. Nevertheless, God would not abandon the city. He would lead His people out of exile in a grand new exodus and bring them back to the promised land. Once again Zion would be inhabited. This vision was only partially fulfilled about 538 B.C., when the Persian ruler Cyrus allowed exiles to go back to Palestine. The full restoration of Israel awaits a future time when covenant renewal is complete (compare Isa 55 with Rom 11:27).

The Servant of the Lord (the focal point of the so-called servant songs of chaps. 42–53) plays a prominent role in the restoration of Israel. Portrayed as a new Moses who mediates a new covenant for the nation, this servant suffers on behalf of God's people and brings them redemption. Subsequent biblical revelation identifies this servant as Jesus Christ. In the earlier chapters of Isaiah we see a more traditional portrayal of the Messiah as a mighty Davidic ruler who conquers the enemies of God and establishes justice in Israel and among the nations.

The book also emphasizes God's sovereignty over the nations. He raised up Assyria and Babylon as instruments to punish His rebellious people but then destroyed them because of their arrogance and cruelty. Time and time again the Lord declared His infinite superiority to the idol-gods of the nations. They were products of human hands and inactive, but He is the sovereign Creator who superintends the universe.

JUDGMENT AND RESTORATION OF GOD'S PEOPLE (ISA 1:1–12:6)

1:1-31
A Divine Ultimatum and Warning

See the introduction to "Isaiah" for a discussion of the heading. The Lord summoned the personified heavens and earth, the ancient witnesses to God's covenant with Israel (Deut 30:19; 31:28), to hear His accusation against His rebellious people. Despite His fatherly concern, they had disobeyed and rejected Him. Though Judah had already experienced the horrors of military invasion and Jerusalem alone had been spared, the nation refused to turn back to God. Comparing His people to the evildoers of Sodom and Gomorrah, the Lord denounced their hypocritical religious acts and demanded that they promote social justice in the land. The Lord delivered an ultimatum. Obedience would bring forgiveness and restored

SYRIA

Syria is the modern translation for the Hebrew term *Aram*, usually referring to the territory northwest of Israel. During OT times small city-states (particularly Hamath and Damascus) vied with one another for control of the area.

Aram encompassed modern Lebanon and Syria with small parts of Turkey and Iraq. In the NT Syria refers to the Roman imperial province centered around its capital at Antioch and including Judea.

Geographically, Syria is an indefinite area. For Tiglath-Pileser III of Assyria it stretched from Mount Lebanon to Ramoth-gilead. Modern Bible students usually think of the area from the Taurus Mountains in the north to Damascus in the south (or even further) and from the Lebanon Mountains in the west to the Euphrates River in the east. From west to east Syria encompasses: (1) a narrow coastal plain, (2) the Lebanon mountains, (3) the rift valley, watered by the Orontes and Leontes Rivers, (4) and the fertile plateau trailing off to the Arabian Desert.

Archaeologists provide valuable information about Syria's early history. Ebla originated about 3500 B.C. and became the capital of a major city-state of about sixty thousand inhabitants around 2500 B.C. It continued to exercise great influence until about 1600 B.C., though at times defeated by Mesopotamian kings.

Yamhad, with its capital at Aleppo, was a major city-state after 2000 B.C. Here a famous Syrian style of art developed, attested on decorations on cylinder seals. Alalakh was another major city in this kingdom. The kingdom fell to Hittite raids about 1630. Qatna ruled central Syria during this period.

The Bible connects the patriarchs with Syria in this period. Aram is listed as a descendant of Shem (Gen 10:22-23; compare 22:20-24). Isaac's wife Rebekah was an Aramean from Paddan Aram (25:20). Jacob was called a "wandering Aramean" (Deut 26:5; compare Hos 12:12). The prophet Balaam was an Aramean (Num 23:7; Deut 23:4).

About 1550 B.C. Egypt began to exercise major control in Syria, battling the Mitanni and then the Hittites for control. During this period Kumidi, Sumur, and Ulasa served as administrative centers. Qatna, Byblos, Tyre, Sidon, Beirut, Arwad, Damascus, and Kadesh remained city-states with local rulers subject as vassals to the Egyptian pharaoh. Hurrians began to mix with the basic West Semitic population.

Ugarit, a major city on the northeastern border of Syria, rose to great importance in this period. Archaeologists trace its origins into the Chalcolithic period (about 6500 B.C.). Excavations there have shown us much about Canaanite language, literature, religion, and life. Despite its size and importance, Ugarit seldom experienced political independence. Rather, its king was a vassal to the Hittites, Egyptians, or to other Syrian cities such as Yamhad. Ugarit fell about 1180 B.C. to the Sea Peoples, from whom emerged the Philistines, among other tribal groups. Nomadic peoples called Arameans began to make their presence felt from Persia to Syria about this time.

About 1112 B.C., Assyria, under Tiglath-Pileser, became Syria's major threat. Success wavered back and forth, Tiglath-Pileser claiming to have crossed the Euphrates into Syria twenty-eight different times. But documents also show Arameans to have invaded Assyria. The Bible shows the rise of Syrian city-states contemporary with Saul and David. Saul faced the king of Zobah (1 Sam 14:47), as did David (2 Sam 8:3; compare the title of Ps 60). Damascus was an ally of Zobah (2 Sam 8:5), but Hamath congratulated David for defeating Zobah. This shows the changing relationships among the small Syrian city-states. Zobah supplied soldiers for the Ammonites in their fight against David (10:6). Defeat only led King Hadadezer of Zobah to bat-

blessings; continued disobedience would result in destruction.

In response to the Lord's denunciation, Isaiah lamented that once-faithful Jerusalem was defiled by social injustice and corruption. The Lord would take up the cause of the oppressed and purify the city of its evildoers. Once again Jerusalem would become a center of justice.

2:1–4:6
Purifying Judgment and Restoration

This section begins and ends with a description of purified and restored Jerusalem of the future. In between Isaiah addressed the situation of his own day, warning of impending judgment and condemning the city's proud residents.

Universal Peace (2:1-5). Following the Lord's purifying judgment, Jerusalem would become the center of His universal kingdom of peace. Rather than resorting to warfare, the nations would allow the Lord to settle their disputes. In anticipation of this coming age of peace, the prophet exhorted his own generation to seek the Lord's guidance.

The Lord's Day of Judgment (2:6-22). Returning to the realities of his own day, Isaiah denounced

---

tle David and suffer defeat again (10:13-19).

Zobah's defeat gave Rezon opportunity to establish Damascus as the Syrian power (1 Kgs 11:23-24). Rezon troubled Solomon (11:25). Excavations point to Damascus as a city before 3000 B.C. Abraham chased kings there to recover Lot (Gen 14:15); and Eliezer, Abraham's servant, came from Damascus (Gen 15:2).

Asa, king of Judah (905–874 B.C.), paid Ben-Hadad of Damascus to break his military alliance with Baasha of Israel and attack the Northern Kingdom (1 Kgs 15:18-22).

Another Ben-Hadad of Damascus formed a large coalition of kings and attacked Samaria under King Ahab (874–853 B.C.). A prophet led Israel to victory, then chastised Ahab for making a treaty with Damascus (1 Kgs 20). Jehoshaphat of Judah and Ahab of Israel attacked the Arameans but lost at Ramoth-Gilead, resulting in Ahab's death (1 Kgs 22). The prophet Elisha also delivered Samaria from Ben-Hadad (2 Kgs 5–7). Elisha then prophesied a change of dynasty in Damascus, naming Hazael as its king (2 Kgs 8:7-15).

Shalmaneser III of Assyria (858–824 B.C.) claimed victory over Ben-Hadad and Hazael at Qarqar in a series of battles between 853 and 838. The 853 battle saw Irhuleni of Hamath, Ben-Hadad of Damascus, and Ahab of Israel stop Shalmaneser's advance. Ahaziah of Judah and Joram of Israel joined forces against Damascus in 841, leading to Joram's murder of Ahaziah (2 Kgs 8:25–9:28).

After 838 B.C. Hazael and Ben-Hadad restored Damascus's strength (2 Kgs 10:32-33; 13:3-25; compare Amos 1:4). But Adad-nirari III of Assyria (810–783) put a stop to that with invasions from 805 to 802 and again in 796. Hazael did attack Jerusalem and force King Joash to pay tribute (2 Kgs 12:17-18), but Jehoash of Israel regained Israelite cities from Damascus (2 Kgs 13:19,25).

Finally, Jeroboam II (798–782 B.C.) asserted Israel's strength, gaining control of Damascus (2 Kgs 14:28). Zakir of Hamath filled part of the power vacuum in Syria, bringing Hamath to its greatest power (800–750 B.C). In 753 Shalmaneser IV of Assyria battled Damascus.

Damascus's final efforts began under its last king Rezin, who became Tiglath-Pileser's vassal in 738 B.C. Rezin joined Pekah of Israel, invading Judah and attacking Jerusalem. Rezin managed to capture Elath and give it to Edom (2 Kgs 16:6).

Ahaz of Judah refused to believe Isaiah's advice that Israel and Aram would not threaten Judah for long (Isa 7). He paid Tiglath-Pileser of Assyria to defeat his enemies (2 Kgs 16:5-18). Tiglath-Pileser claimed to destroy 501 cities in sixteen districts as he captured Damascus and exiled its leadership. He appointed his own governors in Syrian provincial centers at Hauran, Qarnini (or Karnaim), and Gilead in the south; Damascus in the middle; and Subatu in the north. When Damascus rebelled in 720 B.C., Sargon II put down the rebellion and destroyed Hamath. This introduced permanent foreign control to Syria, first by Assyria, then Babylon after 612, Persia after 538, and finally Greece in 321.

In the division of the Greek empire after Alexander's death *Syria* became popular as a name for the Seleucid kingdom centered in Antioch. The Maccabean revolts led to Jewish independence in 167 B.C. In 64 B.C. Rome made Syria a province. A procurator answerable to the Syrian legate ruled Judah (compare Matt 4:24; Luke 2:2). Antioch remained the governmental center of the province.

Paul was traveling to Damascus to persecute Christians there when God intervened to save him (Acts 9). Paul evangelized in Syria (Acts 15:41; Gal 1:21). Antioch became a Christian missionary center (Acts 13:1-3). There the term *Christian* was coined (Acts 11:26). □

A piece of gold jewelry in the shape of a crescent dating from the end of the Bronze Age (1200s B.C.). See Isaiah 3:18.

Judah for its foreign alliances, idolatry, and accumulation of wealth and armaments. He warned that the Lord's Day of judgment was imminent. Like a mighty warrior He would destroy the proud, symbolized here by lofty trees, high mountains, walled cities, and impressive ships. In that day idol worshipers would discard the gods they had formed and flee in terror from God's wrath. Since even the mightiest and most proud could not withstand God's judgment, the prophet urged his contemporaries to no longer place their trust in mortals.

Jerusalem's Injustice (3:1–4:1). The focal point of the Lord's judgment would be Jerusalem's arrogant and oppressive leaders. Ironically, in the aftermath of judgment men would refuse positions once coveted for their power and prestige. Those totally incapable of ruling society would be forced to assume leadership.

The pride of Jerusalem's upper classes was epitomized by its wealthy women. Their demeanor and dress were vivid proof that the wealthy profited at the poor's expense. In the day of judgment the signs of wealth and pride would be replaced by those of deprivation and humiliation. The women would wear mourners' sackcloth, not beautiful garments. With their husbands and sons slaughtered in battle, they would beg the few surviving men to marry them.

Jerusalem's Purification (4:2-6). Despite its horrors, God's judgment had a positive goal of purification. He would "wash away" the "filth" of Jerusalem's women (an ironic reference to their beautiful garments) and burn away the blood stains left by their violent treatment of the poor. Out of the fire of judgment would emerge a remnant of faithful followers, who would at long last fulfill God's ideal for a holy nation (compare Exod 19:6). He would bless them with agricultural prosperity and protect them from all harmful and destructive forces. The imagery of the "cloud of smoke" and "glow of flaming fire" (4:5) alludes to the period of the exodus and wilderness wanderings, when a cloud and fire were tangible symbols of God's protective presence and guidance (Exod 13:21-22; 14:20).

Some see the "Branch of the LORD" (4:2) as a messianic title (compare Jer 23:5; 33:15; Zech 3:8; 6:12). But this seems unlikely in this context, where the phrase corresponds to "fruit of the land." Both phrases probably refer to the agricultural abundance the Lord would give to His restored people. The Hebrew word translated "Branch" (*semah*) can refer to vegetation or agricultural growth (compare Gen 19:25, "vegetation"; Ps 65:10, "crops"; Ezek 16:7, "plant"). Several prophets, including Isaiah, pictured the age of Israel's restoration as one of renewed agricultural blessing (Isa 30:23-24; 32:20; Jer 31:12; Ezek 34:26-29; Amos 9:13-14).

5:1-30
Destruction of the Lord's Fruitless Vineyard

Isaiah marshaled all of his rhetorical skills to emphasize the necessity and inevitability of divine judgment. What begins as a love song quickly hits a sour note. The song tells of a farmer (the Lord, compare 5:3-7) who clears land for a vineyard (God's people, compare 5:7). Having made all the necessary preparations, he expected the vineyard to yield good grapes. Instead it produced only bad. Likewise God established Israel to be a model of justice and righteousness. Israel rewarded God's efforts with violent deeds and injustice. (In the Hebrew text wordplay highlights Israel's perversion of God's ideal. The word translated "bloodshed" in 5:7 [Hebrew *misah*] sounds like the word for "justice" [Hebrew *mispat*], while the word rendered "cries of distress" [Hebrew *seaqa*] sounds like the word for "righteousness" [Hebrew *sedaqa*].) The farmer's only alternative was to destroy a fruitless vineyard. So the Lord had to judge His sinful people.

A series of judgment speeches follows, each of which begins with the word "woe." Ancient Israelites used this word when mourning the death of a friend or loved one. By employing this word, the prophet was, as it were, acting out the nation's funeral in advance and thereby emphasizing the inevitability of judgment.

In these woe-speeches Isaiah condemned several sins, including socioeconomic injustice, corruption of the legal system, the carousing of the rich, and their spiritual insensitivity. Irony highlights the speeches. Those who accumulated land and houses at the poor's expense would not prosper from their acquisitions. Those who wined and dined would die of hunger and thirst in exile and would themselves be devoured by the grave. Those who challenged the Lord to "hurry" (5:19) would soon see

Pictured above is a relief dating from 1000–800 B.C. of a six-winged figure who resembles the seraphim described in Isaiah 6:2.

His instrument of judgment, the Assyrian hordes, advancing "swiftly and speedily" (5:26). Finally, those who "put darkness for light and light for darkness" in moral and ethical matters (5:20) would find their sphere of sinful activity darkened by the clouds of judgment (5:30).

6:1-13
Isaiah's Vision and Commissioning

Isaiah 1–5 describes how God's people rejected their "Holy One" (1:4; 5:24). In Isaiah 6 the prophet tells of his face-to-face encounter with this Holy God. In the year of King Uzziah's death (740 B.C.) Isaiah received a vision of the real King, the Lord, seated on His heavenly throne. Seraphs surrounded Him, chanting "Holy, holy, holy is the LORD Almighty" (6:3). Overwhelmed by God's splendor, Isaiah acknowledged his and his people's sinful condition. After Isaiah was symbolically purified, the Lord commissioned him as a messenger to His spiritually insensitive people. He was to preach until judgment swept through the land and the people were carried into exile, leaving only a remnant.

7:1–12:6
The Lord's Ultimate Deliverance of His Faithless People through the Messiah

The background for these chapters is the Syro-Ephraimitic war (735–733 B.C.), when Aram and the Northern Kingdom invaded Judah and besieged Jerusalem.

Ahaz's Unbelief, Isaiah's Sign Children (7:1–8:22). During the Syro-Ephraimitic war, Aram (Syria) and the Northern Kingdom threatened to replace Judah's king, Ahaz, with a nearby ruler. Isaiah urged the king to trust in the Lord's promises to the Davidic dynasty. While Ahaz was inspecting the city's water system in preparation for a siege, Isaiah and his son, Shear-jashub, met the king. The names of the prophet (Isaiah means *the LORD saves*) and his son (Shear-jashub means *a remnant will return*) were symbolic, indicating that God was fully capable of preserving His people through the crisis.

Isaiah challenged Ahaz to ask for a sign of confirmation. When Ahaz refused, Isaiah announced that the Lord would give the king a sign. In the near future a child would be born and named "Immanuel" (meaning *God is with us*). The name would be appropriate because he would be a living proof of God's providential presence with His people. Before the child could distinguish right from wrong, the Lord would deliver Judah from the Aramean-Israelite coalition, demonstrating His sovereignty over Judah's destiny.

However, due to Ahaz's unbelief, this time of deliverance would be shortlived. To punish the king for his lack of faith the Lord would bring upon the land a crisis far worse than the Aramean-Israelite threat. Ironically, the Assyrians, to whom Ahaz looked for help (2 Kgs 16:7-9), would invade the land and decimate its population. The curds and honey eaten by Immanuel, which at first appeared to be signs of divine blessing (7:15), would now attest to the land's desolate condition (7:21:22).

Matthew 1:22-23 states that the birth of Jesus fulfilled the prophecy of Isaiah 7:14. However, one must not conclude from this that the ancient Immanuel prophecy refers *exclusively* to Jesus. The circumstances surrounding the prophecy demand a more immediate fulfillment as well. The context of Isaiah 7:14 indicates that a child would be born in the days of Ahaz who would serve as a sign to that generation of God's providential control of international events and of His people's destiny. This child, who was a sign of God's presence with His people, foreshadowed Jesus, who is "God with us" in the fullest possible sense. Matthew's use of the Immanuel prophecy is consistent with the way he used the Old Testament elsewhere in the early chapters of his Gospel. Matthew 2:14-15 applies Hosea 11:1, which in its context speaks

MESSIANIC PROPHECIES OF THE OLD TESTAMENT

PROPHECY	OT REFERENCES	NT FULFILLMENT
Son of Man comes in glory	Ps 102:16	Luke 21:24,27; Rev 12:5-10
"Thou remainest"	Ps 102:24-27	Heb 1:10-12
Prays for His enemies	Ps 109:4	Luke 23:34
Another to succeed Judas	Ps 109:7-8	Acts 1:16-20
A priest like Melchizedek	Ps 110:1-7	Matt 22:41-45; 26:64; Mark 12:35-37; 16:19; Acts 7:56; Eph 1:20; Col 1:20; Heb 1:13; 2:8; 5:6; 6:20; 7:21; 8:1; 10:11-13; 12:2
The chief cornerstone	Ps 118:22-23	Matt 21:42; Mark 12:10-11; Luke 20:17; John 1:11; Acts 4:11; Eph 2:20; 1 Pet 2:4
The King comes in the name of the Lord	Ps 118:26	Matt 21:9; 23:39; Mark 11:9; Luke 13:35; 19:38; John 12:13
David's seed to reign	Ps 132:11 Sam 7:12-13,16, 25-26,29	Matt 1:1
Declared to be the Son of God	Prov 30:4	Matt 3:17; Mark 14:61-62; Luke 1:35; John 3:13; 9:35-38; 11:21; Rom 1:2-4; 10:6-9; 2 Pet 1:17
Repentance for the nations	Isa 2:2-4	Luke 24:47
Hearts are hardened	Isa 6:9-10	Matt 13:14-15; John 12:39-40; Acts 28:25-27
Born of a virgin	Isa 7:14	Matt 1:22-23
A rock of offense	Isa 8:14,15	Rom 9:33; 1 Pet 2:8
Light out of darkness	Isa 9:1-2	Matt 4:14-16; Luke 2:32
God with us	Isa 9:6-7	Matt 1:21,23; Luke 1:32-33; John 8:58; 10:30; 14:19; 2 Cor 5:19; Col 2:9
Full of wisdom and power	Isa 11:1-10	Matt 3:16; John 3:34; Rom 15:12; Heb 1:9
Reigning in mercy	Isa 16:4-5	Luke 1:31-33
Peg in a sure place	Isa 22:21-25	Rev 3:7
Death swallowed up in victory	Isa 25:6-12	1 Cor 15:54
A stone in Zion	Isa 28:16	Rom 9:33; 1 Pet 2:6
The deaf hear, the blind see	Isa 29:18-19	Matt 5:3; 11:5; John 9:39
King of kings, Lord of lords	Isa 32:1-4	Rev 19:16; 20:6
Son of the Highest	Isa 33:22	Luke 1:32; 1 Tim 1:17; 6:15
Healing for the needy	Isa 35:4-10	Matt 9:30; 11:5; 12:22; 20:34; 21:14; 7:30; 5:9
Make ready the way of the Lord	Isa 40:3-5	Matt 3:3; Mark 1:3; Luke 3:4-5; John 1:23
The Shepherd dies for His sheep	Isa 40:10-11	John 10:11; Heb 13:20; 1 Pet 2:24-25
The meek Servant	Isa 42:1-16	Matt 12:17-21; Luke 2:32
A light to the Gentiles	Isa 49:6-12	Acts 13:47; 2 Cor 6:2
Scourged and spat upon	Isa 50:6	Matt 26:67; 27:26,30; Mark 14:65; 15:15,19; Luke 22:63-65; John 19:1
Rejected by His people	Isa 52:13–53:12	Matt 8:7; 27:1-2,12-14,38
Suffered vicariously	Isa 53:4-5	Mark 15:3-4,27-28; Luke 23:1-25,32-34
Silent when accused	Isa 53:7	John 1:29; 11:49-52
Crucified with transgressors	Isa 53:12	John 12:37-38; Acts 8:28-35
Buried with the rich	Isa 53:9	Acts 10:43; 13:38-39; 1 Cor 15:3; Eph 1:7; 1 Pet 2:21-25; 1 John 1:7,9
Calling of those not a people	Isa 55:4-5	John 18:37; Rom 9:25-26; Rev 1:5
Deliver out of Zion	Isa 59:16-20	Rom 11:26-27
Nations walk in the light	Isa 60:1-3	Luke 2:32
Anointed to preach liberty	Isa 61:1-3	Luke 4:17-19; Acts 10:38
Called by a new name	Isa 62:1-2	Luke 2:32; Rev 3:12
The King cometh	Isa 62:11	Matt 21:5
A vesture dipped in blood	Isa 63:1-3	Rev 19:13
Afflicted with the afflicted	Isa 63:8-9	Matt 25:34-40
The elect shall inherit	Isa 65:9	Rom 11:5,7; Heb 7:14; Rev 5:5
New heavens and a new earth	Isa 65:17-25	2 Pet 3:13; Rev 21:1
The Lord our righteousness	Jer 23:5-6	John 2:19-21; Rom 1:3-4; Eph 2:20-21; 1 Pet 2:5
Born a King	Jer 30:9	John 18:37; Rev 1:5
Massacre of infants	Jer 31:15	Matt 2:17-18
Conceived by the Holy Spirit	Jer 31:22	Matt 1:20; Luke 1:35
A New Covenant	Jer 31:31-34	Matt 26:27-29; Mark 14:22-24; Luke 22:15-20; 1 Cor 11:25; Heb 8:8-12 10:15-17; 12:24; 13:20
A spiritual house	Jer 33:15-17	John 2:19-21; Eph 2:20-21; 1 Pet 2:5
A tree planted by God	Ezek 17:22-24	Matt 13:31-32
The humble exalted	Ezek 21:26-27	Luke 1:52
The good Shepherd	Ezek 34:23-24	John 10:11
Stone cut without hands	Dan 2:34-35	Acts 4:10-12
His kingdom triumphant	Dan 2:44-45	Luke 1:33; 1 Cor 15:24; Rev 11:15
An everlasting dominion	Dan 7:13-14	Matt 24:30; 25:31; 26:64; Mark 14:61-62; Acts 1:9-11; Rev 1:7
Kingdom for the saints	Dan 7:27	Luke 1:33; 1 Cor 15:24; Rev 11:15
Time of His birth	Dan 9:24-27	Matt 24:15-21; Luke 3:1
Israel restored	Hos 3:5	John 18:37; Rom 11:25-27
Flight into Egypt	Hos 11:1	Matt 2:15

MESSIANIC PROPHECIES OF THE OLD TESTAMENT

PROPHECY	OT REFERENCES	NT FULFILLMENT
Promise of the Spirit	Joel 2:28-32	Acts 2:17-21; Rom 10:13
The sun darkened	Amos 8:9	Matt 24:29; Acts 2:20; Rev 6:12
Restoration of tabernacle	Amos 9:11-12	Acts 15:16-18
Israel regathered	Mic 2:12-13	John 10:14,26
The kingdom established	Mic 4:1-8	Luke 1:33
Born in Bethlehem	Mic 5:1-5	Matt 2:1; Luke 2:4,10-11
Earth filled with knowledge of the glory of the Lord	Hab 2:14	Rom 11:26; Rev 21:23-26
The Lamb on the throne	Zech 2:10-13	Rev 5:13; 6:9; 21:24; 22:1-5
A holy priesthood	Zech 3:8	John 2:19-21; Eph 2:20-21; 1 Pet 2:5
A heavenly High Priest	Zech 6:12-13	Heb 4:4; 8:1,2
Triumphal entry	Zech 9:9-10	Matt 21:4-5; Mark 11:9-10; Luke 20:38; John 12:13-15
Sold for thirty pieces of silver	Zech 11:12-13	Matt 26:14-15
Money buys potter's field	Zech 11:12-13	Matt 27:9
Piercing of His body	Zech 12:10	John 19:34,37
Shepherd smitten—sheep scattered	Zech 13:1,6-7	Matt 26:31; John 16:32
Preceded by Forerunner	Mal 3:1	Matt 11:10; Mark 1:2; Luke 7:27
Our sins purged	Mal 3:3	Heb 1:3
The light of the world	Mal 4:2-3	Luke 1:78; John 1:9; 12:46; 2 Pet 1:19; Rev 2:28; 19:11-16; 22:16
The coming of Elijah	Mal 4:5-6	Matt 11:14; 17:10-12
Seed of the woman	Gen 3:15	Gal 4:4; Heb 2:14
Through Noah's sons	Gen 9:27	Luke 6:36
Seed of Abraham	Gen 12:3	Matt 1:1; Gal 3:8,16
Seed of Isaac	Gen 17:19	Rom 9:7; Heb 11:18
Blessing to nations	Gen 18:18	Gal 3:8
Seed of Isaac	Gen 21:12	Rom 9:7; Heb 11:18
Blessing to Gentiles	Gen 22:18	Gal 3:8,16; Heb 6:14
Blessing to Gentiles	Gen 26:4	Gal 3:8,16; Heb 6:14
Blessing through Abraham	Gen 28:14	Gal 3:8,16; Heb 6:14
Of the tribe of Judah	Gen 49:10	Rev 5:5
No bone broken	Exod 12:46	John 19:36
Blessing to firstborn son	Exod 13:2	Luke 2:23
No bone broken	Num 9:12	John 19:36
Serpent in wilderness	Num 21:8-9	John 3:14-15
A star out of Jacob	Num 24:17-19	Matt 2:2; Luke 1:33,78; Rev 22:16
As a prophet	Deut 18:15,18-19	John 6:14; 7:40; Acts 3:22-23
Cursed on the tree	Deut 21:23	Gal 3:13
The throne of David established forever	2 Sam 7:12-13,16,25-26 1 Chr 17:11-14, 23-27; 2 Chr 21:7	Matt 19:28; 21:4; 25:31; Mark 12:37; Luke 1:32; John 7:4; Acts 2:30; 13:23 Rom 1:3; 2 Tim 2:8; Heb 1:5,8; 8:1; 12:2; Rev 22:1
A promised Redeemer	Job 19:25-27	John 5:28-29; Gal 4:4; Eph 1:7,11,14
Declared to be the Son of God	Ps 2:1-12	Matt 3:17; Mark 1:11; Acts 4:25-26; 13:33; Heb 1:5; 5:5; Rev 2:26-27; 19:15-16
His resurrection	Ps 16:8-10	Acts 2:27; 13:35; 26:23
Hands and feet pierced	Ps 22:1-31	Matt 27:31,35-36
Mocked and insulted	Ps 22:7-8	Matt 27:39-43,45-49
Soldiers cast lots for coat	Ps 22:18	Mark 15:20,24-25,34; Luke 19:24; 23:35; John 19:15-18,23-24,34; Acts 2:23-24
Accused by false witnesses	Ps 27:12	Matt 26:60-61
He commits His spirit	Ps 31:5	Luke 23:46
No broken bone	Ps 34:20	John 19:36
Accused by false witnesses	Ps 35:11	Matt 26:59-61; Mark 14:57-58
Hated without reason	Ps 35:19	John 15:24-25
Friends stand afar off	Ps 38:11	Matt 27:55; Mark 15:40; Luke 23:49
"I come to do Thy will"	Ps 40:6-8	Heb 10:5-9
Betrayed by a friend	Ps 41:9	Matt 26:14-16,47,50; Mark 14:17-21; Luke 22:19-23; John 13:18-19
Known for righteousness	Ps 45:2,6-7	Heb 1:8-9
His resurrection	Ps 49:15	Mark 16:6
Betrayed by a friend	Ps 55:12-14	John 13:18
His ascension	Ps 68:18	Eph 4:8
Hated without reason	Ps 69:4	John 15:25
Stung by reproaches	Ps 69:9	John 2:17; Rom 15:3
Given gall and vinegar	Ps 69:21	Matt 27:34,48; Mark 15:23; Luke 23:36; John 19:29
Exalted by God	Ps 72:1-19	Matt 2:2; Phil 2:9-11; Heb 1:8
He speaks in parables	Ps 78:2	Matt 13:34-35
Seed of David exalted	Ps 89:3-4,19,27-29 35-37	Luke 1:32; Acts 2:30; 13:23; Rom 1:3; 2 Tim 2:8

of the historical exodus of Israel out of Egypt, to Jesus' flight to Egypt as an infant. Matthew presented Jesus as a new or ideal Israel, whose experience in early life is patterned after that of the nation Israel. According to Matthew 2:17-18, Herod's slaughter of the innocent children of Bethlehem fulfilled Jeremiah 31:15, which in its context describes the mothers of Ramah (not Bethlehem) weeping as their children were carried off into exile. Herod's action fulfilled Jeremiah 31:15 in that the event described by Jeremiah establishes a pattern to which Herod's oppressive deeds correspond in their character.

The immediate fulfillment of the Immanuel prophecy is described in chapter 8. Isaiah made careful preparations for the birth of a sign-child. He and "the prophetess"

A bronze relief from Balawat on which is depicted the victory in 848 B.C. of Shalmaneser III over the people of Hamath. Captives are shown being led away by warriors.

Assyria

The Assyrian heartland was a triangular-shaped region whose west side ran along the Tigris River from Nineveh south about one hundred miles to the traditional capital at Asshur. The third point of the triangle was at Arbela about fifty miles east of the Tigris. Assyria's history is commonly divided into three periods: the Old Assyrian (about 2000–1363 B.C.), the Middle Assyrian (about 1363–1000 B.C.), and the Neo-Assyrian (about 1000–612 B.C.).

Old Assyrian Period

Shamshi-Adad I (about 1815–1782 B.C.) united the Assyrian city-states into the first Assyrian kingdom. It stretched from the Zagros mountains in the east to the Euphrates River in the west.

Middle Assyrian Period

After a period of weakness, the Assyrian kingdom reemerged under Ashur-uballit I (about

(presumably his wife) then had a child, who was named Maher-Shalal-Hash-Baz. Though the child was not named Immanuel, the special significance attached to his name and growth pattern parallels the Immanuel prophecy. Maher-Shalal-Hash-Baz' name, which means *quick to plunder, swift to the spoil*, pointed to the destruction of Judah's enemies. Before he could cry out "daddy" or "mommy," Assyria would plunder both the Arameans and the Northern Kingdom (8:4; compare 7:14-16). But the prophecy has its negative side as well. Because of Judah's unbelief, the Assyrians would also invade the Southern Kingdom and, like a flood, bring widespread destruction (8:5-8; compare 7:17-25). This message of judgment concludes with an address to Immanuel, as if

1363–1328 B.C.). They developed their famous military skill and during this period also plundered Babylon. The Assyrians began assimilating Babylonian culture, introducing the worship of its god Marduk and its rich religious literature.

Neo-Assyrian Period

Having been weakened by the Arameans, Assyria rose again in the tenth century. They were "the most successful imperial power the world had ever seen." Ashurnasirpal II (883–859 B.C.) began notoriously savage annual military campaigns. He extended Assyria's effective control as far as Tyre on the Mediterranean coast. He boasted of his cruelty:

> I stormed the mountain peaks and took them. In the midst of the mighty mountain I slaughtered them. With their blood I dyed the mountain red like wool. With the rest of them I darkened the gullies and precipices of the mountains. I carried off their possessions. The heads of their warriors I cut off, and I formed them into a pillar over against their city. Their young men and their maidens I burned in the fire.

It was surely such a policy of "calculated frightfulness" that encouraged Israel and Judah to form alliances with the Arameans (Ben-Hadad of Damascus) and Phoenicians (Ahab's marriage to Jezebel of Sidon). Ashurnasirpal II rebuilt Calah between Nineveh and Asshur as his new capital. His was one of the most beautiful palaces of antiquity, decorated with reliefs of his victories.

On a military expedition into Syria in 853 B.C., Shalmaneser III (858–824) met a coalition of Syrian and Palestinian kings (including Ahab of Israel and Ben-Hadad of Damascus) at Qarqar. Whether he gained a clear victory is uncertain (the battle is not mentioned in the Bible); but he returned in 841 to besiege Damascus and exact tribute from Jehu, the new king of Israel.

There followed another period of relative weakness in Assyria, during which Damascus continually harassed Israel and Judah. Adadnirari III (810–783 B.C.) brought a period of relief to Israel (2 Kgs 13:5) by an expedition against Damascus in 805. Assyria's weakness (the time of Jonah's ministry, 2 Kgs 14:25) was greatest during the expansion of Jeroboam II of Israel (793–753) and Uzziah of Judah (792–740).

Tiglath-Pileser III (also named Pulu, 745–727 B.C.) reestablished Assyrian power and, with a newly formed standing army, began wars of conquest rather than simply plunder. In 743 he began a series of campaigns into Syria and Palestine. Annexing the Aramean kingdoms as Assyrian provinces, He exacted tribute from Israel and Judah (2 Kgs 15–16).

For the rebellion of the puppet king Hoshea of Israel, Shalmaneser V (727–722 B.C.) conquered Samaria in 722 after a three-year siege and deported its inhabitants (2 Kgs 17). In 712 early in Hezekiah's reign (715–687), Judah revolted (Isa 20:1). Sargon (712–705) responded with a show of Assyrian power. A later revolt, supported by the Egyptians (2 Kgs 18–19; Isa 30:1-5; 31:1-3; 37:6-37), caused Sennacherib (704–681) to send an army in 701 that defeated Egypt, captured forty-six cities of Judah, and besieged (but did not capture) Jerusalem.

Esarhaddon (680–669 B.C.) and his son Ashurbanipal (668–627) managed to extend the Assyrian empire into Egypt (compare Nah 3:8-10) but were constantly involved in defensive fighting on all sides. Ashurbanipal seems to have largely expended Assyrian resources in quelling a rebellion of Babylon, Elam, and others (652–639). This resulted in a final waning of Assyrian strength enabling Josiah (641–609) to bring temporary reform and restoration to Judah.

Asshur, the patron city, was lost to the Medes in 614 B.C. Nineveh, the capital, fell (compare Nah 2:8–3:7, probably by flooding [Nah 1:8]) to the Medes, Babylonians, and Scythians in 612. Josiah of Judah attempted in 608 to obstruct the Egyptian army at Megiddo from aiding the Assyrians in their fight against the Babylonians (2 Kgs 23:29). Josiah failed and was killed. But Babylonian forces under prince Nebuchadnezzar pursued and finally defeated the Assyrian armies at Carchemish in 605.

"O king of Assyria, your shepherds slumber; your nobles lie down to rest. / Your people are scattered on the mountains with no one to gather them" (Nah 3:18). □

Isaiah compared the liberation of God's people to the loosening of a yoke and the lifting of a burden (Isa 9:4). In this Assyrian relief captives are shown yoked together and pulling a heavy load.

he were already living. This is best explained by understanding the preceding verses as describing his birth.

If indeed Maher-Shalal-Hash-Baz and Immanuel are one and the same, some explanation must be given for the different names. Perhaps the names emphasize different aspects of the same prophecy. Immanuel focuses on God's involvement in history, while Maher-Shalal-Hash-Baz, the child's actual name, anticipates the destructive effects of God's involvement. (In the same way Immanuel is applied to Jesus, emphasizing God's personal intervention in history through the incarnation. At the same time, the name Jesus, meaning *the Lord saves*, points to the purpose of God's act.)

Following the message of judgment upon Judah, the prophet, in a sudden burst of emotion, abruptly shifted his perspective. Challenging the nations to attack God's people, he announced that God's presence with His people assured their ultimate deliverance.

Before developing this theme in more detail (compare 9:1-7), Isaiah recorded instructions he received from the Lord. The Lord exhorted Isaiah to reject popular opinion and trust in Him. He promised to be a sanctuary for the faithful, but for faithless Israel and Judah He would be like a stumbling block or a snare. In response to the Lord's charge, Isaiah declared his trust in God. He also reminded his listeners that he and his children were God-given signs and encouraged them to look to God's revealed prophetic word, not pagan practices, for guidance.

The Messiah's Deliverance of God's People (9:1-7). Dark days were ahead for God's people, especially for the Northern Kingdom (compare 8:22–9:1). The Assyrians would invade Palestine from the north and humble Israel. Isaiah looked beyond this time of punishment and saw a bright deliverance. Eventually the Lord would save His people from their oppressors, just as He did in the days of Gideon, through whom He annihilated the oppressive Midianites (compare Judg 6–8).

The Lord would accomplish this future deliverance through the Messiah, who would rule on David's throne. The words "For to us a child is born, to us a son is given"

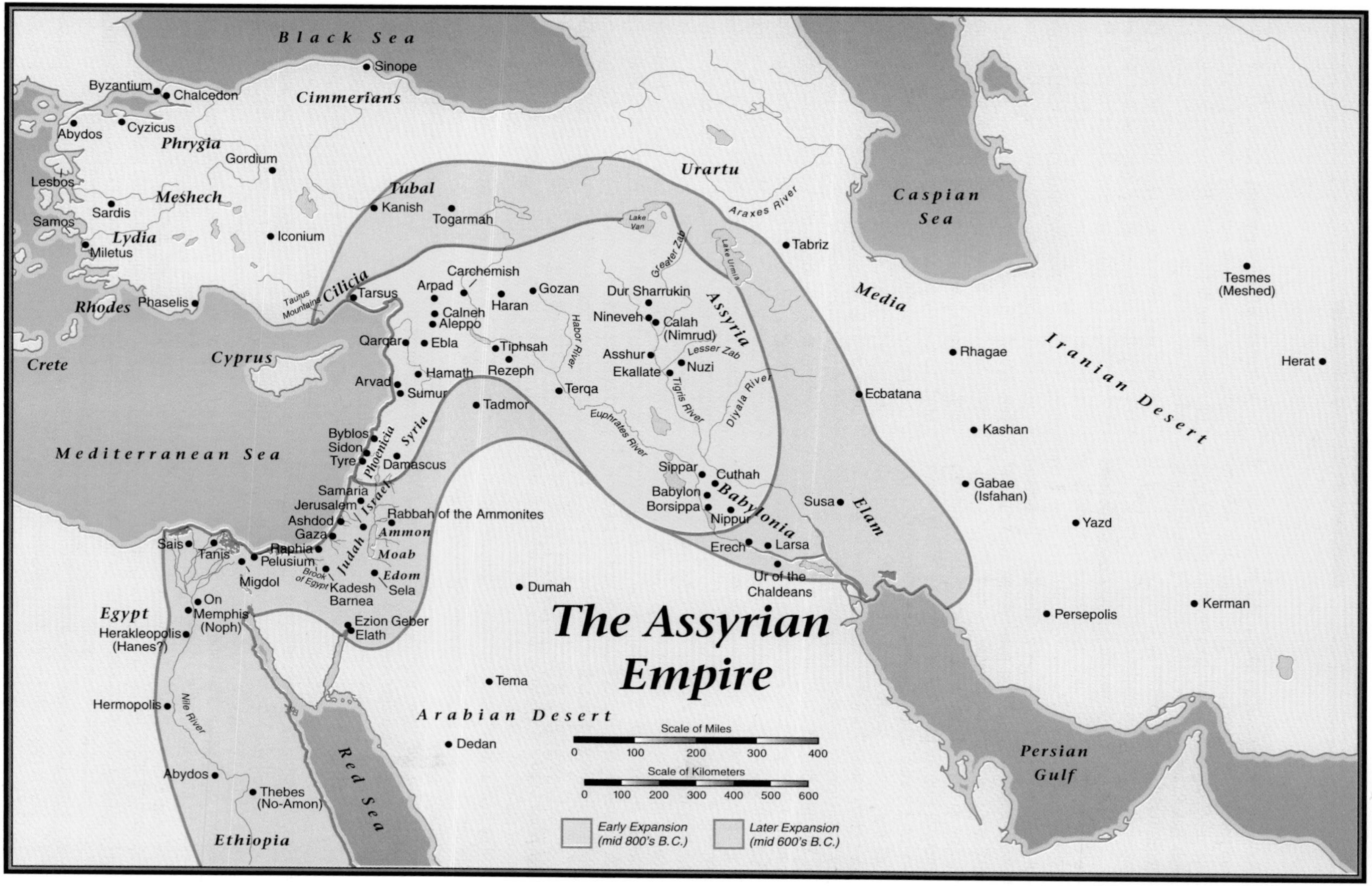

The Assyrian Empire
Black Sea
Caspian Sea
Mediterranean Sea
Red Sea
Persian Gulf
Arabian Desert
Iranian Desert
Cimmerians
Phrygia
Meshech
Lydia
Rhodes
Crete
Cyprus
Tubal
Cilicia
Taurus Mountains
Urartu
Media
Assyria
Babylonia
Elam
Syria
Phoenicia
Israel
Judah
Ammon
Moab
Edom
Egypt
Ethiopia
Sinope
Byzantium
Chalcedon
Abydos
Cyzicus
Gordium
Lesbos
Sardis
Samos
Miletus
Iconium
Phaselis
Kanish
Togarmah
Tarsus
Carchemish
Arpad
Calneh
Aleppo
Haran
Gozan
Qarqar
Ebla
Tiphsah
Rezeph
Hamath
Arvad
Sumur
Tadmor
Terqa
Habor River
Euphrates River
Lake Van
Lake Urmia
Greater Zab
Lesser Zab
Tigris River
Diyala River
Araxes River
Tabriz
Dur Sharrukin
Nineveh
Calah (Nimrud)
Asshur
Ekallate
Nuzi
Sippar
Cuthah
Babylon
Borsippa
Nippur
Erech
Larsa
Ur of the Chaldeans
Susa
Ecbatana
Rhagae
Kashan
Gabae (Isfahan)
Yazd
Persepolis
Kerman
Tesmes (Meshed)
Herat
Byblos
Sidon
Tyre
Damascus
Samaria
Jerusalem
Ashdod
Gaza
Raphia
Pelusium
Migdol
Brook of Egypt
Kadesh Barnea
Sela
Rabbah of the Ammonites
Ezion Geber
Elath
Dumah
Tema
Dedan
Sais
Tanis
On
Memphis (Noph)
Herakleopolis (Hanes?)
Hermopolis
Nile River
Abydos
Thebes (No-Amon)
Scale of Miles
0
100
200
300
400
Scale of Kilometers
0
100
200
300
400
500
600
Early Expansion (mid 800's B.C.)
Later Expansion (mid 600's B.C.)

(9:6) link this messianic prophecy with the prediction of Immanuel's birth (compare 7:14), suggesting that Immanuel/Maher-Shalal-Hash-Baz foreshadowed the Messiah. Isaiah's son was a reminder of God's sovereign presence; the Messiah would be a much more perfect expression of God's presence.

The Messiah's royal titles attest to his close relationship to God and depict him as a mighty warrior capable of establishing peace in his realm. Four titles are listed, each of which contains two elements. The first, "Wonderful Counselor," in this context portrays the Messiah as an extraordinary military strategist.

The second, "Mighty God," indicates that God would energize Him for battle so that He would display superhuman prowess against His enemies. (Some argue that this second title points to the divine nature of the Messiah. Others contend that the doctrine of the Messiah's deity is only clearly revealed in the NT.)

The third title, "Everlasting Father," pictures the Messiah as a beneficent Ruler who demonstrates fatherly concern for His people. In the eighth century B.C. "everlasting" probably would have been understood as royal hyperbole (compare the attribution of "eternal" life to the king in Pss 21:4; 61:6-7; 72:5 [compare NIV]). Of course, in the progress of revelation one discovers that Christ's eternal reign will literally fulfill the language of the prophecy. (The title "Father" must not be understood in Trinitarian terms. In this context it is best taken as an idiom, commonly used in the ancient world, for a benevolent and just official or ruler. For a biblical example of the idiom, see Isa 22:21.)

The fourth title, "Prince of Peace," indicates that the Messiah's kingdom will be characterized by social justice and prosperity.

Judgment of the Northern Kingdom (9:8–10:4). Having described the glory of Israel's future, Isaiah addressed the situation of his own times. The Northern Kingdom, despite experiencing God's increasingly severe discipline, refused to turn back to the Lord. Though suffering the ravages of foreign invasion and civil war, the Northern Kingdom proudly claimed to be the master of its own destiny and antagonized Judah, its neighbor to the south. The nation's corrupt leaders continued to enact unjust laws, depriving the poor of their rights. For such a nation divine judgment was inevitable. The punitive measures taken by God in the past would culminate in a "day of reckoning" (10:3), characterized by exile and slaughter. The words "Yet for all this, his anger is not turned away, his hand is still upraised," which appear as a refrain in this judgment speech (9:12,17,21), picture the relentless approach of this day.

Judgment of the Assyrians (10:5-34). With the appearance of this same refrain in 10:4 one expects a further description of Israel's judgment. But once again the prophet suddenly shifts his perspective by including the Assyrians within the scope of God's Judgment Day. God raised up the Assyrians as His instrument of judgment against Israel and Judah. Obsessed with delusions of grandeur and empire, the Assyrians arrogantly attributed their military success to their own strength and claimed sovereignty over God's chosen city, Jerusalem. From God's perspective this was as absurd as a tool attempting to wield the laborer who uses it or a weapon trying to brandish the warrior who employs it. In anger the Lord announced that He would annihilate Assyria in a single day. Though the mighty Assyrians were comparable to a forest filled with trees, the Lord, like a raging fire, would reduce them to an insignificant number. Like Egypt and Midian, past oppressors of God's people, the Assyrians would experience the harsh judgment of God. When they defiantly marched against Jerusalem, the Lord would cut them down to size, like a woodsman felling a tall tree. This prophecy was fulfilled in 701 B.C. when the Lord decimated Sennacherib's armies outside Jerusalem's walls (compare 37:36-37).

In conjunction with Assyria's demise, the Lord promised to restore the once numerous people of Israel, who had been reduced to a mere remnant by the oppressive Assyrians. In that day God's people would place their trust in Him and in the Messiah (compare "Mighty God," 10:21) rather than in foreign alliances.

The Messiah's Kingdom of Justice (11:1-10). Assyria's destiny was in direct contrast to that of the Davidic throne. The Lord would chop down the Assyrian empire, but He would cause a new ruler, the Messiah, to spring up from Jesse's family tree. Energized by the Lord's Spirit, this King would possess wisdom, executive ability, and loyalty to the Lord, all of which are necessary to rule in a just and effective manner. His legal decisions would be based on truth, not superficial appearances. He would defend the poor and suppress the wicked. His kingdom would be one of justice, equality, and peace, where the strong no longer prey upon the weak.

Restoration of God's Exiled People (11:11–12:6). In the messianic age God's people would also be restored to their former glory. Though exiled throughout the world, God would lead them back to the promised land in a grand new exodus. As in the days of Moses, God would miraculously eliminate all obstacles, prompting His people to once more declare, "The LORD is my strength and my song; he has become my salvation" (12:2; compare Exod 15:2). As in the first exodus, God's people would experience His abundant provision and blessing (compare 12:3 with Exod 15:22-27). Upon returning to the land, the once hostile Northern and Southern Kingdoms would reunite and, as in the days of the Davidic empire, bring their enemies into subjection. In contrast to Isaiah's day, when Israel "spurned the Holy One of Israel" (compare 1:4), the Holy One of Israel would be exalted among His people (12:6).

UNIVERSAL JUDGMENT AND THE ESTABLISHMENT OF GOD'S KINGDOM (ISA 13:1–39:8)

13:1–23:18
Judgment Speeches against Various Nations

Before the prophet's vision of universal peace (compare 2:2-4; 11:1-10) could become a reality, God had to subdue the rebellious nations of the world. Chapters 13–23 contain a series of judgment speeches against various nations of Isaiah's day and pave the way for the message of universal judgment in chapters 24–27. These judgment speeches serve as a reminder to God's people of His absolute sovereignty over all nations, including both their enemies and allies. God's people need not fear the surrounding nations or rely on their aid.

Judgment on Babylon and Assyria (13:1–14:27). Isaiah's first judgment oracle begins and ends with a universal focus (compare 13:2-16; 14:26-27). The speech is specifically directed against Babylon, with a brief message against the Assyrians appended in 14:24-25. Some understand the entire speech against the background of the Assyrian period because the Assyrians controlled Babylon during a large portion of Isaiah's ministry and devastated the city in 689 B.C. However, it is more likely that the Babylonian empire, which replaced Assyria as the Near East's leading power, is in view in 13:17–14:23. Isaiah 13:19 specifically associates the city with the Babylonians, and the "king of Babylon," mentioned in 14:4, is most naturally viewed as a Baylonian (compare 39:1). Furthermore, the Medes are named as the conqueror of the city (13:17).

In Isaiah's days the Babylonians struggling with the Assyrians for control of Mesopotamia, sought an alliance with Judah. But the prophet knew that the Babylonians would eventually become the enemies of his people and take them away into exile (compare 39:1-7). Here he proclaimed judgment against Judah's future oppressor.

The speech opens with a vivid picture of the Lord gathering His armies for war. This coming battle is set against the background of the universal judgment of the Lord's day, which is accompanied by cosmic disturbances and brings widespread terror and slaughter. The Lord would use the cruel Medes as His instrument of judgment and reduce Babylon to an uninhabited heap of ruins.

This prophecy appears to refer to the conquest of Babylon by Medo-Persian forces under Cyrus in 539 B.C. However, Cyrus's takeover of the city, which was relatively peaceful and even welcomed by many Babylonians, fails to satisfy fully the language of 13:17-22. Perhaps the description is a standardized and exaggerated way of emphasizing that the Babylonian empire would be terminated. But the universal and eschatological setting of this speech suggests that a final judgment of Gentile powers, which the downfall of historical Babylon only symbolized and foreshadowed, is also in view (compare Rev 17–18). Since Babylon was a center of Mesopotamian religion and was associated in biblical tradition with rebellion against God (compare Gen 11:1-9), it became an apt symbol of the nations' opposition to God.

The destruction of Babylon would mean deliverance for Israel. In chapter 14 God's people, released from bondage and restored to their land, sang a taunt song against the fallen king of Babylon. They depicted him as descending into the world of the dead, where other deceased kings rose to meet him. These kings ridiculed him, declaring that this once proud world conqueror had been cast down into a bed of worms and maggots. Drawing on their own mythological traditions, these pagan rulers compared the king of Babylon to the petty god "Morning Star, Son of the Dawn," who had had the audacity to think he could ascend the mountain of the gods and rival the high god El's authority. (In 13:13 "God" translates Hebrew *el,* the name of the chief god of the many Canaanite gods. "The sacred mountain" translates Hebrew *sapon,* the name of the Canaanite Olympus, where the gods, here called "stars," assembled.)

It comes as no surprise that words of judgment against Assyria are appended to the oracle against Babylon. Assyria and Babylon were closely associated geographically and in biblical tradition, which attributes the founding of both to Nimrod (compare Gen 10:8-12). As an oppressive Mesopotamian power that ruled Babylon in Isaiah's day, Assyria's decisive judgment foreshadowed that of the coming Babylonian empire and all the hostile nations of the world.

Judgment on the Philistines (14:28-32). God's judgment would also fall upon the Philistines. The oracle, which is dated to the year of King Ahaz's death (about 715 B.C.) warns that the Philistines should not rejoice over the apparent relief from Assyrian oppression that they had recently experienced. Though the Assyrians' attention might be diverted to other trouble spots in their empire, they would again invade the west and bring the rebellious Philistines into subjection. In 712 B.C. Sargon captured the Philistine city of Ashdod (compare 20:1) and made it an Assyrian province. In 701 B.C. Sennacherib conquered Ashkelon and Ekron. In contrast to these Philistine cities, Jerusalem experienced God's supernatural protection.

Judgment on Moab (15:1–16:14). This oracle against Moab is undated, and therefore the time of its fulfillment is uncertain. Like the preceding and following oracles, it probably anticipates one of the Assyrian invasions of the late eighth century B.C. Geographical details and vivid imagery highlight the oracle. In virtually every city the once proud Moabites would lament over their military defeat and its disastrous effects on their land (15:1-9; 16:6-13). With dramatic flair Isaiah urged the Moabite fugitives to look to Jerusalem for aid (16:1-2). He then recited Moab's appeal for help, which includes a statement recognizing that only an ideal Davidic ruler could provide relief from the oppressor (16:3-5).

Judgment on Damascus and Israel (17:1-14). Though directed against Damascus, the capital of Aram (Syria), this judgment speech deals primarily with its ally, the Northern Kingdom. The oracle was fulfilled between 732 and 721 B.C. when the Assyrians conquered both Aram and Israel and made them provinces. Isaiah warned that Damascus would be reduced to a heap of ruins and lose its power. The prestige of the Northern Kingdom would be diminished, like a man who loses weight during a serious illness. Isaiah compared the coming devastation to a harvest, when the grain is stripped from the fields and the olives are beaten and shaken from the trees. Instead of trusting in God's protection, Israel placed its hope in foreign gods and alliances (compare "imported vines," v. 10), which would prove worthless in the day of calamity. At that time people would recognize the futility of idolatry because God is absolutely sovereign.

Isaiah concluded this oracle with a message of hope for Jerusalem. Though the Assyrian hordes would come sweeping down on Paiestine like raging waters, the Lord would only allow them to go so far. When they threatened Jerusalem, He would suddenly sweep them away like chaff or tumbleweed before a powerful wind (compare 10:28-43; 14:25; 37:36-37).

Judgment on Cush (18:1-7). This oracle pertains to Cush (Ethiopia), located south of Egypt. Possibly it alludes to Cushite efforts to enlist Judah's support in an anti-Assyrian alliance. The Lord would not support the Ethiopian effort, causing it to come to ruin, like unfruitful branches that are pruned. Eventually the Cushites would bring gifts of homage to Jerusalem in recognition of the Lord's sovereignty.

Judgment on Egypt (19:1-25). Because the Ethiopians controlled Egypt during Isaiah's time, this oracle is closely related to the preceding one. In the late eighth century B.C. Judah was tempted to ally itself with Ethiopia/Egypt against the Assyrians. Such an alliance was ill-advised, for the Lord was about to bring judgment upon the Egyptians. Following a period of civil strife and turmoil, a foreign ruler would conquer Egypt. This prophecy was fulfilled in the seventh century B.C., when the Assyrian kings Esarhaddon and Ashurbanipal conquered Egypt. Egypt's demise would be accompanied by economic disaster caused by the drying up of the Nile and by a complete breakdown in leadership.

Isaiah foresaw a time when Egypt would recognize the Lord's sovereignty, submit to His rule, look to Him for help, and worship Him. In that day peace would sweep over the war-torn Near East. The rivals, Assyria and Egypt, who oppressed God's people, would join Israel in the worship of the one true God.

Judgment of Egypt and Cush (20:1-6). This brief oracle is a fitting conclusion to the judgment message of the two preceding speeches. The oracle is dated to the year of the Assyrian conquest of rebellious Ashdod (712 B.C.). This event demonstrated the helplessness of Egypt, which had encouraged Ashdod's rebellion but then offered it no assistance against the Assyrians. The message spoken in 712 is found in 20:3-6, while 20:2 records the Lord's words to the prophet three years before. During this three-year period the prophet had walked around indecently exposed as an object lesson on Egypt's and Cush's fate. In the near future the Assyrians would conquer Egypt and carry off exiles, who would be taken away stripped and barefoot. The purpose of the prophet's action and the subsequent oracle is obvious. To trust in Egypt/Cush was foolish, for it would lead only to ruin and shame.

Judgment on Babylon (21:1-10). Babylon (compare 21:9), poetically called "the Desert by the Sea," again takes center stage in Isaiah's vision of judgment (compare 13:1–14:23). The prophet's vision of Babylon's defeat at the hands of the Elamites and Medes had an intense physical and emotional effect upon him. In dramatic fashion he urged the unsuspecting Babylonians to get up from their feasts and prepare for battle (compare Dan 5). The drama continues as imaginary messengers are depicted announcing the news of Babylon's defeat to eagerly awaiting watchmen. In conclusion Isaiah assured his audience, a future generation who would experience Babylon's oppression, that his message was authentic. The fulfillment of the prophecy came in 539 B.C. when

The oracle in Isaiah 20:1-6 is dated by Isaiah to the year that Sargon conquered Ashdod. Pictured above is a relief from Dur Sharrukin (modern Khorsabad) showing an Assyrian general standing before Sargon II.

Cyrus, whose army contained Medes and Elamites, conquered Babylon (compare comments on 13:1–14:23).

Judgment on Dumah (21:11-12). This very brief, riddlelike oracle, concerns Dumah, an oasis in Arabia. Assuming the role of an imaginary watchman, the prophet was asked by an unidentified speaker from Seir (Edom) how long the night would last. Because of its geographical proximity to Dumah, Edom would have taken a keen interest in developments there. The watchman responded that morning was indeed coming, only to be followed again by night. Apparently the night is here a symbol of distress. The prophet was unable to encourage oppressed Dumah. Even though some relief might come, the future remained foreboding.

Judgment on Arabia (21:13-17). In a related oracle the prophet foresaw the defeat of other Arabian peoples. He dramatically described the plight of fugitives from battle. He then officially announced that Kedar in the Arabian desert would fall within one year. This prophecy was probably fulfilled in conjunction with one of Sargon's or Sennacherib's Arabian campaigns.

Judgment on Jerusalem (22:1-25). Chapter 22 concerns Judah and Jerusalem. It contains two judgment speeches, an oracle against the "Valley of Vision" (22:1-14) and a message addressed to the royal official Shebna (22:15-25). The location of the "Valley of Vision" is unknown, though it is clearly associated with Judah and Jerusalem (22:8-14). The historical background of the oracle is uncertain. It may reflect one of the Assyrian invasions of the late eighth century B.C. (either Sargon's in 712 B.C. or Sennacherib's a decade later).

The Lord denounced the people for their improper response to the crisis. Instead of trusting in the One who founded the City of David, they relied on their own efforts, which included fortifying the city walls and building a new water system. Refusing the Lord's call to repentance, they feasted and fatalistically abandoned any hope of deliverance, implying that the Lord was not in control of the city's destiny. For such people judgment was inevitable. While Hezekiah's repentance (Isa 37–38; Jer 26:17-19) and God's decision to demonstrate His sovereignty over the proud Assyrians (10:5-34) postponed Jerusalem's downfall, divine judgment eventually fell upon the city.

The people's lack of devotion to the Lord was epitomized by Shebna, a royal official who displayed inordinate pride by building himself a grand tomb. The Lord announced that Shebna would die in a foreign land and never occupy his specially built tomb. Eliakim would replace him as the royal steward. He would assume responsibility for the nation's care and exercise authority on behalf of the king. For a time his position would be firm and his family honored. However, in due time Eliakim, like all mere human officials, would lose his authority. By the time Sennacherib besieged Jerusalem in 701 B.C., Eliakim had replaced Shebna as steward, and Shebna had apparently been demoted to a scribal office (compare 36:3,11,22; 37:2). Beyond this we have no record of the outworking of these prophecies.

Judgment on Tyre (23:1-18). Isaiah's oracles against the nations conclude with this judgment speech against Tyre, a prominent commercial center on the Mediterranean coast north of Israel. Tyre's many trading partners were told to mourn, for the Lord was about to bring the proud city low. Tyre should not consider it safe, for even the greatest of cities, such as Babylon, could be conquered (23:13 refers to the Assyrian devastation of Babylon in 689 B.C.). Tyre would experience a seventy-year period of decline. This number may be figurative, suggesting completeness and implying that few, if any, of those who saw its decline would live to view its resurgence. Eventually the city would be restored to its former status, but in that day its wealth would be sent as tribute to the Lord.

The precise details of the prophecy's fulfillment are uncertain. Assyria brought Tyre under its control, leading to an eclipse of the latter's prominence. Later both Nebuchadnezzar (in the sixth century B.C.) and Alexander the Great (in the fourth century B.C.) conquered the city.

24:1–27:13 Worldwide Judgment and the Restoration of Jerusalem

Isaiah's message of judgment against individual nations culminates in this section. It describes God's judgment on a universal scale and the establishment of His worldwide rule, using language akin to apocalyptic.

God Judges the Earth for Its Rebellion (24:1-23). The Lord would completely destroy the earth for its rebellion against "the everlasting covenant," probably a reference to God's mandate to Noah (compare Gen 9:1-7). Instead of showing respect for God's image in other human beings, the inhabitants of the earth had shed innocent blood (compare 26:21). In the ancient Near Eastern world curses (threatened forms of punishment often involving loss of fertility and death) were attached to formal agreements. Verses 6-13 describe such a curse sweeping over the sinful earth. While the prophet heard the future praise God's just judgment would elicit from His followers, he expressed his chagrin over the present injustice. This prompted him to once more describe the coming worldwide judgment as inescapable and severe as Noah's flood (compare 24:18b with Gen 7:11). In that day the Lord would defeat all heavenly and earthly opposition and establish His rule from Jerusalem.

God's People Celebrate His Kingship (25:1–26:6). Chapter 25 begins with a song of praise spoken by the future generation of God's people who would witness His worldwide judgment and experience His deliverance. They celebrated His conquest of the hostile nations and declared that He had been their faithful protector.

In that day the Lord would host a marvelous feast at Jerusalem in celebration of His kingship. He would eliminate the curse of death from humankind once and for all and remove the disgrace of His covenant people. The imagery of God swallowing up death is powerful irony, in that death was viewed in the Bible (compare 5:14) and in pagan mythology as the great swallower of humankind. In contrast to Jerusalem's glorious future, the proud cities and peoples of the Gentile world, epitomized here by Moab, would be humiliated.

This section closes with another song of praise, in which a future generation of Judeans affirm their trust in the God of Jerusalem, who protects those who place their faith in Him and humiliates the proud oppressor.

God's People Anticipate His Intervention (26:7-19). These verses date to a time prior to the announced judgment and deliverance of the preceding chapters. God's faithful people lamented the wickedness around them, expressed their confidence in and devotion to God, and asked for His intervention. In response God assured them that He would restore the nation, using the figure of bodily resurrection to emphasize the miraculous revival His people would experience (compare Ezek 37:1-14).

The Restoration of God's People (26:20–27:13). The prophet urged the faithful to hide behind closed doors until the judgment of God passed. The Lord would punish the sinful world for its bloody deeds and subdue those who resist His kingship. These forces are symbolized by the sea monster Leviathan, which in Canaanite myth resisted the kingship of the storm god Baal. Following God's victory over His foes, He would make Israel His "fruitful vineyard" and guard it with unceasing attention (contrast the vineyard image in 5:1-7).

Returned briefly to the present, Isaiah reminded his audience that purifying judgment lay ahead for God's people. Because of their idolatry and lack of spiritual understanding, they would endure warfare and exile and even witness the desolation of Jerusalem. Nevertheless, a day would come when the exiled people would return and worship the Lord in purified Jerusalem.

28:1–35:10
Judgment and Hope for Judah

Much of this section, which contains several woe-oracles (compare 28:1; 29:1,15; 30:1; 31:1; 33:1), is accusatory and threatening, but these chapters also contain words of hope. Though the Northern Kingdom and the Gentile nations were included as objects of divine judgment, the focal point was Judah. Rebellious Judah had to reject the example of the Northern Kingdom and resist the temptation to rely upon foreign alliances. Instead the nations must trust in God alone as the One who is sovereign over the destiny of His people and of the surrounding nations.

Samaria's Impending Downfall a Warning to Self-confident Judah (28:1-29). The chapter opens with a woe-oracle against Samaria, the capital city in which the carousing upper classes of the Northern Kingdom took great pride. However, the Lord would send the Assyrians against it like a destructive storm. Samaria would disappear as quickly as a sweet early fig that one grabs with delight and quickly devours (compare Hos 9:10; Mic 7:1). Eventually judgment would bring God's people to their senses, and they would take pride in Him, not in structures they had made.

Verses 7-13 either continue the description of Samaria's carousers or depict the people of Judah. In either case the religious leaders are portrayed as staggering, vomiting drunkards and the people as sarcastic mockers of the prophet's message. Since they rejected the Lord's offer of true peace, conditioned upon righteous living, He would send against them the Assyrians, whose foreign speech would serve as His mocking response to their jeering mimicry of the prophet.

The remainder of the message is addressed to the leaders of Jerusalem, who boastfully claimed they were safe from harm because they had made a covenant with death (probably an allusion to a foreign alliance in which they were placing their trust). However, the Lord, the only true Protector of the nation and the sovereign Ruler of all things, including death, would bring judgment upon them. He would attack His own people, like He did the Philistines at Mount Perazim (compare 2 Sam 5:20-21) and the Amorites at Gibeon (compare Josh 10:10-11).

Just as a farmer plows, plants, and harvests at the appropriate times and uses the proper methods for each activity, so the Lord would deal with His people in a wise and appropriate manner. While judgment was necessary, the Lord would not allow it to be excessive.

Warning Spiritually Insensitive Ariel (29:1-24). The Lord warned that He would bring a military crisis upon complacent Jerusalem, called here Ariel (the meaning and contextual significance of this name are uncertain). The people were characterized by spiritual insensitivity, religious hypocrisy, and an unwillingness to trust their destiny to God. The coming crisis would be severe, but God would suddenly rescue the city from the armies outside its walls. This prophecy anticipated the miraculous deliverance of Jerusalem in 701 B.C. Eventually God would restore spiritual awareness, justice, and covenantal loyalty to the land.

Warnings against Foreign Alliances (30:1–31:9). The Lord denounced Judah for seeking an alliance with Egypt. Instead of consulting the Lord, the people rejected the prophetic word and sought help from a nation that was incapable of following through on its promises. The Lord warned Judah that continued obstinacy would lead to defeat and humiliation. He reminded them that deliverance could only come through repentance and faith. If they cried out to Him, He would graciously and compassionately give them renewed spiritual direction and restore agricultural prosperity to the land. He would appear in glorious splendor and destroy the Assyrians, causing His people to rejoice over the demise of their enemies.

Chapter 31 begins with another denunciation of the alliance with Egypt. Though the Egyptians had many horses and chariots, their military might could not prevent their defeat at the hands of the sovereign God. Judah had to repent and trust in the Lord, for He, not Egypt, was the true Protector of Jerusalem. He would miraculously destroy the Assyrians, demonstrating again His sovereignty over mere human armies.

Justice and Peace Reestablished in Judah and Jerusalem (32:1–33:24). In another of his messianic visions Isaiah anticipated a day when a just king would reign over the land, assisted by competent rulers who would protect, rather than exploit, the people. The spiritual dullness of Isaiah's generation, which resulted in the exaltation of foolish, unjust leaders, would disappear.

Of course, prospects for the immediate future were not as bright. Urging the nation's complacent women to lament, Isaiah warned that the land's agricultural prosperity would soon be swept away and its cities abandoned. Perhaps he proclaimed this message just prior to Sennacherib's invasion of the land in 701 B.C. However, in

The relief above from the palace of Ramses II at Thebes (1200s B.C.) shows Egyptian chariots as they move into battle. See Isaiah 31:1.

another of his abrupt shifts in perspective, Isaiah promised that restoration would eventually follow judgment. The Lord would again pour His life-giving Spirit upon the land and restore its crops. Justice and genuine security would then return to the land.

Chapter 33 begins with a brief woe-oracle against the "destroyer" and "traitor" (probably a reference to Assyria), whose deeds would one day be punished appropriately.

A model prayer follows, in which the people asked for the Lord's gracious intervention and expressed confidence in His ability to defeat the nations. They praised Him as the sovereign King who would reestablish Jerusalem as a center of justice. In support of their request, they lamented the devastating effects of the enemy invasion. In response to their prayer, the Lord announced He would be exalted over His enemies, whose plans would be self-destructive.

Unfortunately, not everyone in Jerusalem was as godly as those who spoke in 33:2-9. The Lord made it clear to the sinners in the city that only those who promoted justice and order would experience His protection and blessing. The righteous could look forward to a grand new era for Jerusalem. The arrogant, terrifying foreign armies would disappear from outside the city's walls. Jerusalem would again be the religious center of the land, experiencing security and prosperity under its divine King's just rule. A forgiving God would eliminate sin and its effects from the city.

Judgment of the Nations Brings Restoration of God's People (34:1–35:10). The theme of God's sovereignty over the hostile nations (compare 29:5-8; 30:27-33; 31:4-9; 33:1,18-19) culminates in chapter 34 with a vivid description of universal judgment. The Lord would unleash His anger upon the nations, resulting in widespread carnage and bloodshed. Even the heavens would not escape. The stars, perhaps symbolizing heavenly opposition to God (compare 24:21), are pictured as rotting and falling like a leaf or fig to the ground.

The Lord singled out Edom as a representative of the nations (compare 63:1-6; Obad). The prophet compared the bloody slaughter of Edom to a large sacrifice where sheep and cattle are butchered in great numbers. This day of vengeance and retribution on behalf of Jerusalem would reduce Edom to a state of perpetual desolation. By divine decree its weed-covered ruins would be populated only by desert creatures such as owls and hyenas.

In contrast to Edom, God's weakened, discouraged

people would be rejuvenated by His mighty deeds on their behalf. This renewal is compared to the miraculous healing of various physical disabilities and to the blossoming of a hot, dry desert. Where once there was only sand and desert creatures, there would now be flowers, green pastures, abundant water, and thick vegetation. Through this garden land would run a highway, upon which no wicked men or dangerous wild beasts would be allowed to go. The Lord's redeemed people would follow this "Way of Holiness" to Jerusalem, entering its gates with joy. The delightful imagery depicts in a striking way the divine blessings and renewed access to God's presence that would follow the future purification and restoration of His people.

36:1–39:8 Significant Events During the Reign of Hezekiah

These chapters, which repeat 2 Kings 18–20 in many respects, record three significant events of Hezekiah's reign: (1) the Lord's miraculous deliverance of Jerusalem and destruction of the Assyrians, (2) Hezekiah's recovery from a serious illness, and (3) Hezekiah's unwise dealings with the messengers from Babylon. Isaiah played a prominent role in these events, each of which prompted at least one prophetic oracle.

The chapters are not in chronological order. The Assyrian deliverance (chaps. 36–37) followed the events recorded in chapters 38–39. Perhaps chapter 39 comes last because its reference to Babylon provides a frame for chapters 13–39 (compare chap. 13, which also focuses on Babylon). Also, by showing that even godly Hezekiah had his faults and ultimately could not prevent Judah's downfall, it paves the way for chapters 40–66, the setting of which is the Babylonian captivity.

The Lord Delivers Jerusalem from the Assyrians (36:1–37:38). In 701 B.C. the mighty Assyrian army overran the countryside of Judah and, according to Assyrian records, conquered forty-six cities. The Assyrian king Sennacherib sent his field commander to Jerusalem with a message for Hezekiah. With many of the people looking on from the city's walls, the field commander pointed out that Jerusalem's reliance upon its military strategies and its alliance with Egypt was misplaced. He even argued that the Lord would not deliver the city. He erroneously reasoned that Hezekiah's centralization of worship was an affront to the Lord. He claimed that the Assyrians had been commissioned by the Lord to invade Judah.

Troubled by the field commander's use of Hebrew, the language of the people, Hezekiah's officials asked him to use Aramaic, the diplomatic language of the day. He

The wilderness of En Gedi shown above is a good example of the description in Isaiah 35:1 of the blossoming of a redeemed land.

refused, pointing out that the siege would adversely affect all of Jerusalem's citizens. The field commander then urged the people of Jerusalem to reject Hezekiah's appeal to trust in the Lord. He exhorted them to surrender the city, promising them future peace and prosperity (albeit in a new land!). He concluded his speech with an arrogant claim that the Lord could not deliver the city. Jerusalem was no different than other cities, whose gods had been unable to rescue their people from the Assyrians. The people, in obedience to Hezekiah's decree, did not reply to the field commander.

Having torn their clothes in consternation and mourning, Hezekiah's officials reported the message to the king. Hezekiah tore his clothes, went to the temple, and asked Isaiah to pray on behalf of the city. Isaiah sent a salvation oracle back to the king, urging him not to fear, for the Lord was about to punish the Assyrian king for his blasphemy. An alarming report would cause him to return to his own land, where he would be slain by the sword.

Meanwhile the field commander rejoined the Assyrian army, which was now marching to meet an Egyptian army led by Tirhakah. (Though only a prince in 701 B.C., Tirhakah is here called "king of Egypt" in anticipation of his rise to the throne a decade later. Isaiah may have even written or incorporated this account into his prophecy after Tirhakah became king.) Concerned that Hezekiah might derive false hope from this action, Sennacherib sent another message to Hezekiah, assuring him that he still intended to conquer Jerusalem. Once again he emphasized that Hezekiah's God, like the gods of the many lands conquered by the Assyrians, would not be able to deliver the city from his hands.

Upon receiving this letter, Hezekiah went to the temple again, spread the letter out before the Lord, and poured out his heart in prayer. Hezekiah acknowledged that the Lord was the sovereign Ruler of the universe and infinitely superior to the man-made gods of the nations previously defeated by the Assyrians. He asked the Lord to deliver Jerusalem so that the whole earth might recognize His sovereign power.

Through the prophet Isaiah the Lord responded positively to Hezekiah's request. The first part of His response came in the form of a taunt song against Sennacherib. The Lord castigated the Assyrian ruler for his pride, reminded him that his successes were by the Lord's decree, and then announced that He would force the Assyrians back to their own land. In the second part of the message the Lord assured Hezekiah that He would preserve Jerusalem for His own glory and because of His promise to the Davidic dynasty.

The final verses of the chapter record the fulfillment of God's promise. The angel of the Lord struck down the Assyrian hordes in one night, forcing Sennacherib to return home, where two decades later he was assassinated by two of his own sons.

Hezekiah's Life-Threatening Illness (38:1-22). The event recorded in chapter 38 probably occurred the year before Sennacherib's invasion. When Hezekiah became seriously ill, Isaiah announced to him that he would die. Reminding the Lord of his faithful deeds, the king pled for his life. The Lord decided to give Hezekiah fifteen more years of life and also promised He would protect Jerusalem from the Assyrians. In response to Hezekiah's request for a confirming sign, the Lord refracted the sun's rays so that the shadow they cast was

Shown above is a bronze statue (partially gilded) of Tirhakah presenting an offering to the god Hemen of Upper Egypt, who is represented here as a bird. See Isaiah 37:9.

Messianic Prophecies

Messianic prophecies are OT passages that refer to a future anointed King who will bring salvation to Israel. Passages may be regarded as messianic prophecies from two different perspectives.

1. From the perspective of the Christian church, many passages qualify as messianic from Genesis 3:15 to Malachi 4:5-6. From this viewpoint one listing numbers 124 passages, each with a specific NT fulfillment. This method of identifying messianic prophecies begins with NT citations or references connecting the ministry and/or meaning of Jesus' life with the OT.

The method allowed the earliest Christians to witness to Jews by using their Scriptures to prove that Jesus was the goal toward which the Scriptures pointed. It also helped Christians learn more about Jesus and understand His work of salvation. From this point of view the original meaning of the OT passages is not as important as is the contemporary meaning of the passage for the church. The Jews of Jesus' day used a similar method of interpretation to gain the fullest meaning and application of Scripture.

2. From a historical point of view only a limited number of passages qualify as messianic prophecies. To qualify a passage must represent its original author's reference to a future King of salvation. This method begins with the OT historical setting and selects passages that point to the future, refer to an anointed King, and describe salvation of God's people. This method would speak of incomplete fulfillments in the lives of specific Jewish kings such as Hezekiah, major fulfillment in the earthly ministry of Jesus Christ, and final fulfillment in the second coming. Major passages in view here are 2 Samuel 7; 1 Chronicles 17; Psalms 2; 72; 89; 110; 132; Isaiah 2:2-5; 9:1-7; 11:1-10.

This point of view originates with modern understandings of history and with more recent methods of interpreting ancient literature. It seeks to understand ancient Israel's self-understanding at various points in its history. It asks such questions as: When did Israel begin looking for God to send a new deliverer? What did Israel expect this new kind of deliverer to be and to do? How did various changes in Israel's historical understanding affect the understanding of and expectation of a messianic deliverer?

It asks: In what ways did Jesus of Nazareth fulfill the expectations of Israel? Should the average Israelite in Jesus' day have been able to see that Jesus was the expected Messiah? Did Jesus provide a deeper or different interpretation of Messiah than Israel had known until His day? Whose methods of biblical interpretation did the inspired NT writers use as they interpreted Jesus in light of the OT? How can the church today legitimately interpret the OT Scriptures in light of the fulfillment we see in the person of Jesus?

The two points of view thus start with different emphases, different types of questions, and different methods of interpretation. Ultimately they end with the same question: How does the OT help us to understand the life, ministry, and saving work of our Savior, Jesus the Messiah.

Both viewpoints see Jesus as the fulfillment of the religion and hope of the OT. The first viewpoint may find more individual texts pointing to Jesus. The second viewpoint may deem application of some passages to Jesus to be the result of the history of interpretation rather than the meaning of the original author.

Both viewpoints affirm that NT writers effectively used the OT to witness to Jesus of Nazareth as Messiah of Israel and Savior of the world. In so doing they see that an original viewpoint was of an earthly king ruling on the throne of his forefather David and restoring political power to the nation Israel. This historical viewpoint developed within Israel's history. This view culminates in the ministry of Jesus the Messiah and Suffering Servant, dying on a cross and being resurrected to ascend to a heavenly throne at the Father's right hand. There He rules not just Israel but the entire universe. This rule will become clear to all nations and people when Jesus returns in the second coming to establish His kingship on earth as well as in heaven. □

reversed. (Verses 21-22 are misplaced and belong between 38:6-7. Compare 2 Kgs 20:6-9.) Ironically, this sign took place at the "stairway of Ahaz," a structure named for the king who, in contrast to his son, had rejected the Lord's promise of deliverance by refusing to ask for a sign (compare 7:10-17).

In response to the Lord's merciful deliverance, Hezekiah offered a song of thanksgiving, in which he recalled his time of need, acknowledged the Lord's intervention, and promised to praise Him all his days.

This account has a twofold purpose. First, Hezekiah serves as an example to God's people of dependence on the Lord in the midst of a crisis. Second, Hezekiah's recovery was representative of the nation's future. Just as the Lord healed Hezekiah and granted him additional years, so He would give Judah and Jerusalem a new lease on life by miraculously removing the Assyrian threat. Nevertheless, like Hezekiah's briefly extended life, so Judah's and Jerusalem's days remained numbered.

Hezekiah Entertains Babylonian Messengers (39:1-8). Even godly men have their moments of failure. Hezekiah was no exception. Chapter 39 records an event that occurred shortly after his recovery. The Babylonians, who were seeking to form an anti-Assyrian alliance, sent messengers to Hezekiah. Hezekiah proudly (and foolishly) showed them the riches of his storehouses. It was this kind of self-sufficient attitude that would eventually bring the nation's downfall. The Lord used the occasion to announce through Isaiah that the Babylonians would someday conquer Jerusalem and carry the royal riches and even some of Hezekiah's own descendants into exile. Hezekiah readily submitted to the prophet's words, confident that the rest of his reign would be peaceful. His tone of resignation contrasts sharply with his earlier unwillingness to accept the announcement of his own impending death (compare 38:1-3). This may be interpreted negatively (as reflecting self-interest) or positively (as an admission of his own guilt and of God's grace in not bringing immediate punishment).

HOPE AND RESTORATION FOR GOD'S EXILED PEOPLE (ISA 40:1–66:24)

The setting of Isaiah's message shifts to the time of the exile, which earlier passages of the book assumed (11:11-12,15-16; 14:1-2; 27:12-13; 35:10) and prophesied (5:13; 6:12; 27:8; 39:5-7). This final section of the book begins on an extremely positive note, as God affirmed His commitment to His servant nation and promised them deliverance from exile in seemingly unconditional terms. As the section progresses, it becomes apparent that total restoration would not be automatic. Covenantal renewal, mediated through a special servant viewed as an ideal Israel and a second Moses, was necessary. Anticipating that some would reject God's offer of reconciliation, the books' final chapters foresee a final, purifying judgment, out of which a holy community would emerge.

The four so-called servant songs highlight this section (compare 42:1-9; 49:1-13; 50:4-11; 52:13–53:12). For years scholars have debated this servant's precise identity. Some conclude that the servant in the four songs is none other than the personified nation Israel. Throughout chapters 40–48 the Lord calls the nation His servant. Isaiah 49:3, located in the second servant song, specifically calls the servant "Israel." However, the solution is not this simple. One of the major tasks of this servant "Israel" is to restore the nation (compare 49:5-6,8-9) by suffering innocently on behalf of God's sinful people (compare 53:5,8).

These texts require some distinction between the servant "Israel" and the exiled nation. It is best to identify the servant as an individual within the nation who as Israel's representative mediates a new covenant between God and His people (compare 49:8). He also fulfills God's original purpose for the nation in that he becomes a channel of divine blessing to the Gentiles (compare 42:6; 49:6). Because he embodies God's ideal for the nation, he can be called "Israel." In the progress of biblical revelation Jesus Christ emerges as this ideal Israel who restores God's covenant people and takes His salvation to the nations (compare Acts 8:30-35).

40:1–48:22
The Deliverance of the Exiles from Babylon

God emphasized that He was both willing and able to deliver His exiled people. Much of the section focuses on God's superiority to the nations and their idols.

Comfort for Jerusalem and the Exiles (40:1-31). The chapter begins with a message of encouragement for downtrodden Jerusalem. The city had suffered more than enough; its time of punishment was over. Preparations were to be made for the King's glorious return. The city's restoration was certain, for God's decree is reliable, unlike frail persons and their promises, both of which fade like grass before a hot wind. Jerusalem was to proclaim the good news of God's return to the other cities of Judah. Like a shepherd tenderly holding his sheep to his chest, the Lord would carry the exiles back to the land. The same mighty arm that destroys His enemies (compare 51:9-10) would protect His people.

For tired, discouraged exiles this promise of restoration may have seemed like wishful thinking. They felt abandoned by God (compare v. 27) and may have wondered if He possessed the ability to deliver them. Perhaps He was a local deity limited to the borders of Judah. To alleviate such doubts, the Lord reminded His people of His sovereignty and might. He is the Creator of the universe, who demonstrated immeasurable power and wisdom in forming the heavens and the earth. He is sovereign over His world, exercising absolute control over the nations and their puny rulers. He is infinitely superior to idols. The stars of the heavens, made gods in pagan thought (compare Jer 19:13), are mere servants who report for duty when God calls. Because His authority, power, and wisdom are unlimited, God is capable of delivering His people from bondage. He gives superhuman strength to those who rely on Him.

God's Redemptive Program (41:1–42:12). This section briefly outlines God's program for Israel's redemption. Later chapters then develop this program.

The Lord began by asserting His sovereignty over history and the nations. He was raising up a mighty conqueror (Cyrus the Persian, compare 44:28; 45:1) who would subdue the nations and accomplish the Lord's will. Before his relentless march the nations and their idols would be helpless.

Reminding His people of their special position as descendants of Abraham, the Lord assured them that He would protect them and eliminate their enemies. Comparing their distress to the plight of a thirsty man in a desert, the Lord promised to transform their condition. He would, as it were, cause the desert to overflow with abundant waters and blossom into a forest, resulting in universal recognition of His sovereignty.

The Lord challenged the nations' idols to present evidence of their power to predict and fulfill. In response to their silence, He pronounced them to be "less than nothing" and "false." As proof of His own power, He pointed to Cyrus, the "one from the north" whom He was raising up to conquer the nations.

In addition to Cyrus, the Lord would raise up another servant, whose ministry would be characterized by humility and by gentleness toward the downtrodden. Energized by the Lord's Spirit, He would establish justice on the earth, mediate a new covenant for Israel, and release the oppressed. Like Cyrus's conquests, his divinely decreed accomplishments would demonstrate the Lord's sovereignty over history and His superiority to idols. The proper response to this announcement was universal praise.

Blind and Deaf Israel Summoned as Witnesses (42:13–44:23). This section is arranged in two parallel panels (42:13–43:13; 43:14–44:20), each of which contains four parts: (1) an announcement of divine intervention in world events, (2) an exhortation to Israel, (3) a message of salvation for God's people, and (4) a declaration of the Lord's sovereignty over the nations and their gods. The following outline reflects the structure of the section:

	Panel A	Panel B
1.	42:13-17	43:14-21
2.	42:18-25	43:22-28
3.	43:1-7	44:1-5
4.	43:8-13	44:6-20

The section concludes with an exhortation to Israel (44:21-22) and a call to praise (44:23).

Though the Lord had been silent for a lengthy period, He would come like a mighty warrior and lead His people back to their land, demonstrating His superiority to the pagan gods (42:13-17). He made it clear that spiritually unresponsive Israel had experienced His judgment and the hardships of exile because of their refusal to obey His law (42:18-25). Nevertheless, as their Creator He assured them of His continuing presence and supernatural protection (43:1-2). He would raise up the Persians, who would conquer Egypt but allow the Israelites to leave Babylon (43:3-4). Eventually all of God's dispersed people would return to the promised land (43:5-7). Summoning His people as witnesses to His sovereignty over the events of history, the Lord declared His superiority to the gods of the nations (43:8-13).

The traditional tomb of Cyrus the Great located at Pasargadae in Persia.

Speaking as the Redeemer of Israel, who in former times had led His people out of their Egyptian bondage, the Lord announced a new exodus. He would free Israel from their Babylonian captivity and provide for their needs on the journey home (43:14-21). In the past their sinful deeds had invalidated their sacrifices and resulted in severe judgment. (Isa 43:28 is better understood as a reference to past judgment.) But the Lord reminded them that He is the God who forgives sin (43:22-28). The Lord addressed Israel by its ancient name Jeshurun (44:2), which Moses applied to early Israel as the recipient of God's blessings (Deut 32:15; 33:5,26). Like that earlier generation, exiled Israel would experience an outpouring of divine blessing (44:1-5). Again calling His people as witnesses, the Lord reaffirmed His superiority to all other gods (44:6-20). Certainly the nations' idols could not compare with Him. With great sarcasm the Lord ridiculed idol worshipers. After cutting down a tree, people formed idols from some of the wood and with the rest made fires to cook their meat and warm themselves. They never stopped to think that their god and the wood

ELECTION IN THE OLD TESTAMENT

Election is the concept representing the Hebrew verb *bachar* (*select*) or participle *bachir* (*elect* or *chosen*), referring to selection by extending preference from among alternatives.

The biblical doctrine of election refers to God's free and sovereign choice of those whom He has appointed to fulfill His purposes. It has particular reference to His decision prior to creation as to whom He would save and how He would bring about their salvation.

Scripture insists that God's saving work is done neither arbitrarily nor outside of His all-inclusive control. Rather, it is accomplished through His sovereign wisdom and power according to His eternal decree.

Election therefore differs from *predestination*. Predestination is the doctrine that God, as omnipotent Ruler over His creation, has planned everything that comes to pass. While the concept of election is included in that of predestination, the latter is broader. Specifically, the OT uses the term *elect* in relation to three subjects:

1. *The nation Israel* (Isa 45:4). Israel had a unique role as God's elect. God chose them to be His covenant community. He chose them to reveal His sovereignty and holiness to the nations through the prophets and the Scriptures. He chose them to be the vehicle for bringing forth the Messiah.

Israel's election is prominent in Deuteronomy and in Romans 9–11. It was based not on any demonstrated virtue on Israel's part but solely on God's love (Deut 7:7-8).

2. *A select group of prominent leaders in Israel.* To preserve Israel as the covenant community, God chose certain strategic leaders for their unique positions of authority. Among them Moses, as Israel's intercessor, is called the Lord's "elect one" (Ps 106:23). David, as the recipient of the Davidic covenant, is described as God's "elect" (Ps 89:3).

3. *The elect Servant (Isa 42:1-4).* From before the foundation of the world, God ordained that His chosen "Servant" would someday establish justice upon the earth. The NT identifies the Servant as Israel's Messiah, the Lord Jesus Christ. It indicates that not only His reign but His work of redemption was preordained from eternity (Acts 2:23; 1 Pet 1:20). □

used for such everyday tasks were made from the same substance.

In conclusion the Lord exhorted Israel to lay hold of His promise of restoration and forgiveness. In anticipation of Israel's redemption, the prophet urged the entire universe to break out in song.

God Initiates His Redemptive Program through Cyrus (44:24–45:25). Identifying Himself as the sovereign Creator, who alone controls the events of history, the Lord announced that He would use Cyrus the Persian to restore His people to the land and rebuild the ruined cities. A commissioning account follows, in which the Lord promised Cyrus military success in order that he, and eventually the whole world, might recognize the incomparability of Israel's God. The mention of Cyrus by name is startling, since this ruler did not come on the scene until the sixth century B.C., over a hundred years after Isaiah died. However, such a precise prediction is certainly consistent with the theme of God's ability to predict and fulfill (compare 44:26).

Though God had great plans for His exiled people, some grumbled about their condition and questioned God's ways. The Lord reminded such individuals that they had no right to question their Creator's sovereign decisions. To do so would be as absurd as a piece of pottery criticizing the potter who forms it.

The Lord reiterated His plan to use Cyrus as His instrument of redemption. Israel would return from Babylon and rebuild Jerusalem. Foreigners would recognize Israel's privileged position and the incomparability of Israel's God.

Once more declaring His sovereignty and superiority to the pagan gods, the Lord exhorted all nations to turn to Him for salvation. It is wise to submit to God now, for He has issued an unchangeable decree that all will someday bow before Him and acknowledge His sovereignty.

Exhorting Israel in Light of Babylon's Fall (46:1–48:22). Here announcements of Babylon's fall (46:1-2; 47:1-15) are coupled with exhortations to the exiles (46:3-13; 48:1-22).

Babylon's idols would be carried away into captivity, unable to rescue themselves, let alone their worshipers. These useless idols were stationary and a burden to the animals that carried them. In contrast, God had always been active in Israel's history and had, as it were, carried His people. He urged those exiles who remained rebellious in spirit to recall His past deeds and to recognize His sovereign hand at work in the career of Cyrus. For those who were willing to trust His promises, a new era was approaching.

This statue of Nebo, Babylonian god of wisdom and writing, found at Calah dates from the time of Adadnirari III. See Isaiah 46:1.

In chapter 47 Babylon's fall is described in a taunt song addressed by a vengeful God to the city, which is personified as a proud queen. This once "tender and delicate" queen would now do the work of a commoner or servant and be publicly humiliated. Though God had commissioned her to punish His sinful people, she had shown no mercy, severely oppressing even the very aged. Thinking her position secured, she boasted that she would never experience bereavement. However, the Lord announced that she would suddenly loose both her husband and children. The once self-sufficient queen would be deprived of all means of support. Despite her diviners' and astrologers' attempts to ward off disaster, the judgment of God would overtake the city.

The Lord recognized that many of the exiles only possessed an outward form of religion, while others were outright idolaters and rebels. Throughout Israel's history the Lord had announced His actions beforehand so that His rebellious people would not attribute the events to false gods. Now He was announcing another major event in the nations' history. Though He had punished Israel for its rebellion, He would now bring glory to Himself by delivering it through Cyrus. Because of their disobedience, God's people had forfeited peace and blessing. The Lord was now offering them an opportunity to start over. If they responded in faith and left Babylon, He would care for their needs, as He had done during the wilderness wanderings following the exodus from Egypt. However, the Lord warned that the wicked would not participate in this new era of peace and blessing.

49:1–55:13
The Restoration of Jerusalem

Chapters 41–42 introduced Cyrus (compare 41:2-3,25) and the Lord's ideal servant (compare 42:1-9) as important instruments in God's program for Israel's redemption. Chapters 43–48 focused on Cyrus's role, while chapters 49–55 develop in more detail the ideal servant's part in the drama.

This section is arranged in three panels (49:1–50:3; 50:4–52:12; 52:13–54:17), each of which begins with a servant song followed by an encouraging message for personified Jerusalem. A moving call to covenantal renewal concludes the section (55:1-13).

The Lord Commissions an Ideal Servant (49:1-13). Here the Lord's ideal servant, introduced in 42:1-9, recounts his special divine commission. From before his birth the Lord chose him for a special task. The Lord made him an effective spokesman to be used at an opportune time. The servant received the title "Israel" because as an ideal representative of the nation he would restore

Israel's relationship to God. In the role of a new Moses the servant would mediate a new covenant for Israel and lead the people out of captivity and back to the promised land. As "Israel" the servant would also fulfill God's original ideal for the nation by being a channel of blessing to the Gentile nations. Though the servant faced rejection and discouragement, he was confident that the Lord would eventually vindicate him. Someday even kings would acknowledge his greatness.

The Lord Answers Jerusalem's Complaint (49:14–50:3). The servant's work would have important results for Jerusalem. The city is here personified as a woman who complains of being abandoned by her husband (the Lord) and deprived of her children (the exiled residents of the city). Comparing Himself to a nursing mother, the Lord assured Jerusalem that He could never abandon her. Though she and her children had experienced the harsh consequences of their sin, she would again be inhabited. Her exiled children would return en masse, escorted by the Gentiles. The Lord would rescue them from captivity and take vengeance on their oppressors.

The Lord's Ideal Servant Perseveres (50:4-11). In this third servant song the servant declared his confidence in God. He had not drawn back from the Lord's commission, despite severe opposition and humiliation. He persevered, confident that the Lord would one day vindicate him before his enemies. The song concludes with an appeal for the servant's faithful followers to continue to trust the Lord and with a warning of judgment to those who reject the Lord's guidance.

A New Exodus (51:1–52:12). Once more the Lord addressed His people with a message of hope and encouragement. He urged the faithful to consider the example of Abraham and Sarah. From this single individual and his barren wife the Lord formed a nation in fulfillment of His promise. He would do the same for desolate Jerusalem, transforming its ruins into a new Garden of Eden filled with song. God would also extend His blessings to the nations by establishing a just world order.

Overwhelmed by God's reassuring promises, the prophet cried out for and anticipated their fulfillment. He longed for a new exodus, in which God would display the power that destroyed the Egyptians (compared to the mythical sea monster Rahab) and divided the Red Sea.

Speaking as His people's Comforter and as the sovereign Creator of the world, the Lord reiterated His promise to the frightened exiles. He would exert His mighty power on their behalf and release them from their prison.

The Lord would also lift up downtrodden Jerusalem. The city had suffered humiliation at the hands of the nations; now the time of retribution had arrived. The cup of the Lord's wrath would pass from Jerusalem to its oppressors. Never again would the purified city be invaded by foreigners. Though His name had been blasphemed among the nations, the Lord would establish His rule from Jerusalem and reveal His power to the entire earth. The prophet employed vivid imagery, picturing a messenger bringing the good news of God's advent to the watchmen of Jerusalem's walls.

A final exhortation urges the priests to leave the unclean land of exile, implying that the worship system would be reestablished. In contrast to the exodus from Egypt, which was conducted in haste (compare Deut 16:3), there would be no need to hurry because the oppressor would be crushed prior to their departure. As in the first exodus God would accompany His people as their protector.

Suffering and Vindication of the Lord's Ideal Servant (52:13–53:12). This fourth servant song describes in greater detail the servant's suffering and vindication, themes introduced in earlier songs (compare 49:4,7; 50:6-9). The song begins with the Lord's declaration that His servant would be greatly honored. Just as many had been shocked by the degree of the servant's humiliation, so many nations and even kings would be amazed by his glorious exaltation.

In the central section of the song (53:1-10) Israel confessed its former unbelief and acknowledged that the servant's suffering was on their behalf. Responding to the announcement of the servant's future exaltation ("our message" in 53:1 is better translated "the report just heard by us"), Israel confessed that they never had considered such a thing possible for they had not seen God's power revealed through the servant. They regarded him as insignificant and interpreted his intense sufferings as a sign of divine displeasure. Now they were forced to reevaluate their former opinion. They now realized that the servant's suffering was due to their sins and for their ultimate benefit. Like stray sheep all Israel had wandered from the Lord, and the servant had borne the punishment for their rebellion. He was innocent of wrongdoing, yet he silently endured oppressive treatment and a humiliating death. The Lord had decreed that the servant was to suffer; eventually He would vindicate and bless him.

The song ends as it began, with the Lord Himself declaring His pleasure with the servant. Because the servant submitted to suffering and identified with sinful Israel, he would restore many to the Lord and be richly rewarded for his efforts.

Jerusalem's Glorious Future (54:1-17). With Israel's restoration assured by the servant's ministry, Jerusalem's future was bright. Comparing the ruined city to a barren woman, the Lord announced that she would be blessed with an abundance of children (a reference to her returning exiles). Placing her in the role of His divorced wife, He promised a restoration of the marriage. Nothing would ever again separate them. The Lord would adorn the city with beauty and protect it from all assailants.

A Call to Covenant Renewal (55:1-13). Using the imagery of an invitation to a banquet, the Lord exhorted His people to receive the blessings He offered. The Lord desired to make an eternal covenant with the nation, which would parallel His covenant with David. Like David, Israel would be living testimony of God's greatness and would rule over nations. If the nation actively sought the Lord and turned from their wicked ways, He would compassionately forgive their sins. They could depend on this merciful response, for God's word of promise, unlike sinful human plans, is always realized. Just as rain does not reverse its course, but falls to the ground and makes the farmer's crops fruitful, so God does not take back His word of promise but rather brings it to fulfillment. The Lord would shower repentant Israel with abundant blessings, which would be an eternal sign of their renewed relationship.

The Palestinian viper shown above is indigenous to Israel and is highly poisonous. See Isaiah 59:5.

56:1–66:24
The Final Purification of God's People

Despite God's promise of a new era of blessing and His invitation to reconciliation, the reality of Israel's rebellious spirit remained. Isaiah 56–66 indicates that only the repentant would participate in the new era. Those who followed the sinful ways of earlier generations would be excluded. Though many of the promises of chapters 40–55 are reiterated here, the theme of God's purifying, discriminating judgment is also prominent.

Foreigners and Eunuchs Granted New Status (56:1-8). In anticipation of God's coming age of salvation, His people should promote justice, one of the chief characteristics of the new era. Without exception, all who demonstrated loyalty to God by keeping His commands would experience His blessings and enjoy access to His presence. Even those who had once been subject to exclusion and strict regulations, such as eunuchs and foreigners (compare Deut. 23:1,3,7-8), would freely enter the Lord's temple.

Sinners Denounced, the Repentant Encouraged (56:9–57:21). The wicked would have no place in this new community. The Lord warned that judgment was imminent for all the greedy leaders and rebellious idolaters who sought to perpetuate the injustice and spiritual adultery of earlier days. The promised land was reserved for those who trusted in the Lord and displayed a repentant spirit.

God's Righteous Demands, the Nation's Sinful Deeds (58:1-14). The Lord denounced the people's hypocritical claims of loyalty and their empty expressions of repentance. Their unjust and violent deeds made their fasts unacceptable. The Lord demanded righteous living, not meaningless ritual. They were to free the oppressed, feed the hungry, give shelter to the homeless, and clothe the naked. In addition to caring for the needs of others, they also were to demonstrate true devotion to God by honoring His Sabbath Day. Then they would experience the Lord's protective presence, enjoy His blessings, and witness the rebuilding of the land.

Accusation and Confession (59:1-15a). The Lord was able and willing to restore His people, but their persistence in sin had separated them from God. He could not tolerate their violence, deceit, and injustice. Their evil thoughts produced destructive actions. In contrast to the justice and peace demanded by the Lord, their life-style was characterized by bloodshed.

Identifying with and representing the nation, the prophet acknowledged the truth of the preceding accusation. He lamented that justice and truth had disappeared, preventing divine deliverance from becoming a reality. He confessed the nation's many sins and admitted that they had rebelled against and rejected the Lord.

The Restoration of Jerusalem (59:15b–63:6). In response to the prophet's confession on behalf of the nation, a message of salvation now appears (59:15b-21). The Lord would judge His enemies and return to Jerusalem to rule over His repentant people. He would establish a new covenant with them, enabling them by His Spirit to obey His commandments.

The Lord's glorious return would begin a bright new era for Jerusalem (60:1-22). The city's exiled population would return, and nations would bring their wealth as tribute to the Lord. Signs of the Lord's renewed blessing would be everywhere. Foreigners would rebuild the city's walls. Its gates would remain open to accommodate the steady stream of visitors bringing tribute. The splendid trees of Lebanon would be used as building materials for the Lord's temple. Those who formerly oppressed the city would acknowledge its special status. God's glorious presence would assure continual peace and justice. In fulfillment of His promise to Abraham, His people would possess the promised land forever and experience extraordinary population growth.

Chapter 61 begins with an unidentified speaker (the prophet? the servant of chaps. 40–55?) relating his commission to proclaim good news to the city's grieving exiles. The Lord had officially decreed a year of release for His captive people. They would rebuild the cities of the land and serve the Lord as a nation of priests (compare Exod 19:6). Foreigners would serve them and bring them their wealth. The Lord would take away His people's shame and give them a double portion of His blessings. The nations would recognize Israel's special relationship to the Lord. The recipient of God's blessings (personified Jerusalem?) rejoiced in His salvation.

The portrayal of Jerusalem's future continues in chapter 62. The restored city's glory would be apparent to all. Though Jerusalem was deserted and desolate, it would someday be named Hephzibah (*My delight is in her*) and Beulah (*Married*), for the Lord would renew His relationship with her. With the threat of foreign invasion forever removed, God's people would enjoy the fruit of their labors.

The chapter concludes with an exhortation to prepare the way for the return of the Lord (compare Isa 40:3-5), who would bring His exiled people with Him (compare 40:10) and set them apart as a holy community (compare Exod 19:6).

This section ends as it began with a description of the Lord as a conquering warrior (Isa 63:1-6; compare 59:15b-19). He comes from Edom (which here represents the hostile nations, compare v. 6 and 34:5-17) with His garments stained with blood. He announces that He has single-handedly crushed His enemies, as if they were grapes in a winepress. One is reminded again that God's kingdom of peace and justice will only come after a powerful and angry display of His judgment against His foes.

A Prayer for Deliverance (63:7–64:12). In combination with the confession of 59:9-15a, this prayer forms a frame around the message of salvation in 59:15b–63:6. Once again the prophet represented the nation and provided a model response for God's disobedient, exiled people.

The prophet recalled the Lord's faithful deeds for His people throughout their history. He redeemed them from Egypt and protected them. When they sinned, He was forced to treat them as an enemy, prompting them to recall the days of Moses. The prophet was now doing the same. He longed for a new display of the divine power revealed at the Red Sea.

The remainder of the prayer combines lamentation over the people's current situation, confession of sin, statements of confidence, and petitions for God's deliverance. Confident that God remained their Father and Redeemer, the prophet asked that He might respond compassionately to their plight. He lamented that the Lord had given them over to the hardness of their hearts and that the enemies of God had destroyed His temple. He asked that the Lord might break through the heavens and judge the nations, demonstrating once more His ability to deliver those who trusted Him. He acknowledged their punishment was well-deserved, for they had been totally contaminated by sin. Yet the prophet, confident that their relationship with God was not completely severed, begged Him to relent from His anger. Surely the ruined land and temple were proof that their punishment was sufficient.

Separation of the Righteous and the Wicked (65:1–66:24). Chapter 65 contrasts the respective destinies of the righteous and the wicked. Despite the Lord's constant attempts to get Israel's attention, many rejected Him and embraced pagan religious practices. Such stubbornness demanded harsh punishment. However, the Lord would exercise discrimination in judgment. He would preserve the righteous and give them the promised land as a reward. A new world was coming, in which purified Jerusalem would be the focal point. The troubles of the past would be forgotten, and God's blessings would abound. Life spans would dramatically increase; the people would enjoy the fruits of their labor; God would respond immediately to their prayers; all dangers would be eliminated, and peace would prevail.

Chapter 66 begins by contrasting the character of the righteous and the wicked. The righteous were humble, repentant, and showed respect for God's commandments. The wicked were violent, idolatrous, self-willed, spiritually unresponsive, and hostile to the righteous.

A day of retribution was coming, in which the wicked would be purged from the covenant community and the righteous vindicated. The Lord's fiery judgment would destroy the wicked along with their pagan practices. The righteous would take possession of glorified and renewed Jerusalem, where peace and prosperity would abound. The Gentiles would come to Jerusalem on a regular basis to worship the Lord. In the background the smoldering, decaying carcasses of the wicked would serve as a constant reminder of the consequences of rebellion against the Great King.

The Book of Isaiah begins with the Lord accusing His people of rebellion (compare 1:2). It ends with a hideous but sobering description of the total and final destruction of the rebellious.

Theological and Ethical Significance

For Isaiah God was "the Holy One of Israel" and "the Creator of the ends of the earth." Such a God demanded moral purity and justice from His people and all nations. God's people, like other nations, failed to meet His standards of behavior. The Holy One was thus just in punishing their sin by sending them into exile. God, however, desired to play the part of Savior, Redeemer, and Father to those who would turn to Him in repentance. Isaiah called Israel to hope in God, the Creator who brought order from chaos and the Redeemer who rescued Israel from Egyptian captivity. Such a God would surely again act creatively and redemptively in leading his people home to a restored Jerusalem.

Isaiah challenges Christians to hope in God, who is not through with creation. Old Testament Israel only partially realized God's salvation and peace. God, who acted to save Christians in the past through the Suffering Servant Jesus, will act again to bring history to His desired end of a new heaven and a new earth.

Questions for Reflection

1. How did Isaiah portray God? What divine names and titles did he employ? What characteristics did he attribute to God? What effect should Isaiah's teaching about God have on our thinking and behavior?

2. Why were God's people so displeasing to Him in Isaiah's day? Is the modern church like ancient Israel in any ways?

3. How does Israel's judgment serve as a lesson to us? What does God's judgment of Israel teach us about His relationship to His people?

4. Why did God remain committed to Israel? In what ways is His devotion to His people portrayed or illustrated in the book?

5. How did Isaiah portray the ministry and future reign of Jesus Christ?

Sources for Additional Study

Butler, Trent C. *Isaiah. Layman's Bible Book Commentary.* Vol. 10. Nashville: Broadman, 1982.

Martin, Alfred and John. *Isaiah: The Glory of the Messiah.* Chicago: Moody, 1983.

Oswalt, John N. *The Book of Isaiah, Chapters 1–39. The New International Commentary on the Old Testament.* Grand Rapids: Eerdmans, 1986.

Wolf, Herbert M. *Interpreting Isaiah.* Grand Rapids: Zondervan, 1985.

JEREMIAH

According to the book's heading, Jeremiah was a priest from Anathoth whose prophetic career began in the thirteenth year of Josiah (627–626 B.C.) and continued until the final exile of Judah in 586. Chapters 39–44 indicate that Jeremiah continued to minister after the fall of Jerusalem and was forced to accompany a group of exiles to Egypt.

Historical Background

Jeremiah lived during the final days of the Kingdom of Judah. The revival under King Josiah (who ruled from 640–609 B.C.) and the fall of the Assyrian empire (in 612–609) seemingly offered some hope for Judah. The nation's rebellious spirit, however, coupled with the rise of the Babylonians as the new power of the Near East, made calamity inevitable. When Jeremiah denounced Josiah's successors, Jehoahaz (609), Jehoiakim (609–598), Jehoiachin (598–597), and Zedekiah (597–586), he was threatened, imprisoned, and humiliated. Though complaining at times to the Lord, Jeremiah continued to warn of impending judgment.

That judgment came through the Babylonians. In 612 B.C. they conquered Nineveh, the capital of Assyria. In 609 they defeated the last remnant of Assyrian power at Haran. By this time the Egyptians had allied themselves with Assyria in an attempt to stem the Babylonian tide and maintain the balance of power. When they marched northward to help the Assyrians in 609, Josiah tried to stop them and lost his life. His son Jehoahaz took the throne of Judah, but the Egyptians took him into exile three months later and replaced him with his brother Jehoiakim.

In 605 B.C. the Babylonians established themselves as the premier power of the Near East by defeating the Egyptians at Carchemish. Though loyal to Babylon for a time, Jehoiakim eventually rebelled. The Babylonians besieged Jerusalem and in 597 conquered the city. They replaced Jehoiakim's son Jehoiachin, who had only ruled for three months following the death of his father, with his uncle Zedekiah. After remaining loyal to Babylon for a short time, Zedekiah also rebelled.

In 588 B.C. Nebuchadnezzar invaded Judah and began a long siege of Jerusalem that culminated with the fall

The prophet Jeremiah

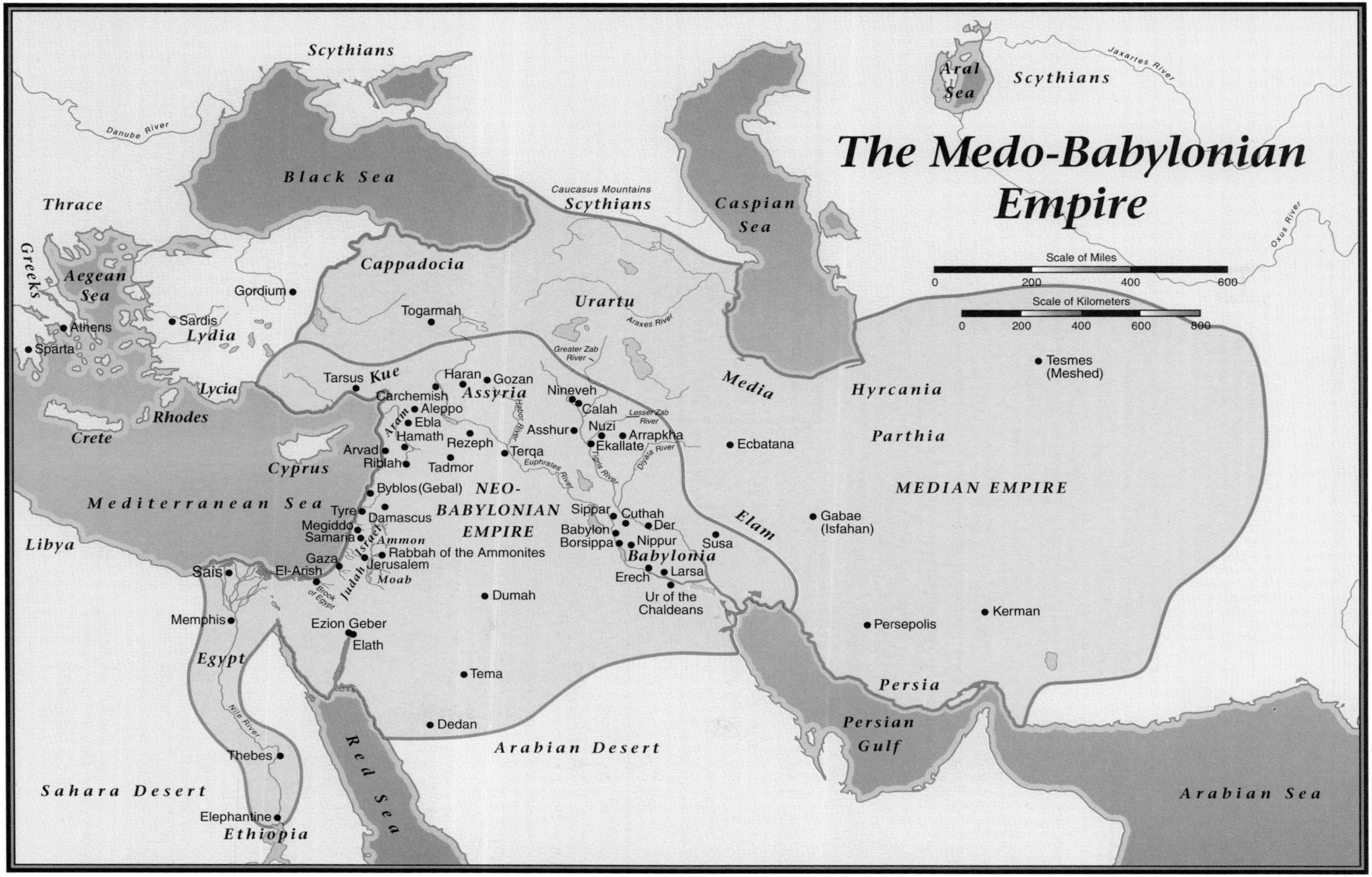
The Medo-Babylonian Empire
Scale of Miles
0
200
400
600
Scale of Kilometers
0
200
400
600
800
Scythians
Danube River
Black Sea
Thrace
Greeks
Aegean Sea
Athens
Sparta
Sardis
Lydia
Gordium
Cappadocia
Togarmah
Lycia
Rhodes
Crete
Cyprus
Mediterranean Sea
Libya
Sais
Memphis
Egypt
Nile River
Thebes
Elephantine
Ethiopia
Sahara Desert
Red Sea
Caucasus Mountains
Scythians
Caspian Sea
Aral Sea
Scythians
Jaxartes River
Oxus River
Urartu
Araxes River
Greater Zab River
Lesser Zab River
Tarsus
Kue
Haran
Gozan
Assyria
Carchemish
Aleppo
Aram
Ebla
Hamath
Rezeph
Arvad
Riblah
Tadmor
Habor River
Terqa
Euphrates River
Nineveh
Calah
Asshur
Nuzi
Arrapkha
Ekallate
Tigris River
Diyala River
Byblos (Gebal)
NEO-BABYLONIAN EMPIRE
Tyre
Damascus
Megiddo
Samaria
Israel
Ammon
Rabbah of the Ammonites
Gaza
Jerusalem
El-Arish
Judah
Moab
Brook of Egypt
Dumah
Ezion Geber
Elath
Tema
Dedan
Arabian Desert
Sippar
Cuthah
Der
Babylon
Borsippa
Nippur
Babylonia
Susa
Erech
Larsa
Ur of the Chaldeans
Elam
Media
Ecbatana
Hyrcania
Parthia
Tesmes (Meshed)
MEDIAN EMPIRE
Gabae (Isfahan)
Persepolis
Kerman
Persia
Persian Gulf
Arabian Sea

of the city in August 586. The Babylonians carried many into exile, but some survivors were allowed to remain in the land under the authority of Gedaliah, a governor appointed by the Babylonians. However, in October 586 a small band of dissidents assassinated Gedaliah. Fearing a Babylonian reprisal, many fled to Egypt. Jeremiah, who opposed this course of action and insisted that the Babylonians would not punish the people, was forced to go with the fugitives to Egypt.

Theme

Like so many of the other writing prophets of the Old Testament, Jeremiah promised that God would ultimately fulfill His ideal for Israel, but only after a time of purifying judgment and exile. God would not tolerate unfaithfulness among His people. Judgment would sweep away covenant violators and pave the way for the establishment of a new covenant.

Literary Form

The book contains a variety of literary types, including prophetic messages given in both poetic and prose style and biographical accounts of Jeremiah's ministry. The first half of the book includes a number of dialogues between Jeremiah and the Lord in which the prophet poured out his heart in prayer. Reports of symbolic acts are also included.

Chapters 1–24 focus on the sin and impending judgment of Judah. The scope of the book broadens in chapters 25–52, where judgment oracles against the nations and messages of Judah's ultimate restoration appear.

A comparison of the Hebrew with the ancient Greek version of Jeremiah suggests that two canonical versions of Jeremiah's prophecies may have circulated in the intertestamental period. The Greek version is about 12 to 13 percent shorter than its Hebrew counterpart, omitting single verses as well as longer sections. The Greek version also arranges the oracles against the nations (chaps. 46–51 in the Hebrew text) differently and places them earlier in the book (as chaps. 25–31).

I. Jeremiah's Call (1:1-19)
II. Guilty Judah's Downfall (2:1–24:10)
III. Messages of Judgment and Restoration (25:1–51:64)
IV. A Historical Epilogue (52:1-34)

BABYLON

Babylon is a country, sometimes called Babylonia, and the major city within that country. Babylon dominated the Near Eastern political scene at several points between 3000 B.C. and 539 B.C. For the Bible student Babylon is most famous as the nation that took Judah into exile in 586 B.C. and that destroyed Jerusalem. In Hebrew the name *Babylon* is closely related to the Hebrew word for Babel (Gen 10:10; 11:9).

Babylon's origins are lost in archaeological levels below the current water line at the ancient city site located about fifty miles south of modern Baghdad. Shortly after 2000 B.C., about the time of Abraham, Babylon's history becomes available for modern study. Amorite kings, such as the famous Hammurabi (about 1792–1750), brought the city to international dominance.

Hittite kings destroyed the city of Babylon, ending this Babylonian dynasty about 1595 B.C. A period of which we know little ensued under the rule of Kassite kings.

About 1350 B.C. Babylon's kings were important enough to correspond with Egyptian kings. Their correspondence shows trouble brewing to the north from Assyria. The Elamites' conquest ended this stage of Babylon's history about 1160 B.C. A brief renewal under Nebuchadnezzar (about 1124–1103 B.C.) gave way to two hundred years of darkness and weakness. Chaldeans and other nomadic tribes settled much of Babylonia. Shortly after 900 B.C. Assyria gained control of Mesopotamia, including Babylon. The Assyrians often allowed Babylonian kings to reign as their vassals, paying tribute.

By 721 B.C. Marduk-apal-iddina (called Merodach-Baladan in the OT), a Chaldean, ruled Babylon. In 710 B.C. Sargon II of Assyria forced Marduk-apal-iddina to flee to his allies in Elam. He returned to Babylon at Sargon's death in 705 and apparently sent messengers to Hezekiah (2 Kgs 20:12-19; Isa 39). Sennacherib of Assyria regained control in 703 B.C., finally destroying the city of Babylon in 689 B.C. in response to revolts backed by Elam.

Nabopolassar, a Chaldean chief, established Babylonian independence in 626 B.C. In 612 with the help of the Medes he destroyed Nineveh, the Assyrian capital. Pharaoh Neco of Egypt marched to Assyria's defense but failed to drive back the Babylonians in 609 B.C. Nebuchadnez-

Purpose and Theology

Jeremiah accused Judah of breaking their covenant with the Lord. He denounced the people's unfaithfulness to God, which was seen most clearly in their idolatry and foreign alliances. The leadership of the nation was particularly corrupt. The kings neglected to ensure justice and even persecuted God's prophet. At the same time, false prophets promised deliverance and prosperity.

Jeremiah warned the people not to listen to these lying prophets. The Lord was about to punish Judah for its breach of covenant by bringing upon the nation the curses Moses threatened (see Deut 27–28). Famine and the sword would destroy multitudes, while many others would go into exile. Jeremiah's warnings of certain doom were fulfilled in 586 B.C., when Jerusalem fell to the Babylonians, an event described in the book's later chapters.

Though much of the book is devoted to the themes of sin and judgment, Jeremiah did see a light at the end of the tunnel. God would someday judge Judah's enemies, including the mighty Babylonians. He would restore His exiled people and make a new covenant with them, enabling them to willingly obey His commandments. The Lord would also restore the Davidic throne and raise up an ideal king who would ensure peace and justice in the land.

JEREMIAH'S CALL (JER 1:1-19)

For discussion of the heading (1:1-3), see the introduction. Before Jeremiah's conception and birth, the Lord had chosen him to be His prophet. When Jeremiah objected that he was too young and inarticulate for the task, the Lord assured him of His protective presence. The prophet's divinely appointed words would determine the destiny of nations.

Through a pun based on a vision, the Lord assured the prophet that the divine message spoken through him would be fulfilled. When Jeremiah identified an almond branch (Hebrew *saqed*), the Lord punned on its name, announcing that He was "watching" (Hebrew *soqed*) carefully to assure the realization of the prophetic word.

Through another vision, that of a boiling pot tilting southward, the Lord revealed that Jeremiah's message would be one of impending judgment. The boiling pot symbolized foreign armies that would invade the land from the north as instruments of judgments against God's idolatrous people.

The Lord exhorted Jeremiah to declare His word

zar, the crown prince, led Babylon to decisive victory over Egypt at Carchemish in 605 B.C. (compare Jer 46:2-12).

When he became king, Nebuchadnezzar forced Jehoiakim of Judah to pay tribute as his vassal in 603 B.C. Temporary Egyptian victory in 601 encouraged Jehoiakim to rebel (compare 2 Kgs 24:1-2). Finally, Babylon retaliated and forced Judah's new young king Jehoiachin to surrender on March 16, 597 B.C. Many Judeans were exiled to Babylon (2 Kgs 24:6-12).

Nebuchadnezzar appointed Zedekiah as Judah's king, but he, too, rebelled in 589 B.C., only to be defeated in 586. This defeat resulted in the destruction of Jerusalem and its temple and the exile of the leading citizens to Babylon (see Jer 37:4-10; 52:1-30; 2 Kgs 25:1-21).

Nebuchadnezzar's death inaugurated Babylon's gradual fall though several kings followed him: Awel-marduk, the Evil-Merodach of 2 Kings 25:27-30 (561–560 B.C.); Neriglissar (560–558 B.C.); Labashi-Marduk (557 B.C.); and Nabonidus (556–539 B.C.). Nabonidus apparently tried to replace Babylon's god Marduk with the moon god Sin and moved to Tema in the Arabian Desert for ten years, leaving his son Belshazzar in charge (compare Dan 5:1). Babylon's population became discouraged and welcomed the invasion of Cyrus of Persia, letting him into the city gates without opposition in 539 B.C.

Babylon established a complex and sophisticated society, worshiping officially over a thousand gods, though only about twenty had strong importance. These included Anu, god of the heavens; Enlil, god of the earth; and Ea, god of the waters. During Babylon's political heyday, however, the major god was Marduk, patron god of the city of Babylon. Marduk was also called Bel, or lord (see Isa 46:1; Jer 50:2; 51:44). Other gods included Shamash, the sun god; Sin, the moon god; Ishtar, goddess of the morning and evening star. Ishtar was known as the Queen of Heaven (see Jer 7:18; 44:17-19).

Archaeologists have uncovered thousands of Babylonian tablets, revealing many narrative texts such as the *Enuma elish*, the creation story, and the *Gilgamesh Epic*, the flood story.

For Jews and Christians, Babylon became synonymous with evil and the enemy above all enemies (see 1 Pet 5:13; Rev 14:8; 16:19; 17:5; 18:2). □

Jeremiah reminded Israel of the care and guidance of the Lord in bringing them through the wilderness (Jer 2:6) and into the land of milk and honey. Shown above is the desolate wasteland of the wilderness of Zin.

boldly and fearlessly, promising him protection from his hostile audience.

GUILTY JUDAH'S DOWNFALL (JER 2:1–24:10)

These chapters contain several judgment oracles against God's people, as well as many of the prophet's emotionally charged prayers to and dialogues with the Lord. The major theme of the section is sinful Judah's coming downfall, yet glimpses of future restoration also appear.

2:1–3:5
God Accuses His Unfaithful People

Israel's history was one of apostasy. Early Israel had faithfully followed the Lord and enjoyed His protection. Later generations turned to idols, forgot the Lord's mighty deeds, and defiled the land God had graciously given them. Even the priests, civil leaders, and prophets abandoned the Lord.

Unlike pagans, who maintained loyalty to their worthless gods, Israel exchanged their glorious God and His blessings for useless idols. Consequently they suffered humiliation at the hands of foreigners. Still they sought protective alliances with these same nations.

The Lord compared rebellious and idolatrous Israel to a prostitute and to a good grapevine turned wild. Their guilt was like an irremovable stain in the sight of God. In their frantic pursuit of false gods they were like a skittish female camel dashing about or a lusty female donkey pursuing a mate. Idolatry can only result in shame. The people's idols would prove futile in the coming crisis.

Despite their unfaithfulness, the people claimed to be innocent and accused the Lord of treating them unfairly. In response the Lord pointed to their blatant rebellion and shameless acts of idolatry throughout the land.

3:6–6:30
Judah's Alternatives: Repentance or Destruction

A Call for Repentance (3:6–4:4). Idolatrous Judah was even more corrupt than their sister, the Northern Kingdom, had been. Though the Lord had swept the Northern Kingdom away into exile, Judah had not learned from their northern sister's example. The time for decision had come. Judah's only hope was to repent. The Lord appealed to His faithless people to confess their sins, turn from their idols, and commit themselves to the Lord with renewed devotion. He promised to give them godly leaders and make Jerusalem the focal point of His worldwide rule. Nations would travel to the city to worship the Lord. Judah would be reunited with the exiled Northern Kingdom and would possess the promised land.

Invasion from the North (4:5-31). The alternative to repentance was destruction. If Judah persisted in its sin, the Lord would bring a mighty army down from the north to devastate the land. Reference is made to the Babylonians, who would attack with the ferocity of a

Shown above is a statue attached to the lid of a copper jar dating from the 400s B.C. It is a horseman at full gallop in traditional Scythian dress and showing great skill in shooting arrows. See Jeremiah 4:29.

lion, the power of a whirlwind, and the swiftness of an eagle. The people would flee for their lives; and Jerusalem, abandoned to its doom by its idol-gods, would cry out in panic. Conditions in the ruined and deserted land would resemble those prior to creation, when the earth was formless, empty, and shrouded in darkness.

Throughout the chapter dramatic speeches and vivid imagery are used to emphasize the urgency of the hour. Calls to alarm (4:5-8,15-17), lamentations (4:10,13b,19-21,31b), denunciations (4:18,22), a taunt (4:30), and an impassioned appeal for repentance (4:14) are combined with striking descriptions of the invaders (4:7,11-13a,15-17) and their effect upon the land (4:20,21-31).

A Sinful Society Condemned (5:1-31). Chapter 5 reiterates why judgment was impending. Without exception the residents of Jerusalem had resisted the Lord's discipline and rebelled against His commandments. Idolatry and sexual immorality were prevalent throughout the land. The people believed the false prophets' message of security. Rich, powerful men exploited others and neglected the cause of the weak and oppressed. Instead of repenting and recognizing God as the source of their blessings, the people stubbornly continued in their sinful ways. Judgment was inevitable for such a nation. The fearsome Babylonians would devour their crops and herds, kill their children, and destroy their cities. Since God's people insisted on acting like pagans, they would serve pagans in a pagan land.

Jerusalem Attacked (6:1-30). The invasion threatened in chapters 4 and 5 now takes on even more frightening proportions as the coming siege of Jerusalem is depicted. In succession one hears the Lord's call of alarm to the residents of Benjamin and Judah, the enemy army's call to war, the Lord's summons to this army, a warning to Jerusalem, and the Lord's authorization of foreigners to "glean" His people (6:1-9).

The prophet then interjected a word. Though the people were obstinate and rejected his message of judgment, he was compelled to continue preaching it. God encouraged him to persevere in his proclamation of coming wrath because judgment was inevitable for such a corrupt nation. Even the religious leaders were greedy and deceitful. They glossed over the nation's dire situation and proclaimed a message of false hope. The people refused to obey God's law or to listen to His prophets. Their empty sacrifices would not prevent the coming disaster. The mighty northern army would march relentlessly forward, causing terror and grief among the people. In conclusion the Lord compared Jeremiah's role to that of a metal tester. Having seen the people's moral character revealed in their response to his ministry, Jeremiah observed that they were rebels in need of the hot, purifying fires of divine judgment.

7:1–10:25
Hypocrisy and Idolatry Condemned

False Confidence (7:1–8:3). The people of Judah believed they were safe because the temple, the Lord's dwelling place, was in their midst. The Lord denounced this false confidence, pointing out that only genuine repentance could save such unjust, violent, and idolatrous people. He reminded them of the example of Shiloh, a former dwelling place of the Lord which had not been spared destruction when God judged His wicked people. Though the people brought Him sacrifices, the Lord rejected them as meaningless and hypocritical. He demanded loyalty, not empty ritual. While the people gave the Lord lip service, they also prepared offerings for the "Queen of Heaven" (the Babylonian goddess Ishtar). They sacrificed their children in the Valley of Ben Hinnom south of the city and worshiped the sun, moon, and stars. Apart from repentance, judgment was inevitable. The Valley of Ben Hinnom would be called the Valley of Slaughter, for there the carcasses of the idolaters would be devoured by scavengers. The invaders would desecrate the tombs of the city, leaving the bones exposed to the light of the heavenly bodies the deceased once worshiped.

Punishment and Lamentation (8:4–9:26). Though the people claimed to be wise because they possessed God's law, their actions contradicted their words. They disobeyed that same law, refused to repent, and believed the religious leaders who promised peace and safety. The Lord would deprive them of their crops and bring into the land a mighty army, likened to deadly serpents. In that day the doomed and despairing people would lament their fate and acknowledge that their previous hope had been misplaced.

Jeremiah was emotionally shaken by this message of judgment. He described the future cry of the exiles, who in bewilderment would try to reconcile their belief in Jerusalem's inviolability with their situation. He lamented that there was no cure for the nation's sickness and that he did not have enough tears to weep around the clock. He longed to run away, for he recognized that wickedness was everywhere. Even the closest human relationships were polluted by deceit and exploitation.

The time for mourning and lamentation had come, for destruction and exile were on the way. Embodied in the Babylonian army, death would invade the cities and houses of the land, robbing the women of their children and robust young men.

In the coming day of judgment, human wisdom, strength, and riches would be of no avail. Security could only be found in loyalty to the Lord, who as a faithful and just God looks for and rewards these same qualities in His people. Traditional outward signs of a relationship with

A scene from a wall painting in a tomb at Thebes (1300 B.C.) depicting women who are professional mourners (see Jer 9:17-18).

God, such as circumcision, would also be worthless, if not accompanied by genuine devotion to the Lord (likened in 9:26 to circumcision of the heart, compare 4:4). Because God's people lacked this devotion, their physical circumcision would be as useless as that of Gentiles who also observed this practice. Israel would be swept away with the nations mentioned in the coming Babylonian invasion of the west.

The Incomparable Lord (10:1-16). The Lord exhorted His people to reject their pagan gods. The man-made wooden and metal idol-gods were inactive and as lifeless as scarecrows. In response Jeremiah praised the Lord, whose greatness infinitely surpasses that of idols. The Lord is the true, living, and eternal God, who created and controls the physical universe and determines the destinies of nations.

Jeremiah's Lament (10:17-25). Since God's people had rejected their sovereign King for idols, judgment remained inevitable and lamentation appropriate. Continuing the mood of earlier chapters, the prophet lamented the nation's incurable sickness and impending doom. Appealing to God's justice, he pled that the coming judgment not be unduly harsh and that God would eventually punish the nations for their mistreatment of His people.

Shown above is an example of a mutual obligation treaty or covenant dating from 672 B.C. between Assyria and one of its vassal kings. It ends with a series of curses. See Jeremiah 11:3.

11:1–13:27
Warnings against Rebellion

Breach of Covenant (11:1-17). The Lord reminded His people of the covenant that was to govern their relationship. After the Lord delivered their forefathers from Egypt, He made an agreement with them. If they obeyed His commandments, He promised to be their God and give them the promised land. However, throughout their history the people disobeyed God's law, bringing the punishment (the "curses") threatened in the covenant. Jeremiah's generation had followed in their forefathers' steps by worshiping Baal and other foreign gods. Consequently, they too had to experience the curses of the covenant.

Opposition to Jeremiah (11:18–12:6). As the Lord's messenger of judgment, Jeremiah faced opposition, even in his hometown of Anathoth, where some plotted to take his life. Though the prophet had not suspected their hostile intentions, the Lord revealed their schemes. Jeremiah trusted the Lord to vindicate and avenge him. The Lord declared that Jeremiah's enemies would be violently and thoroughly destroyed.

The dialogue between the Lord and His prophet continues in chapter 12. Knowing that God is just, Jeremiah was troubled by the prosperity of the wicked. Confident that God was aware of his loyal character, the prophet asked the Lord to judge the wicked so that the land might be released from the curse that the sin of the wicked had brought upon it. This time the Lord offered no messages of judgment (compare 11:21-23). He warned Jeremiah that the situation would become far worse and that even members of his own family would conspire against him.

The Lord Abandons and Reclaims His Inheritance (12:7-17). Though the Lord regarded Judah as His special possession, its hostility forced Him to abandon it. He would allow foreigners to desolate the land. However, He would someday punish these same nations and restore His exiled people to their land. Any nation that then turned to the Lord would be restored, while those that rejected His rule would be annihilated.

An Object Lesson and a Parable (13:1-27). The Lord instructed Jeremiah to purchase, wear, and then bury a linen belt. Days later He told the prophet to dig up the now rotten and useless belt. Just as a fine belt brings its owner compliments, so God had intended to glorify Himself through His people. But their pride, stubborn-

A dark-skinned Nubian presenting a spotted leopard to Thutmosis III (from a tomb painting, 1400s B.C). See Jeremiah 13:23.

would ruin their pride through judgment, just as Jeremiah's belt was ruined by the elements.

The Lord also used a parable to illustrate the coming judgment. Jeremiah was to make the observation that wineskins should be filled with wine. When the people rebuked him for making such an obvious remark, he was to explain the symbolism behind his statement. Just as wineskins were to be used for their designed purpose, so God would deal with His sinful people appropriately. Like wineskins filled with wine, they would be filled with "drunkenness," which is a figurative reference to the staggering effects of God's thorough punishment.

Just as persons cannot change their skin color or a leopard its spots, so the people could not change their propensity for evil. The darkness of judgment would descend on the incorrigible nation, and the people would be swept away into exile like chaff before the wind.

14:1–15:21
God Responds to Jeremiah's Prayers

Famine and Sword Are Inevitable (14:1-18). Jeremiah lamented that a severe drought had swept over the land, confessed the nation's sin, and asked the Lord to restore His favor. In response the Lord pointed to the nation's wickedness, instructed Jeremiah to cease interceding for the people, and announced He would not accept their hypocritical sacrifices. Jeremiah blamed the nation's condition on the false prophets and their promises of peace. These liars would be destroyed with the rest of the nation.

Prophetic Intercession Is Futile (14:19–15:9). Once more Jeremiah interceded for the nation, lamenting its condition, confessing its sin, and asking the Lord to intervene. He acknowledged that the Lord was incomparable to the idol-gods and that He alone was the source of the nation's blessings. The Lord declared that not even Moses or Samuel could effectively intercede for such a wicked people. The sins of King Manasseh had angered Him (compare 2 Kgs 21:1-18), and the people had not changed their ways. God decreed that death, famine, and exile would sweep through the land.

The Lord Vindicates His Prophet (15:10-21). Jeremiah once again lamented the opposition he experienced (compare 12:1-4). Though he was innocent of wrongdoing and had faithfully declared the Lord's word, he suffered reproach. He questioned God's dependability and asked the Lord to take up his cause. The Lord assured him of divine protection and vindication before his enemies. However, the prophet had to confess his lack of faith and persevere in his mission.

16:1–17:27
More Warnings and Exhortations

Jeremiah's Restrictions Foreshadow Judgment (16:1–17:4). The Lord placed several restrictions on Jeremiah that foreshadowed the effects of the coming judgment. Jeremiah was not to take a wife in order to show the devastating effects of judgment upon the nation's families. Many would be left without children and spouses. The prophet was forbidden to attend a funeral, for after the coming disaster people would not even have the opportunity to mourn the dead. Neither was he to attend a feast, for judgment would bring a cessation of joyous celebrations throughout the land.

Once again the Lord pointed out that the people's idolatry had brought this calamity. Though the Lord would someday restore His people to the land through a grand new exodus, the immediate future was only dark. The invaders, like fishermen and hunters, would pursue the people relentlessly. The Lord would repay them double for their idolatry. They would forfeit their place in the promised land and live as slaves in a distant, foreign place.

Contrasting Fates of the Wicked and Righteous (17:5-11). The Lord stopped to contrast the wicked and the righteous. Those trusting in human strength and rejecting the Lord were doomed to experience extreme discomfort and eventual death. But those trusting the Lord would flourish, even in times of crisis. Though people can be exceedingly deceptive, God is capable of piercing their minds and motives and dealing with them in a just manner.

Jeremiah's Prayer (17:12-18). Appealing to this all-knowing and just God, Jeremiah asserted his faithfulness to his commission and asked that he be vindicated before his persecutors.

Sabbath Commands (17:19-27). Once more the Lord offered the people an opportunity to exhibit a repentant attitude. He exhorted the whole nation, including its king, to demonstrate their loyalty to Him by observing His requirements concerning the Sabbath Day. If they kept it holy by refraining from work, the Lord would bless them and accept their offerings. However, if they rejected this test of obedience, the threatened calamity would come in full force.

18:1–20:18
Lessons from the Potter Bring Trouble for Jeremiah

A Marred Pot and an Unpopular Prophet (18:1-23). The Lord sent Jeremiah to a potter's house, where he illustrated His sovereign control over Judah. As Jeremiah watched the potter shaping a pot, the clay was marred. The potter reshaped the marred clay into a different style pot. The Lord explained that His people were like clay in His hands which He is free to reshape in accordance with His desires. When He threatens to destroy a sinful nation, He remains willing to reshape that nation's destiny if they are repentant. When He plans to bless a nation, He will alter His purpose if they are disobedient. Though He had once blessed His people, He was now planning disaster against them because of their idolatry and disobedience. Repentance would reshape their destiny, but they refused God's offer.

Jeremiah's proclamation of these truths was not well-received. The residents of Judah and Jerusalem plotted against the prophet, causing him to protest his innocence and again seek vindication from the Lord.

A Broken Jar and a Disillusioned Prophet (19:1–20:18). The Lord instructed Jeremiah to buy a jar from a potter and then take some of the civil leaders and priests out to the Valley of Ben Hinnom (compare 7:31). Once there the prophet was to pronounce scathing judgment against Jerusalem because of the idolatry and child sacrifice its residents carried on in the valley. He was then to break the jar, illustrating what God would do to the city. This idolatrous valley would become a burial ground for the slaughtered idolaters.

Having carried out his commission, Jeremiah went to the temple and delivered another announcement of judgment. Pashhur, one of the leading temple officials, had

A limestone statue from the mid-2000s B.C. of a potter working at his potter's wheel. See Jeremiah 18:3.

Jeremiah imprisoned and beaten. When released, Jeremiah gave Pashhur the symbolic name Magor-Missabib (meaning *terror all around*) and announced that this official would witness the death of his friends and the exile of the nation. Passhur would die and be buried in a foreign land.

Embarrassed and angry, Jeremiah poured out his heart before the Lord. His words reflect his confused emotions and perspective. He accused the Lord of deception and complained of being caught between a rock and a hard place. When he proclaimed the Lord's word, he was insulted and abused. If he held back from preaching the message, the divine word burned within him until he was forced to declare it. In a sudden burst of confidence Jeremiah affirmed his trust in the Lord. Just as quickly he sunk back into depression and cursed the day of his birth.

21:1–24:10
Messages against Kings and False Prophets

Messages from King Zedekiah's reign begin (21:1-10) and end (24:1-10) this section. In between are oracles concerning the Davidic throne (21:11–22:9; 23:1-8), Zedekiah's predecessors (Jehoahaz [22:10-12], Jehoiakim [22:13-23], and Jehoiachin [22:24-30]), and the false prophets (23:9-40).

Messages against Judah's Final Kings (21:1–23:8). Zedekiah sent messengers to Jeremiah in hopes that the Lord might miraculously deliver Jerusalem from the Babylonian armies. The Lord declared that He was fighting with the Babylonians and would not rescue the city. Jerusalem would be ravaged by plague, famine, and sword. Zedekiah and the city's survivors would be handed over to the Babylonians (compare 2 Kgs 23:5-7). Those who wished to escape the slaughter should surrender to Nebuchadnezzar immediately.

Jeremiah 21:11–22:9 contains two exhortations, addressed generally to the royal house. Both focus on the necessity for justice. They come from a time when repentance was still an option (compare 21:12; 22:3-4) and the people were still boasting Jerusalem could never fall (compare 21:13). The Lord reminded the king of his obligation to promote justice, warning that a failure in this regard would bring severe consequences. He threatened proud Jerusalem with judgment as well.

The next speech (22:10-12) comes after the death of Josiah and the Egyptian exile of his son Shallum (Jehoahaz), both of which occurred in 609 B.C. (compare 2 Kgs 23:29-34). The people were to cease mourning for Josiah and lament Jehoahaz, for the latter's fate (death in exile) was even more foreboding for the nation than Josiah's death had been.

The next oracle (Jer 23:13-23) concerns Jehoiakim, another of Josiah's sons and Jehoahaz's successor. The Lord denounced the unjust practices used by Jehoiakim in building a beautiful new palace. Jehoiakim's exploitation of the citizenry stood in stark contrast to his father Josiah's righteousness. Josiah's concern for justice in his realm was proof that he truly acknowledged the Lord's authority. Humiliation would overtake proud Jehoiakim and his city.

The future was also dark for Jehoiachin, Jehoiakim's son and successor (22:24-30). The Lord would reject him as king and hand him over to Nebuchadnezzar. He would spend the rest of his days in exile (compare 2 Kgs

FALSE PROPHETS

"Thus says the Lord"—a comforting sound, promising direction, authority, and truth. Or is it? Israel knew the words could come from different directions. Thus God's law cautioned Israel, "A prophet who presumes to speak in my name anything I have not commanded him to say, or a prophet who speaks in the name of other gods, must be put to death" (Deut 18:20). Two types of false prophets confused Israel's search to know God's will.

1. Prophets who claimed to announce a message from Yahweh, Israel's God. These prophets met Israel many times in its history. Such prophets proclaimed the word audiences wanted to hear (Mic 3:5). Such words came "out of their own imagination" (Ezek 13:17) and were usually words of peace (Jer 28:5-9).

Isaiah accused such prophets of getting drunk with spirits (beer and wine) rather than inspired with the Spirit (Isa 28:7-8). They were wicked, even adulterers (Jer 23:10-11,14). They spoke in the name of Israel's God, but they lied (27:16-17; 29:20-23). They did not carry out the prophet's role as intercessor for Israel with God (27:18). They used false means to secure God's word (Ezek 13:6; compare Deut 18:9-10,14). Money motivated them, not God's Spirit (Mic 3:5,11). Indeed, God had not sent them at all (Jer 14:14; 23:21; Ezek 13:6-7; compare 22:28).

Such prophets failed to accomplish their basic missions: they did not turn Israel away from wickedness and evil (Jer 23:14,22), nor did they turn Israel away from Baal or call them to loyalty to Yahweh (23:27). They opposed the righteous rather than the wicked (Ezek 13:22).

Clearly, such prophets were false. Still, they preached, and the people applauded. Why? Because no one could prove them wrong. They carried the same title as those we call the true prophets. They often served the king faithfully (1 Kgs 22). Their message of peace sounded good. They made few demands on their listeners.

The true prophet had no clear defense against them. Hananiah could even tear the symbolic yoke off Jeremiah's neck, and Jeremiah had no recourse. He simply walked away until God spoke (Jer 28:10-14).

One thing exposed false prophets: their predictions did not come true (Deut 18:22; Jer 28:9; Ezek 33:33). In the moment of confrontation, that did not help. Only the destruction of Jerusalem and the exile of the people finally revealed who was true and who was false.

2. The second type of false prophet quickly showed that falseness. These prophets prophesied in the name of other gods (1 Kgs 18:22). Israel should have seen their false nature quickly. But Israel was blinded even to the clear signal of false prophecy. Elisha had to perform a miracle to prove himself over against Baal's prophets. Even then the crowds did not follow. The prophet fled alone to the wilderness.

Repeatedly, then, false prophecy won the day in Israel. Only God's destructive acts in Israel's history finally validated His true prophets and led Israel to preserve their words as part of inspired Scripture. ☐

24:8-17). None of his sons would occupy his throne.

In the final oracle of the section (Jer 23:1-8) the Lord announced the impending judgment of the "shepherds" (or rulers) of the nation, who had misled, rather than cared for, His people. Though the people would be scattered in exile, the Lord would eventually restore a remnant to the land and give them competent leaders. In that day an ideal Davidic king would reign in justice and bring peace to the land.

Messages against False Prophets (23:9-40). The Lord's judgment was about to fall upon the false prophets who failed to denounce evil and promised the people peace and security. None of these prophets had access to the Lord's heavenly council or received revelation from Him, yet they claimed to be His messengers.

Two Baskets of Figs (24:1-10). Following the exile of Jehoiachin in 597 B.C., the Lord gave Jeremiah another object lesson. He showed the prophet two baskets, one filled with tasty figs and the other with inedible ones. The good figs represented those already exiled in Babylon. The Lord would care for them and eventually restore the exiles to the land. The bad figs represented Jehoiachin's successor Zedekiah, his officials, those who remained in Jerusalem, and those who had gone to Egypt. They would experience humiliation and eventual destruction.

Head of a terra cotta statue of a local king from the island of Cyprus (550–450 B.C.). See Jeremiah 25:22.

MESSAGES OF JUDGMENT AND RESTORATION (JER 25:1–51:64)

These chapters outline God's future program in detail. The theme of judgment upon Judah, introduced in chapters 1–24, is developed. This section also describes divine judgment on a universal scale, as well as the future restoration of God's people.

The theme of universal judgment begins (chap. 25) and ends (chaps. 46–51) this section, with the downfall of Babylon being highlighted (25:12-14,26; 50–51). In between appear two subsections (chaps. 26–35 and chaps. 36–45), both of which begin and end with material dating from Jehoiakim's reign.

25:1-38
Universal Judgment

This oracle is dated to Jehoiakim's fourth year (605 B.C.). Through faithful prophets like Jeremiah, the Lord had repeatedly called the nation to repentance. They had rejected the offer and persisted in idolatry. The day of reckoning had come. Nebuchadnezzar's armies would sweep down from the north and overrun Judah and the neighboring states. These nations would serve Babylon for seventy years, after which time the Lord would overthrow their oppressor. This prophecy of Babylon's doom was fulfilled in 538 when the Persians defeated the Chaldean empire and conquered Babylon.

The coming judgment of the nations is likened to an intoxicating cup passed from mouth to mouth. Judah would take the first swig, followed by several other nations (25:19-26). Finally Babylon, referred to here by its code-name Sheshach (25:26; compare 51:41), would be forced to take a draft from the Lord's cup. The Lord's judgment is described with other vivid images, including a deafening storm, the slaughter of sheep, the shattering of a pot, and a raging lion.

26:1–35:19
Exile and Restoration

This section begins (26:1-24) and ends (35:1-19) with events from Jehoiakim's time. These two chapters contrast Judah's rejection of God's prophet with the devotion of the Recabites (35:15-16). The intervening chapters date from the time of Zedekiah. Chapters 27–29 and 34, which condemn the nation's corrupt civil and religious leaders, provide a frame around the messages of hope and restoration in chapters 30–33.

Jeremiah's Life Threatened (26:1-24). Early in the reign of Jehoiakim, Jeremiah delivered a message to worshipers at the temple. Disaster was coming if the people refused to repent of their sinful ways. The temple would be destroyed like the shrine at Shiloh, which had once been the Lord's dwelling place (compare 7:12-14).

Those who heard his message, including the priests and false prophets, grabbed Jeremiah and threatened to kill him. When royal officials intervened, the priests and prophets accused him of treason. Jeremiah declared that the Lord had sent him, again issued a call to repentance, and protested his innocence. The officials and the people objected to the religious leaders' charge. Several elders reminded the crowd of an event in the nation's history about one hundred years before. The prophet Micah had announced that the city and temple would be destroyed (compare 26:18 with Mic 3:12). On that occasion Hezekiah repented, and God postponed judgment. The elders warned that Jeremiah's opponents were about to bring a terrible disaster upon the city. Ahikam, a high-ranking official in the royal court, also interceded for Jeremiah, and he was spared.

However, a parenthetical note (26:20-23) informs us that not all of the Lord's prophets were as fortunate as Jeremiah. One of Jeremiah's contemporaries, Uriah, was forced to flee to Egypt when one of his prophecies of judgment angered King Jehoiakim. Jehoiakim had Uriah extradited and executed.

Jeremiah Confronts the False Prophets (27:1–29:32). Early in Zedekiah's reign Jeremiah warned the people not to believe the false prophets' messages of hope and peace. In accordance with the Lord's instructions, Jeremiah made a yoke and placed it on his neck. He then sent messages to the kings of the surrounding nations, informing them that Nebuchadnezzar would subjugate their lands. They were not to believe their lying prophets and diviners who were advocating resistance and predicting deliverance. Resistance would only bring disaster and exile. They should submit to Nebuchadnezzar's authority (symbolized by the yoke) so that they might remain in their lands. The message was the same for Zedekiah. He should reject the messages of hope delivered by the false prophets, who were even promising that the temple articles already carried away to Babylon would be returned. Zedekiah should submit to Nebuchadnezzar's yoke in order to spare the city and the temple further suffering and humiliation.

In that same year Hananiah, one of the false prophets, confronted Jeremiah in the temple (28:1). He declared that within two years the Lord would deliver Judah from the Babylonians, restore the temple articles, and return Jehoiachin and the other exiles. After expressing his personal desire that Judah might experience such blessings, Jeremiah reminded Hananiah that historically the Lord's prophets had been messengers of judgment. Prophets of peace could only be authenticated when their predictions came true. In response Hananiah removed the wooden yoke from Jeremiah's neck, broke it, and once again declared that the Lord would deliver Judah and the surrounding nations from Nebuchadnezzar's yoke. Not to be denied, Jeremiah announced that the Lord would place an unbreakable iron yoke upon Judah and the nations. He then announced that Hananiah would die before the year ended, a prophecy that was fulfilled two months later.

During Zedekiah's reign Jeremiah sent a letter to those who had already been taken to Babylon (29:1). He encouraged them to settle down there, marry and have children, and pray for the prosperity of their new home. In seventy years the Lord would restore them to the promised land. They were not to believe the deceiving prophets among them who were giving them false hopes of a quick return. Even greater calamity was about to fall on sinful Judah, and those still living in the promised land would be driven among the nations.

Jeremiah condemned two of these prophets by name (28:21). Because of their immoral acts and false prophecies, the Lord would deliver them to the Babylonians for execution, probably on charges of rebellion.

Shemaiah, a false prophet in Babylon, sent several letters back to Jerusalem, informing Zephaniah the priest and others of the contents of Jeremiah's letter to the exiles. Calling Jeremiah a madman, Shemaiah urged Zephaniah to imprison the prophet. When informed by the priest of Shemaiah's words, Jeremiah sent another message to the exiles, denouncing Shemaiah as a false prophet and proclaiming that neither he nor his family would participate in the eventual restoration of the exiles.

Hope and Restoration (30:1–33:26). Though dark days were ahead, God would not totally abandon His people. An awful time of frightening judgment would come upon the sin-filled land. Abandoned by its allies and struck down by God, the nation would be like a man with an incurable wound. However, after this time of discipline, God would cure their wound and bring His exiled people back to the land. Exiles from the Northern Kingdom would be reunited with those from Judah, and together they would serve the Lord and His appointed Davidic ruler. The people would increase in numbers and enjoy a renewed relationship with God.

The message of comfort to the exiles continues in chapter 31. Assuring the Northern Kingdom of His everlasting love, the Lord promised to deliver its exiles from their captors. Like a shepherd He would lead them back home and restore their agricultural prosperity and joy. They would come to Jerusalem to worship the Lord and thank Him for His abundant blessings.

Personification highlights 31:15-22. Calling the Northern Kingdom Rachel (the mother of Joseph and grandmother of Ephraim and Manasseh, the two important northern tribes), the Lord exhorted her to cease weeping over her exiled children, for they would someday return to the land. Comparing Ephraim to His son (compare v. 9), the Lord declared that He had heard His child's prayer of repentance. Finally, addressing Israel as a young woman (compare v. 4), the Lord exhorted her to cease her wandering and carefully observe the road signs guiding her back to the land.

The concluding, riddlelike statement of verse 22 has puzzled interpreters. The woman is undoubtedly Israel, and the man, probably the Lord. Perhaps reference is made to Israel's newfound devotion to the Lord or to its renewed worship around the Lord's throne in Zion (compare vv. 4-6,11-13). In that day Judah's devotion to the Lord would also be renewed. The restored exiles would pronounce blessings upon Jerusalem and prosper in their agricultural pursuits.

Chapter 31 culminates with a glorious promise of a new covenant. In days past the Lord had carefully planned and executed the demise of Israel and Judah. In the future He would carefully superintend their restoration. He would forgive their sins and establish a new covenant superior to the Mosaic covenant they had violated. This time God would supernaturally give them the capacity for loyalty that the old covenant had demanded. The Lord took a formal oath that His people would never cease to be a nation or experience His rejection. He promised that Jerusalem would be rebuilt, purified, and never again destroyed.

During the Babylonian siege of Jerusalem in 587 B.C. Zedekiah, who resented Jeremiah's oracles of doom, imprisoned the prophet in the royal palace (32:1-2). When Jeremiah's cousin Hanamel came to visit him, Jeremiah, as commanded by the Lord, redeemed Hanamel's field in accordance with the ancient law of land redemption (Lev 25:25-28).

Having completed the transaction, Jeremiah prayed to the Lord. He praised God as the almighty Creator and just Ruler over all. He recalled God's mighty deeds in Israel's history and acknowledged that the present crisis was the result of the nation's sin. Aware that the city would fall to the Babylonians, he asked why God had instructed him to purchase a field. What good would a field be once the land was destroyed and the people exiled?

In response the Lord asked, "Is anything too hard for me?" (Jer 32:27). Yes, He would allow the Babylonians to conquer the city because of its idolatry. The Lord would someday restore the exiles to the land, transform them into loyal worshipers, establish a new covenant with them, and restore their prosperity. In that day people would again buy and sell fields. Jeremiah's purchase of the field foreshadowed this future restoration.

While confined in the palace, Jeremiah received another encouraging message about the future restoration of the land (33:1). Though the Babylonians would reduce Judah to a wasteland and fill Jerusalem with carcasses, the Lord would someday forgive His people's sins, bring them back to the land, and cause Jerusalem to prosper. In fulfillment of His eternal promise to David (2 Sam 7:12-16), the Lord would raise up an ideal Davidic ruler, who would bring justice and peace to the land. Faithful to His irrevocable covenant with the Levites (Num 25:12-13), He would establish them as His servants.

Zedekiah's Fate (34:1-22). Despite these glowing promises of restoration, the immediate future remained bleak. During the Babylonian siege Jeremiah warned King Zedekiah that the Babylonians would conquer the city and take the king into exile. The prophet assured Zedekiah that he would die a peaceful, not violent, death and would receive an honorable burial.

Jeremiah also denounced the king's unjust treatment of slaves. During the siege Zedekiah and the citizens of Jerusalem pledged on oath to free all Hebrew slaves. Apparently in some cases this was done as an act of repentance for past failures in this regard (Jer 34:13-15). However, ulterior motives must have been involved; for when the Babylonians lifted the siege, the slave owners reneged on their covenant and revoked the freedom of those just released. Jeremiah sarcastically declared that the Lord had granted these covenant violators "freedom" from their deceitful ways so that they might perish. When the Lord was through with them, they would be like one of the calves cut in two in a covenant-making ceremony. The Babylonians would return to the city and destroy it.

Jeremiah and the Recabites (35:1-19). During the reign of Jehoiakim, the Lord instructed Jeremiah to invite the Recabite family to the temple and to offer them some wine. The Recabites were the descendants of Jonadab, son of Recab (2 Kgs 10:15-23), a zealous devotee of the Lord and opponent of Baal worship. Jonadab had commanded his descendants to follow a nomadic and ascetic life-style, which included total abstinence from

wine. Over two hundred years later his descendants were still observing the regulations their forefather established. When Jeremiah set the wine before them, they refused to drink it, faithful to their ancestor's commands.

The Recabites were an object lesson to Judah and Jerusalem. Their unwavering devotion to their ancestor stood in stark contrast to unfaithful Judah's rejection of the Lord's prophets. Judgment would fall on Judah, but the Lord would preserve Jonadab's godly line.

36:1–45:5
Judah's Final Days

This section opens (36:1-22) and closes (45:1-5) with material dating from the fourth and fifth years of Jehoiakim's reign. Baruch, Jeremiah's scribe, plays a prominent role in these chapters that frame the section. The intervening chapters relate in chronological order various experiences of the prophet, beginning with his dealings with King Zedekiah and concluding with his messages to the Egyptian exiles following the fall of Jerusalem.

Jehoiakim Burns the Scroll (36:1-32). The Lord instructed Jeremiah to record all of his prophetic messages on a scroll. Jeremiah dictated his messages to the scribe Baruch. Baruch took the scroll to the temple on an official day of fasting and read the prophecies to the people assembled there. When the royal officials heard the reading of the scroll, they told Baruch they must report its contents to the king. After warning Jeremiah and Baruch to go into hiding, they informed the king. As the scroll was read, Jehoiakim cut it up by columns and burned it. He then ordered the arrest of Jeremiah and Baruch, whom by this time the Lord had hidden. The Lord then instructed Jeremiah to dictate another scroll. He also announced that Jehoiakim would be punished severely for his disrespect.

Zedekiah Imprisons Jeremiah (37:1–38:28). During the siege of Jerusalem in 588 B.C. the Babylonians temporarily withdrew from the city to fight an army sent out by Egypt, one of Judah's allies. Jeremiah warned Zedekiah that the city's relief was only temporary. The Babylonians would push back the Egyptians and then destroy Jerusalem. Jeremiah was arrested as a traitor, beaten, and imprisoned for a lengthy period of time in a dungeon. Zedekiah eventually sent for Jeremiah to see if he had any new word from the Lord. Jeremiah repeated his earlier message of judgment, protested his innocence, and asked the king not to send him back to the dungeon. Zedekiah granted his request and sent him to the courtyard of the guard.

Baruch recording the prophecies of Jeremiah

While similarities between chapters 37 and 38 might suggest they are parallel accounts of the same events, differences in details make it more likely that chapter 38 records events subsequent to those of chapter 37. While in the courtyard of the guard, Jeremiah continued to proclaim his message of impending judgment. Several royal officials complained to Zedekiah, arguing that Jeremiah should be put to death as a traitor. With the king's approval they lowered the prophet into a muddy cistern, where they intended to let him starve. Ebed-Melech, a palace official, objected to the king, who agreed to let Ebed-Melech rescue Jeremiah from the cistern. Zedekiah again met privately with the prophet. The king expressed his fear that the Babylonians would deliver him over to the hostile pro-Babylonian Jewish party. Jeremiah assured the king that if he surrendered to the Babylonians his life would be preserved. At the same time he warned that resistance would result only in humiliation and ruin. Zedekiah warned Jeremiah to keep their conversation a secret and allowed him to remain in the courtyard of the guard.

Jerusalem's Fall and Jeremiah's Release (39:1–40:6). After a long siege Jerusalem fell to the Babylonians in 586 B.C. Zedekiah ran for his life, but the Babylonians captured him near Jericho and brought him to Nebuchadnezzar. Before the king's eyes the Babylonians executed his sons and the nobles of Judah. They then put Zedekiah's eyes out and took him to Babylon. The Babylonians destroyed Jerusalem and carried most of the population away into exile, leaving only the poor behind.

In the midst of this disaster, Jeremiah was not forgotten. By royal order Nebuzaradan, one of Nebuchadnezzar's high-ranking officials, released Jeremiah from the courtyard of the guard and turned him over to Gedaliah.

Details of the prophet's release follow a brief parenthesis indicating that Ebed-Melech was spared (compare 38:7-13). After his initial release Jeremiah somehow got mixed in with those being taken into exile. Nebuzaradan freed him and gave him the option to go to Babylon or stay in the land. Jeremiah decided on the latter and returned to Gedaliah, the newly appointed governor.

Turmoil in the Land (40:7–41:15). During the Babylonian invasion some of the soldiers and men of Judah had managed to avoid capture. They came to Gedaliah, who promised them safety and encouraged them to return to their agricultural pursuits and serve the king of Babylon. Judean refugees from the surrounding countries returned as well and resumed life in their homeland.

However, all was not well. One of the army officers, Johanon son of Kareah, informed Gedaliah that the king of the Ammonites, who was anti-Babylonian in sentiment (compare 27:3; Ezek 21:18-32), wanted the governor dead and had already sent another of Judah's army officers, Ishmael son of Nethaniah, to do the job. Gedaliah refused to believe this report and declined Johanon's offer to kill Ishmael.

Sometime later (41:1 gives the month, but not the year), Ishmael and ten other men visited Gedaliah in Mizpah. During a meal they suddenly arose and killed Gedaliah, as well as the Judeans and Babylonian soldiers who were present. The next day eighty men passed by on their way to Jerusalem to mourn over the temple and present offerings at its ruins. Ishmael enticed them into the city, where he then slaughtered seventy of the eighty (the ten who were spared promised him provisions) and threw their bodies into a cistern. Taking the residents of Mizpah as hostages, he set out for Ammon. When Johanon heard the news, he and his men pursued Ishmael and overtook him in Gibeon. The hostages were rescued, but Ishmael and eight of his men escaped.

Jeremiah's Message to the Survivors (41:16–43:7). Fearing reprisal from the Babylonians for the death of Gedaliah, Johanon and the people of Mizpah started toward Egypt. However, before leaving the land, they asked Jeremiah to seek the Lord's will on their behalf and promised to obey His directions. After inquiring of the Lord, Jeremiah told them to stay in the land and promised that God would cause the Babylonian king to treat them mercifully. He warned that if they disobeyed and fled to Egypt, disaster would overtake them. Jeremiah's warning fell on deaf ears. Johanon and others accused him of collaborating with Baruch in an effort to hand them over to the Babylonians for punishment. With flagrant disregard for the Lord's command, the group fled to Egypt, taking Jeremiah and Baruch with them.

Jeremiah in Egypt (43:8–44:30). Jeremiah's exile to Egypt certainly did not bring his prophetic ministry to an end. At Tahpanhes, the site of an Egyptian royal residence in the eastern delta, the Lord instructed Jeremiah to announce the coming fall of Egypt to the Babylonians. The prophet took some large stones and buried them in clay in the brick pavement at the entrance to the palace. He then proclaimed that Nebuchadnezzar would someday erect a throne over the stones. The Babylonian king would devastate Egypt and its temples. The Lord would prove to the Judean refugees that He, not Egypt, was their only source of strength and protection.

Chapter 44 records another of Jeremiah's Egyptian messages. Addressing all of the Judean exiles living in Egypt, the prophet reminded them that God's judgment upon Jerusalem was due to the people's idolatry. Their persistence in worshiping idol-gods would only lead to a further outpouring of God's angry judgment.

The people responded to Jeremiah's warning with hostility. They declared that they would continue to sacrifice to the "Queen of Heaven," the Babylonian goddess Ishtar. They thought disaster had only come upon Judah because Josiah purged the land of foreign gods (2 Kgs 23).

Jeremiah attempted to correct their faulty reasoning, pointing out that it was idolatry that had brought God's wrath upon the nation. In the face of such obstinacy Jeremiah announced that divine judgment would overtake them in Egypt. As a sign of coming disaster, he prophesied the downfall of Pharaoh Hophra. This prophecy was fulfilled a few years later, in 570 B.C., when Hophra was overthrown by a rival Egyptian party.

Jeremiah Encourages Baruch (45:1-5). This brief message, which dates to Jehoiakim's fourth year (605 B.C.) and concerns the scribe Baruch, rounds off chapters 36–45. These words were spoken to Baruch after he recorded Jeremiah's prophecies on a scroll (compare 36:1-7). Jeremiah told Baruch not to covet a high position, for judgment would surely come upon the land. Yet Baruch could be assured that the Lord would protect him through the disaster.

46:1–51:64
Judgment on Various Nations

These oracles of judgment develop the message of chapter 25. Together with chapter 25 they form a frame around this section of the book.

Judgment on Egypt (46:1-28). In 605 B.C. one of the major battles of ancient history took place at Carchemish, located on the Euphrates River in Syria. The Babylonians under Nebuchadnezzar defeated the Egyptians under Necho and thereby established themselves as the major power in the Near East. On the occasion of this battle, Jeremiah proclaimed an oracle against Egypt (46:2-12). In dramatic fashion he imitated the commands of the Egyptian officers as they prepared their troops for battle. He then described the Egyptians' retreat and downfall. Though the Egyptians marched into battle with chariots and weapons, they were doomed to defeat, for the Lord was fighting with the Babylonians.

Chapter 46 also includes a prophecy of the Babylonian invasion of Egypt, which took place in 568–567 B.C. The Egyptian army would scatter before the swarming northern invaders. The Egyptians would be as helpless as trees of a forest before the axes of woodsmen. Pharaoh and the gods of Egypt, including even their chief deity Amon, would be unable to resist the Lord's judgment.

The chapter concludes with an encouraging message for God's people. Once their time of punishment was over, the Lord would deliver them from exile and restore them to their land.

Judgment on the Philistines (47:1-7). Divine judgment would also fall on the Philistines. The approach of the Babylonians from the north would cause consternation throughout Philistia. The enemy would sweep through the land, bringing death and destruction. This oracle was fulfilled in 604 B.C. when Nebuchadnezzar overran Philistia and conquered Ashkelon.

Judgment on Moab (48:1-47). This lengthy oracle portrays the downfall of Moab, which apparently took place in 582 B.C. at the hands of the Babylonians. This chapter is filled with Moabite place names and vivid imagery. The destruction of their land would cause the Moabites to weep bitterly and flee in panic. In the past Moab had been relatively secure, like wine that had been allowed to settle in one jar. All that was about to change. Moab would be poured out of the jar. Moab's military might would be shattered, causing its pride and joy to be replaced by humiliation and lamentation. Its demise was inescapable. Its people and their chief god Chemosh would be carried into exile. A brief concluding statement promised Moab eventual restoration.

Judgment on Ammon (49:1-6). Ammon, another of the Trans-Jordanian states, would also experience judgment. The Ammonites were proud of their agricultural prosperity and wealth, but the Lord would bring disaster upon their land. They and their god Milcom (compare NIV "Molech") would go into exile. As in the case of Moab (compare 48:47), Ammon was promised eventual restoration.

Judgment on Edom (49:7-22). This oracle, which parallels the Book of Obadiah, threatens Edom with thorough and final destruction. Edom was proud of its wisdom and secure position. Since God's own people were not immune from punishment, then certainly the Edomites would not be spared. Like Sodom and Gomorrah, Edom would become a prime example of devastation and ruin. The Lord would come against them like a lion attacking a helpless flock of sheep.

Judgment on Damascus (49:23-27). Damascus, an important city in Syria, would also experience judgment. Arpad and Hamath, two city-states located in northern Syria, are portrayed as being troubled over the news of the fall of Damascus. The strong warriors of Damascus would fall in the streets as the city went up in smoke.

Judgment on Kedar and Hazor (49:28-33). Nebuchadnezzar, the Lord's instrument of judgment against nations, would also attack the Arabian tribes located east of Palestine, two of which are specifically named here (the precise location of Hazor is unknown). This prophecy came to pass in 599–598 B.C.

Judgment on Elam (49:34-39). The Lord would also judge the distant land of Elam, located east of Babylon. He would shatter Elam's military might and scatter its people among the nations. As in some of the preceding oracles, an encouraging word concludes the oracle (compare 46:26; 48:47; 49:6).

Judgment on Babylon (50:1–51:64). Though the Lord would use Babylon to punish many nations, He would eventually judge this mighty empire as well. In these two lengthy chapters Babylon's downfall is described in detail.

A mighty nation from the north would capture Babylon. The Medo-Persians conquered the Babylonian empire in 539 B.C. (51:11,28). The Babylonians' idol-gods, the chief of which was Marduk, would be unable to rescue the city.

Babylon's demise would be good news for God's people. He had sent them into exile for their sins, but now they would be able to leave Babylon, return to Jerusalem, and enjoy a renewed covenantal relationship with God. Babylon's and Israel's relative positions would be reversed. Like the Assyrians before them, Babylon had mistreated and oppressed God's people. Now the time of reckoning had come. The Lord would overthrow Babylon and regather His scattered people to their land. He would restore Israel's blessings and forgive their sins.

Babylon's fall is vividly portrayed as dramatic calls to battle alternate with descriptions of the city's defeat. The Lord would vindicate His oppressed people before the arrogant Babylonians. Using the invincible northern army as His instrument, the Lord would destroy everything in which Babylon took pride—its civil and religious leaders, warriors, armaments, and wealth. The city would become like Sodom and Gomorrah. (As in Isa 13–14, the problem of harmonizing this portrayal of Babylon's fall with the Persian conquest of 539 B.C. is difficult. See comments there.) Again employing the imagery of a lion ravaging a flock of sheep (compare 50:44-45 with 49:19-20), the Lord declared that the judgment of Babylon would demonstrate He was a God without equal.

The description of Babylon's fall continues in chapter 51. Once more the Lord's vengeance is a major theme. He would vindicate His people before their oppressor, demonstrating His sovereignty over the affairs of individuals and nations. The Lord is the Creator of the universe, who is infinitely superior to the idol gods.

The Babylonians would be unable to stand before the northern army raised up by the Lord. Babylon would be trampled like a threshing floor at harvest time and be reduced to ruins. In response to His people's prayer for revenge, the Lord announced that the Babylonians would reel like drunkards and be slaughtered like sheep. He would humiliate Babylon and its idols, just as the Babylonians had shamed the Lord's people and dwelling place. Before the Lord's retributive judgment all the wisdom, pomp, and might of Babylon would prove futile.

Having recorded his prophecy against Babylon on a scroll, Jeremiah commissioned Seraiah, an officer of King Zedekiah, who was about to travel to Babylon, to proclaim the message when he arrived there. He instructed Seraiah to offer a brief prayer and to drop the scroll into the Euphrates River as an illustration of Babylon's eventual downfall.

A HISTORICAL EPILOGUE (JER 52:1-34)

This chapter is parallel to 2 Kings 24:18–25:30 (see commentary there). The statistical information given in Jeremiah 52:28-30 does not appear in 2 Kings 25, and the account of Gedaliah's death (compare 2 Kgs 25:22-26) is omitted in Jeremiah 52. The chapter gives a detailed account of Jerusalem's fall to the Babylonians. It is probably included to authenticate Jeremiah's message by showing that his prophecies of judgment were fulfilled.

Theological Significance

Jeremiah shows prophecy in full flesh and blood. He wanted to identify with his people and live a normal life. Instead he had to preach against his people and confront other prophets and then ask God, "Why?" Through the prophet's humanity, God spoke to Judah and the nations during Israel's greatest crisis. God showed that obedience, justice, and piety pleased Him and ensured the nation's future. Theological and worship tradition ensured nothing. God could change political sides to discipline His covenant people and then lead them back to Him. Nebuchadnezzar succeeded in conquering Jerusalem because he was God's agent of judgment on His sinful people. In the end, however, the nations in their arrogance, would face God's wrath, while Israel would be a people of a new, heartfelt covenant.

Jeremiah affirmed that God's ultimate plan was to bless His people (29:11). God's plans, however, are conditional on human response (18:7-10). Persistent rebellion can bring punishment when God had promised blessing. Repentance can avert disaster when God had promised judgment.

Jeremiah affirms the faithlessness of God's people and their need for God to intervene to save them. Jeremiah anticipates a time when God would write a new covenant on His people's hearts, when God would be known in intimate fellowship, when God would no longer remember their sins (31:31-34). Jeremiah's hopes find fulfillment in the new relationship with God made possible through Christ's death (Heb 11:12-22).

Questions for Reflection

1. How did Jeremiah portray God? What roles and characteristics did the prophet attribute to God?

2. Why was God displeased with Judah? Is the modern church like Judah in any ways?

3. In what ways does Jeremiah serve as an example for God's people? What were his strengths? weaknesses?

4. How did Jeremiah characterize the false prophets of his day? How did they differ from Jeremiah? How can modern Christians identify false teachers?

Sources for Additional Study

Harrison, Roland K. *Jeremiah and Lamentations. Tyndale Old Testament Commentaries.* Downers Grove: InterVarsity, 1973.

Skinner, John. *Prophecy and Religion: Studies in the Life of Jeremiah.* Cambridge: University Press, 1922.

Thompson, J. A. *The Book of Jeremiah. New International Commentary on the Old Testament.* Grand Rapids: Eerdmans, 1980.

LAMENTATIONS

Though it does not identify its author, tradition has ascribed the Book of Lamentations to Jeremiah. The author of the book, like the prophet, was an eyewitness of Jerusalem's fall and displayed great emotion in his prayers to God. The book was written between the destruction of the city in 586 B.C. and the rebuilding of the temple seventy years later.

Theme

The author lamented the fall of Jerusalem. While acknowledging that the calamity was deserved, he longed for God to restore His favor.

Literary Form

The book contains five poems, corresponding to the chapter divisions. The central poem is sixty-six verses in length, while the others contain twenty-two verses each. All but the last poem are acrostics, in which the form reflects the successive letters of the Hebrew alphabet. In chapters 1; 2; and 4 the first letters of the first words of the twenty-two verses correspond to the successive letters of the Hebrew alphabet (the order of the letters *ayin* and *pe* varies). In chapter 3 the verses are arranged in blocks of three. Verses 1-3 each begin with the first letter of the alphabet (*aleph*), verses 4-6 with the second letter (*beth*), and so on.

The laments follow the standard pattern seen in the Psalms. (See "Psalms" and "Types of Old Testament Literature.") They contain typical lament elements such as complaint, petition, and confidence.

I. **Lamenting Jerusalem's Affliction (1:1-22)**
II. **Lamenting the Lord's Angry Judgment (2:1-22)**
III. **Confidence in the Midst of Disaster (3:1-66)**
IV. **Lamenting Jerusalem's Downfall (4:1-22)**
V. **Prayer for Restoration (5:1-22)**

Purpose and Theology

The author clearly acknowledged the truth of what the preexilic prophets had preached—Judah's sin led to its downfall and to the tragic destruction of Jerusalem and the temple. However, in the midst of this calamity the author acknowledged the Lord's faithfulness and compassion and appealed to these divine attributes. He longed for the day when God would restore His favor and take vengeance on the nations who had tormented them.

LAMENTING JERUSALEM'S AFFLICTION (LAM 1:1-22)

1:1-11
The Author's Lament

Jerusalem had once been a queen; now she was a slave. Foreigners had stolen its wealth, polluted its temple, and carried its people into exile. Abandoned by its allies and no longer visited by religious pilgrims, it was like an inconsolable widow, weeping bitterly over her loss. Because of its sin, Jerusalem had been humiliated, like a woman publicly disgraced by sexual sin.

1:12-22
The Personified City's Lament

Jerusalem, personified as a woman, lamented that the Lord had poured His anger out upon it. It acknowledged that its sins had brought its downfall and that the Lord had caused its military defeat. It lamented that it had no comforters, for its allies had turned against it and its people had gone into exile or perished. In desperation it confessed its sin and asked the Lord to consider its anguish. Humiliated and abused by its enemies, it pleaded with the Lord to take vengeance upon them.

LAMENTING THE LORD'S ANGRY JUDGMENT (LAM 2:1-22)

2:1-10
The Lord's Anger Unleashed

The Lord attacked Jerusalem as if it were His enemy. Rather than protecting the city with His powerful right hand, He turned His might against it and poured His an-

Lamentations 1:6 compares Jerusalem at the time of its destruction to deer who can find no pasture, food, or water. Shown above is an Assyrian relief from the time of Ashurbanipal showing starving gazelles and their young searching for food and water.

gry judgment upon it like fire. Though He once resided in the city, He abandoned His temple and allowed foreigners to pollute it. The city's walls were destroyed and its leaders enslaved, leaving the rest of the population (represented here by the elders and young women) to mourn bitterly over its demise.

2:11-19
The Author's Lament and Call to Prayer

The author lamented the plight of the small children, who were dying from hunger in their mothers' arms. Addressing the personified city, he grieved over its great distress and reminded it that the words of its false prophets had proven to be futile. In accordance with His sovereign decree the Lord had allowed Jerusalem's enemies to humiliate it. In conclusion he urged the people to cry out to the Lord for mercy.

2:20-22
Lady Jerusalem Laments Her Destruction

Responding to the author's exhortation, personified Jerusalem pleaded with the Lord to consider its plight. Women were forced to eat their own children to survive, religious leaders had been killed in the Lord's temple, and the streets were littered with the corpses of the city's inhabitants. The Lord had invited its enemies to attack the city, and no one had escaped.

CONFIDENCE IN THE MIDST OF DISASTER (LAM 3:1-66)

3:1-20
Lamentation over Suffering

Speaking as a representative of the suffering people, the author lamented God's hostile treatment of the nation. This hostility and its effects are compared to a variety of unpleasant and life-threatening experiences, including physical sickness, injury, and imprisonment in a dark dungeon. The author compared Judah's distress to traveling a winding path filled with obstacles, being mauled by vicious predators, having an arrow pierce one's heart, being force-fed bitter food, and having one's face rubbed into the ground.

3:21-42
Confidence in God's Faithfulness

Despite experiencing the Lord's disfavor, the author retained hope. The Lord's love, compassion, and faithful-

Pictured above is the only remaining wall of the temple mount—a small section of the western wall known as the Wailing Wall. In the photo to the right a young Jewish man prays fervently at the wall with phylacteries strapped to his forehead and arm.

ness had kept the nation from total destruction. The Lord would eventually deliver those who trust in Him, even though they might have to endure His discipline for a time. The Lord is sovereign and decrees both calamity and blessing. The author urged his compatriots to acknowledge their sins and come before the Lord with a repentant spirit.

3:43-66
A Prayer for Vindication

After once more describing the horrible effects of the Lord's judgment, the author prayed for divine vengeance upon the nation's gloating enemies. During Judah's abandonment by God, these enemies had taunted and abused God's people. Confessing that God had intervened for

him in the past, the author asked that the Lord might pay back these enemies for their misdeeds and cruelty.

LAMENTING JERUSALEM'S DOWNFALL (4:1–5:22)

4:1-20
Jerusalem's Glory Turned to Ashes

The description of Jerusalem's downfall continues, with emphasis being placed on the contrast between its former condition and present humiliation. The city's children, once considered as precious as gold, were now treated like mere clay pots. As they cried out in hunger and thirst, no one took pity upon them. The once robust princes were shriveled up from lack of food. Starving mothers who used to be filled with compassion even ate their own children. Because of its slow, painful death, Jerusalem's fate was even worse than that of Sodom, which had been destroyed in an instant. Many had thought the city could never fall. But the Lord allowed its enemies to invade it because of the sins of its unjust and corrupt religious leaders. As the people waited in vain for help from Egypt, their enemies scattered them and even captured their king.

4:21-22
Retribution upon Edom

Having described the nation's conquest of the city, the author issued a warning to Edom, one of the nations that participated in and profited from Jerusalem's fall. The tables would someday be turned. Jerusalem's time of trouble and exile would come to an end, but Edom would experience humiliation at the Lord's hands.

PRAYER FOR RESTORATION (5:1-22)

5:1-18
Lamenting Their Downtrodden Condition

After asking the Lord to take note of His people's disgrace, the author described their plight in detail to motivate God to respond in mercy. Foreigners now controlled the promised land, while God's people were as poverty-stricken and helpless as orphans and widows. The people were deprived of life's necessities and suffered horrible atrocities and oppression. Their sin had turned their joy into sorrow and reduced Jerusalem to a heap of ruins.

5:19-22
A Concluding Petition

In a final burst of energy, the author praised God as the eternal King, asked how long they had to suffer rejection, and prayed that God might restore and renew His relationship with His people.

Theological and Ethical Significance

Lamentations says that there is no place like home, especially when it is gone. It shows the honest face of prayer in the midst of tragedy. It frees God's people to question and still experience His presence. It shows that the road to hope is paved with honesty and questioning, mixed with praise. Faith grows in the midst of crisis when God's people take their troubles to Him.

Questions for Reflection

1. What does this book teach about sin's effects?
2. How should God's people respond when they are disciplined for their sins?
3. What do these laments teach about God's character?

Sources for Additional Study

Gordis, Robert. *The Song of Songs and Lamentations: A Study, Modern Translation and Commentary.* New York: KTAV, 1974.

Harrison, Roland K. *Jeremiah and Lamentations. Tyndale Old Testament Commentaries.* Downers Grove: Inter-Varsity, 1973.

Hillers, Delbert S. *Lamentations. Anchor Bible.* New York: Doubleday, 1972.

The people mourning over the ruins of Jerusalem

EZEKIEL

Ezekiel was among the exiles taken to Babylon in 597 B.C. He received his prophetic call in 593 and prophesied between 593 and 571, as the thirteen specific dates given in the book indicate.

Historical Background

For events leading up to the fall of Jerusalem in 586 B.C., see the introduction to "Jeremiah."

Theme

Ezekiel warned his fellow exiles against any wishful thoughts that Jerusalem might be spared. As portrayed in Ezekiel's visions, the glory of the Lord had departed from the city, leaving it vulnerable to destruction. Judah would pay for its rebellion against the Lord. However, the Lord would eventually restore His people to the land and reestablish pure worship in a new temple.

Literary Form

Among the major literary forms appearing in the book are prophetic visions, reports of symbolic acts, parables, and messages of judgment and salvation. Ezekiel used poetic form less than Isaiah and Jeremiah.

Ezekiel 1–24 focuses on the approaching fall of Jerusalem. Chapters 25–32 prophesy judgment upon the surrounding nations, while chapters 33–48 picture the miraculous restoration of the nation and its worship system.

Ezekiel prophesying

I. Judgment upon Sinful Judah (1:1–24:27)
II. Judgment against Surrounding Nations (25:1–32:32)
III. The Restoration of Israel (33:1–48:35)

Purpose and Theology

Like the many prophets who preceded him, Ezekiel denounced God's people for their sins and warned that judgment was imminent. As a priest Ezekiel was particularly interested in the temple. In a vision he saw the glory of God leaving the polluted temple and abandoning the defiled city. Through speeches, symbolic acts, and parables Ezekiel prophesied the fall of the city to the Babylonians and the exile of its people.

God's judgment would not be limited to His people. He would also punish the hostile surrounding nations, especially proud Tyre and Egypt.

Though God's people were scattered in exile, He had not abandoned them. He would miraculously restore them to their land, reunite Israel and Judah under an ideal Davidic ruler, establish a new covenant of peace with them, and annihilate once and for all their enemies. Ezekiel's prophecy ends with an idealized vision of a new and purified temple, out of which flows a life-giving river.

JUDGMENT UPON SINFUL JUDAH (EZEK 1:1–24:27)

1:1–3:27
Ezekiel's Call

Ezekiel's Vision of God's Glory (1:1-28). In 593 B.C. the Lord revealed His glory to Ezekiel through an elaborate vision. Ezekiel saw a storm cloud coming from the north. In the midst of the storm four flaming, winged creatures appeared. Each combined human and animal characteristics (much like some of the minor deities depicted in ancient Near Eastern art). Accompanying each creature in all of its movements was a large wheel, the rim of which was filled with eyes. A sparkling platform stood above the creatures' outstretched wings, which made a deafening sound as they moved. Above the platform was a throne made of precious stone. A human figure, glowing like fire and surrounded by radiant splendor, sat on the throne. Realizing that he was seeing a representation of God's glory, Ezekiel fell with his face to the ground.

Ezekiel's Commission (2:1–3:27). The Lord lifted Ezekiel up and commissioned him as a messenger to rebellious Israel. He encouraged the prophet not to fear, even in the face of intense hostility and danger. Ezekiel was to proclaim the Lord's word, no matter what the

Shown above is a creature, known in Assyrian as lamassu, with the face of a man, body of a bull, and wings of a bird. These and other similar creatures stood at the entrance of the palace of Sargon II at Khorsabad. They are reminiscent of the creatures seen by Ezekiel (Ezek 1:1-10).

response. To symbolize his commission, the Lord instructed Ezekiel to eat a scroll containing words of lamentation and judgment. He promised to give Ezekiel the determination, perseverance, and boldness he would need to stand up to his obstinate audience.

After this encounter with the Lord, the divine Spirit led Ezekiel to the exilic community at Tel Abib in Babylon, where he sat in stunned silence for a week. The Lord then called him to serve as a watchman who would be responsible for warning his audience of God's impending judgment. Ezekiel was to warn both the wicked and the righteous who were tempted to backslide. If he failed to do so, their blood would be on his head.

No sooner was the commission delivered than heavy restrictions were placed upon it. Ezekiel would not be free to deliver messages of warning wherever and whenever he desired. The Lord instructed him to enter his house, where he would remain confined and incapable of speech. He could only leave his house or speak when specifically directed by the Lord to do so. These restrictions would be an object lesson to God's people that their rebellion was making it increasingly difficult for Him to communicate to them.

4:1–5:17
Object Lessons of Judgment

Ezekiel Acts Out the Siege of Jerusalem (4:1-17). The Lord instructed Ezekiel to draw a picture of Jerusalem on a clay tablet (or perhaps a brick) and to stage a miniature siege of the city, complete with siege ramps, enemy camps, and battering rams. The prophet was also to place an iron pan between himself and the city. This action perhaps illustrated the unbreakable nature of the siege or represented the barrier between God and His sinful people.

The Lord also instructed the prophet to symbolically bear the sin (or perhaps punishment) of Israel. He was to lie on his left side for 390 days, corresponding to the years of the Northern Kingdom's sin (or punishment?). He was then to lie on his right side for forty days, corresponding to the years of Judah's sin (or punishment?). (Ezekiel 4:9-17, which describes the prophet conducting various activities, indicates that he did occasionally rise from his symbolic posture.) Whether periods of past sin or future punishment were being symbolized is uncertain. The significance of the figures 390 and forty is also unclear.

At the Lord's command Ezekiel made bread from various grains and stored it in a jar. During the 390-day period (compare 4:5) he was to eat a daily portion of eight ounces of bread, supplemented by two-thirds of a quart of water. This restricted diet would symbolize the food rationing that would be necessary during the coming siege of Jerusalem. The Lord also told Ezekiel to cook his bread over a fire fueled by human excrement. Though the Old Testament law does not specifically prohibit this, Deuteronomy 23:12-14 suggests it would be regarded as unclean. Ezekiel's action would foreshadow the plight of the exiles, who would be forced to eat food in an unclean foreign land. When Ezekiel objected that he had always kept himself ceremonially pure, the Lord allowed him to use cow manure as fuel.

Ezekiel's Hair (5:1-17). The Lord also told Ezekiel to shave all of the hair off his head and face and to divide the hair into three equal parts. He was to burn one third, cut up another third with a sword, and throw the remaining third into the wind. These actions were to symbolize the coming destruction and exile of Jerusalem's residents. At the same time Ezekiel was to preserve a few strands of hair in the folds of his garment, symbolizing the remnant that would survive the judgment. However, to show the severity and extent of God's judgment, he was to throw some of these strands into the fire.

Jerusalem's sin would be the cause of its downfall. Despite their privileged status, God's people rebelled against the Lord's commandments and polluted the temple with idols. God's judgment would be so severe that the starved people would resort to eating their own family members. Two-thirds of the city's population would perish by famine and the sword, while the other third would go into exile. The surrounding nations would hold Jerusalem up as an object of ridicule.

6:1–7:27
Prophecies of Impending Judgment

Judgment on the High Places (6:1-14). Throughout the land the people had erected altars to worship pagan gods. The Lord was about to destroy these altars and litter the pagan shrines with the carcasses and bones of those who worshiped there. From north to south the land would be devastated. (The "desert" refers to the southern wilderness. "Diblah" should probably be read as Riblah, a city in Syria.) However, the Lord would preserve a remnant and scatter them among the nations. These survivors would someday acknowledge the Lord's sovereignty and confess their sin of idolatry.

The Day of the Lord (7:1-27). Judah's day of judgment had arrived. There would be no delay, for the nation's arrogance and violent, bloody deeds demanded punishment. The Lord would repay His people for their sins and show them no mercy. His judgment would be thorough and inescapable. Plague and famine would kill those inside Jerusalem, while enemy swords would slay those in the surrounding country. The few survivors would flee to the mountains in terror and mourn their fate. They would discard their silver and gold, realizing that it could not save them. The enemy would plunder their wealth and desecrate the temple. Not even the nation's religious and civil leaders, including the king himself, would be able to ward off this day of judgment.

8:1–11:25 God's Glory Departs from the Polluted Temple

Idolatry in the Temple (8:1-18). While sitting in his house with some of the exiled elders of Judah, Ezekiel had a startling experience. Transported in a vision to the temple in Jerusalem, Ezekiel saw an idol at the north gate of the inner court. Also present was the glory of the Lord, which he had witnessed two times before (compare 1:28; 3:23). Entering the court through a hole in the wall, Ezekiel saw seventy elders of the land offering incense to the images of unclean animals drawn on the walls. Each of these elders also worshiped his own private idol in secret, thinking that his actions were hidden from the Lord. Going back out to the north gate, Ezekiel saw women weeping for Tammuz, a Mesopotamian fertility god who had supposedly been confined to the underworld. Returning to the inner court, he observed twenty-five men worshiping the sun at the temple's very entrance. Such blatant disregard for the Lord demanded punishment.

God's Glory Leaves (9:1–11:25). Chapters 9–11 describe the gradual departure of God's glory from the polluted temple. The Lord summoned six executioners and a scribe. The Lord instructed the scribe to place a mark on the forehead of every faithful person in the city. He then commissioned the executioners to mercilessly slaughter everyone who was not so marked, beginning in the temple precincts. When Ezekiel expressed his concern that the whole nation would be wiped out, the Lord reminded him that judgment was well-deserved. The land was filled with bloodshed and injustice, and the people had lost faith in the Lord.

When the scribe returned from his task of marking the righteous, the Lord told him to gather coals from among the wheels of His flaming chariot and to scatter them over the city in an act of purifying judgment. Once more the vehicle bearing the Lord's throne is described in detail (compare 10:9-14 with 1:4-21), with the living crea-

Old Testament Apocalyptic

Apocalyptic represents the culmination of Israel's existence as a persecuted people. Apocalyptic proved to be one tool God used to transform Israel from a defeated people bemoaning their fate to a people looking to God with hope for deliverance and mission.

Apocalyptic is a term modern interpreters use to describe a type of thought, a body of literature, and a religious/political movement. The term comes from the Greek word *apocalypsis*, meaning *an unveiling* and is used as the title of the NT Book of Revelation.

As a type of thought, apocalyptic refers to an understanding of human existence as a battle between the forces of God and those of evil leading to a final confrontation. As a body of literature, apocalyptic includes two biblical books—Daniel and Revelation—as well as parts of other books often described as apocalyptic, especially Isaiah 24–27; Joel; Zechariah 9–14.

Similarly, parts of 2 Thessalonians in the NT are apocalyptic. These latter books have apocalyptic subject material but do not exhibit all the literary features of Daniel, Revelation, and other apocalyptic literature outside the biblical canon. Written shortly before, during, and shortly after the ministry of Jesus, the latter include: 4 Ezra, 1 and 2 Enoch, Jubilees, 2 and 3 Baruch, and the Apocalypse of Zephaniah. Christian works, apocalyptic in whole or part, include: Apocalypse of Peter, Shepherd of Hermas, Apocalypse of St. John the Theologian, Book of Elchasar, 5 Ezra, Apocalypse of Paul, Apocalypse of the Virgin Mary, and the Ascension of Isaiah.

As a religious, political movement, apocalyptic encompassed several groups with differing viewpoints concerning the coming kingdom. The perspective on the kingdom determined whether the group became actively involved in seeking to overthrow the foreign rulers and restore Jewish self-rule or whether the group was content to escape to the fringes of civilization to wait for God to act and bring in His kingdom.

The following ideas are common to the apocalyptic thought-world that produced the literature and the religious/political movements:

1. The present world order is so evil that God will act to destroy it.

2. God's people must exercise wisdom in obeying God, following His revealed will, and living ethically and ritually pure lives.

3. God has provided revela-

tures of chapter 1 now being specifically called cherubim. As in the earlier vision a wheel followed each cherub in its movements. The glory of the Lord, which had earlier left the throne above the cherubim and moved to the temple threshold, now mounted the cherubim chariot once more. The cherubim rose up and stopped over the east gate of the temple.

In the gate below were twenty-five men, including Jaazaniah and Pelatiah, two leaders of the people who were giving the city's residents bad advice and assuring them that they would experience no harm (11:1-2). They compared themselves to meat within a pot, which remains untouched by the flames of the fire below. The Lord told Ezekiel to prophesy against them. He would bring the sword against them and drive them out of the city into exile.

As Ezekiel proclaimed the message, Pelatiah died. Again Ezekiel expressed concern that the remnant of the people would be destroyed (compare 11:13 with 9:8). The Lord assured His prophet that He had not totally abandoned His people. He was preserving a remnant among the exiles and would one day bring them back to the land. This restored community would reject the idol-gods and worship the Lord with true devotion.

Following this word of assurance, the chariot carrying the glory of the Lord rose up from the city and stopped on the Mount of Olives, east of the city (11:23). The Lord had abandoned His chosen dwelling place, leaving it unprotected and vulnerable to invasion. At this point Ezekiel's vision ended, and he reported it to his fellow exiles.

12:1-28
Object Lessons of the Exile

Ezekiel Packs His Bags (12:1-16). The Lord instructed Ezekiel to pack his belongings and then, in the sight of his fellow exiles, dig a hole through the wall of his house at evening and pretend he was sneaking away. He was to carry his belongings on his shoulder and cover his face. In so doing he would be acting out the fate of Judah's king, Zedekiah. A few years later, when the Babylonian conquest of Jerusalem became inevitable, Zedekiah would pack his belongings and flee at night from the city. The Babylonians would capture him, put his eyes out, and then take him into exile.

Ezekiel Trembles as He Eats (12:17-20). The Lord next instructed Ezekiel to shake violently as he ate and drank. In so doing he was acting out the fate of Judah's and Jerusalem's inhabitants. When the Babylonians

tions, usually through complex visions filled with symbols, to His chosen leaders.

4. The visions often describe the course of history from a significant moment of the past, through a series of earthly rulers and kingdoms, to the moment of God's intervention to establish His kingdom.

5. A strong contrast is drawn between the stupidity and evil nature of present rulers and the wisdom and intelligence of the heroes of God's oppressed people.

6. Angels and demonic creatures play significant roles.

7. Universal resurrection leading to eternal hope or eternal punishment awaits individuals.

Apocalyptic had roots both in the prophetic and wisdom movements. Israel's prophets pointed beyond the powerful reigns of Assyrian and Babylonian kings to a restoration of a king on David's throne in Jerusalem (Isa 9; 11; Mic 2; Jer 23:5; Zech 9:9).

Isaiah 53 transformed the hope. The suffering by God's people and by His chosen agent of salvation were the means God would use to save His people.

The prophets likewise transformed the common *Day of the Lord* from a significant event in which God saved His people (Amos 5:18) to a future event when God would judge the evil of the world, particularly the evil of His own people. (See Isa 2:10-22; 13:6,9; Ezek 30:3; Joel 2:1-11; Zeph 1:14-18.) This led to apocalyptic collections featuring the Day of the Lord as a day of victory and salvation (Isa 24–27; Zec 9–11).

Wisdom writers showed Israel the normal life-style that pleased God, encouraging Israel to seek God's blessings by living according to their wise directions. They also warned Israel of the results of evil living, particularly of following after sexual enticements. On the other hand, Israel's wisdom writers also dealt with the dark side of life (Job, Ecclesiastes). Apocalyptic used such proverbial teaching to characterize its heroes and use them as examples for all of God's people (note Dan 1–6).

Apocalyptic combines prophetic hope and wise directions for life. It describes the life-style of those who can trust God to lead them out of their present, persecuted state. It provides them hope not only for victory but also for eternal life in the resurrection (Isa 26:19; Dan 12:2). □

Exiles with their packs of belongings on their backs are prodded by a conquering soldier in this relief from the palace of Ashurbanipal at Nineveh. See Ezekiel 12:1-16.

swept through the land, anxiety and despair would overtake them to such a degree that they would not even be able to enjoy a meal.

Faulty Perceptions of Prophecy Corrected (12:21-28). The Israelites had a saying, "The days go by and every vision comes to nothing"(12:22). The proverb seems to reflect their skepticism concerning the messages of the Lord's prophets. The Lord announced that the saying should be changed to "The days are near when every vision will be fulfilled" (12:23), for He was about to fulfill His decrees.

Some also erroneously assumed that the prophetic message of Ezekiel pertained to the distant future and was irrelevant to them. The Lord announced that his prophecies would be fulfilled immediately.

13:1-23
Denunciation of False Prophecy

There were many false prophets in Israel who claimed to be spokesmen of the Lord and assured the people that all would be well. They were like those who whitewash a flimsy wall to hide its defects. The Lord would purge these deceivers from the covenant community. His judgment would come like a torrential downpour, violent wind, and destructive hailstones and batter the whitewashed wall to the ground.

The Lord also denounced the false prophetesses who misled the people with lying messages gained by divination. (Some interpret the barley and bread of 13:19 as their pay, but the items mentioned were more likely used as part of their rituals.) Their activities had a debilitating effect upon the righteous, and these diviners actually encouraged the wicked to continue in their evil ways. The Lord would expose them as frauds and free His people from their negative influence.

14:1-11
Denunciation of Idolatrous Leaders

The Lord denounced several of the elders living in exile because of their hypocrisy. Though they sought a divine oracle from Ezekiel, they harbored an idolatrous spirit within their hearts. The Lord would answer such individuals directly by cutting them off from the covenant community. Any prophet who dared to give an oracle to such hypocrites would be severely punished.

14:12-23
Jerusalem's Certain Doom

The presence of a righteous remnant within Jerusalem would not prevent the city's destruction. Individuals might be delivered, but the city's doom was certain. To emphasize this point, the Lord stated that even if Noah, Daniel, and Job, three individuals famed for their righteousness, were residents of the city, it would not be spared. These men would escape, but they could save no others, not even their children. (The appearance of Daniel in this threesome is problematic. The Hebrew form of the name is spelled differently here than in the Book of Daniel. Furthermore, Daniel was a contemporary of Ezekiel's, while Noah and Job were figures from antiquity. Some have suggested that Danel, a just ruler who appears in a Canaanite tale dating to the second millennium B.C., is in view here. In this case all three examples would be non-Israelites who lived long before Ezekiel's time. However, others object to this identification, arguing that the Old Testament does not mention this legendary figure anywhere else and that the Lord would not use a worshiper of Canaanite gods as a model of righteousness.)

Men and animals would be destroyed by the Lord's judgment, which would come in the form of the sword, famine, wild beasts, and a plague. In addition to preserving any righteous individuals left in the city, the Lord would also allow a few of the wicked to survive and join the exiles in Babylon. When Ezekiel witnessed the degree of their sin, he would then know from firsthand experience that the Lord's judgment of the city had been necessary and perfectly just.

15:1–17:24
Illustrations of Jerusalem's Sin and Judgment

Jerusalem the Useless Vine (15:1-8). The Lord drew a lesson from the wild vine, which is useless for construction purposes. It is typically used for fuel. Once burned, its charred condition makes it even more worthless. One might as well leave it in the fire until it is entirely consumed. Jerusalem was comparable to such a vine. The Lord had already subjected it to His fiery judgment. Like the charred vine it would now be totally consumed.

Jerusalem the Unfaithful Wife (16:1-63). The Lord used an allegory to illustrate the ingratitude and unfaithfulness of Jerusalem's citizens. Originally Jerusalem was a Canaanite city, populated by Amorites and Hittites. It was like an unwanted baby, thrown into a field and left to die from exposure. However, the Lord preserved the child's life. Later, after she had grown into a mature, beautiful young lady, the Lord entered into a marriage covenant with her. He clothed her with beautiful garments, provided her with food, and made her a queen. Her fame spread throughout the nations. Intoxicated by her riches and status, Jerusalem turned to other gods and nations. She built pagan sanctuaries, sacrificed her children to idols, and formed alliances with the surrounding nations. She became worse than a prostitute. Rather than receiving payment from her lovers, she paid them.

The Lord would punish her severely for her ingratitude and unfaithfulness. He would publicly expose her and then execute her. The very nations with which it had formed alliances would turn on it and destroy it.

Developing the allegory further, the Lord pointed out that Jerusalem was no different than her mother and her sisters, who were unfaithful to their husbands and children. Like the Canaanites who resided in the city in its early days, Jerusalem's residents sacrificed their sons and daughters to pagan gods. Like the people of Samaria and Sodom, viewed here as Jerusalem's sisters, they neglected justice and did abominable things in God's sight. Jerusalem's sins even exceeded those of Samaria and Sodom.

Though it would be humiliated for its sins, the Lord would someday restore the city. The Lord would renew His covenant with it and make atonement for its sins.

A Parable of Two Eagles (17:1-24). The Lord used another parable to illustrate truths concerning Jerusalem. A powerful eagle came to Lebanon, broke off the top branch of a cedar, transported it to a city of merchants, and planted it there. This eagle also took some seeds from the land of Israel and planted them in fertile soil, where they grew into a vine with leafy branches. However, when another mighty eagle approached, the vine's roots and branches grew toward him. The Lord then announced that the vine would be destroyed by the east wind. According to the interpretation of the parable (compare 17:11-18), the first eagle represents Nebuchadnezzar, who carried away to Babylon Jerusalem's king and several nobles. Reference is made to the deportation of Jehoiachin and others in 597 B.C. (compare 2 Kgs 24:8-16). The planting of the vine represents the preservation of a remnant in Judah, headed up by Zedekiah, whom Nebuchadnezzar appointed as his vassal king. The second eagle symbolizes Egypt, to whom Judah looked for assistance when it decided to rebel against the Babylonians. The destruction of the vine points to the demise of Judah, which the Babylonians would severely punish for their rebellion.

However, the future was not entirely bleak. The Lord would break a branch from the top of a cedar and plant it on a high mountain, where it would grow into a large and fruitful tree. Since the cedar branch earlier symbolized the exiled king (compare 17:3-4 with 17:12), the branch mentioned here probably refers to a future king whom the Lord would establish in Jerusalem (represented by the mountain).

18:1-32
Individual Accountability

God's people were quoting a proverb that suggested they were suffering unjustly for the sins of earlier generations. The Lord corrected their faulty thinking. He always preserves the righteous and opposes the wicked, regardless of the moral status of their fathers.

To illustrate His point the Lord described a hypothetical righteous man who repudiates idolatry, adultery, and injustice. Such a man can be assured of divine protection. However, if this man has an idolatrous, adulterous, unjust son, this evil child will be destroyed despite his father's righteousness. Again if this wicked man has a son who is righteous, that son will not be held accountable for his father's evil deeds. Instead, like his grandfather, his life will be preserved by the Lord. Each man is judged

Represented here are two examples of "idols of Egypt" (Ezek 20:7). To the left is a statue of the goddess Taweret found at Karnak. She has a heavy body and the head of a hippopotamus. The photo to the right is a grotesque representation of the dwarflike evil god known as Bes.

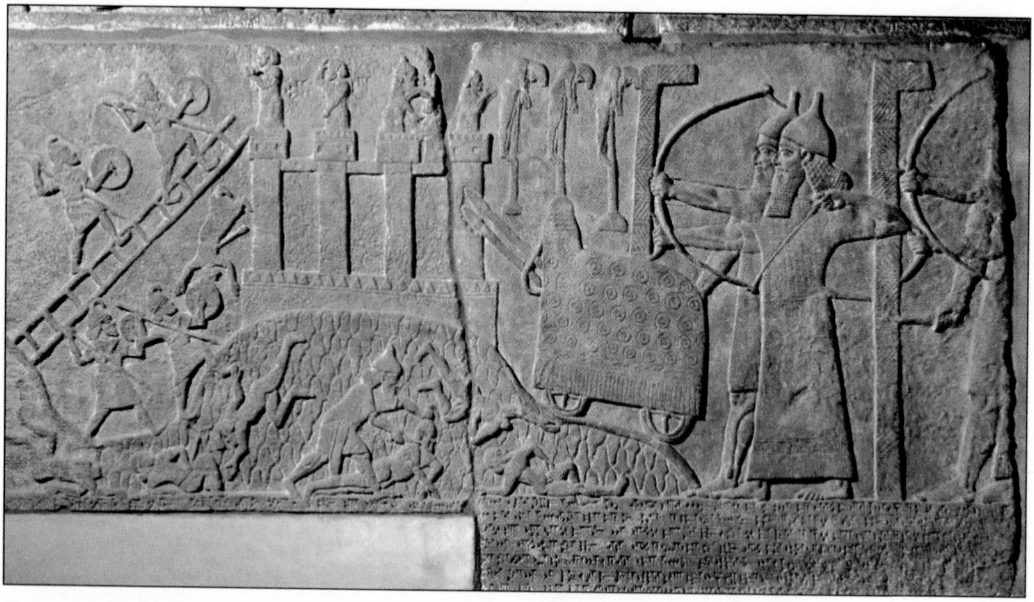

Shown above is a relief from the palace of Tiglath-Pileser III at Nineveh showing the siege of a fortified city with the use of an Assyrian battering ram like the one mentioned in Ezekiel 21:22.

on the basis of his own deeds, not those of his father.

The lesson for Israel was obvious. If they were experiencing divine judgment, it had to mean that they, like their fathers, were evil. Rather than complaining that God is unjust, they had to repent and turn from their wicked ways, for God desired that they live, not die.

19:1-14
A Lament over Israel's Princes

The prophet offered a lament for Israel's princes which, like the previous messages, contains several parabolic elements. The princes' mother (probably the nation Judah or the city of Jerusalem, compare 19:10-14) is compared to a lioness who rears several cubs. One of the cubs grew into a mighty lion who tore people to bits, but he was eventually captured and taken to Egypt. Reference is made to unjust Jehoahaz, whom the Egyptians took captive in 609 B.C. (compare 2 Kgs 23:31-34). Another of the cubs grew strong and brought terror to the land; but he was trapped, put in a cage, and taken to Babylon. Reference is made here to either Jehoiachin or Zedekiah, both of whom were taken into exile (compare 2 Kgs 24:8–25:7).

Switching the imagery, the Lord compared the princes' mother to a fruitful vine which He destroys in His anger and replants in a desert. The nation's (or city's) downfall and exile is in view.

20:1-44
Israel's Past and Present Rebellion

When some of the elders in exile came to inquire of the Lord, He refused to answer them. Instead He told Ezekiel to review the nation's rebellious history. From the very beginning, when the Lord confronted His people in Egypt, they resisted His will by clinging to their idols. After He had delivered them from bondage and given them the law, they rebelled in the wilderness. Though the Lord prohibited that generation from entering the promised land, He preserved their children and warned them not to follow in their fathers' footsteps. However, the children, while still in the wilderness, sinned against the Lord. When He finally established them in the land, they worshiped Canaanite gods at pagan sanctuaries. Ezekiel's idolatrous contemporaries were no different. Consequently the Lord would purify them through judgment and exile. Once He had removed the rebellious worshipers of idols, He would restore the nation to the land. The people then would repudiate their former behavior and worship the Lord in purity.

20:45–21:32
The Fire and Sword of the Lord

Judgment would sweep through Judah like a raging forest fire. In bringing the Babylonians toward the land, the Lord would draw His sharp and polished sword. Flashing like lightning, this sword would bring destruction throughout the land. On his way to Palestine Nebuchadnezzar would reach a fork in the road, with one branch leading to Jerusalem and the other to Rabbah, a prominent Ammonite city. To determine his course of action, he would use various methods of divination, including drawing marked arrows from a quiver, consulting his idols, and examining livers. The Lord would cause all indicators to point toward Jerusalem. Nebuchadnezzar would besiege and conquer the city and take its people into exile. Meanwhile the Ammonites, though arrogant and hostile, were not to think that they would be spared. The Lord's sword of judgment would fall upon them as well (compare 25:1-7).

22:1-31
Jerusalem, a City of Bloodshed

The corruption within Jerusalem made its judgment inevitable. Several specific sins are mentioned here, including idolatry, misuse of power, lack of respect for parents, neglect of widows and orphans, desecration of the Sabbath, incest, bribery, and usury. Violence filled the city. Throughout the chapter reference is made to the shed blood of the innocent (compare 22:3-4,6,9,12-13,27). The princes and civil officials took the lead in this regard by oppressing the poor and helpless. Even the religious leaders were corrupt. The priests failed to instruct the people in the law and made no distinction between the holy and profane. The false prophets proclaimed lies in the name of the Lord. When the Lord looked for a man to stand "in the gap" and intercede for the nation, no one was found. Consequently He would purify the city by judgment and scatter the people among the nations.

23:1-49
An Allegory of Two Sisters

To illustrate the nation's unfaithfulness, the Lord used an allegory in which He compared Samaria and Jerusalem to two promiscuous sisters named Oholah and Oholibah. (Oholah means *her tent* and Oholibah *my tent is in her.* Perhaps the latter name reflects the fact that God dwelt in the Jerusalem temple.) The sisters had been prostitutes from their youth in Egypt. Though belonging to the Lord (whether as wives or children is not clear), they courted the favor of foreign nations.

Oholah (Samaria) sought alliances with the Assyrians. She is portrayed as lusting after the Assyrian soldiers and prostituting herself among their officers. Ironically, her lovers killed her and carried away her children.

Oholibah (Jerusalem) witnessed the fate of her sister but failed to learn from her example. She also lusted after the Assyrians and later turned her attention toward the Babylonians and others. Vivid language and harsh imagery are employed to depict her nymphomania. The Lord warned that her lovers would turn on her. The Babylonians would come against the land with all their military might and cruelly destroy her population. Oholibah would be publicly humiliated and suffer the fate of her sister Oholah.

A woman's toiletries box (Egypt, 1300s B.C.) containing eye makeup, ointments, ivory comb, and sandals. See Ezekiel 23:40.

24:1-14
A Parable of the Cooking Pot

On the very day when the Babylonians began their siege of Jerusalem (January 15, 588 B.C.), the Lord gave Ezekiel a parable illustrating the city's downfall. Jerusalem was like a cooking pot, which had been encrusted with deposits (its bloodshed and idolatry, 24:6-8,13). The inhabitants of Jerusalem were like meat and bones cooking inside the pot. The fire burning beneath the pot (the Babylonian siege) would thoroughly cook the meat and char the bones, both of which would eventually be removed piece by piece (a picture of the exile). The empty pot would then be left on the fire until its impurities were burned away.

24:15-27
The Death of Ezekiel's Wife

The Lord announced to Ezekiel that his beloved wife was about to die suddenly. However, as an object lesson to Israel, the Lord commanded the prophet not to mourn outwardly over her death, as was the custom. Instead he could only groan to himself. When his wife died shortly thereafter, Ezekiel obeyed the Lord's instructions. When the people observed his silence, they inquired about its significance. He explained that they were not to mourn publicly over the downfall of their beloved city and its temple, just as he refused to lament over his wife's death.

When Jerusalem finally fell, a fugitive would bring Ezekiel the news. At that time the Lord would remove Ezekiel's muteness (compare 3:26-27; 33:21-22). He would now speak openly and freely with the survivors of the catastrophe, warning and encouraging them.

JUDGMENT AGAINST SURROUNDING NATIONS (EZEK 25:1–32:32)

The nations surrounding Judah would not escape God's judgment. This section contains oracles against seven specific nations. Though all directions of the compass are represented, Tyre (to the north) and Egypt (to the south) receive special attention. The seven oracles against Egypt conclude the section. The wide geographical distribution of the nations mentioned, as well as the use of the symbolic number seven, convey a feeling of completeness.

25:1-7
Judgment against Ammon

The Lord would judge the Ammonites because they rejoiced over Jerusalem's fall. "People of the East" (25:4, either the Babylonians or marauding tribes from the desert) would plunder Ammon and reduce Rabbah, its most prominent city, to a pasture land.

25:8-11
Judgment against Moab

The Lord would also punish the Moabites, Ammon's neighbors to the south, because they too rejoiced over Jerusalem's fall. The "people of the East" (25:10) would conquer the fortified cities guarding Moab's northern border, opening the land up to invasion.

25:12-14
Judgment against Edom

Judgment would also fall on Edom (already mentioned in 25:8, compare "Seir"), located south of Moab. When Judah fell, Edom displayed a vengeful spirit (compare Obad). The Lord would take vengeance on Edom through His people Israel.

25:15-17
Judgment against Philistia

The Lord would also take vengeance on the Philistines (also referred to here as Kerethites), Judah's neighbors to the west, because they had opposed God's people for centuries.

26:1–28:19
Judgment against Tyre

The Downfall of Tyre (26:1-21). Tyre, located on the Mediterranean coast north of Israel, was a prominent commercial center. Despite its wealth and defenses, it would be unable to withstand the Lord's judgment. Many nations would rage against it, like the turbulent waters of the sea. In the immediate future Nebuchadnezzar's armies would besiege and conquer the city. Tyre would be reduced to a heap of rubble which that never again be rebuilt. All along the Mediterranean coast Tyre's trading partners would lament its demise.

Harmonizing this prophecy with history is difficult. Nebuchadnezzar besieged Tyre for thirteen long years (about 586–573 B.C.) and finally made it a vassal state. However, he did not destroy the city to the degree described by Ezekiel (even 29:18 acknowledges this). Many subsequent conquerors (including Alexander the Great in 332) took the city, but it continued to exist into the Christian era.

Several solutions have been offered, none of which is entirely satisfactory. One possibility is that the description of Tyre's downfall is somewhat stereotypical and purposely exaggerated to emphasize that it would be subjected to the Babylonians and experience a significant decline in prestige. Another possibility is that the description of 26:12-14 moves beyond the time of Nebuchadnezzar and encompasses later attacks on the city. Such subsequent attacks ultimately brought the final downfall of the city. Such a blurring of the immediate future with more distant events is typical of prophetic literature.

The Prophet's Lament over Tyre (27:1-36). To emphasize the certainty of Tyre's judgment, the Lord told Ezekiel to lament the city's doom in advance. Tyre is compared to a large commercial ship made from the best wood, adorned with beautiful sails, and manned by skilled sailors. Tyre bought and sold every conceivable product, including, precious metals and stones, slaves, animals, fabric and clothing, food, and even ivory tusks. Its list of trading partners included virtually every nation and city in the known world. However, a storm (the Lord's judgment) would destroy this great ship. All of its sailors and merchants would sink into the sea, causing its trading partners looking on from the shore to lament over its fate.

The King of Tyre Denounced (28:1-19). Singling out the king of Tyre as representative of the city, the Lord announced that this proud ruler and his city would be humiliated. Because of the city's great success and wealth, its king fancied himself a god and took great pride in his wisdom. (Though some see the "Daniel" of 28:3 as the legendary Canaanite King Danel, the reference to his ability to disclose secrets suggests the biblical Daniel, a contemporary of Ezekiel, is in view. Compare comments on 14:14,20.) When the day of judgment arrived, the king would stand humiliated before his executioners, his delusions of grandeur replaced by the painful reality of his mortality.

In anticipation of the king's downfall Ezekiel pronounced a taunting lament against him. He compared the king to a wise, beautiful, and richly adorned cherub who once dwelt in the garden of Eden and enjoyed access to God's holy mountain. This cherub eventually lost his prestigious position because of his arrogance and oppressive economic practices (Tyre's commercial empire is alluded to here). The Lord threw him down from the sacred mountain and destroyed him with fire in the sight of the nations.

The background for the imagery of this lament is uncertain. The mountain of God has parallels in Canaanite mythology. Use of such mythological imagery might be expected in an address to a Phoenician king. (Compare Isa 14:4-21, where mythological themes and imagery are used in a taunt directed to the king of Babylon.) Verse 13 appears to refer to the garden of Eden of biblical tradition, but the only cherubim mentioned in the Genesis account are those placed as guardians at the gate of the garden following the expulsion of Adam and Eve (Gen 3:24). Perhaps Ezekiel drew his imagery from an extrabiblical Eden tradition.

Because of the references to Eden and to the cherub's pride and fall, some have seen a veiled reference to Satan in 28:12-19. However, the allusion to Eden does not support this view. Satan is not specifically mentioned in Genesis 2–3, let alone portrayed as a cherub. Satan is traditionally associated with the serpent of the Eden account. But even if this interpretation is correct, the serpent is identified as one of the animals created by God (compare Gen 3:1,14), not as a cherub in disguise.

28:20-26
Judgment against Sidon

Sidon, another prominent Phoenician city, would also experience divine judgment. Like Tyre it had treated God's people with hostility. The Lord would destroy the Sidonians with plague and sword.

The Lord would someday restore His people to their land, where they would live in peace, free from the threats of hostile neighbors like Sidon, Tyre, Philistia, Edom, Moab, and Ammon.

29:1–32:32
Judgment on Egypt

The Lord's Opposition to Pharaoh (29:1-16). The Lord announced that He was also opposed to Pharaoh, the proud ruler of Egypt. Comparing the king to a crocodile in the Nile, the Lord warned that He would pull him from the river and drag him to the desert, where he would die and be eaten by scavengers. The Lord would turn the entire land (from Migdol in the north to Aswan in the south) into a ruin for forty years and scatter the Egyptians among the nations. Following the forty-year exile, the Lord would return them to their land, but Egypt would never again experience its former glory. God's people, who had once trusted in Egypt, would no longer rely on its help. When and how this prophecy was fulfilled is not certain. Historical records do not indicate that Egypt experienced desolation or exile to the degree described by Ezekiel.

Booty for Nebuchadnezzar (29:17-21). In 571 B.C., shortly after Nebuchadnezzar had lifted his long siege of Tyre, Ezekiel received another message pertaining to Egypt. Though Nebuchadnezzar had come away from Tyre with relatively little reward for his efforts, the Lord would give him Egypt, from which he would haul away an abundance of riches. This prophecy was probably fulfilled in 568 B.C., when, according to a Babylonian text, Nebuchadnezzar apparently conducted a campaign against Egypt.

The Day of the Lord on Egypt (30:1-19). Egypt's fall is associated with the Day of the Lord, an expression used elsewhere in the Old Testament of those times when the Lord comes as a warrior and swiftly and decisively destroys His enemies. Using Nebuchadnezzar as His "sword," the Lord would destroy both Egypt and its allies. Egypt's great river, the Nile, would dry up, its idols and princes would prove helpless, and all of its famous cities would be conquered.

Pharaoh's Power Broken (30:20-26). Ezekiel received a message concerning Pharaoh in 587 B.C., one year after Nebuchadnezzar had defeated Pharaoh Hophra in battle when the latter had tried to come and aid besieged Jerusalem (compare Jer 37:5-8). By allowing Nebuchadnezzar to defeat Hophra, the Lord had, as it were, broken Pharaoh's arm, a symbol of his military strength. However, the Lord was not finished with Egypt. He would energize the king of Babylon to conquer Egypt. Both of Pharaoh's arms would be broken. When the Egyptians were conquered and scattered among the nations, they would recognize the sovereignty of Israel's God.

A Fallen Cedar (31:1-18). The Lord challenged Pharaoh and his armies to learn a lesson from history. Assyria, the mightiest empire in the Near East from 745–626 B.C., had once been like a mighty cedar of Lebanon. It was well nourished and grew tall. Birds lodged in its branches, and animals sought shelter under its shade. Not even the trees of the garden of Eden could rival its majesty and beauty. However, because of its pride, God delivered it over to a ruthless nation (the Babylonians) who chopped it down. No other trees would ever grow so tall. Pharaoh also was like a great tree, but, like Assyria, he and his armies would come crashing to the earth.

Lamenting Pharaoh's Destruction (32:1-16). The Lord revealed to Ezekiel a taunting lament the nations would someday sing over fallen Pharaoh. Though he was like a mighty lion or a powerful crocodile, he would be captured, destroyed, and eaten by scavengers. Darkness would settle over his land as a sign of judgment and destruction. Babylon would invade Egypt, destroy its people, and steal its wealth.

Egypt's Armies Slaughtered (32:17-32). Pharaoh's armies would be slaughtered and descend into the land of the dead. They would join the armies of other nations who spread terror on the earth but eventually met their demise. These nations included Assyria, Elam (located east of Mesopotamia), Meshech and Tubal (northern nations, compare 38:2), Edom, and Sidon.

THE RESTORATION OF ISRAEL (EZEK 33:1–48:35)

33:1-20
Ezekiel's Commission Renewed

Shortly before the fall of Jerusalem, the Lord renewed Ezekiel's commission as the nation's spiritual watchman (compare 3:16-21). One of a watchman's primary responsibilities was to warn his people of approaching danger. As long as the watchman carried out his duty, he was not responsible for those who failed to take his warning seriously and were unprepared when disaster arrived. Ezekiel was in a similar position. He was to warn both the wicked and backsliders of impending doom and call them to repentance. Even though the nation was weighed down with sin, it was God's desire that they turn from their evil ways and live.

33:21-33
Ezekiel's Prophetic Office Authenticated

In January of 585 B.C., five months after the temple had been destroyed, a fugitive delivered the news to Ezekiel. The evening before, the Lord had opened Ezekiel's mouth, ending his long period of enforced silence (compare 3:26; 24:26-27). Now that Ezekiel's prophecies of judgment had been fulfilled, his ministry would be primarily one of encouragement, and his messages would focus on the future restoration of the exiles.

However, he was to deliver one more judgment speech. The survivors who remained in Judah following the destruction of Jerusalem retained delusions of grandeur, thinking that the land was now theirs. Ezekiel corrected their faulty thinking, pointing out that their idolatry and hypocrisy precluded them from enjoying the land. Another wave of judgment would sweep them away. In the past they had not taken Ezekiel's messages seriously, but in the day of judgment they would finally realize that he was a true prophet of the Lord.

34:1-31
Israel's Shepherd Makes a New Covenant with His People

Israel's leaders, compared to shepherds, had not cared properly for God's flock. These leaders, who were consumed by self-interest, had actually oppressed and exploited the people. The sheep were now scattered and being ravaged by wild beasts (foreign nations such as Babylon). The Lord announced that these incompetent leaders would be eliminated and that He would take over the care of the flock. The Lord would gather His wandering and injured sheep back to Israel, where they would graze peacefully in rich pasturelands. He would reestablish justice among His people and raise up for them a new, ideal Davidic ruler. He would make with them "a covenant of peace," which would assure them of safety from danger and of agricultural prosperity.

35:1-15
Vengeance upon Edom

God would judge those nations that had traditionally sought the destruction of His people. As a prime example of such a nation, Edom was singled out as an object of God's wrath. The Edomites participated in Jerusalem's downfall, with hopes that they might eventually acquire the land of Israel as their own. They arrogantly taunted God's people in their time of calamity. Edom would taste God's vengeance. He would treat them the same way they had treated His people. The Edomites would be slaughtered by the sword and their land left a desolate heap of ruins.

36:1-15
Prosperity Returns to Israel

Foreign armies had overrun the mountains of Israel and boasted of their conquests. The Lord swore that He would bring vengeance upon these nations (Edom is again singled out, compare 36:5). He would also restore His people to the land. Once again crops would grow in the land, and cities would be populated.

Ezekiel's vision of the valley of dry bones

36:16-38
God Cleanses His People

Israel had polluted the land with their sinful deeds and had brought dishonor to God's name. When Israel went into exile, the nations made wrong assumptions about the character of God. To vindicate Himself and restore His reputation among the nations, the Lord would restore the exiles to the land. He would cleanse their sins, create in them a desire for loyalty, and renew His agricultural blessings. At that time both the nations and Israel would recognize His sovereignty.

37:1-14
Israel Comes to Life Again

Ezekiel's vision of the dry bones portrayed in a vivid way Israel's miraculous restoration. In this vision the prophet saw a valley full of dry, disconnected bones, representing the scattered people of Israel. However, suddenly the bones began to come together, and tendons and flesh appeared on them. The breath of life then entered into the corpses, and a multitude of living beings stood in the valley. In the same way the Lord would miraculously revive the nation of Israel. He would deliver them from the grave of exile, place His Spirit among them, and settle them once more in the promised land.

37:15-28
Israel and Judah Reunited

The day of restoration would also be a day of reunification for Israel and Judah. To illustrate this the Lord told Ezekiel to take two sticks, one representing the Northern Kingdom and the other the Southern Kingdom, and hold them as one in his hand. In the same way the Lord would bring the exiles of both Israel and Judah back to the land and make them one kingdom again. He would raise up a new ideal Davidic ruler to lead them, establish a new covenant with them, and once more dwell in their midst.

38:1–39:29
The Final Destruction of the Nations

These chapters describe an invasion of Israel by distant nations, led by "Gog, of the land of Magog, the chief prince of Meshech and Tubal." Attempts to identify Gog with a historical figure are unconvincing. Magog, Tubal, and Meshech are mentioned in Genesis 10:2 and 1 Chronicles 1:5 as sons of Japheth. In Ezekiel's day their descendants inhabited what is now eastern Turkey. According to 38:5-6 the allies of Gog included Persia, Cush (modern Ethiopia), Put (modern Libya), Gomer (another son of Japheth whose descendants resided to the far north of Israel), and Beth Togarmah (according to Gen

10:3, Togarmah was a son of Gomer).

Ezekiel envisioned a time when the armies of these nations would attack unsuspecting Israel. The Lord would intervene in power and miraculously deliver His people. A mighty earthquake would shake the land, and the enemy armies would turn in panic on each other. The Lord would rain down hail and sulfur upon them. The slaughter would be comparable to a great sacrifice. Birds and wild animals would devour the flesh and blood of the enemy warriors. Even with this assistance from the animal kingdom, it would take the people of Israel seven months to dispose of all the corpses. The enemy's weapons would provide God's people with a supply of fuel that would last seven years.

Since this prophecy does not correspond to any known historical event, it is best to understand it as still awaiting fulfillment. Gog and his hordes are symbolic of the end time opposition to God's kingdom which will be violently crushed (compare Rev 20:8-9).

40:1–48:35
Pure Worship Restored

In this section the Lord gave Ezekiel a vision of restored Israel. He saw a detailed picture of the new temple and received lengthy instructions for the future leaders of the nations. The book concludes with a detailed description of the future geographical divisions of the land.

Scholars differ in their interpretation of this section. Some see its language as symbolic and as being fulfilled in the New Testament church, while others interpret the prophecy as applying to a literal Israel of the future. Some understand these chapters as giving a literal description of conditions in the millennial age. Others understand the vision as an idealized, perhaps exaggerated, portrayal of God's future restoration of His people that is filled with symbolic elements.

A New Temple (40:1–43:12). Through the medium of a vision the Lord gave Ezekiel a preview of the new temple. Beginning at the east gate of the outer court, he was given a tour that led into the inner court, its inner rooms, the temple portico, the outer sanctuary, and finally the most holy place. All along the way detailed measurements and descriptions are provided.

Most importantly, God would reside in the new temple. Almost twenty years earlier Ezekiel had a vision of God's glory leaving the Jerusalem temple (compare chaps. 8–10). That temple was subsequently destroyed by the Babylonians. Now through another vision the prophet witnessed God's glory returning to the city and taking up residence in the new temple (compare 43:1-9).

Regulations for the New Temple (43:13–46:24). These chapters contain several instructions and regulations for the priests and rulers who would function in the restored covenant community of the future.

The section begins with instructions for building the temple altar (43:13-17) and for its dedicatory sacrifices (43:18-27). Once the appropriate sin offerings were made for seven consecutive days, the altar would be regarded as purified and would be ready for use. From the eighth day on the altar could be used for burnt and fellowship offerings, which expressed the worshiper's devotion to and communion with God.

Because the Lord's glory returned to the temple complex through the east gate of the outer court (compare 43:4), this gate would remain shut. Only "the prince" could sit inside this gateway, where he would eat in the presence of the Lord (44:1-4). This prince is identified elsewhere as the ideal Davidic ruler, or Messiah, whom the Lord would raise up to lead His people (34:24; 37:24-25).

In the past rebellious Israelites had violated the Lord's covenant by allowing foreigners to bring their detestable

Shown above is a relief from Mesopotamia (700s B.C.) showing a man holding two sets of scales. See Ezekiel 45:10-12.

practices into the temple. These foreigners were "uncircumcised in heart and flesh" (44:7), meaning that they lacked devotion to the Lord as well as the physical sign of being part of the covenant community. Such foreigners were prohibited from entering the new temple (44:5-9).

Because the Levites had been unfaithful to the Lord, they would be demoted (44:10-14). They could tend the temple gates, slaughter sacrificial animals, and assist the people, but they were not allowed to handle the holy objects or offerings of the Lord.

As a reward for their faithfulness the Zadokite line of the Levitical family would function as the Lord's priests (44:15-16). Zadok was a descendant of Aaron through Eleazar and Phinehas (compare 1 Chron 6:3-8,50-53).

In the future allotment of the land a portion must be reserved for the Lord (and His priestly servants) directly in the center of the land (45:1-6). The prince (Davidic ruler) would possess the land bordering the Lord's portion on the east and west (45:7-8).

This mention of the future prince leads to an exhortation to the civil leaders of God's people in Ezekiel's day. They were not to oppress the people but were to promote justice and fairness in the socioeconomic sphere (45:9-12).

The Lord also provided detailed regulations pertaining to offerings and feasts (45:13–46:24), including the New Year festival, Passover, and Tabernacles. Various regulations pertaining to the prince highlight chapter 46. On Sabbath days and New Moons the prince would lead the people in worshiping the Lord by presenting offerings at the threshold of the east gate of the inner court.

The River Flowing from the Temple (47:1-12). Ezekiel envisioned a river flowing from the temple toward the east. The river became increasingly deeper as it flowed through the desert on its way to the Dead Sea. Its fresh water was filled with fish, and fishermen lined its shores with nets. Also lining the river's banks were nourishing fruit trees, the leaves of which possessed healing properties. This life-giving river flowing from God's throne symbolized the restoration of divine blessing which the land would experience.

Boundaries and Land Allotments (47:13–48:35). The Book of Ezekiel concludes with a detailed description of the land's future boundaries and allotted portions. The holy city, constructed as a perfect square in the middle of the land, would have twelve gates (three on each of its four walls) named after the tribes of Israel. The city would be named "Yahweh-Shammah," meaning *the Lord is there.*

Theological and Ethical Significance

Ezekiel was the priestly prophet of judgment and hope. His message to the exiles in Babylon still speaks to hurting, broken people in need of a God-given second chance. Jerusalem's destruction and its people's deportation to Babylon caused some to question God's ability to save and His commitment to His covenants. Ezekiel interpreted these events in light of God's character.

Ezekiel's strange, opening vision pictures God as without equal, perfect in holiness and power. Such a God would not abide with unrepentant people. Jerusalem fell not because God was *unable* to save it but because God *abandoned* His people to their chosen fate.

But judgment was only part of Ezekiel's picture of God. Even in exile, far from home, God was accessible to the prophet. God's faithfulness was Ezekiel's hope. God is the caring Shepherd of His people (Ezek 34). God is the only hope for new life for the dead bones of the nation Israel (Ezek 37).

Christians can learn responsibility from Ezekiel. Like Ezekiel believers are to empathize with the hurt of those around them (3:15). Like Ezekiel Christians are "watchmen," responsible for warning neighbors of sin's consequences (3:16-21). Ezekiel 34 warns believers not to seek their own interests at others' expense. Rather Christians are to model God's love and care in their actions. Believers are to share the good news that God is still the Giver of new life and second chances to those who turn to Him in repentance and faith.

Questions for Reflection

1. In what ways is Ezekiel an example of an obedient, loyal servant of the Lord?
2. How does Ezekiel portray God? What roles and characteristics does Ezekiel attribute to God?
3. Why were Ezekiel's contemporaries displeasing to the Lord? Is the modern church like them in any ways?
4. What do Ezekiel's messages of salvation teach us about God's relationship to His people?

Sources for Additional Study

Alexander, Ralph H. "Ezekiel." *The Expositor's Bible Commentary*. Vol. 6. Grand Rapids: Zondervan, 1986.

Greenberg, Moshe, *Ezekiel 1–20. Anchor Bible.* New York: Doubleday, 1983.

Taylor, John B. *Ezekiel. Tyndale Old Testament Commentaries.* Downers Grove: InterVarsity, 1969.

DANIEL

The Book of Daniel has traditionally been attributed to Daniel on the basis of explicit statements made within its pages (9:2; 10:2) and Christ's testimony (Matt 24:15). Daniel lived in Babylon during the sixth century B.C. and served both Babylonian and Persian rulers.

Modern critics have denied the historical value of the book for several reasons. They regard it as a combination of court legends and apocalyptic visions, the latter being characteristic of intertestamental Jewish literature (see further discussion on "Literary Form").

Only a few observations related to the historical value of the book can be made.

1. The presence of miraculous events, no matter how incredible they may seem (the preservation of Daniel's friends in the fiery furnace and of Daniel in the lions' den), does not necessarily call in question the book's historical value. The sovereign God of the universe does at times intervene in history in supernatural ways, the prime example being the resurrection of Jesus Christ.

2. The book's portrayal of Darius the Mede, while problematic in many respects, does not necessarily prove it is nonhistorical. Some interpreters have used this as proof of the book's fictional nature, pointing out that Cyrus, not this otherwise unknown Darius son of Xerxes, became the king of Babylon following its fall. Others have proposed that Darius may be another name for Cyrus (in this view Dan 6:28 is translated, "So Daniel prospered during the reign of Darius, that is, the reign of Cyrus the Persian"). Still others suggest Darius was Gubaru, who served as the governor of Babylon under Cyrus.

3. Scholars have debated whether the Aramaic used in the book reflects an early date (the time of Daniel) or late date (about 165 B.C.).

4. Chapter 11 is a watershed in the debate over the nature of the book's prophecies. Many modern interpreters understand it as after-the-fact "prophecy" and use it to pinpoint the book's date to 165 B.C. Verses 2-20 contain a rather detailed and accurate account of Palestinian history from the time of Cyrus (about 538 B.C.) to the time of Antiochus Epiphanes (175–164 B.C.). Verses 21-35 accurately reflect Antiochus's career, but verses 36-45 do not. Thus, it is argued, the author must have written in 165 B.C., after the events accurately recorded in the chapter but before the inaccurate predictions pertaining to Antiochus.

Others regard it as a prime example of supernatural, predictive prophecy. These interpreters argue that 11:36-45 does not contain unfulfilled predictions about Antiochus Epiphanes. Instead it describes the career of a yet future ruler who resembles Antiochus. Such foreshadowing and blending is typical of Old Testament prophecy.

Historical Background

Daniel and his friends were taken into exile in 605 B.C. They served mighty Nebuchadnezzar, who ruled the Babylonian empire until 562. Nebuchadnezzar's successors were Evil-Merodach, Neriglissar, Labashi-Marduk, and Nabonidus. Nabonidus spent much of his reign in Tema worshiping the moon god. His son Belshazzar served as his vice-regent. Though the Book of Daniel calls Belshazzar "king," it hints that he was really second in command in the kingdom (5:7,16). Cyrus the Persian conquered Babylon in 539 and made Gubaru governor over the city. Daniel retained a high civil office under the Persians.

Theme

Daniel portrays God as the sovereign Ruler of the universe, who controls the destinies of both pagan empires and His exiled people. He revealed His mighty power to the kings of Babylon and Persia, forcing them to acknowledge His supremacy. He revealed to Daniel His future plans to restore His people Israel once the times of the Gentiles had run their course.

Literary Form

How we classify the narratives of Daniel depends on our view of their historical value. Those who regard the stories as fictional classify them as court legends. Those who accept their historical value regard them as biographical accounts of Daniel and his friends.

Daniel's visions can be categorized as apocalyptic literature. Because later examples of such literature are falsely attributed to some famous person from the past (pseudepigraphic) and contain after-the-fact prophecy, some assume that Daniel shares these characteristics. Others acknowledge some literary similarities but argue for Daniel as genuine prophecy.

The structure of the book can be viewed in different ways. Chapters 1–6 are largely narratives, while chapters 7–12 contain visions of future events. At the same time, 1:1–2:4a; 8–12 are written in Hebrew, while 2:4b–7:28 are in Aramaic. The explanation for the bilingual nature of the book is uncertain. Some observe that the Aramaic section focuses on Gentile rulers and nations, while the Hebrew sections are primarily concerned with Israel. Others explain the variation as a structural device. Daniel 2:4b–7:28 is set off from the surrounding sections because it is a symmetrically arranged unit, displaying a mirror structure (chaps. 2 and 7 correspond thematically, as do chaps. 3 and 6 and chaps. 4 and 5).

I. Experiences of Daniel and His Friends in Babylon (1:1–6:28)
II. Visions and Revelations of Future Events (7:1–12:13)

Purpose and Theology

The God of Daniel is the sovereign Ruler of the world, who raises up and brings down rulers and determines

Persia

The Medes and Persians descended from Indo-European peoples living in ancient Iran since the second millennium B.C. Both were continually harassed by the Assyrians until the Medes and Babylonians conquered and took the Assyrian empire in 612. The Medes dominated the Persians until Cyrus II (559–530). He united the Persian tribes and with Babylonian help seized the Median empire about 550 B.C.

Having extended his empire from Asia Minor to the Indus River, Cyrus conquered Babylon in 539 and decreed the return of deported peoples (including the Jews) to their own cities (compare Isa 44:28–45:7). Since Cyrus valued politics more than religion, he tried to win the favor of his new subjects by encouraging their native religion (Ezra 1:1-4).

Cyrus died in battle in 530, leaving the greatest empire the Near East had ever seen to his son Cambyses, who added Egypt to it in 525. Cambyses died as he returned from Egypt, after learning the Persian throne had been seized by a usurper. A member of his bodyguard, a noble named Darius, showed his political, administrative, and military genius by killing the usurper, assuming the throne, and subduing rebellions throughout the empire.

Darius further developed Cyrus's administrative system, which divided the empire into twenty satrapies (provinces) usually ruled by Persian satraps (provincial governors). Inside the Satrapies the Persians tended to use existing administrators, often employing non-Persian governors of smaller districts. Until about 485 B.C., Syro-Palestine, called Abar Nahara (*Beyond the [Euphrates] River*), formed one satrapy with Babylon. Abar Nahara had a governor who ruled several subprovinces including Judah and Samaria. Darius also developed roads and a "pony express" postal system by which letters could travel between Susa, the capital, and Judah within a week.

In 519 B.C., soon after authorizing the completion of the Jerusalem temple (Ezra 5:3–6:15), Darius marched through Palestine and reestablished Persian authority in Egypt. After successes in Asia Minor, India, Thrace, and Macedonia, his attempt to invade Greece failed at the battle of Marathon in 490.

Xerxes (Ahasuerus in Esther [KJV]; 486–465 B.C.), much less capable than his father, attempted the invasion again in 480 and also failed. He was arrogant, fickle, and was fond of extravagant parties. His harem seems to have been his main interest in life.

Artaxerxes I (465–424 B.C.) murdered and succeeded his father. Probably in response to an Egyptian revolt in 460–454, he sent Ezra to Judah in 458 (Ezra 7:11-26) with an additional group of returnees to bring judicial and religious reform there. When Artaxerxes was told Judah was planning a revolt, he ordered the rebuilding of Jerusalem to cease (Ezra 4:9-22). The subsequent mission of Nehemiah in 445 to continue the work Artaxerxes had just halted (Neh 2:7-8) was perhaps in part due to the chaotic conditions in Abar Nahara following the revolt of the satrap Megabyzus in 448.

Protecting the Persian empire from external threat and internal disintegration occupied the succeeding kings. There was almost continual unrest in Egypt. An invasion of Greek mercenaries employed by a usurper in 401 B.C. almost succeeded. The revolt of the satraps lasted for ten years (368–358). Alexander the Great finally defeated the armies of Darius III (335–330) at Granicus, Issus, and Gaugamela and brought the Persian empire to a close. □

long beforehand the future of nations. He rewards the faithfulness of His devoted servants and protects them, even when they are far from their homeland. His sovereignty is especially apparent in His dealings with Nebuchadnezzar. To him God revealed future history, demonstrated His power to deliver His own, and gave a vivid lesson on the dangers of pride. Nebuchadnezzar was forced to acknowledge the sovereignty of Daniel's God. The Lord also displayed His sovereignty to subsequent rulers. He announced in dramatic fashion Belshazzar's downfall for his arrogance and lack of respect for the temple vessels. He demonstrated to Darius His power to deliver His faithful servants from even the worst crises.

Through Daniel's visions the Lord demonstrates His sovereignty over history. Human empires rise and fall, but the Lord ultimately shatters Gentile opposition to His program and establishes His kingdom on earth.

DANIEL AND HIS FRIENDS IN BABYLON (DAN 1:1–6:28)

1:1-21
Daniel and His Friends Remain Faithful

Daniel and His Friends Chosen to be Court Officials (1:1-7). In 605 B.C. the Babylonians marched against Judah and besieged Jerusalem. They took some temple articles to Babylon, as well as some of Judah's finest young men. Nebuchadnezzar ordered Ashpenaz, his chief court official, to choose the very best of these men and train them for the king's service. Among this group were Daniel, Hananiah, Mishael, and Azariah. They were given Babylonian names, trained in Babylonian language and literature, and placed on a special diet.

Daniel and His Friends Refuse Unclean Food (1:8-16). Daniel regarded the food offered by the Babylonians to be defiling. The Mosaic law forbade God's people to eat unclean animals or flesh that had not been drained of blood. Portions of the wine and meat presented by Ashpenaz may have been offered to idols.

Daniel convinced the Babylonians to allow him and his three friends to follow a different diet, consisting only of vegetables and water. After a ten-day trial period they looked even healthier than those who were following the diet prescribed by the king. Consequently they were not forced to eat the king's food or drink his wine.

God Rewards Daniel and His Friends (1:17-21). In response to Daniel's and his friends' faithfulness, the Lord gave them superior intellect and gave Daniel the ability to interpret dreams and visions. When the king interviewed the trainees, he found Daniel and his friends to be the cream of the crop and appointed them to his service. Their abilities far surpassed those of the king's wise men and diviners.

Daniel and his friends refusing the rich foods of the king's table

2:1-49
Daniel Interprets a Dream

The King Seeks a Dream Interpreter (2:1-16). During the second year of his reign King Nebuchadnezzar had a troubling dream. He summoned his wise men and diviners and, perhaps to ensure credibility, commanded them to reveal the dream's contents, as well as its interpretation. If they failed, they would be executed; if they succeeded, they would be richly rewarded. The diviners, understandably shaken, objected that the king's request was without precedent and that no one could know what another man dreamed. In anger the king decreed that all the royal diviners be put to death.

Daniel Interprets the King's Dream (2:17-49). When Daniel heard what had happened, he and his friends prayed to the Lord for wisdom to know and interpret the dream so that their lives might be spared. When the Lord revealed the dream to Daniel in a night vision, he praised the Lord as the sovereign Ruler of the universe, who is the source of all wisdom.

When Daniel went before the king, he was careful to give God the credit. He told the king that the Lord had revealed to him both the contents and interpretation of the dream. In his dream Nebuchadnezzar had seen a large statue. Its head was made of gold, its chest and arms of silver, its belly and thighs of bronze, its legs of iron, and its feet of iron and clay. A large rock then smashed the feet of the statue, causing it to tumble and shatter. The rock then grew into a large mountain.

Daniel explained to Nebuchadnezzar that the dream pertained to world history. The statue represented successive world kingdoms, which would ultimately be displaced by God's kingdom. Nebuchadnezzar's Babylonian empire was the golden head. The silver chest and arms represented a kingdom that would follow. Just as silver is inferior to gold, so the glory of this kingdom would not match that of Babylon. The bronze portions of the statue symbolized a third world kingdom, while the iron legs represented a fourth empire, which, like iron, would be especially powerful. The mixture of clay and iron indicated that this empire would eventually divide and become vulnerable to attack. God's kingdom (represented by the rock that grew into a mountain) would conquer this empire, bringing human rule to a violent end. Like a mountain His kingdom would be incapable of destruction and would exist forever.

Scholars differ over the identification of the final three kingdoms represented in the vision. Some see the silver portions of the statue as the combined Medo-Persian empire, the bronze parts as Alexander's Greek empire, and the iron legs as Rome. Others see the successive kingdoms as Media, Persia, and Greece.

When Daniel finished, Nebuchadnezzar praised the Lord as the sovereign God who reveals wisdom. He rewarded Daniel and elevated him and his friends to prominent positions in the empire's government.

3:1-30
Daniel's Friends Face Death

Daniel's Friends Refuse to Bow to the King's Image (3:1-18). Nebuchadnezzar made a huge, gold image. The image may have represented his sovereign authority or one of his gods. The king ordered all of his subjects to attend a dedication ceremony for the image. At a designated time they were to bow down to the image. All who refused to worship the image would be thrown into a fiery furnace. When Daniel's friends refused to bow down to the image, the angry king gave them an ultimatum and warned them of the consequences of disobedience. They explained that their loyalty to the Lord prevented them from worshiping images. They also told the king that the Lord was able to deliver them from the furnace if He so desired.

Daniel's Friends Delivered from the Furnace (3:19-30). After ordering the furnace to be heated to its maximum temperature, Nebuchadnezzar had Daniel's friends tied up and thrown in. The fire was so hot that its flames killed the soldiers who threw them in. However, when Nebuchadnezzar looked into the furnace, he saw the three men walking around unbound, accompanied by an angelic being. When the king ordered them out of the furnace, they were completely unharmed. Nebuchadnezzar praised the Lord for delivering His faithful servants, decreed that anyone who slandered the Lord be executed, and promoted the three men.

4:1-37
Nebuchadnezzar's Dream of a Large Tree

This chapter begins and ends with Nebuchadnezzar praising the Lord (4:1-3,34-37). In the intervening verses he related a personal experience through which he came to a greater realization of God's sovereignty and learned the dangers of pride.

The King Reports His Dream to Daniel (4:1-18). While lying in his palace, the king had a terrifying dream. When his wise men and diviners were unable to interpret it, he summoned Daniel. In his dream Nebuchadnezzar

An example of a "harp" like the one mentioned in Daniel 3:5 is seen above painted on this Attic vase dating from the 400s B.C.

saw a large fruit tree with beautiful leaves. Animals found shelter in its shade, and birds lodged in its branches. An angelic being then commanded that the tree be cut down and that the stump be bound with iron and bronze. The angel then announced that the man represented by the stump would be overtaken by insanity and would live outdoors like an animal for a specified period of time ("seven times" may refer to seven years; compare 7:25).

Daniel Interprets the Dream (4:19-27). Daniel informed Nebuchadnezzar that the tree represented none other than the king himself. Though great and mighty, the king would be brought low. For a period of time he would be plagued by an extreme form of insanity (known as boanthropy or lycanthropy) and would actually behave like an animal. Once he was sufficiently humbled, Nebuchadnezzar would be restored to his throne.

The Dream Comes True (4:28-37). One year later, Nebuchadnezzar's dream was fulfilled. As he proudly looked about the great city of Babylon, a voice from heaven announced to him that he was about to be humbled. He began acting like an animal, and his hair and nails grew exceedingly long. Finally, God restored his sanity, causing Nebuchadnezzar to praise Him publicly and warn others of the consequences of pride.

5:1-31
Babylon Falls

The events of chapter 5 occurred in 539 B.C., twenty-three years after Nebuchadnezzar's death. Belshazzar was now ruling Babylon in the absence of his father, Nabonidus (see introduction).

Shadrach, Meshach, and Abednego in the fiery furnace

Hebrew and Aramaic Languages

Hebrew and Aramaic are members of a major grouping of languages once found throughout Mesopotamia, Syria, Phoenicia, Arabia, and Palestine. This collection of languages is called "Semitic" on the basis of Genesis 10:21-32, which indicates the nations that spoke these languages descended from Shem.

The Semitic languages are subdivided on geographic grounds. East Semitic, from Mesopotamia, includes the Assyrian and Babylonian languages which were written in cuneiform script. Each of these symbols represented a syllable, unlike the more flexible alphabet developed later in which each symbol represented a single sound. South Semitic comprised the Arabic language that developed much later than biblical Hebrew and Aramaic. Northern Semitic includes biblical Aramaic (as well as the later forms of this language) and Syriac, which emerged much later using a script influenced by Arabic. Northwest Semitic is the branch of the Semitic family tree that includes biblical Hebrew, Phoenician, Moabite, Edomite, and probably Ugaritic.

Both Hebrew and Aramaic used the same alphabet, the one borrowed from the Phoenicians. The precise date of the invention of the alphabet is unknown, but it surely ranks as one of the most influential inventions in the history of humanity. This script quickly became adopted throughout the ancient Near East. It even served as the precursor of Greek, which in turn served as the model for Latin, the same alphabet we use today. Throughout most of biblical history Hebrew was written in a cursive script called "Paleo-Hebrew." Examples of this script were even discovered at Qumran. The "square" or "Aramaic script" became widely adopted when Aramaic became the official language of diplomacy around the time of the Babylonian exile.

The OT was written entirely in Hebrew, except for Genesis 31:47; Ezra 4:8–6:18; Jeremiah 10:11; and Daniel 2:4–7:28, which were written in Aramaic. Scholars do not always agree why these texts are written in Aramaic instead of Hebrew. The basic reason seems to lie primarily with the language spoken by the audience originally being addressed by the biblical author.

The structure of both Hebrew and Aramaic differs markedly from English, or any other Indo-European language with which the reader might be familiar. Word formation begins with three letters, called the root, which convey the word's basic meaning. For example, *Q-D-S* communicates the idea of holiness. The root is modified by prefixes, suffixes, and infixes to make different types of nouns, adjectives, verbs, infinitives, and participles. The normal word order of the sentence is verb-subject-object. The tense system is much less capable of communicating subtle distinctions in time than is either Greek or English. Both Hebrew and Aramaic are written from right to left.

In addition to the biblical text, we know about Hebrew and Aramaic from numerous inscriptions from during and after the biblical period. Important inscriptions such as the Gezer Calendar, Samaria Ostraca, Lachish Letters, and the Siloam Inscription illustrate Classical Hebrew in nonbiblical texts. Aramaic can be found in such texts as the Elephantine material as well as the later Jewish works such as the Babylonian Talmud. □

A Mysterious Message on a Wall (5:1-12). Belshazzar held a great banquet for all his nobles and their wives. He ordered that wine be served in the golden and silver goblets Nebuchadnezzar had taken from the Lord's temple in Jerusalem years before. While Belshazzar and his guests drank from the goblets, a hand appeared in thin air and wrote a mysterious message on one of the palace walls. The frightened king sent for his wise men and diviners and decreed that whoever was able to interpret the message would be elevated to third in the kingdom. (Technically speaking Nabonidus was still the king, with Belshazzar being his vice-regent.) When they were unable to decipher the message, the queen (or queen mother) reminded Belshazzar of Daniel, who years before had gained a reputation as a skillful interpreter of dreams and riddles.

Daniel Interprets the Message (5:13-31). When summoned by the king, Daniel agreed to interpret the writing, though he declined the king's gifts. Before interpreting the message, however, he reminded Belshazzar of how God had humbled proud Nebuchadnezzar. He also denounced the king for his arrogance and for his disrespect for the temple vessels. Finally, Daniel turned to the cryptic message, which read, "Mene, Mene, Tekel, Parsin." He interpreted the message as being an ominous warning of impending judgment on Belshazzar's kingdom. "Mene," meaning *mina* (fifty shekels), sounds like a related word meaning *numbered.*" Belshazzar's days were numbered and his reign about to come to an end. In similar fashion "tekel," meaning *shekel*, was a play on a related word meaning *weighed.* Belshazzar had been weighed like a shekel on the scales of divine justice and had been found lacking. "Parsin," meaning *half-shekels* (in 5:28 the singular form "peres" is used) was taken as a play on a related word meaning *divided.* Furthermore, it sounds like *Persian.* Belshazzar's kingdom would be divided between the Medes and Persians. This prophecy of Belshazzar's demise was fulfilled that very night (5:30).

6:1-28
Daniel Delivered from the Lion's Den

Daniel Defies the King's Decree (6:1-15). Daniel continued to prosper under Persian rule. Darius the Mede made him one of three administrators over the 120 districts within his jurisdiction. Daniel was so successful that he aroused the jealousy of other administrators and officials. Knowing that Daniel was loyal to his God, they devised a plot by which they hoped to have him executed for treason. Appealing to Darius's vanity,

Daniel interpreting the writing on the wall

Daniel in the den of lions

they convinced the king to issue a decree commanding his subjects to worship him exclusively for one month. Violators would be thrown to the lions. When Daniel defied the decree and openly prayed to the Lord, the conspirators reported him to the king. Realizing he had been tricked, Darius tried to absolve Daniel of guilt; but Daniel's enemies reminded the king that royal decrees could not be altered.

Daniel in the Lion's Den (6:16-28). Darius had no other alternative than to throw Daniel to the lions. A stone was placed over the entrance to the den, and the king sealed it with his own ring so that it might not be disturbed. After a long, restless night Darius returned to the den in the morning. To his amazement Daniel was still alive. Daniel explained that the Lord had miraculously preserved him by closing the lions' mouths. The king ordered that Daniel be lifted from the den and his accusers thrown in. Darius then issued an official statement praising Daniel's God as the sovereign Lord of the universe, who miraculously delivers His servants.

VISIONS AND REVELATIONS OF FUTURE EVENTS (7:1–12:13)

7:1-28
A Vision of Four Beasts from the Sea

The vision recorded in this chapter occurred in Belshazzar's first year of co-regency (about 556–553 B.C.), prior to the events recorded in chapters 5–6.

Daniel Reports the Vision (7:1-14). Daniel saw four beasts emerge in succession from the churning sea. The first resembled a lion but also had the wings of an eagle. As Daniel watched, the creature's wings were torn off, and it stood on two feet like a human. It also was given a heart like that of a person. The second beast resembled a bear with three ribs in its mouth. The third beast looked like a leopard with four wings and four heads. The fourth beast, the most terrifying of all, had iron teeth with which it ripped its victims to bits. It also possessed ten horns, three of which were uprooted before another horn that sprouted up among them. This other horn had human eyes and spoke arrogant words.

In this vision Daniel also saw God, called the "Ancient of Days," seated on His throne with thousands of His servants attending Him. His clothing and hair were white, and His throne, a flame of fire. Books were opened as God prepared to sit in judgment on the fourth beast. The beast, along with its boastful little horn, were cast into the fire and destroyed. A human figure, called "one like a son of man," then appeared in the clouds and approached the divine throne, where he was granted authority to rule the world.

The Interpretation of the Vision (7:15-28). One of the heavenly attendants explained the significance of the vision to Daniel. The four beasts, like the statue seen in Nebuchadnezzar's dream (Dan 2), represented four successive empires that would rule the earth. The ten horns of the fourth beast, which was of particular interest to Daniel, represented ten kings who would arise from the fourth empire. The little horn symbolized another ruler, who would supplant three of the ten. This little horn would oppose God and persecute His people for a specified period of time (perhaps three and a half years, compare "a time, times and half a time," 7:25). After this the Lord would destroy this ruler and establish His kingdom.

As in chapter 2, interpreters differ about the identification of the four kingdoms. On analogy with chapter 2, the lion probably represents Babylon. The bear is often associated with the Medo-Persian Empire, with the three ribs understood as symbols of its three major victims, Lydia, Babylon, and Egypt. The leopard may very well represent Greece, its four heads reflecting the fourfold division of Alexander's kingdom after his death (8:8,21-22). The final beast may represent Rome, with its ten horns symbolizing a later manifestation of this empire prior to the coming of God's kingdom. In this case the little horn may be equated with the New Testament figure of the Antichrist. However, as with chapter 2, others identify the successive kingdoms as Babylon, Media, Persia, and Greece, with the little horn being associated with Antiochus Epiphanes (see Dan 8; 11).

The identification of the "one like a son of man" has also occasioned much debate. Many see the title as messianic. Others understand the figure to represent humanity, God's chosen people, or angelic beings (with Michael sometimes being specified as the angel in view).

8:1-27
A Vision of a Ram and Goat

This vision, like that of chapter 7, came during the reign of Belshazzar.

Daniel Reports the Vision (8:1-14). Daniel saw a vision of a ram with two horns of unequal length, the longer of which grew up after the other. The ram charged westward, northward, and southward, conquering all who opposed it. However, a goat with a long horn then came from the west, shattered the ram's two horns, and trampled the ram into the ground. None could stand before the goat, but at the height of his power his horn was broken and replaced by four small horns. From one of these horns grew another horn that became increas-

In antiquity the ram was a symbol of the Persian Empire. Shown above is a golden ram's head dating from the Persian period.

ingly strong and extended its power southward and eastward. It challenged the hosts of heaven, oppressed God's people, and disrupted the sacrifices in the Lord's temple.

The Interpretation of the Vision (8:15-27). The angel Gabriel revealed the interpretation of the vision to Daniel. The two-horned ram represented the Medo-Persian empire, and the goat, the Greek empire (of Alexander). The four horns reflected the fourfold division of Alexander's empire following his untimely death. The little horn represented Antiochus Epiphanes, the Syrian ruler (about 175–164 B.C.) who opposed God's people and desecrated the temple.

9:1-27
A Vision of Seventy Sevens

Daniel's Intercessory Prayer (9:1-19). In 539–538 B.C., immediately after the Persian conquest of Babylon, Daniel prayed to the Lord on behalf of exiled Israel. Daniel realized that the seventy-year period of Judah's desolation prophesied in Jeremiah 25:11-12 was soon approaching its end. (The prophecy is dated to 605 B.C. [compare Jer 25:1], the year when Nebuchadnezzar besieged Jerusalem for the first time and carried away the first group of exiles to Babylon. If one assumes that the seventy-year period began in that year, then it would be over in 535 B.C.)

Addressing God as Israel's faithful covenant Lord, Daniel confessed the nation's sinful and rebellious condition and acknowledged that they had justly suffered the covenant curses threatened by Moses. He then asked the Lord to forgive the nation's sins and once again look with favor on desolate Jerusalem.

Gabriel Reveals and Interprets the Vision (9:20-27). While Daniel prayed, Gabriel appeared to him and announced that "seventy sevens" (490 years according to many) were decreed for Israel and Jerusalem, after which time atonement would be made for their sins. He then explained the chronology of these "seventy sevens." Sixty-nine sevens would separate the time of the decree to rebuild Jerusalem and the coming of the Messiah ("Anointed One"). Sometime after this the Messiah would be "cut off" and the city destroyed by the "people of the ruler who will come." During the seventieth seven this ruler would make a covenant with God's people, which he would then violate halfway through the period.

Understandably this somewhat cryptic vision poses several difficulties and has been interpreted in a variety of ways. Some view the numbers as symbolic, while others take them quite literally and produce elaborate mathematical explanations of their fulfillment. Among the latter, some even contend that this prophecy pinpoints the date of Christ's crucifixion.

10:1–12:13
An Angel Reveals Future Events

Daniel's Vision of the Angel (10:1–11:1). In 536 B.C. Daniel received his final vision. While standing by the Tigris River, he saw a radiant angelic being whose voice thundered. Totally overwhelmed by the vision, Daniel fell into a deep trance. The angel told Daniel to stand up and encouraged him not to fear. He then explained that he had been delayed in coming by the "prince of Persia," apparently a reference to an angel who exercised jurisdiction over the nation Persia. After a three-week struggle, Michael intervened, allowing this angel to come to Daniel. He would soon be off again to fight against the prince of Persia, but before leaving he revealed to Daniel certain future events.

The Angel Outlines Future Events (11:2–12:4). Daniel 11:2-35 outlines the course of Palestinian history from Daniel's time to the time of Antiochus Epiphanes. Verse 2 refers to the four Persian rulers who would succeed Cyrus: Cambyses (530–522 B.C.), Pseudo-Smerdis (522), Darius I (522–486), and Xerxes (486–465). It alludes to Xerxes' campaign against Greece. Verses 3-4 then refer to Alexander the Great (336–323) and the division of his kingdom. Verses 5-20 outline the relationship between the Seleucids ("the king of the North"), who ruled Syria, and the Ptolemies ("the king of the South"), who ruled Egypt during the period 321–175. Verses 21-35 focus on the career of Antiochus Epiphanes (175–164), mentioning among other things his Egyptian campaigns and mistreatment of the Jews. Verses 32-35 anticipate the Maccabean revolt against Antiochus.

Most of the details of verses 36-45 do not correspond to Antiochus's career. For example, Antiochus died in Persia, not Palestine (compare v. 45). Consequently, some scholars label these verses as unfulfilled "prophecy" and understand the preceding verses (vv. 1-35) as "prophecy" after the fact (see introduction). Others understand a switch in perspective beginning in verse 36. The description merges into a portrayal of the Antichrist, whose hostility to God and His people was foreshadowed in the career of Antiochus.

The final verses of this section (12:1-4) anticipate a time of crisis for Israel in which Michael, the nation's guardian angel, would intervene on their behalf. Reference is made to a general resurrection of the righteous and evil.

Daniel's Final Vision and Instructions (12:4-13). The angel instructed Daniel to seal up the revelation until the end times. Daniel then saw two other angelic beings standing by the river, both of whom were clothed in linen. One asked how long it would be before the revelation was fulfilled. The other responded that "a time, times, and a half a time" (probably three and a half years) would pass between the breaking of Israel's power and the fulfillment of the vision. Verse 11 apparently gives a more exact measurement of this period (1,290 days). The significance of the figure given in verse 12 (1,335 days) is unclear. In conjunction with verse 11, it implies that there would be an additional forty-five-day period before the complete fulfillment of the vision.

Theological and Ethical Significance

Daniel stresses God's sovereignty over world history. History unfolds as part of God's plans and is moving toward God's predetermined goals. Earthly despots wield their cruel power for only a short time. God is in control and has set an end to the time His people have to suffer. God's goals for human history include the deliverance of His people from oppression, the resurrection, judgment, and the establishment of His everlasting kingdom. Daniel thus calls God's people of every time to perseverance and hope. Like Daniel and his friends, today's believers are tempted to compromise their values and worship that which is not God. Daniel calls Christians to live out their faith in a hostile world whatever the cost.

Questions for Reflection

1. What lessons can we learn from Daniel and his friends?
2. In what ways does God demonstrate His sovereignty in this book? What relevance does the doctrine of God's sovereignty have for the modern Christian and for the church?
3. What is the purpose for the book's extensive use of symbolism? How do the symbolism and vivid imagery contribute to the overall message of the book?
4. In what ways does this book offer comfort and encouragement to Christians?

Sources for Additional Study

Archer, G. L., Jr. "Daniel." *The Expositor's Bible Commentary.* Vol. 7. Grand Rapids: Zondervan, 1985.

Baldwin, J. G. *Daniel.* Downers Grove: InterVarsity, 1978.

Wood, L. *A Commentary on Daniel.* Grand Rapids: Zondervan, 1973.

Young, E. J. *The Prophecy of Daniel.* Grand Rapids: Eerdmans, 1949.

THE MINOR PROPHETS

The Hebrew Bible from which our English versions are translated treats the Minor Prophets as a single book. Called *The Book of the Twelve Prophets*, the Hebrew book has the prophets in the same order that we use. Together the Minor Prophets work to present a single message reaffirming God's love and plans for Israel beyond His judgment on their sin.

We are so familiar with the names of the prophets to which these books are attributed that we easily forget that most of them are not mentioned anywhere else. Exceptions are Micah (Jer 26:18), Jonah (2 Kgs 14:25), and Haggai and Zechariah (Ezra 5:1; 6:14). We know little about most of the Minor Prophets and still less about how this information helps us to understand their books.

The Minor Prophets stretch from Hosea (a contemporary of Jeroboam II, 786–746 B.C.) to Malachi (likely a contemporary of Ezra, 458 B.C.). In the mid-700s B.C. the kingdoms of Israel in Samaria and of Judah in Jerusalem were intact and prosperous. But in Mesopotamia, Assyria was growing in power and ambition. It was becoming increasingly interested in Palestine and, beyond that, in Egypt. Its campaigns in 734 and 721 destroyed Samaria and took most of its peoples into exile. Judah survived but became Assyria's vassal and had a troubled history during the following century.

After 655 B.C. Assyria was weakened by a series of rebellions and finally fell to Babylon in 612 and 609. Babylon defeated Egypt and took over Palestine. Jerusalem was destroyed by Babylon in 587, and many Judeans were taken into exile. Then Persia succeeded Babylon in 539 and inherited that empire.

Under Persia's more tolerant attitude toward various religions, permission was received for Jews to rebuild the temple in Jerusalem. It took a long time in view of opposition from their neighbors. But through the work of Zerubabbel in 520–515, of Ezra in 468, and of Nehemiah in 445–427 B.C., the temple and the city were rebuilt, the priestly services were reinstated, the Torah of Moses was recognized as law in Jerusalem, and pilgrims were welcomed for the great festivals.

The Minor Prophets do not follow a strict chronological order. There is a rough chronological outline carried through from Hosea, Amos, and Micah (about 750–701 B.C.); to Zephaniah, Nahum, and Habakkuk (about 628–605); to Haggai and Zechariah chapters 1–8 (520–515); and finally to Malachi (about 500–450). The chronological position of the other books is vague. Obadiah and Habakkuk are apparently related to the fall of Jerusalem in 587, but this is not explicit. Zephaniah's superscription places it in Josiah's time (640–609), but nothing in the book fits that time.

Parts of the Minor Prophets follow a thematic outline rather than a strict chronological order. The six small books relate three themes in reverse order.

1. Joel: Day of the Lord
2. Obadiah: Edom (who was at Jerusalem's fall in 587 B.C.)
3. Jonah: Nineveh
3. Nahum: Nineveh
2. Habakkuk: Babylon (who was at Jerusalem's fall in 587 B.C.)
1. Zephaniah: The Day of the Lord

These seem to be arranged in an order that has little to do with chronology. Instead, they deal with issues related to God's judgment over Israel and the nations. They seem to be particularly related to the terrible happenings at the fall of Jerusalem in 587 (Obadiah and Habakkuk) or to the long rule and fall of Nineveh (Jonah and Nahum) and to the broader theology of God's judgment over all history (Joel and Zephaniah).

Micah's position in the center of the whole seems to be deliberate to shift the center away from 587 B.C., the destruction of Jerusalem, which is the crucial event through the Books of Kings and Chronicles. Isaiah changed that in placing chapters 36–39 in the middle of its vision. Now the twelve Minor Prophets followed suit. They saw the decisive moment, not in an event of history, but in God's decision that would determine all future history. Isaiah had placed this picture of the future temple city at the beginning (chap. 2). The twelve Minor Prophets used the same words at the center of their work in Micah 4 with the same effect.

Both Isaiah and the twelve Minor Prophets pointed the predictions and announcements within their books toward a fulfillment at or near the end of the book. They both looked back to God's word, spoken through prophets and in their pages, in order to celebrate its fulfillment before the end of the book. They did not leave the readers without a future. Quite the contrary. What God has accomplished in history gives the readers a future to be lived with God's written Word (*Torah* in Mal 4:4) and God's living words through prophets (Mal 4:5).

The Books of the twelve Minor Prophets interpret the previous three and a half centuries (about 750 to 430 B.C.) from a viewpoint of God's sovereignty over history. Specifically this includes His covenant people, the nations of Canaan, the Mesopotamian nations, and Egypt.

The central issue was whether the Lord still loved Israel and had a purpose for it after all the terrible times that had passed. Its history is reviewed in terms of the blessings and the curses prescribed in the covenant statements in Leviticus 26 and Deuteronomy 28–30. But the stress is on God's continued love for His people even after the necessary judgments.

Another issue was whether God had controlled this turbulent history or whether chaos had overrun His purpose and control. What was God's relation to a history in which heathen empires had occupied His land and enslaved His people? In a world obviously not controlled by Yahweh's anointed king on Zion, where was God to be found? And what of those who worshiped Him?

The Books of the twelve Minor Prophets, along with the other prophetic books, were written to help their readers or hearers believe their own times to be ones God had willed to be and brought to pass. Knowing this they could ask, "What does God want us to do in this time?" and do it. They had to know that they were surely loved by God. They were privileged heirs of God's great victories. They were responsible to the love of God which spared and restored them. They were still the elect people of God, beloved and blessed, to be guided by His written Word (*Torah*) and by His presence among them, witnessed by inspired preaching like Elijah's.

Taken as a whole, the Books of the twelve Minor Prophets spoke to a people who questioned God's love for them. They were priests who failed to sense the gravity of their service. They were persons who chose to ignore the law and the provisions of covenant. For them the Book of the Twelve reviewed three and a half centuries of God's relation to Israel's bitter history. The lessons of that history follow:

- Hosea: God's love is constant and stubborn. It would not give up despite Israel's apostasy.
- Joel: Sin is great and serious; judgment had to come.
- Amos: Israel's sin and that of their neighbors was full; judgment was near.
- Obadiah: God's rule is shown by judgment on Edom.
- Jonah: God cared about Nineveh too.
- Micah 4–5 (in the center of the whole): God's house (the Jerusalem temple) would be raised above all the mountains. All peoples could come to it for worship. Justice and mercy are more important than sacrifice.
- Nahum: God's wrath was revealed in the destruction of Nineveh.
- Habakkuk: The trials of faith in crisis because of Babylon had to be patiently endured.
- Zephaniah: Joel's theme about the Day of the Lord was resumed.
- Haggai and Zechariah 1–8: Zerubabbel's and Joshua's building the temple showed that the time for fulfillment of God's benevolent purposes for Jerusalem was near. It was happening.
- Zechariah 9–14: The history of preexilic Israel is summarized from the viewpoint of postexilic Judaism under Persia's rule.
- Malachi: God's love has been revealed. Use the opportunity well. Remember God's instruction. Listen for God's prophetic word.

Because of the complexity of the literature, it is important to keep in mind a "map" of the heart of the message. The main points of emphasis are:

- Hosea 1–3: The determined love of God for Israel.

Jonah preaching to the Ninevites

- Micah 4–5: God's goal—a new Jerusalem as a temple city to which all can come for worship.
- Malachi: God's determined love has prevailed. Respond to it.

Because the Book of the Twelve Prophets is preserved in the Jewish canon of the Latter Prophets and in the Christian Scriptures at the end of the Old Testament, modern readers look to it for lessons that continue to be applicable. These include: the love of God for those He has chosen who seek Him and believe in Him; God's control of history to fulfill His plan in which His beloved elect are to play their vital part; and God's primary goal for His people for them to worship Him sincerely and joyfully. (Others can rule the world for Him.) God invites seekers from all nations and peoples to join His people in worshiping Him.

Both Jews and Christians have recognized that the Books of the twelve Minor Prophets affirm the life-style God wants for them. It was not necessary for the Jews returning from the exile to recreate the situations of twelve tribes in Canaan like that in the Book of Joshua or that of the United Kingdom under David. God affirmed their status of being a people dispersed through the known world, offering worship to Him wherever they were. He called them to be unified in their commitment to Him in worship, through their use of a common Scripture, and in looking to Jerusalem's temple.

Christians and Jews today are keenly aware that subsequent history eliminated the temple. The Romans destroyed it in A.D. 70, and it was not to be rebuilt or replaced. The Gospels are aware of this (Mark 14:58; 15:29; John 2:19,21). Part of Christianity later came to look to Rome and St. Peter's basilica as a Christian substitute for Jerusalem's temple. But all Christians have accepted the other forms for the life of the people of God which are taught here: their spread throughout the world, their direction through a common Scripture, and the expectation that God would continue to speak through chosen messengers.

Christians placed the twelve Minor Prophets at the end of the Old Testament. This links the closing message about Elijah with the ministry of John the Baptist in the Gospels. In doing so Christians affirm the books' basic message. The Gospels affirm God's continued love for His people as promised to Abraham. Jesus taught God's concern for the lame, the blind, and the other disadvantaged of His people. Jesus also taught God's bias in favor of the poor, the meek, and the humble among believers. All these are emphases of the twelve Minor Prophets. Acts and the Epistles that follow affirm that God sends His people out to settle in small congregations scattered among the nations, committed to teaching, worship, and care for the poor. And the Book of Revelation pictures Jerusalem and its temple as raised above the earth to be the eternal place of God's presence with His beloved and redeemed people.

The Minor Prophets (the Book of the Twelve) helped the Jews returning from and remaining in exile to come to terms with their turbulent past. They had lost their country, their king, their temple; they were threatened with the loss of their very identity. It helped them see God's consistent love and purpose, still alive and valid for them. They were invited to view that terrible experience as God's way of refining them, preparing them for a new way of fulfilling His original purposes for Abraham and Jacob.

It also teaches that the problems of apostasy and rebellion continue. Not all Jews make it into God's kingdom. But the door is open to them and all others who would join them in seeking God and turning to Him. It teaches that the guide to God's way is in the Scriptures, both the Law and the Prophets.

The word of the Lord to His prophet: Hear, O Israel, the Lord from His holy temple.

HOSEA

Hosea serves as the introduction to the Minor Prophets (the Book of the Twelve). As such Hosea introduces the central question of the Minor Prophets—whether the Lord still loved Israel and had a purpose for them beyond His judgment on their sin. And Hosea provided the answer with his stress on God's continued love for His people and the responsibilities that love placed on them.

Hosea's name occurs in the title verse and in the narrative in Hosea 1:2,4,6. Still, we know little about Hosea apart from those details of his married life used to picture God's love for rebellious Israel. Hosea's ministry to Judah (about 745 B.C.) roughly coincided with Amos's to Israel (about 750) and preceded Micah's to Judah (before 722 to about 701). In the mid-700s B.C. the kingdoms of Israel in Samaria and of Judah in Jerusalem were intact and prosperous. But in Mesopotamia, Assyria was growing in power and ambition. It was becoming increasingly interested in Palestine and, beyond that, in Egypt. Assyria's campaigns in 734 and 721 would destroy Samaria and send most of its peoples into exile. Judah would survive, but it would become Assyria's satellite and have a troubled history during the following century.

1:1–3:5
God Loves His Unfaithful People

Hosea's superscription (1:1) anchors one end of the chronology of the Minor Prophets. Uzziah reigned in Judah from 783 to 742 B.C. Jeroboam reigned in Israel from 786 to 746. The character (or genre) of the material is named: "the word of the Lord." This literature is prophetic in its deepest sense. Hosea means *He has delivered.*

The narrative in 1:2–2:1 and the first-person narrative in 3:1-5 establish the ambivalence in God's relation to Israel that recurs throughout the twelve Minor Prophets.

The prophet Hosea

Hosea disapproved of Israel's kings depending on Assyria for protection. The above relief from the black obelisk of Shalmaneser III shows Jehu of Israel bringing tribute to the king of Assyria.

On the one side Israel's apostasy and violation of covenant agreements merited God's judgment and a "divorce" from God. For this reason the Kingdom of Israel would be terminated (1:4-5) and its people sent into exile. On the other side God's determined love for the people would not allow that estrangement to continue. God's love would find some way to fulfill His promises to Abraham (Hos 1:10a; Gen 13:16) and to Moses (Hos 1:10b; Exod 6:7) of a united people as under David (Hos 1:11; 2 Sam 5:1-5). This hope was that Israel, after judgment, could again know they were God's people and were loved of God. Malachi, at the conclusion of the Minor Prophets, recorded that this had been fulfilled by his time. (Compare Hos 2:1 with Mal 1:2.)

Chapter 2 is a long speech by the Lord on these themes of Israel's apostasy and God's unfailing love. Such speeches (when God speaks and His aids dialogue with Him) pervade the twelve Minor Prophets. Verses 1-13 give reasons judgments (or covenant curses) were necessary and would be carried out.

Verses 14-23 portray a future time, beyond judgment, when God would woo Israel to love Him as in Egypt (v. 15). All of Hosea is characterized by such references to Israel's beginnings. It assumes that the readers know the story found in Exodus through Numbers. This speech, like the covenant sections of Leviticus 26 and Deuteronomy 27–31, proclaims the curses that follow a breach of covenant and the blessings that accompany covenant faithfulness. God's love had established the covenant that made Israel to be God's people. His love would be the basis for reestablishing it with all its blessings.

4:1–10:15
God's Controversy with His People

These speeches by the Lord and His attendants (in Isa 1:2 they are called Heavens and Earth) rehearse the sins of Israel and the inevitable problems that follow. Some of the problems were political: Israel turned to Assyria and Egypt for help (Hos 5:13) instead of turning to God.

Chapter 6 is a choral response that calls for repentance.

Symbolic Actions by the Prophets

The prophetic word became a living word for the prophets. Often God called them to do something beyond preaching. He led them to picture the message in their own lives. They had to live out the meaning and results of God's word to His people. Their actions thus symbolized for the people what God was about to do to and for Israel.

In calling the prophets to symbolic actions, God gave them no easy task. The word had to come alive in their family. For Isaiah the birth and naming of children became acts preaching to the people. He called one son *A Remnant Shall Return* and another *Speedy Is the Spoil, Quick the Plunder* (Isa 7:3; 8:3).

These strange names made people think as they watched the prophet walk down the street carrying his children. Was *Remnant* a sign of disaster in war or a hope for new growth in the future? Did *Return* refer to the aftermath of battle or to spiritual return and repentance? Who was fast to spoil and plunder whom? God's people had to listen to the prophet preach to determine the meaning, but the children's names made them curious enough to listen.

Isaiah gave yet another symbolic name to a more mysterious child—*Immanuel, God with Us* (7:14; 8:8,10). This certainly called the audience to attention when Isaiah announced the birth of yet another child of significance (9:6). Jerusalem's citizens knew the prophet was doing more than acting crazy when he wandered the city's streets minus his clothing for three years pointing to God's actions against Israel's enemies to the south (Isa 20).

Hosea had an even more difficult family task. He had to endure a broken heart and broken marriage along with public indignity and disgrace (Hos 1:1-9; 2:2-9). God called him to marry a prostitute and then name her children *Jezreel* (the sight of a battle), *Not Pitied* (or *Without a Mother's Love,* indicating the withdrawal of God's love and forgiveness from Israel), and *Not My People* (or *Illegitimate,* indicating Israel no longer had a guarantee of God's election and protection).

Later, God used the names to indicate His renewed covenant with His people (1:10–2:1; 2:14–3:5). Israel had to pay attention to Hosea, if only to hear the latest gossip about his family. As they listened, they learned the nature of God's deep, undying love for His people, a love going beyond all human love, even Hosea's (11:8-11). They also found the ups and downs of their relationship to God described in family terms.

Jeremiah had to abstain from the duties and joys of family life to preach God's word and show the imminent danger God's people faced (Jer 16:2). In contrast Ezekiel suffered having to bury his wife without public mourning (Ezek 24:15-27), symbolizing how Israel would have to react at the news their temple was destroyed.

Prophetic symbolism thus ⇨

God replied, "What can I do with you, Ephraim?" Verse 6 is a recurrent theme, "I desire mercy, not sacrifice." (Compare Mic 6:6-8.)

Hosea 9:10 refers again to a story of Israel's beginnings in colorful metaphoric language. Hosea contrasted the Israel of his time (about 745 B.C.) with the patriarchs and the people under Moses. Israel's beginnings were pure, but its contacts with Canaan had brought apostasy.

Hosea 10:3-8 discusses the way kingship became useless and irrelevant for Israel when it was exiled. By the time Malachi wrote, there was no reference to a king at all. In verse 6 the Assyrian dominance of Palestine in the 700s B.C. is clear.

The fate of Bethel (v. 15) is a theme important to the Book of the Twelve Minor Prophets. The historical narratives in the Minor Prophets (Amos 7:10-17 and Zech 7) relate to Bethel. Here in verse 15, and in Amos, Bethel and the king of Israel are closely related (compare 1 Kgs 12:29–13:34).

11:1–14:9
God's Loyal Love

This section begins with another brief account of Israel's beginnings, stressing God's love for them (Hos 11:1-4). Deuteronomy 32:10-21 is a parallel poetical description. There follows an announcement of a return to Egypt (a reversed exodus) and of a submission to Assyria as a result of their rebellion (v. 5).

Hosea is known as the book of God's passion. This is expressed most graphically in 11:8-9, ending with the words "I am God and not man—the Holy One among you."

In chapter 12 God's charges against Israel are again illustrated from stories about Jacob's birth (Gen 25:26), his struggle with God (Gen 32:24-30), and his being found by God at Bethel (Gen 28:10-22; 35).

Chapter 14 called on Israel to return to God, to recognize that Assyria could not solve their problems. It closes with a promise of God's continued openness to them.

reached deep into the prophets' personal relationships. It gave them creative ways to show people God's will without saying a word, though often the prophets did explain the meaning of their actions.

The potter shaping and reshaping a pot on his wheel showed Jeremiah and Israel how God could change course and directions with Israel (Jer 18). Breaking the potter's beautiful jar showed how God could destroy His people (Jer 19). Jeremiah had to wear an oxen's yoke around Jerusalem and summon foreign ambassadors to call them to submit to Nebuchadnezzar. He even had to command his own king of Judah to wear Nebuchadnezzar's yoke (Jer 27). Such action brought quick response. An opposing prophet broke Jeremiah's yoke (28:10-11). False prophets used symbolic actions too. Still, the faithful prophet followed God's calling and continued acting out God's word (compare Jer 32; 43:8-9).

Of all prophets, Ezekiel is most known for his symbolic acts. The first chapters of Ezekiel read almost like modern science fiction at its most bizarre extreme. Ezekiel ate a scroll (3:2). He was tied with ropes and became unable to talk (3:24-27). He drew a map of Jerusalem on a tablet and enacted a military siege against his drawing (4:1-4). He lay down on his left side for 390 days and then on his right side for 40 days (4:4-7). He was called to cook food with human excrement for fuel but allowed to use cow dung when he complained (4:12-15). He cut off his hair and beard and then divided the hair into three parts for separate actions (5:1-4). He packed his bags and left the city by digging a hole in the city wall (12:3-8). He trembled and shuddered as he ate food with the people (12:18).

After the exile Zechariah prepared a crown to symbolize God's messiah (Zech 6:9-15).

The prophets' actions raised many questions for the people. They wondered about the prophets' mental states. They wondered if the prophets were magicians whose power ensured the acts would come true in the real world. They looked to other prophets to cast doubt on the power of the symbolic acts. They even stopped to wonder if God were actually speaking through the prophets and calling them to a faith in a new way of interpreting Yahweh's way with His people.

The prophets themselves knew God had commanded the acts, no matter what suspicions and questions such acts raised for their audiences. The prophets knew they as humans had no power and no magic to give meaning and actual power to the acts. Rather, the prophets depended on God to take the acts, fulfill the message of the acts, and call the people to account for their response to the acts.

Symbolic acts were a vital method for God to speak to His people in warning and hope. In this way He wooed them to return to Him and avoid the judgment their actions had made inevitable. □

Early morning wispy clouds in Israel (like the ones in the above photo of the Dead Sea area as viewed from Masada) disappear as the sun rises (see Hos 6:4; 13:3).

Theological Significance

Nothing can quench God's love for His people. Like a marriage partner, God is deeply involved in their lives and is pained by their rebellion and unfaithfulness. God demands love and loyalty from His own. Often God's people then and now have failed to demonstrate wholehearted love for Him. But God stands ready to forgive and restore those who turn to Him in repentance. In buying Gomer's freedom, Hosea points ahead to God's love perfectly expressed in Christ, who buys the freedom of His bride, the church, with His own life.

Questions for Reflection

1. In what ways are today's believers unfaithful to God?
2. How has God demonstrated His persistent love for us?
3. What demands does God's love place upon us?

Sources for Additional Study

Cohen, G. G. and H. R. Vandermey *Hosea/Amos.* Chicago: Moody, 1981.

Kidner, D. *The Message of Hosea: Love to the Loveless.* Downers Grove: InterVarsity, 1981.

Smith, B. K. *Hosea, Joel, Amos, Obadiah, Jonah. Layman's Bible Book Commentary.* Vol. 13. Nashville: Broadman, 1982.

Wood, L. "Hosea." Vol. 7. *Expositor's Bible Commentary.* Grand Rapids: Zondervan, 1985.

The tall, slender cypress tree was an OT symbol of strength (Isa 37:24; Hos 14:8, NASB).

JOEL

The name *Joel* means *Yahweh is God.* The heading (1:1) does not set the prophet's message in a historical context. The theme of the book is: "The day of the Lord is near" (1:15).

1:1–2:32
Day for Response

Chapter 1 pictures a terrible plague of locusts that signals God's devastating action against the land. Chapter 2 repeats the announcement for Zion and describes the movement of troops (presumably the locusts) across the land (2:1-11). At this time repentance was still appropriate (2:12-17).

There was hope beyond judgment on that day if the people repented (2:18-27). If this occurred, God could restore the land; and the people would know God was present in Israel, that He alone is God (2:27).

After repentance a great outpouring of God's spirit would bring a wonderful renewal "before the great and dreadful day of the Lord" (2:31). All who called on the Lord will be saved. Mount Zion and Jerusalem would be the site of that deliverance (2:32). Postexilic Jewish readers in Jerusalem would have thought these words had been fulfilled in them and in the newly rebuilt city. Later occasions of great spiritual renewal have also claimed these words (Acts 2:16-21). Ten forms of the restoration blessings in Joel 2:18-32 have influenced New Testament writers (Matt 24:29; Mark 13:24-25; Luke 21:25; Acts 21:9; 22:16; Rom 10:13; Titus 3:6; Rev 6:12). In that great time salvation will be available to all who seek God without distinction of age, gender, or social status.

3:1-21
Day of Judgment and Salvation

Chapter 3 pictures a phase of the great day of the Lord when nations are gathered for judgment. Tyre, Sidon, and Philistia are called by name to charge them with selling Hebrew slaves (3:4-6). Such crimes may well have been perpetrated during the entire period described by the Minor Prophets (about 750–400 B.C.). Tyre, Sidon, and Philistia were great trading centers whose commerce was hardly interrupted by the rise and fall of empires.

Verses 9-16 speak of a judgment that would disarm

The prophet Joel

The prophet Joel prophesied the destruction of the city of Tyre. Shown above is a portion of the bronze gates at Balawat that depict the conquering of Tyre by Shalmaneser III (858–824 B.C.).

these peoples and in which the Lord was a refuge for His people, Israel. Verse 17 has Zion recognized as God's holy dwelling, safe from invading foreigners.

Verse 19 speaks of desolation for Egypt and Edom (see Obadiah) because of violence done to Judah. But Judah and Jerusalem were inhabited still, for "the LORD dwells in Zion" (3:21).

This portrayal covers the entire period of the Minor Prophets and ends where the Minor Prophets do: the new temple services proclaimed that the Lord was in Zion and that the city was again prepared to welcome pilgrims for its festivals. Persia's dominance in the 400s B.C. guaranteed peace and safety for travelers, just as it allowed no sovereign nationalism for Canaan's small nations.

Theological and Ethical Significance

God can use crises to sensitize His people to their utter dependence on God and their need for spiritual renewal. Sin is serious and merits God's judgment. Judgment can be avoided by heartfelt prayer and repentance. God is gracious and merciful. God's desire is to forgive His people and pour out His Spirit on them.

Questions for Reflection

1. How do we respond to crises? Do hard times drive us to God?

2. How did Joel's prophecy find fulfillment in the events of Pentecost (Acts 2:16-17)? How did Joel's prophecy find fulfillment in a mixed Jewish-Gentile church (Rom 10:12-13)?

Sources for Additional Study

Allen, L. C. *The Books of Joel, Obadiah, Jonah, and Micah.* Grand Rapids: Eerdmans, 1976.

Price, W. K. *The Prophet Joel and the Day of the Lord.* Chicago: Moody, 1976.

Smith, B. K. *Hosea, Joel, Amos, Obadiah, Jonah. Layman's Bible Book Commentary.* Vol. 13. Nashville: Broadman, 1982.

AMOS

Amos

Amos was not a professional prophet on the king's payroll (7:14). He was just "one of the shepherds of Tekoa," a village about twelve miles south of Jerusalem (1:1), and a tender "of sycamore-fig trees" (7:14). But God's call compelled him to preach so boldly against the sins of King Jeroboam and the upper class of Samaria that Amos was accused of treason (7:7–8:2).

1:1–3:12
Nations Are Subject to God

The title verse of Amos places the prophecies about 750 B.C. Hosea's announcements were moving toward fulfillment. Palestine's small states, including Israel and Judah, sensed that God's decreed fate was inexorably approaching in the form of invading Assyrian armies (6:2).

But Amos's prophecies saw the source of their troubles in the Lord's decisions, not those of the Assyrian king, Tiglath-Pileser. All nations are subject to the Lord. He owns the land of Canaan in a special way (Deut 32:9). In David's reign all these nations became vassals under David and swore loyalty to David's God in Zion (Ps 2). Now they had to stand under His judgment.

This was especially true for Israel. Amos, like Hosea, referred to the Pentateuch. In Amos 2:10 the exodus from Egypt and the wilderness journey are cited, as they are again in 3:1. Amos dealt with a false understanding of election that would prevent Israel's coming under judgment (3:2). Israel's election was not to privileged status but to service.

The nature of prophecy is revealed in 3:3-8. It presumes God's sovereignty over all history. The prophet is gifted to help God's people see the relation between God's will and what happens in history. When Israel asked why they they had to suffer the invasions and destructions between 800 and 600 B.C., the prophets taught that these were due to God's decision; He had had enough of Israel's infidelities and rebellions.

3:13–5:17
Bethel, the Symbol of Judgment

Bethel, which was mentioned in Hosea, appears in Amos as well. In 3:14 its destruction is announced as part of the

Amos compared the weight of the punishment of Yahweh upon the people of Israel to a cart heavily loaded with grain. This is illustrated in the photo above from Anatolia of an oxen-pulled cart filled with sheaves of grain.

judgment. King Jeroboam named Bethel's and Dan's temples as national shrines when his kingdom, Israel, split from the Southern Kingdom, Judah (1 Kgs 12:29). In Amos 4:4 Bethel was a place that God no longer honored. In 5:5 Bethel was listed with Gilgal as useless places of worship. Bethel was the site of Amos's confrontation with Amaziah, the priest, and of his announcement of the coming fall of the royal house now occupied by Jeroboam II (7:10-17).

5:18–6:14
Call to Justice and Righteousness

Amos emphasized sins of injustice and oppression rather than the apostasy through idolatry as did Hosea. He thought of the Day of the Lord as destruction (5:18-20). He rejected sacrifice not accompanied by justice in daily living (5:21-24).

The "woes" in Amos (5:18; 6:1) are covenant curses, witnessing to God's recognition that the covenant was broken and no longer valid.

7:1–9:15
Visions of Judgment and Mercy

Amos has five visions (7:1-3,4-6,7-9; 8:1-14; 9:1-15) that portray God's reluctance to turn Israel over to their executioners. Two times the sentence of judgment was turned back. But finally justice required punishment, and God allowed it.

The story of Amos at Bethel (7:10-17) tells how Amos announced the impending death of Jeroboam II and Israel's exile. The presiding priest, Amaziah, was incensed and ordered Amos to stop preaching. Amos responded with a curse on him and his family for obstructing God's word. This story provides a historical anchor for the first part of the Minor Prophets. It is balanced by a story of Zechariah's meeting with men from Bethel (Zech 7) in the second half of the Book of the Twelve. That story testified to the end of the period of curses and judgments. It proclaimed that it was time for the recognition of blessings and joy in Jerusalem. These narratives form a kind of frame around which all the speeches and other narratives are gathered.

The harsh judgments of the final chapters are summed up in Amos 9:8:

Surely the eyes of the Sovereign LORD
  are on the sinful kingdom.
I will destroy it
  from the face of the earth—
yet I will not totally destroy
  the house of Jacob.

The determined end of the Northern Kingdom was fulfilled in 721 B.C. But God's purpose to spare some for a future purpose is clearly stated.

Amos is a book about the Northern Kingdom. Yet at the very end is a prophecy concerning the restoration of the Davidic dynasty as ruler over a united kingdom with control of all the nations that once were under David's rule (9:11). The verse implies the hope in the 700s B.C. that Assyria's destruction of Samaria might bring some future opportunity of reuniting all Israel. Josiah's reign almost a century later offered the best change for at least partial fulfillment before Judah's final exile.

The very last verses of Amos predicted a time when God would bring back Israel's exiles to live permanently in Palestine (9:13-15). This hope was repeated at the end of Obadiah but was given up before the end of the Minor Prophets.

Ethical and Theological Significance

God will not tolerate sins of social injustice but will punish persistent wrongdoers. God is not pleased by the external worship of those who oppress others. God's past acts of kindness and revelation of His will make His people especially accountable for how they live their lives.

"The lion has roared—who will not fear?" (Amos 3:9). This Assyrian statue of a roaring lion is from Calah (Nimrud).

The eclipse mentioned by Amos (8:9) is listed on the Assyrian king list shown above on clay tablets found at Nineveh.

Questions for Reflection

1. What really pleases God? Are our religious priorities God's priorities?
2. What does Amos teach about the responsibilities of nations before God? How is our nation unjust? How can we work to change it?
3. How just are we in our day-to-day dealings with others?

Sources for Additional Study

Cohen, G. G., and H. R. Vandermey, *Hosea/Amos.* Chicago: Moody, 1981.

McComiskey, T. E. "Amos, Micah." Vol. 7. *Expositor's Bible Commentary.* Grand Rapids: Zondervan, 1985.

Smith, B. K. *Hosea, Joel, Amos, Obadiah, Jonah. Layman's Bible Book Commentary.* vol. 13. Nashville: Broadman, 1982.

OBADIAH

The title verse calls this book "a vision." It portrays God's decisions about Edom, a small mountainous land east of the Dead Sea. Its people were considered descendants of Esau (Gen 36). Judah and Edom lived in tension, sometimes in hostility, with each other throughout Israel's period in Canaan. They both claimed rights to land south of the Dead Sea that changed hands repeatedly during that history.

In 587 B.C., when Nebuchadnezzar's forces closed in on Jerusalem (2 Kgs 25:3-7), the king of Judah attempted to flee toward the Jordan. Lamentations 4:21-22 and Psalms 137:7 with Obadiah 10-14 suggest that Edom helped Babylon in capturing him. In reward the Edomites were allowed to participate in the sack of Jerusalem. In the Minor Prophets, Edom and Assyria are symbols of the enemy that rises up against God and God's people.

Verses 1-17
Deliverance through Judgment

Obadiah graphically portrays God's judgment on Edom (vv. 2-7) when it would be humbled and eventually destroyed. The reason for its doom was "the violence against your brother Jacob" (v. 10). A detailed picture of that cold-hearted betrayal follows (vv. 11-14). Edom's destruction was part of the Day of the Lord (v. 15) that Joel and Amos had already declared. But Edom's destruction would bring deliverance for Zion and Israel (v. 17).

The Nabateans continued the rock dwelling (1:3) of the Edomites with their building of Petra (Petra's "Treasury" is shown above).

Verses 18-21
Kingdom Is the Lord's

Obadiah presents the most complete plan for the resettlement of the Israelite tribes in Canaan to be found in any of the prophets (vv. 19-20). This reoccupation is more complete than even Josiah achieved (2 Chron 34:6). The vision of Obadiah ends with a stirring call to faith in the worst of times: "And the kingdom will be the LORD's" (v. 21).

Theological and Ethical Significance

God is just and holds those responsible who take advantage of others in their time of distress. By forgetting that they and the Jews shared Abraham as an ancestor, the Edomites fell victim to God's promise to Abraham:

"I will bless those who bless you,
and whoever curses you I will curse" (Gen 12:3).

Facing a great distress, the writer of the Book of Revelation found comfort in words that echo Obadiah's: "The kingdom of the world has become the kingdom of our Lord and of his Christ" (Rev 11:15).

Question for Reflection

1. What is our response when others take advantage of our misfortune? Do we trust God to be just, or do we take matters into our own hands?

Sources for Additional Study

Allen, L. C. *The Books of Joel, Obadiah, Jonah, and Micah.* Grand Rapids: Eerdmans, 1976.

Armerding, C. E. "Obadiah, Nahum, Habakkuk." Vol. 7. *Expositor's Bible Commentary.* Grand Rapids: Zondervan, 1985.

Gaebelein, F. E. *Four Minor Prophets.* Chicago: Moody, 1970.

Smith, B. K. *Hosea, Joel, Amos, Obadiah, Jonah. Layman's Bible Book Commentary.* Vol. 13. Nashville: Broadman, 1982.

Watts, J. D. W. *Obadiah.* Winona Lake, Ind.: Alpha, 1981.

JONAH

The Book of Jonah is a narrative about a reluctant Israelite prophet commissioned to prophesy to Nineveh. The purpose of the story and the reason for its position in the Minor Prophets is to discuss God's attitude toward non-Jewish peoples. It balances the Book of Nahum with its message of God's wrath toward Nineveh. Nineveh was the capital of Assyria, the great empire that ruled over Palestine from the days of Tiglath-Pileser (about 750 B.C.) when the kingdoms of Jeroboam II and Uzziah were beginning to wane.

Both Hosea and Amos referred to Assyria. Nahum spoke of the days of Nineveh's collapse before Babylon's armies in 612 B.C.; Habakkuk relates to 609 B.C. when Assyria's last armies surrendered at Haran. Assyria was responsible for Samaria's destruction in 721 B.C., for Jerusalem's humiliation in 701 B.C., and for the generally poor state of Judah's life through Manasseh's reign.

More than any other nation Assyria was responsible for the harassment and exploitation Israel and Judah suffered over more than a century. Assyria took much of Israel's population into exile in order to bring other peoples to colonize its territories. Most Jews who knew that history would have felt that Assyria deserved to be seen as God's prime enemy as well as their own.

Jonah, son of Amittai, was a real prophet. His name means *Dove, son of Truth.* He lived in Gath-hepher, two and a half miles north-northeast of Nazareth early in the reign of Jeroboam II about 780 B.C. (2 Kgs 14:25).

Hosea and Amos pictured Israel and Judah of the generation after Jonah as being apostate, nonreceptive to the word of God, and rebellious against God's covenant. Assyria was pictured as a threat of God's wrath.

In Jonah, Assyria is seen as the recipient of God's word, deserving to be preached to and to receive God's care (4:11a), and as a city capable of profound repentance in response to God's word, even when it is delivered by a reluctant prophet (3:5). The Book of Jonah portrays foreigners, the sailors, and the Ninevites as persons capable of responding to God and ones to whom God responds when they repent. In contrast to the stubborn and rebellious Israelites in Hosea and Amos, the Ninevites appear positively saintly.

God's resistance to the tyrannical power of the great nations does not mean that He hates every foreigner. That lesson was not lost on people in Jerusalem trying to come to terms with the problem of mixed marriages between Judeans and foreigners (Mal 2:10-16). As a whole the Minor Prophets emphasize God's love, which invites all peoples to come to Him. This is particularly clear in Jonah and Zechariah 14:16-21.

1:1-17
Bad Becomes Pious

Jonah resisted God's call and fled in the opposite direction. The storm God hurled at the sea halted his escape. Jonah's stoic offer to leave the ship to save its crew was first refused as the sailors prayed to God. Finally they did as Jonah said. Then God provided a big fish to swallow Jonah. This saved him from certain drowning.

2:1-10
God Hears Distress Calls

Inside the fish Jonah prayed. His prayer was more a reflection on prayer in life-threatening situations than a plea for help. Jonah viewed the fish as a means of deliverance and thanked God for His salvation. There was no repentance or recognition of Jonah's mission.

3:1-10
Compassion Meets Repentance

But God was persistent and ordered Jonah a second time to go to Nineveh. This time Jonah obeyed. His message was terse: "Forty more days and Nineveh will be overturned" (3:4). Despite the meager content of the message and no support for it, the Ninevites accepted God's warning and did works of repentance. Even the king joined in. God took note of their response, had compassion on them, and rescinded His order of destruction.

4:1-11
God's Love Lacks Limits

Jonah observed the results of his preaching from a point outside the city. He was bitterly disappointed that God

Jonah fleeing from God

Joppa, the ancient port city to which Jonah fled to board a ship bound for Tarshish, is seen in this photograph. The ancient tell is surrounded by the modern city.

had not carried out His threat. He protested to God, saying that he knew God was forgiving like that, quoting God's words to Moses (Exod 34:6).

Then he asked God to let him die. Apparently he felt that life under a God so gracious even to Jonah's enemies was not worth living. God challenged Jonah's right to be angry and then provided some shade for him by allowing a vine to grow rapidly over him. Then God sent a worm, which killed the vine, and a very hot sun. Jonah was furious and again begged to die.

Then God showed Jonah that he was upset over something he had nothing to do with making or taking away. On the other hand, God reminded him that He had created everything, the land and the nations. Should not God be allowed to care deeply for a city whose every inhabitant, even every animal, He had created?

Theological and Ethical Significance

God's love was a fundamental of ancient Israel's faith: "The LORD, the LORD, the compassionate and gracious God, slow to anger, abounding in love and faithfulness, maintaining love to thousands, and forgiving wickedness, rebellion and sin" (Exod 34:6-7). The message of Jonah is that the God who revealed Himself to Israel as love desires people of all nations to experience His love. Like Jonah, God's people today have a responsibility to lay aside narrow nationalism and race hatred and to share God's love with those of other cultures.

Questions for Reflection

1. What does God desire for all the peoples of the world?

2. How do we seek to avoid God's command to share our faith with others?

3. How does prejudice compromise our Christian testimony? How do we begrudge God's love for others?

Sources for Additional Study

Allen, L. C. *The Books of Joel, Obadiah, Jonah, and Micah.* Grand Rapids: Eerdmans, 1976.

Ellison, H. L. "Jonah." Vol. 7. *Expositor's Bible Commentary.* Grand Rapids: Zondervan, 1985.

Gaebelein, F. E. *Four Minor Prophets.* Chicago: Moody, 1970.

Smith, B. K. *Hosea, Joel, Amos, Obadiah, Jonah. Layman's Bible Book Commentary.* Vol. 13. Nashville: Broadman, 1982.

MICAH

The title verse calls this book "the word of the LORD" as those of Hosea, Joel, and Jonah have done. *Micah* means *Who is like the LORD?*

Moresheth was a town in Judah. Jotham, Ahaz, and Hezekiah ruled in Judah from 742 to 687 B.C. Between 740 and 700 the Assyrians invaded Palestine repeatedly. In 734 northern Israel and Judah lost their independence and became vassals to Assyria. In 721 northern Israel was invaded; Samaria was destroyed and made an Assyrian province with most of its population being sent into exile. In 716-15 Assyria put down a Philistine rebellion and laid a punishing fine on Hezekiah's Jerusalem. In 701 B.C. the Assyrians laid siege to Jerusalem, only relenting at the last minute by placing a heavy fine on the city rather than destroying it (2 Kgs 16–20). All this was going on during the time that Micah was a prophet (Mic 1:1).

The Book of Micah is the centerpiece of the Minor Prophets (the Book of the Twelve). It contains within it the themes of the books that come before it and of those that follow it. It presents in capsule form the message of all twelve books. The Book of the Twelve uses it as a pivot in balancing the eighth century prophets before it and the seventh to fifth century prophets that follow it.

The book has three parts: chapters 1–2; 3–5; and 6–7. Each begins with the call to hear. All three maintain a balanced message to both northern Israel and Jerusalem of threats of judgment and of potential blessings in the future, both of which were part of God's plan (4:12).

1:1–2:13
God Judges Sin

Chapters 1–2 pick up the themes of judgment that were first heard in Joel and Amos. These are justified by denunciations of sin in both Israel and Judah (1:5-6). Micah used figures of harlotry to describe idol worship as Hosea had done (1:7). These speeches portrayed a devastating end for Samaria (1:6), but they also spoke of danger at Jerusalem's gate (1:9,12). Such danger came in the siege of 701 B.C. (2 Kgs 18–19).

Chapter 2 sounds like Amos in detailing the sins of the people and their unwillingness to listen to prophetic preaching. Micah 2:12-13 ends the section with an ambiguous assurance that God would gather all Israel in one place, open a breach in the restricting wall, and lead them out through it. God and the king would go out before the people. Did this indicate salvation from a prisonlike experience? Or was it a picture of going into exile? Whatever it referred to, God would go with them, indeed before them!

3:1-12
False Leaders Face Doom

This section begins with denunciations against leaders in Jacob, another name for Israel, and the announcement that pleas for God's aid would be of no help at this time. The prophet, however, was strengthened by God's Spirit to declare to Jacob their sins (3:8). His announcements were addressed to leaders in northern Israel but included those who build Jerusalem (3:9-10). Like Amos he condemned them for injustice and for profit-loving priests and prophets. They were too secure in an unjustified confidence (3:11).

Then he announced the destruction of Jerusalem that would leave it a heap of ruins. The mountain of the temple would simply become a tree covered mountaintop (3:12). The fall of Jerusalem to Babylonian troops in 587 B.C. would fit this description.

4:1-13
God's Strategy for Israel

Chapters 4–5 present key views of God's plan or strategy (4:11) for Israel and Judah which looked beyond the disasters. (See "Theological and Ethical Significance" for a summary of these key views.)

Micah 4:1-4 contains the beautiful picture (parallel to Isa 2:1-4) of the restored temple on Zion to which people from many nations would come to learn of God's ways and to hear His word. It heralded a time of peace with no need for fear. The vision previewed the work of Zerubbabel in Haggai and Zechariah 1–8 and the time of Ezra-Nehemiah implied in Malachi.

The promise to assemble the lame and those excluded (4:6-8) uses a common symbol for the return of the exiles. This would come about as the Lord's reign was celebrated in Zion. A new meaning was given to "dominion" through the restoration of God's authority over

Jerusalem.

Verses 9-10 take notice of something missing in these promises. Nothing is said about a human king in Jerusalem. Kings and autonomy were gone in Jerusalem, along with military might or conquest. They were things of the past, an era that was no more. Before this restoration Jerusalem's people would have suffered devastations—even exile to Babylon. From there they would be rescued and redeemed. The theme echoes promises from Hosea and Amos as well as from Joel and Obadiah.

Verses 11-12 are the heart of the section. Like the Book of Isaiah, Micah insisted that God had plans and strategies that He was implementing during these centuries of Israel's history. He was using empires to tear down and destroy those things in Israel which He found most debilitating and divisive. Nationhood and kingship, inevitably accompanied by idolatry, were unacceptable in God's people. Samuel recognized them as such, but God allowed them to be tried (1 Sam 8:6-9). Now experience had proven Samuel right, and God was taking nationhood and kingship away from His people. But God was also using the empires to build His new order for His people. The emperors did not know His plans, but they did His work anyway. Readers of these chapters could not know how God planned and brought it to pass. They could only marvel at His work.

Micah 4:13 was a call for Zion to rise and defeat many peoples, using their wealth to present gifts to the Lord. But this was no promise of future armed power for Israel. This was the age in which Israel was disarmed, a time of peace (4:3-4). Israel's power in that age would be of a different sort, as Haggai and Zechariah illustrated and as Zechariah 9–14 shows.

5:1-15
Bethlehem Revisited

In the meantime there were times of restriction and suffering. Israel's and Judah's kings would be humiliated as Hezekiah, Manasseh, and Josiah were (5:1).

Micah 5:2 is one of the most precious verses in the book. Out of little Bethlehem would come someone with ancient origins to be a ruler in Israel. David came from Bethlehem (1 Sam 16–17), a simple shepherd boy who would do wondrous things, like killing a threatening giant although military arms or armor were not suitable for him. The promise here was that someone from David's house, someone like his early simple origins—not like his later image as lord of Jerusalem's citadel—would be chosen to be a leader in Zion. Within the Minor Prophets that fits the role Zerubbabel plays in Haggai and Zechariah 1–8. Christian readers think of someone later whom God sent to be a Savior for His and for all people, a Savior who would have no use for either arms or armor.

Micah 5:3 speaks of a time of travail while Israel waits for the rest of their brothers to rejoin them. This emphasizes a future united people, while it also calls for patient waiting through a long time of trouble. Habakkuk expresses a similar theme.

Micah 5:4-6 pictures a time beyond Assyria's rule when the Messiah would stand to feed His flock with the strength and majesty customary for Him in times past. The theme of shepherding is found again in Zechariah 9–14 and is parallel to that in Isaiah 40:10-11. Peace despite Assyrian power is pictured in verses 5-6. Deliverance from Assyria through seven or eight leaders is a fairly accurate description of the end of the Assyrian Empire when, over several decades, a coalition of armies from at least three great nations (including Babylonia, Media, and Egypt) took part in ending its long domination. The Book of Nahum pictures the fall of Nineveh, its capital.

Micah 5:7-9 portrays the situation of Israel in exile not as one of weakness and humiliation but of power, even of victory. Daniel 1–6 illustrates this theme. Being without armed forces did not necessarily mean a lack of influence and power. The Jews of the dispersion were taught this lesson.

Micah 5:10-15 describes a part of God's strategy during this period. Hosea had pictured how God's plans for His people in Canaan had gone awry. Israel became like the Canaanites, depending on arms, fortresses, and idols. In Micah God announced His actions to end all of that. The nations who had refused to listen to God's Word or obey His covenant were Israel, Judah, and their vassals in Canaan. God intended to use the invasions of imperial tyrants to get rid of these things so obnoxious to Him.

6:1-16
God's Covenant Curse

The third part of Micah begins as the others do with "Hear!" (6:2). God called for a discussion with His people about their relation to Him in covenant. He asked why they appeared to be tired of Him (6:3), echoing Hosea's story (Hos 1; 3). He reminded them of the great events of the exodus from Egypt and the journey through the wilderness (Mic 6:4-5).

The people responded with a question: What do You want from us? (6:6-7). Someone answered for God, You know; He has shown you: "To act justly, and to love mercy and walk humbly with your God" (6:8). This is the most succinct statement of what the prophets understood to be God's will for His people. It ranks with the Ten Commandments in terms of its terse statement of truth. Sacrifice and priestly services were clearly not God's first or principle concern. A people who acted in justice toward their neighbors, with consistent devotion and love toward God in covenant, and who humbly lived out their piety under God—this was God's goal and supreme wish. Malachi and Hosea 1–3 deal with these issues from other viewpoints.

Micah 6:9-16 returns to the reasons for judgment and for the application of covenant curses. (Compare Deut 28, especially vv. 30-42.) Israel had lived under the laws and standards of Omri and Ahab, the most successful kings of Israel, who were also the most pagan and idolatrous.

7:1-20
Loyal Love Brings Hope

Chapter 7 pictures Israel in their devastated anguish. It parallels Habakkuk. Judgment had come. There was as yet no sign of relief. The advice for such a time, like that in Habakkuk 3:2, was to wait for God in hope (Mic 7:7). That hope was stated in terms of God's turning back toward His people, causing their enemies to fall (7:8-10). The Book of Nahum records the same theme.

That future day would bring a rebuilding of Jerusalem's walls and extension of its territories. People would come to Israel even from Assyria and Egypt (compare Haggai and Zechariah 1–8).

Verse 14 is a prayer for God to shepherd His people back to inhabit all of Palestine as they had long before. God promised to do wonders for them as in the Exodus (v. 15) so that nations would witness God's forgiveness and restoration of His people (vv. 16-18).

The book closes with a profession of faith that God would again have compassion on His people and get rid of their sins completely (v. 19). God would fulfill His pledge to Jacob and Abraham through His love for His children (v. 20; compare Hosea and Malachi).

Theological and Ethical Significance

Micah 4–5 is the key to understanding God's strategy for these important centuries of Israel's history covered by the Minor Prophets. God was changing everything for Israel and Judah except His love and choice of them to be His people. He scrapped the systems of kings (4:9) and fortified cities garrisoned by armed forces (5:10-14). He eliminated the sorceries, idol worship, and symbolic pillars which made Israel a nation like other nations (compare 1 Sam 8:19-20). He was bringing Israel's national existence, that began with Saul, to an end.

At the same time He was beginning a new existence for His people. They would live and prosper scattered

Micah

Micah exhorting the Israelites to repentance

among the nations (5:7-9). But the temple in Zion would remain their rallying point (4:1-4). God would be revealed there for all to see as the Lord in all His glory (5:4). Lacking national autonomy and the protection of a national army, the temple would still have all that it needed (4:13). The people would prosper in peace, and the Lord would be exalted.

This is a fairly accurate picture of the position of Judaism during the Persian Empire. Its people were dispersed throughout the empire with only a small group in Jerusalem. Yet there were Jews in positions of influence and power, like Zerubbabel, Ezra, and Nehemiah, who directed the empire's resources toward the restoration of Jerusalem and its temple. As a whole the Minor Prophets intended to help Israel to understand God's purpose in what was happening to them so that they could adjust to God's strategy. Micah 4–5 is the most concise statement of this strategy to be found in the larger Book of the Twelve Prophets.

Questions for Reflection

1. What does God require of those committed to Him? (See Mic 6:8.) How do we shortchange God?
2. What does Micah teach about the responsible use of power? (See Mic 2:1; 3:1-3,9-12.)
3. What does Micah teach about the qualities of godly leadership? (See Mic 3:8.)
4. What does Micah teach about God's goals for history? (See Mic 4:1-4; 5:2-5.)

Sources for Additional Study

Allen, L. C. *The Books of Joel, Obadiah, Jonah, and Micah.* Grand Rapids: Eerdmans, 1976.

Kelley, P. H. *Micah, Nahum, Habakkuk, Zephaniah, Haggai, Zechariah, Malachi. Layman's Bible Book Commentary.* Vol. 14. Nashville: Broadman, 1984.

McComiskey, T. E. "Amos, Micah." Vol. 7. *Expositor's Bible Commentary.* Grand Rapids: Zondervan, 1985.

NAHUM

The title verse (1:1) calls the Book of Nahum both an oracle of doom and a vision. Both terms are appropriate. *Nahum* means *comfort* or *full of comfort.* The prophet is unknown apart from this verse. The location of Elkosh is unknown.

Although no date or period is provided, the subject of Nineveh's imminent destruction places it late in the 700s B.C. Assyria was a weakened power from 740 to 700. Its kings made fewer campaigns abroad. Its vassals demonstrated more independence, as Josiah's career in Judah demonstrates. Three of its former subject nations were gaining in power and ambition. They were Media, Babylonia, and Egypt. Their efforts became more a contest to determine which of them would inherit Assyria's position than an effort to dethrone it. Finally in 612 Median and Babylonian armies converged on Nineveh, and the city was doomed. The kings of Media and Babylon agreed to divide the empire between them, so they fought as allies against the Assyrian forces. Egypt was not party to the agreement or present at Nineveh's fall.

The Book of Nahum, like the Book of Jonah, is completely concerned with Nineveh. Only two brief speeches concern Judah and Israel (1:15; 2:2). They either note their reactions to Nineveh's destruction or point to what the results would mean to them. In the Minor Prophets the role of Assyrian oppression in the judgment on Israel and Judah has been central, and its removal is of critical importance. Jonah showed that God cared about people in Nineveh as He does about all persons that He has created. Nahum showed God's passion in judgment because of Nineveh's tyrannical rule and unnumbered cruelties against many peoples, including Israel and Judah.

1:1-15
Meet the Sovereign God

Nineveh had become God's enemy (1:2) and earned His wrath (1:3). Now the day for judgment had come. Nahum 1:3b-10 is a poem about God's angry action against His enemies. It does not mention Assyria. It could have been applied just as well to Egypt in Moses' time or to Midian in the time of the judges.

Verse 11 points to a particular villain who had occasioned God's wrath, but the verse does not identify him.

Verses 12-13 note that no one was strong enough to withstand God's wrath and recognized Assyria's past role in punishing Israel, a role which now would end.

Verse 14 addressed Nineveh, pronouncing judgment on it. Its name was to be cut off, and the idols that symbolized its mastery would now be removed from temples.

Verse 15 portrayed the good news of Assyria's fall being brought to Judah. Judah could begin to keep their own festivals again. Their enemy would not oppress them again. (Note the parallel to Isa 52:7, though applied there to a different time.)

2:1-13
Campaign against Nineveh

Nahum 2:1 returns to the military pressure building against Nineveh. Verse 2 parenthetically relates Nineveh's fall to a change in God's attitude toward Israel, whom Assyria had taken into exile a century earlier.

Nahum 2:3-9 pictures the armies breaking in and plundering the city. Verse 7 may refer to the queen or to the goddess Ishtar, whose temple was a central building of the city. Nahum 2:10-12 reflects the meaning of the fall of Nineveh, while verse 13 attributes the turn of events to the Lord of hosts and His decision about its fate.

3:1-19
Curse on Nineveh

Nahum 3:1-4 pronounces a curse on the city for its countless acts of betrayal and cold-hearted broken covenants. Nahum 3:5-6 repeats the Lord's position on the matter. Verses 7-13 compare Nineveh's fall to that of Thebes in Egypt at an earlier date. No nation, no city, no matter how great, was immune to a day of reckoning for the crimes on which its riches and power were built.

Nahum 3:14-17 exhorted Assyrians to prepare for the siege. It noted, however, that Nineveh's greatness was built on constant growth, like that of locusts, in economic power (merchants), in political power (guards), and of administrative apparatus (officials). All of this "growth" evaporated in a time of stress like this.

Nahum 3:18-19 pictured Nineveh's isolation. The empire was spread thin. "Shepherds" were vassal kings,

Nahum prophesied the destruction of Nineveh including vivid descriptions of the enemy horse and chariot forces. In the above section of the bronze gates from Balawat, the Assyrian chariot force is depicted in action.

who like nobles of many lands sensed Assyria's weakness and made no move to defend Nineveh. The empire numbered many people, but they were not there to protect Nineveh's walls. On the contrary, they cheered its enemies on because they had all felt Nineveh's anger and greed in many ways.

Theological and Ethical Significance

Nineveh had been the mistress of the world for a century and a half. Now it crumbled, isolated and hated. No tyrant nation can escape its inevitable "day of wrath." The Minor Prophets reckon this to be the turning point for Israel and Jerusalem, although a long wait of almost a hundred years had to intervene before concrete results would lead to the restoration of Jerusalem. Other books in the Old Testament reckon this turning point to be in 587 B.C., the fall of Jerusalem to Babylon, or 539 B.C., the Persian occupation of Babylon.

Questions for Reflection

1. How did Assyria merit God's anger and judgment? Has our nation been guilty of similar atrocities?

2. How does the fall of Assyria illustrate God's control of history? How did Nineveh's fall contribute to the building of God's kingdom?

Sources for Additional Study

Armerding, C. E. "Obadiah, Nahum, Habakkuk." Vol. 7. *Expositor's Bible Commentary.* Grand Rapids. Zondervan, 1985.

Kelley, P. H. *Micah, Nahum, Habakkuk, Zephaniah, Haggai, Zechariah, Malachi.* Vol. 14. *Layman's Bible Book Commentary.* Nashville: Broadman, 1984.

Maier, W. A. *The Book of Nahum: A Commentary.* Grand Rapids: Baker, 1980.

HABAKKUK

Habakkuk is identified only as "the prophet." Haggai and Zechariah are similarly identified. The meaning of *Habakkuk* is not clear. It may be a foreign word. The book is called "an oracle," which may also be translated *a burden* as several other books or sections of books are called.

The only clue for a date comes in 1:6, which refers to "the Chaldeans" (KJV), another name for Babylonians. They were one of the two nations that overthrew Assyria and fell heir to its territories. Babylonia's share included Mesopotamia, Palestine, and Egypt (if it could be conquered). Babylon defeated the last Assyrian armies at Haran in northern Syria in 609 B.C. and beat back Egypt's challenge at Carchemish the same year.

Babylon established its authority over Palestine, including Judah, in 605 B.C. It campaigned again in Palestine in 598 on its way to Egypt and finally destroyed Jerusalem in 587 B.C. In both of the last two campaigns Judeans were taken into Egypt. The record of these years from a Judean viewpoint is found in 2 Kings 23–25, Jeremiah, and Ezekiel. Babylon continued Assyrian oppression of Judah with renewed vigor. Its ambitions to conquer Egypt made this necessary from its point of view. The Book of Habakkuk relates to the earlier part of the period of Babylon's conquests (around 605 B.C.). The Book of Zephaniah in more general terms portrays the climax of judgment on Jerusalem.

Habakkuk's position in the Minor Prophets, after Nahum and before Zephaniah, is appropriate. It deals with the disappointment of Judeans and Israelites, dispersed in exile, that the fall of Nineveh had not brought immediate relief and restoration for Judah and Israel. Instead, an extended period of almost three decades was a time of greater repression and final disaster. Another half-century under Babylon would follow before Persia would succeed Babylon and bring new hope for Israel and Jerusalem. The Book of Habakkuk deals with the frustrations of that period and teaches how one can maintain faith and hope in an extended period of adversity and trouble.

1:1-17
Perplexed Prophet

The book begins with a cry to God: "How long?" This cry is found repeated in Scripture from Exodus 10:3 to many expressions in the Psalms. The opening speech recognizes chaotic violence all around (1:1-4). God called His people to recognize His hand at work in the situation (v. 5). He had raised up the Babylonians, terrible as they were (1:6-11). The prophet recognized that this had been the divine purpose of judgment (1:12-13), for God could not put up with evil. God makes humans, who like fish and insects know no ruler (v. 14); that is, they do as they please. In verses 15-17 humankind is described as fishermen who worship their nets because they make them rich. The Assyrian Empire did this, worshiping the violence that brought it booty, tribute, and power. Could this kind of idolatry go on forever (v. 17)?

2:1-20
Faith Survives

The prophet took a stand to wait for God's reply to his complaint (2:1). He did not have to wait long before he was commanded to write down his vision and publish it plainly because it still had to be fulfilled (vv. 2-3)

The most meaningful and important verse in Habakkuk follows (2:4). It describes the person who can survive such testing times. First the bad news: He who is puffed up will die. That is, those who are proud, arrogant, and filled with false pretenses cannot survive such testing. Then the good news: But the person in the right [relation to God and to his fellows] *will live* by simply being faithful. That is, people will live by faithfully doing every day what in faith they were accustomed to do. The formula for survival in hard times is faithful humility—standing under the load, as the New Testament puts it. That is why the righteous outlive the tyrants (v. 5).

A series of five woes, or curses, follows against the tyrant and those who work for him. The first cursed anyone who collected wealth that did not belong to him, for someday those who were plundered would demand and get restitution (2:6-8). The second cursed those who built their houses or fortresses with evil gain to try to buy safety because even the stones and beams would rebel (2:9-11). The third cursed anyone who built a town through bloody oppression (2:12). Habakkuk 2:13-14 notes that God can make human striving to be without

result. The knowledge of God—not the fame of emperors or tyrants—is destined to fill the earth at the end. The fourth woe condemned the violent, wrathful person, for the Lord would turn His back on him. This was specifically applied to a violent military campaign against Lebanon (2:15-17). The fifth and final woe cursed those who worshiped idols (2:18-19). In contrast the presence of God in His holy temple was real. All the earth was called to worshipful silence before Him (2:20). How many times have believers given such testimony to the living God while under the heel of arrogant, tyrannical rulers! Here the tyrant was Nebuchadnezzar. At other times it has been Antiochus-Epiphanes, or Nero, or Hitler, or Stalin. The statement holds true: through faithful patience the righteous survive. The tyrant inevitably falls.

3:1-19
Psalm of Confidence

Chapter 3 is Habakkuk's prayer-psalm. The psalmist remembered reverently reports of God's great acts in the past and prayed for Him to bring redemption in this time: "In our time . . . in wrath remember mercy" (v. 2).

Habakkuk 3:3-15 is a poetic portrayal of God's salvation of His people from Egypt (Exod 1–15). Here metaphors of God's actions drawn from many passages of Scripture are mixed together.

Habakkuk 3:16 recounts the psalmist's believing acceptance that God was active in his own moment in time as well as the high points in history. He would "wait patiently" for God's retribution against the tyrants. He recognized that his was a day for waiting, not for action.

The closing verses announced his joy in the Lord despite the deprivations he had to endure. God was his strength (vv. 17-19).

Theological and Ethical Significance

The Book of Habakkuk represents the kind of faith that became the norm for Judaism and later for Christianity. Israel no longer had the means to try to shape their own destiny. Under the empires they were the passive recipients of whatever good or evil the powerful chose to give them. But in faith they could believe that God, through those whom He allowed to rule, would provide what was necessary for His people to serve God. Believing and waiting became essential elements in their way of life. It should still be so.

Questions for Reflection

1. What was Habakkuk's solution to the disappointments and frustrations of life?
2. What did Habakkuk say about the value of faithfulness and hope?
3. According to Habakkuk, what did God have in store for the arrogant and the ruthlessly cruel?
4. What did Habakkuk teach about God's faithfulness to His people throughout their history?

Sources for Additional Study

Armerding, C. E. "Obadiah, Nahum, Habakkuk." Vol. 7. *Expositor's Bible Commentary.* Grand Rapids: Zondervan, 1985.

Gaebelein, F. E. *Four Minor Prophets.* Chicago: Moody, 1970.

Gowan, D. E. *The Triumph of Faith in Habakkuk.* Atlanta: John Knox, 1976.

Kelley, P. H. *Micah, Nahum, Habakkuk, Zephaniah, Haggai, Zechariah, Malachi.* Vol. 14. *Layman's Bible Book Commentary.* Nashville: Broadman, 1984.

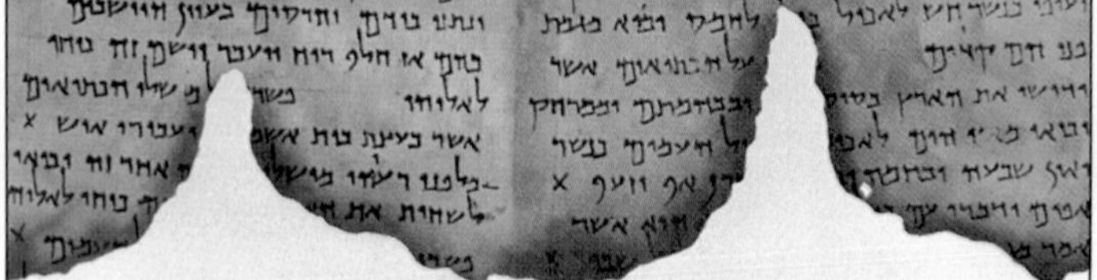

The above photo is of a portion of the Commentary of Habakkuk from the Dead Sea Scrolls. The Qumran community wrote this commentary to apply the words of Habakkuk to their situation.

ZEPHANIAH

The title verse calls this book "the word of the LORD," as those of Hosea, Joel, Jonah, and Micah have done. *Zephaniah* means *Yahweh hides. Cushi* means *the Ethiopian.* Four generations of ancestors is unusual. The fourth name is Hezekiah, probably the king. The date for the book is "the reign of Josiah, king of Judah" (640–609 B.C.). This was prior to the events cited in Nahum and Habakkuk. The theme of the book rather than chronology determines the position of the book within the Minor Prophets.

The theme of Zephaniah is the "day of the Lord." Joel pictured that day as it related to the Assyrian invasions

Zephaniah

that led to the destruction of Samaria and the exile of Israel. Zephaniah returned to the theme of the Babylonian invasions of Palestine, the destruction of Jerusalem (587 B.C.), and the exile of Judah. Thus the two books establish the two poles of judgment within the Minor Prophets in the theme of the Day of the Lord. The Minor Prophets end with reference to future judgments on the Day of the Lord in the last verses of Malachi. As in Joel there are passages of hopeful optimism in Zephaniah, as well as passages announcing disaster. The kingdom was being brought to an end, but Jerusalem and the people received an encouraging word about their future.

1:1-18
Judgment for All

The book opens with a prophecy of total destruction for the whole "land." (The Hebrew word can mean *land* as in the land of Canaan, or it can mean *the earth* as in the whole world.) It would be depopulated (1:2-3). A prophecy against Judah and Jerusalem follows. They were indicted for their idolatry (1:4-6).

Next came a call for silence during the Lord's sacrifice in which He would punish the princes and the overdressed aristocracy (1:7-9). There would be panic in the city (1:10-13). The events that would lead to the end of the population are described (1:14-18).

2:1-15
Righteous Assembly

Chapter 2 calls for an assembly of the humble and religious before the day of judgment arrives to seek the Lord and His will (vv. 1-3). Judgment against ethnic groups in Canaan follows: against the Philistine (Kerethite) cities of Gaza, Ashdod, Ekron, and Ashkelon (vv. 4-7); against Moab and Ammon (vv. 8-11); against Cush (Ethiopia) (v. 12); and against Assyria (vv. 13-15).

3:1-20
Wait on God

Chapter 3 begins with a "woe," or curse, against Jerusalem for its lack of faith, its arrogant officials, prophets, and profane priests (vv. 1-5). The Lord cited His destruction of nations (v. 6) with the hope that Jerusalem might "accept correction" (v. 7). He called for them to "wait" for Him to call (v. 8). The theme of "waiting on the Lord" dominates the Book of Habakkuk.

Beyond the judgment lie God's goals (vv. 9-13). The peoples' lips would be purified so that all might worship the Lord and serve Him together, reversing the curse of Babel (Gen 11:5-9). Scattered exiles might return to the temple for worship. The proud would be removed from Jerusalem. There would be room for the meek, the humble, and for those "who trust in the name of the Lord" (v. 13). It would be a time of right, of truth, and of no fear. The passage foreshadows developments hailed in Haggai, Zechariah 1–8, and in Malachi.

A call to sing follows (vv. 14-17). Zion had every right to sing because the Lord God would be present in it again. He was their king. (Note that nothing is said about a Davidic heir to the throne.)

Verse 18 promises a time when laments for the great destruction would no longer be appropriate (see Zech 7–8). Verse 19 promises God's help for all the oppressed in exile, the lame and the scattered, to be gathered again. Those who remained dispersed would be respected in their far-flung homelands. Verse 20 promises a homecoming and recognition among the nations that it was their God who was restoring them.

Theological and Ethical Significance

The Day of the Lord brought an end to Judean kingship, to Jerusalem's pride, and to the system of small states in Canaan within which Jerusalem had shaped its political existence for more than a thousand years. But the day also cleared the way for restitution of respect and identity for the Lord's people with Jerusalem because they recognized His presence in the city. This foreshadowed a new temple that Zerubabbel would build and the new city that Nehemiah would build. It also points to a revival of true faith in God in postexilic Judaism both among exiles and among people in Jerusalem.

Questions for Reflection

1. How was Zephaniah influenced by the preaching of Amos?
2. What determines how a person fares on the Day of the Lord?
3. Why was it necessary for God to punish Judah? What did God hope to accomplish through those who survived judgment?

Sources for Additional Study

Kelley, P. H. *Micah, Nahum, Habakkuk, Zephaniah, Haggai, Zechariah, Malachi.* Vol. 14. *Layman's Bible Book Commentary.* Nashville: Broadman, 1984.

Walker, L. L. "Zephaniah." Vol. 7. *Expositor's Bible Commentary.* Grand Rapids: Zondervan, 1985.

HAGGAI

Ezra 1 tells of a group of Israel's exiles who returned to Jerusalem under Sheshbazzar in response to a decree by Cyrus, the first of the Persian emperors. This group had already been in Palestine about fifteen years when Haggai's ministry began. They had accomplished very little toward rebuilding the temple.

1:1-11
Materialism Reconsidered

Haggai has no title verse. The information needed is provided in the narrative. This includes a precise date for each prophecy. Darius was the third Persian ruler over the huge empire that succeeded Babylon in 539 B.C. and which controlled territory from India in the east to the Aegean Sea in the west. Darius began his reign in 522. His second year of reign was 520.

Haggai's message is called "the word of the LORD" in the way already familiar from Hosea through Zephaniah. But here it is used for a specific prophecy in verses 1-11.

Haggai probably means something like *festival child,* indicating that he was born on a holiday. He is called "the prophet." That term has not been used frequently in the Book of the Twelve (Minor Prophets). Haggai is mentioned along with Zechariah and Zerubabbel in Ezra 5:1 and 6:14.

Zerubabbel apparently succeeded Sheshbazzar as governor of Judah. He was the grandson of Jehoiakin, former king of Judah, who had been taken to Babylon in 598 B.C. So Zerubabbel was a potential heir to David's throne if there should be one again.

Joshua is called "high priest." That title came into use after the exile. He apparently shared ruling authority with Zerubabbel because Jerusalem was to be a temple-city according to Cyrus's decree. Priests formed a major portion of those who returned under Sheshbazzar (Ezra 2:36).

The occasion for the prophecy was the people's reluctance to start building the temple (v.2). They said that the time was not right. In response the Lord asked if it was time, then, for them to live in luxurious homes while His house remained in ruins (vv. 3-4).

God's people found their labor brought little real result (vv. 5-6). Futility of labor was one of the curses for breaking covenant (Lev 26:16,20; Deut 28:20-41). This curse was already announced for preexilic Israel in passages like Hosea 13:15 and Amos 4:6-12. Despite the fulfillment of judgment and the chance of a new beginning in Jerusalem, the promised reversal of fortunes with outpoured blessings had not occurred. Life was still futile and empty, economically and in every other way.

Verses 7-11 explain that the Lord did this because His house, the temple, remained in ruins with no effort made to rebuild it. Until the people turned their attention to this priority, there would be no prosperity for them.

1:12-15
Motivating God's People

Verses 12-14 report the response of the leaders and the people to Haggai's message. They obeyed the Lord because they recognized that He had sent Haggai. They "feared the LORD" (v. 12), worshiping Him and giving Him due attention. So Haggai announced a new word from God: "I am with you" (v. 13). The Lord's presence was manifested in a revived willingness by all the people

The Behistun Inscription shown above records the political situation under Darius I of Persia (see Hag 1:1; Zech 1:7).

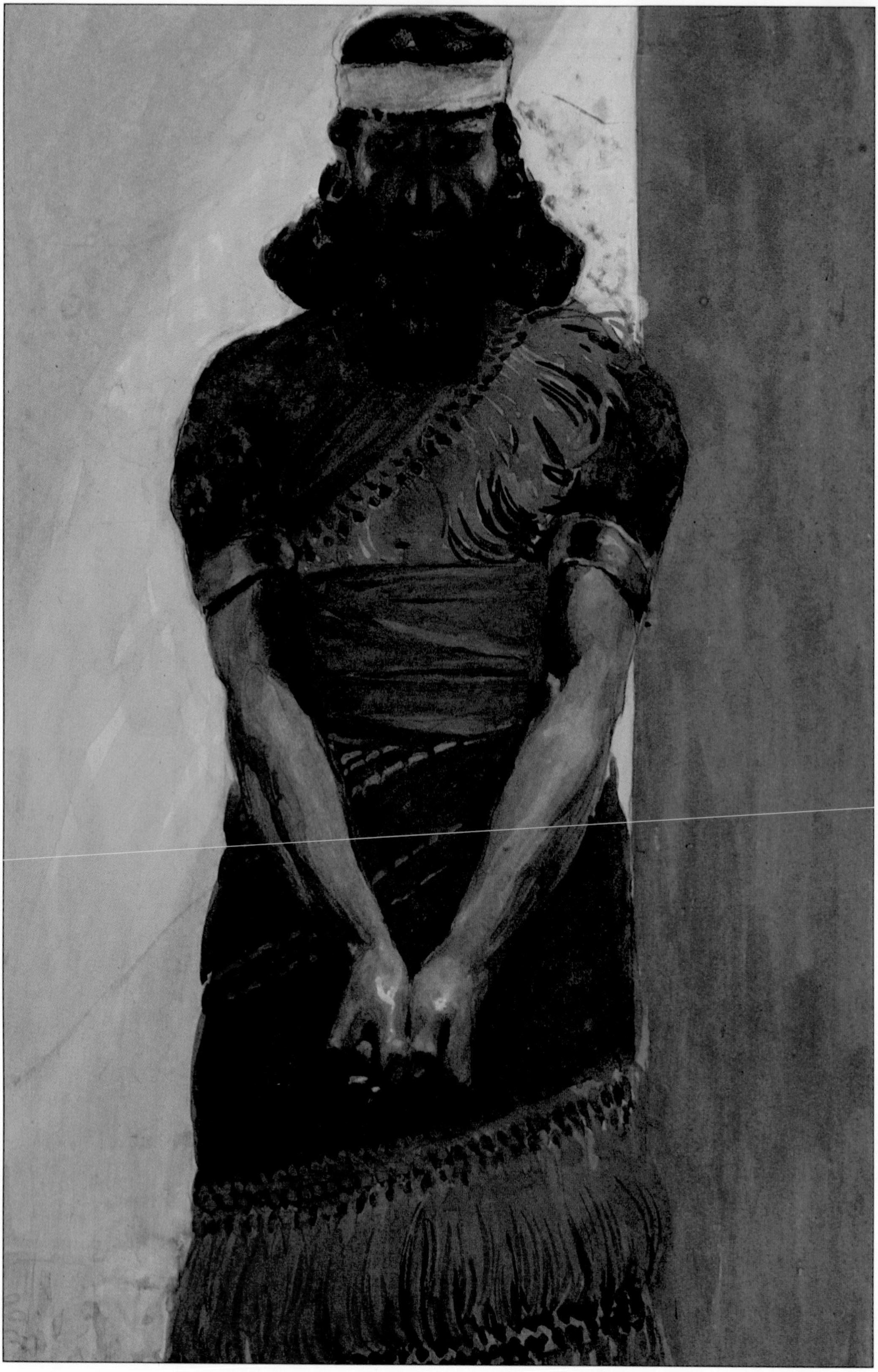

to work on the temple.

2:1-9
God's Emerging Word

A month later God gave an encouraging word to a tiny group which had determined, without adequate resources, to build God's house as He had directed (2:1-9). They might have been discouraged because they had no chance of duplicating the splendor of Solomon's temple that once stood on that spot (v. 3). But God called on all of them to be strong and to work hard because the Lord Almighty was with them (v. 4). The name "the LORD Almighty [or 'the LORD of Hosts']" is used frequently in the last books of the twelve Minor Prophets. The smaller and weaker Israel's own resources, the greater their need for a faith in God as even more powerful than before.

Verses 6-9 portray God's intended use for the new temple. He planned great earthshaking events soon. The "desired of all nations will come" (v. 7). The nations would be shaken and that which they desired would come to pass. Verse 9 suggests that this desire was for "peace." This would come when the temple was filled with God's presence.

God's people did not need to be overly concerned with how they could finance the temple rebuilding. God said, "The silver and the gold is mine" (v. 8). Micah 4:1-5 (= Isa 2:2-4) shows that the new temple was God's goal and that worship there would be related to peaceful life. Haggai said now was the time for that to be fulfilled. As for the needed funding, Ezra-Nehemiah records the specific financial support Cyrus and his successors decreed should be provided for the new temple. He gave back to Sheshbazzar the vessels that were taken away by Babylonian and Assyrian kings. Darius later ordered surrounding peoples through their governors to pay for the work (Ezra 6:8-10). Artaxerxes later ordered even more generous support for Ezra and Nehemiah (Ezra 7).

2:10-23
The Turning Point

Two months later the Lord announced a turning point when the first stones were actually laid for the temple's foundation (v. 15). The passage begins with a parable related to meat consecrated for sacrifice. It had no power in itself to sanctify what it touched and could only be profaned by alien contact. So long as the people had no temple, so long as they were under God's judgment, they were like that. Nothing prospered. Nothing worked for them. But now, from the day the temple began to be a reality, that would change. God would bless them.

Haggai 2:20-23 is a prophecy given on the same day to Zerubabbel that again spoke of earthshaking events in which God would use violence and war. On that day God said He would elevate Zerubabbel. He called him "my servant," a title made great in Isaiah. He promised to make him like God's own signet ring.

The subject turns from building the temple to the question of leadership in Jerusalem, from a position of joint leadership with Joshua, the priest, to the single rule of Zerubabbel. Jeremiah 22:24-25 had announced that God would tear off Yahweh's signet ring from Jehoiakin to give it to Nebuchadnezzar. Now Jehoiakin's grandson was promised that the Lord would "wear him as a signet ring" because God had chosen him. The verse has a messianic sound to it, and Christians have thought of Jesus Christ as its fulfillment. Readers about 420 B.C. must have expected a great deal more from Zerubabbel himself. (See Zech 4 for a further word on Zerubabbel.) It is enough here to note that messianic expectation was not in step with the trend of these later Books of the Twelve Minor Prophets, which expect no restoration of the kingdom of Israel, only restoration of the temple and of the people in the land of Israel.

Theological and Ethical Significance

Haggai calls us to attempt great things for God. Petty selfishness and fears of failure must not prevent God's people from acting. Our actions will reveal whether or not God is the top priority in our lives. If we do not honor God in what we do, we will not be successful no matter how hard we strive. God provides His people with leaders like Zerubbabel to assist His people in serving Him.

Questions for Reflection

1. What does Haggai teach God's people about their use of time and material resources?

2. What evidence was there of God's presence with His people in their work of rebuilding the temple?

Sources for Additional Study

Alden, R. L. "Haggai, Malachi." *Expositor's Bible Commentary*. Vol. 7. Grand Rapids: Zondervan, 1986.

Baldwin, J. *Haggai, Zechariah, Malachi.* Downers Grove: InterVarsity, 1972.

Kelley, P. H. *Micah, Nahum, Habakkuk, Zephaniah, Haggai, Zechariah, Malachi.* Vol. 14. *Layman's Bible Book Commentary.* Nashville: Broadman, 1984.

Verhoef, P. A. *The Books of Haggai and Malachi.* Grand Rapids: Eerdmans, 1987.

Wolf, H. *Haggai and Malachi.* Chicago: Moody, 1976.

ZECHARIAH

Like Haggai, Zechariah 1–8 begins without a title verse. The narrative supplies all the information the reader needs. The date is October 520 B.C., between Haggai's second (Hag 2:1) and third prophecies (2:10). Zechariah was apparently a second prophet active in Jerusalem at this time. His name means *Yahweh remembers* and was a name common among Jews, used by some thirty different persons in the Old Testament.

1:1-6
God's Ways Are Just

The substance of the first account (vv. 1-6) is a call for repentance (v. 3) with a reminder that God had been very angry with their ancestors. The people acknowledged their parents' sins and God's consistency in carrying out the judgment He promised.

1:7-17
Promise of Prosperity

Four months later Zechariah received the first "word of the LORD" in the form of eight visions that extend from 1:7–6:8 (compare the visions in Amos 7:1-9).

In the first vision an angel interpreted for the prophet the appearance of four horsemen who reported to the Lord that they had found "the whole earth at rest and in peace" (v. 11). Persian rule had largely ended wars among the lesser states. So the angel asked the Lord how long He would wait to restore Jerusalem and its neighboring towns. This announcement is important to the plot of the Book of the Twelve (Minor Prophets). The period of judgment was at an end. Persian law and order had made it possible to enter the next phase of God's plan when God's zeal for Zion could be revealed. The prophecy of Micah 4:1-4 was ready to be fulfilled.

1:18-21
Oppressors Punished

The second vision shows the four horns that scattered Judah, Israel, and Jerusalem and the workmen that would demolish them. The motif of "horns" appears in Deuteronomy 33:17 and Psalm 75:10. Isaiah 54:16-17a pictures the workman God uses. The number "four" corresponds to those in the first (Zech 1:7-17) and last (6:1-8) visions, a number of completeness.

2:1-13
God's Glorious Presence

The third vision picks up the theme of a measuring line stretched over Jerusalem from 1:16b. The building had begun. The angel was concerned that the builder would plan too small a city to take care of the scattered exiles (vv. 4-5). Isaiah 40–45 is parallel. God promised to dwell among those who returned from exile, fulfilling the picture of His tabernacling presence in Exodus and Numbers. Many nations would join in Israel's worship (Zech 2:11) in fulfillment of Micah 4:2.

3:1-10
God Wants to Forgive

The fourth vision has a different form: no interpreting angel and no questions from the prophet. Instead Zechariah saw a scene like those of the heavenly council in 2 Kings 22 and Isaiah 6 in which the high priest Joshua was being tried on accusation brought by the official accuser, the Satan. But the Lord refused to hear the accusation, reminding the accuser that He had already chosen Joshua. Joshua was then cleansed, given the new clothes of his priestly office, and charged to do God's will and to walk in His ways. Verse 8 announces God's "servant, the Branch." This usually refers to a king or messiah. Here it appears to mean Zerubabbel (see Hag 2:23). Verse 9 turns back to Joshua. The stone with seven fountains promised blessings for the people. The vision then promised effective priestly service through Joshua. It closes with the promise of peaceful life in fulfillment of Micah 4:4.

4:1-14
Two Messiahs

The fifth vision pictures an elaborate golden lampstand fed by two olive trees. Verse 14 explains these as the two messiahs (or anointed ones), apparently referring to Zerubabbel and Joshua. In the middle of the vision are four words of encouragement to Zerubabbel. "Not by might nor by power" (v. 6) would remind him that he did not need royal authority to succeed. God's Spirit would work through him. The mighty mountain (v. 7) was the obstacle Zerubabbel had to overcome. He would succeed. Verses 8-9 were an assurance that his hands, which had begun the temple, would complete it. A day of small things referred to the slow work of temple building.

5:1-11
Cleansing the Land

The sixth vision (5:1-4) pictured a flying scroll. It was a curse on all who stole and swore falsely. They were to be banished from the land.

The seventh vision (5:5-11) was of a woman in a basket that contained the iniquity of the land's people. Two women with wings took the basket to Babylonia to be left there. These two visions pictured the cleansing of the land of Israel.

6:1-8
Political Stability

The eighth vision showed four chariots driven by spirits emerging from the presence of the Lord to do His will in the world. The one going north was to give God's Spirit of rest to the northern land. That was a sign of political stability in Mesopotamia and therefore in Palestine.

The visions portrayed God's gifts for the struggling Jewish community in Jerusalem that would allow them to rebuild the temple. Dynamic leaders, cleansing for the land, and a promise of political stability provided the necessary setting. Now it was up to them.

6:9-15
Commission for the Branch

Zechariah 6:9-15 recounts the crowning of Joshua as high priest and also as "the Branch" (v. 12). Zerubabbel is not mentioned. Apparently the account was intended to say that now Joshua bore full responsibility for building the temple. The disappearance of Zerubabbel from the scene here and in Ezra 4:5 is nowhere explained and remains a mystery. Joshua's crown was not to be worn, only kept in the temple as a memorial to the promise of help from the exiles far away. Note that the focus here was not on Messiah but on the temple.

7:1–8:23
Righteousness, Not Ritual

Chapter 7 is dated two years later. A delegation from the people of Bethel recognized the authority of Jerusalem in ritual matters and came to ask whether they should continue fasts and mourning. This story is the counterpart of Amos 7:10-17. Both demonstrate Jerusalem's superiority to Bethel (contrast 1 Kgs 12:26–13:33). Apparently the people of Bethel had been more faithful to God than 2 Kings 17 gave them credit for. Or is the story told to demonstrate fulfillment of Micah's prophecy that many peoples would come to worship in Jerusalem? Their question asked whether progress toward restoration of the temple in Zion justified the conclusion that the period of judgment and curse was over.

The question was not answered directly. The prophet spoke of what constituted true worship (Zech 7:8-10; 8:15-17; compare Mic 6:8). Zechariah 8:18-19 finally answers specifically that the fasts were to be transformed into joyful festivals that would celebrate love, truth, and peace.

Zechariah 8:20-23 closes the first half of the book by proclaiming the coming fulfillment of Micah 4:2. Many peoples from many cities would go up to Jerusalem to pray and seek the Lord. (Note the lack of reference to sacrifice.) The ratio of Gentiles to Jews would be ten to one going up to Jerusalem because they would have heard that God was with them. God's presence in Zion would be generally recognized, as would His blessing on those who worshiped there.

9:1-8
Convert the Enemy

Zechariah 9–11 is the first of three "burdens" (or "oracles") that end the Book of the Twelve (Minor Prophets). They are all discourses, more like those found in Hosea, Joel, and Micah than like Haggai and Zechariah 1–8. They summarized the history of preexilic Israel from the viewpoint of postexilic Judaism and applied lessons from that history to their own day. Like Hosea they were aware of Israel's earlier history.

Zechariah 9:1-8 draws a parallel between the Persian period when Judah was trying to reestablish itself in Canaan and restore Jerusalem and the time when Joshua faced the conquest of the land the first time. The people of Canaan named were those ethnic groups still in the land during the Persian period. "The land" was defined in terms such as those promised to Abraham and David, but the local peoples who faced Zerubabbel and Nehemiah between 520 and sometime after 433 B.C. were the troublesome competitors for Persian favor.

God's attention ("the word of the LORD") was on these competing peoples to bring them to heel, at the same time that those going up to the new temple in Zion and "all the tribes of Israel" were turning their attention to the Lord (9:1). The competing nations were Syria, Tyre and Sidon, and the Philistine cities. The passage ends with the promise that the Philistine remnant would belong to the Lord and "become leaders in Judah" (v. 7). The example of Jebusites who were absorbed into Israel through their living in Jerusalem was cited (v. 7). Jerusalem's safety was assured.

9:9-17
Salvation Coming

Zechariah 9:9-13 hailed the coming of Zion's king. "Righteous" might also mean "legitimate" in the Lord's eyes and was a term Isaiah 45 used for Cyrus, the Persian king. "Salvation" was something that Persia brought to Jews in Mesopotamia with rights to worship and to Jerusalem with support for restoration. "Gentle and riding on a donkey" (v. 9) pictures one who comes in peace. The Persians did not conquer Judah. They inherited it through Babylon. Christians applied this text to Jesus' entry into Jerusalem (Matt 21:5; John 12:15).

The speaker in verses 10a and 11-13 appears to be that king, while 10b is spoken about him. He would disarm Ephraim and Judah. He would impose peace on Palestine's troubled peoples. He promised a return and restoration of prisoners. The verses speak of the fulfillment of God's purposes in verses 1-8, but verse 13 has an ominous tone. Persia in the 400s B.C. was locked in war with the Greeks of Athens and the Greek cities of the Aegean area. Verse 13 seems to suggest that men from Ephraim and Judah might be drafted for the war. But verses 14-17 promise God's intervention and salvation that ends with glory and prosperity.

10:1-12
Judgment Explained

The Lord promised rain for the Israelites in Palestine (Lev 26:4; Deut 11:14; 28:12), but they preferred to pray to idols for rain. "The people wander like sheep oppressed for lack of a shepherd" recalls the period of the judges. "Shepherd" means *king*.

Zechariah 10:3-5 pictures the rise of the house of Judah to prominence and victory. Verse 6 pictures the strengths of the two monarchies early on, but then it speaks of restoration and of acceptance which assume the judgment on the kingdoms that has intervened (v. 6b).

The promise then turns to the Ephraimites, people from northern Israel who were exiled in 721 B.C. They would be gathered, redeemed, and multiplied (vv. 7-8). They would remember the Lord when He brought them back to Gilead and Lebanon from Egypt and Assyria (vv. 8-10). Verse 11 suggests a parallel with the crossing of the Red Sea (Exod 15) but goes beyond it: "The Nile will dry up." The people to be returned from Egypt were located in southern Egypt. The Nile rather than the Red Sea would be the barrier to their return. Assyria and Egypt would be humiliated (v. 11). They were both under Persian authority for the first readers of the collection of the twelve Minor Prophets. The passage closes with the promise of strength from the Lord as His people identified with His name (v. 12).

11:1-17
Covenant Failure

Zechariah 11:1-3 returns to a period of violent disorder in northern Palestine (Lebanon and Bashan, vv. 1-2). The kings ("shepherds") and the warriors ("lions") were in deep distress (v. 3).

Zechariah 11:4-17 speaks of a leader or king who had a rebellious and ungrateful people during a time when God had given them over to the results of their unbelief. They were "the flock marked for slaughter" (v. 4). This was the fate of the Canaanites when Israel entered the land (Exod 23:28). It was also their fate in the 700s B.C. when God unleashed the Assyrians against them.

But who is the speaker? The role is larger than any one person could fill. Perhaps it stands for the Davidic line as a whole. Can verse 7 picture the united kingdom of David and Solomon? The names "Favor" and "Union" fit that time. David's conquests could have provided the end of the three shepherds, or kings, of the small nations.

The popularity of the dynasty waned, however, and the kings' attention was diverted to central matters of state and religion (end of Solomon's reign). "Favor" from God was lost. Verses 12-14 picture the rupture of the united kingdom, "breaking the brotherhood between Judah and Israel" (v. 14). The thirty pieces of silver (v. 13) were applied in the New Testament to Judas (Matt 26:15; see also Jer 32:6-15).

Verse 15 speaks of monarchy under an oppressive yoke: a good description of Hezekiah's latter days or those of Manasseh. Verse 17 curses the "worthless shepherd, who deserts the flock." This could describe the last king to sit on David's throne, Zedekiah (2 Kgs 25:4-7).

Zechariah 9–11 has spoken of kingship over Jerusalem and the land. It pictures the benefits of Judah's present, Persian king and portrays the failures of kings when Judah and Israel were independent.

12:1-14
Lord Is Their God

Zechariah 12–14, like 9:1, has a simple heading, "An oracle" or literally, "A burden." It is called "a word of the LORD" and defines the subject, "concerning Israel." This is noteworthy because the chapters speak only of Jerusalem, Judah, and surrounding nations. Yet the note

Zechariah

is not accidental. The Book of the Twelve (Minor Prophets) was concerned to define what it meant to be Israel, the people of God, for the exiles and the little community in Jerusalem. The book and this section called them to focus their attention on God's presence in Zion (Jerusalem).

This section deals with Jerusalem's role and particularly with the way it seemed always to provoke the surrounding peoples: Zechariah 12:2–14:2 applies to the time of the kingdoms; Zechariah 14:3-20, to Jerusalem's role after the exile. It begins by identifying the Lord as Creator of all (12:1) and by quoting His words. He was establishing Jerusalem as a cup that sends people reeling, that is, a drink so strong it would make the nations stagger. He also would make Jerusalem a rock they could not move (vv. 2-3). The frustrated nations would explain their inability to handle Jerusalem by saying, "The LORD Almighty is their God" (v. 5).

Then the passage turns to the role of Judah in subduing the nations in David's time (v. 6). The delicate issue of Jerusalem's prominence versus Judah's pride is mentioned (v. 7), as is the amazing rise of Jerusalem's power under David (v. 8). The extended story is told in 2 Samuel. At that time God subdued the Philistines and all the competing nations. David ruled the whole of Palestine. "A spirit of grace and supplication" (v. 10a) poured on David's line and Jerusalem's people related to the temple and worship there.

Verses 10b-14 speak of ritual mourning in Jerusalem. Apparently God was speaking of Himself as the One "they have pierced" by their sins. John 19:37 related this to the crucifixion of Jesus. Twice in David's reign there were periods of mourning: the death of Bathsheba's first child (2 Sam 12:16-17) and the death of Absalom (2 Sam 18–19). Both instances witnessed to prior sin in David's life.

13:1-9
Responsive Remnant

Jerusalem's long history under David's line was truly by the grace of God (13:1). The kingdom period was the age of prophets. They were often unpopular and mistreated. And some were false prophets (13:2-6).

The chapter closes with an oracle from God calling for the assassination of his shepherd, the Davidic king in Jerusalem (vv. 7b-9). Of those in the land two-thirds would die, leaving one-third alive. Even this third would be tested and refined. But that remnant would be responsive to God, a real covenant people of God (see Lev 26:12; Jer 11:4; 30:22; Ezek 11:20). These words pictured a fulfillment of Zechariah 8:8.

14:1-21
God's Day of Universal Rule

Zechariah 14:1-2 recorded Jerusalem's destruction with half its people exiled. This was the harsh memory of most Jews in exile. Zechariah 14:3-21 pictures a reversal as the Lord fought against the nations. The historical account of God's intervention for the Jews and Jerusalem is told in Ezra-Nehemiah and is pictured in Isaiah 40–66. History records that Persia conquered Babylon and that Persia was friendly to the Jewish restoration of Jerusalem and its temple. Persia did subdue the Palestinian nations and forced them to leave Jerusalem alone. In this passage the process was pictured poetically as earthquake, perpetual light, and healing waters.

The Lord would be King over the whole land (Zech 14:9). He would be one LORD and His name the only one (compare Deut 6:4).

Zechariah 14:10 records the fulfillment of Micah 4:1 with Jerusalem raised high over the land, inhabited, and secure. Zechariah 14:12-15 return to the means God would use to accomplish this. No force of arms would be involved. Wealth of many nations would be collected (compare Isa 60). The decree of Artaxerxes required governors of surrounding territories to support Nehemiah's efforts to rebuild the city (Neh 2:7-8). There was still opposition from surrounding peoples (2:19), but God's intervention would be against them too (Zech 14:15).

Zechariah 14:16-19 pictures survivors from all the nations that had previously attacked Jerusalem, including Egypt, participating in Jerusalem's worship of the Lord as King. This implies recognition that the Lord was God over all the territory. Failure to appear in Jerusalem would bring punishment in rain withheld.

Verses 20-21 picture the entire city of Jerusalem as a temple, all its territory sacred, all its utensils treated as sacred vessels. "Canaanite" may also mean *merchant*. The city would no longer be a mercantile city, no longer an administrative center for government. It would simply be a place to meet God and learn about Him (Mic 4:2-4).

Zechariah 12–14 has dealt with the role of Jerusalem under the Davidic dynasty and its role after it no longer had a king. In both cases it had been and was a special city for God, a city that provoked attention from the nations, formerly hostile but more recently friendly attention.

Theological and Ethical Significance

Zechariah 1–6—like Haggai—called God's people to attempt great things for God, specifically rebuilding the temple. Zechariah 7–8 echoes the message of earlier prophets such as Amos and Micah that God does not value the ritual worship of those who deal unjustly with others. Zechariah 9–14 serves as a reminder that God's plan for Israel's future went beyond the return of a relatively small number of exiles from Babylon and the building of a second temple.

New Testament writers had seen God's plan working out in Jesus. They often applied Zechariah's images to Jesus: the triumphant yet peaceful King (9:9); the pierced One (12:10); and the Shepherd, who was struck down (13:7).

Questions for Reflection

1. According to Zechariah, what must God's people do to experience His blessings?

2. What does the Book of Zechariah teach about God's plans for His people's future? How does Jesus meet these expectations?

Sources for Additional Study

Baldwin, J. *Haggai, Zechariah, Malachi.* Downers Grove: InterVarsity, 1972.

Baron, D. *The Visions and Prophecies of Zechariah.* Grand Rapids: Kregel, 1972.

Barker, K. L. "Zechariah." *Expositor's Bible Commentary.* Vol. 7. Grand Rapids: Zondervan, 1985.

Feinberg, C. L. *God Remembers.* Portland: Multnomah, 1965.

Kelley, P. H. *Micah, Nahum, Habakkuk, Zephaniah, Haggai, Zechariah, Malachi. Layman's Bible Book Commentary.* Vol. 14. Nashville: Broadman, 1984.

Unger, M. F. *Zechariah: Prophet of Messiah's Glory.* Grand Rapids: Zondervan, 1963.

MALACHI

Malachi begins, as Zechariah 9–11 and 12–14 began, with the heading "an oracle." It is expanded with "the word of the LORD through Malachi." *Malachi* means *my messenger.* Whether this is a proper name or a reference to God's messenger in 3:1 is not clear.

The book is a series of dialogues or conversations between the Lord and the people of Jerusalem. Since the issues discussed relate to postexilic experience, the book probably dates to after the time of Ezra (about 458 B.C.). There is nothing in the book to date it more exactly.

1:1-5
Do Not Doubt God's Love

Malachi brings the Minor Prophets (the Book of the Twelve) to an end as Hosea 1–3 began it. Hosea's theme was God's persistent love for Israel despite their apostasy. Malachi 1:1-5 begins this book with the same theme: God's assertion of His unchanging love. The people who had suffered exile asked, "How have you loved us?" (v. 2). God replied, as the Minor Prophets have done so often, by citing a story from the Pentateuch. He spoke of His favoritism for Jacob over Esau (that is, for Israel over the nation Edom). This picked up the themes of Obadiah and reaffirmed the judgment spoken there. God's love for Israel was election love, firmly holding to Israel as His chosen people.

1:6-14
God Deserves Honor

Jerusalem's pious claim that the Lord was their Father did not match their deeds. Their sacrifice was flawed by poor offerings. God objected so much that He wished they would close the temple rather than perform this unworthy worship. Amos had complained about worship at Bethel in similar terms (Amos 4:4-5). God wanted to be recognized and treated like the great King that He is.

2:1-7
Judging Unfaithful Ministers

Inattentive priests neither listened to God's instruction nor took care to honor God's name. They were reminded that God could curse for disobedience as well as bless for obedience. A lesson follows about what it means to be a Levitical priest. (The term *Levi* is collective. Levi himself was not a priest.) They were to revere God and be in awe of His name. Instruction in God's ways was their main task. They were to promote peace and turn people from sin. The priest was a messenger from God with true teaching for the people. The emphasis on teaching how to worship has no reference to sacrifice. This is parallel to Isaiah 66 but different from Leviticus. Their failure to follow God's way led to the priests' being despised and humiliated. In Leviticus 10 the sons of Aaron had their problems, and Eli's sons abused their privileges (1 Sam 2:12-25; 3:14).

2:10-16
Faithful in Marriage

Malachi 2:10-16 deals with instances of "breaking faith" (v. 10). All the Jews recognized God as Father and Creator in their common worship, but not all lived as if God was their Lord.

Judah was faulted for a serious breach of covenant. Note that Judah and Jerusalem were places with populations, but Israel referred to the chosen people gathered in worship. Judah's sin was called "marrying the daughter of a foreign God" (v. 11). This seems to be a pagan religious commitment. The exile had not rid Israel of all their idolatrous practices as God had hoped. Isaiah 65 testifies to the same problem.

Israel was concerned about unanswered prayers (Mal 1:13). The Lord was concerned about divorces. He said, "I hate divorce" (v. 16). The reader is reminded of Hosea 1–3, where God refused to acknowledge a "divorce" between Himself and Israel, despite their infidelity. So the people were urged not to "break faith" in their covenant with God or in their marriage covenants.

2:17
Wearying God

Israel was next accused of wearying the Lord with their whining that God treated evildoers as well as those who do good. Or they asked, "Where is the God of justice?" The Lord was tired of hearing such complaints. This series of discussions about Israel's religious life demonstrat-

Malachi

ed that postexilic life in Jerusalem was far from ideal. The people had learned very little from the judgments of the past three centuries. They were very much like their ancestors.

3:1-15
Unwavering Love

The last two chapters of Malachi (and of the Book of the Twelve Prophets) address the situation of Israelites in Jerusalem after the exile. Their situation was not unlike that of believers, Jewish and Christian, ever since that time. The judgments and saving acts of God leading up to and following the exile had wrought no miraculous change making the people all saints. Some were still idolatrous. Some were simply indifferent. A few were faithful believers. These chapters proclaim God's love and salvation for the believers and teach the style of faith that they should follow.

Malachi 3:1-5 describes a refining judgment still going on that purified the worship of God. The list of sinners (v. 5) runs the gamut from sorcerers to those who oppress the helpless. They obviously did not revere or honor God.

Malachi 3:6-7 restates the basic message of the Minor Prophets: God's commitment in love to His people remains unwavering (Hos 1–3 and Mal 1:2). But those who were building the new city, like their ancestors throughout history, ignored His laws. So the call was repeated, "Return to me, and I will return to you" (v. 7). But the people wanted to talk back. They asked, "How are we to return?" (v. 7). Micah 6:6 asked a similar question about sacrifice. The Lord's reply was blunt: You have robbed God in your tithes and offerings (Mal 3:8c-12). Surely this was only one example of sins that could be corrected, but it was concrete and specific. God showed how they could correct that and how that would change curse to blessing.

Then God provided another example. They had complained that He was not fair and that they saw no advantage in serving Him. God did not appreciate such talk.

3:16-18
They Are Mine

Verse 16 is a key verse that tells of the reaction of a small group of believers "who feared the LORD." They "talked with each other," and the Lord "listened and heard." Their conversation was more effective than prayer. They prepared minutes of their meeting in which they were conscious of the Lord's presence. The names of those "who feared the LORD and honored his name" were recorded. God was pleased. Small groups in Jewish synagogues and Christian churches have been keeping records of persons who have committed themselves to God ever since.

Verse 17 records the Lord's pleased response: "They will be mine." They were His kind of people, and they would be truly His on the day when He makes up His "treasured possession." They would receive His mercy in the judgment. They would clearly see "the distinction between the righteous and the wicked" (v. 18). These had deliberately chosen to worship God in the way He had prescribed. Jesus made the same point about the different kinds of people in His story about the sheep and the goats (Matt 25:32-46).

4:1-6
Healing in His Wings

Malachi 4:1-3 continues to stress the different effect of judgment on believers and nonbelievers. The beautiful expression of blessing as the rising of "the sun of righteousness . . . with healing in its wings" is memorable and appropriate.

Malachi closes with two admonitions that characterize Jewish faith. The first (v. 4) called for readers to remember the law of Moses. The Pentateuch was the Torah of Moses. It came to be the foundation of the Hebrew Bible, the beginning of Christian Scripture. The second (vv. 5-6) spoke of prophecy in the role of Elijah. Such prophetic preaching would prepare the readers for the great day of the Lord, changing attitudes between the generations of believers. The prophetic books of Scripture were part of this tradition of preaching. Christians recognize in this verse the preaching of John the Baptist and of genuine evangelists through the ages.

Theological and Ethical Significance

The central thrust of Malachi is that God had revealed His love for His people through their history. That revealed love made God's people accountable. They were to obey the teaching of God's law (*torah*) and the preaching of God's prophets.

Questions for Reflection

1. How was the situation of the exiles who returned from Jerusalem like that of Christians today?
2. What does Malachi teach about God's commitment to His people?
3. What does Malachi teach about the responsibilities of God's people?

Sources for Additional Study

Alden, R. L. "Haggai, Malachi." *Expositor's Bible Commentary*. Vol. 7. Grand Rapids: Zondervan, 1986.

Baldwin, J. *Haggai, Zechariah, Malachi.* Downers Grove: InterVarsity, 1972.

Kaiser, W. C. Jr. *Malachi: God's Unchanging Love*. Grand Rapids: Baker, 1984.

Kelley, P. H. *Micah, Nahum, Habakkuk, Zephaniah, Haggai, Zechariah, Malachi. Layman's Bible Book Commentary.* Vol. 14. Nashville: Broadman, 1984.

Morgan, G. C. *Malachi's Message for Today.* Grand Rapids: Baker, 1972.

Verhoef, P. A. *The Books of Haggai and Malachi*. Grand Rapids: Eerdmans, 1987.

Wolf, H. *Haggai and Malachi*. Chicago: Moody, 1976.

Between the Testaments

Why study the period between the Testaments? Our Bible skips from Malachi to Matthew. Why should students of the Bible not do the same?

The primary reason for studying this period is that the books of the New Testament were written to speak to people at the time they were written. That they still speak to us is a sign of their inspiration, not an indication of their original purpose.

We live in a different era and thought world from that in which the New Testament was written. In order to be able to appreciate its meaning, we need to immerse ourselves in the world of the New Testament period. Important, world-shaping events occurred in Palestine between the conquests of Alexander (334–323 B.C.) and the destruction of Jerusalem in A.D. 135.

Moreover, Jesus was a first-century Galilean, a Jew. In order to understand aspects of His teachings, we must try to hear Him as first-century Galileans heard Him. Only after we understand the meaning of the New Testament in its original context will we be able to interpret it for our time.

INTERTESTAMENTAL HISTORY

Intertestamental history covers the period between the writing of the final books of the Old and New Testaments. The conquests of Alexander the Great (334 B.C.) and the Bar Kochba Revolt (A.D. 132–135) serve as the outer limits of this period.

Alexander and the Successors

Alexander assumed the Macedonian throne following the assassination of his father, Philip II in 336 B.C. Alexander was twenty, and with Aristotle as his final tutor, he had received the finest education of his day.

At the time of Alexander's rise to power, the Jews were living under the rule of the Persian Empire. Aramaic had become the common language in Palestine. The dispersion of the Jews had already begun. There were significant populations of Jews not only in Babylon and Egypt but also in the major cities of the Mediterranean world also. The numbers of Jews in these cities increased significantly during the period between the Testaments.

Within two years of his coming to the throne, Alexander launched a campaign against the Persian Empire. He would never return to Macedonia. Alexander was a brilliant, resourceful commander. His army was like a traveling city. Under his leadership it won battle after battle in Asia Minor, Phoenicia, Palestine, Egypt, Babylonia, and as far east as the Indus River.

When an officer was wounded, Alexander might appoint him as governor of a city and let him remain there with his family. When an army was overrun, Alexander offered the defeated soldiers the opportunity to fight for him.

As Alexander swept through Palestine in 332, he first took Tyre and then swept down the coast to Gaza. Samaria and Jerusalem offered no resistance. Alexander treated local religions with respect. In Egypt he was even proclaimed as a divine man, the son of their supreme god. Once he had defeated Darius, the Persian ruler, Alexander married Darius's daughter and another royal princess. For Alexander the marriages were a symbol of the union between Macedonia and the Orient.

Alexander's conquests carried with them the spread of Hellenism, Greek culture, and the Greek spirit. Koine Greek became the common language of the eastern Mediterranean. *Koine* means *common* or *profane.* It was not refined, classical Greek but Greek as learned and spoken by those who were not native Greeks. Koine Greek later became the language of the New Testament.

Hellenism emphasized education, physical development, athletic contests, art, sculpture, drama, and philosophy. The theater and the gymnasium were both its landmarks and its legacy. Ironically, some Jews responded to the inroads of Hellenism by establishing a program of universal education. All Hebrew boys would be taught to read the Scriptures in Hebrew. The development of virtue through education, however, was one of the cardinal principles of Hellenism.

Alexander died suddenly in 323 B.C. shortly after his return to Babylon (see Dan 11:3-4). No one could take his place. Indeed, it is doubtful that Alexander himself could have established an effective administration over all

A marble head of Antiochus III, "the Great" (223–187 B.C.), found in Syria.

A mosaic found at Pompeii and dating from the first century A.D. which depicts the battle of Issus in 333 B.C. Alexander the Great is on the left of the mosaic battling his way to the chariot of Darius III on the right center.

the lands he had conquered. For the next twenty years there were constant wars among his would-be successors (the *diadachoi*). By 301 B.C., after the battle of Ipsus, the territories of Alexander's empire were divided as follows:

1. The Antigonids held Macedonia.
2. The Ptolemies ruled Egypt and Libya.
3. The Seleucids controlled Syria and Persia.

Palestine was controlled by the Ptolemies from 301 B.C. until the battle of Panium in 198 B.C., when it fell under Seleucid domination.

Under the Ptolemies, Palestine experienced a century of relatively peaceful development. Political independence, self-sufficiency, prominence, and leadership were the dominant motives for the political conduct of the successors. They sought the greatest measure of economic self-sufficiency as a basis for political independence. They established economic and social patterns that continued into the New Testament period. The parables of Jesus—with their large landowners, tenants, stewards, money lenders, day laborers, tax collectors, grain speculation, and land leasing—must be understood against the background of the economic structures developed by the Ptolemies. The land was regarded as the king's possession, and a portion of its produce was paid to the king. Jerusalem became a temple state governed by a high priestly aristocracy.

At the Battle of Panium (later renamed Caesarea Philippi) in 198 B.C., the Seleucids, under the able leadership of Antiochus III the Great, seized Palestine. Apparently the majority of Jews in Palestine were pro-Seleucid at the time. Antiochus needed the goodwill of the Jews because war with Rome was becoming inevitable as Roman domination spread eastward. Antiochus consequently promised the Jews relief from taxes and relative freedom. The transfer of power in Jerusalem must have created strained relations, however, between Jews in Alexandria and Jews in Jerusalem. Alexandrian Jews may well have been regarded with suspicion by the Ptolemies.

By 188 B.C. Antiochus was forced to sign a peace treaty with the Romans at Apamea. Under this treaty his son, who would later be Antiochus IV Epiphanes, was sent to Rome as a hostage. Territory was taken from Antiochus, and he agreed to pay Rome fifteen thousand talents over a period of twelve years. In effect, Antiochus III was reduced to the role of tax collector for Rome. He died the next year in a foolish effort to plunder treasure from a temple in Elam.

Under his successor, Seleucus IV (187–175 B.C.), Jew-

ish sympathies for the Egyptian Ptolomies seem to have increased as Seleucus raised taxes. Parties began to form with leanings toward one power or the other. Seleucus sent Heliodorus to plunder the temple in Jerusalem, but he returned saying that he had been prevented from doing so by supernatural beings. Shortly thereafter, Heliodorus murdered Seleucus.

Antiochus IV, the brother of Seleucus IV, had been released by the Romans and was residing in Athens. Wasting no time, he acquired an army from the king of Pergamum, attacked Antioch, killed Heliodorus, and seized the throne. He was to become a major—and infamous—figure in Jewish history. Antiochus was marked by his exile. In Rome he had recognized the power of Roman authority. He never opposed Rome. In Athens he had drunk deeply of the spirit of Hellenism. He supported the Greek cults and games and became a proponent of Hellenistic culture. He was also unpredictable, however, and had little knowledge of or respect for Jewish beliefs.

The Maccabean Revolt

The Maccabean revolt was rooted in the longstanding rivalry between two leading pro-Hellenist families in Jerusalem: the Oniads and the Tobiads. Onias III was the rightful Zadokite high priest.

At the time Antiochus came to the throne (175 B.C.), Onias III was in Antioch, apparently to answer charges of disloyalty brought against him by the Tobiads. His brother, Jason, traveled to Antioch and met with Antiochus. Rather than supporting Onias III, however, Jason offered to pay Antiochus more taxes and a one-time tribute if Antiochus would appoint Jason as high priest, establish a gymnasium in Jerusalem, and designate its citizens as Antiochenes. Although no Seleucid ruler had assumed authority to appoint a high priest, Antiochus readily agreed.

In 172 B.C. Menelaus, a Tobiad whom Jason had sent to Antioch with the annual tribute, offered Antiochus twice the annual taxes Jason was collecting. Antiochus agreed and appointed Menelaus as high priest even though he was not from the Zadokite line and had no claim to the office.

Antiochus IV led a campaign into Egypt (169–168 B.C.) but was forced to retreat by the Romans, who ordered him out of Egypt. Bruised and behind in payments to Rome, he plundered the temple in Jerusalem on one and perhaps two occasions. The Jews were outraged at this sacrilege.

In response to the unrest in Jerusalem, and probably in response to the urgings of the Tobiads, Antiochus sought to Hellenize Jerusalem more completely. He tore down

Pictured above is a marble head of Ptolemy I discovered in Egypt.

its walls and built a fortress (probably for defense against the Ptolemies). He also ordered that God be called Zeus Olympius in the temple. He erected altars and ordered that the Jews sacrifice swine to Zeus Olympius. Nothing could have been more abhorrent to the Jews.

When the Seleucid officers attempted to enforce the king's orders in the town of Modein, a Jew by the name of Mattathias killed a fellow Jew who was obeying the orders, killed the officer, and tore down the altar. The revolt had begun.

Mattathias led his five sons into the wilderness. The *Hasidim*, or "pious ones," among the Jews joined forces with them, and they began a guerrilla style warfare against fellow Jews and local Syrian forces. Shortly after the incident at Modein, Mattathias died; and one of his sons, Judas the Maccabee (*the hammer*), became the leader of the rebellion.

The Jews' knowledge of the land, local support, and surprise attacks helped them to win early victories. By 164 B.C. Judas had won a truce with Syria and cleansed the temple. First Maccabees describes the building of a new altar: They deliberated what to do about the altar of the burnt offering, which had been profaned. . . . So they tore down the altar and stored the stones in a convenient place on the temple hill until there should come a prophet to tell what to do with them (1 Macc 4:44-46). There was no prophet in Israel at the time, and some thought there would be no prophet until the end of the age or the coming of the Messiah.

The rededication of the temple in mid-December (the 25th of Chislev) 164 B.C. has been celebrated in Jewish communities ever since. The celebration is called Hanukkah, the festival of lights. John 10:22 refers to Hanukkah as "the Feast of Dedication."

Events outside of Judea influenced the course of events at this point. Judas Maccabaeus was spurred on by his early victories to launch campaigns to gain more land and more power. His efforts were unopposed at first because Antiochus IV was killed at this time and because his officers were locked in struggle over his successor. Judas forced Lysias, the Syrian commander, to make peace. The religious freedom of the Jews was officially recognized, and Menelaus was executed. When Demetrius I, son of Seleucus IV, emerged victorious in the struggle to succeed Antiochus IV, he appointed Alcimus, a descendant of Aaron, as high priest. The first stage of the revolt, the fight for religious freedom, had ended.

In 161 B.C. Judas led his dwindling forces against a vastly superior Syrian army and was killed in battle. Jonathan, his brother and a skillful diplomat, became the leader of the Jewish forces. In the years that followed his astute negotiations with changing leaders brought Judea ever closer to full independence from Syrian control.

Alcimus, the high priest, died in 160/159 B.C. Apparently the office was not filled until 152 B.C., though some scholars contend that there must have been a functioning high priest during this period. In 152 B.C. Alexander Balas, who was contending with Demetrius I for the Syrian throne, appointed Jonathan as high priest. This appointment of one of the Maccabee brothers, who were from a priestly family but were not descendants of Zadok, to the office of high priest by one of the descendants of Antiochus Epiphanes is surely one of the ironies of history. It shows, however, how the high priesthood had been increasingly politicized in the intervening years. By this means Jonathan became the political, religious, and military leader of the Jews and an appointee of the Seleucid Empire.

In 145 B.C. the son of Demetrius I defeated both Alexander Balas and Ptolemy VI in battle. He claimed the Syrian throne and took the title Demetrius II. Demetrius II arrested Jonathan and then killed him in 142 B.C. The leadership of Judea fell to Simon, the last of the sons of Mattathias and the first of the Hasmonean rulers.

The effect of the Maccabean revolt influenced the history of the Jews for years to come.

1. The emergence of the *Hasidim*. Zeal for the tra-

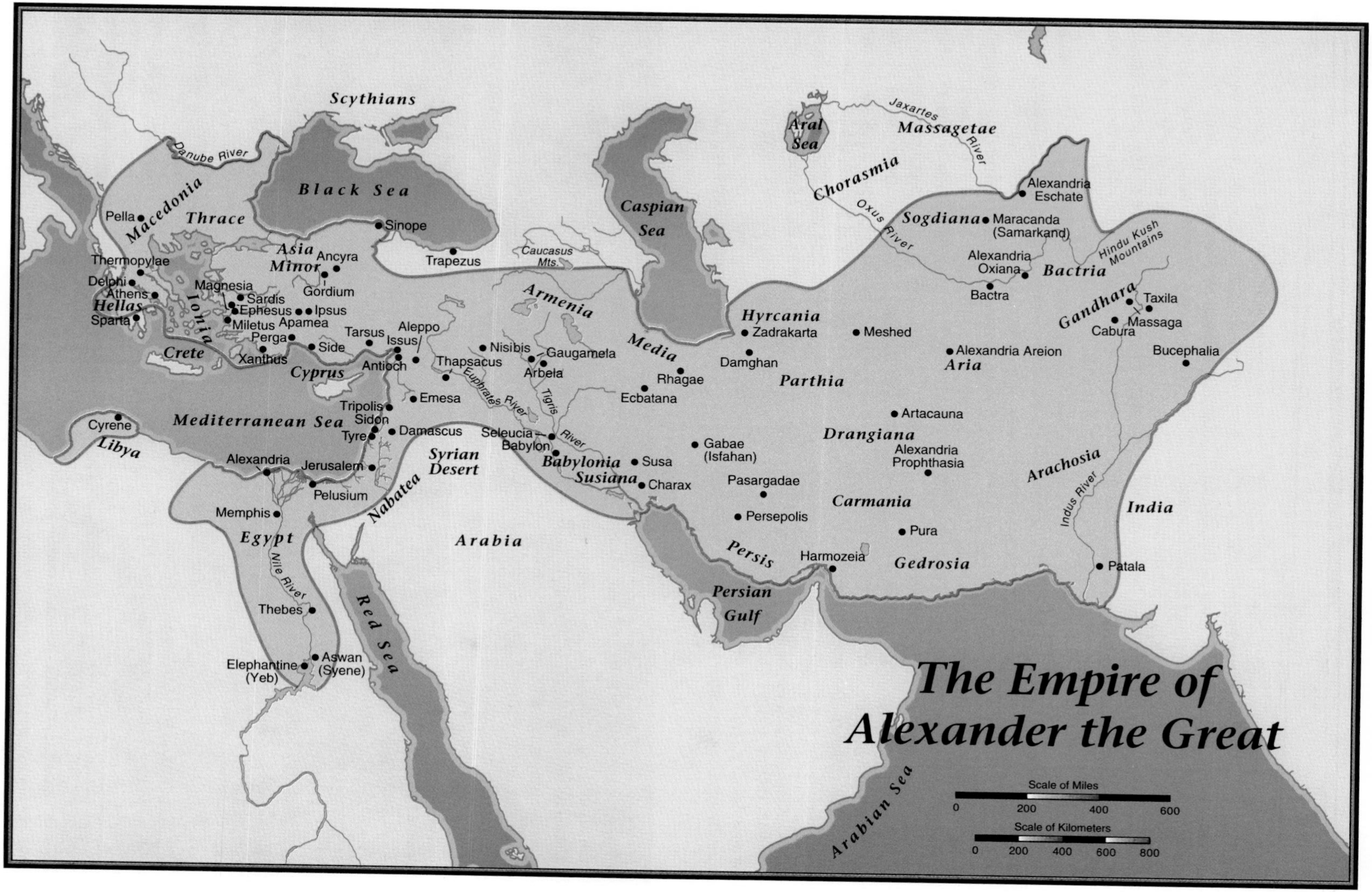

The Empire of Alexander the Great
Scale of Miles
0
200
400
600
Scale of Kilometers
0
200
400
600
800
Scythians
Danube River
Black Sea
Macedonia
Thrace
Pella
Thermopylae
Delphi
Athens
Hellas
Sparta
Ionia
Crete
Magnesia
Sardis
Ephesus
Miletus
Apamea
Ipsus
Asia Minor
Ancyra
Gordium
Sinope
Trapezus
Perga
Side
Xanthus
Tarsus
Issus
Aleppo
Antioch
Cyprus
Mediterranean Sea
Cyrene
Libya
Tripolis
Sidon
Tyre
Damascus
Emesa
Jerusalem
Alexandria
Pelusium
Memphis
Egypt
Nile River
Thebes
Elephantine (Yeb)
Aswan (Syene)
Red Sea
Nabatea
Syrian Desert
Arabia
Caucasus Mts.
Armenia
Nisibis
Thapsacus
Euphrates River
Gaugamela
Arbela
Tigris
River
Seleucia
Babylon
Babylonia
Susiana
Susa
Charax
Caspian Sea
Media
Rhagae
Ecbatana
Gabae (Isfahan)
Aral Sea
Chorasmia
Jaxartes River
Massagetae
Oxus River
Hyrcania
Zadrakarta
Damghan
Parthia
Meshed
Persis
Pasargadae
Persepolis
Persian Gulf
Harmozeia
Carmania
Pura
Gedrosia
Drangiana
Artacauna
Alexandria Prophthasia
Aria
Alexandria Areion
Sogdiana
Maracanda (Samarkand)
Alexandria Eschate
Alexandria Oxiana
Bactra
Bactria
Hindu Kush Mountains
Gandhara
Taxila
Massaga
Cabura
Bucephalia
Arachosia
Indus River
India
Patala
Arabian Sea

ditions of their ancestors and obedience to Torah guided these "pious ones." Although direct connections are difficult to establish, the *Hasidim* were probably the spiritual ancestors of the Pharisees and perhaps of the Essenes.

2. Religious and political freedom. For the first time since the exile the Jews were free from foreign domination. Both a commitment to freedom and a renewed spirit of nationalism were born in the crucible of the Maccabean revolt.

3. Sensitivity to any threat to the law or the temple. The Maccabees had led the struggle for freedom to worship according to the traditions of their ancestors and the deliverance of the temple from "an abomination that causes desolation" (Dan 9:27; 11:31; 12:11). It is not insignificant that Jesus was charged with violating the law (Sabbath law and blasphemy) and threatening to destroy the temple and build another not made with hands (Mark 14:58). Stephen, the first Christian martyr, was stoned because he spoke against "this holy place and against the law" (Acts 6:13). Similarly, Paul was charged both with teaching "against our [Jewish] people and our law and this place" and with defiling the temple's inner courts by admitting a Gentile (Acts 21:28).

4. Forced adoption of Greek ways was stopped, but subtle adaptation to Hellenism continued. The Maccabees interpreted the law for themselves, determining that it was proper for them to fight on the Sabbath (1 Macc 2:41). They proclaimed a festival to honor their victory in retaking the temple. The office of high priest was also politicized to the point that Jonathan accepted appointment to the office by the Seleucid emperor, Alexander Balas. Even the increased efforts to teach the Torah to Jewish children was consistent with the platonic notion that virtue is teachable.

5. Concentration on the law spurred the development of Pharisaism. The martyrdom of the righteous further led to reflection on the righteousness of God, the principle of just retribution, and the acceptance of belief in life after death (Dan 12:1-2). The righteousness of God would not be frustrated. He would vindicate the righteous and punish the wicked, if not in this life, then after death. Belief in resurrection was still so recent that in the first century the Pharisees and Essenes taught the resurrection of the dead, but the Sadducees did not (Acts 23:8).

6. Apocalyptic literature flourished. Daniel and the

Judas Maccabeus pursuing Timotheus (from the Apocrypha, 1 Macc 5:42)

A bronze bust of Seleucus I found at Herculaneum near Pompeii

many apocalypses of the Pseudepigrapha (see "Intertestamental Jewish Literature") testify to the importance of apocalyptic thought during the Maccabean period. Apocalyptic writings taught that history was following a determined course and that after a terrible tribulation, which would come shortly, God would intervene and bring history to an end. The apocalyptic writings were generally written in the name of one of the ancient heroes of Israel (Enoch, Abraham, Baruch). They employed symbolism, animal imagery, tours of heaven, a developed system of angels, and a call for endurance and obedience. The Revelation of John is deeply indebted to the apocalyptic literature of this period.

7. The Maccabean era gave to Judaism a vitality that enabled it to make its two greatest contributions: Christianity and rabbinic Judaism.

The Hasmoneans

Jonathan's and Simon's rise to power marked the beginning of about eighty years of independence for Judea during which it was ruled by the descendants of the Maccabees. These rulers are called "the Hasmoneans." While the name *Hasmonean* is not used in 1 or 2 Maccabees, Josephus said it was a family name that originated with the great-grandfather of Mattathias. It probably was derived from a place name (Heshmon or Hashmonah).

Simon (142–134 B.C.). When Simon succeeded his brother in leadership of the Jewish forces, Syria was in decline. Both external conflicts (with Rome and the Parthians) and internal instability contributed to this decline. Demetrius II and Trypho were locked in conflict over the throne. Simon supported Demetrius II, and in exchange Demetrius agreed to the cessation of all taxes for Judea. In May 142 B.C. Judea became an independent state. Three other prerogatives of independence soon followed. In 140 B.C. the Jewish people elected Simon their high priest, general, and ethnarch forever "until a trustworthy prophet should arise" (1 Macc 14:41). So began the Hasmonean Dynasty. Judea was ruled by a house of priests who also served as their military and political leaders. The Syrian calendar was abolished, and a Jewish lunar calendar was adopted. Shortly thereafter Antiochus VII Sidetes, the Seleucid ruler from 138 to 128 B.C., granted Simon the right to mint his own coinage.

John Hyrcanus I (134–104 B.C.). In 135/34 B.C. Simon was assassinated by treachery while attending a banquet near Jericho. One of his sons, John Hyrcanus, who already had experience in military affairs, succeeded him. Early in John Hyrcanus's rule, Antiochus VII Sidetes invaded Judea and forced him to surrender. The Seleucid dealt with the Judeans benevolently, but he died in battle in 129 B.C. The death of Antiochus VII marks the end of Seleucid domination of Judea.

In a series of military campaigns John Hyrcanus extended his territory north to Scythopolis, south to Idumea, and east into the Transjordan, an area roughly equivalent to that ruled by David. In 128 B.C. he destroyed the Samaritan temple on Mount Gerizim, thus sealing the hostility between Jews and Samaritans (compare John 4:9b,20). The conquered Idumeans were forced to accept circumcision but were never regarded as Jews.

The Pharisees and Sadducees were first mentioned by Josephus during the reign of John Hyrcanus. When the legitimacy of Hyrcanus's birth was questioned, he rebuffed the Pharisees and supported the Sadducees, thus opening a conflict that continued throughout the period of Hasmonean rule.

Aristobulus I (104–103 B.C.). Aristobulus frustrated his father's plans of dividing power between his widow and Aristobulus by having his mother imprisoned and allowing her to starve to death. He also allowed one

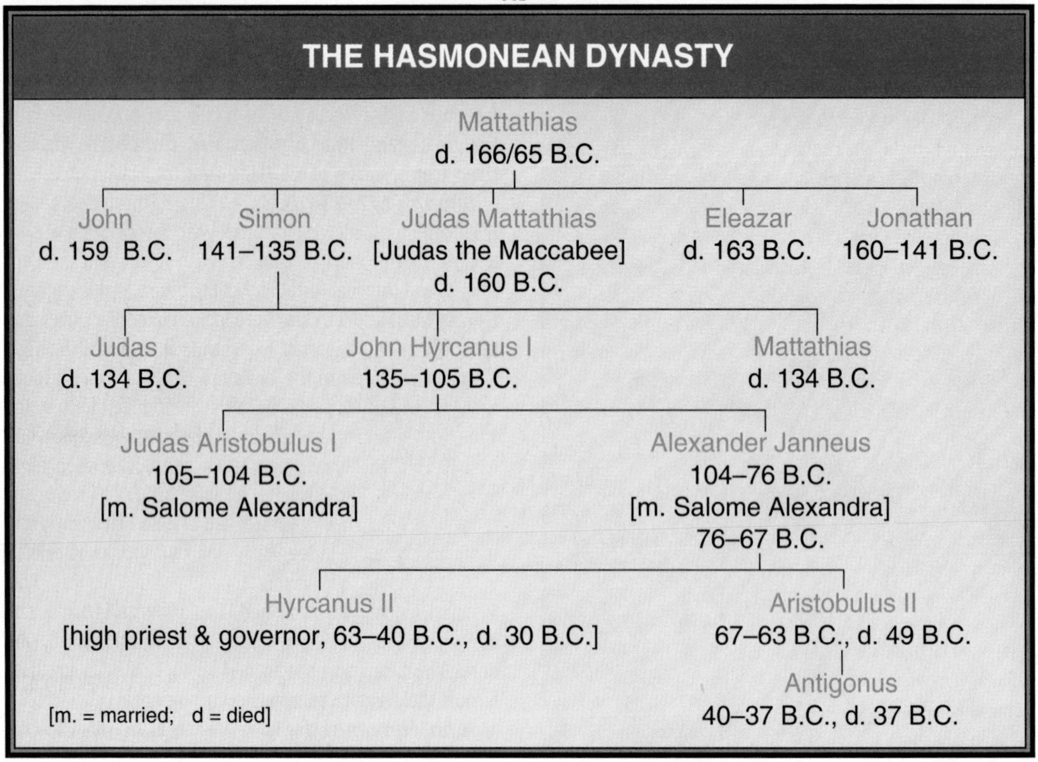

of his brothers to be killed. Within a year he himself had died, some say of grief; others suspect that his wife, Salome Alexandra, may have poisoned him.

Aristobulus was the first of the Hasmoneans to claim the title *king*, even though they were not from the lineage of David. The chief accomplishment of his reign was the extension of his power to Galilee and the Judaizing of its inhabitants by forced circumcision.

Alexander Jannaeus (103–76 B.C.). At the death of Aristobulus, his widow, Salome Alexandra, released his imprisoned brothers and married one of them, Alexander Jannaeus. The reign of Alexander Jannaeus marked the beginning of the end of the Hasmonean Dynasty.

Through continual military campaigns Alexander first suffered defeats at the hands of Ptolemy and Cleopatra III. However, he retained his territory and eventually extended it along the coast from Mount Carmel to Gaza. He also added the Decapolis to the territory controlled by Judea. His heavy-handed administration, however, resulted in a civil war with the Pharisees. It has been estimated that some fifty thousand Jews died in the war. At one point the Jewish people appealed to Demetrius III, the Seleucid descendant of Antiochus IV Epiphanes, for help in their fight against Alexander, the descendant of the Maccabees. At the conclusion of this war Alexander had eight hundred Pharisees crucified and executed their families in front of his dying victims.

Salome Alexandra (76–67 B.C.). At the death of Alexander, his widow, Salome Alexandra, the most powerful woman of the Hasmonean dynasty, reported that Alexander had instructed her to make peace with the Pharisees. She ruled in name, while the Pharisees were the real power behind the throne. To her credit she was able to put an end to reprisals and provide a period of relative peace and prosperity. Because she could not serve as high priest, she had her son Hyrcanus II (a Pharisee) appointed to this office. Aristobulus II (a Sadducee), another of her sons, was not so easily controlled by his mother. At the time of her death, he was raising an army.

Hyrcanus II and Aristobulus II (67–63 B.C.). The forces of the two brothers met near Jericho, and Hyrcanus was defeated. In defeat he found a skillful political ally, Antipater, the son of the governor of Idumea and himself an Idumean. Antipater crafted an alliance between Hyrcanus II and the Nabateans, which enabled Hyrcanus II to defeat his brother.

Overshadowing this provincial sibling rivalry was the

advance of Pompey and the power of Rome through Syria. Both brothers appealed to Pompey for his support, and a group of Jews (probably Pharisees) urged Pompey to put an end to the Hasmonean Dynasty. In 63 B.C. Pompey imposed Roman control over Judea, brought the Hasmonean Dynasty to an end, took Aristobulus II back to Rome as a prisoner, and left the weaker brother, Hyrcanus II, as his vassal high priest in Jerusalem.

While Hyrcanus was high priest, the real power in Judea was Antipater, an Idumean but the son of a Jewish mother. He rose in power by loyally supporting Rome at every turn, working first for Pompey, then for Julius Caesar. Although his political shrewdness worked to the advantage of Judea, the Sadducees and even many of the Pharisees hated him. For his loyalty, Julius Caesar named him procurator of Judea. Shortly before he was poisoned to death in 43 B.C., Antipater appointed his sons as governors: Phasel, governor of Judea; and Herod, governor of Galilee.

Herod the Great

The months following Antipater's death were filled with intrigue and revolt. Herod forcefully put down an insurrection in Galilee, winning Roman favor, an extension of his territory (adding Samaria and Coele-Syria), and the hatred of the Jews. Antigonus, one of the sons of Aristobulus, gained the support of the Parthians and took control of Judea. Phasel was killed. Hyrcanus II was captured, and his ears were cut off, thereby preventing him from ever serving as high priest again (Lev 21:17-23). Antigonus was appointed high priest and king of Judea by the Parthians. Herod fled to Petra, then to Egypt, and finally to Rome, where he was appointed king of Judea in 40 B.C.

Judea, however, was still controlled by Antigonus. With Roman support Herod invaded Judea, and by 37 B.C. he had captured Jerusalem and executed Antigonus. He also pursued the bandits who roamed Judea and Galilee and either exterminated them or drove them off.

Herod's rule is a story of tragic contrasts. He sought to win the favor of the Jews, but he was hated because he was an Idumean, an agent of Rome, and a replacement for the Hasmoneans. In response Herod married Mariamne, the granddaughter of Hyrcanus II. He appointed another Aristobulus, grandson of Hyrcanus II, as high priest, but Aristobulus III drowned shortly thereafter. Herod was blamed, but he was ruthless in defense of his power. By the time of his own death, he had ordered the deaths of everyone suspected of intrigue against him. This included Joseph, his uncle, brother-in-law, and trust-

Herod the Great's extensive building activities included this aqueduct at Caesarea Maritima that was part of an intricate water system built to bring water to the city from the distant mountains.

A view inside the Herodium, a magnificent fortress-palace built by Herod the Great about four miles from Bethlehem.

ed aide; Hyrcanus II; Mariamne, whose death grieved him terribly; two of his sons by Mariamne; and Antipater, his eldest son. Along with these family members, other descendants of the Hasmoneans, suspected leaders of the army, and zealous Jewish leaders were executed. The Gospel of Matthew's stories about Herod's efforts to kill the Christ child, though unsupported by nonbiblical sources, are entirely consistent with what we know of Herod's response to threats against his throne.

Herod was a great builder. He built fortresses throughout his territory: the Herodium, Masada, and Machaerus. He built the port at Caesarea, with its aqueduct to bring water from Mount Carmel, and rebuilt Samaria (Sebaste). He built palaces in Jerusalem and in Jericho. Most important, he built a grand, new temple in Jerusalem. The temple was begun in 20–19 B.C. but completed only in A.D. 64, shortly before its destruction in A.D. 70. The Jewish leaders had so little trust for Herod that they would only let him tear down the old temple in stages as it became necessary to clear space for the next section of the new temple. Neither did they call it the Herodian temple; the entire period is known as "Second Temple Judaism."

Herod died in 4 B.C. Before he died he made his sister, Salome, promise to execute a number of Jewish leaders at his death so that there would be mourning throughout the country. She did not carry out this order. Nevertheless, Herod's son Archelaus violently quelled the riots in Judea, and some three thousand died.

Tetrarchs, Procurators, and Kings

The unrest continued. Herod's will was not effective until it was ratified by the emperor. While the emperor debated what to do with Judea, another revolt broke out there. Varus, the Syrian governor, stamped out the revolt and crucified two thousand rebels. A Jewish delegation appealed to the emperor not to ratify Herod's will. In an apparent compromise, Augustus ratified the will, splitting Herod's territory among three of his sons; but he denied them the title king. Archelaus was made ethnarch of Judea, Idumea, and Samaria. Antipas and Philip were given the lesser rank of tetrarch. Antipas received Galilee and Perea, and Philip was given Batanea (northeast Galilee).

Archelaus (4 B.C.–A.D. 6). Archelaus is remembered as cruel, power hungry, and insensitive to the Jews. The reference to him in Matthew 2:22 is again credible in light of this reputation. So harsh was Archelaus that Augustus removed him from office when a delegation of Jews and Samaritans complained about him. Archelaus was banished to the Rhone valley.

Philip (4 B.C.–A.D. 34). Philip, in contrast, is remembered as a kindly, just, and peaceful ruler. He built Caesarea Philippi (Matt 16:13; Mark 8:27) and Bethsaida (John 1:44). Jesus occasionally withdrew to his territory, which was predominantly Gentile.

Antipas (4 B.C.–A.D. 39). Herod Antipas was the son who played the most important role in the events of the New Testament. Jesus called him "that fox" (Luke 13:32). He built his capital, Tiberias, on the shores of the Sea of Galilee. Because an ancient burial ground was unearthed during the construction of the city, no Jews would live in Tiberias (and it is never recorded that Jesus went there). Instead, it was populated by Gentiles.

On a trip to Rome, Herod Antipas fell in love with Herodias, the wife of Herod Philip. Antipas divorced his Nabatean wife. Herodias divorced Philip, married Herod Antipas, and brought Salome into his court. When Herod, struck by Salome's dancing, pledged to give her whatever she wanted, Herodias prompted Salome to ask for the head of John the Baptist. Josephus said that Herod arrested John the Baptist because he was a political threat and that Herod's defeats in battle with the Nabateans (who were outraged over his divorce from their princess) were God's judgment on him for executing John the Baptist.

Herod Antipas is mentioned in two other New Testament passages. He reportedly thought that Jesus was John the Baptist come back to life (Luke 9:7-9), and he refused to convict Him when Pilate sent Jesus to him (Luke 23:6-12).

When Agrippa I was made king of the area that once belonged to Philip, Herodias became jealous and urged her husband, Herod Antipas, to appeal to Caligula for the title king. Agrippa, however, had already reported charges against Herod Antipas. Instead of elevating Antipas, Caligula removed him, gave his territory to Agrippa, and banished him to Lyons.

The Early Procurators in Judea and Samaria (A.D. 6–41)

When Archelaus was removed from office, Judea and Samaria were placed under the rule of procurators who were responsible to the governor of Syria. Caesarea became the official residence of the procurators.

Under Coponius, procurator from A.D. 6–9, a census was ordered by Quirinius, legate of Syria. Remembering 2 Samuel 24, some Jews refused to take part in the census. A brief revolt was led by Judas of Galilee (compare Acts 5:37). Many scholars believe that this census is the one reported by Luke in connection with the birth of Jesus.

Coponius was succeeded by Ambibulus (A.D. 9–12), Rufus (A.D. 12–15), Valerius Gratus (A.D. 15–26), and then by Pontius Pilate (A.D. 26–36). Pilate is remembered as a harsh ruler, despised by the Jews. When he brought imperial shields bearing the image of Caesar into the holy city, the Jews were outraged. On another occasion he massacred Jews in the temple in Jerusalem. Finally, he was sent to Rome to appear before Tiberius after his soldiers killed a number of Samaritans who had gathered on Mount Gerizim.

The administrations of the procurators were generally heavy handed and harsh. Often they did not understand Jewish customs and sensitivities. The high priest's vestments were kept by the procurators so that they could control the celebrations of holy days in the temple. By Roman law the procurators could also impose the death penalty. Two less significant procurators followed Pontius Pilate: Marcellus (A.D. 36) and Marullus (A.D. 37–41).

At the death of Herod (4 B.C.) the power of appointment of the high priest passed first to his son Archelaus (4 B.C.–A.D.6), then to the Roman procurators in Judea (A.D. 6–41), then Agrippa I (A.D. 41–44), and finally to Agrippa II. Under the Herods high priests were appointed from the family of Boethus. The Roman procurators appointed high priests from the families of Annas (mentioned in the New Testament), Phiabi, and Camithus. Annas, his son-in-law Caiaphas, and three of his sons all served as high priest between A.D. 6 and 41.

Several of the high priests, notably Joazar, Annas, and Jonathan, retained considerable influence even after their terms in office. Hence the role of Annas in the trial of Jesus in the Gospel accounts seems entirely appropriate (see John 18:13,24).

Agrippa I (A.D. 37–44)

Agrippa was the grandson of Herod the Great, son of Aristobulus (who was killed in 7 B.C.), and the brother of Herodias (the wife of Herod Antipas). Raised in Rome, he received a Roman education and befriended Gaius, who later became Emperor Caligula. When his friend became the emperor, Agrippa was in debt and in prison. He was immediately rewarded for his friendship, released from prison, given a gold medallion, and appointed king of the territory that had been ruled by Herod Philip.

When Herod Antipas, encouraged by Herodias, appealed for the title king, Caligula removed him from office, banished him to Lyons, and added Galilee to the territory administered by Agrippa. In A.D. 41 Emperor Claudius added Judea, Idumea, and Samaria to Agrippa's vassal kingdom, thus unifying under his control the territories that had been ruled by Herod the Great. Agrippa was, if not genuinely pious, at least sensitive to the Jews and greatly appreciated by them (Acts 12:3). His death in A.D. 44 is described in similar terms by both Acts 12:21-23 and Josephus's *Antiquities*.

Following the death of Agrippa I, his territory was once again administered by procurators, each seemingly more insensitive, harsh, and greedy than his predecessor. The *sicarii*, or dagger men, assassinated their opponents in Jerusalem, and the whole area degenerated into anarchy.

Fadus quickly put down the revolt of Theudas the Galilean (compare Acts 5:36). Famine plagued Judea during the rule of Tiberius Alexander (Acts 11:28-30). A violent outbreak in the temple resulted in the deaths of twenty to thirty thousand people during the administration of Cumanus, who was eventually removed from office for accepting a bribe. Bribery, mismanagement, and incompetence only increased under his successors.

Felix took strong measures against the Zealots. He caught Eleazar, a Zealot leader, and sent him to Rome. He also held Paul in prison for two years in Caesarea. When Festus assumed office, he sent for Agrippa II and Bernice to help him adjudicate Paul's case. At the death of Festus (A.D. 62), Ananus, the high priest, had James, the brother of Jesus, killed. The last two procurators were the worst of the bunch. War became inevitable.

Agrippa II, the seventeen-year-old son of Agrippa I, was made king of Chalcis in A.D. 50. In A.D. 53 he exchanged his territory for the former tetrarchy of Philip, and he was given the right of appointing the Jewish high priests. Galilee and Perea were later added to his kingdom.

Bernice was widowed by the death of Herod of Chalcis in A.D. 48 and moved in with her brother, Agrippa.

When the scandal of their relationship became public, she arranged a marriage with King Polemon of Cilicia, but it did not last. She resumed her relationship with Agrippa II. She then had a love affair with the Roman general Titus that continued in Rome after the Jewish war of A.D. 66–70. Titus spurned her when the public protested and had nothing to do with her after he became emperor. After the war Agrippa II moved to Rome also, where he died sometime after A.D. 93.

The War of A.D. 66–70

Matters finally came to a head in A.D. 66. The war was the result of anti-Roman sentiment fueled by the incompetent and greedy procurators, growing anarchy, and factionalism among the Jews. The last straw in these developments was Florus's plundering the temple treasury in Jerusalem. Pilate had done the same, but this time the Jews rebelled. They ceased to offer sacrifices on behalf of Caesar. Zealots took the fortress at Masada and then drove the Romans out of Jerusalem. Anarchy prevailed as Jews and Gentiles massacred each other in the towns and villages.

Josephus was sent to Galilee to prepare for the defense against the Romans there. When Vespasian seized the town of Jotapata in A.D. 67, Josephus escaped and then defected to the Romans. John of Gischala, another Zealot leader, escaped to Jerusalem. By A.D. 68 Vespasian was ready to attack Jerusalem. Then Nero committed suicide, and Vespasian delayed the siege. Within the city various groups—Zealots; sicarii; John of Gischala; Simon, son of Gioras; and the Idumeans—fought among themselves. Eventually Vespasian was appointed emperor and returned to Rome, leaving the prosecution of the war in the hands of his son, Titus.

Titus brutally sacked Jerusalem and burned the temple in A.D. 70. Mopping up operations followed at the Herodium, Machaerus, and finally at Masada. When the ramp at Masada was completed and the wall was breached, the Romans found only two women and five children alive. All the rest had chosen death over defeat.

As a result of this costly revolt, Roman deference toward Judaism ceased. Temple worship was terminated, pagan worship was established in Jerusalem, and the temple tax had to be paid to the god Jupiter. Significant changes among the Jews also occurred. The Sadducees, Zealots, and Essenes lost their identity, and the Pharisees became the dominant group.

After the war Johanan ben Zakkai, a student of Hillel, assembled a group of Pharisaic leaders at Jamnia. There they continued to teach Pharisaic traditions. Johanan was succeeded by Gamaliel II. Under his leadership the Pharisees determined the boundaries of the Hebrew Scriptures (the Old Testament) and established the prescribed daily prayers. Synagogues flourished in Jewish communities, and the separation of Christians from Judaism became final at about this time.

The Bar Kochba Revolt (A.D. 132–135)

A final revolt broke out in A.D. 132. Rabbi Akiba proclaimed Simon bar Kochba as the fulfillment of the messianic prophecy in Numbers 24:17-18. Simon won early victories against the Romans in Judea and minted his own coins. The extent of the hellenization of Judea is illustrated by the fact that recently discovered letters of Simon to his officers are written in Greek. Hadrian's troops eventually retook Judea at great cost to the Romans but even greater cost to the Jews. The death toll has been estimated at 985,000. The final battle took place at Bethar, and both Simon and Akiba were killed.

The result of the revolt was equally devastating. Jews were forbidden to enter into Jerusalem. Circumcision was forbidden, as was Sabbath observance and the reading of the Scriptures in Judea. The Jews were dispersed throughout the Roman world; but they survived as a people without a land, held together only by their faith, their Scriptures, and the synagogue.

Sources for Additional Study

Bickerman, Elias. *From Ezra to the Last of the Maccabees: Foundations of Postbiblical Judaism*. New York: Schocken, 1962.

Cate, Robert L. *A History of the Bible Lands in the Interbiblical Period*. Nashville: Broadman, 1989.

Foerster, W. *From the Exile to Christ: A Historical Introduction to Palestinian Judaism*. Philadelphia: Fortress, 1964.

Reicke, Bo. *The New Testament Era: The World of the Bible from 500 B.C. to A.D. 100*. Philadelphia: Fortress, 1968.

Rhoads, David M. *Israel in Revolution: 6–74 C.E.: A Political History Based on the Writings of Josephus*. Philadelphia: Fortress, 1976.

Schürer, Emil. *The History of the Jewish People in the Age of Jesus Christ (175 B.C.–A.D. 135)*. Edinburgh: T & T Clark, 1986.

Welles, C. Bradford. *Alexander and the Hellenistic World*. Toronto: A. M. Hakkert, 1970.

JEWISH INSTITUTIONS, GROUPS, MOVEMENTS

In the midst of the turbulent events of the intertestamental period, institutions, groups, beliefs, and sentiments developed that were to affect both classical Judaism and early Christianity. Josephus characterized the Jewish groups as four philosophies: Pharisees, Sadducees, Essenes, and Zealots. In addition to these groups, the priests and chief priests played an influential role in both religious and political matters. Jewish institutional life in this period centered variously around the temple, the Sanhedrin, and the synagogues. Each of these groups and institutions is treated individually below.

The Pharisees

The *Hasidim* (Hasideans, RSV) mentioned in 1 Maccabees 2:42; 7:13; and 2 Maccabees 14:6 probably included the forerunners of the Pharisees. On the other hand, we know virtually nothing about the diversity or similarity of the *Hasidim* or about their later history.

For our knowledge of the Pharisees we are dependent on Josephus, the New Testament, and later rabbinic sources. According to Josephus, the Pharisees were a politically active group that emerged as a party under John Hyrcanus I (135–104 B.C.). According to the Gospels, the Pharisees were a strict, legalistic group whom Jesus labeled as hypocrites. Acts presents the Pharisees as sympathetic to the Christian witness to the resurrection (5:34-39; 23:6-9). According to the Mishnah and the Talmud, the Pharisees were the scholars and sages of Judaism who devoted their entire lives to living according to the dictates of the Torah. Moreover, it is difficult to determine how much of the oral tradition collected in the Mishnah can be traced back to the early part of the first century. The problem, therefore, is to determine how to use these various sources in constructing our understanding of the Pharisees.

At least this much seems clear. The Pharisees were a lay group—not priests. They maintained their purity by close observance of the law. The Pharisees sought to universalize their adherence to the law through education in the synagogues and school, and at times by means of their political power.

The Pharisees accepted the oral tradition about the interpretation of the law (compare Matt 5:21; Mark 7:3-13). The oral tradition preserved the judgments of the sages regarding how the law should be applied to every aspect of daily life. The sages said three things: "Be deliberate in judgment, raise up many disciples, and make a fence around the law." The oral tradition served, therefore, as "a hedge about the law" so that no one would violate the law in ignorance. The Pharisees also believed in angels and in resurrection (see Acts 23:6-8).

Whereas the Pharisees were politically active during the period of the Hasmoneans, it appears that they shifted their attention from political matters increasingly toward concern with table fellowship, matters of tithing, agricultural laws, and purity under the influence of Hillel (about the time of Jesus' birth). Hillel, who favored a more lenient, freer interpretation of Scripture was frequently opposed by his contemporary, Shammai, who favored a stricter, less tolerant interpretation. According to rabbinic tradition a non-Jew once asked Hillel to teach him the whole law while the Gentile stood on one foot. Hillel responded: "What is hateful to you do not do to your neighbor; that is the whole Torah; the rest is commentary." The early Pharisees also taught that "by three things is the world sustained: by the Law, by the [Temple-]service, and by deeds of loving-kindness."

At the heart of Pharisaism were the *chaburot*, religious associations that maintained ritual purity, observed the oral traditions, ministered to the needs of the synagogue, and probably maintained an interest in charity. The school of Shammai required a period of probation for a full year, while the school of Hillel required a candidate for membership to demonstrate that he could maintain ritual purity for thirty days. After this probationary period, the new member took an oath before a leader of the *chaburah*, generally a scribe, pledging to maintain purity in all matters and to tithe.

In addition to its internal organization and codes of conduct, which provided for expulsion in certain circumstances, the *chaburot* had assemblies and common meals, which were probably held on Friday evening at the beginning of the Sabbath. The Pharisees also distinguished themselves by observing regular prayer times and reciting the Shema (the central confession of Judaism consisting of Deut 6:4-9; 11:13-21; Num 15:37-41) morning and evening.

Following the destruction of the temple in A.D. 70, Pharisaism emerged as the dominant party in Judaism, and the school of Hillel emerged as the dominant school within Pharisaism. It is anachronistic, therefore, to view Judaism in the first part of the first century solely in terms of the teaching of the later rabbis. First-century Judaism was much more diverse, with various groups, practices, and ideals competing with one another for survival and influence.

The Sadducees

The name of this group goes back to Zadok, David's priest (2 Sam 15:24-37). The Zadokites were the ruling priests in Jerusalem from the time of Solomon on. They were linked with Simon II and Onias III, as the legitimate priestly line at the outbreak of the Maccabean revolt. The Zadokites opposed the hellenizing reformers in Jerusalem. There may therefore have been some connection between the Zadokites and the *Hasidim* also. On the other hand, the Zadokites are probably not to be connected directly with the later temple priests, since they seem never to have made peace with the Jerusalem priesthood. At least some of the Zadokite priests left Jerusalem and established the Essene community at Qumran.

The primary difficulty in understanding the Sadducees is that they left no literature. We know the Sadducees only through what the New Testament and the rabbinic (Pharisaic) sources tell us. In the Pharisaic literature "Sadducee" could be used as one who deviated from the Pharisaic norm, so it is difficult to determine what principles they advocated.

Josephus first mentioned the Sadducees during the time of John Hyrcanus. One faction of the Sadducees supported the Hasmoneans and resumed control of the temple cult. The Pharisees and Sadducees represented two different ways Jews responded to the pressure of Hellenism—the adoption of Greek culture. The Sadducees, who were generally aristocrats, had accommodated themselves to a degree of Hellenistic influence. They carefully guarded the prosperity they enjoyed from commerce with the Gentile world. They were religiously conservative in that they supported the temple and the priesthood and held to the traditional faith of the Hebrew Scriptures. They accepted only the Pentateuch as Scripture, but not the Prophets or Writings. They regarded the more recent rulings the Pharisees applied to the Torah as ill-founded, repressive, contrary to the authority of the written law, and contrary to the best interests of the people and the nation. Neither did they believe in angels or in resurrection.

According to Josephus, the Pharisees and the Sadducees also differed over divine providence and human free will. The Pharisees combined various emphases in Scripture to affirm that everything happened according to God's providence but that humanity is free. Therefore God cooperates with humanity in both good and bad. While not denying human freedom and responsibility, the Essenes went further in affirming that God's providence controlled and determined everything; one's destiny and share in the spirits of truth and perversity were foreordained.

The Sadducees—according to Josephus's presentation of Jewish beliefs, which he explained in Hellenistic terms to a Roman audience—solved the problem of God's participation in evil by making evil entirely a matter of human choice. The Sadducees "deny destiny wholly and entirely and place God beyond the possibility of doing and planning evil. They say that good and evil are man's choice and that the doing of the one or the other is according to his discretion."

The Essenes

The Essenes were a sectarian priestly group who withdrew to the desert to study the law and thereby prepare the way for the Lord. The community center at Qumran was established about 130 B.C. under the leadership of the teacher of righteousness. Not all Essenes lived at Qumran, however. The Damascus Document and Josephus refer to Essenes who lived in camps and villages.

Building on the conclusion that the Essenes wrote the scrolls discovered at Qumran, most of what we know about the Essenes comes from the scrolls. They tell us that the Essenes practiced strict ritual purity with periodic washings. The Essenes practiced continual worship, marked by constant study of Scripture, prayers, and praise. There was a hierarchy of leadership and a council. Each member of the community had his own rank.

The Essenes accepted a solar calendar, so their feast days fell on different days from those of the "corrupt" priesthood at the temple in Jerusalem. They also held a sacred community meal. The Manual of Discipline shows that the Essenes expected three end-time figures: the prophet, the messiah of Aaron, and the messiah of Israel. The messiah of Aaron was the priestly messiah, who would take precedence over the royal messiah, the messiah of Israel. The royal messiah would lead the people to victory over the Gentiles, while the priestly messiah would be the final interpreter of the law.

Under the leadership of the teacher of righteousness,

the Essenes wrote the first commentaries on the Scriptures (commentaries on Habakkuk; Nahum; and Ps 37). In these they declared that revelation was a two-stage process: mystery (*raz*) and interpretation (*pesher*). The prophets did not understand the full meaning of what they recorded. Indeed, the writings of the prophets spoke of the Teacher of Righteousness and the early history of the Essenes. This meaning was revealed to the Teacher of Righteousness and the community. This approach to the Hebrew Scriptures is also strikingly parallel to the interpretation of the Old Testament in the New. The early Christians interpreted the Scriptures as having been fulfilled in the coming of Jesus and the early history of the church.

The settlement at Qumran was destroyed in A.D. 68, probably by the tenth Roman legion. We do not know what happened to the Essenes after the destruction of Qumran. Some may have joined the Zealots at Masada. Others were absorbed into Jewish society. Some probably became Christians, but this can be surmised only by parallels to the scrolls in the early Christian writings.

The Zealots

Josephus called the Zealots the "fourth philosophy." The Pharisees, Sadducees, and Essenes were identified as the first three. "Zealot" seems to have been a label that could have been pinned on anyone who advocated violent revolt against Roman oppression.

Judas the Galilean led a revolt in Galilee in A.D. 6. Yet although Judas has been regarded by many as the founder of the Zealot party, it is debatable whether there was actually a party of Zealots between A.D. 6 and the events leading to the Jewish War. During the period of A.D. 6 to 44, a period of relative tranquility, there were only sporadic outbursts against Roman excesses.

Thereafter, passive resistance ceased, and there was a breakdown of law and order in the countryside. The numbers of both sicarii ("dagger men") and prophets predicting God's dramatic intervention in the Jews' struggle against Rome increased.

Zeal for the law and the traditions of Israel characterized many groups. During most of the first century, therefore, not all Zealots were revolutionaries, and not all revolutionaries were Zealots. Josephus named five revolutionary groups and described their roles during the war: the Sicarii; John of Gischala and his adherents; Simon, son of Gioras, and his followers; the Idumeans; and the Zealots. The Zealot party that was active during the war of A.D. 66–70 was composed of lower-class priests and laymen in Jerusalem. Its foremost achievement was overthrowing the provisional government that had been established in Jerusalem.

The Priests and Chief Priests

The priests were vital to the life of the Jewish people. They alone could perform the ceremonies and sacrifices on which the welfare of the people depended. The priests sprinkled blood on the altar and made atonement for sin. The zenith of the priesthood in Israel was reached during the Hellenistic period, when the priest was not only the religious leader but the prince, the political leader, who spoke for the people. He was the link between "native altar and alien throne." A council of elders, the *gerousia* (or Sanhedrin), assisted him in legislative and judicial functions.

Until 175 B.C. the high priesthood was hereditary, and the office was held for life. In that year the rightful high priest, Onias III, was deposed by the Seleucid king, Antiochus Epiphanes. Leading families in Jerusalem supported the more progressive Jason, who promised the king loyalty and great sums of money if he would declare Jerusalem a Greek *polis* and permit him to erect a gymnasium. Within three years Jason was deposed and succeeded by Menelaus, who profaned the sacred vessels in the temple and arranged the murder of Onias III. Shortly thereafter the Maccabees led a revolt against the Seleucids and their supporters in Galilee and Judea.

The last of the pro-Seleucid high priests was Alcimus, who died in 159 B.C. The high priesthood apparently remained vacant for several years. In one of the ironies of history, Jonathan, one of the Maccabean brothers, accepted a Seleucid appointment to the office of high priest in 153 or 152. His brother Simon and his descendants held the joint office of high priest and prince of the Jewish people until 63 B.C. They held the high priesthood until Herod the Great gained control of Jerusalem in A.D. 37.

The priests were responsible for the worship and sacrifices in the temple. The legitimacy of the priestly families was established by their genealogies. Priests were expected to marry only the daughters of other priests. Rank was a matter of pride.

The high priest's duties were largely ceremonial. He was to officiate at the festivals and insure purity. Before taking office, the high priest was examined by the Sanhedrin. The ceremony of consecration involved a bath for purification, putting on the sacred vestments, anointing with oil, further sacrifices and ceremonies, and the laying of portions of the sacrifices on the hands of the priest (Exod 29; Lev 8). The whole ceremony took seven days.

Under Herod (40–4 B.C.) the Hasmonean (Maccabean) control was broken. The high priesthood became an annual appointment, with the high priest being chosen

JEWISH SECTS IN THE NEW TESTAMENT

DATES OF EXISTENCE	NAME	ORIGIN	SEGMENTS OF SOCIETY	BELIEFS	SELECTED BIBLICAL REFERENCES	ACTIVITIES
PHARISEES						
Existed under Jonathan (160–143 B.C.) Declined in power under John Hyrcanus (134–104 B.C.) Began resurgence under Salome Alexandra (76 B.C.)	Pharisees = "the Separated Ones" with three possible meanings: (1) to their separating themselves *from* people (2) to their separating themselves *to* the study of the law ("dividing" or "separating" the truth) (3) to their separating themselves *from* pagan practices	Probably spiritual descendants of the Hasidim (religious freedom fighters of the time of Judas Maccabeus)	Most numerous of the Jewish parties (or sects) Probably descendants of the Hasidim—scribes and lawyers Members of the middle class—mostly businessmen (merchants and tradesmen)	Monotheistic Viewed entirety of the Old Testament (Torah, Prophets, and Writings) as authoritative Believed that the study of the law was true worship Accepted both the written and oral law More liberal in interpreting the law than were the Sadducees Quite concerned with the proper keeping of the Sabbath, tithing, and purification rituals Believed in life after death and the resurrection of the body (with divine retribution and reward) Believed in the reality of demons and angels Revered humanity and human equality Missionary-minded regarding the conversion of Gentiles Believed that individuals were responsible for how they lived	Matt 3:7-10; 5:20; 9:14; 16:1,6-12; 22:15-22,34-46; 23:2-36 Mark 3:6; 7:3–5; 8:15; 12:13-17 Luke 6:7; 7:36-39; 11:37-44; 18:9-14 John 3:1; 9:13-16; 11:46-47; 12:19 Acts 23:6-10 Phil 3:4b-6	Developers of oral tradition Taught that the way to God was through odedience to the law Changed Judaism from a religion of sacrifice to a religion of law Progressive thinkers regarding the adaptation of the law to situations Opposed Jesus because He would not accept the teachings of the oral law as binding Established and controlled synagogues Exercised great control over general population Served as religious authorities for most Jews Took several ceremonies from the temple to the home Emphasized ethical as opposed to theological action Legalistic and socially exclusive (shunned non-Pharisees as unclean) Tended to have a self-sufficient and haughty attitude
SADDUCEES						
Probably began about 200 B.C. Demise occured in A.D. 70 (with the destruction of the temple)	Sadducees = Three possible translations: (1) "the Righteous Ones"—based on the Hebrew consonants for the word *righteous* (2) "ones who sympathize with Zadok," or "Zadokites"—based on their possible link to Zadok the high priest (3) "syndics," "judges," or "fiscal controllers"—based on the Greek word *syndikoi*	Unknown origin Claimed to be descendants of Zadok—high priest under David (see 2 Sam 8:17; 15:24) and Solomon (see 1 Kgs 1:34-35; 1 Chr 12:28) Had a possible link to Aaron Were probably formed into a group about 200 B.C. as the high priest's party	Aristocracy—the rich descendants of the high-priestly line (however, not all priest were Sadducees) Possible descendants of the Hasmonean priesthood Probably not as refined as their economic position in life would suggest	Accepted only the Torah (Genesis through Deuternonomy—the written law of Moses) as authoritative Practiced literal interpretation of the law Rigidly conservative toward the law Stressed strict observance of the law Observed past beliefs and tradition Opposed oral law as obligatory or binding Believed in the absolute freedom of human will—that people could do as they wished without attention from God Denied divine providence Denied the concept of life after death and the resurrection of the body Denied the concept of reward and punishment after death Denied the existence of angels and demons Materialistic	2 Sam 8:17; 15:24 1 Kgs 1:34 1 Chr 12:26-28 Ezek 40:45-46; 43:19; 44:15-16 Matt 3:7-10; 16:1,6-12; 22:23-34 Mark 12:18-27 Luke 20:27-40 John 11:47 Acts 4:1-2; 5:17-18; 23:6-10	In charge of the temple and its services Politically active Exercised great political control through the Sanhedrin, of which many were members Supported the ruling power and the status quo Leaned toward Hellenism (the spreading of Greek influence)—and were thus despised by the Jewish populace Opposed both the Pharisees and Jesus because these lived by a larger canon (The Pharisees and Jesus both considered more than only Genesis through Deuteronomy as authoritative.) Opposed Jesus specifically for fear their wealth/position would be threatened if they supported Him

DATES OF EXISTENCE	NAME	ORIGIN	SEGMENTS OF SOCIETY	BELIEFS	SELECTED BIBLICAL REFERENCES	ACTIVITIES
ZEALOTS						
Three possibilities for their beginning (1) during the reign of Herod the Great (about 37 B.C.) (2) during the revolt against Rome (A.D. 6) (3) traced back to the Hassidim or the Maccabees (about 168 B.C.) Their certain demise occured around A.D. 70–73 with Rome's conquering of Jerusalem.	Refers to their religious zeal Josephus used the term in referring to those involved in the Jewish revolt against Rome in A.D. 6—led by Judas of Galilee	(According to Josephus) The Zealots began with Judas (the Galilean), son of Ezekias, who led a revolt in A.D. 6 because of a census done for tax purposes	The extreme wing of the Pharisees	Similar to the Pharisees with this exception: believed strongly that only God had the right to rule over the Jews. Patriotism and religion became inseparable. Believed that total obedience (supported by drastic physical measures) must be apparent before God would bring in the Messianic Age Were fanatical in their Jewish faith and in their devotion to the law—to the point of martyrdom	Matt 10:4 Mark 3:18 Luke 6:15 Acts 1:13	Extremely opposed to Roman rule over Palestine Extremely opposed to peace with Rome Refused to pay taxes Demonstrated against the use of the Greek language in Palestine Engaged in terrorism against Rome and others with whom they disagreed politically (Sicarii [or Assassins] were an extremist Zealot group who carried out acts of terrorism against Rome.)
HERODIANS						
Existed during the time of the Herodian dynasty (which began with Herod the Great in 37 B.C.) Uncertain demise	Based on their support of the Herodian rulers (Herod the Great or his dynasty)	Exact origin uncertain	Wealthy, politically influential Jews who supported Herod Antipas (or any descendant of Herod the Great) as ruler over Palestine (Judea and Samaria were under Roman governors at this time.)	Not a religious group—but a political one Membership probably was comprised of representatives of varied theological perspectives	Matt 22:5-22 Mark 3:6; 8:15; 12:13-17	Supported Herod and the Herodian dynasty Accepted Hellenization Accepted foreign rule
ESSENES						
Probably began during Maccabean times (about 168 B.C.)—around the same time as the Pharisees and the Sadducees began to form Uncertain demise—possibly an A.D. 68–70 with the collapse of Jerusalem	Unknown origin	Possibly developed as a reaction to the corrupt Sadducean priesthood Have been identified with various groups: Hasidim, Zealots, Greek influence, or Iranian influence	Scattered throughout the villages of Judea (possibly including the community of Qumran) (According to Philo and Josephus) About 4,000 in Palestinian Syria	Very strict ascetics Monastic: most took vow of celibacy (adopting male children in order to perpetuate the group), but some did marry (for the purpose of procreation) Rigidly adherent to the law (including a strict rendering of the ethical teachings) Considered other literature as authoritative (in addition to the Hebrew Scripture) Believed and lived as pacifists Rejected temple worship and temple offerings as corrupted Believed in the immortality of the soul with no bodily resurrection Apocalyptically oriented	None	Devoted to the copying and studying of the the manuscripts of the law Lived in a community sense with communal property Required a long probationary period and ritual baptisms of those wishing to join Were highly virtuous and righteous Were extremely self-disciplined Were diligent manual laborers Gave great importance to daily worship Upheld rigid Sabbath laws Maintained a non-Levitical priesthood Rejected worldly pleasures as evil Rejected matrimony—but did not forbid others to marry

from among the leading families of Jerusalem.

The high priest continued to exercise leadership over the Sanhedrin and to officiate in the temple on certain occasions. In particular, the high priest presided over the sin offerings on the Day of Atonement, when he entered the holy of holies to secure atonement for the people of Israel. On that day the high priest had to be in a state of absolute purity, so in the first century steps were taken to eliminate any possibility of defilement. The high priest took up residence in a room in the temple during the week before the Day of Atonement. This practice may have been instituted following the defilement of Simon, son of Camithus, in A.D. 20. On the evening before the Day of Atonement, Simon was touched by an Arab's spittle. He therefore was prevented from officiating at the ceremonies. In addition, the high priest was kept awake all night before the Day of Atonement to prevent defilement from a nocturnal discharge (Lev 22:4).

At the death of Herod (4 B.C.) the power of appointment of the high priest passed first to his son Archelaus (4 B.C.–A.D. 6), then to the Roman procurators in Judea (6–41), then to Agrippa I (41–44), and finally to Agrippa II. Under the Herods, high priests were appointed from the family of Boethus. The Roman procurators appointed high priests from the families of Annas (mentioned in the New Testament), Phiabi, and Camithus. Annas, his son-in-law Caiaphas, and three of his sons all served as high priest between A.D. 6 and 41.

Several of the high priests—notably Joazar, Annas, and Jonathan—retained considerable influence even after their term in office. Hence the role of Annas in the trial of Jesus in the Gospel accounts seems entirely appropriate (see John 18:13,24).

The plural "chief priests" occurs frequently in the Gospels and Acts and twice in Hebrews. This term seems to refer to those priests who had prominent positions of responsibility over other priests. Some scholars contend, however, that it designates the high priest, former high priests, and members of the aristocratic families from which the high priests were selected (Acts 4:6). Priests from such families, however, were no doubt given positions of influence.

The captain of the temple, who was responsible for oversight of the temple ceremonies, was the head of the chief priests, who included the leaders of the weekly and daily courses of priests and the temple treasurers.

From such a holy heritage and such an exalted position of religious and political influence, the office of the high priest fell to dismal corruption. In the years before the war of 66–70 the high priest surrounded himself by gangs of ruffians who terrorized the city and seized the tithes that belonged to the ordinary priests. The high priestly families also sent their gangs against each other. Mercifully, the power of such high priests ended with the destruction of the temple in A.D. 70.

The priests were organized into twenty-four weekly courses, each of four to nine daily courses. The Levites stood in lower rank to the priests and took no part in offering the sacrifices. The singers and musicians, however, were the upper strata of the Levites and had to have proof of pure descent. Other Levites served as temple servants and guards.

The Temple

The temple was the spiritual center of Judaism. The first temple was built between about 960 and 953 B.C. by Solomon. After the destruction of this temple by the Babylonians, the second temple, Zerubbabel's temple, was built on the same site between 520 and 515; but his temple was not as splendid as its predecessor.

As part of his efforts to gain favor with the Jews and impress the Romans with the importance of Judea, Herod the Great began construction of a magnificent new temple in 20/19 B.C. The temple was built on a massive platform with a circumference of 3,400 feet (which was later extended to the present circumference of 5,000 feet). John 2:20 says that at the beginning of Jesus' ministry the temple had been under construction for forty-six years. It was not completed until the time of Albinus (A.D. 62–64). An army of laborers had been involved in the construction; Josephus reported that there were ten thousand lay workers and a thousand priests. The temple towered over the holy city, and its beauty was dazzling (compare Mark 13:1).

The Golden Gate was the main entrance to the temple from the east. It led directly into the court of the Gentiles, a large open area surrounded by colonnaded walls. At the center of the temple area on the west side, one passed through the Beautiful Gate (Acts 3:2) into the court of the women. No Gentile could enter through the Beautiful Gate (compare Acts 21:28-29). In each corner of the court of the women were small courtlike chambers: the chambers of the wood, of the Nazirites, of the

Reconstruction of Herod's Temple (20 B.C.–A.D. 70) at Jerusalem as viewed from the southwest and from the upper city. The drawing reflects data from archaeological discoveries made since excavations began in 1967 at the southwest corner and along the south end of the temple mount platform. Shown are Wilson's Arch (left center) spanning the Tyropeon Valley, Robinson's Arch and staircase leading up from the lower city, and the now-famous Herodian monumental staircase also leading up to the Double (Huldah) Gate along the south facade.

oil, and the chamber for the purification of the lepers. Ascending fifteen curved steps, one entered through the great bronze doors of the Nicanor Gate into the court of the Israelites.

Only priests were allowed beyond the court of the Israelites to the area of the great altar, the porch, and the sanctuary. The marble facade of the sanctuary was 165 feet high and 165 feet wide. Two columns of reddish marble represented the two columns that had stood in front of Solomon's temple. The entire structure was ornately gilded so that it gleamed in the sun. Inside the sanctuary the priests burned incense (Luke 1:8-11). Once a year, on the Day of Atonement, the high priest entered the holy of holies.

Jesus foresaw the destruction of the temple (Mark 13:2); and in A.D. 70, only a few years after its completion, Herod's temple was destroyed. So much gold was carried off from the destruction of the temple that Josephus said that the gold market throughout Syria was glutted: "The standard of gold was depreciated to half its former value."

The Sanhedrin

The Sanhedrin is mentioned in the Gospels and Acts as a judicial body in Jerusalem. Jesus, Paul, and some of the apostles were brought before the Sanhedrin. The New Testament also mentions sanhedrins elsewhere ("local councils," Matt 10:17; Mark 13:9). The evidence is conflicting, leading scholars to debate whether the Sanhedrin was composed of political leaders, religious leaders, or both. The Mishnah contains a tractate called *Sanhedrin* that speaks of a great Sanhedrin in Jerusalem composed of seventy-one members and presided over by the high priest. The composition and powers of the Sanhedrin changed with the appointment of a procurator in A.D. 6 and again in A.D. 70 in the aftermath of the war. With some variation in the balance of power in different periods, the Sanhedrin was composed of the chief priests, the elders, Sadducees, and Pharisees. Successively, the Hasmoneans, Herods, and procurators controlled and limited the powers of the Sanhedrin. The prerogative of the Sanhedrin to hear capital punishment cases during the time of Pilate is debated, though there are references to several executions during the period between A.D. 6 and 70.

There were also lesser councils of twenty-three members and courts of three. The Mishnah instructs that every town that had 120 males should have a court of twenty-three.

The Synagogue

The synagogue had more influence than any other Jewish institution. It enabled Judaism to survive the destruction of the wars of A.D. 66–70 and 132–135. It provided Jewish communities with a center for worship and learning, and it left its mark on Christianity and Islam. A synagogue was also called a house of prayer or a house of study. The origin of the synagogue is disputed. The earliest archaeological evidence comes from Egypt in the third century B.C. The oldest evidence of a Palestinian synagogue is from the first Christian century, but no Galilean synagogue structure survives from that time.

A view of the reconstructed walls of the Jewish synagogue in the ancient city of Sardis (in modern Turkey).

The theories for the origin of the synagogue have been as follows:

1. Preexilic. The synagogue developed from the schools of the prophets. This view is now generally dismissed.

2. Exilic. The exile would have been a natural climate in which the synagogue might develop. How did the pious Jews continue their worship? Perhaps they met first in their homes during the exile.

3. Postexilic. Ezra introduced the Torah to Judea. It was read publicly and interpreted for the people in Aramaic, which may have led to regular gatherings for worship and study of Torah.

4. Maccabean. The archeological evidence from

Egypt now excludes such a late date. The choice is between the exilic and postexilic positions. The issue is how far back the synagogue can be traced and where it originated. By the first century, however, the synagogue was so well established that it could be found everywhere there were Jews. Paul went first to the synagogues in each of the towns he visited.

The later synagogues, about which we have more information, contained several items of furniture. The Torah was kept in an ark or chest that was screened from the sight of the congregation. A bema or raised platform was used for the reading of Scripture (see Neh 8:4-5). Matthew 23:2 speaks of "Moses' seat," which may have been a seat of honor or the seat where the reader of the Torah would sit. One stood to read or pray and sat down to teach. The synagogues usually contained stone benches around the walls. The congregation stood or sat on mats. It is sometimes said that women were separated from the men and only allowed in their galleries, but the evidence is quite unclear. What is clear is that women played a prominent role in the Hellenistic Jewish synagogues. The menorah was a favorite gift one could make to the synagogue, as rabbinic sources of the second and third centuries indicate.

The head of the synagogue was the *archisynagogos* (compare Acts 13:15). The office seems to have been an elective one, perhaps for a term of one year, though in some instances the head of the synagogue could be elected for life. The head of the synagogue presided in the assemblies and probably later became responsible for the synagogue building and was the head of the council of the community.

The *hazzan* was the assistant. He took the Torah scroll and gave it to whoever was reading. He also announced the advent of the Sabbath and the festivals from the roof of the synagogue.

Although we do not know exactly what transpired in a Jewish synagogue, the following seem to have been elements in the worship there:

1. The Shema, which eventually included Deuteronomy 6:4-9; 11:13-21; Numbers 15:37-41, was recited in Hebrew each morning and each evening (compare Mark 12:29-30).

2. The Decalogue. Although the recitation of the Decalogue was part of synagogue worship in the first century, it was later omitted. Both the Babylonian and the Palestinian Talmuds tell the story of its disappearance from the daily service because of "the fault finding of the heretics" who said that only the Decalogue and not the Shema was given to Moses at Mount Sinai.

3. The Eighteen Benedictions were recited every morning, afternoon, and evening. The prayer was prescribed, but the wording was not always fixed. In the synagogue the congregation responded with "Amen" after each blessing. Probably as a result of the influence of these prayers, the early Christians took over the practice of praying three times daily (compare Acts 2:15; 3:1; 10:9; Didache 8.3).

4. The Scripture lesson was the central feature of synagogue worship. As early as Ezra (Neh 8) we hear of the public reading of Scripture followed by a translation into Aramaic. Any member of the synagogue could be called on to read, though in practice the *hazzan* may have read most of the time. At first the passages were selected freely. Then the readers were prohibited from skipping from place to place. Ultimately the Torah was divided into sections (*sedarim*) so that the reading could be completed in a set length of time. Some have argued that the triennial cycle of readings was established by the first century, but the Mishnah makes no reference to it; so it appears that it did not become standard until the third century.

5. Psalms. Almost certainly the use of psalms in the temple was adapted to the synagogue, but the evidence is not explicit. The daily recitation of psalms was a part of the worship of pious individuals. The Hallel (Pss 113–118), a song of praise to the Lord, was recited in the homes (Matt 26:30) and in the temple and synagogue at Passover and other festivals.

6. The Homily. Scripture readings and homilies (sermons) were confined to Mondays, Thursdays, the Sabbath, and festivals (compare Luke 4:16-30; Acts 13:15-48). The homily can be traced to Nehemiah 8:8, which says that Ezra gave the sense of what had been read. The Mishnah made no attempt to regulate the method or content of the homily. Most of the sermonic expositions (or *midrashim*) that we have come from after A.D. 400. They show that the preachers worked a great deal of Scripture into their sermons, thereby familiarizing hearers with the texts. The preacher normally closed the homily with a brief prayer.

7. The Blessing. At the signal of the *hazzan,* the service would be closed by a priestly blessing if a priest was present to pronounce it. This practice may have developed only after the destruction of the temple.

Sources for Additional Study

Jeremias, Joachim. *Jerusalem in the Time of Jesus.* Philadelphia: Fortress, 1969.

Schürer, Emil. *The History of the Jewish People in the Age of Jesus Christ (175 B.C.–A.D. 135).* Edinburgh: T & T Clark, 1979.

INTERTESTAMENTAL JEWISH LITERATURE

An amazing quantity and variety of Jewish literature has survived from the period of 200 B.C. to A.D. 200. This body of literature sheds a great deal of light on the Jewish origins and context of the early church. It supplies information on the history of this period and the diversity of groups, movements, practices, and beliefs among the Jews of this time. While this literature is of great historical and interpretive value, care must be taken to establish the date, place of writing, and point of view of each document.

The Septuagint

The Septuagint was the earliest Greek translation of the Hebrew Scriptures. According to the Letter of Aristeas, it was translated by seventy-two translators in Alexandria under Pharaoh Ptolemy II (285–247 B.C.). The Letter of Aristeas, however, appears to have been written to promote the accuracy and authority of the Septuagint (often abbreviated LXX). Actually, the Greek translations came into being over a period of time. It was the first translation of Scripture. It was needed because the Greek language was dominant in Jewish communities in Alexandria and elsewhere in the Jewish dispersion.

The Septuagint was widely used among early Christians. It is not always clear which text of Scripture is being quoted in the New Testament. Where differences between the Hebrew and Greek texts allow us to identify the text that is being quoted, 80 percent of the quotations of the Old Testament in the New come from the Septuagint. The Septuagint also provides insight into the Hebrew Scriptures by representing a separate textual tradition, by enabling us to understand what corresponding Hebrew and Greek words meant to the translators, and by study of the way in which the translators worked.

The Apocrypha

Apocrypha now refers to those books in the Septuagint that were not part of the Hebrew Scriptures. In fact, the limits of the Apocrypha are not so clearly defined. The term *Apocrypha* means *hidden.* It came to be applied to books that were either considered to hold hidden teachings or books that because of their teachings should be hidden (see Dan 12:4,9; 2 Esdras 14:4-6; 12:37-38; 14:42-46). These passages reflect the development of *apocrypha* to mean *noncanonical* or *nonscriptural.*

The collection of Hebrew Scriptures was closed about A.D. 100. Thereafter the Apocrypha fell into disuse among the Jews. Prior to this time, however, the situation had been much more fluid. Copies of several books of the Apocrypha (Sirach, Tobit) were found at Qumran along with many books of the Pseudepigrapha. Jerome used *apocryphal* to indicate books that were noncanonical but not heretical. Nevertheless, the term came to mean *spurious* or *heretical.*

Fifteen books or portions of books have been called "apocrypha." Second Esdras did not appear in the Septuagint but did appear in the Latin Vulgate. The Council of Trent in 1546 decreed that the Old Testament canon included the apocrypha except the Prayer of Manasseh and 1 and 2 Esdras. These three books were put in an appendix following the New Testament in subsequent editions of the Vulgate.

Today *Apocrypha* is a Protestant term. Roman Catholics call the books of the Apocrypha "Deuterocanonical," which means that the books are not spurious but *added later to the canon.* The Eastern Orthodox canon includes the "deuterocanonical" books 1 Esdras, Psalm 151, the Prayer of Manasseh, and 3 Maccabees. Fourth Maccabees is added in an appendix. The Slavonic or Russian Orthodox Bibles contain the deuterocanonical books 1 and 2 Esdras, Psalm 151, and 3 Maccabees.

All of the books of the Apocrypha were written by Jewish authors, and all probably were written in Hebrew and Aramaic except for the Wisdom of Solomon and 2 Maccabees. The Hebrew writings were then translated into Greek and circulated with the Writings of the Old Testament, which attests to their wide popularity. The Law and the Prophets had already acquired standing as Scripture, but the Writings circulated with great fluidity. Some writings had authority for one community but not for another. After the collection of Hebrew Scriptures was fixed, the "outside books" were regarded as troublesome or dangerous. Only Sirach, of the apocryphal literature, continued to be used sporadically by Jewish writers.

THE APOCRYPHA					
TITLES (listed alphabetically)	**APPROX-IMATE DATES**	**LITERARY TYPES**	**THEMES**	**IN SEPTUAGINT?**	**IN ROMAN CATHOLIC CANON?**
Baruch	150 B.C.	Wisdom & narrative (composite)	Praise of wisdom, law, promise of hope, opposition to idolatry	Yes	Yes
Bel and the Dragon	100 B.C.	Detective narrative at end of Daniel	Opposition to idolatry	Yes	Yes
Ecclesiasticus (Wisdom of Jesus Sirach)	180 B.C. in Hebrew; 132 B.C. Greek Translation	Wisdom	Obedience to law, praise of patriarchs, value of wisdom; patriotism; temple worship; retribution; free will	Yes	Yes
I Esdras	150	History (621–458)	Proper worship; power of truth	Yes	No
2 Esdras	A.D. 100	Apocalypse with Christian preface and epilog	Pre-existent, dying Messiah: punishment for sin; salvation in future; inspiration; divine justice; evil	No	No
Additions to Esther (103 verses)	114 B.C.	Religious amplification	Prayer; worship; revelation; God's activity; providence	Yes	Yes
Letter of Jeremiah	317 B.C.	Homily added to Baruch based on Jer 29	Condemns idolatry	Yes	Yes
Judith	200 B.C.	Historical novel	Obedience to law; prayer; fasting; true worship patriotism	Yes	Yes
1 Maccabees	90 B.C.	History (180–161 B.C.)	God works in normal human events; legitimates Hasmonean kings	Yes	Yes
2 Maccabees	90 B.C.	History (180–161 B.C.)	Resurrection; creation from nothing; miracles; punishment for sin; martyrdom; temple angels	Yes	Yes
3 Maccabees	75 B.C.	Festival legend	Deliverance of faithful; angels	Some mss.	No
4 Maccabees	10 B.C.	Philosophical treatise based on 2 Macc 6–7	Power of reason over emotions; faithfulness to law; martyrdom	Some mss.	No
Prayer of Azariah and Song of Three Young Men	100 B.C.	Liturgy; hymn & additions to Dan 3:23	Praise; God's response to prayer	Yes	Yes
Prayer of Manasseh	120 B.C.	Prayer of penitence based on 2 Kgs 21:10-17 2 Chr 33:11-19	Prayer of repentance	Yes	No
Psalm 151	?	Victory hymn	Praise to God who uses young & inexperienced	Yes	No
Susanna	100 B.C.	Detective story at end of Daniel	Daniel's wisdom; God's vindication of faithfulness	Yes	Yes
Tobit	200 B.C.	Folktale	Temple attendance; tithing; charity; prayer; obedience to Jewish law; guardian angel; divine justice and retribution; personal devotion	Yes	Yes
Wisdom of Solomon	10 B.C. in Egypt	Wisdom personified; Jewish apologetic	Value of wisdom and faithfulness, immortality	Yes	Yes

Rabbi Akiba stated that among those who have no part in the world to come is "he who reads in the outside books." A midrash or exposition on Ecclesiastes 12:12 states: "Whoever brings together in his house more than twenty-four books [that is, the Jewish enumeration of the books of the Hebrew OT] brings confusion." The preservation of the Apocrypha and Pseudepigrapha is due, therefore, almost entirely to their popularity among Christians.

While approximately 80 percent of the quotations in the New Testament reproduce the Septuagint, there are no quotations from the Apocrypha, which probably indicates that these books were not regarded quite as highly as the Hebrew Scriptures. Still, there are allusions to the Apocrypha in the New Testament (Ecclesiasticus 5:11 in Jas 1:19; 2 Maccabees 6–7 in Heb 11:35-36; Wisdom of Solomon 2:18 in Matt 27:43). Philo adhered to the Hebrew canon. Josephus used 1 Maccabees, 1 Esdras, and the additions to Esther as Scripture in his *Antiquities*.

Among the church fathers, Clement, Origen, and Cyprian believed the Apocrypha was part of the Christian Bible. Cyril of Jerusalem and Jerome were more explicit about separating the Apocrypha from the other books. They were the first to use *Apocrypha* to designate the books of the Greek and Latin Bibles which were not included in the Hebrew Bibles. Because the books of the Apocrypha were commonly accepted, Jerome included them in his translation of the Bible into Latin (the Vulgate), but he carefully marked each work with a note indicating that it was not in the Hebrew Bible. Later copies overlooked the notes. Jerome also wrote that the Apocrypha could be read for edification, but not "for confirming the authority of Church dogmas" (Prologue to Books of Solomon).

Throughout the Middle Ages the Apocrypha was regarded as canonical. When John Wycliffe (about 1382) produced the first English translation of the Bible, it included all of the Apocrypha except 2 Esdras. The prologue to the Old Testament, however, specified a distinction between the Apocrypha and the Hebrew canon. The former, Wycliffe wrote, "shall be set among the apocrypha, that is, without authority over beliefs."

Both doctrinal disputes and a revival of the study of Hebrew contributed to the growing distinction between the Hebrew canon and the Apocrypha. The reformers distinguished between the two because the basis for the Roman Catholic teachings on works and purgatory was contained in the Apocrypha: justification by works (Ecclesiasticus 3:3,14-15,30; Tobit 4:7-11; 12:9; 14:11); merits of the saints (Song of the Three Young Men 12); purgatory and prayers for the dead (2 Maccabees 12:43-45).

When Luther produced his German version of the Bible in 1534, he separated the Apocrypha, placing it in an appendix with the superscription: "Apocrypha, these are books which are not held equal to the sacred Scriptures and yet are useful and good for reading." In this appendix he included Wisdom of Solomon, Ecclesiasticus, Judith, Tobit, 1 and 2 Maccabees, and the additions to Daniel, Esther, and the Prayer of Manasseh (but not 1 and 2 Esdras). He also separated Hebrews, James, Jude, and Revelation to the end of the New Testament because he did not consider them to be among the principal witnesses to Jesus Christ.

The Council of Trent (1546) responded to the reformers' innovations by issuing what the Roman Catholic Church regards as the first infallible declaration on the canon. All of the Apocrypha except the Prayer of Manasseh and 1 and 2 Esdras were accepted as Scripture. In 1592 the official edition of the Vulgate included these three books in an appendix to the New Testament.

The Church of England took a moderating position, quoting Jerome's statement that the books of the Apocrypha should be read for edification but not as a basis for the church's doctrine. The lectionary attached to the Book of Common Prayer has therefore prescribed lessons from the Apocrypha.

As early as 1599 the Puritans began excluding from their Bibles all books that were not regarded as Scripture. The position of the Reformed tradition is succinctly stated in the third article of the Westminster Confession (1647): "The books commonly called Apocrypha, not being of divine inspiration, are not part of the Canon of Scripture; and therefore are of no authority in the Church of God, nor to be in any otherwise approved, or made use of, than other human writings."

The King James Version, being the authorized version of the Church of England, contained the books of the Apocrypha scattered among the canonical books in its first printing (1611). In 1615 the Archbishop of Canterbury directed that no Bibles were to be bound or sold without the Apocrypha. Nevertheless, several printings of the King James Version between 1616 and 1633 lack the Apocrypha. After a bitter struggle the British and Foreign Bible Society announced in 1827 that they would exclude the Apocrypha from their printed copies of the English Bible.

A brief description of each of the books of the Apocrypha follows:

First Esdras. First Esdras traces the history of the Jews from Josiah through the times of Zerubbabel and Ezra, emphasizing their contributions to the reform of Israelite worship. First Esdras 3:1–5:6 is an old Persian or

Babylonian tale of three young men in the court of Darius that has been interpolated into the document. The theme of this segment of wisdom literature is that truth is mighty and prevails. The interpolation can be traced to the Persian period (538–331 B.C.), but 1 Esdras probably was written in the second century B.C. First Esdras is important for our knowledge of postexilic Judaism and supplements the parallel accounts in 2 Chronicles 35:1–36:23; Ezra; and Nehemiah 7:38–8:12.

Second Edras. Second Esdras (or Fourth Ezra) is a profound apocalyptic treatment of God's providence in history. Written about A.D. 100, after the destruction of Jerusalem, it wrestles with the questions: How could God's people hold together the actual facts of history and a belief in a just God who had promised to bless His people? What was the origin of moral evil? How would anyone be justified in the last judgment? Why had God let His people suffer? Was there, then, any basis for hope?

Second Esdras reports seven visions in which the seer was instructed by the angel Uriel. The author knew the traditional answers to the problem of evil: Adam's sin, the evil inclination, or the fallen angels. He rejected all dualistic systems, however, and never mentioned Satan. Instead, he accepted that humanity was responsible for its own destiny. Finally, his thoroughgoing monotheism drove him to the conclusion that God was responsible for the evil in the human heart, and any hope for humanity rested with God. Humankind could not obey the law because of the evil in the human heart, but God loves His creation and has not forgotten His people.

Tobit. Tobit is a delightful folktale written shortly after 200 B.C. that presents a vivid description of Jewish morality prior to the Maccabean era.

A pious Jew named Tobit, living in Nineveh, became blind. Being in need, he sent his son Tobias to collect a deposit he had left in Media. God heard Tobit's prayer and sent an angel, Raphael, to guide him and reveal magic formulas that could heal Tobit's blindness. God also heard the prayers of Sarah, whose seven successive bridegrooms had each been killed by a demon on their wedding night, and guided Tobias to her. Tobias married Sarah, and with one of Raphael's formulas drove off the demon. In the end Tobias completed his mission and returned home with his bride, the money, and a formula that restored Tobit's sight.

The author's religion is primarily personal rather than nationalistic. God is merciful and just. The basis for piety was therefore devotion to God and trust in God's just retribution. Sin and virtue inevitably brought reward or punishment, even if the just suffered temporarily. There is no reference to resurrection, but Tobit's system of angels was well advanced over the Old Testament and comparable to Jubilees and 1 Enoch.

Judith. Judith is a spellbinding story of a heroine who delivers her town from the siege of Holofernes, a Persian general about 350 B.C. The story itself was probably written down or rewritten about 100 B.C. Anachronisms make it difficult to assess the historical value of the story.

When Holofernes laid siege to Bethulia, Judith, a beautiful, pious, and resourceful widow, initiated a carefully devised plan to deliver the town. She made her way to Holofernes's camp and then craftily prepared her escape. When she was alone with Holofernes in his tent and he was thoroughly intoxicated, she decapitated him and returned to Bethulia with her gruesome trophy.

Judith may naturally be compared with Esther. She stands in the tradition of Jael (Judg 4:17-22; 5:24-27), the woman of Thebez (Judg 9:53), Deborah (Judg 4–5), the wise woman of 2 Samuel 20:14-22, and Esther. Judith's religion was vigorously nationalistic, a blend of patriotism and piety. She scrupulously obeyed the law of Moses in regard to dietary laws, fasting, prayer at fixed times, and ritual pollutions. The end of defending her nation and her religion justified her breach of moral law.

Additions to Esther. Additions were apparently added to biblical Esther by Lysimachus, an Alexandrian Jew who translated the book from Hebrew into Greek about 114 B.C., or by others shortly thereafter. The six additions were interspersed at various points in the Greek text. Jerome separated them and placed the additions at the end of Esther, where they received the following chapter and verse numbers in the Latin Vulgate: Mordecai's dream (11:2–12:6); the first royal letter (13:1-7); Mordecai's and Esther's prayers (13:8–14:19); Esther's appearance before the king (15:1-16); the second royal letter (16:1-24); and the interpretation of Mordecai's dream (10:4–11:1).

Canonical Esther contains no reference to God or religious practices. The additions, however, give the book a religious character by introducing fifty references to God, God's providential care for His people, and God's intervention in history. The additions convey an anti-Gentile attitude and emphasize prayer, fasting, and the temple cult.

The Wisdom of Solomon. The Wisdom of Solomon was probably written as a defense of the Jewish belief in God by a Hellenistic Jew about the time of Jesus' birth. It addressed pious Jews to encourage them, erring Jews to call them back to their faith, and Gentiles to convert them. This thoroughly Jewish theme was presented in a thoroughly Hellenized style that appealed to the cardinal virtues of Platonism and Stoicism. Parts of the book are lyrical and poetic; elsewhere its prose is ponderous.

The author personified wisdom and combined it with the Stoic concept of the *logos*. It was only a short step, therefore, from the Wisdom of Solomon to the use of *logos* (*Word*) in the prologue to the Gospel of John, though no direct dependence can be shown. The Wisdom of Solomon encouraged Jews to take pride in their traditional faith and justified their present suffering through the promise of immortality.

Sirach. The Wisdom of Jesus the Son of Sirach, also called Ecclesiasticus, is often called Sirach for short. Sirach shows us a wisdom teacher—Jesus the son of Sirach or Joshua ben Sira in Hebrew—on his way to becoming an interpreter of the law. Like the Book of Proverbs, it opens with a praise of wisdom and closes with an alphabetic acrostic. Ben Sira was a teacher in a wisdom school (compare 51:23-30). There were apparently various wisdom schools in Jerusalem at the time (see Sirach's characterization of other teachers in 37:19-26). Ben Sira cannot be identified with the Pharisees, the Sadducees, or even the Hasidim. Rather, he represented a wisdom teacher reacting to Hellenism during the period immediately preceding the Maccabean revolt.

There are no references to resurrection or immortality, nor is there any reference to a synagogue. On the other hand, Sirach reflects a positive attitude toward the temple and the priesthood and gives a glowing description of Simon, the Oniad high priest (50:1-24). Its hope is completely this worldly and has a political and nationalistic coloring. Sirach represents the tension at the time between political involvement in protest against the liberal aristocracy and the traditional caution of the wise, who counseled subjection to the powerful. Sirach also contains an echo of the prophets. It is concerned about the opposition between rich and poor (13:2-5,15-20) and is especially critical of merchants (26:29–27:3). In opposition to the teaching of determinism, Sirach emphasizes the freedom of the will and holds firmly to the doctrine of divine retribution.

The book was translated from Hebrew into Greek by Ben Sira's grandson after 132 B.C. The title Ecclesiasticus comes from the Vulgate, though it has been used in the Western church since Cyprian (248–258). This title may have been pinned on the book because of its similarity to Ecclesiastes. Rufinus (345–410) explained that it means *The Church's Book*.

Baruch. Baruch purports to be a letter written by Baruch, Jeremiah's scribe (Jer 32:12; 36:4), and sent to Jerusalem to be read at a festival. Actually, the book is a composite of three works, each probably coming from a different author. The three parts probably were compiled between 200 and 100 B.C.

The first part serves as a prose introduction and recites Israel's sins. The second part is a poem on wisdom that bears no relation to the first part except the presumed setting in the exile. The third part is a poem written in a different style that gives a comforting reply to the first two parts. The author drew from Isaiah 40–66 and looked forward to an imminent deliverance of the Jews and a return to Jerusalem.

The Letter of Jeremiah. The Letter of Jeremiah purports to be a letter sent by Jeremiah to those who were about to be carried into exile in Babylon. It is a treatise on the folly of idolatry which dates from the Hellenistic or Maccabean period. The earliest fragment of the letter, dating about 100 B.C., was discovered in Cave 7 at Qumran. Its style is elevated and rhetorical. Following each of its various proofs of the powerlessness of idols, its frequently repeated refrain declares, "This shows that they are no gods."

Additions to Daniel. Both the original language and the date of these legendary additions are debated, though the first has the greatest likelihood of having been written in Hebrew. The additions are saturated with Jewish piety, and they are theologically inoffensive. Other than the assumption that the additions were recognized as additions, and Susanna casts the elders in a bad light, it is unclear why the additions were not accepted as part of the Hebrew canon. The common theme of the additions is how faithful Jews who trusted in the Lord even while in exile in Babylon were delivered from certain death.

Although fragmentary copies of Daniel containing the additions were discovered at Qumran, the additions were not widely attested. Josephus told other apocryphal stories about Daniel, but not these. The Talmud does not refer to them, and Jerome said that he knew of no Semitic text of the additions.

The Prayer of Azariah and the Song of the Three Young Men. This work describes the furnace that the three young men were thrown into. Azariah is the Hebrew name of Abednego. The song of the three young men contains both a liturgy addressed to God and an appeal to the whole creation to join in the praise of God.

Susanna. Susanna is a detective story that may have been composed late in the Persian period. Two elders attempted to ravish the beautiful and innocent Susanna (whose name means *a lily*). When she cried out, the elders accused her of having lain with a young man. God heard her pleas and raised up Daniel (whose name means

The death of Eleazar (from the Apocrypha, 1 Macc 6:43,46)

God has judged). Daniel interrogated the two elders separately and showed that their stories did not agree with each other. They were both lying.

Bel and the Dragon. Bel and the Dragon contains two stories that unmask the impotence of foreign idols. The first is another detective story, though more contrived and less appealing than Susanna. Bel, the Babylonian deity, consumed quantities of food and drink each night. Daniel devised a plan that revealed to all that the priests were slipping into the temple at night to consume the offerings. In the second story Daniel killed a dragon by feeding it a concoction of pitch, fat, and hair. The dragon ate them and burst open. The priests were enraged and had Daniel thrown into the lion's den. The prophet Habakkuk was transported to Babylon to provide for Daniel. The king released Daniel from the lion's den and threw his accusers to the lions, who immediately devoured them.

The Prayer of Manasseh. Manasseh's prayer is a beautiful, penitential prayer of one who had fallen into idolatry. It purports to be the prayer of Manasseh referred to in 2 Chronicles 33:11-13,18-19. There is very little evidence by which to date this prayer. It is a Jewish composition, but verses 7b and 15b have at times been regarded as Christian additions. The Prayer was not in the Septuagint known to Origen or Jerome. It is first attested after A.D. 200 in the Syriac Didascalia and in the later Apostolic Constitutions. It has appeared in the Septuagint since about A.D. 400 in the odes appended to the Psalms. It was subsequently placed in the appendix to the Vulgate at the Council of Trent.

First Maccabees. First Maccabees is a historical writing that records the history of the Jews from the beginning of Antiochus Epiphanes' reign (175 B.C.) to the reign of John Hyrcanus I (134 B.C.). It was written in Hebrew in a style similar to that of the Books of Kings and Chronicles in the Old Testament. The Hebrew original was known to Josephus, Origen, and Jerome but was subsequently lost. First Maccabees survives in a Greek translation and in other versions. This history of the Maccabean revolt was written, probably in Jerusalem, sometime between the death of John Hyrcanus I in 104 B.C. and the Roman conquest under Pompey (63 B.C.).

The apparent purpose of the work was to establish the legitimacy of the Hasmonean Dynasty, just as the books of Samuel proved the legitimacy of the Davidic Dynasty. Although the author attributed the Maccabean victories to divine Providence, he did not record any miraculous interventions.

Second Maccabees. Second Maccabees was not written by the author of 1 Maccabees and differs sharply in character and purpose. Second Maccabees is an abridgment of a five-volume history written by Jason of Cyrene. Both Jason's history and 2 Maccabees were composed in Greek. Jason's work can be dated to about 100 B.C., and 2 Maccabees can be dated sometime later in the same century.

Second Maccabees is generally less reliable than 1 Maccabees as a source for historical information. The sequence of events differs in the two accounts. For example, 1 Maccabees places the death of Antiochus Epiphanes after the dedication of the temple, while 2 Maccabees places it before that event. Second Maccabees covers the period from the high priesthood of Onias III to the defeat of Nicanor's army (180 to 161 B.C.), the period covered by 1 Maccabees 1:10–7:50. The author of 2 Maccabees interpreted history theologically and sought to show that the claims of the Hasmoneans after the death of Judas were illegitimate. Second Maccabees, however, vindicates Daniel and exalts the Oniads.

Second Maccabees reports angelic interventions and affirms the resurrection of the dead and the doctrine of creation from nothing (7:28). Second Maccabees also teaches that the dead intercede for the living (15:11-16) and that the living may pray and offer sacrifices for the dead (12:43-45).

Third Maccabees. Third Maccabees has nothing to do with 1 or 2 Maccabees. Indeed it deals not with the Maccabean period but with the deliverance of faithful Jews in Alexandria during the reign of Ptolemy IV Philopator (221–203 B.C.).

According to 3 Maccabees, Ptolemy IV attempted to enter the holy of holies in the temple after his victory at Raphia (217 B.C.). God prevented him from doing so by striking him with paralysis. Ptolemy was angered by the Jews because they would not open their temple to him and resolved to kill all Jews who would not submit to initiation into the Dionysiac cult. He ordered drunken elephants to be readied so that they could be released on the captive Jews. In response to the prayers of the Jews, God sent a deep sleep on Ptolemy, then struck him with forgetfulness, and finally sent two angels who were invisible to the Jews to turn the elephants on the Egyptians. As a result of the rout, Ptolemy granted the Jews their freedom, and the Jews declared a festival that would be observed each year.

Third Maccabees—like Esther—explains the origin of a festival. It was written in a florid, bombastic style and dates from between 100 and 1 B.C. While this book was not included in the Latin Vulgate, it has been regarded as scripture by the Eastern churches.

Fourth Maccabees. Fourth Maccabees is a philosophical treatise. Its theme is that reason is the mistress of the emotions. Actually, however, the author used the form and theme merely as a way in which to present Jewish piety in the guise of a philosophical address. The writer exhorted Jews to remain resolutely faithful to the law and to their ancestral faith. The power of reason dictates that one should obey the law.

The body of the work deals with the martyrdom of Eleazar and the seven brothers and their mother (2 Macc 6:12–7:42). The writer argued that they were able to uphold the law and meet death courageously because they were guided by reason. Once titled "On the Supremacy of Reason," the book is now called 4 Maccabees because it is based on the martyrologies of 2 Maccabees 6–7.

The origin of the book is difficult to locate. It is dated between 100 B.C. and A.D. 100. It is traced variously to Alexandria or Antioch. The Greek form of the book and its thoroughly Jewish content show that form and content did not always correspond in works of this period. Its theme, the supremacy of reason, is also a favorite Stoic theme. Nevertheless, 4 Maccabees maintains that martyrdom atones for the sins of Israel and teaches that martyrs receive blessing and everlasting life. The wicked, on the other hand, suffer eternal punishment.

Psalm 151. Psalm 151 was included among the psalms of David in the Septuagint and by the scribe of Codex Sinaiticus. A longer form of the psalm was also found on a scroll from Qumran Cave 11 that contains about thirty-five canonical psalms and several noncanonical psalms. Most other manuscripts, however, exclude this psalm. The psalm celebrates David's youth and his victory over Goliath.

The Pseudepigrapha

The definition and limits of the Pseudepigrapha are even more problematic than those of the Apocrypha. Literally, the term *pseudepigrapha* means *falsely attributed,* or *attributed to a fictitious writer.*

R. H. Charles published an English translation of the Pseudepigrapha in 1913 that included seventeen works. Two of them clearly do not belong with the Pseudepigrapha (Pirke Aboth and the Fragments of a Zadokite document). By common agreement the sectarian works among the Qumran scrolls do not belong to the Pseudepigrapha. The rabbinic materials also have been kept separate. The recent English translation of the Pseudepigrapha edited by James H. Charlesworth contains fifty-two books. Charlesworth adopted five criteria for identifying Pseudepigrapha:

1. The work must be, at least partially and preferably totally, Jewish or Jewish-Christian.
2. It should date from the period 200 B.C. to A.D. 200.
3. It should claim to be inspired.
4. It should be related in form or content to the Old Testament.
5. It should ideally be attributed to an Old Testament figure.

Most of these works were preserved through the centuries by groups on the fringe of Christianity. Hence they have come down to us in such languages as Slavonic, Ethiopic, Syriac, Georgian, Coptic, and Armenian. Among the principal works of the Pseudepigrapha are the following: The Letter of Aristeas, Jubilees, the Martyrdom of Isaiah, the Psalms of Solomon, 4 Maccabees, the Sybilline Oracles, 1 Enoch, 2 Enoch, the Assumption of Moses, 4 Ezra, 2 Baruch, 3 Baruch, the Testaments of the Twelve Patriarchs, and the Books of Adam and Eve.

The Dead Sea Scrolls

The designation "Dead Sea Scrolls" is commonly used to refer to the scrolls found in thirteen caves near Qumran. Scrolls also have been found at other sites near the Dead Sea, such as Masada and Wadi Murabba'at. Among the scrolls and fragments found at Qumran were canonical works (including parts of every book of the Old Testament except Esther), apocryphal works, eschatological texts (some of which were previously known and some of which were not), haggadic texts (exhortation and instruction), halakic texts (rules, law codes), hymnic texts, liturgical texts, calendrical and astrological texts, florilegia (verses of Scripture from various contexts drawn together to form a new context), commentaries, and prayers.

The first cave containing scrolls was discovered in 1947 by Muhammed ed-Dib, a Ta'mireh shepherd. It contained the great Isaiah scrolls and some of the most important sectarian texts (the Manual of Discipline, the Hymn Scroll, and the War Scroll). For the next ten years

The Shrine of the Book in Jerusalem is the museum that houses the Dead Sea Scrolls found in the caves of Qumran.

desert-dwelling Arabs continued to find and sell scrolls through middlemen. Archaeologists combed the area searching for new caves, and the settlement at Qumran was excavated.

By 1960 the fragments had been pieced together, and the writings were identified or named. The principal scrolls had been purchased by Israel, and scholarly judgment identified Qumran as the center of an Essene community which had produced the sectarian writings and most of the other texts found in the area. Although Josephus, Philo, Pliny, and Hippolytus refer to the Essenes, little was known about their beliefs and practices until the discovery of the scrolls.

The archaeological data revealed that Qumran was an Israelite fortress from sometime between 800 and 600 B.C. that was resettled around 140 to 130 B.C. The settlement experienced a period of significant growth and acquired its definitive form about 100 B.C. An earthquake partially destroyed Qumran in 31 B.C., but the settlers rebuilt the community after a brief period of abandonment. A century later the community was finally destroyed and burned in A.D. 68, probably by the tenth Roman Legion. The cemetery nearby contains about eleven hundred tombs. Only males were buried in the main part of the cemetery. An extension contains the remains of a few females and children. At its height, therefore, the Qumran occupation probably had no more than two hundred inhabitants.

The Manual of Discipline (1QS), a composite work dating about 100 B.C., contains a description of the purpose and ideals of the community, its ceremony of admission, the annual census, instruction on the two Spirits, regulations for the community, and a hymn. The earliest material in this document (1QS 8:1–16a and 9:3–10:8a) is widely regarded as the manifesto for the community written prior to the foundation of Qumran.

Two manuscripts dating from the 900s and 1100s A.D. were discovered in a Cairo Geniza (*storeroom for discarded copies of Scripture*) in 1896–97. They contained sections of what is now known as the Damascus Document (CD), eight copies of which were discovered at Qumran. It is a composite document written between the death of the Teacher of Righteousness and the Roman conquest in 63 B.C. The writer alluded to various events in the history of Israel up to the founding of the Qumran community and drew encouragement from these events. Other sections contain laws to be observed by those who live in the camps. These laws differ from the laws contained in the Manual of Discipline, which may indicate either that they were written at a later time or that they applied to the camps rather than to the main community at Qumran.

The Hymn Scroll (1QH) is a collection of hymns or thanksgiving psalms. In many ways it is reminiscent of the Book of Psalms and draws heavily from Old Testament imagery. The scroll dates from A.D. 1 to 50 and was written by three scribes. The date of the composition of these hymns is unknown. Six other manuscripts of the hymns were found in Cave 4. Various scholars have suggested that some of the hymns were written by the Teacher of Righteousness; others are regarded as "community hymns."

Five fragments of the War scroll (1QM) were found in Cave 4. The work purports to give the plan of the final war in which God will crush the forces of evil. The scroll blends holy war traditions (Num 2:1–5:4), apocalyptic

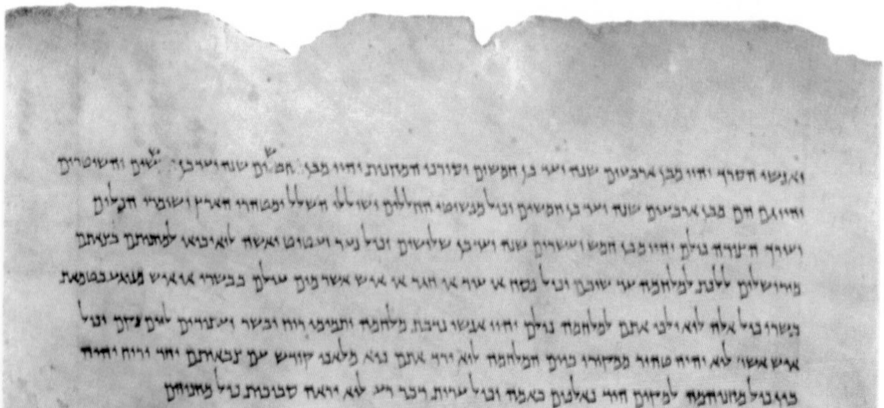

Above is a reproduction of one of the columns of "The War of the Sons of Light against the Sons of Darkness," one of the sectarian scrolls found in the library at Qumran.

imagery, military terminology and strategy, and liturgical and theological pronouncements. All extant copies date from between A.D. 1 and 100, but the document was probably composed sometime after 50 B.C.

The commentaries, or *pesharim,* are marked by a peculiar form of interpretation. The message of the Old Testament prophets was interpreted verse by verse and applied to the history, life, or hope of the Qumran community. Thus the prophets wrote not about their own times but about the Qumran community, which saw itself as living at the end of time. References in the prophets were therefore interpreted allegorically and applied to the community.

The Temple Scroll, the largest of the scrolls, was acquired by Yigael Yadin in 1967. The entire scroll presents its contents as the revealed word of God. Most distinctively, Scripture quotations were changed to the first person. The lost beginning probably dealt with the covenant of Moses on Mount Sinai. The scroll described the messianic temple rather than the existing temple. It strongly argued against practices at the Jerusalem temple. As its name implies, the Temple Scroll described the temple building and moved outward. Related laws were recorded after the description of each installation.

The Qumran scrolls have shed a great deal of light on the life and practices of the Essenes in the first century, thereby revealing even more of the richness and diversity of Jewish life during the New Testament period.

Philo

Philo (about 20 B.C. to A.D. 50) was the most prolific author of Hellenistic Judaism. Philo was a statesman and a philosopher. The only dateable event in his life is a trip to Rome in A.D. 40 when he led an embassy to Gaius. Philo was born into one of the leading families in Alexandria, and his writings defend and interpret Judaism by interpreting Jewish thought in terms of Greek philosophy. His writings are variously mystical, allegorical, homiletical, and didactic. While the New Testament writers never quote Philo, his writings illuminate the larger cultural and philosophical context in which John's Logos Christology emerged. References in Paul's Letters and in Hebrews can also be illuminated by reading Philo.

Josephus

The historian Flavius Josephus is the primary source for much of what we know of the history of the Jewish people during the intertestamental and New Testament periods. He was born in a priestly family in A.D. 37/38 and died about 100. Early in the revolt of 66–70, Josephus was placed in command of Jewish forces in Galilee. In 67 he was captured by the Roman general Vespasian at Jotapata. Thereafter Josephus aided the Romans and prophesied that Vespasian would become the Roman emperor. When the prophecy came true, Vespasian released Josephus and allowed him to spend the rest of his life in Rome, where he produced four major works that interpreted recent events for his fellow Jews and portrayed Judaism in a positive light for Greco-Roman readers.

The Jewish War is an account of the Jewish revolt, written within a decade of the revolt. Josephus placed the blame for the war not on the nation as a whole but on misguided revolutionaries. He further counseled other Jews to accept Roman authority.

The Antiquities of the Jews records the history of the Jewish people up to the war of A.D. 66–70. The first part summarizes and paraphrases the biblical record. The latter part provides a detailed history of the Jews during the intertestamental period.

Against Apion refuted slanders against the Jews, and *Life* is a brief autobiographical account, principally of Josephus's activities in Galilee during the war.

The Mishnah and Talmud

The Mishnah and Talmud are the principal collections of rabbinic scholarship. The Mishnah is a collection of the oral tradition of the rabbis, written about A.D. 200 by Rabbi Judah the Priest. Rabbinic laws are organized in sixty-three tractates and six orders. The commentary (Gemara), additions, and interpretations of the Mishnah were collected in the Babylonian and Palestinian Talmuds that date from about A.D. 550 and 450, respectively. The laws deal with agriculture, feasts, women, and damages, and sacrifices. The Babylonian Talmud is the more extensive and became the standard authority for most of Judaism in the succeeding centuries.

Sources for Additional Study

Anderson, B. W., ed. *The Books of the Bible*. Vol. 2. *The Apocrypha and the New Testament*. New York: Scribner's, 1989.

Charlesworth, J. H., ed. *The Old Testament Pseudepigrapha*. 2 Vols. Garden City: Doubleday, 1983–1985.

Danby, H. trans. *The Mishnah*. Oxford: University Press, 1933.

Dupont-Sommer, A. *The Essene Writings from Qumran*. New York: World, 1961.

Nickelsburg, G. W. *Jewish Literature between the Bible and the Mishnah*. Philadelphia: Fortress, 1981.

Vermes, G. *The Dead Sea Scrolls: Qumran in Perspective*. Philadelphia: Fortress, 1981.

The Gospels

The New Testament begins with four books we call Gospels. Whenever we use the term *Gospels,* we must recall that before the Gospels came the *gospel*, the good news concerning Jesus Christ—His life, death for sins, and resurrection (see 1 Cor 15:3-4). Jesus preached good news (the gospel) when He began His work (Mark 1:1,15).

All four Gospel books—Matthew, Mark, Luke, and John—tell the story of Jesus. At some points the four books are quite similar. At other points they are quite distinctive. The first three Gospels, called the Synoptics (which comes from a Greek word that means they saw the ministry of Jesus from a similar point of view), have much material in common. For example, over 600 of Mark's 661 verses are in Matthew. About 380 verses in Luke are similar to Mark's material. Some have suggested that all three drew upon a common source. Others have suggested that Matthew was written first and that Mark and Luke were influenced by Matthew. Yet others have maintained that Mark was written first and so in turn influenced Matthew and Luke.

We really do not know how the Gospels came into being. Luke offered a hint that he did thorough research of other accounts about Jesus before he wrote his Gospel (see Luke 1:1-4). We really do not know the historical process in which the Gospels came into being. What we do know is that the four books we have called Gospels are inspired of God's Spirit and communicate the story of Jesus to us in a powerful way (see the article "The Order of the Gospels").

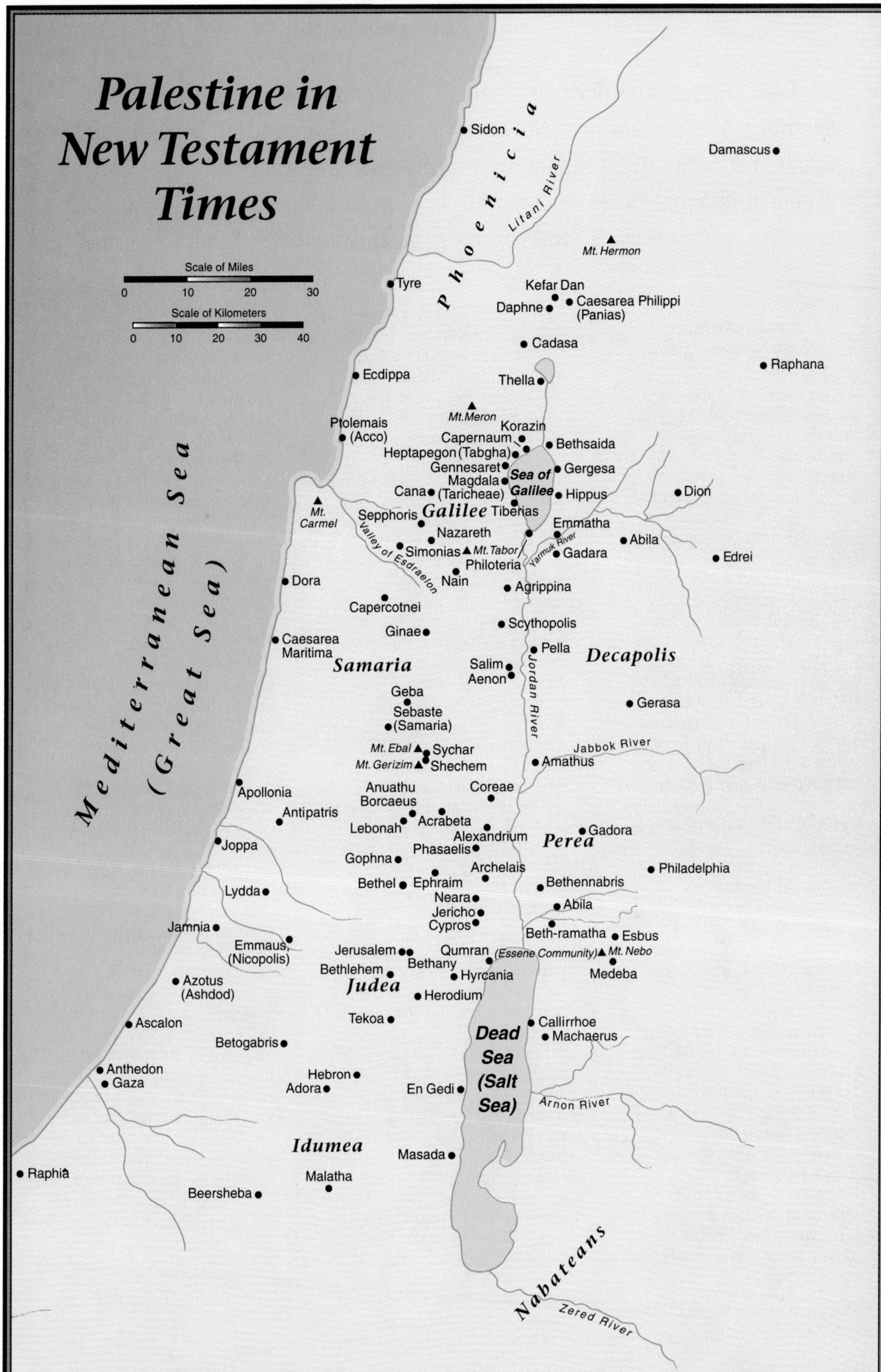

Palestine in New Testament Times
Scale of Miles
0 10 20 30
Scale of Kilometers
0 10 20 30 40
Mediterranean Sea (Great Sea)
Phoenicia
Litani River
Sidon
Damascus
Mt. Hermon
Tyre
Kefar Dan
Daphne
Caesarea Philippi (Panias)
Cadasa
Raphana
Ecdippa
Thella
Mt. Meron
Ptolemais (Acco)
Korazin
Capernaum
Heptapegon (Tabgha)
Bethsaida
Gennesaret
Sea of Galilee
Gergesa
Magdala (Taricheae)
Cana
Hippus
Dion
Mt. Carmel
Galilee
Tiberias
Sepphoris
Emmatha
Nazareth
Valley of Esdraelon
Yarmuk River
Abila
Simonias
Mt. Tabor
Gadara
Edrei
Philoteria
Nain
Dora
Agrippina
Capercotnei
Scythopolis
Ginae
Caesarea Maritima
Pella
Samaria
Decapolis
Salim
Aenon
Geba
Jordan River
Sebaste (Samaria)
Gerasa
Mt. Ebal
Sychar
Mt. Gerizim
Shechem
Jabbok River
Amathus
Apollonia
Anuathu Borcaeus
Coreae
Antipatris
Acrabeta
Lebonah
Alexandrium
Gadora
Perea
Joppa
Phasaelis
Gophna
Archelais
Philadelphia
Bethel
Ephraim
Bethennabris
Lydda
Neara
Abila
Jericho
Cypros
Jamnia
Beth-ramatha
Esbus
Emmaus (Nicopolis)
Jerusalem
Qumran
(Essene Community)
Mt. Nebo
Bethany
Bethlehem
Medeba
Hyrcania
Azotus (Ashdod)
Judea
Herodium
Ascalon
Tekoa
Callirrhoe
Dead Sea (Salt Sea)
Machaerus
Betogabris
Anthedon
Gaza
Hebron
Adora
En Gedi
Arnon River
Idumea
Masada
Raphia
Malatha
Beersheba
Nabateans
Zered River

Each Gospel is ascribed to a person who either witnessed the events described or who obtained eyewitness accounts. Each of the Gospels tells us things that none of the others do. Each Gospel was written by different people at different times in different places with unique situations. All, however, were probably written sometime between A.D. 60–95 (see the

New Testament Apocrypha

Apocrypha is a title given to a number of books that date from the second century until the Middle Ages but were not finally accepted into the canon of Scripture. In modern usage the adjective "apocryphal" connotes something that is spurious or false.

Title

The Greek term *apokryphos,* from which we get the English word "Apocrypha," means *hidden* or *secret* (see Mark 4:22; Luke 8:17; Col 2:3). It is used in several senses: (1) contents that are secret, known only for the initiated and thus hidden from the uninitiated; (2) books that were not suitable for reading in public worship, although some of them could be read in private; and (3) books that were rejected as false and heretical.

It is thought that originally these books were too sacred for every person to handle, thus needing to be limited to the initiated.

Furthermore, many books commanded respect by having some unmerited venerable name attached to them, such as the Gospel or Acts of Peter. Usually it is purported that these books had been concealed for some time by pious believers and were later brought to light. However, the falsity of their claim only brought disrepute to these works, and so they were looked upon as spurious or untrue.

Purpose

The purposes vary with each writing. One common purpose was to fill in gaps left out by the canonical books. Hence, there are works on Mary, Joseph, Jesus' youth, and Pilate, as well as the various apostles—their gospel, passion, or acts.

Another purpose was to promote certain teachings, usually heretical, on the authority of important names of the past such as apostles. Also some of these works attempted to expound what seemed to be sound Christian doctrine, such as the virgin birth or the resurrection, many times with bizarre analogies from nature or history.

Form

Their form parallels the four forms of the canonical NT: gospels, acts, epistles, and apocalypses. In the apocryphal gospels accounts are given of Jesus' birth, infancy, youth, and early ministry. They can be extravagant such as claims made regarding Jesus' miraculous powers in His youth where at times He used these powers for selfish purposes. This, of course, is incompatible with the character description given in the canonical literature.

The apocryphal acts, especially the five major works from the second and third centuries (Acts of Andrew, John, Paul, Peter, and Thomas), were intended to supplement the canonical Acts by giving further information about the apostles. They are noted for their uncurbed imagination of the apostles' great deeds and miracles, normally ending with their martyrdom. Furthermore, they tend to be more romance than history.

There are comparatively few apocryphal epistles, and they never flourished as the other forms. There were such letters as Epistle to the Laodiceans, the Letters of Paul and Seneca, and 3 Corinthians. The apocryphal apocalypses were similar to the thought pattern of the Jewish apocalyptic although there is a shift to Christ and His return. These have descriptions of the blessedness of heaven, the miseries of hell, and delay of Christ's return.

Value

The apocryphal books reflect the thinking of the churches in various geographical locations and time. They give insight on how the early church interpreted some of the NT passages. They give us understanding of the heresies in the early church. We can see how various doctrines and practices, like Mariolatry and celibacy, began. Finally, it gives an understanding about why these works were excluded from the canon, namely, because they are inferior in so many respects.

The NT apocryphal works never gained the status of the OT Apocrypha. However, their influence in the church is seen in areas of doctrine like the veneration of Mary and in architecture like the stained glass of the cathedrals. On the other hand, in reading this material, one is immediately impressed with their dissimilarity to the canonical books of the NT. □

NEW TESTAMENT APOCRYPHA

TYPE	TITLE	CONTENT	PURPOSE	DATE OF COMPOSITION
INFANCY GOSPELS	Protoevangelium of James	Miracles connected with Mary	Glorify Mary	150
	Infancy Gospel of Thomas	Miracles of Jesus as child	Fill in silent years of Jesus' life	200
PASSION GOSPELS	Gospel of Peter	Crucifixion and resurrection unconnected to Jewish history and without notes of salvation through the cross	Prove resurrection; put guilt on Jews; down-play Christ's humanity; emphasize miracles	150
	Gospel of Nicodemus (Acts of Pilate)	Dating of crucifixion; testimonies to innocence of Jesus and of Mary; resurrection appearances; guilt of Jews; Jesus' decent into hell	Prove Jesus innocent and Jews guilty; prove resurrection	150?
JEWISH CHRISTIAN GOSPELS	Gospel of Nazareans	Editing of Matthew; with some expansions	Uncertain; some ethical motivations	135
	Gospel of Ebionites	Abbreviation of Synoptic Gospels; at times Jesus narrates story.	Oppose virgin birth; emphasize union of Christ and Spirit at baptism; oppose temple sacrifice	150
	Gospel of Hebrews	Resurrection appearance to James; James at last supper; Holy Spirit is female; Spirit rests in and unites with Jesus.	Lift position of James; support mystical piety	150
HERETICAL GOSPELS	Gospel of Truth	Homily on Jesus without narrative of His life or sayings	Define gospel in Gnostic terms	160
	Gospel of Thomas	114 secret sayings of Jesus	Gnostic teachings	200
APOCRYPHAL ACTS	Acts of John	Life of John with journey to Rome, life on Patmos, death in Ephesus; teachings of John	Gnostic teaching	225
	Acts of Peter	Disputes between Peter and Simon in Jerusalem and Rome; miracles; Peter's death	God's victory over Satan; information about Peter; moral teachings	185
	Acts of Paul	Acts of Paul and Thecla, correspondence with Corinthians; further missionary work; miracles; martyrdom	Support Paul's image; build up the church; teach sexual continence; hope of resurrection	190
	Acts of Andrew	Journey across Asia Minor into Greece; miracles; martyrdom	Self-knowledge; deny material world; fight Satan	150
	Acts of Thomas	Journeys; miracles; hymns; anointings; Eucharist; conversions; martyrdom	Gnostic salvation doctrine; asceticism; no baptism	215
APOCRYPHAL EPISTLES	Proclamation of Peter	Summary of apostolic gospel	Apology for Christianity	100
	Epistle to Laodiceans	Combination of Pauline passages based on Col 4:16	Supply lost letter of Paul	300?
APOCRYPHAL APOCALYPSES	Ascension of Isaiah	Martyrdom; heavenly journey	Supply prophecy of Christ	225?
	Apocalypse of Peter	Vision of heaven and of hell	Provide explicit teaching on afterlife	135

introductions to Matthew, Mark, Luke, and John).

Each of the writers shaped the telling of his story to accomplish particular purposes. For example, Matthew focused on Jesus as the Messiah foretold in the Old Testament. Mark presented Jesus as an active Person, a powerful Minister, and a Suffering Servant. Luke portrayed Jesus as the Savior for all people. John specifically explained his purpose in writing his Gospel (see John 20:31). He wanted his readers to understand that Jesus is the Christ, the Son of the living God. We can be thankful that we have four different Gospels. Our knowledge of who Jesus is and what He has done is far richer and deeper because we have more than just one Gospel.

The various purposes of the Gospels can help us understand and appreciate their differences and unique features. The way or time an event or saying of Jesus is presented is often shaped by the author's overall purpose. This in no way casts doubt on the reliability or trustworthiness of the writing or the historicity of the event. Instead we recognize that while the Gospels can be read together as complementary stories in *harmony* one with another, we also learn that each Gospel must be read and understood on its own. Together these four books present for us the good news about Jesus Christ, the Son of God.

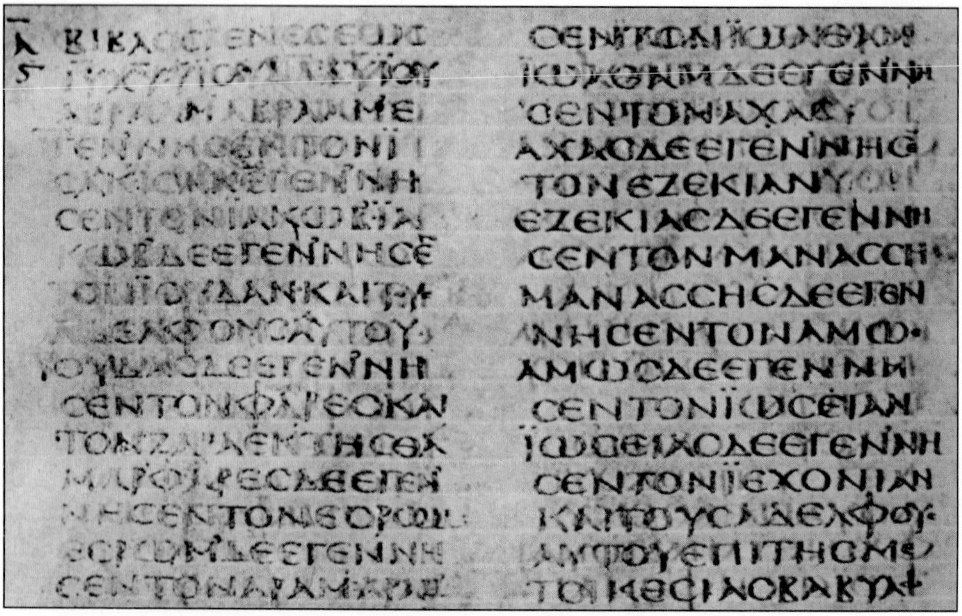

Shown above is a portion of the first page of the Gospel of Matthew in the Codex Sinaiticus, one of the most important manuscripts of the New Testament. It dates from the fourth century A.D. and was discovered on Mount Sinai in 1844.

MATTHEW

Strictly speaking, the Gospel of Matthew is anonymous. The titles of the Gospels were not added until the second century. But early church tradition unanimously ascribes this Gospel to Matthew. Matthew was also known as Levi, one of Jesus' twelve apostles, and a converted tax-collector (9:9-13; 10:3). Although modern scholarship has called this identification into repeated question, there are no persuasive reasons for rejecting this tradition outright.

Recipients

Early church tradition meshes with the style and contents of the Gospel to suggest that Matthew wrote to a Jewish-Christian audience. We have very little way of narrowing down the destination more than that. A few ancient sources favored Palestine, perhaps Jerusalem. Modern scholars often propose Syria, particularly Antioch.

Date

The hostility between Jews and Jesus' followers on the pages of the Gospel has suggested to many that Matthew's Jewish-Christian church had decisively broken from the (non-Christian) Jewish synagogue. This often leads to a dating in the mid-80s or later, after the synagogues allegedly introduced a curse on heretics (including Christians) into their liturgy of prayers. Quotations by the Apostolic Fathers suggest an upper limit for the dating of around A.D. 100. References to the destruction of the temple (most notably 22:7) have convinced many that Matthew was writing after that event (which occurred in A.D. 70).

But none of these considerations proves decisive. It is increasingly doubtful whether a formal break between synagogue and church ever occurred at one specific period of time over a wide portion of the Roman Empire. Arguments based on Jesus' prophecies often rule out the possibility that He genuinely could have foretold the future. How one understands the literary relationship between Matthew, Mark, and Luke will also affect the dating. Matthew probably knew and used extensive portions of Mark in his writing. But Mark may be dated from the late 50s to sometime in the early 70s.

Luke apparently also used Mark, and many have dated Luke-Acts to A.D. 62, since that is when the final events of Acts took place. Mark would then have to be earlier, allowing for Matthew to be as early as the late 50s or early 60s. But there are other explanations for the end of Luke. Repeated references in Matthew to Jewish rituals, which could no longer be performed after A.D. 70, may suggest a date in the 60s, which would dovetail with possible Sadducean persecution of Christians between 58 and 65. In light of all the variable factors, we should allow for any date between A.D. 40 and A.D. 100, but perhaps a slight weight of evidence favors a time before the fall of Jerusalem between A.D. 58 and A.D. 69.

Literary Form

Despite many counterproposals, Matthew, like the other Gospels, is best described as a theological biography. Little if any detail in the book appears out of sheer historical interest. Matthew was trying to commend his understanding of Christianity to his audience. But theological motive does not exclude historical reliability. Ancient historiography regularly valued both accuracy and ideology even if it did not insist on compartmentalizing the two the way modern historians do. Once Matthew's text is interpreted in light of literary conventions of the day, which for the most part do not require modern standards of precision in reporting, we may fairly assume his accounts to be historically trustworthy. But the reason for their inclusion is almost always theological.

I. Introduction to Jesus' Ministry (1:1–4:16)
II. The Development of Jesus' Ministry (4:17–16:20)
III. The Climax of Jesus' Ministry (16:21–28:20)

Purpose and Theology

Matthew most likely wrote his Gospel for several reasons. (1) He wanted to convince non-Christian Jews of the truth of Christianity. (2) He sought to explain to Christians how their religion is the fulfillment of God's promises and patterns of activity in the Old Testament (3) He wanted to give young believers basic instructions in Christian living. (4) He wanted to encourage his church in the midst of persecution from hostile authorities in both Jewish and Roman circles. (5) He desired to deepen Christian faith by supplying more details about Jesus' words and works.

The Gospel's theological emphases mesh with these purposes. Matthew took pains to demonstrate God's work in Jesus to bring the fulfillment of His promises to His chosen people, the Jews. Through (or even in spite of) their response, Matthew wanted to show how God offers the identical blessings and judgments to all humanity (see 10:5-6 and 15:24 with 2:1-12 and 28:19). He depicted Christ as a teacher (through five main sermons in chaps. 5–7; 10; 13; 18; 23–25). But he portrayed Him

Order of the Gospels

The question of relationship between our Gospels is often discussed, but not easily answered. This is especially so when attention is focused on the Gospels of Matthew, Mark, and Luke, the popularly designated "Synoptic Gospels."

The term *Synoptic* means *to see together* or *to view from a common perspective.* The first three Gospels are so identified because they present the life and ministry of Jesus from a common point-of-view that is different from that of the Gospel of John.

In general the Synoptics follow the same outline and record similar material. Sometimes their accounts are almost identical. Yet at other times important differences are observed. This phenomena has given rise, especially in the modern era, to what is called "the Synoptic problem."

How are we to understand and explain the literary relationship of these three Gospels? John's Gospel is usually dated later than the Synoptics (A.D. 80–95), and no extensive literary dependence is readily discerned. Therefore we will note the more popular theories as they pertain to the Synoptic Gospels.

Primitive Gospel Theory

This position suggests that our three biblical or canonical Gospels drew their material from an earlier, more primitive gospel that has not been preserved, probably written in Aramaic. This view has little if any historical support.

Oral Tradition Theory

This view believes that only an "oral gospel" is behind our Synoptic Gospels. This theory emphasizes that the Gospel material was passed along orally or by word of mouth before being written down. There is some truth in this theory, but it is insufficient to account for (a) the possible existence of early written accounts (see Luke 1:1-3), (b) the different order of events discovered in the Synoptics, and (c) the variations in form, content, vocabulary, grammar, and word order that are evident in our Synoptic Gospels.

Markan Priority

This theory is the most popular theory among contemporary Bible students. It was not advocated until the modern era and the rise of historical criticism. This theory initially began as a two-source theory but is now usually expanded into a four-source theory.

Mark is viewed as the first Gospel written and is the foundation of Matthew and Luke, who incorporated almost all of Mark. Matthew and Luke also utilized another source (usually assumed to have been written) commonly called Q, from the German word *Quelle,* meaning *source.* This second source is said to account for about 250 verses of mostly teaching material of Jesus common to Matthew and Luke but that is not in Mark.

Expanding the two-source theory, an M-source is thought to account for material unique to Matthew, and an L-source is hypothetically set forth to account for material peculiar to Luke. Though the most popular theory, this model faces the difficulties of (a) having no early church support and (b) claiming sources (Q, L, M) with no historical support for their existence.

Matthean Priority

Matthean priority was the position of the church from the first century until the Enlightenment. This theory sees Matthew as the first Synoptic, Luke, who utilized Matthew, as second, and Mark as third, being an abbreviated combination of Matthew and Luke.

The preaching of Peter is also seen as a significant influence on Mark's Gospel. The strengths of this theory are that (a) it was the unanimous view of the early church, and (b) it can account for the literary relationship that exists between the Synoptic Gospels without assuming hypothetical documents with little or no historical support.

While we do not know for sure how the Gospel writers possibly interacted with one another or what sources may have influenced their work, we are confident that the result of their work has given us three inspired, truthful, and authoritative portraits of our Lord Jesus Christ. □

as much more than a teacher, the Son of David-Messiah, and Lord of the universe and of human hearts.

Matthew portrays Christian living preeminently as doing the will of God, which is defined as following Jesus in discipleship and obeying all of His commands (7:21-27; 12:46-50; 28:19). Christ does not abolish the Old Testament, but the law can be rightly applied in a believer's life only after one understands how it is fulfilled in Jesus (5:17). Matthew is the only Gospel to use the word "church" (16:18; 18:17). He envisaged his community of followers living on after his death and resurrection and completing his ministry of preaching the kingdom of God so that men and women might enter into a saving relationship with Jesus.

1:1–2:23
Jesus' Origin

Matthew began his story by recounting selected events surrounding Jesus' birth (about 4–6 B.C.). The genealogy establishes Jesus' ancestry by which He was a legitimate descendant of David and rightful candidate for the messianic throne (1:1-17). The rest of Matthew's "infancy narrative" is comprised of five quotations from the Old Testament and the stories that illustrate how those texts were fulfilled in Jesus (1:18–2:23).

In one instance we read of the rather straightforward accomplishment of certain events previously predicted, namely, the Messiah's birthplace in Bethlehem (2:5-6). In two instances texts that were not prophecies at all in the Old Testament are typologically reapplied to events surrounding Christ's birth (2:15,18). Typology is the perception of recurring patterns of action in salvation-history that are too "coincidental" to be attributed to any cause but God. Examples are that the Messiah, like the Israelites of old, was brought out of Egypt and that the mothers in the vicinity of Bethlehem again bewailed the loss of their children. In one instance Matthew quoted a "text" that does not even appear in the Old Testament, but probably he had a more general theme in view (2:23). In the most famous case, he cited the prophecy about a child to be born to a virgin (1:23). This probably combines direct prediction-fulfillment with typology: Isaiah originally had a young woman of his day in view, but the prophecy was not exhaustively fulfilled in her or her child. This left Jews to believe that a great, more complete fulfillment still awaited them.

Two other themes emerge in these opening two chapters. First, Christ would be for all the nations even as He excluded many from His own people who refused to welcome Him. Even before He grew up, the Messiah clearly was not just another Jewish nationalist. His genealogy includes five women, all of whom were shrouded, rightly or wrongly, in the suspicions of having given birth to illegitimate children. The Gentile magi who came to worship the Christ child (2:1-12) are most likely Persian astrologers. They responded properly, however, to God's revelation to them, whereas the political and religious authorities of Jerusalem did not. Second, Herod figures, directly or indirectly, in every passage in chapter 2. Matthew contrasted the one who is truly the King of the Jews by birth (2:2) with the one who actually rules but turns out to be a temporary intruder.

Mary and Joseph fleeing to Egypt with the baby Jesus

3:1–4:16
Jesus' Preparation for Ministry

Matthew jumped abruptly to Jesus' adulthood, passing over in silence the intervening years of His life. The events of this section set the stage for and culminate in Jesus' baptism and temptation, both of which would prepare Him for His approximately three-year ministry (about A.D. 27–30). Jesus' cousin John preceded Him in the public eye, fulfilling the prophecies that one like Elijah would come to prepare the way for the Christ (3:1-12; see 11:7-19, esp. v. 14). He became known as "the Baptist" because he called Jews to repent of their sins and

The Jordan River flows south from Mount Hermon through Israel and empties into the Dead Sea.

demonstrate the rededication of their lives to God by immersion in water, a rite otherwise largely reserved for Gentile proselytes to Judaism. John vividly taught the lesson that one's faith is a matter of personal commitment and not a reliance on ancestral pedigree.

Jesus and John met each other on the banks of the Jordan, where Jesus requested baptism even though He did not need to repent from sin. After initial protests John acceded, recognizing that this formed part of God's will (3:14-15). God used the occasion to testify with a heavenly voice to Jesus' true identity (3:16). Jesus is God's Son, the one whom Isaiah called Immanuel ("God with us," 1:23).

Immediately the Spirit orchestrated the circumstances

The New Testament and Criticism

Scholars who study the Gospels use the many different tools and methods of biblical criticism. "Criticism" in this context is a neutral word, simply meaning *analysis.* The different branches of criticism scholars employ fall into three major categories.

1. *Methods Common to the Interpretation of All Written Texts.* Several things scholars do are exactly the same as what many lay readers of Scripture do, whether or not they realize it. In fact, valid interpretation of any written document requires three important foundational steps.

• If the original document is not available, readers need to know how reliable are the copies they have. Reconstructing, to the best of our ability, what the biblical authors actually wrote is the science of textual criticism. This is extremely crucial for those who believe those that words were inspired by God.

Most modern translations of the Bible include footnotes that alert the reader to the most important textual variants. In the Gospels, for example, scholars have discovered that the earliest and most reliable texts do not contain Mark 16:9-20; John 7:53–8:11; or Matthew 6:13b. (See the article "Differences in Bible Manuscripts.")

• A reliable translation is obviously essential if a reader does not understand the language in which a document was originally written. Most English-speaking people cannot read the Greek of the NT, so they rely on a variety of translations. These range from very literal to highly paraphrastic. Because the Gospels are written in narrative form, smooth, idiomatic renderings (such as NIV) are often the clearest.

• Historical criticism seeks to learn as much as possible about the political, social, and religious background of the author, audience, and general culture of the time of the document being studied. Without this discipline it is too easy to read modern understandings of events into ancient texts in ways that are highly inappropriate. For example, most people today think of Samaritans as "good guys" and Pharisees as "bad guys." But in the Gospels almost everyone except Jesus viewed them as exactly the opposite!

2. *Methods Largely Unique to the Study of the Gospels.* Another three methods of scholarly study focus only on documents that were compiled by combining information gathered from written sources with that which was passed on by word of mouth. Matthew, Mark, and Luke are the clearest examples in the NT of this kind of document.

• The types of similarities and differences among these three "Synoptic" Gospels, along with the testimony of Luke 1:1-4, convince almost all scholars that some kind of literary interrelationship exists among them. The study of the written materials on which a particular writer drew is called source criticism.

The most common explanation assumes that Mark wrote his Gospel first and that Matthew and Luke both used it in writing theirs. Many people also believe that Matthew and Luke had a common source of Jesus' sayings (often labeled Q, from the German *Quelle* for *source*). These theories do not necessarily compete with belief in biblical inspiration. Rather, they may illuminate what processes the Gospel writers used as God's Spirit guided them. They can also help us understand what a particular writer was emphasizing when we see how he reworded his sources. (See the article "Order of the Gospels.")

• Form criticism recognizes

that would permit the devil to test Jesus' understanding of that sonship. Would He use His elevated power and position for self-aggrandizement or for military or political ends? Would He turn out to be another would-be liberator of the Jews from Rome? Or would He follow the way of the Suffering Servant, the way that leads to the cross? The three temptations (4:1-11) epitomize all major categories of human temptation, what the apostle John later would call the "lust of the flesh," "the lust of the eyes," and "the pride of life" (1 John 2:16). Where Adam, the nation of Israel, and indeed all humanity had previously failed, Jesus remained faithful. His ministry proceeded according to plan. As it did, He would continue to fulfill Scripture (4:12-16).

4:17-25
Introduction

"From that time on Jesus began to preach" (4:17) marks the beginning of His major public ministry, mostly spent in Galilee. "Repent, for the kingdom of heaven is near" (4:17) epitomizes His message in one sentence. With Jesus' ministry, death, and resurrection, God's saving reign would be inaugurated in the hearts and lives of those who became His disciples. Universal acknowledgment of God's sovereignty in Jesus must await his second coming, but the kingdom has at least been inaugurated. He began to call to Himself those who would be His most intimate associates and trainees (4:18-22). Matthew then previewed the essence of Christ's ministry with the key

that not all parts of the Gospels are made up of the same kind of material. Jesus' teaching employs parables, proverbs, commands, and a variety of figures of speech. The narratives of His life and action include miracles, controversies with His opponents, object lessons, and so on.

Scholars try to isolate each of these different "forms" and understand the distinctive rules of interpretation each requires. Parables, for example, cannot be treated as straightforward history. Many form critics (sometimes under the heading of "tradition criticism") also go on to try to reconstruct the manner in which each form was passed along orally until it was first written down.

• Redaction criticism focuses on the distinctive emphases of each of the Gospel writers. *Redaction* means *editing.* When one analyzes the unique ways in which the Evangelists edited their sources and arranged their material in different ways, one learns a lot about their particular concerns. If God gave us four Gospels rather than just one, presumably we are to learn something new from each one.

Redaction critics largely agree, for example, that Matthew wanted to stress Jesus as the Son of David and King of Israel, that Mark highlighted His role as miracle worker and suffering servant, that Luke emphasized Jesus as completely human and concerned for the outcasts of society, and that John underlined Jesus as the Son of God equal to the Father Himself.

3. *Newer Methods of Biblical Study Not Limited to the Gospels.* In recent years scholars have begun to use a number of approaches that may or may not become established tools of biblical criticism. Many of these derive from other disciplines of scholarly study but have been widely applied to the Gospels.

• Midrash criticism (from the Hebrew word for *commentary*) seeks to understand the way in which NT writers quoted or alluded to the OT. Often scholars compare the Gospel writers' approaches to those of ancient rabbis. Since Matthew quoted the OT most often of the four Gospels, his work has been especially scrutinized.

• Canon criticism explores the way the interpretation of a book of the Bible has changed once it was included with other writings viewed as Scripture. For example, we often forget to read Luke and Acts as a two-volume unity, since John was inserted in between them in our Bibles.

• From one point of view, nearly all the methods discussed here could be called literary criticism. But scholars usually reserve this label for studies that analyze the plot, themes, motifs, character development, and other literary devices of the biblical narratives. Recent, more esoteric approaches focus more on the readers' responses than on the authors' intentions in analyzing the Gospels.

Still other scholars study the "deep structures" of the texts, exploring the underlying relationships between the various characters and actions that unfold in the Gospel stories.

• People trained in social-scientific approaches often analyze Scripture in terms of the psychology, sociology, anthropology, or economic systems presupposed by Scripture. The Gospels have been viewed as justifying numerous ideologies, including Jungian psychotherapy, Marxist socialism, women's liberation, and Western capitalism!

Every one of the methods discussed here can be and has been abused. The presuppositions of individual scholars play a large part in determining how well or poorly they will employ the tools of Gospel criticism. But each method has given scholars valuable insights into the meaning of the Gospels. □

The pinnacle ("highest point," NIV) of the temple (Matt 4:5) may refer to the southeastern corner of the temple area shown above which in New Testament times towered over the Kidron Valley 130 feet below.

terms "preaching, teaching and healing," which characterized his activity wherever He went (4:23-25).

5:1–7:29
The Sermon on the Mount

Perhaps no portion of Scripture is as well known as Jesus' Great Sermon. It begins with the well-loved Beatitudes (5:3-12), which classically exemplify God's inversion of the world's values. In His kingdom or reign, those who are considered fortunate include the poor, sorrowing, humble, righteous, merciful, pure, peacemakers, and persecuted. These are precisely those categories of people too many of us tend to despise and ostracize.

These countercultural values could suggest that Jesus intended His followers to withdraw from the world and form separate communities. Matthew 5:13-16 immediately belies any such notion. Disciples must be salt and light, arresting decay and providing illumination for a lost and dying world.

Such radical ideas understandably would have raised the question of the relationship between Jesus' teaching and the Old Testament. Jesus addressed this topic next (5:17-48). He had not come to abolish the law, yet neither had He come to preserve but rather to "fulfill" it—to bring to completion everything to which it originally pointed. Some believe that Jesus demonstrated just the opposite with His contrasts in verses 21-48. These verses make plain, however, that Jesus was setting up dramatic contrasts between His teaching and the typical interpretations of the law. In some cases He drastically deepened the requirements. He demanded a greater righteousness (v. 20), as with His discussion of murder, adultery, and divorce. But in other cases He actually set aside certain provisions of the Old Testament in favor of entirely new, internalized regulations, such as with oaths, retaliation, and probably love for enemy.

Throughout these illustrations Jesus used numerous hyperboles (the clearest is vv. 29-30). They were not meant to be applied literally, but we nevertheless can understand why portions of this material have been taken as a manifesto for nonviolence in the church and in the world (particularly vv. 38-47).

Matthew 5:48 closes off this section of the sermon by demonstrating that Jesus was setting forth an ideal. His disciples will never attain to these standards this side of His return, but they are not thereby excused from continuing to strive after those goals.

Matthew 6:1-18 turns to the theme of true versus hypocritical piety. In three closely parallel examples, Jesus treated the practices of almsgiving, prayer, and fasting. In each case the motive for correct religious behavior must be to please God rather than fellow humans. In the middle of the second of these topics, on prayer, Jesus gave the classic disciples' prayer, which has come to be known as the Our Father or the Lord's Prayer (6:9-13). In it He models all the elements of proper prayer in an appropriate sequence. He presented elements such as praise and adoration, leaving room for God's sovereign will to override ours; appeal for kingdom priorities to be manifest on the earth; personal petition and pleas for forgiveness contingent on our practice of forgiving others; and prayer for strength to avoid the tempter and his snares.

Matthew 6:19-34 is united by the themes of wealth and worry. Here Jesus contrasted transient, earthly riches with permanent, heavenly riches. If our priorities correctly reside with the latter, God through His people will take care of the former. The implementation of 6:33 presupposes Christian communities who look after the needy in their own midst as well as throughout the world. Matthew 6:22-24 catches us up short with its bold suggestion that money may be the single biggest competitor with God for ultimate allegiance in our lives, particularly for those who are not in the poorest classes of society. Affluent individuals who call themselves Christians need to read verse 24 again and again and ask themselves who they really are serving.

Matthew 7:1-12 rounds out the body of the sermon by discussing how to treat others. First, Jesus called His followers not to be judgmental in their relationships with others (vv. 1-5). But His illustrations also underline that once we have properly dealt with our own sins, we have the right and responsibility to evaluate others' behavior and to help them deal with their shortcomings (vv. 5-6). Second, He reminds us of God's generosity and desire to give us good gifts (7:7-11), though, after the Beatitudes we dare not define "good" in worldly terms like health and wealth. The well-known Golden Rule (7:12) brings

The Sea of Galilee as viewed from the northwest

BEATITUDES

Beatitudes are words of blessing or congratulations. In the Greco-Roman world blessedness was something associated with the existence of the gods. Everyone assumed the gods were blessed because they were immune to the troubles and sorrows of day-to-day existence. Any human who was thought to enjoy the imagined privileges of the gods was considered to be blessed like the gods. People were therefore saluted for their fortunate external conditions.

The beatitudes in the Old Testament are quite different from the secular blessings. People were proclaimed blessed because of their godly lives. They were to be congratulated because they had divine approval. For example, those who were pronounced blessed were those who had God as Lord (Ps 144:15), who feared God (Ps 112:1-3), who trusted in God (Ps 84:12), who dwelt or took refuge in God (Ps 2:12), and who wisely obeyed God (Ps 119:1-2).

The OT beatitudes were primarily intended to motivate others to develop the same sterling virtues in their lives so that they might also have God's approval. These beatitudes offer practical wisdom for happiness in this life. If you want to have lasting joy in this world, obey God.

The focus of the beatitudes found in the Jewish literature composed during the time between the Testaments reflects the political changes in Israel's historical circumstances. The concern shifted from how to be happy in this life—which seemed impossible— to how to be happy in the life to come. The emphasis was on how to be saved from the last judgment. The blessed are those who will have a share in the age to come. The tone of these beatitudes is one of consolation and assurance.

Jesus' beatitudes are an announcement that the new age of salvation has already dawned. Jesus did not address a past generation or a future one. He told His disciples that they were blessed because they were able to see and hear what the prophets and the righteous longed to see and hear (Matt 13:16-17; Luke 10:23-24). He acclaimed the poor in spirit, the weeping, the hungry and thirsty for righteousness, the persecuted, and the hated because God has acted decisively to make them happy (see Matt 5:1-12).

Despite appearances to the contrary, congratulations are in order because Jesus' presence fulfills all the hopes of the pious. Although the persecuted may still be harassed, they are to know that their redemption has come. Jesus announced that if our lives are marked by the characteristics of those described in the beatitudes we participate in the reign of God that burst in at Jesus' incarnation.

We should note one more important characteristic about Jesus' beatitudes. As announcements of blessing and congratulations, many of the beatitudes are paradoxical. They do not reflect the conventional wisdom of the day that prizes earthly well-being. Jesus said, "Happy are those the world considers unhappy." The poor in spirit, the mourners, the meek, the hungry, and the persecuted are not normally counted as blessed. Most would view them as unfortunate. The same thing that was true in the ancient world may also be said for our culture today. Such is the nature of Jesus' beatitudes. □

the body of Jesus' message to a climax and epitomizes the ethic underlying it all—treat others as you would want to be treated.

Matthew 7:14-27 forms the concluding warning. There are only two possible responses to Jesus' preaching—obedience or rejection. The narrow versus the wide roads (vv. 13-14), the good versus the bad fruit (vv. 15-23), and the wise versus the foolish builders (vv. 24-27) illustrate this warning in three parallel ways. Professions of faith without appropriate changes of life-style prove empty. But mere works by themselves do not save; a relationship with Jesus is needed. On Judgment Day many will cry, "Lord, Lord" and appeal to their deeds. Christ will reply, "I never knew you" (7:23).

8:1–9:34
Pictures of Jesus' Healing Ministry

Chapters 8–9 present nine miracle stories, all but one dealing with Jesus' physically healing the sick. As with His preaching, He astonished people with His authority, this time in working miracles. Matthew interrupted his narrative in two places to present Jesus' teaching on discipleship (8:18-22 and 9:9-17), thus creating three collections of three miracle stories each. The first underlines how Jesus healed the ritually outcast (8:1-17). He deliberately touched the leper, risking defilement, to cure bodily uncleanness (vv. 1-4). Then He rewarded the Gentile centurion's unparalleled faith by curing his servant, transcending Jewish boundaries of ethnic uncleanness (vv. 5-13). Third, He healed Peter's mother-in-law despite conventional taboos based on gender uncleanness (vv. 14-15). Matthew characteristically inserted an Old Testament fulfillment quotation to demonstrate how Jesus was accomplishing the mission of Isaiah's Suffering Servant by all of this (vv. 16-17).

The synagogue at the site of ancient Capernaum on the northern shore of the Sea of Galilee.

The first break in the healings occurs with Jesus' replies to two would-be disciples, both of whom exhibited inadequate responses to His exacting demands (8:18-22). The one man was overeager; the other, undereager. Neither had adequately counted the cost of following Christ. The second group of miracles proves even more dramatic than the first. Jesus stilled a storm (8:23-27), exorcised a Gentile demoniac (8:28–9:1), and healed a paralytic (9:2-8). In so doing He displayed His power and authority over disaster, demons, and disease. The stilling of the storm is the lone miracle in these two chapters that is not a healing. But Matthew's reference to Jesus' "rebuke" (v. 26) employs language characteristic of exorcisms, so perhaps Matthew saw this miracle as a kind of healing of nature.

After this dramatic series of wonders, Jesus could return again to the question of discipleship. This time He received a more adequate response—from Matthew himself (9:9-13). This in turn triggered Jesus' key pronouncements on the new, radical priorities of His ministry (9:14-17). A correct appreciation for who Christ is, disclosed in the miracles, should lead people to serve him in discipleship.

The final series of miracle stories includes one passage with two actual healings in it. En route to Jairus's home, Jesus stopped the flow of blood from a chronically hemorrhaging woman. The delay resulted in His not merely curing Jairus's daughter but actually raising her from the dead (9:18-26). Next He gave sight to two blind men (9:27-31). Finally, He restored speech to a mute person (9:32-34).

Throughout these three accounts, the crowds that observed Jesus' miracles began to take sides. In 9:26 Jesus received widespread positive publicity. In 9:31 this continued, but Jesus hinted at possible danger as well (9:30). In 9:33-34 the antagonism became explicit. Even as His popularity grew, the Jewish leaders accused Jesus of working His wonders by the devil's power. This charge reflects consistent Jewish hostility over the next several centuries. Interestingly, rabbinic Judaism never tried to deny that Jesus worked miracles but merely challenged the source of His authority.

9:35–10:42
Opposition Predicted

Jesus' second major "sermon" in Matthew proceeds at once. One might entitle it "The Sermon on Mission: To the Jew First and Also to the Greek." The sermon begins after introductory remarks explaining the need for workers to help Christ proclaim the good news of the king-

JESUS' MINISTRY AS FULFILLMENT OF SCRIPTURE IN MATTHEW		
Aspects of His Ministry	**Fulfillment Passage in Matthew**	**OT Prophecy**
His virgin birth and role as God with us	Matt 1:18,22-23	Isa 7:14
His birth in Bethlehem and shepherd role	Matt 2:4-6	Mic 5:2
His refugee years in Egypt and role as God's Son	Matt 2:14-15	Hos 11:1
His upbringing in Nazareth and messianic role (the Hebrew term for branch is *nezer*)	Matt 2:23	Isa 11:1
His preaching ministry in Galilee and role as Light to the Gentiles	Matt 4:12-16	Isa 9:1-2
His healing ministry and role as God's Servant	Matt 8:16-17	Isa 53:4
His reluctance to attract attention and His role as God's chosen and loved Servant	Matt 12:16-21	Isa 42:1-4
His teaching in parables and His role in proclaiming God's sovereign rule	Matt 13:34-35	Ps 78:2
His humble entry into Jerusalem and role as King	Matt 21:1-5	Zech 9:9
His betrayal, arrest, and death and role as Suffering Servant	Matt 26:50,56	The prophetic writings as a whole

dom and after a list of the twelve Jesus formally called to this task (9:35–10:4). It divides sharply into two quite different sections. In 10:5-16 Jesus laid down the stipulations that would apply to the immediate mission He was sending His followers out two-by-two to carry out. They were to travel light and unencumbered, depend on others' hospitality for their daily provisions, and not stay long with any who remain unresponsive to their message. They were to limit their mission to Jewish territories and communities. As God's chosen people, the Jews had the right and the privilege of hearing and responding to this latest and fullest revelation from God before the rest of the world did.

From 10:17-42 Jesus broadened His scope far beyond His earthly life and the immediate mission on which the disciples were embarking. He envisaged the prospect of future hostility from both Jews and Gentiles, both frustrated family members and officials in high places with legal authority to persecute and potentially condemn Christ's followers (vv. 17-25). He explained the proper reaction to such hostility: Fear God who can condemn people eternally more than humans who can merely take away one's physical life (vv. 26-31).

As at the end of the Sermon on the Mount, Jesus closed His address by reminding His followers that they have only two options—either to give God ultimate allegiance or not (vv. 32-42). To do so they must acknowledge that they are Jesus' followers (vv. 32-33), put God above family (vv. 34-39), and welcome those who are Christ's emissaries (vv. 40-42). Any other choice will lead to Jesus' disowning them, which results in the loss of eternal life (vv. 33,39).

11:1–12:50
Opposition Experienced

The hostilities Jesus predicted the disciples would later experience now began to chase His footsteps as well. In chapter 11 the opposition is implicit; in chapter 12 it becomes explicit. John the Baptist had been arrested and understandably began to question whether he had correctly identified the Messiah-Liberator after all. After sending his disciples to interrogate Christ, he was told to consider Jesus' mighty deeds and then to make up his own mind (11:1-6).

But if John was doubting Jesus, some in the audience may have been starting to doubt John. So Jesus discussed the Baptist with the crowds. John too came in some unexpected ways but was nevertheless to be viewed as the forerunner, fulfilling Old Testament prophecy about preparation for the Messiah's advent (vv. 7-19). In fact, John was the greatest man to live under the old covenant. But he would not live long enough to see Christ's death and resurrection establish the new covenant, so in that sense even the most insignificant Christian was greater than he (v. 11). The crowds were not to reject the legitimacy of either Jesus or John. Time would vindicate God's wisdom in sending each in unexpected fashion (vv. 16-19). Turning to still a third audience, Jesus began to upbraid, because of their unbelief, the Jewish cities in which He performed most of His miracles (vv. 20-24). A proper response should imitate His disciples, who generally represented the powerless and insignificant of the world but who accepted the spiritual rest available in Christ (vv. 20-25).

In chapter 11 no one opposes Jesus directly. In chapter 12 opposition turns explicit and ugly. First, the Jewish authorities called Jesus on the carpet for breaking their Sabbath laws (vv. 1-14). Although it cannot be proven that Jesus went beyond the infringement of the "oral law" to violating the Old Testament itself, part of the argument Jesus made on His behalf appeals to Old Testament precedent in which the very provisions of the Mosaic law were violated (v. 4). Matthew reasoned that in Jesus something greater than both David and the temple (the king and priestly cult) is present. Surely very serious infractions indeed would be needed to have elicited the Pharisees' extreme response (v. 14). Jesus withdrew from hostilities and in so doing again fulfilled Scripture (vv. 15-21).

But the antagonism quickly resumed and grew to a fever pitch. Another exorcism led to the identical charge as in 9:34. This time Jesus responded at some length (vv. 22-37). The Jews dared not accuse Him of being empowered by the devil. They too cast out demons, so their argument could easily turn back on themselves. In fact, it is absurd to imagine Satan warring against himself in this way. More so than any other kind of miracle, the exorcisms should make plain that God's saving rule had arrived.

Verse 28 offers one of the most crucial texts in all of the Gospels demonstrating that the kingdom had come with Jesus. Having defended Himself, Jesus then unleashed an attack on His accusers. They had better "come clean" and "show their true colors," which would disclose the evil intentions of their hearts. In this context appears the troublesome warning against the one unforgivable sin of which Scripture speaks—blasphemy against the Holy Spirit (vv. 31-32). Probably we are to understand this sin as the prolonged, hostile, and unrepentant rejection of Jesus as one empowered by the Holy Spirit, which eventually dulls a person's spiritual sensibilities beyond a point of no return (cf. Rom 1:18-32). But we dare never play God and pretend we know who such people are; we would invariably err. And all persons fearful of having committed such sin by that very concern demonstrate that they have not.

If the exorcisms prove inconclusive to the Pharisees, what more indisputable sign could Jesus have offered them (vv. 38-42)? "None," Jesus responded, save for His resurrection, which, if the other signs had not proved convincing would not likely seem any more decisive (Luke 16:19-31). As at the end of chapter 11, Jesus concluded with the positive alternative. It is not adequate simply to be exorcised (vv. 43-45). One must replace the emptiness created by the demons' absence with loyalty to Christ. Those who follow Him and do God's will thus form His true family, even while some literally related to Him must take a back seat (vv. 46-50).

Etruscan bronze figurines of a peasant plowing with a yoke of oxen (500s B.C). Jesus used the yoke metaphor in inviting people to come to Him (Matt 11:29-30).

Parables of Jesus

Perhaps the most distinctive style of Jesus' teaching was His use of parables. From the outset of His public ministry until the last days in Jerusalem, one comes across His timeless parables. Matthew's word is appropriate at every juncture: "He told them many things in parables" (Matt 13:3). A parable has been defined as a comparison from nature or daily life designed to teach a spiritual truth.

Parables and Teaching

Everyone loves a good story. Jesus developed stories from familiar images and ideas that reveal truth about the nature of God, prayer, spiritual values, stewardship, judgment, and the kingdom of God. He used parables as a teaching device with His disciples, antagonistic religious leaders, and ordinary people.

The Synoptic Gospels contain between fifty and sixty such stories. Add to that number ten brief stories found in John's Gospel. Some of them are very brief, such as the parables of the pearl of great price, the leaven, the hidden treasure. Some are full-length stories like the parables of the good Samaritan, the talents, the sower and the soils, the rich fool, the prodigal son, and others.

Parables and Daily Life

Jesus was the keenest of observers about daily life. He drew lessons from farmers sowing in the field, from village customs about weddings, from shepherds and sheep, and from banquets. Recall that His audiences were often simple, uneducated people such as fishermen, farmers, and villagers. They could grasp His lessons easily about an unjust judge or a friend who knocked at the midnight hour. Jesus used good storytelling to project divine truths about redemption, the kingdom of God, and ethical values.

There is a timelessness about these stories as well as a haunting beauty. They always present some powerful lesson about God and His will for life today.

Parables of the Kingdom

Many of the parables deal with the kingdom of God, a major message Jesus sought to bring to Israel in His day. Matthew 13 is the great chapter on this theme. There Jesus used a series of parables to proclaim the actions of God in His own ministry.

Parables on God's Nature

Some parables illustrate unforgettably the nature of God as Jesus came to reveal this essential truth. Speaking of the love of God to the Pharisees who were grumbling about tax gatherers and sinners around them, Jesus produced some memorable parables in Luke 15.

These parables of Jesus on the nature of God are excellent examples of His understanding of simple truths from daily living. For example, He related the shepherd's concern about a lost sheep, the peasant woman's loss of a dowry coin, the prodigal's lapse so terrible that he was feeding swine when "he came to his senses" (Luke 15:17).

Themes of the Parables

Though Jesus did not follow a consistent theme in His teachings through parables, He did address some of the major subjects of His ministry through parables. He dealt with the relation of the old covenant with the new covenant in the parables of the barren fig tree and the great feast. His lessons on prayer were highlighted by the parables of the friend who knocked at midnight and the unjust judge. Stewardship was another important theme as portrayed by the stories of the unjust steward and the rich fool.

Jesus' solemn teachings on judgment come through His parables of the wise and foolish virgins and the talents. The parables of Jesus touch movingly on death and resurrection in His parables of the rich man and Lazarus and the wicked husbandman.

Approaches to the Study of Parables

Contemporary Bible studies strongly insist that Bible students who seek the message of Jesus through His parables must understand the setting of the story. It is also important to realize that the parable usually has one major lesson to teach. Using an allegorical approach to the study of parables is both inappropriate and inaccurate. Students of Scripture should seek for one primary lesson from each parable.

Jesus' timeless reputation as a Teacher certainly comes from the substance and content of His inspired and authentic lessons. When we add the unique form of these lessons through the parables, we quickly affirm the conclusion of the centuries regarding Jesus' teaching: they "were amazed at his teaching, because he taught as one who had authority" (Matt 7:28-29). □

13:1-52
Kingdom Parables

With chapter 13 we reach the midpoint of Matthew's narrative and a turning point in Jesus' ministry. The polarization of response to Jesus made it necessary for Him to concentrate on those who remained open to His message. In His third major discourse, He taught by means of parables. Parables are short, metaphorical narratives

PARABLES OF JESUS

PARABLE	OCCASION	LESSON TAUGHT	REFERENCES
1. The speck and the log	When reproving the Pharisees	Do not presume to judge others	Matt 7:1-6; Luke 6:37-43
2. The two houses	Sermon on the Mount, at the close	The strength conferred by duty	Matt 7:24-27; Luke 6:47-49
3. Children in the marketplace	Rejection by the Pharisees of John's baptism	Evil of a fault-finding disposition	Matt 11:16; Luke 7:32
4. The two debtors	A Pharisee's self-righteous reflections	Love to Christ proportioned to grace received	Luke 7:41
5. The unclean spirit	The scribes demand a miracle in the heavens	Hardening power of unbelief	Matt 12:43-45; Luke 11:24-26
6. The rich man's meditation	Dispute of two brothers	Folly of reliance upon wealth	Luke 12:16
7. The barren fig tree	Tidings of the execution of certain Galileans	Danger in the unbelief of the Jewish people	Luke 13:6-9
8. The sower	Sermon on the seashore	Effects of preaching religious truth	Matt 13:3-8; Mark 4:3-8; Luke 8:5-8
9. The tares	The same	The severance of good and evil	Matt 13:24-30
10. The seed	The same	Power of truth	Mark 4:20
11. The grain of mustard seed	The same	Small beginnings and growth of Christ's kingdom	Matt 13:31-32; Mark 4:31-32; Luke 13:19
12. The leaven	The same	Dissemination of the knowledge of Christ	Matt 13:33; Luke 13:21
13. The lamp	To the disciples alone	Effect of good example	Matt 5:15; Mark 4:21; Luke 8:16 11:33
14. The dragnet	The same	Mixed character of the church	Matt 13:47-48
15. The hidden treasure	The same	Value of religion	Matt 13:44
16. The pearl of great value	The same	The same	Matt 13;45-46
17. The householder	The same	Varied methods of teaching truth	Matt 13:52
18. The marriage	To the Pharisees, who censured the disciples	Joy in Christ's companionship	Matt 9:15; Mark 2:19-20; Luke 5:34-35
19. The patched garment	The same	The propriety of adapting actions to circumstances	Matt 9:16; Mark 2:21; Luke 5:36
20. The wine bottles	The same	The same	Matt 9:17; Mark 2:22; Luke 5:37
21. The harvest	Spiritual wants of the Jewish people	Need of labor and prayer	Matt 9:37; Luke 10:2
22. The opponent	Slowness of the people to believe	Need of prompt repentance	Matt 5:25; Luke 12:58
23. Two insolvent debtors	Peter's question	Duty of forgiveness	Matt 18:23-35

PARABLE	OCCASION	LESSON TAUGHT	REFERENCES
24. The good Samaritan	The lawyer's question	The golden rule for all	Luke 10:30-37
25. The three loaves	Disciples ask lesson in prayer	Effect of importunity in prayer	Luke 11:5-8
26. The good shepherd	Pharisees reject testimony of miracle	Christ the only way to God	John 10:1-16
27. The narrow gate	The question, Are there few who can be saved?	Difficulty of repentance	Matt 7:14; Luke 13:24
28. The guests	Eagerness to take high places	Chief places not to be usurped	Luke 14:7-11
29. The marriage supper	Self-righteous remark of a guest	Rejection of unbelievers	Matt 22:2-9; Luke 14:16-23
30. The wedding clothes	Continuation of the same discourse	Necessity of purity	Matt 22:10-14
31. The tower	Multitudes surrounding Christ	Need of deliberation	Luke 14:28-30
32. The king going to war	The same	The same	Luke 14:31
33. The lost sheep	Pharisees objected to His receiving the wicked	Christ's love for sinners	Matt 18:12-13; Luke 15:4-7
34. The lost coin	The same	The same	Luke 15:8-9
35. The prodigal son	The same	The same	Luke 15:11-32
36. The unjust steward	To the disciples	Prudence in using property	Luke 16:1-9
37. The rich man and Lazarus	Derision of the Pharisees	Salvation not connected with wealth	Luke 16:19-31
38. The importunate widow	Teaching the disciples	Perseverance in prayer	Luke 18:2-5
39. The Pharisee and tax-gatherer	Teaching the self-righteous	Humility in prayer	Luke 18:10-14
40. The slave's duty	The same	Man's obedience	Luke 17:7-10
41. Laborers in the vineyard	The same	The same further illustrated	Matt 20:1-16
42. The talents	At the house of Zaccheus	Doom of unfaithful followers	Matt 25:14-30; Luke 19:11-27
43. The two sons	The chief priests demand His authority	Obedience better than words	Matt 21:28
44. The wicked vine-growers	The same	Rejection of the Jewish people	Matt 21:33-43; Mark 12:1-9; Luke 20:9-15
45. The fig tree	In prophesying the destruction of Jerusalem	Duty of watching for Christ's appearance	Matt 24:32; Mark 13:28; Luke 21:29-30
46. The watching slave	The same	The same	Matt 24:43; Luke 12:39
47. The man on a journey	The same	The same	Mark 13:34
48. Character of two slaves	The same	Danger of unfaithfulness	Matt 24:45-51; Luke 12:42-46
49. The ten virgins	The same	Necessity of watchfulness	Matt 25:1-12
50. The watching slaves	The same	The same	Luke 12:36-38
51. The vine and branches	At the last supper	Loss and gain	John 15:1-6

designed to teach truths about spiritual realities in ways that reveal insights to those open to Jesus' claims about Himself but that further alienate those who are not so receptive (vv. 10-17). Even the structure of this sermon reflects the growing polarization. First Jesus addressed the increasingly skeptical crowds (vv. 1-35), then He turned to His more loyal disciples (vv. 36-52). The latter do not always catch on any better at first, but they remain faithful and so eventually achieve more profound understanding.

In the more public half of His message, Jesus narrated and interpreted the parable of the sower (vv. 1-9,18-23), told the story of the wheat and the weeds (vv. 24-30), and recounted the shorter similes of the mustard seed and heaven (vv. 31-33). The "sower" depicts four kinds of seeds, standing for four ways in which people respond to God's word. The only adequate, saving response is that which perseveres until it bears a bountiful crop of fruit, notwithstanding the obstacles that may first intervene. The "wheat and weeds" warns against premature, human attempts to usurp God's role as Judge and Avenger. Despite the attacks of the enemy in the present age, often in the form of professing Christians superficially indistinguishable from the real kind, disciples are not to usurp God's role. The "mustard seed and leaven" promise great endings for God's kingdom despite inauspicious beginnings.

When Jesus went indoors to finish His discourse with His disciples, He interpreted the "wheat and weeds" for them (vv. 36-43). Then He told them a series of short parables. Included are parables of the hidden treasure and pearl of great price (vv. 44-46), the dragnet (vv. 47-50), and the scribe trained for the kingdom of heaven (vv. 51-52). The first two depict the inestimable value of the kingdom and the need to sacrifice whatever it takes to enter it. The dragnet resembles the wheat and weeds but with emphasis on final judgment and the only two destinies humanity faces. Verses 51-52 compare the well-schooled Christian to a homeowner who finds valuable treasures in his storehouse, both old and new. This probably is an allusion to continuities as well as discontinuities between old and new covenants.

View of the harbor at the ancient city of Sidon (in the modern country of Lebanon).

13:53–16:20
From Jew to Gentile

Jesus turned in the midst of His teaching from those who refused to respond adequately to His message to those who proved more receptive. In the same way He then turned from those who rejected His miracle-working ministry, in His hometown and homeland, to those outside Israel who would receive Him more gladly. Matthew 13:53–14:12 opens this section by paralleling Jesus' rejection in His hometown of Nazareth with John's rejection and execution by his own governor, Herod. Both reflect an inadequate understanding of who Jesus is. The Nazarenes thought Him merely a prophet (13:57). Herod thought Jesus was John resurrected (14:2).

The main panel of this section extends from 14:13–16:12. Here Jesus revealed Himself as the Bread of life for Jews and Gentiles alike. First He manifested Himself to Israel (14:13-36). He miraculously fed the five thousand from a few loaves and fishes, reminiscent of manna in the wilderness in the days of Moses and the exodus (vv. 13-21). Jesus was a new and greater Moses, bringing full, spiritual redemption for His people Israel if they would accept it. Then He walked on the water, showing Himself as equal to Yahweh, Lord of wind and waves (vv. 22-33). The innocuous greeting "It is I" (v. 27) exactly echoes God's words to Moses from the burning bush (Exod 3:14). It more literally reads, "I am"—the very meaning of the name of God. Appropriately Jesus' disciples reached a provisional high point in their understanding of Jesus' identity as they acclaimed Him "Son of God" (v. 33). A flurry of healings on the shores of Galilee rounds out this section (vv. 34-36).

Despite all these attestations of Jesus' divine origin, the Jewish leaders remained hostile. Matthew 15:1–16:12 thus portrays Jesus' turning from the Jews to the Gentiles, among whom He received a better welcome. In 15:1-20 Jesus had not left Israel geographically, but He certainly had departed ideologically. Here He challenged all of the Jewish "kosher laws." As with the Sabbath, one cannot prove that He went beyond breaking the oral laws to infringing on the written law of Moses, but verse 11 certainly sets the stage for this conclusion. Food, as something that goes into people from the outside, could no

THE HERODIAN RULERS

Ruler	Family Relationship	Realm of Responsibility	Dates	Biblical Reference
Herod I (the Great)	Son of Antipater	King of Judea	37–4 B.C.	Matt 2:1-22; Luke 1:5
Herod Archelaus	Oldest son of Herod the Great	Ethnarch of Judea, Samaria, and Idumea	4 B.C.–A.D. 6	Matt 2:22
Herod Philip*	Son of Herod the Great and Cleopatra of Jerusalem	Tetrarch of Iturea and Trachonitis	4 B.C.–A.D. 34	Luke 3:1
Herod Antipas	Youngest son of Herod the Great Second husband of Herodias	Tetrarch of Galilee and Perea	4 B.C.–A.D. 39	Matt 14:1-11; Mark 6:14-29; Luke 3:1,19; 13:31-33; 23:7-12
Herod Agrippa I	Grandson of Herod the Great	King of Judea	A.D. 37–44	Acts 12
Herod Agrippa II	Great-grandson of Herod the Great	Tetrarch and king of Chalcis	A.D. 44–100 (Became king in A.D. 48)	Acts 25:13–26:32

*Another Herod Philip is mentioned in the New Testament. He is the son of Herod the Great and Mariamne II and was the first husband of Herodias. (See Matt 14:3; Mark 6:17; and Luke 3:19.)

longer ritually defile them. In 15:21-28 Jesus left Galilee for Syrophoenicia (the regions of Tyre and Sidon) and met a woman Matthew deliberately referred to as Caananite—an archiving label designed to conjure up horrors of Israel's enemies of old. This woman admitted her secondary place in salvation history (Jesus was sent to the Jews first, v. 24). But she nevertheless exemplifies "great faith" (v. 28), reminiscent of the Gentile centurion (whose faith Jesus said surpassed that of all He had found in Israel, 8:10). So Jesus granted her request for her daughter's healing. Even more dramatically, He reenacted the miracle of the loaves and fishes, this time for four thousand Gentile men and their families (15:29-39). Whereas many Jews had scoffed, these Gentiles "glorified the God of Israel," particularly as Jesus again performed a host of healings (v. 31).

Returning to Galilee, His opponents reared their ugly heads at once. Again Jesus met a request for a sign with rebuff (16:1-4). God does not work miracles on demand to satisfy skeptics. Jesus took His disciples and returned immediately to the eastern shores of the lake. En route He warned them against the insidious teaching of the Pharisees and Sadducees (16:5-12). This combination of rival Jewish factions highlights their hostility against Jesus. They willingly set aside their differences in the face of a common enemy.

The concluding portion of 13:53–16:20 contrasts with the introductory section (13:53–14:12). There inadequate understandings of Jesus led to His rejection. Here, still in Gentile territory, His disciples, and Peter in particular, correctly identified Him as "the Christ, the Son of the living God" (v. 16). Matthew 16:13-20 thus forms the famous "confession" on the road to Caesarea Philippi. In response, and only in Matthew's version of the episode, Jesus praised Peter's insight as heaven sent and called him the rock on which He would build His church, promising Peter the keys to the kingdom. Nothing of the Roman notions of the papacy or apostolic succession appears here. But Jesus did predict the preeminent role Peter would play as the leader of the infant church in integrating new ethnic groups into the Christian community (see Acts 1–12).

The main body of Matthew's Gospel and the culmination of Jesus' public ministry end with a strange warning against spreading the word about Jesus' true identity (v. 20). The next verse, with which the final main division of

The Herodian Family

Herodian rulers served as the agents of Rome in various sections of the Palestinian regions from 37 B.C. to A.D. 92/93. This family dynasty, which spans more than a century and a quarter, begins with Herod the Great and includes members of the larger family down to Herod Agrippa II.

1. *Herod the Great* (37–4 B.C.). Herod gained entrance into the political life of Palestine due to the influence of his father, an Idumean (Edomite) who achieved prominence and power by assisting the Romans as they ruled Judea through Hyrcanus, a weak Jewish puppet-king.

Herod was appointed governor of Galilee at the suggestion of his father. He served with distinction under Hyrcanus, bringing the area relief from robbers led by Ezekias. As Roman leaders rose and fell, Herod was loyal first to Cassius, then to Antony, who appointed him king of Judea in 39 B.C.

Judea was in revolt, but Herod established his power by 37 B.C. His rule was beset with problems from 37–25 B.C., mainly resulting from attempts by the Jewish Hasmonean family to regain the control Hyrcanus had lost. The focal point of intrigue was Herod's favorite wife, Mariamne. Meriamne was a Hasmonean who was executed at Herod's order in 35/34 B.C.

From 25–13 B.C. Herod led Palestine into prosperity, spending lavish sums on public works such as the new Jerusalem temple initiated in 20/19 B.C. (see John 2:20). Through Herod's efforts Jerusalem became one of the most impressive capitals in the Eastern empire. Herod's projects included his royal residence, an amphitheater, a hippodrome, three great fortress towers adjacent to the temple, and the restoration of the fortress tower of Antonia. In addition to these projects, Herod built palaces and fortresses at various places throughout Palestine.

The last years of Herod's life (13–4 B.C.) were marked by increasing turmoil centered in the disputes among his ten wives and fifteen children about how the kingdom would be divided at Herod's death.

2. *Herod Archelaus* (4 B.C.–A.D. 6). Assigned by the Romans to rule in Judea (see Matt 2:22), Archelaus demonstrated the worst traits of his father. His brutal role was terminated in A.D. 6, and he was replaced with a procurator.

3. *Herod Antipas* (4 B.C.–A.D. 39). A true son of his father, Antipas governed by Roman appointment the areas of Galilee and Perea. Jesus referred to him as "that fox" (Luke 13:31-32). His disregard for Jewish law emerged in his marriage to Herodias, his brother's wife (Matt 14:3-4), and in his brutality in dealing with John the Baptist (Matt 14:10). He is the Herod of Luke 23:6-12 before whom Jesus appeared. He was deposed by the Roman Emperor Caligula in A.D. 39 on charges that he had cooperated with enemies of Rome.

4. *Herod Philip* (4 B.C.–A.D. 33/34). Philip's assigned territory was north and east of Galilee, including Batanaea, Trachonitis, Auranitis, Gaulanitis, Panias, and Ituraea (see Luke 3:11). Little is known of his reign, other than that it was peaceful, unlike his father's. He died in A.D. 33 or 34.

5. *Herod Agrippa I* (A.D. 33/34–44). Agrippa I was the grandson of Herod the Great. He was educated in Rome, where he cultivated the friendship of Caligula. Caligula gave Herod Agrippa the assignment held by Herod Philip at his death in A.D. 33/34. He then added the areas of Galilee and Perea on the deposition of Herod Antipas in A.D. 39. In A.D. 40 Judea and Samaria were added, making him king over the entire domain ruled by Herod the Great.

Agrippa I is the Herod of Acts 12 who persecuted the church and whose gruesome death in A.D. 44 is described in Acts 12:20-23. Three of his four children are mentioned in the NT: Herod Agrippa II (see below), Bernice (Acts 25:13,23; 26:30), and Drusilla (Acts 24:24).

6. *Herod Agrippa II* (about A.D. 53–92). Considered too young at his father's death to be governor, Agrippa II, who was also educated in Rome, assumed what had been the domain of Herod Philip (see above) in A.D. 53. Soon after Galilee and Perea were added, but Judea and Samaria were not.

Agrippa II is called "King Agrippa" in Acts 25:13, and Paul appeared before him in Acts 25:23–26:32. Agrippa II was Roman in sympathy and pled with the Jews to remain loyal in the revolution of the nation in A.D. 66. When Rome crushed the revolt with the fall of Jerusalem in A.D. 70, Agrippa was given the decimated and ravaged land to govern, but nothing is known of his reign, which ended about A.D. 92/93. □

the Gospel begins, will dramatically clarify why.

16:21–17:27
Correcting Misunderstandings

Immediately on the heels of his triumphant confession of Jesus as Son of God, Peter betrayed a serious flaw in his understanding of that sonship. He was not prepared to hear about the road to the cross, to learn of the suffering Jesus must endure. But a Messiah without an atoning death fits in with the goals of Satan, not the plans of God. In fact, disciples too must be prepared to carry their own crosses, experiencing persecution and even death for

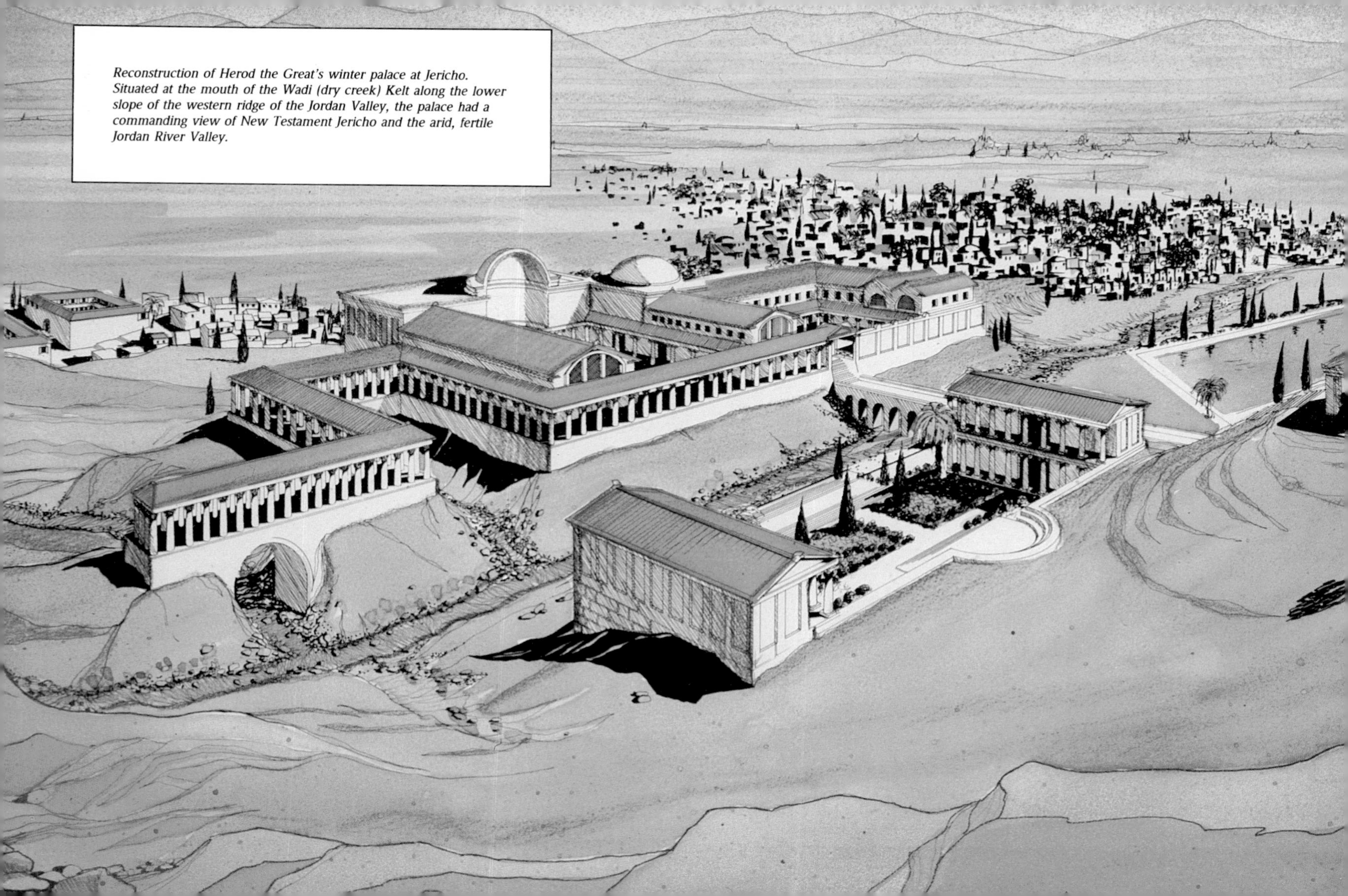

Reconstruction of Herod the Great's winter palace at Jericho. Situated at the mouth of the Wadi (dry creek) Kelt along the lower slope of the western ridge of the Jordan Valley, the palace had a commanding view of New Testament Jericho and the arid, fertile Jordan River Valley.

their Master when need arises (16:21-28). These verses set the stage for the rest of the Gospel, which narrates the unfolding drama of how Christ was in fact crucified but also resurrected. Glory lies ahead, but the cross must precede the crown.

Jesus, nevertheless, gives His three closest disciples a preview of that glory. He provides a glimpse of His majesty no longer incognito, through the miraculous self-disclosure on a high mountain we have come to call the mount of transfiguration. Matthew 16:28 probably predicts this event. Matthew 17:1-9 describes it in more detail. With Jesus appeared Moses and Elijah, key Old Testament prophets and miracle workers, leading the disciples naturally to ask once more about the prophecies of Elijah's return (17:10-13). In striking contrast with the triumph of the transfiguration appears the failure of the other nine disciples to work a "simple" miracle for which they had long ago been commissioned (recall 10:8). Jesus rebuked their paltry faith and reassured them that even confidence of the size of the proverbially tiny mustard seed would have been sufficient (17:14-21).

Matthew 17:22-27 rounds off this section as it began—with Christ again predicting His suffering, death, and resurrection. A question about whether or not Jesus paid the temple tax leads Him to teach a remarkable lesson about the freedom of God's people from the Old Testament laws coupled with the necessity of avoiding unnecessary offense in transgressing them (a balance Paul would repeat in a quite different context in 1 Cor 8:10).

18:1-35
Humility and Forgiveness

In his fourth major sermon in Matthew, Jesus began to outline regulations for life in Christian community under the sign of the cross. This discourse divides naturally into two sections. The first focuses on humility (18:1-14); the second, on forgiveness (vv. 15-35). In verses 1-9 Jesus called His disciples to a humble demeanor. Positively, this means adopting a childlike dependence on God (vv. 1-5). Negatively, it means ruthlessly excising from one's life anything that could cause another believer to sin (vv. 6-9). In verses 10-14 Jesus explained why He can command these things of His followers. God has already demonstrated the ultimate humility in leaving His nearly

Titles of Christ in the Gospels

The Gospels contain two classes of titles: those that go back to Jesus Himself and those that are applied to Him by others. There is considerable scholarly discussion about the exact nature of the first group, but the evidence of Scripture must be allowed to speak for itself. Jesus used certain titles for Himself and allowed His followers to refer to Him in certain ways. From these we gain insight into how He understood Himself and His mission.

Son of Man

This was Jesus' favorite self-designation. It originated in the OT (Dan 7:13-14), was used during the intertestamental period, and was chosen by Jesus to define His messianic mission. It was serviceable because it had messianic overtones. It also was sufficiently fluid to allow Jesus to inject His own meaning into it. He needed to do this because the idea of messiahship current in His day was that of a military hero, whereas He came to be the Savior of the world.

Jesus used the title Son of man in four different ways. First, frequently it was a synonym for "I." Jesus was simply referring to Himself (for example, see Matt 26:24). Second, the Son of man is one who exercises divine authority (for example, see Matt 9:6). Third, the Son of man fulfills His earthly mission by death and resurrection (for example, see Matt 12:40; 17:9,12,23). Fourth, the Son of man will return in great glory to establish His kingdom (for example, see Matt 16:27-28; 19:28). In this way Jesus defined who He, the messianic Son of man, is.

Son, Son of God, Only Son

The title "Son of God," or "Son" for short, was also a messianic title derived from the Old Testament (2 Sam 7:11-16). It assumes a more exalted status, however, when used by or about Jesus. It means in fact that Jesus possesses the qualities of the divine nature. This was quite evident when the heavenly voice cried out to Jesus at His baptism that He was beloved and well pleasing (Matt 3:16-17), an affirmation reiterated at Jesus' transfiguration (Mark 9:7).

Jesus' own understanding of His unique relation to God as Son is reflected in Matthew 11:25-27 and Luke 10:21-22. Jesus expressed the same idea when confounding the Pharisees (Matt 22:41-46). In the Gospel of John, Jesus is referred to as God's "one and only Son" (John 3:16), a term that means *one of a kind* or *unique.*

Lord

This was a title of honor used of Jesus, the equivalent of "Master" or "Sir." However, we can see lurking in it something of greater significance (Matt 8:5-13; Mark 2:23-27). In Judaism "Lord" had become the word pronounced ⇨

complete flock of ninety-nine sheep to seek to recover one stray.

Closely linked with humility is forgiveness. When believers offend fellow believers, they should seek reconciliation at almost any cost. Verses 15-20 describe the appropriate process but recognize that at times one party will still refuse to be reconciled. When all other measures fail, the unrepentant sinner must be "excommunicated" from the fellowship. But even then the goal is rehabilitative and not punitive. Treating people like pagans or tax-collectors suggests first of all that they are not considered as members of the community. But it also indicates that, even as Jesus dealt with the literal pagans and tax collectors of His day, they are continually to be wooed to repent so that they might return. Decisions made by the church in keeping with the procedures of verses 15-18 will be ratified in heaven (vv. 19-20). On the other hand, when believers do repent, forgiveness should be unlimited (vv. 21-22). For in light of the immense sin God has forgiven each of us, a professing Christian's refusal to forgive a fellow believer who requests it (and demonstrates a change of heart and action) proves so callous that one can only conclude that such a person never truly experienced Christ's forgiveness in the first place (vv. 23-35).

19:1–22:46
True Discipleship and Harsh Condemnation

In 19:1 Jesus left Galilee for the final time to begin His fateful journey to Jerusalem, where He met His death. En route He worked but one more miracle, focusing rather on teaching those around Him. He increasingly stressed the nature of discipleship, but as He entered the city, He underlined the theme of impending judgment for Israel.

In 19:1–20:34 Jesus was literally "on the road," journeying to Judea. Matthew 19:1–20:16 describes three encounters with people who accosted Him with various kinds of questions or demands. First, the Pharisees tried to trap Him by asking Him His views on divorce. In His reply Jesus went beyond both competing schools of Pharisaic thought—the Hillelites, who granted divorce "for any good cause," and the Shammaites, who limited it to adultery. Instead, He stressed the permanence of marriage as God's original design. He did agree with Shammai in permitting divorce and remarriage when adultery

when the personal name Yahweh appeared in Scripture. "Lord" thus meant *God.* The church later, in light of Jesus' death and resurrection, used it to mean nothing less than that Jesus was God.

Christ (Messiah)

Jesus was reluctant to acknowledge this title because of the popular misconceptions that abounded about the Messiah, centering on a king to rule on David's throne. Under the proper circumstances, however, He was willing to confess that He was indeed God's Anointed One (Matt 16:13-20; 26:62-64; John 4:25-26). This title was used so commonly later on in the church that it became virtually a name for Jesus; so "Jesus the Christ" became simply "Christ." (See as an example the shifting use of names and titles in 2 Cor 1–2.)

The Word

In the Gospels this title is found only in John (1:1-14). The expression "word of God" is common in both the Old and New Testaments as defining how God expressed Himself and what the content of that communication was. When referring to Jesus, it makes that self-revelation of God personal. Jesus as the Word of God supremely reveals who God is. If we would know God, we are to look at Jesus, the very expression (Word) of God. "Anyone who has seen me has seen the Father" (John 14:9), said Jesus.

Savior

It is self-evident in the OT that just as there is only one God, so there is only one Savior (for example, see Isa 43:3,11; 45:21). This is also true in the NT (1 Tim 2:3; 4:10; Titus 1:3; 2:10). It is all the more significant, then, that Jesus is announced as the Savior of Israel (Luke 2:11) and the world (John 4:42) in the Gospels. Jesus was understood to be divine redemption incarnate and was proclaimed as such by the early church (Acts 5:31; 13:23; 1 John 4:14).

Holy One of God

This is a term used specifically by supernatural evil beings of Jesus as the one who is pure and holy (Mark 1:24; Luke 4:34; John 6:69). As such He sealed their doom in that He is wholly righteous and they are wholly evil. It identified Jesus with the Holy God (compare Isa 6).

Son of David

Son of David is a messianic title frequently used to refer to Jesus in the Gospels (Matt 1:1; 9:27; 15:22; 20:30-31; 21:9,15). The title expresses hope. The Son of David, who was greater than David (22:41-45), would bring deliverance for those hopelessly in bondage. □

has already ruptured a union. But unlike Shammai, He did not require it. And very much out of keeping with conventional Jewish sympathies, He pointed out God's call to some to lead a single, celibate life-style (19:1-12).

Second, He dealt with His disciples' impatience at certain individuals who asked Him to bless their children. As in 18:1-5, He used this opportunity to teach about childlike dependence on God (19:13-15). Third, He responded to the rich young man's question about how to receive eternal life. His call to this man demanded that he sell his possessions, give to the poor, and follow Him in discipleship. He called other people to deal with their money differently (see Luke 19:1-27); but whenever something becomes an obstacle to doing God's will, it must be jettisoned. This third encounter led Peter, on behalf of the Twelve, to ask what reward they would receive inasmuch as they *had* left families and possessions behind in their itinerant ministries. Jesus' answer points to their eternal reward but also hints at manifold compensation in this life, presupposing that fellow disciples share their possessions and functions as a large, extended family (see Mark 10:30).

In 20:17-34 Jesus centered further attention on His "passion," eliciting contrasting responses from His audiences. Verses 17-19 form the third and final passion prediction. Verses 20-28 illustrate an inappropriate response. James and John, two of the apostles, through a request by their mother, sought status in Jesus' kingdom and were rebuked. Verses 29-34 illustrate an appropriate response. Two blind men recognized Jesus as Son of David, the legitimate Jewish Messiah, and merely begged for mercy. Christ was gracious and healed them of their malady, leading them to follow Him in discipleship.

Chapters 21–22 find Jesus arriving in Jerusalem itself. There He taught about the imminent destruction of the Jewish temple, capital, and nation if its people as a whole and leaders in particular did not repent. Matthew 21:1-22 introduces this topic by a series of object lessons or enacted parables. Jesus began with what has been improperly termed "the triumphal entry." Six days before the Passover, on what we now call Palm Sunday, He rode a donkey into the city. He was acclaimed by the crowds as Messiah and ushered into town in a fashion reminiscent of conquering warriors and kings of Old Testament and intertestamental times (vv. 1-11). But the crowds did not recognize what kind of Messiah Christ is. They had no place in their plans for Him to be presented on such a humble animal nor to be arrested and suffer. Hence, the howling mob merely five days later clamored for His crucifixion. As Jesus entered the temple precincts, He did the entirely unexpected. He overturned the benches of the moneychangers, drove out the sacrificial animals, and accused the Jewish leaders of having corrupted a place of prayer by turning it into an extortionary marketplace (vv. 12-17).

This judgment of the temple by "purification" is followed immediately with judgment by threatened destruction (vv. 18-22). The strange miracle of cursing the fig tree is best interpreted by Jesus' parable that uses identical imagery (Luke 13:6-9). Fig trees often stood for Israel in the Old Testament. Jesus was showing what would happen to the nation if it did not repent.

Matthew 21:23–22:46 presents a series of controversies with the Jewish leaders. Various individuals and groups approached Jesus, each with a question in keeping with their own commitments. But they were not seeking enlightenment. Rather, again they were trying to trap Jesus so as to be able to arrest and condemn Him. The temple authorities understandably asked about Jesus' authority. How dare He come in and so disrupt their proceedings? Recognizing the trap, He posed a counterquestion. How do they account for John the Baptist's ministry? They could not reply without either conceding Jesus' divine authority, since His message parallels John's, or falling out of favor with the crowds who applauded the Baptist. So they refused to answer, and Jesus did likewise (21:23-27). But He recounted a series of three parables that clearly imply His (and John's) God-given authority, even as they successively depict God's indictment, sentence, and execution of Israel.

The parable of the two sons (21:28-32) makes the point that performance takes priority over promise. The parable of the wicked tenants (21:33-46) predicts that "the kingdom of God will be taken away from [the Jewish leaders] and given to a people who will produce its fruit" (v. 43). The parable of the wedding banquet (22:1-14) prophesies the destruction of Jerusalem in response to the Jews' rejection of Jesus (vv. 1-10) but also threatens judgment on any would-be Christians who refuse to come to Christ on His terms (vv. 11-14).

The series of controversies resumed as the Pharisees and Herodians questioned Jesus about paying taxes to the Roman emperor. The former did not support doing so; the latter did. No matter His reply, Jesus would alienate one of the two groups—except that He found a way out! Both God and human governments deserve allegiance, each in its rightful sphere of influence (22:15-22).

The Sadducees took the stage next and ridiculed the resurrection by means of a worst-case scenario. This Jewish sect refused to believe in any doctrine that could not be established from the five books of Moses. So Jesus replied by proving the resurrection from Exodus 3:6 after

TITLES FOR JESUS IN SCRIPTURE

TITLE	SIGNIFICANCE	REFERENCE
Alpha and Omega	The Beginning and Ending of all things	Rev 21:6
Bread of Life	The one essential food	John 6:35
Chief Cornerstone	A Sure Foundation of life	Eph 2:20
Chief Shepherd	Gives guidance and protection	1 Pet 5:4
Christ	The Anointed One of God foreseen by Old Testament prophets	Matt 16:16
Firstborn from the Dead	Leads us into resurrection	Col 1:18
Good Shepherd	Gives guidance and protection	John 10:11
High Priest	The Perfect Mediator	Heb 3:1
Holy One of God	Perfect and sinless	Mark 1:24
Immanuel	God with us	Matt 1:23
Jesus	His personal name meaning Yahweh Saves	Matt 1:21
King of Kings, Lord of Lords	The Sovereign Almighty	Rev 19:16
Lamb of God	Offered His life as a sacrifice for sins	John 1:29
Light of the World	One who brings hope and gives guidance	John 9:5
Lord	Sovereign Creator and Redeemer	Rom 10:9
Lord of Glory	The power of the Living God	1 Cor 2:8
Mediator	Redeemer who brings forgiven sinners into the presence of God	1 Tim 2:5
Prophet	One who speaks for God	Luke 13:33
Rabbi/Teacher	A title of respect for one who taught the Scriptures	John 3:2
Savior	One who delivers from sin	John 4:42
Son of David	One who brings in the Kingdom	Matt 9:27
Son of God	A title of Deity signifying Jesus' unique and special intimacy with the Father	John 20:31
Son of Man	A divine title of suffering and exaltation	Matt 20:28
Word	Eternal God who ultimately reveals God	John 1:1

correcting their mistaken assumption that humans would retain sexuality in heaven (22:23-33).

A lawyer approached Christ to ask about the greatest commandment in the law. Jesus gave not one but two answers, combining Deuteronomy 6:5 and Leviticus 19:18. The lawyer had no dispute with Jesus' reply. The questions ceased as the crowds remained amazed at Jesus' responses (22:34-40). Jesus concluded this round of teaching in the temple by turning the tables on His questioners and baffling them with a question about Psalm 110:1: How can David's son (the Messiah) be merely human if David (king of all Israel) also calls Him his Lord (22:41-46).

23:1–25:46
Judgment on the Temple and Nations

Jesus' final discourse takes place in two parts. First, while still in the temple He unleashed a series of warnings against the scribes and Pharisees, in view of God's judgment on Israel (chap. 23). Then with His disciples on the Mount of Olives He predicted the destruction of the temple but also the final judgment of all peoples (chaps. 24–25). The temple invective divides into three sections. In 23:1-12 Jesus warned against imitating various kinds of undesirable behavior the Jewish leaders too frequently exemplified. In 23:13-36 proceed seven woes decrying their hypocrisy. Matthew 23:37-39 changes the tone as Jesus more compassionately lamented Israel's downfall and hinted at a future restoration.

Chapters 24–25 comprise Jesus' predictions of what will unfold after His death to usher in the end times. Its structure and interpretation are notoriously complex; the following is but one of several viable options. Matthew 24:1-35 describes the signs and times of the temple's destruction and of Christ's return. The disciples asked about both events (v. 3), probably thinking of them as occurring simultaneously.

Jesus made clear in His reply that they are distinct. First, He reviewed a series of signs that do not herald the end but consistently characterize life in the Christian era (vv. 4-14). Second, He described the horror of the actual destruction of the temple (vv. 15-20). Third, He alluded to the subsequent "great tribulation" (vv. 21-28), which for Matthew, at least, seems to embrace the entire period between Christ's two comings (compare "then" in v. 21 and "immediately" in v. 29). Fourth, He described Christ's actual return, an unmistakable, universally visible event (vv. 29-31). Fifth, and finally, He drew a series of conclusions or implications from this scenario of events (vv. 32-36).

Of these, two remain crucial in the face of many false prophets, ancient and modern. First, no one, not even Jesus, knows or can predict when He will come back (v. 36). Second, all of the preliminary signs leading up to but not including Christ's actual return were fulfilled in the generation immediately following Christ's death (vv. 33-34). This is why Christians ever since have been able to believe Christ could come back in their day. No modern event (such as the restoration of the nation of Israel) can carry any special significance in pointing to the end of the last days; all the things necessary for Christ to come back were completed by A.D. 70. We now must merely remain faithful and expectant.

Verse 36 may also be seen as the first of many implications that form the second half of the Olivet discourse (24:36–25:46). Here Jesus strung together a series of parables and metaphors to underline one central theme—believers must always be prepared for Christ's return whenever it may occur. Matthew 24:37-44 describes how it will catch many by surprise. Matthew 24:45-51 warns disciples not to assume Christ will stay away longer than He actually does. Matthew 25:1-13 warns them against assuming that He will return more quickly than He actually does. Matthew 25:14-30 teaches proper behavior however long that interval turns out to be—faithful stewardship of every resource with which we have been entrusted.

Whenever Christ does come back, He will judge all humanity, separating people into one of only two categories—sheep and goats, disciples who will be rewarded with eternal life and unbelievers who will be eternally separated from God (25:31-46). The criterion for determining who goes where is how a person has responded to "the least of these brothers of [Jesus]" (vv. 40,45). A popular, modern interpretation is that Jesus was teaching judgment on the basis of response to the poor and needy of the world, whoever they are. But the more common view throughout the history of the church, which is supported by Matthew's uniform usage of the words "brothers" and "least" or "little ones" elsewhere, is that Jesus' brothers refer to fellow Christians. Those who welcome itinerant Christian missionaries by providing for their physical needs (as in 10:11-14,40-42) demonstrate that they have also accepted the Christian message.

26:1–27:66
Passion and Crucifixion

From here on events move quickly to the climax of the Gospel—Jesus' death and resurrection. Chapter 26 outlines the events that set the stage for Jesus' condemnation and execution. Chronologically, the items narrated in 26:1-16 precede "Maundy" Thursday night, the night of

Jesus clearing the temple (see Matt 21:12-13)

His arrest. These include a final reminder that Jesus knew exactly what was going to happen to Him (vv. 1-2). When He submitted, He would do so voluntarily and thoughtfully. The Jewish leaders plotted against Him (vv. 3-5). Mary of Bethany (see John 12:1-8) anointed Jesus with precious perfume, symbolizing, possibly inadvertently, His coming death and burial. Judas prepared to betray Him (vv. 14-16).

Matthew 26:17-46 details the final hours Jesus and His disciples shared. They were celebrating the Passover meal, the Jewish festival that commemorated the Israelites' liberation from Egypt at the expense of the Egyptian firstborn. Lambs were slaughtered, special meals celebrated, and an elaborate liturgy rehearsed. Extended families ate together on this joyous occasion. Jesus and the eleven (minus Judas) constituted such a "family," and Jesus Himself would soon become the sacrificial Lamb to spiritually liberate all people from their sins. During this "Last Supper" Jesus ate with His followers, He turned the Passover meal into the first celebration of what Christians have come to call the Lord's Supper (or Holy Communion or the Eucharist). As He broke the loaf of bread and drank the cups of wine that formed part of this festive meal, He invested them with new and deeper significance. They symbolized His soon-to-be-broken body and shed blood for the forgiveness of the sins of all humanity, inaugurating God's new covenant, which fulfills the prophecies of Jeremiah 31:31-34. Christians must repeat this ceremony to commemorate Christ's atoning death but also to anticipate His glorious return (Matt 26:26-29).

After celebrating this meal in an "upper room" somewhere in Jerusalem, the little troupe adjourned for the Mount of Olives to the east of town across the Kidron Valley. On its western slopes lay the garden of Gethsemane—a wooded olive grove. Here Jesus took His three closest companions aside and asked them to stay awake and pray with Him. Three times they failed Him, even as He had predicted Peter would shortly deny Him three times (vv. 31-46).

Christ, who alone remained awake, nevertheless teaches profound lessons for us through His praying. As fully human, He no more wanted to endure His coming torture than any of us would. He asked of God if there were any way possible that He might be spared this ordeal. But He left room for God's sovereign will to override His natural human inclinations. It became increasingly clear as He prayed that God required Him to die for the sake of the world, and so He submitted compliantly. Here if ever is proof that all human prayers must include the condition "if it be God's will" (recall 6:10) and that God does not always grant the desires of those who pray even when those prayers are uttered with complete faith and every good motive.

Suddenly Judas arrived with a combination of Jewish and Roman guards. Matthew 26:47-75 narrates the proceedings taken against Jesus by the Jewish authorities. He was arrested, but Jesus made plain that He would countenance no fighting on His behalf (vv. 47-56). He was bound and led away to the home of the high priest, Caiaphas, where a hastily called nighttime gathering of the Sanhedrin, the Jewish "supreme court," had been convened (vv. 57-68).

The proceedings that followed broke many later Jewish laws. Perhaps not all of these were yet in effect; perhaps desperate men were willing to set aside legal provisions so as not to let Jesus escape from their hands. Despite the various illegalities, there was a pretense of due process, which itself almost stymied the authorities.

TRIAL OF JESUS

With the traitorous kiss of Judas Iscariot at the garden of Gethsemane, Jesus was arrested and brought before Jewish leaders (Matt 26:49-57; Mark 14:45-33; Luke 22:54; see John 18:2-13). Subsequently, He was tried by the Jewish and Roman leaders.

Jewish Trial

John recorded a preliminary examination by Annas (high priest A.D. 6–15), the father-in-law of the high priest Caiaphas (A.D. 18–37; see John 18:13-15). Annas questioned Jesus about His disciples and His teaching. Jesus did not answer his question, was then abused, and was sent as a prisoner to Caiaphas (John 18:19-24).

At Caiaphas's house there was the gathering of the chief priests, elders, and scribes, the first of the two phases of Jesus' trial before the Sanhedrin (Matt 26:57-68; Mark 14:53-65; Luke 22:54,63-65).

The chief priests sought for those who would falsely testify against Jesus in order to put Him to death. Finally, two agreed to testify that Jesus had stated that He would destroy the temple and build it in three days. The high priest questioned Jesus on this, but He made no reply. Next, the high priest asked Jesus if He would make a claim that He was the Christ, Son of God. Jesus replied by stating that He was the Christ and further elaborated by referring to Himself as the "Son of Man" and predicting His future role from Daniel 7:13 and Psalm 110:1 as being seated at the right hand of Power and coming on the clouds of heaven.

Caiaphas, tearing his robe, interpreted Jesus' claim as putting Himself on par with God and thus a blasphemy worthy of death. The soldiers mocked Jesus and spat on Him. Immediately after this it is recorded that Peter three times denied that he was a disciple of Jesus (Matt 26:69-75; Mark 14:66-72; Luke 22:55-62).

A second meeting of the Sanhedrin occurred the next morning, Friday, in order to find some semblance of legality to the verdict reached in the previous night trial and make an official brief for the Roman prefect Pontius Pilate (Matt 27:1-2; Mark 15:1; Luke 22:66–23:1).

According to Luke's account the morning trial rehearsed the previous night's trial with the exclusion of calling for false witnesses. The only charge they had against Jesus was one of blasphemy. However, the Sanhedrin lacked the power to carry out the death penalty, which was the Roman prefect's prerogative (John 18:31). Hence, they brought Jesus to Pilate.

Roman Trial

Death may have been a valid punishment for blasphemy in ▷

Finally they found some testimony that led the high priest to confront Jesus directly with the question of His self-understanding. Did He claim to be the Christ, the Messiah? He answered with a qualified affirmative, which might be paraphrased, "That's your way of putting it" (v. 64). But since the council was anticipating a merely human liberator, He went on to clarify. He is a heavenly Son of man who will sit at the very right hand of God and return on the clouds of heaven. *Son of man* for Jesus is a heavenly, Christological title based on Daniel 7:13-14. Such claims made Jesus seem too clearly to have been usurping prerogatives reserved for God alone. Caiaphas tore his clothes in grief and cried "blasphemy!" Little did he know it was he and not Jesus who was scandalously rejecting God's true revelation.

The council condemned Jesus to be sentenced to death; blasphemy was a capital offense. The Romans had taken the right to execute criminals away from the Jews, however, so they had to appeal to the imperial authorities in town (John 18:31). Before they did, Matthew returned outside to where he had left Peter and narrated the pathetic account of Peter's denial, just as Jesus had prophesied (Matt 26:69-75). Peter provided a sad contrast with Jesus, who remained stalwart under life-threatening pressure.

Chapter 27 moves quickly to Jesus' sentence and execution, the events that occurred on the day we now call Good Friday. Verses 1-31 unfold His sentencing. In verses 1-2 the Jews, more legally now that morning had broken, confirmed their verdict. They then sent Jesus to Pilate, the Roman governor. Pilate did not care if Jesus had blasphemed God according to Jewish law, but he would take careful notice if the Jews charged Him with treason against Rome (as, for example, if Jesus claimed to be king, v. 11).

Again Matthew interrupted the chronology to sandwich another event that offers a bitter contrast—Judas' remorse and suicide (vv. 3-10). Not only did Judas and Jesus dramatically differ, but also Judas and Peter provided instructive contrasts. Both betrayed their master, even if in differing ways. Both were deeply grieved afterwards. But Peter apparently demonstrated true repentance, which would permit him to be reinstated (John 21:15-18), whereas Judas sought absolutely the wrong remedy by taking his own life.

Verses 11-26 proceed with the Roman sentencing of

terms of the Jewish law, but that would have been of little interest to Rome. New charges had to be formulated for Pilate (Matt 27:11-14; Mark 15:2-5; Luke 23:2-5; John 18:29-38).

Three accusations against Jesus were presented to Pilate: perverting the nation, forbidding the payment of tribute to Caesar, and proclaiming His kingship (Luke 23:2). Only the last one was of concern to Pilate. He questioned Jesus directly on this point, but Jesus did not answer him.

Being suspicious of the Jewish leaders' motive for their accusations (Matt 27:13,18; Mark 15:4,10), Pilate found Jesus innocent. The Jewish leaders insisted that Jesus stirred up the people in Judea and Galilee. When Pilate heard that he was a Galilean, he sent Jesus to Herod Antipas, who was in Jerusalem for the Passover (Luke 23:5-7).

Although according to Roman law the accused was to be tried in the province of his misdeeds and not the province of his home, Pilate nevertheless sent Jesus to Herod Antipas, who ruled over Galilee. The reason for this was that Herod Antipas had recently reported to Tiberius that Pilate had caused an unnecessary riot in Jerusalem (Philo, *Legatio ad Gaium,* 299-305). Pilate did not want to make another wrong move that Herod Antipas could relate to the emperor.

On the other hand, Herod Antipas did not want to make a wrong move so that Pilate could tattle on him. In fact, both Pilate and Herod Antipas realized that any reporting done by either could jeopardize either or both of them, thus they made peace and became friends (Luke 23:8-12). It is not difficult to understand why there was no progress in this trial.

Jesus was returned to Pilate (Luke 23:13-16). Since the Jewish leaders were not placated by Pilate's sending Jesus to Herod Antipas, Pilate tried to extricate himself by flogging and releasing Jesus (Luke 23:16,22). Finally he attempted to release Him as an act of clemency at the Passover (Matt 27:15-23; Mark 15:6-14; Luke 23:17-23; John 18:39-40).

Although Pilate repeatedly confessed Jesus' innocence (Luke 23:14-15,22), the crowd was not satisfied until he released Barabbas, scourged Jesus, and delivered him to be crucified (Matt 27:24-26; Mark 15:15; Luke 23:24-25; John 19:16).

Responsibility for the trial, or mistrial, of Jesus rests squarely on both the Jewish and Roman authorities. □

A view of the garden of Gethsemane looking west toward the city wall of old Jerusalem. It was to this garden that Jesus went with His disciples to pray after the last supper.

our Lord. Pilate seems to have been convinced that Jesus had committed no crime against the empire but found himself in a delicate position. If the Jews rioted, he could have been in trouble with the emperor for not preserving the peace. What did it matter to him if the price of peace was the life of one Jewish religious fanatic? Despite his own instincts and warnings from his wife, he acceded to the request of the Jewish leaders and the mob they had whipped up into an irrational frenzy.

Verse 25 climaxes this section with a ringing acceptance of the responsibility for Jesus' death on the part of the Jewish crowds present. "His blood be on us and on our children," however, cannot be taken to refer to all Jews of all times. Matthew doubtless envisaged "our children" as the next generation, which was indeed judged by the destruction of Jerusalem in A.D. 70. But Jesus' blood would also be on the heads of Jewish people for good if they turned to Christ for the salvation His shed blood makes available. Meanwhile Pilate handed Jesus over to his soldiers, who mocked Him and then prepared to lead Him to His execution site (vv. 27-31).

Matthew offered few details about the nature of crucifixion in general or Jesus' experience on the cross in particular (vv. 32-56). He was more interested in the reactions of other people and of nature itself. The crowds and Jewish leaders mocked and misunderstood. Two who would have alleviated Jesus' suffering were rebuffed. Jesus would endure the agony to the fullest and to the end. An excruciating death that often lasted several days until slow asphyxiation was completed ended abruptly. Jesus sensed alienation from God in a way we can scarcely explain or imagine, yet He seemingly still chose the moment to stop fighting for life.

Even more remarkable was nature's testimony. Darkness accompanied Jesus' final three hours on the cross (from 12:00 to 3:00 p.m.). After His death the temple curtain was ripped open, signifying the new, intimate access with which Jew and Gentile alike may approach God. An earthquake disrupted the cemeteries, and after Jesus' own resurrection other Old Testament saints were raised, apparently demonstrating that Christ's resurrection is indeed the firstfruits of the destiny of all believers (see 1 Cor 15:20).

The Gentile commanding officer keeping watch at the

cross climaxed Matthew's account of the crucifixion by confessing what most of the Jews had failed to accept—Jesus' divine sonship (Matt 27:54). The burial scene emphasized the reality of Jesus' death (vv. 57-61), while the guard at the tomb vv. 62-66) accounted for the standard Jewish explanation of the Christian resurrection claim (28:13).

28:1-20
Resurrection!

Matthew's Gospel fittingly concludes with the most dramatic and glorious miracle in all of Scripture—the resurrection of Jesus Christ. With this event stands or falls Christianity's claim to be the one true way to God (1 Cor 15:12-19).

Verses 1-10 describe how the women who had watched where Jesus was buried (27:55-56,61) went to the tomb after the Sabbath (Saturday) was passed to give His corpse a more proper anointing. To their astonishment they found an angel instead, beside an open door revealing an empty burial cave. The angel commanded them to go tell Jesus' disciples that He was risen. On the way they met Jesus Himself, who repeated the command. Verses 11-15 comprise the sequel to 27:62-66 and disclose how flimsy alternatives to belief in the resurrection inevitably proved to be.

Verses 16-20 summarize all the major themes of the Gospel—Christ's divine sovereignty and authority, the nature of discipleship, the universal scope of Christian faith, the importance of doing the will of God, and the promise of Christ's presence with His followers in everything they may experience. Verse 19 has understandably come to be known as the Great Commission. Believers' task in life in essence is to duplicate themselves in others, leading men and women in every part of the world to faith, baptism, and obedience to all of Christ's commands. But the final word of the book (v. 20) properly returns our focus to Christ rather than keeping it on ourselves. Even when we are faithless, He remains faithful.

Theological Significance

Matthew's Gospel shows the essential unity between the Old Testament and the New. The prophesied Messiah of the Old Testament has come in the person of Jesus of Nazareth. Matthew presents Jesus Christ as the One who fulfills the Old Testament promises and predictions (1:18–2:23; 5:17-18). While Jesus is presented as the promised King, He is portrayed as a Servant King, whose kingdom is established on His redemptive work.

The garden tomb is one site offered by tradition as the burial place of Jesus' body (see Matt 27:57-61).

The kingdom is presented as both present and future. The rule of God over the earth is inaugurated in the person and ministry of Jesus. Its present manifestation is expressed through the moral transformation of its citizens. Followers of Christ reflect an ethical vision of the kingdom as presented in the Sermon on the Mount (5:1–7:29). They are people who seek first the kingdom of God and His righteousness (6:33). The kingdom awaits its consummation at the return of Christ (24:1-51). In the present time kingdom citizens are to live out their calling as obedient disciples. Disciples express their allegiance to Jesus by obeying His Word (28:19-20).

Questions for Reflection

1. What are the themes of Matthew's Gospel?
2. What is the significance of the title "Son of Man"?
3. What is the importance of Jesus' statement that He has come to fulfill the law, not to abolish it?
4. What do we learn about the meaning of discipleship from Matthew's Gospel?
5. How can we best understand and apply the Sermon on the Mount for our lives?

Sources for Additional Study

Blomberg, Craig L. *Matthew. The New American Commentary.* Nashville: Broadman, 1992.

Carson, D. A. "Matthew." *The Expositor's Bible Commentary.* Grand Rapids: Zondervan, 1984.

France, R. T. *Matthew. Tyndale New Testament Commentaries.* Leicester: InterVarsity, 1985.

MARK

Unlike Paul's letters, the Gospel of Mark does not identify its author or first audience. According to church tradition, John Mark wrote the Second Gospel from Rome, using Peter as his primary source. John Mark's mother hosted a Jerusalem house church (Acts 12:12), and he ministered alongside his cousin Barnabas (Acts 12:25; 15:37,39), Paul (Col 4:10; 2 Tim 4:11; Phil 24), and later Peter (1 Pet 5:13). Jewish-Christians were likely in Rome in A.D. 45 when Claudius expelled the Jews over the "Christos" disturbance (see Acts 18:2). About A.D. 55 Paul wrote to a Roman church composed of both Gentile and Jewish believers (Rom 11:17-24). Mark shows signs that it was written to a largely Gentile church; for example, explanations of Aramaic expressions (5:41; 7:34; 14:36; 15:34) and the Pharisees' traditions (7:3-4). If Mark was known and used as a source by both Matthew and Luke, as seems probable, the Gospel was likely written before A.D. 70 and perhaps even a decade earlier.

Theme

Discipleship is the central theme of Mark's Gospel. Of all the Gospels, Mark is at once the most frankly realistic in assessing the difficulties of discipleship and the most hopeful. Discipleship is costly (8:34-37; 12:44; 14:3-5), and persecution comes with the territory (10:30; 13:9-13). Mark was not blind to the disciples' misunderstandings (4:40; 6:52; 8:17,33; 9:6; 10:38) and failures (10:13; 14:37,43,50,71). Nevertheless, he expressed hope that beyond failure, those first disciples—and contemporary disciples—experience forgiveness (16:7) and fulfillment of Jesus' promises to be "fishers of people" (1:17, NRSV) and Spirit-inspired witnesses (13:11; compare 10:39). Mark's hope was grounded in Jesus, who both trusted in God's goodness and love for Him (1:11; 9:7; 10:18) and submitted to the necessity of His suffering and death as a prelude to His resurrection.

Literary Form

Before Mark the early Christians had passed on the story of Jesus orally as isolated stories, short sayings collections, and some longer narrative, such as the passion. Mark was likely the first Christian to write a "Gospel," not a mere biography but an extended treatment of the significance of Jesus' life, death, and resurrection for believers. Most scholars believe that Matthew and Luke, writing ten to twenty years later, based their Gospels on Mark's. Indeed Matthew reproduced about 90 percent of Mark. Mark's distinctives include his fast-paced adventure style ("immediately," thirty-five times); his use of blunt language ("the heavens torn apart," 1:10, NRSV; "the Spirit . . . drove him out into the wilderness," 1:12, NRSV); his appreciation of the humanity of Jesus (1:41; 3:5; 4:38; 6:6; 11:12; 14:33), and his emphasis on the difficulty of discipleship.

I. Introduction (1:1-13)
II. Jesus' Authority Revealed (1:14–3:6)
III. Jesus' Authority Rejected (3:7–6:6a)
IV. Gathering a New Community (6:6b–8:21)
V. Equipping the New Community (8:22–10:52)
VI. Judgment on Jerusalem (11:1–13:37)
VII. Judgment on Jesus: Passion and Resurrection (14:1–16:8)

Purpose and Theology

Though Mark doubtless wrote with the needs of his own church in mind, his Gospel is not an occasional document such as Paul's letters. The concerns Mark addressed were typical of Christians of his generation and are pertinent to ours. Mark wrote to preserve the story of Jesus after the deaths of first-generation Christians such as Peter. Mark, however, was not a mere archivist, for he used the story of Jesus for pastoral purposes.

1. Mark wrote to encourage Christians to persist in faithful discipleship, particularly in the crisis of persecution. Sometimes Mark encouraged perseverance through Jesus' sayings (8:34-38; 13:11). More often he encouraged faithful discipleship through the examples of his characters: *Jesus*, who by His exorcisms and healings triumphed over evil but who committed Himself to a life of humble service, suffering, and death. *John the Baptizer*,

Forms of New Testament Literature

The NT contains four main literary forms—Gospels, the Acts, Epistles, and an apocalypse. Proper interpretation of each type of writing requires an understanding of the nature of its form.

Gospels

The word *Gospel* means good news. By itself it does not indicate what form that news will take. The casual reader might first be inclined simply to label the Gospels as biographies of Jesus' life.

Yet they do not look like biographies we are used to reading. Two of them say nothing about Jesus' first thirty years, and the two that do focus almost entirely on His birth. All of them spend a disproportionate amount of time on the last few days of His life.

Matthew, Mark, Luke, and John were clearly not trying to write accounts of everything Jesus did or to reflect the perspective of disinterested observers. Rather, they wrote what may be called *theological biographies*. Each event, each teaching of Jesus was carefully selected because of its relevance for the readers to whom the Gospels were addressed. As long as the Gospels are interpreted by historical canons of the first century, they may be said to be historically reliable. But theology rather than history is their primary focus.

The Acts of the Apostles

This title is somewhat misleading. Apart from Peter, Acts tells us almost nothing about the activities of the twelve apostles. Over half of the book focuses on Paul's travels. If the Gospels are theological biographies, then Acts is a *theological history* of selected events in the life of the first generation of the Christian church. Luke chose to retell key episodes in the transformation of an exclusively Jewish sect into a major, Gentile-dominated, empirewide religion.

Epistles

Most of the NT Epistles conform to many of the conventions of Greco-Roman letter writing. The general structure—greetings, thanksgiving, body, exhortations, and closing—was widely used for many kinds of correspondence in the NT world.

Paul's Epistles tend to be longer and more literary than the average personal letter of his day but less flowery and elaborate than models of classical rhetoric. Hebrews and the so-called "Catholic Epistles" or "General Epistles" (James, 1–2 Peter, 1–3 John, and Jude) tend not to have all of the features of a standard letter. Instead they often resemble sermons or homilies of various kinds.

Individual Epistles may frequently be classified more specifically. Galatians, for example, closely parallels certain Greco-Roman "apologetic letters"—tracts designed to convince an audience of the truth of some contested proposition.

The Apocalypse

The very title of the Book of "Revelation" in Greek means *apocalypse*—the disclosure of something previously hidden. Numerous Jewish writings (including parts of Daniel and Zechariah in the Old Testament) were apocalyptic. These words usually described periods of world history, especially those relating to the end times, in highly symbolic language. Bizarre and even grotesque imagery paints the picture of the world going from bad to worse until God supernaturally intervenes to establish peace and justice. Revelation, in fact, combines three forms. In addition to a large dose of apocalyptic, it also contains more straightforward forms of prophecy and a series of seven epistles (chaps. 2–3). □

who was Jesus' forerunner in proclamation and death. *Those first disciples,* who left all to follow Jesus but who often lacked faith and understanding and who failed Jesus through their rebuke, betrayal, denial, and abandonment. *The women*, who anointed Jesus for His death, who accepted the suffering, dying Christ of the cross and tomb. *Bartimaeus,* who once was blind but then through the mercy of the Son of David saw and followed Jesus in the way of the cross.

2. Mark encouraged Christians to courageous witness. The call of the first disciples included Jesus' promise to make them "fish for people" (1:17, NRSV; compare 6:6b-13). Mark encouraged witness in the face of Jewish opposition through the thirteen "conflict stories" illustrating Jesus' authority (2:1-3:6; 3:20-35; 7:1-23; 10:1-12; 11:27-12:37). Mark likewise encouraged witness through the example of his characters: *the friends of the paralytic* who brought him to Jesus; the former demoniac who proclaimed how much Jesus had done for him; the Syrophoenician women who envisioned a gospel that reached the Gentiles; the people of Bethsaida who brought a blind man to Jesus for healing; those who brought their "little ones" to Jesus; and ultimately Jesus before the Sanhedrin (14:62; see 13:11). The oldest manuscripts of Mark end with the fear and silence of the women in 16:8. This puzzling ending reminds contem-

porary disciples that the Jesus story is unfinished until we share the message boldly with our generation.

3. Mark encouraged Christians to hope in the promises of Jesus. Mark might be termed "the Gospel of loose ends." Mark often pointed ahead to promises that were only fulfilled *outside* his story. For example, John promised one who "will baptize with the Holy Spirit" (1:8); Jesus promised that the disciples would "fish for people" (1:17, NRSV), that God's "mustard seed" of a kingdom would become "a great shrub" (4:30-32), and that disciples would be given grace to share Jesus' cup of suffering and baptism of death (10:39). Also John promised that the Spirit would enable disciples to withstand persecution and witness boldly (13:9-13) and that Jesus would meet His disciples in Galilee after the resurrection (14:28; 16:7). Mark doubtless knew traditions such as those Luke incorporated in Acts that related the fulfillment of such promises. That Mark left these "loose ends" suggests that for Mark the "Jesus story" is not finished until it is finished through the bold witness and costly discipleship of His followers.

1:1-13
Introduction

Already in Mark 1:1 the titles applied to Jesus point to His suffering and death. The Greek term "Christ" corresponds to the Hebrew "Messiah," meaning *anointed king.* Jesus would be anointed in preparation for His burial (14:3,8). "Son of God" was used as a title for kings descended from David (2 Sam 7:14; Ps 2:6-7). Jesus is, however, a king unlike other kings. By some mystery Mark did not explain, Jesus is both "Son of David" and "David's Lord" (12:35-37). Though the demons discerned Jesus' mysterious identity from the start (1:24,34; 3:11), only the cross opened human eyes to the "Son of God" (15:39).

For Mark the "good news of Jesus Christ" began with John the Baptizer (1:1-11). John's God-authorized ministry (see 11:29-32) fulfilled Scripture (Mal 3:1; Isa 40:3). Both John's clothing (2 Kgs 1:8) and his preaching of repentance and forgiveness (Mal 4:5-6) recall the prophet Elijah. John's baptism symbolized an inner commitment to lead a changed life. Mark's audience doubtless understood Jesus to be the more powerful Coming One John anticipated (1:7). On receiving John's baptism, Jesus was confirmed as the beloved Son who pleased God by His identification with sinners (1:9-11).

The experience of God's affirmation quickly gave way to Satan's temptation (1:12-13). God's Spirit is not just a comfort; here the Spirit thrust Jesus into the situation of testing. Though Mark did not indicate Jesus' triumph over Satan, the exorcisms that follow demonstrate that Jesus had bound the Satanic "strong man" and was plundering his human possessions (3:27).

In this painting from Pompeii a slave removes the sandals of a visitor to the home. See Mark 1:7.

1:14-20
Jesus' Authority Revealed

The first major section of Mark highlights Jesus' role as authoritative teacher, healer, and exorcist. Jesus began His ministry following John's arrest (see 6:14-28). The "fulfilled time" was the era the prophets anticipated when God's rule would become a reality. The necessary response to God's work in Jesus was repentance (a change in life direction) and trust in the good news of God's reign.

Jesus' call to the first disciples (1:16-20) included both a demand, "Follow me," and a promise, "I will make you fish for people" (1:17, NRSV). In the Old Testament fishers caught persons for God's judgment (Jer 16:16-18). Here persons are caught for salvation. The immediate response of leaving nets and father illustrates the sacrificial commitment of those first disciples.

1:21-45
Response to Jesus

Jesus, like Paul, frequently taught in the synagogue (1:21,39; 3:1). There Jesus surprised the crowds by teaching "as one having authority," not like the scribes

Seen above is the traditional site of Simon Peter's home in Capernaum. This is the location of Jesus' healing of Simon Peter's mother-in-law (Mark 1:29-34).

who taught on the basis of legal precedents (1:22). Ironically, only the "unclean spirit" knew Jesus' true identity, and His authority exposed it for what it was (1:24). This exorcism evidenced the power of Jesus' words, which broke the power of evil and changed lives (1:27).

The incident in Simon's home (1:29-34) clarifies that discipleship does not necessarily involve severing family ties and abandoning possessions. The grateful service to Jesus by Simon's mother-in-law represents the first of many women modeling proper responses to Jesus (1:31).

Jesus' response to His newfound popularity was solitary prayer (1:35). Already Simon Peter emerged as the leader of the disciples ("Simon and his companions," 1:36, NRSV). For the first time Jesus had to clarify His mission for His disciples (1:38). "The message" Jesus proclaimed to "the neighboring towns" was the good news sketched in 1:15. By His dual ministry of preaching and exorcism, Jesus established the pattern for the disciples' subsequent mission (6:12-13).

Mark affirmed Jesus' full humanity by portraying the scope of His emotions. According to a few ancient manuscripts, Jesus was moved to anger, not pity, by the leper's request that expressed doubt that Jesus—and the God active in His ministry—willed his healing (1:40-41). Jesus' response and reference to the cleansing laws (Lev 14) underscored God's willingness to heal. The "free proclamation" of Jesus' authority to heal hindered Jesus' mission to the neighboring towns by forcing Him into the open country.

2:1-17
Guiding Bold Witness

The healing of the paralytic is the scene of the first of five "conflict" stories in 2:1–3:6. Mark likely included these stories and a later five-part collection (11:27–12:37) as a "guidebook" for bold witness to the Jewish community. The people who brought the paralyzed man to Jesus were fulfilling their role as fishers of people. Earlier the crowds had recognized Jesus as one who taught with authority (1:22,27). Here Jesus demonstrated His authority to proclaim God's forgiveness of sins (2:5). The scribes were experts in the Jewish traditions. They objected to Jesus' acting the part of God. In contrast the crowd "glorified God," whose reign was evidenced by Jesus' offer of relationship ("son," 2:5), forgiveness, and healing.

In 2:10 Jesus identified Himself for the first time as "the Son of Man," an ambiguous designation that can mean simply *I* or *human being*. But it also recalls the "supernatural" Son of man to whom God entrusted dominion, glory, and kingship in Daniel 7:13. In Mark, Jesus retained this ambiguity, sometimes using the title in connection with His human experience of suffering and death and sometimes in connection with His future glory.

The toll-collector Levi, like the earlier disciples, abandoned his livelihood—here the customs table—to follow Jesus. "Sinners" (2:15) included not only immoral persons but those whose occupations prevented their keeping the strict Pharisaic interpretation of the law. Jesus' association with such persons recalls His identification with sinners at His baptism (1:4,9). This table fellowship occasioned the second "conflict" with the scribes, culminating in Jesus' defense of His—and His disciples'—mission: "I have not come to call the righteous, but sinners" (2:17). Only sinners could respond to Jesus' call to "repent and believe in the good news" (1:15) of God's forgiveness and acceptance.

2:18–3:6
Jesus the Revolutionary

Mark's third "conflict" concerns fasting (2:18-22). Jesus argued that the time of His ministry was a time of joy, like a wedding party, when fasting was inappropriate. The images of new cloth and new wine illustrate the "revolutionary" affect of God's new work in Jesus. What the Jewish leadership feared was true: Jesus was bursting the old categories of Judaism.

Mark's fourth (2:23-28) and fifth (3:1-6) "conflicts" concern Sabbath observance. The Pharisees interpreted plucking grain as "reaping," an illegal activity on the Sabbath (Exod 34:21). Jesus' response was twofold. The goal of Sabbath observance was human benefit, and Jesus' "Son of Man" means *I* had authority over the Sabbath.

Life of Christ

Christ's birth is recorded in both Matthew (chaps. 1–2) and Luke (chaps. 1–2). In each report the coming of Jesus is announced beforehand. Furthermore, both authors present genealogies, thus affirming Jesus' descent from Abraham and David. Except for the discussion of the twelve-year-old Jesus at the temple (Luke 2:41-50), the Gospels are silent about Jesus' years of development in Nazareth.

A brief preparatory period preceded the beginning of Jesus' public ministry. This period included the appearance of John the Baptist. John was a forerunner (Mark 1:2-13) who announced the imminent coming of the kingdom of God. The starting point of Christ's public ministry came at His baptism when He was thirty years old (Luke 3:23). This was followed by the temptations of Satan, which demonstrated Jesus' obedience as the Son of God.

John is the only Gospel that records Jesus' ministry in Judea following His baptism. However, Christ's ministry in Galilee is described by all of the Gospel writers. This period included the calling of the disciples (Mark 3:13-19). It was also a time of extensive public teaching. Christ challenged His audience with the ethical demands of the Sermon on the Mount. He preached the need for repentance (Mark 1:15) and the arrival of the kingdom of God (Luke 11:20).

During this phase, Christ was very popular with the people (Matt 4:23-25). Nonetheless, this popularity did not indicate that the people understood Christ's mission. They simply marveled at His ability to work miracles. Christ's powers were revealed in healings (Matt 8:1-9:34), exorcisms (Matt 8:28-34), and nature miracles (for example, the stilling of a storm, Mark 4:35-41). These events showed Christ's control over the natural and supernatural realms.

As news of Christ's deeds dispersed, rising opposition developed. For example, the Pharisees charged Jesus with casting out demons by the power of Beelzebub, the prince of demons (Matt 12:24). Despite Christ's widespread activity, He was also preparing His disciples for their responsibilities. Each of the Synoptic Gospels recalls Jesus' instructions to the disciples before sending them out on a preaching campaign (for example, Mark 6:7-13).

The turning point in Jesus' ministry came at Caesarea Philippi (Matt 16:13-20; Mark 8:27-38; Luke 9:18-27) when He acknowledged that He was the Christ. He then informed His disciples of His ensuing death. Jesus' true identity was confirmed by the transfiguration, when He was transformed in the presence of Peter, James, and John (Matt 17:1-8).

The journey back to Jerusalem marked the next period in Christ's life. Luke devoted more than half of his Gospel to the events that followed Jesus' departure from Galilee. A major feature of this stage is Christ concentrated ministry with His disciples. All the Gospels relate Christ's triumphal entry into Jerusalem. The finai days before His crucifixion included further controversies with religious leaders (Matt 21:23–22:46), instructions to the disciples about the future (Mark 13), and the last supper (Matt 26:17-30).

On the night He was betrayed, Christ was arrested in the garden of Gethsemane. He was later tried before Annas, the Sanhedrin, Herod Antipas, and finally Pontius Pilate. Condemned for claiming to be Messiah (Mark 15:26), Jesus was crucified on the eve of the Sabbath at a place called Golgotha (Mark 15:22). Buried in the tomb of Joseph of Arimathea (John 19:38), He arose on Sunday, which was the third day (Luke 24:1-7). After appearing to His followers, He remained on earth forty days and then ascended into heaven (Acts 1:1-11). □

The Pharisees likewise took the law to prohibit healing unless life was in danger. Mark again recorded Jesus' anger, anger at callousness toward human need and at willful blindness to the deeper goals of the Sabbath—doing good and saving life (3:5). The five "conflict" stories conclude with an unlikely coalition of Herodians and Pharisees—political collaborators and orthodox religionists—rejecting Jesus' authority and plotting His destruction (3:6).

3:7-35
Jesus' Authority Rejected

The Herodians' and Pharisees' rejection of Jesus contrasts with the common people's acceptance. Jesus' popularity exceeded John's (3:7-8; see 1:5), extending into the Gentile areas of Lebanon and Transjordan. Such acclaim occasioned some inconvenience. The silencing of demons suggests that the time was not yet right for the revelation of Jesus' brand of divine sonship (15:39; see 9:9).

Their number points to the Twelve's foundational role in the new people of God (3:13-19a). Their responsibility as disciples was twofold: to be with Jesus and to be sent out to preach His message and exercise His authority over demons.

Mark 3:19b-35 is the first of the "sandwiches," texts where Mark inserted one narrative—the "meat" (3:22-30)—into another—the "bread" (3:19b-21,31-35)—to highlight their common emphasis. Here both accounts concern the legitimacy of Jesus' ministry: Jesus' family thought Him "out of his mind" (3:21); the Jerusalem scribes supposed He was in league with the "ruler of demons" (3:22). Jesus was the "stronger one" who had entered Satan's world and was "plundering his possessions" through His exorcisms (3:27).

Blasphemy against the Holy Spirit involves a stubborn refusal to acknowledge God at work in Jesus and attribution of that work to Satan (3:30). Repentance and forgiveness are not possible for those who *consistently* reject God's saving work in Christ. In the "top slice of bread," Jesus redefined His family as the community of those who enter into a student-Teacher relation with Him ("those who sat around him," 3:34; see 4:10) and who obey God's will (3:35; see 1:20; 10:29-31).

4:1-34
Mystery of Jesus

The parable of the soils provides a framework for interpreting responses to Jesus' message. Jesus' preaching evoked (1) the disciples' obedient following (1:18,20; 2:14); (2) the crowds' amazement (2:22,27); (3) His family's suspicion of insanity (3:21); (4) the Jewish leaders' opposition (2:7,16,24; 3:6,22). As Mark's story unfolds, a rich man has his opportunity to follow Jesus "choked" by love of wealth (10:17-25; see 4:18-19). And the crowds "who received the message with joy" (4:16) join Jesus' opponents in time of persecution (14:43; 15:15). Beyond Mark's conclusion, the disciples—like seed sown on good soil—come to maturity in which they endure persecution (see 13:9-13) and bear much fruit.

Jesus was not a "secret" (He preached and healed in public) but a mystery waiting to be unraveled by the disciples (4:10-11). Jesus' teaching in parables resulted in many not perceiving what He was about and responding with repentance (4:12; see 1:15). Strangely, Jesus was simultaneously a riddle and a shining lamp (4:21-22). Disciples who "have" some understanding of Jesus and His mission are "given more." "Outsiders" who refuse to see understand less and less of Jesus and ultimately reject Him completely (4:24-25).

The parable of the growing seed (4:26-29) emphasizes that God gives the kingdom growth in ways that are beyond human understanding. Having sown the seed, disciples must trust God to give the growth. The parable of the mustard seed (4:30-32) stresses that God's rule, which became real in a small way in Jesus' tiny circle of followers, is destined for a glorious end.

4:35-41
Jesus' Faith in God

Jesus demonstrated His absolute trust in God by sleeping through the storm on Lake Galilee. The disciples mistook Jesus' trust for apathy: "Don't you care?" (4:38). Strangely, their fear is not mentioned until Jesus had quieted the storm (4:40-41). Here faith is courage based on trust in God's care no matter what. The disciples' question, "Who is this?" suggests their awe stemmed from the realization that somehow their Teacher did what only God could do.

5:1-20
Life out of Control

The Gerasene demoniac (5:1-5) pictures the horror of a life out of control: isolation, violence, painful cries, self-destructive behavior, and powerlessness of neighbors to intervene or heal. Only Jesus could confront the oppressive forces and leave him "sitting . . . dressed and in his right mind" (5:15). A Roman legion consisted of between four thousand and six thousand men. Again the crowds' fear comes at the end (5:15; see 4:40-41). They feared the power at work in Jesus more than the demonic forces that had worked in their neighbor. They valued swine more than another human being.

Though Jesus denied the man's request to be with Him (5:18; see 3:14), Jesus commissioned the Gerasene to fulfill another disciple task: to tell how much the Lord had done for him.

5:21-43
Faith and Fear

Mark's account of a girl restored to life and a woman healed (5:21-43) is a second example of his "sandwich" technique. He juxtaposed two examples of faith: a synagogue ruler, a highly respected community member, with a now-impoverished woman who lived as an outcast because of her hemorrhage. The woman in the "inner" story "had heard about Jesus" and exemplified faith in daring to touch the fringe of His garment.

Again Mark noted fear at the end of her story (5:33). Her fear of illness and death was surpassed by her awe at this one who knew He had healed her. Like the Gerasene she told her story of God's mercy to her (5:33). Jesus' address "Daughter" brought her into relationship with Him based on her saving faith (5:34). This new relationship makes going in God's peace possible. In the "outer" story Jesus called Jairus to faith that did not fear even death (5:36) but trusted that God was at work in Jesus to restore life to his daughter. The laughing crowd of mourners viewed as ridiculous a faith that trusted God no matter what. Those who trusted God had the last laugh (5:42).

6:1-6a
Scandal of Familiarity

At Nazareth Jesus experienced the scandal of familiarity (6:1-6): He's just a carpenter, just Mary's son—who knows who His father really is? We know His brothers and sisters.

A view of the modern city of Nazareth with the Church of the Annunciation in the center of photo.

But Mark's readers will recall that Jesus' family is now the community of those who do God's will. The Greek term rendered "took offense" (v. 6) is the polar opposite of "believe in" and is often used for the Jewish rejection of Jesus (Matt 11:6; Rom 9:33; 1 Cor 1:23; Gal 5:11). Jesus "was amazed at their lack of faith" (Mark 6:6) and "could not do any miracles there"except heal a few people. Jesus' miracles were God's response to human need and faith, not magic tricks performed to impress the crowds. John 1:11-12 perhaps provides the best commentary on this account: "He came to what was his own, and his own people did not accept him. But to all who received him, who believed in his name, he gave power to become children of God" (NRSV).

6:6b-44
Danger of Preaching Repentance

Jesus' rejection by "his own" (6:4) prepares for the gathering of His new people anticipated in 3:35. The mission of the Twelve "sandwiches" the account of John's martyrdom (6:14-28), underscoring the danger of preaching repentance. Jesus set the pattern for the mission of the Twelve by His preaching, healing, and exorcisms. Though the authority given the disciples to heal and exorcise demons was a sign of the kingdom, Jesus only commissioned them to preach repentance, not the good news of the kingdom (see 1:15). The mission instructions (6:8-11) evidence absolute dependence on God for support and allude to the exodus. The disciples, like Jesus before them (6:2-3), were to experience rejection as well as welcome (6:11).

The question of Jesus' identity introduces the account of John's death (6:14-16). John's full significance is seen only later (9:12) in relation to Jesus, whose fate he foreshadows. Like Jesus, John was arrested, recognized as righteous and holy, nevertheless executed, and laid in a tomb. Jesus' end, however, distinguishes Him as the more powerful Coming One, whose sandals John counted himself unworthy to tie (1:7).

"Sheep without a shepherd" (6:34) serves as an image for God's people without spiritual leadership. Jesus' initial response to the crowd's need was teaching. The details of the crowd seated on "green grass" (6:39) and fully satisfied (6:42) recall the shepherd of Psalm 23 who made his sheep lie down in green pasture (Ps 23:2,5). The miraculous feeding of the five thousand establishes Jesus as the true Shepherd of God, but it also points to the future ministry of the disciples. Jesus' use of the Twelve to feed the crowd of five thousand suggests a pattern for future ministry in which Jesus provides the disciples with resources for ministry.

6:45-56
Hope in Life's Storms

Jesus saw the disciples' struggle at the oars and came to them walking on the water (6:48). Jesus did not call disciples into the storm to abandon them there. The disciples characteristically failed to "see clearly." They thought He was a ghost (v. 49). "It is I" (v. 50) suggests the covenant name of God (Exod 3:14; Isa 43:10). The reassurance "Do not be afraid" is common in God's Old Testament appearance (for example, Gen 15:1; 21:17; 26:24). Mark did not clarify just what the disciples did not understand "about the loaves" (Mark 6:52). Perhaps they thought Jesus was the Shepherd who would care for their needs and lead them through the dangers of death or that He was a new Moses who would lead them across the sea just as He had miraculously fed them. The disciples' failure to recognize Jesus (vv. 49-50) contrasts sharply with the Gennesaret crowd who recognized Jesus "at once" and appealed to Him for aid (vv. 54-55).

7:1-23
Conflict with Tradition

The "conflict" with the Jerusalem Pharisees and scribes occasioned by the disciples' eating with unwashed (ritually defiled) hands prepares for the following three narratives in which Jesus and the disciples overcame barriers to ministry to the Gentiles (7:24–8:10). Verses 3-4 are Mark's explanation for his Gentile readers. This "conflict" was of crucial importance to the later mission of the church: would Jesus' disciples be bound to follow "the tradition of the elders" (v. 3)?

Jesus' response to the Jewish leaders was twofold: the leaders invalidated God's laws in order to keep their human traditions; and sin is a matter of the heart, not the diet. Mark again explained an Aramaic term—*corban*—for his Gentile readers. Apparently such an offering to God could be retained during the giver's lifetime but could not be used for any other purpose, somewhat like an irrevocable living trust. In calling His disciples to heed the weightier matters of God's law, Jesus affirmed God's Old Testament revelation as the heritage of the church. Verse 19b is Mark's comment, which the disciples did not immediately grasp (Acts 10), on the significance for the Gentile mission of Jesus' teaching on what really defiles.

7:24-37
Jesus and the Gentiles

Jesus' response to the Syrophoenician woman (7:27) has a harshness that leaves us uncomfortable: Jews used "dogs" as a derogatory term for Gentiles whom they re-

Jesus and the Syrophoenician woman

garded as unclean as "muts" searching streets for garbage. Interpreting the diminutive as "puppy" does not solve the dilemma either, for a "house pet" does not share the family status of a child. Status in God's household is not a matter of race. Mark 3:35 has already paved the way for a larger family of those who do God's will. The key word in the narrative is "first" (7:27), which leaves open later ministry to Gentiles. Jesus' role was first Jewish Messiah and then Savior of the world (compare Paul's bringing the gospel to the Jews first and then to the Greeks, Acts 13:46). Jesus commended the persistent faith of this "unclean" woman who *knew* there must be a place for her in God's grace (7:29). In 8:1-10 Jesus would feed a Gentile crowd with bread as He had God's Jewish children (6:30-44).

As a resident of the Decapolis, the league of ten Greek-speaking cities, the deaf-mute probably was a Gentile (7:31). As with the Jewish paralytic, friends brought him to Jesus (7:32). Experiencing God's grace makes it impossible to keep the good news of Jesus secret (7:36). Ironically, the Gentile crowd recognized that Jesus met the expectation of the Jewish Messiah (see Isa 35:5).

8:1-21
Seeking to Understand Signs

Feeding the four thousand represented Jesus' miraculous provision for the Gentiles much as the feeding of the five thousand represented His care for the Jews (6:30-44). Mark's Roman readers doubtless saw that those who came "a great distance" (8:3) to be with Jesus foreshadowed the church's mission to the ends of the earth.

The Pharisees' demand for a sign from heaven (8:11-13) recalls the Israelites' testing God in the wilderness (Deut 6:16; 33:8). Jesus perhaps refused to give a sign because ample opportunity had already been given for those with eyes to see what He was about.

The yeast of the Pharisees and of Herod (8:15) represents their bad influence. The disciples again lacked understanding. Mark did not specify just what the disciples should have "seen" about Jesus—perhaps that they had no need to worry about bread with Jesus there to provide for their needs.

8:22-26
Suffering Discipleship

Mark's central section is "sandwiched" by two accounts of Jesus giving sight to blind men (8:22-26 and 10:46-52). The "meat" in between consists of teaching on the costliness of discipleship and the suffering/glorification of the Son of man.

The healing of the blind man at Bethsaida (8:22-26) is distinct from other miracles in the gospel traditions as a two-part healing. The man at first saw distorted images—people who looked like walking trees. Only after a "second touch" from Jesus did he see clearly. Similarly the disciples would soon see that Jesus was the promised Messiah (8:29), but their understanding of messiahship would be badly distorted, even Satanic. In this larger section of Mark, Jesus would remind them repeatedly of the necessity of His suffering and death (8:31; 9:31; 10:32,45).

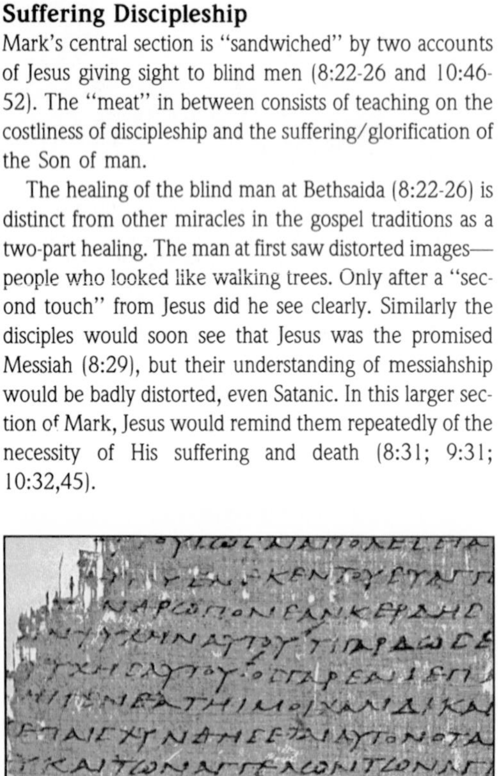

The above photo is a portion of the Chester Beaty papyrus fragment of Mark 8:34–9:1—the earliest remaining manuscript of Mark dating from A.D. 200s.

8:27-38
Who Am I?

Jesus' first question at Caesarea Philippi is merely preparatory; the crucial question then, as now, is, "Who do *you* say I am?" (8:29). Peter, as usual, spoke for all the disciples in declaring, "You are the Christ" (8:29). In Mark's account Peter received no "pat on the back" (compare Matt 16:17-19). English translations obscure the harshness of Jesus' response (using the same Greek verb translated "rebuked" in Mark 8:33). Jesus taught plainly that as the Son of man He must suffer rejection and death (8:32; contrast 4:11,33-34). About this central truth of the necessity of the Messiah's suffering, death, and resurrection there was to be no misunderstanding. But disciples had a way of calling Jesus "Lord" and then telling Him what kind of Lord to be. Peter's rebuke of Jesus serves as a warning to modern disciples: one can mouth the correct titles and still have a false understanding of who Christ is (8:33). To accept Jesus as Lord is to accept not just His glory but also His suffering, rejection, and death (8:34). Peter, realizing the deeper implications for his own discipleship said No thank you to Jesus' brand of suffering messiahship. He knew that those who follow this Christ will experience more of the same.

Faithful discipleship in persecution depends on the grace of seeing circumstances from God's perspective rather than in terms of human cost (8:35-37). On the cross Jesus would be tempted to follow the world's way and save Himself (15:30). Though He felt abandoned by God, Jesus did not seek an easy way out. True life is lost by failing to follow Christ in the way of the cross. Just as Christ endured the cross by setting His gaze beyond the pain (see Heb 12:2), believers are called to endure present sufferings for the gospel in hope of future glory (9:1; see Rom 8:18).

9:1-13
God's Kingdom Comes

Jesus encouraged the crowds (8:34) and His disciples that some of those listening to His teaching on costly discipleship would not die ("taste death," 9:1) until they saw that God's kingdom had come in power. The two most probable interpretations of this difficult saying are that (1) God's kingdom came in power at the resurrection and at Pentecost (Rom 1:4; Acts 1:8), or (2) the transfiguration served as an anticipation of the powerful coming of God's kingdom at Christ's second coming.

Jesus' altered appearance at the transfiguration offered the disciples a preview of His resurrection glory. Peter again spoke for the disciples who desired to build booths so they could "package" the experience of glory. That

The Kingdom of God in the Gospels

The kingdom of God is the heart of the New Testament's message. It was announced by John the Baptist (Matt 3:2). It formed the essence of Jesus' teaching—we are to seek it first and foremost (Matt 6:33). It constitutes the life of the church—"The kingdom of God is not a matter of eating and drinking, but of righteousness, peace, and joy in the Holy Spirit" (Rom 14:17). It was the evangelistic message of the early believers (Acts 8:12; 14:22; 19:8; 20:25; 28:23,31). It will someday be all in all when the kingdom of this world is become the kingdom of our Lord and of His Christ, and He shall reign forever and ever (Rev 11:15; 1 Cor 15:23-28).

The kingdom of God, also called the kingdom of heaven by Matthew, is not defined geographically by Jesus or the Gospel writers. But along OT prophetic lines, it is seen as the realm where God's will is being done. It is God's sovereign rule and, in principle, embraces all of the created order. In some respects it parallels God's providential control of the world, but this idea does not predominate in the Gospels. The primary focus is on God's redemptive work. The kingdom of God is the realm where God's saving will is known and experienced. It is the realm where God's will is done. Some are attracted to it, some are on the fringe of it, and some are actually in it (Matt 13:24-30,36-40,47-50). We are not, however, to say who is and who is not—it is God's kingdom, not ours. We must be careful not to drive people away if they are trying to make their way into it. Those who are in God's kingdom are saved, and Jesus is the one who leads them in it.

It is interesting to note that although God's kingdom is the central point of Jesus' teaching and of the Gospels, God is nowhere called a king. This ties in with another prominent element of what Jesus said, namely, that God is our Heavenly Father. Taken together we have a description of God's sovereign, saving rule. He is the Ruler who exercises His sovereignty as a benevolent Heavenly Father, who opens the door of salvation to all who would enter.

The kingdom is both present (Matt 11:11-12; 12:28; 18:1-5; Luke 17:21) and future (Matt 6:10; 26:29; Luke 19:11-27; 21:29-31). The saving power of the age to come has broken into this age, and we may be saved now; but the kingdom has not yet fully come. This age grinds on until the end arrives, until God alone is supreme, and we are fully saved.

The Gospels say a great deal about the entrance requirements of the kingdom. To enter into the kingdom and be saved, we must repent and believe the gospel (Mark 1:15). Jesus' preaching of the kingdom was the preaching of the gospel (Matt 4:23; 9:35). We must do the will of our Heavenly Father to enter (Matt 7:21), and our righteousness must exceed that of the scribes and Pharisees (Matt 5:20). We must repent and become as little children to enter (Matt 18:3; Mark 10:15; Luke 18:17).

Those who have no faith, even if they are children of the kingdom (that is, Jews), will not participate in it (Matt 8:10-13). We must sell all that we have to purchase the kingdom, which is a treasure beyond comparison (Matt 13:44-45). If necessary, we must be willing to make extraordinary sacrifices to enter (Matt 19:12; Mark 9:42-48). Jesus epitomizes all the above by saying that we must be born anew (John 3:3-9).

Because God's kingdom is not of this world (John 18:36), life in the kingdom is a total reversal of this world's values. The Beatitudes define its fundamental principles (Matt 5:3-12). In addition, we are to be forgiving (Matt 18:23-35), humble (Matt 18:4), generous (Matt 20:1-16), self-effacing (Matt 20:20-28), and totally committed (Luke 9:57-62).

In sum, those who by faith in the gospel of Christ have become members of the kingdom are God's children, and they are to live their lives accordingly as those redeemed by Him and who will ultimately inherit eternal life. □

God's seal of approval comes on the heels of Jesus' commitment to the way of the cross is no accident. Only after Jesus had risen from the dead would the disciples be able to share God's vindication of the Suffering Servant-Son.

Jesus' reference to the resurrection perhaps sparked the disciples' interest in the coming of Elijah. Jesus shifted their focus to the crucial question: not why Elijah must first come but why the Son of man must suffer. A suffering servant is what the Scriptures demand—other than that Mark did not answer this question any more than he did Jesus' "Why?" (15:34). "Elijah" (John the Baptist) finds his significance as forerunner of the suffering and death of Jesus (9:13).

9:14-37
Price for Not Praying

The disciples learned that their inability to exorcise a demon—and fulfill their commission (6:7)—resulted from their failure to pray (9:18,29). The father of the afflicted boy expressed doubts about Jesus' ability to help him.

An intricately carved stone pillar in the ruins of ancient Capernaum on the shore of the Sea of Galilee.

Jesus responded that "everything is possible for him who believes" (9:23). The father's plea captures the dilemma of many hesitant believers: "I do believe; help me overcome my unbelief!" (9:24). Jesus responded to the man's feeble faith. Healing of the boy who resembled a corpse sets the stage for further teaching concerning Jesus' death and resurrection.

The disciple's discussion of who was the greatest indicates their misunderstanding of the destination of "the way" of the cross they traveled with Jesus. The measure of true greatness is service. In this Jesus set the standard, coming not "to be served, but to serve" (10:45). The child (in 9:37) is not a model for discipleship (see 10:15) but an illustration that no insignificant one should be neglected in the disciples' service.

9:38–10:16
The Absolute Value

The Twelve's narrow view of "authorized" disciples prompted Jesus to affirm that all ministering in His name would be rewarded (9:38-41). Intolerance of the work of fellow believers can prove a stumbling block to nonbelievers looking to see our love and unity (John 13:35; 17:23). That the warnings that follow (9:42-49) concern common sins is unlikely. This sin prevents one from entering eternal life and results in one suffering in "Gehenna" (9:43,45,47). Earlier Mark noted that *all* sin can be forgiven except rejecting God's saving work in Jesus (3:28). Jesus' warning is to avoid causing anyone else to reject Christ (9:42) and to reject whatever leads one to reject Christ (9:43-48). Hand, foot, and eye—like possessions, family, and physical life—are not absolute values. God's future kingdom is *the* absolute value. To be "salted with fire" (9:49) is to undergo persecution. The disciples' "saltiness" (9:50) is their loyalty to Jesus and the gospel that results in their effective witness.

The presence of Christ leads to peace in the community rather than bickering over who is greatest (9:33-34). Jesus noted that Moses permitted divorce because of stubborn hearts that refuse to be reconciled (10:5). God's plan for marriage at creation was, however, one man and one woman sharing their lives together for life (10:6-9).

Though Jesus promised to make the disciples "fishers of men" (1:17), when others brought children to Jesus (10:13) the disciples interfered. Jesus not only permitted the children to come to Him but used them as an example for those needy ones who would receive the kingdom (10:14-15).

10:17-45
Inheriting Eternal Life

The rich man's question (10:17) follows naturally on 10:15: "What must I do to inherit eternal life?" What is involved in receiving "the kingdom of God like a little child"? Jesus challenged the rich man to trust that God alone was good (v. 18). Jesus did not dispute the claim to have kept external requirements of the law (see Phil 3:6): one can keep rules and still miss the heart of the matter. One essential thing was missing in the rich man's life: "Sell what you own . . . then come follow me" (10:21).

Above is an example of the heavy millstone of Mark 9:42. It is attached to an oilpress and is turned by harnessed animals.

Jesus welcoming the children (see Mark 10:13-16)

The rich man's problem was not wealth per se but the failure to trust that God—not wealth—was the only good and that God's radical call to discipleship was for his own good. Only radical trust in God's goodness makes possible abandoning wealth and following Jesus in the way of the cross. Such absolute trust in God's goodness that is the prerequisite for entering the kingdom is impossible without a work of grace in one's life (10:24-27). And God does the impossible in conversion, radically reordering human values. Jesus promised a reward—and persecution—for those like Peter who left all to follow Him (10:28-30).

At 10:33 Jesus specified the destination of His way—Jerusalem, where He would face condemnation, torture, and death. Jerusalem has already been depicted as the home base of Jesus' opponents (3:22; 7:1). Jesus' acceptance of His role as Suffering Servant stands in sharpest contrast with James and John's demand: "Teacher, . . . do . . . whatever we ask" (10:35). Our prayer requests say much about us. Later Bartimaeus would ask Jesus for sight so he could follow Jesus in the way of the cross (10:51-52). Here James and John's request for the seats of honor at Jesus' coming in glory (10:37) confirms that Peter was not the only disciple interested in sharing only the Messiah's glory (8:32) and that the lesson of "greatness through service" (9:35) was not easily grasped. Jesus promised James and John that they would fulfill their calling as disciples by sharing His cup of suffering (see Ps 75:8; Isa 51:17,22) and baptism of death (10:39). Christian leaders are to be distinguished from secular leaders who "lord it over" (10:42-43). Jesus, who came not to be served but to serve, sets the pattern for Christian leaders. His costly "ransom" frees us for service.

10:46-52
A Model for Disciples

Mark's section on discipleship concludes as it began with the healing of a blind man (10:46-52; compare 8:22-26). Bartimaeus models true discipleship. His plea for help, "Son of David, mercy me!" (10:47-48), is the cry of a dependent, childlike spirit (see 10:15). He asked Jesus not for a "glory seat" (see 10:37) but to see, and all disciples need eyes that see/perceive (see 4:12). By throwing aside his cloak, Bartimaeus evidenced readiness for mission (see 6:9). By following Jesus on the way to Jerusalem, Bartimaeus accepted the way of his suffering Lord. Finally, Jesus had a disciple who saw.

11:1-33
The Servant Messiah

Jesus entered Jerusalem as one coming in the name, that is, the authority, of the Lord (11:9-10) with a God-given mission of salvation ("Hosanna" means *save now*). By riding a colt, Jesus laid claim to His own brand of messiahship—not conquering hero but humble servant (see Zech 9:9).

The cursing of the fig tree (11:12-14,20-21) was a prophetic act meant to illustrate God's judgment upon the

The ancient city of Bethany—the hometown of Mary, Martha, and Lazarus—probably visited often by Jesus. See Mark 11:11-12.

temple (11:15-17), which had proved unfruitful by not realizing its mission as a place of prayer for all people (11:17). What is necessary for experiencing God is not the temple (cf. 13:1-2) but "faith in God" (11:22). Indeed, faith makes the temple obsolete. The one who believes can cast the temple mount into the sea (11:23; contrast 1 Kgs 8:29-30). Forgiveness of sins is not experienced in temple sacrifice but in sharing God's willingness to forgive. The "forgiveness requirement" warns believers not to turn their prayer time into a robbers' retreat (Mark 11:17).

Understandably, the religious leaders questioned Jesus' authority because cleansing the temple was the responsibility of the Messiah or the end-time prophet (Mal 3:1-5; Zech 14:20-21). Leaders had earlier questioned Jesus' authority to announce God's forgiveness (2:1-12), celebrate God's new work (2:18-22), and do good on the Sabbath (3:1-6). Jesus' question suggests that His authority was God given (see 11:30).

12:1-17
Who Tends the Vineyard?

The Jewish leadership took the parable of the wicked tenants as a direct attack on them. The parable builds on several common Old Testament images: the vineyard representing God's possession Israel (Isa 5:1-7); the harvest as judgment time (Jer 51:33; Hos 6:11a; Joel 3:13); and the servants as spiritual leaders (Exod 14:31; Judg 2:8; 1 Sam 3:9; 2 Sam 3:18). Jesus stood in continuity with the ministry of John and the prophets, yet as "beloved Son" He represented more. His special relation to God was deserving of special respect (12:6), and through Him God made His ultimate appeal to Israel (see Heb 1:1-14). This parable—like the passion predictions (Mark 8:31; 9:31; 10:32)—witnesses Jesus' awareness of a special role in God's plan that would end with His death. Mark's Gentile readers likely saw the Gentile mission reflected in the giving of the vineyard to others (12:9).

Ironically, the Jewish leadership recognized Jesus' qualifications as a Teacher/Judge of Israel. They saw Him as one who had integrity, who was not swayed by people (11:32; 12:12), and who was truly teaching God's way (12:14). By using Roman coinage, Jesus' adversaries witnessed their dependence on that government. Christians should fulfill legitimate responsibilities to their government (Rom 13:6-7). We bear God's image (Gen 1:27) and must fulfill our responsibilities to God.

12:18-44
Priority of Love

The Sadducees illustrate that one can know something of

CONTROVERSY STORIES IN MARK

Controversy	Reference in Mark
Over Jesus' right to forgive sins	2:1-12
Over Jesus' fellowship with tax collectors and "sinners"	2:13-17
Over the disciples' freedom from fasting	2:18-22
Over the disciples' picking grain on the Sabbath	2:23-27
Over Jesus' right to do good on the Sabbath	3:1-6
Over the nature of Jesus' family	3:20-21,31-35
Over the source of Jesus' power to exorcise	3:22-30
Over the disciples' eating with unwashed hands	7:1-5,14-23
Over the Pharisees' and teachers' of the law setting aside the commands of God in order to observe their own tradition	7:6-13
Over the legality of divorce and God's intention for marriage	10:1-12
Over Jesus' authority to cleanse the temple and John's authority to baptize	11:27-33
Over paying taxes to Caesar and giving God His due	12:13-17
Over marriage at the resurrection, the power of God, and the witness of Scripture	12:18-27
Over the most important commandment	12:28-34
Over the nature of the Messiah—son of David or David's Lord	12:35-37

Scripture (the law of brother-in-law marriage, Deut 25:5-6) and still miss its central message of God's redemptive love. Resurrection relationships are transformed relationships. Indeed Jesus' disciples already experience transformed relationships as God's children (3:34-35; 10:29-30; 13:12-13). God is the God of the living (12:26) not because humans are by nature immortal but because God in His love does not abandon us to death.

Not all Jewish leaders opposed Jesus. One authority in Jewish law asked Jesus which commandment takes priority (12:28). When Jesus replied that love of God and neighbor were the priorities of the law, the leader concurred that these obligations were more important than all the sacrificial system (12:29-33; compare 11:15-17). Jesus answered that this scribe was near allowing God to rule in his life (12:34); all he lacked was to follow Jesus as a disciple (10:21).

In Mark 12:35-37 Jesus took the offensive in asking the religious leaders a question (see 8:27). The riddle of David's son who is David's Lord expresses the mystery of the incarnate Lord, "who as to his human nature was a descendant of David, . . . and who through the Spirit of holiness was declared with power to be the Son of God by his resurrection" (Rom 1:3-4).

Jesus warned the scribes who used religion to get ahead and to take advantage of others (12:38-40). A widow evidenced characteristics of true discipleship (12:41-44). She showed devotion to God first (12:30), freedom from materialism (10:21), and total trust in the good God who would care for her (10:18b).

13:1-13
Destruction Coming

Jesus' teaching on the destruction of the temple/Jerusalem and the coming of the Son of man in Mark 13 are difficult to untangle. Despite this difficulty, two primary pastoral emphases are clear in the warnings to beware of deception and to be prepared for Christ's return. The disciples' amazement at the temple complex (13:1) demonstrated they did not appreciate the prophetic acts of 11:12-21 and prepared for Jesus' prediction of the utter destruction of Jerusalem's temple (13:2). Notable among events preceding the destruction of the temple (13:4-8) is the appearance of messianic pretenders (13:6). Believers are warned not to be taken in by such pretenders or to mistake "the beginning of the birth pains" (13:8) for God's judgment on Jerusalem.

Acts and Paul's letters witness that the events related to the early Christian community in 13:9-13 were fulfilled before the destruction of the temple in A.D. 70. Paul, for example, was beaten in synagogues five times (2 Cor 11:24), testified before governors (Acts 18:12-13; 24:1-2; 25:7-8) and kings (Acts 9:15; 26:1-2.). And he was accused of spreading the gospel throughout the known world (Acts 17:6; compare Rom 15:19). Peter and others bore Spirit inspired witness (Acts 4:8-22).

13:14-37
An Event without Equal

The events of 13:14-23 concern the Roman campaign against Judea. "Never to be equaled again" in verse 19 suggests an event within human history rather than its conclusion. The "abomination that causes desolation" (v. 14) refers to the defiling of the temple. As before (vv. 5-6), Jesus cautioned believers about false messiahs and false prophets (vv. 21-22). In the midst of judgment, God "has shortened" (v. 20) the days of war for the sake of believers ("the elect".

The events surrounding the coming of Christ (13:24-27) belong to a time after the destruction of Jerusalem. The coming of Christ in power and glory (see 9:1) is an event whose cosmic repercussions echo Old Testament descriptions of the coming of God for judgment (for example, Isa 13:10; 34:4). Jesus here emphasized His coming to save the elect.

The fig tree lesson (13:28-31) is likely a warning to be prepared for Christ's coming, though "this generation" (13:30) suggests that the destruction of Jerusalem was in view. "That day," which was unknown even to the Son (13:32), is the time of Christ's return. Christians' duty in the interim is to perform assigned tasks (13:33-37) rather than speculate about God's timetable. The church must not repeat Israel's failure to be found fruitless when visited by Christ (see 11:12-21).

The western slope of the Mount of Olives on which Jesus gave His Olivet discourse (see Mark 13:3-37).

14:1-11
Approaching Death

Mark's final section concerns events surrounding the human judgment *against* Jesus (14:1–15:47) and God's judgment *for* Jesus (16:1-8). The plotting of the Jewish leadership to secure Jesus' death sets the somber tone (14:1-2). A woman was again a model of discipleship. Anointing Jesus with expensive perfume was a "beautiful" act (v. 6) demonstrating freedom from wealth (see 10:21-25) and acceptance of Jesus' suffering and death (see 8:31-33). Ironically, Mark preserved the names of those who sought seats of honor for themselves (10:37) and not this woman, who sought only to pour love on Jesus. The section concludes by telling the readers that Judas agreed to betray Jesus to the chief priests for money (14:10-11).

14:12-31
The Lord's Supper

Mark's account of the Lord's Supper repeatedly emphasizes its Passover setting (14:12,14,16; see 14:18,20). As "Son of Man' (14:21) Jesus would go to His death in accordance with Scripture just as the Passover lambs were sacrificed. As in the account of the entry into Jerusalem (11:1-6), the instructions regarding preparations underscore the significance of the event (14:13-16). What Jesus meant by giving His body (14:22-23) is clarified by His comments on the cup. His blood would establish a new covenant (see Jer 31:31) by being "poured out for many" (14:24). The Lord's Supper also looked beyond the cross (14:25,28). Jesus would experience the blessedness of God's kingdom and would be reunited with His

The dipping dish (Mark 14:20) used at the last supper may have been similar to the one above covered with red glaze and imported to Samaria from a pottery center in the west.

disciples in Galilee after the resurrection.

Jesus' acceptance of His God-ordained fate is contrasted with the disciples' denial of theirs. Distressed at the thought of a traitor in their midst, first one then another dismissed the possibility of his own betrayal (14:19). Later Peter spoke for the group: "Even if all fall away, I will not" (14:29). The prediction of his denial (14:30) points to the difference in the lives of faithful witnesses under pressure after Easter (see 13:9-13).

14:32-53
Prayer in Crisis

At Gethsemane Jesus responded to crisis with prayer (14:32-42). Gethsemane called into question Jesus' foundational beliefs. Jesus addressed God as "Abba," His "Papa," who loved Him (1:11; compare 9:7). Gethsemane threatened faith in such a Father. Jesus taught that everything was possible for one who believed and prayed (9:23; 11:23-24). Gethsemane raised the awful possibility that something was not possible for God—the passing of Jesus' hour of suffering and death (14:35). Mark shows a frankly human Jesus, "deeply distressed and troubled" (14:33), repeatedly falling on the ground in anguished prayer (14:35). Despite the test of faith, Jesus emerged reaffirming faith in God's possibilities and recommitting Himself to God's will (v. 36). The disciples' repeated failure warns contemporary believers to be alert and pray in time of temptation (14:37-41).

Judas, one of the Twelve, betrayed Jesus (14:43-45). His betrayal cautions that it is not enough to be near Jesus, to have been called to discipleship, to have received Jesus' love. Discipleship entails commitment of life to this suffering Christ. Another disciple responded to the arresting mob with violent resistance (14:47). The response is inappropriate: Jesus had already accepted the necessity of His suffering and death (8:31; 9:31; 10:32,45). In a real sense the betrayer and arresting mob were unnecessary; Jesus did not run from His fate. He would die to satisfy Scripture rather than human plans. Though the disciples were called to be with Jesus (3:14) and had promised to die with Him (14:31), they all abandoned Him (14:50).

14:54-72
Witness unto Death

The picture of Peter following "at a distance" and warming himself at the fire (14:54) contrasts sharply with that of Jesus on trial for His life (14:55-56). The shadow of the cross was heavy when Jesus revealed the mystery of His identity to the high priest. Yes, He was the Son of God ("the Blessed One," 14:61) and the Son of man, to whom God had entrusted judgment (Dan 7:13). Jesus' faithful witness under pain of death contrasts with Peter's denial of discipleship (14:66-72). The servant girl's charge, "You also were with . . . Jesus" (14:67) echoes Jesus' commission that the disciples "might be with him" (3:14). Peter's concern for comfort and safety led him in the end to brokenness and weeping (14:72).

15:1–16:8
The King of the Jews

Jesus was doubtless brought before Pilate on charges of being a revolutionary. Jesus' response to Pilate's question, "Are you the King of the Jews?" was guarded, "So you say" (15:2, NRSV). Jesus was a king, but not the kind to which Pilate was accustomed (see 10:42-45). Ironically, Pilate released Barabbas, a real terrorist, and sentenced the innocent Jesus to death (15:6-15).

The soldiers mocked Jesus with a purple robe and crown of thorns (15:16-17). The symbols are both awful and beautiful. Jesus embraced His role as suffering, dying Messiah with royal dignity. The inscription above the cross defined the charge: "THE KING OF THE JEWS" (15:26). The cross redefined the meaning of Messiah.

Jesus taught His disciples that "those who want to save their life will lose it" (8:35). At the cross the crowds jeered for Jesus to do just that—save His own life (15:30). But Jesus believed what He taught His disciples: Those who lose their life for the sake of what God is doing in the world will save it (8:35). Jesus could face the cross because He trusted God with His life. Ironically, the Jewish leaders confessed that Jesus had saved others (15:31). Their insult, "He can't save himself," was a great half truth. Jesus could not save Himself and still trust God and submit to the necessity of His death. Jesus' cry, "My God, my God, why have you forsaken me?" (15:34) points to the sense of abandonment Jesus experienced when He bore our sins (15:34). It would be a mistake to think God aloof from the cross event. The tearing of the temple veil "from top to bottom" (15:38) demonstrates that "God was reconciling the world to himself in Christ" (2 Cor 5:19). Strangely, when Jesus felt God was farthest from Him, a centurion saw clearly that Jesus was God's Son (15:39). God doubtless was pleased with Him (1:11; 9:7).

The women who had followed Jesus from Galilee accepted His suffering and death but "from a distance" (15:40). Joseph of Arimathea exhibited boldness when the most a disciple could do was see to Jesus' proper burial (15:42-46).

The women's desire to anoint Jesus' body though appropriate at another time (14:3-9) was not the proper response for Easter morning disciples (16:1-2). The "young man" seated at the empty tomb said it all (16:5-6): "You're looking for Jesus in the wrong place; God has raised him from the dead; he's not here!" (author's translation). God had vindicated Jesus. The message for the disciples (16:7) points to restoration after they had denied and abandoned Jesus.

The oldest manuscripts of Mark end at 16:8 with the women silent and fearful. As noted in the introduction, Mark might be termed "the Gospel of loose ends," for Mark often pointed ahead to promises that are only fulfilled outside his story. That God would raise Jesus from the dead following His suffering and death and that Jesus would then meet His disciples in Galilee are but two such promises. Mark doubtless knew traditions relating the fulfillment of such promises; he would have had no reason to write a Gospel had he doubted these promises. That he left these "loose ends" suggests that for Mark the "Jesus story" is not finished until it is finished in you and me through our bold witness to the resurrection.

Theological and Ethical Significance

The Jesus who confronts us in Mark makes us uncomfortable. He is hard to understand and even harder to follow. This is the Jesus most clearly seen to be God's Son only when He has suffered and died on the cross. What those first disciples were so slow to understand, what the centurion and Mark grasped, and what Paul preached is this: "Christ crucified . . . the power of God and the wisdom of God" (1 Cor 1:23-24).

Mark challenges his readers to open our eyes and see Jesus for who He really is. Mark dares us to follow the example of this suffering, dying Servant of the Lord. Our discipleship will be costly. It may call for leaving families, giving up horded resources, even giving up life itself. All too often we, like those first disciples, will fail Jesus. We too misunderstand; we too lack faith; we too retreat under pressure; we too remain silent and comfortable while others wait to hear that we have been with Jesus. Our stories of discipleship, like Mark's story, are incomplete. But Jesus' promises stand sure. Like those first disciples, Jesus will forgive our failures and make us into what He desires—bold witnesses and followers in His way of costly discipleship.

Questions for Reflection

1. What does Mark teach us about suffering and discipleship?

2. What does Mark teach about the full humanity of Jesus?

3. What can we learn from Mark's positive and negative examples of discipleship?

4. What role do suffering and death play in Jesus' messiahship?

5. Why do we sometimes live as though we are ashamed of Jesus' example and clear teaching on suffering?

Sources for Additional Study

Brooks, James A. *Mark. The New American Commentary.* Nashville: Broadman, 1991.

Lane, William L. *The Gospel of Mark. The New International Commentary on the New Testament.* Grand Rapids: Eerdmans, 1974.

Marshall, I. Howard. *Mark: A Bible Study Book. Understanding the New Testament.* Philadelphia: A. J. Holman, 1970.

Schweizer, Eduard. *The Good News according to Mark.* Richmond: John Knox, 1970.

LUKE

The Gospel of Luke according to church tradition was written by the sometime companion of Paul, Luke. (This is indicated by the "we" passages in Acts 16:10-17; 20:5-15; 21:1-18; 27:1–28:16.) He likely was a medical doctor, possibly from Antioch of Syria. Though he was not Jewish, it is not known whether he was a native Syrian or a Greek. No one knows the locale from which Luke wrote his Gospel.

The date when the book was written is disputed. Two possibilities exist: a date about a decade or so after A.D. 70 and a date in the sixties of the first century. Those who favor a date in the seventies or eighties suggest that Luke knew about the destruction of Jerusalem in A.D. 70, but this is not certain since there is no specific reference to this event in any text. The best one can do is see possible allusions to it in 19:41-44 and 21:5-24. The decision is linked to the date of Acts, which ends with events in A.D. 62. If these books were written later, it is curious why later events are not explicitly narrated in Acts. It is also curious why Jewish and Gentile relations form such a central portion of dispute in Acts. This was a problem for the early church and was less a problem in the eighties. These factors slightly favor a date for the Gospel in the sixties.

Recipients

Luke was explicitly written to Theophilus (1:1-4). Theophilus appears to have had some exposure to the faith, as Luke's introduction makes clear. In fact, it is quite likely that he was a Gentile believer struggling with his association in a movement that had Jewish origins. Indications that Theophilus was Gentile are reflected in Luke's explaining certain Jewish customs or names (Acts 1:19).

Did God really plan to include Gentiles among His people? Why do the Jews, for whom the promise of God was originally intended, reject the gospel so strongly? Theophilus may have been wondering if he was in the wrong place. So Luke wrote to reassure Theophilus about God's plan. Luke may also have been writing with an eye on those who were raising doubt for Theophilus. Luke showed how God legitimized Jesus and attested to Him as the one sent to bring God's promise.

Sources

Luke said that he had predecessors, but he did not name them for us (Luke 1:1-4). Three views of sources exist.

1. Many scholars regard it as likely that Luke used Mark, some special source material only Luke had, and tradition (or, better, a collection of traditions) which he shared with Matthew.

2. Others prefer to suggest that Luke used Matthew and had his own special source material. This means that in terms of order Mark is last of the Synoptic Gospels and that Luke did not know or use Mark. In this view Mark is seen as a summarizing Gospel of the other Synoptics.

3. A few see Luke as the last of the Synoptic writers, with Matthew and Mark preceding him.

Any of the options is possible, but it is hard to explain Luke 1–2 if Luke knew Matthew's infancy account. Lukan rearrangements of parables and accounts from Matthew are also hard to account for if the second or third hypothesis is taken. Against the second option is explaining how Mark is a summary Gospel and yet omits so much of Jesus' teaching and parables. So it is slightly more likely that the first option holds.

Themes

Luke highlights God's plan. It explains how Jesus was not only Messiah but also the Prophet like Moses (see Deut 18:15), the Suffering Servant, and the one who is Lord. Luke gradually reveals this view of Jesus, bringing the reader from a messianic, prophetic understanding of Jesus in Luke 1–2 to a view that reveals the total authority Jesus bears (Luke 22:69). It is often said that Luke presents Jesus as the "Son of Man," but this emphasis is not, strictly speaking, unique to Luke's Gospel and should be avoided in summarizing Luke. Luke is interested in Jesus as Messiah-Servant-Prophet-Lord. A full portrait of Jesus is a major concern of Luke's work.

Luke details how many in Israel became hostile to Jesus and His teaching. The bulk of this discussion comes in chapters 9–13. Many of the parables unique to Luke touch this question. The nation holds a large degree of blame in slaying Jesus as Luke 23 makes clear. But there is always hope for the nation. Luke never gave up on

Israel as even in Acts 28 Paul was speaking to Jews about the promise.

Luke also spent much time explaining the proper response to Jesus. His favorite description is "repent." This picture comes in the mission statement of 5:31-32, the picture of the prodigal in 15:11-32, the picture of the tax collector in 18:9-14, and in the picture of Zacchaeus in 19:1-10. Repentance reflects a humble reception of what God offers on God's terms. It means "agreeing with God" about sin and Jesus and thus involves a genuine turning from sin toward God. This is something Paul called faith. But the opportunity Jesus brings requires that believers be committed to pursuing the lost, even the tax collector and sinner.

Luke highlighted the walk of the believer. He noted the danger of excessive attachment to wealth (12:13-21). He warned about the cost of following Jesus (14:25-35). He called for believers to love God and other people, even those who persecute (6:20-49; 18:18-30). In fact, the disciple's love is to stand out as something distinct from the love the world gives by its love for enemies and its care for every type of person. Disciples are to persist in

THEMES IN LUKE

THEME	EXAMPLES FROM LUKE	REFERENCE
Theology	Word of God	5:1; 6:47; 8:11,13-15,21; 11:28
	Jesus as Savior	1:69; 2:11; 19:9
	The present kingdom of God	11:20; 19:9
	The Holy Spirit	1:35,41,67; 2:25-27; 3:22; 4:1,14; 11:13; 24:49
Concern for women	Elisabeth	1:5-25,39-45,57-66
	Mary	1:26-56; 2:1-20,41-52
	Anna	2:36-38
	The widow of Nain	7:11,12
	The "sinner" who anoints Jesus' feet	7:36-50
	Women disciples	8:1-3
	The woman searching for her lost coin	15:8-10
	The persistent widow petitioning the unjust judge	18:1-8
	The sorrowful women along the way to the cross	23:27
Concern for the poor/warnings to the rich	Blessings on the poor	6:20-23
	Woes on the rich	6:24-26
	The rich fool	12:16-20
	The rich man and the beggar Lazarus	16:19-31
Concern for social outcasts	Shepherds	2:8-20
	Samaritans	10:25-37; 17:11-19
	Tax agents and "sinners"	15:1
	Gentiles/all people	2:32; 24:47
The Christian life	Gratitude and joy	1:46-55,68-79; 2:14; 15:7,10,24,32; 17:16,18; 24:53
	Prayer	3:21; 6:12; 9:18; 11:1-13; 18:1-14
	Proper use of material possessions	6:32-36; 10:27-37; 12:32-34;16:1-13
	Changed social behavior in imitation of God	9:3-5,16; 10:2-16,38-42; 12:41-48; 22:24-27
	Repentance/faith	3:7-14; 5:32; 10:13; 11:32; 13:3-5 15:7-10; 24:47

suffering (9:23; 18:8; 21:19), watch for God's return (12:35-48; 17:22-37; 21:5-38), rejoice (1:14; 2:10; 10:17; 24:41,52), and pray (11:1-13; 18:1-8).

Literary Form

Luke is a Gospel, a form unique to the Bible. The account operates like a narrative. It is more than a biography because it is selective and has a theological message to convey. It is history but only a selective history (see "Types of New Testament Literature"). We are told nothing about the details of Jesus' childhood. Rather, we move from Jesus' birth directly to His ministry with only one incident at the age of twelve and the ministry of John the Baptist intervening briefly. A Gospel is a theological, pastoral explanation of the significance and impact of Jesus' life, death, and resurrection. So characters, setting, movements of time and location, mood, and the arrangement of events are all a part of telling the account of Jesus' ministry.

All the Gospels tell the events surrounding Jesus in their own way, sometimes presenting events not in their historical, chronological order but according to topical concerns. A *synopsis* easily reveals these rearrangements (compare Mark 6:1-6 and Luke 4:16-30 or the order of the temptations in Matt 4:1-11 versus Luke 4:1-13). Luke's narrative is dominated by two features: the gathering of disciples in Galilee (4:14–9:50) and the journey to Jerusalem. During the journey, rejection heightens, and Jesus prepares His disciples for His departure (9:51–19:44). Here one can find the central elements in Luke's Gospel.

Luke also has many miracle accounts and parables. These emphasize the power and teaching of Jesus. Luke has more parables than any of the other Gospels. Most parables deal either with God's plan or the walk of the disciple. The explanation of His miracles and their significance comes in Luke 7:18-35 and 11:14-23.

Theology

When we look at Luke's portrait of God, the major feature is that He is the God of design and concern. Many texts allude to God's plan or to what must be (1:14-17,31-35; 2:9-14; 4:16-30; 24:44-49). The major scheme Luke applies to make this point is promise and fulfillment. Luke's use of the Old Testament often involves descriptions of Jesus (1:46-55,68-79; 3:21-22; 4:17-19; 7:22; 9:35; 13:31-35; 19:27; 20:41-44; 21:27; 22:69; 24:43-47). Other texts emphasize the immediacy of the realization of the plan "today" (2:11; 4:21; 5:26; 13:32-33; 19:5,9,42; 23:42-43). John the Baptist is the bridge in the plan (3:1-19; 7:18-35). So God's work is central to Luke. Nothing that happens to Jesus takes God by surprise.

The emphasis on Jesus has already been noted. He had many roles: teacher, prophet, prophet like Moses, Messiah, Servant, Son of man, and Lord. Luke wanted to stress the person of Jesus. He said little about how Jesus saved on the cross. In fact, only one text tackles the issue of the cross directly (22:18-20), though allusions to Jesus as the Servant occur as Jesus' baptism shows (3:21-22). Luke wanted his reader to appreciate who does the saving.

Also important to Luke is the arrival of the kingdom. In fact, the kingdom in Luke has two stages. It has already come in the authority Jesus shows over the forces of evil and in the hope of the coming of the Spirit or in the arrival of new covenant promise (10:9,18; 11:9; 17:20-21; 22:18-20; 24:49). Yet there comes a time when the kingdom will come in even more splendor (17:22-37). This combination is known as the kingdom already and not yet. Jesus will manifest His rule in stages. What comes now is but a foretaste of what will come. Part of what Jesus brings now is the Spirit (3:15-18). Though this is more emphasized in Acts, the promise is stated in Luke (24:49).

When one looks at who benefits from Jesus' coming, the simple answer is to say all people. But Luke drew attention to the poor, tax collectors, sinners, and women, since these neglected groups indicate the comprehensive nature of God's salvation. The makeup of God's new community includes all who come in faith and repentance to Christ.

When Luke discussed the blessings of salvation, he used terms like forgiveness, life, peace, the kingdom, and the Spirit. These are various ways to state that God blesses the one He saves, not with material wealth, but with spiritual riches. When Luke sought to assure Theophilus, he made sure that Theophilus was aware of how much he had received from God. The promise of God is rich in benefits.

The outline of Luke breaks down largely into geographical divisions to show the progress of Jesus' ministry.

I. John the Baptist and Jesus (1:1–2:52)
II. Preparation for Ministry (3:1–4:13)
III. Galilean Ministry (4:14–9:50)
IV. Jerusalem Journey (9:51–19:44)
V. Jerusalem (19:45–24:53)

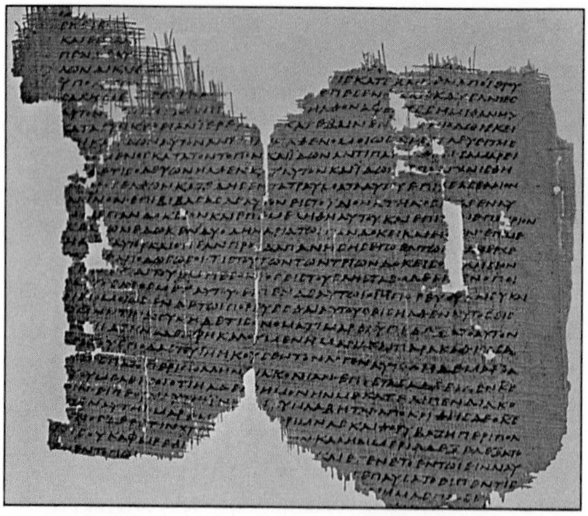

The Chester Beaty papyrus fragment of Luke 3:8-20—the earliest extant manuscript of Luke dating from A.D. 200s.

Purpose

Luke wrote his Gospel for a wide variety of reasons.

1. Luke wanted to confirm the message of God's promise and salvation through Jesus.
2. He wished to portray God's faithfulness both to Israel and to all persons while explaining why so many in Israel tragically rejected Jesus.
3. He wanted to lay the foundation in Luke for his defense in Acts of the full membership of Gentiles as a part of God's people and promise.
4. He wished to offer a word of conciliation and explanation to Jews by showing how responding to Jesus is the natural extension of Judaism.
5. He wished to show that God's promise extends to all men and women by showing the variety of social classes and people who responded to Jesus.

Luke is an extremely personal Gospel, showing how people can be related to God and share in the full blessing of His promise. It is also a cosmic Gospel, since it reveals and explains God's plan. The question of fulfillment is tackled both at the racial (Jew, Gentile) and individual level. God's plan is shown as wise, thought out, and on course. The death of Messiah was always expected, and so was His resurrection. Now the call of God's people involves the commission to take the message of repentance for the forgiveness of sins to all the nations in the power of the Spirit (24:43-49).

1:1-80
God's Faithful Fulfillment

After a crucial preface in which Luke explained his task

Virgin Birth

The angel Gabriel declared that "no promise is impossible with God" (Luke 1:37). To cause the elderly Zechariah and Elizabeth to conceive was as easy for God as to cause Mary of Nazareth to conceive a child without a human father. The "virgin birth" is the theological term for Mary, a virgin, becoming pregnant with the child Jesus through the power of the Holy Spirit. Luke, the careful and accurate compiler of eyewitness events (1:1-4), included several details that describe Mary's pregnancy as being without a human father.

1. Mary is described as a virgin (*parthenos*) betrothed to a man called Joseph (1:27).
2. Mary said she could not bear a child because "I do not know a man" (1:34).
3. The angel said the pregnancy would come about when the Holy Spirit came over Mary and "the power of the Most High" overshadowed her (1:35).
4. Jesus is described as "the son, so it was thought, of Joseph" (3:23).

Matthew in addition recounts:

5. Joseph, when he discovered that his betrothed Mary was pregnant, intended to terminate their engagement (1:18-19).
6. The virgin birth was a fulfillment of Isaiah 7:14 (Matt 1:22-23).
7. Joseph did not have any sexual relations with Mary until after Jesus' birth (1:25).
8. The rest of the NT has several possible allusions to the virgin birth. Jesus' enemies questioned His father (John 8:19,41). Some of Jesus' neighbors in Nazareth described Him as "the son of Mary" (Mark 6:3). Paul described Jesus as "born of woman" (Gal 4:4) and as the human "from heaven" (1 Cor 15:45-48).

Usually *parthenos* refers to a young woman who is unmarried and therefore who has had no sexual relations with a man. For instance, Philip's four daughters are called *parthenos* (Acts 21:9). *Parthenos* was also used to describe young unmarried men who had had no sexual relations with a woman. Paul contrasted a virgin with a married person (1 Cor 7:25-28), and the 144,000 in Revelation 14:4 are virgin men.

Matthew cited the pregnancy of Mary and the birth of Jesus as a fulfillment of Isaiah 7:14. When King Ahaz of Judah refused to ask a sign of God, God gave him a sign: "A virgin in the womb shall conceive and bear a son, and you shall call his name Immanuel." Before this child was of the age of accountability (twelve?), the land of the two kings who threatened Ahaz would be deserted (Isa 7:17).

Isaiah and his wife, the prophetess, shortly had a child whom

The annunciation (announcement to Mary of Jesus' coming birth, Luke 1:26-38).

they named Mahershalalhashbaz (*The spoil speeds, the prey hastes*) as a sign that soon Damascus and Samaria would be conquered by the Assyrians (Isa 8:4,18). Both Damascus and Samaria fell within thirteen years of the original prophecy (732–722 B.C.). Thus the prophecy in Isaiah has at least two fulfillments, one in Mahershalalhashbaz and one in Jesus. Isaiah may have expected a more perfect future fulfillment because he and his wife did not call their child "Immanuel," even though "God" had been "with them" to protect Judah from its adversaries.

The virgin birth of Mary's child early became an important aspect of Christian doctrine because it insured that Jesus was indeed "holy, Son of God" (Luke 1:35). Having had a human mother, Jesus was fully human. Having had the Holy Spirit cause conception, Jesus was fully God. Therefore Jesus could truly be the perfect intermediary between, and representative for, God and humanity (Heb 2:17; 4:15; 7:26-28).

The bishop of Antioch, Ignatius, who lived during the first century A.D., mentioned the virgin birth at least five times in his eight letters that have been preserved for us. For example, to the Smyrneans he wrote: The Lord Jesus Christ "is in truth of the family of David according to the flesh, God's Son by the will and power of God, truly born of a virgin" (1.1; see also *Ephesians* 7.2; 18.2; 19.1; *Trallians* 9.1).

Justin Martyr, who lived in the second century A.D., explained in his *First Apology* that Jesus "was begotten by God as the Word of God in a unique manner beyond ordinary birth" (22). "For 'behold, the Virgin shall conceive' means that the Virgin would conceive without intercourse . . . God's power . . . caused her to conceive while still remaining a virgin" (33).

The NT does not present the virgin birth of Jesus as some outlandish event but as simply the fulfillment of a promise by Almighty God made to a poor but devout Hebrew woman. Even as the shekinah glory filled the tabernacle and as an eagle shelters its young under its wings (Exod 40:35; 19:4; Ps 91:4), God's Spirit "overshadowed" (*episkiadzo*) and filled Mary (Luke 1:35). Although a Jew would consider for God to "change into a human" or "a human into God the "most grievous impiety" (Philo, *Embassy to Gaius* XVI), Mary believed (even if she may not have fully understood) because she agreed that "no promise is impossible with God." □

(1:1-4), the author launched into a unique comparison of John and Jesus by showing how both represent the fulfillment of promises made by God. John was like Elijah (1:17), but Jesus had Davidic roles to fulfill and possessed a unique supernatural origin (1:31-35). John was forerunner, but Jesus was fulfillment. Everything in Luke 1–2 points to the superiority of Jesus over John, who obediently prepared the way.

Mary's hymn (1:46-56) praises the faithfulness of God to His promise and His blessing of those who are humble before Him, setting up a major Lukan theme. Her praise is personal in tone. Zechariah reiterated the hope in national, Davidic terms and set forth the superior relationship of Jesus to John (1:67-79). In doing so, Zechariah links spiritual promises and national promises to Davidic hope, another theme Luke would develop in the Gospel. The goal of salvation is to free God's people to serve Him without fear and to enable them to walk in God's path of peace. In these accounts Mary pictures the one who trusts God (1:36-38), Elizabeth is the one who rejoices in God (1:39-45), while Zechariah learns to trust God (1:17-19,61-66).

The New Testament and History

There are at least three ways to approach the question of the NT and history. The first is to examine the historical perspectives in the NT writings themselves. Jesus, for instance, lived and died in the specific historical context of first-century Palestine.

The Gospels, however, show little concern with the events of the time, except as they bear directly on Jesus. It is in the story of Jesus' death and resurrection that historical references are most apparent with Jesus' appearance before the Roman procurator Pilate. For the most part, the Gospel writers were most concerned with Jesus Himself, His teachings, and His ministry rather than the larger social and political movements of the time, which are the characteristic concerns of historians.

Among the Gospel writers, Luke was the exception. He showed a definite historian's perspective. He was careful to set Jesus within the framework of world history, listing the Roman Emperor and the Syrian governor at Jesus' birth (Luke 2:1-2). He gave all the relevant rulers when John the Baptist began his ministry: the emperor, the Judean governor, the minor Jewish kings, and the Jewish high priests (Luke 3:1-2).

This historian's viewpoint is perhaps even more pronounced in Luke's second volume, Acts. He related the death of the Jewish King Herod Agrippa I (Acts 12:20-23). He showed Paul encountering the political leaders of his day: the Roman proconsul of Cyprus (Acts 13:4-12), the proconsul of Achaia (Acts 18:12-17), the governors of Syria, Felix and Festus (Acts 24:24–25:5), and the Jewish King Agrippa II (Acts 25:13–26:32). Luke wanted to make clear that the events involving the young Christian movement were of worldwide significance. They were "not done in a corner" (Acts 26:26).

An equally strong concern with history is found in Revelation. The theme of the book in a real sense is that God holds the keys to all history. All the affairs of nations and their leaders stand before God's ultimate judgment. He is the Alpha and the Omega. All time, all history, begins with His creation, and in His own time He will draw the final curtain on it.

A second approach asks, What do the non-Christian historians of the first century have to say about Christianity? Actually, there are not many such references, but the few that exist are significant. The Roman historian Suetonius, in his biography of the emperor Claudius, related that Claudius in A.D. 49 expelled all the Jews from Rome because of a riot instigated by a certain "Chrestus." In addition to explaining a reference in Acts to this event (Acts 18:2), Suetonius's remark probably also is good evidence that Christianity had reached Rome by A.D. 49, for "Chrestus" most likely refers to Christ (Latin *Christus*). In his writings the Jewish historian Josephus referred to three NT figures—Jesus, John the Baptist, and James the brother of Jesus. Although the present form of Josephus's reference to Jesus has been somewhat reworked by later Christian scribes, the latter two accounts are considered reliable and confirm the impact early Christianity had on the larger Jewish community.

A final approach deals with the historical setting in which the NT came into being. Jesus was a historical figure whose birth, ministry, and death occurred in first-century Palestine under Roman occupation. Paul wrote to actual congregations in Asia Minor, Greece, and Rome. Revelation was written during a period when Christians were being persecuted for their refusal to participate in Roman emperor worship. In short, God sent His Son to redeem the world at a definite time in human history. All the NT writings are in a sense "historical documents," for they reflect the faith and mission of the early Christian movement. To understand the NT in light of the larger backdrop of its own contemporary world enhances our understanding of its message and our ability to communicate that message effectively in our own day. □

2:1-52
The Pious Praise Jesus

Jesus' birth took place in humble circumstances, but all the figures surrounding His birth were pious and responsive to the hope of God. Jesus was praised by a priest, by a humble virgin, by shepherds, and by a prophet and prophetess at the temple (2:1-40). All reflect high expectation from people who are portrayed as walking with God. Only the word of Simeon to Mary gives an ominous ring. The old man noted that Jesus would be a "light for revelation to the Gentiles and for glory to . . . Israel" (2:32). In fact, Jesus would be a cause of grief for Mary and division in Israel (2:34-35). Jesus is the "salvation" of God (Luke 2:30), but in the midst of hope is the reality that fulfillment comes mixed with pain and suffering.

Jesus' own self-awareness concludes the introductory overture in the Gospel (2:41-52). Here the young boy declares that He must be about the work of His father in the temple. Jesus notes His unique relationship to God and His association with God's presence and teaching.

This section, dominated by Old Testament allusions, opens the Gospel with notes of fulfillment and indications

The only known extrabiblical mention of Pilate's name is shown above in a Latin dedicatory inscription on a stone slab found at Caesarea Maritima. See Luke 3:1.

Twelve-year-old Jesus in the temple (see Luke 2:41-50)

of God's direction. These emphases continue through the entire Gospel. John and Jesus are placed side by side in the stories of Luke 1, and then Jesus has the stage in Luke 2. The structure imitates the theology of forerunner-fulfillment.

3:1-38
Well-pleasing Divine Son

John and Jesus remain side by side in this initial section on Jesus' ministry. John was the "one who goes before" (Isa 40:3-5; Luke 3:1-6), while Jesus is the "One who comes" (Luke 3:15-17). Only Luke among the Gospel writers lengthens his citation of Isaiah 40 to make the point that salvation is seen by all persons. In addition, only Luke contains the section where the ethical dimensions of John's call to repentance in terms of compassionate response to others is made clear (Luke 3:10-14). John also warns about judgment, calls for repentance, and

The mount of temptation as photographed from the top of Old Testament Jericho. See Luke 4:1-13.

promises the coming of One who brings God's Spirit. John baptized Jesus, but the main feature of the baptism is one of two heavenly testimonies to Jesus (3:21-22: 9:35 has the other).

John had promised that Jesus would bring the Spirit, but in 3:22 Jesus was anointed with the Spirit. The first hints of fulfillment occur here. The heavenly testimony calls Jesus "my son, whom I love; with whom I am well pleased." This fusion of Isaiah 42:1 ("one in whom I delight") and Psalm 2:7 ("my Son") marks out Jesus as a regal, prophetic figure who as a chosen Servant of God brings God's revelation and salvation. The universal character of Jesus' relationship to humankind is highlighted in the list of His ancestors (Luke 3:23-38). He is "son of Adam, . . . son of God." Jesus not only has connections to heaven but also connections with those created from the dust of the earth.

4:1-13
Faithful in Temptation

Jesus' first actions were to overcome temptations from Satan, something Adam had failed to do. So the section shows Jesus as anointed by God, representative of humanity and faithful to God. God's promise comes in through a man who is able to deliver what God offers and who can deal with sin by being faithful to God.

4:14-30
Who Is Jesus?

Jesus' teaching and miracles dominate this section. Major teaching blocks include His declaration of the fulfillment of God's promise in the synagogue (4:16-30) and the Sermon on the Plain (6:17-49). Both passages are unique to Luke in that the synagogue speech represents Jesus' self-description of His mission, while the sermon represents His fundamental ethic presented without concerns about Jewish tradition that Matthew's Sermon on the Mount possesses.

The section's fundamental question is, Who is Jesus? The unit pictures the growth of faith that comes to those whom Jesus gathered around Himself. Their discovery is the vehicle Luke used to answer the question of Jesus' identity. The reader is to identify with the disciples and the crowds who witness and discuss Jesus. The reader is to share in the reflection their discussions and reactions raise. Jesus followed up the disciples' response in faith with the first discussions of the hard road of discipleship. The section shows that following Jesus is full of blessing, but it is not easy.

In the synagogue speech (4:16-30), Jesus raised the note of fulfillment through the appeal to Isaiah 61:1 and 58:6. He said that the anointing of God promised in this passage is fulfilled today. In the context of Luke, the anointing looks back to the anointing with the Spirit in Luke 3:20-22. As such the appeal to Isaiah was not just to the picture of a prophet, as allusions to Elijah and Elisha in verses 24-28 suggest but also asserts Jesus' regal role. Jesus would bring salvation to all those in need: poor, blind, and captive. His presence means release from bondage, particularly bondage rooted in the activity of Satan, as His subsequent miracles in 4:31-44 show. Rejection, like that in Nazareth, will not be met with failure but with the taking of the message to others, an indirect allusion to the inclusion of Gentiles (vv. 24-30). The mission's scope is summarized here.

4:31–6:11
Jesus' Authority and Mission

Jesus' ability to bring salvation is pictured in a series of miracles (4:31-44). These miracles show the authority of Jesus, even over evil spirits that oppress people and cause them suffering. The healings are a metaphor for the spiritual obstacles Jesus can overcome. Jesus healed, but His

DISCOURSES OF JESUS

Where Delivered	Nature or Style	To Whom Addressed	The Lesson to Be Learned	References
1. Jerusalem	Conversation	Nicodemus	We must be "born of water and the Spirit" to enter the kingdom	John 3:1-21
2. At Jacob's Well	Conversation	Samaritan Woman	"God is spirit" to be worshiped in spirit and truth	John 4:1-30
3. At Jacob's Well	Conversation	The Disciples	Our food is to do His will	John 4:31-38
4. Nazareth	Sermon	Worshipers	No prophet is welcomed in his own hometown	Luke 4:16-31
5. Mountain of Galilee	Sermon	The Disciples and the People	The Beatitudes; to let our light shine before men; Christians the light of the world; how to pray; benevolence and humility; heavenly and earthly treasures contrasted; golden rule	Matt 5–7; Luke 6:17-49
6. Bethesda—A Pool	Conversation	The Jews	To hear Him and believe on Him is to have everlasting life	John 5:1-47
7. Near Jerusalem	Conversation	The Pharisees	Works of necessity not wrong on the Sabbath	Matt 12:1-14 Luke 6:1-11
8. Nain	Eulogy and Denunciation	The People	Greatness of the least in heaven; judged according to the light we have	Matt 11:2-29; Luke 7:18-35
9. Capernaum	Conversation	The Pharisees	The unforgivable sin is to sin against the Holy Spirit	Mark 3:19-30; Matt 12:22-45
10. Capernaum	Conversation	The Disciples	The providence of God; nearness of Christ to those who serve Him	Mark 6:6-13; Matt 10:1-42
11. Capernaum	Conversation	A Messenger	Relationship of those doing His will	Matt 12:46-50; Mark 3:31-35
12. Capernaum	Sermon	The Multitude	Christ as the Bread of life	John 6:22-71
13. Capernaum	Criticism and Reproof	The Scribes and Pharisees	Not outward conditions, but that which proceeds from the heart defiles	Matt 15:1-20; Mark 7:1-23
14. Capernaum	Example	The Disciples	Humility the mark of greatness; be not a stumbling block	Matt 18:1-14; Mark 9:33-50
15. Temple–Jerusalem	Instruction	The Jews	Judge not according to outward appearance	John 7:11-40
16. Temple–Jerusalem	Instruction	The Jews	To follow Christ is to walk in the light	John 8:12-59
17. Temple–Jerusalem	Instruction	The Pharisees	Christ the door; He knows His sheep; He gives His life for them	John 10:1-21
18. Capernaum	Charge	The Seventy	Need for Christian service; not to despise Christ's ministers	Luke 10:1-24
19. Bethany	Instruction	The Disciples	The efficacy of earnest prayer	Luke 11:1-13
20. Bethany	Conversation	The People	Hear and keep God's will; the state of the backslider	Luke 11:14-36
21. House of Pharisee	Reproof	The Pharisees	The meaning of inward purity	Luke 11:37-54
22. Beyond Jordan	Exhortation	The Multitude	Beware of hypocrisy; covetousness; blasphemy; be watchful	Luke 12:1-21
23. Perea	Object Lesson	The Disciples	Watchfulness; the kingdom of God is of first importance	Luke 12:22-34
24. Jerusalem	Exhortation	The People	Death for life; way of eternal life	John 12:20-50
25. Jerusalem	Denunciation	The Pharisees	Avoid hypocrisy and pretense	Matt 23:1-39
26. Mount of Olives	Prophecy	The Disciples	Signs of the coming of the Son of man; beware of false prophets	Matt 24:1-51; Mark 13:1-37
27. Jerusalem	Exhortation	The Disciples	The lesson of humility and service	John 13:1-20
28. Jerusalem	Exhortation	The Disciples	The proof of discipleship; that He will come again	John 14–16

healings picture much more than physical resuscitation.

Beyond deliverance there also is mission. Disciples are called to be fishers of men (5:1-11). Unlike the fisherman, who catches fish to devour them, disciples fish to snatch people from the grip of death and damnation. But the offer of hope will yield negative reaction. The first hints of official opposition came with the miracles of divinelike authority, when the Son of man claimed to be able to forgive sins and healed on the Sabbath (5:12-26). This healing of the paralytic is significant because it shows the "picture" quality of miracles. Jesus healed the paralytic, but more importantly it "pictured" His absolute authority to forgive sin.

In contrast to the negative reaction came the positive responses. Levi, a hated tax gatherer, was called (5:27-28). And four controversies emerged, one of which involved the type of company Jesus kept, while the others centered on the Sabbath (5:29–6:11). In the midst of this debate, Jesus gave some mission statements: His task was to call the sick to repentance (5:32). His authority was such that to do good on the Sabbath is the requirement (Luke 6:5,9).

6:12-49
Love Like Christ

So Jesus organized the disciples who were responding and issued a call. The Twelve were chosen (6:12-16). Then Jesus offered blessing to the humble and poor while warning the rich and oppressive (6:20-26). His Sermon on the Plain is a call to love others in the context of accountability of God. Such love is to be greater than the love a sinner shows. It is not conditional love. It is love shown to the one who persecutes. Jesus' death for sinners will be the prime example of such love. If the world is to recognize God's disciples, their love will have to be different. Such love recognizes sin in the self before it hastens to deal with sin in others. Real wisdom is to respect the authority of Jesus' teaching and respond with obedience (6:27-49). The mission and message of Jesus are introduced here, as well as the fundamental elements of a disciple's ethic.

7:1–8:3
Messiah for All People

Luke 7:1–8:3 concentrates on who Jesus is and the ap-

Prayers of Jesus

Jesus was preeminently a person of prayer. There are at least seventeen references in the four Gospels to His practice of prayer. Most of these refer to the act of prayer rather than the content of His prayer.

The Gospel of Luke focuses on this aspect of Jesus' earthly life more than the others. Only in Luke is mention made of Jesus' praying at His baptism (3:21), at the transfiguration experience (9:29), before the choosing of the apostles (6:12-13), at the identification at Caesarea-Philippi (9:18), and on the cross (23:34).

In addition to these major moments in Jesus' life, the Gospels teach us that there was prayer at the feeding of the five thousand, at the raising of Lazarus from the tomb, and the institution of the Lord's Supper. Jesus' agony of prayer in the garden of Gethsemane is well-known. All the Gospels refer to Jesus' prayers from the cross.

Jesus' Practice of Prayer

The Gospels contain many references to Jesus' practice of prayer in the morning, often by Himself. Mark's Gospel records the first account of this discipline: "Very early in the morning, while it was still dark, Jesus got up, left the house and went off to a solitary place, where he prayed" (1:35).

Some key examples of Jesus' prayers include those recorded in Matthew 11:25-26 and John 17. Luke 11:1-13 is a beautiful treatise on prayer for His disciples. It came as a response to the disciples' asking to be taught more about prayer. These three references are worth serious searching in any study of the prayers of Jesus.

Jesus and the Fatherhood of God

Jesus' prayer in Matthew 11 is a good example of His addressing God as Father. Almost without exception Jesus began His prayers with this salutation. To Him, God was His Heavenly Father who loved Him, guided Him, and assisted Him in His divine mission of revelation and redemption. "I praise you, Father, Lord of heaven and earth" (Matt 11:25).

This verse reveals Jesus' concept of the fatherhood of God, a fundamental plank in Jesus' practice and teaching of prayer. Jesus' use of the word *Father,* though not a new idea in biblical tradition, stressed both complete obedience to God as well as total responsiveness to His love. A major premise is apparent that what we believe about God is what we will ultimately believe and practice about prayer.

Lord, Teach Us to Pray

In Luke 11:1-13 is listed the only specific teaching request the disciples ever made, "Lord, ▷

propriate response to Him. A Gentile centurion understood faith better than those in the nation, as the contrast between Israel and the nations surfaced (7:1-10). The crowd believed that Jesus was a prophet when He raised the widow of Nain's son much like Elijah and Elisha had done (7:11-17). John the Baptist wondered whether Jesus was the Coming One, probably because Jesus' style of ministry did not reflect the ruling, judging Messiah John had anticipated. Jesus replied that His eschatological works of healing and preaching give the affirmative answer (7:18-35; Isa 29:18; 35:5-6; 61:1). He is the One who brings the time of fulfillment. The difference in the two ages is so great that John, as the best of men born up to the day of Jesus, is less than the least of those who share in the age to come (Luke 7:28).

An exemplary faith is displayed by the woman who anoints Jesus and by those women who contribute to His ministry (7:36–8:3). Here the breadth of Jesus' ministry is emphasized as women, who were held in low esteem in the first century, are raised up as examples of faith. Here also in two scenes poor women, wealthy women, and women oppressed by Satan are all brought to equal honor by Jesus.

The grape vine produces delicious fruit and raw material for juice. See Luke 6:44.

8:4-56
Jesus Can Be Trusted

Jesus can be trusted. With the parable of the seed and the

teach us to pray" (11:1). Following this request is a paragraph of helpful teachings on prayer. Matthew placed the Lord's Prayer and some subsequent texts on our persistency and God's responsiveness in the Sermon on the Mount (see Matt 6:9-13; 7:7-11).

The teachings in Luke illustrate many of Jesus' own practices of prayer. He stressed again the fatherhood of God, the coming of the kingdom, dependence upon God for daily food, both the forgiveness of sins from God as well as the giving of forgiveness to others, and the seeking of strength from God in prayer to withstand temptation, regardless of its source.

The parable of the friend who knocked at midnight illustrates Jesus' strong teaching about persistence in prayer life, something He both taught and practiced. The final analogy of the father and son encourages prayer as an integral part of the Christian life because of the readiness of God to hear the disciples' prayers and to grant the best response. "How much more shall your heavenly Father give the Holy Spirit to those who ask Him?" (Luke 11:13).

Jesus and Intercessory Praying

John 17 records the longest prayer of Jesus. This prayer evidently was given somewhere between the establishment of the Lord's Supper and the Gethsemane experience on the night before the crucifixion. The timing of these great words is significant. In the shadow of the cross, Jesus revealed in His prayer an intimate relationship with God the Father. His prayer illustrates prayerfully some lessons He wanted His disciples to know.

Prayer was a means of fellowship with the Father. Prayer confirmed the direction of Jesus' work and ministry. Prayer gave Him a sense of timing about His actions. Jesus' prayer focused on unity among disciples. Throughout the chapter is the necessary emphasis on intercessory prayer. "My prayer is not that you take [the disciples] out of the world but that you protect them from the evil one" (John 17:15). In fact, the entire paragraph (vv. 9-19) deals with Jesus' prayer for His disciples. Praying for one another is one of the finest privileges of the Christian life.

Jesus' praying brought Him fellowship with the Father. It produced strength for the hours of temptation, discernment about the will of God, both in its content and timing. Jesus' prayer life is still a matchless guide for His disciples everywhere because it shows His complete confidence in God's love, power, and wisdom. □

Disciple

The term *disciple* implies several important ideas in the Scriptures. The primary emphasis of the word points to the various aspects of one's entire Christian experience. The actual English term is derived from the Latin word *discipulus.* In the first century this simply meant a *pupil* or a *learner.* It was often used in the philosophical world to speak of a philosopher's understudy. The exact equivalent of the term in NT Greek carries the same idea of *learner* or *pupil.*

In the Septuagint the term is used in its root form in Isaiah 8:16 and 1 Chronicles 25:8. The idea of *learner* predominates in those OT passages. The term finds its full meaning, however, in the NT.

We see the word used extensively in the four Gospels. Moses' disciples (John 9:28) and the followers of John the Baptist (Mark 2:18) are classic examples. It is also used to denote the disciples of the Pharisees (Matt 22:16). Of course, the NT usage is primarily concerned with the disciples of the Lord Jesus Christ. Here it is used once again as a *learner* or *pupil.* Those who encountered Jesus and became His committed followers and learners were known as disciples.

It is clear that the many who came to our Lord had varying degrees of conviction and loyalty. Thus there is a broad as well as a narrow connotation to the term as used in the four Gospels. The highest concept of *disciple* in the Gospels relates to the Twelve (Luke 6:12-18).

In the Acts of the Apostles, the word takes on a definite absolutist connotation. It was the accepted description of those who had come into full faith and commitment to Jesus Christ.

By the second century it was common for people to call themselves disciples in the context of martyrdom. A classic case in point is that of the Ignatius, where he spoke of himself in that setting. The primary idea seems to be that death for Christ would prove one to be a true disciple of the Lord.

The entire theme can be summarized by saying that a disciple was (1) a person who became a believer (Acts 11:26), (2) one who became a learner of Christ and thus His follower or pupil, (3) a believer who is committed to suffering and living a sacrificial life-style for the sake of Jesus Christ (Luke 14:26,27,33), and (4) one who fulfills the ultimate obligation of discipleship—to make disciples of others (Matt 28:19-20). This involved leading them to faith in Jesus Christ, baptizing them, and teaching them the truths of Christ. Disciples are those who have identified with Jesus Christ in baptism and been instructed in the community of faith.

Quite clearly, *disciple* is a most significant term. It implies repentance and faith for salvation, dedicated, sacrificial Christian living, identification with and service to Christ, and telling the good news to others. □

image of the word as light, a call is made to trust God and His word, as revealed by Jesus (8:4-21). Those who yield fruit cling to the word patiently and with a good heart, while the obstacles to fruitfulness include wealth, persecution, and the worries of life. Jesus then showed His total authority by exhibiting sovereignty over nature (8:22-25), over demons (8:26-39), and over disease and death (8:40-56). All the forces of life bow at His feet.

9:1-17
The Center of Promise

In the context of such authority, He sends out the message of promise. He sends out a mission of proclamation of the kingdom (9:1-6), as word about Him reaches as far as Herod (9:7-9). The picture of Jesus' ability to provide comes in the multiplication of loaves (9:10-17). Jesus is the source of life and resides at the center of promise.

9:18-50
Listen and Follow Jesus

At this point the story moves from teaching and demonstration of authority to confession and call to discipleship. Peter confessed Jesus to be the Christ (9:18-20). Then Jesus explained what kind of Messiah He would be; He would suffer (9:21-22). Those who follow Him must have total and daily commitment in order to survive the path of rejection that comes with following Jesus (9:23-27). The second heavenly testimony to Jesus comes at the transfiguration (9:28-36). The divine voice repeats the endorsement made at the baptism with one key addition, the call to "listen to him" (9:35; see Deut 18:15). Jesus was a second Moses, who marked out a "New Way."

The section closes with the disciples failing, thus showing their need for Jesus to instruct them. Jesus issued calls to trust and be humble, two basic characteristics of discipleship (9:37-50). If one is to learn and grow, one must listen to Him.

9:51–12:48
Trusting on the Way

Over 40 percent of this section contains material unique to Luke. There is a high concentration of teaching and parable. In fact, seventeen parables are in this unit, fifteen of which are unique to Luke. The "journey" is not a chronological, straight-line journey, since Jesus in 10:38-42 was near Jerusalem, while later in the section He was back in the north. Rather, it is a journey in time, in the context of the necessity of God's plan.

Jerusalem and the fate that met Jesus there drew near. The section explains how Jerusalem and the cross happened. Journey notes dot the section (9:51; 13:22; 17:11; 18:31; 19:28,44). Jesus traveled to meet His appointed fate in Jerusalem (13:31-35). The section's thrust is that Jesus gives a new way to follow God, which was not the way of the Jewish leadership. Its theme was "listen to him" (9:35). So this section discusses how Jesus' teaching related to current Judaism. Jesus fulfilled the promise and is the Way, but His way is distinct from that of Israel's leadership. The difference surfaces great opposition, a theme dominating Luke 9–13. All are invited, but some refuse. As the new way is revealed, the seeds of discontent leading to Jesus' death are also made manifest.

The journey starts with the disciples learning the basics of discipleship: mission, commitment, love for God, love for one's neighbor, devotion to Jesus and His teaching, and prayer (9:51–11:13). Here we see the call to be a neighbor in the example of the Good Samaritan. The choice of the Samaritan is a surprise, since Samaritans were not respected in Israel. Here again Jesus showed His racial breadth. Here is the example of Mary choosing the "better" thing, which was to sit and listen to Jesus. Here Jesus revealed devotion and submission to God as He taught the disciples the Lord's Prayer, which is really to be the Community's Prayer. Also raised are notes of challenge to Judaism's leadership (11:14-36) and a scathing indictment of them by Jesus (11:37-52). Their way is not God's way. Discipleship is fundamentally trusting God, not people or riches, for everything while remaining faithful to Him (12:1-48). If God is sovereign and cares for creation, fear Him and trust Him.

12:49–14:24
Narrow Way of Repentance

Jesus called on the crowd to know the nature of the times of His ministry (12:49–14:24). Israel was turning

DISCIPLES OF JESUS

Matthew 10:2-4	Mark 3:16-19	Luke 6:13-16	Acts 1:13-14
Simon Peter	Simon Peter	Simon Peter	Peter
Andrew	James son of Zebedee	Andrew	John
James son of Zebedee	John	James	James
John	Andrew	John	Andrew
Philip	Philip	Philip	Philip
Bartholomew	Bartholomew	Bartholomew	Thomas
Thomas	Matthew	Matthew	Bartholomew
Matthew the tax collector	Thomas	Thomas	Matthew
James son of Alphaeus	James son of Alphaeus	James son of Alphaeus	James son of Alphaeus
Thaddaeus	Thaddaeus	Simon who was called the Zealot	Simon the Zealot
Simon the Zealot	Simon the Zealot	Judas son of James (compare John 14:22)	Judas son of James
Judas Iscariot	Judas Iscariot	Judas Iscariot	(Judas Iscariot) Matthias (v. 26)

The good Samaritan (see Luke 10:25-37)

away; and the time for them to respond, without facing judgment, was short (13:1-9; 31-35). The only sign Jesus would give was the sign of Jonah, the message of repentance (12:29-32).

The Lukan focus on repentance here is unique to his Gospel, for in Matthew the "sign" was resurrection. For Luke the comparison was with the preaching of Jonah and the message of Jesus. Israel was like a fruitless tree that the owner of the garden was ready to remove (13:6-9). But tragedy is the end of all people unless they repent (13:1-5). Israel's house would be desolate until they recognized Jesus as sent by God (13:31-35). Nevertheless, blessing would still come to the earth regardless of how the nation responded. Jesus wanted His people, the Jews, to repent but knew their refusal.

Renewed Jewish condemnation of Jesus' Sabbath healings shows that the warnings and divine authentication were unheeded (13:10-17; 14:2-6). Jesus said the door was closing, so be sure to enter the narrow way (13:23-30). He also warned that those at the table would not be those who were expected to be there (14:1-24). Israel ran the risk of missing out on blessing, but the table would still be full with the blessed from the corners of the earth.

14:25–15:32
Seek the Lost

With Israel duly warned, most of the journey section concerns discipleship. Disciples in the face of rejection need absolute commitment (14:25-35). Their mission, even though others grumble at it, is to seek the lost, just as God does (15:1-32). God rejoices in finding lost sinners, so Jesus' call is to pursue them as one would a lost sheep, a lost coin, or a wayward son. When the lost come, open arms are to await them. Celebration and joy greet them in heaven.

16:1–18:30
Serve and Wait Humbly

Beyond mission is discipleship. Discipleship expresses itself in service to others, so the disciple is generous with resources (16:1-31). He is not like the rich man, who ignored Lazarus (16:19-31). Though false teaching is a threat, it is overcome with forgiveness of the brother, deep faith, and service (17:1-10). Disciples are to see themselves as slaves who do their duty (17:7-10), something Paul also knew (Rom 1:1).

Disciples are to live, looking for the hope of the King's return, when the promise of the currently inaugurated kingdom is consummated with judgment and the expression of Jesus' total authority (Luke 17:11–18:8). That coming will be sudden, so be ready. It will be visible, so no one will have to hunt for it. The return will be a time of severe judgment but also a time of vindication for the saints. So in the meantime, disciples should live lives of humility, should devote themselves completely to God because disciples trust all to the Father (18:9-30).

18:31–19:44
Messianic Authority

Now Jesus turned to Jerusalem. He again displayed His authority when He predicted His suffering and healed as the "Son of David" (18:31-43). The last miracle before Jerusalem returns to Jesus' Davidic, regal association, returning to the theme of Luke 1–2 and the issue of His trials.

Zacchaeus pictures the transformed sinner and rich man (19:1-10). He is a picture of the mission of Jesus, the lost who can be sought and saved (19:10). The parable of the pounds shows the need for faithfulness and the reality that the disciple, as well as the nation of Israel, is accountable to the king (19:11-27). Jesus entered Jerusalem as a king, but the leadership rejected the claim (19:28-40). Jesus warned the nation that they had failed to respond to God's promise and faced judgment (19:41-44). Their tragic fall drew near. Though opposition resulted in death for Jesus, opposition resulted in something much worse for the nation. Jesus predicted the nation's terrible defeat by Rome in A.D. 70. Thus the nation was the loser, while God's plan advanced in triumph.

The prodigal son returns home (see Luke 15:20-24)

19:45–21:4
God's Commitment to His Plan

In this concluding section, Luke explained how Jesus died and why apparent defeat became victory. Luke showed how God revealed who Jesus was. In addition, the task of disciples in light of God's acts becomes clear. Luke mixed fresh material with that present in the other Gospels.

The final battles in Jesus' earthly ministry occur here, recalling earlier confrontations in Luke 11–13. Jesus cleansed the Temple, signaling His displeasure with official Judaism (19:45-48). The leaders failed to embarrass Jesus in various controversies concerning His authority to act as He had, concerning an individual's political-economic responsibilities, and concerning resurrection (20:1-8,20-26,27-40). Jesus' source of authority is like that of John the Baptist; it comes from God. That which is to be rendered to God is to be given to God and is to be separated from the rights God has granted to government to operate. Resurrection changes people, so that life in the next world is different from and transcends life in this world.

In the midst of these controversies and at their end, Jesus told a parable and asked a question, which give an overview of God's plan. They revealed God's commitment to His Son despite Jewish rejection. The nation's rejection would cost them. The kingdom would go to new tenants. The question about Psalm 110 gives the reason. The Messiah is not just David's Son; He is David's Lord, who is to be seated at God's right hand. When we see Jesus, we see more than a king; we see the person God has chosen to share His authority and His rule. Jesus' death is a transition, not an end to God's plan. Jesus reveals how things stand when He condemns the scribes' hypocrisy, while praising a poor widow's simple, generous, and sacrificial faith (20:45–21:4). Blessing is not a matter of position but of the heart. The widow may have been poor, but in terms of life she was wealthier than the wealthy because her priorities were right.

21:5-38
Looking to the End

In light of the nation's refusal, Jesus predicted the fall of the temple and of Jerusalem, events that themselves are a foretaste of the end (21:5-38). The fall of Jerusalem will be a terrible time for the nation, but it was not yet the end, when the Son of man returns on the clouds with authority to redeem His people (Dan 7:13-14). This discourse on the end is hard to understand because it describes events that lead up to the fall in A.D. 70 and the events of the end together. In Luke the events of the fall of Jerusalem are largely in view from verses 5-24. But these events are like those of the end. Disciples are to watch and be faithful. The events of A.D. 70 are a guarantee that the end also comes, since the one set of events does picture the other.

22:1–23:25
Christ's Exaltation

Luke 22–23 describes the moments before Jesus' death. Jesus directed where the Last Supper was held and told the disciples to prepare it (22:1-13). Jesus, though betrayed, was innocent, but His death would bring the new covenant and was a sacrifice on behalf of others (22:14-20). In His last discourse Jesus announced the betrayal, pointed out that greatness is in service, appointed eleven to authority, predicted Peter's denials, and warned of rejection (22:21-38). Jesus was in control, even as His death approached.

As Jesus prayed, He exemplified trust in the face of rejection, something He had exhorted the disciples to possess (22:47-53). The trails centered on who Jesus is. The crucial answer comes in 22:69. Jesus "from now on" would be manifest as the exalted Lord, who is seated with authority at the side of God. The allusion to being

Jerusalem in New Testament Times

Jerusalem is mentioned frequently in the four Gospels and in Acts. The name also occurs in Romans, 1 Corinthians, Galatians, Hebrews, and Revelation. The name is the OT designation for the city, as is the expression "the holy city" used in Matthew 4:5; 27:53.

Location and Setting

Jerusalem was the largest city in Palestine and one of the largest in Syria. It had a first-century population of about twenty thousand within the city walls and about ten thousand outside. The city owed its size and prosperity to the Jewish temple rather than location on a major trade route, a wealth of natural resources, or agricultural productivity.

The temple—with its thousands of workers, sacrifices of hundreds of animals daily, subsidy from all Jews in the temple tax (see Matt 17:24-27), and thronging visitors (see Luke 2:41; Acts 8:27)—was the enterprise that brought Jerusalem its prosperity.

The city, whose walls enclosed an area about one mile long and half a mile wide, was located on the end of a ridge with valleys surrounding it on each side. The Hinnon Valley was to the south and west (Josh 18:16), and the Kidron Valley was to the east (John 18:1). The Kidron Valley was the site for the Gihon spring, which King Hezekiah diverted (2 Chron 32:30) through a tunnel to flow into the Pool of Siloam (John 9:7) to supplement the rainwater supply stored in pools and cisterns.

Major Buildings and Sites

The high priest's home (John 18:15) was located in the southwestern section of the city. Pilate's "palace" (John 18:28) was either the lavish residence of Herod the Great in the northwestern corner of the upper city or the older residence of the Hasmonean king in the northeast. Herod had converted the latter into a fortress called Antonia. This fortress was the place where Paul was taken when he was arrested in Jerusalem (Acts 22:23-29). The site of the crucifixion was outside the city walls (Mark 15:20; Heb 13:12) to the north as was the rock tomb (John 19:41-42) where Jesus was buried.

The Mount of Olives, which was across the Kidron Valley directly east of the temple, was where Jesus taught on occasion (Mark 13:3), where the garden of Gethsemane was (Matt 26:30-36), and where Jesus ascended (Acts 1:9-12). ⇨

seated at the right hand repeats the allusion to Psalm 110, a passage to which Luke would return in Acts 2:30-36. Messiahship means lordship, that is, authority over God's plan and salvation. No judgment the leadership makes can prevent that from happening. In fact, ironically and unwittingly they help bring this authority to pass. Jesus was on trial, it seems; but, in fact, He was the Judge (Luke 22:54-71).

But it was not only the leadership that was guilty. As Pilate and Herod debated what to do about Jesus, the people were given the final choice (23:1-25). Despite Pilate's repeated protestations of innocence and Herod's similar reaction, the people asked for Jesus to be slain and Barabbas to be freed. Justice was absent, both in the request and in the failure of the leaders to carry out their impression. Passively and actively, the responsibility for Jesus' death widens. Everyone, whether actively or passively, shares in the responsibility of Jesus' death (Acts 4:24-28).

23:26-56
God Triumphs over Injustice

So the innocent died, while a criminal was freed. Here is the first cameo of the significance of Jesus' death as He prepares to face His departure. Next a second image of

The hill of Golgotha, or Place of the Skull (see Luke 23:33)

the significance of Jesus' death follows. Jesus was crucified between two thieves. One derides, but the other believes and receives the promise of life in paradise. Here is a picture of division of opinion and of eternal fate, which Jesus brings. A centurion confesses the righteousness of Jesus, the final word at the scene of the cross (23:47). Luke made clear that Jesus died unjustly, yet in the face of injustice God still works. Luke describes Jesus' death with Old Testament allusions that picture Jesus as an innocent sufferer who relied on God (23:26-56; Pss 19;

The Temple

The temple was located in the northeastern corner of the city directly west of the Mount of Olives. The temple area, which was approximately three hundred yards wide and five hundred yards long, was entirely walled with the main gates being in the south wall.

Immediately inside the temple walls a portico existed with three rows of massive marble columns on the north, east, and west and four in the south. The eastern portico was known as "Solomon's Colonnade" (John 10:23; Acts 3:11; 5:12). All of the colonnades were fully open to the large, open area paved with variously colored stones and known as the court of the Gentiles. There animals were sold, and money was exchanged (Mark 11:12-19).

Making one's way through the area of the Gentiles toward the temple building itself, one passed through a low stone fence (Eph 2:14). This fence marked the limit for the Gentiles, and through its openings only Jews could pass (Acts 21:27-29).

The temple building was within a walled enclosure with one large entrance opening to the east, called the Beautiful Gate (Acts 3:2). Inside the gate was the area called the court of the women, where the temple offerings were received (Mark 12:41).

Only male Israelites could proceed to the next area closer to the building itself. The area immediately adjacent to the front of the building where the great altar was set was open only to the priests. The facade of the building was approximately 150 feet wide and 180 feet high.

The temple itself contained two main rooms. First was the holy place, where the seven-branched lampstand and the altar of incense (Heb 9:2; Exod 30:6) were and where only priests chosen by lot could enter (Luke 1:9). The inmost room, called the holy of holies, was entered only once each year and only by the high priest in the ceremony of atonement (Heb 9:25).

Christian Symbol

The author of Hebrews used imagery drawn from the temple and its ritual to explain what Jesus accomplished: He entered into the holy of holies to win our redemption (9:11-14) and gives to all Christians the spiritual privilege limited to the high priest (10:19-22) in Jewish ritual. □

Jerusalem in the Time of Jesus

1. *The Temple (Herod's Temple)*
2. *Women's Court*
3. *The Soreg*
4. *The Court of the Gentiles*
5. *Royal Porch*
6. *Eastern Gate (the present-day Golden Gate)*
7. *Antonia Fortress*
8. *The Double Gate (the Western Huldah Gate)*
9. *The Triple Gate (the Eastern Huldah Gate)*
10. *Monumental Herodian Staircase (sections still remain today)*
11. *The City of David (established by David, the oldest part of the city)*
12. *Earliest defense wall (destroyed and constructed many times)*
13. *Herodian outer defense wall around the expanded city*
14. *Herodian wall separating the Upper City (or affluent district) from the Lower City (or lower economic district)*
15. *The Second North Wall (possible location)*
16. *Garden of Gethsemane (the west side of the Mount of Olives)*
17. *Mount of Olives*
18. *Kidron Valley*
19. *Gihon Spring*
20. *Pool of Siloam*
21. *Tyropoeon Valley (Lower City)*
22. *Herodian aqueduct (possible location)*
23. *Shops and marketplace of Jesus' day*
24. *Additional shops and marketplace (probably added at a later time)*
25. *Staircase (Robinson's Arch) leading up from the Lower City*

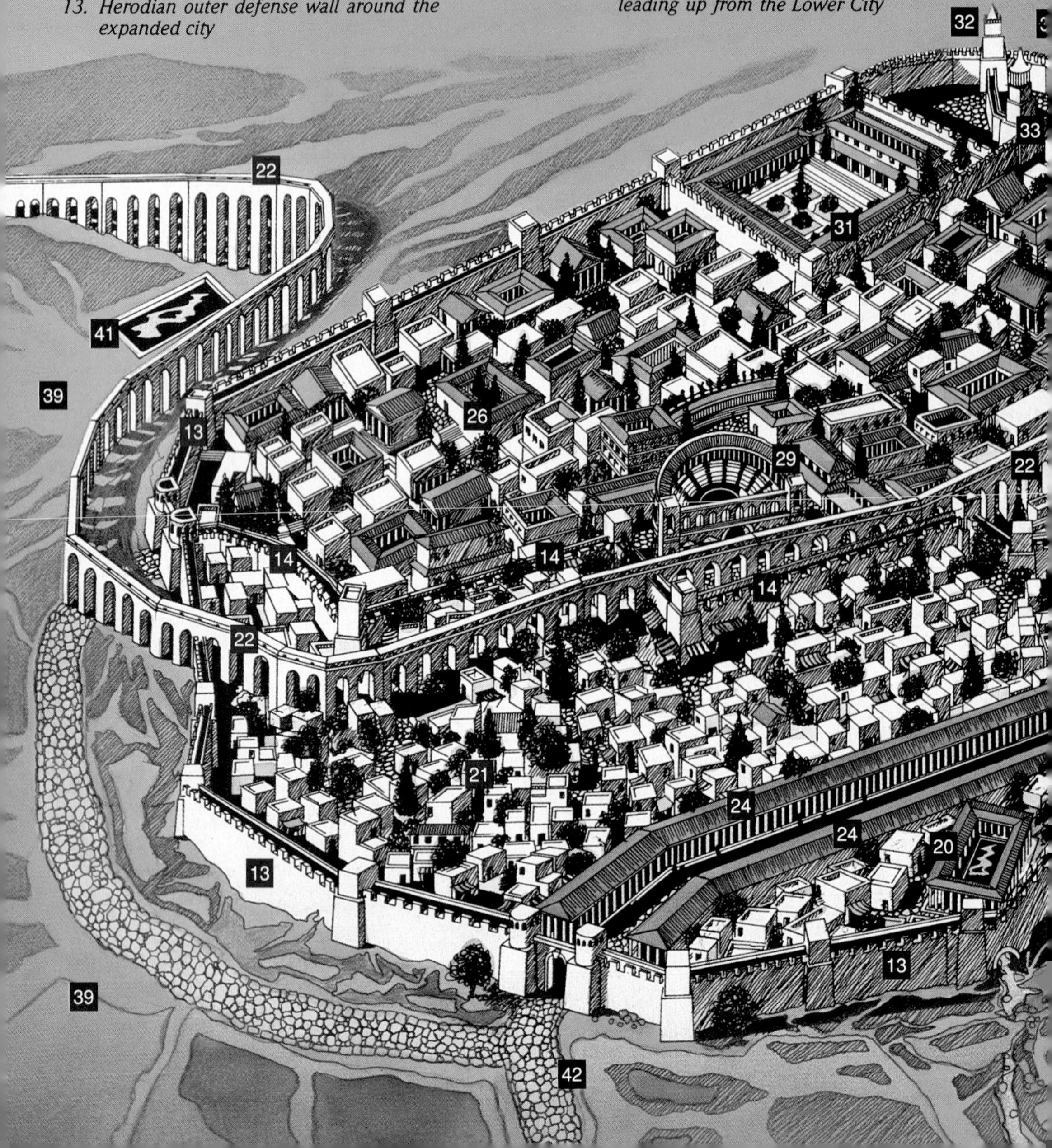

26. *Upper City*
27. *Causeway (Wilson's Arch) leading from the Upper City to the Temple*
28. *Residential houses*
29. *Roman Theater (structure mentioned by Josephus but whose location remains unverified)*
30. *Hippodrome (structure mentioned by Josephus but whose location remains unverified)*
31. *Herod's Palace*
32. *Phasael Tower*
33. *Mariamne Tower*
34. *Hippicus Tower*
35. *Sheep Pool*
36. *Traditional Golgotha (Calvary)*
37. *Traditional tomb of Jesus*
38. *Pool of Bethesda*
39. *Hinnom Valley*
40. *Gennath Gate*
41. *Serpent's Pool*
42. *Road to the Dead Sea*
43. *Road to Sebaste (Samaria)*

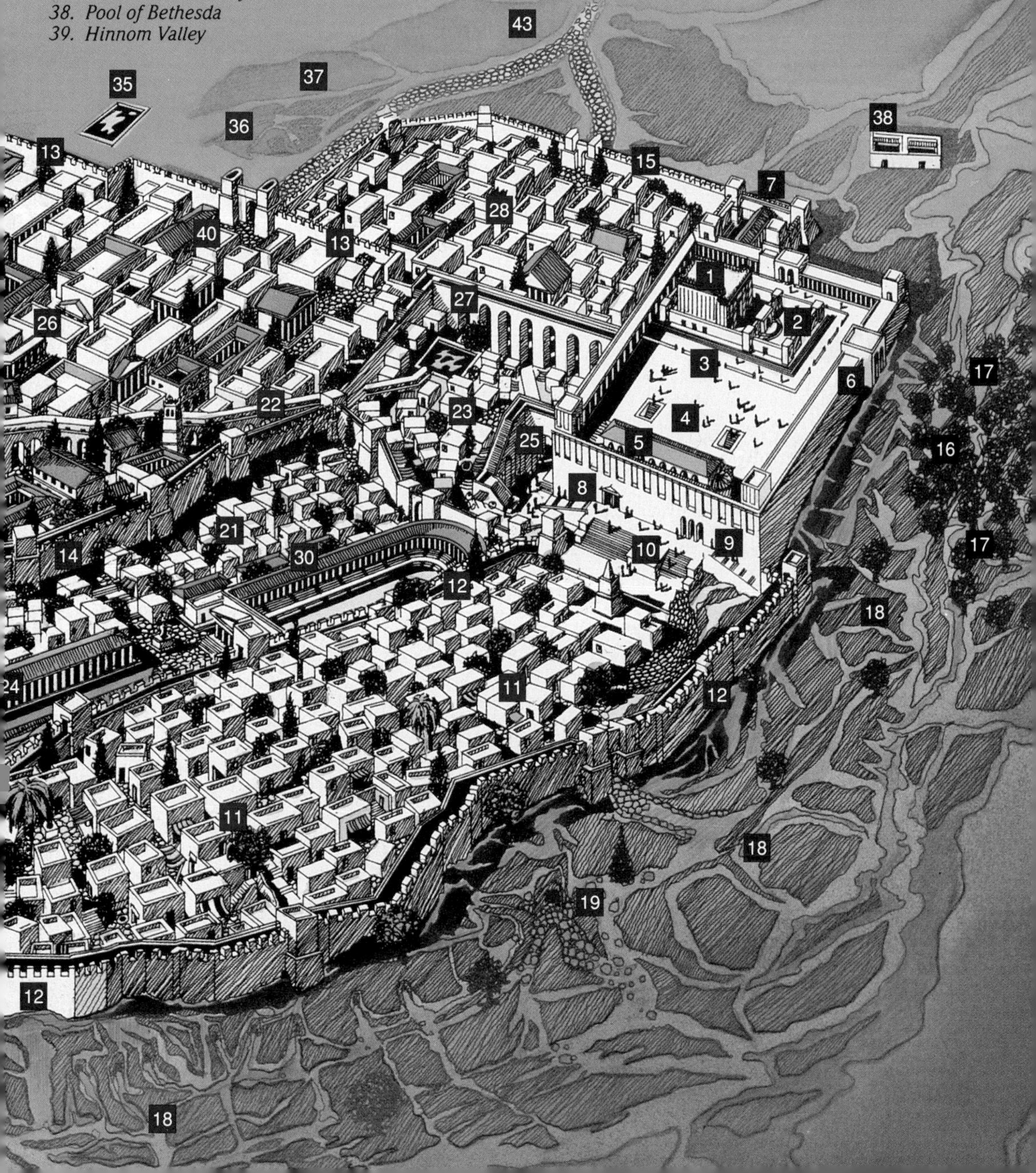

Accounts of the Resurrection

The resurrection of Jesus Christ is the central event of the Christian faith. Its importance is well stated by the apostle Paul in 1 Corinthians 15:17: "If Christ has not been raised, your faith is futile; you are still in your sins."

The reality and nature of the resurrection has been debated from the time of Jesus until the present. A number of different theories have been set forth to explain exactly what happened. These can be summarized as follows:

1. *Swoon theory.*—Jesus did not actually die. He passed out on the cross and was later revived and appeared to His followers.

2. *Spirit theory.*—Jesus appeared only in a spirit form to His disciples. His body remained in the tomb.

3. *Hallucination theory.*—The disciples experienced mass and personal hallucinations. They thought they saw the risen Jesus, but they were mistaken.

4. *Legend/Myth theory.*—This is the most popular view among people with antisupernatural biases. In it the idea of "resurrection" is considered simply a first-century prescientific metaphor that expresses that in Jesus something significant was present. "Resurrection" is not to be understood as a literal bodily event of rising from the dead.

5. *Stolen body theory.*—The body of Jesus was illegally removed from the tomb by the (a) Jews, (b) Romans, or (c) disciples of Jesus (see Matt 28:11-15).

6. *Wrong tomb theory.*—The followers of Jesus went to another tomb by mistake, found it was empty, and erroneously assumed Jesus had risen.

7. *Hoax theory.*—The early church deliberately and knowingly fabricated the resurrection for personal profit.

8. *Mistaken identity theory.*—The disciples mistakenly identified someone else as Jesus after His crucifixion and burial.

9. *Literal/Bodily resurrection theory.*—Jesus of Nazareth was supernaturally resurrected from the dead bodily. The tomb was actually empty, and Jesus on numerous occasions appeared to His followers up until His ascension (see Luke 24:50-53; Acts 1:6-11).

No one actually saw the resurrection event within the tomb. The evidence is overwhelming, however, in pointing to theory 9, a literal bodily resurrection, as the best explanation of the biblical and historical data. The following evidences are noted:

1. Naturalistic theories are weak and forced to manipulate the evidence due to their antisupernaturalism.

2. The birth of the church during this time period.

3. The transformation of the disciples into bold witnesses who were willing to die for their faith.

4. The change in the day of worship by people raised as devout Jews from the Sabbath to Sunday.

5. The testimony of women as the first to see the risen Lord. (A woman's testimony carried little if any official or legal value in the first century. That they actually saw Christ first is the best explanation for Scripture's testimony to the historicity of the event.)

6. The empty tomb and the articles of clothing left.

7. The unlikely nature of mass hallucinations.

8. The fact that the reported appearances lasted forty days and then suddenly and completely stopped.

9. The fifty-day interval between the resurrection and the proclamation of it at Pentecost in Jerusalem (see Acts 1–2).

10. The unexpected nature of the resurrection.

11. The character of Jesus and His claims that He would indeed rise.

12. The fact that neither the Romans nor the Jewish leaders could disprove the resurrection event by producing the body of Jesus.

13. The conversion of a skeptic like James (the half brother of Jesus) and the subsequent conversion of an antagonist like Saul of Tarsus (see Acts 9:1-31).

It is extremely difficult in all of these cases, and impossible in some, to explain these thirteen events, and others that could be listed, apart from the resurrection of Jesus Christ. When all the information is gathered and evaluated, the bodily resurrection of Jesus can be concluded to be both a historical reality and the foundation of the Christian faith. □

22:8-9; 31:6; 69:22). The injustice is transcended in God's plan through the coming resurrection.

24:1-12
Resurrection and Vindication

Luke closes with three scenes of resurrection and vindication. First, 24:1-12 announces the empty tomb, but the news of the excited women is greeted with skepticism. The angelic announcement told the women to recall the predictions of suffering proclaimed during the journey to Jerusalem. Luke 24 often notes that such events *must take place* (Luke 24:7,26,44). God's plan emerges at the end of the Gospel, just as refrains of its presence began the Gospel in the various hymns and announcements declaring its presence.

24:13-35
Overcoming Despair

Second, the experience of the Emmaus disciples pictures the reversal the resurrection brought to the disciples' despair (24:13-36). These two disciples mourned the departure of the Prophet of Israel who might have redeemed the nation. But instruction in Scripture and the revelation of Jesus Himself shows that God had a plan, which included Jesus' death. God has indeed raised Jesus, vindicating both Jesus and the plan. Despair turns to joy upon understanding the nature of God's plan and Jesus' role in it, a major note in Luke. Events that on the surface appeared devastating to Jesus' claims, in fact, were foundational to what God was doing. Jesus' death should not cause despair because it allowed heaven to open its gates to humankind.

24:36-53
God's Plan Fulfilled

Third, Luke reported Jesus' final commission, instruction, and ascension (24:36-53). Just as Luke 1–2 opened with the hope of Old Testament promise fulfilled, so Luke 24:43-47 returns to the central theme of Jesus the Messiah as the fulfillment of God's plan and promise. Jesus' final Gospel appearance yields a commission, a plan, and a promise. The disciples were reminded again that Scripture taught the suffering and exaltation of Messiah. Jesus also told them that they were called as witnesses to preach repentance. The plan was to go to all the nations, starting from Jerusalem. The promise was the gift of the Father, the Holy Spirit (24:49; 3:15-17). As the Baptist promised, so it had come to pass. Enabling power from heaven, from on high, would come in the distribution of the Spirit upon those who had responded to the message of Jesus (Acts 2:16-39).

Jesus' ascension (Luke 24:50-53) pictures the exaltation He predicted at His trial (22:69). God's plan does not involve a dead Messiah but one who sits at God's side. In exaltation Jesus is vindicated, and the plan to reach all nations of people goes on. Jesus, the Messiah, is Lord of all, so the message can go to all (Acts 2:14-40; 10:34-43).

The Gospel of Luke closes with the disciples rejoicing that out of the ashes of apparent defeat, victory and promise arose. The new way was still alive, and the risen Lord showed the way. Theophilus could be reassured (1:1-4), while the history continues in Acts.

Theological and Ethical Significance

How does God want people to receive the message? The centrality of repentance as a summary term for responding adequately to God's message is prominent throughout Luke's message. The fundamental dynamic of responding to God is agreeing with Him about the seriousness of sin, turning to Him to forgive it, and trusting Him to forgive sin and deal with it. In short, we know that God has dealt with the sin problem so we can walk with God (1:77-79; 5:31-32).

As disciples follow Christ, they can count on rejection. They are to hold to the word and endure (8:1-14) and watch for the Lord's return, being faithful until He comes again (12:35-48; 18:1-80; 17:22-37; 21:5-38). The fact of Jesus' return and the reality that He returns bringing judgment should bring perspective to the temporary suffering endured by His disciples. Though some rejection exists now, reception in heaven awaits in the future (23:42-43; Acts 7:55-56). This truth has been called Luke's individual eschatology, where Luke described how heaven receives the individual faithful to Jesus.

Luke's Gospel is pastoral, theological, and historical. The reality of God's plan affects how individuals see themselves and the community to which they belong. Old barriers of race are removed. New hope abounds. The message of Jesus is one of hope and transformation. Anyone, Jew or Gentile, can belong. At the center is Jesus, the promised Messiah-Lord, who sits at God's right hand exercising authority from above. He will return one day, and all are accountable to Him. His life, ministry, and resurrection/ascension show that He can be trusted. He can bring God's promises to completion, just as He has inaugurated them. In the meantime being a disciple is not easy, but it is full of rich blessing that transcends anything else this life can offer. This is the reassurance about salvation Luke offered to Theophilus and others like him.

Questions for Reflection

1. What are the themes of Luke, and what additional ones did you find in your own reading of the Gospel?
2. What various roles does Jesus Christ have according to Luke?
3. What elements are part of the disciple's walk?
4. What attitudes should a disciple have about money, suffering, the poor, the rejected, and the lost?
5. What role does hope and looking for Jesus' return play in the disciple's walk?

Sources for Additional Study

Evans, Craig. *Luke. New International Bible Commentary.* Peabody, Mass.: Hendricksen, 1990.

Stein, Robert. *Luke. The New American Commentary.* Nashville: Broadman, 1992.

Tiede, David L. *Luke. Augsburg Commentary on the New Testament.* Minneapolis: Augsburg, 1988.

JOHN

The Gospel of John is perhaps the most intriguing of the four accounts of the life and teaching of Jesus found in Scripture. More of a theological treatise than a historical narrative, John put the challenge of the incarnation before his readers—God in human flesh.

Authorship and Date

The authorship of the Gospel of John has been traditionally ascribed to the apostle John, the son of Zebedee and the brother of James. The Gospel itself, however, does not put forth the author's name (which has made the authorship of John a much-debated issue among interpreters). The only reference to the author is the "disciple whom Jesus loved" (21:20,24). The apostle John is usually seen as the author because the Gospel exhibits many marks that intimate it was written by one who was an eyewitness to the life and ministry of Jesus, such as the aroma of the broken perfume jar in the house at Bethany (12:3).

Even individuals who were anonymous in the Synoptics are given names in John's Gospel (6:7-8; 12:3; 18:10). Many other aspects of the Gospel point toward the apostle John. Examples are the author's knowledge of Palestinian geography, Jewish customs, and the author's inclusion within the inner circle of disciples (listed by the Synoptic Gospels as Peter, James, and John). Writers in the earliest periods of Christian history, such as Irenaeus and Tertullian, also attribute the Gospel to the apostle John.

Who was John the apostle? John was "the disciple whom Jesus loved" (13:23; 19:26; 20:2; 21:7,20,24). John's brother was James, and together they were called the "sons of thunder" by Jesus (Mark 3:17). John's mother was Salome, who served Jesus in Galilee and later witnessed His crucifixion (Mark 15:40-41). Formerly a follower of John the Baptist, the apostle John was perhaps only twenty-five years of age when called to be a follower of Christ.

Beyond this Gospel, John has been traditionally understood to have written the three epistles bearing his name as well as the Book of Revelation. After Christ ascended to heaven, John became one of the principal figures of the church at Jerusalem, along with Peter and James (Acts 3:1; 8:14; Gal 2:9). Second only to the apostle Paul in the number of books written that are included in the New Testament canon, John served as the pastor of the church at Ephesus. The emperor Domitian later exiled him to Patmos, where he wrote the Book of Revelation (Rev 1:9). Most interpreters have concluded that John's was the last of the four Gospels to be written, most likely between A.D. 60 and 90.

Literary Form

The literary form of the Gospel of John is just that—a gospel. What is a gospel? The word itself comes from the Anglo-Saxon word "godspell," which literally means *good news.* In reference to the four Gospels in the New Testament, what we have is a narrative of the good news of Jesus Christ.

John made use of many features of Hebrew poetry, most notably parallelism. The Gospel of John does not contain parables, as do Matthew, Mark, and Luke, but rather brings forth the many allegories present in the teaching ministry of Jesus.

Purpose and Theology

The theme of John's Gospel is that God had taken human form in the person of Jesus Christ. For this reason John's Gospel is often seen as the most evangelistic of the four Gospels. John's emphasis on the nature of Christ—as opposed to the more chronological, historical accounts of Jesus' life in Matthew, Mark, and Luke—has fostered the popular classification of Matthew, Mark, and Luke as "Synoptic" Gospels. This means they put forth a similar view and emphasis, while the Gospel of John falls into a class all to itself.

Virtually every reader of the four Gospels finds the Gospel of John unique in its approach and treatment of the life of Jesus. For example, note the omissions from the Synoptic accounts of the life of Jesus: the genealogy of Jesus, His birth, His boyhood, His temptation, His transfiguration, His appointing of the disciples, His ascension, and the Great Commission. Yet we find uniquely in John Christ called the Word, the Creator, the Lamb of God, and the great "I AM." The contrasts between John and

COMPARISON OF THE GOSPELS

Event or Point of Comparison	In Synoptic Gospels?	In Gospel of John?	Scripture Reference
Wedding at Cana	No	Yes	John 2:1-11
Encounter with Nicodemus	No	Yes	John 3:1-14
Encounter with Woman at the Well	No	Yes	John 4:1-45
Washing of the Disciples' Feet	No	Yes	John 13:1-17
Last Supper	Yes	No	Luke 22:7-23
Jesus' Final Priestly Prayer	No	Yes	John 17:1-26
Extensive Prologue to the Gospel	No	Yes	John 1:1-18
Concluding Epilogue to the Gospel	No	Yes	John 21:1-25
Birth Narratives	Yes	No	Luke 2:1-20
Jesus' Use of Parables	Yes	No	Matt 13:1-52
Casting Out Demons	Yes	No	Mark 1:21-28
Jesus with Tax Collectors	Yes	No	Luke 6:27-32
Jesus Heals Lepers	Yes	No	Luke 17:11-17
Jesus with Children	Yes	No	Mark 10:13-16
Sermon on the Mount	Yes	No	Matt 5:1–7:27
Discourses on the End Times	Yes	No	Matt 24:1-51
Emphasis on Miracles	Yes	No	Matt 8:1–9:8
Emphasis on Interpretation of Miracles/Signs	No	Yes	John 5:1-47
Jesus' Teaching on Hell	Yes	No	Matt 23:1-39
Temptations of Jesus	Yes	No	Matt 4:1-11
"I AM" Sayings	No	Yes	John 14:6

the Synoptics have been framed in many different angles by a host of interpreters. Perhaps the most succinct statement of their distinctions is to say that the Synoptics present theology from a historical point of view, while John presents history from a theological point of view.

The purpose of John's Gospel is not a question for speculation. It contains the most clearly stated purpose statement in all of Scripture: "That you may believe that Jesus is the Christ, the Son of God, and that by believing you may have life in his name" (20:31). The key word here is "believe," found in John close to one hundred times. This gives the Gospel two primary purposes. First, John's Gospel sought to confront individuals with the life and claims of Christ in order that they might surrender their lives to Christ's rule. Therefore the first purpose of John's Gospel is evangelistic. Second, it is possible to translate "may believe" in John's purpose statement as "may continue to believe," which would intimate the purpose of not only winning individuals to faith in Christ but also that of strengthening the family of faith that is already walking with Christ.

The central theological theme of John is the nature of Jesus Christ. This Gospel teaches us that the Word was God, and that Word became flesh (1:1,14). John's Gospel presents Jesus as God Himself in human form. This is perhaps presented most clearly in the seven "I am" statements found in chapters 6–15, which portray Christ as the "bread of life" (6:35,48), "the light of the world" (8:12; 9:5), "the door" (10:7,9), "the good shepherd" (10:11,14), "the resurrection, and the life" (11:25), "the way, the truth, and the life" (14:6), and "the true vine" (15:1-5). There are even moments in John's Gospel where Jesus equated Himself directly with the Old Testament name for God Himself, "I AM" (Yahweh), such as in 8:58. When one has seen Jesus, one has seen the Father (chaps. 12; 14).

The ancient heresy of Docetism, however, is not to be found in this account of the life of Jesus. The Docetic view emphasized Christ's divinity to the exclusion of His humanity. John's Gospel balances the proclamation that Jesus was God in human form with the equal proclamation that Jesus was fully human (2:24; 4:6-7; 6:51; 11:35; 19:5,28,34-35). Other unique features in the Gospel of John in relation to the purpose of showing that Jesus was God in human form include the "seven witnesses" (John the Baptist, Nathanael, Peter, Martha, Thomas, John, and Christ Himself) who proclaim the divinity of Jesus and the "seven miracles" (turning water into wine, healing the nobleman's son, healing the man at Bethesda, feeding the five thousand, walking on the water, healing the blind man, and the raising of Lazarus), which demonstrate the unique person of Jesus Christ as the Son of God.

Many other theological themes present themselves in

Religious Background of the New Testament

The background of the New Testament involves two realms of religious thought and practice: Palestinian Judaism and Hellenistic culture. The life of Jesus and the development of the church in Jerusalem embrace the four Gospels and almost the first half of Acts, and they unfold in the center of Palestinian Judaism. Paul's ministry and the establishment and growth of churches outside Jerusalem, which embrace nearly all the rest of the New Testament, are set in the context of the Hellenistic cultural climate that prevailed in the Roman Empire outside Palestine.

Palestinian Judaism was based on the revelation God gave Israel, and the Old Testament was its heart. It was not its entire body, however. Historical developments in Jewish religious thought and practice resulted in institutions (such as the synagogue and Sanhedrin), parties (such as the Pharisees and Sadducees), and feasts, (such as Hanukkah or Dedication) that are not mentioned in the OT.

Pharisees

Understanding the parties or basic alternatives for religious lifestyles is the best way to enter the world of Palestinian Judaism. The most popular party in the time of Jesus was that of the Pharisees. They believed that the purity rule for the priests on duty in the temple should be extended to embrace every aspect of life, hence their emphasis on ritual cleanliness.

To attain this goal, the Pharisees developed rules called "the tradition of the elders" (Mark 7:3). They felt these traditions were as authoritative as the OT laws themselves because their rules applied the law. Jesus was accused of breaking the Sabbath because He healed on that day, and the Pharisees' "law" defined healing as work (Mark 3:1-6).

Study of the OT and their own traditions, which were legalistically imposed, was the essence of Pharisaism. Those who did not follow their rules were viewed as sinners and outcasts (Luke 15:1-2).

Sadducees

Sadducees were the priestly party. The heart of this movement

this Gospel, such as the clear choice to accept or reject Christ. This decision, placed before every individual, permeates the Gospel (1:11-13; 3:36; 5:24-29; 10:27-29). Sin is treated primarily as unbelief, the rejection of Christ, which leads to judgment and death (chap. 8). The Gospel of John contains more teaching about the Spirit than any other Gospel. The unity and witness of the church is also a theme that is given careful attention.

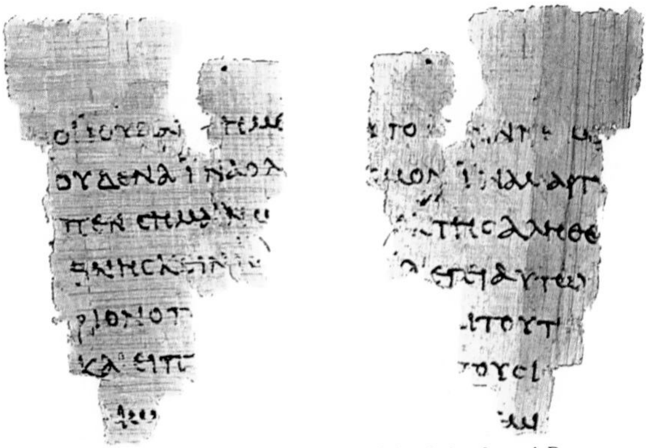

Two papyrus fragments of the Gospel of John dating from A.D. 100–150. They are in the John Rylands Library and are the earliest extant manuscript of any part of the New Testament.

I. Introduction (1:1–2:11)
II. Public Ministry of Christ (2:12–4:54)
III. Opposition to Christ (5:1–12:50)
IV. Final Words and Deeds of Christ (13:1–21:25)

1:1-18
The Word Became Flesh

No other book in the Bible has a prologue as overtly theological as does the Gospel of John. First, John made a clear and decisive statement regarding the nature of Jesus: "the Word was God" and that "Word became flesh" (1:1,14). John wanted it known that Jesus Christ was fully God in human form. That is the meaning of "incarnation," from the Latin *incarnatus,* which means *made flesh*. God has made Himself known through Christ (1:18-19). Christ was both "Word" and "flesh," not one to the exclusion of the other, and thus was the perfect and only God-man. Christ made His "dwelling" with us, a word associated with "tent" or "tabernacle," intimating the literalness of God's coming to humanity. This word usage should not be lost on the reader, for the tabernacle of the Old Testament was an earthly building filled with the glory of God (Exod 40:34-35).

In using the term "Word" (*logos*), John was using a term familiar to both Jews and Greeks, though each attributed a different meaning to the term. For the Greek

was dedication to the temple and its preservation. To accomplish this, the Sadducees cooperated with the Roman authorities and were more open to their cultural influences than the Pharisees, who were devoted to preserving the traditional way.

Zealots

The Zealots were much like the Pharisees except that they felt to accept Roman domination was to deny the domination of God as the Ruler of Israel. They felt that paying Roman taxes denied God's rule, and they advocated revolt against the Romans.

Essenes

The Essenes were much like the Sadducees in their devotion to the temple. But they felt that cooperation with the priests in Jerusalem was impossible because of their political compromises. They moved to the deserted area at the northwest tip of the Dead Sea to await God's coming according to Isaiah 40:3 (Mark 1:3).

Hellenistic culture, which was the world of Paul's ministry, was marked by a unity of language (the Greek in which the NT was written), by an openness to new ideas and life-styles (Acts 17:21), and by a tolerance of cultural and religious diversity.

The heart of Hellenistic culture was a question: How should a person live, act, and believe to get the most from life? The diversity of the Hellenistic world reflects the various answers given to this question and the passion with which the answer was pursued. Religions that offered answers, such as the Isis Cult of Egypt, thus spread all over the empire. Hellenistic cities thus had large numbers of temples dedicated to the worship of various gods (1 Cor 8–10). In addition, there were gods who were thought authoritative in various areas of life: birth, agriculture, business, illness, marriage, home, travel, and others.

Philosophy also offered answers. The Stoic view, that one should simply accept one's life, was the most popular. The Epicurean view found the best life to be a simple one with friendship as a treasured ingredient, but it was popularly understood to be the pursuit of pleasure (see Phil 3:19). Paul faced the Hellenistic world with one message—Jesus is the source of life and salvation. □

mind the "Word" referred to the rational principle that supervised or governed the universe. To the Jew, "Word" was a reference to God. Thus John wanted to equate the "Word" with God while noting that the Word was distinct from the Father. John stated that Jesus was with God "in the beginning" and that through Christ "all things were made" (1:2-3). Jesus is therefore seen as co-eternal with God and as the Creator.

John then discussed the purpose of the Word becoming flesh, namely that Christ brought life, a life that serves as the "light" for all people (1:4). The life Christ offers is beyond that of mere human life; it is life eternal with God. Therefore Jesus brought the light of truth and the life of salvation. The questions and concerns of this world that find no ultimate answers are met by the Light that pierces all darkness with the brilliance of truth, yet this truth has been rejected.

The bitter irony of this should not be lost on the reader. John emphasized this irony, stating that though He created the world, the world did not recognize Him. Though He came to His own, His own did not receive Him (1:10-11). God has come to the world for acceptance and relationship. Those who accept the Light, who believe in the message Christ proclaimed about Himself, are given the "right to become the children of God" (1:12). To be born into the kingdom of God is not something achieved on human energy (1:13; compare Eph 2:8-9) but by the grace of the living God through Christ Jesus. This is to be balanced by the emphasis on the need to "receive" Christ (1:12). Though we bring nothing to God and contribute nothing to our salvation, the gift itself is dependent on our willingness to receive it from the one who offers it.

1:19-28
John's Role

The role of John the Baptist is explained with clarity in relation to Christ. John the Baptist was sent from God (1:6). John was not himself the Light (1:8). He came as a witness to Christ (1:7,15).

John the Baptist offered the words of the prophet Isaiah about the nature of his identity: "I am the voice of one calling in the desert, 'Make straight the way for the Lord' " (1:23; see Isa 40:3). Some had thought he might be Isaiah, the great prophet who had never died but had been taken to be with God (2 Kgs 2:11). Many believed that Elijah would return to the earth in order to announce the coming end of the world. John denied being Elijah. A word should be mentioned, however, regarding Jesus' reference to John as Elijah in the Synoptics (Matt 11:14; 17:10-13). What was at hand in Jesus' mind was how John was a fulfillment of the prophecy recorded in Malachi 4:5 (compare Luke 1:17).

What was the purpose of John's testimony? First, to fulfill prophecy (Isa 40:3). Second, to call people to repentance. Third, to draw people's attention toward the coming of the Messiah, Jesus Christ (1:31). What was the purpose of John's baptism? Clearly it was not Christian baptism, for that is the mark of one's acceptance of Christ as personal Lord and Savior. John's baptism was "a baptism of repentance for the forgiveness of sins" (Luke 3:3). It looked forward to the coming of the Messiah and served to prepare the people for the coming of the kingdom of God.

1:29-34
The Lamb of God

John the Baptist's confession upon seeing Christ, that here was "the Lamb of God, who takes away the sin of the world!" (1:29), is of great significance. The Jews used a lamb as a sacrifice for the Passover Feast, which celebrated Israel's deliverance from bondage in Egypt (Exod 13:1-10; compare John 13:1). Isaiah offered the idea of the Suffering Servant in terms of a sacrificial lamb (Isa 53). John was declaring that Jesus was the true sacrificial lamb for the passover; His death would now serve as the deliverance of God's people from their sins. As Paul wrote in his letter to the church at Corinth, "Christ, our Passover lamb, has been sacrificed" (1 Cor 5:7).

John the Baptist then gave testimony that he saw "the Spirit come down from heaven and rest" on Jesus (1:32). This confirmed to John that Jesus was the Messiah. For he then declared: "I have seen and I testify that this is the Son of God" (1:34).

1:35-42
Witnessing about Jesus

The calling of Andrew, Simon Peter's brother, was the direct result of John the Baptist's testimony concerning Jesus as the Lamb of God (1:36-37). The second person mentioned in this account is not named, but many surmise that it was the author of this Gospel, the apostle John. Andrew immediately sought his brother, Simon Peter, and proclaimed that the Messiah had been found (1:41). Upon encountering Simon, Jesus declared that he would " 'be called Cephas' (which, when translated, is Peter)" (1:42). Both "Cephas," which is Aramaic, and Peter, which is Greek, mean *rock*.

That Peter would be given this name is interesting in light of the fact that he was anything but "rocklike." Peter was impulsive and undisciplined in spirit, a rough-hewn man of raw emotion. Yet Christ was calling those whom He would develop, and Peter would indeed become the pillar of the church, the "rock" upon which the early church would depend (Matt 19:18; Acts 2).

1:43-51
The Son of Man

Jesus used the term "Son of Man" as His favored description for Himself. It has been suggested that the title "Son of God" is Jesus' divine name (Matt 8:29); "Son of David," His Jewish name (Matt 9:27); and "Son of Man," the name that ties Jesus to His earthly mission. The term itself is based on Daniel 7:13-14, where it served as a reference to God.

2:1-11
Providing Pure Wine

Jesus' first miracle was at a wedding at Cana of Galilee where He turned water into wine. A wedding feast during this period of history might last as long as a week, with poor hospitality treated as a serious offense; and this celebration had run out of wine. The symbolism of this event should not be lost on the reader, for the water used for purification was replaced by wine, that which would come to symbolize the blood of Christ. The blood of Christ did indeed supplant the Jewish ceremonial system in regard to the predicament of sin in light of a holy God.

That Jesus was aware of His "time" and the progress of His mission is evident throughout this Gospel (7:6,8,30; 8:20). The cross was ever before Jesus, and His movement toward that inevitable moment was to remain on God's timetable (12:23,27; 13:1; 16:32; 17:1). As is the pattern of this Gospel, miracles are referred to as "signs" (Greek *semeion*), intimating that they served as authentication for Jesus' nature and mission. In the Synoptics the most commonly used word for miracles is *dunameis,* which refers to mighty works that demonstrate the power of God.

2:12-25
God's Standard of Conduct

In the clearing of the temple, Jesus brought forth God's standards of what is right and what is wrong. Present for the Passover, a time of remembrance for Israel's deliverance from Egypt, Jesus encountered individuals who were profiteering from the religious festival. Jews who had traveled great distances needed to purchase animals for sacrifice, as well as exchange their money into local currency. They encountered entrepreneurial individuals who offered both services. While legalism was denounced by Jesus, holiness was maintained. The issue at hand was not business or profit making as such but the

A view of the church in traditional Cana which commemorates the miracle of the water being changed into wine (John 2:1-11).

mockery of the entire sacrificial system of the temple and the exploitation of devout men and women by greedy individuals who were capitalizing on religious sentiment.

This spectacle aroused the indignation of the Jews. Their concern was not the moral issue of whether the sellers and money exchangers should have been there in the first place but on what grounds Jesus took it upon Himself to expel them. The Jews called for a "sign," and Jesus responded, "Destroy this temple, and I will raise it again in three days" (2:19). Jesus was referring to the temple of His body, but his Jewish antagonists associated His comments with the temple building, providing the groundwork for some of the mockery and ridicule Jesus was subjected to while hanging on the cross (Matt 27:40; Mark 15:29).

3:1-21
God's Saving Love

There can be little doubt that this section in John's Gospel is the most renowned in all of Scripture, with verse 16 serving as the most familiar single verse in all of the Bible. There is good reason for this, for John 3:16 presents the clearest, simplest statement of the good news Christ came to bring to the world. What is that good news? First, that God loves you. Second, that God's love was so great that He sent His only Son to tell the world about God's love. Third, that anyone who will believe in God's Son will never die but will live forever with God. Belief, of course, means far more than mere intellectual assent. Rather, it means placing one's life and trust in complete surrender to the one in whom you believe.

The heart of Jesus' message to Nicodemus is that men and women, in order to come to God in faith, must be "born again" (3:3). This is not optional, according to Jesus, but a necessity. By this Jesus meant being "born of the Spirit" (3:8). The reference to "water and the Spirit" (3:5) has many possible interpretations, such as (1) water referring to purification; (2) synonymous with "born of the Spirit"; (3) baptism, either John's or Christ's. The latter of these three interpretations, that baptism is necessary for salvation, is the least desired understanding (Eph 2:8-9). To be considered as well is that the Greek manuscript does not have an article ("the") with the word "Spirit," therefore it would be grammatically incorrect to separate Spirit from water. What is to be maintained is that to be "born again" is a gift from God through the Holy Spirit as a result of the death, burial, and resurrection of Christ. To be born again is to become a member of God's family through faith in Jesus Christ, initiated by repentance and the desire to lead a new life to the honor and glory of Christ (1 Pet 1:23; 2 Cor 5:17). Jesus' purpose was never to condemn the world, for that is something we do to ourselves through our own willful choice to reject Christ, but rather Jesus' purpose was to save the world (3:17-19).

3:22-36
Jesus the Discipler

When students of the life of Christ list the priorities of His ministry, many items come to mind: the miracles, the crucifixion, and of course, the resurrection. But one of the most significant items on Jesus' agenda is found in this: "Jesus and his disciples went out into the Judean countryside, where he spent some time with them" (3:22). Jesus took twelve men and poured His life into theirs, discipling them in thought and deed in order that they might become the foundation of the church following His death, burial, and resurrection.

THE SEVEN SIGNS IN JOHN

SIGN	REFERENCE	CENTRAL TRUTH
1. Changing water to wine	2:1-11	Points to Jesus as the Source of all the blessings of God's future (see Isa 25:6-8; Jer 31:11-12; Amos 9:13-14)
2. Healing the official's son	4:43-54	Points to Jesus as the Giver of life
3. Healing the invalid at Bethesda	5:1-15	Points to Jesus as the Father's Coworker
4. Feeding the five thousand	6:1-15,25-69	Points to Jesus as the life-giving Bread from heaven
5. Walking on water	6:16-21	Points to Jesus as the divine I AM
6. Healing the man born blind	9:1-41	Points to Jesus as the Giver of spiritual sight
7. Raising Lazarus	11:1-44	Points to Jesus as the Resurrection and the Life

During this time an argument developed between some of John's disciples and a certain Jew over ceremonial cleansing. The appropriate means of achieving ceremonial purification was of great interest to many in the Jewish community. In coming to John over the matter, the question of Jesus' ministry in relation to John's ministry was surfaced. The loyalty of these disciples to their master, John, is evident as they allowed envy to enter their thinking regarding Jesus. John's reply affirmed his previous testimony about Jesus, as well as providing an important insight into John's character.

Knowing a teachable moment had presented itself, John informed his students that one "can receive only what is given him from heaven." The point of this affirmation is clear. Knowing God has given everything, one who loves God will not envy another person's gifts, abilities, or accomplishments. John understood his role in relation to Jesus to be that of the "best man" to the groom at a wedding. John instructed those that had supported and followed his ministry that Jesus must become greater, while he "must become less" (3:30).

John knew that he was "from the earth," while Jesus, as God's son, was "from heaven" (3:31). John taught his disciples that their relation to Jesus determines life itself, for rejection of Jesus brings about God's wrath. Therefore the one who accepts Jesus and the truth of His message avoids God's wrath, participates in the life of the Spirit, and has life eternal. That life is not as a gift in the future but life eternal as a present reality that begins at the moment Jesus is accepted in faith and engaged in relationship.

4:1-26
The Source of Life

Not wanting to be seen in competition with John's ministry, Jesus returned to Galilee. In that journey "he had to go through Samaria" (4:4). It should be noted that Samaria was not a geographic necessity for Jesus' trip but a necessity for His mission. The division between Jews and Samaritans was legendary, a division Jesus did not and would not recognize. Samaritans were rejected because of their mixed Gentile blood and their differing style of worship, which found its center on Mount Gerizim. On this mountain Samaritans had built a temple that rivaled the Jewish temple in Jerusalem.

Jesus' excursion into Samaria resulted in one of the most fascinating dialogues recorded in Scripture. Resting by a well, Jesus encountered a Samaritan woman who had been living a life of habitual immorality. Their conversation proceeded upon two levels, the spiritual and the temporal, with the woman constantly finding excuses for

Two bedouin women drawing water at a well in the Negev in the same way as would the woman Jesus met at a well in Sychar.

Jesus' probing of her inner world. Her first shock was that Jesus would even speak to her, an act unheard of for that day between a Jewish man and a Samaritan woman. Jesus continually responded not to her questions but to her needs, offering her the opportunity of receiving "living water" (4:10).

Here we see much regarding the intent of Jesus' ministry, to bring persons to a realization of the state of their life in order to lead them to repentance and a new life in Him. This new life is a life that honors and worships God in spirit and truth in daily life. The location of worship is not important, but the Object is! The English word "worship" is from the Anglo-Saxon *weorthscipe,* literally reading "worthship." Worship is attributing worth and honor to the living God.

4:27-38
The Christ's Mission

When the disciples rejoined Jesus, they did not dare ask Him about His conversation with the Samaritan woman but rather inquired about His physical well-being. Perhaps they thought hunger had deprived Him of the sense necessary to know better than to talk with such a woman. Jesus then continued the education of the disciples, instructing them that His "food" was to "do the will of him who sent me and to finish his work" (4:34).

Jesus was clearly on a mission, a mission that was God-informed and God-directed (5:30; 6:38; 8:26; 9:4; 10:37-38; 12:49-50; 14:31; 15:10; 17:4). What was that mission? To confront people—all people, as the Samaritan woman demonstrated—with the truth of Himself. Jesus told them that the "fields are ripe for harvest" (4:35) and that in entering that field for work, it makes no different whether one plants the seed or brings in the crop. This is an important truth, for there should never be competition among Christians regarding differing fields of service. All should share in the joy of seeing the kingdom of God extend.

4:39-42
Savior of the World

Jesus' encounter with the woman at the well, and her subsequent sharing of that conversation, resulted in many Samaritans believing in Jesus. After they met Jesus themselves, they believed not because of what the woman said but because they had come to believe themselves "that this man really is the Savior of the world" (4:42). This confession of the Samaritan believers, that Jesus was the "Savior of the world," is only found in the New Testament here and in 1 John 4:14. Only through Jesus is the world able to be saved, and that salvation is indeed for everyone in the world.

4:43-54
True Belief

After his time in Samaria, Jesus returned to Galilee. There he met a royal official whose child was near death. Jesus commented how the belief of the Galileans was tied to His production of miraculous signs and wonders. This provides an interesting contrast, for the Samaritans believed "because of his words" (4:41), while the Jews believed because of "miraculous signs and wonders" (4:48). As Jesus would later say to Thomas following His resurrection, "Blessed are those who have not seen and yet have believed" (20:29).

5:1-15
Seeking Good Health

After an unspecified period of time, Jesus traveled to Jerusalem for a "feast of the Jews" (5:1). The name of this feast is not mentioned, but it was probably one of the three pilgrimage feasts that Jewish males were expected to attend: Passover, Pentecost, or Tabernacles.

There Jesus passed by the Bethesda pool, where a number of invalids had placed themselves. The waters, when stirred, supposedly had miraculous powers of healing. A man who had been there for thirty-eight years was asked an interesting question by Jesus: "Do you want to get well?" (5:6). Many depended on their condition for financial support given by healthy individuals out of pity. Another possible reason for this question relates to the man's spirit; many who have experienced prolonged pain or misfortune have surrendered even the will to attempt to overcome their situation in life. When the invalid shared with Jesus his difficulty of getting into the pool for healing, Jesus proclaimed: "Get up! Pick up your mat and walk" (5:8). The man was instantly healed.

This healing took place on a Sabbath. The Jews' response was not joy over his healing but concern that he was violating the Sabbath by carrying his mat! The law of Moses did not forbid such a practice, only the Jewish interpretation of the law of Moses forbade it. Jesus found the healed man, and as with the Samaritan woman at the well, addressed the deeper condition of the man's relationship with God. Jesus' words are interesting: "Stop sinning or something worse may happen to you" (5:14). This injunction could be easily misinterpreted, either into a perspective that equates health with spiritual obedience or an idea that God bestows calamity upon the disobedient. For Jesus the consequences of sin are far more serious than any form of physical illness. He did not say that one can actually stop sinning but, in accord with the entire biblical witness, that believers should not purposefully live a life of sin.

5:16-30
The Son of God

John then informs his readers that because of this healing on the Sabbath, the Jews began to persecute Jesus. Legalism is a dreadful distortion of God's will for those whom He created to live in fellowship with Him. Not outer deeds but inward postures matter to God. When the inner world is ordered around God's dictates, then the outer world will exhibit utter holiness, a holiness defined by the life and ministry of Jesus. At this rebuke the Jews were outraged, not because Jesus was wrong (they didn't answer His reply regarding healing on the Sabbath) but because "he was even calling God his own Father, making himself equal with God" (5:18). The Jews did not object to the idea of God as Father but that Jesus somehow was in a special relationship to God as His Father, thus intimating that Jesus was equal with God.

Jesus then gave a clearly defined response about the relationship between the Father (God) and the Son (Himself). First, the Son can do nothing without the Father (5:19,30). Second, the Father loves the Son and reveals everything to Him (5:20). Third, the power to bestow life itself is shared by the Father and the Son (5:21). Fourth, God has given all judgment over to the Son (5:22). Fifth, the Father and the Son share equal honor (5:23). Sixth, belief in the words of the Son result in

MIRACLES OF JESUS

MIRACLE	BIBLE PASSAGES			
Water Turned to Wine				John 2:1
Many Healings	Matt 4:23	Mark 1:32		
Healing of a Leper	Matt 8:1	Mark 1:40	Luke 5:12	
Healing of a Roman Centurion's Servant	Matt 8:5		Luke 7:1	
Healing of Peter's Mother-in-law	Matt 8:14	Mark 1:29	Luke 4:38	
Calming of the Storm at Sea	Matt 8:23	Mark 4:35	Luke 8:22	
Healing of the Wild Men of Gadara	Matt 8:28	Mark 5:1	Luke 8:26	
Healing of the Lame Man	Matt 9:1	Mark 2:1	Luke 5:18	
Healing of a Woman with a Hemorrhage	Matt 9:20	Mark 5:25	Luke 8:43	
Raising of Jairus's Daughter	Matt 9:23	Mark 5:22	Luke 8:41	
Healing of Two Blind Men	Matt 9:27			
Healing of a Demon-possessed Man	Matt 9:32			
Healing of Man with a Withered Hand	Matt 12:10	Mark 3:1	Luke 6:6	
Feeding of 5,000 People	Matt 14:15	Mark 6:35	Luke 9:12	John 6:1
Walking on the Sea	Matt 14:22	Mark 6:47		John 6:16
Healing of the Syrophoenician's Daughter	Matt 15:21	Mark 7:24		
Feeding of 4,000 People	Matt 15:32	Mark 8:1		
Healing of an Epileptic Boy	Matt 17:14	Mark 9:14	Luke 9:37	
Healing of Two Blind Men at Jericho	Matt 20:30			
Healing of a Man with an Unclean Spirit		Mark 1:23	Luke 4:33	
Healing of a Deaf, Speechless Man		Mark 7:31		
Healing of a Blind Man at Bethesda		Mark 8:22		
Healing of Blind Bartimaeus		Mark 10:46	Luke 18:35	
A Miraculous Catch of Fish			Luke 5:4	John 21:1
Raising of a Widow's Son			Luke 7:11	
Healing of a Stooped Woman			Luke 13:11	
Healing of a Man with the Dropsy			Luke 14:1	
Healing of Ten Lepers			Luke 17:11	
Healing of Malchus's Ear			Luke 22:50	
Healing of a Royal Official's Son				John 4:46
Healing of a Lame Man at Bethesda				John 5:1
Healing of a Blind Man				John 9:1
Raising of Lazarus				John 11:38

eternal life (5:24). Finally, the very consummation of the age will be by and through the Son (5:25-30).

The Jews' objection was in light of their staunch monotheism (the belief in one God). Christians are monotheists as well yet maintain that the nature of the One True God is that He is Triune—three Persons, one God. To the Jewish mind Jesus' claim to be God was blasphemous in view of the fact that it intimated two Gods. Of course, nothing of the sort was in mind in Jesus' self-declaration as the Son of God. Rather, Jesus was proclaiming that He was God in human form, the second Person of the Trinity.

5:31-47
Testimony to Jesus

Testimony regarding Jesus includes John the Baptist (5:33), the works of Jesus (5:36), God Himself (5:37), the Scriptures (5:39), and Moses (5:46). In this Jesus clearly distinguished the worth of human testimony from God's testimony concerning that which is of worth (5:34) and the worth of human praise compared to the praise that flows from God (5:41,44).

6:1-15
No Earthly King

The feeding of the five thousand is the one miracle, apart from the resurrection, that occurs in all four of the Gospels. The number was far greater than five thousand, for this figure refers only to men, since woman and children were not counted (Matt 14:21). This miracle led the people to try to make Jesus king by force. God's design was not that Jesus manifest Himself as an earthly king but as the Suffering Servant who would give His life as a ransom for many (Mark 10:45).

6:16-24
Jesus' Divine Acts

This "sign" pointed to the divine nature of Jesus, demonstrated by His power and authority over the natural, created world. The crowds seemed more interested in Jesus' "signs" than in Jesus' truth.

6:25-59
Bread of Life

After the feeding of the many thousands, it is not surprising that these same numbers sought Jesus out again. When they found Him, Jesus read their hearts and confronted them with their motive: "You are looking for me, not because you saw miraculous signs, but because you ate the loaves and had your fill" (6:26). Jesus then encouraged them not to devote themselves to such pursuits but rather to "food that endures to eternal life" (6:27).

This eternal food is the teaching of Jesus. When asked about what works were necessary to appease God, Jesus replied in a decidedly different fashion than they anticipated. Rather than outlining a list of do's and don'ts, Jesus replied, "The work of God is this: to believe in the one he has sent" (6:29). Salvation is not something that is attained through human effort, but instead it is a freely

"I AM" SAYINGS IN THE GOSPEL OF JOHN

SAYING	REFERENCE IN JOHN
I am the Bread of Life.	6:35
I am the Light of the World.	8:12
I am the Gate for the Sheep.	10:7
I am the Good Shepherd.	10:11,14
I am the Resurrection and the Life.	11:25
I am the Way, the Truth, and the Life.	14:6
I am the True Vine.	15:1,5
I am a King.	18:37

given gift. The only "work" necessary is to receive the gift of God for eternal life through His Son, Jesus Christ.

The crowd then asked for a sign, as Moses gave with the manna, that Jesus was indeed the One sent from God (6:30-31). This revealed that their primary interest was food, attempting to goad Jesus into giving them bread in exchange for their faith.

This interchange resulted in the first of the seven "I am" statements found within the Gospel of John. Jesus replied, "I am the bread of life" (6:35). The Greek language at this point is strongly emphatic, reminiscent of God's own "I AM" recorded in Exodus 3:14. Jesus stated that all who come to Him in saving faith will never be driven away and that it is God's will that all should so come (6:37,40). Such statements did not please the Jews. Jesus was claiming to have come from heaven, and this was unacceptable for them to bestow upon one "whose father and mother we know" (6:42).

In reply Jesus maintained the following: first, that no one can come to the Father through Christ except as the Father wills (6:44). Second, to be in relationship with God is to be in a relationship with Jesus (6:45). Third, only the Son, Jesus, has seen the Father (6:46); Fourth, the bread of life (Jesus) is that which comes from heaven, and only by eating of that bread, given for the world, can life eternal be gained (6:48-51). The Jews understood this to mean that Jesus was going to give of His actual flesh for them to eat (6:52). Jesus added to their confusion by stating that "unless you eat the flesh of the Son of Man and drink his blood, you have no life in you" (6:53).

This verse is subject to many misinterpretations, such as thinking that it refers to the Lord's Supper, or Eucharist. Nowhere, however, is it taught in Scripture that the taking of the Lord's Supper is the single requirement for salvation. The sole requirement for salvation is not partaking of the elements of the Lord's Supper but faith in Christ (6:35,40,47,51). So what is the flesh and blood of which Christ spoke? Clearly it is the flesh and blood He offered to the world at the moment of His death, an offering made to the world for acceptance, resulting in eternal life for those who accept His death on their behalf as an atonement for their sin.

6:60-71
The Holy One of God

Jesus knew from the beginning which disciple would eventually betray Him. At this point many who had followed Jesus ceased to do so. When Jesus asked the Twelve if they too wished to depart, Peter responded for them all: "Lord, to whom shall we go? We believe and know that you are the Holy One of God" (6:69).

7:1-13
God's Time

Some might wonder why Jesus would purposefully stay away from Judea because the Jews there were waiting to take His life, especially in light of the fact that Jesus willingly went to His death at the time of the crucifixion. Simply put, it was not time (7:6-8). The time for surrendering of His life would come, but not now; there was more God desired to be accomplished through His life. All would transpire at the moment God intended.

7:14-24
Authoritative Teacher

At the appropriate time, halfway through the Feast of the Tabernacles, Jesus revealed Himself and began to teach. The crowds were surprised that Jesus had not studied under any of the noted Jewish scholars. Jesus responded to their amazement. His teaching was not his "own" but "comes from him who sent me" (7:16). This interchange should not be taken as a disparagement of education or learning. Jesus was uniquely empowered and gifted by God for His mission, and His words were God's words.

7:25-44
The Spirit Promised

Many falsely understood that no one would know the origin or birthplace of the Messiah, and since they knew of Jesus' origins, He could not be the Messiah (7:27). This is to be understood in light of the Jewish tradition, though not a biblical idea, that the Messiah would be a man of mystery. As a result they tried to seize Jesus, but apparently they were unable to lay even a single hand upon Him because "his time had not yet come" (7:30). On the last day of the feast, Jesus promised to all who would believe in Him "streams of living water," which the author of the Gospel interpreted for us as the Spirit given later at Pentecost (7:38b-39).

7:45-52
A Prophet from Galilee?

The temple guards sent to arrest him exclaimed, "No one ever spoke the way this man does" (7:46). The Pharisees simply dismissed them as deceived, arguing that since none of the Pharisees had expressed belief in Jesus, then He was not to be accepted. The Pharisees elevated their own sense of learning and understanding. In so doing, they exaggerated the ignorance of the average person. This produced a spiritual pride that led them to believe that true understanding rested solely with their own musings. Then Nicodemus, who had spoken with Jesus earlier (3:1-21), reminded them all that no one was to be judged without a hearing. The response was the adamant stance that no prophet could come from Galilee, which was patently false, since Jonah the prophet was from Galilee.

7:53–8:11
A Sinless Judge

This story is certainly in line with Jesus' character and teaching, but it does not appear in the earliest and most reliable manuscripts. This does not deny the story's authenticity, only that it may have been added at a later date. (See NIV note.)

The teachers of the law and the Pharisees had brought a woman who had been caught in adultery to the feet of Jesus in order that He might pronounce the proper judgment upon her. The purpose was to trap Jesus, for if He neglected to suggest stoning, as the law required, He could be charged with being a lawbreaker. (The actual law prescribed stoning only if she was a betrothed virgin; the man was to be stoned as well, compare Lev 20:10; Deut 22:22-24.) If however, Jesus did advocate stoning, then He would bring the wrath of the Roman government to bear upon Himself. How did Jesus handle the dilemma? "If any of you is without sin, let him be the first to throw a stone at her" (8:7). Brilliantly, He did not break the law; yet He ensured the woman would not be stoned. When all had left, Jesus addressed the woman's two greatest needs, self-esteem and a new life. For her self-esteem, He assured her that He, who was without sin, did not condemn her. For her deepest need, that of a new life, Jesus said, "Go now and leave your life of sin" (8:11).

8:12-30
Light of the World

The second of Jesus' seven "I am" statements occurs here: "I am the light of the world" (8:12). The relationship between Jesus and His Father is of such a nature that Jesus could say that if "you knew me, you would know my father also" (8:19).

Teaching about His identity and nature, Jesus revealed that He is from above and not of this world (8:23). Further, "if you do not believe that I am the one I claim to be, you will indeed die in your sins" (8:24). Such a statement could only elicit a shocked, "Who are you?" (8:25). Jesus answered that He was who He had always claimed to be, the One sent from the Father, the Son of man.

Many have wondered how a loving God can condemn persons to hell. Our response should be that He does nothing of the sort. Individual persons condemn them-

The Pool of Siloam in the old city of Jerusalem where Jesus told the blind man to go and wash (see John 9:1-7).

selves by choosing to reject Jesus Christ and the truth He came to share with the world.

8:31-41
Truth That Sets Free

Jesus made clear that holding to His teachings is essential in order to claim to be one of His disciples (8:31). Further, His teachings should be accepted as absolute truth. This truth, and no other, has the power to set a person free (8:32). Many philosophies and ideologies make the claim for truth, but all truth is God's truth, and therefore all claims for truth must be judged in light of God's revealed truth and knowledge. To adhere to a false view of reality is to be held captive to ignorance. To live a life apart from God's rule is to be held captive to sin. The truth of Jesus sets individuals free from all such bondage (8:34). The Jews refused to listen to the truth of Jesus, instead insisting on clinging to their own understandings. Perhaps the most telling verse is when Jesus stated that they had "no room" for His word (8:37).

8:42-47
Who Is Your Father?

If God was truly their Father, then they would love Him. Jesus' made clear that His origin was divine, His mission God planned, and His purpose God willed.

People cannot hear what God has to say if they do not belong to God (8:47). If people choose to listen to the evil one in terms of what is considered truth (8:43-44), then they close out the voice of God. The basic disposition of Satan is that of a liar, a perverter of truth, one who deceives all who will allow him to direct their lives and thoughts.

8:48-59
The Eternal I Am

Desperate to discredit Jesus, the Jews accused Him of being a Samaritan as well as demon possessed (8:48). Jesus denied the charge and immediately resumed His charge that they were living apart from God (8:49). He added that if anyone kept His word, "he will never see death" (8:51). At this the Jews were outraged. Jesus was placing Himself above even Abraham. With one voice they asked in indignation, "Who do you think you are?" (8:53). Jesus responded that God glorified Him, that He knew God, and that He kept God's word. Further, Abraham "rejoiced at the thought of seeing my day; he saw it and was glad" (8:56). This brought utter incredulity to the crowd. They challenged Him, for here Jesus—far from even the fifty-year-old mark—was claiming to have seen Abraham.

Jesus gave one of the most important answers to any question posed to Him in the entire Gospel of John. " 'I tell you the truth,' Jesus answered, 'before Abraham was born, I am!' " (8:58). What was Jesus saying? That He was God Himself! The only other time the phrase "I am" was used to describe someone was in Exodus 3:14, where God used that very phrase as His name. Here Jesus claimed that name for Himself. No identity statement could be clearer. Jesus claimed to be God Himself in human form. The Jews did not respond with words but picked up stones to kill Him for blasphemy (see Lev 24:16). Jesus hid Himself and slipped away from the temple grounds (8:59).

9:1-12
Sin and Sickness

Jesus performed more miracles related to giving sight to the blind than any other miracle. Such an activity was forecast in prophecy as a messianic act (Isa 29:18; 35:5; 42:7). Jesus came to clear the sight of human beings who had become blinded to the things of God.

The disciples of Jesus, espousing a common perspective of the day, desired to know who sinned in regard to this man's affliction. They understood that such things occurred either as a result of an individual's personal sin or because of sin in the life of one's parents. The rabbis taught that no one died unless there had been sin, and no one suffered unless there had been sin. Even a child could sin in the womb, they suggested, or even in the preexistent state prior to conception. Refuting this entire system of thought, Jesus proclaimed that neither "this man nor his parents sinned" (9:3). Instead, this man was there at that moment for God to work in His life in order to glorify Jesus.

Jesus suggested that there would come a time when the work of the kingdom of God will not be able to continue. That time is not the end of His life, as the "we" in verse 4 suggests, but when the consummation of the age takes place. Until that day God's people must do all they can to combat evil and do good in the name of Christ.

9:13-34
Power of Personal Testimony

The man who had been healed testified that his own perspective was that Jesus was a Prophet (9:17b). This was not the answer the Pharisees wanted to hear. Questioning the formerly blind man again, he said "One thing I do know. I was blind but now I see!" (9:25). This simple testimony has been the incontrovertible evidence for the Christian faith for centuries. His final words carried the greatest sting: "If this man were not from God, he could do nothing" (9:33). The Pharisees became enraged, accused the man of being a sinner, and excommunicated him from the synagogue.

9:35-41
Sight Means Guilt

The healing of this blind man took place on two levels: at the physical level his sight was restored. On the spiritual level he had come to faith in Christ. This man serves as a paradigm for Jesus' entire ministry. The Pharisees who witnessed this event responded only in indignation that Jesus would intimate that they were blind (9:40). Masterfully, Jesus responded that if they were truly blind, they would be guiltless, but since they claimed sight, their guilt remained (9:41).

10:1-21
The Good Shepherd

One of the great images of Jesus is as the "good Shepherd" (10:11). First, He is the gate to the sheep pen, meaning that no one can enter the fold through any oth-

Jesus is described as the "Good Shepherd" (John 10:14-16). Shown above is a shepherd in Israel tending his flock of sheep.

er means than Jesus Himself (10:1,7-9). Only through Jesus Christ can anyone be made right with God leading to eternal life. Second, Jesus leads His sheep. No other voice is the true voice of leadership (10:3b-5). Third, as the good Shepherd, Jesus protects His flock—even to the point of death (10:11). Unlike someone who watches sheep for employment, Jesus is a Shepherd motivated by love for His sheep (10:12-13).

As the good Shepherd, Jesus mentioned that there are other sheep that will listen to His voice and will one day be brought into the fold. More than likely what is in view are the Gentiles who would come to believe in Christ. The idea is not many shepherds with many flocks but one Shepherd joined together as one flock (10:16; compare Eph 2:16). Jesus was not forced into being the good Shepherd; He willingly took the role upon Himself, and for this He is loved by God (10:17-18).

10:22-42
One with the Father

The Feast of Dedication was the celebration of the dedication and subsequent reopening of the temple by Judas Maccabeus in December of 165 B.C., after it had been desecrated by the Syrian ruler Antiochus Epiphanes in 168 B.C. (compare Dan 11:31). This event is commonly referred to as "Hanukkah" or "The Feast of Lights."

Jesus stated that His sheep are given eternal life and that no one can "snatch them out of my hand" (10:29). When a person comes to Christ as Savior and Lord, nothing can remove that person from the state of salvation against their will. If one is truly saved, then that person can rest assured that they are held in the hand of God, protected from any assault to their state of redemption.

Jesus also declared that "I and the Father are one" (10:30). Jesus and God are not, according the Christian doctrine of the Trinity, identical persons but separate persons who are of identical nature.

At this the Jews picked up stones to kill Him, for it was blasphemy for a man to claim to be God (10:33). Jesus responded to their anger by pointing back to the Old Testament where, in accord with the worldview of the ancient Near East, rulers and judges, as emissaries of the heavenly King, could be granted the honorary title "god" (Ps 82). If they could be culturally comfortable with that title for those to whom the Word of God came, why did they rebel against the idea that the Messiah would be God's Son (10:34-37)? And if this does not make sense, Jesus argued, then simply look at my life and the miracles performed (10:37-39). This did not persuade the Jews, and again they tried to seize Jesus for execution.

11:1-16
Dying with Jesus

Lazarus was the brother of the sisters Mary and Martha. Mary had poured perfume on the feet of Jesus and wiped them dry with her hair (12:3). Jesus loved all three of them (11:5). His two-day delay was probably to ensure that the miracle He was about to bestow would be clearly understood to be a resurrection from the dead, not a resuscitation from a severe illness. His disciples urged Him not to go, for there were individuals there who desired to seize and kill Him. Thomas, often known as the doubter, here revealed the depth of his personal commitment to Jesus when he said to his fellow disciples: "Let us also go, that we may die with him" (11:16).

11:17-37
The Emotions of Jesus

One of the most moving scenes in the life of Jesus is the death of Lazarus. Here we see not only the power of Jesus to raise the dead, but the emotions of Jesus moved by the grief of those around Him. Martha's faith is evident as she approached Jesus, four days after the death of

Lazarus, and professed belief that He could save her dead brother. When Mary came as well and Jesus saw her grief and the grief of those with her, he was "deeply moved in spirit and troubled" (11:33). Scripture then tells us that Jesus wept (11:35).

11:38-44
The Resurrection and Life

What could testify more to the divine nature of Jesus than to exhibit the power needed to raise someone from the dead? Wishing to teach an important truth about how God hears and answers the prayer of belief, Jesus prayed aloud. Note that the raising of Lazarus serves as something of a foreshadowing of the power to resurrect all believers one day to fellowship and eternal life in Christ. Unlike Lazarus, who was raised only to die again, Christians will be raised to eternal life.

11:45-57
One Man for the World

The resurrection of Lazarus caused many to place their faith in Jesus. It also led to a meeting of the Sanhedrin. The Sanhedrin was the high court of the Jews. In the New Testament period, it was composed of three groups: the chief priests, the elders, and the teachers of the law. Its membership reached seventy-one, including the high priest, who served as the presiding officer. Under Roman jurisdiction the Sanhedrin was given great power, but it could not impose capital punishment (18:31).

Their concern was self-preservation. If Jesus continued as He had, then people would continue to place their faith in Him as the Messiah. If the Romans then heard that a Messiah was being heralded by the Jews, they would come and destroy the threat, including the Sanhedrin (11:48). Therefore much of the opposition to Jesus was

New Testament Signs and Miracles

From a biblical perspective, a miracle is an extraordinary work of God that may transcend the ordinary powers of nature. Throughout Scripture miracles are most prevalent at crisis points in salvation history. They authenticate God's presence in historical acts. The basic NT terminology used to describe these events includes "signs" (John 2:11; 10:41), "wonders" (Matt 24:24; Mark 13:22), "power" (Matt 7:22; Luke 10:13), and "work" (Luke 24:19; John 5:20).

Jesus underscored the relationship between His miraculous ministry and the arrival of the kingdom of God (Matt 12:28). His supernatural activity signified the coming of a new age in God's program (Luke 4:18-21). Despite the revelatory nature of Christ's miracles, their testimony was not always recognized; they had to be interpreted by faith.

The miracle accounts in the Gospels reveal different theological themes. Mark placed more emphasis on Christ's deeds than the other Gospel writers. Consequently, of the four Gospels, Mark contains the highest proportion of miracles. In Mark the focus of miracles involves tension and confrontation as Christ interacted with His opponents and His own disciples. While Matthew stressed healing miracles, Mark centered on exorcisms; Christ is the one who "binds" Satan (3:27).

However, despite the power evident in Christ's activity, miracles can only be comprehended by faith; they do not produce faith. The disciples misunderstood the miraculous elements of Christ's ministry (4:40; 6:52). They needed Jesus' teaching and His person to comprehend these events properly (4:40; 5:34).

While Mark stressed Jesus' deeds, Matthew highlighted Christ's teaching. Thus miracles are organized around instructive sections for theological purposes. In Matthew miracles reveal Jesus' sovereign power and His ability to forgive sins (chaps. 8–9). They also show His authority over the law and over Satan (chap. 12).

Furthermore, Matthew used miracles to show transition in Christ's ministry. The disciples were involved in Christ's activity (chaps. 14–15). As they learned from His actions, they became a means by which Jesus' ministry was extended.

Miracles do not play as great a role in Luke as they do in Mark. Primarily they express Jesus' authority over natural forces and the demonic realm. In Luke miracles have more of a validating force than they do in the other Gospels. They authenticate faith in Jesus (7:16; 9:43). As people witnessed the power of God operative in Jesus, they both "saw" (10:23-24; 19:37) and "feared" (5:26; 8:35) the divine truth in Him.

The Gospel of John records only seven miracles or "signs" from Christ's ministry. (See chart "Seven Signs in John.") As signs these miracles serve as symbols of the true significance of Jesus. However, while many marveled at Christ's supernatural exploits, only true believers saw the spiritual implications of the signs. The signs confronted Jesus' audience with the necessity of decision. While some rejected the actual meaning of the signs (2:23-25; 4:45), others grew in understanding because of these events (2:11; 11:42). □

sociopolitical in nature.

The remark by Caiaphas about their ignorance was one of rudeness. He understood the political dimension more fully than the others, who were actually thinking in terms of guilt or innocence. For Caiaphas it did not matter whether Jesus was guilty or innocent of wrongdoing. What was important was that the death of one man was worth the viability of the Jewish nation under Roman rule (11:50). Historically, Caiaphas was in error; for despite the death of Jesus, the Jewish nation perished in A.D. 70.

The prophecy of Caiaphas was truer than he could have imagined. He prophesied the death of Jesus for the Jewish nation in order to alleviate political tensions, not knowing that Jesus' death would be for the spiritual salvation of the Jewish nation and for the world.

12:1-11
Devotion or Death

This portion of John's Gospel contains a host of important elements. First, there is the devotion of Mary. The perfume used was expensive, a luxury item for herself, selflessly given in devotion to Jesus. That she poured it on the feet of Jesus was an act of humility, for attending to the feet of another person was the work of a servant. Wiping the oil with her hair was also unusual, for respectable women did not unbraid their hair in public. Mary exhibited unrestrained love and devotion to Jesus that went against personal cost and concern for perception.

Second, is the deceit and corruption of Judas. This is the sole passage that reveals the wicked character of Judas prior to his betrayal of Jesus. While the author of this Gospel relates Judas's dishonesty in hindsight, at the time Judas must have been highly esteemed, for he was trusted with caring for the money bag (12:6). All too often individuals have been able to deceive people regarding their relationship with God, but never is God Himself deceived, for He sees into the very heart of every person.

Third, is the judgment of Jesus on both Mary and the poor. Jesus affirmed Mary's act of devotion and linked it to His own burial. Mary did not intend for this to be the significance of her act, but it was perceived by Jesus in this manner, knowing of the growing shadow of the cross. In discussing the use of the expensive perfume on Himself rather than selling it to assist the poor, Jesus said, "You will always have the poor among you" (12:8). Unfortunately, many throughout the centuries of Christian history have misinterpreted this statement by Jesus as an excuse to neglect the poor. This was far from the intent of Jesus, who exhibited care and concern for the poor throughout His ministry. The point Jesus was making was that Mary's act of devotion at that particular time and place was worthy of the cost.

12:12-19
Praising the King

The triumphal entry into Jerusalem coincided with the Passover Feast. The palm branches were symbolic and used in celebration of victory. The response of the crowds to Jesus was spectacular. The shout of "Hosanna!" is a Hebrew term meaning *save* which had become an expression of praise.

The Gospel of John emphasizes the royalty of Jesus. Here is the only Gospel that records that the people also shouted, "Blessed is the King of Israel!" (12:13). The crowd's exultation, as well as Jesus' riding a colt, was not seen by the disciples until after His death, burial, and resurrection as the fulfillment of prophecy (12:16). This moment, perhaps more than any other, was the high mark of Jesus' popularity and influence. In only a matter of days, however, the "Hosanna!" would turn to "Crucify him!" (19:15).

12:20-36
The Hour Is Come

The request of some Greeks to interview Jesus occasioned a lengthy response from Jesus regarding the road that lay before Him. Throughout the Gospel, Jesus had avoided situations that would hasten His death. But now the "hour" had come for "the Son of Man to be glorified" (12:23). Jesus' death and subsequent resurrection is what is in mind by the term "glorified." Jesus presented Himself as a role model for our perspective on life. Life should not be loved from a temporal perspective but hated as that which represents our sinful separation from God our Creator (12:25). This is not, as the life of Jesus demonstrated, a rabid asceticism but an attitude that puts more importance on the world to come.

Jesus understood that His death would bring life to many (12:24). Nonetheless, Jesus' heart was "troubled," which is all John wrote in relation to the Gethsemane passages of Jesus' final hours recorded in the Synoptics (12:27). Jesus' troubled heart surely came more from the idea of bearing the weight of the sin of the world as a sinless Being than the mere physical and emotional agony that awaited Him. While Jesus contemplated praying to God for deliverance from that which awaited Him, He remained on the course God had willed for His life.

Not only would Jesus' death offer liberation to men and women from the bounds of sin, but it would bring judgment upon the world and drive the prince of the world from its midst (12:31). The cross achieved salvation for those who would believe, brought judgment upon the world for the refusal to believe, and defeated Satan's rebellion once and for all. The lifting up of Jesus on the cross would be the beacon that would draw all persons—meaning without regard to sex, race, social status, or nationality—to Himself for deliverance from sin (12:32).

12:37-50
God or the World

How could the Jews have witnessed so many miraculous deeds and remain in unbelief? The answer is found in prophecy. Jews both would not and could not believe. They would not believe when they should have according to what they had witnessed. They could not believe, not because they had freedom of choice removed from them, but because they had purposely rejected God and chosen evil. Thus God turned them over decisively to their choice (12:40). Those who had chosen to believe were afraid to make their decision public for fear of excommunication (12:42). Even these believers were indicted for caring more for the approval of others than for the approval of God (12:43).

What is Jesus' relation to those who reject Him? John made clear that it is not judgment (12:47). It is not that judgment for unbelief will not take place (12:48), only that the primary mission and role of Jesus was not judge but Savior (12:47b). Again, the close relationship between God and Jesus is clearly exhibited in regard to thought and deed (12:44-45,49-50).

A word should be given regarding the difference between "last day" and "last days." The latter refers to the current period of time, begun when Christ entered the world (Acts 2:17; Heb 1:2; 1 Pet 1:20; Jude 18). The "last day" (singular), however, refers to the consummation of time and history when the great resurrection and judgment will occur of all persons (1 John 2:18).

Foot washing was a gracious and humble act for a host to provide (see John 13:1-17). The Attic pottery above (A.D. 400s) shows Odysseus having his feet washed by his aged nurse.

13:1-17
The Humble Servant

The love of Jesus for His disciples, and those who would come to be His disciples, is shown in the washing of the disciples' feet. The servant motif, so prevalent in the Gospel of Mark (Mark 10:45), is here revealed as well in the Gospel of John. Servanthood is a direct extension and representation of love (13:1). What enabled Jesus to perform this act of utter humility was a keen understanding of who He was, where He had come from, and where He was going (13:3). This is a key to humility in all persons—a healthy and balanced understanding of who they are.

If Jesus, Lord and Teacher, washes our feet, how much more should we wash one another's feet (13:14). What is at hand is not the institution of an ordinance of foot-washing, as this passage has sometimes been interpreted, but the life-style of humble servanthood.

13:18-30
Satan and the Betrayer

At the moment that Jesus identified Judas as His betrayer, Scripture tells us that "Satan entered into him"; and Jesus said, "What you are about to do, do quickly" (13:27). This is the only use of the name "Satan" in the Gospel of John, and it is unclear whether here is actual possession or simply the motivation from Satan to evil. The fellow disciples, however, did not realize what Jesus was referring to, thinking that it had something to do with Judas's responsibilities as keeper of the money bag (13:28). Jesus had to be betrayed, but Judas did not have to be that betrayer. It has often been commented that the difference between Judas and Peter, both of whom betrayed Christ, is that Peter sought forgiveness, but Judas did not.

13:31-38
The Mark of Discipleship

After Judas's departure, Jesus made clear that His time with the disciples was short (13:33). The heart of this passage is found in verses 34-35: " 'A new command I give you: Love one another. As I have loved you, so you must love one another. By this all men will know that you are my disciples, if you love one another.' " Here Jesus was saying that love among Christians must be in the vanguard of all that we are about. Further, if we fail in this endeavor, then the world will be given the right to deny that we are disciples of Christ. Our love for one another will be the distinguishing mark of authenticity that we truly follow Christ.

14:1-4
Remedy for Anxiety

Such words from Jesus regarding His upcoming departure, not to mention the forecast of Peter's betrayal, cast a net of depression upon the meal. Now come words of comfort from Jesus: "Do not let your hearts be troubled. Trust in God; trust also in me" (14:1). Trust in God is the one true remedy for anxiety. Jesus completed the remedy for their concern by painting a beautiful portrait of the life that awaits them upon their reunion (14:2-4).

14:5-14
The Way, Truth, Life

Jesus responded that a life given in belief and faith in Him will pave the way to eternal fellowship with Him (14:6). Jesus' claim to be the way, the truth, and the life is of great importance. Jesus is not one among many ways to God but the only way to God. The early church was even called "The Way" because of its insistence upon this point (Acts 9:2; 19:9,23). That Jesus embodies and proclaims the truth is a theme throughout the Gospel of John. Jesus also offers life itself, life through God the Father, the Creator and Giver of all life.

The last verse in this section has been fuel for much debate regarding proper interpretation and application. Was Jesus saying that we have unlimited power over God in determining what He will or will not do for us if we simply pray in Jesus' name? Clearly not, for this would be out of accord with the rest of the scriptural witness. God is sovereign over all and subject to none. We are to pray in accordance with the will of God as exhibited in the life and teaching of Jesus. When we pray in that manner, surely it will be answered. To pray in Jesus' name is to pray in accord with Jesus' will and mission. Such a prayer request is far different from an idea of prayer as some type of shopping list handed to God that He is then bound to perform. Yet the enormous spiritual power that courses through the spiritual veins of the believer should not be underestimated in light of our involvement with the growing kingdom of God. The Holy Spirit empowers believers to do and to be all that Christ would have us to do and to be.

14:15-31
The Counselor

John's Gospel pays much attention to the Holy Spirit. This is the first of several passages that teach about the nature and role of the Holy Spirit in the life of the church and the individual believer (15:26; 16:7-15).

Here the Holy Spirit is referred to as the "Counselor" who will be with the disciples forever (14:16). Note that Jesus called the Holy Spirit "another" Counselor, suggesting that the work of the Holy Spirit would take the place of His role in their lives. The word "Counselor" is a legal term that goes beyond legal assistance to that of any aid given in time of need (1 John 2:1). The Greek word is *Paraclete,* which suggests adviser, encourager, exhorter, comforter, and intercessor. The idea is that the Spirit will always stand alongside the people of God. The Holy Spirit is also referred to as the "Spirit of truth" (14:17). This means that truth is that which characterizes the nature and mission of the Spirit. The Spirit testifies to the truth of God in Christ and brings people toward that truth through conviction leading to repentance and faith. The Spirit will continue to bring the presence of Christ into the lives of the disciples (14:16-18,20).

To love Jesus is to obey Jesus (14:15,23). If one does not obey Jesus, it is an act of lovelessness (14:24). Obedience and love cannot be separated for the believer. The Holy Spirit will also serve as a reminder to the disciples of all that Jesus has taught (14:25), sent forth by both God and the Son (14:26). The role of the Holy Spirit as the One who "reminds" the disciples of what Jesus said and taught should not be overlooked in regard to its importance in relation to the writing of the New Testament and for the ongoing life of the church. Jesus' effort is one of comfort as He prepares to leave His disciples for the agony of the cross. Here Satan would be allowed to stir people's hearts toward great evil, but never is that to be understood as Satan having power over Jesus (14:30). Jesus willingly submitted to the cross in order to fulfill God's will (14:31).

15:1-17
The True Vine

Here Jesus put forth another declarative "I am" statement, this time asserting that He is the "true vine" and that God is the gardener (15:1). In the Old Testament the "vine" is frequently used as a symbol of Israel (Ps 80:8-16; Isa 5:1-7; Jer 2:21). This symbol was often used when Israel was lacking in some way. Jesus, however, is the true Vine.

Two scenarios are presented that should be seen as representative for the Christian life: first, the one who is on the vine and producing fruit (Matt 3:8; 7:16-20) and second, the one who is on the vine who is not producing fruit. The productive vine is pruned for greater production, while the nonproductive vine is cut off for destruction. The key to producing fruit is one's relationship to the vine, to "remain in the vine" (15:4-5,7). Apart from Christ nothing can be accomplished (15:5). The verse "Ask whatever you wish, and it will be given you," as with 14:13, needs to be seen in the context of one who is firmly part of the vine (15:16). When one is in such a close and dynamic relationship with Christ, requests coincide with His will. In other words, asking whatever you wish and having it granted is dependent upon the first clause of the verse: "*If* you remain in me and my words remain in you" (15:7).

15:18–16:4
Planted in Christ

What is the result of a life that remains firmly planted in Christ? Here the suggestion is that you will be hated by the world (15:19). Christ was hated and rejected because of the conviction that pierced the heart of every person He encountered. Because of the life and teaching of Christ, individual persons know the truth and therefore have no excuse for those choices which deny God's rule (15:24).

This conviction will not end with the life and ministry of Jesus, for the Counselor, or Holy Spirit, will continue to testify to the hearts and minds of persons through truth of Christ and the claims of Christ (15:26), as will the disciples (15:27). Why did Jesus share this with His disciples? "So that you will not go astray" (16:1). Jesus prepared His followers for the reality of the cross they too would bear because of His name.

16:5-16
The Work of the Spirit

Jesus chided His disciples for their concern over their own situation upon His departure rather than concern over where Jesus was going to be (16:5). Again turning to His discussion of the Holy Spirit, Jesus made clear that His departure was worthwhile if only to allow for the coming of the Counselor whom Jesus Himself would send (16:7).

In a carefully detailed statement, Jesus outlined the convicting work of the Holy Spirit, all related to the work and person of Christ. First, the Holy Spirit will convict the world in the area of sin that results from disbelief in Jesus (16:9). Second, the Holy Spirit will convict the world in the area of righteousness in light of the life of Jesus (16:10). Third, the Holy Spirit will convict the world in the area of judgment because Jesus defeated the prince of the world who now stands condemned (16:11). Only through the Holy Spirit can an individual be brought to repentance leading to faith. It is not good works that elevate our status before God but the cross-work of Christ. The Holy Spirit enables the follower of Christ to live out the Christ life.

The Spirit of Truth will guide the disciples into all truth (16:13). His purpose will be to reveal Christ (16:14). The mark of the work of the Holy Spirit, then, is whether Christ is made central and glorified.

16:17-33
I Have Overcome

The disciples were experiencing understandable anxiety and confusion regarding all that Jesus had shared with them. Jesus comforted them by proclaiming that no matter how dark the hour may prove to be, the dawn will follow! Two "dawns" seem to be at hand, the first being the resurrection and the second being the day they will be with Jesus forever in heaven.

Prior to Jesus' death, the disciples had no need to pray in His name, for Jesus was there to be asked personally! This dynamic element of conversation was not to be lost, only now it would be through the Counselor that Jesus would send. The death, burial, and resurrection of Jesus serves as the intercession on our behalf before God, thereby eliminating the need for Jesus' direct intercession (thus not a contradiction of Rom 8:34; Heb 7:25; 1 John 2:1). Persecution will surely come, including trials from living in a fallen world, difficulties in life, and even discipline from God. But Jesus' words of comfort are paramount with His passionate plea to "take heart! I have overcome the world" (16:33).

17:1-5
The High-priestly Prayer

Here we have the beginning of the longest recorded prayer of Jesus (17:1-26). Many interpreters have called it Jesus' "high-priestly" prayer. In the first section of the prayer, Jesus noted that the cross would bring glory to Himself, for it was the will of God and the means of salvation for all who would believe.

17:6-19
Praying for the Disciples

Most of this portion of Jesus' prayer is devoted to the welfare of the disciples. Jesus prayed specifically for their protection in the area of unity (17:11), emphasizing again the importance of the unity of the body of Christ, the church. This is not organizational unity but interpersonal, relational unity. Jesus also prayed that they would be protected from the evil one, or Satan (17:15), who is more than active in the world and bitterly opposed to the things of God (1 John 5:19). Finally, Jesus prayed that God would sanctify them through the word of truth (17:17). Sanctification is the divine process whereby God molds us according to His holiness. It is the bringing to bear upon our lives the moral absolutes of the living God in such a way that they affect how we live and think. Sanctification and revelation are inextricably intertwined, for without God's revelatory word to our life the process of sanctification cannot begin.

17:20-26
The Church's Unity

Here Jesus' prayer turns specifically to those who would come to believe through the disciples' message and testimony (17:20). Again the theme is unity (17:21-23). Christians form the body of Christ (1 Cor 12:13) and the household of faith (Eph 2:19).

Some divisions and controversies are necessary and unavoidable. The purification of the church is as insistent a theme as the unity of the church. Jesus Himself said that He came not bearing peace but a sword. What He meant was that the truth of God can never be neutral, but it divides truth from that which is false by its very nature. Jesus' plea for unity has to do more with the petty controversies and bitter divisions that often plague relationships. The love that binds Christians together should overcome all such grievances, demonstrating to the world that the people of God are unique and unprecedented in their fellowship, drawing the nonbelieving world to faith in Christ.

18:1-11
Embracing the Cup

John is the only Gospel that records that the attack on the servant of the chief priest was carried out by Simon Peter on a man named Malchus (18:10). Luke recorded Jesus' healing of the man's wound (Luke 22:51).

A view of modern Jerusalem looking south through the Kidron Valley from Mount Scopus (see John 18:1).

His concern for the disciples at the moment of His own arrest is evident (18:8). Peter's effort at defending Jesus was rebuked by Jesus Himself, for despite Peter's good intentions, the "cup" that was before Jesus had to be embraced. It should be noted that "cup" was often used as a reference to suffering (Ps 75:8; Ezek 23:31-34), as well as the wrath of God (Isa 51:17,22; Jer 25:15; Rev 14:10; 16:19).

18:12-18
Peter's Denial

The two interrogations may have been enacted to give the semblance of a fair trial for Jesus, though it was far from just by any stretch of the imagination. Peter's first denial, all four Gospels report, came as the result of the challenge of a slave girl. She asked Peter if he was one of the disciples of Jesus, which Peter promptly denied (18:17).

18:19-24
The Jewish Trial

The interrogation of Jesus by the high priest brought out Jesus' response that what He had taught had been taught publicly and that nothing had been taught in private that was not openly said to the crowds. This brought a blow to the face as if such a reply was improper when answering the high priest (18:22). This blow was illegal for such questionings. Jesus' reply was that what He had said was simply the truth and should not be rejected or reacted to with such violence. Note that John treated the Jewish trial with great brevity, devoting the majority of his narrative to the Roman trial.

18:25-27
Drama of Betrayal

Peter's second and third denials, followed by the prophesied crow of the rooster, are recorded just before John recorded Jesus' interaction with Pilate (13:38). Two plots are being simultaneously revealed by John, (1) Peter's denials and (2) Jesus' interrogations and mock trial. Both constitute a drama of betrayal, one by the people who should have received Christ as King and one by a person who should have remained loyal to Christ as King.

18:28-40
Jesus the King

One of the most ironic observations in all of Scripture is made by the apostle John. In order to avoid ceremonial uncleanness, the Jews who had plotted to kill an innocent

Peter denying Jesus (see John 18:12-18,25-27)

man and were now executing that plan did not enter the palace of the Roman governor (18:28). The decision to take Jesus to Pilate was to ensure that He would be killed.

This Gospel records three major conversations held between Jesus and an individual person who was being confronted with the truth and the claims of the gospel. In John 3 Nicodemus was a religious man who sought Jesus in order to pursue his spiritual questions. The Samaritan woman in John 4 was neither religious nor a skeptic but rather one who represented worldliness in its most common form. She was indifferent to the spiritual, living a life of moral self-indulgence. Pilate, however, is indicative of the modern secularist. Hardened to that which would speak to his soul, he was neither open nor inquisitive about the gospel.

Pilate's first question was perfunctory, almost a leading question in order to investigate the nature of the Jewish complaint. Jesus' answer was disarming and brought about a transparent reply from Pilate regarding the political tensions that had led Jesus to his feet. Speaking in terms Pilate would understand, Jesus admitted being a King but a King of far more than an earthly, temporal realm. Many individuals throughout Christian history have misinterpreted the kingdom of God in earthly terms.

As was His custom, Jesus then turned the discussion toward His mission. He informed Pilate that His kingly role was identified with testifying "to the truth. Everyone on the side of the truth listens to me" (18:37). Pilate's response has become legendary: "What is truth?" (18:29). Was it a serious question? sarcastic? We simply do not know. What is clear is that upon voicing the question, Pilate went out to the Jews and dismissed their charges against Jesus and offered to release Him in celebration of the Passover. The Jews, however, demanded Barabbas, a man who was both an insurrectionist and a murderer (Luke 23:19).

19:1-16a
The Source of Power

The physical and emotional torment that Jesus suffered is beyond description. He was not only physically beaten but ridiculed and mocked. Perhaps as one last effort to have Jesus released, Pilate presented Him before the crowd after His beating in order to see if now they could accept His liberation (19:4). The Jews, however, insisted on His death because Christ claimed to be the Son of God (19:7).

Pilate's claim that he had the power to free or crucify Jesus brought the following response: "You would have no power over me if it were not given to you from above. Therefore the one who handed me over to you is guilty of a greater sin" (19:11). What should perhaps be noted here is Jesus' intimation that Pilate, though not the initiator of the death of Jesus, was not without sin.

19:16b-27
The Hour

Every word of John's Gospel leads to this moment, for the "hour" had finally come. As if one last effort to

PILATE

Pontius Pilate was the Roman procurator in Judea from A.D. 26–36. Procurator was the title for a governor of a Roman province under direct imperial rather than senatorial control. Pilate was thus responsible to the emperor, Tiberias Caesar, for the military, financial, and judicial operations in Judea.

The emperor personally supervised some provinces, such as Judea and Egypt, because of their instability or crucial importance to Rome. Judea qualified on both counts as the land bridge to Egypt, Rome's breadbasket, and as a rebellious population longing for independent Jewish rule (see John 8:31-33 and Mark 15:7).

A procurator held an authority by delegation from the emperor, called the *imperium*. The *imperium* was the power of life or death over persons in a subject population. Pilate reflected this with accuracy when he said to Jesus, "Don't you realize I have power to free you or to crucify you?" (John 19:10).

Pilate's responsibility for maintaining peace and order was the reason for his being in Jerusalem at the time Jesus was arrested. Passover season commemorated the deliverance of the Jews from Egypt (Exod 12:1-36) and was the time of year when Jewish patriotism was at its height.

Pilate, whose residence was at Caesarea on the Mediterranean coast, was in Jerusalem to take personal command of the resident Roman forces in the event of any uprising or act of rebellion in Judea's largest Jewish city. He personally interrogated Jesus rather than delegating it to a regular judge (for example, see Matt 5:25 and Luke 18:2-6) because Jesus was accused of claiming to be a king—a charge that assumed He was trying to recruit revolutionary forces to launch a rebellion against Roman authority (see Matt 27:11-14; Mark 15:2-5; Luke 23:2-5; and John 18:33-38). Pilate sentenced Jesus to death even though he knew the charge was fallacious (Matt 27:18), but the soldiers clearly believed they had a revolutionary leader in custody and mocked Jesus (Matt 27:27-31; Mark 15:16-20; Luke 23:11; John 19:2-3).

Pilate was certainly less than noble in dealing with Jesus as he did, revealing both an indifference to human life and an ugly willingness to cooperate with the Jewish leaders in an execution on the basis of a false charge (Matt 27:18). See the article "Trial of Jesus."

Additional information about Pilate from non-Christian sources supports the picture of Pilate's character revealed in the NT. Philo reported that Tiberius was infuriated with Pilate for his insensitivity in governing and accused him of taking bribes as well as performing numerous executions without any trials (*Embassy to Gaius,* 302-4).

Josephus recounted two incidents in which Pilate himself sparked Jewish demonstrations in Jerusalem—one by flaunting Roman images of the emperor on military equipment and the other by attempting to confiscate temple funds for works he wanted done related to the water supply for Jerusalem (*Antiquities,* 18.55-62).

The incident that resulted in Pilate's being returned to Rome in A.D. 36 by Tiberias was his ordering the unwarranted execution of a number of Samaritan villagers for a religious march to Mount Gerizim (*Antiquities,* 18.85-87). Nothing is known of Pilate after his recall in A.D. 36, but several fictional accounts of his later years appeared during the ensuing centuries. Some of these accounts have Pilate becoming a Christian while others stress his despondency over the way he treated Jesus. □

cleanse Himself from guilt, Pilate had the title "Jesus of Nazareth, the King of the Jews" fastened onto the cross where Jesus was crucified in Latin, Aramaic, and Greek (19:19). Every prophecy regarding the Messiah, even to the gambling for His clothing, was fulfilled (19:24; compare Ps 22:18).

Crucifixion was the Roman means of execution for slaves and criminals. The victim was nailed to a cross shaped either in the traditional form, or in the shape of a *T, X, Y,* or *I.* The nails were driven through the wrists and heel bones. Present at the cross were Jesus' mother, His mother's sister, Mary the wife of Clopas, and Mary Magdalene (19:25). Also present was the author of this Gospel, the apostle John, whom Jesus instructed to care for His mother (19:27).

19:28-37
It Is Finished

The actual death of Jesus was preceded with words fitting the narrative John had written: "It is finished" (19:30). What was finished? The mission of Jesus, the Son of God, to die a substitutionary death for sinful persons. As a result of His death on our behalf, our sin was atoned for, and eternal life through Jesus became attainable through trusting faith.

With these final words Jesus "bowed his head and gave up his spirit" (19:30). This rather unusual way of describing someone's death intimates that Jesus died voluntarily as an act of the will. After the death of Jesus, a soldier pierced His side, "bringing a sudden flow of blood and water" (19:34). From a medical standpoint the mix of blood and water from the spear's thrust was the result of piercing of the sac that surrounds the heart (the pericardium) as well as the heart itself. The author of the Gospel, the apostle John, then offered his testimony that he was a witness to this event and that even to the final moment every detail fulfilled the prophecies concerning the Messiah (19:35-37; compare Exod 12:46; Num 9:12; Ps 34:20; Zech 12:10).

19:38-42
The Burial

After the death of Jesus, most of the disciples were nowhere to be found, yet at that moment two individuals who had previously been afraid to make their allegiance known came boldly forward to care for the body of Christ. These two were Nicodemus (John 4) and Joseph of Arimathea, a rich member of the Sanhedrin who had agreed to the condemnation of Jesus (Matt 27:57; Luke 23:51). Jesus was laid in a tomb following a traditional Jewish preparation.

20:1-9
The Resurrection

The first person to the tomb of Jesus was Mary Magdalene. Upon seeing the stone removed from the tomb, she ran to Peter and John, exclaiming that they had taken Jesus from the tomb. Mary did not understand that Jesus' body had not been stolen but that He had been raised from the dead. Peter and John ran to the tomb, finding only the strips of Jesus' burial clothes. Peter and John, as did Mary, failed to understand that the resurrection had taken place (20:9).

20:10-18
The First Appearance

Commentators often have suggested that Mary Magdalene was the first to see Jesus following His resurrection because she was the person who needed to see Him the most. After all the others had left the empty tomb, she stood alone by its side weeping. Two angels appeared to her, asking her why she was expressing such grief. After answering that someone had taken her Lord away and she didn't know where He was, she turned and saw Jesus.

The tenderness of the moment when he said "Mary" and her recognition of Him and cry of "Rabboni!" (teacher) is one of the emotional highlights of the entire Gospel. Jesus' warning not to "hold on" to Him for He had "not yet returned to the Father" is at first confusing (20:17). When Jesus spoke of not having returned to the

Thomas the doubter (see John 20:24-29)

Belief in the New Testament

The linguistic usage of the words translated "belief" are quite varied. The OT root, from which the NT meaning of belief is developed, signifies *firmness* or *stability.* The verb used often means *to believe, to trust,* or *to say amen to.* Implied is a relationship, ultimately a personal relationship. God is the primary object of that personal faith; hence, belief points to a personal, saving, helping relationship. At times the concept of faithfulness is the prominent idea. At other times the sense is true religion and is often associated with grace, steadfast love, and righteousness.

In classical Greek the verb meant *to trust, have confidence in* whether of persons or of things. The noun conveyed the idea of *trust, reliance, be confident that.* It can also be used in the concrete sense of pledge, guarantee, or proof.

The root word for "belief" in NT Greek (*pistis,* noun; *pisteuo,* verb) abounds with meaning. In the NT it can signify belief in God as almighty, self-revealing, and benevolent. In the Synoptic Gospels (Matthew, Mark, and Luke) it can mean *trust* or *give credence to.* But the Synoptics do not use it in this fashion as frequently as the rest of the NT does.

In noun form in the Synoptics, it mostly carried the meaning of confidence in God and trust in His power to heal and save. Jesus constantly used the word in this manner: "Your faith has healed you" (Mark 5:34).

For Paul faith was the foundational Christian attitude, the core of the divine-human encounter. The Pauline corpus presents no really radical development of the basic ideas outlined above. For Paul faith meant utter dependence on God and belief in His power (see Rom 4:16-20; Col 2:2). The idea of power in Paul was, however, something of a development and was meant to show true faith is not mere words or a shallow, intellectual grasp of Christian ideas. Faith has power to change life radically. As seen so often in Paul, true faith justifies a person before God (Rom 3:1).

John at times used the word in a rather distinctive manner. John spoke of the belief that Jesus is the Messiah and was sent by the Father. By believing one receives life. In John we have something of an identification of believing with knowing, emphasizing the intellectual or theological content of faith.

In substantive form the term was at times coupled with the definite article "the faith." This quite clearly designated the whole of accepted Christian teaching. □

Father, clearly the ascension is in view. Also to be considered here is the idea that Jesus was not to be held to in the same sense as before the resurrection, for now Mary's relationship with Him would be through the Holy Spirit (16:5-16).

20:19-23
Forgiveness of Sins

Jesus encountered a group of frightened disciples behind locked doors and gave them what they needed most—Himself. He showed them His hands and His side in order to dispel any doubt that they were seeing anything but their crucified Lord (20:20). As with the "Great Commission" recorded in Matthew 28, Jesus decisively gave His followers the command to go into all the world and continue His ministry. To enable them to respond to this task, they received a precursor of the full coming of the Holy Spirit at Pentecost—almost as a deposit for that which was to come fully fifty days later—breathed to them now from the very mouth of Jesus (20:22).

Jesus stated that if the disciples forgave anyone, they were forgiven, and if they did not forgive them their sins, they were not forgiven. At first glance this is a remarkable statement that seems out of step with the role and authority of the disciples. It was not the disciples who could forgive sins but Jesus. The literal reading from the Greek is more clear, stating: "Those whose sins you forgive have already been forgiven; those whose sins you do not forgive have not been forgiven." God's forgiveness is not dependent upon human forgiveness, but rather forgiveness is extended by God as a result of individual responses to the proclamation of the gospel by fellow human beings.

20:24-31
Do You Believe?

Thomas's doubt was that of many in the modern world. Unless he could see, taste, touch, and hear what was being presented as reality, he would not accept it as the truth. As Jesus noted, however, "blessed are those who have not seen and yet have believed" (20:29).

John's purpose statement is included here, following the resurrection, in order that the reader may know the reason for this carefully detailed narrative of the life and teaching of Jesus. This Gospel was "written that you may believe that Jesus is the Christ, the Son of God, and that by believing you may have life in his name" (20:31). The purpose of the Gospel of John is to present Jesus as God in human form and that through faith in Jesus, individuals would embrace salvation to eternal life.

21:1-14
Miracles Continue

The miraculous catch of fish, an almost casual appearance and fellowship of the risen Christ with the disciples, constitutes the third recorded appearance of Jesus following His resurrection. Here Jesus demonstrated again His power over the natural world.

21:15-25
Do You Love Me?

Following their breakfast meal on the shores of the Sea of Tiberias, Jesus turned to Peter and asked a series of questions related to Peter's devotion. The first word for love, used in Jesus' first two questions, refers to a love that involves the will and personality. The second kind of love, indicated by the word for love used in the third question of Jesus, refers more to the emotions than to the will.

Regardless of whether or not much is to be made of these word distinctions, the key issue is that of love for Christ, and this Peter surely expressed. His earlier three denials are here answered in three affirmations of love and service. Jesus clearly wanted love for Him to include both will and emotions, demonstrated in a life of discipleship and devotion to the church.

Then Jesus forecast the kind of death Peter would die in order to glorify God. The early church understood the "stretching out of hands" mentioned here to mean crucifixion. Tradition understands the death of Peter to have been by upside-down crucifixion.

The final words of the Gospel of John change from firsthand narrative to that of a plural perspective. It would seem that the Gospel of the apostle John was preserved and then another author, equally inspired by the living God, added his own testimony on behalf of a community of faith as witness to the truth of all that the apostle had written. Not everything from the life of Christ was recorded but only those things the author felt supported the goal of leading individuals to belief in Jesus as the Son of God who came to take away the sins of the world.

Theological and Ethical Significance

From this Gospel we learn much about God as Father. Contemporary believers are indebted to John for their habit of referring to God simply as "the Father." The Father is active (5:17), bringing blessing on those He has created. He is love (3:16; see 1 John 4:8-10). We know love because we see it in the cross; it is sacrificial giving, not for deserving people but for undeserving sinners. He is a great God whose will is done in bringing about our salvation (6:44).

The Gospel throughout focuses on Jesus Christ. It is clear that God in Christ has revealed Himself (1:1-18). God is active in Christ, the Savior of the world, bringing about the salvation He has planned (4:42).

John's Gospel tells us more about the Holy Spirit than do the other Evangelists. The Spirit was active from the start of Jesus' ministry (1:32), but the Spirit's full work was to begin at the consummation of Jesus' own ministry (7:37-39). The Spirit brings life (3:1-8), a life of the highest quality (10:10), and leads believers in the way of truth (16:13). The Spirit thus universalizes Jesus' ministry for Christians of all ages.

In response to the work of God in their lives, Christians are to be characterized by love (13:34-35). They owe all they have to the love of God, and it is proper that they respond to that love by loving God and other people.

Questions for Reflection

1. John presented a portrait of Jesus as fully God and fully man. What are the dangers in emphasizing either Christ's humanity or divinity to the exclusion of the other?

2. John presented a challenging call to believe in Christ as Savior and Lord. What did John mean when he said to believe in Christ and you will be saved? Is it mere intellectual assent or something that involves one's entire life?

3. Essentially Jesus' final recorded prayer was for believers to be unified. What does it mean for believers to be unified? What did Jesus say happens to our witness to the world regarding His truth and claims if we are not unified?

4. What is the relationship between the risen Jesus and the Holy Spirit? How does the Holy Spirit make Jesus present in our lives?

Sources for Additional Study

Barrett, C. K. *The Gospel According to St. John*. Second Edition. Philadelphia: Westminster, 1978.

Bruce, F. F. *The Gospel of John: Introduction, Exposition and Notes.* Grand Rapid: Eerdmans, 1983.

Carson, D. A. *The Gospel of John*. Grand Rapids: Eerdmans, 1991.

Morris, Leon. *The Gospel According to John. New International Commentary.* Grand Rapids: Eerdmans, 1971.

The Acts of the Apostles

The Book of Acts is an exciting and powerful portrait of the history of the early Christian church. From the upper room to the Roman capital, this narrative chronicles the spread of the gospel. Without it we would know little about the apostles and their mission to the Jewish and Gentile world.

Acts follows the activities of two apostles in particular: Peter and Paul. For this reason it has been named after their activity. The book might better be named "The Acts of the Holy Spirit," however, for the Spirit is the one who provides the power and motivation for the missionary activity of the apostles. Through Acts we follow the unhindered movement of the gospel around the shores of the Mediterranean Sea. We move from Jerusalem to Samaria, from Palestine to Asia, from Greece to Rome. By the time Acts ends, the gospel has been proclaimed throughout the Roman world with miraculous success.

ACTS

Acts is a familiar book to most students of the Bible, but we must try to understand this book in its ancient context. Who wrote the book? Why was Acts written and to whom? What are the major themes of Acts? Answering these questions will aid our understanding of the book in its context.

Authorship

Acts was designed to complete a two-volume work and is the companion volume to the Gospel of Luke. In fact, for much of its early history, the two volumes circulated together. When the early church decided on the form of the New Testament we now have, Acts was separated from Luke by John. This was due to the desire to begin the New Testament with the four Gospels.

Acts, like the Gospel of Luke, is anonymous. Neither narrative refers to its author by name. Traditionally, Luke has been seen as the author of both the Gospel and Acts. We know little about Luke. He is referred to as a doctor in Colossians and a dear friend to Paul. From other places in the New Testament, one can conclude that Luke was a Gentile. Some have suggested that Luke came from Macedonia and was part of Paul's vision to preach the gospel in Greece (Acts 16). Others have suggested that Luke was a native of Antioch in Syria.

What is clear from the text of Luke-Acts is Luke's knowledge of Greek literature and language. His books are well written. Luke's writings also display signs of his education and his ability to suit his writing style to the subject.

Date

Ancient literature is notoriously difficult to date. Acts is no exception. Some have suggested an early date for Acts. This date is based on the ending of Acts, since the book ends before Paul appeared before Caesar. If this were the case, Acts would have been written sometime around A.D. 60–64.

Acts certainly was written after the third Gospel. Some people date Luke's Gospel sometime after the destruction of the temple (A.D. 70), around A.D. 75–80. If that were the case, Acts would be dated sometime after that, A.D. 80–85. Certainty about the date for Luke-Acts is impossible. Too little information is available. A conservative approach to the problem would be to give a rather wide range of possibility, somewhere between A.D. 62 and 85. While this may strike some as too broad, it has the value of giving us a general idea of the time period without placing too much emphasis on precise dates.

Audience

To whom did Luke write this book? Was it one person? Was it a great many people? What were they like? What information about the early Christian church did they need in order to live strong and committed Christian lives in a pagan world?

Acts gives us a place to start. Unlike many other biblical books, Acts addresses a specific person: Theophilus. Significant energy has been spent speculating about the identity of Theophilus. Most people start with the possibility that Theophilus was a wealthy Roman citizen. Perhaps Luke addressed both of these books to Theophilus in the hope that Theophilus would pay for their publication. Perhaps Theophilus was a Roman official whom Luke was trying to convince that Christianity posed no threat to the Roman Empire. Some have even suggested that Acts was intended to be used for Paul's defense before Caesar.

The word "Theophilus," while a man's name, also means *lover of God.* Many have suggested that Luke addressed not just one man but all those who love God. This would explain the inclusive nature of Luke-Acts and Luke's emphasis on Christian faith and its development.

Whether Luke addressed one prominent Roman or all those who loved and followed God, one must assume that Luke-Acts was meant to be read by a number of people. We know little about these readers. We do know that they were able to read a form of Greek that is more difficult than most of the New Testament. They also seem to be more familiar with the Roman Empire and Asia Minor than with Palestine. Luke had to give them information about places in Palestine; they appear to have known the places elsewhere in the Empire. Luke's emphasis on women and wealth has led some to conclude that many of his readers were either wealthy, women, or both. Most of all, Luke's readers were in need of information about the gospel and the church.

Themes

Two major themes run through Acts. The first of these themes is that of the *universal, unhindered spread of the gospel.* With the constant aid of the Holy Spirit, the gospel grew from a small group of followers in Jerusalem to encompass the "ends of the earth" (Acts 1:8). Along the way the Spirit removed barriers to the spread of the gospel. Religion, race, physical handicaps, philosophy, and magic fell before the power of the Spirit manifest through the apostles. Luke highlighted this theme throughout the book. The last word in the Greek text is "unhindered," as Luke described Paul's preaching in Rome. The gospel is triumphant in Acts; nothing could stop its spread.

The second theme of Acts concerns the *separation of Christianity from the Jews.* Luke took great care to insert some distance between the church and the Jews. At crucial points Paul rejected the Jewish people—just as they had rejected the gospel. Even though the beginning of Acts portrays the church as continuing to worship in the temple and synagogue, Acts chronicles an increasing separation between the two groups. Luke also makes clear that the Jews had rejected Christ; Christians had not rejected Jews. A significant part of this theme is the portrayal of Christianity as the true heir of Israel rather than as a heretical sect. Christians are the "true Israel." This theme also assures Luke's Roman readers that the conflict that involves the Christians is religious (with the Jews) rather than political (with Rome).

Literary Form

Acts is narrative. It has a beginning and an end. It has characters and plot. Acts tells a story.

Much of the discussion of the form of Acts concerns the question of Luke's historical accuracy. Such questions are difficult to answer conclusively, since Acts is unique within the New Testament. Some people use parts of Acts to prove Luke's historical accuracy; others use the same material to attack Luke's historical accuracy.

Perhaps the most important sections of Acts in this regard are those known as the "we" sections (Acts 16:10-17; 20:5-15; 21:1-18; and 27:1–28:16). The author's use of the pronoun "we" in narrating these sections suggests that Luke was a traveling companion of Paul, who used the pronoun to indicate those times in which he was part of Paul's entourage. These sections have also been interpreted as evidence that Luke used a diary of one of Paul's companions as the source for his narrative concerning Paul's missionary journals. Perhaps these passages were an attempt by the author to give himself eyewitness authority through the strategic placement of pronouns.

Another difficult question has been Luke's use of sources in general. Unlike the Gospels, we have no way to compare Acts with any other similar material. Therefore we can only conjecture as to which sources, if any, Luke used in writing Acts.

The question of Luke's historical reliability cannot be answered solely on the basis of one's conclusions about the "we" sections or his use of sources. Acts, especially in comparison with other ancient historical narratives, consistently proves itself to be reliable by ancient standards.

We do not have enough information to know for sure what sources Luke used or how he used them. Within God's providential oversight and under the inspiration of the Holy Spirit, Luke was able to bring together a variety of sources to communicate the important events in the life of the early church. The recent focus on Acts as a literary work, however, has affirmed the literary unity of the work. Acts can and should be read as a whole.

Purpose and Theology

Luke's prologue to Acts suggests his reason for writing. He specifically related this second volume to the first, noting that in his "former book" he "wrote about all that Jesus began to do and to teach" (Acts 1:1). With the guidance of the Holy Spirit, the disciples continued to do and to teach as Jesus had done. Luke narrated their activity with a number of purposes in mind.

His first purpose was to *inform.* The prologue to Luke's Gospel clearly states his intention to present "an orderly account" (Luke 1:3). Luke was a historian. He had researched the events and written them down for the benefit of his readers. This purpose became even more vital with Acts. Luke's history of the formation and spread of the early church provided important information to his readers.

His second purpose was to *convince.* History rarely records mere facts. The process of deciding which facts to record reflects a desire to convince on the part of the historian. In Luke's case this desire is, again, made evident in the prologue to the Gospel. Luke stated that his reason for writing this orderly account was that his reader or readers might "know the certainty" of that which they had been "taught" about the Christian faith (Luke 1:4). This is a theological purpose. Luke wanted his readers to be confirmed in their faith. His readers probably knew enough about the message of Christ to have become Christians. Their need was for confirmation. Luke's information is designed to convince them of the truth of the gospel they had accepted, to strengthen their faith. He might also have written to correct their misunderstandings about the things Jesus did and taught. Certainly Luke's history has a theological message. Not only that, Luke's history conveys a social and religious message. One of the results of Luke's writing is the defense of the Christian way of life. On the one hand, Luke defended the church against the Jewish accusation that Christianity was anti-Caesar. On the other hand, Luke countered the suggestion that Christianity was merely a Jewish sect.

A book can be informative and convincing without being readable. It will not, however, be widely read. Acts is historically and theologically accurate; it is also extremely interesting literature. This is due in great part to the nature of Luke's subject. One must give credit as well to the literary artistry of Luke, who narrated the spread of the gospel in an exciting manner.

The Acts of the Apostles may be divided into two major sections. The first section narrates the spread of the gospel from Christ's ascension and Pentecost to Cornelius's conversion and the commissioning of Saul and Barnabas to preach to the Gentiles. The major apostolic figure in this first section is Peter, the one responsible for the church's mission to the Jews.

Ascension of Christ

The ascension of Christ is that occasion when at the close of His earthly ministry the risen Christ Jesus was take up into heaven. It was a moment of joy for the disciples, for He said they were to be His witnesses among all the people of the earth. It was a moment of worship, for He blessed them with His outstretched hands and promised His power for the mission He had assigned to their care (Luke 24:47-51; Acts 1:2-3,8-9).

Some have a problem thinking of Jesus "going up" into heaven. But for Luke to note that from the disciple's perspective Jesus was taken up from them is completely natural. Jesus was taken up, much as a father picks up his child and carries him away. Luke described the event this way, "After he said this, he was taken up before their very eyes, and a cloud hid him from their sight" (Acts 1:9). The cloud symbolized the mysterious, majestic presence of God with His people (compare Luke 9:34-35 and Exod 13:21-22).

A careful reading of Luke and Acts raises the question about when the ascension occurred. Luke 24 seems to imply that Jesus was taken up into heaven in the late evening of the day He arose. But Luke's account in Acts clearly says the ascension happened forty days after the resurrection (Acts 1:3). Though several suggestions have been made to harmonize these accounts, two explanations provide the most plausible solution.

1. Jesus did in fact ascend to to heaven on Sunday evening as Luke 24 indicates. However, He returned to the earth for special appearances throughout the forty days until a second public ascension happened as described in Acts 1:3. John's account of the resurrection appearance lends weight to this line of reasoning. On Easter morning Jesus said to Mary Magdalene, "Do not hold on to me for I have not yet returned to the Father" (John 20:17). One week later He invited Thomas: "Put your finger here; see my hands. Reach out your hand and put it into my side" (John 20:27). Apparently He had ascended on Sunday night and returned to be with the disciples a week later (John 20:26).

2. Others suggest that Jesus was raised up and glorified in one great exaltation early on Sunday morning. He returned for each of the appearances throughout the day and through the forty days as the risen and glorified Son of God. Peter Toon calls this the "secret and invisible" ascension that was followed for the benefit of the disciples forty days later by the "visible symbolic demonstration" of that earlier ascension.

The ascension means that the humanity of God's creation into which He emptied Himself at the incarnation (Phil 2:7) has been taken into glory. All things human can be redeemed from the effects of sin, so that what God intended from the beginning (see Gen 1:31, "It was very good") can now be fully achieved. The ascension means that Christians are never without a voice before the Father. Jesus, the Great High Priest, lives now in glory to intercede for His brothers and sisters (Rom 8:34; Heb 7:25).

The ascension means that the heavenly reign of our Lord has begun, and one day what is now dimly seen will be fully realized as He becomes all in all (see Eph 1:20-23; Rev 3:21). It means that God the Father is fully satisfied with the Son and has seated Him at the Father's right hand, where He reigns as our Great High Priest (Heb 1:3; see 1 Pet 3:22).

The ascension is a visible reminder that Jesus has left the task of world missions to His disciples, empowered by the Holy Spirit whose work would not start until Jesus went away (John 16:7; Acts 1:8). The ascension is the sign that Jesus will come again to receive His people unto Himself (Acts 1:11). The description of the ascension is the dramatic assertion that Jesus was taken up into heaven to be with the Father with whom He reigns then, now, and forever. □

I. Peter: Missionary to the Jews (1:1–12:24)
II. Paul: Missionary to the Gentiles (12:25–28:31)

1:1–5:42
The Apostles Minister in Jerusalem

1:1-11
Prologue: Ascension

Acts begins where the Gospel of Luke ended. Luke began his second volume with a prologue that explicitly linked Acts with Luke's Gospel (Acts 1:1). It also reminded Luke's readers of the events that ended the Gospel, especially Jesus' ascension and promise of the Holy Spirit. The first section also contains what is often considered the "programmatic" statement for Acts (1:8). This verse provides an outline for the rest of Acts, a "map" for the spread of the gospel. Jesus told His disciples that the power of the Holy Spirit would give them the ability to witness "in Jerusalem, and in all Judea and Samaria, and to the ends of the earth." It is no coincidence that Acts narrates the unhindered movement of the gospel message from Jerusalem to Judea and Samaria, and ultimately throughout the Roman Empire.

Finally, this section closes with a note of hope for the disciples at the ascension. As they stood on the mountaintop, peering into the heavens for one last glimpse of Jesus, they were reminded of Jesus' return.

1:12-26
Replacing Judas

The disciples returned to Jerusalem after the ascension. The distance from the Mount of Olives to Jerusalem is given as "a Sabbath day's walk" (1:12), slightly more than one-half mile. The disciples were waiting for the coming of the Holy Spirit. In the interim, though, they had important business at hand. The loss of Judas left the ranks of the apostles in serious imbalance. Luke listed the apostles still left, the Eleven. The number of twelve apostles is a significant number. The church was to represent the "new Israel." Therefore it was important that there be twelve apostles, one to represent each tribe of Israel.

In the midst of Peter's speech in the upper room, Luke interrupted with information about the fate of Judas. Luke translated the Aramaic term "Akeldama" as "Field of Blood," for the benefit of his non-Palestinian audience. Note that Luke's account of Judas's end needs to be read in conjunction with Matthew (Matt 27:1-10) so we can fill in details in both accounts. In Matthew, Judas hanged himself, and the authorities used the "blood" money to buy the field of which both Matthew and Luke wrote.

The text returns to Peter's speech and to the business of electing a successor to Judas. The qualifications for such a witness related to his time spent with Jesus, "beginning from John's baptism to the time when Jesus was taken up from us" (Acts 1:22). The election of Matthias to witness to the resurrection showed a unity and power within the community that was a direct result of their dependence on the Holy Spirit.

2:1-13
Pentecost and Peter's Sermon

The second chapter of Acts begins with a reference to "the day of Pentecost" (2:1). The term "Pentecost" (meaning *fifty days*) was a term used by Diaspora Jews and the New Testament to refer to the Jewish Festival of Weeks. This festival celebrated the firstfruits of the harvest; it was an early summer festival. The Jewish people offered loaves of bread baked from the first harvested grain in thanksgiving for the harvest to come.

The giving of the Spirit at Pentecost represented that idea of firstfruits. The resurrection of Christ is the promise of resurrection (1 Cor 15); the Spirit is the promise of power and the kingdom. The events of Pentecost evoked Old Testament images. The violent wind (2:2) and tongues of fire (2:3) were familiar signs of the presence of God, especially connected with Mount Sinai. The miracle of communication in many languages reversed the curse of Babel (Gen 11).

This miraculous phenomenon is probably not what Paul referred to in his Epistles as *glossolalia,* or the gift of tongues (1 Cor 12:28). Later references indicate that the Spirit-filled language requires an equally Spirit-filled interpretation. Here the miracle was the ability to speak languages not previously learned. At Pentecost, Jews from every Diaspora nation were amazed that Galileans were able to speak in their languages. The list of nations encompassed the Roman world. Pentecost meant that the gospel was now able to reach the world through the power of the Spirit. The Jewish people who heard were not converted to faith through the message of the tongues. They were motivated to ask what all of this meant; they offered Peter an opportunity to share the gospel.

Peter's sermon is the first of many sermons and speeches in Acts. Luke recorded both the content and the tone of these sermons. One should not expect exact transcripts of these sermons. Like Jesus, the apostles spoke

The Holy Spirit and Acts

The Acts of the Apostles might as accurately have been named the Acts of the Holy Spirit. While the Gospels describe the ministry of God the Son, Acts describes the ministry through the church of God the Holy Spirit. Rather than a strict contrast between the work of Son and Spirit, however, Acts shows the continuity of the work of the incarnate God through His Holy Spirit. Christ Himself is present in His church through His Spirit.

The Holy Spirit is not an "it" but the very presence of God in the life of a Christian. Peter made the understanding clear in the episode of Ananias and Sapphira. Peter charged them with lying to the Holy Spirit (5:3), with lying to God (5:4), and with tempting the Spirit of God (5:9). He did not refer to three things they had done. He spoke of the Spirit in three ways, but he meant the one Spirit who proceeds from the Father and the Son. Likewise, the "Spirit of Jesus" is used to refer to the Holy Spirit when Paul and Timothy were not allowed to go into Bithynia (16:6-7).

The Book of Acts begins with the resurrected Lord promising the gift of the Spirit to His disciples. With the Spirit would come the power to carry out the mission of taking the gospel to the world (1:8). Jesus declared the mission in a geographic progression beginning in Jerusalem, spreading to the region of Judea, crossing the cultural barrier to Samaria, and on to the rest of the world. As the book unfolds, the Holy Spirit bore testimony to the advance of the church at each of these crucial stages.

On the day of Pentecost, the Holy Spirit fell on the church in power (2:1-4). As a result of that day's preaching and witnessing by all the church (2:4,6,14), about three thousand people were added to the church (2:41). The early church understood the baptism of the Holy Spirit (1:5) as the fulfillment of the promise of God through the prophets. Peter preached the first gospel sermon based on the prophecy concerning the coming of the Holy Spirit in Joel 2:28-32 (2:16-21). Furthermore, Peter stressed the gift of the Holy Spirit as a central element of salvation (2:38).

When Philip carried the gospel to Samaria, the church in Jerusalem sent Peter and John to pray for the converts to receive the Holy Spirit (8:14-17). Likewise, the conversion of Paul reached its climax when Ananias came to him that he might regain his sight and be filled with the Holy Spirit (9:17). The gift of the Holy Spirit to Cornelius and other Gentiles as they heard the gospel convinced Peter and the other apostles that God had granted salvation to the Gentiles (10:44–11:18; 15:8).

When he met a group of disciples of John the Baptist in Ephesus, Paul asked them about the Holy Spirit as a diagnostic question. The fact that they had never heard of the Holy Spirit demonstrated to Paul the need to preach the gospel of Jesus to them. Paul baptized those who believed, and when he laid hands on them, they received the Holy Spirit (19:1-6).

Acts contains no fixed order of sequence related to baptism, laying on of hands, and the reception of the Spirit. Some conversion accounts make no reference at all to laying on of hands. The governing principle seems to be that those who have faith in Jesus receive His Holy Spirit to apply the benefits of salvation. Thus baptism and laying on of hands have no sacramental significance for salvation. Instead, they symbolically declare faith in what God has done. □

and preached many times, far too often to record each word of each speech.

2:14-36
Beginning of Evangelism

Peter's speech (Acts 2:14-36) is the heart of this chapter. The controversial and exciting nature of the pentecostal experience has claimed tremendous attention. The true focus of the chapter, however, is the beginning of Christian evangelism. Here from the mouth of Peter is the story and significance of Christ's life, death, and resurrection, the "meaning" of the pentecostal event.

Two themes run through Peter's sermon. Peter's primary theme is that Jesus' life, death, and resurrection happened according to God's plan. Peter supported this affirmation by quoting the prophet Joel and two psalms. Joel's prophecy was considered to be apocalyptic (figurative language referring to the appearance of the Lord or the Day of the Lord). This prophecy was fulfilled in the coming of the Spirit and the signs of God's presence just revealed. Peter used this prophecy to move on to the real meaning of the event: these are the last days; the Day of the Lord is at hand. The two Psalms are used to prove God's hand in the resurrection of Jesus and show Jesus' superiority to David.

A second theme is the Jewish responsibility for Jesus' death. Twice Peter accused his audience of direct responsibility for the murder of Jesus. As Jews they were responsible for the actions of their fellow Jews.

2:37-41
Overwhelming Acceptance

Peter's sermon "cut [them] to the heart" (2:37). Once again Peter had an opportunity for evangelism. The sermon evoked a response, a question. Peter's answer was an offer to enter the church through repentance and baptism. The response to Peter's invitation was overwhelming; about three thousand people "accepted his message" and were baptized (2:41).

2:42-47
Summary

Acts contains many summary passages. On the surface these summaries separate the narrated activities of the apostles. They provide transitions between those narratives. Usually they prepare the reader for events that will follow. The summaries focus attention on the church itself and offer information about what is happening to the Christian community.

This first summary in Acts provides a picture of the church immediately after its beginnings. The picture is one of maturing discipleship. The new converts were being taught, they continued to worship in the temple, and they were unified economically and spiritually. Finally, God was continuing to add "to their number daily" (2:47). The church was not only surviving, but it also was growing.

3:1-10
Conflict with Jewish Authorities

Since the Christians continued to worship in the temple, the presence of Peter and John at the temple during the

The Birth of the Church

When was the church born? In a sense we could trace it back to God's call of Abraham and the history of Israel as the people of God.

In the more restricted sense of the church as the new people of God, the body of Christ, its roots are certainly to be found in the mind and ministry of Jesus Himself. His intention to establish a community of faith is clearly reflected in His response to Peter's confession (Matt 16:13-19) and in His words about a new covenant at the last supper (Luke 22:20).

Jesus' intention also is reflected in His choosing an inner circle of twelve disciples in continuity with the twelve tribes of Israel, the original covenant people of God. The twelve did not constitute a church, however, for the basis of His new covenant was Jesus' own death and resurrection. The people of the new covenant were to be redeemed and forgiven of sin, a people with God's law written on their hearts (see Jer 31:31-34).

That act of forgiveness and deliverance took place on the cross. Only through God's decisive atoning work in Jesus' death could a new covenant people come into being. Ultimately, Calvary gave birth to the church.

A community needs organization and direction, and this was no less true for that original band of disciples who witnessed the appearances of their risen Lord. More than anything else, it was the Holy Spirit who gave them this sense of direction. The coming of the Spirit is anticipated by Jesus in His words to the disciples at the last supper (John 13:31–17:26). There He promised not to leave them desolate after His departure from this world (14:18). He promised instead to come to them in the person of the Spirit (Paraclete), who would teach them, guide them, and be His own abiding presence in their lives (14:6; 15:26; 16:7-15).

In the Pentecost narrative of Acts 2, this coming of the Spirit is vividly depicted as the foundational event in the constitution of the new community of Christian believers. The risen Christ strictly charges the eleven apostles to wait in Jerusalem for the coming of the Spirit (Acts 1:5). At His ascension He commissioned them as witnesses to the world, but this was to take place only through the power of the Spirit (1:8).

So the apostles and larger band of disciples gathered together in an upper room, some 120 in all, awaiting this promised event (1:12-14). Their minds were certainly on the community, for their main undertaking during this waiting period was to choose a twelfth apostle, filling the vacancy left by Judas and completing the apostolic leadership necessary for the young Christian community (1:15-26).

Then at Pentecost, some fifty days after Jesus' resurrection, the Spirit came, apparently on the whole band who had gathered in the upper room (2:1). The Spirit's coming was both audible, like the sound of the wind, and visible, as a flame with tongues of fire lapping on the head of each one present (2:2-3).

The result was that all were "filled with the Spirit" and began "to speak in tongues" through the Spirit's leading (2:4). Scholars are sharply divided as to whether the phenomenon was that of *glossolalia* (unintelligible ecstatic speech) such as Paul described in 1 Corinthians 14 or whether it was a miracle

time of prayer was not a surprise. Neither is what happens next! One of the messages of Acts is that the apostles inherited the ministry of Jesus. Therefore, confronted with a beggar who had been lame from birth, they healed him. They did in the name of Jesus what Jesus did so many times. The formerly lame man became remarkably active. He jumped, walked, and leapt, calling attention to himself as he accompanied Peter and John into the temple courts (3:8). Those looking on were amazed at what the lame man could do.

One question raised by Luke's narrative is the identification of the beautiful gate (3:2,10). No other literature from this period of Jewish history refers to such a gate. Perhaps this gate was a doorway on the eastern side of the temple between the outer court and the inner court otherwise known as the gate of Nicanor. This gate, according to other sources, was covered with bronze and considered very beautiful.

3:11-26
Call to Repent

The scene of Peter's next speech, Solomon's Colonnade, was probably a covered area located on the eastern side of the temple, within the Temple walls. As in the case of Pentecost, an apostolic action raised questions that gave Peter an opportunity to preach. This sermon is remarkably like his first sermon in both organization and content. Peter noted the will of God in the life, death, and resurrection of Jesus. He also emphasized the power of God to raise Jesus and the Jewish responsibility for Jesus' death.

unique to Pentecost of speaking in foreign languages.

The latter seems more likely because Luke gave a long catalog of the many nationalities present in Jerusalem who witnessed this event (2:5-13). He stressed that each of these heard the Christians speaking "in their own language" (vv. 6,8). Some would appeal to a "miracle of hearing" in which the Christians would have spoken in ecstatic language that would have been miraculously transformed into the native language of the foreigners as they listened. But this would require almost a greater activity of the Spirit on the nonbelievers than the Christians, and that seems most unlikely.

In a real sense Pentecost witnessed the birth of the church. Its mission began then. The three thousand converted on that day (v. 41) drew from the whole crowd of Pentecost pilgrims and in a real sense anticipated the worldwide mission the remainder of Acts details. At Pentecost all the converts were Jews (v. 5), but they came from all parts of the civilized world, and many doubtless returned to their homeland witnessing to Christ.

The key factor at Pentecost was the gift of the Spirit. In OT times the Spirit of God had often been active in the lives of inspired individuals like the prophets. The new phenomenon, however, was the universal nature of the gift of the Spirit. The Spirit was poured out on *all* the Christian band gathered in the upper room. The gift was to the *whole* church. See the article "The Holy Spirit and Acts."

Peter saw this clearly. So he began his Pentecost sermon by citing Joel's prophecy of the final times in God's saving activity. At that time the Spirit would be poured out on *all* flesh, and all who called on the Lord's name would receive the Spirit and be saved (2:17-21). Hereafter in the Acts narrative the Holy Spirit is a vital part of the conversion experience and a permanent gift to those who are saved (Acts 2:38; 8:17; 9:17; 10:44).

If Pentecost relates the foundation of the church, then the remainder of Acts spells out the implications. In Acts the role of the Spirit is above all that of empowering the church for its witness.

The Spirit gave Peter the courage to address the Jewish Sanhedrin (4:8) and Stephen courage to debate in the Diaspora Jewish synagogues of Jerusalem (6:10). In fact, the Spirit led in every major breakthrough in the expanding Christian mission—with Philip as he witnessed to an Ethiopian eunuch (8:29,39), with Peter's conversion of the Gentile Cornelius (11:12), and with the Antioch church as it commissioned Paul and Barnabas for their missionary journey (13:2).

The Spirit prevented Paul from working in Asia and Bithynia and provided the vision of the Macedonian call that led him to Philippi and his first work on European soil (16:6-10). Paul's courage to undertake the risky trip to Jerusalem and his resolve to witness in the capital city of Rome—these too are the work of the Spirit (19:21; 20:22). Indeed, some would call Acts "the Acts of the Holy Spirit." Luke probably would not reject such a title as inappropriate to his book. Were one to ask him what gave birth to the church, he would undoubtedly point to Pentecost and the gift of the Spirit there and quickly add that the same Spirit constitutes not only the birth but the continuing vitality of the church. □

4:1-31
Prison Leads to Power

Unlike the first sermon the Jewish officials intervened before Peter had an opportunity to issue an invitation. Even though the apostles were arrested and placed in jail overnight, many believed. The number of Christians had now increased to about five thousand (4:4).

The next scene of this section took place before the Sanhedrin, the Jewish governing body composed of priests, Pharisees, and Sadducees. Before the destruction of the temple, the Sadducees were the most powerful party, especially in political terms. The Pharisees, due to their popular support and their relationship with the synagogue, would gain power after the destruction of the temple removed priests from their position of religious power. The Sanhedrin did not play a large role in the trial of Jesus, since the Gospels indicate that Jesus' trial was an illegal appearance before the high priest and his advisors, not before the Sanhedrin itself.

Peter and John had been ordered to appear before the Sanhedrin and account for their actions. They were probably in trouble as much for Peter's message in the temple as for the healing of the lame man. Peter answered with the aid of the Spirit. The power by which the lame man was healed was that of Jesus of Nazareth (4:10). Not only that, but Peter accused the Sanhedrin of responsibility for rejecting and killing Christ. He also noted God's power in raising Jesus from the dead. Peter's speech to the Sanhedrin summarizes his other two sermons to this point.

The response of the council was a political one. Although they were unable to deny the apostolic miracle, the Sanhedrin felt compelled to curtail the apostolic preaching. Before the power of God that transformed "unschooled, ordinary men" (4:13) into powerful proclaimers of the gospel, the Sanhedrin was unable to punish the apostles.

This section ends with a report of the church's prayer in gratitude for God's deliverance of the apostles from the Jewish authorities. Luke recorded again the content of the Gospel: God foretold Jesus' death, both Jews and Gentiles conspired to kill Jesus, and God will empower His church with a resurrection power. In response to their prayer for power and strength, their meeting place was shaken with the presence of the Spirit. The result of His presence was a renewed boldness in proclaiming the gospel.

4:32-37
Summary

This second summary amplifies one of the ideas introduced in the first: their common possessions. The Christians were living in harmony and unity. The proof of their unity was their willingness to share resources with one another. Through the charity of wealthier members, those who were poor received enough. No one among them was "needy" (4:34). This summary prepares the reader for the following story, noting both the encouragement of Barnabas and the fact that some were selling property to support the church.

5:1-11
Ananias and Sapphira

Ananias and Sapphira, like Barnabas, sold some property and gave the proceeds to the church. Unlike Barnabas, they agreed to lie about their profit from the sale. The sin of Ananias and Sapphira was not that they kept some of the profit. Their sin was in lying to God and to the apostles by misrepresenting their giving.

This event had a powerful effect on the church. The moral of the story has little to do with the amount one gives; the importance of giving lies with one's attitude. Ananias and Sapphira gave this offering in order to impress the congregation. The fact that they held money back and asserted that they had given the entire sale price reflected a self-serving attitude, not one that serves God. Also God's quick and decisive punishment threw great fear into the church. Sometimes the New Testament writers used "fear" as a synonym for *worship*. In this case, however, one must assume that the other church members were terrified, a natural response to the power of God.

5:12-42
Conflict with the Sanhedrin

Luke's summary and the story of Ananias and Sapphira have provided an interlude within the larger story of the conflict between the apostles and the Jewish authorities. In the previous section (Acts 3:1–4:31) the Sanhedrin had instructed the apostles not to teach and preach the Gospel. Now the apostles were back in the temple, in Solomon's Colonnade, teaching and performing miracles.

As a result many were being "added to their number" (5:14). The apostles had become quite well known because of their healing.

Luke noted that the persecution of the apostles was motivated by jealousy (5:17). Luke also distinguished between Sadducees and Pharisees. Acts presents some Pharisees in a positive light as believers and protectors of the Christian faith. The Sadducees, the priestly party who did not believe in the resurrection, are presented as the enemies of Christianity. In this case the Sadducees and priests initiated the persecution of the apostles. The apostles were arrested again and placed in jail. This time the jail could not hold them. An angel released them, commanding the apostles to return to the temple courts and to preach the gospel.

The next morning the Sadducees called the Sanhedrin into session in order to try the apostles. Luke identified the Sanhedrin as "the full assembly of the elders of Israel" (5:21). Some have suggested that this note was designed to inform the reader that both Pharisees and Sadducees were fully represented in this council. Others have suggested that Luke was offering a point of comparison to the Roman Senate for his Gentile readers. In either case this trial was a formal one with significant importance.

The trial could not begin without the accused, who had disappeared from prison. In fact, the cell doors were locked, the guards were still in place, but the prisoners were not in the cell. The puzzlement of the chief priests and the captain of the guard (5:24) probably refers both to their wonder at the escape and their questions about the guards' responsibility. Their questions were answered by an unidentified observer, who informed the council that the apostles had returned to the temple. The subsequent rearrest of the apostles was accomplished without force, for fear of the crowd (5:26).

The apostles were accused not only of speaking and preaching, but also of disobeying the Sanhedrin in order to do so. In response the apostles echoed Acts 4:19: "We must obey God rather than men!" (5:29). Again Peter accused the Jews of murdering Jesus, and he proclaimed the resurrection. Peter's words were met with murderous anger.

At this point Gamaliel, identified as a Pharisee, intervened. A respected Pharisee and Paul's teacher, Gamaliel was a student and teacher of the law. Gamaliel was also the voice of moderation. He urged the Sanhedrin to spare the apostles, appealing to the history of other messianic movements.

Josephus, a first-century Jewish historian, mentioned both Theudas and Judas the Galilean as leaders of Jewish uprisings. Josephus, however, dated the uprising of Judas around A.D. 6 and that of Theudas at about A.D. 44 (some ten years after Gamaliel's speech). Either Luke misread Josephus or was not aware of any historical tradition that contradicted his own tradition about Gamaliel's speech.

Persuaded by Gamaliel's speech, the Sanhedrin decided to spare the apostles. They did remind the apostles of the command not to speak and preach. The apostles also received a flogging, probably the traditional thirty-nine lashes (a punishment of forty lashes was considered too harsh, since forty was considered the limit of one's endurance and often caused death). Undaunted by this punishment, the apostles continued to preach and worship, praising God for their ability to suffer for the "Name" of Christ (5:42).

This ends the first major section of Acts. Luke's two major themes have been skillfully interwoven throughout these narratives. The gospel, through God's power, had overcome the barriers of language and persecution. The Spirit had been poured out on the church and empowered the church to minister and grow. The Christian church has been portrayed as a group of devout Jews who wanted nothing more than to be able to worship and minister without obstruction. The Jewish authorities, however, were unwilling to allow the Christians free reign. Therefore the Jews began the process of separation by rejecting the Christian claim to full standing within the Jewish faith.

6:1–8:40
The Seven Spread the Gospel

6:1-6
Appointment of the Seven

The second set of stories about the ministry of the church in the Jewish world concerns the chosen helpers of the apostles: the seven.

The phrase "In those days" links this passage firmly with the accounts of the apostles' ministry in Jerusalem. For the first time a major division confronted the church. Conflicts had arisen between two factions of the disciples: Hellenists and Hebraists ("Grecian Jews" and "Aramaic-speaking Jews"). The Hellenists seem to have been Jewish Christians who spoke only Greek. Their inability to speak Aramaic, the native language of Palestine, would have presented problems in worship. These people also would have been instantly recognized as foreigners or newcomers. The language differences between Greek- and Aramaic-speaking Christians would have rekindled some of the conflict existing within the larger Palestinian Jewish culture.

The conflict came to a head because a large number of Hellenistic widows needed assistance. One of the ministries of the synagogue (and the church) was to provide food and assistance to those widows and children not supported by their relatives. The migration of elderly Jewish couples to Palestine seems to have increased at this time. Women were outliving their husbands, and they had no close relatives who would support them. Thus they fell within the care of the church. Perhaps most of the widows who needed the help of the church were Hellenistic widows, and conflict arose over the proper distribution of food.

The apostles proposed a solution that pleased the entire Christian community. That solution involved selecting a group of men to administer the church's welfare system. Like the apostles, these men were chosen for their wisdom and their spirituality. Their job was considered a ministry as well. The church selected their ministers; the apostles confirmed that choice and set "the seven" apart for their ministry.

This passage never refers to these seven men as "deacons." The word is used as a verb to refer to their ministry; it is also used as a noun to refer to the apostles' "ministry of the word." All seven of those chosen have Greek names and probably were Hellenists. Their ministry seems to have been to the entire church however. The church adapted its structure to the needs of the congregation rather than attempting to squeeze the congregation into an already existing structure. The ministry of the seven was vital to the church. The "deacons" did little serving; they were as involved in the mission activity of the church as the apostles themselves.

Apostolic Preaching

While the many letters in the NT give a full account of the teaching of the apostles, only the Book of Acts actually gives a record of apostolic preaching. In their public preaching, the apostles directed their message to the unconverted. They stressed the gospel of Jesus Christ and preached for conversions. The apostles reserved their doctrinal and ethical instruction for the church (Acts 2:42).

Though only lengthy accounts of preaching by Peter, Paul, and Stephen appear in Acts, their preaching represents the commonly held concept of the gospel. The same basic message of the gospel occurs in the full accounts of preaching. Where only a commentary on preaching occurs, the comment tends to highlight one of the essential elements of the gospel common to full messages.

Peter preached five major sermons in Acts: outside the house where the Holy Spirit fell upon the church (2:14-40), at Solomon's Colonnade (3:11-26), before the rulers and elders (4:8-12), before the Sanhedrin (5:29-32), and before Cornelius and his guests (10:34-43).

Paul preached numerous sermons in Acts, but only three appear in substantial form: at Antioch of Pisidia (13:16-41), at Athens (17:22-31), and before Agrippa (26:2-23). In addition to these, however, a brief commentary on other of his preaching appears: in Damascus (9:20), in Lystra (14:15-17), in Thessalonica (17:2-3), in Corinth (18:5), and in Ephesus (19:14; 20:21).

Acts also makes reference to the content of the preaching of Stephen (7:1-56), Philip (8:5,12,35), and Apollos (18:28). Other places in Acts mention only that the apostles preached the word. Because of the consistency of the message in the other passages, we may assume that when they preached the word, they proclaimed the gospel of Jesus Christ.

The message preached by the apostles had several essential elements in common.

1. They proclaimed that Scripture had been fulfilled. They consistently proved Jesus was the Christ in accordance with, rather than in contradiction to, Scripture. Their message of salvation had continuity with all God had been doing from creation on to save people. They did not bring a new religion but the climax of all God had promised.

2. The fulfillment came in the person of Jesus, whom they proclaimed as Messiah or Christ: Son of David and Son of God.

3. Salvation comes through the death, burial, and resurrection of Jesus, who has ascended to the right hand of God from whence He will come again to judge the world.

4. Salvation consists in the forgiveness of sins and the gift of the Holy Spirit. When sin is taken away and the Holy Spirit comes in, a person has received eternal life.

5. The appropriate response to this gospel is repentance toward God and faith in the Lord Jesus. Believers made this response public through baptism.

When the apostles took the message beyond the Jews, they had to lay a foundation that was unnecessary where people shared the same theological presuppositions. At Lystra and Athens, Paul had to begin by declaring the Creator God (14:15-17; 17:22-31).

Peter could speak to Jews in Jerusalem of Jesus as Lord, a holy title among the Jews. The Gentiles used the term "lord" very loosely.

To express the same divine title, Paul spoke of Christ as the Son of God. Peter did not explain the relationship between the death of Christ and the forgiveness of sins. The Jewish law made clear that atonement came through blood sacrifice. Peter did not need to explain it. For the Gentiles, however, Paul explained the relationship, especially in his letters, that Christ died for our sins (1 Cor 15:3). □

6:7
Summary

Like other summaries in Acts, this verse concludes one section and begins another. Often people were introduced in Acts before they became major characters in the narrative. In this section Luke introduced Stephen and Philip; both would play major roles in the spread of the gospel. His introduction of the seven and Hellenists also provided backdrop for Saul's presence at the stoning of Stephen. Luke's reference to the continuing growth of the church and the conversion of priests continued the theme of church growth. It also set the stage for Stephen's speech in the next passage.

6:8-15
Stephen on Trial

Stephen's important role in Acts was foreshadowed by the way Luke introduced him in 6:5 ("a man full of faith and of the Holy Spirit"). Stephen had been acting more like an apostle than a deacon. He had been doing miracles, and none of the Hellenistic Jews could win an argument with him. The reference to the Synagogue of the Freedmen and the national groups that follow in 6:9, may refer to as many as five separate synagogues. One synagogue that held all of these groups, however, makes considerably more sense. The name "Freedmen" may refer to their identity as former slaves or descendants of captives taken from Palestine during the Diaspora.

These men were disturbed by Stephen's preaching and ministry. Their plan to stop him included conspiracy, perjury, and mob psychology. They charged Stephen with blasphemy against the temple and the law. The trial provided a forum for Stephen to speak with passion and persuasion in the triumph of the Spirit. Before Stephen spoke, Luke reminded us of his power; for his face looked like that of an angel, a true sign of God's presence with him.

7:1-53
Stubborn Denial

Stephen's speech was an important part of Luke's narrative. On the one hand, the speech explained Stephen's execution and showed him to be an eloquent and effective speaker. The speech also provided the theological foundation for the gospel's movement into the Gentile world. Stephen did not address the charges as such but used them as a springboard for this message so important to the early church and to Acts.

Three main ideas were addressed by Stephen. The first was the Jewish reverence for the "holy land." Most Jews were convinced that the land was God's greatest gift to

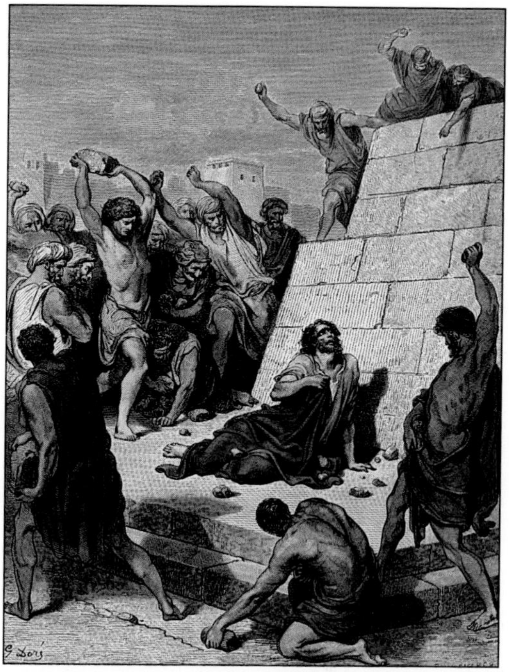

The stoning of Stephen (see Acts 7:54-60)

them, and they considered Palestine to be the place where God lived and worked. Stephen denied that God was tied to the land, recounting the history of the patriarchs (Abraham, Isaac, Jacob/Israel) and showing that God worked in their lives much more outside the promised land than within (7:2-36). Second, Stephen showed that Moses, the one venerated by the Jews as the great giver of the law, had been constantly disobeyed by the Jews. Stephen cited the idol worship of the Israelites at Mount Sinai as proof. Finally, Stephen noted that God allowed Solomon to build the temple because the Jews demanded it; God Himself was satisfied with the nomadic life of the tabernacle.

Stephen's speech climaxed in strong words toward the Jews. He termed them "stiff-necked" (a common Old Testament reference to stubbornness) and accused them of denying God's prophets, Spirit, and Messiah. In response to the charge that he had blasphemed against God, Moses, and the temple, Stephen accused the Jews of failing to obey the law of which they were so proud.

7:54–8:3
Prayer for Forgiveness

By this time the scene had ceased to resemble a trial. The crowd reacted to Stephen's words with hostility and anger. Stephen was filled with the Spirit and had a vision of

Jesus in heaven. At this the crowd rushed at Stephen, "dragged him out of the city, and began to stone him" (7:58). Paul witnessed and approved this "execution" (7:58; 8:1). Stephen died with the words of Jesus on his lips, asking God to receive his spirit and to forgive the crowd.

This speech is important as one attempts to understand the way in which the gospel moved from its Jewish beginnings to a Gentile world. That the Jews rejected the gospel should be no surprise. Stephen's speech asserted that they had rejected the will of God throughout their history as chosen people.

8:4-8
In Samaria

In the face of the persecution following Stephen's death, the Christians were scattered. As they spread throughout the area, they also spread the gospel. Philip, one of the seven, found his way into Samaria. As with Stephen, the power of the Holy Spirit was present in the work of Philip. Philip's words and deeds produced a tremendous outpouring of faith among the Samaritans.

Jews and Samaritans did not like each other. Their rivalry had its roots during the time when David's kingdom split into the Northern Kingdom of Israel and the Southern Kingdom of Judah. The captivity of Israel by Assyria and resulting intermarriage between Assyrians and northern Jews produced the racial mix known as Samaritans. The Samaritans worshiped on Mount Gerazim and accepted only the first five books of the Old Testament. The conflict between Jews and Samaritans had religious and political overtones. The two groups simply avoided each other. Philip's work in Samaria was a bold step in the spread of the gospel.

8:9-25
Ineffective Magic

Simon the Sorcerer (sometimes called Simon Magnus) stands in contrast to Philip and his works. Simon had held power in Samaria "for some time" as a result of his ability to do miracles (8:9-11). Simon was a magician, and magic was a significant form of religious expression in the ancient world. As a result of Philip's ministry, many Samaritans came to faith, including Simon. The first portion of this passage reveals the power of the Holy Spirit to overcome any other kind of religious expression. Philip's miracles were done by the power of the Spirit, not through the power of magic or pagan religions.

In order to make the Samaritans full members of the Christian church, the apostles prayed and laid hands on them. The Samaritans received the Holy Spirit, an activity portrayed as separate from baptism. This separation has provided a mandate for the tradition of separating baptism from confirmation and the Pentecostal doctrine of a baptism of the Holy Spirit subsequent to water baptism. In context, however, Luke seems to have focused more on the significance of the Holy Spirit's manifestation than on the chronological order of the events. The animosity that characterized the relationship between Samaritans and Jews would have hindered the acceptance of Samaritan converts by the church in Jerusalem. Peter and John, pillars of the Jerusalem church, were sent to investigate the reports of Samaritan converts. Their approval of Philip's evangelistic efforts would effect a smooth entry of Samaritan converts into the fellowship of the Christian church. The outpouring of the Spirit in this passage (probably manifested by their speaking in tongues) added the witness of the Spirit to the validity of their salvation.

Not all of the Samaritans had experienced a valid salvation. Certainly Simon, even though he had been baptized (8:13), was not a model Christian. Seeing the power of the apostles to confer the Holy Spirit through the laying on of hands, Simon offered to buy that power. Perhaps he considered it to be another kind of magic. Peter's response was harsh; he consigned Simon and his money to hell. We are left to draw our own conjectures about Simon's future actions and eternal destiny. This passage provided the name for the practice of buying offices within the hierarchy of the church. "Simony" was common enough to be outlawed at many points during the history of the church.

8:26-40
Salvation for a Eunuch

Philip's evangelistic activity did not end with Samaria. He was also chosen to participate in another advance of the gospel beyond the precincts of the Jewish people. In response to the prompting of an angel, Philip went to a certain road in the desert and met an Ethiopian traveling home from a visit to Jerusalem. Philip was offered the chance to explain Scripture to the Ethiopian, witness to him about Jesus, and baptize him before being transported to another region by the power of the Spirit. On the surface this passage seems an inspiring narrative about the power of the gospel.

The Ethiopian was called a eunuch. This name was used of highly placed bureaucratic officials as well as those with the actual physical deformity, since eunuchs had traditionally filled the most sensitive spots within governments. This person's physical condition is unclear. Our uncertainty about the physical condition of the eunuch (was he really emasculated or merely described that

Wall from the New Testament time period in the city of Damascus. The window on this wall is traditionally accepted as the opening from which Paul was lowered to escape from the city. See Acts 9:25.

way because he was a high official?) leads to uncertainty about his spiritual standing. The Jewish law did not allow eunuchs to enter the temple to worship (Deut 23:1), although Isaiah 56:3-5 mitigated the law somewhat by referring to eunuchs as recipients of God's love.

Perhaps the context of this story gives us the clearest indication of its importance. The conversion of the Ethiopian is situated between Philip's work in Samaria (in which one racial barrier is overcome) and the conversion of Cornelius in Acts 10. From a literary standpoint we would assume that these stories serve as steps in the gospel's transition from the Jews to Gentiles. If this were the case, then we would consider the Ethiopian to have been a true eunuch, whose ability to worship God would always be limited by his physical deformity under the Jewish law. The Spirit, having broken down the racial barrier that denied Samaritan half-breeds religious access to God, now had broken down a physical barrier to faith as well. None will be judged based on racial or physical characteristics; entry into the kingdom depends solely on spiritual relationship with God.

Stephen and Philip might be overlooked in deference to the importance of the apostles, but Luke set the stage through them for the conversion of the first Gentile. The gospel has been proclaimed through the power of the Spirit "in Jerusalem, and in all Judea and Samaria" by the twelve and the seven (1:8). Preparations were being made to carry the gospel unhindered to the "ends of the earth."

9:1-30
God Calls Saul

9:1-19a
Persecuting the Church

Saul played a large part in God's plan to take the gospel to the Gentile world. We have already met Saul at the stoning of Stephen. He was the person who held the coats of the crowd and assented to Stephen's death (7:58–8:1). In addition, Saul has been portrayed as a ravager of the church (8:3). He represents everything wrong with the Jewish response to Christianity. Saul was a Hellenistic Jew, perhaps one of those who spent so much time disputing with Stephen. He was also full of energy and zeal, characteristics God would use for the spread of the gospel.

The miracles done by Philip and the success of the gospel in both Samaria and with the Ethiopian have been exciting stories. The gospel seems to be overcoming even the persecution the Christians were experiencing just two chapters before. In reality, though, all was not well; Saul was still seeking out Christians to put them in prison. In fact, he had made "murderous threats" against the members of the church (9:1). On a trip from Jerusalem to Damascus, Saul met the risen Christ. The brilliant light that accompanied the voice of Jesus was a common Old Testament symbol of God's presence. This voice left no doubt in Saul's mind that he was in the presence of the Christ. This encounter left Saul physically blind for three days.

After that time Saul was visited by Ananias, a disciple living in Damascus. Ananias had the most difficult job in this story. He was charged with the task of sharing God's message and mercy with Saul, the most hated enemy of the Christians. In fact, Ananias argued with God until God revealed His plan for Saul (9:15-16). Through the ministry of Ananias, Saul was cured of his blindness and brought into the family of faith.

The traditional house of Simon the tanner in Joppa where Peter received his famous vision from God (see Acts 9:43).

9:19b-30
Call to the Gentiles

Immediately Saul began to preach in the synagogues, serving the gospel with all of the zeal he had formerly used to persecute it. In fact, Saul was so successful that the Jews in Damascus plotted to kill him, forcing him to escape over the wall and go to Jerusalem. There the disciples were still afraid of Saul's reputation, until Barnabas, still acting as an encourager, vouched for Saul's sincerity and effectiveness in Damascus. Saul's custom of sharing the gospel and debating "Grecian Jews" forced him to leave Jerusalem and return to his home of Tarsus.

Saul was not "converted" in the way we tend to think of conversion. Saul was forced to accept Jesus as the risen Christ, the culmination of the Jewish religion. We would be much more correct to think of this experience as God's call of Saul into the service of Christ. When Paul referred to this experience in Galatians, he used the language of the prophetic call. As it had with the prophets, the word of the Lord came to Paul in that personal encounter. The Lord's words to Ananias clarified Saul's task as that of prophet and evangelist. Saul would be responsible for taking the gospel to the Gentile world.

9:31–12:24
Peter Ministers in Syria

9:31-43
Peter Performs Miracles

This section of Acts begins with one of Luke's summary statements. The activity of the apostles and the seven had resulted in the spread of the gospel throughout Judea, Galilee, and Samaria. This summary statement also prepares the reader to resume the narrative of the gospel's spread, a narrative interrupted by the story of Paul's call.

The only area yet to be evangelized is that of "the ends of the earth" (1:8). The mission to the Gentiles was Paul's special task; introducing the gospel to a Gentile audience had been reserved for Peter. Peter had been "traveling about the country" encouraging the disciples in their faith (9:32). During that time he healed both Aeneas, an invalid for eight years, and Tabitha/Dorcas, a recently deceased disciple. Both of these miracles strengthened the faith of the disciples (9:35,42).

Peter had been staying with Simon, "a tanner" (9:43). Some have suggested that Peter had little concern for keeping the demands of the law, since Jewish lawyers considered those who tanned skins to be "unclean." Peter's place of lodging fits into the pattern of the passage, however, working with other clues to prepare the reader for a Gentile conversion.

10:1-8
Cornelius's Vision

Cornelius's conversion is recounted in four steps. Significant emphasis is placed on the power of God and the work of the Holy Spirit that brings this event to completion. Peter had been led to the right place at the right time. Luke began with Cornelius's encounter with the angel of God (10:1-8). Cornelius was a Roman centurion, but he and his household were "devout and God-fearing" (10:2). He was generous and had a good reputation within the Jewish community of Caesarea. Luke may have meant to characterize Cornelius as one of those Gentiles who practiced the Jewish faith. The term "God-fearing" in this case, though, does not necessarily imply anything more than devout, moral, and monotheistic behavior. Cornelius's religious practices had been acceptable to God, whether or not Cornelius was worshiping as a Jew, for the angel mentioned Cornelius's gifts and work with the poor as the reason for God's favor. Cornelius's vision was only a prelude to conversion, since it ended with the command to send to Joppa for Peter.

10:9-23a
Nothing Unclean

On the day after Cornelius's vision, Peter climbed to the top of Simon's house around noon, perhaps to rest between meals. Noon in Palestine was not necessarily a time for eating; often noon would be a midway point between the meals of the day. Peter's presence on the roof probably indicated his desire to find a cool sea breeze and escape the heat of the day.

As Peter waited for the meal, he "fell into a trance" and had a vision (10:10). Jews followed strict rules concerning religious purity. Eating was an area in which these rules were especially important, for God had called many foods "unclean" and had forbidden Jews to eat them. Jews and Gentiles rarely ate together, since Gentiles could not be relied upon to eat only those foods that were "clean." Peter's vision denied any distinction between "clean" and "unclean." Peter had no sooner awakened from his vision than the messengers arrived to request his visit to Cornelius. Again Cornelius's religious credentials and the content of his vision were narrated, this time to Peter.

10:23b-48
The Gospel for Gentiles

The third episode of this narrative occurred at the home of Cornelius. Peter and some Jewish-Christian representatives from the community at Joppa had journeyed to Caesarea (about thirty miles) to visit Cornelius. Because

Artist's reconstruction of ancient Caesarea Maritima where Paul was imprisoned for two years (Acts 23:31–26:32). See also Acts 10:1.

of his vision on the roof of Simon's house, Peter was willing to share the gospel message, even with Gentiles (10:27-29).

Peter's sermon is similar to those in Acts 2 and 5, although it contains more information about the life and teaching of Jesus than do those addressed to Jewish audiences in Jerusalem. Peter and his Jewish companions watched in amazement as the Holy Spirit filled Cornelius and the other Gentiles with unmistakable signs of His presence, "while Peter was still speaking" (10:44). Peter had no choice but to offer them baptism and full fellowship in the community. This passage affirmed the power of God to break down even the strongest barriers of prejudice.

This passage also teaches us to be careful of being too positive about the methods of the Holy Spirit. One of the most common arguments in Christendom concerns the way in which a Christian receives the Holy Spirit. Many believe that the Spirit comes sometime after one's confession of faith and may even necessitate a second baptism. Many events in Acts, such as Pentecost, can be interpreted to support such a view. The conversion of Cornelius, though, must be taken into account to offer a more balanced picture of the events surrounding conversion and full acceptance into the kingdom of God. For Cornelius the gift of the Spirit preceded baptism. In fact, this gift was a necessary proof of the validity of Cornelius's conversion. We cannot separate a Christian's confession of faith from the reception of the Holy Spirit. The only valid salvation experience must include both.

11:1-18
Who Can Oppose God?

The final episode happened in Jerusalem. The events in Caesarea were soon reported to the Jerusalem church.

The Cilician Gates through the Taurus Mountains northwest of Antioch of Syria through which Paul passed on his journeys.

The Jewish Christians accused Peter not of preaching improperly but of going "into the house of uncircumcised men" and eating with them (11:3). Peter responded by recounting the events surrounding the conversion of Cornelius, including his vision and the presence of the Spirit. The testimony of Peter and his six companions convinced those in Jerusalem.

The conversion of Cornelius was the crowning achievement of Peter's mission to the Jews. Peter's involvement in breaking down this final barrier to a worldwide spread of the gospel was no coincidence. No other leader commanded the same respect as Peter; his testimony was undeniable. Peter's words provide a fitting summary of this vital passage: "Who was I to think that I could oppose God!" (11:17). Luke's message is that no one can oppose God or the spread of His gospel. The stage was now set for the work of Paul, who would carry the gospel beyond the boundaries of Palestine.

Luke followed the conversion of Cornelius with two stories. The first reintroduced Saul/Paul, Barnabas, and the church at Antioch, the "home" church that supported their journeys into Asia Minor and Greece. The second of these stories provided a sense of closure to the ministry of Peter, relating his miraculous escape from Herod's prison.

11:19-30
Called Christians

The church at Antioch of Syria represented another step in the movement of the gospel beyond Judea and Syria. Soon after the news and acceptance of Cornelius's conversion, the church at Jerusalem received word of a community in Antioch. This community was founded by disciples dispersed after the martyrdom of Stephen and included both Jewish and Gentile Christians. In order to confirm and strengthen their faith, Barnabas was sent to them by the church in Jerusalem. When he saw the potential for growth in Antioch, Barnabas found Saul in Tarsus and returned to Antioch. Together they worked with the first people called "Christians" for about a year (11:26).

Luke dated the famine in Jerusalem squarely within the chronology of the Roman Empire. In fact, Luke's dating of this empirewide famine within the reign of Claudius has been confirmed by a number of other ancient sources, including the Roman historian Suetonius. Luke's main reason for mentioning the famine, though, was to show that the Gentile Christians in Antioch participated in the famine relief effort.

12:1-24
Believing God's Miracles

During this period, Herod touched off another round of persecution. This time the persecution of Christians was as much political as religious, since Herod could hardly have been considered a religious man. Such a persecution could have had religious motivations, though, if only for the political attempt to please the Jewish authorities. James, the brother of John and one of the pillars of the Jerusalem church, was executed. Peter was arrested.

Peter anticipated a fate similar to that of James as he awaited the "public trial" Herod planned for him (12:4). Herod's plans were thwarted, however, by God's deliverance of Peter from prison. Unquestionably a miracle was involved in Peter's release, since Herod had commanded that Peter be guarded by "four squads of four soldiers each" (12:4). Ironically, no one in this story was able to comprehend or believe that Peter had escaped from prison. Those gathered at the house of Peter's sister and nephew (John Mark) were unwilling to believe that Peter has escaped (even though their purpose for gathering had been to pray for Peter's release). Even the soldiers and Herod had no idea what had happened to Peter. Only the servant girl, Rhoda, was willing to believe, and no one

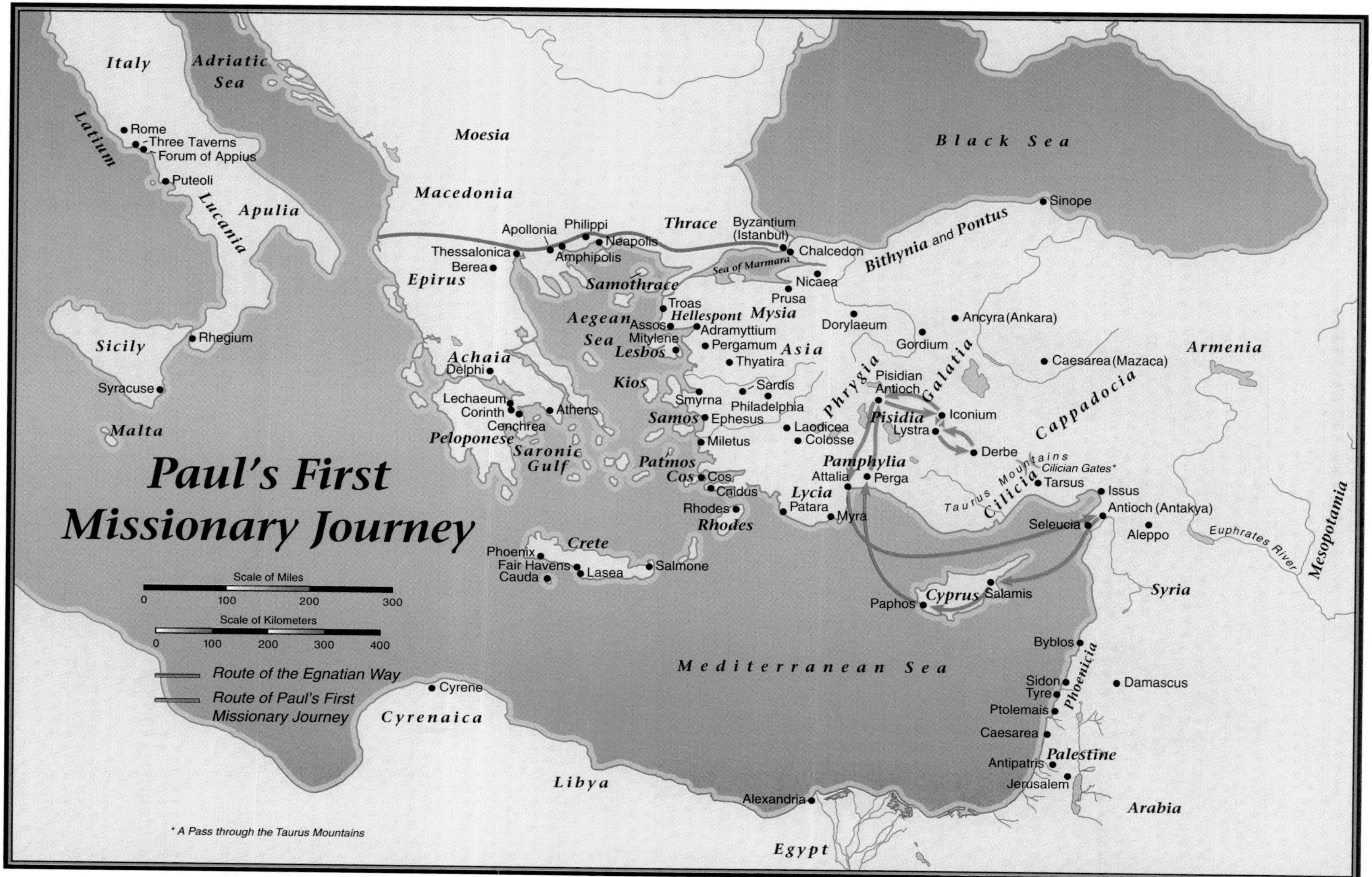

Paul's First Missionary Journey
Italy
Adriatic Sea
Latium
Rome
Three Taverns
Forum of Appius
Puteoli
Lucania
Apulia
Sicily
Rhegium
Syracuse
Malta
Moesia
Macedonia
Epirus
Apollonia
Philippi
Thessalonica
Amphipolis
Neapolis
Berea
Thrace
Byzantium (Istanbul)
Chalcedon
Sea of Marmara
Samothrace
Nicaea
Prusa
Bithynia and Pontus
Black Sea
Sinope
Troas
Hellespont
Mysia
Aegean Sea
Assos
Mitylene
Lesbos
Adramyttium
Pergamum
Asia
Thyatira
Achaia
Delphi
Kios
Sardis
Smyrna
Philadelphia
Lechaeum
Corinth
Cenchrea
Athens
Peloponese
Saronic Gulf
Samos
Ephesus
Miletus
Laodicea
Colosse
Patmos
Cos
Cnidus
Rhodes
Lycia
Patara
Myra
Attalia
Perga
Pamphylia
Phrygia
Pisidia
Pisidian Antioch
Galatia
Iconium
Lystra
Derbe
Dorylaeum
Gordium
Ancyra (Ankara)
Caesarea (Mazaca)
Cappadocia
Armenia
Taurus Mountains
Cilician Gates*
Cilicia
Tarsus
Issus
Antioch (Antakya)
Seleucia
Aleppo
Euphrates River
Mesopotamia
Syria
Crete
Phoenix
Fair Havens
Lasea
Cauda
Salmone
Cyprus
Salamis
Paphos
Byblos
Phoenicia
Sidon
Tyre
Ptolemais
Caesarea
Damascus
Palestine
Antipatris
Jerusalem
Arabia
Mediterranean Sea
Cyrene
Cyrenaica
Libya
Alexandria
Egypt
Scale of Miles
0
100
200
300
Scale of Kilometers
0
100
200
300
400
Route of the Egnatian Way
Route of Paul's First Missionary Journey
* A Pass through the Taurus Mountains

Pictured above is the south Hellenistic gate of the ancient city of Perga in Pamphylia (modern Turkey). It was at this point in the first missionary journey that John Mark left Paul to return to Jerusalem. See Acts 13:13.

would believe her testimony (12:15).

This first major section of the Book of Acts ends with the death of Herod and a summary statement. Luke implied that Herod's death was also related to his persecution of the Jewish Christians. This first section announces the spread of the gospel, even in the face of tremendous barriers and persecution. The missionary ministry would continue that same trend through the power of the Holy Spirit.

With the help of the Holy Spirit, the gospel spread with amazing results throughout "Jerusalem, and in all Judea and Samaria" (1:8). Peter was instrumental in beginning the transition from a Jewish church to one composed of Jews and Gentiles. The rest of Luke's history relates the missionary activity of Paul, apostle to the Gentiles.

12:25–15:41
Paul Journeys through Asia Minor

12:25–13:3
Paul and Barnabas Commissioned

Acts portrays Paul as the great missionary, blazing trails for Christianity in areas that have never heard the gospel. Each new journey finds Paul further away from the geographical roots of the faith. His activity was vitally important to the advance of the gospel.

The church at Antioch was important to Paul and to the Gentile ministry. In fact, mention of the church reminds the reader of the connection between Paul and Barnabas and the Christians at Antioch (11:26). Antioch served as a base from which Paul's journeys began, and he maintained close ties to the believers there throughout his missionary career. In this respect we must note that those in Antioch (that Luke recorded their names indicates their importance) were open to the leadership of the Holy Spirit. Once again we are reminded of the role of the Spirit in the advance of the gospel. Here the Spirit's command to call and commission Paul and Barnabas was quickly obeyed.

13:4-12
Cyprus

The evangelization of Cyprus paralleled that of Samaria. First, Paul and his companions were chosen by the Spirit. Second, Paul and the gospel had to overcome opposition in the form of magic. Elymas the sorcerer was as formida-

Shown above is the traditional site of the mythical birth of the goddess Aphrodite in the ocean just off the coast of the island of Cyprus visited by Paul (see Acts 13:4-12).

ble an opponent for Paul as Simon Magnus was for Peter. In Elymas, Paul faced not only the threat of magic but that of Jewish opposition as well. Paul's triumph in this event showed the power of the gospel (and the Spirit) to deal with any opposition, especially that of magic. This event also resulted in faith on the part of the Roman proconsul, Sergius Paulus (13:12). Finally, almost as a footnote, Luke said that Saul's other name is Paul. Up to this point Luke had referred to Paul by his Hebrew name, without any indication of the social status Paul enjoyed. As Paul moved closer to the center of the Roman Empire, Luke switched names.

13:13-52
Antioch of Pisidia

The split between Paul and John Mark poses one of the more puzzling questions in the New Testament. Commentators have offered solutions that range from physical illness and homesickness on John Mark's part to significant disagreement among the missionaries over who would lead the party, where they would go, and to whom the gospel would be preached. Perhaps John Mark was opposed to the conversion of Sergius Paulus and the inclusion of Gentiles in the church. Whatever the case, John Mark returned to Jerusalem at this point. The schism was so deep that Paul was unwilling to allow him to accompany them on a subsequent journey. Paul's Epistles indicate that he and John Mark were later reconciled (Col 4:10; Phil 24; 2 Tim 4:11).

Certainly the basic focus of their mission had not changed. As in Cyprus, Paul and Barnabas began their evangelistic activity with the Jews in Antioch of Pisidia. In fact, Luke's narrative of their mission there would provide a pattern of missionary activity Paul and his companions followed in almost every case. They began their ministry by preaching in the synagogue, a privilege

Ruins of the Roman aqueduct at ancient Antioch of Pisidia visited by Paul (see Acts 13:13-52)

Stone slab with the Latin inscription "LUSTRA" found at the ancient site of Lystra that helped archaeologists identify the site. Now at the museum at Konya, Turkey (ancient Iconium).

accorded them as traveling teachers. Many Jews and Gentile "God-fearers" were intrigued by their message and desired to hear more. The Jewish leaders, jealous and angry at Paul's success, would stir up the crowd and reject Paul, leaving him no other option than to present the gospel to the Gentiles and any who would accept his message. Usually this resulted in persecution and the need to move to another place of ministry, where the pattern would begin again.

Just as Paul's activity in Antioch provided a pattern for other evangelistic activity, so his address to the synagogue in Antioch provided an example of Paul's gospel. Paul's presentation was remarkably like that of Peter and Stephen, designed to prove that Jesus was the Messiah who had been promised in the Old Testament, that Jesus had risen from the dead in spite of His crucifixion, and that those who believed in Jesus had a chance for forgiveness and reconciliation with God. Paul's speech was so effective that many "followed Paul and Barnabas," and "almost the whole city" returned to hear him on the next Sabbath (13:13-14). The Jewish leaders responded to Paul's popularity with jealousy and abuse. Since the Jews had rejected the gospel, Paul and Barnabas made it clear that the gospel would be given to the Gentiles.

The Jews responded to the spread of the gospel by inciting "the God-fearing women of high standing and the leading men of the city" (13:50) and persecuting the missionaries. Paul and Barnabas, forced to move on, symbolized their rejection of the unbelievers by shaking the dust from their feet. One must take careful note of the mention of women in Acts, especially as women became targets for Paul's evangelism. Romans were very nervous about the combination of women and religion. Many of their religions were dominated by women as participants and leaders. Even prostitution had religious overtones, since most of the prostitutes were "priestesses" in pagan temples. Women were essentially powerless in Roman society, and religion gave them an arena in which they could wield some influence and authority. Pagan religious ceremonies offered more than a place of power for women, however. They often resulted in alcohol-aided celebrations. Husbands of women involved in these religious ceremonies took great care to ensure that men and women did not "worship" together and became uneasy at any hint of impropriety. Paul and the Christian church often struggled to convince people that their worship was different from other religious ceremonies. Therefore when the Jews incited leading women, that posed a serious problem for Paul.

14:1-7
Iconium

Paul and Barnabas left Antioch of Pisidia to go eastward to Iconium. There the pattern of evangelism was essentially the same as that in Antioch. Once again the way in which the missionaries spoke in the synagogue provided access to many of the people in the town, both Jews and Gentile. Once again the Jews "stirred up the Gentiles" (14:2) and tried to have Paul and Barnabas stoned. The missionaries discovered the plot and fled to the southern part of the province of Galatia, to Lystra and Derbe.

14:8-20
Lystra

In Lystra the pattern of evangelism was different. Paul's influence in the town did not begin with speaking in the synagogue. In fact, Paul was speaking in the marketplace when he healed a man who had been lame from birth (14:8). This miracle caused the local people to confer divinity on Paul and Barnabas, considering Barnabas to be Zeus in human form and Paul to be his messenger, Hermes. This went so far that the priest from the temple of Zeus tried to worship Barnabas.

Two things are interesting about this passage. The first is Luke's note that the people spoke in the "Lycaonian language" (14:11). This reference not only explained why it took Paul and Barnabas so long to understand what was going on, but it also implied that these people were ignorant, uneducated, and superstitious. Therefore we should not be surprised at their pagan reaction to the miracles of God. A second note about this passage concerns the parallel between this miracle and that of Peter in 3:1-8. In both instances an apostle healed a man "lame from birth" in a public place. Here is an indication not only of the power of the Holy Spirit but of Paul's status as an apostle equal to Peter.

Paul's ministry in Lystra ended as other ministries

ended. Jews from Antioch and Iconium, having followed Paul to Lystra, stirred up the crowd who stoned Paul and left him for dead. Luke's matter-of-fact narration obscures the fact that the ministrations of the other believers miraculously revived (or resurrected) Paul, and he returned to the city. This must have been a great encouragement to the believers and a great surprise to those who thought they had killed Paul!

14:21-28
Return to Antioch of Syria

Paul and Barnabas ended their mission work by retracing their steps through all of the churches that had been established. Importantly, they "appointed elders" for each of the churches (14:23). More than likely these were men who had shown wisdom and the ability to motivate the churches to continue the work begun by Paul and Barnabas. These verses give no indication that Paul and Barnabas established any kind of church hierarchy or ordained these men into a professional ministry. The missionary journey ended where it began, at Antioch of Syria. Paul and Barnabas reported all that had happened in Asia Minor, with special emphasis on the way God "had opened the door of faith to the Gentiles" (14:27).

15:1-35
Jerusalem Council

Acts 15 is a transitional passage, giving closure to the first journey and laying the foundation for Paul's second missionary journey. Because the Jerusalem council resolved a conflict that was created through Paul's work in his first journey, however, Acts 15 seems to fit more clearly as a final part of Paul's initial work among the Gentiles.

One issue faced this council of Christian leaders in Jerusalem, Gentiles in the church. While Paul and Barnabas were in Antioch after their journey, others came from Judea to teach the necessity of circumcision for salvation. One learns from Paul's Letters that he was often opposed by such people, whom he termed "Judaizers." The dispute between Paul and the Judaizers became the central issue that confronted the mother church in Jerusalem. In spite of a challenge to Paul's gospel in the assembly from some believers who were also Pharisees (15:5), the decision of the elders and apostles was affected by the testimony of Peter, Paul, and Barnabas. Peter's speech reminded the council of the work of the Holy Spirit in the conversion of the first Gentile, Cornelius. Paul and Barnabas also referred to the miraculous work of God in their experiences with the Gentiles. To James, the brother of Jesus and the leader of the Jerusalem church, was left the final statement. Theologically, the Gentiles would not be hindered from becoming Christians; they would not be required to undergo circumcision. Practically, however, the council requested that Gentile Christians refrain from practices that would put a strain on their relationship with Jewish Christians.

15:36-41
Paul and Barnabas Split

After some time in Antioch, Paul and Barnabas made ready to return to Asia Minor and check on the churches they had established. They were unable to agree on traveling companions, for Barnabas suggested taking John Mark again. Luke gave little more idea of Paul's objections to John Mark's presence than he did the first time (13:13). Barnabas and Mark went to Cyprus, but Paul chose Silas and began the second journey through Asia Minor and Greece.

16:1–18:22
Paul Journeys through Greece

16:1-5
Lystra

The second missionary foray from Antioch began as an attempt to retrace Paul's earlier journey. It led Paul even further away from Palestine, into Greece itself.

Paul's first evangelistic tour went as far as Lystra and Derbe. When Paul and Barnabas left that area of Asia Minor the Jews were so opposed to their ministry that the missionaries had been forced to leave rather hurriedly. Now Paul returned to this area as a foundation for the work that was to be done. Paul's stated purpose for this trip was to strengthen the churches that had been established in the earlier journey. The focus of his visit to Lystra, however, was upon one previously made a disciple in

A view of the tell of ancient Lystra (see Acts 14:8-20)

that town: Timothy. Paul accepted the recommendation of the believers in the area and took Timothy as a companion. Paul circumcised Timothy in order to make his presence acceptable to Jewish Christians. This circumcision was justified on the basis that Timothy was, by virtue of his mother's family, Jewish. By the decision of the Jerusalem Council, Timothy's circumcision should not have been necessary; obviously Paul found Timothy's circumcision to be an asset to his ministry.

16:6-40
Philippi

Paul and his companions had been traveling throughout the western half of Asia Minor, strengthening existing

Roman Provinces

Rome's primary administrative division for its overseas territories was that of the province. Although the use of the term *province* is rare in the New Testament (only in Acts 23:34; 25:1), there are many references to the provinces by name.

The Roman provincial system was set up over subject territories as a means of maintaining peace and collecting tribute. In the NT period (mid-first century A.D.) there were thirty-two such provinces in all. Eleven were designated as senatorial provinces under the jurisdiction of a proconsul, who usually served a one-year term of office.

Senatorial provinces were those territories where the peace was secure, and the proconsul usually had only a small military detachment under his command. In contrast were the twenty-one imperial provinces. These were under the jurisdiction of an imperial legate (or governor) who was appointed by the Roman emperor and served an open-ended term of office.

Full Roman legions (six thousand soldiers) were maintained in imperial provinces, since these were territories along the frontiers of the empire or places where revolt against Roman rule might arise.

In addition to the provinces were territories under the rule of a client-king, who was loyal to Rome and paid tribute to the empire. Many of the first-century provinces originated as such client-states, which were eventually ceded to Rome by the rulers. Thus Bithynia became a province in 74 B.C. when its king turned it over to direct Roman rule.

In the same manner Pamphylia became a province in 189 B.C.; Galatia, in 25 B.C.; and Cappadocia, in A.D. 17. Other territories were organized into provinces after Rome conquered them in war, such as Macedonia and Achaia in 148 B.C.

The official status of Judea is somewhat unclear. It was a client-state under Herod and his sons but later came under Roman procurators during the ministries of Jesus and Paul. During this period it still may have maintained its client-state status, with the procurator sharing jurisdiction with the Jewish high priest and being subject to the governor of Syria. See the article "Pilate."

After the Roman suppression of the Jewish revolt in A.D. 70, Judea was definitely organized as a Roman imperial province.

One often encounters provincial names in Paul's Letters and in the Pauline portion of Acts. Paul himself was born in Tarsus, a city of Cilicia, which in his day was a part of the province of Syria. Likewise in Syria were Damascus, where Paul was converted, and Antioch, where the church was located that sponsored him on his missionary journeys.

On his first mission Paul worked in the senatorial province of Crete and converted the Roman proconsul there (Acts 13:12). From Crete, Paul went to Perga in the imperial province of Pamphylia and from there to Lystra, Antioch, and Iconium, all cities in his day belonging to the imperial province of Galatia.

On his second missionary journey Paul worked in the Greek-speaking senatorial provinces of Macedonia and Achaia. Philippi and Thessalonica are located in Macedonia; Athens and Corinth are located in Achaia. The primary focus of his journey was Ephesus, capital of the senatorial province of Asia. Other provinces mentioned briefly in the Acts narrative of Paul's journeys are Bithynia, along the Black Sea, and Lycia, just west of Pamphylia and under joint provincial administration with it.

Paul preferred to use provincial names when referring to these churches rather than the cities where the churches were located. "Achaia" was his word for Corinth, and "Asia" was his word for Ephesus. When he spoke of "Macedonia," it was not always clear whether he had Philippi or Thessalonica in mind.

Other NT writers referred to the Roman provinces. First Peter is addressed to the Christians in the provinces of Asia Minor—former Bithynia, Galatia, Asia, and Cappadocia (1:1). Revelation is addressed to seven churches in the province of Asia (1:4). The geographical term "Italy" also appears in the NT (Acts 27:6; Heb 13:24). Italy is the term used for the territory under direct Roman jurisdiction as distinct from its foreign territories. In the first century all Italians from just north of Florence to the boot of Italy were considered citizens of the city of Rome. □

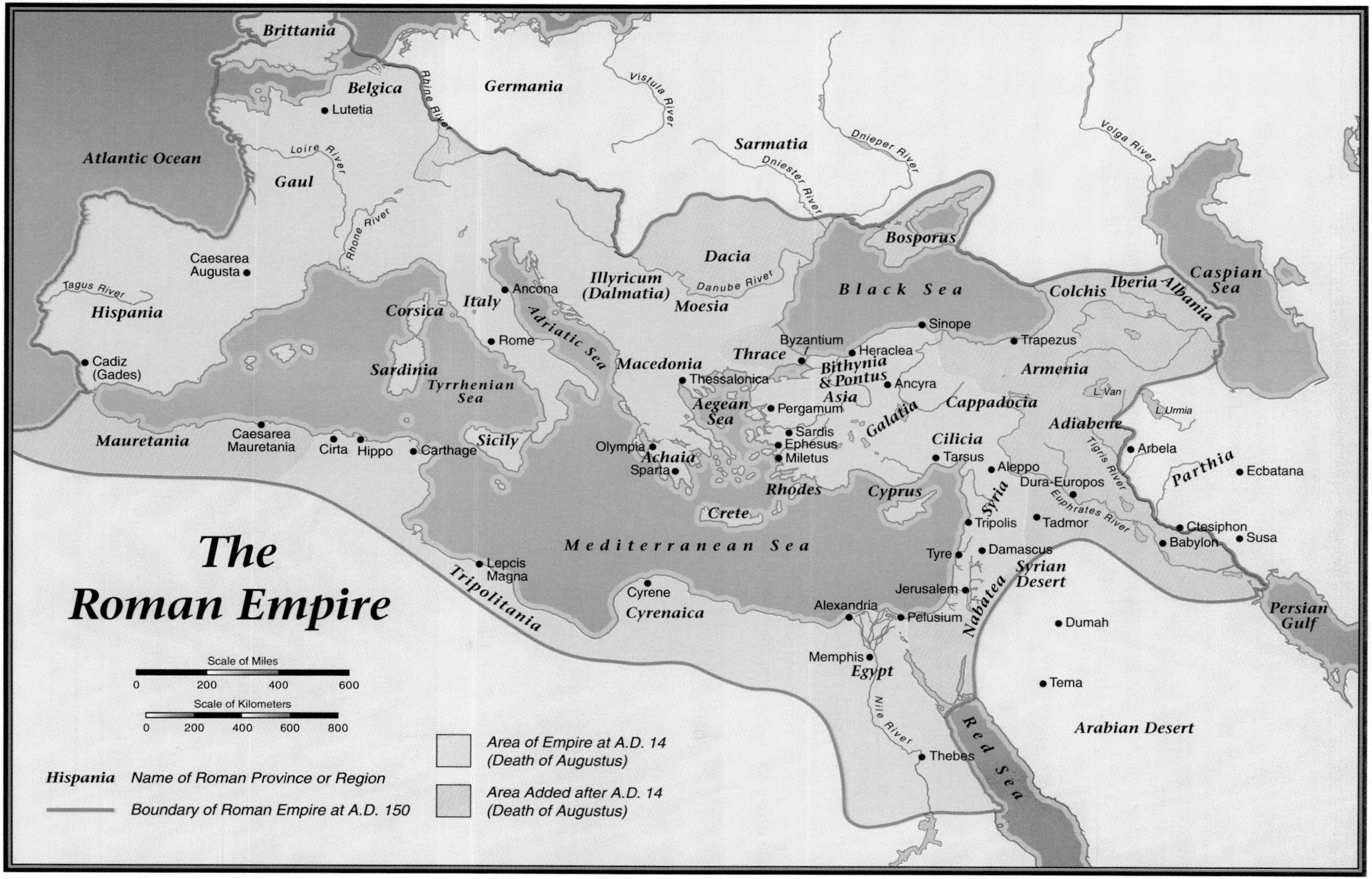
The Roman Empire
Brittania
Belgica
Lutetia
Germania
Vistula River
Rhine River
Atlantic Ocean
Loire River
Gaul
Rhone River
Sarmatia
Dnieper River
Dniester River
Volga River
Caspian Sea
Caesarea Augusta
Tagus River
Hispania
Cadiz (Gades)
Corsica
Sardinia
Tyrrhenian Sea
Italy
Ancona
Rome
Adriatic Sea
Sicily
Mauretania
Caesarea Mauretania
Cirta
Hippo
Carthage
Illyricum (Dalmatia)
Dacia
Danube River
Moesia
Macedonia
Thessalonica
Thrace
Byzantium
Bosporus
Black Sea
Sinope
Heraclea
Bithynia & Pontus
Ancyra
Asia
Aegean Sea
Pergamum
Sardis
Ephesus
Miletus
Olympia
Achaia
Sparta
Rhodes
Crete
Galatia
Cappadocia
Cilicia
Tarsus
Cyprus
Colchis
Iberia
Albania
Trapezus
Armenia
L. Van
L. Urmia
Adiabene
Tigris River
Arbela
Parthia
Ecbatana
Aleppo
Dura-Europos
Euphrates River
Syria
Tripolis
Tadmor
Ctesiphon
Babylon
Susa
Mediterranean Sea
Lepcis Magna
Tripolitania
Cyrene
Cyrenaica
Tyre
Damascus
Syrian Desert
Jerusalem
Nabatea
Alexandria
Pelusium
Dumah
Persian Gulf
Memphis
Egypt
Tema
Nile River
Red Sea
Thebes
Arabian Desert
Scale of Miles
0
200
400
600
Scale of Kilometers
0
200
400
600
800
Area of Empire at A.D. 14 (Death of Augustus)
Area Added after A.D. 14 (Death of Augustus)
Hispania Name of Roman Province or Region
Boundary of Roman Empire at A.D. 150

The ruins of the marketplace at ancient Philippi (see Acts 16:6-40).

churches and beginning new ones. They traveled all the way to the Black Sea in the north, and Paul wished to enter the Roman province of Bithynia in order to spread the gospel. He was prohibited from doing so by the Spirit. Instead, at the city of Troas (an important city on the western coast of Asia Minor) Paul had a vision of a man from the Greek province of Macedonia, who begged him to come to Greece and "help" the citizens of Macedonia (16:9).

Once again the Spirit had guided the movement of the gospel. Rather than moving toward the northern part of Asia Minor, as Paul desired, the gospel had now been pointed toward the western world.

The narrative changed from third person to first person with 16:10. This begins one of the "we" passages that have been so puzzling to scholars. Some have explained the switch as the use of a source; Luke perhaps had an itinerary of Paul's movements. Others have suggested that the switch from third person to first person was merely a literary device, designed to lend more authority to the narrator. Noting that this "we" section begins and ends with Philippi, the second of the "we" sections begins again when the missionaries return to Philippi (20:5-15), and that Philippi receives a great deal of attention and detail, others have concluded that Luke was a part of Paul's vision and a resident of Philippi.

The jailer trembling before Paul and Silas (see Acts 16:25-34)

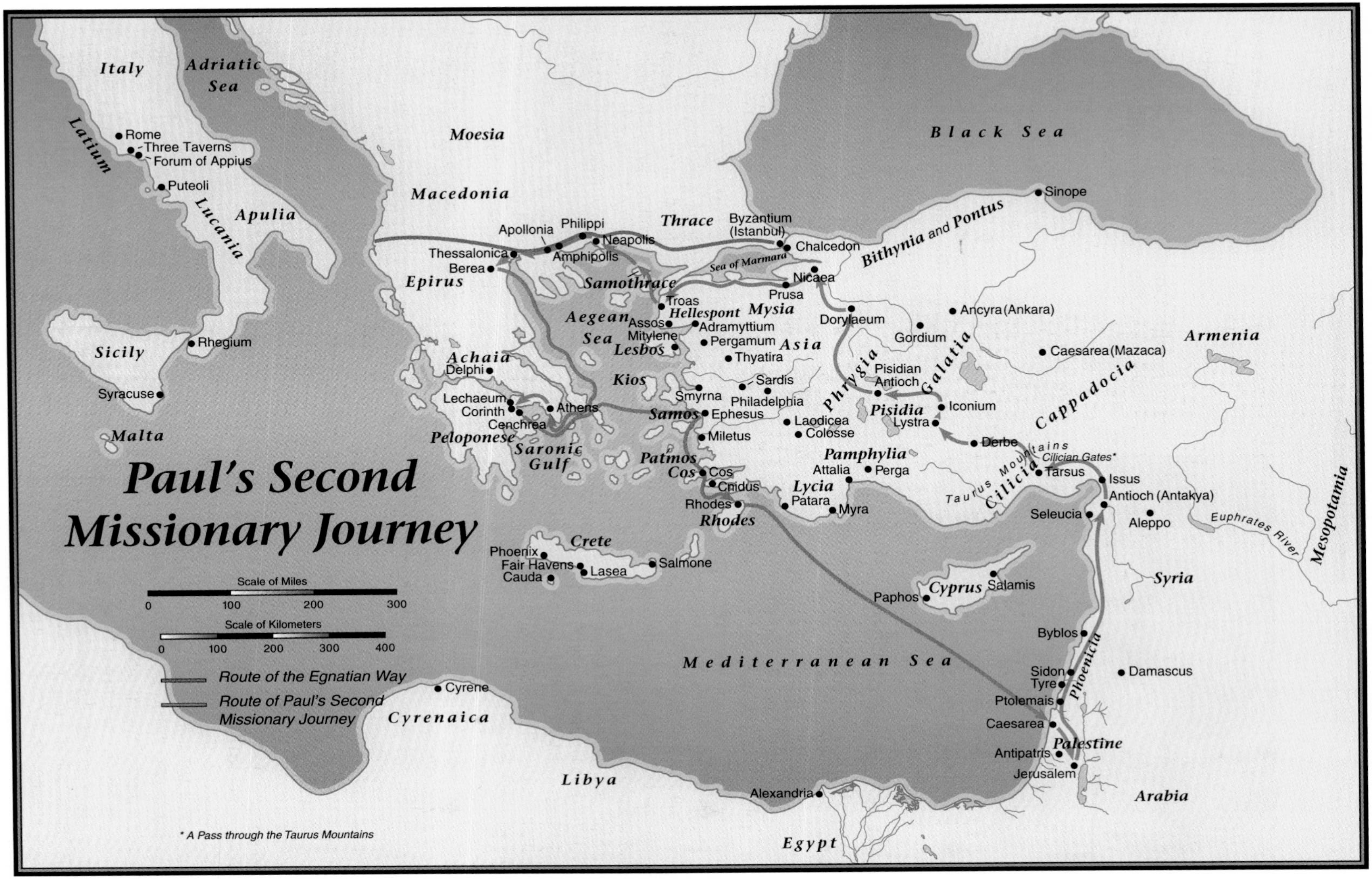

Paul's Second Missionary Journey
Italy
Adriatic Sea
Latium
Rome
Three Taverns
Forum of Appius
Puteoli
Lucania
Apulia
Sicily
Rhegium
Syracuse
Malta
Moesia
Macedonia
Epirus
Achaia
Delphi
Lechaeum
Corinth
Cenchrea
Peloponese
Saronic Gulf
Athens
Thessalonica
Berea
Apollonia
Amphipolis
Philippi
Neapolis
Thrace
Samothrace
Aegean Sea
Byzantium (Istanbul)
Chalcedon
Sea of Marmara
Nicaea
Prusa
Troas
Hellespont
Mysia
Assos
Adramyttium
Mitylene
Lesbos
Pergamum
Thyatira
Asia
Kios
Smyrna
Sardis
Philadelphia
Samos
Ephesus
Miletus
Patmos
Cos
Cnidus
Rhodes
Laodicea
Colosse
Black Sea
Sinope
Bithynia and Pontus
Dorylaeum
Gordium
Ancyra (Ankara)
Phrygia
Pisidian Antioch
Galatia
Pisidia
Iconium
Lystra
Derbe
Caesarea (Mazaca)
Cappadocia
Armenia
Pamphylia
Attalia
Perga
Lycia
Patara
Myra
Taurus Mountains
Cilician Gates*
Cilicia
Tarsus
Issus
Antioch (Antakya)
Seleucia
Aleppo
Euphrates River
Mesopotamia
Syria
Crete
Phoenix
Fair Havens
Lasea
Cauda
Salmone
Cyprus
Salamis
Paphos
Byblos
Phoenicia
Sidon
Tyre
Ptolemais
Caesarea
Damascus
Palestine
Antipatris
Jerusalem
Arabia
Mediterranean Sea
Alexandria
Egypt
Libya
Cyrene
Cyrenaica
Scale of Miles
0
100
200
300
Scale of Kilometers
0
100
200
300
400
Route of the Egnatian Way
Route of Paul's Second Missionary Journey
* A Pass through the Taurus Mountains

Ruins of a Roman wall at ancient Thessalonica (see Acts 17:1-9)

Luke described Philippi as "the leading city of that district of Macedonia" (16:12). Since Thessalonica was the capital city of the province, Luke's description of Philippi probably was an attempt to show the relative importance of the city. It was a Roman colony that had been given the legal status of an Italian city, a unique honor. The Philippians were proud of their citizenship.

Philippi did not have a synagogue. Instead, those Jews who wished to worship met outside the city for prayer. In the case of Philippi, many of these were women. Paul and his companions sought out these women "on the Sabbath" and spoke to them (16:13). A woman named Lydia (or perhaps from the province of Lydia) and her household responded in faith to Paul's message. Their baptism established the church in Philippi. The church was increased through the addition of the Philippian jailer and his family. Paul and Silas were in jail, accused of rebellion against Roman law. God gave them the opportunity to escape (a clear parallel to Peter's experience in Acts 12), but they chose, instead, to lead the jailer and his family to salvation.

Two things should be noted about Paul's ministry in Philippi. First, the church was very influential in the ministry of Paul. It was strategically located, and the members of the church had significant social and economic influence. Second, the charges against Paul and Silas were serious. Here was another barrier to the spread of the gospel; Christians could not be accused of rebellion against Roman religious and social customs. The conversion of women in Philippi added an element of uncertainty to the proceedings. As soon as the magistrates had a chance to review the charges, Paul and Silas were released (16:36). Paul found it necessary however, to make sure that he and Silas were fully exonerated of any accusation of wrongdoing. The success of his mission demanded that the gospel be recognized as legitimate by the Roman government.

17:1-15
Thessalonica and Berea

In Thessalonica Paul resumed the missionary pattern established in the first missionary journey. Again his ministry in the synagogue engendered belief on the part of many Jews and Gentiles and opposition from leading Jewish citizens. Here, as in Philippi, Paul and Silas were accused of sedition, but they were released and asked to leave the city rather than jailed.

In Berea the atmosphere was more conducive to Paul's gospel. Luke stated that "they received the message with great eagerness" (17:11). Perhaps the most interesting part of this passage is the fact that Greek men believed in Berea, not just women (17:12). Paul was forced to leave Berea as well, due to persecution by Jews from Thessalonica. Leaving Silas and Timothy behind, Paul went south to Athens.

17:16-34
Athens

Athens was a center for learning and philosophy. Luke's characterization of the Athenians in 17:21 as people who "spent their time doing nothing but talking about and listening to the latest ideas" was a common description. Paul was unwilling merely to wait for Silas and Timothy. He spent his time debating in the synagogue and in the marketplace. Paul's speech on the Areopagus was an attempt to present the gospel in a setting different from any that Luke had described before. This speech is a masterpiece of Hellenistic rhetoric. Paul did not begin with the Old Testament; his starting point was Greek philosophy

A view from the Acropolis in Athens of the Hill of Pynx where the citizens of ancient Athens gathered to vote, thus creating the first democracy (on Paul's visit to Athens, see Acts 17:16-34).

and literature. Paul and his presentation of the gospel can hold their own, even in the midst of cynical intellectualism. Note also that some who heard Paul were moved to salvation by his speech.

18:1-17
Corinth

From Athens, Paul went to Corinth, a city famous for its immorality. Paul ministered in Corinth for about eighteen months. Because Luke was so precise in his narrative and because scholars have been fortunate enough to find reference both to the expulsion of the Jews from Rome (about A.D. 49) and to the time Gallio held the political office of proconsul in Corinth (about A.D. 51), we are able to have some idea of the time Paul spent in Corinth. Not only that, but this dating aids us in projecting the chronology of Paul's other movements.

Three things about this passage are worthy of note. The first is Paul's encounter with Aquila and Priscilla. In these Jewish Christians, Paul found company and encouragement when he needed both. Paul was also able to strengthen their faith and their understanding of the

The Corinthian canal built in the late A.D. 1900s to connect the Saronic Gulf and the Gulf of Corinth near ancient Corinth (see Acts 18:1-17).

Greco-Roman Cities

Paul's ministry was primarily conducted in the great cities of the Roman Mediterranean. Paul came from an urban background, having been born in Tarsus, the major city of Cilicia.

Tarsus had been under Roman rule since 67 B.C. and had the status of a free city, which afforded it considerable local autonomy. The leading citizens of free cities held Roman citizenship, and Paul's family enjoyed this status (Acts 22:28).

Growing up in Tarsus, Paul would have encountered all the characteristic marks of a Greco-Roman city—its temple, its theater, its bustling agora (marketplace), and its noted school of philosophy. Through the latter, Paul may well have been first exposed to the Stoic philosophical language and argumentative methods he employed extensively in his Epistles.

Paul was converted in another great city of the Roman Empire: Damascus. Damascus was an ancient city dating well back into the second millennium before Christ. In the fourth century B.C. it came under Greek rule by Alexander and his successors and under Roman rule in 64 B.C. During this period the city was completely rebuilt on the Greek grid-system city plan, which consisted of streets crisscrossing at right angles.

Like all Greco-Roman cities, Damascus was surrounded by a defensive wall, had a prominent temple (to the Roman Jupiter), and extensive marketplace. The Jewish king Herod the Great built a Greek-style gymnasium there. The main street, "Straight Street," was where Paul lodged when Ananias was sent to him (Acts 9:11) and is still in use in modern Damascus. The city wall proved instrumental in Paul's bizarre escape in a basket (Acts 9:25; 2 Cor 11:32).

Paul's sponsoring church for his mission work was located in Antioch in Syria. The church had been established by Greek-speaking ("Hellenist") Jewish Christians who had already begun to witness to the Gentiles of the city (Acts 11:19-26; 13:1-3).

Antioch was a Greco-Roman city from the very beginning, having been established in 300 B.C. by the Syrian king Seleucus I as his capital city. In Paul's day it was a bustling commercial center, the third largest city of the Roman Empire. Like many of the major cities of the day, it was a harbor city, located sixteen miles upstream on the Orontes River with the Port of Seleucia at the mouth where the river flowed into the Mediterranean.

The city had been under Roman rule since 64 B.C. Fortified by both inner and outer walls, it had a palace, a colonnaded forum (civic center), a theater, a splendid main street with polished stones and colonnades on both sides built by Herod the Great. It had an aqueduct that brought water from springs in the south of the city, a gymnasium, Roman-style public baths, an amphitheater, a theater, and an impressive temple. Though the latter was dedicated to the Greek Artemis, the ancient fertility cult of Daphne still flourished in Antioch whose sacred prostitution probably contributed to

gospel, to the extent that they would later inform Apollos. Second, Paul's experience with the Jews in the synagogue was such that he rejected them openly and without guilt. Finally, Gallio, the Roman provincial governor, considered Christianity to be a part of Judaism, with all of the rights and privileges the Jewish religion enjoyed in the Roman Empire. In fact, Gallio refused to take jurisdiction over the dispute.

18:18-22
Return to Antioch

With his eighteen-month ministry at Corinth completed, Paul and his companions (including Aquila and Priscilla) traveled to Ephesus. Paul left Aquila and Priscilla there and returned to his home base, Antioch of Syria. Paul had "his hair cut off at Cenchrea because of a vow he had taken" (18:18). This probably was a Nazirite vow, which required persons not to cut their hair for a specified length of time. At that time the hair and another offering would be made at the temple in Jerusalem. Usually the vow was considered a sign of increased devotion to God for a specific task. In Paul's case the necessity to return to Jerusalem and complete the vow would explain his unwillingness to spend more time in Ephesus.

Paul's third missionary journey took him back through area previously evangelized, and the narrative of this activity focuses primarily on Paul's work in the area of Ephesus. His fourth journey (to Rome) actually went through Jerusalem (19:21).

18:23–19:20
Ephesus

This trip began with Paul "strengthening all the disciples" (18:23). While Paul was absent from Asia Minor and Greece, Apollos had come from Alexandria (near the site of modern Cairo, Egypt) to Ephesus. There he met Aquila and Priscilla, who encouraged him and deepened his understanding of the gospel. Apollos had already

the city's reputation for immorality.

Paul's first missionary journey was primarily conducted in the Roman province of Galatia, where he preached in many Greco-Roman cities (Acts 13:13–14:28). Among these was Antioch in Pisidia, where the ruins of its Roman-style temple, aqueduct and theater are still visible today.

To the south-east of Antioch, the city of Iconium lay on the main east-west highway. Along with Derbe, Lystra is as yet unexcavated, but official inscriptions in Greek found in the vicinity of both testify to the dominant Greco-Roman culture pervasive in that area in Paul's day.

On Paul's second missionary journey he worked in the major cities of the Greek world. His first stopping place on Greek soil was Philippi (Acts 16:11-40). Since Philippi was located some thirteen miles inland from the Aegean Sea, its port city was Neapolis, where Paul landed.

Philippi had been settled in ancient times because of the extensive copper and gold mines in the region. Originally named Krenides, it was rebuilt in the fourth century B.C. by the father of Alexander the Great, Philip of Macedonia, for whom it was named. It was again reorganized and rebuilt by the Romans beginning in 42 B.C. after the successful defeat of Caesar's assassins by Antony and Octavian on the plains just outside the city.

At this time Philippi was given the status of a Roman colony, which meant that it had a nucleus of Roman citizens for its population, many of these "colonists" having come from the ranks of the soldiers who shared the victory there. A colony enjoyed many privileges, such as being under Roman law, election of their own officials, and exemption from provincial taxes.

This explains why Paul so enjoyed demanding the personal apology of the Philippian magistrates for beating and imprisoning him without a hearing (Acts 16:37-39). It was illegal to treat a Roman citizen in such a fashion, and loss of their colony status could result from such an infraction. Prominent among Paul's first converts was Lydia, a "seller of purple" (Acts 16:14). A Latin inscription excavated at Philippi refers to merchants of purple goods, thus giving further testimony to the prominence of that trade in Philippi.

Thessalonica was the second major city of Macedonia in which Paul worked (Acts 17:1-9). Some ninety miles southwest of Philippi, Thessalonica was capital of one of the four major political divisions of Macedonia. Like Tarsus, it had the status of a free city. Like Philippi, the via Egnatia, the main east-west Roman highway, ran through it. Located on an inlet of the Aegean, it was a major port city. Because of opposition from the Jews of Thessalonica, Paul had to flee to the smaller town of Berea some fifty miles to the southwest.

Paul next went to Athens, the city that epitomized Greek culture. Like many Greek cities, Athens was dominated by a hill known as the acropolis. This hill overlooked the city. (There were similar acropolises at Philippi

shown his willingness and ability to preach in the synagogues and marketplaces. The Ephesian church supported Apollos's mission trip into Achaia, the area around Corinth.

Meanwhile, Paul had returned to Ephesus. His ministry there lasted around three years. When Paul first arrived in Ephesus, he discovered some disciples who had been baptized with John's (the Baptist's) baptism alone and not with the Holy Spirit (19:3). Perhaps a group of people around Ephesus followed John the Baptist. Just as the Gospel of John took great care to prove that Jesus' power and authority superseded that of the Baptist, Acts indicated that Paul was forced to share the gospel with these "disciples" in order to bring them to true faith.

After a short account of Paul's miraculous and successful ministry in Ephesus, we read of a family of Jewish exorcists who were trying to capitalize on the magical power of Jesus' name. In a fairly humorous fashion, Luke related the punishment of these exorcists who misused

The Great Theater of ancient Ephesus (see Acts 19:1-41)

Jesus' name. Not only were they unable to drive out the demon, but they were beaten naked and bloody. The significance of their failure was obvious to the residents of the area. Christian faith was more powerful than magic,

and Corinth.)

On the acropolis stood several temples, the most notable being the Parthenon, dedicated to Athene, the patron goddess of the city. Northwest of the acropolis was the agora (marketplace) where Paul may have observed the idol dedicated "TO AN UNKNOWN GOD" (Acts 17:23). It was here in the agora that he debated with the curious Athenian philosophers (Acts 17:16-21).

On the west side of the acropolis was the Areopagus (Latin "Mars' Hill") where from ancient times a court was held that governed matters of religion and morals. The court itself eventually took on the name of its original meeting place. So there is some question about whether Paul's appearance before the Areopagus was on the actual hill itself or some other location where the court met.

Paul evidently did not start a major Christian community in Athens at this time but departed for Corinth, where he worked for some eighteen months (Acts 18:1-18).

Corinth probably was the most important commercial center of Greece in Paul's day, located on the Peloponnesus, the southern portion of Greece connected to the northern mainland by a narrow isthmus just to the north of Corinth. Corinth thus had two ports, one on each side of the isthmus. Lechaion to the west gave access to the Adriatic Sea; and Cenchreae on the east, to the Aegean.

Although this region was settled as early as 3000 B.C., the city of Paul's day was less than a hundred years old. The ancient city had been leveled in 146 B.C. as the result of a war with Rome. It was reestablished as a Roman colony in 44 B.C. by Julius Caesar. Corinth was excavated in the nineteenth century and is an excellent example of a Roman city.

At the main entrance to the city stands the temple to Apollo, the patron god of the city. On the acropolis overlooking the city stands a temple to Aphrodite, goddess of love. Along the wall of the city is a temple to Asklepius, god of healing. A Jewish synagogue has been excavated, and this may be the same site where Paul preached. A large theater that seated eighteen thousand people has a plaza outside dedicated to Erastus, the treasurer of the city. Erastus may have been the same person Paul sent greetings from to the Romans (Rom 16:23).

Corinth had a large agora. A large *bema,* or judgment seat, of blue and white marble was discovered on its southern side. This may be the same bema from which the proconsul Gallio heard the Jews' case against Paul (Acts 18:12-17). As a major port city, Corinth was particularly cosmopolitan, and it is easy to see why Paul had to deal so extensively with both religious and moral problems when writing the Corinthian Christians.

Paul's third missionary period was mainly conducted in Ephesus, where he spent two and a half to three years. Ephesus was capital of the province of Asia, having been under Roman dominion since 133 B.C. The site was extensively excavated in the nineteenth century. Among the

and many disciples in Ephesus publicized their decision to stop practicing magic.

This section ends with a summary statement about the spread of the gospel, summarizing Paul's ministry in Asia Minor and Greece.

19:21–28:31
Paul Journeys to Jerusalem and Rome

19:21-41
Ephesus

Paul's final missionary journey parallels Jesus' passion narrative. Like Jesus, Paul turned his face to Jerusalem, where he was captured, taken before Jewish and Roman officials, and placed in Roman hands. Luke's narrative plays on these parallels, letting the reader know of Paul's danger.

Before Paul could leave Ephesus for a final visit to the Greek churches, a riot broke out. This riot was economically motivated, for Christianity had made great inroads into pagan worship and caused financial loss for the makers of idols. In Ephesus the silversmiths incited a riot against the Christian leaders, seizing some of Paul's companions and accusing them of illegal practices. The riot itself is the most illegal activity among these events, and the mob was dispersed by a city official. The clerk reminded the crowd of their legal recourse and noted that the Christian leaders had done nothing wrong or illegal. Paul was advised by "officials of the province" (Asiarchs) not to speak before the crowd for safety's sake. These officials were fairly important politically and socially, and Luke's mention of them lends further respectability to Paul and his group.

20:1–21:16
Missionary Farewell

Paul left Ephesus for a final swing through Greece, back to Asia Minor, and finally to Jerusalem. Four aspects of

---

ruins uncovered are a stadium that Nero built in Paul's day, a theater with a capacity of twenty-four thousand, and a main street thirty-five feet wide with colonnades fifteen feet deep on either side. Its most impressive edifice was the Temple to Artemis (Latin Diana), with dimensions of 180 feet by 360 feet. It had sixty-foot columns and was extensively overlaid with gold leaf.

Artemis worship had its roots in the ancient Asian fertility cults of the Mother Goddess. The temple in Ephesus was considered one of the wonders of the ancient world and attracted many visitors to its spring festival. Small wonder Paul attracted the ire of the local merchants when he criticized the cult's idolatry (Acts 19:23-41).

Ephesus was an important commercial center, located on a natural harbor and the main Roman highway. By now it should be apparent that Paul carried on his main work in the metropolitan centers, the major Greco-Roman cities.

Two further Greco-Roman cities held prominence in Paul's career, Caesarea and Rome. He was imprisoned in Caesarea for more than two years (Acts 23:31–26:32). In Paul's day the Roman governors kept their residence in that city. Although there had been some settlement in the vicinity at least as early as the fourth century B.C., the city of Caesarea was primarily the contribution of Herod the Great, who desired a major harbor in that area. It was built entirely in the Greco-Roman style, complete with a theater, a hippodrome for chariot races, and an amphitheater for athletic events and gladiatorial combat.

Most impressive was Herod's harbor, with its two massive stone breakwaters. He also built himself a palace or praetorium there, and this subsequently became the governor's residence and the place of Paul's imprisonment (Acts 23:35).

The most impressive city of all was the last Paul visited—Rome, the largest city of the empire, the city that ruled the world. Paul, of course, was a prisoner, waiting to appear before Caesar. He was under house arrest (Acts 28:30-31) but definitely with freedom to preach and perhaps to move some about the city.

The ancient world was comprised largely of city-states. The more powerful of these often carved out for themselves empires—Nineveh, Babylon, Carthage. No matter how extensive the empire, the city always remained the central governing power.

In Paul's day, Rome's power embraced the entire Mediterranean world. Knowing the importance of cities, Paul especially wanted to witness to *the* city of his world. He wrote a letter to the Christians who preceded him there to prepare the way (Rom 15:14-29). He reached his goal, even if it was as a prisoner. Paul's missionary work may thus be characterized as urban evangelism, for he worked almost exclusively in the metropolitan centers of his day. □

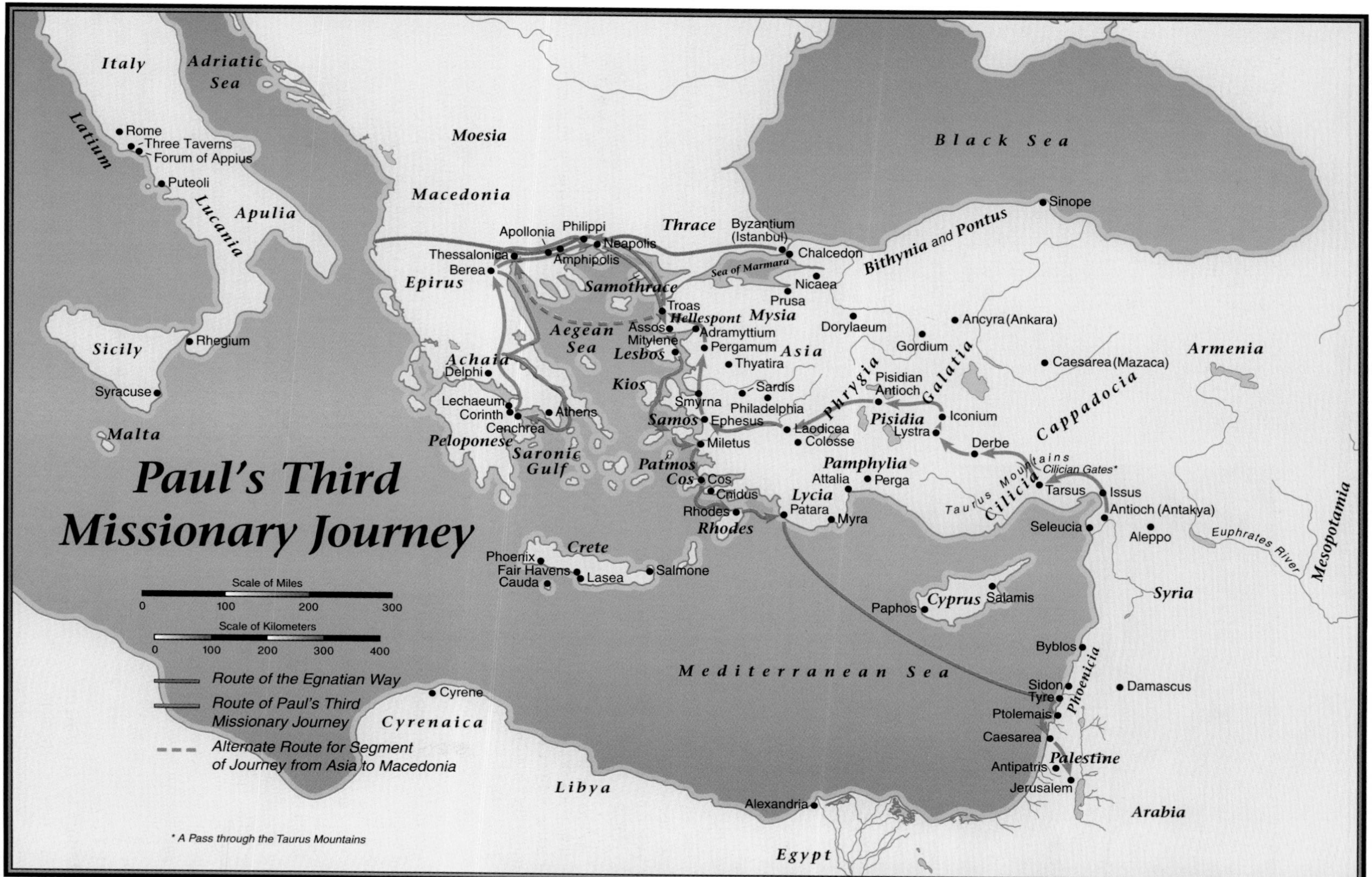

Paul's Third Missionary Journey
Italy
Adriatic Sea
Latium
Rome
Three Taverns
Forum of Appius
Puteoli
Lucania
Apulia
Sicily
Rhegium
Syracuse
Malta
Moesia
Macedonia
Epirus
Thrace
Apollonia
Philippi
Thessalonica
Amphipolis
Neapolis
Berea
Byzantium (Istanbul)
Chalcedon
Sea of Marmara
Nicaea
Prusa
Samothrace
Troas
Hellespont
Mysia
Assos
Mitylene
Adramyttium
Pergamum
Aegean Sea
Lesbos
Asia
Thyatira
Achaia
Delphi
Kios
Sardis
Smyrna
Philadelphia
Lechaeum
Corinth
Athens
Cenchrea
Samos
Ephesus
Peloponese
Saronic Gulf
Miletus
Laodicea
Colosse
Patmos
Cos
Cnidus
Rhodes
Patara
Myra
Lycia
Attalia
Perga
Pamphylia
Crete
Phoenix
Fair Havens
Caudа
Lasea
Salmone
Black Sea
Sinope
Bithynia and Pontus
Dorylaeum
Gordium
Ancyra (Ankara)
Caesarea (Mazaca)
Armenia
Phrygia
Pisidian Antioch
Galatia
Pisidia
Iconium
Lystra
Cappadocia
Derbe
Taurus Mountains
Cilician Gates*
Cilicia
Tarsus
Issus
Antioch (Antakya)
Seleucia
Aleppo
Euphrates River
Mesopotamia
Syria
Cyprus
Salamis
Paphos
Byblos
Phoenicia
Sidon
Tyre
Ptolemais
Caesarea
Damascus
Palestine
Antipatris
Jerusalem
Arabia
Mediterranean Sea
Cyrene
Cyrenaica
Libya
Alexandria
Egypt
Scale of Miles
0
100
200
300
Scale of Kilometers
0
100
200
300
400
Route of the Egnatian Way
Route of Paul's Third Missionary Journey
Alternate Route for Segment of Journey from Asia to Macedonia
* A Pass through the Taurus Mountains

A view of the harbor of ancient Rhodes showing the area where the ancient Colossus stood. Paul visited Rhodes on his third journey (see Acts 21:1).

the passage stand out. The first is the story of Eutychus at Troas. Paul, on his way back to Ephesus, left Greece and stopped in Troas to say farewell. The story is quite humorous; Paul literally "talked" Eutychus to death (20:9). All was well, however, for Paul had the power to bring the boy back to life, and he left the community rejoicing over the resurrection of Eutychus.

The second event in this passage which stands out is Paul's speech to the elders at Ephesus. Paul wanted to bypass Ephesus (to reach Jerusalem by Pentecost [20:16]), and his speech serves as a summary of his ministry in Asia Minor and Greece. From Paul we get a sense of the responsibility he was leaving with the Ephesian elders, as well as a defense of his gospel and ministry in their midst for so many years.

Third, the detail in this passage is incredible. Another "we" passage has begun in 20:6, and the narrative is full of details about the trip. Such detail not only gives the reader the feeling of being with Paul and his companions but lends an air of authority to the narrative. Furthermore, such detail serves to slow down the action of the narrative and increase the tension felt by a reader who is aware that Paul was entering dangerous territory.

Finally, the prophecy of Agabus at the house of Philip the evangelist heightens the sense of impending doom we feel for Paul. During Paul's trip to Jerusalem, disciples tried to dissuade him from continuing the journey. Now we are fully aware of the danger into which Paul was going, yet we have a sense of the Spirit's leading. Paul and God had a larger plan: to spread the gospel to Rome.

21:17-36
Report to Jerusalem

Paul's time in Jerusalem may be divided into four episodes. First, Paul reported to the church in Jerusalem about his missionary activity. He presented an offering from the Gentile churches to the church in Jerusalem designed to aid the Judeans in their time of famine. In response to the success of Paul's mission, James asked that Paul sponsor four men in the completion of their Nazirite vow. This was to show the Jewish population that Paul (and Christianity) had not abandoned the Jewish religion. This sponsorship allowed those unable to provide their own offering to reap the spiritual benefits of a vow. It was a fairly common practice. Luke's mention of seven days (21:27) refers to the time necessary for Paul's own purification, since he had recently come into the country from abroad.

The second episode chronicles Paul's encounter with the mob and his arrest. The crowd took Paul's presence in the Temple and the presence of his Gentile companions in the city as evidence that Paul had brought Gentiles into the temple courts reserved for Jews. This was a capital offense. Paul was accused by Jews from Asia Minor, not natives of Jerusalem. A Roman tribune, in an effort to keep the peace, came to Paul's rescue, but he could not "get at the truth because of the uproar" (21:34). As the Roman soldiers were taking Paul away, he asked to address the crowd. Perhaps the tribune was surprised to hear Paul speak fluent Greek. Certainly he was mistaken in identifying Paul as one of the messianic figures who caused much unrest within Palestine.

21:37–23:35
Before the Sanhedrin

Paul's speech to the crowd was in Aramaic, the common language of Palestine. The speech itself was autobiographical, but its purpose was to defend Paul's gospel and mission. Paul informed the crowd that he was a Jew from the Diaspora, a Pharisee educated in Jerusalem, and a persecutor of Christians. All of that changed, however, with his call on the Damascus road. He concluded by narrating God's command to him to share the gospel with the Gentiles. At this point the crowd demanded Paul's execution again.

In the aftermath of Paul's speech, as he was about to be flogged and questioned, he invoked his Roman citizenship. The tribune was again surprised at Paul. Paul's citizenship would play a large role in his final trip to Rome.

The third episode is rather humorous. The tribune, in order to make his report to his superiors, had to determine the accusations against Paul. To do so he convened the Sanhedrin to examine Paul! Some scholars assume the tribune's power to call the Sanhedrin into session; others disagree. In either event this session of the

TEN MAJOR SERMONS IN ACTS

Reference in Acts		Audience	Central Truths
Peter's mission sermons	1. Acts 2:14-41	An international group of God-fearing Jews in Jerusalem for Pentecost	The gift of the Holy Spirit proves now is the age of salvation. Jesus' resurrection validates His role as Messiah.
	2. Acts 3:11-26	A Jewish crowd in the Jerusalem temple	The healing power of Jesus' name proves that He is alive and at work. Those who rejected the Messiah in ignorance can still repent.
	3. Acts 10:27-48	The Gentile Cornelius and his household	God accepts persons of all races who respond in faith to the gospel message.
Stephen's sermon	4. Acts 7:1-60	The Sanhedrin	God revealed Himself outside the Holy Land. God's people capped a history of rejecting the leaders He had sent them by killing the Messiah.
Paul's mission sermons	5. Acts 13	Jews in the synagogue in Pisidian Antioch	Paul's mission sermons illustrate the changing focuses of early Christian mission work: first Jewish evangelism, second Gentile evangelism, third development of Christian leaders.
	6. Acts 17	Pagan Greeks at the Areopagus in Athens	
	7. Acts 20	Christian leaders of the Ephesian church	
Paul's defense sermons	8. Acts 22:1-21	Temple crowd in Jerusalem	Paul's defense sermons stressed that Paul was innocent of any breach of Roman law. Paul was on trial for his conviction that Jesus had been raised from the dead and had commissioned him as a missionary to the Gentiles.
	9. Acts 24:10-21	The Roman Governor Felix	
	10. Acts 26	The Jewish King Agrippa II	

Sanhedrin was highly unusual and perhaps as illegal as the one that questioned Jesus. The narrative is full of irony. Not only did the High Priest (Ananias) act in an unacceptable manner (we read in other ancient sources that such violence was in character for this particular High Priest), but the council ended on a note of confusion worthy of slapstick comedy. The members of the council seemed unaware that the resurrection of which Paul spoke (23:6) was that of Jesus rather than a philosophical concept. The council meeting turned into a mob scene, forcing the tribune to remove Paul to safety without learning any more about the accusations against Paul.

This section of the narrative has revolved around Paul's desire to preach in Rome. We are reminded of that end as we hear God's voice assuring Paul that he would "testify in Rome" (23:11). The first step of that journey from Jerusalem to Rome is the subject of the final episode in this passage. Paul's nephew uncovered a Jewish plot to kill Paul. This plot involved at least forty men and the Sanhedrin. When Lysias, the tribune, was informed of the plot, he made plans to move Paul from Jerusalem to Caesarea, there to appear before Felix, the governor.

EARLY CAESARS OF ROME

Caesar	Dates	Biblical Reference
Julius Caesar	49–44 B.C.	
Second Triumvirate	44–31 B.C.	
Augustus (Octavion)	31 B.C.–A.D. 14	Luke 2:1
Tiberius	A.D. 14–37	Luke 3:1
Caligula (Gaius)	A.D. 37–41	
Claudius	A.D. 41–54	Acts 11:28; 17:7; 18:2
Nero	A.D. 54–68	Acts 25:11; Phil 4:22
Galba, Otho, and Vitellius	A.D. 68/69	
Vespasian	A.D. 69–79	
Titus	A.D. 79–81	
Domitian	A.D. 81–96	
Nerva	A.D. 96–98	
Trajan	A.D. 98–117	
Hadrian	A.D. 117–138	

Ironically, the military might of the Roman presence in Palestine was mobilized to protect Paul from forty Jewish revolutionaries. Lysias commanded that Paul be accompanied by 472 men on his trip. Surely such a number was sufficient to face forty conspirators. Paul was in protective custody, since the tribune could find "no charge against him that deserved death or imprisonment" (23:29). Paul arrived safely in Caesarea, where he and Felix awaited accusers from Jerusalem.

24:1-27
Before Felix

For more than two years Paul was imprisoned in Caesarea. Roman justice moved slowly or not at all; the corruption of the Roman legal system was well-documented in ancient literature.

Paul's first trial took place before Felix. Felix was a former slave who had been elevated to this powerful political position because his brother was a close friend of the emperor Claudius. Jewish lawyers came from Jerusalem to accuse Paul of worldwide insurrection among the Jews and of messianic political connections. Paul defended his actions, noting that he had done nothing in Jerusalem deserving of punishment. In fact, his behavior in Jerusalem was an example of true Jewish piety. Paul also called on the Jews from Asia Minor who were his true accusers to appear, a right that was his by law. Paul's trial before Felix ended on an uncertain note because Felix kept Paul in prison until the end of his term of office. Felix was waiting for Paul to pay for his release.

25:1–26:32
Before Festus and Agrippa

Paul also appeared before Festus, who had been sent to replace Felix. Once again Jews came from Jerusalem to charge Paul with "many serious charges . . . which they could not prove" (25:7). Paul denied having broken any Jewish or Roman law. Festus, like Felix before him, desired to please his Jewish subjects. Therefore he suggested a trial in Jerusalem. Paul feared for his life in Jerusalem; he appealed to Caesar. Such an appeal was the legal right of any Roman citizen charged with a capital offense. Paul would be taken to Rome, where his accusers would come to present their evidence before the emperor.

For a third time Paul appeared before the authorities. This time Festus called for Agrippa's aid in making a report to Caesar. Agrippa, a descendant of Herod the Great, had been raised in Rome and appointed as ruler of the province to the north of Judea. Agrippa had the reputation of being an expert in Jewish culture and religion.

Three aspects of Paul's appearance before Felix and Agrippa stand out. The first was the public nature of this hearing (25:23). The first two had been legal trials; this time Paul defended himself in a formal audience before these two officials. Second, both officials declared Paul's innocence. Festus's preliminary comments to Agrippa indicated that the Jews' charges were religious rather than political. Before Paul spoke, Festus repeated the words of Lysias the tribune, declaring that Paul had done nothing "worthy of death" (25:25). After speaking to Paul, even Agrippa declared his innocence. The third interesting aspect of this passage is the nature of Paul's defense. Like the other two occasions, Paul proclaimed his innocence of any wrongdoing. In this case, however, he went on to share his own personal experience and to call Agrippa and all those who heard to faith in God.

Three times Paul appeared before Roman officials; each time no official verdict was rendered. Paul was about to realize his desire to preach the gospel in Rome.

27:1–28:31
Rome

This passage begins another "we" passage, with all of the detail and narrative skill we have come to expect from such passages. Paul and his group sailed for Rome, but they were in danger from winter weather. "It was after the Fast" (27:9), that is, the Jewish Day of Atonement, which occurred in late September or early October. Paul warned them not to sail on, but the captain and soldiers were determined to winter in a different harbor. Paul's ominous prediction came true; the ship ran into a hurricane that eventually destroyed the ship. (Luke called the wind "Northeaster" [27:14]. The winds that blew from the points of the compass were considered beneficial; those that blew from the corners were famed for their destructive force.) God preserved Paul and his companions, however, along with the crew and the soldiers.

Everyone on the ship reached Malta safely, although Paul was bitten by a serpent soon after landing. The natives of Malta considered this to be divine judgment. When Paul did not succumb to the poison, they tried to make him a deity, a pattern reminiscent of his early ministry. Paul's stay on Malta was an opportunity for ministry that set the tone for his time in Rome.

The remainder of the trip was uneventful. Paul came to Rome in triumph, met and accompanied by Roman Christians who had come out along the road from Rome. Luke gave no indication that Paul was harshly treated; Paul lived at his own expense under a loose house arrest. Paul met with the Jewish leaders, explained the circumstances of his arrest and his innocence, and shared the gospel message with them. The result was similar to his other missionary endeavors. Some believed; others did not. For their disbelief Paul assured them that the gospel would go now to the Gentiles who "will listen" (28:28).

Acts ends abruptly. Luke gave no indication of what happened to Paul. Some have suggested that Luke meant to write a third volume, which would narrate the further spread of the gospel. Others have suggested that Luke did not know the outcome of Paul's trial when he wrote Acts. Perhaps the most cogent argument suggests that Paul was never tried because the accusers from Jerusalem never showed up. This theory would take Luke's reference to "two whole years" (28:30) to refer to some statute of limitations, after which the charges would be dropped.

The book does end with a sense of closure however. We must remember that neither Peter nor Paul is the main character of the book. The book is concerned primarily with the spread of the gospel and the activity of the Holy Spirit. Paul's ministry in Rome fulfilled Jesus' statement that the disciples would be witnesses "to the ends of the earth" (1:8). Our final picture of Paul is of him preaching the gospel "boldly and without hindrance" (28:31). Luke's entire narrative has brought out the fact that the gospel has overcome all the barriers. The gospel has been victorious throughout the entire Roman world.

Conclusion

The themes of Acts have come to fruition. Paul's presence in Rome underscored the spread of the gospel throughout the world and the gospel's ability to overcome any barrier. The fact that no Roman official could find any evidence of illegal or immoral action affirmed Luke's claim that Christianity was no threat to society. Finally, Paul's missionary activity made the separation between Christianity and Judaism plain.

Theological Significance

Luke's primary purpose for writing Acts may be seen as theological. While he sought to inform, convince, and entertain, his primary concern was that his readers learn something about God. Luke emphasized the work of the Holy Spirit. Luke's message is not just that the gospel spread from Jerusalem to the ends of the earth; his message is that God caused the spread of the gospel. At each step of the way, the reader is confronted with the working of God in the world. Missionaries are guided to new fields of endeavor by the word of God. Their words are confirmed by the miraculous deeds of God done through the apostles. The faith of new believers is affirmed by the unmistakable presence of the Holy Spirit. From beginning to end in Acts, the apostles are providentially protected and directed by the work of God in their lives. The missionary imperative for the church continues for each generation. By the enablement of the Spirit we must be obedient witnesses as the gospel message is taken to the whole world (1:8).

Questions for Reflection

1. Discuss the themes of Acts. Why were they important to Luke? Why were they important to Luke's readers? What themes can you find in Acts other than the ones mentioned in this article?

2. Discuss the place of Acts in the New Testament. How does Acts relate to the Gospels? How does it relate to the Epistles? How important has Acts been to you in your study of the New Testament?

3. Look at the church in Acts. What were its characteristics? How did the church adapt to the needs of the Christian community? What can we learn from Acts about the way our churches should be organized? What can we apply to our own situation?

4. How did Luke portray Peter? Does Peter seem to have changed since the Gospels? How? What was Peter's role in Acts? What was Peter's role in the early church?

5. How did Luke portray Paul? Does Acts paint a different picture of Paul's life than the one we find in Paul's Epistles? If so, why? What was Paul's role in Acts? What was his role in the early church?

Sources for Additional Study

Longenecker, Richard. "The Acts of the Apostles." *The Expositor's Bible Commentary.* General editor Frank E. Gaebelein. Grand Rapids: Zondervan, 1981.

Polhill, John B. *Acts. The New American Commentary.* Nashville: Broadman, 1992.

Stagg, Frank. *The Book of Acts: The Early Struggle for an Unhindered Gospel.* Nashville: Broadman, 1955.

Stott, John R. W. *The Spirit, the Church, and the World: The Message of Acts.* Downers Grove: InterVarsity, 1990.

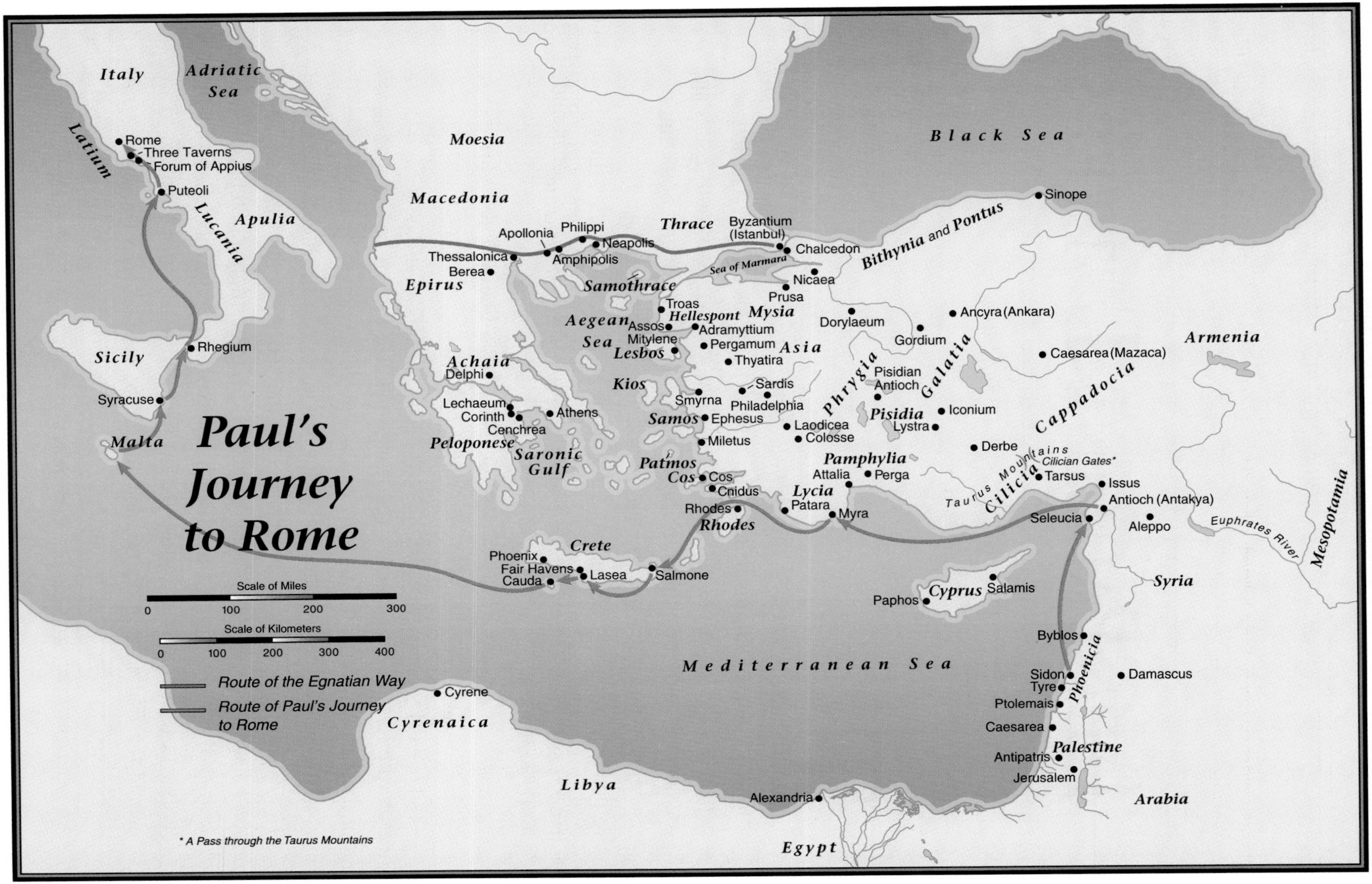
Paul's Journey to Rome
Italy
Adriatic Sea
Latium
Rome
Three Taverns
Forum of Appius
Puteoli
Lucania
Apulia
Sicily
Rhegium
Syracuse
Malta
Moesia
Macedonia
Epirus
Thessalonica
Berea
Apollonia
Philippi
Amphipolis
Neapolis
Thrace
Samothrace
Byzantium (Istanbul)
Chalcedon
Sea of Marmara
Nicaea
Prusa
Bithynia and Pontus
Black Sea
Sinope
Troas
Hellespont
Mysia
Aegean Sea
Assos
Adramyttium
Mitylene
Lesbos
Pergamum
Asia
Thyatira
Achaia
Delphi
Kios
Smyrna
Sardis
Philadelphia
Lechaeum
Corinth
Cenchrea
Athens
Peloponese
Saronic Gulf
Samos
Ephesus
Miletus
Patmos
Cos
Cnidus
Rhodes
Dorylaeum
Gordium
Ancyra (Ankara)
Phrygia
Galatia
Pisidian Antioch
Pisidia
Iconium
Lystra
Laodicea
Colosse
Derbe
Pamphylia
Attalia
Perga
Lycia
Patara
Myra
Caesarea (Mazaca)
Cappadocia
Armenia
Taurus Mountains
Cilician Gates*
Tarsus
Cilicia
Issus
Antioch (Antakya)
Seleucia
Aleppo
Euphrates River
Mesopotamia
Syria
Crete
Phoenix
Fair Havens
Lasea
Cauda
Salmone
Cyprus
Paphos
Salamis
Byblos
Phoenicia
Sidon
Tyre
Ptolemais
Caesarea
Damascus
Palestine
Antipatris
Jerusalem
Arabia
Mediterranean Sea
Cyrene
Cyrenaica
Libya
Alexandria
Egypt
Scale of Miles
0
100
200
300
Scale of Kilometers
0
100
200
300
400
Route of the Egnatian Way
Route of Paul's Journey to Rome
* A Pass through the Taurus Mountains

The Pauline Letters

Thirteen letters in the New Testament bear the name of Paul. They inform us about Paul, his beliefs, his ministry, and his activity. The letters generally focus on issues within the life of the church. As various issues and problems developed, help from the apostles was often sought. Sometimes messengers brought word to Paul of problems in the churches. His letters responded to these concerns. As a result the writings contain instruction; advice; rebuke; and exhortation in theological, ethical, social, personal, and liturgical matters.

Paul's Letters were written over a span of less than twenty years. His place among the writing apostles came by virtue of his intimate relationship and personal encounter with the risen Christ and the instruction he received from the Lord. These special experiences qualified him to be classified as one of the apostles, equal in authority to the twelve appointed by Jesus.

The Acts of the Apostles traces the key events in the life of Saul of Tarsus, the persecutor, who became Paul the apostle to the Gentiles. That story starts with his approving presence at the martyrdom of Stephen (Acts 7:58–8:3). He had studied the Jewish law with the great rabbi Gamaliel in Jerusalem (Acts 22:3). He surpassed his peers with a tremendous zeal to uphold the traditions of his people (Acts 26:5; see Gal 1:13-14; Phil 3:5). As he traveled to Damascus to persecute the believers there, he encountered the exalted Christ, and his life was radically changed (Acts 9:1-31).

Paul in prison writing to the Ephesians

Later he spent time alone with God in Arabia (Gal 1:17). Here he came to realize that the crucified Jesus was raised from the dead, and He is Lord of all (Acts 9:5). The good news of salvation accomplished by Jesus' death and resurrection was the message to be proclaimed to all (Gal 2:15-21). Surprisingly, Paul learned that this good news applied equally to both Jews and Gentiles (see Gal 3:28). Paul's mission was specifically focused on the Gentiles, whom Paul had previously rejected (see Acts 9:15; Gal 1:15-17). Paul ministered in Antioch from where his mission work (with Barnabas) began (Acts 11:25-26; 13:1-3). Three mission journeys took him across the four Roman provinces of Galatia, Asia, Achaia, and Macedonia. From these various locations he wrote his Letters (see the chart showing the relationship between his writings and his mission work).

PAUL'S MISSION TRAVELS AND LETTERS

Book of Acts	Activity	Approximate Date	Writing
9:1-19	Paul's Conversion	34–35	
9:26-29	Visit to Jerusalem	37–38	
11:27-30	Second Visit to Jerusalem	48	
13-14	First Mission (Cyprus and Galatia)	48–50	Galatians
15	Jerusalem Council	50	
16:1–18:22	Second Mission (Galatia, Macedonia, Greece)	51–53	1, 2 Thessalonians
18:23–21:14	Third Mission (Ephesus Macedonia, Greece)	54–57	1, 2 Corinthians Romans
21:15–26:32	Arrest in Jerusalem, Trials and Imprisonment in Caesarea	58–60	
27–28	Roman Imprisonment	60–63	Philemon Colossians Ephesians Philippians
	Release, Further Work, Final Imprisonment, and Death		1 Timothy Titus 2 Timothy

ROMANS

Romans has been called the most important letter ever written. Paul wrote his Letter to the Romans from Corinth during his third missionary journey around A.D. 56–57 (see Acts 20:2-3).

Setting

Paul had never been to Rome, but Christians had been there for several years. We do not know how the church began in Rome. Most likely it started sometime shortly after Pentecost when new believers returned home and started to spread the Gospel (see Acts 2:10-11).

Paul understood the importance and influence of a strong church in Rome. He wanted to strengthen the existing work in that place initially through the letter and secondly by visiting them (1:8-15; 15:14-33). For this reason Paul methodically and systematically outlined the foundational meaning of salvation in Jesus Christ, the foundation of Christianity. He described the human condition, the meaning of the gospel, God's plan for men and women, God's purpose for Israel, and the responsibilities of the Christian life and ministry.

Phoebe carried the letter to Rome. She was a "servant," or minister, of the church at Cenchrea (16:1), a marine suburb of Corinth.

Literary Feature

Romans is both a systematic theological treatise on central themes and a missionary document that applies those themes to practical issues in the Roman church.

The authenticity and integrity of this letter has rarely been doubted. Some have questioned whether chapters 15–16 were a part of the original letter. Four reasons have been suggested for this division.

1. Some manuscripts ending at chapter 14 circulated in the late second and early third centuries.

2. The letter has three doxologies that could possibly serve as endings (15:33; 16:24; 16:27).

3. Chapter 14 includes 16:25-27 in some manuscripts.

4. The so-called inappropriateness of the personal greetings in chapter 16.

The shorter version ending at chapter 14 indicates an influence from Marcion whose bias against Judaism and the Old Testament would have led him to find the discussion of the preparatory work of Judaism (15:1-29) to be offensive. As for the so-called misplaced endings, it was not uncommon for Paul to interject a doxological emphasis at any point in his writings (for example see 11:33-36). Finally, the people mentioned in chapter 16 probably were people with whom he had worked before and now were located in Rome.

All sixteen chapters of this grand epistle should be viewed as a literary whole. The letter is not only a summary of the apostle's thought on salvation in Jesus Christ, but also an expression of his desire to fellowship with the Roman Christians and recruit their support for his mission work to Spain.

Purpose and Theology

It is clear from the last two chapters of the letter that Paul planned to take the contribution from the Gentile churches to the Christians in Jerusalem (see 1 Cor 16:1; 2 Cor 8–9; Rom 15:25-29). From Jerusalem he planned to sail for Rome (15:23-24). One important purpose for the letter was to alert the Romans of his coming so they could help him with his journey to Spain (15:24,28). Paul wanted to inform them of his plans and have them pray for their fulfillment (15:30-32).

In addition to this missionary purpose Paul stated the means by which the righteousness of God had been revealed (1:17). The thematic statement of chapters 1–8 is found in 1:16-17 (see Hab 2:4). The theme of God's righteousness is paramount throughout the book. The first three chapters show that both Jews and Gentiles are under sin and that the atonement of Christ is applicable to both (3:21-31). Chapter four shows how the Old Testament promises to Abraham and David are significant for both since Abraham is the spiritual father of believing Gentiles and Jews.

In chapters 5-8 Paul expounds the meaning of this gift of righteousness. Whether Jew or Gentile, those who trust in the redemptive work of God in Jesus Christ will have "peace with God" (5:1) and will live free from the wrath of God. They will be freed from the penalty and power of sin (chap. 6) but will still struggle experientially with reality of sin and the power of the law (chap. 7).

DOCTRINAL EMPHASES IN THE LETTERS OF PAUL

Paul's Letters	Purpose	Major Doctrine(s)	Key Passage	Other Key Doctrines	Influence of the Letter
Romans	To express the nature of the Gospel, its relation to the OT and Jewish law, and its transforming power	Salvation	Rom 3:21-26	God Humanity The Church	Martin Luther (1515), through preparing lectures on Romans, felt himself "to be reborn."
1 Corinthians	To respond to questions about marriage, idol food, public worship; to discourage factions, to instruct on resurrection	The Church The Resurrection	1 Cor 12:12-31 1 Cor 15:1-11	God Humanity	The hymn on love in Chapter 13 is among the most familiar and loved chapters in Paul's writings.
2 Corinthians	To prepare readers for Paul's third visit and to defend Paul and the gospel he taught against false teachers	The Church Jesus Christ Salvation	2 Cor 5:11–6:2	God	Called by C.K. Barrett "the fullest and most passionate account of what Paul meant by apostleship."
Galatians	To stress freedom in Christ against Jewish legalism while avoiding moral license	Salvation	Gal 2:15-21	Christian Ethics The Church Election	A sermon on the Book of Galatians brought peace of heart to John Wesley. "I felt I did trust Christ alone for salvation."
Ephesians	To explain God's eternal purpose and grace and the goals God has for the church	Salvation The Church	Eph 2:1-22	God Jesus Christ	Called by Samuel Taylor Coleridge "one of the divinest of compositions."
Philippians	To commend Epaphroditus; to affirm generosity; to encourage unity, humility, and faithfulness even to death	Christian Unity Joy in Salvation	Phil 1:3-11	Christian Ethics The Church Prayer	Bengel (1850) described as "Summa epistlae, gaudes, gaudete," which means "The sum of the epistles is 'I rejoice; rejoice ye.' "
Colossians	To oppose false teachings related to a matter and spirit dualism and to stress the complete adequacy of Christ	Jesus Christ	Col 1:15-23	The Church Prayer God	Arius of Alex. (318) used Col 1:15, from a hymn on the supremacy of Christ, to undermine Christ's deity. Arianism pronounced heretical at Councils of Nicea (325) and Constantinople (381).

Paul's Letters	Purpose	Major Doctrine(s)	Key Passage	Other Key Doctrines	Influence of the Letter
1 Thessalonians	To encourage new converts during persecution; to instruct them in Christian living and to assure them concerning the second coming	Last Things	1 Thess 4:13-18	Evangelism Prayer God	Every chapter of 1 Thessalonians ends with a reference to the second coming.
2 Thessalonians	To encourage new converts in persecution and to correct misunderstandings about the Lord's return	Last Things	2 Thess 1:3-12	Prayer The Church Evil & Suffering	With only three chapters, the letter is one of Paul's shortest yet because of 2:3-10 one of the most extensively studied.
1 Timothy	To encourage Timothy as minister, to refute false doctrine, and to instruct about church organization and leadership	Church Leaders	1 Tim 3:1-15	God Christian Ethics Salvation	Known as a "pastoral epistle" since the early part of the eighteenth century, Thomas Aquinas (d.1274) described 1 Timothy as a "pastoral textbook."
2 Timothy	To encourage Christians in the face of persecution and false doctrine	Education	2 Tim 2:14-19	Evil & Suffering Jesus Christ Prayer	Used by Augustine (d.430) in book four on *Christian Doctrine* to support the importance of Christian teachers.
Titus	To instruct church leaders, to advise about groups in the church, and to teach Christian ethics	Salvation	Titus 2:11-14	God Christian Ethics The Church Sin	Called the "Magna Charta" of Christian liberty.
Philemon	To effect reconciliation between a runaway slave and his Christian master	Christian Ethics	Phlm 8–16	Prayer The Church Discipleship	Called by Emil Brunner (d.1965) a classic testimony to what is meant by Christian justice.

Chapter 8 gloriously describes the believers' freedom from death.

A third emphasis is related to the possible conflict between the Jewish and Gentile segments in the church at Rome. Whether the Judaizers, who had hounded Paul's ministry elsewhere (see Galatians), had reached Rome we do not know. Paul emphasized the historical and chronological priority of the Jews (see 1:16; 2:9-10). He stated the "advantage" in being a Jew (see 3:1-2; 9:4-5) and pointed out that "since there is only one God," He is the God of the Gentiles and Jews (3:29-30). "Jews and Gentiles alike all are under sin" (3:9) and are redeemed by the sacrifice of Christ (3:21-31).

In chapters 9-11 Paul explained Israel's place in the future purposes of God. Believing Gentiles had been brought into God's program of salvation, but God did not cast off Israel (11:1,2). God will graft them back into the tree from which they have been temporarily separated because of their unbelief. This God will do if they trust in Jesus as the true Messiah and Savior (11:23). God continues to have a believing "remnant" (11:5) "until the full number of the Gentiles has come in" (11:25).

The final theological theme runs throughout the letter. It is a defense and vindication of God's nature.Paul refuted those implied undertones that questioned God's goodness, justice, and wisdom as seen in His plan of salvation.

Backgrounds of the New Testament

The Roman Empire was the world of the New Testament. Until 27 B.C. Rome was a "republic," governed by two consuls and the senate. However, only the "patricians" (the upper class) had full legal rights to participate politically.

"Plebeians" had only limited rights; slaves and foreigners had virtually none. The aspirations of these underprivileged classes and territorial expansion led to revolution and movement toward more centralized government (thus to break the power of the ruling families).

In 49 B.C. Julius Caesar established himself as sole ruler. He was assassinated (44 B.C.) by supporters of patrician republicanism. The defeat of these conspirators led to ascendancy of Ocatvian. He took the name "Augustus" and ruled as "Emperor." Throughout the NT period, although the titles and governmental forms of the republic were maintained, Rome was actually a monarchy.

Augustus divided the empire into thirty-two provinces. The older, more stable ones were designated as "senatorial provinces." These were governed by a "proconsul" who was answerable to the senate, but he commanded no troops.

"Imperial provinces" were usually more difficult to govern and often contained revolutionary elements. Their rulers held both civil and military authority and were answerable directly to the emperor. "Legates" were placed over larger imperial provinces; "prefects," over the smaller.

There were also a number of semi-independent kingdoms presided over by native rulers called "king," who held office at the pleasure of Rome. Other petty subject princes were called "tetrarch" or "ethnarch" (a slightly higher title). Additional governmental officers and titles were found in specific locations—such as "asiarchs" (Ephesus), "strategoi" or "magistrates" (Roman colonies such as Philippi), and "politarchs" (Thessalonica).

The affairs of each province were strictly regulated by Roman law. However, Roman citizens (a status to which one was born, given, or bought) enjoyed special rights and privileges not available to others. The provisions of Roman law were often interpreted quite differently by individual rulers. The system was open to abuses and injustice, as illustrated by the popular distrust of "publicans," who were charged with collecting taxes for Rome.

The stability of the Empire and the famous *Pax Romanae* (Roman Peace) depended upon the army. Officers were named from the roll of citizens; other soldiers were freedmen and sometimes mercenaries. A "centurion" commanded a hundred foot soldiers in the Roman army. There were ten centurions in a "cohort" and sixty in a "legion."

When Jesus was born, Palestine was ruled by Herod the Great as "king." At Herod's death Palestine was attached to the province of Syria. Herod's three sons—Archelaus, Herod Antipas, and Herod Philip—were permitted to rule Judea and Samaria, Galilee and Perea, and Gaulantius and surrounding areas respectively. Antipas (called Herod) and Philip were tetrarchs, and Archelaus was an ethnarch. When Archelaus was deposed in A.D. 6, his area was placed under the direct control of Roman procurators.

At one time or another the rest of Palestine was also under procurators. From A.D. 37–44 Herod Agrippa I ruled as "king" over all or a part of Palestine as did his son, Herod Agrippa II, from A.D. 53–66. The suppression of the Jewish revolt against Rome, A.D. 66–70, brought an end to all semblance of native rule in Palestine. Paul's travels took him across a number of different provinces and into contact with officials of various rank and office. □

God is "just and the justifier" of those who believe in Jesus (3:26). Paul exulted in "the depth of the riches of the wisdom and knowledge of God" (11:33). He challenged the questioners, "Let God be true, and every man a liar" (3:4).

I. Introduction and Theme (1:1-17)
II. The Human Condition and God's Wrath (1:18–3:20)
III. Righteousness by Faith (3:21–4:25)
IV. God's Righteousness Explained (5:1–8:39)
V. God's Faithful Purposes for Jews and Gentiles (9:1–11:36)
VI. Righteousness in Christian Living and Service (12:1–15:13)
VII. Conclusion (15:14–16:27)

1:1-15
Introduction

Paul identified himself as a "servant" of God, an "apostle" who was "set apart for the gospel of God" (1:1). He offered greetings to the Christians at Rome. Paul told them of his prayers for them and his eagerness to proclaim the Gospel there.

1:16-17
The Theme

The theme is summarized in these two verses as the revelation of a righteousness of God. "The righteous will live by faith" is as some have suggested a summary of Pauline theology as a whole.

The negative manner is a sober reflection of the reality that the gospel is something of which Christians will, while still in the world, continually be tempted to be ashamed (see Mark 8:38; Luke 9:26; 2 Tim 1:8).

The gospel is the almighty power of God directed toward the salvation of men and women. Paul's understanding of the gospel made him not yield to the temptation to be ashamed of the gospel but live to proclaim it.

For Paul, eternal issues were at stake. Those whose minds were blinded and failed to believe and obey the gospel were perishing (2 Cor 4:3). They would ultimately fall under the divine wrath (2 Thess 1:9). Everyone who believes, whether Jew or Gentile, the gospel effectively becomes the power of God for salvation.

This gospel reveals "a righteousness of God." (1:17). Righteousness denotes the right standing God gives to believers. Believers are righteous (justified) through faith and by faith but never on account of faith. Faith is not itself our righteousness, rather it is the outstretched empty hand that receives righteousness by receiving Christ. Paul's concept of righteousness or justification is a complete and total work of God, and we can do nothing to earn it. (See article on "Justification by Faith.")

1:18-32
God's Wrath Revealed

Before Paul set forth his message of righteousness by faith (3:21–8:31), he showed the need for it. The human race stands condemned, helpless, and hopeless apart from God.

Even though God had given sufficient revelation of his existence and power in the world through creation, men and women had nevertheless become idolatrous and polytheistic with resulting moral degradations. Paul claimed that God gave them up to their dishonorable lusts (1:24), passions (1:26), conduct (1:28), and all kinds of evil. The refusal to acknowledge and glorify God results in a downward path: worthless thinking, moral insensitivity, and religious stupidity.

2:1-16
All Face Judgment

The focus of this section is on the fact that God will judge *all* people. Obviously some Gentiles had high ethical standards and moral life-styles. They were not characterized by the blanket judgment expressed in 1:18-32. They condemned the widespread idolatry and corruption among those around them. But Paul insisted that God's judgment applied to them as well. They were responsible because they too were guilty of the same kinds of things. The judgment is based on God's revelation in creation (1:18-32) and in their consciences (2:1-16). Paul's emphasis is on God's just judgment.

2:17-29
Jews Are Guilty

The Jews had no better standing even though they had received God's special revelation through the law of Moses. Though they knew the will of God expressed in the law, they had not kept the law. One's heritage does not make one a true Jew with right standing before God. Rather, true Jews are only those who have received the regenerating work of the Spirit in their hearts.

3:1-20
Judgment Is Just

Paul described the advantages of the Jews: primarily they have been "entrusted with the very words of God" (3:2).

The tomb relief above dating from A.D. 200s shows a teacher with students at either side and one entering on the right. (See Rom 2:20.)

To suggest that God is unfair (as the questions of 3:5,7 appear to do) is to blaspheme God. Those who question God's judgment are therefore themselves condemned (3:8). Paul brings together a series of Old Testament quotations to show that Jews and Gentiles have all sinned, and therefore all are held accountable to God (3:9-20).

3:21-31
Justified by Faith

The gravity of the situation is summarized in 3:23: "All have sinned and fall short of the glory of God." God thus has provided a righteousness for unrighteous people through the atonement of Jesus Christ. The way of forgiveness and freedom has been offered to all, Jews and Gentiles, through the sacrificial death of Christ.

Four words need special explanation. In verse 24 he said that all who believe "are justified." *Justified* is a legal term meaning to *declare righteous*. On the basis of what Christ has accomplished for sinners on the cross, God now views those who believe in Christ from an eschatological perspective. That is, He sees them not as they are but as they will be in Christ. He sees them as He sees Christ: perfect, holy, and without sin (compare 2 Cor 5:21).

God's justification of those who believe is provided "freely by his grace" (3:24). *Grace* points to God's free and unmerited favor by which God has without charge to believers declared them to have a right standing in His sight.

God could declare persons righteous only by dealing with their sin. This He did in the "redemption that came by Jesus Christ" (3:24). The term *redemption* means a *price was paid*. The death of Christ on the cross was the payment price for human sin that secured release from the bondage to sin, self, and Satan.

In verse 25 Paul stated that Christ Jesus was presented as "a sacrifice of atonement" (sometimes translated "propitiation" or "expiation"). Perhaps the idea of satisfaction best illuminates this Pauline concept for us. In Jesus Christ His Son, God has graciously satisfied His own holy demands and directed against Himself His own righteous wrath that the sinner deserves. By Christ's sacrifice God has satisfied, or propitiated, His own wrath.

As a result God is both "just and the one who justifies" those who have faith in Jesus (3:26). Therefore Jew and Gentile alike stand justified not by their works but by their faith in the finished work of Christ (3:27-31).

4:1-25
Faith Always the Plan

The apostle had shown that God declares Jews and Gentiles righteous by their faith in Jesus. How was this different from God's dealings with His people in former times? Paul demonstrated the unity and continuity of God's plan by illustrations from Abraham and David. Paul showed that God declared Abraham righteous by faith, not by works or ritual or the law (4:1-17). Neither Abraham nor any other person had anything to boast about before God

Justification by Faith

Justification is the act of God whereby He declares that a sinful person is righteous, based on a belief and trust in Jesus Christ rather than in the person's own good works. It is a change of state from guilt to righteousness.

Biblical Overview. The concept of justification has its background in the OT. The Hebrew term for *to justify* or *to be righteous* indicated that one was declared free from guilt. The idea carried legal connotations. This can be seen in usages where justification is contrasted with condemnation (see Deut 25:1; Prov 17:15; Isa 5:23). It can also be found in settings that imply a process of judgment (see Gen 18:25; Ps 143:2).

Justification was not merely an ethical quality of character. Rather, it emphasized being righteous; that is, having a right relationship to a certain standard. This standard was God's very own nature and person. As such only He could could perfectly judge whether a person had lived up to the criterion for the relationship. Therefore justification in the OT involved declaring that a person had been faithful to the requirements of the relationship in accordance to the standard given by God.

The NT further advances this idea, mainly in Paul's writings. His understanding of justification is the starting place for developing the implications of the central truth of the gospel, namely, that God forgives believing sinners.

From justification flows the understanding that God gives grace and faith equally to all people (Rom 1:16; Gal 3:8-14). The concept of grace is defined in accordance with justification (Rom 3:24). Paul's explanation for the saving significance of Christ's life, death, and resurrection arises from justification (Rom 3:24; 5:16).

The revelation of God's love at the cross of Jesus (Rom 5:5-9), human liberation from sin's bondage (Gal 3:13; Eph 1:7), a reconciled relationship with God (2 Cor 5:18; Gal 2:17), adoption into God's family (Gal 4:6-8), and assurance in the Christian life (Rom 5:1-11) are also examined in light of justification.

Theological Considerations. Imputation is an act of God whereby He credits Christ's righteousness to sinners who believe and accept His gift. They are then pronounced by God as righteous.

This is not to say God considers believers merely as if they had never sinned. This would only indicate they were innocent. Justification goes beyond this understanding. Christ has paid the penalty for sin and guilt and has fulfilled the just requirements of the law. God the Father applied Christ's perfect work to the believer's life in such a way that he or she is restored to a right standing with God. In this way God declares a person *righteous*.

The basis for a believer's justification is the death of Jesus Christ. People are not able to justify themselves by performing good works (Rom 3:28; Gal 2:16). Christ was "made sin" (2 Cor 5:21) in the place of sinners, dying as their substitute. God'sjustice was demonstrated by punishing sin through the death of Christ (Rom 3:21-26). In Christ's death God justified Himself (by punishing sin), as well as justifying believing sinners (by crediting Christ's righteousness to them).

The way a person receives God's justification is through faith. Faith is an absolute reliance in Jesus Christ and His work for salvation. Faith should not be considered a good work (Rom 3:28), for it rests on grace (Rom 4:16) and excludes works (Eph 2:8-9). Faith is a condition that has no merit in itself; rather, it rests upon the merit of the person and work of Jesus Christ. Justification is something that is completely undeserved. It is not an attainment but the gracious gift of God. Not every sinner is justified, only those who believe in Jesus Christ.

Good works do not procure justification. Works, however, are the way people demonstrate that they are justified by faith (Jas 2:18).

Paul is the only NT writer to use "justify" as a term for God's act of accepting people when they believe. When James spoke of being justified, he used the word in a general sense of proving a genuine and right relationship before God and people. James wanted to deny the character of a superficial faith that does not produce works for God's kingdom. If there are no good works, there has been no valid justification. □

because of what he had done but by his faith in God's promise (4:18-25; see Gen 15:6).

5:1-21
Grace Abounds

Paul argued that by the impact of this righteous gift believers are given salvation from the wrath of God (5:9). God has reconciled godless and unrighteous enemies to Himself (5:10-11). Thus they "have peace with God through our Lord Jesus Christ" (5:1). Paul, by way of a typology, demonstrated that sin and death came to men and women through Adam; righteousness and life, through Jesus Christ (5:11-21). Sin had been intensified by the transgression of the law. Thus greater grace was needed. But where sin abounded, grace abounded all the more (5:20).

6:1-14
New Life in Christ

God's provided righteousness involves more than declaring believers righteous on the basis of faith. He declared the duty to reject sin and do what is right because of the new life received in Christ.

Paul argued that it would be a perversion of grace to argue that since grace results in freedom and [grace] increases where sin increases, people should continue in sin so that grace can abound. Paul contended that those who have been justified by Christ have died to the power of sin, which no longer has enslaving power. Believers have been identified ("baptized") with the death and resurrection of Christ, the source of their spiritual life (6:2-7). Since believers are dead to sin and its power, they must realize they have new life in Christ and not yield themselves to unrighteousness (6:8-14).

6:15-23
Slaves of Righteousness

Paul stated that sin results in death (6:16,21,23). Believers have been set free from sin (6:18,22) and no longer are in bondage to it (6:20). Now believers are slaves of righteousness (6:16-19) and alive to God (6:11,23). They are now to reject sin and do what is right by serving God.

Chapter 6, like chapters 3–5, asserts the importance of Christ's death. Again the death of Christ is reasserted, but not in isolation as the death of the righteous for the unrighteous. Here the believer has been joined to Christ. Death to sin calls for resolute separation from sin, and

Glory

Paul's use of glory is determined by two factors—the OT and the revelation of Christ to Paul on the Damascus road. The OT and Jewish traditions form the proper context for interpreting glory in Paul. The appearance of the resurrected and exalted Christ to Paul was the key for understanding Paul's specific appropriation of glory language.

In glory (*doxa*) Paul inherited a word already invested with meaning. The OT refers to God's glory (*kabod*), His visible presence, in several different contexts: (1) the revelation to Moses on Mount Sinai and in the tabernacle (Exod 24–40); (2) the regular celebration of God's revelation of glory in creation and at the temple in Jerusalem; and (3) the promised revelation of God's glory which will inaugurate the recreated kingdom of God (see Isa 40–66; Ezek 40–48).

In particular the graphic description of God in Ezekiel 1:28 (and to a lesser extent Isa 6) exerted a powerful influence on the development of glory in the Jewish traditions.

In line with this longstanding glory tradition, Paul closely connected, if not actually identified, Christ as glory. Paul entitled Christ the "Lord of Glory" (1 Cor 2:8; see Eph 1:3,17). The crucified, resurrected, and exalted Jesus reveals God's glory (for example, see Eph 1:18; 3:16; Col 1:27). The gospel that Paul preached—a gospel that features the death, resurrection, and future coming of Jesus—is a "gospel of glory" (see 2 Cor 4:4; 1 Tim 1:11).

Paul's close connection of Jesus and glory is tantamount to claiming that Jesus was the special agent of God— that He is the Son of man, the Messiah, the Son of David, the Suffering Servant, or even God Himself. What was it that allowed Paul to make such a bold identification?

The revelation of the resurrected Jesus on the Damascus road was the catalyst for Paul's identification of Christ as glory. Like the revelation to Moses on Mount Sinai, God revealed His glory to Paul in a special appearing (2 Cor 3:4–4:6). And like the call of the prophets Isaiah and Ezekiel, Paul was commissioned by God's glory (Gal 1:11-17). Further, the revelation of God's "glory" to Paul in the Damascus Road experience signals the inauguration of the promised new age of salvation and re-creation (see Acts 9:1-31; 1 Cor 15; Rom 8). In short, Christ's appearance to Paul was a revelation of God's end-of-time "glory" in the resurrected person of Jesus.

Paul's use of "glory" is not without importance for the followers of Christ. Believers share the future of Jesus and thus live in anticipation and hope of their transformation into "glory," that is, resurrection life in the unmediated presence of God.

To hear and believe the gospel is to possess the "hope of the glory of God" (Rom 5:2). To be changed into the likeness of Christ is to be changed "into his likeness with ever-increasing glory" (2 Cor 3:18).

Through Christ God calls the believer to His own "kingdom and glory" (1 Thess 2:12,14), while through the "glory" of Christ, God furnishes the enabling power to live the life of a disciple (Col 1:11).

The future sharing of Christ's "glory" eclipses any suffering experienced in the earthly life (Rom 8:17-18; 2 Cor 4:16-17). The exchange of suffering for "glory" occurs at Christ's second coming (see Phil 3:21; Col 3:4; 2 Thess 1:9; Titus 2:13). On that day believers, and creation itself, will experience the fullness of God's glory in Christ. □

Baptism

The term *baptism* translates the Greek noun *baptisma;* the verb is *baptizo. Baptizo* means to *immerse* or *dip.* Besides the practice of baptism, *baptizo* is used in the NT for ceremonial washing (Mark 7:4; Luke 11:38). It is also used metaphorically in a number of ways (Matt 20:22; 1 Cor 10:2; 1 Pet 3:19-21).

1. *Background.* Christianity was not the only religion to practice baptism. In fact, during the NT era several different groups used some form of baptism in their religious rites to attain the removal of guilt, moral cleansing, and a new birth or start.

The Oriental mystery religions of that day used some form of immersion, at times in blood, as an initiation rite into their communities. The Jews began at about the time of Jesus to require a ritual bath, or baptism, of its Gentile converts seven days after circumcision. Also the sectarian Jewish community of Qumran (famous for the Dead Sea Scrolls) had a highly developed practice of religious washings, which included baptisms.

2. *John the Baptist.* Although the Gospels demonstrate a close connection between John's baptism and the early Christian practice, it would be wrong to make John's baptism equivalent to Christian baptism. John's baptism had a dual focus.

First, his was a baptism of repentance, calling the Jews back to faithfulness and commitment to the law of God (Matt 3:5-12; Luke 3:3). John was undoubtedly influenced by his own Jewish context, which saw the washings of water as an agent of moral or ethical purification (Mark 1:4; Matt 3:11). However, he did not envision the water of baptism acting to purify apart from repentance (Matt 3:7-8).

Second, John's baptism was in anticipation of the coming of God's Messiah (Matt 3:2; Mark 1:7-8; Acts 10:37). It served as a prophetic symbol of the OT's pronouncement of the inauguration of God's messianic salvation (Isa 4:4; 40:3; Mal 3:1-6). John consciously linked his baptism with the expected messianic baptism of Spirit and fire, new life and judgment, brought about in Jesus Christ (Matt 3:11; Mark 1:8; John 1:33).

3. *Jesus and Baptism.* The practice of baptism is, for the most part, noticeably absent from the ministry of Jesus. Early in Jesus' ministry He may have baptized in a way similar to John (John 3:22-23), but later He seemed to discontinue the practice (John 4:1-3).

Jesus' own baptism by John was extremely significant for His ministry. It identified Him with the righteous concerns of John (Matt 3:15) while it demonstrated His own solidarity with sinful humanity, whom He came to serve (2 Cor 5:21; Phil 2:7).

The descent of the Spirit and the voice from heaven showed this to be the beginning of God's work of salvation through His Son, Jesus, and the promise of the coming of God's kingdom on earth.

Jesus' command to baptize given in the Great Commission (Matt 28:18-20) is the foundation for the church's practice of baptism. Christian baptism takes place in light of Christ's redemptive death, resurrection from the dead, and ascent to glory and authority at the right hand of God.

4. *The Early Church.* Baptism in the early church was performed "in the name of Jesus" or "into Jesus" (Acts 2:38; see Gal 3:27). In Acts this involves the believers' calling on the name of Christ for salvation (Acts 22:16) in light of the forgiveness brought about by Christ (Acts 2:38). Hence, baptism identifies believers with the new messianic community called into worship and missionary effort by the risen Lord (Acts 2:41).

Baptism was an integral part of the earliest proclamation of the good news, even though the early church had to struggle with its implications and to whom it was to be administered (see Acts 2:38; 8:14; 10:44; 19:1).

Paul's basic understanding of baptism was that the believer is baptized "into Christ." Baptism serves to illustrate the union with Christ brought about through faith (Gal 3:26-27).

Paul employed this basic understanding of baptism in a number of ways. The Christian's baptism is "into his death" and unites the believer with Christ's death and resurrection (Rom 6:3). Because of this, Christians share in Christ's victory over sin and death (Rom 6:4; Col 3:3).

Baptism is related to the baptism of the Spirit (1 Cor 12:13), since the new life in Christ is inseparable from the presence of the Spirit (Rom 8:9-17). Baptism further relates the believer to the body of Christ, the church (Gal 3:27-29; 1 Cor 12:12-13).

Therefore baptism in the NT has a rich symbolism and vital purpose. It was the first public act for believers identifying them with Christ's saving death, saved people, and saving mission. □

resurrection means a new type of life in response to God.

7:1-13
The Human Contradiction

In chapter 7 Paul pictured himself in a representative way as one wanting to live righteously and fulfill the demands of the law but frustrated by sin that still indwelt him. Nowhere else in Paul's Letters, and nowhere else in ancient literature, is there such a penetrating description of the human plight and contradiction as in 7:1-25. There is a remarkable parallelism between what chapter 6 says about sin and what chapter 7 says about the law.

Paul addressed the issue of the believer and the law by a somewhat imperfect analogy with the husband and wife. These verses demonstrate the character of the law. It is "holy, righteous, and good" (7:13). Paul described the role of the law in his transitional experience before his conversion.

7:14-25
The Christian Struggle

The interpretation of these verses is as difficult as any in the New Testament. The text is gripped with tension. Paul painted for the readers a picture of the Christian life with all its anguish and its simultaneous hopefulness. This is the ongoing struggle with which believers are involved throughout their lives. Deliverance is promised. Victory is sure; but it is an eschatological hope (7:24-25).

Paul described one who hates sin and judges it in his or her life. In this struggle the believer constantly continues to strive for the good. Both the struggle of chapter 7 and the deliverance of chapter 8 are true and real in the believer's journey. Though Paul spoke autobiographically of the tensions of life as he experienced them, it remains apparent that he spoke by implication for all who have the struggle and need for God's enablement and blessing.

8:1-17
No Condemnation

Paul's exposition shifted to a focus on the role of the Holy Spirit, who brings pardon and power for the children of God. Those who have been justified have been freed from death. "Therefore, there is now no condemnation for those who are in Christ Jesus" (8:1). God will give life to their mortal bodies through His spirit, who indwells believers (8:11). If believers live according to the sinful nature, they will die; but if by the Spirit believers put to death the misdeeds of the body, they will live (8:13).

In contrast to the control of sin, which enslaves to the point of fear, believers have received the Spirit of adoption. So instead of retreating in fear, Christians can approach God in an intimate way, calling Him "Abba, Father" (8:15-17). "Abba" is a transliteration of the Aramaic term for father, implying great familiarity and intimacy (see Mark 14:36; Gal 4:6). The portrait is one of solidarity and relatedness through the Spirit.

Verse 17 concludes and climaxes a list of conditional "ifs" (see 8:9-11,13). He lifts the issue of suffering beyond their own inner moral struggle to suffering together with Christ as a prelude to being glorified together with Him.

8:18-27
Redemptive Suffering

Hope transforms suffering. Paul pointed to creation's longing for its redemption (8:18-21) and believers' eagerly awaiting their ultimate adoption and redemption (8:22-25). Here we see God's plan of redemptive suffering moving to its fulfillment at the end of the age.

The Spirit Himself groans for believers as they pray and anticipate their glorification (8:26-27). Even though the Spirit groans with words that cannot be expressed, the Father knows what the Spirit is thinking. Though believers during this in-between time are often unsure and unaware of what to pray, the Holy Spirit communicates their concerns for them.

8:28-39
More Than Conquerors

Paul's conclusion to the first half of the book emphasized the majesty and glory of God and pointed to the certainty of God's redemptive plan. All that happens to them rests in the sovereign hand of God, who in all things "works

The photo above is a page from a codex of the Pauline Epistles (dating from A.D. 200s) that shows Romans 8:15-25.

for the good of those who love him" (8:28). Believers gain assurance knowing that God is for them (8:31). In all the testings and sufferings that confront believers, they can be confident that they are more than conquerors through Christ who loved them (8:37). Believers can expect difficulties in this age (8:35-36); yet they can be certain that nothing will be able to separate them from the love of God that is in Christ Jesus" (8:39).

9:1-5
Israel's Place

The apostle could not deal with the issue of men and women, whether Jew or Gentile, being given a right standing before God without addressing the place of Israel in God's plan. Paul stated with great emotion his concern for the Jews, his own people. They had a special place in God's purposes in the past. They were the recipients of adoption, glory, covenants, the law, the promises, temple worship, and the patriarchs.

9:6-13
God Is Faithful

Paul here described God's sovereign choice of His people. Everything that has taken place in redemptive history has been due to God's faithfulness to the promise He gave to Abraham and his descendants. With Jesus, Paul could affirm that "salvation is from the Jews" (John 4:22). The problem for Paul was, How could Israel, as the recipient of all these blessings, fail to receive and recognize the promised Messiah?

Paul answered that God elected Abraham, but not all the descendants of Abraham receive his promises (9:6-13). The choice of God had nothing to do with their character or worth; it was a matter of God's purpose.

SUFFERING

Nearly all discussions of suffering revolve around suffering's origin, nature, scope, and meaning. According to Paul, all such questions are bound up with suffering's close connection with the destructive powers of sin and death. The origin and presence of suffering in the world is linked to the powers of sin and death. Like sin and death, suffering is universal in scope. And like sin and death, suffering profoundly alters the quality of human life.

Paul roots the universality and intensity of suffering in humanity's willful complicity with the powers of evil. Suffering as loss, illness, violence, fear, and failure—both socially and individually—can be traced to the power of sin (Rom 1:18–3:20). The ultimate end of sin, and thus the greatest suffering, is death, the eternal separation from God (Rom 6:23).

Only Christ's work on the cross counteracts the suffering in this world (Rom 5:12-21). Through His humble life of service, painful trial, and sacrificial crucifixion, Jesus patterns a response to suffering (Phil 2:5-11). As the unique Son of God, Jesus' death also provides the possibility of atonement, forgiveness, and reconciliation (Rom 3:21-26; 2 Cor 5:16-21). Furthermore, in His suffering death, Jesus conquered the very powers that enslave and estrange: on the cross Christ defeated the powers of evil (Col 2:13-15).

Through Spirit incorporation into Christ, the believer has solidarity with the new age, an age in which sin, death, and suffering will disappear (Rom 8). The preached gospel rehearses the cross-resurrection events, and a faith response ensures ultimate victory over evil, death, and suffering.

Faith in Christ does not automatically erase suffering's presence, however. Paul strongly opposed any notion of the Christian life as free from suffering. Quite the contrary, for Paul suffering was one of the marks of true gospel ministry (2 Cor 4:7-17; 11:23-28) and discipleship (Phil 3:10-11; Col 1:24). As children of God, sharing in the sufferings of Christ translates into sharing future glory (Rom 8:17-18; Col 3:1).

The focus upon future glory rescues suffering from meaninglessness in the present. In response to suffering, Paul called on the believer to live a life of joyful hope—a "hope of the glory of God" (Rom 5:2). A life of hope in response to suffering enacts a process of Spirit-led perseverance and character transformation (Rom 5:3-5). The believer is to rejoice in suffering and resist any temptation to submit to a life of resignation. Such a life will receive special divine comfort (2 Cor 1:3-7).

The life of hopeful suffering is not to be lived in isolation from others. Christians experience a foretaste of the release from the bondage of suffering through participation in life of Christ. Nowhere is this more evident than in the church. The life of hope comes to expression in the community of faith, the church.

A life of hope recognizes the presence of evil and suffering—be it just or unjust, social or individual. And yet through the power of the Spirit it seeks to redeem tragedy and loss for the kingdom of God. According to Paul, present suffering is rescued from meaninglessness through hope for the future kingdom. Paul called all Christians to live in hope, refusing both resignation and denial. Thereby, through the process of discipleship, Christians permit God to give meaning to the reality of suffering. □

9:14-33
God Chose Israel

Paul contended that there is no injustice with God. His choices show forth his power so that His name might be proclaimed in all the earth (9:14-17). He had chosen Israel to serve His purposes as Lord over all. Only by faith are people declared righteous before God. Those who attempted to establish their righteousness on any other basis stumbled over the Messiah (9:27-33).

10:1-21
Believe and Confess

Paul argued that only a remnant of Israel ever believed (9:27-29). In rejecting Christ Israel was following a precedent already at work in earlier days. The Jews' zeal was commendable but nevertheless misguided (10:1-4). The only way of acceptance before God was faith in Christ and was (and is) within the reach of all (10:5-13). Those who believe in their heart and confess with their mouth "Jesus is Lord" will be saved (10:9-10). People cannot believe unless they can hear, and they cannot hear without a preacher (10:14-21). Though Israel heard, they still rejected God's message.

A relief from the Roman period showing a potter working at his wheel attaching a handle to a vase. (See Rom 9:21.)

11:1-24
Call to Humility

Next, Paul claimed that since a remnant of Israel had believed the gospel, it was a clear indication that Israel as a whole will yet believe. Though God may have temporarily rejected Israel, He has not finally or irrevocably rejected them. When Israel rejected God's message, the opportunity was given to the Gentiles, who were grafted into the tree (11:17-21). Gentiles, however, were warned not to be proud of their acceptance but humbly to rely on God's grace (11:22-24).

11:25-36
Israel in His Purpose

Israel's alienation is not necessarily final. God still has a future and purpose for Israel (11:25-26). The Gentiles are saved by a temporary hardening of Israel, which will continue until the "full number of the Gentiles has come in" (11:25). Still, within God's purposes "all Israel will be saved" (11:26-27). Paul concluded this section by praising the marvelous wisdom of God demonstrated in His purposes for both Jews and Gentiles (11:33-36).

12:1-2
Be Transformed

Paul appealed for the dedication of the whole of life to God. The basis of the appeal rested in the mercy of God (12:1). As believers are transformed in their minds and conformed to the image of Christ, they will be able to discern, desire, and approve the will of God. God's will is good and holy; it is sufficient for every need. Only through spiritual renewal can believers do the will of God.

12:3-21
Spiritual Gifts

Believers' dedication to God and the accompanying transformed life-style is lived out through the exercise of spiritual gifts (see 1 Cor 12–14 and the article "Spiritual Gifts"). Christians are to live together in love as members of Christ's body, the church. With their various gifts they are to serve one another (12:3-8). The rest of the chapter (12:9-21) consists of a series of short exhortations that focus on the outworking of love in all relationships and under all circumstances.

13:1-14
Christians and Rulers

Christians should recognize that civil government is ordained of God. Government is God's servant to discipline the disobedient (13:4) and carry out His righteous will

(13:1-7). Love is the sum of the Christian's duty (13:8-10). Christian conduct is vitally related to the hope of Christ's return and the believer's ultimate transformation (13:11-14).

14:1-23
Relationships among Believers

Harmonious relationships are important. Believers should live without judging others (14:1-12) and without influencing others to violate their consciences (14:13-23). Not only should the mature not hinder the weak with their freedom, but the weak must avoid restricting those who have discovered Christian freedom. Mutual love and respect are the marks of true disciples of Christ.

15:1-13
Please Others

The apostle described how Christian living involves the desire to please others and not oneself. A need exists to welcome others as Christ Himself has received Gentiles as well as Jews to be His people.

15:14–16:27
Conclusion

This concluding section contains Paul's travel plans and his role as a minister to the Gentiles. He stated his aim to proclaim the gospel where it had not been preached. He wanted to go to Rome in order to extend the Christian mission westward to Spain (15:14-29). He requested prayer from the church for his mission (15:30-33).

Chapter 16 closes typically with greetings and commendations from various individuals. Greetings are offered to twenty-seven people, including a significant number of women (16:1-16). Paul appealed for the church to avoid divisions and disunity (16:17-20). He offered greetings from his colleagues (16:21-23) and closed with an appropriate doxology: "To the only wise God be glory forever through Jesus Christ. Amen" (16:25-27).

Theological Significance

Paul's message to the Romans means that the church must proclaim that God is the giver of salvation, the gift of righteousness, and this gift is for all who will receive it by faith. The church must not call for a faith that can be separated from faithfulness. Assurance must be grounded not in human decision but in the atoning and justifying work of Jesus Christ.

The thematic emphasis of the believer's righteousness in Christ means that our acceptance and worth before God cannot be earned but only received. When we feel depressed, discouraged, or defeated, we must remind

An interior view of the house of Livia, wife of Caesar Augustus, on Palatine Hill (site of several Caesars' palaces) in the city of Rome.

ourselves that God has reconciled us, accepted us, and given us value and significance in His sight because of the work of Jesus Christ for us.

When troubled from all sides, we are reminded that God is for us, and nothing can separate us from the love of Christ (8:31-39). When divisions occur in the church, we must turn to Paul's exhortation for mutual love, concern, and service for one another. No one has a superior place in Christ's body because of inherent worth, heritage, accomplishments, or background. There is, therefore, no place for human boasting or claim of special privilege. All nations are invited to come to Christ, in whom there is no condemnation for those in Christ Jesus.

Questions for Reflection

1. How did Paul express the idea of right standing before God?

2. How are believers to understand their relationship to the law?

3. How are believers to live with the tensions of struggle, suffering, and victory as described in chapters 7–8?

4. How does Israel's unbelief relate to God's redemptive purpose?

5. What did Paul say about the responsibilities of Christians in their service in the church and relationships with one another (12:1–14:23)?

Sources for Additional Study

Cranfield, C. E. B., *Romans: A Shorter Commentary.* Grand Rapids: Eerdmans, 1985.

Hendriksen, William, *Exposition of Paul's Epistle to the Romans. New Testament Commentary.* Grand Rapids: Baker, 1980.

Moo, Douglas J. *Romans 1–8.* Chicago: Moody, 1990.

Vaughan, Curtis and Bruce Corley. *Romans: A Study Guide Commentary.* Grand Rapids: Zondervan, 1976.

1 CORINTHIANS

The letter (1:1-2; 16:21) as well as church tradition acknowledge Paul as the author of 1 Corinthians. This affirmation generally has gone unchallenged. The letter was written around A.D. 55 near the end of Paul's three-year ministry in Ephesus (see 1 Cor 16:5-9; Acts 20:31).

The City of Corinth

Corinth was one of the chief commercial cities of the Roman Empire. Its location made it a natural center of commerce and transportation. It had two ports: Cenchrea, six miles to the east of Corinth on the Aegean Sea (see Rom 16:1), and Lechaeum, a port on the Corinthian Gulf that opened westward to the Adriatic Sea. Sailing in those days was very hazardous, and rounding the southern tip of Greece was a troublesome voyage. To avoid this detour, eastbound shipping between Rome and Asia used the isthmus at Corinth as a portage, unloading their cargoes and carrying them overland to be reloaded at the opposite port. Corinth was thus called the bridge of the seas. It was also a gateway for north-south routes between the Peloponnesus and mainland Greece. As a commercial center it was famous for arts and crafts.

Ancient Corinth was completely destroyed in 146 B.C. by the Roman General Mummius because it had taken the lead in an attempted revolt by the Greeks against the rising power of the Roman Empire. At that time its art treasures and wealth were said to have equaled those from Athens. For nearly one hundred years the city lay in ruins. In 44 B.C. Julius Caesar sent a colony of soldiers to rebuild it, making it the seat of the Roman province of Achaia. Almost immediately it assumed the former prominence it had as the richest and most powerful city of Greece.

Corinth had two patron deities. Poseidon, god of the sea, was appropriately reflected in the naval power and devotion to the sea. The other deity, Aphrodite, goddess of sexual love, was reflected in the city's reputation for immorality. The temple was central to the worship of Aphrodite. It boasted one thousand female prostitutes available to the people of the city and to all the visitors. Most of these women were famous for their great beauty. The income of the temple prostitutes provided a major source of the city's income. This practice, coupled with the looseness often characteristic of a port city of a mixed and transient population, gave Corinth a reputation far beyond the cities of its day.

To demonstrate this fact, the Greeks invented a term, *to Corinthianize,* which meant *to live an immoral life*. To call a young woman "a Corinthian" meant she was an immoral person. Paul wrote what perhaps was a descriptive account of Corinth in his Letter to the Romans (see Rom 1:18-32).

The Church at Corinth

The church was a picture of converts who had come out of this background (see 1 Cor 6:11). The church had several problems, among them a leadership problem producing divisions in the church (1:10-17). Immoral practices were not being dealt with (5:1–6:20). An enthusiastic group in the church flaunted their spiritual gifts (12:1–14:40). A legalistic group was concerned about dietary laws (8:1–10:32). Some were abusing the Lord's Supper (11:17-34), and others were offering false teachings regarding the resurrection (15:1-58). These matters—in addition to its multiethnic makeup of Greeks, Romans, and Jews and a mixture of social classes including rich, poor, and slave—made for a unique and troubled congregation.

Occasion

Paul had been to Corinth and stayed for eighteen months (see Acts 18). During this time he had established the church. He possibly visited again for a short time between the Letters to the Corinthians and the time he was in Corinth when he wrote Romans. Some have conjectured four visits and have rearranged the order quite a bit.

The apostle had received information from different sources concerning the conditions in the Corinthian church. Members of Chloe's household had informed him of the various factions in the church (1:11). Stephanus, Fortunatus, and Achaicus came to Paul in Ephesus to bring a contribution to his ministry (16:17).

Purpose and Theology

Paul dealt with several problems in this letter. He learned of these matters through the report from Chloe's people (1:11), common rumors (5:1), and from information received from the church (7:1; 8:1; 12:1; 16:1). Paul wrote to answer the questions the Corinthians had put to him, but he had other concerns as well. Although the church was quite gifted (1:4-7), it was equally immature and unspiritual (3:1-4). Paul wanted to restore the church in its areas of weakness. Through the inspiration of the Holy Spirit, he expounded the Bible's clearest exposition on the Lord's Supper (11:17-34), the resurrection (15:1-58), and spiritual gifts (12:1–14:40).

Yet the focus of 1 Corinthians is not on doctrinal theology but pastoral theology. This letter deals with the problem of those who bring division to the body of Christ (1:11–3:4), with the treatment of fellow Christians who sin (5:1-13), with matters of sexuality in marriage and divorce (7:1-40), with propriety in church worship (11:2-34), and with disputes about food (8:1–11:1).

I. Introduction (1:1-9)
II. Concerning Divisions (1:10–3:4)
III. Concerning Leadership (3:5–4:21)
IV. Concerning Immorality (5:1–6:20)
V. Concerning Marriage (7:1-40)
VI. Concerning Food Offered to Idols (8:1–11:1)
VII. Concerning Orderly Worship (11:2-34)
VIII. Concerning Spiritual Gifts (12:1–14:40)
IX. Concerning the Resurrection (15:1-58)
X. Concerning the Collection and Closing Remarks (16:1-24)

1:1-9
Introduction

Paul began this letter in customary fashion, identifying himself (with Sosthenes) as the writer. The recipients were primarily "the church of God in Corinth" (see Acts 20:28; 2 Cor 1:1). Generally, however, the letter was addressed to "all those everywhere who call on the name of the Lord Jesus Christ" (1:2). The greeting is followed by a typical Pauline salutation (see Gal 1:3; Eph 1:2) and a lengthy expression of thanksgiving (1:4-9). Here he offered thanks for their reception of the gospel, their giftedness, and particularly for God's faithfulness.

1:10-17
Concerning Divisions

Paul's first major topic was the problem of divisions in the church. Some were claiming to follow Paul, some Apollos, others Cephas (Peter), and yet others Christ (1:12). The leaders themselves were not the cause of division. Most likely the superspiritualists claiming to follow Christ were the major source of the problem.

Paul disclaimed responsibility for the situation and showed its sinfulness and folly. God does not act in the way human wisdom might expect. God redeemed men and women by the foolishness of the cross, not by anything that would enhance human pride. The gospel message did not originate in profound human thought but in the Holy Spirit Himself.

1:18–3:4
Infants in Christ

The Corinthian church showed a great misunderstanding of the essential truth of the gospel. The Corinthians evidenced a wrong concept of wisdom (1:18–2:5), a wrong concept of the gospel (2:6-13), and a wrong concept of spirituality (2:14–3:4). It must be remembered that God's wisdom is something that those "without the Spirit" cannot accept (2:14-16). The Corinthians had an improper attitude regarding church leaders. They demonstrated they were "mere infants in Christ" (3:1-4).

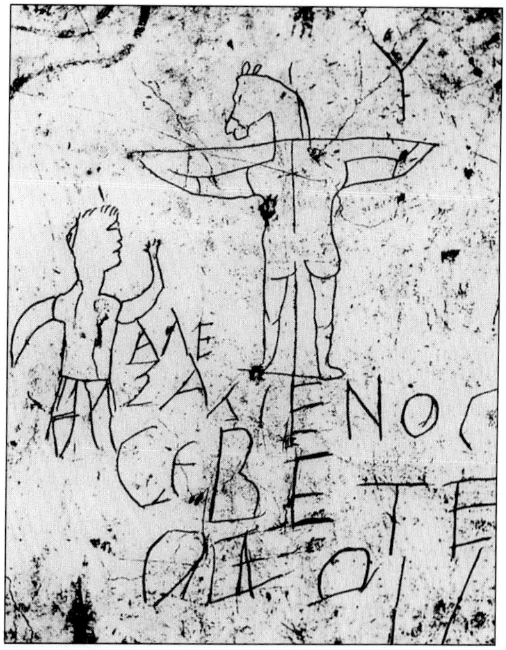

The above graffiti found in Rome (A.D. 200–250) shows a man kneeling before a crucified figure with a donkey's head. This is an example of the contempt shown toward the importance placed by Christians on Christ's crucifixion (see 1 Cor 1:20).

The Cross of Christ

The crucifixion of Jesus of Nazareth is the central event of the New Testament. The term "Cross of Christ" has come to stand for all that went into and flows out from that event. The cross of Christ points to the violent death of Jesus by means of a heinous Roman method of execution reserved for slaves and enemies of the state. This central event, therefore, is at the same time the "scandal" (Gal 5:11) of the Christian faith.

Torturous executions of the ancient world had found their worst form in crucifixion. Josephus called it "the most wretched of deaths." Already in Jesus' own ministry "bearing your cross" was a mark of discipleship (Mark 8:34; Matt 10:38; 16:24; Luke 9:23; 14:27) and seemed to mark a readiness to follow even unto death for Christ's sake.

Jesus probably was stripped of all clothing and nailed to something like rough hewn boards that would have elevated Him but a few feet once secured in the ground. This elevation, or lifting up, Jesus also anticipated, referring to it in His conversation with Nicodemus (John 3:14).

To the Jew, hanging was a sign of cursedness (Deut 21:23) and so the usefulness of the cross in God's saving plan representing a turning around of the law and all the habits that had grown up around the law. To the Jews the "word of the cross" (1 Cor 1:18) was a scandal and not to be believed (1 Cor 1: 28). To the Greeks it was madness and not to be believed (1 Cor 1:21). But to Paul the cross of Christ was the power and wisdom of God and alone was to be preached about Christ in the world (1 Cor 2:2-5; see Gal 3:1).

In view of the victorious resurrection of Jesus, the cross now signifies atonement (Col 1:20; 2:4); unity of Jew and Gentile (Eph 2:16); baptism (Rom 6:3-11); self-denial of the believer (Phil 3:8); the believer's self-identification with Christ and rejection of the world (Gal 2:20). Indeed, the living out of Christian faith has and must always see earthly existence through the cross of Christ.

If anything, the Christian "world view" is cruciform: Christians live in a suffering world and remind themselves that even the goods they may hold are perishing and often promote death (see 1 Cor 7:29-31). Christians at the same time are filled with joyful hope because Christ's victory was already secure even while he hung upon His cross of suffering. □

3:5-9
Partners in God's Work

Paul and Apollos were not in competition with each other. They were partners in the work of God. One "planted" while another "watered." Each one did his part, but God brought about the growth (3:5-9).

3:10-23
Christ the Foundation

The foundation of the church was not the church leaders but Jesus Christ. Each person builds on this foundation. What is built may be something valuable or something worthless. Final evaluation of the value of one's work will be revealed at the day of judgment. Paul explained the condition for rewards (3:10-17) with appropriate warnings for leaders and followers (3:18-23).

4:1-21
Christian Leaders

Paul's warnings do not mean human leaders are unimportant. People are saved only by Christ, and there is no other basis for salvation. Church leaders build on the foundation. From this thought Paul appealed to the Corinthians to act on what he had written. The apostle emphasized both the responsibility of leaders (4:1-5) and the importance of their example (4:6-21). They were "entrusted with the secret things of God" (4:1). These secret things granted to these leaders are things that human wisdom cannot discover but can only be revealed by God to His people.

5:1-13
Concerning Immorality

The apostle had heard reports of sexual immorality among them (5:1). He reminded the church that incest was considered a reprobate act even by pagans. The Corinthians, however, had apparently done nothing to deal with the detestable evil. Worse than that they were proud of this situation (5:2). Paul urged them to discipline the man involved by handing him "over to Satan so that the sinful nature may be destroyed and his spirit saved on the day of the Lord" (5:5). This abandonment to Satan was to be accomplished not by some magical incantation but by expelling the man from the church (see 5:2,7,11,13). To expel him meant to turn him over to the devil's territory, severed from any connection with God's people.

Paul ordered the church not ever to eat with such a

man. This means that intimate association with an immoral person, especially together at the Lord's table, would cause the unbelieving world to think that the church approves such ungodly living. The church must exercise spiritual discipline over the members of the church (see Matt 18:15-18).

6:1-20
The Spirit's Temple

Paul then chastised them for their factious spirit. Their active part in lawsuits before heathen judges evidenced their carnality (6:1-8). Sexual relations outside the marriage bond are a perversion of the divinely established marriage union. Believers have been bought by Christ. The body is a temple of the Holy Spirit. Christians must glorify God in their bodies (6:9-20).

7:1-40
Concerning Marriage

The Corinthians had raised a series of questions for Paul. He responded to their concerns by addressing the issue and then offering principles for them to deal with the issue. Paul maintained marriage as the normal rule of life (see Eph 5:21-33). He offered general principles for marriage (7:1-7). He then gave advice to the unmarried (7:8-9) and then to the married (7:10-11). People should lead the kind of life God assigns them. He did note a definite value in celibacy because celibates are free to serve the Lord without the cares that are inseparable from marriage (7:32-35). In verse 10 Paul had appealed to Jesus' teaching regarding the permanence of marriage. If a believer is separated from her spouse, Paul argued that in light of Christ's command she is not to marry again. Rather, the separated couple should be reconciled (7:11). Verses 12-16 offer advice concerning separation/divorce when an unbeliever abandons a believer. In this case the abandoned believer is under no obligation to remain married to the unbeliever.

Paul offered further advice concerning contentment (7:17-24). He concluded this topic with counsel for virgins and widows (7:25-40).

8:1-13
Concerning Food Offered to Idols

Most meat that was available in the marketplace came from animals sacrificed in the temple. To the more scrupulous in the community all of this meat would be suspect. Some Corinthians felt more mature because they were convinced that idols had no reality—"for there is but one God" (8:6). Therefore any food offered to idols was still fit to eat. Love, not knowledge, is the key to Christian conduct (8:1-13). It would be better not to eat

A tombstone from Rome (first century A.D.), from the grave of Aurelius Hermia and his wife Aurelia Philemation, shows the couple clasping hands. It is inscribed with words of praise from each for the other. (For Paul on marriage, see 1 Cor 7; Eph 5.)

A statue of the emperor Claudius who was worshiped as a god in the Roman Empire (see "so-called gods" in 1 Cor 8:5).

meat, even if one's conscience allows, than to lead a fellow believer into sin.

9:1-27
Christian Discipline

Paul practiced the principles he described. As an apostle he had certain rights and privileges. One of these rights was to be maintained by those to whom he preached. But Paul stressed that one should subordinate one's own interests to those of others, especially those of Christ and His gospel (9:1-23).

It is not necessarily who begins but who completes the Christian life that counts. Thus it is a life of discipline, not license, that is important (9:24-27).

10:1-13
A Way of Escape

The apostle showed how the Israelites, despite their rights and privileges, suffered in the wilderness. Through the use of typological interpretation of the Old Testament events, Paul warned the Corinthians not to grumble or dabble with idolatry (10:6-12). Christians, however, need not be fearful in the face of temptation, for God has provided help and a way of escape for those who will take it (10:13).

10:14–11:1
Christian Freedom

Spiritual fellowship at the Lord's table served as a stern reminder that the Corinthians should have nothing to do with idols. One cannot share simultaneously in the Lord's table and in the table of demons (10:14-22).

A summary of the discussion (10:23–11:1) brings chapters 8–10 to a conclusion. The food had not been affected even if it previously was offered to idols, since all food belongs ultimately to God. It is not that the meat had been contaminated. The problem remained with the weak Christian whose conscience was tainted. The strong believers should have passed the meat by out of concern for the good of the congregation and other believers. Believers must always act in a spirit of love, in a spirit of self-discipline, with the good of the community in mind, and with God's glory uppermost in mind.

11:2-34
Orderly Worship

The next issue Paul addressed concerned the different head coverings that appropriately distinguish women and men as they pray or prophesy in worship (11:2-16). Paul praised the church at this point because they had not departed significantly from the substance of what he had previously taught. He had no praise for what he heard about their behavior at the Lord's Supper (11:22). Their action did more harm than good. The Lord's Supper should be a celebration of unity; instead divisions among the church were magnified (11:18).

Paul repeated the words of institution to point out they are participating in Christ's body and blood (see 10:16-17). To participate in an unworthy manner, with divisions among them, profanes the supper and invites God's judgment (11:29). Paul exhorted them to examine their motives, their methods, and their manners as they gathered to worship the Lord at His supper (see the article "The Lord's Supper").

12:1-3
Jesus Is Lord

The exercise of spiritual gifts in the church was a subject on which the Corinthians had asked for advice. Many of them were attracted by the more spectacular gifts. All spiritual gifts are given by the Spirit. No one speaking by the Spirit's power will use derogatory words about Jesus.

The Lord's Supper

The Lord's Supper was instituted by the command of Christ and by His example as well. On the night before His death, Christ gathered with His disciples to eat the Passover meal (see Matt 26:26-29; Mark 14:22-25; Luke 22:17-20).

Since the Supper was celebrated in connection with the Passover, we may assume the bread was unleavened. Jesus gave thanks (*eucharisteo,* from which the idea of Eucharist comes) for the meal. That the institution of the Lord's Supper was connected with the Passover meal is clear in the phrase "after the Supper" (1 Cor 11:25), meaning after the Passover meal. It is practically certain that 1 Corinthians was written before the completion of the Gospels, which means that Paul's account is the earliest record we have have of the institution of the Lord's Supper.

The Names of the Supper. The Supper is identified six different ways in the NT: (1) Lord's Supper (1 Cor 11:20); (2) Lord's Table (1 Cor 10:21); (3) Breaking of Bread (Acts 2:42; 20:7); (4) Communion (1 Cor 10:16); (5) Eucharist (1 Cor 11:24); and (6) Love Feast (some manuscript readings of 2 Pet 2:13; Jude 12).

The Meaning of the Supper. The Supper's initial focus was table fellowship around a common meal. As the bread and wine were taken, the Lord's presence was to be recalled in the words "in remembrance of me" (1 Cor 11:24). To recall means to transport an action that is buried in the past in such a way that its original potency and vitality are not lost but are carried over into the present. It is a remembrance of the life and death of the Lord.

Just as the Passover was the means that dynamically allowed Jews to relive the past experience of their forebears in the land of Egypt, the Lord's Supper takes believers back to the scenes of the Lord's redemption, leading them again to receive the blessings of the Lord's passion.

The bread symbolizes His sinless life that qualified Him to be a perfect sacrifice for sin. It represents His body in which He actually bore our sin on the cross (1 Pet 2:24). His shed blood is represented by the wine. Believers are to look upon these elements as taking them back to the scenes of the Lord's death.

The believers' participation in the Supper represents their response to the Lord's love that bore the cross.

The Supper is a basic announcing of the gospel (1 Cor 11:26), a sermon by the entire church in silence. The Supper tends to quicken the anticipation for the second coming (see Matt 26:29). It thus points beyond itself to a future hope in the kingdom of God.

As believers participate in the Supper, they are reminded of the oneness within the body of Christ and of the fellowship that is shared among fellow believers. The observance is one that is so simple a believing child can partake with a sense of understanding. Yet it also contains so many doctrinal ramifications that even the most mature believer will not fully comprehend its meaning.

The Practice of the Supper. The church is commanded to continue the ordinance of the Lord's Supper (1 Cor 11:24). The Supper provides a needed emphasis on the death and resurrection of the Lord that established the new covenant (1 Cor 11:25; see Jer 31:31-34).

There are no specific guidelines about how and when the Supper should be observed. Yet the implications from the NT teach us that the Supper should be regular, frequent (1 Cor 11:20), and normally on the first day of the week (see Acts 20:7).

Conclusion. Past, present, and future are thus gathered up in one sacred and joyful festival of the Lord's Supper in apostolic practice and teaching. Indeed, in this ordinance the whole of what Christianity means is expressed. One Lord, incarnate, atoning, and triumphant is the sum and substance of the observance.

Here is seen a dramatic interrelationship between human relationships and relationship with God. The essence of the experience is fellowship and worship, eating together, while at the same time remembering the death of the Lord Jesus Christ in our behalf. □

The confession 'Jesus is Lord" is the touchstone of the Spirit's genuine work in the community.

12:4-31a
Gifts of the Spirit

Paul named nine gifts of the Spirit. Their use is compared to the functioning of the various parts of the human body for the good of the whole. All believers have been "baptized by one Spirit into one body" (12:13). The same Spirit brings refreshment and unity to the whole body. Paul emphasized the unity of the church expressed in variety. As chaos would take over in the human body if each part tried to do the work of other parts, so problems will break out in the church unless each member makes his or her proper contribution for the good of the whole (see the article "Spiritual Gifts").

12:31b–13:13
Grace of Heavenly Love

Paul now explained the right way to exercise all spiritual

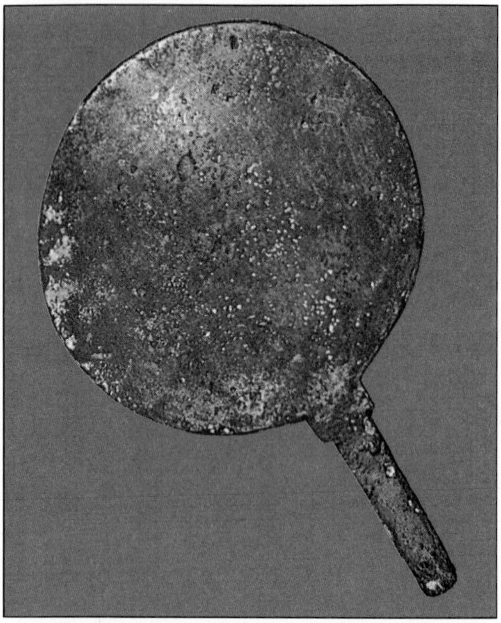

"Mirror" in 1 Corinthians 13:12 refers to a bronze mirror like the one above, which could be polished to obtain a dark reflection.

gifts. Higher than all the gifts of the Spirit is the grace of heavenly love. Paul declared that even the most spectacular manifestations of the gifts, even tongues or prophecy, mean nothing unless motivated by love. Christians may be talented, gifted, devoted, generous in their giving, or endowed with mountain-moving faith; but it is of no value if love is not present (13:1-3).

Spiritual gifts have their place for a time, but love endures forever. Above all else love is the one thing needful. Faith, hope, and love form a heavenly triad of spiritual graces that endure forever, but "the greatest of these is love" (13:4-13).

14:1-25
The Way of Love

Paul applied this grand truth to the Corinthian church by exhorting them to "follow the way of love" (14:1). While all gifts should be desired, Paul maintained that prophecy should be the gift of choice in the church meetings (14:1-12). The Corinthians desired tongues more than other gifts. Paul claimed that tongues without interpretation is of little value to anyone except to the speaker. The goal of the practice of any spiritual gift is the edifica-

Spiritual Gifts

To the community of faith spiritual gifts, *charisma,* are given (Rom 12:6; 1 Cor 12-14; 1 Pet 4:10). Specific gifts of the Spirit for the building up (edification) of the body of Christ are listed in Romans 12:5-8; 1 Corinthians 12–14; Ephesians 4:11-16. Although it is the same Spirit who gives these nurturing gifts (1 Cor 12:4), the gifts are different in kind and in purpose concerning what they are supposed to accomplish. One might distinguish three categories of the gifts of the Spirit.

1. *The essential gifts that all Christians must have.* These are the gifts of the Spirit's presence and the highest gifts, namely, faith, hope, and love. The presence of the Spirit enables the spirit of humans to open their lives to God through the gospel. The gift of faith (Eph 2:8-9) is the gift that appropriates the Spirit. The gift of hope enables believers to anticipate the full redemption the Spirit of God will accomplish (Rom 8:18-39). The gift of love enables Christians to demonstrate the presence of the Spirit (Rom 5:5).

2. *The dynamic gifts of the Spirit.* These have proved most difficult for Christians to interpret. A list of the dynamic gifts would include: a heroic kind of faith (1 Cor 12:9), the gift of healing (1 Cor 12:9), miracles (1 Cor 12:10), discerning the spirits, speaking in tongues, and the interpretation of tongues (1 Cor 12:10).

These gifts are particularly in dispute in contemporary Christendom. Questions arise: What are they? How are they to be used? Are they normative?

For example, miracles in the NT are of four types: healing the sick, casting out evil, raising the dead, and nature miracles. Are all of these viable today? Three basic answers are found among contemporary Christians to this question about miracles.

1. Some say these miracles were intended to be confined to the first century as an evidence of the coming of the Spirit.

2. Others say these miracles are supposed to be normative in the church in every generation.

3. A third perspective is that these NT mighty works are tokens of what God will do at the last days. In the meantime such miracles might occur in any age, but if they were to do so, it would have to be for some special redemptive purpose of God.

Another example of a disputed dynamic gift is the gift of tongues, which has been much discussed in the twentieth century. Many scholars would agree that tongues are ecstatic utterances. Another interpretation is that the tongues in NT days referred to foreign languages. Some charismatic Christians want to make this gift normative for all Christians. Other interpreters believe that the gift of

tion of others. When tongues speakers speak only to themselves, they edify no one (14:17). The confusion seems like madness to those outside the church.

Outside there is perhaps a role for tongues, either for private devotion (14:17) or as a sign of judgment (14:21). Inside the church tongues should not be used unless an interpreter is present. Prophecy, however, should be exercised inside the church or outside the church because it both builds up and convicts (14:22-25).

14:26-40
Strengthen the Church

All gifts are allowed to function with the goal of mutual edification in mind, not selfish demonstration (14:26). Both tongues speakers and prophets must speak in turn. Each utterance should be properly evaluated (14:27-33). Women should refrain from interrupting with their questions (14:33b-36).

Two principles remain valid for the church of any place or time period: (1) all "must be done for the strengthening of the church" (14:26), and (2) "everything should be done in a fitting and orderly way" (14:40).

15:1-19
The Resurrection

Paul knew that at Corinth there were doubts about the resurrection. He affirmed that the resurrection of Jesus is essential for the gospel message (15:1-11). The consistent testimony of the church was that Jesus died for our sins, rose again, and appeared to numerous witnesses. Paul pointed out that if the Corinthians consistently maintained their antiresurrection argument, Christ could not have been raised. If Christ has not been raised, there is no hope, and all gospel proclamation is in vain.

15:20-34
Resurrection for Believers

The resurrection of Christ carries with it the promise of resurrection from the dead for all believers. Just as the firstfruits presented to God on the first day of the week following Passover guaranteed the coming harvest (Lev 23:9-11), so Christ's resurrection guarantees the resurrection of believers (1 Cor 15:20-28).

The hope of the resurrection encourages men and women to become Christians. The same hope provided

tongues ceased in the NT era. Some interpreters see tongues as a gift for some Christians as a way to remind the whole body of Christ of the need to use human emotion as a way of developing spiritually.

The gift of healing also is often variously understood by contemporary Christians. "Faith healing" means to some direct healing without medical intervention. Most Christians today would affirm the healing gift of the Spirit through and with medical therapy. These are only a few of the interpretations of the dynamic gifts of the Spirit.

The third class of gifts of the Spirit, the functional gifts of the Spirit, are necessary to the structure and the ongoing ministry of the church. The major functional gifts of the Spirit to the NT church were:

1. Apostles, the founding circle of witnesses to the Christ event—historical apostles (the twelve and Paul).

2. Prophets, those who proclaim the word of the Lord clearly and courageously.

3. Evangelists, the ones who seek to declare the salvation of God to those outside the faith.

4. Pastors or shepherds who guide and guard the people of God.

5. Teachers, those who nurture and encourage believers.

6. Ministry, service to others.

7. Exhorting, the task of encouraging the church.

8. Supervising, the role of planning and implementing plans.

9. Showing mercy, special care for those with special needs (Rom 12).

10. Word of wisdom, awareness from experience enlarged by the Spirit.

11. Word of knowledge, facts of learning applied by the Spirit.

12. The gift of administration (government).

13. The gift of helps, the understanding of problems and bringing spiritual resolutions to them (1 Cor 12).

The gifts of the Spirit lead to the fruit of the Spirit (Gal 5:22-25). The "offices" of ministry—such as pastors, evangelists, prophets, and teachers, elders, bishops, deacons—provide leadership for the body of Christ. All believers are the priests of God who, as living stones, make up the temple of God (1 Pet 2:5,9).

Spiritual gifts are given to the people of God so that they might build up the church, bear witness to Christ, and become light to all persons (Matt 5:14). It is not appropriate to glory in gifted individuals and give them undo praise. The purpose of the gifts of the Spirit is for the use of the whole body of Christ and for the enlarging nurture of the church and its witness in the world. □

PAUL'S LISTS OF SPIRITUAL GIFTS					
Spiritual Gift	**Rom 12:6-8**	**1 Cor 12:8-10**	**1 Cor 12:28**	**1 Cor 12:29-30**	**Eph 4:11**
Apostle			1	1	1
Prophet	1	5	2	2	2
Teacher	3		3	3	5
Pastor					4
Miracles		4	4	4	
Discernment of Spirits		6			
Word of Wisdom Knowledge		1			
Evangelists					3
Exhorters	4				
Faith		2			
Healings		3	5	5	
Tongues		7	8	6	
Interpretation		8		7	
Ministry/Serving	2				
Administration			7		
Rulers	6				
Helpers			6		
Mercy	7				
Giving	5				

Seven of the original thirty-eight columns of the Temple of Apollo remain standing at the site of ancient Corinth.

Paul with boldness to proclaim the gospel and endure the suffering that accompanied his calling (15:29-34).

15:35-58
Resurrection Body

The resurrection body will be one adapted to its new spiritual environment. The physical body is weak, dishonorable, and perishable. It will be raised in Christ as spiritual, glorious, powerful, and imperishable (15:35-50). The resurrection will take place when the last trumpet sounds. With genuine excitement the apostle shared his real hope: the transformation of the dead who will be raised. Those alive at Christ's coming will also be transformed "in the twinkling of an eye" (15:52). Thanks to the victory of Christ, death will be finally abolished. This is great encouragement for all believers to persevere faithfully in the Lord's service, knowing that "labor in the Lord is not in vain" (1 Cor 15:51-58).

16:1-24
Closing Remarks

Paul told them to set aside some money week by week so that it would be ready to be taken to Jerusalem for the needs there (see 2 Cor 8–9).

Paul planned to remain at Ephesus to make use of ministry opportunities there. In the meantime the Ephesians could expect a visit from Timothy (16:5-14). A closing formal exhortation to firm faith and love led Paul to conclude with his customary greetings and benediction (16:19-24).

Theological Significance

If Paul were to write a letter to the average church today, he probably would rewrite much of 1 Corinthians. The Corinthians' world was much like our modern world. The people had the same thirst for intellectualism, the same permissiveness toward moral standards, and certainly the same fascination for the spectacular. The church resembled our churches—extremely proud, affluent, and fiercely eager for acceptance by the world.

In doctrine there existed a mixture of orthodoxy and error. In ethics the church manifested widespread immorality and worldliness. Two valuable contributions come from this letter. First, we have the doctrinal and pastoral expositions of the topics discussed. Second, we have Paul's approach to the problems. Paul carefully defined each issue and then offered helpful principles to deal with them. What we learn from the apostle's method is as important for the contemporary church as the solutions he articulated.

Questions for Reflection

1. What are the problems Paul addressed in this letter?
2. What are the principles Paul developed to deal with the problem of food sacrificed to idols?
3. What is the significance of the resurrection for believers?
4. What is the goal of spiritual gifts?
5. How does God's wisdom compare and contrast to human wisdom?

Sources for Additional Study

Fee, Gordon D. *The First Epistle to the Corinthians. The New International Commentary.* Grand Rapids: Eerdmans, 1987.

Gromacki, Robert G. *Called to Be Saints: An Exposition of 1 Corinthians.* Grand Rapids: Baker, 1977.

Lea, Thomas D. and Curtis Vaughan. *First Corinthians.* Grand Rapids: Zondervan, 1983.

Morris, Leon. *The First Epistle of Paul to the Corinthians. Tyndale New Testament Commentaries.* Grand Rapids: Eerdmans, 1958.

2 CORINTHIANS

Paul is the author of this letter (1:1; 10:1). It is the apostle's most personal and pastoral letter. While it is a different kind of letter than Romans or even 1 Corinthians, it is characterized by his style. It contains more autobiographical material than any of his other writings.

The letter is difficult to date, for we do not know the amount of time that separated 1 and 2 Corinthians. It has been variously dated between A.D. 55 and 57.

Destination and Situation

See 1 Corinthians.

Purpose and Theology

The primary purpose of 2 Corinthians was to prepare the church at Corinth for another visit from Paul. The letter was penned at a difficult time between Paul and the Corinthians. Paul communicated his thankful relief that the crisis at Corinth had somewhat subsided. Moreover, Paul wrote to them concerning the collection that he wanted to gather for the church at Jerusalem.

Paul exercised extraordinary vigor in declaring his role and authority as an apostle. His opponents, the so-called "super apostles" (see 2 Cor 10–13), had challenged Paul's apostolic status and leadership. In return Paul authenticated his apostolic calling and ministry.

The self-portrait of Paul is one of the most fascinating features of this letter. Second Corinthians gives invaluable autobiographical information. Dominant motifs include Paul's gratitude to God and Christ (1:3; 5:14) and his ministry as a continuing triumph in Christ (2:14). Paul shared the risen life of Christ (4:10-11). Simultaneously he gloried in infirmities and was content with weaknesses, persecutions, and calamities for the sake of Christ (12:9). His ministry was characterized by integrity and suffering (1:8-12; 6:3-10; 11:23-29), marks of a true apostle. His message as an ambassador of Christ focused on the message of reconciliation (5:11-21) and Jesus Christ as Lord (4:5).

Paul's collection for the church at Jerusalem had an important role in his missionary efforts. He devoted two chapters to this matter (chaps. 8–9). They provide some of the most helpful teaching on Christian stewardship found in the New Testament.

Events between 1 and 2 Corinthians

The reconstruction of these events is helpful for understanding the issues addressed in the letter. However, there is no universal agreement on these matters.

1. The Corinthians probably rectified most of the practical abuses Paul addressed in 1 Corinthians.

2. However, because of the arrival of the intruders (Paul's opponents), conditions at the church had deteriorated, thus calling for Paul's painful visit (see 2:1; 12:14; 13:1-2).

3. Titus was sent from Ephesus to Corinth with the severe letter in which Paul called for the discipline of the wrongdoer (2:3-9; 7:8-12). Paul instructed Titus to organize the collection for Jerusalem (8:6). Titus was to meet Paul in Troas or in Macedonia (2:12-13; 7:5-6).

4. Paul left Ephesus, then suffered his affliction in Asia (1:8-11), and then crossed to Macedonia to organize the collection in the churches there (2:13; 8:1-4).

5. Titus arrived in Macedonia with the report of the Corinthians' response to the severe letter (7:5-16).

6. On returning to Macedonia and hearing of new problems at Corinth, the apostle wrote 2 Corinthians.

7. Paul spent several months at Corinth (Acts 20:2-3), at which time he authored Romans.

Unity of the Letter

Some have suggested that chapters 10–13 were the severe letter, written prior to chapters 1–9; but strong evidence for this hypothesis is lacking. Most likely the severe letter has not survived. The letter, as we now have it, forms a coherent whole as the structure and outline indicate. The history of the church has been nearly unanimous in affirming the letter's unity. No existing Greek manuscripts present the letter in any other form.

I. Introduction (1:1-2)
II. Apostolic Experience (1:3-11)
III. Apostolic Explanation (1:12–2:11)
IV. Apostolic Ministry (2:12–7:16)
V. Apostolic Fellowship (8:1–9:15)
VI. Apostleship Defended (10:1–13:14)

The Lechaion Road at Corinth with the Acrocorinth (mountain) in the background.

1:1-2
Introduction

The letter begins with a standard greeting. The identification of Paul as an apostle, one specially commissioned by Christ, is significant for Paul's defense of his calling and ministry.

1:3-11
Apostolic Experience

Paul knew what it meant to suffer, but it was in suffering that Paul experienced God's comfort. Paul uniquely described the value of an experience of suffering (1:4-7) before relating the experience from which the value came (1:8-11). Paul praised God as the source of all comfort, the comfort he wished to pass along to the Corinthians. The apostle thought he might not survive the difficult experience (1:8). God's intervention seemed like a resurrection in his life. This reinforced Paul's conviction that God's resources alone, not human effort, can provide comfort and refuge.

1:12–2:11
Apostolic Explanation

Paul's opponents suggested that Paul really had no desire to visit them. Paul's first explanation was an appeal to his clear conscience before God (1:12-14). He claimed he was not ambivalent about his intentions; he truly wanted to visit them (1:15-16). Paul's purpose was for vindication, not accusation (1:17-22). This meant he desired their joy, not their pain (1:23–2:4). Thus the apostle called for redemption, not retaliation (2:5-11).

2:12–7:16
Apostolic Ministry

2:12-17
Triumph of the Ministry

At this key transitional point in the letter, Paul began to explain the nature of apostolic ministry. He began to recount his journey from Ephesus to Philippi, when he sought news of the Corinthians' response to the severe letter (2:12-13). At this key transitional point in the letter, Paul explained the nature of apostolic ministry (2:14–7:1). This was followed by further explanation of his ministry and motives (7:2-16).

The apostolic ministry follows the ministry of Jesus, in that it includes both suffering and glory. Even in suffering there is triumph in Christ. Paul borrowed a picture from the Roman army. The perfumes of a Roman triumph were joy to the triumphant victors and death for the defeated prisoners. Similarly, Jesus' triumph is a sweet aroma of triumph for believers, but it is a symbol of death for unbelievers.

3:1-18
Testament of the Ministry

Paul noted that the true minister does not need human endorsement (3:1) because changed lives are the authentic endorsement of genuine ministry (3:2). Paul could not validate his own ministry. The certainty of a valid ministry is only from Christ (3:3-6).

Paul's boast was not in himself but in the new covenant in the Spirit, which unlike the old covenant is not fading away. Paul followed the Jewish interpretation of Exodus 34:29-35, which taught that Moses put a veil over his face so the people would not see the glory fade. The new covenant does not veil the presence of God; it is permanent, and through the Spirit of God it reveals God. The old covenant of the letter was a ministry of death. The new covenant gives life. The old covenant was external, engraved on stones. The new covenant was internal, engraved on human hearts (3:7-18).

4:1–5:10
Testimony of the Ministry

There was no deceit in Paul's ministry, for the ministry was received, not achieved (4:1). Paul's message was not about himself but about Jesus, who is the Light (4:2-6). The apostolic ministry is a manifestation of light. Paul himself was only a weak container that held the priceless pot: the message that "Jesus Christ is Lord" (4:5-7). The only power in the gospel is God's power. The contrast between weakness and power was typified by the apostle's ministry, modeled on the sufferings of Jesus that flowed to others (4:7-15).

Yet the ministry was a continuation of renewal. Even in the midst of suffering, Paul exemplified courage. This was possible because he looked beyond the decay of the outer person to the renewal of the new person. Paul's life was one of faith, focusing on unseen realities (4:16–5:5). Because the future includes Christ's judgment, Paul exerted great effort to please Christ in all things (5:6-10).

5:11–6:13
Service of the Ministry

Now the apostle claimed that the motivation for service is the love of Christ. No one should live for himself or herself but for Christ (5:11-15). Paul's job, like ours, was to proclaim the reconciliation accomplished by Christ. We who are the recipients of divine reconciliation have the privilege, like Paul, to be heralds to minister God's message throughout the world (5:16-20). Reconciliation is the removal of human enmity toward God. This was accomplished by Christ, who "had no sin" but was made to "be sin for us, so that in him we might become the righteousness of God" (5:21).

Following this train of thought, Paul stated that from his side he was reconciled to the Corinthians. Paul had nothing against the Corinthians. If there was any blockage in the relationship with him, it must have been on their side (6:1-13).

6:14–7:1
Separation of the Minister

Paul seemed to suspect the block in the relationship was brought about by the Corinthians' love of the world. Paul pointed out that the light cannot be a part of the darkness. Christians must not be bound to unbelievers in a way that will affect their moral purity.

7:2-16
A Concluding Explanation

This section of the letter concludes with one more appeal to the Corinthians and another explanation of his ministry and motives. Paul was not criticizing them but appealing to them in love. Thus he asked them to "make room for us in your hearts" (7:2-6).

8:1–9:15
Apostolic Fellowship

In the context of restored relationships Paul turned to the topic of the collection for the church in Jerusalem. These two chapters deal exclusively with the subject of the church's need for renewed stewardship. In 1 Corinthians 16:1-4 Paul had appealed for help in the Jerusalem relief fund. Jerusalem had been impoverished through the famines in Judea in the 40s. The collection was both an act of charity as well as a symbol of unity between the Gentiles and Jews in the church (see Acts 11:27-30; Gal 2:10). The Corinthians had promised to give and had failed to participate. Paul now appealed for the Corinthians to complete what they said they would do.

Paul taught that believers should give sacrificially (8:1-2) and spontaneously (8:3-4), with spiritual motives (8:5-9). Paul taught that they should give freely, for God values the eagerness to give, not necessarily the amount of the gift (8:10-15).

Paul explained that Titus and two men from the Macedonian churches would handle the money. Paul would have nothing to do with money himself. The handling and administration of the money is as important as the giving of the money. It is important for the church and the world to see the honesty with which the church handles its finances (8:16–9:5).

Paul then reminded them of the extent of God's giving for them. Out of appreciation for God's gift, believers should give joyfully (9:6-15).

10:1–13:14
Apostleship Defended

10:1-11
Accusations against Paul

There is not only a subject change at this point but an abrupt change in tone. Paul's apostleship had been attacked. Here he vigorously defended it.

Paul was accused of being two-faced (10:1-2) and worldly (10:2-5). Paul's opponents claimed to have a closer relationship with Christ than Paul had (10:6-9). These accusers said Paul's presence was contemptible.

10:12-18
God's Commendation

Paul would not enter the game of comparing himself with these other ministers. He noted that God had used him, not the interlopers, to plant the Corinthian church. Whatever ministry his opponents might have had was dependent on his work. Paul's concern was not with the commendation of others. In the end only God's commendation counts.

11:1-33
Credentials of Genuineness

The Corinthian rebellion was serious enough to force Paul into the corner of self-defense. The apostle was shocked at how quickly they had turned away from apostolic teaching (11:1-6). Paul's pastoral concern was evidenced by his godly jealousy for the church.

Paul proclaimed the gospel in Corinth without payment, although he had the right to receive their support. He refused payment to avoid suspicion concerning his motives. The critics judged Paul for refusing payment, for they quickly received it. Paul was surprised that the Corinthians could not see through the hypocrisy of the opponents (11:7-21).

The irony is that his tenderness and pastoral concern was used against him as a supposed weakness. They claimed Paul was a false apostle and knew it; thus he did

The excavations at Corinth showing some of the many shops found in the agora (or market).

not receive their money. Paul turned the argument around and suggested the true sign of an apostle was a form of weakness, for true apostles suffer. Paul then chronicled his experiences of suffering (11:21-29). This was repulsive to Paul, so he related one particular experience of weakness. Yet that weakness was indeed his glory (11:30-33).

12:1-10
Ecstasy and Agony

The opponents' criticisms forced Paul to say what he did in this chapter. They claimed true apostles had special revelations. Paul knew this boasting was senseless, but he related a time around A.D. 42 when he experienced the inside of heaven. Paul disliked sharing this account, for he knew that God's strength is more easily seen in the apostle's weakness. In fact, God allowed Satan to afflict Paul to keep him humble and to demonstrate the power of God in his life. If vulnerability revealed God's power, Paul gladly accepted the weakness (12:1-10).

12:11-21
Concern for the Corinthians

Paul found this all distasteful. His ministry was not validated by special experiences but by his concern for the church. Paul planned to come to them again. He would again refuse their money. Paul's ministry was characterized by constant concern for people and a consistency in actions and motives.

13:1-14
Conclusion

Paul claimed he would without fail make another trip to visit them. He warned them at this time that he would have to deal with their sin. He would do so firmly with the power of God (13:1-4). He admonished them to examine their faith and to restore fellowship with him and with one another (13:5-10). The letter concludes without the usual greetings but with a beautiful benediction (13:11-14). The benediction is Trinitarian in form and has played an important role in the worship of God's people through the centuries.

Theological Significance

In this letter we learn of the importance of restoring relationships in ministry. An important lesson on dealing with opponents and appealing to God for confirmation of one's ministry is contained herein. The most important aspect of this letter is Paul's inspired insights regarding the nature of ministry. Ministry involves suffering, joy, comfort, and hard work. Primarily ministry is the power of God working in and through us to accomplish God's purposes.

The "bema," or judgment seat, at Corinth, where Paul probably was brought before Gallio (see Acts 18:12-17).

We learn of the importance of sacrificial and spontaneous giving. These important principles regarding Christian stewardship need to be expounded in every congregation. Believers are to follow Christ in giving freely with joy and love.

Finally, we learn of the significance of Christ's reconciling work in restoring our broken relationship with God. Because of what He has done for us, we are a new creation, participants in the new covenant, and His ambassadors to proclaim the message of reconciliation. Because we have been reconciled to God, we should be reconciled to other believers. The importance of the unity of the church cannot be neglected.

Questions for Reflection

1. What is the spiritual value of times of suffering in our lives?
2. What are the primary characteristics of an authentic ministry?
3. What does it mean to be reconciled to God?
4. What principles concerning Christian stewardship can be applied to our own situations?
5. How is God's power revealed in our weakness?

Sources for Additional Study

Bruce, F. F. *1 and 2 Corinthians. New Century Bible.* London: Oliphants, 1971.

Harris, Murray J. "2 Corinthians." *Expositor's Bible Commentary.* Vol. 10. Grand Rapids: Zondervan, 1976.

Hughes, Philip E. *Paul's Second Epistle to the Corinthians. New International Commentary.* Grand Rapids: Eerdmans, 1962.

Robertson, A. T. *The Glory of the Ministry.* New York: Revell, 1911.

GALATIANS

There can be little doubt that the apostle Paul wrote the Letter to the Galatians. This conclusion has seldom been called into question because the circumstances portrayed in the epistle, the details concerning Paul's life found in Galatians, and the theology of the book all coincide closely with information found in Acts and Paul's other letters. Galatians may have been written from Syrian Antioch in A.D. 48–49 or from Antioch, Corinth, Ephesus, or Macedonia in the early to mid-50s.

The Recipients and Location

The ethnic Galatians of Paul's day were descendants of the cults who had migrated from Gaul to north-central Asia Minor several centuries before. By the New Testament era, however, the Roman province of Galatia included territory well to the south of the original Galatian kingdom. It is difficult to determine in which of these areas "the churches of Galatia" (1:2) were located.

If Paul was writing to churches in North Galatia, the only possible occasions when he could have been that far north are found in Acts 16:6 and 18:23. Both of those passages make passing mention that Paul had traveled through the region comprising Phrygia and Galatia, providing no additional information about ministry. It is quite possible that this was when Paul planted and revisited churches in North Galatia, near what is today Ankara, the modern capital of Turkey. It is also unusual, however, that Acts would give virtually no background.

On the other hand, if Paul wrote to churches in South Galatia, the beginning of those congregations is prominently displayed in Acts 13–14. Much of the apostle's first missionary journey is focused in the southern Galatian cities of Pisidian Antioch, Lystra, Derbe, and Iconium. Even details about the evangelism, disciple making, teaching, and appointing of leadership in the new congregations is available (Acts 14:21-23).

One other consideration must be weighed in attempting to determine who were the recipients of the Book of Galatians. The primary subject developed in Galatians is "the truth of the gospel" (Gal 2:5,14), which was also the focus of the Jerusalem Council in Acts 15. Therefore we must ask whether the letter was written before or after the Council met. That question becomes even more necessary to address because Paul made mention in Galatians 1–2 of two trips he had earlier taken to Jerusalem.

If Paul wrote sometime after the Jerusalem Council, the visit in Galatians 2 is referring to the Council, though that is not readily apparent from a comparison of the passages. Also no mention of the pertinent findings of the Council in Galatians casts doubt on the later dating and North Galatian recipients.

Placing Galatians before the Jerusalem Council does not answer all possible questions. But it is quite plausible to parallel Galatians 2 with Paul's earlier visit to Jerusalem in Acts 11–12. Also the apostle's subject and purpose in writing Galatians fit well in the situation prior to the Jerusalem Council's addressing the issues surrounding the gospel. If that conclusion is correct, Galatians is the earliest of Paul's epistles.

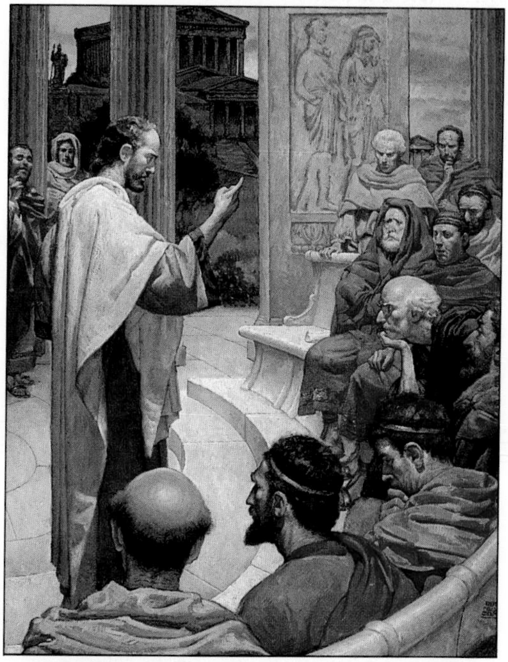

Paul preaching the "truth of the gospel" to the Athenians as he did in all cities of his journeys.

Theme

The hub that holds Galatians together is its treatment of the gospel. Much like a scientist approaching data from every conceivable angle, so the apostle Paul considered "the truth of the gospel" (2:5,14): its origin, content, reception through justification by faith in Christ, scriptural support, and practical outworking. Considering its shorter length, Galatians actually is proportionately more saturated with "gospel truth" than even Romans. Perhaps the key verse of this power-packed letter is Galatians 2:16: "Know that a man is not justified by observing the law, but by faith in Jesus Christ."

Literary Form

In most respects the Letter to the Galatians is quite similar to Paul's other letters, as well as the standardized epistles of the day. It has a well-defined introduction (1:1-5), body (1:6–6:10), and conclusion (6:11-18). There is not, however, the characteristic thanksgiving section, as in most of Paul's other letters (compare Phil 1:3-11). Paul probably could find nothing to be thankful for in connection with the Galatians' rapid defection from the true gospel (Gal 1:6-9).

From a literary standpoint there is one more issue of a longstanding nature, plus a quite recent one, that are worthy of note. Paul's use of the allegory about Abraham's sons in Galatians 4:22-31 has been debated throughout church history. The meaning of the allegory is not in question but whether Paul was sanctioning the use of allegorical interpretation of Scripture. By and large the conclusion has been that the apostle was turning the false teachers' own brand of allegorizing back on them to make his point and was not other otherwise recommending the allegorical approach.

The recent issue has to do with whether Galatians is purposefully structured like a formal "apologetic letter" of that day. Certainly there are interesting parallels, especially related to 1:6-9 and 2:15-21. But there is not enough evidence presently to draw the firm conclusion that Paul crafted Galatians as an apologetic letter. Besides, the hurry in which Paul composed the epistle argues against such a highly stylistic framework for composition.

Purpose and Theology

Paul had three closely related purposes in mind in writing Galatians.

1. He was defending his authority as an apostle against those who claimed otherwise.

The Law in the New Testament

How the OT law should be applied was one of the most debated issues during the ministry of Jesus and in the early church. The Jewish authorities constantly were offended by Jesus' actions and teachings on the law (for example, see Matt 12:1-8).

The early church had a major disagreement over whether circumcision should be required of Gentile Christians (Acts 15). Paul even had to warn against useless quarrels about the law (Titus 3:9).

Law in the Teaching of Jesus. The popular notion that Jesus set aside the OT law is wrong. In Matthew 5:17 Jesus stated explicitly that He did not come to destroy the law but to fulfill it.

The discussions of the law in Matthew 5:20-48 show that obeying the law is not accomplished by some external act. Rather, obedience to the law of God includes the "heart," what people think and feel at the core of their being.

Jewish teachers understood the focus of the law to be on proper religious observances and on separation from unclean foods and unclean people. Jesus had little concern for such ritual purity. He focused instead on mercy and love for all people (Matt 9:9-13). Jesus summarized the law with the two greatest commandments, the commands to love God and neighbor (Matt 22:34-40).

The Law in the Early Church. For the early church the law was still the word of God and a guide for life, but it was no longer the center of attention. Jesus was now the focus of Christian thinking. In light of Jesus' coming, early Christians concluded that certain parts of the law were no longer in effect. Still, all of the Ten Commandments are reaffirmed in the NT except the command to keep the Sabbath holy.

Such decisions about how to apply the law took time and often caused disagreement, as the Book of Acts shows. Stephen deemphasized the role of the Jerusalem temple (Acts 7:47-50). Peter had a vision about unclean foods from which he concluded that neither food nor people should be called unclean (Acts 10:9-16,28; compare Mark 7:19).

The Jerusalem Council decided that Gentiles did not have to keep the Jewish law to be Christians (Acts 15). Gentiles did not have to be circumcised. This was a crucial decision that made mission activity easier and kept Christianity from being a sect of Judaism. ⇨

2. He was stating, explaining, and proving the gospel message.

3. He was applying the gospel message to daily Christian living by the power of the Holy Spirit.

The basic theology of Galatians is related to the truth of the gospel and its implications. Its ultimate ramifications are as clear-cut as that turning from this gospel equates with deserting God and deserving "accursed" status (1:6-9), while faith in Christ is the only grounds for justification in God's eyes and for eternal hope (2:16; 5:5).

The false "gospel" (1:6-7) the Jewish teachers in Galatia were proclaiming relied upon "the works of the law" (2:16; 3:2), apparently emphasizing distinctives like circumcision (5:2-3). Paul made it clear that the motivation behind such "works" is "the flesh" (3:3; 5:19-21), that aspect of humankind that struggles against the Lord (5:17). Tragically, there is no saving power in the pursuit of fleshly works (2:16; 5:21).

Much of the emphasis on the gospel in Galatians has to do with its proper reception and application (2:16–6:10). But Paul also presented a strong historical foundation for his message. At the very beginning (1:1), the apostle stated his basic assumption concerning the resurrection of Jesus Christ (1:1), which validated Christ's redemptive work and deliverance of believers (1:4). This "good news" of justification of faith in Christ's death alone (3:1-2) is the only means of salvation. Also faith in God's promises has always been God's means of pardon and blessing (3:6–4:31). Thus the only aspect of the gospel that is new since Abraham (3:6-9) was Christ coming to live and die in "the fullness of the time," God's perfect timing (4:4).

An amazing transformation takes place when a person trusts Christ and is justified eternally (2:16; 5:5). Paul called this change "a new creation" (6:15; compare 2 Cor 5:17) and deliverance from the present evil age (1:4). This incredible new status of salvation came about because Christians have been crucified with Christ (2:20), freed from bondage to sin (3:22-25), adopted as children and heirs of God (3:26–4:7), and given the Holy Spirit to dwell within (3:2; 4:6).

After becoming a Christian, the need for faith in Christ does not diminish. In living daily by faith, the power of Christ (2:20) and His Spirit (4:6) allows believers to have God's guidance (5:18) and to avoid the sinful behavior promoted by the flesh (5:13,16,19-21). Living by faith harnesses the Holy Spirit's power (5:5) for a loving, radi-

---

The Epistle to the Hebrews set aside the ineffective priesthood of the OT with its animal sacrifices (7:11-18). Jesus is viewed as the eternal Priest whose death and resurrection were once and for all effective. The sacrifices mentioned in the law are only shadows of what is now a reality in Christ (9:11-14).

The Law in the Writings of Paul. Paul wrote most of the explicitly negative statements about the law in the Bible. He viewed the law as in some sense temporary (Gal 3:19-25). He argued it did not lead to salvation or a righteous life. In fact, Paul thought the law was powerless to bring life (Rom 8:3). That is the work of God through Jesus and the Holy Spirit. Rather, the law created an opportunity for sin and led to death (Rom 7:7-13; also see 5:20).

However, Paul still valued the law as holy, good, and spiritual and as an indication of the will of God to be lived (Rom 7:12,14; 8:4,7). Even while saying that Christians are not under the law, Paul also expected Christians to fulfill the law by loving their neighbors as themselves (Gal 5:14-18; Rom 13:8-10).

Paul's conflicting statements have created frequent debate about how he viewed the law. For example, does Paul's statement "Christ is the end of the Law" (Rom 10:4) mean "Christ is the goal of the Law" or "Christ is the setting aside of the Law"? Probably his intention is "Christ is the goal of the Law." (Compare the use of the same word translated "end" in the KJV in Rom 6:22.)

For Paul the important point was not law itself but whether God's Spirit is at work in a person's life. Without God's Spirit the law is an occasion for sin and rebellion and leads to death (Rom 7:5-13). With God's Spirit the law is an occasion for obedience and showing love to one's neighbor.

Relevance for Modern Christians. The OT law cannot be ignored by modern Christians. The focus can never be on its ritual and ceremonial practices or on legalistic observance. Christians should study the law in light of Jesus' life, death, and resurrection to learn about God's relation to humans and His desire for them to live in love. They can then understand why James 1:25 refers to the law as "the perfect Law that gives freedom." □

ant life (5:6) that produces a spiritual "bumper crop," both short-term (5:22-23) and over a lifetime (6:8-9).

I. Salutation and Preview of Themes (1:1-5)
II. Occasion: Condemnation of Error (1:6-9)
III. Defense of the Apostolic Authority of the Gospel Message (1:10–2:14)
IV. Statement of the Gospel Message against the Backdrop of Jewish Legalism (2:15-21)
V. Explanation of the Meaning and Scriptural Basis of the Gospel Message (3:1–4:31)
VI. Implications of the Gospel Message for Christian Living (5:1–6:10)
VII. Conclusion: Signature, Summaries, Salutation (6:11-18)

1:1-5
Salutation and Preview of Themes

Like the introduction of most letters in the New Testament era, the name of the writer ("Paul") and readers ("The churches of Galatia") are given, as well as Paul's standard greeting ("Grace to you and peace"). There are also several distinctive elements that are linked to the development of thought in the rest of the epistle. For example, the resurrection of Christ is mentioned only here, then assumed throughout the letter. Also the capsule summary of the gospel in terms of redemption and deliverance from "this present evil age" is uniquely worded, though similar thought patterns emerge later in Galatians. Paul's divinely granted apostleship will become the first theme developed at length in the body of the letter (1:10-2:14).

1:6-9
Occasion: Condemnation of Error

Paul was astounded that so soon after his ministry among the Galatians they had defected from the gospel of grace in Christ. To turn away from Paul's message was, in effect, to turn away from God and to turn to a perversion of the true gospel. It was being passed off by the false teachers as an alternate gospel but was, in reality, merely a confusing counterfeit. Paul was so concerned by this development that he twice pronounced a curse ("anathema") on any being, including an angel, distorting the gospel among his readers.

1:10-2:14
Defense of the Apostolic Authority

The apostle was well aware that his strong criticism would be unpopular with his readers. It was not his intention to be a people pleaser but to please God and to serve Christ, from whom he received his gospel message by direct revelation on the Damascus Road (Acts 26:12-18).

To back his authority as an apostle (1:1) and to show that he had wrestled with the issue of the gospel of grace repeatedly before, Paul presented a selective overview of his own experience. First, he recalled his own misguided zeal for the Jewish law and traditions and his intense persecution of the church. Certainly no one among the Galatian churches, or even the Jewish false teachers, could rival the unsaved Paul's works, if that were the true issue of the gospel (Phil 3:4-6).

In his great care to demonstrate that his apostleship, and specific role as apostle to the Gentiles, came from God, Paul next recounted his conversion and what happened in regard to the gospel over the following years. He noted that his call to salvation was independent of human agency and that he did not immediately consult the other apostles in Jerusalem to verify, or even clarify, his calling or message. After three years Paul did travel to Jerusalem for a brief conference with Peter. But he remained largely unknown among Jewish Christians, except for reports of his ministry in Tarsus and Syrian Antioch (Acts 11:25-26), which were joyfully received by the churches in Palestine.

Next Paul described what would have been the decisive opportunity for the leadership of the Jewish church in Jerusalem to correct his gospel of grace if it needed to be corrected. Well over a decade later Paul revisited Jerusalem, accompanied by Barnabas and Titus, a ministry associate who was a Gentile. If circumcision were really part of the "truth of the gospel," the inner circle of leaders—Peter, John, and James, the half-brother of Jesus—would necessarily have required Titus to be circumcised, especially given the pressure exerted by some Paul called "false brethren." The outcome of this important meeting was apparently full recognition of Paul's gospel message and primary mission field among the Gentiles and a request for Paul and the churches he worked with to continue support of the poor.

A final incident is presented in this section to clear up apparent confusion among Paul's readers. Sometime after the cordial agreement reached in Jerusalem, Peter visited the church in Syrian Antioch, then under the leadership of Paul and Barnabas (Acts 11:26–13:1). While there, criticism from other Jews who had arrived from

A great Roman aqueduct at Antioch of Pisidia, a city in south central Asia Minor (or Galatia) visited by Paul.

the church in Jerusalem pressured Peter into hypocritical behavior. Peter's actions strongly implied that it was necessary for Gentiles to observe Jewish distinctives, although God had decisively taught him at a much earlier point that was not true (Acts 11:1-18). As a result, Paul found it necessary to confront Peter because of his dangerous hypocrisy.

2:15-21
The Gospel Message

This section not only crystallizes the essence of the gospel of grace versus the counterclaims of the Jewish false teachers, but it also serves as a major hinge in the letter. The argument appears to either continue or emerge directly out of Paul's face-off with Peter at the end of the long preceding autobiographical portion. It also prepares for the following exposition of justification by faith alone by stating the central thesis to be proven.

Paul's logic was tight, so as to make his conclusions virtually undeniable. He answered key objections: Jews do not have to sin in the same gross ways as Gentiles to be sinners (Rom 1–3). Nor does a message of grace provoke more and more sin (Rom. 6:1-14). Having corrected such common misperceptions, the apostle proclaimed that no one can be justified by God by "the works of the Law," although the law of Moses does play an important role in convincing of "deadness" in sin (Gal 3:10-25; Rom 7:7-12). Rather, the only channel of justification is faith in Jesus Christ, and the road of growth in the Christian is also full identification with the death and resurrection of Christ by faith (5:5).

3:1–4:31
Scriptural Basis of the Gospel Message

Because the distorted "gospel" being propagated by the Jewish false teachers was based on an understanding of the law of Moses and other Jewish distinctives, Paul now wisely expanded and backed his gospel of justification by faith in Christ from the Old Testament. Paul moved back and forth from personal appeal to more formal argument

Opponents of Paul

Everywhere Paul went, he met opposition. At times the opposition came from official sources; at other times it came from riot. Perhaps the best way to understand the opposition Paul faced is to review the complementary evidence from Acts and the relevant Pauline Letters.

The Book of Acts

The Book of Acts describes Paul's opponents more from historical and sociological perspectives than theological. The early opposition came from Jewish sources in Damascus (Acts 9:23) and Jerusalem (Acts 9:28-30). That trend continued as Paul and his companions conducted their missionary journeys.

In almost every city there was a violent reaction to Paul's preaching. Most of the time it arose from his preaching in the synagogue (see Acts 13:44-45; 14:1-6,19; 17:5,13; 18:12; 21:27; 23:12). On some occasions, however, Paul appeared before civil courts to explain his activities, sometimes as a result of Jewish uproar in the city and sometimes because of Gentile opposition to his message (Acts 16:19-40; 19:23; 23:12). Generally, the opponents objected either to Paul's Christocentric gospel or to its broad implications. The gospel changed people's social, economic, and religious values. In Acts, Luke emphasized that reactions to Paul arose in religious circles, primarily Jewish, and that ultimately Paul was no threat to Rome.

Paul's Letters

Paul's Letters reveal a more directed theological attack against him and the gospel. The opponents apparently organized, hoping to counter Paul wherever he went. The primary passages to study are Galatians, 1,2 Corinthians, Philippians, Colossians, and 1 Timothy.

Galatians. Opposition to Paul's early ministry is recorded in Galatians. Paul expressed surprise that the new converts embraced a "different gospel" so quickly after he left them (Gal 1:6-8). Traditionally, the opponents, called Judaizers, have been identified with a group of Jewish people who called new converts back to Judaism. Since Paul stated that they wanted to avoid the persecution of the cross (Gal 6:12), it seems possible that they were nominal Christians who were uncomfortable with Paul's emphasis on freedom from circumcision and the law. A few scholars identify them as Gentiles, and others view them as Jewish-Christian Gnostics. Most, however, conclude they are Jewish.

The debate in Galatians supports the interpretation that they were Jews who had an exposure to Christianity. Primarily the opponents taught about Jewish law and ritual. They hoped Paul's converts would accept a full gospel that included circumcision (Gal 5:2-3; 6:13), ritual feasts (Gal 4:10), celebrations, and probably Jewish dietary regulations (Gal 2:11-16). As a means to this end they undermined Paul's authority, claiming that his apostleship was as flawed as his gospel.

Paul responded by affirming his call from the Lord and the gospel he preached. He accused them of fearing persecution (6:12) and desiring to return to elementary aspects of religion, the OT legal code (Gal 4:9).

The opponents were not Paul's converts as is clearly seen in the interchange of third-person address for the opponents and second-person address for the church. The opponents at Galatia, therefore, seem to have been Hellenized Jews from outside the church. They called Paul's converts to what they considered a full gospel, mixing elements of Judaism and popular Greek religion. It included a return to the legalism of the law. Paul had concluded that their message was not the gospel (Gal 1:6-7).

Corinthians. Paul also faced severe attack at Corinth. The Corinthian Epistles reveal a general church disorder, a questioning of Paul's integrity, and an organized opposition from outside the church. In 1 Corinthians, however, the problems encountered arose from within the congregation. Groups within differed about how best to build the church, and they appealed to various leaders who had left their mark on the congregation (1 Cor 1–3). Although this situation demanded a strong word, the proponents of this division did not attack Paul and the church as severely as outsiders did.

In 2 Corinthians the opponents resembled those who opposed Paul elsewhere. Second Corinthians is the primary source for understanding the opponents at Corinth. The issues in 2 Corinthians involve Paul's character and calling.

The opponents used several avenues of approach in undermining Paul's authority. They said he had no credentials (2 Cor 3; 11). Paul responded by saying that the Corinthian Christians stood as his credentials. They said he had no confidence (2 Cor 10). Paul responded with a theology of personal weakness that allowed the power of Christ to appear. They said he had no character (2 Cor 1:17; 11:7). He responded by informing them that he followed the will of God for his life. Neither did he wish to burden them financially when he preached. They said he had no charisma (2 Cor 11:5-6), to which he responded that he would not use the wisdom of the world to manipulate conversions. Finally, they claimed Paul had no calling (2 Cor 3:12; 12:11). The apostle replied that his ministry was from God Himself (2 Cor 5:20).

Additional attacks came from ⇨

those concerned about Paul's seeming carelessness about the law. Some have interpreted Paul's opponents to have been Gnostic. The immediate issues, however, focused on the place of the law in the believer's life. These include the relationship of law and grace (2 Cor 3:1-18).

Further, Paul defended himself against an attack on his true Jewishness by a comparison to other Jewish apostles (2 Cor 11:22). The concern for the law was mixed with a concern for some of the finer points of oratory that were practiced so well at Corinth.

Paul defended himself because the purity of the gospel was at stake. He would not allow anyone to capture his converts and bring them under a legal code. The gospel would not be trivialized by using rhetorical devices of manipulation. At Corinth, therefore, Paul's opposition came from both Jewish and Gentile sources. The primary opposition, however, came from Jews with some exposure to Christianity intent on reaffirming the law as a vital part of Christian faith.

Philippians. The Letter to the Philippians contains some of the most directed attacks against Paul's opponents.

The profile of the opponents must be developed from 1:12-30 and 3:1-21. Historically, scholars have determined that the passages reflect two different groups of people. In 1:12-30 Christian preachers opposed Paul. They hoped that by their preaching they would bring an unfavorable court verdict against Paul. Although they had insincere motives (Phil 1:15-17), they preached a gospel that Paul affirmed. These opponents were motivated by (1) jealousy of Paul, (2) opposition to Paul's calling as the apostle to the Gentiles, or (3) opposition to Paul's message of freedom from law. Perhaps more than one motivation characterized them.

In contrast to chapter 1, the opponents mentioned in chapter 3 came from outside the Christian community and preached a different message. Paul's attitude changed as he characterized them as unethical scavengers (Phil 3:2) who were preoccupied with dietary laws and circumcision (Phil 3:19). They failed to realize that Christ delivers from such earthly concerns (Phil 3:19-20). In their place He offered an eternal perspective for living. Paul countered them by recalling his experience as one under law but who disavowed personal achievements in order to gain Christ (Phil 3:7-11).

These people, like the opponents of Galatians, feared Paul's apparent disregard of the legal code and sought to educate the Philippians in this area.

It is possible that these opponents believed they had already reached the ultimate spiritual experience, perhaps by already experiencing the spiritual resurrection. Some even may have denied a physical resurrection, arguing God only promised a spiritual resurrection. Since Paul acknowledged his need to mature and develop in the Christian life (see 3:12-16), the opponents argued that his apparent immaturity made him inferior to them.

Colossians. This letter has produced the most discussion of the opponents of Paul. In 2:6-19 the issues raised by the opponents were the law and circumcision. Paul argued that in Christ believers already experience a spiritual circumcision and that the law's demands have been satisfied. Christians are not to focus on such earthly matters as the elements associated with the law (Col 2:20).

The specific doctrines of the opponents, however, cannot be easily and clearly identified with the same issues as those at Philippi and Galatia. In the last 150 years many scholars have argued for a Gnostic or pre-Gnostic environment.

Gnosticism was a philosophy that emphasized spiritual deliverance through an experience of insight or knowledge. The name of the movement comes from the Greek word for *knowledge* (*gnosis;* see the article on "Gnosticism").

Both Gnosticism and the Colossians Letter share similar vocabularies. Paul's teaching may certainly be understood to counter that movement if Colossians is understood as a response to Gnosticism. One problem with this, however, is that there is no concrete evidence that Gnosticism existed in the first century A.D. Some have therefore suggested a pre-Gnostic environment in Colosse.

On the other hand, others have offered the Jewish Essenes as possible identification of the opponents in Colosse. This group of Jewish teachers promoted a Christian gospel mixed with ascetic tendencies. Their community and worship patterns resembled the Essenes of Palestine. Understood this way, these Jewish opponents advocated an inferior Christianity. They taught that Jesus was less than God and that all persons must adhere strictly to the law and its demands. Paul countered them by teaching that Jesus was indeed God in flesh (2:9-10) and that His sacrifice on the cross provided for a total and complete salvation (2:11-19).

First Timothy. In 1 Timothy Paul countered a similar heresy as that in Colosse, but it came in a slightly different form. He combatted a preoccupation with "myths and genealogies" (1 Tim 1:2-4) and the law (1 Tim 1:8-11). The advocates had a quarrelsome temperament that involved the minutia of words and controversies (1 Tim 6:4). These were Jewish concerns, and the general tenor of the letter reinforces that idea. Paul stated that these teachers were motivated by greed (1 Tim 6:5) and pride (1 Tim 1:7). The language Paul used to counter them differed from the earlier writings. However, similar themes such as the law, spiritual maturity, and asceticism were present.

Since Timothy served in Ephesus, probably in the mid-60s, the same opponents had access to him as they did to the church at Colosse. Again, some have looked to Gnosticism and Greek philosophy to describe the opponents.

The issues, however, are clearly suited to Jewish interests. Since the other letters give evidence of similar problems from those outside the Pauline churches, it seems Paul countered a mature form of those issues in 1 Timothy. These opponents appear to have been Jews with an interest in the legalistic type arguments of the OT law and its application to Jewish congregations.

Summary

Some general conclusions provide direction. First, historically scholars have reached different conclusions regarding Paul's opponents. Until the eighteenth century the consensus was that Paul opposed Jewish teachers called Judaizers who sought to bring his liberated Christians back under the law. In the eighteenth century, however, some scholars advanced the theory that Paul opposed many Gentile philosophers. This theory grew into an assumption by many that Paul countered the Gnostics. Later, however, it was demonstrated that Gnosticism did not exist until the second century, so people began to think of what is called incipient Gnosticism. That view still prevails in many circles.

Others hold to the predominantly Jewish identity of the opponents. Few hold to the earlier view that they were pure Judaizers. More likely they were Jews who held a theology containing a mixture of Essene, Jewish, and Christian ideas. Throughout his ministry Paul, the champion of Gentile Christianity, faced opposition from Jews who shared his background, but not his theological insights.

Second, Paul's opponents attacked him, his credentials, and his message. The attacks were vicious and varied (see 2 Cor 10–13; Gal 1–2; Phil 3). Equally, the attempts to undermine his theology were systematic and well conceived. In defending himself Paul first defended the gospel and then himself only as an apostolic proponent of that gospel. Personal attacks mattered only if they hindered the message. The gospel mattered supremely; it was Paul's very life.

Third, although at times the identification of Paul's opponents depended on wild speculation, the study brings many benefits. Biblical readers must look for a textual context to bring the text to life. The opponents provided an occasion for some of the loftiest theology, especially Christology.

Further, as is true in many other disciplines, history repeats itself. Many heresies encountered throughout Christian history share doctrinal tenets with these early heresies. The better we know them, the more effectively we can counter others.

Finally, knowing Paul's opponents provides insights into how to defend the gospel and its representatives today. Since Paul faced constant theological controversy, his life models a Christian response. Each generation of Christians bears the same responsibility. □

throughout this lengthy section.

Initially, the apostle pointedly inquired whether the Galatians received the Holy Spirit at salvation by doing the works of the law or by believing the gospel message they had heard from Paul. He then posed an important follow-up question: Is your progress in the Christian life by such works or by faith? Since they had heard the message of the cross so clearly portrayed by Paul, their "foolish" attraction to the false gospel of the Jewish teachers was without any real excuse.

In order to counter any possibility of different answers to those questions, Paul referred to the example of Abraham, father of the Jewish nation, and the relationship of that example to the law. Abraham's faith was credited to his account as righteousness, and all who follow that classic example are Abraham's spiritual children and are similarly blessed.

On the other hand, those who try to attain righteousness through observing the law are cursed (1:8-9), according to the law itself. Fortunately, Christ's death on the cross, in which he was cursed for us, according to the law, provided the payment by which anyone might receive the blessing of Abraham and the Holy Spirit by faith. This is seen to be true because the fulfillment of the promises to Abraham are in Christ, his ultimate descendant, not in the law, which did not invalidate the earlier covenant God made with Abraham.

That does not mean the law was without divine purpose. The law convicts all people of sin, holding them in captivity until the message of faith in Christ was revealed. The law played the role of both a jailer and a guardian of underage children in preparing for believers to be full-fledged children of God, on equal footing spiritually and joint heirs of God's promise no matter their ethnic, social, or sexual gender backgrounds.

Paul then developed a cultural illustration to underline how amazing it is that because Christ became a man at just the right point in history, now any person can, by faith, become an adopted adult child of God. Each believer has full rights and privileges, including the indwelling Holy Spirit. In being freed from the virtual slavery of spiritual "childhood" outside of Christ, the apostle then ironically asks how the Galatians could return to slavery to such weak principles, which cannot provide spiritual strength, such as the law.

He wanted them to know he was concerned for them in their time of spiritual weakness just as they had shown great concern for Paul in his earlier time of physical infirmity. The apostle reminded them how, in initially receiving the gospel from him, the Galatians had honored him and nursed him back to health. He wanted them to know he was risking a fellowship he valued greatly by telling them the hard truth, unlike the false teachers, who were courting their favor for an improper purpose. He related to his beloved spiritual children his deep agony and confusion over their misguided spiritual status.

As the capstone of his argument concerning justification by faith from the Old Testament, Paul created an allegory from the two sons of Abraham: Ishmael and Isaac. In this twist on the method of the false teachers, Paul paralleled Ishmael, the child of a slave, to the covenant of the law made at Mount Sinai and the current spiritual slavery of Jewish legalism. He presented Isaac, the child of free Sarah, in line with the promise to Abraham and the New Jerusalem, the Jewish future hope. He concluded by implying that persecution of those in line with the promise by those in spiritual slavery is to be expected. But that will not last because those in spiritual slavery will be banished by the "father." Paul intended to leave little doubt that the doom of the false teachers and their message is certain before the Lord.

5:1–6:10
Christian Living

Having secured the argument for freedom in Christ through justifying faith alone, Paul examined the nature of that liberty. While again rebuking the tendency to turn back to legalism, he also deplored the opposite extreme

Adoption

References to adoption in the OT and NT occur primarily where personal relationship between God and persons is described. Sonship or the family of God is in view here.

The identity of "God's son" may be the king of Israel or the descendants of Israel who have been called into this relationship with Him. Of course, Jesus Christ Himself is supremely "Son of God." This title most probably is drawn from Jewish intertestamental literature. Son of God is carried on as a special title for Christ in the epistles (see Rom 8:29; Col 1:15; Rev 3:4).

The biblical theological backdrop to the concept of adoption by God is clearly that of human sin and estrangement from God. The nations of the earth have "adopted" to themselves, as it were, "strange gods" and have become strangers to the only true and living God. Out of all the nations of the earth God has very particularly chosen and adopted Israel as His "son" and people.

When we move into the NT, adoption with reference to Israel is used only one time (Rom 9:4). Otherwise, it is a term used exclusively by Paul to refer to everyone whom God draws into permanent saving relation with Himself.

Christ had promised in the Upper Room discourse (John 13–17) that He would not leave His disciples orphaned but by His spiritual indwelling would make them offspring of God. In view of Christ's unique sonship, He is the elder brother, as it were, of all those who have been adopted by God.

In Galatians this theme is set forth poignantly when the confirmation by the "Spirit of his Son" sent into the heart which cries out, "Abba! Father!" (Gal 4:4-7; see Rom 8:16,23). To belong to Christ is to belong to the offspring of Abraham (Gal 3:29). And so, all of those whom God saves, Jew and Gentile, become one family composed of His sons of every kind of humanity.

In addition, the idea of inheritance as a metaphor for salvation enters in here. Christ, who is and will be Lord over all, will have believers as his "co-heirs" in the glory of God. The vital faith that appropriates this truth now, however, must also stand in readiness to accept the suffering that faithfulness to him always entails. ("We share in his sufferings in order that we also may share in his glory," Rom 8:12-17.)

Thus the concept of adoption includes a forward-looking, eschatological dimension. Believers will be raised in the likeness of Christ's bodily resurrection on the last day. And until that time the efforts of believers to live out the sanctification to which they are called are supported by the constant reassuring testimony of the Holy Spirit within the heart. □

of license. Paul expertly showed that freedom in Christ is a Spirit-guided life-style within the limits of a new "law" given by Christ: the law of love.

Paul quickly warned against circumcision, which has no spiritual value in Christ. He reminded them that they could not keep part of the law and ignore the rest. And to attempt to be justified by keeping the law of Moses is to turn completely away from God's grace. The route of spiritual freedom in Christ is faith, faith that shows love (5:13-14,22) in the short run and that waits eagerly but patiently for the Christian's eternal hope.

The apostle next laments how the false teachers had confused the Galatians, halting their forward progress in Christ. He longed for an end to the leaven of false teaching spreading among them, wishing that the agitators would do away with themselves. Still, he displayed confidence that the Galatian churches would return to a proper viewpoint.

The danger of misunderstanding freedom in Christ is a tendency toward self-indulgence, which can express itself in destructive words and actions toward other believers. True spiritual freedom manifests itself in love, both for God and for one another. Such loving behavior is against the grain of the flesh. Thus it is necessary to live in the power of the Holy Spirit and thus be guided by the Spirit in our attitudes, decisions, and actions. To fail to follow the lead of the Spirit as a Christian is to manifest a sinful life-style that is unworthy of the kingdom of God. On the other hand, the believer who is controlled by the Spirit shows forth qualities that reflect supernatural godliness beyond the requirements of the law.

Such a life of Spirit-prompted love does not go on automatically however. It is necessary to remain consciously in step with the Holy Spirit, and it is easy to do otherwise. Even though the flesh was, in a very real sense, crucified with Christ, the tendency to pride, and even to gross sin, still exists. Mature Christians must, in the power of the Spirit, restore such errant believers. Also they must be available to support Christians overloaded with cares or responsibilities. It is right for every person to work up to their capacity, but not go beyond it. Nor is it proper for a person to boast because someone else has fallen under a load within that person's capacity.

The life of love even includes support of biblical teachers who have financial needs. These are the kinds of good works that bring about a long-term harvest of eternal worth. The opposite route of sowing to the flesh only eventuates in corrupt fruit. The difference in the two final outcomes is whether we choose to do what is right in all situations, especially toward fellow believers, here and now.

6:11-18
Conclusion

At this point Paul began the conclusion to Galatians by taking the manuscript from his unnamed scribe and writing with large, bold script. He then effectively summarized the issues of the entire letter by setting the pridefulness of those pushing circumcision on the Galatians over against the cross of Christ and the new creation that begins when a person becomes a believer. The apostle then pronounced a benediction of peace and mercy upon all Gentile and Jewish believers with proper perspective. He requested peace for himself in regard to the persecution he had suffered for the sake of the message of the cross and new creation. He ended as he began, and proceeded throughout, with a note of grace (1:3; 2:21).

Questions for Reflection

1. Why did Paul say that to turn away from the gospel of salvation through faith in Jesus Christ is "desertion" from God and pronounce a curse upon each behavior?

2. How did Paul's own personal background serve as important evidence supporting his message of justification by faith in Christ without works?

3. How does the Old Testament, especially the foundational example of Abraham, back the truth of the gospel, as proclaimed by Paul?

4. How should Christians relate to such precious unseen realities as being crucified with Christ, being adopted children of God and rightful heirs, and having the indwelling Holy Spirit?

5. How can the believer draw upon the resources of the Holy Spirit for guidance and victory over the flesh, as well as a loving, fruitful life in both the short term and over the long haul?

6. How can you discern the difference between someone shouldering their proper responsibility and one who is overburdened? How can you support the person crushed by the overload?

Sources for Additional Study

Fung, Ronald Y. K. *The Epistles to the Galatians. New International Commentary.* Grand Rapids: Eerdmans, 1988.

Guthrie, Donald. *Galatians. New Century Bible.* Grand Rapids: Eerdmans, 1973.

Stott, John R. W. *The Message of Galatians. The Bible Speaks Today.* Downers Grove: InterVarsity, 1968.

EPHESIANS

Paul referred to himself by name as the author of the Book of Ephesians in two places (1:1; 3:1). Today some scholars think the book contains a writing style, vocabulary, and even some teachings that are not typical of the apostle. Yet others regard the book as the crown of all of Paul's writings. If that is the case, then it would mean a disciple of Paul had surpassed him in theological insight and spiritual perception. Of such an erudite disciple the early church has no record. Furthermore, pseudonymity (a writer writing with someone else's name) probably was not practiced by early Christians. We can conclude, in line with the undisputable acceptance of Pauline authorship in the early church, that there is no reason to dispute the Pauline authorship of Ephesians.

Paul penned the letter while in prison (3:1; 4:1; 6:20). Disagreement exists concerning whether Paul was imprisoned in Caesarea (Acts 24:22) around 57–59 or in Rome (Acts 28:30) about 60–62 when he wrote this letter. Paul most likely wrote Colossians, Philemon, and Philippians during the same imprisonment. The evidence for a Roman imprisonment seems more likely. Tradition confirms this conclusion. This being the case, it is plausible to suggest that Paul wrote the letter from Rome around 60–61. This would have transpired while Paul was housed in guarded rental quarters (Acts 28:30).

Destination

In spite of the traditional heading (1:1), relatively little is known about the recipients of the letter called Ephesians. (Several important and early manuscripts do not contain the words *in Ephesus* [1:1].) The letter was carried to its destination by Tychicus, who in Ephesians 6:21 and Colossians 4:7 is identified as Paul's emissary. Both letters probably were delivered at the same time since in both letters the apostle noted that Tychicus would inform the churches concerning Paul's situation.

We can suggest the following possible scenario. While Paul was imprisoned in Rome, the need arose to respond to new religious philosophies influencing the Asia Minor area. The impetus to write the letters came to Paul from Epaphras, who informed him of the threats to Christianity in the Lycus Valley. In a response Paul wrote a letter to the church at Colosse. About the same time, either shortly before or shortly thereafter, he penned a more expansive and general letter intended for churches in Asia Minor, including Laodicea (see Col 4:16) and Ephesus.

What we call Ephesians was probably a circular letter, with Ephesus being the primary church addressed. Paul stayed at Ephesus, the capital city of the province of Asia, for almost three years (see Acts 20:31). These factors help explain the absence of personal names of Ephesian believers. After the Ephesians read it, the letter would have been routed to Colosse, Laodicea, and other churches in the area.

Literary Features

The salutation and structure of Ephesians is quite similar to Colossians. Many topics are commonly treated in both

The entryway into the Basilica of St. John at the site of ancient Ephesus.

Election in the New Testament

Election is the operative principle of God's covenant with Israel. The background for the doctrine of election in the NT is the OT.

Old Testament Background. In the OT "election" relates directly to Israel's understanding of its own origins. Election signifies the meaning and expression of Israel's destiny: God's giving of Himself to be their God and His selection of them to be His people. With this election they will know the blessing of His abiding presence.

In nonreligious biblical usage, election indicates the "choice" of an individual person, place, or thing out of a wide selection. When pertaining to persons, election points to their selection for or appointment to an office (see Gen 13:11; Exod 18:25; 1 Sam 8:18). Thus there can also be a passive use of the word *elected,* which often indicates the great worth and usefulness of something or someone.

Theologically, election signifies God's selecting His people from the nations to be holy and wholly for Himself. They have been chosen to be His inheritance (see Deut 7:6; 10:5). Outside of Deuteronomy, "election" is used frequently by Isaiah: "You are My Servant, I have chosen you and have not rejected you; fear not!" (Isa 41:9). The object of God's choice, the Servant of God, names him "Chosen." But the idea here is much more one of office rather than personal condition to which God's servant is called.

Within the elected community God chose individuals for specific duties (for example, see Deut 18:5, the Levites; Ps 105:26, Aaron) and in an extended sense Judah (Ps 78:68) and Abraham (Neh 9:7).

The election of the king is special in this regard (Deut 17:15). Above all, David was elected by the Lord (1 Sam 10:24). Also according to Deuteronomy and other related OT literature, God elects the place for the holy of holies (Deut 12:18)—particularly Jerusalem (1 Chron 6:6; Zeph 1:17).

New Testament Teaching. In the NT election has several different usages that correspond to the usages of the OT. Jesus chose the twelve from the group of His disciples (Luke 6:13) and told them that He had chosen them "out of the world" (John 15:19).

Election is entirely a work of God. He claims persons for Himself and His own purpose: this is His glory. Indeed, our knowledge of election always comes as an already accomplished fact. "He chose us in Christ before the foundation of the world" (Eph 1:4) and "the elect whom he chose" (Matt 13:20) indicate that election is an action of God prior to and independent of any human action or condition. Through the means of God's gracious election, He actually bestows all spiritual blessings that accompany salvation (see Eph 1:4-14).

Characteristically, however, the NT teaching of election is always descriptive and never discloses God's reasoning behind this action. One fact is unmistakable: the mystery of God surrounds this gracious expression of His almighty will.

Where the NT indicates a basis for election, grace and love are mentioned to the exclusion of any righteous works or superior value of an individual. Faith is the means by which God's work of election is made known. A most serious and holy consequence is connected with the knowledge of election: the renunciation of all pride and the pursuit of a righteous and holy life before the Lord.

Faith matures in the knowledge of election, and every Christian virtue flourishes (Col 3:12). This understanding certainly supplies believers with confidence in the promise of the sanctifying power of the Holy Spirit (1 Pet 1:2). Obedience to all of Christ's commands serves to confirm election (2 Pet 1:10). This knowledge builds within the believer an understanding of a shared faith within a large community of spiritual people of God.

Personal security in salvation is also an outcome. But this is based upon the fact, first of all, of God's securing a people for Himself who will be living witnesses of His electing grace to the whole world. Election then is that will and action of God to call undeserving persons to share in His glory.

We should note finally the most special case of election, that of Jesus, the Son of God (Luke 9:35). This designation of Christ seems to relate to the fact that believers are elect through Him; and remaining "in Christ," they enjoy every spiritual blessing (Eph 1:3). □

letters. The message is strikingly similar. Of the 155 verses in Ephesians over half contain identical expressions with those in Colossians. Colossians, however, is abrupt, argumentative, and seemingly compressed. Ephesians presents a bigger, finished picture that is meditative, instructive, and expansive.

Though Colossians and Ephesians contain many similarities, it is important to observe the distinctives of Ephesians. When the content of Ephesians that is common to Colossians is removed, there remain units of material unique to Ephesians.

1:3-14	an expanded benediction
2:1-10	a confessional statement on the new life
3:14-21	a prayer to understand the mystery of Christ
4:1-16	an extended exhortation to Christian unity
5:8-14	a section on walking in the light
5:23-32	a theological expansion on the household roles
6:10-17	a unique picture of the Christian's spiritual warfare

Purpose and Theology

The book hints at several purposes. The apostle taught that Jewish and Gentile believers are one in Christ. This oneness was to be demonstrated by their love one for another. Paul used the noun or verb form of love (*agape*) nineteen times (about one-sixth of the total uses in all the Pauline Letters). Ephesians begins with love (1:4-6) and ends with love (6:23-24).

Paul implicitly addressed matters raised by the mystery religions in the Lycus Valley. The letter has much to say about the mystery of redemption (1:7) and the divine intention for the human race (1:3-14). Other themes treated include grace (1:2), predestination (1:4-5), reconciliation, and union with Christ (2:1-21).

Central to the message of Ephesians is the re-creation of the human family according to God's original intention for it. The new creation destroys the misguided view that God accepts the Jew and rejects the Gentile. Paul claimed that this distinction was abolished at Christ's sacrificial death. Thus no more hindrance remains to reuniting all humanity as the people of God, with Christ as the head (1:22-23). The new body, the church, has been endowed by the power of the Holy Spirit to enable them to live out their new life (1:3–2:10) and put into practice the new standards (4:1–6:9).

In sum we can say that the overall emphasis of Ephesians is on the unity of the church in Christ through the power of the Spirit.

I. Introduction (1:1-2)
II. God's Purposes in Christ (1:3–3:21)
III. God's Purposes in the Church (4:1–6:20)
IV. Conclusion (6:21-24)

1:1-2
Introduction

Paul identified himself by name and calling. He offered greetings in the manner common to the Pauline Letters. Absent is the usual mention of Paul's companions.

Excavations of the Roman Harbor Baths and Gymnasium at the ancient port of Ephesus in western Asia Minor.

1:3-14
God's Purpose in History

Paul offered praise to God for his glorious blessings in Christ. This section is one long sentence in the original text made up of carefully balanced clauses. This extended benediction surveys the redemptive activity of the Triune God. Some have seen here a hymn of three stanzas of uneven length (1:3-6,7-12,13-14). Each stanza concludes with a reference to the praise of God's glorious grace. The theme of this section is God's eternal purpose in history (1:9).

Paul theologized about God's purposes. In Christ, God "chose us . . . before the creation of the world to be holy and blameless in his sight" (1:4). The spiritual blessings granted to believers (1:3) are the work of the Trinity: the Father's electing (1:4-5,11), the Son's redemptive work (1:7), and the Spirit's sealing (1:13). God now has made known His purposes (1:9), has forgiven our sins (1:7), and granted hope to His own (1:12).

God the Father loves His Son, and believers who have been redeemed by the Son are also the object of God's love.

1:15-23
Know God and His Power

The entire letter was written within a framework of prayer. This section (1:15-23) is an extended prayer. Paul prayed that his readers would have the spiritual insight to perceive the truth that is hidden in God. It can be unlocked only in the experience of life and fellowship with Him. The prayer issues from his opening section, constituting a request that believers may appropriate all that is contained in that beautifully rich sentence.

Paul's prayer began with thanksgiving for their faith and love (1:15-16). In 1:17-23 he made four requests for them: (1) to know and experience God; (2) to know the hope of His calling; (3) to know of His glorious inheritance; and (4) to know of His great power. Paul expounded on this great power available to believers exhibited in Christ's resurrection, ascension, rule, and headship.

2:1-10
Redeemed by Grace

Chapter two continues Paul's thoughts about God's eternal purposes in Christ. In 2:1-10 Paul discussed how sinful people who deserve nothing but God's wrath can be redeemed by His grace.

Paul described the human condition in 2:1-3. He explained how people were "dead in transgressions and sins" (2:1), cut off from the life of God and controlled by their own selfish desires (2:3). Beyond this they were ensnared by the power of Satan (2:2). As a result men and women apart from Christ are without life, without freedom, and without hope.

By His grace He has granted new life to believers (2:4-6). The basis for the new life is God's great love and mercy. Believers have been united with Christ in His resurrected life. Formerly people apart from Christ were dead, enslaved, and objects of wrath. In Christ believers are now alive, enthroned, and objects of grace.

The ancient Curetes Street in Ephesus with the Library of Celsus in view in the distance.

God's purpose for believers is spelled out in 2:7-10. He has restored us, "expressed in his kindness to us in Christ Jesus" (2:7). The memorable words in verses 8-9 express a central idea in Paul's theology. He declared that the nature of God is to give freely because of His own love. God does not deal with people on the level of human achievement but on the level of their deepest needs.

He provides salvation as His gift to men and women. He then creates a disposition of faith within them so that they may receive His gracious gift. Salvation is completely God's achievement, a pure gift of God (2:8-9). Salvation is His workmanship. We are saved to live a totally different life "to do good works, which God prepared in advance for us to do" (2:10).

2:11-18
Reconciliation

Paul explained Christ's peace mission in this section. Those who were separated from the covenant have been united, those who were alienated have been reconciled, and those who were far off have been brought near.

The first ten verses of chapter 2 dealt with personal reconciliation. The remainder of the chapter turns to corporate reconciliation, particularly the reconciliation of Gentiles. For centuries the Jews (the "circumcision") looked with contempt on the Gentiles (the "uncircumcision"). The Jews thought they were participants in God's covenant by their heritage. They believed the Gentiles were distant from this covenant. Thus Paul described the Gentiles with the term "without."

They were without Christ, without citizenship, without covenants, without hope, and without God. Their condition was not due to their heritage or even to God but to their own sinfulness and spiritual bankruptcy.

Paul exclaimed the good news in verses 13-18. Apart from Christ the Gentiles were hopeless. "But now in Christ Jesus" (v. 13) Gentiles and Jews are reconciled to God and to one another. The enmity, the barrier, has been broken down. This is the meaning of reconciliation—*to bring together again.* In Jesus Christ, Jew and Gentile became one because of His crosswork. The law and its accompanying barriers created the barriers. Now those barriers have been nullified. Not only has Christ made peace, "He himself is our peace" (2:14). Jews and Gentiles are no longer strangers; they are called in one hope as one people of God.

2:19-22
The New Society

Some modern theologians assert that God has acted in

Christ to reconcile all the world to Himself. Consequently, the church's primary concern is not to seek to effect the reconciliation of all people to Christ but merely to proclaim that all have already been reconciled. This type of universalism is not what Paul taught in this chapter. In fact, the apostle opposed that kind of thinking.

It is only in response to the cross of Christ (called faith in 2:8) that peace exists vertically between humans and God and horizontally between humans. This new society, called the church, is depicted at the end of chapter 2.

The church is pictured as a nation ("fellow citizens," 2:19), a family ("a household"), and a "building" (2:21). This new building is "built on the foundation of the apostles and prophets, with Christ Jesus himself as the chief cornerstone" (2:20). The purpose of the church is for believers to be "built together to become a dwelling in which God lives by his Spirit" (2:22).

3:1-13
The Divine Mystery

After discussing the union of Jewish and Gentile believers in the church (2:11-22), Paul began to offer a prayer on their behalf (3:1). However, he stopped unexpectedly in the middle of the sentence and digressed on the subject of the divine mystery. He explained the meaning of the mystery and returned to his prayer in 3:14.

Paul was assured that his readers understood something about his unique ministry. He indicated this saying, "Surely you have heard about the administration of God's grace that was given to me" (v. 2). Paul described the details of his unique and privileged ministry in 3:3-12. The word "administration" that he used to refer to this ministry has the sense of *a stewardship or trust to be shared* (translated "trust" in 1 Cor 9:17 and "commission" in Col 1:25). Paul was to administer God's grace, which had been granted to him, particularly to the Gentiles.

The apostle identified the unique aspect of his ministry as a "mystery" in 3:6. A mystery is *something previously concealed but now made known in the gospel.* In 1:9 "mystery" spoke of God's purpose of gathering together all things under the headship of Christ. In chapter 3 it refers to one aspect of that ultimate goal, the inclusion of Gentiles in the blessings of the gospel and the terms on which this is done.

Paul then moved another step in verses 7-12 to declare his unique role as a minister of the good news of salvation to the Gentiles. His service was carried out in the church in the service of the gospel. The church is the agency of the divine mission. Thus the church is central to history, to the gospel, and to Christian living.

A baptismal pool in the Double Church of Mary at the site of ancient Ephesus. The pool dates from the Roman period.

3:14-21
United in His Love

Paul now continued the prayer he started in 3:1. What he described in 2:11-22 is now the subject of his prayer. He desired for the church to be united experientially. He wanted them to know and experience Christ's love and share it with one another.

Paul addressed his prayer to the Father (3:14). He expressed his aspiration for the saints to be strengthened, grounded, and filled. He asked that they comprehend Christ's love and be filled unto God's fullness (3:16-19). His confidence in prayer was grounded not in his abilities or his readers' but completely in God's abundant power. Astoundingly he claimed that God can do abundantly more than we can ask or even imagine (3:20). Following these majestic words the apostle concluded with a beautiful doxology (3:21)

4:1-6
God's Purposes in the Church

Ephesians is the perfect balance between doctrine and duty. The first three chapters deal with doctrine, the believers' spiritual blessings in Christ. The last three chapters focus on the church's responsibility to live in unity, variety, maturity, purity, and victory. We learn from Paul's balanced perspective the need for both orthodoxy (right belief) and orthoproxy (right living).

Commentators have suggested that the pivotal verse of the entire letter—indeed, the key that unlocks its structure—is 4:1. It brings together the themes of chapters 1–3 and in a stirring appeal announces Paul's emphasis of chapters 4–6. The church's privileged position and calling carries with it weighty responsibilities. Paul exhorted the church to worthy living. He emphasized the character and effort required for such exemplary living (4:1-3).

Christian Unity

Christian unity is founded on each Christian's commitment to the one God. Common submission to His person and will should result in a church united in worship, fellowship, and service. Both this fact, and the conflicting fact of churches frequently fractured, is the testimony of the NT.

The Gospel of John reminds the church that oneness was the Lord's design for His followers (John 17:20-23). Jesus' prayer for every generation of believers was that "all of them may be one" (John 17:21). This unity with one another stems from a shared oneness with the Father and Son. The stated intent is that "the world may believe" in Jesus through the united testimony of His disciples.

John made a similar point to a church in turmoil. Those in fellowship with God (those who "walk in the light") share a resultant fellowship of love (1 John 1:5-7). The absence of this Christlike love, which should characterize the "light," is no small matter. A loveless, divisive Christianity is not Christianity at all. It is a type of heresy (1 John 2:9-11,15,19).

Paul also prayed for unity in the church and often exhorted believers to maintain oneness. His prayers identify the basis of unity as the one Father, the work of the one Spirit, and believers' common bond to Christ (Rom 15:5-6; Eph 4:3-6; Phil 2:1-2). Frequent references to unity reveal both its importance and the challenge of maintaining it in the church.

It is important because it glorifies the Father and the Son. Thus it is appropriate for believers, and it provides a witness to unbelievers (Rom 5:6-7). Paul's actions illustrate how crucial this was to him. His conflict with Peter (Gal 2:11-14), the Jerusalem Council (Acts 15), and the offering for the saints in Jerusalem (2 Cor 8–9) were all attempts both to defend the truth of the gospel and to maintain the unity of the church.

Yet the church experienced divisions. Selfishness, immaturity, conceit, and an unforgiving attitude are identified as common, root causes (Rom 15:7; 1 Cor 3:1-4; Phil 2:1-4; Jas 4:1-12). Even apparently mature Christians could place personal feelings or interests ahead of the good of the gospel and thus generate divisions. Individuals in conflict could also gather into warring factions and endanger the life and witness of the church (Acts 6:1-4; Gal 2:11-13; Phil 4:2-3; 3 John 9–10).

Believers were exhorted to recognize these pitfalls and avoid them. They were to emphasize the church's common purpose rather than focus on the ambitions of individuals (John 17:21; Phil 2:2). They were to accept others (forgiving faults and accepting differences) as Christ had accepted them (Rom 15:7; Col 3:13-14). Also, like Christ, they were to promote the well-being of others, not narrowly pursue their own goals (Phil 2:3-4). The true "yokefellow" was exhorted not only to govern his own actions but also to promote unity where there was conflict (Phil 4:2-4).

The NT makes clear the basis for unity in the body of Christ. Jesus, Paul, John, and others frequently emphasized its importance and its rewards. The church, therefore, in every generation bears the responsibility of making unity a reality. □

Then with characteristic Trinitarian emphasis the apostle claimed the church could so live because it is energized by the Spirit, established by the Lord, and empowered by the Father.

4:7-16
The Church's Gifts

Borrowing an illustration from Psalm 68:18, Paul described the gifts given to the church. God is both sovereign and generous in His distribution of the various gifts (4:7-10).

The gifts in fact are gifted persons: apostles, prophets, evangelists, pastors, and teachers (or pastor-teachers). Apostles and prophets were already mentioned in 2:20 and 3:5 as the foundational gifts to the church. In a strict sense apostles were witnesses of Christ's resurrection and were commissioned by Him to preach. It broadly included those associated with such men, who also were commissioned for ministry (for example, see Acts 14:4,14; 1 Thess 2:6). Prophets, under the direct inspiration of God, carried out a preaching ministry that included both foretelling and forthtelling.

Evangelists ministered in a manner itinerant and external from the church. They were missionaries to the unconverted empowered with special insight into the gospel's meaning. Pastors and teachers most likely constituted two sides of one ministry. This ministry was indigenous and internal to the church. Persons with this gift shepherd the flock and instruct them in divine truth.

All of these gifted people carry out equipping ministries so that service ministries can be actualized. Or as Paul put it, "to prepare God's people for works of service, so that the body of Christ may be built up until we all reach unity in the faith" (4:12-13).

The Great Theater of Ephesus as photographed from the Arcadian Way on the way to the harbor.

Paul stated the goal of the church in 4:13-16. The church is to grow up in Christ so it will avoid spiritual immaturity, instability, and gullibility. The atmosphere of spiritual maturity is described in terms of truth and love (4:15). Maturity is defined totally in relationship to the corporate Christian body. Maturity is an ongoing process of being "joined and held together" in relationship with the body of Christ.

4:17–5:21
Holy Living

In this very practical and challenging section Paul focused on holy living. Believers are to walk in purity as well as unity. The apostle first showed negatively how believers should not walk. Then he provided positive aspects of Christian conduct.

Paul distinguished between those characterized by rebellion, obstinacy, and darkened understanding (4:17-18) and those who respond to Jesus Christ as both subject and teacher (4:19-21). The first group is called the "old self" or unregenerate self (4:22). The second group is called the "new self" (4:23-24). Paul exhorted believers to live out the reality of their new position with an inward renunciation and restoration.

The conclusion of chapter four includes ethical exhortations grounded in theological truth. Believers are to rid themselves of vices like "bitterness," "anger," and "slander" and instead imitate the compassionate kindness of Christ (4:25-32).

Believers are to walk in love (5:1-7), please God by avoiding evildoers (5:8-14), and walk in wisdom (5:15-17). The church is enabled to do this by the empowering (filling) of the Holy Spirit (5:18). When this happens, believers can together praise God, constantly offer thanksgiving in all things, and mutually submit one to another (5:19-21).

5:22–6:9
New Relationships

Paul now applied his teaching to particular life relationships. Wise believers filled with the Spirit who mutually submit one to another are to live out these truths in household relationships. Three relationships are addressed: wives and husbands, children and parents, servants and masters. In each of these relationships the first partner is exhorted to be submissive or obedient (5:22; 6:1,5). The second person in the relationship shows submissiveness by Christlike love (5:25) and concerned care (6:4,9). All relate to one another as service to the Lord. All concerned experience personal worth, value, security, and significance when these reciprocal relationships are exercised under the lordship of Christ.

In the above Attic vase painting (from about 490 B.C.), depicting Odysseus giving the armor of his father Achilles to Neoptolemos, can be seen the essential Roman armor to which Paul referred in Ephesians 6:13-17—helmet, breastplate, shield, and spear.

6:10-20
The Warfare of the New People

Paul made sure believers recognized that as new people who have been granted new life in a new family with new relationships they still would endure spiritual warfare. The closing portion of Paul's letter explained his account of the Christian's conflict with evil forces.

Believers must adorn themselves with the armor of God in order to stand against the devil's schemes. Five defensive weapons are identified: (1) the enabling nature of truth that resists lying and false doctrine; (2) the covering quality of righteousness that resists accusations of conscience and despondency; (3) the stabilizing quality of peace that resists slander and selfishness; (4) the protective ability of faith that resists prayerlessness and doubt; and (5) the encouraging nature of salvation that resists fear and disappointment.

Two offensive weapons are included in the armor of God: (1) the sword of the Spirit, which is the word of God, and (2) prayer. It is fitting that this prayerful and meditative letter concludes with an exhortation to prayer (6:18) and a request for prayer (6:19-20).

6:21-24
Conclusion

We learn that Tychicus was the bearer of the letter (6:21). Paul concluded the letter with words of grace and peace (6:23-24). The unusual benediction provides a fitting benediction to Paul's majestic letter.

Theological Significance

This letter lifts us to a new vantage point from which we are united with the risen and ascended Christ. Believers are not to have a limited or merely earthly perspective. When we view life from the heavenly realms (1:3), we can understand that the church's strength is not in human resources but in the grace and strength of God alone. The church's warfare is not with people but with spiritual powers (6:10-17). The church, the people of God, does not function merely to carry out routine activities. It is to reveal the wisdom of God and to proclaim the rich redemption provided by Jesus Christ (1:3-11; 3:2-13). This grand book gives us a purpose for living in line with God's purposes in history (1:10). This is accomplished as we live in submission to Christ, the head of the church, indeed the head over all things (1:22).

Questions for Reflection

1. What is important for Paul's concept of the new life?
2. What did Paul identify as his special ministry? How does the church today carry out this ministry?
3. How do spiritual gifts (gifted people) contribute to the unity and maturity of the church?
4. Why do contemporary Christians often ignore the evil forces at war against the church? How can the church apply Paul's teaching on spiritual warfare?

Sources for Additional Study

Bruce, F. F. *The Epistle to the Ephesians. The New International Commentary.* Grand Rapids: Eerdmans, 1984.

Stott, John, R. W. *God's New Society: The Message of Ephesians. The Bible Speaks Today.* Downers Grove: InterVarsity, 1979.

Vaughan, Curtis. *Ephesians: A Study Guide Commentary.* Grand Rapids: Zondervan, 1977.

PHILIPPIANS

The Letter to the Philippians was written while the apostle Paul was in prison probably from Rome about A.D. 62, though we cannot know for sure. Other possible locations for the writing of the letter could have been Ephesus or Caesarea (sometime between A.D. 54 and 62).

The Recipients

The Philippian church was founded about A.D. 50–51, approximately a decade before the writing of the letter, during Paul's second missionary journey (Acts 16:12-40). Paul and Silas arrived in Philippi and apparently found no Jewish synagogue. There was, however, a place of prayer by the riverside where some women met on the Sabbath to pray. One of these women, Lydia, believed the gospel message Paul preached. As a result of her gratitude to God and to the missionaries, she opened her home to them.

After the missionaries had settled in Philippi, they were arrested when Paul exorcised a demon from a slave girl because her masters aroused opposition against the preachers. They were beaten, thrown into prison, and fastened in stocks. Yet Paul and Silas were still able to praise God and sing hymns. While they were in prison, there was an earthquake, and all the doors were immediately opened. The events of the evening set the stage for the conversion of the jailor and his household. Through the ministry of Paul and Silas, many in Philippi became Christians, and a church was established (see Acts 16).

When Paul and Silas, along with Timothy, left Philippi, Luke, the doctor, remained. Luke apparently did much to help stabilize the young congregation and enhance its outreach ministry.

Philippi was a Roman colony located on the great northern east-west highway, called the Egnatian Way. Philippi took its name from Philip II, Alexander the Great's father. Just west of town near the Gangitis River, Antony and Octavian defeated Cassius and Brutus in 42 B.C. In 30 B.C. Octavian made the town a Roman colony for retired soldiers and bestowed upon Philippi the full privileges of Roman citizenship. The Philippians took great pride in their privileges as Roman citizens and lived as faithful citizens of Rome, a point to which Paul appealed for illustration purposes in 3:20.

Women in this colony, as in most of the province of Macedonia, were treated with respect. As reflected in the church (Phil 4:2-3), the women in this area were active in public life.

Ruins of the agora (marketplace) at the site of the ancient city of Philippi in Macedonia.

Theme

A continuous note of joy in Christ is sounded throughout the letter. Despite Paul's testings and the difficulties encountered by the church (Phil 1:27-30), the theme of joy in Christ is echoed eighteen times in the four chapters of this letter. An exemplary text of this theme is Philippians 4:4: "Rejoice in the Lord always. I will say it again: Rejoice!"

Literary Form

As the letter now stands, there is some question concerning its unity and sequence. This has led some scholars to hypothesize that Philippians contains two or three letters joined together by the collector of Paul's Letters. The questions involve the placement of the matter concerning Timothy and Epaphroditus (2:19-30), which might be expected to come at the end of the letter rather than the middle. Also the farewell and benediction (4:4-9) seem appropriate for the letter's closing. The conclusion, however, does not occur until after the section concerning the Philippians' generous gifts (4:10-20), which some might expect to begin the letter. In addition there is an emotional outburst (3:2) that is surprising.

While some expect Paul to have been more logical and orderly, the literary structure of the book reveals the hypothesis, however interesting, to be unprovable. The fact that Philippians is an informal letter, probably produced over a period of time, helps explain the roughness of style and the questionable sequence of the letter.

Much discussion has also centered around the origin and interpretation of 2:5-11. It is widely held that this section exemplifies an early Christian hymn or confession that Paul used in support of his appeal for humility. Whether or not this is the case, there is no reason to doubt that Philippians 2:5-11 formed a part of the epistle as originally composed by Paul.

Purpose and Theology

Paul wrote this letter for several reasons:

1. He wanted to explain why he was sending Epaphroditus back to them (2:25-30).
2. He wanted to let them know of his plan to send Timothy to them (2:19-24).
3. He wanted to thank the Philippian church for their concern for him and their generous gifts to him (4:10-20).
4. He desired to inform them of his own circumstances and the advancement of the gospel (1:12-26).
5. He wanted to exhort the church to live in humility, fellowship, and unity (1:27–2:11; 4:2-3).
6. He also needed to warn them concerning the false teachings of legalism, perfectionism, and careless living (3:1–4:1).

The letter is extremely practical, but the guidance and warnings are theologically based: Paul's joy was grounded in Christ, as is all of life. In this sense the letter is thoroughly Christ-centered. The preexistence, incarnation, and exaltation of Christ is set forth in 2:5-11. Christ's incarnation is offered as an example for Paul's appeal to humble living and Christian unity (2:1-4).

Paul explained his doctrine of justification by faith in contrast to a false legalism (3:1-9). He contended for a sanctified life by identification with Christ through faith, sharing in His sufferings, death, and the power of His resurrection (3:10-11). Paul exhorted the church to set its mind on heavenly, rather than earthly, realities because Christians are destined for life in the age to come (3:17–4:1).

I. Greetings (1:1-2)
II. Paul's Joyful Concern for the Church (1:3-11)
III. Paul's Joyful Response in the Midst of Difficult Circumstances (1:12-26)
IV. Paul's Personal Plea for Christian Unity and Humility (1:27–2:18)
V. Paul's Pastoral Commendation for His Coworkers and Their Examples of Humility (2:19-30)
VI. Paul's Warning against the Error of Self-righteousness (3:1-11)
VII. Paul's Single-Minded Exhortation to Christian Maturity (3:12–4:1)
VIII. Paul's Gentle Advice for Joy and Peace Among the Saints (4:2-9)
IX. Paul's Genuine Thanksgiving for the Church's Generosity (4:10-20)
X. Conclusion (4:21-23)

1:1-2
Greetings

The letter addressed the church in Philippi. Paul and Timothy, who were servants of Christ Jesus, wrote to the saints. "Saints" refers to all believers set apart for God's service. The mention of overseers and deacons indicates a developing maturity in the organization of the young church. (See the article on "Models of Church Government.")

1:3-11
Paul's Joyful Concern for the Church

Paul's concern and love for the church was evidenced by his thanksgiving and prayer for them. His prayer is full of joy because of their fellowship in the gospel, the confidence of God's continued work in their lives, and because they also shared in God's grace along with Paul. Paul desired for them to abound in richer and deeper spiritual understanding so that they will be blameless until the day of Christ. The day of Christ will be a time of judgment of the believers' works at the Lord's appearing when their faithfulness will be rewarded.

1:12-26
Difficult Circumstances

Paul demonstrated a confident joy in the midst of his situation. If Paul was writing from Rome, his tribulations included mob violence, imprisonment, shipwreck, personal stress, and long detention under the palace guards (2 Cor 11:23-33). Paul rejoiced that in spite of his circumstances the gospel was being preached, even by those opposing him.

Paul informed them of his past and present situation and consciously weighed the alternatives for his future. The joy of Paul's life was grounded in his Christ-centered life. He stated, "For me, to live is Christ and to die is gain" (1:21). Dying was gain because it meant to be with Christ, the better by far. Yet it was the Lord's will for Paul to remain in this life because it was more helpful for the Philippians' progress and joy in the faith.

1:27–2:18
Christian Unity and Humility

In this very significant section of the letter, Paul urged the church members to dismiss their pride and to live and serve together in unity. Anything less falls short of the gospel's standards. True unity will be realized by authentic meekness and selflessness, ultimately exemplified in the earthly life of Jesus. The attitude the church should exhibit was the one Jesus maintained.

Jesus' self-emptying served as the basis for the apostle's exhortation. Philippians 2:5-11, possibly a quotation from an early hymn in praise of Christ, taught that Jesus' self-emptying led to His exaltation by the Father. Jesus existed in the very nature of God and made Himself nothing, not giving up His deity but His heavenly glory and privileges. He lived a life of humble obedience and humbled Himself even to the point of dying for sinners on the cross. He was then gloriously exalted in His resurrection and ascension. (See the article on "Jesus Christ" in the section on "Christian Faith and Christian Community.")

Paul's exhortation to unity involved Christians working out their salvation with fear and trembling. This action brings about a spiritual community void of complaining and friction. They are encouraged to live as lights in the world, thus holding out the word of life to others and providing joy for the apostle on the day of Christ.

2:19-30
Their Examples of Humility

Paul was willing to sacrifice himself in service for the church at Philippi and warmly commended his coworkers, Timothy and Epaphroditus, for their humble and sacrificial service as well. He told of his plan to send Timothy to them when there was further news for him to give. Also he offered an explanation for Epaphroditus's return to them. Paul wanted to be sure the Philippians did not think that Epaphroditus failed in his task to serve Paul.

3:1-11
Error of Self-righteousness

Paul warned of the dangers of turning aside to depend on legalistic standards rather than on the grace of God in Christ. Paul labeled these false teachers "dogs, those who do evil, mutilators of the flesh" (3:2). The church must have been aware of these false teachers, Judaizers, who followed Paul everywhere, insisting that Gentile believ-

The agora at Philippi with the ruins of an early Christian church in the background.

ers should be circumcised and keep the ceremonial law in order to be saved. Instead, Paul taught that true circumcision involved faith in Christ. He offered himself as an example of one who in his past trusted in human achievement instead of the justifying grace of God and the all-sufficiency of Christ. (See the article on "Justification.")

The object of joy, of concentration, indeed of all of life is Christ. Paul's purpose in life was to know Christ experientially, becoming like Him in His death and attaining to the resurrection from the dead.

3:12–4:1
Christian Maturity

Like an athlete who does not waste time looking around or looking back, Paul exerted his all-out effort to reach the finish line of Christian maturity. He did not presume to have attained perfection and therefore fully pursued the goal of God's upward call in Christ Jesus. He likewise called for the Philippians to move forward in their Christian lives.

Simultaneously in this exhortation he strongly denounced the false teachings of careless living, on the one hand, and spiritual perfectionism on the other. He appealed for unity and maturity by reminding them that they were citizens of heaven. Because the Philippians were intensely proud of their Roman citizenship, they would have quickly grasped all that Paul meant. Finally, he reminded them that they would be transformed at the coming again of the Lord Jesus Christ.

4:2-9
Joy and Peace

There was some hint of division in the church. Paul appealed to Euodia and Syntyche to agree with each other and for the entire church to stand firm in the Lord. Paul offered them a prescription for receiving God's peace, to rejoice in the Lord, and to let their thoughts be filled with that which is good, lovely, and true.

4:10-20
Thanksgiving for Generosity

Paul rejoiced and offered thanksgiving for the Philippians' generous care for him. He had learned to be satisfied in whatever situation he found himself in the Lord's service. This word of contentment and thanksgiving came from a man in prison facing death, a man who had been beaten, stoned, and hounded by his enemies. The basis for such contentment was found in his confidence that he could do everything through Christ who gave him strength (4:13). Paul commended them for their generosity. From the first, even at great cost to themselves, they had shared with the apostle. In all of this Paul displayed his attitude toward material things and urged them to realize that God would meet all their needs according to His glorious riches in Christ Jesus.

4:21-23
Conclusion

Paul concluded his letter with a benediction and personal greetings. He also sent greetings from Caesar's household, which included Christian members of the emperor's staff.

Theological Significance

In this letter we learn the importance of church unity (1:27-30) and Christian humility (2:1-4). Christ's humility serves as the basis of Christian humility, which is the key for genuine Christian unity. Paul's suffering during his imprisonment also serves as a foundation for teaching abasement and humility (1:12-18; 4:10-13). Alongside abasement and suffering is joy, the great theme of the letter. In all of life's circumstances believers can experience joy. For it is in suffering and sacrifice that true joy is found. Paul's exhortation to rejoice is a much-needed and practical word for believers at all times in all situations.

Questions for Reflection

1. What does this letter teach us about hardship and suffering?
2. What should be our attitude concerning material things?
3. What can we learn about what Jesus has done for us in providing our salvation and offering us an example of selfless living?
4. How can we demonstrate unity in our churches so as to avoid conflict and bickering?
5. What can we learn through the examples of Timothy and Epaphroditus?

Sources for Additional Study

Bruce, F. F. *Philippians, A Good News Commentary*. San Francisco: Harper and Row, 1983.

Martin, Ralph P. *The Epistle of Paul to the Philippians. Tyndale New Testament Commentaries*. Grand Rapids: Eerdmans, 1959.

Melick, Richard R., Jr. *Philippians, Colossians, Philemon. The New American Commentary*. Nashville: Broadman, 1991.

Motyer, J. A. *The Message of Philippians*. Downers Grove: InterVarsity, 1984.

COLOSSIANS

Tradition supports the letter's claim that Paul was the author (Col 1:1). Paul had never been to Colosse, but he wrote to them to address matters raised by Epaphras (1:7). The letter would have been written about the same time as Ephesians and Philemon (around 60–61). (See the discussion of dates in Philippians and Ephesians.)

Some people today doubt Pauline authorship on the grounds of the book's theology and style. But some obvious differences in the theological perspective do not force one to conclude that someone other than Paul wrote Colossians.

Destination

Colosse was an important city in Phrygia on the upper Lycus River in what is today South Central Turkey. It served as a trading center at a crossroads on the main highway from Ephesus to the east. In Roman times relocation of the road leading north to Pergamum brought about both the growth of Laodicea, a city ten miles away, and Colosse's gradual decline.

In New Testament times Colosse was a small city with a mixed population of Phrygians, Greeks, and Jews. Paul may have instructed some from Colosse during his stay in Ephesus (see Acts 19:10). Epaphras, a leader in the church at Colosse, visited Paul in prison in Rome and told him about the church's situation (Col 1:7; 4:12). Epaphras was later imprisoned with Paul (Phlm 23). Paul wrote to the Colossians to address the concerns raised by Epaphras at the same time he wrote to the church about Onesimus (Phlm 16).

Purpose

Paul's purpose was to address the false teaching in the church. To identify the false teaching has been a puzzling problem for students of Paul's letters. Some think the problem was basically a form of Gnosticism. Others think it was a Jewish mystical asceticism. Still others suggest a type of legalistic separatism. Some think it was a syncretistic (combined forms) movement with aspects of each of these ideologies. What we do know is that the false teaching

- attacked the centrality of Christ (1:15-19; 2:9-10);
- focused on speculative philosophical traditions (2:8);
- observed dietary prescriptions and prohibitions (2:16,21);
- observed certain religious rites of a Jewish nature (2:16);
- venerated angels (2:18);
- tended toward asceticism (2:20).

(See the article on "The Opponents of Paul.")

The readers were admonished to "see to it that no one takes you captive through hollow and deceptive philosophy, which depends on human tradition and the basic principles of this world rather than on Christ" (2:8). Paul countered this false teaching with correct teaching, focusing on the supremacy of Christ (1:15-23), ministry and the church (1:24–2:7), and other exhortations (3:1–4:6).

Theology

Paul's major teaching centered around the question Who is Jesus Christ? The apostle insisted that no chasm existed between the transcendent God and His material creation. Christ is both the Creator and Reconciler (1:15-23). He is the exact expression of God and brings together heaven and earth. A need for a hierarchy of angelic powers is nonexistent since Christ is fully divine and fully human. Indeed "in Christ all the fullness of the Deity lives in bodily form, and you have this fullness in Christ, who is the head over every power and authority" (2:9-10).

Second, he dealt with the issue of genuine spirituality. Paul developed the basis for genuine worship and spirituality by refuting the false spirituality that encouraged an unspiritual pride (2:6-23). He exhorted them to abandon sins of the old life and cultivate the virtues of the new life (3:5–4:6).

I. Introduction (1:1-14)
II. Explanation of the Supremacy of Christ (1:15-23)
III. Ministry for the Church (1:24–2:5)
IV. Warnings against False Spirituality (2:6–3:4)
V. Exhortations for Ethical Living (3:5–4:6)
VI. Conclusion (4:7-18)

Gnosticism

Gnosticism is difficult to define because it is used of a collection of divergent movements. The term is derived from the Greek word for knowledge (*gnosis*). Usually Gnosticism is used of a second-century Christian heresy that was a major threat to the church. The main ideas in Gnostic systems include the following:

1. A dualism in the universe between God and a lesser, evil being usually called the Demiurge.
2. God is unknowable and is neither concerned about the world nor has anything to do with it.
3. Various beings emerge from God and join in male and female pairs to form concentric barriers around God.
4. The female being in the last barrier, without her male partner, gave birth to the Demiurge.
5. The Demiurge created the world, and therefore anything material (including the body) is evil.
6. But a spark of the divine was also placed in humans (or at least some of them) that needs to be awakened and called back to the divine.
7. A revealer calls humans and shows the way through the barriers. Christ was viewed as the revealer, but He was not truly human. He only took over the body of Jesus at the baptism and left before His death.
8. Knowledge of one's true self and of the character of the universe is the way to salvation. Salvation is achieved when at death or the end of the world a person passes through the barriers and is reintegrated into God.

With these core ideas a variety of Gnostic systems developed with different emphases. Some of them had very strict rules, while some had no rules.

Origins of Gnosticism. Little is known about the origins of Gnosticism. It had no one founder, even though the name Simon Magus (see Acts 8) was often associated in church traditions with the rise of Gnosticism. Gnosticism had no founding text, nor can a specific time of beginning for the movement be identified. Some of the ideas in Gnosticism were already current in NT times. But although debated, there is no evidence that Gnosticism existed before Christianity.

Some facts about the origin of Gnosticism are clear. This religion arose because of a deeply felt spiritual need. One of the main concerns was the problem of evil. The Gnostic understanding of the universe was a way to protect God from any responsibility for the evil in this world. Ideas were gathered from various religions, especially Judaism. The focus on knowledge and light is present in nearly every religion.

Until recently most of what was known about Gnosticism was obtained from quotations of church fathers. In 1945 the discovery of a Gnostic library at Nag Hammadi, Egypt, provided firsthand evidence of Gnostic beliefs.

Relevance of Gnosticism. Gnosticism is obviously important for an understanding of church history. It is also important theologically. We too must deal with the problem of evil. Many of the errors of Gnosticism are still dangers. Often there is a tendency to reject God's created world and to view the body as evil or to view Christ as not fully human. Or, like the famous Gnostic Marcion, many people are tempted to reject the authority of the OT.

Gnosticism is also important for reading the NT.

Already the ideas of Gnosticism were emerging. First John 4:2 stresses the necessity of acknowledging that Jesus Christ has come *in the flesh.* Timothy was warned against a "falsely called knowledge" (1 Tim 6:20). Gnostic tendencies are sometimes identified as the problems in 1 Corinthians and Colossians, but other explanations of the difficulties in these churches are more likely.

Also an awareness of Gnosticism reminds us that in Christianity knowledge does not save; a faith relationship with Christ does. □

Theme

The theme of this letter centers on the supremacy of Christ in all things.

1:1-14
Introduction

Paul followed a standard form of salutation, thanksgiving, and prayer in the first part of the letter. It is perhaps longer than some of his other letters because Paul was not personally acquainted with the people of Colosse. The salutation carried greetings from both Paul and Timothy (1:1-2). Words of high commendation and thanksgiving follow for the well-being and spiritual health of the Christian community at Colosse (1:3-8).

These opening words are followed by Paul's prayer for their knowledge and godly conduct (1:9-14). The prayer centered on spiritual blessings, not on physical or material things. He prayed for spiritual insight (1:9), genuine obedience (1:10-11), and moral excellence (1:12-14). The prayer went right to the heart of the false teaching invading the church.

The false teachers promised a special insight and a superior spirituality. Terms like knowledge, wisdom, and spiritual understanding were a part of the false teachers' vocabulary. So Paul employed these types of words in his prayer. The prayer requested that God "fill" them "with the knowledge of his will" (1:9). The term "filled" is a key word in Colossians. It was likewise an important term for the false teachers. Paul used it here and in 1:19,25; 2:2,9-10; 4:12,17. It carries the idea of *being fully equipped or controlled*. Paul's prayer then was for the Colossians to be controlled by the full knowledge of God's will, which would lead to obedience and moral excellence.

1:15-23
Explanation of the Supremacy of Christ

The false teachers challenged the true nature and deity of Jesus Christ. Their teaching possibly involved the worship of angels or some other beings (2:15,18,20) who

SALVATION IN PAUL'S THOUGHT

The message of salvation was central in Paul's thought. He addressed the issue from the perspective of Christ's work on the cross for us. Common themes include justification by faith, new life in Christ, freedom, grace, and assurance. We will examine Paul's thought with a focus on the doctrine of justification by faith.

Justification (or righteousness) by faith summarizes Paul's teaching that faith in Christ now secures the vindication of the believer in the final judgment. It represents Paul's understanding of the gospel. Paul emphasized that Christ's giving of Himself on the cross on behalf of us and our sins was necessary and sufficient for the salvation of all, both Jew and Gentile.

Paul's pronouncements on this matter always appear in contexts in which relations between believing Jews and Gentiles are at issue. In Galatians the question at hand was whether Gentile believers must be circumcised and adhere to the law of Moses in order to be assured of salvation. Paul vigorously attacked this suggestion and those who would press it upon the Galatian churches (Gal 5:1-12; see Phil 3:1-11).

In Romans Paul addressed a predominantly Gentile church with a Jewish minority, who were in danger of rejecting one another. Here Paul's aim in unfolding his understanding of justification by faith was to secure allegiance to his gospel. This would provide the basis for mutual acceptance by the opposing groups (Rom 15:7-13). In all these instances Paul's claim that righteousness was given through faith opposed the idea that it was given through the law (Rom 3:21; Gal 3:11), works (Rom 4:2,6), or works of the law (Rom 3:20,28; Gal 3:2).

Variations on the theme of justification appear in the Corinthian correspondence. In these letters Paul stressed that it is Christ and the shame and suffering of His crucifixion that effects our righteousness (see 1 Cor 1:22-25,30).

In Ephesians Paul developed the topic further. The apostle taught that grace was the ultimate and faith the mediate means to salvation (Eph 2:8-9). Similarly in the Pastoral Letters we find the formulation "justification [or salvation] by grace" (2 Tim 1:9; Titus 3:7). All of these statements elaborate the theme of justification by faith for Gentile readers. Paul did this also in Romans, where in speaking to Gentile readers he explained that being justified by faith means possessing peace with God and the assurance of salvation (Rom 5:1-11).

It is important to bear in mind that justification by faith was only one aspect of Paul's gospel. For Paul participation in Christ involved more. It also meant being made new in Christ, indwelt and empowered by the Spirit for obedience to God (Rom 6; 8:1-17).

According to Paul it is impossible to share in one aspect of salvation without sharing in all of them. Those justified by faith manifest the fruit of the Spirit in their lives (Gal 5:16-26). The freedom that the gospel brings is not a freedom for oneself or one's sinful desires but a freedom for service to God and love for one's neighbor (Gal 5:13-14). Paul did not expect believers to be sinless, but he did expect to see progress and evidence of the presence of Christ in the believer's life (see 2 Cor 13:5).

The basis for Paul's exhortation to believers lies in what God has done for them in Christ, including justification. They obey not in order to become new persons but because Christ has made them new persons already (see Gal 5:25; 1 Cor 5:7).

Christians must again and again by faith appropriate God's saving promises made in the gospel (Gal 3:3; 5:5-6). Our appropriation of this teaching must always be guided by the purposes for which Paul's arguments were formed. They were not intended to provide an excuse for sinful behavior or a lax spiritual life. They were given instead to shatter all human pretense at righteousness before God, to expose the ultimate sickness and depravity of human nature, and to apply the saving cure of Christ and His cross. □

The ruins of a Roman bridge built over a brook near the site of ancient Colosse.

negated or minimized the supremacy of Christ. The false teachers declared that salvation was achieved by knowledge rather than faith. Paul's answer to these matters begins in this important section.

Many think that 1:15-20 was a pre-Pauline hymn that Paul used and applied for the Colossian situation. Regardless, whether reworked or original, Paul presented Christ as preeminent in relation to the entire creation (1:15-17) and in relation to humanity and the church because of His resurrection (1:18-20). This hymn or early creed celebrated Christ as the sovereign Creator and Redeemer of all things.

Paul described Jesus as Lord of creation, the "firstborn" (1:15). The term "firstborn" stresses uniqueness and sovereignty rather than priority in time. Jesus is the "firstborn" because He is the agent of creation and the heir of creation.

Paul developed a physiological metaphor to establish the relationship of head over the body. As the head Christ sends life into the whole body. The church responds in humble adoration, acknowledging that Christ is head over all. God was pleased for His fullness to dwell in Christ and through Him to reconcile all things to Himself (1:19-20). The reconciliation spoken of in verses 19-20 is discussed with reference to humankind. Through Christ's physical death they have been reconciled to God (1:21-23). The purpose of Christ's reconciliation is to achieve a new creation in which estranged people may know and approach God. (See the feature article "Reconciliation.")

1:24–2:5
Ministry for the Church

The second major part of the letter described Paul's apostolic ministry for the church. Paul's ministry task involved making known the mystery of God concerning Christ to the Gentiles in general (1:24-29) and to the churches of Colosse in particular (2:1-5). Paul's service was to make known to Gentiles the "mystery" that God had kept hidden from the world but has now revealed to people like Paul (1:26). Paul worked to bring about the inclusion of the Gentiles into the church so he could "present everyone perfect in Christ" (1:28).

Paul's efforts on behalf of the Gentiles were intended to help them know the meaning of God's "mystery" about Christ (2:2). By mystery Paul meant that God has now revealed something formerly concealed. The mystery is the fact that Gentiles are now made fellow members with Jewish Christians.

2:6-15
Christ Is Divine

Paul wanted to make sure the Colossians did not follow those who set forth Christ as merely an important visionary or religious leader. Christ is uniquely divine and preeminent. This is the foundation for true spirituality. The exhortation to live in him [Christ] is surrounded by themes that are clearly a response to the false teaching that threatened them (2:6-7). The context emphasizes "as you received Christ Jesus" and "as you were taught." Paul obviously considered the false teachers a real threat to the church. He warned, "See to it that no one takes you captive through hollow and deceptive philosophy" (2:8).

The right antidote for false teaching is right teaching about Christ, in whom "all the fullness of Deity lives in bodily form" (2:9). In Christ believers have received all they have and all they need (2:10-15). Christians are not subject to any forms of legalism, nor does legalism do them any good spiritually. Jesus Christ alone is sufficient for our every spiritual need, for all of God's fullness is in Him. The believers' covenant relation (2:11), their life (2:12-13), their freedom (2:14), and their victory (2:15) are all in Him.

2:16–3:4
Captive to Christ

The spiritual life has its dangers and its warnings. Paul warned the church against those who would make the Christian life just a set of rules. The basis for resisting legalism (2:16-23) involves focusing on the believer's relationship with Christ (3:1-4). Believers no longer are captive to religious tradition or human bondage. Instead, they are captive to Christ. In view of this privileged identification with Christ (3:1), the church must realize its great responsibility: "Set your minds on things above" (3:2).

The life in Christ is a profound reality (see Gal 2:20). It is a life that draws its existence from the very center of all reality, Jesus Christ Himself. The admonitions that follow are controlled by the thought of the full life that belongs to all who are in Christ (see Rom 6:4-5).

3:5-11
Put Sin to Death

Paul exhorted the Colossians to put to death whatever belonged to their "earthly nature" (3:5). This suggests that they had not been living consistently with the principle of a spiritual death and resurrection in their conversion. Some think it is only coincidental that Paul listed five vices in 3:5 and five more in 3:8 and then five virtues in 3:12. More likely Paul was responding to the heretics' list of vices and virtues. The list initially focused on sexual sins. Those who commit such sins bring the wrath of God on themselves (3:5-6). In their former way of life the Colossians practiced this kind of sin. Now they were commanded to differentiate themselves from such conduct (3:7-11).

3:12-17
Put on Love

This section completes Paul's exhortation to the Colossians to maintain a holy life-style. Paul admonished them "to clothe yourselves with compassion, kindness, humility, gentleness and patience" (3:12). Over all these they should "put on love, which binds them all together in perfect unity" (3:14).

The heretics were obviously causing divisions in the church. The way to unity included letting the peace of Christ and the word of Christ rule in their hearts (3:15-16). This required obedient application. So Paul said, "Whatever you do, whether in word or deed, do it all in the name of the Lord Jesus, giving thanks to God the Father through him" (3:17).

3:18–4:1
Family Life

Paul turned to the issue of household relationships. He addressed husbands and wives, parents and children, and slaves and masters. As in Ephesians 5:21–6:9, Paul arranged his discussion to treat the subordinate person first (wife, child, or slave; see 3:18,20,22). Paul immediately followed each statement with a reminder of the responsibility of the second member of each pair (see 3:19,21; 4:1). The distinctly Christian contribution to the ordering of family life was the stress on reciprocal responsibilities. Even in culture where family relationships were given an importance and significance not widespread in antiquity, it was generally assumed that husbands and fathers had *rights* to be exercised but few duties. Wives and children assumed they had *duties* but no or few rights. Paul stressed that all household members had rights and duties. Paul here taught a picture of family life implicit in Jesus' teaching concerning marriage (see Mark 10:2-16).

4:2-6
Conduct and Speech

This section concludes with further instructions to con-

A view of the tell of Colosse

tinue in prayer (4:2-4) and to conduct themselves in a worthy manner toward others (4:5-6). Believers' conduct and speech should be carefully controlled and used with great wisdom and love (4:6).

4:7-18
Conclusion

Paul's lengthy conclusion included personal news, greetings, and final instructions. The conclusion gives the letter, which is strategically polemical in places, a real personal touch. The apostles referred to Tychicus, who carried this letter plus Ephesians and Philemon, and to Onesimus, the runaway slave who accompanied him. They were to give a report to the church concerning Paul and Epaphras (4:7-9) as well as pertinent information regarding Onesimus's situation.

Paul often sent greetings from those with him. He mentioned Aristarchus, Mark, Jesus (Justus), Epaphras, Luke, and Demas. Mark (referred to in 4:10) was the cousin of Barnabas and companion with Paul and Barnabas on the first journey (see Acts 12:12,25; 13:4). But Mark had turned back before the journey was finished, and Paul did not want to take him on future journeys (see Acts 13:4,13; 15:37). Evidently Mark had reconciled himself with Paul.

The reference to a Laodicean letter in 4:16 has called forth numerous suggestions. Some have identified Paul's Letter to the Ephesians as this letter. Others have suggested that Philemon was the letter to which Paul referred. Still others have identified the reference to a lost letter to the Laodiceans. We cannot know for sure. Archippus was encouraged to fulfill the temporary ministry he had received (4:17). He fittingly asked to be remembered in prayer. Paul concluded with a brief benediction written in his own hand (4:18). This probably implies that Paul dictated the letter to a secretary and then signed it himself (see Rom 16:22).

Theological Significance

In Colosse a religious philosophy appeared that challenged the essence of Christian teaching. It contained Jewish elements (2:16), had an aspect of angel worship (2:18), and had a strong ascetic emphasis (2:20-23). This philosophy brought divisions to the church. It had some parallels with Christianity, but its teaching about Christ was wrongheaded. Today similar movements exist that confront the church's theology about Christ as well as its spirituality. The proper response needed in the church then is the same today. These contemporary New Age teachings must be recognized for what they are. The church must readily affirm that "in Christ all the fullness of the Deity lives in bodily form" (2:9). Any effort to approach God through angelic or human intermediaries is not only misguided, but it is a denial of Christ and authentic Christian teaching.

Questions for Reflection

1. How is the gospel threatened by combining portions of truth and portions of error from various theological traditions?

2. How does the church deal with false ascetic movements? legalistic movements?

3. What is involved in a distinctively Christian understanding of Jesus Christ?

4. What are the implications of Paul's teaching in Colossians for the church's contemporary response to New Age movements?

Sources for Additional Study

Bruce, F. F., *The Epistles to the Colossians to Philemon, and to the Ephesians. The New International Commentary.* Grand Rapids: Eerdmans, 1984.

Martin. R. P. *Colossians and Philemon. New Century Bible.* Grand Rapids: Eerdmans, 1981.

Melick, Richard R., Jr. *Philippians, Colossians, Philemon. The New American Commentary.* Nashville: Broadman, 1991.

1 THESSALONIANS

Galatians probably was the first of Paul's letters to be written, and 1 Thessalonians was the second. Paul traveled to Thessalonica, the capital city of Macedonia, on his second missionary journey around A.D. 51. Luke reported the brief visit, Paul's preaching ministry there with Silas, and the subsequent persecution that drove them out of the city (see Acts 17:1-9). Many people believed in Jesus Christ before they were compelled to leave. From Thessalonica, Paul went to Berea, Athens, and then Corinth. Timothy and Silas, who had been with Paul at Thessalonica, rejoined Paul in Corinth (see Acts 18:5; 1 Thess 3:6). Paul wrote 1 Thessalonians in response to Timothy's report shortly after his arrival.

The Purpose of the Letter

Paul received the report that the Thessalonians were strong in faith and were making favorable progress. He wrote this letter to defend himself against enemies who spread false rumors and to answer the Thessalonians' questions. Paul's experience with the opposition of the Jews in Corinth, terminating in his expulsion from the synagogue, may well have been the reason for his strong condemnation in 1 Thessalonians 2:14-16. The controversy over the law had plagued the churches of Macedonia. Paul's Jewish adversaries had accused him of being a heretic, a deceiver, and a religious adventurer who made a living by victimizing an ignorant public. The Letter to the Thessalonians was Paul's answer to these issues.

The Theology of the Letter

Paul's basic theology about salvation, Christ, and His return make up the essence of the letter. Here we learn there is one living and true God (1 Thess 1:9) who has loved men and women (1 Thess 1:4) and has revealed Himself to them (1 Thess 2:13). This revelation concerned His Son, the Lord Jesus Christ (1 Thess 1:3,8,10) who died and rose again (1 Thess 4:14) for our salvation (1 Thess 5:9). The Holy Spirit imparts joy, authoritative truth, and prophetic wisdom (1 Thess 1:6; 4:8; 5:19). The apostle taught that holiness of life is required of all Christians (1 Thess 4:3; 5:23).

Paul often mentioned the gospel (1 Thess 1:5; 2:2-4,8; 3:2), though not in the framework of justification by faith. He affirmed that Jesus' death and resurrection are the core of the gospel, but the greatest single doctrinal emphasis of this letter concerned the return of Christ (1 Thess 1:10; 2:19; 3:13; 4:13-18; 5:23). This teaching indicates that the expectation regarding the return of Christ was the hope of the earliest church. The motivation for Christian living was based on this anticipation. The hopelessness of death was reversed and abandoned because of this confident hope.

I. Salutation (1:1)
II. Personal Relations (1:2–3:13)
III. Church Problems (4:1–5:11)
IV. Concluding Exhortations (5:12-28)

1:1
Salutation

The salutation included the identification of the writer, the recipients, and a Christian greeting. Paul, Silas, and Timothy were the authors, though obviously Paul was the primary writer. The letter is addressed "to the church of the Thessalonians, who are in God the Father and the Lord Jesus Christ." This opening word describes the church's union with the Godhead, which meant a new sphere of life on an infinitely higher plane.

1:2-10
Faith, Hope, and Love

The first part of the letter deals primarily with the response of the church and the nature of Paul's ministry.

Paul offered thanksgiving for the Thessalonians' faith. This letter started Paul's practice of beginning his letters by thanking God for his readers (all of his letters except the first Letter to the Galatians contain such a statement). Paul's words were not mere rhetorical flattery. He was giving credit to One who brought about their spiritual progress (1 Thess 1:2-3).

The apostle's trilogy of faith, hope, and love is introduced at this early part of the letter. Paul described the church service as "work produced by faith, labor prompted by love, and endurance inspired by hope in our Lord Jesus Christ" (1 Thess 1:3). He commended their courageous service that excluded self-pity. The early church associated faith with work (see Gal 5:6; Jas 2:18), love with labor (see Rev 2:2,4), and hope with endurance (see Rom 5:2-4; 8:24).

Paul found in the fruitfulness of their lives an adequate proof that God loved them (1 Thess 1:4-5). The knowledge of God's prior choice of these believers was the root of Paul's thanksgiving. The heart of divine election is God's sovereign decision to choose a people for Himself, making them peculiarly His own.

The power of the gospel to bring about conviction and transform lives encouraged the apostle. He knew the Holy Spirit was the source of that power (1 Thess 1:5-7). The Thessalonians welcomed the message and were converted. In spite of difficult circumstances and severe suffering, they had a joy that could only be supplied by the Spirit. They rapidly became imitators of Paul and the Lord and thus became a model to all believers throughout Macedonia and Achaia.

The apostle affirmed that these converts played a substantial part in the ever-widening scope of Christian witness. Their testimony echoed the preaching that had undergirded the mission to Thessalonica. They had turned (been converted) from idol worship to the worship of God. They turned to serve the living God and to wait for His Son from heaven. Early Christianity universally maintained that the resurrected and ascended Christ would return. Their expectancy of this event implied its imminency. Ultimately the faith, hope, and commitment of all believers should be focused on the person of Jesus, in whom God's gracious favor found its most pointed expression.

2:1-9
God-Approved Ministry

Chapter 2 is new material, but it is closely related to chapter 1 as the following chart shows:

2:1-6	expands	1:4-10
2:7-12	restates	1:5,9
2:13-16	echoes	1:6-8,10

Chapter 2 is a defense against insinuations about his alleged ulterior motives. The apostle was subjected to a constant barrage of accusations. The Thessalonians themselves may have begun to question Paul's sincerity. No evidence of organized opposition on a wide scale exists (though see the article "The Opponents of Paul"). Estrangement could have developed unless treated immediately. So Paul addressed his readers most affectionately.

Paul claimed their ministry (Paul as well as Timothy and Silas) was above suspicion. It was bold and powerful because God had approved their ministry to preach the gospel. The success of their mission, in spite of sustained opposition, was due largely to their courage inspired by God. The approval of God was more significant for Paul and his team than the success of the mission. Yet the success of the work offered important validation of his motives and message (1 Thess 2:1-6). Verses 7-8 picture Paul as one who had found sufficient reason to endure suffering and the questions surrounding his character. He denied that flattery was the means of his ministry. Also greed and human praise were not the motivations for his ministry.

2:10-16
Worthy of God

Paul appealed to the sensitive nature of their ministry in order to silence those who attacked him. To the hesitant he offered exhortation; to the weary he offered encouragement; to the weak he offered strength and direction. His motivation was to help each convert see what it meant "to live lives worthy of God, who calls you into his kingdom and glory" (1 Thess 2:10-12).

Christian ministers are expected to offer practical guidance to fellow Christians, but not as dictators. Christian leaders cannot rule by decree. If they are to be true to the Spirit of Christ, they must lead by example. The example must be modeled after the Lord Jesus Christ (see 2 Cor 1:12; Phil 2:7).

Paul returned to the theme of thanksgiving in verse 13. His thanksgiving for them was an aspect of his vindication and served as a demonstration of his guileless interest in them. They had listened to him and welcomed his message as "the word of God, which is at work in [those] who believe" (1 Thess 2:13). The manner of speech was Paul's. At the same time God was uttering His own powerful, creative word through him. The word had evidenced its power in their daily experience.

The words of verses 15-16 have been the source of careful scrutiny. Some think Paul spoke mistakenly about the Jews. Others reject Pauline authorship of these verses. These options are hardly worthy of Holy Scripture. Certainly the words here reveal Paul's heartfelt concern and exasperation with his countrymen. Yet to read this as personal vindication is to misunderstand Paul's point. It is the rejection of the gospel that moved Paul to bitter denunciation reminiscent of the prophets of God.

2:17–3:5
My Glory and Joy

Paul again expressed deep feeling for the Thessalonians. He described himself in sharp contrast to the persecutors just mentioned in 2:14-16. He declared that the Thessalonians were his glory and joy—not only at Christ's return but even at that very time (2:17-20).

We are allowed to see into Paul's heart in 3:1-5. Paul's deepest concerns for the church are here expressed. He needed to know how the Thessalonians were doing in the midst of persecution. Paul's mission was to strengthen and encourage them in their faith (see Rom 1:11; 16:25; 1 Thess 3:13). He knew dependence on God in faith was their only recourse in adversity.

3:6-13
Faith That Lacks

Timothy's report of the favorable feelings of the Thessalonians toward him assured Paul that the church had not cast him off as one who exploited them. The encouraging report rejuvenated Paul (as it did elsewhere; see Rom 1:12; 2 Cor 7:4; Phlm 7). Along with rejoicing, Paul prayed continually for the believers in Thessalonica that God would supply what was lacking in their faith.

The prayer reflects the transition in Paul's life from anguish to exhilaration. The prayer served to conclude what he had said in this section (2:1–3:13) and prepared the readers for what Paul had to say in the second half of the letter. He prayed that God would enable him to visit his friends. Then he asked the Lord to perfect and enlarge the love the Thessalonians had already displayed toward one another.

Love toward God and toward others turns us away from selfish concerns and opens the way to moral perfection that is the condition of holiness. This radical transformation of character Paul desired for the church then and God desires for believers today so that they may face Christ's return without fear or shame. Daringly Paul set himself as a standard of love to be emulated, a step he could take only because of his imitation of Jesus (see 1 Thess 1:5-7).

4:1-12
Sexual Morality

The second section of the letter shifts to ethical or doctrinal issues. Up to this point the letter has been intensely personal. Now it shifts to instruction and exhortation.

Paul encouraged his readers to purity of life, love, and faithful work. The word "finally" was used to indicate the transition in Paul's thought. He addressed matters of moral irregularities (4:1-8) and brotherly love (4:9-12).

Pagan culture looked upon sexual immorality either indifferently or favorably. Had church members slipped into immorality they probably would not have thought it strange. Paul gave general guidelines concerning pleasing God and then specific ones focused on sexual morality.

A modern highway near Salonica (ancient Thessalonica) going toward Athens.

To please God is to do His will, and His will is the sanctification of the believer (1 Thess 4:3-5).

Verses 6-8 provide theological reasons for his ethical exhortations. These include the judgment of God and God's calling on their lives; the words themselves are God's words. To reject these words is to reject God.

Paul turned from negative commands in verses 1-8 to positive concerns in verses 9-12. The manner of the believer's life-style should be characterized by mutual edification. God's will includes the necessity of moral purity and love relationship with people, which demands openness and self-sacrifice on the part of believers.

4:13-18
Hope in Grief

This important paragraph holds out hope for believers during times of sorrow. The believing community should not grieve over those who have died in Jesus because God will bring them with Jesus at the return of the Lord (1 Thess 4:13-14). Paul desired that these believers not grieve as those who are without hope.

The "Lord's own word" further confirmed the fact that the Christian dead will experience no disadvantage at the Lord's return (1 Thess 4:15-17). Paul said the living believer will not have an advantage at the Lord's appearing. In fact, the Christian dead will rise first. After that those "who are still alive" will be "caught up with them in the clouds to meet the Lord in the air" (1 Thess 4:17). These encouraging words provided great comfort to those whose family members had already died. Also it served as the basis for an evangelistic appeal to those who have no hope. Paul exhorted the believers to comfort one another with these words (1 Thess 4:18).

5:1-11
Day of the Lord

In this section Paul continued his discussion about the Lord's return with particular emphasis on the meaning of the Day of the Lord. Since the Day of the Lord will come suddenly and unexpectedly, bringing destruction on those who are spiritually insensitive, believers should maintain spiritual alertness. The good news for the Thessalonians and for all believers is that their destiny is not wrath but eschatological deliverance through Jesus Christ. Again Paul exhorted believers to comfort one another (1 Thess 5:11).

Believers should encourage and build up one another in the faith because one day we will live with Christ. The simultaneous truths concerning the return of Christ and the resurrection of believers offer hope and meaning for living. The flip side is that at the Day of the Lord, God's wrath will be revealed. There is no universalism in this text. People need to be saved from the wrath to come by placing their faith and hope in the Lord.

5:12-28
Concluding Exhortations

The concluding section stresses the responsibilities to the different people in the Christian community. Paul told them they were responsible to church leaders (1 Thess 5:12-13). Leaders were to guard against abusing their authority.

Verses 14-15 focused on their responsibilities to others. They were to warn when necessary, encourage the timid, and show kindness to one another. Responsibilities to oneself and to one's spiritual relationship with God can be seen in 1 Thessalonians 5:16-18. Compliance with other commands and exhortations in the book is impossible apart from personal communion with God. To "be joyful always; pray continually; give thanks in all circumstances" is possible even in the midst of persecution when one recognizes God's superintendence over all things (see Rom 8:28).

Paul shifted the focus from the personal to the community in 1 Thessalonians 5:19-22. Here Paul reflected on the believers' responsibilities in Christian worship. They were not to underestimate the importance of prophecy while holding "on to the good." Finally they were to be free from every kind of evil that attempts to parade itself as a genuine representation of the Spirit.

Paul offered edifying words of blessing for the church. These comments underscore the importance of prayer in carrying out the purposes of God. Paul's signature theme—"the grace of our Lord Jesus Christ"—concludes this pastoral and encouraging letter.

Theological Significance

The letter is more practical than theological. It is God-centered throughout. God chose them unto salvation (1 Thess 1:4). His will is the guide for all believers (1 Thess 4:3). He calls His people to holy living (1 Thess 4:7) and imparts sanctification to them so they can live obediently. He raised Jesus from the dead (1 Thess 4:14) and will raise believers to be with Him at the Lord's return (1 Thess 4:13–5:11).

The letter was written specifically to reassure those who were concerned about believers who had already died. Words of comfort and hope from Paul about the resurrection of believers provide equally good news for the church of all times in all places. This good news serves as a basis for practical and godly living.

Questions for Reflection

1. How does what Paul says about the nature of ministry speak to church leaders and church members today?

2. What is the relationship between the promise of the Lord's return and holy living?

3. How can the true character of Christian love be communicated in a secular world that has degraded the idea of love?

4. In what way is Paul's teaching about the Christian life in 1 Thessalonians 4:1-12 binding on Christians today?

Sources for Additional Study

Bruce, F. F. *1 and 2 Thessalonians. Word Biblical Commentary.* Waco: Word, 1982.

Hiebert, D. E. *The Thessalonian Epistles.* Chicago: Moody, 1971.

Marshall, I. Howard. *1 and 2 Thessalonians.* Grand Rapids: Eerdmans, 1983.

Stott, John R. W. *The Gospel and the End of Time.* Downers Grove: InterVarsity, 1991.

2 THESSALONIANS

Paul's authorship of 2 Thessalonians has been questioned frequently in recent years in spite of the fact that it has extremely strong support throughout church history. The objections to Pauline authorship are threefold: (1) The style of 2 Thessalonians is said to be more formal than 1 Thessalonians. (2) The vocabulary is supposedly too different from the rest of Paul's writings (ten words in 2 Thessalonians are not used elsewhere in Paul). (3) The unique approach to eschatology in 2 Thessalonians (the "man of lawlessness" is not mentioned elsewhere). However, these arguments are not convincing in light of the similarity of content between 1 and 2 Thessalonians.

The interval between 1 and 2 Thessalonians must have been rather short, for the second epistle does not presuppose major changes in the inner constitution of the Thessalonian church or in the conditions under which Paul was writing (see introduction to 1 Thessalonians).

The Occasion of the Letter

The second letter was apparently evoked by alarm on the part of the Thessalonians who had been informed that the Day of the Lord had arrived.

The agitators who had confused the Thessalonians apparently appealed for authority either to the utterances of inspired prophets within the church, or to some phrases from Paul's writings, or possibly to a forged epistle (2 Thess 2:1). Some who anticipated the Lord's soon return had ceased working and depended on others to supply them with life's necessities (3:11).

The church members were uncertain of their position because of inexperience. They needed reassurance in order to cope with opposition of pagan culture and their own doubts raised by their own misunderstandings (2:15). Discipline was needed to keep the lazy ones from disrupting the community life (3:13-15).

Purpose and Theology

Paul's purpose in writing 2 Thessalonians paralleled his first letter to them.

1. He wrote to encourage the persecuted church (1:4-10).

2. He attempted to correct the misunderstanding about the Lord's return. (Much of the letter, 18 out of 47 verses, deals with this issue.)

3. He exhorted the church to be steadfast in all things (2:13–3:15).

4. Paul's emphasis was on the return of Christ when the church will be gathered to Him (2:1) and the wicked will be judged (1:6-9; 2:8).

5. Paul instructed the church concerning the man of lawlessness (2:1-12).

The man of lawlessness has no exact parallel in history. The mystery of lawlessness was already at work but was restrained by some "secret power" (2:7) so that it might burst forth at any time in uncontrollable fury. The man of lawlessness is a human being possessed by demonic power who claims for himself the prerogatives of deity. The end times will be accompanied by a rise of organized evil. A blasphemous attempt to supplant the worship of God by the worship of a man who will be the final manifestation of Satanic power will culminate the final apostasy. The force that holds back (2:6) the completion of the mystery of lawlessness has been variously interpreted as (1) the Roman imperial rule, (2) the Jewish nation, (3) the church, or (4) the Holy Spirit.

I. Salvation (1:1-2)
II. Encouragement for the Church (1:3-12)
III. Instructions to Correct Misunderstandings (2:1-12)
IV. Injunctions to Steadfastness (2:13–3:18)

1:1-2
Salvation

The letter started by identifying Paul, Silas, and Timothy as its senders. No doubt Paul was the primary author. The letter's beginning followed the pattern of most Pauline Letters (see 1 Thessalonians).

1:3-12
Encouragement for the Church

The Thessalonians were commended for their growing faith and their maturing love and patience (1:3-4). Paul offered praise and thanksgiving to God for their lifestyles.

Paul offered hope to his readers by noting the forthcoming reversal in God's judgment of the present roles of the persecuted and the persecutors. While the Thessalonians were at that time facing persecution, the persecutors had to face judgment at the coming of the Lord Jesus Christ (1:5-7). Those who reject the good news of the gospel "will be punished with everlasting destruction and shut out from the presence of the Lord" (1:8-9). God's people can be encouraged by knowing they will be vindicated at the Lord's coming and will realize they have neither believed nor suffered in vain (1:10).

The first chapter concludes with Paul's prayer that God's purposes for the church will be fulfilled in them. Paul expressed his desire that glory will be ascribed to Christ for all He will do in the lives of the believers (1:11-12).

2:1-12
Instructions to Correct Misunderstandings

Some were wrongly teaching that the Day of the Lord had already occurred. Paul countered these false teachers by noting things that must precede the second coming of Christ. Before the Lord's coming the "man of lawlessness" must be revealed (2:3). Paul spoke of one who would hold back the mystery of lawlessness. The identification of this person or power remains unclear. Since the second century many have understood the restraining force as the Roman Empire. Others have suggested a supernatural power such as an angel; others have identified this power with the gospel message, the church, or the Holy Spirit. We cannot be sure about such an identification, but we can know that the coming of Christ will mean the overthrow of evil and those who oppose the gospel and take pleasure in unrighteousness (2:4-10).

Because of their deliberate rejection of the truth, God will send them "a powerful delusion so that they will believe the lie" (2:11). The "lie" is not just any lie but the great lie that the man of lawlessness is God (2:12; see 2:4).

The Via Egnatia (which passes through Thessalonica) was a Roman road that ran from Bysantium in the east to the western coast of Italy. The section of the ancient road shown in this photo is near Philippi.

2:13-17
Remain Faithful

Before taking up the discussion of the power of evil in people's lives, Paul offered thanksgiving for the Holy Spirit's work in the life of the church. He also encouraged them to remain faithful to all they had been taught. In typical Pauline style the apostle prayed that God would encourage their hearts and strengthen them in every good word and deed.

3:1-5
Pray for Me

Paul in turn requested that they pray for him. He wanted God to bless and prosper the proclaimed word. He also expressed his concern to be delivered from wicked and evil men.

Paul noted that these evil men did not have faith. In sharp contrast to their faithlessness God is faithful (3:2-3; see 1 Cor 1:9; 2 Cor 2:18). The apostle expressed confidence that God would continue to direct their paths. Before Paul's rebuke of the idle, he prayed that God would direct their hearts into God's love. There should be no hard feelings among those who are completely indebted to the love of God.

3:6-15
Why Quit Working?

Some in Thessalonica had ceased working in light of the imminent return of the Lord. While Paul maintained his confidence in the Lord's return, he rebuked the idleness of those who passively waited. Paul instead urged them to be examples in the community, to earn their own living, and not to grow weary in well doing.

The problem was mentioned in the first letter (1 Thess 4:11-12; 5:14) and had apparently grown worse. Paul responded in a most serious fashion, giving more attention to this matter than any in the book except for Christ's return per se. Christians must not be loafers or busybodies. Worse than being idle, they were interfering in other people's lives. Paul strongly urged the faithful believers not to associate with those who rejected his teaching. They, however, should not be treated as enemies but admonished as brothers.

3:16-18
Conclusion

Paul concluded the letter with words of grace and peace

The Return of Christ

The Lord Jesus, who was raised from the dead and ascended to the Father, will return. This conviction is expressed repeatedly in the NT.

The church used several terms to refer to the return of Christ. *Parousia,* meaning either *coming* or *presence,* often described the Lord's return (see Matt 24:3; 1 Cor 15:23; 1 Thess 2:19). *Epiphaneia* in religious usage described the *appearing* of an unseen god (see Titus 2:13). The revelation (*apocalypsis*) of the power and glory of the Lord was eagerly anticipated by the church (for example, see Luke 17:30; Rom 8:18).

The phrase "the day of the Lord" (an OT theme) is also common in the NT. "That day," "the day of Christ," and similar phrases were used as synonyms.

Often the writer implied that he was living in the last days (Acts 2:17; 1 John 2:18). The reference to time in many passages listed above, however, is ambiguous (see 1 Cor 1:8; 5:5; Phil 1:6,10; 1 Thess 5:2; 2 Thess 1:10). The character of that "day" is clearer than its timing. It is a day of judgment.

The Gospels. Jesus taught His disciples to expect a catastrophic conclusion to history. At that time God would effect a general resurrection and a final judgment with appropriate rewards for the just and the unjust (Matt 7:21-27; 24:1-51; Mark 12:24-27; 13:1-37; Luke 11:31-32; 21:5-36).

Although the signs of the end receive considerable attention in the Gospels (Matt 24; Mark 13; Luke 21), the time of the end remains obscure. Some sayings imply the end is near (Matt 10:23; Mark 9:1; 13:30). Others imply a delay (Matt 25:5; Mark 13:7,10). The clearest statements indicate that the time cannot be known (Matt 24:36,42,44; Mark 13:32-37; Luke 12:35-40).

Acts 1:6-8 expresses the same conviction: the time cannot be known. According to Jesus, the disciples' task was to bear witness to the gospel. The time was left in the Father's hands.

The Epistles. As the church aged, questions arose. What happens to those who die before Jesus' return (1 Thess 4:13-18)? What will His return be like, and when will it occur (1 Thess 5:1-11; 2 Thess 2:1-12)? What will happen to us and our world (1 Cor 15:12-13,23-28)? Does His delay make His promised return a lie (2 Pet 3:3-10)?

The NT answers these questions with a strong affirmation concerning Christ's return. The NT is not as clear regarding the time of His appearing. Yet the Epistles clearly reveal a persistent faith in the return of Christ (Rom 8:19-39; 2 Tim 4:1). His lordship is real. His victory is assured. His people will share His glory at His return (Rev 19:6–22:17). Thus the responsibility of the church is patience, faithfulness, and witness (see Acts 1:7-8; 1 Cor 15:58; 1 Thess 4:18). □

and with his personal signature. Paul normally dictated his letters (see Rom 16:22). Probably Silas penned the letter, but Paul added something in his own handwriting (see 1 Cor 16:21; Gal 6:11; Col 4:18). The book included encouragement, instruction, rebuke, and admonishment. But it is a word of grace from beginning to end, concluding with "the grace of our Lord Jesus Christ be with you all" (3:18).

Theological Significance

The emphasis on the second coming of Christ reminds us to be ready for Christ's coming at any time. We must be prepared, for He will come as suddenly as a thief in the night. Those who have died and those who are still alive will be united with Christ at His return. These words provide hope and encouragement for the church at all times.

Likewise, we must be alert to the evil schemes of the man of lawlessness. The church gains strength from the instruction about the wicked activity of Satan with all power and pretended signs and wonders. Believers are empowered with the truth that the man of lawlessness will be finally destroyed by the Lord Jesus at His coming (2:12). In the meantime the church must remain faithful and steadfast to the goodwill and providential purposes of God.

Questions for Reflection

1. What should our attitude be concerning the return of the Lord?

2. Compare and contrast the different features in Paul's teaching regarding the second coming in 1 and 2 Thessalonians.

3. Why must believers avoid idleness in their expectancy of the Lord's coming?

4. How is Paul's teaching about the return of Christ relevant for pastoral and evangelistic ministry today?

Sources for Additional Study

See 1 Thessalonians.

1 TIMOTHY

Paul's three letters to Timothy and Titus are called the *Pastoral Letters*. These letters were written near the end of Paul's life to guide his two younger associates.

Some have suggested that Paul did not write these letters. Arguments against Pauline authorship are basically threefold. (1) These letters cannot be placed within the framework of the chronology of Acts and are thus assumed to have been written after Paul's death. (2) The content of the letters is said to be different from Paul's teaching elsewhere. (3) Differences in vocabulary are said to be so great that the same author could not have written these three letters and Paul's earlier works.

In response it should be noted that Acts 28 and Philippians 1:25-26 imply that Paul was released from his first Roman imprisonment. Several writers in the early church indicate a release, a further period of activity (during which 1 Timothy and Titus were written), and reimprisonment (when 2 Timothy). Also, the different subjects addressed and the needs of the recipients account for the differences in style, vocabulary, and doctrine. The characteristics discussed are not those of the second century and the contents of the letters are appropriate continuations of Paul's earlier concerns. If Luke was the one who wrote down Paul's thoughts, as was certainly possible, then Luke's input may explain some of the unique vocabulary. There is no compelling reason to deny the claim of Paul's authorship of these letters written sometime between A.D. 64 and 67.

Occasion

The letters were written to deal with the false teaching which was negatively impacting the young churches. The churches were apparently in more danger from internal threats than from external persecution. Paul urged his apostolic associates to counter the internal danger with sound teaching, by providing an example of godly living, and by organizing and training leaders for the congregations.

First Timothy suggests Timothy was at Ephesus while Paul wrote from Macedonia (1 Tim 1:3). Timothy probably was still located in Ephesus when he received 2 Timothy (2 Tim 1:18). The second letter was written from a Roman prison. Titus received his letter in Crete (1:5,12). Paul's whereabouts between Macedonia (1 Tim) and Rome (2 Tim) cannot be known for certain. The order of the letters then was 1 Timothy, Titus, and 2 Timothy.

Purpose and Theology

The letters to Timothy and Titus share many similar characteristics. Unlike Paul's other letters the letters to Timothy and Titus are personal words to his apostolic helpers. These letters address the need for pastoral oversight in the churches (thus the name *Pastoral Letters*, a name given to these three letters in the eighteenth century). They focus on church organization, the importance of apostolic doctrine, and the refutation of false doctrine. First Timothy and Titus carefully describe the qualifications of Christian leaders.

Not only is there emphasis on orthodox doctrine (1 Tim 1:8-11; 2 Tim 1:13-14; Titus 2:1) and church leadership (1 Tim 3:1-15; 2 Tim 2:22-26; Titus 1:5-9), but other important matters are addressed as well. Paul wrote to give Timothy and Titus guidance in their ministries (1 Tim 1:18-2:7; 2 Tim 2:1-7; Titus 2:7-8,15; 3:9). An emphasis on godly living also characterizes the letters (1 Tim 1:3-7; 2:8-10; 2 Tim 1:3-12; 2:14-19; Titus 3:1-11).

I. Introduction (1:1-2)
II. Warning against False Teachers (1:3-20)
III. Guidelines for Church Worship (2:1-15)
IV. Instructions for Church Leadership (3:1-13)
V. Maintaining the Truth (3:14–4:16)
VI. Miscellaneous Instructions for the Church (5:1–6:10)
VII. Personal Charge to Timothy (6:11-21)

1:1-2
Introduction

The letter begins like other Pauline letters. Paul the apostle is named as the author, Timothy is named as recipient, and then follows a greeting. Timothy is affectionately called "my true son in the faith" (1:2). The phrase indicates the spiritual relationship between Paul and Timothy. We cannot be sure whether Timothy was a convert of Paul, but certainly Timothy had a special role on the Pauline mission team (see 1 Tim 1:18; compare 1 Cor 4:17; Phil 2:19-24; 2 Tim 1:2; 2:1).

1:3-20
Warning against False Teachers

1:3-11
Paul emotionally warned Timothy about the danger of false doctrine (1:3-11). Timothy was urged to stay in Ephesus, indicating perhaps some inclination on Timothy's part to leave Ephesus to rejoin Paul. Timothy's assignment was to restrain those in the congregation who were teaching false doctrine.

These false teachers were probably forerunners of second-century Gnostics (see 6:20). In this letter Paul characterizes these false teachers as: (1) teachers of Jewish myths and fictitious stories based on obscure genealogies (1:4; 4:7; see Titus 1:14; 3:9); (2) conceited (1:7; 6:4); (3) argumentative (1:4; 6:4; Titus 3:9); (4) desiring to teach OT law, yet they knew not what they teach (1:7); (5) full of meaningless talk (1:6; Titus 3:9); (6) teaching false ascetic practices (4:3); and (7) using their positions of religious leadership for personal financial gain (6:5).

1:12-20
Paul's measuring rod for evaluating what is and is not sound teaching was the message of God's grace in Christ with which he had been entrusted. At this point Paul's inventory of sinners, of which he knew he was the chief, initiated a powerful sense of gratitude. Paul's thanksgiving developed from the fact that God in His grace had provided Paul a privileged place of service. Paul expounded the doctrine of God's grace as experienced in his life (1:12-17) and as seen in Timothy's ministry (1:18-20).

2:1-15
Guidelines for Church Worship
From his concerns about false teachers Paul turned to issues relating to the worship of the church. Paul began with instructions concerning prayer (2:1-7) and then moved to matters regarding the roles of men and women (2:8-15).

2:1-7
Paul urged that "requests, prayers, intercession and thanksgiving be made for everyone" (2:1). Prayer is an exceedingly important part of the church's worship. The apostle stresses the importance of special prayer for persons in high places of authority in the state.

Prayer is addressed to God "who wants all men to be saved" (2:4). Paul here cited three basic truths of the gospel. (1) There is only one God. (2) God can only be approached through the Man who was God in the flesh, the man Christ Jesus. (3) This man gave himself as a ransom for the human race. Paul was not teaching universalism for salvation is possible only for those who know the truth through a relationship with Jesus Christ (2:4-6).

2:8-15
Christian men and women should pray to God. Women should adorn themselves modestly and sensibly (2:8-10). Some maintain that Paul's teaching about women here is historically conditioned. Others see these verses as normative teaching for every age. Some type of prohibition remains. Some believe that Paul prohibited teaching only by women who had not been properly taught themselves. Such women tended to domineer over men. Others suggest that Paul did not allow women to be official teachers in the Christian community, meaning they could not function as overseers (see 3:1). Christian churches differ about the role of women in the church, but the abiding authority of Scripture must not be jettisoned in the ongoing discussion.

Timothy was admonished to pray "for kings and all those in authority" (1 Tim 2:1-2), including the emperor Nero (above).

Models of Church Government

Church government refers to the structures used by a church or denomination to organize its work. Since examples of church government in the NT are meager and often localized, we should not expect a uniform pattern of church government in Scripture.

Paul appointed leaders wherever he planted churches. Sometimes these leaders carried unofficial designations, such as "those . . . who are over you in the Lord" (1 Thess 5:12). At other times they had official titles such as "elder" (*presbyteros,* Titus 1:5), "bishop" (*episkopos,* Titus 1:7), or "deacon" (*diakonos,* 1 Tim 3:8).

In the NT the terms *elder* and *bishop* are interchangeable and describe the same function. The qualifications for each are the same (Titus 1:5-9; 1 Tim 3:1-7). This fluidity of function and office is typical of NT church government.

Most churches and denominations today are characterized by one of three major types of church government. The episcopal model of church government is centralized in structure and hierarchical in ministry. This pattern finds its biblical model in Paul's appeal to apostolic authority and the orderly appointment of formal leaders in the churches. A contemporary example of this model is the Episcopal Church.

Authority in the presbyterian model of church government is in a governing body. For biblical support this model points to the plurality of ministers in the NT (1 Cor 12:28) and the use of the word *elder*. The term *elder* came from the Jewish practice of using a council of elders to settle important matters. A current example of this form of government is the Presbyterian Church.

The congregational model of government calls for government by the entire membership of the church. This model highlights the autonomy of the local church, free of external controls or a centralized government. Leaders are chosen by the membership. Cooperation with other congregations is voluntary. The biblical precedence for this model is the self-governing churches established by Paul. Baptists are an example of this form of government. □

3:1-13
Instructions for Church Leadership

3:1-7

Continuing his instructions on how the church should conduct itself, Paul turned to the matter of leadership. Paul said that church leadership is a noble task. Here Paul described the qualifications for those who aspire such leadership.

The term "overseer," one of several terms used for church leaders, was used to refer to the presiding officials in civic or religious organizations. Here it refers to those who provided leadership for local congregations, rather than leaders over a group of churches, such as the office of episcopal bishop developed in the second century. The term "elder" and "overseer" are used interchangeably in Acts 20:17,28; Titus 1:5-7; and 1 Peter 5:1-5. These leaders are to teach the Scriptures (1 Tim 3:2; 5:17), and to provide direction and administration for the church (3:5; 5:17), to shepherd the flock of God (Acts 20:28), and to guard the church from error (Acts 20:28-31).

An overseer must be a person of noble character. These leaders should be respected by other members of the church and by those outside the church. The overseer must be above reproach, should conform to a high view of sexual morality, should be able to discipline the family, should not be a new Christian, and should not be under the domination of strong drink. Only a person of excellent character should serve as an overseer (1 Tim 3:1-7).

3:8-13

Then Paul moves to discuss the qualification of deacons. The qualifications for deacons are virtually the same as those for elders. Generally the service of deacons (the word means one who serves) was meant to free the overseers to give full attention to prayer and the ministry of the Word (see Acts 6:2-4). The two church offices mentioned in the NT are overseer and deacon (see Phil 1:1). Before being elected as deacons they should have experience in church work (1 Tim 3:8-10,12-13)

First Timothy 3:11 applies the same qualifications for women. The Greek for the phrase "wives" simply means "the women" and therefore could refer to deacons' wives or female deacons (see Rom 16:1).

3:14–4:16
Maintaining the Truth

3:14-16

Paul informed Timothy of his hopes to come to see him and the church at Ephesus. He majestically described Christ in words many scholars believe were adopted from an early hymn of adoration to Christ (3:16).

4:1-10

As the repository and guardian of the truth, the church continually must be aware of the strategies of the enemies of the truth (4:1-5). Paul stressed that Timothy's pastoral duties involved guarding the truth and refuting the heretics. The church was instructed to confront the false teaching by teaching correct doctrine (4:6-7) and by godly living (4:8-10).

The false teachers taught a false asceticism, forbidding marriage and the eating of various foods. But Paul maintained that God has given these things to be appreciated and used for God's glory.

4:11-16

The apostle moved from the general concerns of the church to personal exhortations specifically for Timothy. Paul recognized that Timothy was a young man and that some of the older believers might be tempted to look down on his youth. Timothy was to be an example for the church "in speech, in life, in love, in faith and in purity" (4:12). He was to give himself to the public proclamation of the Scriptures (4:13) through the use of gift given to him (4:14). Since God had called Timothy and the church had sanctioned his ministry through the laying on of hands, Timothy was to strive to live up to these high responsibilities (4:15-16).

5:1–6:10
Miscellaneous Instructions for the Church
5:1-16

From the instructions about how Timothy was to live out his call to pastoral ministry, Paul turned his attention to the various groups that make up the church. The general principle passed on by Paul was to treat different people as one would treat the members of one's own family.

First, Paul addressed the care of widows (5:3-16). Specifically he offered guidelines for helping widows in need (5:3-8), for enabling widows as workers in the church (5:9-10), and suggestions for the younger widows (5:11-16). Younger widows were to be encouraged to marry again and get new husbands to support them. The church, then, would have the responsibility to care for the older widows who have no families to take care of them.

5:17-25

The overseers/elders were not only to teach but to provide oversight for the church. These leaders who do double duty are worthy of "double honor" (5:17). That such honor involves financial support is indicated by the two illustrations in v. 18.

Early church leaders, like modern ones, were not perfect. Their imperfections need to be dealt with. Criticisms of leaders should be rejected unless they can be proven to be conclusively true. Formal discipline should be exercised with care and caution when needed (5:19-21). These leaders must be examined thoroughly. They should not be chosen or ordained too quickly (5:22-25).

6:1-10

This section gives advice for slaves and masters (6:1-2) and the rich and poor (6:3-10) in the congregation. Paul recognized that money could be made into a false god and bring all kinds of evil to those with misplaced affections (6:9-10). However, money rightly used can advance the work of God and be changed into a heavenly treasure.

6:11-21
Personal Charge to Timothy

Finally, Paul urged Timothy to do his very best to a man of God. Timothy had been a partaker of eternal life since he had first believed the gospel, but Paul encouraged Timothy to claim the gospel's benefits in greater fullness. Timothy should fight a good fight as a soldier of God in his pursuit of holiness, his persistence in service, and in the protection of the gospel. In order to do this Timothy, like all believers, must focus his adoration on the glorious Christ.

The letter concludes with a brief benediction, "Grace be with you" (6:21).

Theological Significance

The letter to Timothy develops a theology of the church. The church needs organization to do its work effectively. Church leaders give guidance and enablement for the Christian community to carry out its service. The church is to be a pillar and bulwark, a custodian of the truth. The church must strive always to avoid heresy and to teach the truths of the gospel to succeeding generations.

Questions for Further Reflection

1. What are practical ways for the church to guard the gospel?
2. What are the responsibilities of church overseers?
3. How can false doctrine be recognized? How should it be refuted?
4. What is the church's responsibility for the care of widows?

2 TIMOTHY

1:1-7
Introduction

Paul began this letter in a similar way to 1 Timothy. In the first letter Paul greeted Timothy as "my true son in the faith." Here it is "my dear son."

Paul offered thanks for Timothy's heritage (1:3-5) and for God's gift to Timothy (1:6-7). Paul appealed to helpful reminiscences and urged Timothy to stir up his gift. Gifts are not given fully developed; they need to be strengthened and matured through use.

1:8-18
Suffering and the Gospel

In light of the gift that had been divinely given to Timothy, Paul urged him not to be ashamed "to testify about our Lord" (1:8). Paul also urged Timothy not to be ashamed of "me his prisoner." The aged apostle wanted to strengthen the courage of his young colleague.

Paul offered a strong admonition to Timothy to keep the faith in the midst of suffering. The apostle's appeal was based on his testimony of God's grace in his own experience (1:9-12). Timothy was to guard the gospel that Paul had entrusted to him (1:13-14). This was possible only through the enabling "help of the Holy Spirit who lives in us" (1:14).

During this time the apostle had been deserted by Phygelus and Hermogenes (1:15). Perhaps this took place when Paul was arrested and taken to Rome for his final imprisonment. In contrast to the actions of the majority, some, such as Onesiphorus, helpfully befriended Paul. Those must have been difficult days for Paul, forsaken by friends and facing imminent death. It is hard to understand why God's servants suffer like this, but for Paul it was a privilege not only to believe in Christ "but also to suffer for him" (Phil 1:29).

2:1-13
Encouragement to Faithfulness

In this section Paul provided special advice to Timothy. After exhorting Timothy to "be strong in the grace that is in Christ Jesus, Paul declared his frequent message about preserving and passing on the truth (2:1-2).

Paul gave three examples for Timothy to follow: (1) a soldier who wants to please his commander, (2) an athlete who follows the rules of the game, and (3) a farmer who toils faithfully. The three figures of speech used here are found in 1 Corinthians 9:6,24-27. Paul encouraged Timothy to faithful devotion and self-discipline in his service for the Lord (2:3-7). Again the apostle's exhortations were grounded in his own experience of suffering (2:8-13).

2:14-26
Contrasts in the Church

Paul then offered advice regarding false teachers in the church. Positively, he urged Timothy to be an unashamed workman (2:14-15). Negatively, Timothy was to avoid godless chatter (2:14-19). Paul contrasted true and false teachers (14-19), noble and ignoble vessels (2:20-21), and the kind and the quarrelsome (2:22-24).

Not only was Timothy to refute the heretical teachers, but he also was to practice and encourage godly behavior and attitudes. Paul concluded this section by saying that a good minister must gently instruct "those who oppose him" so that God might grant them a "change of heart" (2:25-26).

3:1-9
Godlessness in the Last Days

Like his remarks in the first letter (see 1 Tim 4:1), Paul predicted the moral decline that would come in the last days. This does not at all deny that these conditions have been and will be present throughout the church age. It does say that the characteristics enumerated here (3:1-5) will be more intensive and extensive as the end approaches.

In verses 2-4 Paul listed almost twenty different vices that will characterize people in the last days. Generally they all describe those who place self in the place of God as the center of their affections. These people are to be avoided, even though they have "a form of godliness" (3:5).

Paul began the chapter by pointing out the characteristics of those who love money and pleasure (3:1-5). Then he focused on their depraved living and thinking. These false teachers preyed on "weak-willed women" (3:6). Such women were apparently easy prey because they wanted to pose as learned people. They were "always learning but never able to acknowledge the truth (3:7). Paul compared the false teachers to "Jannes and Jambres." (3:8-9). Neither of these men is mentioned in the Old Testament, but according to Jewish tradition they were the Egyptian court magicians who opposed Moses (see Exod 7:11).

3:10-17
God-breathed Scripture

Paul again appealed to his own experience (3:10-13) and exhorted Timothy to continue the work (3:14–4:5). Paul urged Timothy not to be led astray by these imposters. Instead, Timothy should continue in what he had learned and had "become convinced of" (3:14). Timothy could be convinced of the truth taught in the Scriptures because (1) it had made him "wise for salvation through faith in Christ Jesus" (3:15), and (2) the Scripture is "God-breathed" (3:16). Paul affirmed God's active involvement in the writing of Scripture. The Lord's superintending work is so powerful and complete that what is written is God's truthful and authoritative word (see the article "Inspiration and Authority of Scripture").

4:1-18
Preach the Word

Paul's concluding charge stressed the need to preach the word (4:1-5). Like Timothy, all believers are to be prepared in any situation to speak a needed word, whether of correction, rebuke, or encouragement. Christian workers must be ready to endure hardship as Paul had done.

Paul viewed his approaching death as the pouring out of a "drink offering" (4:6). A drink offering referred to the offering of wine poured around the base of the altar during the Old Testament sacrifices (see Num 15:1-12; 28:7; Phil 2:17).

Paul's plea to Timothy closed with personal requests and reference to his "first defense" (4:16). An important lesson can be learned here about divine support in the midst of human opposition (4:14-18).

This illustration shows a farmer on the right overseeing the bringing in of his harvest (see 2 Tim 2:6).

4:19-22
Final Greetings

The letter concludes with greetings to Priscilla and Aquilla and the household of Onesiphorus. The household of Onesiphorus was mentioned with great appreciation in 1:16-18. But we know little about this devoted believer.

Paul then sent greetings from four members of the church at Rome and all the brothers. Paul pronounced a personal benediction on Timothy ("your spirit" in 4:22a is singular) before concluding with a corporate blessing "God be with you all" ("you" in 4:22 is plural).

Theological Significance

Second Timothy teaches us about the importance of our theological heritage (1:14). Paul had much to say about what God has done in Christ, our Savior. Jesus Christ has been revealed, destroyed death, and given us life and immortality (1:8-10). The foundation of the Christian life is what God has already done for us in Christ. We should live boldly, for we have received "a spirit of power, of love and of self-discipline" (1:7). These truths about the gospel and Christian living are available to us in God's inspired Scripture (3:15-17). Now we, like Timothy, should pass on these truths to faithful men and women who can teach others also (2:2).

Questions for Reflection

1. What does it mean to guard the faith?
2. What is the significance of the three examples of Christian living listed in chapter 2?
3. What advice did Paul offer regarding false teachers?
4. What can we learn about the nature of Scripture from this letter?
5. Why is it important to preach the word?

Sources for Additional Study

See Titus.

TITUS

1:1-4
Introduction

Paul had been released from Rome. He probably then went to the island of Crete, as well as to Ephesus and Macedonia. Titus, Paul's colleague in ministry, was left behind to work. The letter to Titus was written later to offer him advice and encouragement.

Paul began the letter by identifying himself as "a servant of God" (1:1). Only here did Paul use this phrase. Elsewhere he used "servant of Christ" (see Rom 1:1; Gal 1:1; Phil 1:1). Paul's salutation is quite long for such a short letter. In the salutation Paul emphasized the purpose of his letter.

Titus is identified as "my true son in our common faith." This designation points to the endearing and intimate relationship between writer and reader. This special relationship assured that in Crete, Titus rightly represented the aged apostle.

1:5-9
The Appointment of Elders

The first subject of this letter provided Titus with instructions concerning church leaders. Verse 5 states Titus's task, and the following verses in the paragraph (1:6-9) identify the character qualities needed in the new leaders.

Titus was to appoint leaders in every place where there was a group of believers. Probably the entire congregation selected these leaders with the encouragement of Titus. He had the official responsibility, as a representative of Paul, to appoint them to office.

The character qualities identified here corresponds closely to 1 Timothy 3:1-7. Yet differences should be noted. These differences help us see how Paul applied general truths to particular situations. Unlike 1 Timothy, no deacons were mentioned here, suggesting that the organizational structure was not as advanced in Crete. The leaders' character should be blameless (1:6-8), and their doctrinal commitments must be faithful to the biblical message (1:9).

1:10-13
The Rebuke of False Teachers

The elders were needed to defend the truth (1:9) being attacked by the false teachers. Paul described the false teachers in 1:10-13. They were (1) "rebellious" because they rejected the demands of the gospel message; (2) "mere talkers" because they tried to use impressive speech, even though it accomplished nothing; and (3) "deceivers" because they were leading astray the church members. These false teachers could not and should not be trusted because they were "liars," (1:12-13). Paul's own observations about these people confirmed the negative assessment of one of Crete's own prophets. Just as Paul gave principles with which to appoint church leaders, so he also provided Titus with guidelines to deal with the false teachers.

The error is described in terms of "Jewish myths" or "the commands of those who reject the truth" (1:14). These false teachers should be rebuked from the perspectives listed in 1:15-16.

Believers who have been purified by the work of Christ can perceive all things as pure. Unbelievers, especially legalistic ascetics, do not enjoy true freedom in Christ. These false teachers were attempting to set up human standards against which matters of purity and impurity could be judged. But Paul identified these standards as corrupt.

2:1-15
The Different Groups in the Church

Paul turned his attention to the various groups in the congregation. He gave instructions for the older men (2:1-2), the older women and younger women (2:3-5), young men, including Titus (2:6-8), and slaves (2:9-10). To all of these Paul stressed the importance of building up the spiritual life of believers as the best defense against error.

Verse one serves as the basis for Paul's instructions. Paul told Titus to "teach what is in accord with sound doctrine." Sound doctrine must lead to ethical conduct in the lives of all the people in the church.

God's grace provides the foundation for Paul's instructions and exhortations. God's grace has saved us, and it teaches us both by teaching us what to do and by providing enablement to live appropriately. God's grace flows from the work of Jesus Christ who "gave himself for us" in order "to redeem us from all wickedness and to purify for himself a people that are his very own, eager to do what is good" (2:14). God's grace enables us to live rightly in the present while giving us a future perspective as well (2:13). We eagerly await for the appearing of Jesus Christ, who is our Savior and our great God. These are the truths Titus should teach to encourage the church and rebuke the heretics (2:15).

3:1-11
The Responsibility of Christian Living

Paul moved his thoughts to the duties of all believers, especially in relation to the government and the non-Christian world. Verses 1-2 remind Christians of their duty to government leaders and authorities. It is important to note that early Christian teaching was not limited to the way of salvation, but included exhortations concerning the practical implications for daily life (see Rom 13:1-7; 1 Pet 2:13-17).

Some might suggest that such a response to ungodly leaders was inappropriate. Paul met this objection by reminding them of their own pre-Christian condition (3:3-4). It is only by God's "mercy" that we are saved (3:5). God brought about our salvation by changing our lives through the work of the Holy Spirit who was "poured out on us" (3:6) By God's gracious gift of Christ's righteousness to us God now declares us justified in His sight and heirs of eternal life (3:7-8). (See the article "Salvation in Paul's Thought.")

Paul concluded his letter with further instructions about false teachers. Their stubborn refusal to listen to correction revealed their inner corruption.

3:12-15
Personal Concluding Requests

Paul announced his plans for the future. Another worker, Artemas or Tychicus, would be sent to replace Titus in Crete. Titus did not need to carry the burden alone. This transition situation offered Paul one more chance to stress the idea that believers need to be characterized by noble deeds. All the workers with Paul joined in sending greetings (3:15). Paul's typical closing blessings are addressed to all to whom Titus was to share Paul's greetings.

Theological Significance

Like the other pastoral letters, Paul's letter to Titus focuses on keeping the faith and refuting heresy. Especially significant, considering the nature of the Cretan heresy, are the repeated emphases on doctrinal fidelity (2:11-14; 3:4-7) and faithful living (1:16; 2:7,14; 3:1,8,14). The letter makes it plain that the Christian life is grounded in the grace of God (2:11-14). Believers must recognize this truth and rebuke heresy and avoid legalism (1:10-16). This can be done only by grace; grace that saves, grace that teaches, grace that strengthens, and grace that enables. In so doing we can see the relationship between doctrine and practice.

Questions for Reflection

1. What are the primary qualifications for a church leader?

2. How can we avoid the trap of legalistic Christianity?

3. What is the relationship between Christian doctrine and Christian living?

4. What duties do believers have as citizens? Why should believers be subject to rulers and authorities?

5. How does a focus on Christ's glorious appearing affect Christian living?

Sources for Additional Study

Fee, Gordon D. *1 and 2 Timothy, Titus.* San Francisco: Harper and Row, 1984.

Guthrie, Donald. *The Pastoral Epistles.* Grand Rapids: Eerdmans, 1957.

Kent, Homer A., Jr. *The Pastoral Epistles.* Chicago: Moody, 1982.

Lea, Thomas D. and Hayne P. Griffin, Jr. *1, 2 Timothy, Titus. The New American Commentary.* Nashville: Broadman, 1992.

Stott, John R. W. *Guard the Gospel.* Downers Grove: Intervarsity, 1973.

PHILEMON

Paul's authorship of the letter has strong support in all spheres of the church. It is closely linked with the Epistle to the Colossians. The letter was carried by Onesimus to Philemon with Tychicus (Col 4:7-9; Eph 6:21-22). The letter was written near the end of Paul's first Roman imprisonment at the same time as Ephesians and Colossians, about 60–61.

Destination

The recipient of the letter was Philemon, a wealthy resi-

Paul writing from a Roman prison

Slavery in the First Century

Slavery, the legal possession of an individual by another, was the primary "energy source" for the Greco-Roman world. Slaves were employed in agricultural and manufacturing enterprises, construction, mining, governmental positions, education of children, cultural and entertainment activities, as well as many routine household duties.

In the Roman Empire slavery was unrelated to race. It probably began as generals chose to enslave conquered enemies rather than liquidate them. It was also a form of punishment for crimes or a means of dealing with debtors unable to repay loans.

Unwanted, exposed children were frequently rescued, raised, and sold as slaves. Children of slaves were themselves slaves. Some kidnap victims were sold into slavery. Some voluntarily became slaves for religious reasons or chose security in benevolent bondage over insecurity in freedom and poverty.

By the first century there were thousands of slaves in all parts of the Empire. Their status and treatment differed greatly. Slaves were not completely without legal rights. They were free from taxation and military service, had the right to common-law marriage, and could join social groups or associations.

Yet their lot was determined by the will of their masters. Essentially they were nonpersons, property, "human tools" (Aristotle). Abuse, harshness, and brutality were frequent. Runaway slaves could be subject to torture and death. Kind and considerate treatment was extended if not on humanitarian grounds, then because it was prudent to care for one's "property." Slaves were valuable property. In NT times the price of a slave was about nine times the wages paid a laborer for a year. A slave could be sold privately or at public auction at the will of the owner.

Slaves had the hope of freedom. Some bought their freedom. More often it was given, either formally in the will of the owner, by pronouncement of an official, or informally. In the latter case former slaves had no legal proof of their new status. Slaves might gain freedom by being sold to a god; the walls of some ancient temples contain hundreds of names of such individuals. As a "freedman" the former slave had basic civil rights, the possibility of achieving citizenship, but retained some obligations to the former owner.

The NT attests that slaves were members of the early church. Both Christian slaves and masters are told their relationship must be controlled by their common relationship in Christ. Philemon was enjoined to receive the runaway slave Onesimus "as a beloved brother" (v. 16), thus elevating the nonperson to the status of an equal. Slavery furnishes NT imagery for the status of the sinner under sin and of the Christian to God. In his incarnation Christ accepted the role of slave (Phil 2:7). Terms such as "ransom" and "redeem" reminded NT readers of the parallels between the purchase of their spiritual freedom and that of the physical freedom of the slave. □

dent of Colosse. The church members of Colosse who met at Philemon's house were among the first readers (Phlm 2). Archippus possibly had some official capacity at the church (see Col 4:17).

Purpose

Philemon had a slave, Onesimus, who had run away from his master and who perhaps had stolen money from him as he went (Phlm 18). Somehow Paul met Onesimus in prison. Onesimus became a believer in Christ and repented of his past deeds. Onesimus was responsible to return to Philemon. Paul wrote to Philemon to intercede for Onesimus, asking Philemon to allow him to return. Paul asked Philemon not only to receive him but to receive him as a brother.

Theology

This short letter teaches much about the sense of brotherhood that existed in early Christianity. We see the tension between the sense of equality in Christ (see Gal 3:28) and the societal differences. Paul did not endorse slavery, nor did he want slaves to rebel against their masters. The teaching of this letter has served as an impetus for the abolition of slavery.

I. Introduction (vv. 1-3)
II. A Good Word about Philemon (vv. 4-7)
III. A Good Word in Behalf of Onesimus (vv. 8-22)
IV. Conclusion (vv. 23-25)

Verses 1-3
Introduction

Paul identified himself as a "prisoner of Christ Jesus."

This introduction also identified Paul with Onesimus (v. 1). Although the letter is obviously directed to one person, Apphia, Archippus, and the church in Colosse are also mentioned. Apphia was most likely a relative of Philemon, perhaps his wife. Archippus may have been the pastor of the church. Verse 3 follows the pattern of Paul's usual benedictions (see Col 1:2).

Verses 4-7
A Good Word about Philemon

The situation that had developed between Philemon and Onesimus required the mediation of an advocate. Paul needed to speak effectively for Onesimus and with respect to Philemon. Paul offered good words of commendation and appreciation about Philemon. Whether or not this was intended to help Paul win a hearing through the psychology of commendation we cannot know. Verses 6-7 include a prayer for Philemon.

Verses 8-22
A Good Word in Behalf of Onesimus

A transition occurs at verse 8. Paul offered five appeals for Onesimus. He started with Philemon's reputation as a person who brought blessing to others. Paul could have appealed to Philemon, but instead he appealed in love. The third basis of his argument focused on the conversion of Onesimus. Paul then explained how valuable Onesimus had been to him. The final appeal related to God's providence over the entire situation.

Legally Philemon could have punished Onesimus. Some slave owners were cruel; others, more merciful in these situations. Paul carefully convinced Philemon that he should receive his disobedient slave and forgive him. This situation was quite difficult for Philemon. How should he respond? If he were too easy on Onesimus, his other slaves might rebel or try to "become Christians" to receive special treatment. If he were too hard, it might disrupt the church. Paul recognized this dilemma and offered a helpful suggestion.

Paul volunteered to become a business partner with Philemon and help him deal with the Onesimus situation. Two suggestions followed: (1) "Welcome him as you would welcome me." (2) "If he has done you any wrong or owes you anything, charge it to me" (vv. 17-18). Philemon was then able to receive Onesimus as though he were receiving Paul. Paul did not suggest that Philemon ignore the slave's crimes and forget about the debt Onesimus owed. Instead Paul offered to handle the debt himself. The apostle assured Philemon his debts would be paid.

Obviously we see here many things that remind us of our relationship with Jesus Christ. God's people are so identified with Jesus Christ that God receives them as He received His Son (see Eph 1:6).

Paul hinted that Onesimus should be treated as a free person. He asked Philemon to receive Onesimus "as a dear brother" (v. 16). Philemon was implored to do "even more" than Paul asked (v. 21).

Verses 22-25
Conclusion

Paul concluded the letter with his usual greetings from those with him, including Epaphras, a leader in the Colossian church. One final request (v. 22) and a benediction bring the letter to a close.

Theological Significance

Early Christians did not mount an open crusade against slavery. They focused on the message of the gospel but did not ignore its social implications. In other places Paul seemed to accept slavery as a reality in the Roman Empire (see 1 Cor 7:20-24; Eph 6:5-9; Col 3:22–4:1), but he did not endorse it. There are no indications that Paul had any thoughts of abolishing it. We cannot impose issues from the nineteenth or twentieth centuries back into the New Testament, but the importance of Philemon as a social document cannot be neglected. The expression of Christian love melted the fetters of slavery and counted master and slave alike as *brothers* and *sisters* in the family of God. More importantly the gospel message is beautifully illustrated in Philemon.

Questions for Reflection

1. What is the relation between the church's evangelistic and social ministry?

2. What can we learn from Paul about dealing with conflict situations?

Sources for Additional Study

See Colossians.

The General Letters

The "General Letters" are those writings in which the author designated the recipients in general terms rather than with a specific location. Exceptions to this are 2 and 3 John, addressed to specific individuals. Some New Testament scholars do not regard Hebrews as a General Letter, pointing out that the author spoke to a specific group of believers (Heb 5:11–6:12). Most of the General Letters take the name of the writer as the title. By contrast most of the Pauline Letters take the name of the recipients as the title. We can clearly observe the difference between the specific address of the Pauline Letters ("To all the saints in Christ Jesus at Philippi," Phil 1:1) and the broad address of the General Letters ("To the twelve tribes scattered among the nations," Jas 1:1).

The Letter to the Hebrews addresses a warning to Jewish-Christian believers who were considering abandoning the riches of Christ and returning to the empty rituals of Judaism (5:11–6:6). James penned a warning to Jewish Christians who were neglecting obedience to the practical commands of the Bible (2:1-13). The apostle wrote 1 Peter to steady both Jews and Gentiles against painful persecution that threatened to consume them (4:12-19). The readers of both 2 Peter and Jude faced challenges from heretical teaching that threatened to sap their spiritual vitality (2 Pet 2:1-3; Jude 3-4).

John wrote his first letter to urge his readers to right action (2:6), a right attitude (4:11), and right belief (4:1). In his second letter he warned against false teachers (vv. 7-11), and in his third letter he dealt with a church dispute (vv. 9-10).

In the ancient Greek manuscripts of the New Testament, the General Letters usually appear before the Pauline writings. In modern listings of New Testament books that order is reversed. The dates of the General Letters, which are later than most Pauline Letters, make this arrangement best.

With the possible exception of James, all the General Letters appeared near the end of Paul's life or after his death. They discussed problems the church faced in its later growth and expansion. Such writings as 2 Peter, Jude, and 1 and 2 John touch on the subject of false teaching. This was a normal problem in a growing church encountering alien ideas and viewpoints. Hebrews, James, 1 Peter, and 3 John provide encouragement for Christians who faced harassment and persecution.

All the writers presented a picture of a Savior whose strength could sustain them (Heb 4:14-16). They called for a demonstration of new stamina and steadfastness (Jas 1:2-4; 1 Pet 4:19). Some of the writers called on the readers to show compassion for one another (1 John 3:16-20) and basic practices of honesty and integrity (Jas 5:1-6). Because modern Christians also face these problems, the words of the General Letters can provide us strength and help in our spiritual battles today.

John—author of three epistles and the Book of Revelation

HEBREWS

The Book of Hebrews is anonymous in that the name of the author is not mentioned in the book. The original readers knew who the writer was, but he remains unknown to us. Despite the difficulties in determining the author of Hebrews, its majestic picture of Christ commended its contents to the early church.

The writer of Hebrews presented Christ as superior to the Old Testament prophets, angels, Moses, Joshua, and Aaron. He laced magnificent discussions of Christ's person and work into frightening passages warning against apostasy (1:1–2:4). The superiority of Christ led the writer to appeal for faith (chap. 11), stamina (12:3-11), and good works (13:16).

Authorship

The early church historian Eusebius quoted the biblical scholar Origen as saying, "Who it was that really wrote the Epistle [Hebrews], God only knows" (*Eccelesiastical History* 6.25). Despite this verdict many varied opinions about the authorship have arisen.

Christians in the Eastern Roman Empire regarded Paul as the author. Hebrews contains statements similar to Paul's view of the preexistence and creatorship of Christ (compare Heb 1:1-4 with Col 1:15-17). Both Hebrews 8:6 and 2 Corinthians 3:4-11 discuss the new covenant. These factors inclined some observers to consider Paul as the author.

Christians in the Western Roman Empire originally questioned Pauline authorship of Hebrews. They observed that the statement of 2:3 suggested that the author was not an apostle. Also the Old Testament quotations in Hebrews come from the Greek Septuagint, but Paul used both the Hebrew text and the Septuagint. Further, none of Paul's other writings are anonymous; and the polished Greek style of Hebrews does not resemble the explosive, dynamic style of most of Paul's writings. Shortly before A.D. 400, Christian leaders in the West extended acceptance to the Book of Hebrews. They absorbed it into the Pauline collection of writings without distinguishing it from the rest.

Tertullian advocated Barnabas as the author of Hebrews. Barnabas's background as a Levite would qualify him to write the book, but support for his authorship is lacking in the early church. Martin Luther suggested Apollos as the author. In Apollos's favor is his reputation for eloquence (Acts 18:24), but against him is the absence of early church tradition accepting him as author. Some have suggested Luke as the author. His knowledge of Greek would favor him, but Luke was a Gentile. The outlook of Hebrews is definitely Jewish. The nineteenth-century church historian Adolph Harnack mentioned Priscilla, the wife of Aquila, as the author. She and her husband would have known Pauline theology and Jewish practice, but the early church was silent about nominating her as author.

Modern Greek texts of Hebrews bear the title "To the Hebrews." It is best to accept this title and recognize that we cannot know for sure who wrote Hebrews. Despite our ignorance of the author, we can use and understand what he wrote.

Date

The date of writing Hebrews is difficult to determine. We must date the book before A.D. 95, when Clement referred to it. The writer used present tense verbs in 10:11 ("performs" and "offers") to describe the ministry of the priests in the Jerusalem temple. This indicates that sacrifices were still being offered in the days of the writer.

The Roman army destroyed the temple in A.D. 70. Persecution intensified as that day drew near (see 10:32-34). Timothy was still alive (13:23). The best option for the date is the mid to late 60s before the Romans destroyed the temple.

Recipients

The above title for Hebrews reflects the conviction that Jewish Christians were the original readers of the writing. Frequent appeal to the Old Testament, extensive knowledge of Jewish ritual, and the warning not to return to Jewish ritual support this conviction.

One might feel that the Jewish Christians who read Hebrews lived in Palestine. According to 2:3, however, the readers may not have seen nor heard Jesus during His earthly ministry. The verse suggests that the readers had been dependent on the first hearers of the Christian message to share it with them. Doubtless, most Palestinian Christians had heard Jesus' preaching and teaching. According to 6:10 the readers of Hebrews had resources enough to assist other believers. Palestinian Christians were poor and needed aid (Acts 11:27-30; Rom 15:26). These facts indicate that the readers were not from Palestine.

The statement in 13:24, "Those from Italy send you their greetings," sounds as if Italians away from their home were returning greetings to friends in Rome. If this is true, Rome is the probable destination of the writing. A second fact favoring this view is that a knowledge of Hebrews first appears in Clement's First Epistle, which was written in Rome.

Purpose

Wherever the recipients lived, they were well-known to the writer. He described them as generous (6:10) but immature (5:11-14). He was aware of their persecution (10:32-24; 12:4), and he planned to visit them soon (13:19,23).

The writer rebuked the readers for not meeting together often enough (10:24-25). They were in danger of lapsing into sin (3:12-14). Perhaps the readers were a Jewish-Christian group who had broken away from the chief body of Christians in the area. They were considering returning to Judaism to avoid persecution. The author wrote to warn them against such apostasy (6:4-9; 10:26-31) and to help them return to the mainstream of Christian fellowship.

Theme

The writer of Hebrews presented Jesus Christ as the High Priest who offered Himself as the perfect sacrifice for sins (8:1-2; 10:11-18). Christ had superiority over every aspect of Old Testament religion. Understanding this principle could prevent the readers from abandoning Christ and returning to Judaism (10:26-29).

Literary Form

The language of Hebrews is elegant and carefully constructed. Its excellent Greek does not clearly show up in English translations that strive for readability.

Was the writer penning a letter to a specific group of Christians, or was the letter a summary of a sermon made available to several Christian congregations? The reference to "I do not have time to tell" in 11:32 seems to indicate a sermon; however, the writer knew specific details about the congregation (5:11-12; 6:9-10; 10:32-34; 12:4; 13:7). This suggests a letter written to a specific location. The statement in 13:22 also requires that we view the writing as a letter penned in the style of an earnest warning to a specific congregation.

Theology

The Letter to the Hebrews emphasizes the person of Christ. It presents a Jesus who is truly human (2:18), realistically tempted (4:15), and obedient to death (3:2; 13:12). The suffering of Jesus taught Him the value of obedience (5:8).

Hebrews also emphasizes the finality of Christ's work. The sacrifices offered by Jewish priests in the temple reminded the worshipers of sin, but the sacrifice of Christ removed sin (10:1-4). The priests of Judaism repeatedly offered sacrifices that did not take away sin (10:11). Christ's single offering of Himself forever removed the sin that hindered fellowship with God (10:12-14).

I. The Superiority of Christ over the Old Testament Prophets (1:1-3)
II. The Superiority of Christ over Angels (1:4–2:18)
III. The Superiority of Christ over Moses (3:1-19)
IV. The Superiority of Christ over Joshua (4:1-13)
V. The Superiority of Christ over Aaron (4:14–10:18)
VI. The Practice of Spiritual Endurance (10:19–12:29)
VII. Final Exhortations (13:1-25)

1:1-3
The Superiority of Christ over the Old Testament Prophets

The author emphasized that God had spoken in the past through the prophets at many different times and in varied ways. He stated that the revelation God had given through Jesus was superior to that through the prophets. This was true because Jesus was the Heir, Creator, divine Reflection, Image of God, and Sustainer of the world. Jesus had cleansed our sins and then taken His seat at God's right hand as a token of His finished work.

1:4–2:18
The Superiority of Christ over Angels

Our writer presented angels as servants God created to minister to believers (1:14). He portrayed Christ as God's Son, who received the worship of angels and had an eternal existence (1:5-6,10-12). The superiority of Christ made the failure to believe on Him a fearsome experience (2:1-4). The author concluded that Christ's incarna-

New Testament Use of the Old Testament

A study of the NT's use of the OT must include not only an assessment of OT quotations as they are found in the NT. It also must include matters of a broader scope, such as the relationship of the two Testaments, the nature and meaning of prophecy and fulfillment, methods of interpreting the OT used by NT writers, and their development of biblical themes. These aspects of such an important study can only be touched upon in a survey article of this nature.

The relationship of the two Testaments is foundational to our understanding of the NT's use of the OT. Without question, the NT authors attributed full authority to the OT Scriptures. The NT is never viewed as being in conflict with the OT but rather as the fulfillment of what God had begun to reveal in the OT (see Heb 1:1-2). The NT writers viewed the OT as invested with divine authority, and in their use of it by way of quotations they treated it as the very Word of God.

We are surprised to discover that 250 quotations of the OT are in the NT. In addition, there are a number of allusions to the OT that are not specific quotations but where it is obvious that an author was employing OT phraseology. Eliminating all allusions that are not of a direct nature, there are at least 278 different OT verses cited in the NT: ninety-four from the Pentateuch, ninety-nine from the Prophets, and eighty-five from the Writings.

Something of the authority with which the NT authors quoted the OT can be seen in their use of citation formulas. Sometimes the NT authors used citation formulas such as "it is written" or "Scripture says." The former emphasizes the permanent nature as well as the binding character of that which has been written. Jesus withstood the temptation of Satan in the wilderness by three times introducing OT quotations with the phrase "it is written." The latter emphasizes the fact that Scripture "speaks" (present tense) to us today. The desire of the author of Hebrews to emphasize the continuity of the old and new covenants is seen in the fact that eighteen of our twenty-five OT citation formulas appear in the present tense.

Many times God is referred to as the Author of Scripture, emphasizing its divine origin. The joint nature of the origin of Scripture is attested in the use of the names of the human authors as well as the divine Author. For example, Matthew 1:22 reads, "What the Lord had spoken through the prophet." In Acts 1:16 we read, "The Holy Spirit spoke long ago through the mouth of David."

In the Gospels there are approximately thirty-nine OT quotations attributed to Jesus. Many times Jesus' use of the OT reflects a literalist interpretation. At other times He used the OT in a "this is that" or fulfillment type of interpretation. For example, in Luke 4:16-21 the fulfillment theme is prominent in our Lord's use of the OT. Jesus treated the OT as the very Word of God, giving it the highest authority when He said of it that "not the smallest letter, not the least stroke of a pen, will by any means disappear from the Law until everything is accomplished" (Matt 5:18).

In Acts there are twenty-seven OT quotations attributed to various Christian leaders. Their use of the OT reveals that they understood it from a Christocentric perspective. In the Pauline Epistles there are no less than eighty-three quotations (excluding allusions).

As in Acts, Paul's understanding and use of the OT was couched in a Christological setting as well. Oftentimes Paul's OT quotations can be found in clusters as he would seek to bolster an argument with quotations from many parts of the OT (see for example, Rom 3:10-18 and 9:12-29).

The NT writers interpreted many of the events concerning Christ and the church as having been prophesied in the OT. In addition, the NT writers, under the inspiration of the Holy Spirit, have taken many OT passages and interpreted and applied them in a greater perspective beyond their original context. For example, Habakkuk 2:14, "The righteous will live by faith," is quoted three times in the NT: Romans 1:17; Galatians 3:11; and Hebrews 10:38.

Sometimes a question arises when one compares the NT citation with the OT original in that it would appear the NT writers used some freedom in their quotations both in respect to form and meaning. Several factors should be kept in mind. First, modern-day rules of precision in quotation did not apply to the biblical writers. Second, as a result, OT quotations were oftentimes paraphrased by the NT writers. Third, quotations had to be translated from Hebrew to Greek. Fourth, NT writers often simply alluded to an OT passage without intending to quote it verbatim. These and other reasons account for the fact that some quotations are not "exact."

In conclusion, the NT writers believed the OT to be directly relevant to them, and they used it accordingly. Their statements indicate that the OT in its entirety is meaningful and relevant for the first-century church as well as for us today. □

tion and crucifixion enhanced His superiority and qualified Him to become a spiritual trailblazer for believers (2:5-13). This was true because the sufferings of Christ better equipped Him to help us as we suffer (2:17-18).

3:1-19
The Superiority of Christ over Moses

Christ was God's Son who reigned over the household of God's people (3:6). He was superior to Moses, who was merely a servant within God's household (3:5). Jesus' superiority to Moses made it a more serious matter to reject Jesus than to reject Moses (3:12-19). Our writer referred to the experience of Israel in Numbers 14:1-35 as an illustration of the seriousness of unbelief.

4:1-13
The Superiority of Christ over Joshua

The writer showed that Joshua failed to lead the people of God to rest because of their unbelief (4:1-2,8). Jesus promised rest to His people if they believe and follow the promises of the gospel (4:9-10). This rest is not fully available in this life, but by faith we may experience a portion of its blessings now (see chap. 11).

4:14–10:18
The Superiority of Christ over Aaron

4:4–5:10
Christ Represents Us

Our writer began with a summary of Christ's work as

Apostasy

Apostasy: Defection; rebellion. The classical Greek term *apostasia* brought to mind a military or political context and referred to rebellion against established authority. In the major English translations the actual word *apostasy* occurs seldom (NASB 6; RSV 3; NEB 2; NIV 0; KJV 0), but as a reference to rebellion against the Lord, the idea is widespread. In the OT it is Israel's greatest national sin, that is idolatry, or forsaking the worship of the Lord (Exod 20:3; Deut 6:5,14; 29:14-28).

The Greek term *apostasia* occurs twice in the NT. In Acts 21:21 it refers to an accusation against Paul that he had encouraged Jews to "forsake" Moses. In 2 Thessalonians 2:3 it refers to the great defection or falling away from the faith that will precede the return of Christ.

Various other NT contexts point to religious defection, the causes of which vary: affliction or persecution (Matt 13:21; 24:9-13), false teachers (Matt 24:11; 2 Tim 4:30), erroneous views of Christ (1 John 2:18-23; 2 John 7-9), and unbelief (Heb 3:12-14).

The theological issue raised by the question of apostasy is of paramount importance. The historic doctrines of Christian assurance and the security of the believer are not, however, nullified by the fact that there are those who make Christian professions and/or attend Christian worship who later forsake, either by word or deed, their earlier confession.

The Pauline doctrine of the Spirit is an unequivocal scriptural affirmation of the security of the believer. Paul's references to the Spirit as "firstfruits" (Rom 8:23) and "pledge" (2 Cor 1:22; Eph 1:14) indicate that Christians have already begun to experience the gift of eternal life.

For Paul all who hear and believe the gospel receive the gift of the Spirit, which is God's pledge (promise, guarantee, earnest) of the resurrection (Eph 1:13-14; Rom 8:11,23,38-39). In this connection the Pauline verb "to predestine" (Rom 8:28-30; Eph 1:5,11) is not so much a reference to what God decided before the world began (though Paul certainly affirmed Christ's death and the mystery of the gospel as part of God's eternally predestined purpose; see 1 Cor 2:7-8; Acts 4:27-28). Rather it is a reference to God's unalterable promise to resurrect unto glory the one who believes in Jesus. Christians are predestined to be raised like Christ. Thus, "having been justified by faith" (Rom 5:1), having received the Spirit as God's pledge of love (Rom 5:5; 8:35,39), we may know that "we shall be saved from the wrath of God through him" (Rom 5:9; compare 5:10).

Hebrews 6:1-8 (esp. v. 6) is interpreted by some to refer to the realistic possibility of losing one's salvation, but the argument is hypothetical. Just as it is impossible for Christ to be crucified twice (see 9:25–10:18), so also is faith a once-for-all experience (see 6:4). Furthermore, Hebrews 6:13-20 is one of the strongest affirmations in the NT of the certainty of our future hope, which is grounded in the faithfulness of God.

Certainly the fact of sin is a Christian tragedy, but even extremes of sin cannot nullify the promise of God (note that even the incestuous man of 1 Cor 5:1-5, who is to be "handed over to Satan," will "be saved in the day of the Lord Jesus"). As for those who make Christian confessions only later to renounce them and defect from the faith, we may perhaps say with John, "They went out from us, but they were not really of us" (1 John 2:19). □

ASSURANCE, WARNING AND PERSEVERANCE

For many Christians who struggle to understand their faith and the meaning of salvation, the question of security looms very large. Texts like John 10:27-29 affirm that no one will pluck them out of the hand of the Lord. They seem to provide assurance concerning security.

Texts like Hebrews 6:4-6 and 10:26-27, however, with the warnings of the impossibility of being renewed, seem to offer insecurity. Because this issue of security touches Christians at a deep level, a few would like to reword the texts of Hebrews or dismiss the entire book from their authoritative canon.

This way of dealing with the NT will not work because such disturbing texts can be found throughout other parts of the Bible (see 1 Cor 10:6-22). Instead, we must realize that there is a built-in tension written into the biblical texts. Remember that God knows what people are like and that Jesus was not confused by their "believing" (John 2:23-25). Remember also that in Hebrews 6 there is not just one "impossible" but two (6:4,18): the one a warning and the other an assurance.

This built-in tension in the Bible reminds us that when God sent Jesus, He was not playing a game. The cross was the most serious moment in the history of the world. God expects us to treat it with utmost seriousness. Believing is not just a matter of words; it involves the way we live (see Jas 2:14-26). Therefore the entire Bible is laced with warnings about the way we live.

Nevertheless, we must also understand that we do not save ourselves, whether it is at the beginning point of justification (Rom 3:21-31) or throughout our lives to the point of death and our glorification (Rom 6:22-23). It is by the gracious working of God that we are renewed daily (2 Cor 4:16). Our security then is not rooted in our ability to save or uphold ourselves. Our security is in the power of God to save and to forgive us repeatedly since we all continue to sin (1 John 1:8-10).

This life therefore is a pilgrimage with God. It is a pilgrimage that takes seriously both assurance and warning. In this pilgrimage we have a sense of security outlined in the classical definition of the "perseverance of the saints." This means that those who struggle on earth to live with God *will* attain their heavenly rest (Heb 4:9-13; 2 Thess 2:13-15).

The contemporary popularized statement "once saved, always saved," however, creates a problem because it is an unfortunate oversimplification of this classical doctrine. It makes God's gracious working with us a static momentary action that loses the emphasis of pilgrimage and the great struggle of Christian life reflected throughout the NT, to say nothing of the similar OT messages about God and His people.

The purpose of the Bible is twofold. (1) Everything possible is done in the midst of a hostile world to call Christians to a faithful life. (2) Everything possible is done to remind Christians of the assurance of God, who calls them to draw near to the throne of grace (Heb 4:16).

This tension between assurance and warning is the context for Christian living. Tension is present throughout the Bible because the Bible deals with the intersection of human weakness and divine strength. Genuine Christians take seriously the warnings of the Bible and rely firmly upon its gracious assurances. □

our High Priest. Christ is our great High Priest who represents us in God's very presence (4:14-16). God appointed Aaron as a high priest to represent people before God. Because Aaron was surrounded with weakness, he was able to have compassion on other weak, sinful people (5:1-4). Christ also faced hardship, and He learned the value of obedience by His commitment to God's will. God called Christ to serve as a high priest after the order of Melchizedek (5:5-10). Our author explained this idea more fully in chapter 7.

5:11–6:20
Warning against Apostasy

The immaturity of the readers prevented their usefulness and skillful performance for God (5:11-14). The writer warned his readers that no one could ever repeat the experience of repentance and conversion if he committed apostasy (6:1-8).

Some see this warning as a teaching that a true Christian can lose his salvation. That position would contradict the teaching of such New Testament passages as John 10:27-29; Romans 11:29; and Philippians 1:6. Others see the warning as hypothetical and not a realistic possibility. The repetition of the warning here and also in 10:26-31 makes this interpretation less likely. Others see the warning as directed at those who are almost Christians but not genuine Christians. In opposition to this view is the fact that a passage such as "shared in the Holy Spirit" (6:4) could not be used of one who was not a Christian. The preferred interpretation is to view this passage as addressed toward professing Christians. The writer urged them to show the reality of their faith by enduring in their commitment to Christ without falling away (6:6). The writer spoke to his readers in accordance with their profession, but he urged them to show their true faith by producing real works.

The work and love the readers showed convinced the writer that none of them were apostates. However, he wanted all of them to press on to achieve full maturity by obeying the promises of God (6:13-18).

7:1-28
Order of Melchizedek

The writer reached back to the story of Melchizedek (Gen 14:17-20) to explain the nature of Jesus' priesthood. Melchizedek's name and hometown suggest that he was the "king of righteousness" and the "king of peace." The Bible did not record any beginning or ending for his life. His eternal priesthood of righteousness was like that of Christ (7:1-3). Abraham's action of giving tithes to Melchizedek showed that the priest was a great man (7:4-10).

Because the priesthood of Aaron did not bring people into obedience to God, He changed the priesthood. He installed Christ as the Priest after a new order, that of Melchizedek. Our writer felt that the priesthood of Christ was superior to that of Aaron for three reasons. First, God initiated this priesthood with an oath, not merely by some worldly rules (7:16-17). Second, Christ's priesthood was permanent. Christ would never deliver His office to someone unqualified to handle it (7:25). Third, the character of Christ was superior to that of the Aaronic priests. Christ was exactly the type of high priest weak believers needed (7:26-28).

8:1–9:28
A New Covenant

Our author indicated that in addition to beginning a new

OLD AND NEW COVENANT

Definitionally, a covenant is an agreement between two parties, whether equals or not, that signified a relationship whereby the two bound themselves to each other, either conditionally or unconditionally.

Theologically, the term was used to describe the relationship God initiated by His grace between Himself and humankind to those who were willing to bind themselves through a personal commitment of faith. This is reflected in the oft-occurring phrase in the OT "I will be their God and they shall be my people."

A covenant was made by a sacrifice. Hence the Hebrew idiom for its establishment was "to cut a covenant" (Gen 15:7-21). From God's perspective His covenant is unconditional and unilateral in establishment, but from humankind's perspective it is conditional and two-sided. God commands His people to keep His covenant through obedience and alternatively judges and blesses them according to their response.

The word *covenant* in the NT is *diatheke,* and it functions as the equivalent for the OT *berit.* It occurs thirty-three times, nearly half of which are either OT quotations or references to the OT covenants. But the concept of the "new covenant" did not originate in the NT, for Jeremiah 31:31-34 speaks of God's intention to establish a new covenant.

The phrase "new covenant" is found six times in the NT: 1 Corinthians 11:25; 2 Corinthians 3:6; Hebrews 8:8; 9:15; 12:24. The new covenant is the fulfillment of the old in that it is identified with the death of Jesus and the Christian age. It is superior to the old covenant according to Hebrews 7:20-22; 8:6 and displaces the old according to Hebrews 8:13; 10:9.

The new covenant was established by the shed blood of Jesus on the cross. In the Gospel accounts of the last supper, it was Jesus Himself who related His coming death to the establishment of the new covenant. He is, by virtue of His death, the Mediator of a new covenant (Heb 9:15; 12:24). The sacrificial offering by Jesus on the cross constituted the beginning of the new covenant and is complete and unrepeatable. Entrance into the covenant relationship is by faith in Christ.

The Book of Hebrews is the NT epistle most concerned with the relationship between the old and new covenants. The writer's intent was to show both continuity and discontinuity between the two covenants.

Continuity can be seen in that God is the initiator of both covenants, and both are based on sacrifice. Discontinuity can be seen in that the new covenant supersedes the old due to the final nature of the death of Christ.

The old covenant was enacted upon inferior promises, lacked finality, and lacked efficacy in that it provided no power to keep its conditions. In contrast, the new covenant is unconditional, final, and spiritually efficacious. □

order of priesthood, Christ inaugurated a new covenant. Jeremiah 31:31-34 foretold this new covenant. It provided three benefits for those who lived under it. First, it provided a new awareness of God's laws and a new nature by which to obey God. Second, it gave a personal knowledge of God that inspired a loyalty and commitment to Him. Third, it provided a complete forgiveness of sins (8:8-12). Christians today have inherited the benefits of this new covenant in their relationship with God.

The old covenant made provision for removing external pollution by the use of animal sacrifices and familiar rituals (9:6-10). Under the new covenant Jesus surrendered His life to God in sacrifice for sin. The sacrifice of Christ is more effective for us today in three ways. First, it did not limit itself to the mere removal of ceremonial pollution. It cleansed the conscience from guilt and thus inspired holy living (9:11-14). Second, it resulted in the removal of sin by the shedding of Christ's blood (9:15-22). Third, by entering God's presence, Christ showed that He has offered a perfect sacrifice (9:23-28). Because Christ has fully removed all sins, Christians have the hope that He will one day return to complete their salvation by taking them to be with the Father.

10:1-18
Christ's Permanent Sacrifice

The author explained the permanence of Christ's sacrifice. The repetition of the sacrifices offered by the Jews on their Day of Atonement (Lev 16) could never make the worshipers perfect. Their sacrifices served as an annual reminder of the sins of the people (10:1-4). What God truly wanted was not merely the offering of an unthinking animal but a conscious, volitional choice to follow Him. That is what Jesus gave when He came to do God's will. Jesus' choice to offer Himself as a sacrifice for our sin earned for Christians acceptance in God's sight (10:5-10). The constant offering of Levitical sacrifices testified that sins still remained. The once-for-all death of Christ forever took away all sins. When these sins are removed, no further need for sacrifice remains (10:11-18).

10:19–12:29
The Practice of Spiritual Endurance

10:19-39
Stamina in Obedience

The writer of Hebrews found the readers tempted to pull away from Christ. Hebrews attempted to call them to God and to fellowship with one another by describing a veil by which all believers could enter God's presence (10:20). This veil symbolized the life of Jesus presented

This stone carving found at Caesarea is thought by some to be an early representation of the tabernacle (see Heb 8:2).

to God when He suffered for our sins (1 Pet 3:18). Because Christians had complete access to God, they could draw near to Him with an inward and outward cleansing. They also needed to consider how to stimulate one another to good works by meeting together (10:25).

In no instance should Christians fall into a pattern of neglecting fellowship with one another. The author warned his readers that turning away from Christ would expose them to divine judgment (10:26-31). He insisted that his readers show genuine faith by continued commitment to Christ. They had already suffered for their faith, but they needed to demonstrate stamina in obeying God (10:32-39).

11:1-40
Heroes of Faith

As an incentive to endurance before God, the writer presented a gallery of Old Testament heroes of faith. Faith gives reality to things that cannot be seen. By this faith the Old Testament believers received a positive witness from God (11:1-2). In the generations before the flood, Abel, Enoch, and Noah all responded by faith to demonstrate obedience to God. Their faith pleased Him. Abraham demonstrated his faith by forsaking the comforts of Ur and Haran to follow God to the promised land. By faith Abraham and Sarah bore Isaac as a child of their old age (11:8-12). Moses showed his faith by leaving the wealth of the Egyptian palace to suffer hardship with the Hebrew people (11:23-28). The writer presented Gideon, Samson, David, Samuel, and many other heroes as

This Coptic painting from Egypt (A.D. 400s) shows the prophet Isaiah being "sawed in two" (Heb 11:37) by two executioners.

examples whose faith Christians should follow. The promises the Old Testament believers had expected were coming true in the events New Testament Christians were experiencing (11:39-40).

12:1-29
Encouraged to Endure

The writer also found encouragement for endurance from Jesus' example (12:1-11). Jesus had already run the race of faith, and God had placed Him on the throne. When Christians consider the hardship He faced, they can find strength and fresh courage. God allows all Christians to experience hardship so that they might develop holiness. Even though God's chastisement seems hard for the time, it will eventually produce righteousness in those who follow Him.

The character of God provided another incentive for endurance. God desires that all persons seek after holiness (12:14). God will not tolerate a disobedient, self-serving life-style. The presence of God at Sinai caused thunder, lightning, and fright among the people who saw Him. If God's speaking on earth at Sinai produced fear, how much more would His words from heaven through Jesus produce fear! The writer showed that God's kingdom was unmovable. This gives Christians the grace to serve Him with stamina and reverence (12:25-29).

13:1-25
Final Exhortations

Christians have practical duties with one another. They must show sympathy to those in prison, and they must avoid all immorality. God has promised never to leave Christians, and that promise helps to banish greed (13:1-6).

Christians must follow the faith of their leaders. When Christians submit to those who care for their spiritual needs, this allows the leaders to do their jobs with joy and not with hardship or frustration (13:7-8,17).

God is pleased with spiritual sacrifices that Christians offer. These sacrifices are commitment, praise, and unselfish sharing of goods (13:9-16).

In the last section of Hebrews the author urged prayer for himself and reported on Timothy's release from prison. He shared a doxology in 13:20-21 and an expression of greeting in 13:24-25.

Theological Significance

The author of Hebrews points us to the superiority of Jesus Christ. He is superior to the prophets (1:1-3), superior to the angels (1:4–2:18), and to Moses (3:1–4:13). He provides a superior priesthood on the basis of a superior covenant (4:14–10:31). Not only is Jesus superior to the foundational aspects of Judaism, but He also is superior to any aspect of contemporary religion. This means that Jesus is not just one good option among many ways of drawing near to God; He is the only way. Because of the superiority of Jesus we must not neglect such a great salvation that He has provided with His sacrificial death (2:3; 10:1-18).

Jesus, the superior Savior, is also the superior Priest. We can come to Him in times of trouble, suffering, and struggle. In Him we will find a sympathetic Priest (4:14-16) who offers grace in time of need. Thus we can and should draw near to Him in worship (10:19-25), live by faith (11:1-40), persevere to the end (12:1-29), and live a life of love (13:1-25).

Questions for Reflection

1. In what way is Christ superior to the angels (1:5-14)?
2. What is the significance of suggesting that Christ is a priest after the order of Melchizedek (7:1-10)?
3. Why was the sacrifice of Christ more effective than that of the Old Testament priests (10:1-18)?
4. What were some of the specific deeds of faith the Old Testament heroes in Hebrews 11 performed?
5. How does the writer of Hebrews explain God's purpose in chastisement (12:4-11)?
6. What are some of the sacrifices that please God (13:9-16)?

Sources for Additional Study

Brown, Raymond. *The Message of Hebrews.* Downers Grove: InterVarsity, 1982.

Bruce, F. F. *The Epistle to the Hebrews. The New International Commentary on the New Testament.* Grand Rapids: Eerdmans, 1964.

Guthrie, Donald. *Hebrews. Tyndale New Testament Commentaries.* Grand Rapids: Eerdmans, 1983.

JAMES

Martin Luther, whose vigorous voice led to the birth of Protestantism during the Reformation, described the Book of James as a strawy writing. The epistle's emphasis that a believer was justified by works (2:24) clashed with Luther's conviction that the believer becomes just by faith.

Most Christians would feel that Luther erred in his evaluation. The firm demands of the Book of James call wandering Christians back to obedience to God's Word. It is especially useful in pointing out ethical application of the gospel of grace. With the concern of a pastor, James spoke to his readers in urging them to face trial with stamina (1:2-18). He also spoke with the firmness of a prophet in urging them to show evidence of their genuine faith (2:14-26).

Authorship

The Book of James came slowly into widespread circulation in the early church. Many factors contributed to this. Its brevity and practical nature made it seem of small significance in comparison to a book like Romans. Christians in the early church also disagreed concerning the identity of James, the author of the epistle. Those who identified the name with the Lord's brother tended to view the book as genuine Scripture. Those who rejected the link between James and Jesus tended to ignore the Book of James. Church councils meeting at Rome (A.D. 382) and Carthage (A.D. 397) accepted James as Scripture. This acceptance gave support to the view that James, the Lord's brother, was the author.

The text of James provides little information about the author other than his name, but the mention of the name provides an important clue to his identity. Few persons with the name of James could succeed in identifying themselves merely by their first name. The writer must have been an important James.

Four persons in the New Testament have the name of James. James, the father of Judas (not Iscariot), is mentioned in Luke 6:16 and Acts 1:13. James, the son of Alphaeus, appears in Matthew 10:3 and Acts 1:13. Both are obscure figures who lacked the importance to have been recognized by the mere designation "James." James the apostle was martyred under Herod Agrippa I in A.D. 44 (see Acts 12:2). He died before the time in which most people feel the Book of James appeared. The Lord's brother was an unbeliever during Jesus' earthly ministry (John 7:2-5), but an appearance of the risen Christ to him apparently led him to become a believer (1 Cor 15:7; Acts 1:14). He rapidly became a leader in the early church (Gal 2:6-9). The New Testament pictures him as a committed Jew who recognized Jesus as Messiah and Lord and showed spiritual sensitivity to the

James

working of God. James the Lord's brother would be important enough in the early church clearly to identify himself by the designation "James."

Other features of the Epistle of James also confirm the likelihood of identifying the author with Jesus' brother. James 1:22 and 5:12 contain echoes of Jesus' teaching in Matthew 7:20-24 and 5:34-37, respectively. The brother of the Lord could have heard this teaching. James 5:14-18 portrays our author as a man of prayer, and this agrees with the extrabiblical portrait of James, the Lord's brother. The tradition is that the Lord's brother spent such time in prayer that his knees became as hard as those of a camel (Eusebius, *Ecclesiastical History* 2.23). It is not possible clearly to prove that the Lord's brother is the author of this epistle, but he is the most likely candidate from among the Jameses in the New Testament.

Date of Writing

Many scholars feel the Book of James is one of the earlier New Testament writings. Three features suggest an early date. First, James described a large gap between the rich and the poor (5:1-6). When the war against Rome broke out in A.D. 66, the rich suffered great losses, and conflict between rich and poor ceased. The impact of this observation pushes the writing to an earlier time rather than later. Second, the church organization mentioned in James seems undeveloped as seen in the mention only of elders as church leaders (5:14). Third, Christians were fervently expecting the return of Christ (5:7-9). It is felt that such fervor would be more true of the initial generations of Christians. All of these features support the acceptance of an earlier date.

Recipients

The address of the Epistle of James to "the twelve tribes scattered among the nations" (Jas 1:10) suggests that the readers were Jewish Christians who lived outside of Palestine. Several features confirm the truth of the suggestion. First, the term for "meeting" (2:2) is the Greek word for "synagogue." The word does not suggest that the readers met in a Jewish synagogue, but it indicates that Jewish Christians used this name to describe their place of meeting. Second, the statements of 5:1-6 present the picture of poor believers being intimidated by the wealthy. These rich people may have attended church meetings (2:1-3), but their presence did not indicate conversion. Third, the term "scattered among the nations" (1:1) reflects a single Greek word that referred to Jews who lived out of their homeland. All of these facts suggest that the Lord's brother directed a message to Jewish believers who had left their native country of Palestine.

Theme

The Epistle of James makes a unique contribution in the New Testament with its strong ethical emphasis. Its ethical teaching is scattered throughout the writing. James clearly taught that a faith that lacked works was empty, vain, and useless. James's frequent use of the imperative mood indicates his passionate feeling about the issues he faced. His fiery words resemble those of an Old Testament prophet. He shared ethical commands that touched upon both personal morality and social justice.

Literary Form

James's writing is similar to the Old Testament wisdom literature in Proverbs and Psalms. Both sources treat such subjects as the use of the tongue, the dangers of wealth, and the need for self-control. Some students of James have also pointed out a similarity with synagogue homilies or sermons.

James's writing reflected a vivid imagination. We can see his use of vigorous figures of speech in his comparison of the wavering man to "a wave of the sea, blown and tossed by the wind" (1:6). He also was a close observer of nature. We can see this from his description of the effects of the sun's heat (1:11), horticulture (3:12), and rainfall (5:7,18).

I. Greeting (1:1)
II. How to Face Trial (1:2-18)
III. A Correct Response to God's Word (1:19-27)
IV. The Avoidance of Partiality (2:1-13)
V. The Production of Works of Mercy (2:14-26)
VI. The Practice of Personal Discipline (3:1-18)
VII. The Avoidance of Worldliness (4:1-17)
VII. The Demonstration of Justice (5:1-6)
IX. The Practice of Endurance (5:7-12)
X. The Proper Use of Prayer (5:13-18)
XI. The Reclamation of Straying Christians (5:19-20)

Purpose and Theology

James wrote to Jewish Christians facing trials and persecution. Under the threat of persecution the readers considered compromising their Christian commitment and accommodating themselves to worldliness. James spoke as a pastor to urge his friends to develop spiritual stamina in facing persecution. He also spoke as a prophet to urge those who considered compromise to give evidence of their faith.

Some students of James suggest that the book lacks doctrinal emphases. It is true that James assumed some doctrinal similarity between himself and his readers and did not elaborate on all his beliefs. He did affirm the unity of God (2:19; 4:12) together with an emphasis on divine goodness (1:17), graciousness (4:6-8), and judgment (2:13). He emphasized strongly the return of Christ (5:7-11). In 1:12-15 he presented an analysis of temptation and sin, suggesting that human desire was the source of sin. Much of the content of James represented an effort to call individuals and the church back to full commitment to God and to complete concern for one another.

1:1
Greetings

It is significant that James chose not to mention his relationship to Jesus. His statement that he was a servant of Jesus indicated his humility. The expression "twelve tribes" represented the children of Israel (Acts 26:7). The fact that they were "scattered" suggested they were Jews living outside their Palestinian homeland. James spoke to his readers as Christians, for only believers would see Jesus as the "Lord Jesus Christ."

1:2-18
How to Face Trial

James urged his readers to look at trial from God's attitude. The trial itself was not an occasion of joy, but it could promote joy by becoming an occasion for producing stamina in the life of a committed believer (1:2-4).

In trial the believer must ask for an understanding of the purpose behind the divine permission of the difficulty. An incentive to do this is that God will give generously to those who ask and will not humiliate them for asking (1:5-8). Those who face trial with perseverance receive a crown of life from God as a reward for their stamina (1:12).

James moved from a discussion of trial to a discussion of inward enticement to sin in 1:13-18. First, he warned believers not to blame God for temptation in their lives. God does not dangle evil before people to entice them to sin. Second, he stated that the desires of his readers were responsible for luring them to disobedience. Third, he taught that God gave only "good and perfect" gifts to believers and would not vary from that principle.

1:19-27
A Correct Response to God's Word

Because his readers might compromise under trial, James warned them of the urgency for demonstrating their faith with works. His appeals can be summarized under the command, "Be doers of God's Word and not mere listeners."

In 1:19-25 James presented three figures of speech that explained how God's Word could help believers. First, he compared God's Word to a seed that could be planted within each Christian to grow into salvation (1:21). Second, he pictured God's Word as a mirror that clearly reflected the condition of the one who looked into it (1:23-24). Third, he described God's Word as a law that provided freedom (1:25). Listening to God's Word could provide the strength to produce obedient living.

In 1:26-27 James indicated that a true response to God's Word involved both outward activity and inward control. Ministry to orphans and widows was the outward activity. Separation from the world was evidence of inner control.

2:1-13
The Avoidance of Partiality

In 2:1-4 James rebuked his readers for demonstrating favoritism to the rich who attended their services while ignoring the poor. The display of partiality for the rich was contrary to their own interests, for the rich were actually their oppressors (2:6-7). Such partiality was also contrary to God's law (2:8-10). James reminded his audience that they would be judged for their inconsistency (2:12-13).

2:14-26
The Production of Works of Mercy

James warned that a faith that merely spoke kind words to the poor without offering them help was not a saving faith (2:14-17). Just as Abraham and Rahab demonstrated their obedience to God by works, James urged his friends to show their faith by works (2:21-25). James explained that a faith that merely affirmed correct belief without producing a changed life was lifeless (2:19-20).

The horse's bit shown above is from Pompeii. James wrote of the control exercised by a bit in a horse's mouth upon the movement of the entire body of the animal (Jas 3:3-4).

Above is a ship on a Late Roman sarcophagus. The two oars used for steering are in the center of the illustration (see Jas 3:3-4).

3:1-18
The Practice of Personal Discipline

James insisted that Christians show their obedience to God by controlling their tongues and all of their desires. He explained that the tongue had great power for both good and evil (3:3-6). He also pointed out the stubbornness (3:7-8) and inconsistency of the tongue (3:9-12). He urged his readers to demonstrate heavenly wisdom rather than earthly wisdom. Earthly wisdom produced envy and selfish ambition. Heavenly wisdom produced peacemakers who were merciful and considerate of one another (3:13-18).

4:1-17
The Avoidance of Worldliness

James saw an epidemic of worldly living among his readers. In 4:1-10 he warned against worldliness and showed its effects on the prayer life of his recipients. In 4:11-12 and in verses 13-18 he showed, respectively, that worldliness produced a critical spirit and a godless self-confidence.

In describing the effect of worldliness on the prayer life, James showed that his friends resorted to scheming, quarreling, and striving in order to obtain their wishes. They failed to receive what they truly needed because they did not ask. Whenever they did ask, they failed to receive because their request was tinged with self-will (4:1-3). James's description of God in 4:5 demonstrated that God tolerated no rivals and wanted complete commitment from His followers. God could make heavy demands on His followers, but He could also provide the grace to meet those demands (4:6). In 4:7-10 James uttered in rapid-fire fashion ten imperative appeals to submit to God and avoid worldliness.

One evidence of worldliness James cited was the presence of a critical spirit (4:11-12). He saw that Christians were defaming one another in the same way that the ungodly defamed Christians (4:11; 2:7). James warned that those who belittled fellow Christians had set themselves up as judges and had assumed a position that rightly belonged only to God (4:12).

Probably the arrogance James denounced in 4:13-17 came from self-confident Jewish businessmen who planned their lives without reference to God's will. James warned his readers that life resembled a transitory vapor and that all of life must be planned with reference to God's will (4:14-15). The sin James described in this paragraph is an example of a sin of omission.

5:1-6
The Demonstration of Justice

James leveled harsh warnings against wealthy landowners who valued the dishonest accumulation of material goods above the demonstration of justice (5:1-3). He accused the rich of the sins of dishonesty (5:4), wanton living (5:5), and injustice (5:6). He implied that God had heard the cries of the oppressed and would punish the unjust treatment meted out by the rich (5:4).

5:7-12
The Practice of Endurance

James used three illustrations to encourage a life-style of persistent devotion in serving the Lord. First, he spotlighted the farmer who planted and then waited for rains in order to produce a crop (5:7). Second, he mentioned the Old Testament prophets who spoke boldly for God despite suffering (5:10). Third, he commended Job, who faced tragedy, family misunderstanding, and physical suffering in obeying the Lord (5:11).

In times of distress Christians could easily use God's name in a careless, irreverent way. James warned against invoking God's name to guarantee truth and instead called for truthfulness so consistent that no oath was needed (5:12).

5:13-18
The Proper Use of Prayer

James urged believers to use prayer in all the seasons of life. In times of affliction Christians are to pray to God for help and strength (5:13a). In times of blessing believers are to praise God instead of congratulating themselves (5:13b). In instances of critical sickness the sick person was to summon the leaders of the church for prayer. Prayer for the sick could result in either physical healing or spiritual blessing (5:14-15). In times of sin and struggle mutual intercession could promote spiritual victory (5:16). Elijah prayed with such force that God withheld rain from the earth for three and a half years and gave it again at his request (5:17-18).

5:19-20
The Reclamation of Straying Christians

James operated with a realism about the spiritual life. He insisted that those who continue in sin show their lostness despite their profession of faith. He promised that the believer who won back a wanderer would save the sinner from eternal death and win blessings for himself.

Theological Significance

James reminds us in a forthright way that faith involves doing. It is not enough to be hearers of the word; we must be doers as well. We cannot just say we are believers; we must show it in our lives. This must be evident in the way we control our tongues and the way we relate to others. The rich must share with the poor. The Christian community must live out its faith by demonstrating love and a working faith to those inside and outside the body of Christ.

The above relief is from a Roman sarcophagus dating from A.D. 359 and shows Job (admired by James in 5:11 for his perseverance).

Questions for Reflection

1. What does James 1:2-8 teach about a correct response to trials and afflictions?
2. Refer to James 2:14-26 for a discussion of the question, Can a faith without works produce salvation?
3. Explain James's ideas concerning the power, stubbornness, and inconsistency of the tongue.
4. Explain how worldly living affects the prayer life of the Christian.
5. How does the certainty of the return of Christ provide stamina for facing suffering?
6. Does James promise that prayer for the recovery of the sick should always produce healing? Use such passages as 2 Corinthians 12:7-10 and 2 Timothy 4:20 in arriving at an answer.

Sources for Additional Study

Davids, Peter. *Commentary on James. Good News Commentary.* San Francisco: Harper and Row, 1985.

Moo, Douglas J. *James. Tyndale New Testament Commentaries.* Grand Rapids: Eerdmans, 1985.

Motyer, Alec. *The Message of James. The Bible Speaks Today.* Downers Grove: InterVarsity, 1985.

Vaughan, Curtis. *James: A Study Guide.* Grand Rapids: Zondervan, 1969.

1 PETER

The Epistle of 1 Peter was written to Jewish and Christian believers living in the northern part of Asia Minor. They faced persecution because of their commitment to Christ. Peter wrote to urge them to show stamina and commitment. Peter also wanted his readers to show a Christian life-style that would convert pagan sneers and accusations into appreciation and respect. To accomplish this, he urged all Christians to obey their leaders, servants to be subject to their masters, and husbands and wives to demonstrate honor and submission to one another. The vivid descriptions of Christ's suffering and death (2:21-25; 3:18) could serve as an encouragement for Christians to conquer evil and endure to the end.

Authorship

Leaders of the early church made frequent reference to 1 Peter, and there is no evidence of any dispute about authorship at this time. In the twentieth century some students of 1 Peter have questioned whether the apostle wrote the book.

Some have pointed out that the polished Greek of 1 Peter could hardly come from a man viewed as "unschooled" and "ordinary" (Acts 4:13). However, it is certainly possible that Peter could have developed ability in Greek in the years after Jesus' death. Also, Silas (5:12) may have served as a secretary, or amanuensis, to assist Peter in the expression of some of his ideas. Other students of 1 Peter have felt that the type of persecution mentioned in 4:14 refers to a time when it was a crime merely to be a Christian. They generally locate this time in the 90s or in the second century A.D. Peter would have been dead by this date. However, the expression "insulted because of the name of Christ" may mean only that believers were insulted because of their loyalty to Christ, not that it was a crime to be a Christian.

It is best to accept Peter's claims for authorship in 1:1. Added support for this acceptance comes from recognizing the similarity between statements in 1 Peter and the Petrine speeches of Acts (see Acts 10:42 and 1 Pet 4:5). Such statements as those of 1 Peter 2:13-17 sound as if Peter could have learned them by listening to Jesus' words in Matthew 17:24-27. The similarity to Jesus' teaching provides added support for Petrine authorship.

Date

Each chapter of 1 Peter contains a reference to suffering by someone (1:6-7; 2:21-25; 3:13-17; 4:12-19; 5:10). It is known that Nero brought persecution on Christians in Rome in the early 60s. Many feel that the Neronian persecutions caused a ripple effect in outlying provinces such as those in Northern Asia Minor.

The Neronian persecutions probably did not reach such an intensity that Christians were forced to choose between obedience to God and obedience to the state. Peter had articulated the Christian position concerning this choice in Acts 5:29. The teaching of the Christian attitude toward the state in 2:13-17 more resembles the response to the government we would expect during Nero's time. When persecution intensified in the late 90s and the early second century A.D., the Christian response would be to call for commitment to God rather than the state.

Recipients

The area in which Peter's readers lived, mentioned in 1:1, was far off the beaten path of travel and commerce. The Bible contains no record of how the gospel reached this area. Although the area contained colonies of Jews, Gentiles were numerically predominant. The order in which the provinces are mentioned might suggest the route followed by the letter carrier. He could have landed in Pontus, followed a circuit through the provinces, and left the area at Bithynia.

Peter's references to preconversion sins of idolatry (4:3) and evil desires they had when they lived in ignorance (1:14) suggest a way of life more true of Gentiles than Jews. The statement in 2:10 that they "were not a people" could not be made of Jews. Although the term "strangers" is the Jewish term for those dispersed from the homeland of Palestine (1:1), it is likely that Peter used it to refer to the church. Peter saw believers as a pilgrim people on earth who had been set apart by God to do His will.

Theme

Peter elaborated upon the subject of suffering throughout the entire epistle. He offered words of hope to his readers as they faced suffering (1:4-5; 5:4). He pictured suffering

Peter

as purposeful (3:14; 4:14). Christians were to endure it patiently (2:21; 3:9), and they were to demonstrate joy despite hardship (4:13). They could draw encouragement from following the example of Christ in suffering (2:21-25). God's will often demanded that believers endure suffering (4:19).

Literary Form

Students of 1 Peter have discussed widely the literary forms within the book. Many find extensive evidence of the presence of hymns, creeds, or fragments of sermons in such passages as 2:4-8 and 2:21-25. Some view the entire writing as a sermon preached at the baptism of a group of Christians. They view the opening section through 4:11 as a message spoken to candidates for baptism. They locate the performance of baptism at 1:21-22 and feel that the "Amen" at 4:11 concludes the address to the candidates.

The concluding section beginning with 4:12 is viewed as an address to the entire church gathered for the rite of baptism. Although these discussions are enlightening and enriching, they are often inconclusive and unconvincing. Peter may have used material from different sources in writing this book, but it is best to see that he made it his own material under the leadership of the Holy Spirit.

Peter made frequent reference to the Old Testament, sometimes by quotation (2:6-8) and sometimes by allusion (3:6,20). This frequent use suggests that Jewish readers were at least among the recipients of the letter. Some of Peter's emphases resemble those of Paul. For example, there is a similarity between Peter's words about relationships between wives and husbands in 3:1-7 and Paul's discussion in Ephesians 5:22-33.

I. Greetings (1:1-2)
II. The Method and Nature of Salvation (1:3-12)
III. A Demand for Holiness (1:12–2:3)
IV. A Description of the People of God (2:4-10)
V. The Christian Witness in the World (2:11–3:12)
VI. Appeals and Promises to the Persecuted (3:13–4:19)
VII. Assurances for Faithful Servants (5:1-9)
VIII. Praises to God and Greetings to the Church (5:10-14)

Purpose and Theology

Peter urged his readers to live in accordance with the hope that they had received in Christ (1:3). He gave guidance for them to use in their relationships with one another (3:1-12), and he urged them to endure suffering joyfully for Jesus' sake (4:19). His chief aim in writing was to provide them encouragement in Christian living.

Peter often used theological ideas to drive home his ethical demands. He presented the death of Christ as a stimulus for Christians to endure suffering (2:21-25). He also affirmed the resurrection as a chief source of Christian hope and confidence (1:3). He presented the return of Christ as an incentive for holy living (1:13). He portrayed the nature of the Christian call (2:9-10) as a basis for individual Christians to obey Christ at home (3:1-7), to obey Him as servants (2:18-20), and to follow Him as citizens (2:13-17).

1:1-2
Greetings

Peter addressed his readers as "God's elect" and "strangers" who were "scattered." Although such terms as "chosen" were sometimes used in reference to the Jews (Isa 43:20), Peter designated the church as a special people temporarily away from their heavenly home. Election began with the foreknowledge of God the Father, included the sanctifying work of the Holy Spirit, and was sealed by the redemptive work of Jesus Christ.

1:3-12
The Method and Nature of Salvation

Peter's First Epistle alternated between teaching and preaching, between proclamation and application. In this initial section Peter pictured salvation as based on the hope inspired by Jesus' resurrection (1:3). This salvation produced an unfading and imperishable inheritance given to them by God. The believers are promised protection with God's power through faith (1:4-5).

The faith of Peter's readers was deepened by their trial. These trials came because of their commitment to Jesus, they were a necessary part of their experience, and they could deepen their faith (1:6-7). The faith of the believers filled them with joy and brought them into living contact with Jesus (1:8-9).

In 1:10-12 Peter indicated that the prophets had reported the grace and glory of salvation. Peter stated that the prophets understood that Messiah must suffer, but they tried to learn the time and circumstances when this would occur.

1:13–2:3
A Demand for Holiness

Peter explained that the character of God and the high cost of redemption were incentives to produce holiness in his readers. He also demanded that holiness show itself in earnest love for other believers and in a forsaking of all malicious attitudes.

Peter's words in 1:13 are equivalent to saying, "Roll up your sleeves and go to work." He mentioned that the return of Jesus Christ was to give them hope and stability in the face of persecution. Christians would show their response to God's holiness by leaving the "evil desires" of their past ignorance (v. 14) and by adopting God's own behavior as their pattern.

In 1:17-21 Peter indicated that a proper reverence for God and an appreciation of the high cost of redemption demanded holy living. The readers would understand redemption as the freeing of a slave by paying a price. The payment that released Christians from an "empty way of life" was the "blood of Christ." Peter noted that God had determined the performance of this work of Christ before the beginning of time. He had only recently made His plan evident in the incarnation, passion, and resurrection of Jesus (v. 20).

Peter urged his readers to express their holiness by genuine love for one another (1:22-25). The quotation of Isaiah 40:6-8 (vv. 24-25) showed that the experience of this love came from the creative activity of God. Peter directed his readers to put aside malice and hypocrisy in their response to God's holiness (2:1-3). He also encouraged them to grow as believers by appropriating the nurture inherent in the gospel message.

2:4-10
A Description of the People of God

Peter used three images to describe the church in this section. First, he portrayed the church as a living body that gave sacrificial service to God (2:4-5). Christ was a life-giving Stone who enabled His followers to produce such spiritual sacrifices as obedience (Rom 12:1), praise, and practical ministry (Heb 13:15-16). Second, he described the church as a building or structure founded on Christ as the cornerstone (2:6-8). He quoted Old Testament passages from Isaiah 8:14; 28:16 and Psalm 118:22 to show that Christ was a foundation stone for believers and a rock which caused tripping for unbelievers. Third, he used the language of Exodus 19:5-6 and Hosea 2:23 to portray believers as a select nation reflecting the glories of God (2:9-10). God had fashioned special recipients of His mercy from those who previously never belonged to anyone.

2:11–3:12
The Christian Witness in the World

Peter was eager for God's people to demonstrate distinctive, obedient behavior in order to convince critics of their faith. He urged them to apply this behavior in relation to their rulers, their earthly masters, in their families, and to one another.

In 2:11-12 Peter suggested three reasons Christians must discipline their lives. First, Christians were foreigners to their pagan environment and were not adjusted to it. Second, if Christians yielded to the flesh, they would wage battle against their best selves. Third, self-discipline and obedience had a wholesome influence on unbelievers.

In relation to the government Peter urged voluntary submission for the purpose of commending Jesus' lordship (2:13-17). In relation to their owners slaves were to be subject. An incentive for showing this subjection even in the presence of provocation was the moving example of Christ's obedience (2:21-25). In the home women were to win their unsaved husbands to Christianity by serving them and showing them respect (3:1-6). Husbands in return were to live in an understanding way with their wives and treat them as full heirs of God's grace (3:7). Peter concluded this section by urging all

Church and State

Throughout church history the Christian community has sensed a somewhat ambiguous relationship to civil government. This relationship tends to follow a variant of three basic models. The first is characterized by a close link between the two realms almost to the point of fusion, sometimes with the state co-opting the church for its own purposes.

In the second model this situation is reversed, as the church seeks to utilize the civil power to its own benefit. The third model maintains that church and state are to exist side by side, each exercising authority in its own sphere and not interfering with the other. Advocates of each model claim the support of the Bible and the Christian heritage.

Similar to other ancient nations, the Hebrew commonwealth saw no division between the civil and religious spheres. Israel was in some sense a theocracy, for Yahweh was to be the sole sovereign over the nation. Yahweh exercised rulership through various representatives, including judges, prophets, and kings, who for this reason exercised both political and religious authority. Nevertheless, these two aspects of national life were not completely fused, as was the case among Israel's neighbors. This is evidenced, for example, by the prophetic movement, which provided a religious critique of the monarchy.

The NT was written in a quite different context. For the Christian church, in contrast to Israel, was an entity quite separate from the Empire. As a response to this situation, the NT writers offered two basic principles, one positive and one negative, for the proper Christian relationship to the state.

The Pauline Epistles and 1 Peter enjoin believers to be good citizens. This includes submitting to and honoring those in authority (1 Pet 2:13-17), paying taxes (Rom 13:7), and praying for leaders (1 Tim 2:2). For this they appeal to the function of government in acting as God's agent in punishing persons who do wrong. Yet the underlying motivation appears to be the authors' interest in the good reputation of the Christian community, and this for the sake of the gospel proclamation.

At the same time, believers must always follow a higher allegiance—to God. Peter and John articulated this during their conflict with the Jerusalem authorities (Acts 4:19-20). This principle likewise lies behind the conflict presented in Revelation, as the martyrs defied the injunctions of the satanically influenced civil order (see Acts 6:9; 13:7-8).

Both principles build from Jesus' response to the Pharisees' tricky question concerning paying taxes (Matt 22:15-21). In external matters—taxes and perhaps social conventions—disciples are to honor civil laws because these matters fall under the jurisdiction of civil authority (the coin carries Caesar's imprint). But the emphasis of Jesus' response rests with the matter of personal allegiance. Here God alone has claim to lordship, as indicated by the implied but unstated parallel: the human person carries the imprint of the Creator.

In keeping with these principles and as a result of historical experience, certain Protestant groups (such as the Baptists) have generally advocated the third model, the separation of church and state. This outlook places restrictions on both spheres. It denies the civil government the prerogative of seeking to shape the religious beliefs of its citizens, of meddling in the church's internal affairs, or of determining the nature of the church's message. The separation model, however, is not intended to eliminate religion from national life or to silence the voice of the church in matters of civil concern. □

Christians to practice compassion and forgiveness (3:8-12). They were to treat others not as they had been treated by their accusers but as God had graciously treated them.

3:13–4:19
Appeals and Promises to the Persecuted

In this section Peter directly faced some of the difficult suffering of his readers. He encouraged them to respond righteously to those who had caused their suffering (3:13-17) by reflecting on Christ's vindication despite His suffering (3:18-22). He urged a full commitment to God's will (4:1-6), and he presented Christ's return as an incentive for watchful action (4:7-11). He demonstrated that a knowledge of future glory provided an additional encouragement to obedience (4:12-19).

Paul instructed his recipients that even if they suffered for righteous living God would bless them (Matt 5:10). He urged them to serve the Lord even in the face of unjust treatment, for that unjust treatment might be a part of a divine plan to glorify Himself (3:17).

In 3:18 Peter presented Christ's suffering as mediatorial because through it He brought believers to God. The death of Christ took place in the realm of the flesh, but the resurrection of Christ occurred in the realm of the Spirit.

Christ's experience in 3:19-20 took place at a time after Christ was made alive in the realm of the Spirit. The "spirits in prison" refer to supernatural beings or wicked angels who opposed the work of God (see Gen 6:1-4; 2 Pet 2:4-5; Jude 6). Preaching to them was not an offer of an additional chance for repentance but an announcement of doom.

The exact location of these disobedient spirits is not specified. Some interpreters have seen this as a description of Jesus' descent into hell. Peter stated that Jesus went to the place where these spirits were confined, an unnamed location. If we equate the spirits in prison with the angels who sinned in 2 Peter 2:4, then their location is Tartarus ("cast them down to Tartarus," 2 Pet 2:4). In Greek thought this place of punishment was lower than Hades. Peter's readers would understand that evil spirits lay behind their persecution. The coming defeat and doom of these spirits would be a source of encouragement to the readers. The knowledge of their ultimate vindication would give believers an additional incentive to obey. The judgment of the flood served as a warning of God's coming judgment on the world (3:20). The ark that saved a few through water illustrates the salvation available in Christ.

In verse 21 Peter presented baptism as a copy of the Old Testament deliverance from judgment. The conviction of sin calls for a faith response to Christ. The act of baptism portrays this response. Salvation comes to believers because Christ has arisen from the dead. Not only has He arisen from the dead, but He has also been installed in a place of power and authority over all His enemies.

In 4:1-6 Peter issued a further call to holy living. He called on his readers to arm themselves by a cocrucifixion with Christ so that sin would no longer be an option for them. Some who had received the gospel message earlier had since died (4:6). Their death showed that they experienced the common judgment that sin brings on all people. Despite their death they had entered into life eternal.

Shown above is a painting on an Attic vase (450–359 B.C.) depicting the idolatrous and orgiastic dancing of nymphs in honor of the god Dionysus. (Peter condemned such actions, 1 Pet 4:3.)

In 4:7-11 Peter presented the return of Christ as an incentive for disciplined, watchful behavior. The fact of Christ's return should promote love, hospitality, and a proper use of spiritual gifts.

Peter urged his friends to prepare themselves for a coming trial by commitment and stamina (4:12-19). Instead of offering complaint, they should rejoice that their suffering allowed them to share in Christ's glory. Peter warned his readers against disgracing Christianity by evil deeds or indiscreet action. Peter argued in 4:17-18 that even if believers must face difficulty, the fate of unbelievers would be absolutely terrifying.

5:1-9
Assurances for Faithful Servants

In 5:1-4 Peter outlined the duties of elders and assured them of divine rewards for faithful service. Peter urged the elders to assume their tasks for the right reasons, not because they felt obligated but because they freely chose to do it. At Christ's return the faithful leaders were promised an unfading crown of glory.

In 5:5-9 Peter urged Christians to practice humility and endurance. Christians were to show this humility to one another. They were also to demonstrate a lowliness in the face of circumstances that God allowed (5:6-7). Christians needed to avoid carelessness because their adversary Satan could overpower them (5:8-9).

5:10-14
Praises to God and Greetings to the Church

Peter expressed praise for God's grace, which allowed Christians growth even after suffering (5:10-11). Silas (5:13) is probably the same as Paul's helper in Acts 15:40. "She who is in Babylon" is a reference to the church at Rome.

Theological Significance

First Peter calls the contemporary church to faithfulness in Christian living and Christian duty. Peter provided guidance for the church in times of persecution and suffering and offered hope for difficult situations. This hope is grounded in the death and resurrection of Christ. The sufferings and sacrifice of Christ on the cross were central for Peter's theology and ethics. He called for the church to be holy since Christ has redeemed us from an empty way of life (1:18). The church must respond to persecution and oppression with patience and perseverance "because Christ suffered for you, leaving you an example, that you should follow in his steps" (2:21). The church must do good and live for God in all situations since "it is better if it is God's will, to suffer for doing good than for doing evil. For Christ died for sins once for all, the righteous for the unrighteous, to bring you to God" (3:17-18). The church can take heart and gain courage from this stirring letter that encourages us by testifying about "the true grace of God" (5:12).

Questions for Reflection

1. Explain how trials develop genuineness in faith. Does genuineness automatically develop through trial? What response on our part promotes the development of faith through trial?

2. Read 1:17–2:3 and then list some of the results a commitment toward holiness should produce in the life of a Christian.

3. Write a definition for the various terms used in reference to Christians in 1 Peter 2:9. How should an understanding of these terms contribute to growth in our Christian life?

4. Harmonize the behavior mentioned in 1 Peter 2:13-17 with the principle spoken in Acts 5:29.

5. Using Peter's words in 1 Peter 3:1-7, explain responses of a husband and a wife within a home. Does Peter's description suggest that the wives and husbands are Christians or non-Christians?

6. What instruction about spiritual gifts does Peter provide in 1 Peter 4:10-11?

7. List the motives and incentives for effective ministry Peter gave in 1 Peter 5:2-3.

Sources for Additional Study

Davids, Peter. *1 Peter. New International Commentary.* Grand Rapids: Eerdmans, 1990.

Grudem, Wayne. *1 Peter. Tyndale New Testament Commentaries.* Grand Rapids: Eerdmans, 1988.

Kelly, J. N. D. *A Commentary on the Epistles of Peter and Jude.* Grand Rapids: Baker, 1981.

Vaughan, Curtis and Lea, Thomas D. *1, 2 Peter, Jude. Bible Study Commentary.* Grand Rapids: Zondervan, 1988.

2 PETER

Peter wrote his Second Epistle to counter the influence of heresy within the church (2 Pet 2:1). He appealed for spiritual growth as an antidote to defeat heresy, and he urged his readers to live holy lives in anticipation of Jesus' return (2 Pet 3:11-12).

The brevity of the letter resulted in its being ignored for centuries by the church. Few Christians made use of it until the time of Origen (A.D. 250), and today many feel that the name Peter is a pseudonym.

Authorship

The author claimed to be Peter in 1:1 and asserted that he was an eyewitness of Jesus' transfiguration (1:16-18). His claim to be an apostle and the admission of friendship with Paul (3:15) clearly indicate that the writer intended to be seen as Peter.

Several features have contributed to the questioning of the genuineness of Petrine authorship. The epistle was little used in the early church. No clear second-century usage of the book appears. There are few usages in the third century, and only in the fourth century did it gain general acceptance. Origen's use of the book indicated that he knew of it, but he classified it among the disputed books of the New Testament. Despite these difficulties the church eventually accepted it as genuine and as worthy of inclusion in the canon.

Some have questioned the relationship of 2 Peter to Jude. Second Peter 2 and Jude have sections that are almost identical. Did one copy the other, or did both copy a common source? Many feel that Peter copied Jude, and this would lead to dating the book far beyond Peter's lifetime. Some evidence exists that the false teachers are seen as future in 2 Peter (2:1) but already present in Jude 4. This feature would point to an earlier date for 2 Peter.

Still others have found that the cumbersome language of 2 Peter is unlike that of 1 Peter. Some of the words used in 2 Peter are difficult, unfamiliar words which a Galilean fisherman might not know. It is possible that a helper assisted Peter with the writing and that this fisherman had learned better Greek with the passing of time.

Peter's reference to Paul in 3:15-16 is interpreted by some as a suggestion that Paul's epistles had been written, collected, and distributed. This would obviously have been at a time long after Peter's death. A reading of Peter's statements in 3:15-16 demands only that Peter had read those writings of Paul available up to the time of Peter's own writing. Peter could have found these writings through his widespread travels.

Those who deny Petrine authorship of 2 Peter have not succeeded in showing how a pseudepigraphical author could avoid being called dishonest. Despite some difficulties it is better to accept the claim of the epistle for Petrine authorship.

Date

Peter anticipated that his death would be soon (1:14-15). Assuming Peter wrote both 1 and 2 Peter, we can observe that Peter called this his second writing to the same readers (3:1). There is little specific information by which to arrive at an exact date, but it seems likely that 2 Peter was written shortly after 1 Peter. A time in the mid to late 60s shortly before Peter's demise seems acceptable.

Recipients

This letter lacks a specific address as 1 Peter contains. If we assume that Peter wrote the letter, "my second letter" (2 Pet 3:1) would indicate that he was writing to the same group that received the first letter. The statement of 1:16 suggests that Peter had spoken or preached to this group, but we have no knowledge of when or how this occurred. It seems best to suggest that Peter wrote to churches located in the northern part of Asia Minor.

The letter contains little indication of Peter's location as he wrote. We may leave this as an open question, for a decision on this issue does not affect our interpretation of the book.

Theme

Peter centered his emphasis on an exposure of the work of malicious false teachers (2 Pet 2). Whereas the First Letter of Peter dealt with external opposition to the readers, this letter focuses on internal opposition within the church.

In chapter 1 Peter urged that his readers grow in the virtues of faith, goodness, knowledge, self-control, perseverance, godliness, kindness, and love (2 Pet 1:5-9). Growing Christians would not be susceptible to heretical influence.

In 2 Peter 2 he described the moral errors of the heretics, and in 2 Peter 3 he exposed their doctrinal error in the denial of Jesus' return. He concluded with an appeal for growth as an antidote to pernicious heresy.

Literary Form

Several passages in 2 Peter indicate that Peter wrote to a specific congregation (2 Pet 1:16; 2:1; 3:1). The entire letter is an earnest warning against false teachers and an appeal for growth in maturity. Peter made little use of the Old Testament in quotations (but see 2 Pet 2:22), but there is frequent allusion to Old Testament characters and events (2 Pet 2:4-8).

I. Greetings (1:1-2)
II. Provisions for Spiritual Growth (1:3-21)
III. The Danger of False Teaching (2:1-22)
IV. A Reminder of God's Hope (3:1-13)
V. Closing Commands (3:14-18)

Purpose and Theology

Peter felt strongly that his death was near (2 Pet 1:14-15). He wanted to leave a spiritual testament that would provide helpful instruction after his departure. He provided warning against the character and false teaching of heretics who would infiltrate the church (2:1-19; 3:1-4). To provide protection against their errors, he urged a development of proper Christian virtues (1:3-11) and a constant growth in God's grace (3:17-18).

Peter held to a high view of Scripture (1:19-21), and he viewed Paul's writings as "Scripture" (3:16). He designated Jesus Christ as "Savior" and "Lord" (1:1-2), and he outlined his observation of Jesus' transfiguration (1:16-18). He affirmed the return of Christ (3:1-4) and asserted God's sovereign control of the events of history (3:13). He used the certainty of Christ's return as an incentive to appeal for godly living (3:14).

1:1-2
Greetings

Peter identified himself as a servant and an apostle of Jesus Christ. He addressed his words to those who had received faith in Christ. His references in 1:16; 2:1; and 3:1 suggest that he had a specific congregation in mind. Peter wanted his readers to experience God's loving favor and spiritual wholeness because of their clear, personal knowledge of Jesus.

1:3-21
Provisions for Spiritual Growth

Peter presented four sources of power for spiritual development in his readers. He wanted the commitment of his readers to be a throbbing, pulsating experience that was maturing in its understanding.

First, he assumed the calling and election of his readers (1:3-11). Their special position in God's plan had provided a union with Christ which allowed them to overcome the moral corruption of the world (1:3-4). The new birth of these readers and their receipt of God's blessings provided an incentive to nurture eight qualities of Christian character in their lives (1:5-7). If Peter's readers developed these Christian graces, they would not fall into spiritual ruin, and they would have a glorious entrance into God's presence (1:10).

Second, Peter mentioned his own witness as an incentive for spiritual growth (1:12-15). Peter's use of the future tense (v. 12) may suggest that he was considering writing a document in the future that would remind his readers of his teaching. Peter felt that his coming death made the writing of this testament imperative (1:14-15). He intended, as long as he was alive, to stimulate his friends to devoted commitment by repeated reminders (1:13).

As a third source of power Peter mentioned the majestic glory of Christ (1:16-18). The recipients of 2 Peter had likely encountered those who mocked the idea of a powerful, heavenly Christ who could strengthen them for godly living. Peter had been an eyewitness of Christ's majesty in the transfiguration. He could testify that the glory of Jesus was a reality they could experience.

A final source of power for the readers was the prophetic message of Scripture (1:19-21). Peter felt that the transfiguration and other events in Jesus' life made the scriptural picture of Jesus more sure and certain. Christians are able to find guidance from this word until Christ returns in person. Peter stated that the Scripture was reliable because it had a divine rather than human origin.

2:1-22
The Danger of False Teaching

Peter used pictorial words to warn his readers of the danger they faced from the false teachers. In 2:1-3 he pictured the immorality and greed of the false teachers. In 2:4-9 he used Old Testament examples of judgment on sin in order to show the certainty of punishment for followers of the false teachers. He described God's condemnation of the angels who sinned (v. 4), the judgment of the world of Noah (v. 5), and the destruction of the cities of Sodom and Gomorrah (v. 6). He promised deliverance for the godly by referring to the preservation of Noah and Lot (vv. 5,7,9). He denounced the pride, lust, and greed of the heretics (2:10-16). He indicated that those who followed the empty teachings of the heretics were deluded by empty promises (2:17-19).

In 2:20-22 Peter warned that those who had made a superficial commitment to Christ and had turned back to sin were in a more culpable state than before their response. The false teachers had experienced some knowledge of Christian truth which had given them short victory over worldly corruption. A true knowledge of Jesus would have affected them permanently. They were in a worse condition because they had turned from the truth about Christ which they had once received. Their condition of willful rejection made their disobedience a more blameworthy experience. The two proverbs in verse 22 show the folly of returning to a life-style of disobedience after an initial response toward Christ. Peter would scarcely use the terms "dog" and "sow" of believers. The passing of time had demonstrated that the false teachers had made a pretense of faith in Christ, but their faith was not genuine.

3:1-13
A Reminder of God's Hope

Peter discussed a doctrinal failure of the false teachers, their denial of Jesus' return. In 3:1-4 he reminded his readers of the incentive to obedience provided by the promise of Jesus' return. False teachers were looking skeptically at such promises because the stability of the universe did not indicate that God was about to break again into history (3:3-4).

Peter responded to the denials of the heretics by suggesting that the present regularity of the world was not an argument for permanent continuance in the same form. The God who held the universe together by His word could alter it with the same word (3:7). In favor of a belief in Jesus' return, Peter also argued that God viewed time differently from human beings (3:8). The true explanation for the delay in Christ's return was to allow an opportunity for sinners to respond in faith to Jesus (3:9). Peter believed that Christ's promise to return would be fulfilled with destructive power at a time when sinners would least expect it (3:10).

The fact of Jesus' promised return could provide strength for a new attitude of holiness and commitment (3:11). Peter hinted that Christians could "speed" Jesus' return by renewed vigor in evangelism and devout living (3:12).

3:14-18
Closing Commands

Peter reminded his readers that an anticipation of Christ's future return carried with it the incentive to produce a holy life (v. 14). He referred to Paul's writings as a support for Peter's belief that divine patience was a factor in the delay of Jesus' return (vv. 15-16). Many see a reference by Peter to Romans, but Peter left his Pauline source unstated. Peter acknowledged the difficulty of some of Paul's teachings, but he suggested their authority by naming them as "Scripture" (3:15-16). Peter boldly stated that his recipients could protect themselves spiritually by mature Christian growth. The "knowledge" they needed was a development in personal acquaintance with Christ (3:18).

Theological Significance

The abiding emphases in 2 Peter, with its call for spiritual growth (chap. 1), its warning of false teaching (chap. 2), and its call for holy living in view of the Lord's certain return (chap. 3) are just as relevant for our generation as they were for Peter's. Such features as these have commended it to the consciousness of the church as an inspired writing. Peter's two letters help the church focus its response to external opposition (1 Peter) as well as to evildoers who have come into the church (2 Peter).

Questions for Reflection

1. Was Peter suggesting that works earn salvation from God, or was he suggesting that they prove the possession of salvation? What is the difference between these options (1:5-11)?

2. What did God do in order to deliver Noah and Lot from a compromise with temptation? Has God helped you in a similar way?

3. Do the proverbs of 2:22 teach that actions demonstrate the nature of an individual or that actions change the nature of an individual?

4. In 3:1-7 Peter argued that both he and the false teachers saw that there was regularity in nature. What opposite conclusions did both draw from that regularity?

5. According to 3:10-13, what should the hope of Christ's return produce in the life of a Christian?

Sources for Additional Study

Green, Michael. *The Second Epistle of Peter and the Epistle of Jude. Tyndale New Testament Commentaries.* Grand Rapids: Eerdmans, 1968.

Vaughan, Curtis and Lea, Thomas D. *1, 2 Peter, Jude. Bible Study Commentary.* Grand Rapids: Zondervan, 1988.

1 JOHN

Leaders in the early church assumed that John the apostle wrote this letter although the author never identified himself by name. Polycarp, Irenaeus, and Tertullian all argued for apostolic authorship of this epistle.

Evidence supporting apostolic authorship is the similar vocabulary between the Gospel and the Epistle. Such terms as "light" and "eternal life" appear in both writings. The author claimed that he was a companion of Christ during His earthly ministry (1:1-4). His description of his readers as "dear children" (2:1) indicates a person of sufficient authority to address his audience in this man-

John

ner. All of these features point toward apostolic authorship. Some who question apostolic authorship favor an authorship by "John the elder" mentioned in Eusebius (*Ecclesiastical History* 3.39). Some feel that the term "John the elder" is merely an alternate way of referring to John the apostle.

Date

Little specific material is available for a precise dating of 1 John. Tradition indicates that John later spent a significant ministry in Ephesus. The epistle is usually dated during that ministry. The close link with the Fourth Gospel demands a date during the same period as the writing of that Gospel. Most who assume a common authorship for Gospel and Epistle will date the epistle in the mid-90s.

Recipients

The letter has no named recipients mentioned within it. Identification of the readers as "dear children" (2:1) and "Dear friends" (2:7) suggests they were a group well known by John. It is best to view the letter as addressed to a group of people perhaps in more than one Asian community. John personally knew them and wrote to warn them of the infiltration of false teaching (4:1-2).

Theme

The Epistle of John presents three criteria for testing the Christian profession of teachers and individual Christians. First, professing Christians needed to present righteousness as the right behavior (2:3-4). Second they must demonstrate love as the correct attitude of Christian living (4:8). Third, they needed to hold to the correct view of Christ as the proper teaching of Christians (4:3). Those who demonstrate these three traits have eternal life. John would repeat these three themes several times in the epistle as tests to determine the presence of eternal life.

Literary Form

The letter lacks an introduction and greeting from the author. It expresses no thanksgiving and lacks a concluding salutation. The author never mentioned the name of another Christian in the writing. He never quoted the Old Testament. The epistle reads like a sermon, but there are sections in which there are clear indications that John wrote to specific people with specific problems (2:1,26).

The style of writing involves much repetition, often with deceptively simply phrasing of words. John alternated emphases on the necessity of right attitude, right action, and right belief. John believed that the practice of these patterns demonstrated the possession of eternal life and distinguished believers from unbelievers.

I. Basis of Fellowship with God (1:1–2:6)
II. The New Commandment of Love (2:7-17)
III. The Christian and False Teaching (2:18-28)
IV. The Need to Practice Righteousness (2:29–3:10)
V. The Priority of Love for One Another (3:11-24)
VI. Exposure of False Teaching (4:1-6)
VII. The Importance of God's Love (4:7-21)
VIII. The Victory of Faith (5:1-12)
IX. Assurance of Eternal Life (5:13-21)

Purpose and Theology

John wrote to strengthen the joy (1:4) of his readers and to give them assurance of their relationship with Jesus Christ (5:13). He also wanted to prepare them for dealing with false teachers (4:1-3).

John advocated the genuineness of Christ's humanity (1:1-2), and he called those who questioned the reality of Jesus' incarnation "Antichrists" (4:1-3). He presented the death of Christ as an atoning sacrifice for sins (2:2), and he taught the return of Christ (2:28). He denied the idea that Christians could make a practice of sinning (3:8-9), and he called for a demonstration of the reality of faith by ministry (3:16-18).

He opposed both moral laxity and theological errors centering around the person and work of Christ. He opposed Docetism, the denial of the reality of Christ's body, by teaching that he had heard, seen, and touched Christ (1:1). He also emphasized that the same Jesus Christ appeared at both the baptism and the crucifixion (5:6).

1:1–2:6
Basis of Fellowship with God

John began the epistle with a proclamation of the apostolic message. He proclaimed the preexistence and genuine humanity of Christ. He expressed that he was a reliable witness of Jesus' message (1:1-4). In verse 4 he expressed that producing joy in his readers was one of the purposes of this letter. John emphasized that a full experience of joy depended on genuine fellowship with Christ.

In 1:5–2:6 John emphasized the importance of right action in the Christian life. He began with a declaration of the divine character in 1:5-7. John stated that God had revealed Himself as a God of perfect purity. Anyone who

ATONEMENT

The English word *atone* means *to make reconciliation*. It is based on the English phrase *at one*. Generally the word *atone* refers to the condition "at-oneness" or "reconciliation." Specifically the word is used to refer to the process by which obstacles to such reconciliation are removed. The entire Bible demonstrates that outside of some atoning action, humankind is estranged from God. This alienation, brought on by sin, must be remedied.

In the OT *atone* and *atonement* are based on the Hebrew *kpr*, which means *to cover* or, as some have suggested, *to wipe clean*. Words based on *kpr* are found primarily in the Pentateuch with a few references elsewhere. The Septuagint translated *kpr* and its derivatives primarily by the word family containing *exilaskomai, exilasmos,* and *hilasterion.*

The word *atonement* is not found in most translations of the NT. (However, the NIV has "atone," "sacrifice of atonement," "place of atonement," and "atoning sacrifice." Also note that Romans 5:11 in the KJV has "atonement," but it renders *katallage* and is properly translated "reconciliation," as seen in all modern translations.)

The *concept* of atonement pervades the fabric of NT thought. In the NT atonement is centered in Christ's incarnation and especially His work on the cross. The NT presents human beings in their natural condition as totally estranged from God. They are "alienated and hostile in mind, engaged in evil deeds" (Col 1:21). This alienation and hostility outside of Christ is the basic presupposition of NT anthropology. It graphically presents humanity's need for atonement. The cause for human estrangement is persistent rebellion to the will of God. God's holiness and righteousness make clear that sin cannot be ignored; sin has its retribution. "The wages of sin is death" (Rom 6:23). Outside of God's intervention and provision, humanity is absolutely helpless to remedy the situation (Rom 5:6,8). The sinner is "dead in . . . trespasses and sins" (Eph 2:1).

God provides deliverance from that which held humankind away from Him. In His infinite compassion and love, He provides atonement in the person of Jesus Christ. The stated purpose of the incarnation was that Jesus came "to seek and to save that which was lost" (Luke 19:10). Christ's atoning work is particularly connected with His death on the cross. "We are reconciled to God through the death of His Son" (Rom 5:10). This death provided "propitiation in His blood," which must be accompanied "by faith" (Rom 3:25).

God is the source of atonement. In the OT God had provided the sacrificial system to effect reconciliation, but in the NT God not only initiates atonement but He also brings it to completion. In no sense is the merciful Son championing the rights of humankind against the severe Father who gives forgiveness only grudgingly. "God was in Christ reconciling the world to himself" (2 Cor 5:19).

The result of the atonement is that the breach between God and humanity is bridged. Fellowship with God is restored because that which has disrupted that relationship has been removed. Through Christ's sacrifice not only is humanity's sin removed, but we also are delivered from our former "futile way of life" (1 Pet 1:18). Another consequence of the atonement is that the individual in Christ is delivered from selfishness and enabled to live with Christ as Lord (Rom 14:9; 2 Cor 5:15).

The NT presents a rich and varied treasury of expression concerning the atonement. The words *hilasterion, hilaskomai, and hilasmos* are from a root word meaning *appease* or *propitiate*. In Romans 3:25 the word *hilasterion* is rendered "propitiation" in the KJV and NASB. It is translated "sacrifice of atonement" in the NIV and "expiation" in the RSV. In Hebrews 9:5 the same word is translated "mercy seat" in the KJV, NASB, and RSV and "place of atonement" by the NIV. In Hebrews 2:17 the word *hilaskomai* is translated "reconciliation" by the KJV, "propitiation" by the NASB, "atonement" by the NIV, "expiation" by the RSV. The same word in Luke 18:13 is rendered "be merciful" in the KJV, NASB, and RSV and "have mercy" in the NIV.

In both 1 John 2:2 and 4:10 the word *hilasmos* is translated "propitiation" by the NASB, "atoning sacrifice" by the NIV, and "expiation" by the RSV.

A second word family containing *lytron, lytroo, apolytrosis,* and *antilytron* should be explored. The first of these words is fairly consistently understood as "ransom" by the KJV; the second is given as "redeem" or "redeemed"; the third and fourth are "ransom." The Bible student should also consider the sacrificial terminology applied to Christ.

Sin effectively keeps people from God. In His atoning work God has secured reconciliation through the work of Jesus Christ. "For he himself is our peace, who . . . broke down the barrier of the dividing wall, by abolishing in his flesh the enmity . . . establishing peace, and might reconcile them both in one body to God through the cross, by it having put to death the enmity" (Eph 2:14-16). In Christ atonement for the believer has been made complete. □

desired fellowship with Him must walk in obedience to His revealed will. John explained that those who denied the practice of sin were deceived, but those who admitted their sin experienced forgiveness and cleansing (1:8-10).

John wrote these words in order to prevent his readers from committing sin. He felt that whenever we commit sin, Christ functions as our advocate in the Father's presence and assures our standing before Him (2:1). Christ functions for believers both as a defender and as an atoning sacrifice. The sinlessness of Jesus qualifies Him to be our defender or advocate.

Christ volunteered to serve as our atoning sacrifice for sin. The term translated "atoning sacrifice" (2:2) is sometimes rendered "propitiation." The term suggests that our sin against God demands that some form of sacrifice be given to satisfy God's offended holiness. Something in God's nature demanded this propitiation, but something in that same nature was moved with love to provide it. The love of the Father led Him to provide the sacrifice of His Son.

The revelation of God's purity and holiness led John to emphasize that obedience to God's commands provides fellowship with God. Those who would enjoy fellowship with God must follow in the love, holiness, and service that characterized Christ (2:3-6).

2:7-17
The New Commandment of Love

John emphasized the importance of right attitude as an evidence of genuine Christianity. A believer will love Christian brothers and not the world.

John indicated that the command to love others was a new command (v. 7). It is new in that Christ's own example of love filled the command with new meaning and application. The response to the command of love is a clear indicator of character (vv. 9-11). One who habitually fails to love others shows that he lives in the darkness of sin and not in the light of God's presence.

In 2:12-14 John assured his readers that they were recipients of strength and help from the Word of God to assist in their spiritual struggles. In 2:15-17 John urged his readers not to love the pagan, self-centered life-style that surrounded them. Such a worldly love excluded love for God and also led the Christian to focus on a style of living that was slowly dying.

2:18-28
The Christian and False Teaching

John emphasized the importance of right belief as an indication of genuine Christianity. The term "antichrist" described those who disrupted fellowship in the churches by holding the wrong doctrine about Christ. The distinctive beliefs of these false teachers appear in verses 22-23.

Believers stood secure against the false teaching of the antichrists because of three sources of strength. First, they had the anointing of the Holy Spirit. This provided the capacity to understand spiritual things (v. 20). Second, they had made a personal commitment to the Christian message (vv. 24-25). Third, they were living in union with Jesus Christ (v. 28).

2:29–3:10
The Need to Practice Righteousness

John again emphasized the importance of right action as a demonstration of Christian commitment. Christians who had been divinely begotten of God had the privilege of experiencing God's love and living as members of His family (2:29–3:2). They were to demonstrate their family membership by righteous living. John indicated that Christ had come to take away our sins (3:5). Jesus had died for the purpose of causing us to stop sinning.

John pointed out that the person who made a practice of sinning had never known Christ (v. 6). In verse 9 he indicated that the experience of a believer in conversion rendered the practice of sin a moral impossibility. John was not suggesting that a Christian will never commit an act of sin. He did indicate that a believer could not live in the practice of sin.

The conclusion in verse 10 pointed out the importance of righteous behavior and also underscored the significance of loving other believers. It makes a good transition from discussion of right action to another presentation of the proper attitude, an attitude of love.

3:11-24
The Priority of Love for One Another

John mentioned the importance of the demonstration of a proper attitude, love, as evidence of genuine faith. John presented love as the proof that we have passed from death into life (3:14). He located the chief revelation of love in the sacrificial death of Jesus Christ (v. 16). The chief manner in which we as believers demonstrate our love is by our kindness and mercy in ministry to others (vv. 17-18).

In verses 19-24 John indicated that our love brought with it an assurance of our standing with God. If we demonstrate this love, we are able to set our hearts at rest in God's presence. The assurance that love brings will carry with it an experience of boldness before God (v. 21) and also an assurance of effectiveness in the practice of prayer (v. 22).

THE VALUE OF HUMAN LIFE

What does it mean to be human? What is personhood? Is it ever morally justifiable to take human life? These and other emotionally charged questions, all of which revolve around the perennial issue of the value of human life, are being raised anew in the current debates concerning a host of complex ethical issues.

The Bible clearly puts forth what may be termed a high view of the value of human life. In contrast to many contemporary outlooks, however, the Scriptures do not ground this evaluation in society or even in the human person, as important as that is, but squarely in the creative activity of God. This activity gives a special place in creation to human beings as those who bear the image of God.

These themes are sounded in the opening chapters of the Bible. The first creation account reports God's intent as expressed on the sixth day of the creative week: "Let us make man in our image" (Gen 1:26). God's purpose comes to fruition in the creation of human beings—male and female—each of whom, as a result, is to share in the divine image. Genesis 1 and 2 indicate that the image of God is a multisided concept. It refers to the responsibility of acting as stewards over creation. It includes as well the relational nature of human beings: we are created to live together in community with one another and with God. As a result, human life is of value because God has entered into a covenant with humans, entrusting them with a special purpose, a specific role in the divine plan for creation.

Creation in God's image subsequently became an integral part of the Hebrew mind-set. It forms a basis for biblical injunctions concerning fair treatment of others. God's covenant with Noah after the flood, for example, includes a serious penalty for murder, based on an appeal to the creation of each person in the divine image (Gen 9:6). So ingrained was this idea that James could matter-of-factly state to his original Hebrew-Christian readership, "With the tongue we praise our Lord and Father, and with it we curse men, who have been made in God's likeness" (3:9). He appealed to human creation in the divine image as a basis for respecting other humans even in our speaking to and about each other.

Creation in God's image and the resulting value of human life is incomplete, however, without the future orientation given to it by the NT. For Paul, Jesus Christ is preeminently the image of God (2 Cor 4:4; Col 1:15).

Believers truly participate in the image in that they are being transformed into Christ's likeness (2 Cor 3:18), a process directed toward the coming of God's kingdom at Christ's return (1 John 3:2). As a result, the value of human life is ultimately based on God's salvation purpose, which is directed toward the future completion of all God's activities. At that point God's purposes in the creation of humans will find its full realization.

On the basis of these considerations, the value of life can and should be seen as bestowed on all humans by God as God's gift. Because all persons are the objects of God's love in Christ and are all potential participants in God's kingdom, all human life is valuable. God calls all humans and human society to acknowledge the value God and God alone has placed in each human being. □

4:1-6
The Exposure of False Teaching

John expressed the importance of right belief as an evidence of genuine Christianity. John was speaking of people who claimed to be Christians but who spoke as deadly opponents of Christianity. He was also referring to church services much more informal than our own. In these early services visitors could stand and claim to speak by the Spirit of God. John wanted to provide direction to distinguish between the true and the false.

John directed his readers to test the words of those who claimed to speak for God because of the possibility of the presence of false prophets (v. 1). The test by which the utterances were to be judged was the acceptance of Jesus Christ as God's incarnate Son (vv. 2-3). As his readers struggled with the presence of false teaching, John assured them that the victory ultimately belonged to them (v. 4). He also indicated that the worldly message of the false prophets would attract an audience that was gullible in their acceptance of falsehood (v. 5).

4:7-21
The Importance of God's Love

In this section John again underscored the importance of a demonstration of love. He presented love as a disposition that originated in the divine nature.

John appealed for believers to love for two reasons. First, such love has its source and dynamic in God (v. 7). Second, God is characterized by love (v. 8). Both reasons blend together so that one runs into the other. The greatness of the divine love for us leaves us with an incentive to love one another (v. 11). Our practice of love for one another provides evidence that God's love for us has attained its goal (v. 12).

In verses 13-16 the apostle discussed the relationship between love and the indwelling of God. He suggested that it is not enough merely to know that God is love. Believers must live daily in the sphere of divine love. In so doing they genuinely live in God's presence and have God living in them.

In verses 17-21 John mentioned two evidences of the presence of a ripened fruit of love in a Christian's life. First, such love provides confidence on the day of the coming judgment (vv. 17-18). Second, this love leads to a genuine concern for fellow Christians (vv. 19-21).

5:1-12
The Victory of Faith

John began this section by stating the chief confession of faith that should characterize Christians. Christians are those who believe that Jesus is the Messiah, the Son of God (v. 1). Those who are genuine believers demonstrate it by their love for God and obedience to His commandments (vv. 2-3). The faith that provides strength for spiritual victory is the faith that Jesus is God's incarnate Son (v. 5).

In verse 6 John outlined more specifically who Jesus is as the Son of God. John's opponents held that Jesus was a mere man to whom the divine Christ spirit came at baptism and from whom this spirit departed before crucifixion. John taught that Jesus was the divine Son of God at both baptism and crucifixion, throughout the entire course of His life.

In verses 7-12 John showed that our faith in Jesus Christ has a good foundation. The KJV text makes a reference to the Trinity in verse 7 that most modern translations omit. The best texts of verses 7-8 suggest that the Spirit, the water, and the blood all unite in their witness to Christ. The Spirit presented His witness at Jesus' baptism and throughout the totality of Jesus' ministry. The terms "water" and "blood" are a reference, respectively, to Christ's baptism and death. John also referred to the witness of the Father and to the witness of personal experience (vv. 9-10). The truth to which all of the preceding witnesses testified was that eternal life is available only through God's Son, Jesus (vv. 11-12).

5:13-21
The Assurance of Eternal Life

In 5:13 John indicated that he had written this epistle to lead believers to an assurance that they possessed eternal life. John suggested that assurance that we have been accepted with God provides an assurance toward receiving answers in prayer (vv. 14-15). He urged that Christians practice intercessory prayer, particularly for fellow believers caught in the trickery of sin (vv. 16-17). He concluded with the statement that Jesus' death had made possible holiness in the life of each Christian (v. 18), the new birth (v. 19), and a genuine knowledge of God (v. 20).

Theological Significance

This letter speaks to contemporary Christians in a significant way. Today there are many people who profess to know God and have fellowship with Him but do not demonstrate such faith at all. John's tests concerning obedience, love, and belief provide warnings for the unfaithful as well assurance for genuine believers. To be sure that we know God, we must keep His commandment. If we lack love for others, it indicates we do not know the love of God in our hearts. Foundationally we must believe rightly about Jesus Christ. He is the Christ, the Son of God, who has come in the flesh. This important triad calls the contemporary church to a strong, balanced faith. We must grow stronger and stronger in all areas of our Christian life.

Questions for Reflection

1. List the three evidences of eternal life John focused on in this epistle.
2. Who were the "antichrists"? What special doctrinal truth did they deny?
3. List the purposes for the writing of 1 John according to the statements of 1:3-4 and 5:13.
4. When John urged his readers to show love for a Christian brother (3:17-18), what type of demonstration of love was he seeking?

Sources for Additional Study

Marshall, I. Howard. *The Epistles of John. The New International Commentary on the New Testament.* Grand Rapids: Eerdmans, 1978.

Stott, J. R. W. *The Epistles of John. Tyndale New Testament Commentaries.* Grand Rapids: Eerdmans, 1964.

Vaughan, Curtis. *1, 2, 3 John. Bible Study Guide.* Grand Rapids: Zondervan, 1970.

2 JOHN

The brevity and lack of a specific address for 2 John led to its neglect in the early church. Few early Christian leaders made reference to it, but some knew of the epistle. Eusebius placed it and 3 John among the disputed books of the New Testament, but after his time both writings were generally received with little dispute.

The writer described himself as "the elder," and many have seen this as an affectionate title for the aged apostle John. This epistle has a similarity of style and vocabulary with 1 John and with John's Gospel. The false teaching of 2 John 7 is similar to that of 1 John 4:1-3. Some have felt that an unknown "John the Elder" penned this writing, but this elder is a shadowy figure whose existence is uncertain. It is best to see John the apostle as the elder who wrote these words.

Date

The interval between the writing of 1 John and 2 John was not great. The false teaching John had mentioned in 1 John 4:1-3 was still a problem for the readers of 2 John. A date in the mid-90s seems most likely.

Recipients

John wrote to "the chosen lady and her children." This may be a reference to a personal friend of John. Some have pointed to the use of "lady" in verses 1,5 and the description of her children in verses 1,4 as evidence to take the term in reference to a person. Some have even named the woman as "Kyria" (the Greek word for "lady") or "Electa" (the Greek word for "chosen").

Another more likely interpretation is to see "lady" as a personification for a local church and its members. The Greek word for "church" is feminine in gender. This gender is normally used in speaking of the church. Also a church would more likely have a reputation for truth than a single family (2 John 4).

Theme

John mentioned twin themes in writing 2 John. First, he urged his readers to practice love with one another (2 John 5). Second, he called them to practice truth in affirming the correct doctrine about Jesus (2 John 7-11).

Literary Form

This writing is more clearly in letter form than 1 John. John mentioned specific recipients and also included a final greeting. He wrote to a specific community with a doctrinal problem. The epistle contains no reference or allusion to the Old Testament.

I. Greetings (vv. 1-3)
II. Encouragement to Christian Love (vv. 4-6)
III. Warning against False Teaching (vv. 7-11)
IV. Conclusion (vv. 12-13)

Purpose and Theology

The false teachers whom John denounced denied the true humanity of Jesus Christ. Their specific error was likely Docetism, a denial of the reality of Jesus' human body. The false teachers traveled among the churches and took advantage of Christian hospitality. John expected his readers to offer hospitality to traveling Christians, but he urged his readers to refuse such hospitality to itinerant heretics (vv. 10-11).

John also urged his readers to practice love with one another. This love would lead them to walk in obedience to God's commands (vv. 5-6).

Verses 1-3
Greeting

John described himself as an "elder." The term may refer either to an official title (see 1 Pet 5:1), or it may describe John affectionately as an old man.

John designated his recipients as "the chosen lady and her children." Some have felt that her name was "Kyria" and others have chosen "Electa." If her name were "Electa," we would have to say that she also had a sister of the same name (v. 13). If the recipient were an individual, she would likely be anonymous. The phrase is more likely a reference to some local church over which the elder had authority. The "children" were members of that church. John's statement of love (vv. 1-2) and the command to love (v. 5) would be more suitable for a church than for a person. The command not to host false teachers (vv. 7-11) is also more suitable for a local church than for a single home.

The feature that united John with his readers was their common love for the truth (vv. 1b-2). Grace indicated God's provision of salvation, and God's gift of mercy demonstrated the depth of human need of it. Peace is a description of the character of salvation.

Verses 4-6
Encouragement to Christian Love

John had met some of the children of the lady, perhaps members of the church, in his travel. Their conduct had impressed him. The meeting led to a single request: Love one another. That request led John to consider the link between love and obedience. If we love God, we will obey Him. Our love for Him expresses itself in our obedience.

Verses 7-11
Warning against False Teachers

John warned against deceivers who led others astray. The doctrine they stressed involved a denial of the incarnation. Christians affirmed the genuine humanity of Jesus when they said, "Christ has come in the flesh." Jesus did not become Christ at the baptism or cease to be Christ before His death. He was Christ come in the flesh.

John warned his readers against losing their reward for faithful service by falling into doctrinal error (v. 8). He affirmed that one who erred at this important point did not have God (v. 9).

John included an additional warning in verses 10-11. He warned against providing any sort of official welcome for those who erred in their doctrine of Christ. John was not promoting intolerance, nor was he violating his earlier appeal to "love one another." He was warning against extending any form of support for those who erred at the point of the genuine humanity of Christ. We should not apply John's words to cause us to separate from those whose opinions we happen to dislike.

Verses 12-13
Conclusion

Although John had much he desired to communicate to his readers, he did not want to use another sheet of papyrus for writing. He preferred to speak face to face so that he could not be misunderstood. He anticipated a time of future visitation so that they might experience a future completion of joy.

The burial of Jesus Christ—another affirmation of His humanity.

John's concluding word in verse 13 sounds more like a message of greeting from members of one church to the recipients to whom he wrote.

Questions for Reflection

1. What is the relationship between our love for God and our disobedience to Him (see John 14:15)?

2. Many Christians today use the term "Antichrist" to refer to a powerful leader at the end time. How does John's use of the term contrast to this?

3. Did John suggest that we should be rude to those with whom we disagree doctrinally?

Sources for Additional Study

See the list at the conclusion of 1 John.

3 JOHN

There is little evidence for the use of 3 John before the third century. The brevity and lack of a specific address for the letter would have contributed to its neglect. Eusebius classified the letter among the disputed writings of the New Testament, but the church came to accept it as a product of the apostle John.

The use of the term "elder" in common with 2 John makes it likely that both writings came from the same writer. Both letters also make reference to the practice of walking in the truth (2 John 4; 3 John 3). These similar practices plus the opinion of early Christian leaders make the acceptance of apostolic authorship the wisest choice.

Date

The similarities just mentioned make it likely that both 2 John and 3 John were written near the same time. It is possible that the writer referred to 2 John in his description of writing to the church in 3 John 9. No clear scriptural evidence exists, however, of the order of writing the two letters. A date in the mid-90's seems most likely.

Recipients

John named the recipient of 3 John (v. 1), but we have no idea of the specific location to which he wrote. Church tradition has placed John at Ephesus during the latter years of his life. It seems reasonable that this is a letter to some churches in Asia for which John had pastoral responsibilities. It is not certain from 3 John that both Gaius and Diotrephes belonged to the same church, but both men probably lived close together.

Theme

This letter presents a contrast between the truth and service demonstrated by Gaius and the arrogance shown by Diotrephes. John emphasized that "truth" was a type of behavior that agreed with the doctrine Christians professed (3 John 8). The autocratic behavior of Diotrephes violated this behavior. John wanted to bring his domineering practices to an end.

Literary Form

This writing has the form of a typical letter. Both the author and recipient are identified. A conclusion with a collection of Christian greetings appears at the end. The misbehavior of Diotrephes provided a specific occasion for the writing of the letter.

I. Greeting (v. 1)
II. Commendation of Gaius's Hospitality (vv. 2-8)
III. Condemnation of the Rebellion of Diotrephes (vv. 9-11)
IV. Prospects of a Future Visit (vv. 12-14)

Purpose and Theology

John wrote both to commend and rebuke. He commended Gaius for his unselfish behavior and Christian hospitality. He rebuked the domineering Diotrephes for his dictatorial practices. He also praised Demetrius (v. 12), who probably carried the letter. The length of the letter allows little opportunity for theological expression.

Verse 1
Greeting

John's use of the term "elder" duplicates that of 2 John. It is impossible to determine whether Gaius was the same as others mentioned by that name in the New Testament (see Acts 19:29; 20:4). It was one of the most common names in the Roman Empire.

Verses 2-8
Commendation of Gaius's Hospitality

John acknowledged that the spiritual growth of Gaius was progressing well and wished that his physical health might be in the same condition. Some traveling missionaries ("brothers," vv. 3,5), probably sent out by John, had commended Gaius for his loyalty to the truth of the gospel (v. 3) and his demonstration of love (v. 6). John regarded Gaius as his spiritual child (v. 4) and indicated that a report of his spiritual growth filled him with joy.

John was fearful that the aggressive opposition of Diotrephes might lead Gaius to refrain from showing hospitality to traveling believers (vv. 6b,9-10). He urged Gaius

First John 5:21 warns against idolatry. In the above painting children are shown worshiping the goddess Diana—those on the left honoring her statue and those on the right forming a procession.

to continue what he had been doing.

Since we cannot know whether Gaius and Diotrephes attended the same church, we are uncertain of the nature of John's warning about Diotrephes. If both men were in the same church, John may have commended Gaius for not buckling under to Diotrephes. If they were in nearby churches, John could have warned Gaius about the high-handed actions of Diotrephes.

Verses 9-11
Condemnation of the Rebellion of Diotrephes

John denounced Diotrephes for his pride (v. 9), his wicked words, and his inhospitable treatment of traveling Christian missionaries (v. 10). The motives for Diotrephes' actions do not seem to have been theological but personal and moral. Diotrephes was dominated by personal ambition.

John may have feared that Gaius would follow carelessly the bad example of Diotrephes. This led him to warn Gaius to choose his examples carefully. Gaius was to follow those who practiced good, not evil (v. 11).

Verses 12-14
Prospects of a Future Visit

John commended Demetrius to the care of Gaius. He complimented Demetrius with the statement that "everyone" spoke well of him (v. 12).

John's heart was full of thoughts and ideas to convey to his readers, but he withheld them in anticipation of a future visit. He had much more to say than he could include on a single sheet of the writing material known as papyrus.

Questions for Reflection

1. For what actions did John commend Gaius? How can we duplicate his actions today?

2. For what actions did John rebuke Diotrephes? What forms would his disobedient actions take today?

Sources for Additional Study

See books listed for 1 John.

JUDE

The author identified himself as "a servant of Jesus Christ and a brother of James." In presenting himself as a brother of the Lord's half-brother (Jas 1:1), he modestly neglected to mention his own relationship to Jesus (Matt 13:55; Mark 6:3). Some have identified Jude as "Judas son of James" (Luke 6:16), but the author did not claim apostleship. He was initially an unbeliever (John 7:3-5), but he here displayed a vigorous faith.

The frequent use of the book in the early church, especially references by Tertullian and Origen, made it less controversial than 2 Peter. Some found its reference to apocryphal books a cause for questioning its genuineness.

Date

Suggestions for dating this letter vary widely. Little evidence is available for making a conclusive decision. We cannot be certain whether Jude was younger or older than the Lord, but it is likely that he was younger. If Jude were born during the early part of the first century, the letter could be dated from A.D. 65 to 80.

Some claim that the reference to "the salvation we share" (v. 3) implied a time in which Christians had agreed upon a body of widely accepted doctrine. This would be later than the likely lifetime of Jude. The reference to this common faith need mean no more than the common beliefs held by all Christians.

Others have suggested that the wickedness of the false teachers described in verses 5-13 represented a Gnostic viewpoint that appeared only during the second century. Jude's description would fit any heresy in which immorality was prominent. It is possible to link Jude's references clearly with a specific sect.

Recipients

No address for the readers appears in Jude. The readers might have been Jews or Gentiles who lived anywhere. Jude had a concrete situation in mind, but it is impossible to locate it precisely. The statements of verses 17-18 have led some to suggest that the readers knew apostles within the region of Palestine. This is a possible but unproven hypothesis.

Theme

Jude began with the intention of discussing the theme of "salvation." Awareness of the infiltration of false teachers led Jude to emphasize two features. First, he warned against and condemned false teachers who were heavily influencing his area. Second, he urged his readers to greater firmness and commitment.

Literary Form

Despite the lack of a specific address, Jude's Letter is directed to a specific situation. It is more impersonal than John's Epistles. Jude was fond of mentioning items in triads (v. 2: "mercy, peace, and love"; v. 11: Cain, Balaam, and Korah). The majestic doxology provides a moving conclusion to Jude's words (vv. 24-25).

I. Greetings (vv. 1-2)
II. Occasion for Writing (vv. 3-4)
III. Description of the False Teachers (vv. 5-16)
IV. Resisting the False Teachers (vv. 17-23)
V. Doxology (vv. 24-25)

Purpose and Theology

Jude intended to produce a message about the common salvation he shared with his readers (v. 3). His awareness of the appearance of heresy led him to change his emphasis to a denunciation of the heresy surrounding him. Jude gave direction for halting the advance of heresy among his readers in verses 17-23.

The epistle contains little theological content because the purpose was largely practical. One controversial feature of the book is the references to the apocryphal books of First Enoch (v. 14) and the Assumption of Moses (v. 9). Some have seen these references as a liability to accepting the authority of Jude, but Paul quoted a heathen poet in Acts 17:28. He also referred to a noncanonical writing in 2 Timothy 3:8. Jude appears to have viewed his references to the Apocrypha as authoritative, and he apparently accepted the historicity of the incident in the

Assumption of Moses. He used his references more as an illustration to substantiate his points.

Verses 1-2
Greetings

Jude identified himself as a follower of Jesus Christ and "a brother of James." Jude was listed among the brothers of Jesus (Mark 6:3). His brother James is the probable author of the Epistle of James. Jude gave no geographical designation to his readers, but he presented them as those who were "called," "loved by God," and "kept by Jesus Christ." Jude wished his readers an experience of mercy that would allow them to know the benefits of peace and love.

Verses 3-4
Occasion for Writing

Jude had prepared to write a letter on the theme of "salvation" when he learned of the entrance of false teachers. He urged his readers to contend for the faith by living godly, obedient lives. He described the false teachers as "godless men," who stood condemned before God because of their denial of Jesus' lordship.

Verses 5-16
Description of the False Teachers

Jude pictured the heretics as deserving to receive God's judgments just as the unbelieving Jews, the sinning angels, and the cities of Sodom and Gomorrah had merited judgment (vv. 5-7).

He showed that the false teachers were arrogantly defying God by their perverse moral behavior. They disdained angelic creatures whom they failed to understand. Jude commended the example of the angel Michael, who did not deal with the devil's protests on his own authority (v. 9). Jude used this story from the apocryphal Assumption of Moses to demonstrate a proper attitude toward the supernatural.

In verses 10-13 he used historical examples from the Old Testament to characterize the false teachers as materialistic and immoral. They were as greedy as Balaam and as rebellious as Korah.

In verses 14-15 Jude cited a statement from 1 Enoch to prove the reality of divine judgment upon the ungodly. Jude was not necessarily viewing 1 Enoch as inspired, but he was referring to a book his readers would know and respect.

Verses 17-23
Resisting the False Teachers

Peter reminded his readers that the apostles had warned against the divisiveness and spiritual emptiness of the coming false teachers (vv. 17-19). The recipients were to build themselves up with prayer and obedience (vv. 20-21). They also were to offer help to wandering believers who need both an experience of divine mercy and the wisdom to avoid corruption (vv. 22-23).

Verses 24-25
Doxology

Jude's mind focused on the power of almighty God who alone could provide the strength needed for full obedience. In verse 24 he praised God for His sustaining power toward believers. In verse 25 he ascribed "glory, majesty, power and authority" to God because of the work of Jesus Christ.

Theological Significance

Jude's warnings regarding false teachers need to be sounded again in today's churches. The people of God must contend for the faith that has been entrusted to them. Jude reminds us of the seriousness of the Christian faith and Christian teaching. False teachers who oppose the truth must be prepared to face the judgment of God. True believers must faithfully maintain the truth and keep themselves in the love of God. The exhortations to watch, pray, convince the doubters, and lead others into the way of salvation must be heard and obeyed.

Questions for Reflection

1. What is the best way to "contend" for the Christian faith? See Jesus' words in John 13:34-35; 14:21.

2. List some of the characteristics of the false teachers Jude mentioned in verses 5-16. How common are these traits today?

3. List some of the truths about God Jude mentioned in verses 24-25.

Sources for Additional Study

See books listed for 2 Peter.

THE REVELATION

The Book of Revelation is a work of intensity. Forged in the flames of the author's personal tribulation, it employs the language of biblical allusion and apocalyptic symbolism to express the heights and depths of the author's visionary experience. The result is a work of scriptural and prophetic magnitude.

To encourage Christian faithfulness, Revelation points to the glorious world to come (a world of "no more mourning, no more crying, no more pain," 21:4; compare 7:16) at the reappearing of the crucified and risen Jesus. This now-enthroned Lord will return to conclude world history (and the tribulations of the readers) with the destruction of God's enemies, the final salvation of His own people, and the creation of a new heaven and a new earth.

The intensity of the prophet's experience is matched only by the richness of the apocalyptic symbolism he employs to warn his readers of the impending disasters and temptations that will require their steadfast allegiance to the risen Lord. To be sure, the Lord will come in power and majesty, but not before His enemies have exercised a terrible (albeit limited by the divine mercy) attack upon those who "hold to the testimony of Jesus" (6:9; 12:17; 20:4).

The author's situation was one of suffering. He was a "fellow-partaker in

Apocalyptic Literature

The Greek word *apokalypsis* ("apocalypse"), found in Revelation 1:1, provides the title for the final and climactic book of the Bible. In modern literary study Revelation, Daniel, several other biblical books (to a lesser degree), and a wide range of extrabiblical Jewish writings have been characterized as examples of biblically related apocalyptic literature. Similarities in thought and form have also been noted with certain Persian apocalyptic writings and elsewhere.

The Age of Apocalyptic Literature. It is almost universally agreed that the first full-blown example of biblical apocalyptic is the Book of Daniel. Other limited OT inclusions of apocalyptic may be seen in Ezekiel and Zechariah. Certain scholars place Daniel during the Maccabean period of Jewish history, specifically about 165 B.C. But there is no compelling evidence against dating it in its stated sixth-century B.C. setting along with Ezekiel or viewing Zechariah as having a fifth-century B.C. point of origin.

Differences in the literary characteristics and thought patterns between earlier biblical apocalyptic and that of the intertestamental period must be viewed as a further, and only partly related literary, development. That conclusion becomes even clearer when we realize that Daniel, Ezekiel, and Zechariah all contain numerous characteristics of biblical prophecy as well as apocalyptic. They could be categorized as "prophetic-apocalyptic," perhaps more as a hybrid of the two types of literature than as a transitional form, especially considering that the NT Apocalypse (Revelation) also describes itself as prophecy (see Rev 1:3; 22:18-19).

There is a sense in which the period between the early second century B.C. and the later second century A.D. represented the "flowering" of apocalyptic in Jewish circles. That is true even if only because so many apocalyptic books or portions, mostly extrabiblical, were written during that time. A number of such works have been traced to separatist groups like the Qumran community, famous for most of the Dead Sea Scrolls.

It is also accurate to refer to the latter part of that period as the high point and climax of biblical apocalyptic. The emergence of the Book of Revelation as well as Christ's Olivet discourse, often referred to as a "little apocalypse," represent the end of canonical apocalyptic literature. Jewish apocalyptic of a somewhat different style continued on in earnest for another century or so before beginning to give way to more formal mainstream Judaism.

Overall it seems fair to say that apocalyptic flourished during periods of foreign domination, starting with the Babylonian exile. The Maccabean era and the persecution of the church under the Roman Empire during the latter first century A.D. were similar historical contexts. After the second Jewish revolt against Rome in A.D. 135, apocalyptic began to decline and eventually ceased after the fourth century A.D.

Characteristics and Theology of Apocalyptic. There are several literary characteristics common to apocalyptic, as well as a relatively consistent pattern of theological thought. That does not mean that there may not be significant differences between various apocalyptic books. But the strikingly similar characteristics and theology marks them as legitimate examples of the apocalyptic form.

One agreed-upon characteristic is that all apocalyptic works claim to have been written by significant biblical characters. Books like Daniel and Revelation almost certainly were written by historical figures, as supported by strong internal and external evidence. However, most other apocalypses only assert that they were authored by important OT (and some NT) figures (for example, Enoch, Ezra, Solomon) to gain a hearing, a feature called ⇨

the tribulation" that is "in Jesus," who because of his testimony to Jesus was now exiled to the island of Patmos (1:9). The situation of the recipients, that is, "the seven churches that are in Asia" (1:4), seems not yet so dire. To be sure, a faithful Christian in Pergamum had suffered death (2:13), and the church in Smyrna was warned of a time of impending persecution (2:10). But the persecutions described in Revelation, though a very real and threatening prospect for the churches of the Roman province of Asia, are still

pseudonymity. Thus the actual writers of the bulk of apocalyptic works are unknown.

Apocalyptic writing is also known by its use of visions and symbolism. The revelations, dreams, and visions were often narrated or interpreted by an angelic figure. Sometimes the writer is even caught up into the heavenly realm. The striking symbolism of Daniel's visions is found to accurately portray the sweep of history in advance by its interpretive sections and later fulfillments. But such symbolism was taken to bizarre extremes by much of later apocalyptic. Also many of the pseudononymous apocalypses are little more than history that has been recast to appear to be futuristic prophecy, with the actual uncertainty about what was still future masked by vague symbolism.

In addition, apocalyptic focused side by side on the movement of world history, especially as it related to the Jewish people and coming of the Messiah. Apocalyptic writers were not just predicting the future but fitting its development into a theological framework, frequently with a climax of messianic intervention on behalf of God's people. For example, Daniel 7 builds upon the earlier vision in Daniel 2. But it clarifies the wider progression of beastlike world empires (7:3-8) by showing that the messianic figure, "The Son of Man," will gain everlasting victory through God's power (7:9-14), delivering and vindicating "the saints," God's people (7:21,25-29).

The above consistent literary characteristics are paralleled by a broader theological pattern. Several interlocking theological emphases show up again and again in these writings, making vivid use of the literary style of apocalyptic. Again biblical and extrabiblical apocalypses are comparable at a number of points but also quite different at others.

Studies of apocalyptic often note that it is "dualistic" (God versus Satan) and "deterministic" (history is determined in advance in moving toward God's ultimate victory). These outlooks have been used to compare biblically related apocalyptic to other types, such as the Persian form. However, the much more specific emphasis on what could be called spiritual warfare at its highest level and the loving but just sovereignty of God over history marks Jewish and Christian apocalyptic as truly distinctive. For example, the unseen angelic conflict in Daniel 10 leads into the movement that climaxes in the resurrection and divine judgment in Daniel 11–12. Also the climactic stratagems of the devil, his ongoing war against God, are ended by the appearing of Christ in Revelation 19:11–20:3.

Two other related theological perspectives can be called "eschatological realism" and an "imminent expectation" (possible near occurrence) of the final events. Some scholars describe the conclusion that the end times will be a time of "great tribulation" (Dan 12:1; Matt 24:21; Rev 7:14), suffering, and catastrophic events as pessimism. However, because that is the straightforward conclusion of what the apocalyptic works set forth, and because there is an inarguable, optimistic conclusion (God's victory), it is better to view this overall pattern in terms of biblical realism.

With many of the extrabiblical apocalypses, this combination of anticipated suffering and possible near-term divine intervention combined to produce an ethically passive attitude. It apparently seemed to such apocalypticists that there was nothing that could be done except to hang on until the Lord intervened. However, biblical apocalyptic is marked by numerous challenges to godly living in light of the possible soon arrival of the climactic events of history (Dan 13:2-3; Rev 1:3; 21:7-8). □

largely anticipated at the time of John's writing.

John's readers might have felt secure, but John knew such security would be short-lived. He called them to faith in the coming Christ and loyal obedience to Him during the time of persecution and tribulation to come. "To him who overcomes I will give the right to sit with me on my throne. . . . He who has an ear, let him hear what the Spirit says to the churches" (3:21-22).

REVELATION

According to early Christian traditions, the Gospel of John, the three Epistles of John, and Revelation were all written by the apostle John. Revelation is the only one of these books that actually claims to be written by someone named John.

The author does not claim to be the *apostle* John. Given the authority and prestige of the Twelve, no other first-century Christian leader was associated closely enough with the churches of Asia Minor to have spoken so authoritatively and to have referred to himself simply as John unless he were, in fact, the apostle. There are certainly differences of style and language between the Fourth Gospel and Revelation—as well as some remarkable similarities of thought and terminology. Regardless of the problems related to the authorship of the Fourth Gospel, however, it is not implausible to assume that the John of Revelation was, in fact, John the apostle, the son of Zebedee.

Date

Scholars have traditionally suggested two possible dates for the writing of Revelation. Suggested dates are based upon the repeated references to persecution (1:9; 2:2-2,10,13; 3:9-10; 6:10-11; 7:14-17; 11:7; 12:13–13:17; 14:12-13; 19:2; 21:4). It is well-known that the Roman emperor Nero (54–68 A.D.) persecuted Christians, and many think that a persecution took place under Domitian (81–96 A.D.) as well.

From the middle of the second century A.D., Christian authors usually referred to Domitian's reign as the time of John's writing, but there is no historical consensus supporting a persecution of Christians under Domitian, while hard evidence does exist for a persecution under Nero. In this century most New Testament scholars have opted for the later date under Domitian (about A.D. 95), though there has been a resurgence of opinion arguing for a setting just following the reign of Nero (about A.D. 68). The reference in 17:10 to "seven kings," of whom "five have fallen, one is, and the other has not yet come," fits well with this later dating. Nero was fifth in the line of Roman emperors beginning with Augustus (then Tiberius, Caligula, Claudius, and Nero). The evil Nero, who persecuted Christians, died of a mortal wound (13:3,14; 17:11). His name yields the number 666 when put into Hebrew from Greek, (13:18), thus for John it would stand as the ultimate exemplar and prototype of the coming antichrist.

Whichever date is chosen, however, the setting must be clearly related to a time of persecution for the author and an anticipated expansion of persecution for the original audience.

Literary Forms

Revelation has traditionally been called an "apocalypse." Although the kind of literature was not known in the first century, what modern scholars now call "apocalyptic literature" certainly existed (see the article "Types of New Testament Literature"). In any case, John called himself a "prophet" and his work a "prophecy" (1:3; 22:10,19). But he also gave it some of the features of a letter, or epistle, including an epistolary "greeting," an epistolary "conclusion" (22:21), and the overall tone of a Christian letter of "instruction," designed to be read aloud in worship (1:3,11; 2:7,11,17,29; 3:6,13,22).

Within Revelation we find other forms of literature as well, especially hymns. Perhaps more so than any other book in the New Testament, the Book of Revelation may be called a book of Christian worship. Vision, symbol, prophecy, sermonic exhortation, Scripture citation, narrative, prayer, and dialogue are all frequently interspersed with heavenly (and sometimes earthly) choruses of praise and adoration. The Father is worshiped in hymnic praise for His creative power and sovereign purposes (4:8-11). The Lamb (Christ) is worshiped at His enthronement for His faithfulness unto death, a sacrifice of great redeeming power for the redemption of His people (5:8-14). Or, again, the Lord God, the Almighty, is worshiped for His triumph over evil through Christ (11:15-18). Heaven rejoices at both the expulsion of Satan upon the enthronement of Christ (12:10-12) and at the judgment of the great harlot upon the coming of Christ (19:1-7). The saints also rejoice with a "new song" of salvation (14:1-5) and at their redemption from the beast (15:2-4). Then, as now, God is worthy of all worship and devotion, for He has mercifully accomplished salvation for all who approach Him through Christ.

I. Introduction (1:1-8)
II. John's Vision on the Island of Patmos (1:9-20)
III. Letters to the Seven Churches (2:1–3:22)
IV. The Sovereignty of the Creator God Committed to the Crucified and Now Enthroned Lamb (4:1–5:14)
V. The Enthroned Lamb's Judgments Via the Seven Seals (6:1–8:5)
VI. The Enthroned Lamb's Judgments Via the Seven Trumpets (8:6–11:19)
VII. The Dragon's Persecution of the Righteous (12:1–13:18)
VIII. A Summary of Triumph, Warning, and Judgment (14:1-20)
IX. The Enthroned Lamb's Judgments Via the Seven Cups (15:1–16:21)
X. The Fall and Ruin of the Immoral City of the Beast (17:1–18:24)
XI. The Rejoicing of Heaven and the Revelation of the Lamb (19:1–22:5)
XII. Conclusion (22:6-21)

Theology

The Book of Revelation is often treated as if it constituted a world of its own within the canon of the New Testament. Certainly its status as apocalyptic literature, with its exceedingly strange symbolic images, its angelic guides, visionary experience, and cosmic as well as earthly catastrophes, justifies the commonly held perception of it as "strange" and "unusual." But the extraordinary images, symbols, and experiences reflected in Revelation should not mislead us into isolating the book from the world of New Testament theology.

The Book of Revelation, in spite of its unusual language and symbolic traditions, has the basic apostolic theology at its core. The rest of the New Testament speaks profoundly about the same crucified, risen, and exalted Jesus who is variously portrayed in the Book of Revelation. Some of these portraits include: the strangely dressed, apocalyptic Son of man of chapter 1; the Lord of the churches of chapters 2 and 3; the Lamb/Lion of Judah of chapter 5; the Lord of judgment who pours out woes upon the earth by way of the seals, trumpets, and cups of chapters 6–19; the Child who is to rule the nations and who is exalted to the right hand of God of chapter 12; the Lamb and Son of man of chapter 14; the Word of God, who is the King of kings and Lord of lords who comes to do battle riding a white horse and having a robe dipped in blood of chapter 19; and the One who reigns upon the throne of God and is likewise the heavenly Temple of chapters 20–22.

The focus of Revelation clearly falls upon the future coming of Christ. His coming will defeat the powers of Satan, those evil forces that oppress the people of God. The One who will come is none other than the same crucified and risen Jesus. The churches and those within them who have devoted themselves to the lordship of Jesus Christ are exhorted to remain faithful in the hour of affliction to Christ the crucified and risen Lord. Such exhortations to perseverance are widespread in the New Testament. (See Matt 10:22; John 15; Acts 14:22.) They represent still a central need and obligation of authentic Christian living.

The Book of Revelation thus reflects the basic, apostolic theology that may be attested throughout the New Testament. This "apostolic theology" may be summarized as follows:

1. The events accomplished by God, particularly as they pertain to the person of Jesus Christ, have all been done in fulfillment of Scripture (Matt 1:22-23).

2. God has powerfully acted for our salvation, especially through the death and resurrection of Jesus (Acts 2:23-32).

3. This same Jesus is now the exalted Lord. Having ascended to the right hand of God and taken His place on God's throne, He now executes the purposes of God as the Living Lord of the cosmos (Acts 2:32-36).

4. All who believe and confess the person of Jesus Christ will experience the salvation of God (Acts 2:38).

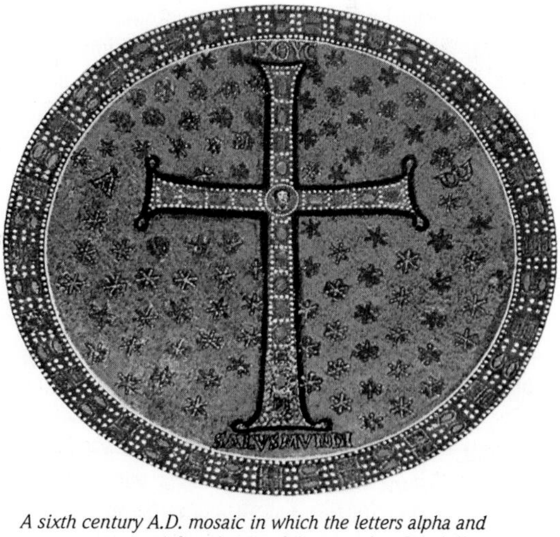

A sixth century A.D. mosaic in which the letters alpha and omega appear to left and right of the cross (see Rev 1:8).

The Island of Patmos to which John was exiled and on which he received from God the vision that became the New Testament Book of Revelation.

5. God's Spirit has been poured out on all those who name the name of Christ (Acts 2:38; Rom 5:5; 8:9).

6. Commitment to God through Christ means participation in a fellowship of worship and instruction (Acts 2:41-42; Rom 9:24-26).

7. This same Jesus will come again to rescue those who have confessed Him in faithfulness (see Mark 13:24-27).

1:1-8
Introduction

Written to "the seven churches" of the Roman province of Asia, John's work is a "revelation" of "what must soon take place." Given to John by Jesus Christ, it is a message committed by God to the Lord to show to His "servants." John wrote his prophecy in the form of a letter, beginning with a greeting of grace and peace from each person of the triune God (1:4-5). The theme of John's work is clear: the Lord God, the Almighty One Himself, has guaranteed the final vindication of the crucified Jesus before all the earth (1:7-8). The victory of Christ is assured. His people will rejoice in their final deliverance, but those who have rejected Him will mourn His coming, for it will mean judgment for them.

1:9-20
John's Vision on Patmos

While in exile on the island of Patmos, John saw the risen Lord (1:9-20). It happened as he was in the Spirit on the Lord's Day. Suddenly he heard behind him a loud voice like the sound of a trumpet. The voice declared that John should write down what he would see and send it to the seven churches: to Ephesus, Smyrna, Pergamum, Thyatira, Sardis, Philadelphia, and Laodicea. John turned to see the source of the great voice. Interestingly enough, before mentioning Christ, he said he saw first of all "seven golden lampstands" (v. 12). We read later on (v. 20) that the seven golden lampstands are "the seven churches."

Thus the significance of John's visions, a message to the seven churches, should not be overlooked. Indeed, not merely in chapters 2–3 do we find the seven letters in which the churches are addressed but in the entire Book of Revelation (1:3; 22:10,16-19). There is certainly no textual evidence that the letters, either individually or as a collection, circulated apart from the rest of John's literary work. It is a serious mistake to think that certain portions of Revelation were not important for, or relevant to, the original audiences. The whole of the Revelation is relevant to the churches (then and now), for they are fellow partakers with John in "suffering and kingdom and patient endurance that are ours in Jesus" (1:9). Each church must heed not only its own letter, but all of the letters, and indeed the entire Revelation (22:18-19), since it warns of coming judgment and pronounces a blessing on all those who persevere in the hour of affliction and die in faithfulness to the Lord (14:13). John's authoritative book is not a literary mystery for those struggling to live in a difficult time of persecution and

Hymns and Creeds in the New Testament

The NT is a virtual hymnbook setting forth the praise songs and creeds of the early church. The major problem for modern scholars has to do with the criteria one might use in pinpointing a hymn in the biblical text. Contemporary scholars have set forth certain stylistic and contextual criteria.

Criteria for Hymns. Under stylistic characteristics we find a definite use of the verb *to be* in the second and third persons: *you are* and *he is.* The verses are carefully constructed with numerous parallelisms and relative clauses affirming praise to God. The vocabulary of the hymns also includes words not found elsewhere in the NT. The hymns also tend to make use of the term "all."

Certain contextual criteria include the use of introductory formulas such as verbs of saying (*lego*). The content of the hymns involves Christological elements and assertions of God's saving deeds or pleas for God to render help. Many of these hymns end with the phrase "forever and ever."

The Philippian Hymn. One of the best known of the NT hymns is found in Philippians 2:6-11. This hymn is written in the third-person style, and the praise of the believing community remains in the background. No Christological title is used except that of Lord Jesus Christ in verse 11.

One encounters a brief outline of the basic Christological facts: He humbles Himself, takes on the form of a servant, becomes a human being, humbles Himself, dies, is elevated and given a name above every other name. In the Greek text one can sing this hymn to the modern church tune "Man of Sorrows."

Some scholars divide this hymn into six stanzas with three lines in each. Others in contrast see three stanzas. The first speaks of the preexistence (vv. 6-7a), the second the incarnation (vv. 7b-8), and the third the exaltation (vv. 9-11). Many scholars conclude that Paul took over a hymn as a unit from the early church and made use of it in his Philippian Letter.

Revelation Hymns. The Book of Revelation is also filled with hymns. The twenty-four elders serve as a choir that sings many hymns of praise to God. In chapters 4–5 alone we find five hymns. The four living creatures begin the music by singing softly, "Holy, holy, holy" in 4:8. There follows three hymns that all start with the phrase "worthy."

In 4:11 the twenty-four elders join the living creatures in praising God as the creating God. In 5:9-10 they sing a hymn of praise to Christ as a lamb appears on stage. The choir grows to thousands of angels, and they join in singing 5:12, another worthy hymn. Finally everyone in the universe comes together to sing 5:12, a hymn of praise to God and the Lamb.

1 Timothy Hymn. The early church often used these hymns for teaching and training new members. In 1 Timothy 3:16 we find a hymn that contains the early Christological teaching of the church. From such hymns the church developed its early creeds:

Who was made manifest in the flesh;
who was made righteous in the Spirit;
who was seen by the angels;
who was preached in the world;
who was taken into glory;
(this can be sung in Greek to the tune of "Rock of Ages").

Thus in a simple hymn the church could teach some of the most important aspects of its faith in Christ. The passages reflect hymns of the faith that were used for training and teaching.

Singing Greek Hymns. The music dimension of the NT needs to be rediscovered. The tunes used two thousand years ago remain unknown. Yet one can set them to modern church tunes and rediscover some of the thrill of singing words used by the early Christians. □

suffering. John's book is an exhortation to the churches to remain faithful to Jesus Christ, to persevere in the hour of trouble knowing that Christ, who is the Lord of the churches, the One who walks among the seven golden lampstands (1:13; 2:1), will return to rescue and vindicate His people.

Having seen the seven golden lampstands, John then saw in the middle of the lampstands a glorious human figure. He saw none other than the heavenly Son of man Himself, clothed in a robe reaching to His feet, having a golden girdle worn high around His breast (in contrast to the workman who wore his belt in a lower position around the waist, so he could tuck his robe about it while at work). Like the Ancient of Days in Daniel 7:9-10, this glorious figure had hair "like white wool, as white as snow" (Rev 1:14). His eyes, which were penetratingly powerful to judge and discern, were like a flame of fire. His feet, alluding probably to Daniel 10:6, were like burnished bronze. His voice, which John had already likened to the sound of a trumpet, was also like the sound of a mighty waterfall, similar to the description in Ezekiel 43:2 of the voice of God.

In His right hand He held seven stars, which are the angels of the seven churches (Rev 1:20). Proceeding from the mouth of the Glorious One was a sharp two-edged sword with which He would smite the nations (19:15), but which also stood as a reminder even to the churches that He is the Lord of judgment (2:12). Overwhelmed with this vision of the glorious Son of man, John fell down as a dead man. But the Glorious One laid His right hand upon John and said: "Do not be afraid. I am the First and the Last. I am the Living One" (1:17-18). This description is virtually synonymous with the title of Alpha and Omega given to the Lord God in 1:8. It combines the sacred name revealed at the burning bush of Exodus 3:14 with the description of the Lord, the King of Israel, beside whom there is no other God, given in Isaiah 44:6.

This Living One, this One who possesses the absolute life of God, was Himself once dead but now is alive forever more (Rev 1:18). This is, of course, none other than the crucified and risen Lord Jesus Christ. Though "born of a woman, born under law" (Gal 4:4) and Himself thus susceptible and vulnerable to death, this Jesus, having endured the pangs of death, has now been raised to absolute life and can never die again (Rom 6:9; Heb 7:16-25).

Saints and martyrs in early Christian art usually were represented as "dressed in white" (see Rev 3:5).

Every feature in John's description of the Risen One suggests the presence of power and majesty. The Living One then instructed John to write an account of the things he both had seen and would see, that is, an account of "what will take place later" (Rev 1:19).

2:1–3:22
Letters to the Seven Churches

The letters to the churches of Ephesus, Smyrna, Pergamum, Thyatira, Sardis, Philadelphia, and Laodicea have a fairly consistent format. First, after designating the recipients, the risen Lord as Sender introduces and describes Himself using a portion of the visionary description of the glorious Son of man found in 1:9-20. There follows an "I know" section of either commendation or criticism. Next appears typically some form of exhortation. To those who received criticism, the usual exhortation was to repent. However, to the churches of Smyrna and Philadelphia, for whom the Lord had only praise, the exhortation was one of assurance (2:10; 3:10-11). Each letter concludes, though the order may vary, with both an exhortation to "hear what the Spirit says to the churches" and a promise of reward to the "overcomer," that is, the one who conquers by persevering in the cause of Christ.

The church at Ephesus (2:1-7) was told to return to its first love or else its lampstand would be removed out of its place, a judgment implying the death of the church, though not the individual loss of final salvation. The church at Smyrna (2:8-11) was tenderly encouraged to be faithful unto death, while the churches of Pergamum (2:12-17) and Thyatira (2:18-29) were sternly warned to beware of false teaching and the immoral deeds that so often accompany erroneous theology.

The church at Sardis (3:1-6) was told to wake up and complete its works of obedience. The church at Philadelphia (3:7-13) was promised, in the face of persecution by the local synagogue, that faith in Jesus would assure access into the eternal kingdom. Christ alone has the key of David and has opened the heavenly door that no one else can shut. And the church at Laodicea (3:14-22) was told to turn from its self-deception and repent of its lukewarmness.

These warnings and encouragements were sent to seven real churches. No doubt the fact that "seven" are referred to has some symbolic significance and may well mean that the seven churches represented many Christian communities in Asia Minor. However representative the seven churches may have been, they were nonetheless seven very real churches to whom John was known and for whom he was instructed by the Risen Lord to write these words of warning and hope.

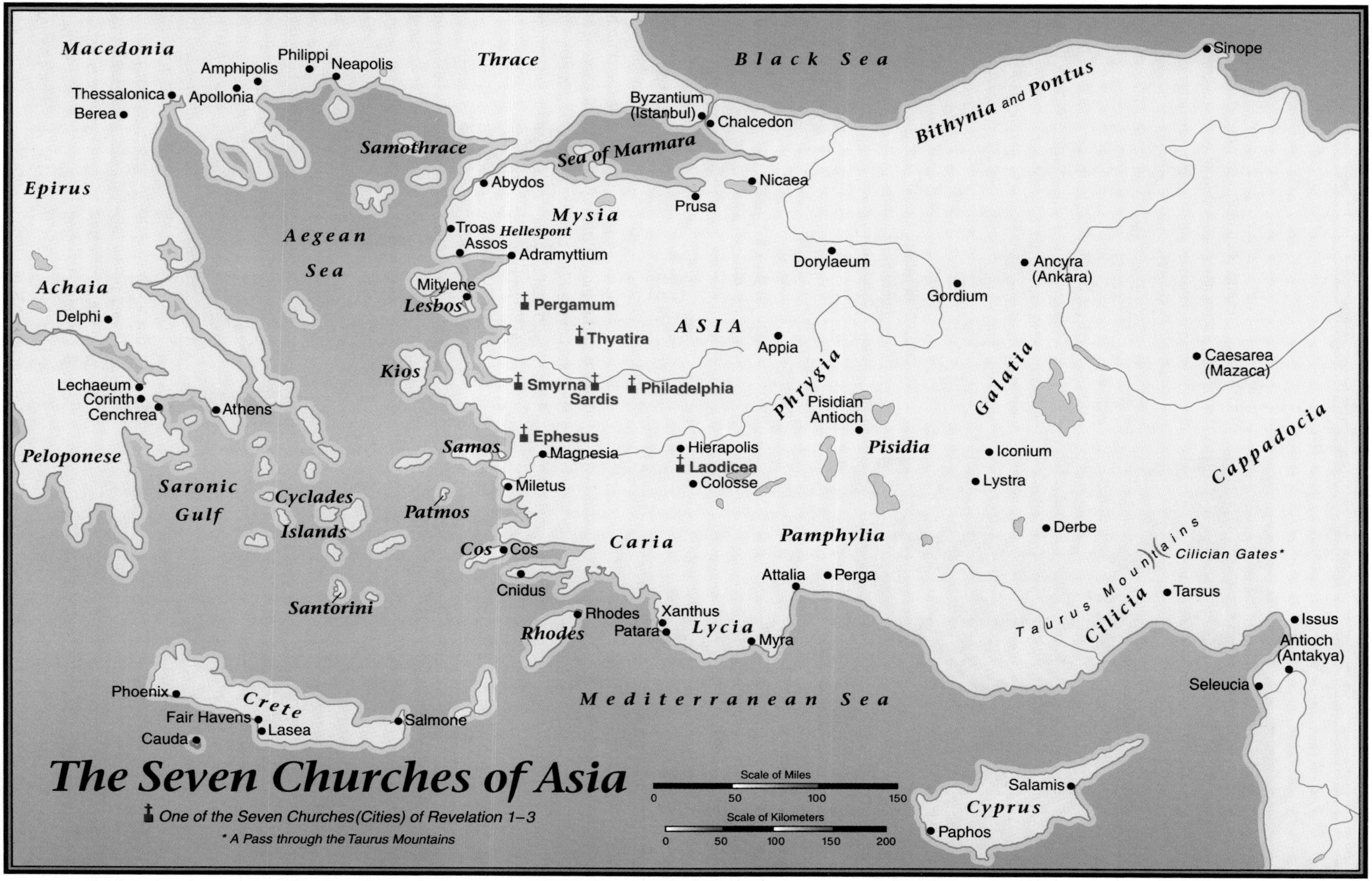
The Seven Churches of Asia
One of the Seven Churches (Cities) of Revelation 1–3
* A Pass through the Taurus Mountains
Scale of Miles
0
50
100
150
Scale of Kilometers
0
50
100
150
200
Macedonia
Thrace
Black Sea
Bithynia and Pontus
Sinope
Amphipolis
Philippi
Neapolis
Thessalonica
Apollonia
Berea
Byzantium (Istanbul)
Chalcedon
Samothrace
Sea of Marmara
Epirus
Abydos
Nicaea
Prusa
Mysia
Troas
Hellespont
Assos
Adramyttium
Aegean Sea
Dorylaeum
Ancyra (Ankara)
Gordium
Achaia
Mitylene
Lesbos
Pergamum
Delphi
ASIA
Thyatira
Appia
Caesarea (Mazaca)
Kios
Phrygia
Galatia
Lechaeum
Corinth
Cenchrea
Athens
Smyrna
Sardis
Philadelphia
Pisidian Antioch
Ephesus
Samos
Magnesia
Hierapolis
Laodicea
Colosse
Pisidia
Iconium
Lystra
Cappadocia
Peloponese
Saronic Gulf
Cyclades Islands
Miletus
Patmos
Pamphylia
Derbe
Caria
Cos
Cnidus
Attalia
Perga
Taurus Mountains
Cilician Gates*
Tarsus
Cilicia
Santorini
Rhodes
Xanthus
Patara
Lycia
Myra
Issus
Antioch (Antakya)
Seleucia
Phoenix
Crete
Fair Havens
Lasea
Cauda
Salmone
Mediterranean Sea
Salamis
Cyprus
Paphos

The custom of writing on pillars was widespread in the ancient world (see Rev 3:12). Shown above is a pillar in the synagogue at Capernaum that bears a dedicatory inscription in Greek.

Some commentators refer to the seven churches as seven epochs of world history, but there is not the slightest hint in the text that the seven churches are to be understood in such a way. In fact, it is only a very forced and erroneous reading of church history that can make the letters to the seven churches appear as prophecies regarding seven epochs of world history.

Again, there is absolutely no hint in the text that John intended for us to understand these seven letters in that way. Instead, it is abundantly clear that the letters were written to real congregations, engaged in the very real struggles of faith and perseverance in the midst of impending, and sometimes actual, persecution. God's word to one situation clearly had relevance for other situations in the first century. It is therefore not surprising that we, too, may read these letters, and indeed the entirety of the Revelation, and hear the voice of God in them. Thus, we read Revelation in the same general way that we would read Paul's Letters to the Corinthians. That is, after doing our best to understand the historical situation of and the inspired message to the intended, first-century audience, we then seek, as a people who continue to stand under the authority of God's Word, to apply the ancient message to our lives and situations today.

4:1–5:14
The Sovereignty of the Creator God

Chapters 4–5 represent the pivot point of the book. They tie the risen Lord's opening exhortations to the churches (chaps. 2–3) to the judgments and final triumph of the Lamb (chaps. 6–22). Seen in this way the exhortations to the churches are in fact warnings of both the coming afflictions and God's ultimate triumph, the latter of which may serve as a spur of hope to enable the recipients of the prophecy to endure the former. These chapters also provide the historical and theological basis of the risen Lord's authority over both the church and the world by depicting His enthronement and empowering to carry out the judging and saving purposes of God.

Chapter 4 asserts the sovereign authority of the Creator God. Surrounded by the adoring and powerful four creatures and twenty-four elders, the Lord God the Almighty is holy, sovereign, and worthy of all worship. For He has created all things, and all things exist because of His gracious, sovereign will (4:11). John's vision of God upon His throne is reminiscent of Daniel 7 (especially vv. 9-10) and Ezekiel 1, each of which is calculated to impress the reader with the God of might and glory.

Chapter 5 depicts the delegation of the divine authority to the risen Lord by introducing a sequence of events again reminiscent of Daniel 7. In Daniel 7 the people of God were oppressed by four terrible beasts, symbolic of evil empires and kings. Similarly, Revelation is written to people who either were, or soon would be, experiencing persecution from powers of evil. In Daniel 7 the heavenly thrones of judgment are established, the books of judgment are opened, and authority to carry out God's judgment, and thus to rescue the people of God from the evil nations, is committed to a human figure. This human figure, a glorious "son of man," mysteriously appears before the throne of God in the clouds of heaven.

Similarly, in Revelation 5 we see both a book of judgment (in this instance one with seven seals held in the right hand of God) and a glorious, redemptive agent of God. But now, instead of an unidentified human figure, we learn that the exalted agent of God is none other than the crucified Jesus, the Lamb and Lion of God. This Jesus, because of His conquering obedience to the will of God, is now (being) enthroned and therefore is worthy to take the book and break the seals.

The events portrayed here are highly symbolic but are not for that reason to be regarded as sheer myth. For the scene readily suggests an otherwise well-known and important historical and theological moment within biblical history, namely, the ascension and enthronement of Jesus. Besides explaining the visible absence of Jesus and/or the end of the resurrection appearances, the ascension of Jesus is His enthronement as heavenly Lord (see Acts 2:33-36; Eph 1:20–2:31; Col 1:18), His empowering now to execute the judgments of God. He is worthy to

MILLENNIAL PERSPECTIVES ON REVELATION

POINT OF INTERPRETATION	AMILLENNIAL	HISTORICAL PREMILLENNIAL	DISPENSATIONAL PREMILLENNIAL	POSTMILLENNIAL
Description of View	Viewpoint that the present age of Christ's rule in the church is the millennium; holds to one resurrection and judgment marking the end of history as we know it and the beginning of life eternal	Viewpoint that Christ will reign on earth for a thousand years following His second coming; saints will be resurrected at the beginning of the millennium, nonbelievers at the end, followed by judgment	Viewpoint that after the battle of Armageddon, Christ will rule through the Jews for a literal thousand years accompanied by two resurrections and at least three judgments	Viewpoint that Christ will return after a long period of expansion and spiritual prosperity for the church, brought about by the preaching of the gospel; the Spirit's blessing; and the church's work toward righteousness, justice, and peace. The period is not a literal thousand years but extended time of spiritual prosperity.
Book of Revelation	Current history written in code to confound enemies and encourage Asian Christians; message applies to all Christians	Immediate application to Asian Christians; applies to all Christians throughout the ages, but the visions also apply to a great future event	"Unveiling" of theme of Christ among churches in present dispensation, also as Judge and King in dispensations to come	Written to encourage Christians of all ages, but the visions also apply to a great future event.
Seven candlesticks (1:13)	Churches		Churches, plus end-time application	Churches
Churches addressed (chaps. 2–3)	Specific historical situations, truths apply to churches throughout the ages; do not represent periods of church history		Specific historical situations and to all churches throughout the ages; shows progress of churches' spiritual state until end of church age	Specific historical situations, truths apply to churches throughout the ages; do not necessarily represent periods of church history
Twenty-four elders (4:4,10; 5:8,14)	Twelve patriarchs and twelve apostles; together symbolize all the redeemed	Company of angels who help execute God's rule (or elders represent twenty-four priestly and Levitical orders)	The rewarded church; also represents twelve patriarchs and twelve apostles	Symbolizes all the redeemed
Sealed book (5:1-9)	Scroll of history; shows God carrying out His redemptive purpose in history	Contains prophecy of end events of chapters 7–22	Title deed to the world	Portrays God carrying out His redemptive purpose in history
144,000 (7:4-8)	Redeemed on earth who will be protected against God's wrath	Church on threshold of great tribulation	Jewish converts of tribulation period who witness to Gentiles (same as 14:1)	Redeemed people of God
Great tribulation (first reference in 7:14)	Persecution faced by Asian Christians of John's time; symbolic of tribulation that occurs throughout history	Period at end time of unexplained trouble, before Christ's return; church will go through it; begins with seventh seal (18:1) which includes trumpets 1-6 (8:2–14:20)	Period at end time of unexplained trouble referred to in 7:14 and described in chapters 11–18; lasts three and a half years, the latter half of seven-year period between rapture and millennium	Symbolic of tribulation that occurs throughout history
Forty-two months (11:2); 1,260 days (11:3)	Indefinite duration of pagan desolation	A symbolic number representing period of evil with reference to last days of age	Half of seven-year tribulation period	A symbolic number representing an indefinite time and evil influence
Woman (12:1-6)	True people of God under old and new covenants (true Israel)		Indicates Israel, not church; key is comparison with Gen 37:9	True people of God under old and new covenants
Great red dragon (12:3)	All views identify as Satan			

MILLENNIAL PERSPECTIVES ON REVELATION

POINT OF INTERPRETATION	AMILLENNIAL	HISTORICAL PREMILLENNIAL	DISPENSATIONAL PREMILLENNIAL	POSTMILLENNIAL
Manchild (12:4-5)	Christ at His birth, life events, and crucifixion, whom Satan sought to kill	Christ, whose work Satan seeks to destroy	Christ but also the church (head and body); caught up on throne indicates rapture of church	Christ at His birth, life events, and crucifixion, whom Satan sought to destroy
1,260 days (12:6)	Indefinite time	Symbolic number representing period of evil with special reference to last days of age	First half of great tribula- after church is raptured	Indefinite time
Sea beast (13:1)	Emperor Domitian, personification of Roman Empire (same as in chap. 17)	Antichrist, here shown as embodiment of the four beasts in Dan 7	A new Rome, satanic federation of nations that come out of old Roman Empire	Roman Empire
Seven heads (13:1)	Roman emperors	Great power, shows kinship with dragon	Seven stages of Roman Empire; sixth was imperial Rome (John's day); last will be federation of nations	Roman Emperors
Ten horns (13:1)	Symbolize power	Kings, represent limited crowns (ten) against Christ's many	Ten powers that will combine to make the federation of nations of new Rome	Symbol of power
666 (13:18)	Imperfection, evil; personified as Domitian	Symbolic of evil, short of 777; if a personage meant, he is unknown but will be known at the proper time	Not known but will be known when time comes	Symbol of evil
144,00 on Mount Zion (14:1)	Total body of redeemed in heaven		Redeemed Jews gathered in earthly Jerusalem during millennial kingdom	Redeemed people of God
River of blood (14:20)	Symbol of infinite punishment for the wicked	Means God's radical judgment crushes evil thoroughly	Scene of wrath and carnage that will occur in Palestine	Symbol of judgment on the wicked
Babylon (woman—17:5)	Historical Rome	Capital city of future Antichrist	Apostate church of the future	Symbol of evil
Seven mountains (17:9)	Pagan Rome, which was built on seven hills	Indicate power, so here means a succession of empires, last of which is end-time Babylon	Rome, revived at end time	Pagan Rome
Seven heads (17:7) and seven kings (17:10)	Roman emperors from Augustus to Titus, excluding three brief rules	Five past godless kingdoms; sixth was Rome; seventh would arise in end time	Five distinct forms of Roman government prior to John; sixth was imperial Rome; seventh will be revived Roman Empire	Roman emperors
Ten horns (17:7) and ten kings (17:12)	Vassal kings who ruled with Rome's permission	Symbolic of earthly powers that will be subservient to Antichrist	Ten kingdoms arising in future out of revived Roman Empire	Symbolic of earthly powers
Bride, wife (19:7)	Total of all the redeemed		The church; does not include Old Testament saints or tribulation saints	Total of all the redeemed

MILLENNIAL PERSPECTIVES ON REVELATION

POINT OF INTERPRETATION	AMILLENNIAL	HISTORICAL PREMILLENNIAL	DISPENSATIONAL PREMILLENNIAL	POSTMILLENNIAL
Marriage supper (19:9)	Climax of the age; symbolizes complete union of Christ with His people	Union of Christ with His people at His Coming	Union of Christ with His church accompanied by by Old Testament saints and tribulation saints	Union of Christ with His people
One on white horse (19:11-16)	Vision of Christ's victory over pagan Rome; return of Christ occurs in connection with events of 20:7-10	Second coming of Christ		Vision of Christ's victory
Battle of Armageddon (19:19-21; see 16:16)	Not literally at end of time but symbolizes power of God's word overcoming evil; principle applies to all ages	Literal event of some kind at end time but not literal battle with military weapons; occurs at Christ's return at beginning of millennium	Literal bloody battle at Armageddon (valley of Megiddo) at end of great tribulation between kings of the East and federation of nations of new Rome; they are all defeated by blast from Christ's mouth and then millennium begins	Symbolizes power of God's Word overcoming evil forces
Great supper (19:17)	Stands in contrast to marriage supper		Concludes series of judgments and opens way for kingdom to be established	Stands in contrast to marriage supper
Binding of Satan (20:2)	Symbolic of Christ's resurrection victory over Satan	Curbing of Satan's power during the millennium		Symbolic of Christ's victory over Satan
Millennium (20:2-6)	Symbolic reference to period from Christ's first coming to His second	A historical event, though length of one thousand years may be symbolic, after Armageddon during which Christ rules with His people	A literal thousand-year period after the church age during which Christ rules with His people but especially through the Jews	A lengthy period of expansion and spiritual prosperity brought about by the preaching of the gospel
Those on thrones (20:4)	Martyrs in heaven; their presence with God is a judgment on those who killed them	Saints and martyrs who rule with Christ in the the millennium	The redeemed ruling with Christ, appearing and disappearing on earth at will to oversee life on earth	Saints and martyrs who rule with Christ
First resurrection (20:5-6)	The spiritual presence with Christ of the redeemed that occurs after physical death	Resurrection of saints at beginning of millennium when Christ returns	Includes three groups: (1) those raptured with church (4:1); (2) Jewish tribulation saints during tribulation (11:11); (3) other Jewish believers at beginning of millennium (20:5-6)	The spiritual presence of the redeemed with Christ
Second death (20:6)	Spiritual death, eternal separation from God			
New heavens and earth (21:1)	A new order; redeemed earth			
New Jerusalem (21:2-5)	God dwelling with His saints in the new age after all other end-time events			

Vision of death (Rev 6:8)

take the book, *for He was slain* (5:9,12). His redemptive death, that is, His obedience to the will of God, has revealed Him as qualified for the role of heavenly Lord. He has "triumphed" (5:5), a word which for John referred to Jesus' triumphal suffering and subsequent enthronement (see 3:21) and may therefore now as the heavenly Lord assume the role of divine Agent and Executor. All power in heaven and on earth has been given to Him (Matt 28:18). He may take the book and break the seven seals of judgment and thereby execute the purposes of the sovereign, Creator God. At His enthronement the heavens rejoice (5:8-14; 12:5-12), for He truly is worthy, and the people of God now have their reigning Savior.

6:1–8:5
The Seven Seals

The breaking of the first four seals brings forth four horsemen of different colors (6:1-8). These riders, paralleling the chaos predicted in Mark 13, represent God's judgments through the upheavals of war (6:2) and its devastating social consequences: violence (6:3-4), famine (6:5-6), pestilence, and death (6:7-8). The fifth seal (6:9-11) is the plea of martyred saints for divine justice upon their oppressors. For now they are told, they must wait, for the number of the martyred of God's people is not yet complete.

A careful look at the sixth seal (6:12) is important for understanding the literary structure and episodic sequence of Revelation. When broken, the sixth seal brings forth the typical signs of the end: a great earthquake, the blackening of the sun, the reddening ("blood red") of the moon, and the falling of the stars of heaven (Matt 24:29-31; Mark 13:24-27). Though Revelation is but a few chapters old, we are brought to the end of world history. The sky is split apart like a scroll; mountains and islands are moved. And the mighty as well as the lowly of the earth realize that the great day of God's (and the Lamb's) wrath has come, and nothing can save them (6:14-17).

The earthquake is a consistent sign in Revelation for the destruction that immediately precedes the end (see 8:5; 11:13,19; 16:18-19) of history and the appearance of the Lord. The repeated references to the earthquake at strategic spots in Revelation do not mean that history itself repeatedly comes to an end but that John employed the well-known literary technique of "recapitulation" (see Gen 1–2), that is, the retelling of the same story from a different "angle" so as to focus upon other dimensions of and characters in the same story.

Thus, in Revelation we are repeatedly brought to the end of history and the time of Christ's return. But John withheld his final (and fullest) description of this world's end until the end of his document (19:1–22:5). In the meantime he used the literary technique (among others) of retelling to prepare his readers for both the traumas and hopes of human history. He wanted to prepare his readers for the fact of judgment coming at the hands of the enthroned Lamb of God (6:1-17), for both His protection of His people (7:1-17; 11:1) and their responsibility to bear witness to the earth regarding Him (10:1–11:13), for the redemptive purposes of judgment (8:6–9:21), for the coming persecution (11:7; 12:1–13:18), and for the finality of God's judgments (15:1–18:24). There was much for John to explain regarding the suffering of the saints and the apparent triumph of evil, facts that seem to deny the Christian confession that Christ has been raised and enthroned as Lord. Does He protect His people? Will He truly come again? Why must we suffer, and "how long, Sovereign Lord" (6:10), must we wait? The merciful but mysterious ways of God with human-

In the photo above a Parthian horseman at full gallop shoots his bow and arrow. (See Rev 6:2.)

kind require, for the sake of completeness, the retelling of the story of human history from several points of reference, replete with the certainties of both judgment and salvation through Christ.

The description of the judgments initiated by the breaking of the first six seals would no doubt tend to overwhelm John's audience, but final wrath is not the lot of the people of God (see Rom 8:35,39; 1 Thess 5:9). Therefore John interrupted the sequence of judgments leading to the seventh seal to remind us that the people of God need not despair, for "the servants of our God" (7:3) have the promise of heaven.

Chapter seven is actually two visions (7:1-8,9-17), with the second both interpreting and concluding the first. The sealing of the 144,000 (7:1-8) employs starkly Jewish symbols to describe those who know God through Jesus Christ. Clearly John was referring to Christians as the 144,000. For 7:3 refers to the "servants" of God, a term consistently used throughout Revelation to refer either to Christians in general or the Christian prophet, but *never* to the non-Christian Jew (or Gentile). Language employed in the Old Testament to refer to the Jews is characteristically used in the New Testament to refer to those who know God through Jesus Christ (for example, 2 Cor 6:16-18; Gal 3:29). Those who are in Christ are the beneficiaries of the promises made to Israel (Rom 4:13-17; Gal 3:8-9,15-29).

The number 144,000 is an intensification (12 x 12 x 10 x 10 x 10) of the original number twelve (itself an obvious allusion to the twelve tribes). This indicates that the 144,000 comprise the full number of God's people, God's people now being all (Jew or Gentile) who are followers of Jesus. (Note 12:1-17; the woman who has a crown of *twelve* stars and brings forth Christ is *Israel*. Her true offspring is first Jesus—the fulfillment of Israel's his-

The scales and balance shown above were found at the site of ancient Pompeii. See Revelation 6:5.

tory—and His followers, that is, Jews and Gentiles "who obey God's commandments and hold to the testimony of Jesus," v. 17.)

In the second vision (7:9-17) the 144,000 have become "a great multitude, which no one could count." Who are they? Using his favorite descriptions of heaven (see 21:3-4,23; 22:1-5), John said that they are those who have "come out of the great tribulation," now to experience the joys of heaven and relief from the tribulations they have endured. Compare 7:14-17 with 21:1-6; 22:1-5. The numberless multitude of 7:9 is not a reference to non-Christian Jews (or Gentiles); it refers rather to all who have trusted Christ. It is the Lamb's bride, the holy city, the new Jerusalem (20:2). To have "come out of the great tribulation" (7:14) does *not* mean that they exited the earth *before* the hour of tribulation. To the contrary, they did indeed experience the tribulations of this evil age; but now in heaven they enjoy the presence of God (7:15), where they will hunger *no more* nor thirst *any more* (7:16). No longer subject to death (21:4), they will drink of the water of life (7:17), will no more experience the oppressive heat of the sun (7:16), and will have every tear wiped from their eyes (7:17). As the true Israel of God, Christians ("the servants of our God," 7:3) have the seal of *God*. Having refused the mark of the beast (13:16-17), they hold to the testimony of Jesus in spite of persecution and therefore have the promise of final heavenly deliverance from this evil age of great tribulation.

Revelation 8:1-5 describes the seventh seal and again the traditional signs of the end, including "peals of thunder, rumblings, flashes of lightning and an earthquake" (8:5). These signs represent the very end of human history and the coming of the Lord, but the prophet was not yet ready to describe the Lord's return. He still had too much to say (based on what he saw) about the nature of judgment, the mission of the church, and the persecutions of the beast to bring his prophecy to an end. Therefore, before describing fully the end, John had to start over. Using the symbolic vehicle of the seven trumpets, he declared that the judgments of God also have a redemptive purpose because they are signs, partial expressions, of the coming final judgment.

8:6–11:19
The Seven Trumpets

The seven seals were divided between the four horsemen and the remaining three seals, with a narrative break between the sixth and seventh seals to remind the people of God of the Lord's promise of final protection and their hope of eternal glory. A similar pattern occurs with the seven trumpets (8:7–11:19).

The first four trumpets describe partial judgments ("a third," 8:7) upon the earth's vegetation, the oceans, fresh waters, and the heavenly lights. The last three trumpets are grouped together and are also described as three "woes" upon the earth, emphasizing God's judgment upon humankind. The fifth trumpet (and first woe) releases hellish locusts who will sting those not having the seal of God (9:1-12). The sixth trumpet (and second woe) brings forth a mighty army of infernal horsemen who kill a third of humankind (9:13-19). But all these judgments have no redemptive effect, for the rest of humankind who are not killed by these plagues refuse to repent of their immoralities (9:20-21). The warnings have fallen on deaf ears.

Just as the interlude between the sixth and seventh seals assured the recipients of Revelation that the people of God are safe from the eternally destructive effects of God's wrath, so also between the sixth and seventh trumpets we are reminded of God's protective hand on His people (10:1–11:14). But in the trumpet interlude we also learn that God's protection during these days of tribulation does not mean isolation, for the people of God must bear a prophetic witness to the world.

In 10:1-18 John's call (after the pattern of Ezek 2:1–3:11) is reaffirmed. He is told to eat a bittersweet book and "prophesy again about many peoples, nations, languages and kings" (10:11). The note of protection and witness is again struck in 11:1-13, where the measuring of the temple of God alludes to God's protective hand upon His people during the hour of turmoil. These persecutions will last for forty-two months, but His people, the "holy city" (11:2), will be neither destroyed nor silenced. For the "two witnesses" (11:3) will bear witness during this time, also called "1,260 days," to the mercy and judgment of God. Note well: the "42 months" and the "1,260 days" refer to the *same* time period seen from different perspectives, for the days of witness are also days of opposition (11:2-7; 12:6,13-17). Negative references to persecution and the activity of Satan and the beasts are consistently called "42 months" (11:2; 13:5), whereas positive references to the sustaining hand of God or the prophetic testimony of His two witnesses are called "time, times and half a time" (12:14), or "1,260 days" (11:3; 12:6).

It seems unlikely that the "two witnesses" ("two" suggests a confirmed, legal testimony) are two individual persons, for they are also called "two lampstands" (11:4), terminology already interpreted in 1:20 to mean the church. Also we must note that the "1,260 days" of the woman's flight and protection from Satan in 12:6 is as well a reference to the protection of God's people, though under a different image or symbol. Note, too, that in 13:5-7 the same beast from the abyss, who here in 11:7 attacks the two witnesses and overcomes them, is said in 13:7 to "make war against the *saints*" and "to conquer them."

Though engaged in great spiritual warfare, the church, like Moses and Elijah of old, must faithfully maintain a courageous and prophetic witness to the world, a witness even unto death. Although the earth rejoices that the testimony of the church is in the end apparently snuffed out (11:7-10), the temporary triumph of evil ("three and a half days," 11:9) will turn to heavenly vindication as the two witnesses (the people of God) are raised from the dead. Though John was not yet ready to describe more fully the resurrection of Christ's followers and the bliss of heaven, we have in the resurrection of the two witnesses (11:11) the depiction of the church's great hope: the resurrection of all those who hold to the testimony of Jesus (compare 11:7-11 with 13:15; 20:4-6).

The seventh trumpet (and third woe) again introduces the earthquake, lightning, thunder (11:15-19). The end of history has come, the time for the dead to be judged and the saints to be rewarded (11:18). Clearly the very end has come, for the heavenly chorus now treats the coming of the reign of God (and Christ), as well as the day of judgment, as *past* events (11:17-18). The chorus sings, "The kingdom of the world *has become* the kingdom of our God and of his Christ, and he will reign for ever and ever" (11:15).

John has again brought us to the point of our Lord's return and, indeed, has begun to describe the rejoicing that will accompany His return (19:1-10). But he is not yet ready to describe the actual coming of the King of kings and Lord of lords. There is (sadly) more to relate regarding "the beast that comes up from the Abyss" to make war with the two witnesses, the people of God (11:7). It is that awful forty-two months, the period of persecution (and protection/witness), that John must now unfold.

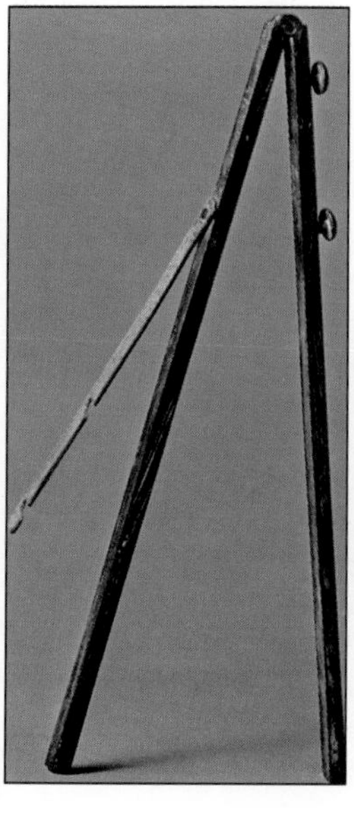

In the photo to the left is a Roman measuring rod probably similar to the one seen by John in his vision (see Rev 11:1).

An ancient censer of the open type is shown above. It consists of a flat shovel on which hot coals were heaped and a handle coated with a heat-resistant material. See Revelation 8:3.

12:1–13:18
The Dragon's Persecution of the Righteous

Chapter 12 is crucial for understanding John's view of the sequence of history. The number three and a half was associated by Christians and Jews with times of evil and judgment (see Luke 4:25). John variously referred to the three and a half years as either "42 months" (11:2; 13:5) or "1,260 days" (11:3; 12:6) or "a time, times and half a time" (12:14). For John it was the period of time when the powers of evil will do their oppressive works. But during this time, God will protect His people (12:6,14) while they both bear witness to their faith (11:3) and simultaneously suffer at the hands of these evil powers (11:2,7; 12:13-17; 13:5-7).

All commentators agree that this terrible period of tribulation will be brought to an end with the coming of the Lord. The critical question, however, is when the three-and-a-half-year period of persecution and witness *begins*. Though some scholars have relegated the three and a half years to some as-yet-unbegun moment in the future, chapter 12 unmistakably pinpoints its beginning with the ascension and enthronement of Christ (12:5). When the woman's (Israel's) offspring is "caught up to God *and to His throne*" (12:5), there is war in heaven, and the dragon is cast down to the earth.

Heaven rejoices because it has been rescued from Satan (12:10-12), but the earth must now mourn (12:12) because the devil has been cast down to earth, and his anger is great. He knows that he has been defeated by the enthronement of Christ and that he has but a short time (12:12). The woman, who (as Israel) brought forth the Christ (12:1-2) and also other offspring (those who hold to the testimony of Jesus), now receives the brunt of the frustrated dragon's wrath. As the enraged dragon now seeks to vent his wrath upon the woman, she is nonetheless nourished and protected for "1,260 days" (12:6), that is, for a "time, times and half a time" (12:14).

John's altogether brief description of the life of Christ (only His birth and enthronement are here specifically referred to) should not mislead the reader into thinking that it is the *infant* child who is "caught up to God and to His throne" (12:5). This passage does not have for its main purpose the telling of the life of Christ, for John knew his readers to be familiar with the decisive events in Christ's history. Rather, the passage seeks to show the *continuity of persecution* as inaugurated by Satan against the woman (Israel) and her child (Christ) and continued against the woman and the rest of her offspring (Christians).

It is, of course, the crucified and risen Lord who is enthroned and whose accession to the throne brings the defeat of the powers of darkness (see Eph 1:19-23; 1 Pet 3:22; compare Rom 1:4; Col 4:15-20; 1 Tim 3:16). The account of the dragon's defeat in, and expulsion from, heaven clearly commences with, and is caused by, the *enthronement* of the woman's offspring. Likewise, *note well* that the story of 12:6, where the woman flees to the wilderness and is protected by God for "1,260 days," has two unmistakable plot "links" in the developing story line of chapter 12. First, the woman's flight and the "1,260 days" of protection in 12:6 clearly commence with the enthronement of 12:5. But in 12:14-17 it is the *persecution of the dragon,* who has now been cast down from heaven to earth, that motivates the woman's flight to the wilderness. Thus what we have in 12:14-17 is the resumption and amplification of the woman's story which was begun in 12:6.

Note the parallel references in 12:6 and 12:14 to the "desert," nourishment, and "time, times and half a time" (12:14), or it's equivalent, "1,260 days" (12:6). This dual plot connection—where two events are seen in connection with the woman's flight—between the *enthronement* of the woman's offspring (Christ) and the *dragon's pursuit* of the woman is neither odd nor surprising. It is the enthronement that (virtually simultaneously) produces the war in heaven, which results in the dragon's expulsion and which then immediately causes the now-enraged dragon to persecute the woman and "the rest of her offspring" (12:17). It is not only clear that the "1,260 days" of 12:6 is the equivalent of the "time, times and half a time" of 12:14 but that the one particular period of persecution/protection in question commences both with the enthronement of Christ and the subsequent—and, for all practical purposes, simultaneous—expulsion of the dragon from heaven.

The dragon then brings forth two henchmen (chap. 13) to help him in his pursuit of those who believe in Jesus. Satan is thus embodied in a political ruler, the beast from the sea (13:1), who will speak blasphemies for "forty-two months" (13:5) and "make war against the saints" (13:7), while the second beast (or "false prophet," 19:20), who comes up from the earth (13:11), seeks to deceive the earth so that its inhabitants worship the first beast.

Thus, in chapters 12–13 each of the various ways of referring to the three and a half years is a reference to a single period of time that began with the enthronement of Christ and will conclude with His return. The time period is not a literal three and a half years but the *entire time between the ascension and the return of Christ,* which will permit the dragon to execute his evil work upon the earth (compare Gal 1:4; Eph 2:2). Almost two

Shown above is a mosaic from Beth-Shan (dating from A.D. 500s) depicting the grape harvest. Shown in the right center is a man holding a sharp sickle in one hand and a cluster of grapes in the other. See Revelation 14:18.

thousand years have elapsed since our Lord ascended to the right hand of God, but the evil period known as the three and a half years continues. Satan still rages, but his time is short, and his evil will cease at the return of Christ.

14:1-20
A Summary of Triumph, Warning, and Judgment

After the depressing news of the ongoing persecutions of God's people by the unholy trinity, John's readers need another word of encouragement and warning. Chapter 14 therefore employs seven "voices" to relate again the warnings and promises of heaven. First is another vision of the 144,000. The 144,000, as before, are the full number of the people of God. It is certainly a reference to Christians, for they "were purchased from among men and offered as firstfruits to God and the Lamb" (14:4).

Using the common biblical imagery of sexual immorality as a reference to idolatry, John called these followers of the Lamb "blameless" (14:5). That is, they did not "defile themselves" with the beast. They are the men and women who have been faithful in their worship of the one true God through Jesus Christ and have not been seduced by the Satanic deceptions of the first beast and his ally, the false prophet. They will be rescued and taken to heaven's throne, where with one voice they will sing a new song of salvation (14:1-5).

Another voice is heard (14:6-7), that of an angel announcing the eternal gospel and warning the earth of coming judgment. The remaining "voices" (or oracles) follow in rapid succession. The fall of "Babylon the Great" (14:8), an Old Testament symbol for a nation opposed to the people of God, is announced. Then the people of God are warned not to follow the beast, and those who follow him are warned of the coming torments of their separation from God (14:9-12). After that a blessing is pronounced on those who remain faithful (14:13). Finally, two voices call for harvest. One calls upon the Son of man to reap the earth as a giant wheat harvest (14:14-16), while the last voice likens the reaping of the earth to a grape harvest, for the coming of the Lord will mean the treading of the winepress of the fierce wrath of God the Almighty (14:17-20).

15:1–16:21
The Seven Cups

Just as the seven seals and the seven trumpets depict different aspects of God's judgments through Christ, so now another dimension of His judgment must be revealed. The seven cups of wrath are similar to the seven trumpets and the seven seals, but they also are different; for there comes a time when the wrath of God is no longer partial or temporary but complete and everlasting. The outpouring of the seven cups of wrath means that God's judgment is also final and irrevocable. The partial judgment ("one-third") of the trumpets suggests that God uses the sufferings and evils of this life as a warning to draw humankind toward repentance and faith. But such tribulations also foreshadow the final hour of judgment, when God's wrath is finished and there is delay no longer.

The seven cups of wrath represent the judgments of the Lamb on the earth, especially on those who have received the mark of the beast. Between the sixth and seventh seals and the sixth and seventh trumpets we were told of God's protection of, and mission for, the people of God. But with the seven cups there is no break between the sixth and seventh outpourings of judgment. Now only wrath is left; there is no more delay. Babylon the Great, the symbol for all who have vaunted themselves against the Most High God, will fall. With the pouring out of the seventh cup of wrath, there is again the great earthquake accompanied by "flashes of lightning, rumblings, peals of thunder" (16:18), for the end has come.

The notion of God's wrath is not always a welcome subject to the Bible reader, but its reality as a clear-cut teaching of both Old and New Testaments is inescapable. The reality of evil, the reality of human freedom, the righteousness of God, and the longing of God to have creatures, who though distinct from Him as real creatures nonetheless freely relate to Him in trust and love, make inevitable the notion and reality of God's wrath. A righteous God responds to those who persist in their evil refusal to acknowledge their rightful Lord.

God longs to see His rebellious children lay down their arms and come home to Him. God has mercifully acted by all possible means—even to the extent of taking to Himself, through His Only Begotten Son, the very penalty that He has prescribed for sin—to bring His wayward children home. Wrath brings grief even to the heart of God, but God will not coerce our love of Him. He has given His children their freedom, and He will not destroy their humanity by removing that freedom, even when His children stubbornly persist in using that freedom in rebellion against Him. Incredibly enough, in spite of the overwhelming mercies of God revealed through Jesus Christ, there will be those who refuse His mercies. In such cases the faithful God of creation and redemption will faithfully respond in keeping with His own nature and word by giving His rebellious sons and daughters what they have stubbornly insisted upon, namely, everlasting separation from Him. Surely, as God's wrath, this is the height of torment and misery—to be separated from the One who is the true source of life, to be cut off from one's merciful Creator and thus to experience everlastingly the eternal death that comes from the rejection of Him who is the source of everlasting life. But we must neither deny nor even lament the wisdom of God for His past or future assertions of wrath. Our God evidently loves righteousness, justice, and mercy to such an extent that He will not brook our cowardly tolerance of evil. We may not lightly dismiss the fact that heaven is neither silent nor embarrassed when evil is punished. Heaven *rejoices* at the justice and judgment of God (19:1-6).

17:1–18:24
Fall and Ruin of the Immortal City and the Beast

Chapter 17 retells the sixth cup, the fall of Babylon the Great, and chapter 18 gives a moving lament for the great city. She has not fulfilled God's purposes for her. All of her mighty works, industry, craftsmanship, political power, and artistic skill are brought to nothing, for she has played the harlot and worshiped the beast rather than devoting her skills and energies to God and to the Lamb.

19:1–22:5
Rejoicing of Heaven and Revelation of the Lamb

Heaven now begins to rejoice because Babylon the Great has fallen and it is time for the appearing of the Lamb's bride. The great marriage supper of salvation is ready to

A relief found near Venice shows two men treading and stomping grapes in a large vat (see Rev 19:15).

commence. Although he has withheld a description of the coming of the Lord on at least three earlier occasions, John is now prepared to describe the glories of the Lord's appearance.

All of heaven rejoices over the righteous judgment of God upon evil (19:1-6). The Lamb's bride, the people of God, has made herself ready by her faithfulness to her Lord through the hour of suffering. Therefore "it was given her" (salvation is always a gift of God) to clothe herself in fine linen, for "the wedding of the Lamb" has come (19:7-8).

Heaven is opened, and the One whose coming has been faithfully petitioned from ages past, the Word of God, the King of kings and Lord of lords, appears to battle the enemies of God in a conflict whose outcome is not in doubt (19:11-16). When the Lamb comes with His heavenly armies, the first beast and the second beast are thrown into the lake of fire from which there is no return (19:20). The dragon, who is the serpent of old, the devil and Satan, is cast into a hellish abyss that is shut and sealed for a thousand years (20:1-3). Since the powers of evil reigned for "three and a half years" (the period of time between the ascension and return of our Lord), Christ will reign for a "thousand years." The dead in Christ are raised to govern with Him (20:4-6), and God's rightful rule over the earth is vindicated.

This thousand-year reign is called the millennium. The term *millennium* is derived from the Latin (*mille,* one thousand, *annum,* year) and means *a period of one thousand years.* The biblical words for *thousand* are *eleph* in Hebrew and *chilioi* in Greek. In multiple Old Testament instances the term is used in counting, even as it is in the New Testament (see Gen 24:60 and Luke 14:31). Occasionally the term is used to mean a large number without specific units being intended (see Mic 5:2; 6:7; and Rev 5:11). The particular references used to establish a doctrine of a thousand years associated with Christ's final coming are found in Revelation 20:2-7.

The biblical materials do not present a systematic eschatology in which all of the diverse references about the end times are brought into one teaching. Therefore in Christian history differing strands of interpretation have emerged. Christian interpreters seeking a coherent systematic doctrine of the last things relate the apocalyptic elements of Old Testament prophecy (especially the Book of Daniel); the apocalyptic elements in the New Testament (especially Matt 24–25; Mark 13; 2 Peter; Jude; and the Book of Revelation); Paul's writings about the final coming (especially 1 Thess 4:13-18 and 2 Thess 2:1-11—the man of lawlessness); Paul's views about the relationship of Jews and Gentiles (Rom 9–11); and the references to antichrist(s) in 1 John.

Our concern with millennial issues, that is, whether the return of Christ is before the millennium (premillennialism) or after the millennium (as in either postmillennialism or amillennialism), is a concern whose significance is greatly exaggerated with respect to the interpretation of the Book of Revelation. What ultimately mattered for John is that the followers of Christ, those who have suffered the afflictions and persecutions of this present evil age, will one day be rescued and vindicated by the appearance of Christ, whose coming will destroy the powers of evil. It is abundantly clear in the New Testament that the shape and promise of the future hope should exert an influence upon our present behavior and moral devotion to Christ (compare Rom 8:18-25). Indeed, the very point of Revelation is to encourage Christian perseverance in the present in light of the coming triumph of God through Jesus Christ.

The interpretation of the relationship of the thousand-year kingdom to the return of Christ given in the commentary above could be called a form of premillennialism. For millennial views see the chart "Millennial Perspectives on Revelation" and the article "God's Rule and Reign: The Doctrine of Last Things."

Each of the views has something to commend it. Postmillennialism is wrong in its placement of the return of Christ at the conclusion of the thousand-year kingdom. Yet postmillennialism has accurately captured a significant motif in biblical prophecy in both the Old and New Testament. That is, we must live and preach in hope. We must preach the gospel not in the expectation that no one will believe, but we must proclaim the gospel to the ends of the earth, believing that God will somehow use our witness to His glorious salvation through the person of Jesus Christ to bring about a mighty triumph for the kingdom of God. Though we certainly cannot bring the kingdom of God on earth through human means, the preaching of the gospel does indeed offer hope for the transformation of life.

Amillennialism is to be commended for its emphasis upon the current reign of Jesus Christ. Indeed, the Book of Revelation makes abundantly clear (see the exposition above of chaps. 5 and 12) that Christ indeed has overcome and as such has been raised and exalted to the right hand of God. He is currently Lord of the churches. He is indeed currently Lord of the cosmos. He is the one into whose hands all power in heaven and on earth has been given. He has been raised far above all rule and authority and power and every name that is named (Eph 1:19-21).

Still, only premillennialism can properly explain the episodic sequence of Revelation 19–20.

At the conclusion of the "thousand years" (20:7), the dragon is to be released. He is permitted another brief time of deception, but his time is short-lived. Following this final episode of deception at the conclusion of the thousand years, the dragon is recaptured and this time cast into the lake of fire and brimstone, "where the beast and the false prophet are also" (20:10). The fate given to the beast and the false prophet at the return of Christ is also finally meted out to the dragon at the close of the reign of Christ. Then the final judgment takes place, at which all not included in the Book of Life are thrown into the lake of fire (20:11-15).

Chapter 21 is often thought to refer to the period following the thousand-year reign, but it is more probably a retelling of the return of Christ from the viewpoint of the bride. Here we have clear-cut clues about the fact of a literary "retelling." Just as chapter 17 was a recapitulation of the seventh cup and the fall of the harlot, Babylon the Great (compare the language of 17:1-3, which clearly introduces a "retelling" with the language of 21:9-10), so chapter 21 recapitulates the glorification of the bride of the Lamb (21:1–22:5). Now the story is told with the focus upon the bride. To be the bride is to be the holy city, the New Jerusalem, to live in the presence of God and the Lamb, and to experience protection, joy, and the everlasting, life-giving light of God (21:9-27). The tree of life grows there, and there the river of the water of life flows. There will no longer be any night; there will no longer be any curse, for the throne of God and of the Lamb is there. And there His bond-servants will serve Him and reign with Him forever and ever (21:1-5).

22:6-21
Conclusion

John concluded his prophecy by declaring the utter faithfulness of his words. Those who heed his prophecy will receive the blessings of God. Those who ignore the warnings will be left outside the gates of God's presence (22:6-15). Solemnly and hopefully praying for the Lord to come, John closed his book (22:17,20). The churches must have ears to hear what the Spirit has said (22:16-17). Under the threat of an everlasting curse, the hearers are warned to protect John's sacred text: neither to add to nor to take away from the words of his prophecy (22:18-19). The people of God must, by His grace (22:21), persevere in the hour of tribulation, knowing that their enthroned Lord will soon return in triumph.

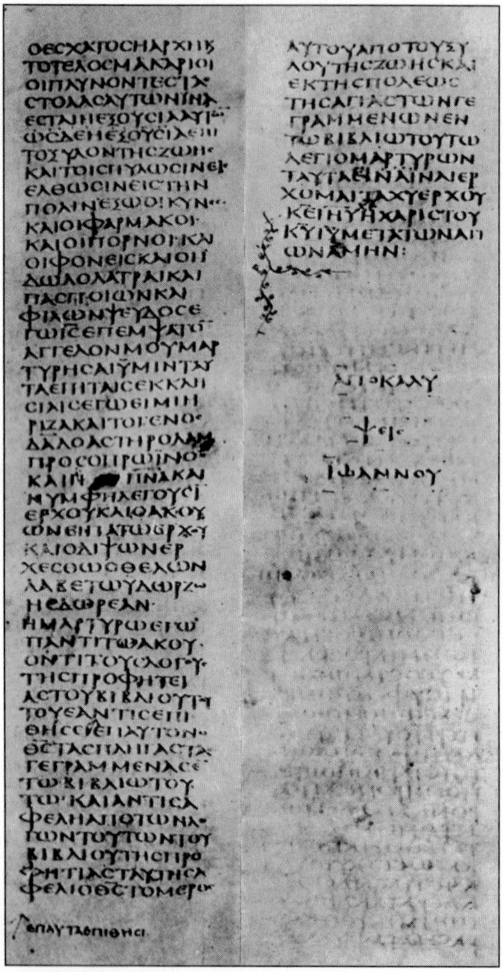

Shown above is the last page of one of the earliest and most important manuscripts of the Greek Bible—the Codex Sinaiticus (from A.D. 300s).

Theological Significance

It is extremely helpful to remember what the very first verse of the book says about this book. It is a revelation that God gives to His church, a revelation of Jesus Christ. The greatest purpose of the book is to show us Jesus Christ. A suffering church does not need a detailed forecast of future events. It needs a vision of the exalted Christ to encourage the weary and persecuted believers. We see Jesus Christ standing in the midst of the churches. We see Him portrayed as the Lamb of God who died for the sins of the world. We see Him as one who rules and reigns. He is the one who takes His church to be with Him in the new heavens and the new earth, where we will worship Him forever and ever. Amen.

Questions for Reflection

1. How does Revelation differ from other New Testament books?
2. How is Revelation like other New Testament books in terms of basic Christian doctrine?
3. What is the central theme of Revelation?
4. What is the central exhortation of Revelation for Christians?
5. What events in the experience of Jesus are referred to in Revelation 12, and how do the "1,260 days" and "42 months" relate to those events?
6. How does the message of Revelation relate to our current situation?
7. How do the "42 months" or "1,260 days" and the "1,000 years" relate to the return of Christ?

Sources for Additional Study

Beasley-Murray, George R. *The Book of Revelation. New Century Bible.* Grand Rapids: Eerdmans, 1981.

Ladd, George E. *A Commentary on the Revelation of John.* Grand Rapids: Eerdmans, 1972

Mounce, Robert H. *The Book of Revelation. New International Commentary on the New Testament.* Grand Rapids: Eerdmans, 1977.

Newport, John P. *The Lion and the Lamb: A Commentary on the Book of Revelation for Today.* Nashville: Broadman, 1986.

Walvoord, John. *The Revelation of Jesus Christ.* Chicago: Moody, 1976.

PART V

THE BIBLE AND CHRISTIAN FAITH

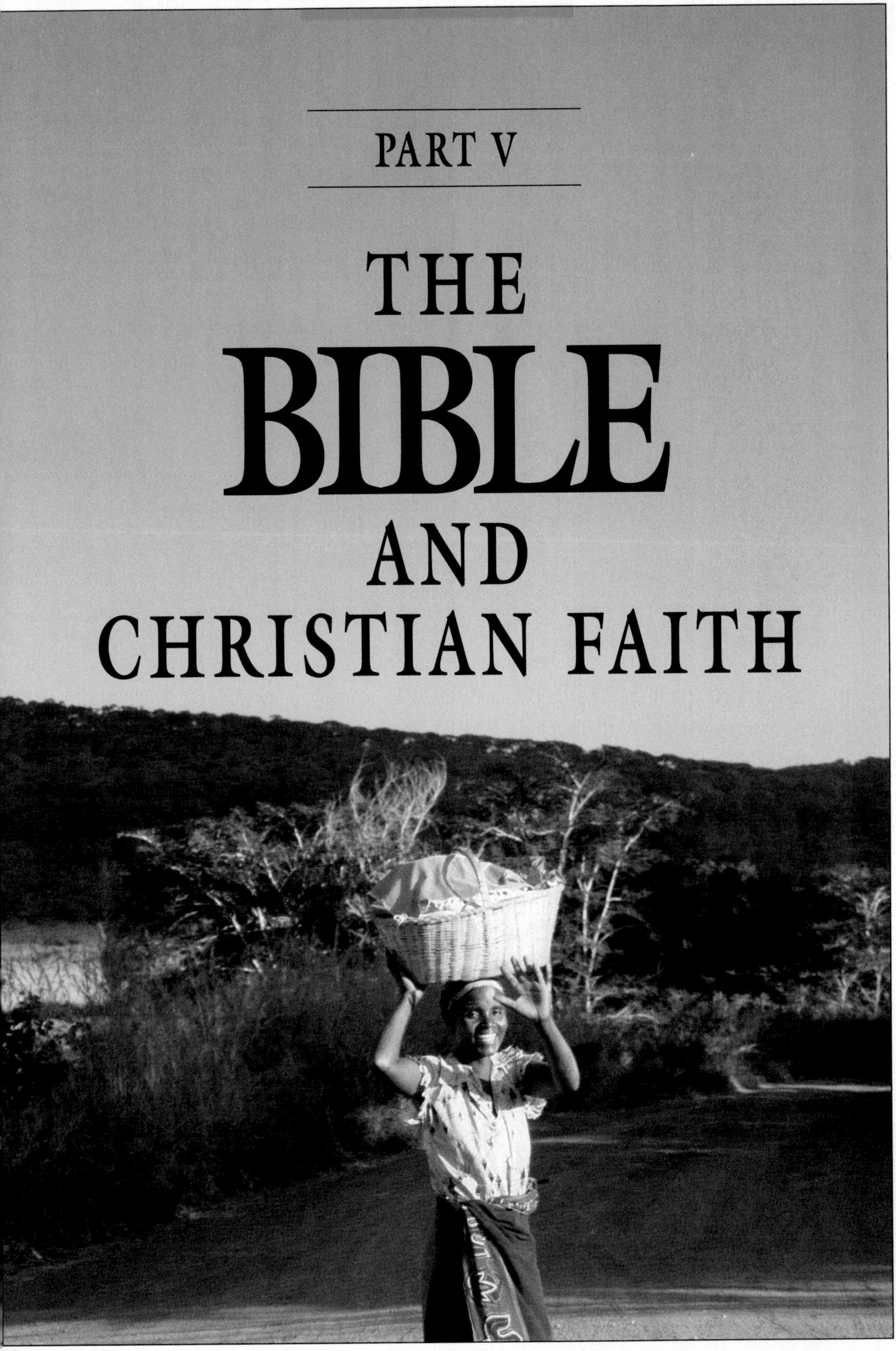

Christian Faith and the Christian Community

Jesus' ministry with His followers followed general principles of first-century instruction. The students listened to, questioned, learned from, and imitated their teacher. Jesus stated that a student "who is fully trained will be like his teacher" (Luke 6:40). Jesus challenged His followers to teach others what they had learned from Him and had been commanded by Him (see Matt 28:18-20).

Similarly, the Epistles stress the importance of teaching and living "in accord with sound doctrine" (Titus 2:1). Christian truth must be formulated and articulated in such a way as to inform and shape beliefs, values, and life-styles. The earliest form of Christian doctrine or theology focused on Jesus and the teachings of the apostles. It was the responsibility of the first generation of Christians and every following generation to "encourage others by sound doctrine and refute those who oppose it" (see Titus 1:9; Jude 3).

Christian theology is thinking about and articulating thoughts about God based on His revelation to us. Christian theology should engage and impact academic worlds, society at-large, and the church. Primarily, however, theology is for the church. Every Christian is called to think lofty thoughts about God and to love God with all of one's mind, as well as one's heart, soul, and strength. Christian theology forms the foundation of the church's beliefs, proclamation, and ministry. Christian theology involves not only believing revealed truth, but it includes calling the church to purity and ethical holiness.

The articles that follow summarize the basic truths of the Christian faith concerning God, His Word, His world, His Son, His Spirit, the salvation of God's people, and the reign and rule of God. Not only do they discuss how these truths are shaped, but also how they are applied for Christian worship, Christian living, and Christian families.

The crucifixion

DENOMINATIONAL PERSPECTIVES ON MAJOR DOCTRINES

	Baptist	Catholic	Church of Christ	Episcopal	Lutheran	Methodist	Pentecostal	Presbyterian
GOD	There is one and only one living and true God who reveals Himself to us as Father, Son, and Holy Spirit, with distinct personal attributes but without division of nature, essence, or being.	The one God is three by reason of three inner personal principles, Father, Son, (Word), and Holy Spirit. One God beyond time and space is perfect and and changeless. God created freely from love.	Speaking where the Bible speaks and remaining silent where the Bible is silent, Churches of Christ prefer not to use the word "Trinity." While believing in Father, Son, and Holy Spirit, stress is on the Son, Jesus Christ.	"In unity of this Godhead there be three persons of one substance, power, and eternity, the Father, the Son, and the Holy Ghost."	There is one Divine Essence, God; and yet there are three Persons of the same essence and power, co-eternal—Father, Son, Holy Ghost.	The three persons of the Godhead are "one in substance, power and eternity. God is infinite in power, wisdom, and goodness." He is spirit and personal, creator and sustainer, and has revealed Himself as Father, Son, Spirit.	God is ultimate authority. The one true God has revealed Himself in three personalities: Father, Son, and Holy Spirit. All three are essential in revealing the one, inseparable God.	God made Himself known to us in three Persons: Father, Son, and Holy Spirit. The three Persons are one true, eternal God, the same in substance, equal in power and glory, though distinguished by personal properties.
HOLY SCRIPTURE	The Holy Bible was written by men divinely inspired and is the record of God's self-revelation to humanity. It has God for its author, salvation for its end, and truth without mixture of error for its matter.	The Bible teaches without error those truths which God wishes to reveal to all people for their eternal salvation. The church in her creeds summarizes basic doctrines of the Bible. Both Old and New Testaments and Apocrypha are believed divinely inspired.	Scripture is true, inspired, and completely sufficient for doctrine. Both Old and New Testaments are canonical, but the New Testament is primary since it reveals Christ.	The Word of God is the written record of God's self-revelation and of God's acts in history. Must be seen in the context of reason and tradition. Includes Old and New Testaments and Apocrypha.	The Scriptures are the Word of God, reliable, trustworthy, and understood through the Holy Spirit. Several confessional statements interpreting Scripture "participate in the normative authority of Scripture."	The sixty-six books of the Bible contain all things necessary to salvation. The Bible is the primary source and guideline for doctrine. Tradition, experience, and reason interact with Scripture in understanding God's Word.	The Bible as the written revelation of God in Christ is inspired by the Holy Spirit and is authoritative.	The sixty-six books of the Bible are the primary source of knowledge about God and His intentions for persons. As the inspired record of God's revelation, Scriptures contain instruction to salvation.
SALVATION	Salvation involves redemption of sinners who accept Jesus Christ as Lord and Savior. In its broadest sense, salvation includes regeneration, sanctification, and glorification.	Original sin interfered with God's plan for humanity. God sent His Son to save humanity from original sin and sins committed. Jesus saved humanity by His life and death and by rising from the dead and ascending into heaven. All who believe Jesus and are sorry for sins are saved.	All persons are sinful and need salvation but do not merit it. God offers salvation, and persons may decide to accept or reject it. Salvation comes through faith in Bible teachings and Jesus, repentance, and baptism. Apostasy is an option.	Redemption was wrought and wholeness of life is seen in the life, death, and resurrection of Jesus Christ. Individuals respond to God's salvation through baptism and spend a lifetime appropriating God's grace.	Salvation is God's gift offered to all people by the Holy Spirit through the preaching of God's Word.	Salvation comes by the the grace of God upon a person's decision to say yes to God's gracious offer of salvation. Good works are a sign of salvation. Christians may renounce salvation (commit apostasy) or achieve a temporary state of holy perfection.	All persons need salvation to restore relationship with God because of sin. Salvation involves three stages including repentance and salvation, sanctification, and baptism of the Holy Spirit evidenced by speaking in tongues.	All persons are sinful and need salvation. We do not earn salvation; rather God elects some persons to salvation. These cannot refuse His offer (irresistible grace). God saves those who by faith repent and put their trust in Christ.

DENOMINATIONAL PERSPECTIVES ON MAJOR DOCTRINES

	Baptist	Catholic	Church of Christ	Episcopal	Lutheran	Methodist	Pentecostal	Presbyterian
BAPTISM	Christian baptism is the immersion of a believer in water in the name of the Father, Son, and Holy Spirit, symbolizing the believer's death to sin, burial of old life, and resurrection to new life in Christ.	Baptism is the sacrament of spiritual regeneration by which a person is incorporated into life with Christ and His church, given grace and cleansed from original and personal sin. It is administered by pouring water over the person, or the person is immersed in water.	Baptism is necessary for the remission of sins, to place one in Christ, and to place one in the church. The mode is immersion for believers only.	Baptism is the sacrament in which we say yes to God's prior act of grace toward us in Jesus Christ. Baptism is the preferred form, though pouring is often used. Both adults and infants are baptized.	Baptism plants the seed of salvation and may be administered by sprinkling. Other means of baptism using water and the Word of God are also accepted.	Baptism is a sacrament, a sign of God's grace by which He works within us to strengthen and confirm our faith. Infants are baptized as an initiation into Christian community by sprinkling, pouring, or immersion.	Baptism is a sacred ordinance to be obeyed, but it does not save. Believers are baptized by immersion.	A visible sign of God's word portraying Christ's redemption, baptism is administered by sprinkling or pouring water on adults. Baptism is the sign and seal of our ingrafting into Christ.
LORD'S SUPPER	The Lord's Supper is a symbolic act of obedience whereby members of the church, through partaking of the bread and fruit of the vine, memorialize the death of Christ and anticipate His second coming.	The Eucharist or mass is the central act of worship. The sacrament reenacts Christ's death and resurrection in ritual form. The actual body and blood of Christ are believed to be present in the elements (transubstantiation). Celebrated daily.	The Lord's Supper is an ordinance with a threefold meaning including: memorial meal commanded by Christ, proclamation of Christ's death for sins, and a time for examination of commitment to Christ. Observed only on Sunday at the church each week.	The Holy Eucharist is the sacrament commanded by Christ for the continual remembrance of His life, death, and resurrection until His coming again. The elements of bread and wine are received by those claiming Christ as Savior.	Holy Eucharist is one of three sacraments including baptism and absolution. Celebrated corporately, Eucharist is the Real Presence of the body and blood of Christ through sacramental union. When received in faith, grace through the Eucharist works forgiveness of sin, life, and salvation.	The Lord's Supper is a sign of love that Christians should share and a sacrament of our redemption by Christ's death. As a symbol the Lord's Supper represents Christ's work of atonement. As a sacrament the Spirit of God works through the bread and grape juice to call to mind Christ's death. Open to all Christians.	The Lord's Supper is a command of Christ to be obeyed in remembrance of Christ's death and sacrifice on the cross. The elements are symbolic of the spilled blood and the broken body. The supper is a time for individual examination and may be accompanied by foot washing.	The Lord's Supper is a sacrament in that the Spirit of God works in the believer who recalls Christ's work of redemption, reflects on his or commitment to Christ, and participates in the priesthood of believers by passing the bread and cup. The Lord is the host of the supper, and all who trust Him may partake.

THE TRIUNE GOD HIS EXISTENCE, NATURE, AND ATTRIBUTES

The study of God is the fundamental doctrine of Christian theology. Some would suggest that the study of humankind or sinfulness is the proper starting point for doing theology. We would suggest, however, that humankind as creation is only understood in light of God as Creator and that sinfulness is understood only in light of God's holiness and grace (Isa 6:1-8).

Approaches to the Study of God

There are two primary methods of approaching the study of God: (1) a philosophical approach and (2) a biblical approach. The philosophical approach begins with the rational arguments for the existence of God. This approach begins with creation and attempts to argue for the existence of God.

The five basic arguments while unique are all similar in that they argue from the standpoint of cause and effect. These arguments are called the cosmological, the teleological, the anthropological, the moral, and the ontological. Each argument attempts to find and understand God through general revelation. But as we will see in our next section, general revelation is in need of special revelation to be rightly understood (Ps 19). This approach might be able to conclude that there is a Creator or an uncaused cause, but the Trinitarian God of biblical Christianity can only be discovered through special revelation.

This leads us to the second approach: the biblical starting point. This starting point brings us into the presence of God without delay. The biblical approach presupposes the existence of God and recognizes that only through special revelation is God truly revealed (Gen 1:1). From this starting point it is recognized that the central affirmation of Scripture is not that there is a God but that God has acted and spoken in history.

Thinking about God

The Westminster Shorter Catechism describes God as Spirit, infinite, eternal, and unchangeable in His being, power, holiness, justice, goodness, and truth.

The Belgic Confession of Faith affirms we all believe with the heart and confess with the mouth that there is one simple and spiritual being we call God and that He is eternal, incomprehensible, invisible, immutable, infinite, almighty, perfectly wise, just, good, and the overflowing fountain of all good.

The Baptist Faith and Message confesses that there is one and only one living and true God. He is an intelligent, spiritual, and personal being, the Creator, Redeemer, Preserver, and Ruler of the universe. God is infinite in holiness and all other perfections.

Finally, all we can say, however, is that God is God. He cannot be exhaustively described or defined. Yet the following foundational principles can be helpful in our thinking about God.

1. God has spoken to men and women, and the Bible is His Word, which has been given to us to make us wise unto salvation.
2. God is Lord and King over this world, ruling all things for His own glory, displaying His perfections in all that He does in order that humans and angels may worship and adore Him.
3. God is Savior, active in sovereign love through the Lord Jesus Christ to rescue believers from the guilt and power of sin, to adopt them as His children and accordingly to bless them.
4. God is Triune; there are within the Godhead three persons: the Father, Son, and Holy Spirit. And the work of salvation is one in which all three act together, purposing, providing, and applying forgiveness.

Godliness means responding to God's revelation in trust and obedience, faith and worship, prayer and praise, submission and service. True Christianity is seeing life and living it in light of God's written word (adapted from J. I. Packer).

To think wrongly about God is idolatry (Ps 50:21). Thinking rightly about God is eternal life (John 17:3) and should be the believer's life objective (Jer 9:23-24). We can think rightly about God because He is knowable (1 Cor 2:11), yet we must remain mindful that He is simultaneously incomprehensible (Rom 11:33-36). God can be known, but He cannot be known completely (Deut 29:29).

The names for God is that all reveal God as personal in contrast to the philosophical terms such as "Ground of Being," "Unmoved Mover," and "First Cause," which are abstract and nonpersonal. See article under Pentateuch.

Personal Nature of God

God is personal and is differentiated from other beings, nature, and the universe. This is in contrast to current philosophical approaches to God that say that God is in a part of the world, creating a continual process, and the process itself is the actuality. These approaches speak of God as being and becoming, primarily becoming as part of the cosmic process, seeing God for what He was and will become.

The Bible, however, proclaims God as Spirit (John 4:24), alive (Deut 5:26), intelligent (Rom 11:33), purposive (Eph 1:11; 3:11), active (John 5:17), and free (Ps 135:5-9). God is free in that His actions are determined *solely by His own nature and pleasure.* Only an absolutely free person can limit himself, and God has chosen to limit Himself. He cannot do anything prohibited by His own nature. As a personal God, He is self-conscious (Exod 3:14), knowing Himself completely. He is emotional; yet these emotions, unlike human emotions, are not mixed with imperfections and weaknesses. We learn that God rejoices (Isa 62:5), loves (Jer 31:3), shows compassion (Ps 145:8), demonstrates pity (Ps 103:3), hates (Ps 5:5), is jealous (Deut 5:9), and can suffer and be grieved (Judg 10:16).

The Attributes of God

When we talk about the attributes of God, we are affirming something true about God that has been revealed in creation, Scripture, or Christ. The study of the attributes of God, far from being dull and heavy, may, for God's people, be a sweet and absorbing spiritual exercise. For the soul that is thirsty for God (Ps 42:1), nothing could be more enjoyable or delightful.

Theologians have distinguished the attributes of God in a variety of ways. Some of these include: God's constitution and God's personality; absolute attributes and relational attributes; natural attributes and moral attributes; divine love and divine freedom; incommunicable attributes and communicable attributes; holiness and love. All of these approaches can be helpful in different ways. Whatever way we choose to distinguish and categorize these, we must avoid antithetical views of God's attributes that attempt to pit God's love against His holiness or His mercy against His righteousness. Likewise, we must be cautious not to adopt an exclusionary principle that will leave out certain attributes in favor of others. For the purposes of our study, we will adopt the classifications of *greatness* and *goodness* (following the work of Millard Erickson) as handles by which we can discuss these truths about God.

Attributes of Greatness

Self-existent. When we confess that God is self-existent, we mean He is totally self-sufficient, depending on nothing external to Himself. The source of God's existence is completely within Himself (Ps 36:9; John 5:26).

Infinite. We gladly affirm that God is infinite in relation to time, space, knowledge, and power. When we say God is infinite, we mean that God is not only unlimited but unlimitable.

God's infinity and time (eternality). God is eternal, and His existence is not measured by time. This does not mean that God is timeless but rather that He is above time or over time. We must acknowledge that He is aware of what has happened, what is happening, and what will happen at each point in time. Yet there is no time in His action or willing. He has from all eternity known what He is doing and will do (Ps 90:2; Isa 57).

God's infinity and space (omnipresence). God created space, and He cannot be localized. He has access to the whole of creation at all times (Ps 139:7-12; Acts 17:24-25).

God's infinity and knowledge (omniscience). God always acts with all the facts. His knowledge is all inclusive (past, present, and future) and complete. He does not grow in knowledge (Ps 147:4; Rom 11:33).

God's infinity and power (omnipotence). God can do all things consistent with His nature. We confess biblical affirmations about God's power, not philosophical abstractions. God's energy is constant and never will be diminished. Where the Bible maintains that all things are possible (Matt 19:6), it is primarily a confession about God's relation to people, although it also has reference to God's power over nature (Isa 40:28; Jer 32:15-17).

Sovereign. God is the Supreme Being and Ruler in the universe, is total and absolute, and is in control of all things (Eph 1:11).

Constant and Consistent. Some theologians refer to God's consistency as His immutability. We prefer to speak of God as consistent because immutability is often misunderstood as meaning immobility. An unchanging

The birth of Jesus Christ

God must change or respond in His dealing with humanity (such as His negative response to Adam and His positive response to Nineveh) in order to remain unchangeable in His character (Num 23:19; Jas 1:17). There is no change in God's nature, character, or purpose, though there are changes or responses in His actions and dealings. To affirm that God is consistent means He never becomes greater, better, or worse; He never learns, grows, develops, improves, evolves, or gets younger or older. While He is consistent, He is not static or isolated from His creation but dynamic and involved with His creation. He does feel, sympathize, and express emotion and passion; but He does so perfectly and consistently.

Attributes of Goodness

Holiness. To affirm God is holy means He is both completely unique and absolutely pure. God is unique, separate from the ordinary sense of life. He is majestic in holiness. The expression of God's love is regulated by His holiness, and His holiness is related to His faithfulness and the surety of His covenants (Ps 105:42; Num 20:6-13). It is right to see God's holiness as a controlling attribute in relation to His other attributes of goodness (Isa 6:1-4; 57:15; 1 Pet 1:15-16).

Righteousness. God is absolutely right beyond all comprehension in reference to His law (Ps 19:7-9), His actions (Gen 18:25), and in His relationships. God's actions are right not just because He pronounces them right but because He acts consistently with His nature, thus His actions are objectively right.

Justice. The application of His righteousness and the administration of righteousness to others is God's justice. Because He is just, He must punish sin (Gen 2:17; Rom 6:23), which includes the exercise of His wrath (Rom 1:18). Apparent injustices in society will be made right by God's eschatological justice (Ps 73). But we, as God's people, are to seek justice in society (Amos 5:12-15; Jas 2:9).

Truth. God makes good His every word and promise (John 17:17-19). God can always be trusted because He conforms exactly in His being to the highest ideal of what He ought to be. This assures us that He will respond to all true worship (John 4:24).

Faithfulness. God's faithfulness is closely related to His consistency. His will and actions are always found true, reliable, and steadfast. He will never commit Himself to do something He is not capable of doing (Lam 3:23-24; 1 Thess 5:24).

Love. God's love includes fatherly benevolence (Matt 5:45), motherly care (Isa 49:14-16), and a parental discipline (Heb 12:6) because His love is a holy love. There is in God no thought of personal benefit since He seeks only the good of the ones loved (Jer 31:3; John 3:16). God's love is an initiating love (1 John 4:7-8) and does not wait for a reciprocal response to be expressed.

Grace. God deals with women and men on the basis of His goodness and generosity, not on any merit in us but according to our need. God could love unselfishly and insist that His love be deserved, but His grace requires absolutely nothing. Grace is giving us what we do not deserve (Eph 1:7; 2:8; Titus 3:4-7). God is truly righteous and holy as well as truly loving and gracious.

Mercy. God is likewise tenderhearted and demonstrates loving compassion for His people (Exod 3:7; Ps 103:13). This includes His slowness toward anger and wrath which is His persistent love (Rom 2:4; 2 Pet 3:9). If grace is giving us what we do not deserve, God's mercy includes not giving us what we deserve.

We can conclude that all of God's attributes work together. Between His attributes there are no contradictions. One attribute does not need to be suspended to demonstrate another. His attributes are not added together to make up His total being. Rather, in Him all His attributes are one. All of God does all that He does, and He does not divide Himself to act. He works in the complete unity of His being. Thus we can speak of His holy love. To see God for who He is gives believers a God-centered perspective of life and ministry. It also enables us to see theology not from the standpoint of the needs of men and women, which produces an inverted theology, but from the viewpoint of God's majestic glory.

The Triune God

Scripture reveals the unity of God (Deut 6:4; Eph 4:6; 1 Tim 2:5). It also asserts or implies the deity of three Persons: Father (John 6:27), Son (Heb 1:8), and Holy Spirit (Acts 5:3-4). Also the Bible pictures the Trinity in action at the birth (Luke 1:35) and baptism (Matt 3:16) of Jesus. The Trinity is associated together in benedictions, doxologies, and baptismal formulas (Matt 28:19-20; 2 Cor 13:14).

We can say that God is one in His nature and three in His Persons. More specifically we can confess that there is only one God, but in the unity of the Godhead there are three eternal and coequal Persons, the same in substance yet distinct in function. The members of the Trinity are equal, yet they may functionally subordinate at times. Without the Trinity we have no final and perfect revelation of God. God is perfectly infinite, and only God can reveal God perfectly and adequately. Thus Christ perfectly reveals an infinite God to finite and imperfect humanity while the Spirit makes known to us the fullness of Christ.

The teaching regarding the Trinity is incomprehensible. It is truth for the heart. The fact that it cannot be satisfactorily explained, instead of refuting such a truth, rather underscores it. No one could have imagined this doctrine; such a truth had to be revealed. As the church fathers affirmed, the Trinity is divinely revealed, not humanly constructed. It would be absurd if it were a human invention. It is not self-evident or logically consistent, but it is a mystery that God has revealed.

Without the Trinity there could be no salvation from sin in the biblical sense. If there had been no incarnation, there would have been no Savior. Without a Savior there would have been no atonement and no salvation for the Spirit to apply. All analogies to explain the Trinity fall short, resulting in functional understandings of the Trinity, resulting in either modalism or tritheism (one person manifesting himself in three ways or three different gods, respectively). Try to explain it and we might think we are losing our minds. Far worse, try to deny it and we will lose our very souls.

Conclusion

God is not physical but spiritual, not dead but living, not passive but active, not impersonal but personal. As a personal Spirit, God has intellect, emotions, and will. He enjoys fellowship with persons created in His image. The Trinitarian God acts consistently with His nature; He cannot deny Himself. God is absolutely free, holy, loving, gracious, and infinitely wise in all He does. God has fully revealed Himself in the person and ministry of the Lord Jesus Christ (John 1:14,18; 14:9).

A right response to these truths will create a God-centered life that focuses on the majesty and glory of God. God desires our worship in spirit and truth (John 4:24). He initiates relationship with His creatures, and our worship is an encounter with God that only He can make possible by His grace.

Questions for Reflection

1. Is it possible to define God? How would we describe Him?
2. Should we speak of love as more central in God than His other attributes?
3. What is meant by the holiness of God? Should we speak of God's holiness as more central than His other attributes?
4. Does the biblical idea of the Trinity teach that there are three Gods or three functions of God or three Persons yet one God? Which one? Why? Why not?
5. Can the Trinity be discovered from nature/general revelation?
6. How does our thinking about God affect our worship and praying (individually and corporately)?
7. How can we reflect or "incarnate" the attributes of God to our contemporary culture so as to bring love, peace, mercy, and justice to this world?

Sources for Additional Study

Bickersteth, E. H. *The Trinity.* Grand Rapids: Kregal, 1959.

Packer, J. I. *Knowing God.* Downers Grove: InterVarsity, 1973.

Tozer, A. W. *The Knowledge of the Holy.* New York: Harper, 1961.

GOD'S WORD THE DOCTRINE OF REVELATION AND INSPIRATION

All Christians recognize that God has acted and spoken in history, thus revealing Himself to His creatures. God's revealing or disclosing of Himself is called His revelation. God has disclosed Himself in a variety of ways (Heb 1:1-3) including nature, history, human experience, human reason, human conscience, the church, Jesus Christ, and Holy Scripture.

Revelation is God's manifestation of Himself to humankind in such a way that men and women can know and fellowship with Him. If human beings are to know God, such knowledge must come about by God's self-revelation to them because humans are finite, and God is infinite. Theologians generally distinguish between *general* and *special* revelation. In this presentation we will look carefully at how God has revealed Himself and also survey the concepts of inspiration and inerrancy as they relate to Holy Scripture, which for today is the source of God's revelation.

Revelation

General Revelation. The apostle Paul tells us in Romans 1:18-23 that God has made Himself known through general or natural means. This echoes an affirmation made by the psalmist centuries earlier. He observed, "The heavens are telling of the glory of God" (Ps 19:1). The psalmist saw the glory of God clearly because he knew God from special revelation, but what he saw had been objectively and genuinely there.

These statements can be rephrased to say that all that can be known about God in a *natural* sense has been revealed in nature. We can say that *general revelation is God's disclosure of Himself in a general way to all people at all times in all places.* Jesus confirmed in Matthew 5:45 that God sends the sun and the rain upon *all* people, both righteous and unrighteous, thus revealing His goodness to all.

Of course, we must acknowledge that although available to all, this is a limited revelation. In fact, Paul limited this knowledge of God to God's power and deity. God exists, and human beings know it. When men and women subsequently refuse to acknowledge and worship God, as they do, the fault is not in a lack of evidence but in their irrational and resolute determination not to know Him. God's revelation in nature is sufficient to convince anyone of God's existence and power if individuals will receive what has been made known to them.

Not only has God revealed Himself in nature but also in what might be called an internal revelation. This internal revelation involves human reason, human experience, and human conscience. This means that each person has been given the capacity for receiving God's general revelation. In Romans 1:19-21 and 2:12-16, Paul talked about this capacity and confirmed that humans know right from wrong and thus are responsible for their actions. The combination of human experiences makes up human history, another source of God's general revelation. In Acts 17:22-31 it is asserted that God has made Himself known in history and that He is no unknown God; rather, He is the true God who commands all people everywhere to repent. God's general revelation is *plain.* No one, no matter how weak minded or seemingly insignificant, can be excused for missing it. There is enough knowledge of God made known in a flower to lead a child or a scientist to acknowledge God and worship Him. There is sufficient evidence in a tree, a fingerprint, a snowflake, or a grain of sand to cause us to glorify the true God. But people *will not* do this. Instead, they substitute nature or parts of nature, or their own experience, for God and find their hearts darkened.

Even though men and women lack the will to come to a pure and clear knowledge of God, all excuse is cut off because the fault of rejection is within them. It is impossible to pretend to be ignorant of God's revelation without human conscience itself convicting humankind of rejection and ingratitude. Men and women suppress God's truth because they do not like the truth about God. They do not like the God to which the truth leads them, so they invent substitute gods instead.

The universality of religion on earth is evident of both truths just discussed. God has revealed Himself to all people in all places at all times; thus people everywhere express a need for God. This expression may be found in sophisticated laws of culture, in materialism, in the gods and goddesses of world religions, or in bestial images of paganism. Yet these expressions are equally evident of the fact that human beings in history have consistently and willfully rejected God because they will not have God and, therefore, need something to take God's place (Rom 1:18-32).

According to Paul, the act of suppressing the awareness of God and His demands warps our reason and conscience. Because of this rejection of God, God righteously reveals His wrath against humankind. God's general revelation does not bring one into a saving relationship with God; it does reveal God to His creatures, and they are therefore *responsible* for their response.

Special Revelation. God has revealed Himself in nature, history, and human experience, but sin's entrance into the world has changed that revelation and the interpretation of it. What is needed to understand fully God's self-disclosure is His special revelation. Indeed, it can be said that special revelation provides the spectacles through which we can fully understand and appreciate God's general revelation. There is divine truth outside of special revelation, but it is consistent with and supplemental to, not a substitute for, special revelation. General revelation is consistent with special revelation but yet distinct from it.

In contrast to God's general revelation, which is available to all people, *God's special revelation is available to specific people at specific times in specific places, which is available now only by consultation of sacred Scripture.* In recognition of the human predicament, God chose at the very beginning to reveal Himself in a more direct way. God has entered our world throughout the course of history. He has disclosed Himself to us within time and space. In this special revelation, God both acted and spoke to redeem the human race from its own self-imposed evil. Through miracles, the exodus, and ultimately through Jesus Christ, God has made Himself known in history. God's revelation includes not only these *acts* in history but also the prophetic-apostolic interpretation of these events.

We can thus affirm that this special revelation has three stages. There is, first of all, redemption in history as mentioned in the previous paragraph. This ultimately centers in the work of the Lord Jesus Christ. He died in the place of sinners and rose as proof of their divine justification. Second, there is the written source of God's revelation, the Bible. God has, in Holy Scripture, provided interpretive records of what He has done for the redemption of men and women. Third, there is the work of the Holy Spirit in the lives of individuals and the corporate life of the church. The Spirit applies God's revelation to the minds and hearts of His people. As a result men and women receive Jesus Christ as Lord and Savior and are enabled to follow Him faithfully in a believing, covenant community until life's end.

For today it is evident that the Bible is of crucial importance. For it is in the Bible alone we learn of God's redemption of sinners in Christ Jesus. It is through the Bible that the Spirit speaks to individuals and believing communities. There, as John Calvin has said, "our wisdom ought to be nothing else than to embrace with humble teachableness, and at least without finding fault, whatever is taught in Sacred Scripture."

General revelation is inferior to special revelation in clarity and in range of subjects considered. The insufficiency of general revelation requires special revelation. It is important to note that general revelation provides concepts of God that enable God's people to know and understand the God of special revelation. These concepts have a common subject matter and perspective that bring about a mutually harmonious and complementary understanding.

We have mentioned the *modes* of God's special revelation, which involve the words and deeds of God primarily focused in Jesus Christ and Holy Scripture. It is necessary also to note the *nature* of this revelation. Special revelation is both personal and propositional. God has revealed Himself personally as "I AM" (Exod 3:14). This is also consistent with the manifestation of Himself in the covenants. Likewise, it is propositional in that God's self-disclosure made known to His people reveals truths about Him. Yet the primary purpose of revelation is not to enlarge the scope of one's knowledge. Rather, the knowledge *about* was for the purpose of knowledge *of.* The primary purpose of special revelation is redemptive so that people may enter into a salvific relationship with God.

Special revelation is not generally speculative. It only speaks on matters on cosmology and history when these issues touch the nature of faith. God has revealed Himself incarnationally through human language, human thought, and human action as ultimately demonstrated in the incarnation of Jesus Christ. Revelation was made known in diverse ways, but this diversity was progressive and developing. Such progressive revelation was complementary and supplementary to what had been revealed prior, not contradictory in any fashion.

In sum, we can say that God has initiated the revelation of Himself to men and women. This revelation is understandable to humankind and makes it possible to know God and grow in relationship with Him. God's self-manifestation provides information about Himself for the purpose of leading men and women into God's presence. Therefore we can identify God, know and understand something about Him and His work, and point others to Him.

Inspiration

God's Inspired Word. *Through the superintending influence of God's Spirit upon the writers of Holy Scripture, the account and interpretation of God's revelation has been recorded as God intended so that the Bible is actually the Word of God.* In writing, these men of God used their own ordinary languages and literary forms that were typical of their day. Yet within this very human activity God was at work. God chose to convey His Word through their words. This divine-human activity is truly the concursive inspiration of Holy Scripture.

When God's Word came to us through human authors, the humanity of the instrument God chose to use can be seen in the product. It is possible to actually see different personalities as we look at various books of the Bible. The style, vocabulary, and particular purposes of the apostle John are distinct from those of Luke. Yet both final products of their writings are equally the inspired Word of God.

In the history of the church, the divine character of Scripture has been the great presupposition for the whole of Christian preaching and theology. This is readily apparent in the way the New Testament speaks about the Old Testament. That which appears in the Old Testament is cited in the New Testament with formulas like "God says" and "the Holy Spirit says" (Acts 4:24-25; 13:47; 2 Cor 6:16). Scripture and God are so closely joined together in the minds of the New Testament authors that they naturally could spoke of Scripture doing what it records God as doing (Gal 3:8; Rom 9:17). The introductory phrase "It is [stands] written" is also used of the New Testament writings.

Because of the apostolic word's divine origin and content, Scripture can be described as "certain" (2 Pet 1:19), "trustworthy" (1 Tim 1:15; Titus 3:8), "confirmed" (Heb 2:3), and eternal (1 Pet 1:24-25). As a result those who build their lives on Scripture "will never be put to shame" (1 Pet 2:6). The Word was written for instruction and encouragement (Rom 15:4), to lead to saving faith (2 Tim 3:15), to guide people toward godliness (2 Tim 3:16b), and to equip believers for good works (2 Tim 3:17).

The Bible affirms its own inspiration in 2 Timothy 3:16-17: "All Scripture is God-breathed and is useful for teaching, rebuking, correcting and training in righteousness, so that the man of God may be thoroughly equipped for every good work."

Second Timothy 3:16-17 focuses primarily on the *product* of inspiration, the final writing of Scripture, though it also includes the secondary aspects of purpose and process. What is being asserted is the activity of God throughout the entire process, so that the completed, final product ultimately comes from Him. It is a mistake to think of inspiration only in terms of the time when the Spirit moves the human author to write. The biblical concept of inspiration allows for the activity of the Spirit in special ways within the process without requiring that we understand all of the Spirit's working in one and the same way. In the processes of creation and preservation of the universe, God providentially intervened in special ways for special purposes. Alongside and within this superintending action of the Spirit to inspire human writings in the biblical books, we can affirm a special work of the Spirit in bringing God's revelation to the apostles and prophets. God's Spirit is involved both in revealing specific messages to the prophets (Jer 1:1-9) and in guiding the authors of the historical section in their research (Luke 1:1-4).

We can assert that inspiration extends to the choice of words, even though Scripture's meaning is located at the sentence level and beyond. Thus our understanding of inspiration affirms the dual nature of Holy Scripture—it is a divine-human book. This recognition enables us to have a healthy understanding of the diverse literary genres represented in Scripture. The Holy Spirit is the one who, in a mystery for which the incarnation provides the only analogy, causes the verbal human witness to coincide with God's witness to Himself.

It is necessary to view inspiration as extending to all portions of Holy Scripture, even beyond the direction of thoughts to the selection of words. We must recognize the element of mystery involved in the process, which does not fully explain the how of inspiration. This understanding of inspiration seeks to do justice to the human factors in the Bible's composition and avoids any attempt to suggest that the Bible was mechanically dictated. We affirm both the divine character of Scripture and the human circumstances of the Bible's composition. (See the article "Inspiration and Authority of the Bible.)

God's Inerrant Word. Inerrancy is the corollary and result of our affirmations about a full view of inspiration. We believe the idea of an inerrant Scripture is important and adequately describes the results of inspiration. Inerrancy means that the Bible is fully truthful, trustworthy, and reliable. More completely, it means that *when all the facts are known, the Bible (in its autographs) properly interpreted in light of which culture and communication means had developed by the time of its composition, will be shown to be completely true (and therefore not false) in all that it affirms, to the degree of precision intended by the author, in all matters relating to God and His creation.*

This definition recognizes our need to approach Scripture in humble submission in awareness to God's omniscience and our own finiteness. Instead of maintaining the critic's relative omniscience, we think it best to admit our own fallibility as critics and trust the omnipotent and omniscient work of God over the writers.

Inerrancy is the proper implication of inspiration. It is an important doctrine not because inerrancy is necessary for salvation but because it is important to continue to affirm an orthodox and biblical confession of salvation and other doctrines as well. Inerrancy, as the corollary of inspiration, yet remains a foundational issue for all of Christian theology. Inerrancy as the result of the Spirit's inspiration primarily stresses the truthful and trustworthy character of God's faithful revelation to humanity.

Inerrancy does not imply an exhaustive knowledge of God or any other subject. Neither does it deny human authorship, promise a correct interpretation of Scripture, nor guarantee an accurate preservation of Scripture so as to produce inerrant translations. It does, however, set certain limits upon the range of acceptable answers in the matters of biblical interpretation and criticism and also provides a solid foundation for trustworthy translations of Scripture.

As many orthodox theologians have observed, theology that is not built upon an inerrant view of Scripture operates within the circle of human concepts and experience and has no reference point. A renewed commitment to biblical inerrancy is the first step toward healing the deadly sickness in today's theological trends. Believing the Bible to be inspired and true, we can joyfully and confidently commit our lives to its message and gladly proclaim this truth to others.

Conclusion

God's revelation has made it possible for men and women to know God truly and salvificly. This knowledge of God is not exhaustive, but God has revealed Himself in acts and words in various times and diverse ways. The Bible is the primary place of God's self-disclosure for people today. While acknowledging the historical situation of the human authors and the time-relatedness of the biblical text, we still affirm the normative character of Scripture.

Because of the basic needs shared by men and woman of all ages and races in all times and cultures, the central message of Scripture can be known in a normative and authoritative way. Beyond this we acknowledge that Scripture speaks to the spiritual needs of humankind but also reveals the truth of and about God. We confess that all Scripture is inspired and is the true, reliable, and inerrant source of God's revelation for today. Beyond these affirmations and articulations about the Word of God, we willfully and happily commit ourselves to it by placing our trust and confidence in the truthful, trustworthy, reliable, inspired Word of God.

Questions for Reflection

1. How do general and special revelation differ?
2. Why was specific revelation necessary?
3. What is meant by biblical inspiration?
4. What is meant by biblical inerrancy?
5. Why should the Bible be considered a special book?
6. How do these truths about the Bible influence our desire to read, study, and obey it?

Sources for Additional Study

Boice, James M., ed. *The Foundation of Biblical Authority.* Grand Rapids: Zondervan, 1978.

Bush, L. Russ and Tom Nettles. *Baptists and the Bible.* Chicago: Moody, 1980.

Carson, D. A. and John D. Woodbridge, eds. *Scripture and Truth.* Grand Rapids: Zondervan, 1984.

Dockery, David S. *The Doctrine of the Bible.* Nashville: Convention, 1991.

Garrett, Duane A. and Richard R. Mellick, Jr., eds. *Authority and Interpretation: A Baptist Perspective.* Grand Rapids: Baker, 1987.

God's World
Creation and Providence
Angels and Demons

In this section we will discuss the topics related to God and the world. The beginning point for our study will be the doctrine of creation. We will also examine the matters of providence, miracles, and preservation. As a related topic to God's providence, we will view the outworking of the plan of God. It will be important for us to look at God's creation of spiritual beings including holy angels, Satan, and demons.

Creation

We confess that God brought into being everything that is without the use of any preexisting material. Both the opening verse of the Bible and the initial sentence of the Apostle's Creed confess God as Creator. The theme of God as Creator of the heavens and earth is clearly taught in Scripture from beginning to end (Gen 1:1; Isa 40:28; Mark 13:19; Rev 10:6). The Bible affirms that God is the direct Creator of men and women (Gen 1:26-17; Mark 10:6), of His covenant people Israel (Isa 43:15), and in fact of all things (Col 1:16; Rev 4:11). With Scripture we maintain that creation occurred by God's Word (Gen 1:3; Ps 33:6-9; 148:5). The spoken word that brought creation into being is vitally related to the eternal Word who was with God and who was God (John 1:1). According to John's Gospel (John 1:3), all things were made through the Word and without this Word nothing was made that was made. This Word was Jesus.

Creation is the work of the Trinitarian God (Gen 1; Heb 11:3). God the Father is the source of creation (1 Cor 8:6), the Son is the agent of creation (Col 1:16), and the Spirit of God was lovingly hovering over the work of creation (Gen 1:2). Creation was by the wisdom of God (Jer 10:12), the will of God (Rev 4:11), and, as previously noted, the Word of God (Ps 33:6-9). Creation reveals God (Ps 19:1) and brings glory to Him (Isa 43:7). All of creation was originally good (Gen 1:4,31) but is now imperfect because of the entrance and effects of sin on creation (Gen 3:16-19). This is, however, only a temporary imperfection (Rom 8:19-22), for it will be redeemed in the final work of God, the new creation (Isa 65; Rev 21:1-5).

The biblical doctrine of creation affirms God as Creator, Redeemer, and Ruler. The Creator God is not detached from the God who works out our salvation in Jesus Christ through His Holy Spirit. God is the source of all things. This means that God has brought the world into existence *out of nothing* through a purposeful act of His free will. We thus affirm God as the sovereign and almighty Lord of all existence. Such an affirmation rejects any form of dualism, that matter has eternally existed, that matter must, therefore, be evil since it is in principle opposed to God, the source of all good.

The doctrine of creation also maintains that God is set apart from His creation and that all His creatures are dependent and good. It also maintains that God is a purposive God who creates in freedom. In creation and in God's provision and preservation for creation, He is working out His ultimate purposes for humanity and the world. Human life is thus meaningful, significant, intelligent, and purposeful. This affirms the overall unity and intelligibility of the universe. In this we see God's greatness, goodness, and wisdom. The creation account finds its full explication in Jesus as the God-Man, the light and life of the world who will bring creation under His domain at the consummation of the world, leading to the ultimate praise and glory of the Creator God.

Preservation and Providence

Preservation. God's work of preservation includes His intervention into the affairs of history. This biblical affirmation of preservation must be distinguished from a deistic view of a distant and nonintervening God. Yet God's work of maintaining and protecting the existence of the created universe is accomplished through the nature of His creative work and by His continuing providential care and intervention. In Colossians 1:16-17 the verb form (perfect tense) emphasizes the ongoing result of God "holding together all things" (also Heb 1:3).

Providence. Closely related, and even larger in scope, is God's work of providence. Providence involves the continuing work of the Triune God whereby all things in the universe are directed and controlled by God, thereby assuredly bringing about His wise plan (Rom 8:28). This is carried out, generally, by the establishment and outworking of natural laws and principles that are part of God's good and wise creation. It can, however, also include *God's unique, purposeful, and special intervention into the natural process to accomplish His will,* which we refer to as a miracle. Miracles, while an aspect of God's providence, must be seen for their uniqueness.

God's providence at times also transcends the affairs of women and men. In so doing, God can take actions intended as evil and use them for His good (Gen 50:20). Such work on the part of God can only bring a response of praise from believers for God's greatness. At the same time, this raises one of the most difficult questions in Christian theology: why do evil and suffering continue in this world?

Some have proposed that God either does not exist or is not powerful enough to do anything about evil or is not loving enough to be concerned about suffering. In contrast to this, we want not only to confess that God exists but that He is indeed infinitely powerful and absolutely loving. Yet we do not want to deny evil and suffering either, for it is obviously present around us.

Ultimately we want to answer this question by confessing that God has a plan and a purpose and puts all things into perspective (Eccl 9:11). In light of this we would say that evil still exists because Satan, a completely evil creature, still exists and continually opposes and attempts to thwart the plan of God. Also we would suggest that evil exists to further and broaden God's revelation (Ps 107:28). Apart from sin, evil and suffering and God's love, mercy, and grace are not fully understood. It is possible that God uses suffering to bring about discipline or punishment among His creatures. We can maintain that evil presently exists, but this is just a probationary period and that God, while temporarily permitting evil, will redeem all things in His final plan.

Finally, we must confess our limited knowledge at this point and say that the problem of evil remains a mystery. We can, with scriptural affirmation, be assured that God can and does use sin, evil, failure, and suffering for His eternal good. The ultimate example is the crucifixion of Christ, which pictures Christ in His suffering state because of the sinful, evil actions of humanity. Yet through the triumph of the resurrection, the greatest act of evil (the crucifixion of the God-Man Jesus Christ) became the greatest good, the provision of forgiveness of sin, and the salvation of humankind. All of this points to God's wise and wonderful plan for this world, part of which has been revealed to us but which is finally incomprehensible in its totality to God's creatures.

The Plan of God

Perhaps prior to a discussion of God's creative acts and His providential oversight is an understanding of God's plan. This refers to the consistent and coherent intention of God's will, an eternal decision rendering certain all things that will come to pass. God's plan not only relates to His creatures, men and women, as moral agents but also to any and all matters in the realm of cosmic history.

God is a loving covenant God who cares for and sustains His people. For Old Testament believers it was almost inconceivable that anything could happen independently of God's plan and the outworking of it. The Hebrew Scripture does not say the rains came and then the sun began to shine but that God sent the rains and then caused the sun to shine. Throughout it reveals God's faithfulness in bringing about and directing His plan in history as well as the futility of opposing it (Isa 46:10-11; Prov 19:21).

God's plan is from all eternity (Eph 3:11) and is therefore free from chronological sequence; it is free and purposive (Eph 1:11-14); it is for His good pleasure (Rev 4:11). The plan, as with all of God's thoughts and acts, is always consistent with His nature. While God's plan is inclusive, it primarily relates to His work of creation, preservation, and redemption. Also God's plan is effective but does not force His creatures to act in a certain way. Yet the plan of God renders it certain that they will freely act in those ways. When discussing the plan of God, it is important not to emphasize the sovereignty of God over His other attributes. Ultimately the plan of God is for His own glory (Eph 1:6,12,18; Rev 4:11); it exalts God (Ps 29:1-2) and affirms that God is in control of the events of history (Acts 4:23-28).

Angels, Satan, and Demons

Angels. Angels are the messengers of God, powerful beings that inhabit the heavenly spheres. The angels were present to praise God at creation as implied by Job 38:6-7 and Psalm 148:2-5. They were created good because God cannot create anything evil. Angels, as free moral agents, are responsible for their actions and may choose evil rather than obedience (Matt 25:41).

Angels are intelligent beings evidencing understanding (Matt 18:10) and curiosity (1 Pet 1:12). As emotional beings they are capable of praise (Luke 2:13-14), rejoicing (Luke 15:10), and anger (Rev 12). They are volitional

The angel with the flaming sword

beings who can plan (Jude 9) and choose to sin (2 Pet 2:4); thus they are also responsible for their actions (Matt 25:41; Jude 6). Angels are creatures who do not create, marry, or propagate (Mark 12:25). As spirit beings, they serve those who will inherit salvation (Heb 1:14). They are immortal (Luke 20:36) and are innumerable (Job 38:7; Rev 12:4).

The Bible classifies angels into elect angels and fallen or nonelect angels (Mark 8:38; Matt 25:41). Apparently some of these are already bound (2 Pet 2:4), though perhaps some, as demons, are loose (Matt 12:22). The elect angels have forms of organization including archangels (Michael, Dan 10:13), thrones, dominions, principalities, authorities, powers, cherubim, seraphim, and living creatures. It is difficult to know the full meaning of these distinctions or if there is some hierarchy among them beyond the archangel. These angels bring revelation (Dan 9:21-22), strengthen and minister to God's people (Heb 1:14), protect (Matt 2:13), and dispense judgments (Rev 8; 9; 16). Angels were present at primary events of revelation and redemption such as creation (Job 38:7), the giving of the Law (Gal 3:19), the birth of Christ (Matt 1:20), and the inauguration of the church (Acts 1:10). They will be present during Christ's reign (Rev 20).

Satan and Demons. The devil is a high angelic creature who before the creation of the human race rebelled against the Creator and became the chief antagonist of God and humankind. At the time of Satan's fall, many angels (demons) fell with him. As mentioned above, some of these roam free while others are bound.

Satan is an intelligent and powerful being. His power extends not only over the angelic realm (Matt 25:41) but is also exerted in the physical realm of men and women (2 Cor 12:7), in their hearts and thoughts (Matt 16:23), in government (John 12:31), in the spiritual realm (Matt 13:19), in the church (1 Tim 4:1), and even in death (Job 1:19). Scripture gives numerous titles and pictures of Satan (2 Cor 11:3,4; 1 Pet 5:8-9; Rev 12:3-4). These titles and pictures describe Satan as a murderer and a liar (John 8:44) who violates the sacredness of life and truth, a sinner (1 John 3:8), an accuser of the saints (Rev 12:10), and extremely prideful (1 Tim 3:6). While Satan, as a powerful being, is active in these areas, it is important to remember that he is accountable (Matt 25:41) and is not infinite in space or knowledge (Job 1:7) or power (Revelation). Thus he can be resisted (Eph 6:10-17; Jas 4:7).

Satan's activities include counterfeiting (2 Cor 11:14-15), slandering (Gen 3:4-5), deceiving (Rev 20:3), attempting to destroy the work of Jesus (1 John 3:8), blinding (2 Cor 4:4), and accusing believers (Rev 12:10). Also he hinders ministry (1 Thess 2:18), incites persecution

(Rev 2:10), and tempts to sin (Acts 5:3). The purpose of Satan is not primarily to establish a kingdom of crime and confusion but to establish a permanent kingdom that supplants and coexists with God's kingdom. In so doing, he focuses attention upon God's restrictions and tempts believers to doubt the goodness of God. He presents attractive counterfeits for God's will and true worship such as piety, religious practices, money, power, and prestige. Constantly Satan places our attention on the present instead of God's eternal values (Matt 4:1-11).

Believers should respond with total dependence on the Lord Jesus Christ. One should not overestimate or underestimate Satan's tactics. Instead, members of the community of faith must draw upon the spiritual resources available to them, stand firm, ultimately submit to God, resist the devil, and draw near to God. He will in turn draw near to His people (Jas 4:7-8).

Conclusion

It has been affirmed that God as the transcendent Lord of all space and time is not indebted to the world or bound to it. God does not need this universe in order to be God. The world is in dependence on God for its origin, unity, and continuity. God who is Creator is also Redeemer and Ruler, and He sustains the world as Preserver by His providential care. Such a view of providence shows history moving toward its consummation in the purposes of their Creator. God's purposes in the world are being realized through the general laws of nature, historical events, the actions of humans, as well as special times of gracious intervention.

God's plan is purposeful, effectual, and pleasing to God. There are invisible spiritual beings (angels, Satan, and demons) that influence God's world both for good and for evil either as God's ministering spirits (angels) or God's opponents, attempting to usurp the kingdom of God (Satan and demons). Even though there is evil in the world, God's goodness will ultimately triumph over evil, and His providential care can take that which was intended for evil and use it for good, advancing the kingdom of God and bringing eternal glory to the name of God.

Questions for Reflection

1. What is the importance of the Bible's teaching that God created "out of nothing"?

2. How can we distinguish between providence and preservation?

Satan wounded in battle with the angel Michael (as envisioned by Milton in Paradise Lost*)*

3. What is biblical miracle? Can examples be offered?

4. How do we relate the plan of God and the free agency of men and women?

5. How should our praying be impacted by our understanding of God's providential plan?

6. How should the church respond to the attacks of Satan and his demons?

7. What place do angels play in our daily lives and spiritual development?

Sources for Additional Study

Berkouwer, G. C. *The Providence of God.* Grand Rapids: Eerdmans, 1952.

Dickason, C. Fred. *Angels, Elect and Evil.* Chicago: Moody, 1975.

Ramm, Bernard. *The Christian View of Science and the Scripture.* Grand Rapids: Eerdmans, 1954.

God's Son: The Person and Work of Jesus Christ

Jesus Christ, who was eternally the second Person of the Trinity sharing all the divine attributes, became fully human. In entering the world as a human, Jesus took on human characteristics while voluntarily choosing to exercise His divine powers only intermittently in order to fulfill His redemptive mission. The biblical writers indicate who Jesus is by describing the significance of the work He came to do and the office He came to fulfill. In this section we shall look at the person and life of Jesus; His titles in Scripture; and the importance and meaning of His ministry, death, and resurrection.

The Person of Jesus Christ

When we point to Jesus, we see the whole man Jesus and say that He is God. This man Jesus Christ does not only live through God and with God, but He is Himself God. The confession of the Christian church has maintained Christ as one Person having two natures, the one divine and the other human. This is the great mystery of godliness, God manifested in the flesh (1 Tim 3:16).

The Humanity of Jesus

Jesus' humanity is taken for granted in the Synoptic Gospels. But in other parts of the New Testament, it seems to be witnessed to in particular as if it might have been called into question or its significance neglected (1 John 1:1-2; 4:2-3). In Mark's Gospel there is concentration on the humanity of Jesus as much as in any New Testament book. Matthew and Luke focus on Jesus' birth stories as aspects of His humanity, including the temptation accounts. John pictures Jesus as the eternal Word who took on full humanity (John 1:1,14; 4:6-7; 11:33-35). He is a real man yet sinless and different from other humans (Rom 8:3). His significance is not found through comparison alongside others but in contrast with others (Heb 2:9,14-18; 5:7-8; 10:10). This uniqueness is especially seen in His miraculous birth and sinless life.

Virgin Birth. The birth of Jesus resulted from a miraculous conception. He was conceived in the womb of the virgin Mary by the power of the Holy Spirit without male seed (Matt 1:18-25; Luke 1:26-38). This does not in any way teach Mary's continual virginity or any type of biological-divine involvement in the incarnation without affirming the virginity of Jesus' mother.

While the biblical writers do not amplify upon the theological significance of the birth of Christ, such significance cannot be overlooked. God's deliverance has come, and it calls to mind a sign (Isa 7:14) of God's great Old Testament promises. The unique birth affirms Jesus' true humanity and His deity. It reveals that Jesus was really born, really one of us, but that this birth was a supernatural event.

The Sinlessness of Jesus. The Gospels present Jesus as participating in John's baptism, which was a baptism of repentance. Also we see Jesus rebuking Peter, cleansing the temple, confronting the Pharisees, and sending pigs into the sea. Jesus was baptized not for repentance from sin but in order to fulfill all righteousness and to identify completely with fallen humanity. The other examples are pictures of righteous anger, not sinful anger (see Eph 4:26). The Bible carefully confesses the sinlessness of Jesus (Rom 8:3; 2 Cor 5:21; Heb 4:15; 1 Pet 2:22). The Bible stresses the true emptying of Jesus in becoming like us (Phil 2:5-8), His full humanity, the reality of the temptations, his Spirit-enabled rejection of the temptations, and His resulting sinlessness.

The Deity of Jesus

Paul affirmed that Jesus existed in the form of God from all eternity past (Phil 2:5-11). This means Jesus possessed inwardly and demonstrated outwardly the very nature of God Himself (Col 1:15-16; 2:9). Also the opening verse of John's Gospel is a categorized affirmation of Jesus' full deity (John 1:1-2; 14:9; 17:5). Pictures of Jesus' deity also are in the unique "I am" statements of John's Gospel (John 6:35; 8:12; 10:7-9,11-14; 11:25; 14:6; 15:1-5). We see this particularly in Jesus' statement about His eternal existence that comes during the confrontation with the Jews (John 8:58). Finally, we see Jesus receiving the worship of Thomas (John 20:28) in his confession, "My Lord and my God." These passages, along with others in the New Testament (see Rom 9:5; Titus 2:13; Heb 1:1-8) cut across all lesser confessions of Christ's person, showing that any view that would make Him merely a great teacher or a great prophet is not adequate.

Unity of the Two Natures

It is necessary that Christ should be both God and man. Only as man could He be a redeemer for humanity; only as a sinless man could He fittingly die for others. Only as God could His life, ministry, and redeeming death have infinite value and satisfy the demands of God so as to deliver others from death.

Christ has a human nature, but He is not a human person. The person of Christ is the God-man, the second person of the Trinity. In the incarnation He did not change into a human person or adopt a human personage. He assumed a human nature in addition to His eternal divine nature. With the assumption of the human nature, He is not a divine person or a human person but a divine-human person possessing all the essential qualities of both the human and divine nature. This is a mystery beyond full comprehension. Also it is confessed that Jesus has both a divine and human consciousness as well as a human and divine will, yet clearly a unity of person. He is always the same person, Jesus Christ the Lord.

We can also learn about Jesus from His titles, such as Christ, Lord, and others ascribed to Him in Scripture. See article "Titles of Christ" in the Gospels. Other meaningful titles include:

Servant. The idea of servant acts as an umbrella term in the New Testament, speaking to many aspects of the person of Christ based upon the servant motif in Isaiah 53 (Mark 10:45; Phil 2:5-11; 1 Pet 2:21-25).

Prophet/Teacher. We find references to Jesus as the voice of God or a teacher who has come from God several places in the New Testament. The emphasis is upon Jesus' preaching ministry and the authority associated with His work (Deut 18:5; John 3:2; Acts 3:22).

Last Adam. The title given to Jesus by Paul in Romans 5:12-21 and 1 Corinthians 15:22,45-47 evidences the solidarity of Adam with the human race and of Christ with His people. Paul showed Jesus' importance and uniqueness by contrasting Him with Adam. Adam's disobedience is contrasted with Christ's obedience; what Adam lost, Christ regained; what Adam failed to do, Christ did. Through Adam's one sin, condemnation came to all, bringing death; through Jesus' act of obedience, grace was provided for all, bringing life. Adam was a living being, a man of dust; Jesus was a life-giving Spirit, a man from heaven.

God. The early church did not hesitate to ascribe full deity to Jesus with the title God (Rom 9:5; Titus 2:13; Heb 1:5-8).

The titles affirm the uniqueness of Jesus and the exalted view of Him by the early church. The total impression gained after reflecting upon the titles and their significance is that Jesus was recognized in His person as fully God and fully human.

The Work of Christ

The Cross of Christ

Christ's life and death exemplified divine love and exerted an influence for good by providing a model of servanthood and sacrifice. But, more importantly, Christ's death provided for sinners a sinless substitutionary sacrifice that satisfies divine justice, an incomprehensibly valuable redemption delivering sinners from enslavement and reconciling and restoring sinners from estrangement to full fellowship and inheritance in the household of God. In this section we shall look at the cross of Christ primarily from the viewpoint of atonement, redemption, and reconciliation.

Atonement. The idea of atonement is the focal point of the New Testament idea of the saving work of Christ (Isa 53:10; Rom 3:25; 1 John 2:2; 4:10; Heb 2:17). This understanding of Christ's work on the cross has reference to the effecting of satisfaction on God while effecting the same satisfaction on the guilt of sin. Atonement can only be rightly understood in light of the holiness and justice of God, the severity of the reaction of God's holiness to sin. This concept affirms that God's holiness must be satisfied and the sins of humanity must be removed. Atonement is realized when God Himself takes upon Himself, in the person of Jesus, the sinfulness and guilt of humankind so that His justice might be executed and the sins of men and women forgiven. It is mandatory to underscore this idea by affirming that God is moved to this self-sacrifice by His infinite compassion.

Redemption. The idea of redemption is vitally related to the themes of liberation, deliverance, and ransom. Within this model there is seen a struggle between the kingdom of God and the hostile powers enslaving humankind. Redemption is the idea of bringing sinners out of such hostile bondage into authentic freedom (Col 2:15). As Redeemer Jesus breaks the power of sin and creates a new and obedient heart by delivering us from the powers of sin, guilt, death, and Satan, thus bringing about a people who have been bought with a price (1 Pet 1:18).

Reconciliation. Reconciliation involves bringing fallen humanity out of alienation into a state of peace and harmony with God. Jesus, as Reconciler, heals the separation and brokenness created by sin and restores communion between God and humankind. Reconciliation is not a process by which men and women become ever more acceptable to God but an act by which we are delivered from estrangement to fellowship with God. Because of Christ's work on the cross, God has chosen to treat men and women in sin as children rather than transgressors (2 Cor 5:18-20; Eph 2:12-16; Col 1:20-22).

Throughout church history Christian thinkers emphasized some or all of these ideas, including some and rejecting others. It is important to see that all of these ideas, as well as the example Jesus provided for us (1 Pet 2:21), are necessary. Other religions have a martyr, but Jesus' death was that of a Savior. It brings salvation from sins for men and women as Christ took our place and died our death. In this His work on the cross was substitutionary. By His obedient life He fulfilled the law for us, and by His death on the cross He satisfied the demands of the law for us. The cross of Christ is the actual execution of justice of God's unrelaxed penalty revealed in the law (Gal 3:10-13). This means that Christ suffered for our sins (2 Cor 5:21). In Jesus, God's holy love is clearly demonstrated (1 John 4:10). As Martin Luther said, "This is the mystery of the riches of divine grace for sinners, for by a wonderful exchange, our sins are not ours but Christ's and Christ's righteousness is not Christ's but ours." Thus, as P. T. Forsythe has so richly stated, "The work of Christ stands not simply for the stain of sin, but the scourge of God on sin, not simply God's sorrow over sin, but for God's wrath on sin." Therefore we cannot rightfully understand the cross unless we perceive both God's anguish over sin and His invincible holiness that refuses to tolerate sin.

The Resurrection of Christ

The resurrection is the core of the Christian message (1 Cor 15:3-4) showing that the hope of the gospel is eschatological in nature (Luke 24:45-48; Acts 2:27,35). The resurrection tells us that the God who raised Jesus from the dead exists. Also it establishes Jesus' lordship and deity as well as the justification of sinners, which was accomplished at the cross (Rom 1:3-4; 4:24-25). The resurrection provides promise as well as guarantee of final judgment.

It promises that believers can be accepted by God, live a life pleasing to God, and have assurance of victory over death (1 Cor 15:55-57). On the other hand, it is a pledge of God's final judgment for those who reject Christ as Lord and Savior (Acts 17:31).

The Ascension and Exaltation of Christ

Following the resurrection, Christ ascended into heaven (Acts 1:9-11), where He is exalted at God's right hand (Heb 1:3), a position of honor. Having sat down, Christ demonstrates that His cross work is finished. His position at God's right hand signifies His sharing in God's rule and dominion and the power and authority to which He is entitled. At God's right hand Jesus exercises His priesthood, interceding for His own (John 17; Rom 8:34; Heb 7:25). Here He serves as the defense advocate (1 John 2:1) of His church, over which He is head (Eph 1:20-21). From here He will return to consummate God's redemptive plan.

Conclusion

We trustingly confess and affirm that Jesus Christ as the God-man has fully revealed God to men and women. Having lived a sinless life, Christ died in our place for our sins. He now sits exalted at God's right hand, a position of honor and exaltation, exercising His rule and dominion. We gladly acknowledge Jesus as Lord, our Prophet, Priest, and King, who has completely revealed God, reconciled humankind with God, and who sits enthroned as ruler of God's kingdom and head of His church. In Him we place our trust and hope, offering our thanksgiving for the salvation He has provided for us.

Questions for Reflection

1. What is the theological significance of the virgin birth?
2. What is the nature of the person of Christ? Can we say it is divine? human? divine-human? Does the doctrine teach one Person with two natures? one Person with one nature? two Persons with two natures?
3. What are some (at least five) of the most important titles of Christ? What is the theological significance of the titles relating to the humanity and deity of Christ?
4. Distinguish between the meanings of atonement, redemption, and reconciliation.
5. What is the theological significance of the resurrection?
6. How do these truths influence our evangelistic zeal and our evangelistic message?

Sources for Additional Study

Erickson, Millard J. *The Word Became Flesh.* Grand Rapids: Baker, 1991.

Henry, Carl F. H., ed. *Jesus of Nazareth: Savior and Lord.* Grand Rapids: Eerdmans, 1966.

———. *The Identity of Jesus of Nazareth.* Nashville: Broadman, 1992.

Morris, Leon. *The Cross in the New Testament.* Grand Rapids: Eerdmans, 1965.

Stott, John R. W. *The Cross of Christ.* Downers Grove: InterVarsity, 1986.

GOD'S SPIRIT THE HOLY SPIRIT AND THE SPIRITUAL LIFE

Our purpose in this section is to examine the primary meaning given to the Holy Spirit in the Old Testament and intertestamental period as well as the person and work of the Holy Spirit in the New Testament, with emphasis given to the apostle Paul. The Bible reveals the Holy Spirit as the third member of the Trinity (John 14; 16; Acts 5:3-4), a distinct entity from the Father and Son.

The Holy Spirit in the Old Testament

The Spirit's Ministry in the Old Testament

In the early sections of the Old Testament, the Spirit of God is an intermittent power that came upon a person and enabled him or her to accomplish God's purposes. In Genesis 1:2 the Spirit was hovering over the face of the waters as a mother hovers over her young. This same relation is expressed further in Genesis 2:7, where God breathed the Spirit of life into human nostrils. The early period of Scripture pictures the Spirit as the perfect symbol of the mysterious nearness and activity of God. The continuing dependence of humankind upon God is expressed by the Spirit's presence (Gen 6:3).

During the period of the judges and the young monarchy, the Spirit's purposes can be understood as the empowerment of a person to accomplish the will of God (Judg 3:10). During the monarchy, the institutional aspects began to predominate over the charismatic, and dependence upon the Spirit became less visible.

During the prophetic period, the work of the Spirit seems to have become more personal, both in the experience of the prophets themselves and in their vision of the future. It would seem that the prophets were at times caught up in ecstatic experiences with the Spirit. The primary aspect of the Spirit in the prophet's ministry is an ethical context. It is more personal and takes on a potential influence that is more universal than in prior times. The visions of the prophets spill over the narrow banks of the nation of Israel and reach out to the ends of the earth. The Spirit is the promise that will be poured out in the age to come, the messianic age.

Spirit in Rabbinic Judaism and the Intertestamental Period

The background of New Testament thought is best located in Palestinian Judaism. During this time the Spirit's activity was basically regarded as a past phenomenon in Israel's history, a phenomenon that had indeed given Israel its Torah, its prophets, and the whole of its Scriptures but had ceased when the prophetic office ended. Yet there were individuals who were conscious of the Holy Spirit as still active in their lives.

The Holy Spirit in the New Testament

Jesus and the Spirit

The Holy Spirit was present at the beginning of the messianic age. This is evidenced by the Spirit's ministry with John the Baptist (Luke 1:15) as well as the Spirit's manifestation to Mary (Matt 1:18) and Simeon (Luke 1:25). Most important in this regard is the Spirit's unique involvement in the miraculous birth of our Lord (Luke 1:35). As we observe the ministry of Jesus, we can make the following notations:

1. The Spirit was present at the baptism of Jesus. The Spirit appeared in the form of a dove at the inauguration of Jesus' messianic ministry. In a sense the Spirit's ministry is very similar to that which we have seen in the Old Testament, as Jesus' ministry is empowered by the Spirit. Within the Godhead the Son needs the empowerment of the Spirit to carry out the ministry because of His voluntary submission to the Father.
2. The Spirit was present at the temptations of Jesus.
3. The Spirit was the power involved in the exorcising of demons.
4. The Spirit anointed Jesus to preach and gave to the messianic ministry a sense of urgency and priority.
5. The Spirit provided authority for Jesus' teaching.

6. Jesus rejoiced in the Spirit's power, which made it possible for Him to focus on the messianic mission. Likewise, Jesus was the giver of the Spirit to His disciples. In this sense the phenomenon seen in John 14 and 16 is not dissimilar from when Joshua received the Spirit from Moses and Elijah received the Spirit from Elisha.

Jesus taught in the latter days of His ministry that His departure was necessary for the Spirit's ministry to be fully manifest. The following parallels can be drawn concerning the ministry of Jesus and His teaching concerning the ministry of the Spirit during the new age:

1. Jesus was sent by the Father (John 3:16); the Spirit was sent by Jesus (John 14:26).

2. Jesus is Himself the truth (John 14:6), so the Spirit of truth (John 15:26) was to guide the new believers into all truth (John 16:13).

3. Just as Jesus glorified the Father and not Himself (John 17:4), so the Spirit glorified Jesus (John 16:14).

4. Jesus still had much to teach the disciples, so the Spirit continued the teaching function (John 16:13).

5. As the world did not accept Jesus (John 1:10-11), so those who have the Spirit can expect that the world would neither accept the Spirit's ministry (John 16:8). The Gospel writers are agreed that Jesus was the unique bearer of the Spirit, in whose power He ushered in the messianic age. Yet these writers agreed that the Spirit also was given by Jesus. One cannot get the Spirit except through Jesus; but at the same time, one cannot get to Jesus except through the Spirit.

The Spirit and the Mission of the New Church

With the coming of the Spirit at Pentecost (Acts 2), there was a universalizing of the ministry and mission of Jesus. Jesus was God's final word to humanity, and the Spirit's role was not to give some new revelation of His own but to bear witness to Jesus and to interpret and bring out all the final implications of God's final Word. When the Spirit came in full at Pentecost, there was the inauguration of the church. With the coming of the Spirit, there was created a quality of life in individuals and the church that was beyond their own natural powers. The Spirit came in order to unite believers in an unparalleled manner. The Spirit came as promise, not as law; as gift, not as challenge; and He came sovereignly, not conditionally.

The Spirit's coming brought not an emotional frenzy but a new, sovereign gift of power to the young church. Yet with the Spirit's coming was the accompanying sign of tongues of fire. Tongues were not necessary to advance the mission but to authenticate the mission's message and messengers. The tongues were given to the apostles; they were not taught. The ultimate purpose of the giving of the Spirit was for enablement of the church's mission, which was the spreading of the good news and to exalt the name of Christ.

After Pentecost the Spirit was active in many aspects of the Christian community. But the Spirit was active primarily in (1) preaching, (2) teaching, (3) prophecy, (4) witnessing, (5) bringing love and guidance to the new community, and (6) the continuation of the church's mission. The Spirit was involved in the early church in Jerusalem (Acts 2–5), in the prophetic proclamation of Stephen (Acts 6–7), in the spreading of the gospel to the Gentiles (Acts 10), in the sending out of Paul and Barnabas (Acts 13), and in the establishment of the transition to the church's mature state (Acts 19).

The Spirit used various means to advance the new mission. Some of these means included trances (Acts 10), prophetic word (Acts 11), worship services (Acts 13), church councils (Acts 15), and inner constraint (Acts 16). What is obvious is that the Spirit always remained the unpredictable, mysterious, sovereign third member of the Trinity.

Paul's View of the Spirit and Spiritual Life

The Pauline view of the spiritual life can be summarized by the statement in 2 Corinthians 3:17, "Where the Spirit of the Lord is, there is liberty." The Spirit's activities so widely permeated the apostle's thought that there hardly was any aspect of Christian experience outside of the sphere of the Spirit's activities. Paul's understanding of the Spirit must be seen from two perspectives: the Spirit in the life of the believer and the Spirit in the life of the community. We could not do justice to Paul's thought without a brief look at life in tension, including the nature of suffering in relation to life in the Spirit.

The Work of the Spirit in the Individual Believer. The apostles, especially Paul, maintained certain expectations that would accompany the coming of the age of the Spirit. Entering into a new community and the pneumatic power that characterized it in its enthusiasm, they recognized evidence of the advent of the age to come. The active presence of the Spirit was a mark of the last days. As will be seen, the ministry of the Spirit authenticated the claims of Jesus as Messiah.

Paul was convinced that it was the responsibility of the Spirit to draw attention to the glories of the risen Christ in the preaching ministry (1 Thess 1:5; 1 Cor 2:1-4). Equally true was the Spirit's task in enabling persons to respond to the message of the glorified Christ. Indeed, it is

The descent of the Spirit at Pentecost

a fundamental assumption of Paul's theology that all believers are possessors of the Spirit. In other words, no one can respond to the claims of Christ without being activated and indwelt by the Holy Spirit.

Paul told the Thessalonians that God had given them the Holy Spirit (1 Thess 4:8). In his first Letter to the Corinthians, he stated that no one can confess Jesus as Lord except by the Holy Spirit (1 Cor 12:3). It can be assumed that all believers have the Spirit since "anyone who does not have the Spirit of Christ does not belong to him" (Rom 8:9). The Spirit has transformed persons from unrighteousness to those who are washed, sanctified, and justified (1 Cor 6:10-11). In this passage is a strong contrast between the former life and the change the Spirit's ministry performs.

The regenerating work of the Spirit brings about new life in Christ. The new life in Christ is summarized in Paul's classic statement, "If anyone is in Christ, he is a new creation; the old has passed away, behold the new has come" (2 Cor 5:17). The point is that the coming of the new age brought about by the Spirit creates a new person. The passing of the old does not mean the end of the old age; it continues until the return of Christ. But the old age does not remain intact; the new age has broken in. Without discussing the full ramifications of the new age, it can be said that while believers live in the old age, because they are in Christ they belong to the new age with its new creation (indicative), and they are to live a life that is expressive of the new existence (imperative).

In addition to the Spirit's initiating and regenerating work is the Spirit's work in adoption and sanctification. Two primary passages show that the believer's conviction of being God's child is directly induced by the Holy Spirit (Rom 8:14-17; Gal 4:6). It is the Spirit who leads the children of God to cry out, "Abba! Father!" Adoption describes the new relationship between believers and their God.

The term *sanctification* can be used comprehensively to describe the overall process by which the new believer moves toward a life of holiness. The standard of sanctification is a holiness acceptable to God; that is, a holiness in line with the Spirit's own character (Rom 15:16; 1 Cor 6:11). The Spirit of God is not only active in revealing the gospel but is likewise involved in bringing the believer to further understanding (1 Cor 2:13). This is referred to as the Spirit's work of illumination and guidance. Paul went into considerable detail in 1 Corinthians 2:10-16 in order to establish the distinction between human wisdom and the Spirit's understanding. He affirmed that without the enablement of the Spirit, a salvific knowledge of God is unattainable. After receiving the gift of the Spirit, there is a capacity for understanding that was previously denied. The Spirit penetrates to the deepest understanding of God in Christ.

The Spirit guides believers into a new way of thinking and gives them a new set of values: "Those who live according to the Spirit set their minds on the things of the Spirit" (Rom 8:5). The mind of the Spirit is the place of reason, feeling, and will patterned after and controlled by the Holy Spirit. The renewal of the mind (Rom 12:2), which was formerly hostile to God (Rom 8:7), can only be achieved by and through the Spirit in opposition to carrying out the desires of the sinful flesh (Gal 6:15; Rom 8:4). The concept of total dependence on the empowering of the Spirit shows how utterly indispensable the Spirit is for Christian living, and it demonstrates the impossibility of any Christian not possessing the Spirit.

Paul spoke of the Spirit in contrast to the life controlled by the flesh. In Galatians 5:22-23 Paul gave his understanding of the fruit of the Spirit as "love, joy, peace, patience, kindness, goodness, faithfulness, gentleness, and self-control." These virtues must be compared with the similar lists in Philippians 4:8 and Colossians 3:12-15. These Spirit-prompted virtues go beyond the cultural bounds of virtue so that, for example, believers demonstrate love by loving their enemies. The outworking of these virtues is a demonstration of the Spirit at work in the believer. The Spirit breaks the shackles of the flesh and delivers the believer from bondage to sin and the law. The bringing of liberty is one of the great outworkings of the Spirit in the new age.

The Work of the Spirit in the New Community. Paul viewed the Holy Spirit as the basis for true unity in the body of Christ. Fellowship in the Johannine Epistles seems to be "with the Father and with his Son" (1 John 1:3). But Paul stressed "fellowship in the Spirit" (Phil 2:1-4; 2 Cor 13:14). The passage in Philippians enlarges on the theme of unity and suggests a mutual participation of believers through the common bond of the Spirit. It is the Spirit who binds Christians together and enables them to be of the same mind, which is the "mind of Christ" (Phil 2:5).

The community of faith is to maintain the unity of the Spirit (1 Cor 12; Eph 4:1-6). The basis of unity is identified by Paul as the baptism in the Spirit (1 Cor 12:13). The baptism of the Spirit is the way of initiation into the new corporate life of the community. This underscores the Spirit-dominated character of the corporate Christian life. The concept of "all were made to drink of one Spirit" shows the basic solidarity of all Christians in the Spirit. It is a transformation for all believers by which they are placed into the body of Christ, made possible by the

Spirit. The Spirit has been given by the exalted Christ to form a new people, to join believers together in the baptism of the Spirit to constitute the body of Christ.

Similarly, the new community should be filled with the Spirit (Eph 5:18-20). Instead of finding empowerment and illumination in wine (Eph 5:17-18), the church finds the basis for such in the Spirit's control and filling. The result is a worshiping community, giving thanks, singing songs of mutual edification to each other and mutually submitting one to another in the fear of Christ.

Tension in the Spiritual Life. Life in the Spirit is to be lived out in the tension between what has been accomplished by the historical achievement of Jesus and what is yet to be fully realized in the second coming. The believer lives in this temporal tension. Believers live in this age, but their life pattern, their standard of conduct, their aims and goals are not those of this human-centered and prideful age. They are of the age to come. Yet the struggle with indwelling sin continues (Rom 7:14-25), and the flesh continues to war against the Spirit (Gal 5:16-21).

While living in the Spirit as a citizen of the new age (Phil 3:21), believers will suffer in this age (Phil 1:29-30). Believers live conscious of life "in Adam" (Rom 5:12-21) and "in Christ" (Rom 6:1-11). Such life is characterized as a tension between freedom and responsible living (Rom 14). Yet life in the Spirit awakens the believer to the prospects of present and ultimate victories. The basis for life in the Spirit must never be forgotten. It is through the death and resurrection of Jesus Christ that the Spirit applies justification, regeneration, sanctification, and ultimate glorification to the lives of believers. Life in the Spirit is living out, by the Spirit's empowerment, what believers are because of Christ.

For Paul, Christianity was essentially spiritual. That is, Christianity is interpreted through the category of the Spirit. This makes it inevitable that Paul should also give greater significance to the ethical aspect of the spiritual life. The Spirit enables the believer to obey in the midst of struggling and suffering.

The most genuine utterance of the Spirit in the assembly of believers is not ecstatic speech but prophecy, since the intention and criterion of the worship service was that God should become manifest for the people (1 Cor 14:23-25). Individual believers experience the Spirit primarily in prayer when they call upon God as Abba! Father! (Gal 4:6; Rom 8:15). The Spirit provides divine enablement to the believer struggling in prayer (Rom 8:26-27). The immediacy of devotion to God does not come forth from innate human capacity but from the Spirit. In prayer the Spirit gives a deep awareness that one has been accepted through the love of God. When the Spirit reaches to God's children, the love of God reaches out (Rom 5:5).

The Spirit is ultimately made known as the power that generates openness before God, enablement in struggle, and openness in prayer. The Spirit is the down payment of future glory (Eph 1:13; 4:30) that will be inherited at the second coming. Until then the community experiences life in the Spirit in such a way that can be characterized as liberty. In the spiritual life liberty comes through obedience, and glory comes through suffering.

Conclusion

We have seen that almost every aspect of the Christian experience is influenced by the Spirit's actions. The Spirit was dominantly viewed as the source of empowerment in the Old Testament and performed a similar function in the ministry of Jesus. After the ascension of Jesus, the Spirit came at Pentecost in His fullness to universalize the ministry of Christ while exalting Him in the expansion of the church's new mission. It was observed that the Spirit characterizes the life of the individual believer as well as the life of the new community of faith. Life in the Spirit brings freedom to believers, a freedom from sin and law and toward obedience that must be exercised in responsible living.

Questions for Reflection

1. What is the relationship between Jesus and the Spirit?
2. What is the Spirit's work regarding the church's mission?
3. What are some differences between the Spirit's work in the individual believer and the corporate community of faith?
4. What is the relationship of suffering to spirituality? How is obedience involved in spiritual development?
5. How does the Spirit's work affect our prayer life?
6. What is the relationship between personal spiritual development and our responsibilities in worship, ministry, evangelism, and social witness?

Sources for Additional Study

Brunner, Frederick Dale. *A Theology of the Holy Spirit.* Grand Rapids: Eerdmans, 1970.

Green, Michael. *I Believe in the Holy Spirit.* Grand Rapids: Eerdmans, 1975.

Packer, J. I. *Keep in Step with the Spirit.* Old Tappan, N.J.: Revell, 1984.

GOD'S SALVATION THE DOCTRINES OF HUMANKIND, SIN, AND SALVATION

Men and women are the highest forms of God's earthly creation. All other aspects of creation are for the purpose of serving men and women; men and women are created to serve God and are thus theocentric. In this section we will discuss the subjects of humankind, their fall into sin, and God's salvation of men and women from their estranged, guilty, and dreadful plight.

Humankind

The Position and Nature of Humanity

Men and women are complex creatures of God composed not only of a physical body but also an immaterial self, called a soul or spirit. In the present life men and women function as whole persons, though it is a type of conditional unity because the material and immaterial aspects interact upon each other in such intricate ways that they are not easily distinguished. Yet as has been expounded by many in the history of the church, the characteristics of the immaterial (soul/spirit) cannot be attributed only to the physical. They remain distinct, but not separated until death, closely related and interacting with each other. Humans were a unity at creation and will again be a complete unity at glorification, but during the present time we can affirm a type of conditional unity brought about by the entrance and effects of sin. The primary reason for the importance of men and women in creation, over against the rest of God's creation, is related to their creation in God's image (Gen 1:26-27).

The Image of God

God has created us in His image and likeness. At first this might appear to refer to our physical makeup—that we look like God. That is not what the Bible means by the terms "image and likeness of God." Men and women, because they are created in the image of God, have rationality, morality, spirituality, and personality. They can relate to God and other humans while rightly exercising dominion over the earth and the animals (Gen 1:26-28; Ps 8).

Nothing in us or about us is separable, distinct, or discoverable as the divine image. Each person individually and the entire race corporately are the image of God. But no single aspect of human nature or behavior or thought pattern can be isolated as the image of God.

Male and Female

In creation there is a complete equality between men and women; neither sex is given prominence over the other. Again this is related to the fact that male and female are both created in God's image. Also "in Christ" in our redeemed state there is neither male nor female (Gal 3:28). We cannot, however, bypass the teaching that a distinction between the roles or functions carried out by men and women is addressed in Genesis 2:18-25.

Sin and the Fall

Even though men and women are created in God's image, the entrance of sin into the world has had great and negative influences upon God's creation, especially humans, created in God's image. As a result of sin the image of God was not lost (Gen 9:6; Jas 3:9) but was severely tarnished and marred. The role of exercising dominion (Gen 1:28) has been drastically disturbed by the effects of sin on humans and the curse on nature. The ability to live in right relationship with God, with others, with nature, and with our very own selves has been corrupted. All attempts at righteousness are as filthy rags in God's sight (Isa 64:6), and humans are ultimately spiritually dead and alienated from God (Eph 2:1-3). Therefore we are unable to reflect properly the divine image and likeness (Rom 1:18-32).

It is necessary to see that the sin of Adam and Eve (Gen 3) was not just a moral lapse but a deliberate turning away from God and rejection of Him. The day that they disobeyed God, they died spiritually—which ulti-

Satan as a serpent approaching Eve in the garden of Eden

mately brought physical death (Gen 2:17). The consequences were many as Paul described in Romans 1:18–3:20; 5:12-21; and Ephesians 2:1-22. Important among these consequences are the effects upon our wills, the volitional elements of men and women. Sin's entrance has brought about a sinful nature in all humanity. People act in accord with their sinful nature. No one ever acts in a way that is contrary to his or her own inner nature apart from regeneration.

This idea is significant when reflecting upon the matters of our relationship to God. Because of the entrance of sin into the world and our inheritance of Adam's sinful nature (Rom 5:12-19), we are by nature hostile to God and estranged from Him (Rom 8:7; Eph 2:1-3). We then have wills that do not obey God, eyes that do not see, and ears that do not hear because spiritually we are dead to God.

While we function as free moral agents with free wills, our decisions and actions are always affected by sin. In day-to-day decisions we have the ability to make free and rational choices, but these choices are always influenced by our sin nature. In regard to our relationship with God, we do not genuinely repent or turn to God without divine enablement because we are by nature hostile to God.

An awareness of these ideas helps to clarify frequently misunderstood concepts about the nature of sinful humanity. Our nature is depraved, but this does not mean we are as wicked as we can be. Rather the idea of depravity refers to the fact that all aspects of our being are negatively impacted by sin. Men and women still can and still do right and good things as viewed by society, but these thoughts and actions no matter how benevolent are sinful if not done for the glory of God. People choose to do good, but not the ultimate good that is the goal of pleasing God and seeking His eternal glory. Thus depravity involves our total willful rejection of the will and glory of God.

We are therefore totally depraved, but we cannot say that we are totally corrupt. Other factors such as environment, emotional makeup, heritage, and, of course, the continuing effect of our having been created in God's image influence the degree of corruption. The degree of wickedness, corruption, and deceitfulness differs from individual to individual and from culture to culture; but certainly some are more noble than others (Acts 17:11). Still, sin is inevitable because all in this world are estranged from God, but the biblical answer is that Jesus Christ has regained what was lost in Adam (Rom 5:12-21). The grace of God has provided our restoration and brought about a right relationship with God, with one another, with nature, and with ourselves.

Salvation

Grace

Salvation is a *free gift of God,* and it cannot be merited by our good behavior (Rom 3:22-24). Grace declares that salvation is not the culmination of humanity's quest for God but that it resides in the initiative of God toward men and women (Eph 1:4-7). Even our faith is a gift of God (Eph 2:8-9), and, as a matter of fact, all of life is such (Jas 1:17). If grace brings us to God, it also enables us to continue and complete our spiritual pilgrimage. This does not deny human involvement in salvation, but it does affirm the primacy of grace. When men and women receive the grace of God, it is a testimony to the impact of grace itself; but when grace is rejected, it is attributable to the hardness and sinfulness of the human heart.

Grace comes to us while we are still in our sins and brings spiritual transformation based on the accomplished cross work of Jesus Christ. Even the sanctifying work of the Spirit is enacted in those who do not merit or deserve it. In reality *grace is God's free and loving favor to the ill-deserving.*

God does not graciously accept us because He sees our

change for the better, as if conversion were the basis for receiving God's grace. Instead, the Bible pictures God coming into our lives, taking us just as we are because He is abundantly merciful (Eph 2:1-10).

Salvation is of God and is not based on the human response, yet men and women must respond to God's grace. Only persons who receive and are transformed by divine grace can make a favorable response to God's salvific invitation, but only those who do respond are indeed transformed by grace. Thus we affirm the priority of initiating grace without neglecting simultaneously to maintain our responsibility to believe.

Far from violating our wills or personalities, God's grace appeals to our deepest yearnings. Therefore when we are exposed to grace, intrinsically we are drawn toward it. We therefore affirm that in salvific grace, we are not merely passive. Neither do we want to imply that God does some and we do the rest; rather, God does all, and we do all. God does not override the will but releases the will for believing response. It is certain that convicting grace can be rejected (Matt 23:37; Luke 7:30; Heb 12:15); yet when we receive the gracious gift of regeneration, our wills are turned in a completely new direction. When God extends His grace to us, He is the active agent, but He always extends grace through various means. The means of grace include the preached gospel, the written Word of God, the invitation to respond to grace, the prayers of other believers, and the faith of the respondent. This leads to the need to understand further the meaning of faith.

Faith

The Bible maintains that faith is the means by which we receive and appropriate the salvation purchased for us by the cross work of our Lord Jesus Christ (Gal 2:16; Eph 2:8-9). *Faith includes a full commitment of the whole person to the Lord Jesus, a commitment that involves knowledge, trust, and obedience.* Faith is not merely an intellectual assent or an emotional response but a complete inward spiritual change confirmed to us by the Holy Spirit. Faith is altogether brought about by God, and it is altogether the human response bringing about complete enslavement to God and full liberation from the snare of sin.

The object of faith is not the teaching about Christ but Christ himself. Though faith is more than doctrinal assent, it must include adherence to doctrine. In our belief in and commitment to Jesus Christ, we acknowledge Him as Savior from sin and Lord of our lives, even Lord of creation (Rom 10:9). True conversion definitely involves a belief in Christ's person as the God-Man and in His work as Savior. We must remember, however, that it is possible to have orthodox understanding of Christ without a living faith in Him.

Conversion and Repentance

Conversion signifies our turning to Christ initiated by God. It is a great work of God's power changing the heart and infusing life into our dead spirits. It is important to recognize that the outworking of this grace in the conversion experience displays itself differently in some than in others. Not all have a "Damascus road experience" like the apostle Paul. Some are converted quietly like Lydia and others dramatically like the Philippian jailer (Acts 16). But for all it involves a turning away from sin to righteousness, and it issues in service to the world and separation without withdrawal from it.

The *turning away from sin, renouncing, and changing our minds about sin and Christ is what we mean by repentance.* It is not merely feeling sorry for ourselves but forsaking sin.

True conversion does not just stimulate our natural abilities to do better, to "turn over a new leaf "; rather it is the impartation of a new nature. Conversion must be differentiated from reformation of character; it is a radical yet progressive alteration of our very being.

Salvation Metaphors

Briefly we must mention some of the important biblical themes and metaphors or models that picture our salvation. None of these concepts completely present the full understanding of salvation. See articles in the Pauline Letters on "Adoption," "Justification by Faith," and "Salvation in Paul's Thought."

Regeneration. This is the most frequently discussed term within popular Christianity. It is *a spiritual change by which the Holy Spirit imparts divine life*. The idea is familiar in the writings of John, Peter, and Paul and is not without Old Testament precedent. The classic presentation is found in John 3:3-8 (see also 1 Pet 1:23; Titus 3:5-7). From John 3 comes the popular term "born again"—which is better translated as "born from above"—whereby God imparts righteousness to us. It is the experiential picture of our entrance into God's family, whereby adoption refers to our position in this family.

Sanctification. Sanctification involves different aspects of our salvation and is in some sense an umbrella term. The Bible speaks of positional sanctification (1 Cor 6:11), progressive sanctification (Rom 6:14–7:25), and ultimate sanctification (1 John 3:1-3). It is a work of the Father (John 17:17), the Son (Gal 2:20), and primarily of the Spirit (2 Cor 3:17-18). Yet it is also a work of the believer (Rom 12:1-2). The Bible does not teach a "letting go and letting God" approach to sanctification; rather, we are to strive after holiness, working out our salvation with fear and trembling. This is accomplished through the Bible's transforming effects in our lives (1 Pet 2:2), prayer (Col 4:2), fellowship and worship (Heb 10:19-25), and the circumstances of life (Rom 8:28).

Glorification. The arrival at the state of absolute righteousness is our glorification. *Justification is a declaration of righteousness; sanctification is the process of becoming more righteous; and glorification is the final consummation of our righteousness* (Rom 8:28-30).

Forgiveness. The putting away of sin and its penalty is forgiveness. It includes a gracious forgetting (Eph 4:32), a sending away of our sins (Matt 26:28), and a putting aside or disregarding of all sin (Rom 3:25). The Bible is the only religious book that emphasizes total and complete forgiveness (Heb 10:17), as pictured in the account of the wayward son (Luke 15:11-32). Scripture presents the bases of forgiveness as the shedding of blood (Heb 9:22-26), as well as our faith and repentance (Luke 17:3-10).

Union with Christ. The result of the concepts of adoption, forgiveness, and justification is pictured as the believer's new sphere of union with Christ (John 15; Rom 6:1-11; Eph 1:3-14). Positionally, our union with Christ presents us in a new position before God. Experientially, the union of believers with God is one of the most tender concepts expressed in Scripture: it is invisible and imperceptible to the senses; it is unfathomable, escaping all inward vision. Yet this mystery (Col 1:27-28) cannot be dissected or denied.

Eternal Security

God is the Author and Finisher of our faith (Heb 12:2). Salvation is from sin, for the world has primarily a need of a sin bearer (John 1:29). This involves disarming believers from the rulers and authorities of this world (Col 2:14-15). Salvation is only in Christ (John 14:6; Acts 4:12), is imperishable (1 Pet 1:4), and is the source of all spiritual blessing (Eph 1:3).

Our salvation is secured in Christ, and nothing can separate us from the love of Christ (Rom 8:31-39); yet our response to this truth brings our assurance. Eternal security is an objective truth, but our response to it is experiential and subjective. It is based on the work of Christ (Heb 7:25), the witness of the Spirit (Rom 8:14-17), and our obedience (1 John 5:11-13). God has promised to keep us from stumbling (Jude 24), having sealed us until the day of redemption (Eph 4:30). Thus we are responsible to persevere and hold on to God. Ultimately our security in Christ comes because He has a hold on us (John 10:28-30).

Conclusion

We affirm that God has created men and women in the image of God. Humans have sinned and are alienated from God apart from salvific grace. In grace God takes the initiative in bringing sinners to Christ through the proclamation of the gospel and the human response of faith. As a result of God's grace, believers experience salvation from sin which involves conversion to God. All of salvation is of God, yet we respond in faith and commitment. The Bible expresses these truths in various metaphors, underscoring throughout that God is the Author and Finisher of our salvation.

Questions for Reflection

1. What is the significance of the teaching that men and women are created in the image of God?
2. Define grace. What is the relationship between divine grace and human faith in our salvation?
3. What is meant by conversion? Is it always a crisis experience? Point out some differences between the conversion accounts in Acts 16.
4. Distinguish between justification, sanctification, and glorification. Define each one as you distinguish them.
5. What is meant by eternal security? What is assurance of salvation? Are these the same? How do they differ?
6. Is the salvation experience identical for everyone?
7. What do these truths indicate for us regarding our relationships and ministry with unbelievers?

Sources for Additional Study

Berkouwer, G. C. *Man: The Image of God.* Grand Rapids: Eerdmans, 1962.

Butler, Trent C., ed. *Disciple's Study Bible.* Nashville: Holman, 1988.

Morris, Leon. *The Apostolic Preaching of the Cross.* Grand Rapids: Eerdmans, 1956.

Packer, J. I. *Evangelism and the Sovereignty of God.* Chicago: InterVarsity, 1961.

Tozer, A. W. *The Knowledge of the Holy.* New York: Harper, 1961.

God's Church
The Nature and Mission of the Church

The church is the community of men and women who have responded to God's offer of salvation. It provides order, organization, and mission directives for the people of God. As far as humanly possible, all believers in the Lord involve themselves in the visible, organized church of Jesus Christ, and every person in the church should be rightly related to Jesus Christ by faith. The people of God on earth at any one time plus all believers in heaven and earth make up the true, invisible, universal church. In this section we will examine the nature and mission of the church including the order and organization of the church, its worship, ministry, fellowship, ordinances, and discipline.

The Nature of the Church

The Inauguration of the Church

The word *church* can be used in a variety of ways. It can be used to talk about a place where believers gather, a local organization of believers, a universal body of believers, a particular denomination (like the Presbyterian Church), or an organization of believers related to a particular area or nation (like the Church of Scotland).

The biblical idea of church must be understood from the usage of *ekklesia* (the Greek word for church) in the New Testament. The basic idea means *a gathered group of people.* In the Bible *ekklesia* has a variety of meanings, but most references point to a local body of believers. The term occurs 114 times in the New Testament, of which 109 refer to the local or universal church of Jesus Christ. In Acts 19:32,41 there is reference to an unruly mob, and in Acts 19:39 the term is translated as a lawful assembly. First Thessalonians 1:1 points to a specific church, 1 Corinthians 4:17 indicates a nonspecific church, while Galatians 1:22 refers to a group of churches. Ephesians 1:22-23 and Colossians 1:18 look beyond the local churches to the spiritual unity of the universal church. We can see that there are several usages of the word *church* in the New Testament.

The church was inaugurated at Pentecost (Acts 2) as God's new society (Eph 2:15). It was founded upon the finished work of Christ (Acts 20:18) and the baptizing work of the Spirit (1 Cor 12:13). The church was a mystery, was prophesied by Christ (Matt 16:18), and was revealed at the Spirit's coming at Pentecost (1 Cor 2:7; Eph 3:13). The church was built upon the foundation as Christ's apostles with Christ Jesus Himself the Cornerstone (Eph 2:20-21).

Characteristics of the Church

What the believing community *is* precedes an understanding of what the church *does.* The church is both in origin and in end God's church. We do not create the church by our efforts but receive it is a gift of God. It is constituted by Him and for Him. Membership is by divine fellowship of those indwelt by the Holy Spirit, a community of believers who have been called as saints.

The New Testament presents several models or images of the church, reflecting more of a Judaistic than of a Hellenistic background. The church was presented through pictures and images rather than logical proposition. Some of these images include the church as the fellowship of the Spirit (Phil 2:2), the household of God (Gal 6:10), the new creation (Eph 2:15), the body of Christ (Eph 1:22), the temple of the Holy Spirit (Eph 2:21), the pillar of the truth (1 Tim 3:15), and the bride of Christ (Rev 19:7).

The church is multisided as these images demonstrate. The idea of the church as people of God pictures its universality, that is, believers who cross all segments of society are in touch with one another (Gal 3:28). The image of the new creation pictures Christ's victory over evil as a new humanity in the midst of the old. The household of God points to the visible form of God's people who relate to each other in community and constitute the new creation. The body of Christ shows the presence of Christ in the world, though it is mystically experienced and known. The church is more than a human organization but is a visible and tangible expression of the people who are related to Christ.

Joining with the church throughout the ages, we maintain that the church is *one, holy, universal,* and *apostolic.* The church's oneness includes unity one with another, visible and invisible (John 17:1-26; 1 Cor 12:4-6; Eph 4:1-6). The completed holiness of the church will be completed in Christ. It reminds the church it is to be visibly holy in spite of its present sinfulness, thus the need to be tolerant with one another's weaknesses (1 Pet 1:15-16). Confessing the church as universal points to the need to be inclusive of all branches of the church rather than to maintain an exclusivistic view that one branch contains the whole truth (John 16:13; 1 Tim 3:15). Also it says that the church's mission is to all nations (Matt 28:19-20). Apostolicity calls the church to remain continuous with the past and to recognize the normative nature of apostolic doctrine and practice and practice (Matt 16:16-18; Eph 2:20).

To this point our discussion has focused on general truths about the universal church, the *community of believers of all time in heaven and on all parts of the earth.* Our focus in the remainder of this section will concentrate primarily on the nature and ministry of the local church, which is a specific group of God's people in a specific place. More definitely we can say that a *local* church *is a group of baptized believers banded together for worship, edification, service, fellowship, and outreach; accepting spiritual leadership; willing to minister to all segments of society through the various gifts in the body; and regularly practicing ordinances.*

Order and Organization of the Church

The church is to do everything decently and in order (1 Cor 14:40). For the church to function in this way, there is a need for leadership (Acts 14:23; Titus 1:5; Heb 13:17). The leadership of the church includes two offices: overseers (referred to as pastors, elders, or bishops in the NT: Acts 20:17,28; 1 Tim 3:1; Titus 1:5; Jas 5:14; and 1 Pet 5:2-3) and deacons (Phil 1:1; 1 Tim 3:8).

The first group of leaders are responsible for general oversight, administration, teaching, and shepherding. The second group of leaders have the responsibilities of service, helping, family care, and visitation. The distinction in function can be determined from the differences in the purposes and qualifications listed in Scripture. Generally speaking, the overseers are responsible for teaching and administration while the deacons are responsible for care and service.

The qualifications of leadership are listed in 1 Timothy 3:1 and Titus 1. The great degree of detail in the lists should point to the high demands to be placed upon the church's leaders. If persons desire the office of overseer, it is a fine work they desire to do (1 Tim 3:1). The primary qualification is that overseers should be "blameless" or "above reproach." The lists from the two passages include twenty character qualities and one requirement concerning ability ("able to teach"). This should say much to the contemporary emphasis upon personality and ability and the little concern given to spirituality and character in many congregations. The standards in today's churches are often backwards from the guidelines presented in Scripture.

The list for deacons (1 Tim 3:8-13) is similar, though it does not contain the same detail. Two obvious differences are present. The first is that the deacons are not required to be able to teach. This does not mean that deacons are unable to teach or should not teach but merely that it is not a requirement for the functions of the deaconal office. The second is that deacons should not be double-tongued. This seemingly implies that deacons are responsible for the offering; visitation and counseling; care of the sick, the poor, and the needy; and the distribution of the Lord's Supper. This type of ministry demands personal involvement, and deacons will have access to information about the private lives of the church members. Thus deacons must not be gossips or those who distort the truth.

Additional order and organization in the church develops from needs among the congregation and the spiritual gifts available for ministry in particular settings (1 Cor 12; Eph 4:11-16). The function of the church is more important than its form as the entire congregation submits to Jesus Christ as Lord and head of the church (Eph 1); so that there is no authoritarian leadership (1 Pet 5:1-3) in the local congregation. Instead, there is mutual participation, admonition, and encouragement (Rom 1:12; Heb 10:24-25), as well as mutual submission one to another (Eph 5:21).

The Mission of the Church

The Church in Praise and Worship

Worship is central in the existence and continuation of the church as presented in the New Testament. The ultimate purpose of the church is the worship and praise of the One who called it into being (Eph 1:4-6). To worship God is to ascribe to Him the supreme worth which He alone is worthy to receive. Worship is desired by God (John 4:24) and is made possible by His grace. To worship God includes reverence and adoration (Rev 4:11). It also involves the expression of awe (Acts 18:7,13), as

The Last Supper

well as the Spirit-enabled service expressed in prayer (Acts 13:2-3), giving (Rom 15:27), or the ministry of the gospel (Rom 15:16). Worship in the community produces a total ministry of life that is pleasing to God (Rom 12:1-2). There is, thus, a close relationship between worship and a life of service to God.

The elements of Christian worship are similar to those found in the Old Testament, yet there are two new factors at the very heart of the New Testament that bring about a decisive reorientation. The first of these is that Christian worship is in its very core and essence the worship of God the Father through the Son. The Christological orientation is new although the essential elements remain. The worshiping community stands in a personal relation to God on the basis of adoption in Christ. Prayer is made in the name of the Son (John 16:23). The works of God in the Son are the theme of this praise (Eph 1:2). The confession is the confession of Jesus as Lord (Rom 10:9; 1 Cor 12:3). Preaching is setting forth the work of Christ (2 Cor 4:5), and the Lord's Supper is the celebration of the new and final exodus, the showing forth of the one sacrifice for sin (1 Cor 11:26). Giving is on the basis of God's gift in His Son (2 Cor 9:15). The focus of the church's worship upon the exalted Christ gives a new depth and content to the worshiping community.

The first new aspect is grounded in the person and work of Christ, while the second new aspect of the church's worship is influenced by the Holy Spirit. The church's worship of God the Father is through the Son, in and by God the Holy Spirit. Prayer comes with the divine aid of the Spirit (Rom 8:26). Praise is rejoicing in the Spirit (Eph 5:18-20). Confession of sins is under the conviction of the Holy Spirit (John 16:8), and confession of Jesus as Lord is by the Holy Spirit (1 Cor 12:3). Holy Scripture is inspired by the Holy Spirit and illumined by the Spirit as well (2 Tim 3:16; 1 Cor 2:14). Preaching is in the power of the Holy Spirit (1 Cor 2:4), and the Lord's Supper is in the fellowship of the Spirit (Acts 2). Liberty flows from love, which is a fruit of the Holy Spirit (Gal 5:22), and a life of worship flows from walking in the Spirit (Gal 5:16). Fitting and acceptable worship can only be offered by and through the Holy Spirit.

The Church in Ministry

Every member of the local church is a believer-priest before God and for one another. Jesus Christ is the head of the church as well as its High Priest (Heb 3:1). Each member functions as a priest who worships, offers praise and thanksgiving (Heb 13:15-16), and offers himself or herself as a sacrifice for ministry (Rom 12:1). Each believer is to function in his or her office of priest within the church. To enable us to do so, the Spirit of God has equipped believers with spiritual gifts for the purpose of ministry. Spiritual gifts are God-given abilities for service (Rom 12; 1 Cor 12; Eph 4).

Paul gave lists of the gifts (see article "Spiritual Gifts") but proceeded to the more excellent way of Christian love (1 Cor 21:31). Paul did not deny that spectacular gifts have a place, but he insisted that the important thing is the manifestation of ethical qualities, especially love, which the presence of the Spirit in the heart of the believer makes possible. The apostle assumed that all believers share in the gifts of the Spirit and that all are for the common good (1 Cor 12:4-7). It is the concept of the edification of the body of Christ (1 Cor 14:13) that is primary in understanding Paul's view of the place of gifts in the churches. Gifts are for the enablement of believers so that the primary ministries of the believing community can be effectively accomplished. These ministries include evangelism (Matt 28:19-20), edification and teaching (Eph 4:11-16), and social service (Jas 1:27).

The Church in Fellowship

The church is a community of men and women who relate to each other because of their relationship to Jesus Christ (Acts 2:44-45; 1 John 1:3; 3:11-18). When genuine fellowship takes place, intercommunication is encouraged, authenticity is increased, intimacy is developed, freedom of expression is encouraged, mutual burden bearing is primary, and prayer becomes specific, creating a sense of belonging. Belonging creates identity, bringing about true spiritual community among the family of God.

The Ordinances of the Church

The ordinances of the church are two: baptism and the Lord's Supper. Both have been commanded by our Lord to be continued as symbols of the Lord's ongoing presence in His church.

Baptism. Christian baptism has its background in the Old Testament act of ritual purification, proselyte baptism, and the baptism of John. Jesus began His public ministry by association with John's baptism, probably not as a sign of repentance but as the King of the kingdom (Matt 3:13-17; John 1:19-34). According to John 4:2, Jesus Himself probably did not baptize. Jesus was baptized to identify with sinners in order to fulfill all righteousness. The church is commanded to continue the practice of Christian baptism as an aspect of discipling the nations (Matt 28:19-20).

In the early chapters of Acts, beginning with Pentecost, baptism is closely associated with repentance as a qualification for salvation and membership in the Christian community (Acts 2:37-41). The references to baptism "in the name of Jesus" are probably attempts to distinguish Christian baptism from Jewish proselyte baptism rather than a specific baptismal formula (Acts 2:38; 8:16).

For Paul baptism was primarily an act of identification with the death, burial, and resurrection of Christ. Also it serves as a sign of covenant relationship with Christ and His people (Rom 6:1-4; Col 2:9-13). Paul did not conceive of baptism as an essential saving ordinance or sacrament as is clearly indicated in 1 Corinthians 1:10-18. For the worshiping community baptism is the initiation act whereby one was made a member of the community, the body of Christ, identifying with Christ and His people. The act of baptism is not restricted to any class of people (Gal 3:27-28). There is not distinction of race (Jew or Greek), sex (male or female), or social status (slave or free). All are regarded as having been "baptized into Christ" as a result of "having put on Christ" (Eph 4:24; Col 3:10).

Baptism is essentially connected with death and resurrection and not with cleansing. Baptism signifies burial with Christ in His death, but baptism also means new life, sharing with Christ's risen life. It exhibits the transition that has occurred, having moved from death to life. This involves the believer in the actual dying and rising of Christ in a kind of reenactment. Also it shows that death has taken place in the life of the believer and a new life has begun. In addition, it demands a crucifixion of the flesh and a new life in the Spirit. The new life in the new community requires a whole new set of values. The act is a valuable teaching medium for candidates and the entire church in order for the symbolic meaning of baptism to be communicated.

Lord's Supper. See the article "Lord's Supper" in 1 Corinthians commentary. When the church celebrates the Supper and the bread and wine are taken, the Lord's presence is to be recalled in His remembrance. It is a remembrance of the life and death of the Lord. The Christian community, following the dynamic example of the Passover, is to look upon the elements of the Supper as taking believers back to the scenes of redemption, as leading them to receive again the benefits of the Lord's passion, and as representing His response to the love that bore the cross.

The celebration of the Supper is central to the church's worship and thus should be a regular and frequent occurrence (Acts 20:7; 1 Cor 11:24). Only believers who are a part of the body of Christ are entitled to partake of it.

The Discipline of the Church

Perhaps the most neglected practice in the contemporary Christian community is the discipline of the church. Discipline rests upon the fact that God Himself disciplines His children (Heb 12:6). God disciplines His own, but He has ordained mediate discipline by the church concerning those affairs that concern the life and walk of the local body. Discipline is based on the holiness of God (Heb 12:11), the command of Christ (Matt 18:18), and the practice of the apostles (1 Cor 5).

The practice of discipline must be done with great care. We should remember that the apostle Paul had much to say about the sins at Corinth, yet He only singled out one sin among the community for discipline in 1 Corinthians 5. The categories for discipline in the New Testament are many (Matt 18:15-17; Rom 16:17-18; 2 Thess 3:14-15; 1 Tim 1:20). Often public rebuke is called for at these times (Matt 18:17; Rom 16:17; 1 Cor 5:4-5; 1 Tim 1:20).

The forms of discipline include warning and admonition (1 Thess 5:12-14), withholding of fellowship (2 Thess 3:6,17), abstaining from association (1 Cor 5:11-15), and excommunication (1 Tim 1:20). The act of discipline is to be performed in love and humility. The purpose of all discipline must be to win back the erring (2 Cor 2:4; Gal 6:1). The ultimate goal is restoration to fellowship, but the immediate goal must be shame (2 Thess 3:14) and sorrow (2 Cor 2:7). Yet there is warning against excessive punishment that produces excessive sorrow (2 Cor 2:7), though there is need for godly sorrow that brings about repentance (2 Cor 7:10). Discipline protects the church from further decay (1 Cor 5:6). Finally, it serves as a reminder of the propensity toward sin on behalf of all (2 Cor 7:11).

Conclusion

God called the church into being for fellowship with Himself and with other believers. The church has a dual purpose in the world; it is to be a holy priesthood (1 Pet 2:5) and to declare the wonderful deeds of God, who called the believing community out of darkness into His marvelous light (1 Pet 2:9). We confess the church as one, holy, universal, and apostolic and believe that God intends for all believers to be involved in local churches, worshiping, ministering, serving, fellowshiping, and celebrating together. In addition to these functions, the church has a missionary task that is not optional and is for the world, not merely for itself.

Questions for Reflection

1. How does the New Testament use the term *church?*
2. When was the church brought into being?
3. What is the significance of the metaphors used for the church in the New Testament?
4. What are the offices of the church? What are the responsibilities of each office?
5. What is the purpose of church discipline?
6. What is signified when the church participates in the Lord's Supper?
7. How can the New Testament emphasis upon the corporate and covenant people be emphasized properly in our individualistic culture?
8. How can churches balance concerns for worship, fellowship, edification, and outreach ministry?

Sources for Additional Study

Martin, Ralph P. *The Worship of God.* Grand Rapids: Eerdmans, 1985.

Saucy, Robert. *The Church in God's Program.* Chicago: Moody, 1972.

God's Rule and Reign The Doctrine of Last Things

Our final section will discuss God's rule, reign, and ultimate victory. This study of last things in relation to individuals and corporate groups is called *eschatology,* from the Greek word for *last* (*eschatos*). The topics to be examined include death, resurrection, judgment, and the eternal state. The consummation of God's plan will be brought about by the return of the Lord Jesus Christ—this is the hope of the church!

Individual Eschatology

Individual eschatology examines the phenomenon of death as an individual experience and the question of the intermediate state, which is the state of the dead in the period between death and the final resurrection.

We must be more cautious in our interpretation of the Bible's reference to future matters. Our confidence in the trustworthiness of the Bible is the same, though our confidence and certainty in our interpretation of such matters is more guarded. Whether concerning the second coming, death, the resurrection, or judgment, teaching on these matters in the New Testament *is presented as an incentive for obedient and holy living.*

Death

No escape avails. Sooner or later, unless the Lord Jesus Christ should return, we all will die (Heb 9:26-28). Physical death is variously represented in Scripture. It is spoken of as the death of the body, as distinguished from the soul (Matt 10:28) or as the separation of body and soul. Never is it spoken of as annihilation but rather as the termination of physical life. According to Scripture, however, death is not merely a biological phenomenon but is a consequence of disobedience to the command of God (Gen 2:16-17; Prov 8:35-36).

Instead of being something natural, it is an expression of divine anger, a judgment on sin (Rom 6:23). Adam's sin brought death not only upon himself but also upon his descendants (Rom 5:12-29). Since death is a punishment for sin and believers are redeemed from sin and its guilt and penalty, we must ask why Christians still die. It is clear that death cannot be a punishment for them but must be considered as an aspect of the sanctification process leading to ultimate glorification. It is the consummation of believers' dying unto sin. Death's ultimate defeat has been manifested in the resurrection of Jesus Christ (1 Cor 15:54-57).

The Intermediate State

The idea of the intermediate state refers to the state of the dead during the period after death and prior to the final resurrection. The soul/spirit, the immaterial aspect of believers, will at death be made perfect in holiness and pass immediately into glory (2 Cor 5:6-8; Phil 1:21-24). The body, the material portion, remains in the grave after death until the final resurrection (1 Thess 4:14). At death the soul consciously rests in the presence of God (Luke 16:22-23) or in torment until the body is raised. Then the whole person exists eternally in a condition established by God's just and righteous judgment. Those who suffer are punished to the degree of divine truth that they refused (see Matt 11:21-22). Those glorified with Christ receive His inheritance as a gift and will dwell in the new heavens and new earth (Rev 21–22).

Corporate Eschatology

Throughout the history of humankind, people have sought, worked, and died attempting to bring about peace and justice on the earth. It is the responsibility of the church to work for and pray for peace and justice on earth, but ultimate peace and justice are precluded by the sinfulness of humanity. Only when God's rule and reign comes to its full manifestation will history know true peace. Corporate eschatology deals with those events that will occur at the close of human history. Included in this discussion will be the topics of the second coming of Christ, the millennium, the general resurrection, the final judgment, and eternal state. It is to the return of Christ that the church has expectantly looked since the Lord's ascension (Acts 1:9-11).

The Return of Christ

Christ came first in the form of a servant. He will return as the Judge of all humankind (1 Thess 5:1-3; John

The Last Judgment

5:24-27). At the first coming He inaugurated His kingdom; at His second coming He will consummate His kingdom. The second coming will be physical and personal, as were His resurrection and ascension (Acts 1:10-11).

The coming of Christ will be immediately preceded by a cosmic and terrestrial distress (Luke 21:25-27). Christ's return will bring a judgment upon the world that is sudden, unexpected, and inescapable (Matt 24:42-44). The Antichrist figure is to arise prior to the second coming. He will be decisively overthrown (2 Thess 2:1-8).

The kingdom of God, God's rule and reign, will be consummated and fully established at the return of Christ. In some sense Christ's redemptive kingdom is already realized in His church through the hearts and lives of believers (Rom 14:17; Col 1:13). There is also a future sense of Christ's kingdom that is not yet realized throughout the earth and awaits the fullness of His kingship (Isa 11:9; Rom 8:18-27; Rev 20:1-6). The fullness of the kingdom, the future rule of Christ, is not identical with the final, eternal state after the establishment of the new creation, the new heavens, and the new earth (Isa 65; Rev 21). We can affirm that while the ultimate Christianization of the world will never occur, there will be a great outpouring of God's grace in the end times as the gospel is proclaimed throughout the world (Matt 24:3-31; Rom 11:35-36). These grand truths have been systematized in four major ways referred to as postmillennialism, amillennialism, dispensational premillennialism, and historical premillennialism. (See the chart "Millennial Perspectives on Revelation.")

The Millennium

The term *millennium* is derived from the reference to the thousand-year reign of Christ with the saints in Revelation 20:4-6. The various millennial views reflect different understandings of the nature of this period and different interpretations of the chronological relationship of the second coming of Christ to the millennial period and other events of the last days.

Postmillennialism. According to this view, Christ will return after (post) a long period of expansion and spiritual prosperity for the church, brought about by the preaching of the gospel; the Spirit's blessing; and the church's work toward righteousness, justice, and peace. The period is not a literal thousand years, but this extended time of spiritual prosperity in this system includes:

1. The kingdom of God is primarily a present reality.
2. A conversion of all nations will take place prior to Christ's return.
3. A long period of earthly peace will occur.

4. The kingdom expands gradually through the proclamation of the gospel, bringing about a kingdom of peace and light.

5. The kingdom is primarily understood in qualitative, not quantitative, terms.

6. At the end of the kingdom, there will be a time of spiritual falling away.

7. The kingdom will end with the personal, bodily return of Jesus.

8. The Lord's return will be followed immediately by the resurrection of all the righteous and unrighteous and the judgment of all.

9. What is true of the gospel's spread from individual to individual is likewise true of its spread through society's institutions and activities, physical environment, houses, education, politics, and both national and international affairs. In this way the whole mass of humanity will be imbued with and governed by Christian principles and support.

Amillennialism. Amillennialists believe there will be no (the negative "a") literal thousand-year reign of Christ with the saints on earth. The return of Christ is followed by the general resurrection of both the righteous and the wicked, the last judgment, and the passage into the eternal state. Some specific beliefs include:

1. The two resurrections in Revelation 20:4-5 are interpreted whereby the first is spiritual and the second is physical.

2. The thousand years in Revelation 20 is symbolic.

3. The Book of Revelation is understood in a cyclical fashion.

4. Revelation 20 must be understood historically in relation to the rest of the book.

5. There is no expectation of revealed prophecy to be fulfilled in the future, except for the general beliefs about the Lord's return. Basically this viewpoint holds that all has been fulfilled in Christ or will be fulfilled in the new earth.

6. Generally there is a lack of prophetic interest in contrast to premillennialism.

7. There is a sense of imminency that is shared by premillennialists.

8. Like premillennialism and contrary to postmillennialism, there is a general view that things will get worse before Christ's triumph in the end times.

Dispensational Premillennialism. This system teaches that Christ will return prior (pre) to the millennium, understood as a literal thousand-year period, and prior to the seven-year period, known as the great tribulation (Dan 9:27; Rev 7:14; 11:2). Christ will come secretly for the church and then publicly with His church to institute the millennial kingdom. The church does not go through the tribulation period. More specifically, some primary beliefs include:

1. The Bible is to be interpreted literally, including the passage in Revelation 20.

2. There is a difference between Israel and the church in the plan of God.

3. The promises and covenants given to Israel will find their ultimate fulfillment in ethnic Israel.

4. Jesus came to offer the kingdom to Israel, but it was rejected.

5. The church is a parenthesis between this rejection and the millennium.

6. The church will not go through the tribulation. The saints in Matthew 24 who are pictured in the tribulation refer to ethnic Israel.

7. The coming of Christ has two aspects: (1) the rapture of the church at the first aspect when Christ appears in the clouds and (2) the second coming of Christ when He comes with the church to the earth.

Historical Premillennialism. This position teaches that Christ will return prior (pre) to the millennium, which may or may not be understood as a literal thousand-year reign of Christ; but it is after the great tribulation (posttribulation). Historical premillennialists believe that the church will go through the tribulation period. Some of their beliefs include:

1. Christ will come back to earth to reign over His kingdom, which will be an earthly one.

2. The two resurrections of Revelation 20 are *both physical* (contrary to amillennialists' view).

3. Christ will reign with righteousness and justice over His subjects.

4. The standard of life in the Sermon on the Mount while applicable teaching for the church today will become a reality in the kingdom.

5. The return of the Lord will be a unitary event (not two stages as in dispensationalism).

6. The thousand-year reign of Revelation 20 is understood as a qualitative period without specifics regarding its length.

7. The church will go through the tribulation, and then Christ will return.

8. Imminency refers to an impending coming rather than an any-moment coming.

9. The church's hope is not for deliverance from the tribulation but in the Lord's coming.

10. The church has in some sense replaced national Israel (though there is still a future for Israel) as God's covenant people.

11. The kingdom is present and future and is primari-

ly understood as the rule and reign of God rather than the realm of God.

All positions agree that Christ will come again physically and visibly, and the church's hope is focused in Him. When He returns, He will consummate God's kingdom. The rule and reign of God will be completely expressed as God's victory over sin, evil, Satan, and death is accomplished.

The Resurrection

Scripture teaches that at the return of Christ, the dead will be raised up (Dan 12:2; John 11:24-25; 1 Cor 15). The resurrection will be a bodily resurrection similar to the resurrection of Christ. The redemption of the body will occur at this time (Rom 8:23; 1 Cor 15). Both the righteous and the wicked will be raised (various millennial viewpoints see the chronology of the resurrection(s) differently). For the wicked, the reunion of body and soul will issue in the penalty of eternal death and for the righteous an act of deliverance and glorification forever.

The Last Judgment

The teaching of the resurrection leads to the throne of final judgment (again the chronology and types of judgments differ according to millennial views). In the first coming of Christ, He came as Savior; in His second coming He will return as Judge of all humankind (John 12:47-48; Acts 17:31). God's judgment will come according to the standard revealed in God's word and will vary based upon the revelation available to different groups of people (Matt 11:20-24). Those who have not heard the gospel, the heathen, will be judged by the law of nature and conscience (Rom 2:12); Jews, by the Old Testament (Rom 2:17-28). Those who have heard the full gospel revelation will be judged by it (Rom 3:19-20). God will give every person his or her due. Every individual of the human race will have to appear before the judgment seat (Matt 25:32; Rev 20:12). Satan and demons will be judged (Matt 25:41; Jude 6), and believers will appear before the judgment seat of Christ to be judged for their works (2 Cor 5:10).

The Eternal State

The last judgment determines the final state of those who appear before the judgment seat. Their final state is either one of everlasting misery and separation from God or one of eternal blessedness. In the final state the wicked are consigned to the place of condemnation called hell, an eternal lake of fire (Rev 20:14-15). They will for all eternity be deprived of divine favor and will suffer punishment for sins. The final state of believers will be preceded by the judgment of the present world and the establishment of a new creation. The abode of the righteous will be heaven, a place prepared by Christ (John 14:2). Heaven is not merely spiritual but is the establishment of the new heavens and new earth (Rev 21–22). In the eternal state, creation itself will be freed from the effects of sin and the curse upon the earth (Gen 3). This fullness of life is enjoyed in communion with God, which is really the *essence* of eternal life (Rev 21:3). All will enjoy perfect bliss, but apparently there will be degrees in the enjoyments of heaven (Dan 12:3).

Conclusion

God's final rule and reign brings victory when Christ returns to establish and consummate His kingdom. Regardless of the positive and industrious attempts by men and women to bring about righteousness and peace to earth, true peace and righteousness will occur only when Christ returns. The age-long quest of the nations can only be fulfilled by the work of Christ. We have seen that sincere believers differ over their understanding of the nature and chronology of Christ's return as well as the kingdom itself. But all agree that following His return will be the resurrection of the dead, both the righteous and the wicked. This leads to judgment, which leads to the eternal state: condemnation for the wicked and eternal bliss for believers as God's eternal glory is manifested in His victorious rule and reign.

Questions for Reflection

1. What is the millennium? What passage in the New Testament refers to the millennium? What are the four major views on the subject?
2. What is the intermediate state?
3. What is the goal of Christ's return?
4. By what standard is God's judgment exercised?
5. How do truths about God's rule and reign impact the spiritual life and mission of the church?

Sources for Additional Study

Clouse, Robert G., ed. *The Meaning of the Millennium.* Downers Grove: Intervarsity, 1977.

Hoekema, Anthony. *The Bible and the Future.* Grand Rapids: Eerdmans, 1979.

Ladd, George E. *The Blessed Hope.* Grand Rapids: Eerdmans, 1962.

Smith, Wilbur. *The Biblical Doctrine of Heaven.* Chicago: Moody, 1968.

THE BIBLE FOR CHRISTIAN LIVING

Doubtless the kind of question most frequently asked by Christians concerns biblical teaching about some current issue or problem. That kind of question reflects two extremely critical facts. (1) Nearly all Christians regard the Bible as the only sufficient and authoritative guide for Christian living. (2) Most Christians have some difficulty understanding exactly *how* the Bible can, or should, serve as guide.

The Bible as a Book for Living

The purpose of the Bible as guide for Christian living can be seen in the nature of the Bible itself. Its distinctiveness lies first in the remarkable way it came into being. It grew piecemeal (Heb 1:1) as God revealed Himself in specific times and cultural situations. He spoke to farmers and business people, poor and wealthy people, philosophers, fishermen, and kings. He addressed people in times of prosperity and adversity, war and peace, obedience and rejection. He came to Eastern cultures and Western. He involved Himself in every category of human need, longing, and failure.

The Bible thus possesses authority as the expression of God's will for human life. It is like the authority of loving parents actively involved in the lives of their children, not of a dictator issuing orders without regard for their effect. The message of the Bible is in touch with the most meaningful aspects of life—marriage and family; joy and love; sorrow and death; right living, thinking, and feeling.

Not only in terms of origin and scope but also in terms of form, the Bible shows itself to be a book for living. The Bible betrays almost no interest in itself merely as literature, although it is literature of the first order. Modern efforts to read, interpret, and appreciate the Bible only as great literature distort the true purpose of Scripture, which is to engender faith and obedience.

What is more, the message of the Bible is intended for all persons, not just the learned. The church of the Middle Ages tended to obscure this common appeal of the Bible by restricting its use to clergy. The Reformers of the sixteenth century helped to restore Scripture to common life by emphasizing (1) the authority of Scripture and (2) its intelligibility to all believers. As a result, and thanks to technological advances, the Bible is more accessible now to more people than at any time in history.

Indeed, it is a tragic irony of the modern era that biblical literacy has not kept pace with biblical accessibility. Christians may choose from some three dozen English translations; many Christians own more than one. Yet the evidence suggests that actual use of the Bible is declining and that many Christians are woefully unacquainted with it. While Medieval Christians were separated from the Bible by ecclesiastical authority, many modern Christians are separated by apathy.

Herein lies the first and most vital principle about the Bible for Christian living. In order to guide faith and life, the Bible must be read and used. The most potent enemy of Christian life has always been neglect of Scripture.

Granted that the Bible is a book for living, a more serious problem arises. *How* does the Bible function as a guide for life?

Such a question really has two answers. One concerns the *reader*—attitude, personality, background, and the like. The other concerns the *Bible* itself—its applicability, scope, authority, and so forth. The Bible therefore functions as guide only when it is both approached and understood responsibly.

A Responsible Approach to the Bible

Jesus once warned certain Jewish leaders that their use of the Scriptures was invalid since these bore testimony of the Christ they were unwilling to acknowledge (John 5:39-40). Such distortions of the Bible through improper motives have continued for centuries.

Personal Faith and Devotion. As Nicodemus learned (John 3:1-12), the Bible is first a book of faith rather than of learning. For Nicodemus and his colleagues among the Pharisees, Scripture was essentially philosophy. But Jesus made clear to him that their message was meant for belief, obedience, and transformation, not for academic discussion.

Particularly since the Middle Ages, the *speculative* and *theological* use of the Bible has tended to overshadow the *pastoral* and *devotional*. This has led to increasing emphasis on study as an end in itself and sometimes to a strict division between study and devotion. No such divisions or emphases appear in the Bible itself. Everywhere the biblical testimony is that persons must approach God's Word in order to hear and obey God (see Ps 119).

In this seminary class the professor suggests several biblical reference books to his students to aid them in their Bible study.

Those who approach the Bible in a spirit of personal devotion are distinguished in several ways. First, they respect the authority of Scripture. They receive it as morally binding. They acknowledge the implications of biblical teaching for thought and behavior. They grasp the seriousness of the Bible. They do not trivialize it, nor do they relegate it to the world of scholars.

Second, they approach the Bible to respond, to learn, and to act on the Word, not simply to hear it (Jas 1:22-25). They involve themselves actively in the Scripture so that it becomes personally significant.

Third, they regard the Bible as a personal message from God for the purpose of leading one into a deeply devoted relationship with Him. The Bible is less like a "how-to" manual than a letter. It testifies of Christ and leads persons to Him (John 5:39-40).

Personal Honesty and Self-examination. No one ever approaches a situation with total openness. The mind is never completely blank. A person brings to every single experience a long history; a set of attitudes; and a variety of fears, hopes, habits, and perspectives.

A reverent approach to Scripture demands an honest recognition of these psychological forces. Indeed, this is part of the Bible's own purpose: "For the word of God is living and active. Sharper than any double-edged sword, it penetrates even to dividing soul and spirit, joints and marrow; it judges the thoughts and attitudes of the heart" (Heb 4:12). It has been rightly said that when one opens the Bible honestly and asks what it is, the question is reversed: The Bible asks who the reader is!

As a guide for living, the Bible cannot be used to rationalize disobedience. Nor can only part of Scripture be permitted to speak. Nor must it be chosen to speak only in selected instances. An honest approach to the Bible implies a recognition of biases and a willingness to receive scriptural judgment from the whole of Scripture for the whole of life.

When personal bias leads to dishonest, inaccurate, or selective use of the Bible, the consequences are predictably disastrous. Any number of cultic groups, for example, have appealed to Scripture to justify the gratification of desires for sex, money, or power. Even among orthodox Christians, Scripture has been used not to guide living but to exercise control (legalism) or excuse disobedience. Several influential Christian movements utilize the biblical materials in these distorted ways. The modern stress on psychological wholeness and self-realization, for example, has encouraged many believers to interpret the Bible as a self-help manual. The effect is often to de-emphasize self-sacrifice or even fundamental doctrine. In so-called "situation ethics," to take another example, generic biblical principles such as "love" are said to replace the restrictive "rules" for proper behavior. Since love may require different responses from one situation to another, right behavior is relative.

Such approaches to Scripture are not necessarily dishonest. However, they do characteristically neglect, distort, or supplement portions of the Bible for the sake of a predetermined agenda. As guide for living, the Bible must be allowed to speak for itself.

Cultural Awareness. A person also comes to Scripture surrounded by an environment, a culture that has helped shape his or her life and that continues to do so. This culture-boundedness can affect the use of the Bible profoundly.

It can encourage neglect or skepticism of the Bible. Especially in modern society, the gap between "then" and "now" can seem intimidating. The Bible may appear irrelevant, out-of-fashion, or impossible to apply to contemporary needs. Scientifically minded people may be skeptical of the Bible's nontechnical point of view or simply ignore the Bible in favor of "hard" data from research.

It can generate confusion or distortion. Biblical injunctions about extramarital sexual behavior, for instance, might seem hopelessly antiquated to a person in a culture that not only excuses but encourages pleasure. In Europe and America materialism is so pervasive that many Christians are inclined to equate economic well-being with Christianity. Even sincere believers may struggle to accept biblical mandates in areas where cultural norms differ radically.

It can lead to selective emphasis on certain doctrines or themes in Scripture to the neglect of others. Biblical concepts like suffering and servanthood, for example, nowadays attract very little attention. Liberation theology, one of the most potent movements in world Christianity, is another excellent example. Most liberation theologians advocate freedom from injustice along the lines of Marxist economic and political philosophy. They frequently draw on "liberation" themes in the Bible (such as the exodus) to support programs of dramatic social change.

In one of the most influential books ever written on the subject, theologian Richard Niebuhr argued that Christians have historically responded to culture in one of five ways (*Christ and Culture* [New York: Harper, 1951]). Some Christians have completely *renounced* their cultures (some monks, for example). Others have *identified with* their cultures ("all Americans are Christians"). Still others have claimed *dual citizenship*, in the kingdom of God and the kingdom of this world. A fourth way Niebuhr called "Christ above culture," where the church exercises *authority over* culture and where those who serve the church live at a higher level than those who work in the secular arena. Finally, some Christians have advocated the *transformation of* culture.

These categories show the complexity of living "in the world but not of the world" (John 17:14-16). Yet the Bible is meant to guide Christians into godly and responsible behavior within their culture. They must neither renounce nor accommodate. They must not allow culture to judge Scripture. Instead they must permit Scripture to confront and evaluate culture. Christians must realize that culture affects their perspective and then come to Scripture for direction in living within that culture.

A Responsible Understanding of the Bible

The second prerequisite for proper use of the Bible has to do with the nature and function of the Bible itself. What should Christians expect from the Bible? What kinds of help can it give and how much? The Bible's testimony concerning itself suggests a threefold answer to these questions.

The Book of the Church. Second Peter 1:20 warns that Scripture is not a private affair. While personal Bible reading and devotion are certainly enjoined in Scripture, full understanding is often linked with corporate reading and explanation (Luke 10:26; Acts 8:28-32; Eph 3:4; Col 4:16). Moreover, the Holy Spirit is promised to the church to illumine Scripture (John 14:26; 16:13; 1 Thess 1:5).

Bible study has entered the computer age with the availability of a wide variety of computer software programs involving both Scripture text and reference material.

There are several important practical implications of this fact. First, Christians should not neglect the acquired wisdom of the church. For two millennia devoted Christians have grappled with the application of Scripture to the issues of living. Their conclusions provide a wealth of information for contemporary believers.

Second, Christian living is meant to be a shared experience. Scriptural discipleship assumes a church context of mutual encouragement, enlightenment, accountability, and discipline.

Third, God's revelation is given for the life and mission

Even a young child who does not understand all of the words of the Bible can be touched by God as he turns through its pages.

of the church, the body of Christ (Eph 3:1-6). The counsel of God is not in the first place for personal benefit. It is for the good of all persons in and through the church.

A Book of Growth. Jesus described His own words as "spirit" and "life" (John 6:63) because they are food that nourishes the spirit (John 6:54-58). Likewise in His encounter with Satan, Jesus rejected bread in favor of "every word that comes from the mouth of God" (Matt 4:4). The writer of Hebrews likened mature doctrine to solid food (Heb 5:11-14).

The food metaphor suggests a process of incorporation resulting in growth and energy. The Bible functions for Christian living as food does for biological living.

This kind of metaphor helps to correct certain misconceptions about the power of the Bible for living. First, it is not symbolic power. A copy of the Bible lying on a desk may communicate something positive to visitors. Taking an oath on a Bible might lend solemnity to the ritual. But the symbolic use of the Bible cannot empower Christian living. Second, it is not magical power. Some Christian groups have attached great significance to the physical presence, reading, or recitation of the Bible. Third, it is not intellectual power. Bible study has no inherent value. It can produce interesting discussion or even insight with no life change whatsoever.

A Book of Wisdom. For many Christians the thorniest problem of all is the application of Scripture to specific situations. There are several explanations for this problem. (1) The Bible obviously fails to address every contemporary issue, such as smoking or genetic engineering. (2) Some commandments, like Old Testament civil and ceremonial laws, seem not to be applicable to modern society or to New Testament doctrine. (3) Some biblical injunctions seem to reflect cultural practice, not universal principles. A warm handshake might be the modern equivalent of greeting "with a holy kiss" (1 Cor 16:20), for example.

In Psalm 119 the psalmist called himself a "stranger on earth" who needs God's commands (v. 19). The law is the standard for guiding his life (v. 8). It is a light for his path (v. 105), it preserves his life (vv. 25,37,40), and gives him understanding beyond his years (v. 101). Throughout this psalm and elsewhere the Bible is a book of wisdom that gives (1) understanding, that is, a proper *worldview* (cosmology) and (2) direction, that is, a proper *standard* (ethics).

Positively, immersion in the Bible enables Christians to think in a Christian manner (2 Pet 3:1). The doctrine of creation, for example, demands a high view of life. Negatively, it enables Christians to evaluate claims and values in light of revelation (Acts 17:11; 1 Thess 5:21-22). The fall, for example, means that no person can be truly good and whole apart from redemption (Rom 13:21-23).

The Bible also gives direction. It urges believers to ground themselves in the truths that Scripture plainly teaches. The Psalms stress this repeatedly. Godly people are to "walk" in the law, "delight" in it, "mediate" upon it, "cling" to it, "live" it, and "keep" it. Proverbs has similar urgings to seek wisdom and keep the commandments (Prov 2:1-22 and many others). The New Testament constantly encourages attitudes and behavior that should characterize the Christian life (Phil 4:8). There are likewise warnings of attitudes and behaviors to be renounced (Gal 5:18-21).

Scripture also teaches discernment. Believers are to avoid conformity with the values of the age (Rom 12:1-2). They are to examine claims and values in light of revelation (Acts 17:11; 1 Thess 5:21-22). Discernment requires full understanding of an issue. Christians should therefore become fully informed in order to interpret cultural practices or values in biblical terms.

Above all, to be a guide for Christian living, the Bible must be a living book. Christians who come to it for answers to isolated questions will find it occasionally helpful. Those who immerse themselves in it will find it "a tree of life" (Prov 3:18).

THE BIBLE FOR CHRISTIAN WORSHIP

Through the words they speak, the ministry they fulfill, and the symbols they create, Christians declare God to be worthy of honor, praise, and devotion. To declare God's worthiness through word, deed, and symbol is the essence of worship.

Scripture plays an indispensable role in both private and public worship. Our response to God through worship presupposes God's revelation of Himself through Scripture. When the Bible is used in worship, the Christian is made aware of God's interaction with His people through the ages. The New Testament especially puts us into contact with the testimony of the original eyewitnesses to God's historic revelation through Jesus Christ. Moreover, Scripture provides us with a sure word from God that stands apart from the vicissitudes of either excessive rationalism or emotionalism.

Worship and Scripture in the Old Testament

Christians are indebted to Jewish worship for many of its forms and patterns, especially in the importance attached to Scripture. Jewish worship centered primarily in two institutions: the temple and the synagogue. Each of these institutions had its own focus in worship, and each would significantly contribute elements to Christian worship. Both would continue to be important in Judaism until the destruction of the temple in A.D. 70 by the Romans.

The central act of worship in the temple was the animal sacrifices. The elaborate ceremonies associated with the sacrifices and feast days provided for a dramatic and highly symbolic style of worship. Emphasis was placed on the dramatic enactment of symbolic rituals.

Along with sacrifices, temple worship also provided for prayers, singing of psalms, reading from the Law, and rabbinic teachings. In fact, the public reading of Scripture originated in the tabernacle and temple worship of the Jews (Deut 31:10-11). The great reform under King Josiah was a direct result of the rediscovery of the Law, and its immediate impact was a gathering of all people at God's house to hear the public reading of Scripture (2 Kgs 23:2).

Temple worship was brought to an abrupt halt in 586 B.C. with the destruction of the temple by the Babylonians and the deportation of the Jews. Jewish worship was so closely tied to the temple that the Jews questioned their ability to worship God apart from that familiar environment. "How can we sing the songs of the Lord while in a foreign land?" (Ps 137:4), they lamented.

As a result of their isolation from the sacrificial worship at the Jerusalem temple, a different kind of worship took preeminence. Location became less important, and a new appreciation for the use of Scriptures in public worship developed.

After the Jews returned from exile, the synagogue arose as a worship and teaching institution. The word *synagogue* is a Greek word. It appears often in the Greek version of the Old Testament to describe the place of Jewish assembly for worship and instruction. Synagogues allowed Jews scattered throughout the known world to worship apart from the temple at Jerusalem. Many Jews still made annual pilgrimages to Jerusalem, especially during Passover. But for most, worship routinely took place in the local synagogue.

During the time of our Lord synagogues were scattered throughout Palestine and the Hellenistic world. Even Jerusalem had several synagogues. Jesus and Paul customarily worshiped and taught in the synagogues (Luke 4:15-16; John 6:59; Acts 13:15).

Synagogue worship included praise, prayers, readings from the Law and Prophets, and exposition of Scripture. As the community gathered for worship at the synagogue, the ruler of the synagogue (chosen from among the elders) would select readers. Since synagogue worship was lay oriented, any qualified male Jew might read the Scriptures. Following the readings, an explanation or exposition of the meaning of the Scripture would be given. The exposition of the Word also was a task shared by the worshipers. The one who preached or explained the Scripture might even be a visitor. Such was the case with Paul (Acts 13:15). Jesus also fulfilled this task at his home town in Nazareth (Luke 4:16-30).

Not all Jews understood Hebrew. Thus, the readings would sometimes be translated into Aramaic, the common language of Palestine in Jesus' day. This practice goes back to the times of Ezra. After the Jews returned from exile, many no longer understood Hebrew. Thus Ezra read the Scripture but had to give "the meaning so that the people could understand what was being read" (Neh 8:8).

Two pieces of furniture in the synagogue indicates the

importance of Scripture in synagogue worship. The *ark* was a repository for the scrolls. The *bema* was an elevated podium used for the reading of the texts. The use of a podium can be traced back to Ezra's reading of the Law from "a high wooden platform" (Neh 8:4).

Scripture passages from the Law read in synagogue worship were not always chosen at random. Jewish feasts required certain appointed readings. By the first century B.C. in Palestine, the Law was divided into about 155 sections with designated readings for each Sabbath. This permitted a triennial cycle of readings so that once every three years the Pentateuch would be read in its entirety in public worship.

During the time of Jesus there were no prescribed passages from the Prophets. The choice of Scripture was made by the priest or attendant, who took the scrolls from the ark and invited persons to read and comment on Scripture.

Worship and Scripture in the New Testament Church

The earliest church was established in Jerusalem. Its first members were Jewish Christians. Naturally, these first Christians brought to their Christianity many of the Jewish patterns of worship. The use of Scripture in worship was one such pattern.

The initial setting for worship among these first Christians was the Jewish temple (Luke 24:52-53; Acts 2:46; 3:1). In fact, many Jews must have thought of Christianity at first as a sect within Judaism, much like the Pharisees or Sadducees. These early Jewish Christians, however, sensed the need for occasions for separate worship apart from the temple. Therefore they held special meetings in homes for the apostles' teaching, fellowship, prayers, and the breaking of bread (Acts 2:42,46).

The church grew rapidly, expanding beyond Jerusalem. Both Jews and Gentiles were converted and baptized into the church. For the Jews outside Palestine, the chief mode of worship had always been the synagogue, not the temple. In fact, Paul commonly used the synagogue as a point of contact for the evangelization of non-Palestinian Jews (Acts 13:5; 14:1,10,17; 18:4,19).

Jewish Christians finally had to break away from the synagogue. This break did not occur uniformly in time and place, and we know that in Paul's life he preached in both synagogues and house churches. Eventually, however, Jesus' warning that his followers would be put out of the synagogue came to pass (John 16:2).

Since the reading and exposition of Scripture was such an important part of synagogue worship, it is logical that Jewish Christians would make these elements a vital part of Christian worship. In addition to Scripture and preaching, the early church incorporated into their worship blessings, prayers, and the breaking of bread (Acts 2:42,46; 20:7). All of these elements of worship were interpreted in light of the person and work of Christ.

The use of Scripture in Christian worship is attested to in the Bible when Paul admonished Timothy to give himself to the public reading of Scripture (1 Tim 4:13). The Scriptures initially used in worship were those of the Old Testament. Special attention was given to Psalms and hymns (Eph 5:14; Col 3:16; 1 Cor 14:26). Some of the hymns recorded in Revelation may have been sung by the early church (Rev 5:9; 5:12-13; 12:10-12; 19:1-2,6-8.). It is logical to assume that these early Christians selected for their reading those portions of the Prophets and Psalms which found their fulfillment in Christ.

Even though the Gospels appear first in our New Testament, Paul's letters were written earlier. Eventually Paul's letters came to be accepted as Scripture, equal to the Old Testament.

We see the initial stages of this process at work even on the pages of the New Testament itself. Though Paul may not have known that all of his letters would become Holy Scripture, he nonetheless instructed churches to read his letters aloud to the brethren. Even before they were recognized as Scripture, they were held in high esteem (2 Pet 3:15-16) and were probably read in the context of worship (1 Thess 5:27; Col 4:16).

Worship and Scripture in the Early Church

One of the earliest documents detailing Christian worship in the period after the New Testament is the *Apology* of Justin Martyr (written about 150 AD). According to Justin, the gathering of the community of faith included the readings of "the memoirs of the apostles [the gospels] or the writings of the prophets."

The sermon or exposition of Scripture immediately followed. "After the reader has finished, the president in a discourse urges and invites [us] to the imitation of these noble things." Other elements included in this early order of worship were prayers, the Lord's Supper, the pronouncing of the Amen, and an offering for orphans, widows, prisoners, strangers, and "all those in need."

Clearly, Scripture played a vital function in the worship of the early church. As time went on, it seemed appropriate to the church to include readings from different parts of Scripture. These readings (known as *lections* or *lessons*) were numerous and diverse prior to the early fourth century. They usually included selections from the Old Testament, the Psalms, and the New Testament.

Later, it became common to have only three lections:

the Old Testament, the Epistle, and the Gospel. Unlike the synagogue worship which used a descending order of importance in the readings (beginning with Law which the Jews considered most important, then the Psalms and Prophets), the church used an ascending order of importance beginning with the Old Testament, then the Epistle, and finally the Gospel. Special attention was given to the Gospels since they record the life and words of our Lord.

By the fifth century in the East (Constantinople) and the sixth century in the West (Rome) the number of lections had been reduced to two: the Gospel and the Epistle. In this period of transition the Psalms continued to be an important part of worship, but they were chanted or sung. Between the readings of the Epistle and Gospel a single cantor or soloist would chant Psalms from a raised pulpit called an *ambo.* Later, this practice would give way to the chanting of Psalms antiphonally (alternately) by two choirs.

Gestures related to Scripture and worship also became important in this period. Some of the gestures used in the early centuries of the church and still used today by some congregations include the so-called Gospel procession, kissing the Gospel, the congregation standing for the reading of the Gospel, and the Gospel as the climax of the three readings. Though these gestures are subject to misunderstanding and abuse, their original intention was to show respect and reverence for God's Word. Many evangelicals also stand for the reading of Scripture as a sign of reverence.

How did the church choose the passages of Scripture to be used in worship? At first readings were taken from the Bible itself. A particular book would be read in segments until its completion (called a *lectio continua*). Eventually, the church began to commemorate annually significant seasons of the year such as Christmas, Easter, Pentecost, and the death of martyrs. As a result, texts were assigned to be read to coincide with these special events. Still later, the readings were gathered into single books called *lectionaries.*

Evangelical Christians have also used lectionaries, often without calling them such. The hymnal, the only liturgical book routinely used by evangelicals apart from the Bible, contains Scriptures for individual, unison, responsive, or antiphonal reading. Some hymnals relate Scripture to specific holy days and/or secular holidays,

CHURCH CALENDAR

The church year calendar does not follow the secular calendar but begins with Advent four weeks before Christmas. This season is the time of expectation and preparation both for the first coming of Christ into this world but also for His second coming in glory.

The season of Christmas marks the incarnation of God into human flesh. It also points to the fundamental need that Christ also be born within every single human heart.

Christmas is followed by the season of Epiphany, which means *manifestation* in Greek. During this season Christ began to be manifested to the world for who He is, first to the shepherds and magi, then as the Son of God at His baptism, and finally as the Messiah beginning with the first miracle at the wedding in Cana of Galilee and culminating on the mount of transfiguration.

The manifestation of Christ, however, resulted in struggle and confrontation with the forces of darkness. So the next season, Lent, marks the beginning of the work of God in Christ to overcome the powers of evil both within the world and in ourselves. That great struggle reacheds its climactic encounter in Holy Week, where evil was vanquished by the death of Christ upon the cross. Though only one week long, the season of Holy Week and its central focus, the atoning death of Jesus, is magnified and extended throughout time and history, bringing the offer of salvation and redemption to the whole world.

The season of Easter immediately follows and celebrates the victory of Christ over death and the lifting of the whole creation into the kingdom of God. The themes and readings for Easter speak of this great triumph, which is promised us as a hope and fulfilled in Jesus Christ, who has gone before us.

The final season of the church year is marked by the ascension of Christ into heaven and the outpouring of the Holy Spirit upon the church at Pentecost. This season is a new beginning because of the gift of life the risen Christ has given to the church for its task of missions and ministry to the whole world. The readings for the season following Pentecost emphasize the greater work of the Holy Spirit ministering to the world through the church. These seven seasons, therefore, provide an extremely rich and fruitful context for the daily reading of Scripture whereby the whole plan of salvation can be grasped in its fullness. □

College students in the country of Zambia (on the continent of Africa) engage in a time of Bible study and worship led by Southern Baptist missionaries Lonnie and Fran Turner.

others index the passages topically.

In the quotation from Justin cited earlier, we saw that the reader of Scripture was not the same person as the worship leader. At first the church followed the pattern of the synagogue in using lay persons to read Scripture. The worship leader would appoint persons from the congregation whom he considered apt for reading.

In the manuscripts used by the early church, words were run together, and little punctuation was used. Thus not everyone would have the expertise to read in public. As a result, an order of readers or *lectors* developed who eventually formed a part of the clergy. Though the evolution of this order indicates how important Scripture reading was to worship in the church, the laity was effectively cut off from the Word of God.

Worship and Scripture in the Reformation

In the early church it is very likely that the service of the word (Acts 5:42) and the service of the Lord's Supper (Acts 2:26) formed two parts of the same gathering. Scripture gives no indication that the church considered one more important than the other. After the close of the New Testament period, however, the Lord's Supper, not the reading and exposition of the Word of God, became the central part of the worship service.

By the time of the Reformation (sixteenth century), the Mass had become the center of Roman Catholic worship. The Mass focused principally on the "bloodless sacrifice of Christ." This sacrifice was enacted when the Priest said the words of consecration, transforming the bread and wine into the body and blood of Christ. Since the Lord's Supper had taken on such a central position in the worship service, the service of the Word became peripheral.

The Word of God was not understood by ordinary people because the language used in worship was Latin and only the clergy were proficient in Latin. Moreover, the sermon fell into disuse as many clergy were biblically illiterate and unable to expound the Word of God. Thus, Scripture ceased to be a significant part of worship.

Out of this setting God raised up reformers, three of whom were especially important: Martin Luther, John Calvin, and Ulrich Zwingli. Each argued in his own way for the centrality of the Word of God. "This is the sum of the matter: that everything shall be done so that the Word prevails" stated Luther. The priority of the Word would also lead to the priority of preaching. Both Luther and Calvin would magnify the exposition of the Word, and each wrote lengthy commentaries on Scripture.

In an attempt to reestablish the importance of the preaching of the Word of God, unfortunately some vital elements of worship practiced by the early church were lost or minimized. For example, the reading of Scripture tended to be a prelude for the sermon and not a separate part of worship. Calvin's order of worship called for Scripture to be read immediately prior to the sermon.

Both Luther and Calvin believed the service of the Word should occur in conjunction with the Lord's Supper. Even though the evidence indicates that the early church celebrated the Lord's Supper each time it gathered, the reformer Zwingli separated the two. He did so out of reaction to Roman Catholic abuses in the Mass, and because he considered the Lord's Supper as a means of preaching. Many evangelical churches have traditionally followed the pattern established by Zwingli, celebrating the Lord's Supper only quarterly.

One of the results of the Reformation was to make Scripture available to believers in their native tongue. In fact, the availability of Scripture in the vernacular was such a novelty that the six volumes of the 1539 English translation of the Bible had to be chained throughout the sanctuary lest it disappear. Moreover, the clergy requested that the king issue a decree forbidding the people to read the Bible aloud while the pastor was delivering the sermon!

Worship and Scripture Today

As a result of the influence of the Reformation, most evangelical congregations have made the Word of God the center of worship. This pattern follows Paul's high regard for the Word when he wrote, "faith comes from hearing the message, and the message is heard through the word of Christ" (Rom 10:17). The centrality of the Word is underscored architecturally in evangelical churches by locating the pulpit at the center of the chancel rather than to the side. Also, an open Bible is usually found on the Lord's Supper table.

It would be improper, however, to magnify the service of the Word in worship to the detriment of the Lord's Supper. Since the Word appeals to the understanding, an overemphasis on the sermon, for example, can easily result in worship that is too rationalistic.

The Lord's Supper is a dramatic enactment and symbolic representation of the gospel. It incorporates into worship more than the mind, appealing to the senses of sight, smell, and taste. Just as Christ is made known through verbal communication, so He is revealed in the breaking of the bread, as He was to the two disciples on the road to Emmaus (Luke 24:13-35). Early in the church's history this dual pattern of Word and Lord's Supper was established in order to proclaim the gospel through both Word and symbol.

Though Evangelicals have tended to magnify the importance of the Word and are sometimes called a "people of the Book," Scripture itself is often strangely silent in our worship services. We need to recapture the early church's practice of reading Scripture aloud in worship. During the Reformation Scripture became little more than a prelude for the sermon. If we believe the "word of God is living and active" (Heb 4:12) and does not depend on the exposition of a preacher, then Scripture must be allowed to speak for itself.

In a visually oriented society, congregations today are not as disciplined to listen to Scripture read aloud. The fault, however, does not always lie with the congregation. Often Scripture is poorly or hurriedly read. Sometimes passages are ill-chosen, or repetitious, or chosen with little sensitivity to special seasons in the Christian year.

Evangelical churches today should reinstitute some of the practices of the early church concerning Scripture and worship. For example, standing for the reading of Scripture is appropriate since it is God's Holy Word. Also, laypersons should be involved as readers in worship services. Scripture passages should be prayerfully selected to reflect special concerns and emphases, and not chosen simply as a starting point for the sermon.

Scripture reading, no less than Scripture exposition, is a way to minister the Word of the Lord to the congregation. Those who read Scripture publicly should read with a sense of holy responsibility. Appropriate to such ministry is a concluding statement, such as "may the Lord add His blessings to the reading of His Word," or "The Word of the Lord." The congregation in turn can affirm the Word by saying "Amen," or "Thanks be to God" or "Glory to Thee, O Lord."

This active participation of God's people in the reading of Scripture is attested to in Scripture itself. When Ezra read the Law before God's people, they stood, lifted their hands, responded with the Amen, and bowed their faces to the ground (Neh 8:5-8).

Conclusion

In the worship of God through Word and symbol, our lives become "living sacrifices." The offering of ourselves to God is a "spiritual act of worship" that is "holy and pleasing to God" (Rom 12:1).

THE BIBLE FOR THE FAMILY AND SOCIETY

In sociology an "institution" is an established pattern of social life. Sociologists typically identify five institutions: (1) government, (2) economics, (3) education, (4) religion, and (5) family. But to a greater degree than any other institution, the family incorporates all the functions of a society. It exhibits patterns of authority and organization (government). It receives and disperses funds (economics). It teaches skills and knowledge (education). It teaches some knowledge of God (or ultimate reality) or some form of devotion (religion). The family is thus the basic unit of society.

Families are both personally and socially necessary. Persons need families for intimacy, belonging, and security. Societies need families to ensure their continuity and to prepare responsible members. Not surprisingly, then, more than 95 percent of all persons marry. And despite some differences in form, marriage and family are foundational to every known culture.

Recent years have brought radical changes to family life in most Western countries. In the United States the number of single-parent families has more than doubled since 1965. More than 20 percent of all families with children are now single-parent families. The crude divorce rate hovers at about 5.5 per 1,000 (compared to 2.5 in 1965). Marriages last, on average, less than ten years. There are strident calls for homosexual marriage and adoption. Premarital sexual activity seemingly is the world's norm. Approximately 70 percent of all college students report that they have engaged in sexual intercourse. A like proportion of married persons report extramarital infidelity.

Calls to redefine the family have accompanied these changes. In the face of such calls, the Bible remains a source of constancy and hope by (1) teaching a normative *model* for family living, (2) addressing the major *issues* that confront the family in its society, and (3) providing resources and guidance for *building* the family.

A Biblical Model of Family

The Bible recognizes that every culture needs the family. The family replenishes the population (Gen 1:28). It establishes control on the sexual drive (1 Thess 4:3-6; Heb 13:4). It gives its members an identity (Ps 127:3-4). It provides basic training for social living (Prov 4:1-27).

The main concern of the Bible, however, is to relate the family properly to God. The biblical teaching is organized around three key concepts: (1) the absolute primacy of marriage, (2) the function of the family, and (3) the role relationships of the family.

The Priority of Marriage. Scripture strongly affirms the primacy of marriage as the basic unit of social living. This is done in at least three ways.

Psychologically. The most fundamental marriage principle is complementarity, the interdependence of male and female in marital intimacy. It is an important theme in the creation accounts.

Genesis 1:27 records that "God created man in his own image . . . male and female he created them." Some scholars have suggested that the "image of God" consists in the union of male and female. The image of God seems to include more than maleness/femaleness. And of course, the Bible allows for, at times encourages, singleness (Matt 19:12; 1 Cor 7:8,32). Nevertheless, marriage does permit the full expression of sexual identity.

The principle of complementarity is more explicit in the account of the creation of the woman: "The Lord God said: 'It is not good for the man to be alone. I will make a helper suitable for him' " (Gen 2:18). Man's aloneness was "not good" (compare Gen 1:31), so God provided a "suitable helper." The Hebrew word for "suitable" literally means "set opposite him so as to be compared to him." It suggests a correspondence or a fitting together, an interdependence of different yet similar kinds of persons.

The climactic statement of complementarity comes from Genesis 2:24: "For this reason a man will leave his father and mother and be united to his wife, and they will become one flesh." In Hebrew thinking, "flesh" can refer not only to biological matter but to what is nowadays called "personality." A married couple thus does not only become one biologically but one emotionally, spiritually, and psychologically. They give and take of each other's inner selves. This may partly explain the frequent biblical euphemism of "know" for sexual intercourse (Gen 4:1; 19:8).

Sociologically. Marriage also has primacy as the basic *social* unit. Marriage is a "creation ordinance," not a church ordinance. This means that marriage is valid for, and binding upon, all persons, irrespective of faith in Christ (1 Tim 4:3-5).

Scripture presents marriage as God's provision for the regulation and sanction of sexual activity (Heb 13:4; Gen 2:24). This is crucial for any society. In the Bible all of the privileges, responsibilities, and consequences of sexual life are entrusted to the marital environment of mutual commitment and social approval.

Theologically. Marriage is a formally committed relationship as the familiar terms of "leaving" and "cleaving" show (Gen 2:24; also Matt 19:5; Mark 10:7; Eph 5:31). This commitment results in social approval for the union of marriage.

For believers, biblical marriage carries the commitment ideal further. It is a "covenant" between the partners (Mal 2:14) and with God (Mal 2:10). Christian marriage is thus to be "in the Lord" (1 Cor 7:12-16; 2 Cor 6:14-18). It also has theological significance, symbolizing the relation of Christ and the church (Eph 5:32).

The Family as Functional Unit. The Bible uses two groups of words to describe a family. By far the more common of the two is "house" or "household" (Greek *oikos;* Hebrew *bayit*). In the Old Testament it occurs more than one thousand times; in the New, more than three hundred.

The words frequently refer simply to a dwelling place. But typically they refer to persons who live together in family relationship. Often the words have an extended sense, like the "house of Israel" (Exod 40:38) and "house of Levi" (Num 17:8) or the "house of Saul" (2 Sam 3:1). Sometimes they denote a nuclear or immediate family (Mark 6:4; 1 Tim 3:5).

These words define the family in terms of *function*. An *oikos* (*bayit*) is a functioning group. It is a system, or an environment, characterized by certain essential activities. The English word "economy" gives a good illustration. It comes from *oikos* and *nomos* ("law"), hence its earliest meaning is *the law of the household.* In Greek *oikonomia* denotes the management or administration of the household (Luke 16:3).

The *oikos* (*bayit*) is a social unit to which certain responsibilities are assigned by God. These include the provision of basic needs (1 Tim 5:8), rearing of children (1 Tim 3:12), protection (Matt 12:25), and enhancing the quality of life for parents and children ("building a house," Prov 24:3). The Bible assumes that these tasks demand a certain structural order both within the family, and with respect to the family in society.

Within the family, order must prevail (1 Tim 3:5,12; Prov 11:29). Legitimate authority is recognized but carefully qualified. The husband is charged to lead his family in love (Eph 5:24), understanding, and respect (1 Pet 3:7; Col 3:18-19). The wife is charged to respect that leadership responsibility (Eph 5:22; Col 3:18), to encourage her husband in it (Titus 2:4; Prov 31:10-11), but with no sense of fear of intimidation (1 Pet 3:5-6).

The tasks of maintaining and building the house thus establish spheres of primary responsibility. The husband's sphere is care and leadership for the household. In 1 Timothy 5:8, for example, he is held accountable for "providing" for his house. The wife's sphere is care and leadership within the household. In 1 Timothy 5:14 women are instructed "to manage their homes" (also Titus 2:4-5; Prov 31:27).

Of course these areas are not exclusive. The difference is one of *focus*. The husband's focused responsibility is the provision and direction for the household. The wife's is the care and management of the household.

Not only must families have order within, but they must have order with respect to the society. Scripture regards the family as the primary caregiving unit for its members. Responsibility for the training of children (Ps 78:4-6; Prov 22:6) and the care of the elderly (1 Tim 5:4), for instance, belongs to the family, not to other social institutions. In a highly complex society these tasks are usually performed indirectly. But Scripture clearly lays them to the family's charge.

Moreover, the Bible speaks of the family as the strategic contact point between the individual and the larger community. The family is a buffer, offering refuge and peace (Prov 25:24; Luke 10:5; Mark 3:20-21). It is an environment for developing relationships (compare 1 Tim 5:1-2), meeting needs (Rom 12:13), and communicating ideas (especially the gospel) in a selective but liberal way (Matt 9:10-11; 10:12-13; Phlm 2). It is noteworthy that homes were the primary instruments of evangelization and ministry in the early church (Acts 2:46; 1 Cor 16:15; Col 4:15). It is the training ground for responsible citizens (Deut 11:19-21), who can impact a society for good (Ps 127:3-5; Mal 2:15). It is above all a nurturing environment for living faith (Deut 6:7; 2 Tim 1:5).

The Family as Relational Unit. The second word group for "family" is *patria* (and the related *genos*) in the New Testament (Hebrew *mispahah*). They occur less than twenty-five times in the New Testament, while *mispahah* occurs in the Old Testament about three hundred times. These words emphasize the *relationships* that bind families together, that is, kinship.

Loose associations sometimes called "family" in contemporary culture are unknown in Scripture. The family is formed by marriage, then birth or adoption (Gen 15:3). Biblically a relationship is not an emotional attachment. It involves a set of responsibilities required by covenant (marriage) and natural (children) bonds.

Biblical principles for building relationships must be interpreted in these terms. Scripture betrays little interest in such modern concerns as relational skills or interpersonal dynamics. Family relationships primarily rest on responsibility *to* spouse, children, parents, and kin (Eph 5:22-6:4).

The Bible and Family Issues

As the basic social unit, every social issue impacts the family in some way. Clearly, however, some issues lie close to the center of family identity and well-being. In contemporary society these would include gender roles (see above), the extent and type of sexual behavior, and marriage patterns.

The Bible and Human Sexuality. The first biblical principle of human sexuality is that sex is legitimate *exclusively* within the marriage covenant. The concise statement of that principle in Genesis 2:24 is the court of appeal throughout the New Testament in questions related to marriage and sexual behavior (see Matt 19:5-6; Mark 10:8; Eph 5:31). The implications of this guiding principle are also explored in Scripture.

First, all sexual deviations are condemned (Gal 5:19; Rom 1:24). These include child molestation (pedophilia, see Matt 18:6), incest (Lev 20:11-21), and homosexual behavior (Lev 18:22; Rom 1:26-27).

Second, sexual activity is always related to family-building. This does *not* mean that the only purpose of sexuality is children, important as that is (Pss 127:3-5; 128:3-6). It does mean that the Bible places sex within the framework of family-building. Every sexual act ordinarily has the potential for conception. And sexual intercourse is the means by which God's mandate to bear children is carried out (Gen 1:28). It also expresses love (Heb 13:4), nurtures companionship (Prov 5:18-19), and strengthens commitment (1 Cor 7:3-4). As an operational principle, therefore, any sexual activity that cannot be said to enhance family-building is unscriptural. Pre-marital sex, for instance, places sexual intimacy before the covenant of marriage. It also has the potential of producing children for whom a secure home (marriage) environment has not already been prepared. Therefore it fails to build a family.

Third, sexuality has powerful psychological consequences. Sex is the mode of union in marriage (Gen 2:24). It brings two persons together into "one flesh" (see above). Sex in marriage enhances the personality. But outside of marriage it distorts and damages emotionally (1 Cor 6:18; Mal 2:16).

Fourth, marriage is God's provision for sexual expression (1 Cor 7:9). As such it is normal and good (John 2:1-11; 1 Tim 4:3; 5:14). The Bible certainly allows singleness and commends it for a life of complete devotion (1 Cor 7:7-9,32-34). But the notion of selfish or pleasure-seeking singleness is alien to Scripture. Biblical singleness always includes celibacy and devotion (Matt 19:10-12; 1 Cor 7:32-34; 1 Tim 5:9-11).

The Bible and Divorce/Remarriage. As is true today, divorce was common throughout the Greco-Roman world and in Israel after the exile (about 536 B.C.). This explains the stern warnings in Malachi (about 430 B.C.) and throughout the New Testament concerning divorce and remarriage. As divorce has grown more acceptable socially, Christians have increasingly questioned the biblical teaching on this subject.

The questioning involves four key passages in the Gospels (Matt 5:32; 19:3-12; Mark 10:2-12; Luke 16:18), one in Paul's Letters (1 Cor 7), and several in the Old Testament (especially Deut 24:1-4). The decisive issue in these passages is whether allowances are made for divorce and, if so, what.

Extensive debate has yielded different conclusions among evangelical Christians. Some find no allowances for divorce at all. Some argue for one, two, or several. Others allow for divorce, but not for remarriage.

An important crux in these debates is Matthew 19:3-9 (also Mark 10:2-12), where Jesus cited Moses' allowance of a "certificate of divorce" in the context of His own teaching. Jesus stated that Moses "permitted" this practice because of hardened hearts. The practice is described in Deuteronomy 24:1-4 which, however, does not prescribe any grounds for divorce at all. Rather, it prohibits the remarriage of a previously divorced couple.

The reason for the divorce ("he finds something indecent about her") is ambiguous in Hebrew. Yet during the New Testament era, Jewish rabbis divided over the meaning of the clause. The followers of Rabbi Shammai limited the meaning to "adultery." The followers of Rabbi Hillel included anything displeasing. The Pharisees' question reflects this debate (19:3). Jesus avoided the intended trap and, at the same time, elaborated three important points about divorce.

First, He declared that the divorce question was misplaced. God intended marriage as a covenant relationship and a lifelong "one-flesh" union (19:4-6).

Second, Moses did not institute divorce, nor did he provide grounds for divorce. He only permitted and regulated divorce as a social reality resulting ultimately from sin.

Third, the Lord designated sexual immorality as the only ground for divorce (19:9). The word used is *porneia* (compare the English "pornography"), a rather broad term including other sorts of immorality as well as adultery.

Paul's teaching in 1 Corinthians 7 has long been held to add a second "exception" for divorce. In this case a believer "is not bound" if an unbelieving spouse leaves the marriage relationship (1 Cor 7:12-15). Taken in their natural sense, these words seem to indicate release from the marital bond and thus freedom to remarry (compare 7:39). In 7:10-11 Paul reiterated the Lord's teaching on the marriage ideal. Husbands and wives "must not divorce." If they do "separate," they are to seek reconciliation or remain single. The word for "separate" here (*chorizo*) may include divorce.

It seems most natural to assume that the Bible accepts remarriage in cases of sexual immorality and abandonment. In 1 Corinthians 7:8-9 Paul said it is better for the "unmarried" to marry than to risk sexual immorality. In 1 Corinthians 7:27-28 Paul gave an even more general guideline dealing with such persons. The word for "unmarried" (*agamos*) does *not* refer exclusively to persons never married ("virgin," *parthenos*) or to widows (*chera*). It seems to encompass singleness resulting from some other condition. Note the contrast between "unmarried" and both "widows" (7:8,39) and "virgins" (7:27-28).

The Bible emphasizes that God Himself intends marriage to be a lifelong covenant relationship between one man and one woman. God declares His hatred of divorce (Mal 2:16). Both the Lord and Paul appealed consistently to the creation ordinance of marriage for their teaching. The Bible *nowhere* demands or even recommends divorce. Instead, forgiveness and reconciliation are urged (1 Cor 7:11). Any exceptions are given grudgingly, as a way of regulating sinful conditions. In short, the easy acceptability of modern divorce is foreign to the Bible.

The Bible as Resource for Family-building

The well-known inspiration passage 2 Timothy 3:16 is a statement not only of the Bible's origin but of its usefulness in "teaching, reproving, correcting, and training in righteousness." Interestingly, the verse was a link between Timothy's ministry at the time and his upbringing (2 Tim 3:15). Paul reminded him that the Scriptures that had molded his character in childhood now provided the foundation for his life's work. Scripture played the crucial role in the impartation to Timothy of the same "sincere faith" possessed by his mother and grandmother (2 Tim 1:5).

A worn and well-used Portuguese Bible held tenderly in the lap of an elderly Brazilian woman during Bible study.

Ancient writers like Tertullian (died about A.D. 215) affirmed that the reading of the Bible formed the core of early Christian home life (*To His Wife* 2.8). Augustine (died A.D. 430) mentions the family's reading of Psalm 101 for comfort in his mother's home at her funeral (*Confessions,* 10.12). Polycarp, a disciple of the apostle John (died about A.D. 155), commended the church in Philippi for constancy in family devotion: "I am confident that you have been well-versed in the holy Scriptures and have forgotten nothing" [*To the Philippians,* 12.1].

Unfortunately much of this emphasis on family devotion dissolved during the Middle Ages. The Bible was restricted to the clergy, and more stress was placed on the scholarly study of the Bible. The Reformation (about 1500) did much to revive family devotional life, though not to the levels of the early Christian centuries. In recent years the practice has again fallen into neglect.

Biblical family-building, however, depends on family *devotion*. God's statutes and commandments are to be taught constantly. Children are to be raised to fear God and live obediently (Deut 6:1-8). Lovingly they are to be instructed and guided "in the Lord" (Col 3:21; Eph 6:4).

Scripture encourages the family to create an atmosphere of devotion (Exod 12:25-27; Deut 12:7; Ps 78:1-8; Isa 38:19), where the Word of God is *taught* and consistently *obeyed*. Thus in Deuteronomy 6 children are taught as the parents make God's statutes the *constant* subject of family attention. Negatively, this implies that the Bible must not be used inaccurately or improperly. Positively, it implies that the reading of Scripture takes place regularly. More importantly it implies that the Bible must be obeyed; and the Savior of whom it speaks, worshiped.

Christian Faith in History

The first real church historian was Eusebius of Caesarea, a bishop of the church in the fourth century. In his *Ecclesiastical History,* Eusebius set forth the value of studying the apostles, martyrs, missionaries, and church fathers who had preceded him. As we retrace their steps, he said, we hear them, as it were, "raising their voices as a man holds up a torch from afar, calling to us from on high as from a distant watch-tower, and telling us how we must walk, and how to guide the course of our work without error or danger" (*Ecclesiastical History* 1.1).

Church history is a vital link between the biblical roots of the Christian faith and its contemporary expressions. It is the story of the people of God, recalled and recounted in its many variations from the perspective of faith. Church history is participatory history. It is not merely the "objective" study of the Christian past but rather the investigation of that past in light of the revelation of God in Jesus Christ.

Church historians thus identify with the believing community they describe. The great Puritan divine Cotton Mather referred to church historians as "the Lord's remembrancers." Christians believe that all history witnesses to a divine purpose and is moving toward a divine destiny. Church historians have the crucial task of placing the story of the people of God in the context of the history of salvation. Thus the bounds within which church historians work are not only the political, social, and economic factors that shape all human events but also the biblical affirmations "In the beginning God" and "I will come again."

The church historian does not always have a lovely, heartwarming story to tell. The historian must honestly face the available records from the past and display the church in all its greatness and also in all its selfish pride and bigotry. The heroic faith of Anselm, Augustine, John Wycliffe, Martin Luther, John Calvin, Charles Spurgeon, Karl Barth, and Billy Graham exemplifies courage, honesty, and hope. The gory stories of the Crusades, fights over the papacy, indulgences, and defense of segregation and injustice shame the church into renewal and repentance. The modern church repeats both sides of its history to learn how to be the church with new heroes of faith in new cultural conditions.

Dr. Billy Graham—one of the great leaders of the faith in the twentieth century.

Just as individuals suffering from amnesia cannot know their true identity, so a community of faith cut off from its historic roots drifts aimlessly on the sea of modernity. Church history shows Christians today that we are part of a people, members of a body, subjects of a kingdom called into being by God and sustained by His divine grace throughout the ages. We belong to the communion of saints, the church, the family of God, which lives in memory and hope and walks by faith, not sight.

The Early Church

The church of Jesus Christ was born at Jerusalem in a blaze of power on the Day of Pentecost. The Book of Acts describes the first Christian community. It was marked by close fellowship, fervent preaching, earnest prayer, and evangelistic outreach. Spurred by persecution from without, the followers of Jesus soon burst out of their Jewish environs. They carried the good news of their crucified, risen, ascended, and soon-returning Lord into every nook and cranny of the Roman Empire.

Saul, later Paul, of Tarsus was the greatest theologian of the early church and the key figure in transforming Christianity from a small Jewish sect into a world religion. The following description of Paul is from the second century: "A man small in size, with meeting eyebrows and rather large nose, bald-headed, bow-legged, strongly built, full of grace; for at times he looked like a man, and at times he had the face of an angel."

Paul's letters reveal that he was often opposed by those who saw him as a threat to the very gospel he was striving to advance. Unlike many Jewish Christians who saw Christ through the lenses of the law, Paul interpreted the law, and all of history, in light of Christ. By the time of his execution at Rome in A.D. 64, Paul had established flourishing churches in many cities of the Roman Empire. He also left the church a permanent legacy in his letters, which were collected and later absorbed into the canon of the New Testament.

The earliest surviving Christian literature outside of the New Testament is a body of writings ascribed to the "Apostolic Fathers." The first of these is a letter written by *Clement of Rome* to the church at Corinth. In it Clement referred to the martyrdom of Peter and Paul and described the church and its ministry at the turn of the first century. *Second Clement* is an early Christian sermon that stresses the need for repentance and reflects a high Christology, "Brethren, we must think of Jesus Christ as of God" (1.1). *The Epistle of Barnabas* interprets the Old Testament in a highly figurative way and calls for the absolute separation of Christianity from Judaism. *The Shepherd of Hermas* contains the visions of a Christian slave who had been set free. This writing became a textbook for catechumens and was regarded as a part of Scripture by some. The *Didache* or *Teaching of the Twelve Apostles*, discovered in a monastery at Constantinople in 1875, is a brief church manual that sets high ethical standards, condemns abortion, and contains instruction on prayer, fasting, baptism, and the Eucharist.

Ignatius, bishop of Antioch, wrote seven letters while en route to Rome, where he was thrown to the wild beasts in the arena. He faced the prospect of martyrdom with great eagerness: "Suffer me to be eaten by the beasts that I may be found the pure bread of Christ." He exalted the office of bishop, which he saw as a vital link between the apostles and the ongoing church. He defended both the humanity and deity of Christ against tendencies to disparage one or the other aspects of the Savior's reality. Jesus Christ, he insisted, was "truly [*alethos*] born, both ate and drank, was truly persecuted under Pontius Pilate, was truly crucified and died . . . was truly raised from the dead" (*Trallians* 9).

One of Ignatius's letters was addressed to Polycarp, bishop of Smyrna in Asia Minor. Polycarp had been a disciple of the apostle John and transmitted this legacy to a later generation of church leaders such as Irenaeus. He was burned at the stake around A.D. 155 when he was eighty-six years old. An account of his trial and execution, "The Martyrdom of Polycarp," has survived. The annual celebration of this event by the church at Smyrna became a model for the veneration of martyrs and the commemoration of their deaths.

The Apologists

The New Testament admonishes Christians to be ready to give an *apologia* to anyone who asks a reason for the faith they hold (1 Peter 3:15). "Apology" in this sense does not mean an expression of regret but rather advocacy, a vigorous speech for the defense. In the second century there was an urgent need to vindicate Christianity against false charges and common misperceptions. While the Apostolic Fathers had addressed their letters to members within the Christian fold, the Apologists defended Christianity to those outside.

Unfriendly critics leveled many false charges against the Christians: cannibalism, because of their talk about "eating the body and drinking the blood" of their Lord; atheism, because they denied the existence of Roman deities whom they regarded as demons; subversion, because they refused to worship the emperor or serve in the Roman army. The Apologists showed that such charges were distortions of the truth. They also sought to make Christianity intelligible in terms of the current Hellenistic philosophies of the day.

The greatest of the Apologists was Justin Martyr (about 100–165), who became a Christian after a long search for truth in pagan philosophy. He claimed that Jesus was the fulfillment not only of the Old Testament prophecies but also of the Greek philosophies he had studied. Both Moses and Plato had foreshadowed Christ. Justin sought to reconcile faith and reason by presenting Christ as the cosmic Word (Logos), the source of all truth, who had become incarnate in Jesus of Nazareth. Other important Apologists included Tatian, a pupil of Justin Martyr, who wrote a life of Christ based on the Four Gospels (*Diatessaron*); Athenagoras, the "Christian philosopher of Athens," who defended Christian belief in the resurrection; and Minucius Felix, an African Christian who wrote on providence and monotheism.

Orthodoxy and Heresy

From its earliest days Christianity had been forced to define itself over against certain doctrinal deviations that if carried to their logical extreme would have undermined the gospel itself. Thus 1 John (4:3) equates denial of the incarnation with the "spirit of the Antichrist," while Jude urges believers to contend for "the faith that was once for all entrusted to the saints."

Christians of the second century faced an enormous challenge from a movement known as Gnosticism, so called from the Greek word for knowledge, *gnosis*. Gnosticism was the New Age movement of the early church. Drawing on religious symbols from Persia and Babylon, as well as on Greek philosophy and Jewish and Christian symbols, it appealed to the God-consciousness within while playing down the essential facts of historic Christianity. Since all matter was inherently evil, there could be no unity between creation and redemption. The object of salvation was the return of all the lost "sparks of divinity" back into an original unity that had been shattered. On a personal level, this could be accomplished only by sloughing off the world of matter and by being awakened through the true *gnosis* to one's real identity. In the Gnostic system Jesus was the divine revealer who had come to impart this secret truth. His body was merely a phantom, and He neither truly was born nor truly died.

Gnosticism made great inroads into early Christianity and called forth vigorous refutations by church leaders such as Irenaeus. His *Against Heresies* defended the fundamental doctrines that were under attack by Gnosticism: that the world was created by a good God; that Jesus of Nazareth, Son of the Creator, was truly human and died on the cross to redeem the lost; that God had a plan for human history which would culminate in a final judgment and resurrection.

For many years our knowledge of Gnosticism was

The ancient Colosseum in Rome—place of martyrdom for many Christians in the early church.

based largely on the works of Christian writers such as Irenaeus. However, in 1946 an entire library of Gnostic writings was discovered near Nag Hammadi in upper Egypt. This collection contains the works of the famous Gnostic leader Valentinus, along with many other Gnostic writings. These Gnostic works, translated now from the Coptic, have shed much new light on the belief and practices of this ancient heresy.

Canon and Creed

Theologians such as Irenaeus and Tertullian defended Christianity against Gnosticism. In part they did so by pointing out the novelty of the heretics' ideas in contrast to the acknowledged tradition of apostolic truth passed down through an unbroken succession of authorized teachers within the church. Irenaeus himself had studied with Polycarp, who had studied with John, who, of course, had studied with Jesus.

The office of bishop, already magnified by Ignatius of Antioch, assumed greater and greater importance for defining the parameters of the true church. The seeds of apostolic succession and papal infallibility are found in this development. Later deviations, however, should not obscure this early Christian appeal to the unity and antiquity of the gospel message.

Of still greater importance was the appeal to the authority and verbal inspiration of the Bible. A heretical teacher named Marcion forced the church toward a decision on the canon when he excluded the entire Old Testament and most of the New (he kept only the Gospel of Luke and some of Paul's letters) from his Bible. Like many of the Gnostics, Marcion had a docetic view of Christ (that is, he believed Jesus was not actually human) and denied that any Scriptures that stressed the humanity of Jesus were genuine.

Eventually the church arrived at a consensus concerning the main contents of the canon, although several books such as Hebrews and Revelation continued to be questioned in some circles. In the year 367 Athanasius's Easter Letter listed the twenty-seven books of the New Testament. Just as the Holy Spirit inspired the prophets and apostles to write the Scriptures in their original form, so likewise He providentially guided the church to ratify and preserve precisely those books He wished to be accepted as His infallible Word.

Another safeguard of the true faith was the confession new converts were required to make at their baptism. Hippolytus's description of baptism at Rome around the year 200 reveals the origin of what later developed into the Apostles' Creed:

> When the person being baptized goes down into the water, he who baptizes him, putting his hand on him, shall say: "Do you believe in God, the Father Almighty?" And the person being baptized shall say: "I believe." Then holding his hand on his head, he shall baptize him once. And then he shall say: "Do you believe in Christ Jesus, the Son of God, who was born by the Holy Spirit of the Virgin Mary, and was crucified under Pontius Pilate, and was dead and buried, and rose again the third day, alive from the dead, and ascended into heaven and sat at the right hand of the Father, and will come to judge the living and the dead?" And when he says: "I believe," he is baptized again. And again he shall say: "Do you believe in the Holy Spirit, in the Holy Church and the resurrection of the body?" The person being baptized shall say: "I believe," and then he is baptized a third time.

This creed or symbol, as it was called, was eventually used at celebrations of the Lord's Supper and in regular services of worship. Recited in these contexts, the creed was a both a witness against false teaching and a testimony of personal faith in Jesus Christ.

Persecution and Martyrdom

During the first three centuries of its existence, the Christian church was subject to outbursts of violence and persecution by the Roman authorities. Later Christians looked back on the "ten great persecutions" beginning with the emperor Nero in the first century and culminating under Diocletian in the fourth. Tertullian regarded martyrdom as the highest accomplishment of the Christian life and referred to it as the "second baptism." No doubt, martyrdom was also a great tool of evangelism in the early church, for Tertullian also remarked that "the blood of the martyrs is the seed of the church."

Martyr stories such as those of Perpetua, a noble woman who had just given birth to a child, and her slave girl Felicitas, who also left behind her newborn child in order to suffer for Christ with her Christian sisters in the arena, encouraged believers to remain steadfast in the face of persecution and death. Such stories were also an important source of devotional reading in the early church.

A major problem arose concerning the *lapsed*, those Christians who had compromised their faith rather than face persecution. Should they be restored to the church once peace had returned? The laxists believed that penance and forgiveness should be extended to the *lapsed*, while rigorists insisted on their permanent exclusion.

A major revolution occurred in the fourth century with the conversion of the emperor Constantine to Christianity. Whether his conversion was genuine or contrived, it brought about a great change in the status of the church. Christianity, formerly a persecuted sect, became at first tolerated and then recognized as the official, established religion of the Roman Empire. The melding together of church and empire brought many advantages to the Christians, such as the erection of great buildings of worship. However, the church also lost something of its earlier zeal and stand over against its surrounding culture. During this period infant baptism became the normal rite of initiation into the church, and the civil punishment of heretics was begun by Christian emperors. A protesting monk declared that, following the conversion of Constantine, there were more Christians but less Christianity!

Trinity and Christology

The word *Trinity* is not found in the Bible. It was coined by Tertullian to refer to the threefold nature of the one true God who knows and reveals Himself as Father, Son, and Holy Spirit. A great dispute arose in the early fourth century when Arius, a presbyter in the church of Alexandria, claimed that the Son of God was a creature who had come into being at some point prior to the creation of the world: "There was when he was not," Arius said.

This view was strongly challenged by the great theologian Athanasius, who insisted that Christ as the eternal Logos was *homoousios*, "of the same essence as," the Father. Athanasius believed that the very foundation of Christianity rested on this affirmation, which he defended along several lines. (1) Cosmological: since the Logos was the One through whom all creation came into being, He must belong to the eternal and not the temporal realm. (2) Liturgical: Christ is worshiped by both the saints on earth and the angels in heaven, an act that would be sheer idolatry were He not truly divine. (3) Soteriological: if Jesus Christ were not fully God, He could not have redeemed lost humanity from their sin.

In 325 the emperor Constantine convened the Council of Nicaea, which excluded the heresy of Arius by declaring that "Jesus Christ, the Son of God, is God from God, Light from Light, Very God from Very God, begotten not made, of one substance with the Father." After much dispute within the church, the Council of Constantinople in 381 reaffirmed the Nicene view of Christ while extending the word *homoousios* to the Holy Spirit as well.

The struggle for the doctrine of the Trinity was one of the most important chapters in the history of the church. By affirming both the oneness and "threeness" of God, the Christian church remained faithful both to the Old Testament declaration "God is One" and the New Testament confession "Jesus is Lord."

Closely related to the doctrine of the Trinity is the question of Christology, the relationship between the divine and human natures in the incarnate Christ. The Council of Constantinople had condemned the teaching of Apollinarius, who denied that Christ had a human soul. A new challenge arose when Nestorius, a famous preacher and church leader, so sharply separated Christ's divinity from His humanity that the unity of His person was obscured. The Council of Ephesus in 431 condemned the Nestorian position.

An opposing error, called Monophysitism (the doctrine that Christ had only one nature, and that entirely divine) arose in the church of Alexandria. Eutyches, a monastic leader in Constantinople, suggested that Christ's humanity had been absorbed by His divinity like a drop of wine in the sea. The Christological controversy came to a head in 451 at the Council of Chalcedon. Here Jesus Christ was declared to be "truly God and truly man." The heresies of both Nestorius and Eutyches were condemned, and the Incarnate Christ was acknowledged to be in two natures, "without confusion, without change, without division, or without separation." While some Eastern Christians refused to accept the consensus of Chalcedon, it has remained a benchmark of Christological orthodoxy to the present day.

Augustine

The life of Augustine (354–430) marks the end of the early church and the beginning of the Middle Ages. Born at Tasgate in North Africa, Augustine was the son of a pagan father and a Christian mother, Monica, who prayed fervently for her son's conversion.

After he became a Christian, Augustine wrote a book of *Confessions* in which he traced the steps that led to his newfound faith. As a young man he was guilty of sexual indiscretions that he could never overcome by his own willpower. Trained in Roman law and literature, he dabbled in the leading philosophies of the day. Like Justin Martyr before him, he undertook a pursuit of truth that would lead to that true wisdom found only in God. For some nine years Augustine was attracted to Manichaeism, a radically dualistic religion of Persian origin. Frustrated with the materialism of this worldview, Augustine then became a skeptic, doubting the possibility of any sure knowledge of the truth. He next embraced the philosophy of Neo-Platonism. This brought him closer to Christianity by teaching him to seek for truth in the spiritual realm.

The preaching of Ambrose, bishop of Milan, forced Augustine to reconsider the validity of the biblical record. "In my misery I kept crying, 'How long shall I go on saying "Tomorrow, tomorrow"? Why not now? Why not make an end of my ugly sins at this moment?' " While crying in a garden, he heard the voice of a child saying, "Take and read." He picked up a Bible, which fell open to Romans 13:12-14: "Take up the weapons of the Lord Jesus Christ; and stop giving attention to your sinful nature, to satisfy its desires." He commented: "I had no wish to read more and no need to do so. For in an instant, as I came to the end of the sentence, it was as though the light of faith flooded into my heart and all the darkness of doubt was dispelled" (*Confessions* 8.12).

Augustine was baptized by Ambrose on Easter in 387. After a time of prayer and study, he gave himself to the monastic life and later was made bishop of Hippo, where he served with great distinction as a theologian and leader of the church.

Augustine lived at a time when Christians were forced to deal with new challenges to their faith. How could a religion with Jewish roots and a history of persecution be adapted to the new culture of the "converted" empire without losing its very soul? This question involved four issues, each of which Augustine addressed at length in his writings: The relation between philosophy and theology, the boundary between the church and the world, the balance between nature and grace, and the understanding of salvation history in light of world events.

Augustine continued to respect the principles of the Neo-Platonists even after he became a Christian, but he knew that philosophy alone could never lead anyone to God. His axiom "Believe in order to understand" stresses the primacy of faith over reason. He used this principle to defend the gospel against his former comrades, the Manichaeans. It is also the basis of his great work *On the Trinity*. "We speak," he said, "in order not to be silent about so great a mystery." Augustine was a strong advocate of the inerrancy and verbal inspiration of the Bible. His treatise *On Christian Doctrine* set forth the rules of interpretation that would govern the study of the Bible during the next thousand years.

The Donatists posed a major problem to Augustine's vision of a united Catholic church in North Africa. The Donatists refused to have fellowship with the mainline Christians because the latter included within their number ministers who had been ordained by bishops who had compromised with the authorities during an earlier period of persecution. They believed that the sacraments were valid only when administered by a priest who was himself pure and unspotted.

Augustine opposed the Donatist schism and insisted that the sacraments were valid by virtue of Christ's promise and presence. At first he tried to persuade the Donatists to return to the Catholic fold; but when this failed, he called on the civil authorities to use force in assuring unity. He based this injunction on the biblical mandate "Compel them to come in" (Luke 14:23). Thus in seeking to preserve the unity of the church by means of civil coercion, Augustine sanctioned a theory of religious persecution that would later bear fruit in the Inquisition and medieval crusades against heresy.

Augustine is known as the "doctor of grace" because of his emphasis on the sovereignty of God in salvation. His many writings on this topic grew out of his encounter with Pelagius, a British monk, who believed that salvation, even perfection, was possible through the exercise of free will. Against this view, Augustine stressed the universal consequences of original sin, the opposition of grace to nature, and the mystery of divine predestination.

While salvation involves a genuine human response to grace mediated by the sacraments, repentance, and faith, its ultimate basis is the good pleasure of God alone. Augustine's doctrine of grace would be ratified by the Council of Orange in 529 and taken up, with varying emphases, by later theologians such as Thomas Aquinas, Gregory of Rimini, Martin Luther, and John Calvin.

Although Pelagius has had few defenders in the history of Christian thought, his views have had a subtle corrosive effect on Augustinian theology and have been openly championed by humanistic thinkers in the modern period. Although Augustine's theology of grace would be refined along biblical lines by the Protestant reformers, he saw himself as merely restating the doctrine of salvation set forth by the apostle Paul, a truth he had experienced personally in his own rescue from a life of sin and darkness.

Augustine's *The City of God* was written in the wake of the sack of Rome by the barbarians and the impending fall of the Roman Empire. Augustine denied that this catastrophe had happened because of the spread of Christianity. He contended that there were two "cities" coexisting throughout history: the *City of God,* which consisted of all true believers on pilgrimage toward their heavenly destiny, and the City of Man, pagan society, which sought only glory and gain in the earthly realm.

In the present age, these two communities coexist. The City of Man, however, is under judgment and doomed for destruction, while the City of God will be united in eternity with its Creator and Redeemer. In this panoramic view of human destiny, Augustine provided the first Christian philosophy of history. When the Roman Empire finally fell in 476, Augustine's perspective guided the church through the difficult centuries of adjustment and transition known as the Middle Ages.

THE MEDIEVAL CHURCH

The early Middle Ages witnessed the fall of the old Roman Empire, the invasion of the barbarians, and the gradual emergence of a new political and social order known as feudalism. During this time the bishop of Rome played an increasingly important role in the conversion of the barbarian tribes and the establishment of a new political order.

Although the title "pope" was not applied solely to the bishop of Rome until the eleventh century, a major papal figure had already emerged much earlier in the person of Pope Gregory I, who occupied the See of Peter from 590 until 604. Gregory was the first pope who had also been a monk. He welded a powerful alliance between papacy and monasticism. In 597 he sent one of his fellow monks, Augustine, on a missionary venture to Britain. From this mission Roman Christianity spread to that important island kingdom. At the Synod of Whitby in 664 the authority of the pope was recognized over the older Celtic brand of Christianity. Within a few years England became a beachhead of missionary activity, sending monastic evangelists such as Willibrord and Boniface to convert the peoples of northern Europe and to establish churches and monasteries loyal to the bishop of Rome.

A new era began on Christmas Day 800 when Pope Leo III crowned Charlemagne, the ruler of the Franks, as "the deputy of God . . . set to guard and rule all his members and . . . render an account for them on the day of judgment." This event, which would be replayed many times throughout the Middle Ages, marked the beginnings of the Holy Roman Empire.

Under Charlemagne there was a minor revival of literature and religion led by the scholar Alcuin. The so-called "Carolingian Renaissance" stimulated new theological controversies over Christology, predestination, and the Lord's Supper. After Charlemagne his empire was plunged into civil war, and the church was thoroughly corrupted by abuse. A fresh wave of barbarian attacks by the Vikings plunged Europe into what is known as the Dark Ages. Many people believed that the end of the world was near as the year 1000 approached.

The Eastern Church

In 330 Constantine had established a new capital city for the empire and named it after himself, Constantinople. This city became the center of a thriving civilization and the home of the Eastern Christian tradition. From this "New Rome" the emperor, seen as "the living image of Christ," exerted great influence over the life of the church. In the East the emperor came to be seen as the earthly reflection of the heavenly Potentate. The emperor controlled the election of high church officials and spoke with great authority on matters of theology and worship. The most famous of the Eastern emperors was Justinian (527–565), who built the great church Saint Sophia, expelled the barbarians, and established orthodoxy throughout his realm. He also consolidated the Roman Law in the Justinian Code which became the basis for the medieval system.

In a sense the Eastern Church never went through the "Middle Ages," since Constantinople withstood all external invasions until 1453. The only exception was the sack of the city by the (Christian!) crusaders in 1204. This meant that Eastern Christianity, also known as the Orthodox Church, became a bulwark of the historic Christian faith and a custodian of classical Christian culture.

The Orthodox Church accepts the decisions of the first seven great church councils, concluding with Nicea II in 787, as definitive and binding statements of Christian dogma. Several of these councils dealt with controversial matters such as the nature of Christ's will and the role of icons, that is, images, in the church. In the eighth century, Emperor Leo III launched an attack on the use of icons, contending that such religious practice was idolatry. The use of icons was defended by the great theologian John of Damascus, who argued that to deny that Christ could be depicted on an image was, in reality, to deny the possibility of the Incarnation. Still, he declared, icons should not be worshiped but simply honored and venerated as outward symbols of the faith.

The rise of Islam posed a tremendous threat both to the empire and the church. Based on the teachings of Mohammed, the Muslim faith is built around five "pillars," or basic doctrines. (1) There is no God but Allah, and Mohammed is his prophet. (2) The will of Allah is written down in the Koran, a divine book that shows the way to salvation. (3) There are six great prophets: Adam, Noah, Abraham, Moses, Jesus, and Mohammed, who surpasses all the others. (4) Prayer, five times a day in the direction of the holy city of Mecca, along with almsgiving and fasting are required of all true Muslims. (5) Pilgrimage to Mecca, either in person or by proxy, is an expected act of devotion. Armed with these beliefs, the followers of Mohammed fanned out from the deserts of Arabia in a series of violent holy wars capturing the ancient Christian centers of Jerusalem, Antioch, Alexandria, and Carthage. They entered Europe through the Iberian Peninsula (Spain) and were only turned back in France by Charles Martel at the famous Battle of Poitiers in 732. The interaction of Christianity and Islam is a major theme of the Middle Ages leading to the Christian efforts to recapture the holy land during the Crusades.

While the Eastern Church was besieged by hostile forces during this entire period, it developed a vigorous spiritual life and displayed a missionary concern. The two brothers Cyril and Methodius carried the gospel to the Slavic peoples, giving them the Scriptures and liturgy in their own language. In 989 the Russian people embraced the Orthodox faith, thus inaugurating a rich heritage of Christian life in that land. When Constantinople fell to the invading Turks in 1453, Moscow emerged as the "third Rome," that is, the new center and bulwark of Eastern Christianity. Even earlier, in 1054, the Eastern Church had broken fellowship with the Christians of the West. To this day this schism remains one of the major divisions within the body of Christendom.

Monasticism

After the conversion of Constantine, when martyrdom was no longer a possibility, many zealous Christians retreated to the desert to embrace the "white martyrdom" of the monastic life. As successors to the martyrs, the monks registered a vigorous protest against the laxity and lukewarmness of "mainline" Christianity. The father of monasticism was Anthony, an Egyptian hermit (about 250 A.D.) whose biography by Athanasius influenced many others to take up the solitary life. The early monks lived alone and gave themselves to a life of prayer, fasting, and solitude. Most of them were laypersons, not priests; and their practice of strict discipline, called asceticism, was an important witness to the entire church.

After Anthony the three most important leaders of the monastic movement were Pachomius, Basil the Great, and Benedict of Nursia. Pachomius believed that monks should live and work together in community. While his ideas were rejected by those who preferred to retreat alone to the desert or remain perched high atop a stone pillar, in time cenobitic (from the Greek *koinos bios*, "life in common") became the norm in both East and West.

In the East the monks followed the rule of Basil, which stressed obedience, prayer, and a life of service. Benedict is known as the "Patriarch of Western Monasticism." The rule of Benedict, drawn up around 480, became the normative guideline for monks throughout the Middle Ages. It set forth the ideals of obedience, humility, daily prayer, and manual labor. The motto of the monastic life was *ora et labora*, pray and work. Benedict avoided some of the extreme asceticism of the early hermits, believing that the monastery should more resemble a family than a penitentiary. He also advised that "great care and concern should be shown in receiving poor people and pilgrims, because in them more particularly Christ is received."

Throughout the Middle Ages there were many forms of the monastic movement. One of the most important of these was associated with the influential monastery of Cluny in eastern France. Founded in 909, this monastery became the "mother house" of over one thousand affiliated communities. A series of strong abbots, including Odo and Peter the Venerable, called for a stricter observance of the monastic life and imposed a uniform liturgy of prayer on the monks under their control.

Bernard of Clairvaux (1090–1153) was perhaps the leading monastic figure of the entire Middle Ages. Bernard founded a new order of monks, the Cistercians, and called for a return to a literal observance of Benedict's rule. Bernard was a great preacher whose eighty-six sermons on the Song of Solomon presented a beautiful picture of the soul's longing for God. Some of Bernard's hymns, such as "Jesus, The Very Thought of Thee," are still sung by Christians today. Bernard also wielded great power in the church politics of his day. He helped to place several popes in power and preached sermons urging knights to fight in the second crusade.

The rise of the mendicant (beggar) orders in the thirteenth century marked a new stage in the spirituality of the Middle Ages. Whereas traditional monks were expected to stay in one place and devote themselves to manual labor and prayer, the mendicants, or friars (brothers) as they were also called, moved freely about in the world and depended on the charity of others for their survival.

The Dominican order was founded by a Spaniard, Dominic de Guzman (1170–1221), whose mission focused on winning heretics and heathen to the true faith through vigorous preaching and a life-style of poverty and simplicity. Because of their concern to insure ecclesiastical orthodoxy, the Dominicans were known as "the Lord's dogs" (the literal meaning of their name in Latin, *domini cani*). The Dominicans produced many great scholars, the most notable of whom was Thomas Aquinas.

A very different legacy was forged by Francis of Assisi,

who founded the Order of Friars Minor (lesser brothers) in 1209. The son of a wealthy cloth merchant, Francis abandoned a life of ease to identify himself with the deprived. Unlike Dominic he was wary of too much "book learning," which he felt would lead to pride. Above all else, Francis's desire was to imitate his Lord, Jesus Christ. Near the end of his life, he was reported to have received the *stigmata*, bleeding wounds that resembled the nail and spear prints on Jesus' crucified body. Although Francis's order was approved by the pope, his way of life challenged the power and wealth of the church of his day. He was a great promoter of peace and made a missionary journey to the East, where he appeared before a Muslim sultan and sought to convert him to Christ. Shortly after his death in 1226, there was a major split in the Franciscan Order between the "spirituals," who insisted on following Francis's rule and example literally, and the more moderate majority, who accepted joint ownership of property and a liberal interpretation of the rule. In the sixteenth century the Protestant reformers rejected monasticism as a valid Christian life-style. More recently, however, some Protestant groups, such as the Church of England, have permitted the emergence of monastic orders within their ranks.

Scholasticism

Through their intense study of the Bible and their preservation of ancient manuscripts, the monks did much to keep the spirit of learning alive during the Dark Ages. The cathedral and monastic schools were centers of study that served as seed beds for the later universities. Scholasticism refers both to the revival of learning that occurred during the Middle Ages and the method of study by which it occurred—the process of careful, rational scrutiny, logical deduction, and the systematic ordering of truth.

Anselm (1033–1109) is known as the "Father of Scholasticism." A devout monk and churchman, he became Archbishop of Canterbury in 1093. Building on the earlier work of Augustine, Anselm suggested three levels of theological insight: faith, where all Christian thinking begins; understanding, the effort to think and speak clearly about that which we believe; and vision, face-to-face communion with God, which is the ultimate goal of all our theology.

In his treatise *Proslogion*, Anselm put forth a simple proof for the existence of God, known as the ontological argument, which he believed could be reduced to one sentence: God is that than which none greater can be conceived. The reality of God, he said, was bound up with this definition of His existence. It is significant, however, that Anselm's proof of the existence of God is contained in the form of a prayer. In other words, he had already been grasped in faith by the One he was seeking to understand. Again echoing Augustine, he wrote, "I believe in order that I might understand."

Anselm is also remembered for setting forth a major understanding of the atonement in his treatise *Why God Became Man*. Since humans incurred an infinite debt to God when they sinned, and since only God could pay this great debt, God became human in Jesus Christ to offer satisfaction for sinful humanity through His death on the cross. This understanding of the cross, later clarified by John Calvin, has remained an important part of the evangelical understanding of atonement.

Between Anselm and Thomas Aquinas two important teachers influenced the development of scholasticism. Peter Lombard (1100–1160) summarized the existing body of theology which he arranged in four books on (1) the Trinity, (2) the creation and sin, (3) the incarnation and the virtues, and (4) the sacraments and last things. Lombard's *Books of Sentences*, as they were called, became the standard theological textbooks of the Middle Ages.

Peter Abelard (1079–1142) was a brilliant scholar who emphasized the role of reason in understanding the Christian faith. His most famous work, *Sic et Non* (Yes and No), was a collection of apparently contradictory excerpts from the Scriptures and the Church Fathers on a large number of questions. Although he tried to resolve these differences by means of logic, Abelard's ideas seemed to go beyond the bounds of historic Christian orthodoxy on several important points. He challenged Anselm's understanding of the atonement by claiming that the cross was primarily a moral display of divine love rather than a required satisfaction for human sin. In applying reason to the mystery of the Trinity, he also seemed to undermine this foundational principle. At the urging of Bernard of Clairvaux, among others, Anselm was condemned for heresy. Nonetheless, his method of doing theology contributed much to the scholasticism of later generations.

Thomas Aquinas (1225–1274) was known as the "dumb ox" during his days as a school boy because he seldom spoke in class. However, he proved to be one of the most brilliant scholars of all time and the greatest theologian between Augustine and Martin Luther. A member of the Dominican Order, Thomas served as a professor at the universities of Cologne and Paris. His *Summa Theologica* was a masterful synthesis of Christian revelation set forth in the Scriptures and interpreted by the church fathers with the newly rediscovered

A painting of Thomas Aquinas enthroned between the doctors of the Old and New Testaments.

philosophy of Aristotle. Thomas believed that reason could show us many truths about God such as His existence, His eternity, and His providence, while other fundamental truths such as the Trinity and the incarnation could only be known through revelation. Thomas accepted the Aristotelian maxim that "there is nothing in the mind which is not first in the senses." This led him to seek empirical proofs for the existence of God that he set forth in his famous "Five Ways." One could show, he believed, the existence of God by examining His effects in the external world in things such as motion, causation, contingency, degrees of perfection, and design. Although some of his ideas were condemned shortly after his death, Aquinas has remained the most authoritative theologian for the Roman Catholic tradition. He was declared to be a saint in 1323 and a Doctor of the Church in 1557. In 1879 his writings were made required reading for all Catholic students of theology and philosophy.

Other important scholastic theologians such as Bonaventura, Duns Scotus, and William of Ockham extended and developed Thomas's teachings in different directions. None of them could ignore the contribution he had made.

The Seven Sacraments

One of the most enduring contributions of scholastic theology was the systematizing of the seven sacraments of medieval Catholicism. Peter Lombard was the first theologian to insist that there were only seven sacraments. Other thinkers such as Hugh of St. Victor and Thomas Aquinas discussed the meaning of these sacraments and their role in the Christian life.

Two of the sacraments were for a restricted group within Christendom: ordination or holy orders for those who were called to a priestly ministry in the church and marriage for those who were wedded as husband and wife. The other five sacraments—baptism, confirmation, the Eucharist, penance, and extreme unction—were intended for everyone. The sacraments were believed to have a direct affect on salvation; they not only signified grace, but they contained and conferred it. Not all of the sacraments were of equal necessity. Baptism, the Eucharist, and penance contributed most directly to the process of salvation.

By the Middle Ages the rite of infant baptism had become almost universally practiced throughout the church. Augustine's doctrine of original sin, which implied that unbaptized babies dying in infancy went to limbo, the outer region of hell, contributed to this practice. It was believed that baptism removed the taint of original sin and disposed the one baptized to receive the grace of the other sacraments. The high rate of infant mortality prompted the practice of baptism by midwives when newborn infants were in danger of death. The doctrine of baptism was reflected in the structure of certain cemeteries: a section of hallowed ground for those dying in the state of grace, unconsecrated soil for those dying unrepentant of mortal sin, and a third parcel of ground for those infants dying without benefit of baptism.

The Eucharist or sacrament of the altar was called the crown of the sacraments and received extensive theological treatment. The Fourth Lateran Council in 1215 approved the dogma of transubstantiation. This teaching held that at the moment of consecration the bread and wine of the Eucharist became the actual body and blood of Christ. This doctrine gave rise to new forms of eucharistic piety in the late Middle Ages: the saying of private masses, the veneration of the consecrated hosts outside the context of the Lord's Supper, and the denial of the cup to the laity (to prevent the spilling of the transubstantiated wine).

Baptism and the Eucharist were supplemented by the sacrament of penance, which was the means of removing the penalty of sin and preparing oneself for the full benefits of the sacrament of the altar. Penance consisted of four stages: (1) contrition, that is, being sorry for one's sin; (2) confession, the making known of sin to a priest, an act required at least once a year by the Fourth Lateran Council; (3) satisfaction, an act of compensation to God for offenses done against Him; (4) absolution, pronounced by the priest who, it was believed, had the authority of Christ to formally remit sins. During the late Middle Ages the sacrament of penance was continually threatened by the abuse of indulgences, that is, the promise of forgiveness in exchange for a sum of money. In effect, this meant that absolution could be attained without contrition, confession, or satisfaction. It was Luther's protest against the abuse of the penitential system that triggered the Reformation in 1517.

The Quest for the True Church

The last two centuries of the Middle Ages were a time of ferment and upheaval. Popes and emperors vied with one another for control of Europe; the crusades introduced new ideas and new social conditions to the world of feudalism; plagues such as the Black Death ravaged the countryside; and the church was beset by new forms of nationalism, heresy, and dissent. All of this presented a crisis of confidence in the identity and authority of the church.

The question of whether the pope or the emperor would be sovereign over the church went back to the eleventh century when Pope Gregory VII had resisted the efforts of the emperor Henry IV to nominate bishops and induct them into office. He asserted papal supremacy and insisted that "the Roman Church has never erred, nor ever, by witness of Scripture, shall err to all eternity."

The pope who came closest to putting into effect Gregory's designs was Innocent III, who presided over a vast world empire from 1198 until 1216. However, even more extravagant claims for papal sovereignty were set forth by Boniface VIII in 1302. He declared that "it is altogether necessary to salvation for every human creature to be subject to the Roman pontiff." By the fourteenth century, however, these words sounded hollow since the papacy had been greatly weakened by its seventy-year exile in France, the so-called Babylonian Captivity (1309–1377).

In addition there followed the shocking confusion of the Great Western Schism (1378–1417) when for a while two, and then three, popes claimed at once to be the supreme head of the church.

The great schism was ended by the Council of Constance which named a new pope, Martin V, and affirmed the supremacy of a general council over the papacy. By the end of the fifteenth century the papacy had lapsed again into great moral decadence and seemed unable to inaugurate reform.

In England John Wycliffe had attacked the abuses in the church. His followers, the Lollards, translated portions of the Bible into English and spread the ideas of their teacher across the land. A similar movement of reform in Bohemia centered on the martyred John Hus, who had been burned at the stake at the Council of Constance. The Waldensians represented still another alternative to the established religious system. They met secretly in the mountain caves and valleys of Europe. They rejected the ministrations of worldly priests and called into question many rituals that were common to the Roman Church, such as indulgences, purgatory, relics, and pilgrimages. There was a great hunger and thirst for God on the eve of the Reformation.

One of the most popular books during this time was Thomas a Kempis's *The Imitation of Christ*. In Germany mysticism was thriving, and from Italy the revival of learning known as the Renaissance was recovering the classical sources of Christian antiquity. The Dutch scholar Desiderius Erasmus, who transmitted much of the Renaissance spirit to northern Europe, believed that he could see "a golden age dawning in the near future." The Reformation, however, unleashed far more virulent energies than even Erasmus could foresee.

The Reformation Church

The Reformation of the sixteenth century came at the end of the Middle Ages and the beginnings of modern times. The Reformation was both a revival and a revolution. The political, social, economic, and religious upheaval that occurred at that time has forever changed the landscape of Western Christianity. The two burning questions of the Reformation were: What must I do to be saved? Where can I find the true church? Just as the early church wrestled with the questions of the Trinity and Christology, so the reformers of the sixteenth century struggled to understand salvation and its meaning for the Christian life.

Luther and Lutheranism

More books have been written about Martin Luther (1483–1546) than any other figure in history except Christ. Yet the last thing Luther wanted to do when he entered the Augustinian monastery at Erfurt in 1505 was to start a new church. He was overwhelmingly concerned to reform himself, not anything else. *How can I find a gracious God?* he wondered. *How can I know that God is for me, not against me?* He gave himself vigorously to the monastic routine of prayers, fasting, confession, and good works. None of this, however, brought peace with God. After many trials he turned to the Bible. He came to see that the righteousness of God that Paul described in Romans 1:17 could not be earned or merited by any works he might do. Rather, it was a free gift accounted (imputed) to lost sinners on account of Christ's vicarious death on the cross. Luther's "evangelical breakthrough," that is, his discovery of justification by faith alone, was the cornerstone on which the entire Reformation movement was built.

Luther was drawn into conflict with the Roman Church through his public stand against the abuse of indulgences, which he attacked in his Ninety-five Theses of 1517. At a debate in Leipzig in 1519, Luther denied the supremacy of the pope and the infallibility of general councils. Scripture alone, he contended, should be our infallible rule of faith and practice. In 1520 Luther wrote three treatises that set forth his positive program of reform. The *Freedom of the Christian* applied the doctrine of justification to the realm of ethics, urging Christians to serve their neighbors out of sheer joy and gratitude for the unmerited love of God revealed in Christ. The *Appeal to the German Nobility* was a patriotic appeal to the princes of Germany and a biting attack against the wealth and power of the papacy. *The Babylonian Captivity* undercut the medieval sacramental system, leaving only baptism and the Lord's Supper as valid Christ-instituted sacraments of the church. Pope Leo X issued a bull of excommunication against Luther which led to his dramatic stand at the Diet of Worms in 1521. There Luther refused to recant his ideas—unless they could be refuted on scriptural grounds. Protected by his prince, Frederick of Saxony, Luther was taken from the Diet to the Wartburg Castle, where he translated the New Testament into German. His experiences in this castle may also be echoed in his famous hymn "A Mighty Fortress Is Our God."

Turbulent days followed as Luther sought to reform the church on the basis of the Word of God. An evangelical Lord's Supper with communion in both kinds was introduced. Luther repudiated his monastic vows and took a wife, Catherine von Bora. In 1524/25 Luther and Erasmus came to a parting of the ways over the doctrine of predestination and the freedom of the will. Erasmus could not accept Luther's strong identification with Augustine's theology of grace. At the same time, Luther revealed his inherent conservatism as he sided with the German princes against the peasants who had risen up in revolt. He also opposed some of his own followers—he called them "swarmers" because they reminded him of bees around a hive—who wanted to carry his own ideas much further and much faster than he deemed wise.

Although Luther preferred for his followers to be called Christians rather than Lutherans, he soon found himself at the center of a church movement that needed direction and support. The Lutheran churches in Germany were established by the authority of the territorial princes. However, it was Luther and his younger colleague, Philip Melanchthon, who guided the churches to reform their worship, teaching, and polity. Luther's *Large* and *Small Catechism* (1527) became the basis of religious instruction in Lutheran homes, schools, and churches. In 1530 Luther approved the *Augsburg Confession,* which had been drawn up by Melanchthon. This document became the guiding confessional standard of

Martin Luther burning the Papal Bull

all Lutheran churches. It defined a true church as that place "where the Word is rightly preached and the sacraments rightly administered."

By the end of the sixteenth century, Lutheranism had spread across Germany and had captured all of Scandinavia. In 1555 the Lutheran churches had acquired a legal basis in the Peace of Augsburg, which established the principle "whose the region, his the religion." This settlement enabled the prince of a given territory to impose his own confessional preference on his subjects. It signaled that the deep division between Protestant and Catholic was not likely to be healed soon.

A recent interpreter of his theology has summed up Luther's thought in the phrase "Let God be God." By insisting on the sovereignty of God in salvation (justification by faith alone) and in the church (submission to the authority of Holy Scripture), Luther was able to recover the heart of New Testament Christianity.

Zwingli and the Swiss Reformation

While Luther's reform took root mostly in territories governed by a single prince, in southern Germany and Switzerland the Reformation broke out first in the cities. Huldrych Zwingli (1484–1531) was a Swiss priest who had served on the field of battle as a chaplain to the troops. Well trained in the classical disciplines, he memorized much of the New Testament in Greek and was greatly influenced by the writings of Erasmus.

On January 1, 1519, Zwingli began his ministry as "people's priest" at the famous Great Minster church in Zurich. He began a program of preaching first through the Gospel of Matthew and then through successive books of the Bible verse by verse. By the early 1520's Zwingli could no longer retain his status as a priest in the Roman Church. Following a public disputation in 1523, the city council declared that the church in Zurich would follow the Scriptures as proclaimed by its pastor. From Zurich the Reformation spread to other cities in Switzerland such as Bern and Basel.

For Zwingli the Reformation was essentially a movement from idolatry to the service of the one, true God. "I call it the depth of impiety," he said, "when we accept the human for the divine." Like Luther, Zwingli believed in predestination and stressed the providence of God in creation and history. He also stressed the priority of Holy Scripture over human tradition and purged the church at Zurich of images, organs, priestly vestments, and other such "hodgepodge of human ordinances." The second of the Ten Conclusions of Bern (1528) captures the spirit of Zwingli's reforming work: "The Church of Christ makes no laws or commandments apart from the Word of God; hence all human traditions are not binding upon us except so far as they are grounded upon or prescribed in the Word of God."

Zwingli's views on baptism and the Lord's Supper led him into major disputes during the last years of his life. Although he opposed a sacramental understanding of baptism, Zwingli defended the practice of infant baptism against the Anabaptists, who had abandoned this rite in favor of believer's baptism in 1525.

One of the great tragedies of the Reformation was that so much strife and hurt occurred around the meal Jesus intended as a supper of peace. Zwingli and Luther disagreed sharply over the meaning of the words "This is my body" in the Lord's Supper. Zwingli understood "is" to mean "signifies," while Luther interpreted it more literally. Important differences on Christology and biblical interpretation were reflected in this dispute. The two great leaders met at the Colloquy of Marburg in 1529 but were unable to reach agreement on this decisive point. Thereafter the Lutheran and Reformed churches developed along separate lines in terms of worship and polity.

Zwingli had always been more concerned than Luther with the reform of society. He saw the Christian church as the new Israel of God, a holy community that should pattern its social structure after the will of God as set forth in the Bible. This commitment led Zwingli to be deeply involved in the political fortunes of Zurich. In 1531 he was captured and slain on the battlefield of Kappel, fighting as a militant crusader for the cause of Christ. A statue of Zwingli in Zurich shows him standing with a Bible in one hand and a sword in the other. This image symbolizes his desire to bring every realm of life, church and state, theology and ethics, into conformity with the will of God.

Calvin and the Reformed Tradition

Zwingli and John Calvin were the coparents of the Reformed tradition that spread far beyond the bounds of its native Swiss context to become the most international form of the Protestant movement. Calvin, a French lawyer and scholar, embraced the Protestant gospel in the early 1530s, thus becoming a reformer of the second

John Calvin

generation. His book *Institutes of the Christian Religion* was published at Basel in 1536. Patterned after Luther's *Small Catechism,* this book offered the most systematic exposition of Protestant theology to date. Calvin continually revised and expanded this work until the definitive edition of 1559. It remains today the single greatest masterpiece of Protestant theology.

Calvin's name is linked with the Reformation in Geneva, where he served as pastor and teacher from 1536 until his death in 1564, apart from a brief period of exile at Strasbourg. In his *Ecclesiastical Ordinances* of 1541, Calvin set forth the basic structure of Presbyterian church polity with its fourfold office of pastor, teacher, elder, and deacon. Calvin insisted on the independence of the church from the state. He also sought to establish a rigorous Christian discipline in the city of Geneva. Calvin's influence was exported to many other lands through the Academy of Geneva, established in 1559, and through the many pastors sent forth from Geneva to evangelize other lands. John Knox, a refugee from Scotland, described Geneva as "the most perfect school of Christ on earth since the days of the apostles." Calvin, like Zwingli, sought to prune the worship service of unedifying features. He encouraged the frequent celebration of the Lord's Supper, public reading from the Old and New Testaments, and the hearty singing of psalms as a standard form of praise to God.

The first two questions of the Genevan Catechism (1541) sum up the heart of Calvin's theology. They are: "Teacher: What is the principle end of human life? Student: It is to know God. Teacher: Why do you say that? Student: Because He has created us and put us on earth to be glorified in us. And it is surely right that we dedicate our lives to His glory, since He is the beginning of it."

Calvin is best remembered for his doctrine of predestination, but predestination was not the central theme of his theology. He emphasized God's positive revelation in Holy Scripture, the person and work of Jesus Christ, justification, regeneration, and especially sanctification. He called sanctification "the principal work of the Holy Spirit," and prayer he defined as "the chief exercise of faith and the means by which we daily receive God's benefits." He also stressed the importance of church discipline, which he saw as integrally related to the church's worship and mission.

If Luther was the theological genius of the Reformation, Calvin provided its clearest theological expression. Through his commentaries, letters, and treatises, as well as through *Institutes,* he offered guidance and support to martyrs, underground churches, struggling pastors, and reform movements from Hungary and Poland in the East to The Netherlands, Scotland, and England—and eventually New England—in the West.

The English Reformation

The English Reformation is often regarded as an act of state since it began in 1534 with Henry VIII's break with Rome over the matter of his divorce and remarriage. However, the seeds of a true revival had already been sown by the work of William Tyndale, who had translated the New Testament into English in 1525. Although Tyndale was eventually martyred for this illegal act, his Bibles were smuggled into England and led to the eventual publication of an official English Bible.

After Henry's death in 1547, his young son, Edward VI, sought to instill a more explicit form of Protestantism among the English people. Thomas Cranmer, Archbishop of Canterbury, supervised the revision of the liturgy into the English language. The final product of this work was the *Book of Common Prayer.* There was a swing back toward Catholicism when Edward's half-sister, Mary Tudor, ascended the throne in 1553. Known in history as Bloody Mary, she sent many Protestant leaders, including Cranmer, to their deaths at the stake. John Foxe recorded the stories of many of these martyrs in his *Acts and Monuments of the Christian Church,* one of the most popular books published during the Reformation. Some Protestant leaders went underground, while others fled to the Continent during the reign of Mary.

With the accession of Henry's other daughter, Elizabeth, in 1558, a new era in English church history began. The Elizabethan Settlement offered a middle way between the Church of Rome and the reforms of Calvin. A new prayer book was approved, and an Anglican theology was set forth in the Thirty-Nine Articles of Religion. Richard Hooker defended this approach in his famous *Treatise on the Laws of Ecclesiastical Polity.* However, many of Elizabeth's subjects were unhappy with the slow pace of reform. This feeling gave rise to an indigenous dissenting movement known as Puritanism. While some of the more radical Puritans separated from the Church of England to pursue, as one of them put it, "a Reformation without tarrying for any," most remained within the church and worked for changes in liturgy, polity, and spiritual life. Although the Puritans had some success during Elizabeth's reign, the movement reached its highest level of influence in the seventeenth century during the time of Oliver Cromwell and the Commonwealth.

The Anabaptists

All of the mainline reformers, including Luther, Zwingli, Calvin, and Cranmer, depended on the civil authorities to establish and enforce their reforming work, whether that authority be prince, city council, or king. Over against the state-supported churches, the radical reformers sought to restore the primitive New Testament church as a voluntary society of convinced believers. Although some of the radical reformers such as Thomas Munzer resorted to violence to bring in the kingdom of God by force, many others were peace-loving people who sought to embody a pattern of reform at odds with both Protestant and Catholic models.

Following the example of leaders such as Conrad Grebel, Felix Manz, and Michael Sattler, the evangelical Anabaptists of Switzerland and South Germany set forth their beliefs in the Schleitheim Confession in 1527. They insisted on believers baptism, the Lord's Supper as a simple meal of Christian fellowship, strict church discipline, and separation from the world. They also refused to take the oath in obedience to Jesus' command in the Sermon on the Mount, and they would not allow any member of their fellowship to bear the sword. These stands set them apart from the surrounding culture and brought severe persecution from the religious and civil authorities.

At the Diet of Speyer in 1529, both Catholics and Protestants agreed to impose the death penalty for the practice of rebaptism. Some Anabaptists had already been drowned by the Protestant reformers in Switzerland, and many others were burned by the Catholic authorities throughout the Holy Roman Empire. The Swiss Anabaptists survived by retreating into the coves and valleys of the Alps. The Amish, who later emigrated to America, came from this group.

The peaceful Anabaptists of the Netherlands found a strong leader in Menno Simons. While still a Catholic priest, Menno came to question both the Roman Mass and the practice of infant baptism. He left the church to take up an itinerant ministry among the persecuted Anabaptists of the Low Countries. He published a fine summary of his theology in the *Foundation Book* that was highly valued by the Mennists, as his first followers were called.

Another important document to emerge from this movement was the *Martyrs' Mirror.* It recorded the sufferings and deaths of hundreds of Anabaptist martyrs, many of them common people who were drowned, beheaded, or burned at the stake because of their refusal to conform to the religious uniformity of their day. There were more martyrs among the Anabaptists in the sixteenth century than in all of the persecutions in the early church. Just as before, however, their public witness on the rack and scaffold and at the stake called forth new disciples who were willing to forsake the world and follow the "bitter Christ." By insisting on the necessity of preaching the gospel outside the boundaries imposed by the political authorities, the Anabaptists recovered an important dimension of the witness of the early Christians, even as the mainline reformers reestablished the foundational doctrines of biblical faith.

Catholic Renewal

While the term Reformation usually refers to the Protestant movement, there was also a strong quickening of religious life and reforming zeal among those who remained loyal to the church of Rome during the sixteenth and seventeenth centuries. The roots of this "Catholic Reformation" go back to the late Middle Ages and to the emergence of new orders that called for a renewal of piety within the church. In the same year that Luther posted his Ninety-Five Theses on the castle church door at Wittenberg (1517), a new reforming group was founded in Rome. The Oratory of Divine Love, as it was called, was dedicated to prayer, preaching, and works of compassion for the poor and the sick. In 1528 the Franciscan Order saw the emergence of the Capuchins, ascetic followers of the Rule of St. Francis. The Ursulines and the Daughters of Mary were new orders of Catholic women dedicated to teaching and caring for children.

By far the most visible and most powerful new order to emerge during the sixteenth century was the Society of Jesus, also known as the Jesuits, which was founded by Ignatius Loyola in 1534. A Spanish soldier, Ignatius, was wounded in battle and experienced a conversion during a long period of convalescence. Dedicating himself to being a soldier of Christ, Ignatius gathered about him a group of like-minded followers who pledged themselves to a life of poverty, chastity, missionary work, and unquestioned loyalty and obedience to the pope. In 1540 Pope Paul III officially approved the Society of Jesus.

The Jesuits soon became a major force in the efforts of the papacy to recapture the ground lost to the Protestant reformers. The Jesuits were pioneers in education. By 1750 they had founded nearly one thousand colleges and seminaries throughout the world. They were also possessed of a world missionary vision and carried the Christian message to faraway lands such as China, Japan, Ceylon, as well as to the newly discovered peoples of North and South America. Ignatius's program of disciplined devotion was set forth in his famous *Spiritual Exercises,* a handbook on prayer and meditation which remains one of the most influential books of the Catholic tradition.

The reforming movement within the Catholic Church was defined and consolidated by the Council of Trent, which met in three different periods from 1545 until 1563. One of the major concerns of this Council was to respond to the challenge of the Protestant Reformation. It defended the doctrine of purgatory, reaffirmed all of the seven sacraments, denied the evangelical understanding of salvation by grace and justification by faith alone, and asserted that Scripture and tradition were equally authoritative in setting forth the teaching of the church.

The decisions of the Council were implemented by a revived Inquisition, also known as the Holy Office, which conducted trials of heresy, and the Index of Prohibited Books, which published an official list of heretical writings that all good Catholics were expected to spurn. The Council of Trent set the tone for the development of Catholicism during the modern period. Since Trent, two subsequent councils have helped to define the contours of the Catholic faith: Vatican I (1871), which affirmed the dogma of papal infallibility, and Vatican II (1962-65), which issued innovative decrees on ecumenism, worship, and the role of bishops in the governance of the church.

The Modern Church

While the Catholic Church consolidated its position based on the achievements of the Council of Trent, the Protestants developed the theology of the reformers into new systems of thought and rallied their churches around new confessions of faith. In 1577 the Lutherans settled their internal disputes and published a common consensus of faith, the *Formula of Concord.* Among the Reformed churches the Synod of Dort (1618-19) defined the doctrines of grace that were to characterize the theology of orthodox Calvinism: unconditional election, total depravity, irresistible grace, particular redemption (limited atonement), and perseverance of the saints. In England the Westminster Confession (1647) echoed the same affirmations for the Presbyterian tradition. Jacob Arminius, a Dutch theologian, had challenged the high Calvinist understanding of these doctrines. Arminianism continued to have great influence both in England and on the Continent.

Post-Reformation theology is sometimes referred to as "Protestant Scholasticism." This term recalls the logical rigor and rational ordering of truth that marked the various systematic theologies of the day. No religious thinker of the caliber of Luther or Calvin emerged during this epoch. However, the Age of Orthodoxy was a time of great cultural flourishing. In the Lutheran tradition Johann Sabastian Bach (1685–1750) developed church music and hymn singing to a refined height. The Dutch Reformed tradition produced the great art of Rembrandt, while England boasted its greatest poet in John Milton.

The seventeenth and eighteenth centuries also witnessed a great intellectual awakening that is commonly known as the Enlightenment. The Enlightenment was marked by the conviction that by the light of reason human beings could find true happiness quite apart from the "props" of revealed religion. This period is also known as the Age of Reason because it was widely believed that reason and nature had displaced revelation as the final source of authority in the church as well as the state. The Enlightenment grew out of the scientific and philosophical work of scholars such as Francis Bacon, Rene Descartes, and Isaac Newton.

Deism was an English brand of enlightenment religion. Its chief architects were John Toland, the author of an important book entitled *Christianity Not Mysterious* (1696), and Matthew Tindal, who wrote the "Bible of Deism," *"Christianity as Old as the Creation"* (1730). The Deists rejected the miracles of the Bible as well as the sacraments of the church. The great doctrines of the faith such as the incarnation, the Trinity, and salvation by grace were repudiated in favor of a "natural" religion that consisted in a code of morality and an emphasis on salvation through human achievement. In France scholars such as Voltaire, under the influence of Enlightenment ideals, subjected the Bible to scurrilous satire, while in America even Thomas Jefferson produced a version of the New Testament from which he had deleted "offensive" passages.

There were many Christian responses to the attacks of the Enlightenment. Some apologists such as John Locke sought to meet the critics on their own ground. In 1695 Locke published his *Reasonableness of Christianity*, arguing that Christianity was in harmony with the findings of reason. Joseph Butler, a bishop of the Church of England, published a counterattack to the Deists in his *Analogy of Religion* (1736). Another response to the mood of the age came from Blaise Pascal, a French thinker who had been dramatically converted to Christianity. He denied that rational proofs of God's existence could ever displace the gift of faith. "What a vast distance there is," he said, "between knowing God and loving Him!" Paschal emphasized God's grace over human reason. "We shall never believe with a vigorous and unquestioning faith unless God touches our hearts; and we shall believe as soon as He does so."

Evangelical Awakenings

The greatest challenge to skepticism of the Enlightenment, however, did not come from learned treatises or reasoned debates. Rather, it came from a great spiritual renewal that stemmed the tide of unbelief and brought true revival to God's church. The winds of awakening swept from the Continent to England and thence across the Atlantic to America in three great movements: Pietism, Methodism, and the First Great Awakening.

In 1675 Philipp Jakob Spener published the manifesto of the Pietist movement, *Pia Desideria* (which means *Pious Wishes*). In this book Spener called for a return to a true, living faith based upon the reading of the Bible and

and Thomas Coke carried the movement to America. These men soon became bishops of an independent Methodist movement. They embodied many of Wesley's ideals, including his strong emphasis on justification by faith alone. They also emphasized his Arminianism and his doctrine of perfection. These characteristics became hallmarks of the Wesleyan tradition which, in time, spawned new denominational groups that emphasized holiness as a distinct mark of the Christian life.

Despite his tremendous influence, Wesley was superseded by an even greater preacher of his age, George Whitefield. Both men were good friends, although Whitefield was a strong Calvinist and debated Wesley over the doctrine of predestination. Whitefield carried the Great Awakening to America, preaching up and down the eastern seaboard. Whitefield assisted many of the revival leaders in America, the greatest of whom was Jonathan Edwards. In 1737 Edwards published a detailed account of a great revival that had broken out in his church at Northampton in Massachusetts, *A Faithful Narrative of the Surprising Works of God.* Edwards, like Whitefield, was a staunch Calvinist and saw the revival as the result of God's sovereign work. The First Great Awakening had a decisive effect on religious life in America. It produced new denominations, educational reforms, and stimulated interest and support for missions.

Sects and Denominations

The era of the Great Awakening saw the expansion of the major colonial denominations that had been transplanted from their place of origin in Europe. The Anglican Church had become the established religious tradition of Virginia and the Southern colonies. Presbyterians flourished in New Jersey and the Middle Colonies, while Congregationalism reigned supreme in New England. English Catholics had secured a foothold in the new world through the patronage of George Calvert, first Lord Baltimore, who negotiated their settlement in Maryland.

The Baptist tradition had made meager gains in New England under the leadership of John Clarke and the famous Roger Williams. Williams, who defended the right of the Indians against the English settlers, also argued for the strict separation of church and state. In founding the colony of Rhode Island as a haven of religious dissent, he left behind a great legacy of religious liberty.

The real Baptist stronghold in colonial America, however, was Philadelphia. The Philadelphia Association, organized in 1707, became a major organizing force in the establishment of Baptist congregations throughout the colonies. In 1742 they secured the services of Benjamin

the priesthood of all believers. He also believed that theological education should be reformed to bring it more in line with devotional studies and practical Christianity. Spener emphasized the importance of the new birth and the living out of the Christian faith in deeds of love and mercy.

Other leaders such as August Hermann Francke put into practice what Spener had called for. Francke was a professor at the University of Halle, which became the center of the Pietist movement. Among other things Francke sponsored an orphanage, a Bible school, a publishing house, and a pharmacy. He also supplied the first Protestant missionaries to India.

A Lutheran nobleman, Count Ludwig von Zinzendorf, embodied the Pietist movement in the Moravian Brethren, who carried out great evangelistic and missionary enterprises. Most Pietists remained within the Lutheran church where they hoped to serve as a leaven within the stale Christianity of their day. Some, however, were forced to separate and begin their own independent churches.

Both John and Charles Wesley, leaders of the Methodist movement in England, were deeply impressed Moravians. Following John Wesley's "heart-warming" experience at Aldersgate on May 24, 1738, he gave himself to a ministry of fervent preaching and evangelistic work. He later described the experience that had changed his life: "About a quarter before nine, while he was describing the change which God works in the heart through faith in Christ, I felt my heart strangely warmed. I felt I did trust in Christ, Christ alone, for salvation; and an assurance was given me that He had taken away my sins, even mine, and saved me from the law of sin and death."

When he was refused permission to preach in the parish churches of England, Wesley declared that "the world is my parish." His *Journal* records his remarkable ministry as a traveling evangelist, covering more than 250,000 miles in the cause of the gospel. One of Wesley's great contributions was his organization of Methodist societies and his insistence on discipline in the Christian life. He also showed great compassion for the poor and oppressed peoples of England. Some scholars have claimed that Wesley's success in offering hope to the poor masses of Britain prevented a violent reaction in England such as happened during the French Revolution. Charles Wesley was a great supporter of his brother and made a tremendous contribution to the Evangelical Revival through his many hymns.

Although Wesley never intended to leave the Church of England, Methodism as a separate denomination emerged shortly after his death in 1791. Francis Asbury

Franklin to publish the first Baptist confession of faith in America. The Philadelphia Confession of Faith was thereafter adopted by the Charleston Baptist Association in South Carolina from which it was commended to Baptist churches throughout the South.

The Philadelphia-Charleston Baptist tradition was marked by a high Calvinist theology, an emphasis on a learned ministry, and support for associational and missionary endeavors. A new impetus in Baptist life came from the Separate Baptists, many of whom had been former Congregationalists recently awakened by the preaching of George Whitefield. They brought the zeal of revivalism and a distrust of structured institutions into the Baptist family. Baptists managed to absorb these various streams until the issue of slavery brought a division within their ranks in 1845.

A smaller denomination that had also been transplanted from England was the Society of Friends, also known as the Quakers. Founded by George Fox in the seventeenth century, the Quakers were hounded out of New England by the Puritans and found refuge in Pennsylvania under the friendly protection of William Penn. Like the Anabaptists, the Quakers were pacifists and refused to participate in military affairs. They discarded both the Lord's Supper and baptism and even played down the importance of the written Word of God in favor of the "inner light" within. Led by John Woolman, the Quakers became known for their opposition to slavery and their devotion to social and educational work. A Quaker woman, Elizabeth Fry, was perhaps the major prison reformer of the nineteenth century.

From 1800 until 1850 the churches in America experienced another blaze of revival, which is known as the Second Great Awakening. This movement began with campus revivals in the East, particularly at Yale College under the leadership of Timothy Dwight. On the frontier it took the form of sensational camp meetings such as the one held at Cane Ridge, Kentucky, in 1801. Peter Cartwright, a pioneer evangelist and church planter, helped spread the fires of revival throughout the frontier regions of the nation. A new form of revivalism was pioneered by Charles G. Finney, who devised "new measures" to persuade unwilling converts to yield to the gospel message. Among other things, Finney introduced the "mourner's bench" during his many citywide crusades throughout America. Finney was not only the leading evangelist of his age but also perhaps the leading social reformer of his time. He advocated temperance, prison reform, and the abolition of slavery. His mantle would later fall on noted evangelists Dwight L. Moody, Billy Sunday, and Billy Graham.

America was not only fertile soil for the major Protestant denominations, but it was also the spawning ground of numerous cults and sectarian groups. Some of these, such as the Shakers, founded by Mother Ann Lee, had roots in the Old World. Many others, however, were indigenous to America, where they prospered in the free air of religious diversity.

The Church of Jesus Christ of Latter-day Saints, or Mormon Church, as it is popularly known, was founded by Joseph Smith, the Mormon prophet, in western New York state, an area of intense revival activity known as the "burned over" district. Smith claimed to be restoring the true church of Jesus Christ that had lapsed into apostasy following the death of the apostles. Along with latter-day prophesy there was also a latter-day scripture, the *Book of Mormon*, which Mormons claim Smith miraculously translated from golden plates. Led by Brigham Young, the Mormons marched across the American desert and established their new Zion in the valley of the great Salt Lake in Utah. Since then they have grown to over six million members worldwide, claiming adherents in numerous countries around the globe. Certain beliefs and practices, such as polygamy and the doctrine of racial inferiority, have been abandoned, but the basic Mormon mythology remains intact.

Mary Baker Eddy's Christian Science and Charles Taze Russell's Jehovah's Witnesses were also successful in winning numerous converts to their radical religious views. Adventism, Campbellism, Swedenborgianism, the Harmonists, and Unitarianism were only a few of the religious movements that took root and flourished in nineteenth-century America.

Missions and Modernity

In 1792 the British cobbler William Carey preached a powerful sermon before a gathering of London ministers, urging them to "expect great things from God, and attempt great things for God." In that same year the Baptist missionary society was launched. Carey's pioneering ministry in India paved the way for thousands of missionaries who spread the gospel to the far corners of the earth during the next one hundred years.

Adoniram Judson and Luther Rice followed in Carey's footsteps and were able to see the formation of a Baptist Missionary Society in America in 1814. The story of David Brainerd, Jonathan Edward's son-in-law, who worked tirelessly among the Indians, inspired others to carry on this outreach to the American natives. Other missionary heroes, such as David Livingstone in Africa and Hudson Taylor in China, inspired a new generation of missionaries to identify themselves with the national peoples to whom they had been sent.

By the end of the nineteenth century, so successful was the effort to Christianize the world that it seemed that every part of the globe might be evangelized within the foreseeable future. The great missionary statesman John Mott expressed this hope in his call for "the evangelization of the world in our generation." The modern ecumenical movement, despite its recent departures from evangelical ideals, was born on the mission field. The World Missionary Conference at Edinburgh in 1910 led to a series of meetings that eventually resulted in the formation of the World Council of Churches in 1948. In 1961 the World Council undertook a major study and discussion of "Jesus Christ, the light of the world." More recently evangelicals of many denominations have found a more suitable forum of missionary cooperation through the Lausanne conferences sponsored by evangelist Billy Graham.

The church in the modern world has been beset by many secular ideologies and worldly philosophies that would undermine its witness and integrity. Since the eighteenth century, the church has been grappling with major new changes that stem from such a secular world view cut loose from the traditional theological moorings of Patristic and Reformation Christianity. Destructive biblical criticism, a naturalistic understanding of humans, historical relativism, and theological modernism have all taken their toll on how the church understands its mission and how it carries out its witness.

In the early twentieth century, American Christians engaged in a bitter debate over the fundamentals of the faith. These basic beliefs seemed to be threatened by an unbelieving theology based on an uncritical accommodation to the prevailing scientific and philosophical world views. A twelve-volume set of tracts called *The Fundamentals* was published between 1909 and 1915. The authors of these works upheld the "five fundamentals" of the faith: the virgin birth, biblical inerrancy, bodily resurrection, Christ's substitutionary atonement, and the visible return of Jesus.

The modernist position was upheld by Harry Emerson Fosdick, one of America's most popular preachers, while the fundamentalist view was set forth with great learning by J. Gresham Machen, professor at Princeton Theological Seminary. Following the 1920s the fundamentalist movement splintered off into competing separatist sects, while the modernists gained control of the major American denominations. The post-World War II era has seen the emergence of a new evangelical movement, faithful to the theological legacy of the fundamentalists but socially and politically engaged and more intellectually sophisticated than their predecessors. During the 1970s and 1980s two major American denominations, the Lutheran Church-Missouri Synod and the Southern Baptist Convention, tilted noticeably in a more conservative direction, reversing some of the losses suffered by evangelicals earlier in the century.

While American Christians were struggling with internal issues at home, churches in Europe were coming to grips with authoritarian state regimes and religious persecution. In Nazi Germany a group of Christians, known as the Confessing Church, banded together to resist Hitler's efforts to suppress their faith. In 1934 a group of confessing church Christians led by theologian Karl Barth set forth the Barmen Declaration, which rejected any identification of the Christian message with the prevailing Nazi ideology. Article One of this statement declared: "Jesus Christ, as He has testified to us in the Holy Scripture, is the one Word of God, whom we are to hear, whom we are to trust and obey in life and in death. We repudiate the false teaching that the church can and must recognize yet other happenings, images, and truths as divine revelation alongside this one Word of God, as a source of her preaching."

Barth was expelled from Germany, and many other resisting Christians were executed or placed in concentration camps. Among the martyrs of the Nazi regime was Dietrich Bonhoeffer, a brilliant theologian and church leader whose opposition to Hitler led to his execution in 1945.

Trends for the Future

As the church of Jesus Christ approaches its third millennium, it is faced with formidable challenges and great opportunities. In four special areas it must strive to be true to its own identity, that is, to be faithful to its Lord, while adapting itself to new ideas and changing circumstances.

1. *Currents of Theology.* The twentieth century has seen an astonishing variety of theological systems and approaches. Shortly after World War I, Karl Barth and Emil Brunner, among others, reacted to the theological liberalism of their teachers and called the church back to its biblical and Reformation roots. The most enduring monument of this theological movement, frequently but misleadingly called Neo-Orthodoxy, is Barth's massive *Church Dogmatics.* Barth stressed the transcendence of God and the character of Christianity as a matter of divine revelation rather than as an example of human religiosity.

While Barth was challenged by evangelicals on his right, he was also confronted with more liberal approaches from Paul Tillich, Rudolph Bultmann, and others. Still, no theologian of our century has attained the stature of Barth, whose influence can yet be seen in theologians such as Jurgen Moltmann, Wolfhart Pannenburg, and Eberhard Jungel.

Among evangelicals the issue of the Bible has generated more discussion than any other theological topic. The Chicago Statement on Biblical Inerrancy (1978), a carefully crafted doctrinal affirmation, has presented a cogent case for an error-free Bible. Carl F. H. Henry's *God, Revelation, and Authority* remains the most ambitious undertaking of an American evangelical theologian. New challenges to historic Christian orthodoxy have appeared in the form of process theology, which questions the omnipotence of God and His sovereignty in creation, history, and providence; liberation theology, which in some forms reduces Christianity to a social critique of society guided by Marxist principles; and approaches to world religions that de-emphasize the uniqueness of the Christian gospel and tend toward universalism. As never before the church stands in need of theological renewal based on a high view of Scripture and the doctrinal fundamentals of evangelical Christianity.

2. *Social Action and Evangelism.* True evangelism implies a genuine social concern. This principle stems from the ministry of Jesus Himself, who fed the hungry and then declared Himself to be the "Bread of Life come down from heaven." The dichotomy between social ministry and evangelistic witness stems from the Fundamentalist/Modernist controversy when these two dimensions of the church's witness were pulled apart. Walter Rauschenbusch's *Theology for the Social Gospel* lacked a proper theological foundation, while many evangelists ignored the social implications of the message they proclaimed. More recently there has been a sustained effort to present a more holistic gospel. It is not coincidental that one of the most creative prison ministries of our day is headed by "born-again" evangelist Charles Colson, while evangelical Christians are in the forefront of those protesting the genocidal slaughter of the innocent unborn.

3. *New Forms of Christian Community.* Much of the phenomenal growth of the church during the twentieth century has taken place outside of traditional institutional structures. Christianity in the Third World has experienced great revival and produced flourishing Christian communities in Africa, Latin America, Indonesia, Korea, and even in China. Black Christians in America have developed their own unique communities of faith and patterns of worship. Pentecostals and other charismatic Christians have infiltrated all of the mainline denominations and emerged as a "third force" within Christianity. Their enthusiastic brand of faith and worship has reintroduced the element of joy into many Christian communities.

4. *Eschatology.* Nearly two thousand years after Jesus said to His little band of followers, "Upon this rock I will build my church," Christians are called to live out their faith in a world ablaze with violence, war, mass starvation, heinous social evils, and the possibility of nuclear self-annihilation. Not surprisingly, a leading evangelical theologian has referred to this era as "the twilight of civilization." In such a world the church of Jesus Christ is called to bear a faithful and consistent witness to the redeeming grace of God, which alone can transform human lives and give hope for the future.

A well-known document of our time expresses the heart of that hope to which the church of Jesus Christ bears witness: "To those who ask, 'What may we expect?' we answer, 'We are not standing before a pathless wilderness of unfulfilled time, with a goal which no one would dare to predict; we are gazing upon our living Lord, our Judge, and Savior, who was dead and lives forevermore; upon the One who has come and is coming, and who will reign forever. It may be that we shall encounter affliction; yes, that must be if we want to participate in Him. But we know His word, His royal word: "Be comforted, I have overcome the world."

Sources for Additional Study

Bainton, Roland. *Christendom.* 2 Vols. New York: Harper and Row, 1964.

Dowley, Tim, ed. *Eerdmans' Handbook to the History of Christianity.* Grand Rapids: Eerdmans, 1977.

George, Timothy. *Theology of the Reformers.* Nashville: Broadman, 1988.

Leith, John H., ed. *Creeds of the Churches.* Atlanta: John Knox, 1982.

Manschreck, Clyde L. *A History of Christianity in the World: From Persecution to Uncertainty.* Englewood Cliffs, N.J.: Prentice-Hall, 1974.

Walker, Williston. *A History of the Christian Church.* New York: Scribner's, 1985.

Christian Faith World Religions Christian Missions

The Christian faith stands apart from all others including the other monotheistic faiths. The Christian gospel is unique, complete, effective, and final. The Bible is different from all other Scriptures in its origin, content, and authority. To many, claims of exclusiveness such as these bespeak intolerance, prejudice, and even bigotry. Those who deny such claims find themselves on the horns of a dilemma. It was Jesus Christ Himself who accepted Peter's words, "You are the Christ, the Son of the living God" (Matt 16:16), and who claimed to be the one and only way to God the Father (John 14:6). Therefore one must conclude either that the master Teacher and holy Example misled humankind at that point or that He was speaking the truth. Christians, of course, believe that He was speaking the truth.

Many arguments can be and have been presented for the truth of Christianity, the veracity of the Bible, and the efficacy of the Christian gospel. In the final analysis no argument is more convincing than the life and ministry, the works and teachings, and the death and resurrection of Jesus Christ. For that reason one would be hard pressed to devise an apologetic that is more compelling than those found in books such as Robert Speer's

The Finality of Jesus Christ, Max Warren's *The Uniqueness of Jesus Christ,* and Charles Braden's *Jesus Compared*. Of all earth's sons, He alone fully reveals God the Father (Matt 11:27; John 14:7), redeems humankind from sin (Mark 10:45), and restores a fallen creation (Col 1:20). It follows that Christianity is inevitably and intrinsically a missionary faith.

The God of the Bible is by His very nature both just and loving. As such He condemns sin and commends righteousness. He also seeks erring humanity and clothes those who respond in repentance and faith with His own righteousness through the sending and sacrifice of His Son (Isa 53:6; Rom 5:17-21).

Faces of the Islamic world who desperately need to hear the gospel message.

Both the Old and the New Testaments evidence the missionary heart of God. The emphasis of the Old is on an invitation to the nations to recognize and worship the God of Israel (Ps 67). Genesis 12 and Isaiah 66 show God's desire to bless and save all nations. The emphasis of the New is on Christ's commission to make disciples of the nations (Matt 28:16-20).

The story of the church is a story of heroic and humble individuals acting in faith to carry out Christ's commission by living out Christ's love and proclaiming His gospel of salvation.

World Religions

Religion is the attempt to relate one to something or someone beyond his or her immediate consciousness. In some cases that which is "beyond" is a governing *principle* such as in Marxist dialectical materialism. In other cases a *personal* God or gods are in view as in most traditional religions. In still other cases that which is "beyond" cannot be adequately described as either a personal deity *or* an impersonal principle—for example, the Brahman or Ultimate Reality in some forms of Hinduism.

The word *religion* can be used with reference to any or all of these cases. More commonly, however, the word is used with reference to a Divine Person or persons and is thought of as one or another system of faith and worship.

The Origin of Religion

What is the source of religion? Logically, there are four possible answers to the question of source. Religions find their source in humans, God, Satan, or some combination of these three.

Humankind as the Source. With the rise of such disciplines as anthropology, sociology, psychology, and comparative religions in the nineteenth century, much attention was given to the origin of religion. In keeping with the growing bias against supernaturalism, many theorists located the source of religion in human beings themselves. E. B. Tylor and James George Frazer taught that religion originated in early man's *reason*—in his attempt to explain otherwise inexplicable phenomena such as lightning, earthquakes, and disease. Max Muller and Herbert Spencer thought that religion originated in the *emotions*—in man's sense of awe, wonder, respect, or fear. Sigmund Freud located the origin of religion in a projection of the human psyche—to control the women of the tribe males did away with their fathers and then projected a father god or spirit in order to expiate their guilt. It was further conjectured that whether religious ideas and practices emanated from man's reason or emotions, different groupings of people developed these ideas in their own way, and this accounts for differences between religions.

Contemporary naturalists as well as their predecessors are confined to the theory that, in one way or another, religion can be accounted for on the basis that it is a projection of human wishes or ideas.

God as the Source. In opposition to these ideas, Wilhelm Schmidt and Andrew Lang emerged as two of the nineteenth century's most strenuous proponents of the view that God Himself is the source of true religion. They insisted that the true God revealed Himself to people, but some accepted that revelation and worshiped God and others rejected it and substituted deities of their own making. God is the source of true religion but of true religion only.

More liberal theologians have inclined toward a somewhat different view. William Hocking, Hans Kung, Raymond Panikkar, and others conclude that God has been at work not only in the biblical religions but also in other religions (such as Hinduism, Buddhism, Zoroastrianism, and so forth). From the very first and down to the present day, they say, God has been revealing Himself, His way, and His salvation in and through these religions. Differences among the various religions occur because God has revealed Himself in a variety of ways, because His revelation has been interpreted in different ways, and because people are at various stages in their religious understanding. The Christian faith may indeed represent the most true and complete understanding. Nevertheless, in and through the various religions people can find the true God because in some significant sense He is the source of all of them.

More in line with Schmidt and Lang, and indeed with the biblical understanding, are those who draw a sharp distinction between the revealed faith of the Bible and other faiths and who attribute only the former to God. *Satan as the Source.* Most scholars who subscribe to the uniqueness of the Christian faith ascribe competing faiths to humankind *and* Satan. But some emphasize the primary role of Satan in the development of competing faiths as when Edmund Perry defines religion as "a generic term comprehending the universal phenomenon of men individually and collectively being led away from God in manifold ways by diverse claims and systems" (*Gospel in Dispute*).

The question of source can be a complex one. However, on the basis of Exodus 20; Deuteronomy 7; Isaiah 44; John 1; 14; Romans 1–3, and similar passages one

RELIGIONS OF THE WORLD*

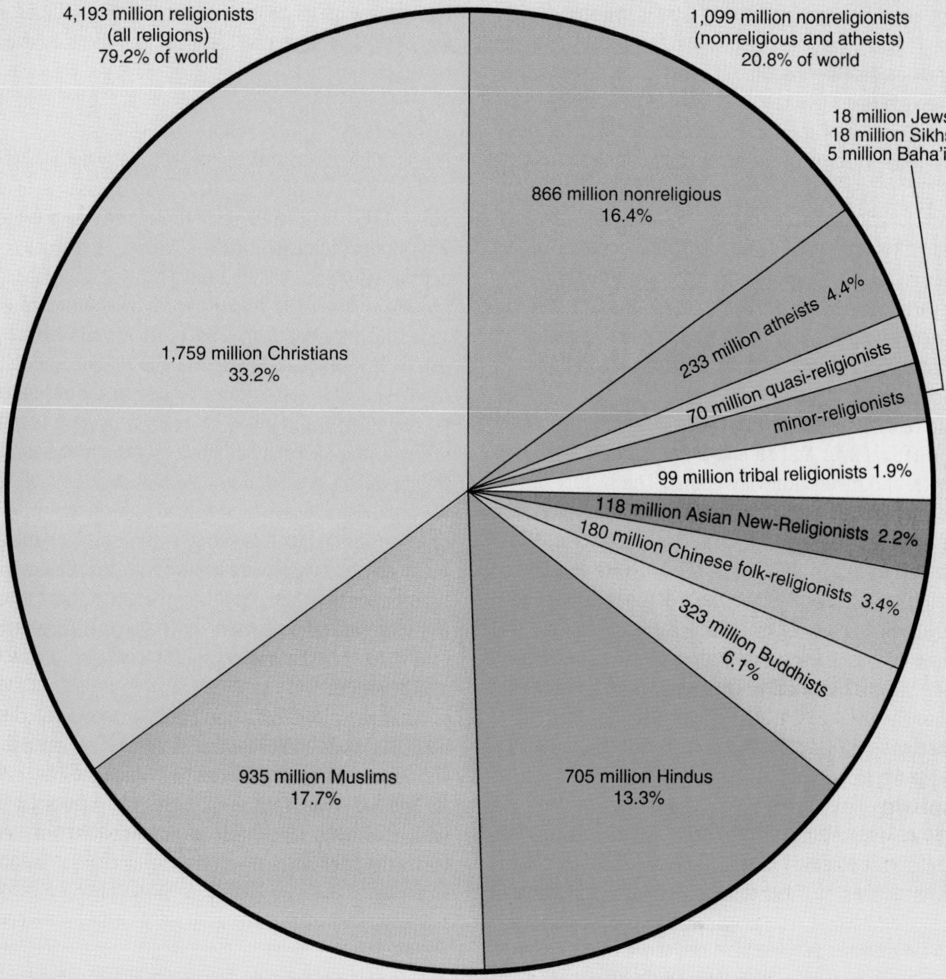

RELIGION (30,000 religions, analyzable into 33 major religious and antireligious blocs)

ADHERENCE TO RELIGION IN 1990

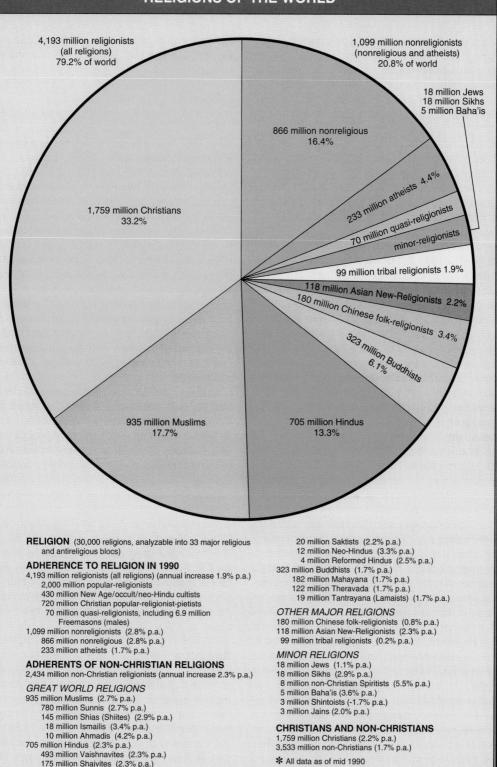

4,193 million religionists (all religions) (annual increase 1.9% p.a.)
- 2,000 million popular-religionists
- 430 million New Age/occult/neo-Hindu cultists
- 720 million Christian popular-religionist-pietists
- 70 million quasi-religionists, including 6.9 million Freemasons (males)

1,099 million nonreligionists (2.8% p.a.)
- 866 million nonreligious (2.8% p.a.)
- 233 million atheists (1.7% p.a.)

ADHERENTS OF NON-CHRISTIAN RELIGIONS

2,434 million non-Christian religionists (annual increase 2.3% p.a.)

GREAT WORLD RELIGIONS

935 million Muslims (2.7% p.a.)
- 780 million Sunnis (2.7% p.a.)
- 145 million Shias (Shiites) (2.9% p.a.)
- 18 million Ismailis (3.4% p.a.)
- 10 million Ahmadis (4.2% p.a.)

705 million Hindus (2.3% p.a.)
- 493 million Vaishnavites (2.3% p.a.)
- 175 million Shaivites (2.3% p.a.)
- 20 million Saktists (2.2% p.a.)
- 12 million Neo-Hindus (3.3% p.a.)
- 4 million Reformed Hindus (2.5% p.a.)

323 million Buddhists (1.7% p.a.)
- 182 million Mahayana (1.7% p.a.)
- 122 million Theravada (1.7% p.a.)
- 19 million Tantrayana (Lamaists) (1.7% p.a.)

OTHER MAJOR RELIGIONS

180 million Chinese folk-religionists (0.8% p.a.)
118 million Asian New-Religionists (2.3% p.a.)
99 million tribal religionists (0.2% p.a.)

MINOR RELIGIONS

18 million Jews (1.1% p.a.)
18 million Sikhs (2.9% p.a.)
8 million non-Christian Spiritists (5.5% p.a.)
5 million Baha'is (3.6% p.a.)
3 million Shintoists (-1.7% p.a.)
3 million Jains (2.0% p.a.)

CHRISTIANS AND NON-CHRISTIANS

1,759 million Christians (2.2% p.a.)
3,533 million non-Christians (1.7% p.a.)

* All data as of mid 1990

cannot avoid the conclusion that God is the sole Author of true religion and that persons and Satan collaborate in the creation of false religion. Of course, it can be successfully argued that since God has created humans (and Satan!), reflections of the *imago Dei,* or divine image, are discoverable in some of the noble aspirations and ethical teachings that are to be found in almost all religions. However, ultimately the various religions must be seen as being "totalitarian"—that is, as unified and indivisible entities and not as the sum total of unconnected and separable parts. Viewed this way, it is easy to see that even the admittedly desirable aspects of the various religions can be used by Satan to deceive people and draw them away from Christ.

The religions of the world can be studied from a variety of perspectives and should be studied from at least historical and theological viewpoints. The history of religions provides us with the religious options that have been proposed through the centuries. At its best, theology introduces us to the God of the universe and tells us what He has to say about the whole of the religious enterprise. Confining ourselves to the basics, then, we will proceed by first characterizing some major non-Christian world religions historically. Then we will underscore the uniqueness of the Christian faith from a theological perspective.

Animism

Animism, dynamism, tribal religion, traditional religion, folk religion—a variety of terms are used to describe the polytheistic religions that tend to prevail in sub-Saharan Africa and the island world. Animism is the *practiced* religion of numerous adherents of the more developed religions. Strictly speaking, animism cannot be classified as a world religion as such because it is not a unified system. But animism tends to exhibit certain basic characteristics wherever one finds it. Most often one god is more prominent than the others, but attention is accorded to numerous deities, spirits, and powers. Prominent religious personages include priests, shamans, witchdoctors, sorcerers, astrologers, and fortune tellers. Fundamental features include sacrifices, witchcraft, magic, fetishes, amulets, talismans, augery, and the like. The basic motivation is fear. And the quest is not so much for the *meaning* of existence as it is for the *maintenance* of existence in a world of capricious spirits and opposing powers. It has been popularly thought that this kind of religion is confined to untutored and backward peoples, but the widespread resort to some of these practices in the Western world belies that thinking.

There are about 99,200,000 animists in the world. But some experts believe that as much as 40 percent of the world's population is essentially animistic in everyday belief and practice.

Hinduism

Hinduism developed in India over many centuries, especially from the time of the Aryan invasions of about 2000–1700 B.C. In its earliest form it was polytheistic, worshiping numerous nature deities. Eventually three deities—Brahma, Vishnu, and Shiva—emerged as most important (the latter two especially have numerous consorts and incarnations). The most prominent scripture corpus is the Vedas, which are the productions of early sages with later elaborations by priests and philosophers. Several doctrines came to be basic in most of Hinduism: *samsara,* the idea that all life is essentially the same and caught up in a cycle of birth and rebirth; karma, the belief we reap what we sow and accordingly are reborn higher or lower on the scale of being; and *moksha* or enlightenment and eventual reabsorption into the Brahman (not Brahma) or the Ultimate Reality in which there is release from *samsara* (and no more individuality). Three primary routes to *moksha* are recognized: works, knowledge, and devotion.

After about 600 B.C. (though their roots preceded that date) six basic philosophical systems developed within Hinduism, the most important of which are Yoga, Vedanta, and Sankhya. Yoga emphasizes techniques for union with Brahman. The most prominent form of Vedanta views the phenomenal world as being *maya* (illusion) and Brahman as the only Reality. Sankhya philosophy teaches that spirit and matter are separate and eternal and is especially important because Gautama Buddha was nurtured in this philosophy.

Various reform movements breathed new life into Hinduism in the nineteenth century. Presently there are about 705 million Hindus in the world. The preponderance of Hindus are in India. However, Hindu ideas and practices are prominent in other Eastern religions and in the New Age and similar movements in the Western world.

Buddhism

Siddhartha Gautama was born in northeast India, perhaps in 560 B.C. At the age of twenty-nine he set out on a religious quest. He tried philosophical speculation and then extreme asceticism. Both failed. Finally, he experienced enlightenment while seated under a Bo tree and thus became the Buddha or Enlightened (Awakened) One. He spent the rest of his life promulgating his "Middle Path" teaching.

Christianity and Its Contemporary Rivals

In a pluralistic age reflecting a shrinking global village, the concept of absolute truth is viewed with increasing suspicion. In no area is this more evident than with regard to religious truth. "The faith once for all delivered to the saints" is viewed by many as, at best, one of a host of competing belief options all seeking the same god. At worst, Christianity is dismissed as an anachronism of the past—a disposable crutch no longer needed in the brave new world of human autonomy.

Some Christians, eschewing "vain philosophy," would reject any formal attempt at an apologetic. Certainly the Gospel is the only cure for the spiritual needs of humanity. However, a Christian response to the challenge of various non-theistic philosophical belief systems, other world religions, and the eclectic and syncretistic trends in popular psychoreligious orientations is indispensable if the church is to "give an answer for the hope that lieth within."

The Christian world-view includes several key elements. First, God exists, is related to (via creation and providence), and yet transcends the universe. Second, humanity, though fallen, bears the image of God. Third, the Lord Jesus Christ is the ultimate revelation of God and is God's response to human sin. Fourth, the record of God revelatory activity is the Bible. Finally, the universe is moving to an omega point dictated by God. The existence of God, confidence in a Divine purpose for life, and the redemptive basis for relationship to God, are foundational to the idea of absolute spiritual and moral value.

Modernity has been labeled the "post-Christian era." The Kantian epistemological divide has removed the classical proofs for the existence of God from many philosophical discussions. Projectionist theories regarding theistic belief (Feuerbach, Marx, Freud) have further weakened the claims for religious truth. A pervasive naturalism has been manifest in various strands including secular humanism, dialectical materialism, and nihilism.

The metaphysical picture has also been clouded by an increased awareness of and encounter with the multiplicity of living religious options. As east and west meet, religious syncretism and universalism have become more predominate. Further, modern culture seems more than ready to assimilate pop trends as exemplified by the emergence of the "new age" movement.

The standard philosophical queries regarding the value of any belief system may be of some help in adjudicating these disputes regarding "ultimate truth." The test of coherence examines the connection between a claim or system of claims and the external world. Naturalism is ultimately not self-explanatory. Any system that excludes the possibility of a metaphysical is to be found wanting. While many Christians affirm the positive interests of humanism, the exclusion of the concept of the *imago dei* is viewed as undermining the basis for a true humanism. Materialism, Marxist or capitalist, is a perpetual reminder that the world is too much with us. Christians should appreciate many aspects of the Marxist critique of capitalism and the escapism of some religious tendencies. We should also encourage the "word ethic" of capitalism without advocating greed. Nihilism, the view that life is meaningless, is a dominate theme of the drug sub-culture and aspects of the entertainment media.

Definitions of "religion" abound and none are fully satisfactory. Some, such as Confucian thought, are ethical in tone and are non-theistic. Others, such as Hinduism, are polytheistic. These and other eastern religious options are committed to a cyclical view of history. Buddhism denies the existence of a substantial human self and the objectivity of this world. The "new age" movement is a loose hodge-podge of ideas with a pragmatic bent. This movement combines pantheism, eastern mysticism, holistic medicine, and self-help psychology in a system espousing human autonomy and self-sufficiency. Christian must avoid excessive labeling of all that is "new age" as wrong (that is, music, and so forth). However, these and other religious world-views frequently offer a fractured perspective on external reality. The world-view offering the fullest and simplest explanation is accorded the status of passing the test for coherence.

The test of internal consistency also demonstrates the weaknesses of the various rivals to Christian faith. The internal logic and consistency of any belief system should be examined. The unique status of the Christian faith as a revealed religion attested to by an historically reliable record (the Bible) accords it a unique status among the major living religions of the world. The Christian account of the nature and purpose of the universe accords it a unique status as a coherent and consistent world-view.

The existential fit of various belief options must also be examined. The collapse of Marxist ideology provides incontrovertible proof of the unsatisfactory nature of this brand of atheism. The seminihilism of modern culture demonstrates modern persons are unable or unwilling to take Nietzsche's leap to the absurdity of thoroughgoing nihilism. Christian provides the basic for fulfillment of the humanistic tendencies of other belief options within a more satisfying ethical and metaphysical framework. □

A young Jewish boy sits quietly on a step in a courtyard in the old city of Jerusalem.

Gautama accepted most of the basic ideas of Hinduism, but he had little or nothing to say about its gods and demons and replaced its rituals with "right conduct." He also denied the existence of the "self" or soul as a permanent entity. At the heart of his teaching were Four Noble Truths: (1) All of life is "suffering" (the realization that all existence including the self is impermanent). (2) Suffering is caused by desire (especially the desire for a permanent and individual existence). (3) Desire can be stopped or overcome. (4) It can be overcome by following the Eightfold Path (right views, aims, speech, action, livelihood, self-discipline, self-mastery, and contemplation). This leads to Enlightenment and, ultimately, to Nirvana, or the state of passionless peace.

The teachings of Gautama were handed down orally from his disciples until they were incorporated into the Tripitaka, or Three Baskets, several centuries after his time. They did not flourish in India but gained wide acceptance elsewhere in Asia and developed into the Lamaism of Tibet; the Hinayana Buddhism of Ceylon (Sri Lanka), Burma, Thailand, Cambodia, Laos, and Viet Nam; and the Mahavana Buddhism of Nepal, China, Korea, and Japan. Hinayana (also called Theravada, or Southern Buddhism) is in many respects closer to Gautama's teaching in that it accepts only the Tripitaka, emphasizes the disciplines, and places the monk in a central position, though it has added numerous deities. Mahayana (Northern Buddhism) worships the Buddha himself, emphasizes mercy and faith, and has developed numerous scriptures and bodhisattvas, or savior-beings. Lamaism is categorized as a form of Mahayana but is a unique combination of Tantrism, shamanism, and sorcery. As Mahayana moved from China to Korea and Japan, it developed a variety of sects such as the Pure Land, Zen, Shingon, Nichirenism, and others—some of which have now attained international prominence. Buddhists now number 323 million worldwide.

Taoism and Confucianism

Lao-tse (born about 600 B.C., though some scholars doubt that he was a historical person) is held to be the founder of Taoism in China, though his teachings were more philosophical than religious. Utilizing the age-old Chinese concepts of the Tao and Yin and Yang, he advocated a form of naturism. Behind everything that exists is the Tao, the eternal, impersonal principle of nature. The Tao operates through two interacting energy modes: the yang (which is masculine, positive, active, light, warm, and dry) and the yin (which is feminine, negative, passive, dark, cool, and wet). By eschewing society, education, and travel and returning to nature, it is possible to get in tune with the Tao and achieve goodness. Lao-tse himself left his native area for such an existence but was required to write down his teachings in the brief and enigmatic Tao-Teh-Ching, which became the scripture of Taoism. Taoism was one of the three officially recognized religions of pre-Communist China (along with Confucianism and Buddhism). As a religion, however, it has borne but superficial resemblance to Lao-tse's philosophy and is characterized by superstition and animistic practices.

Also often thought of as a philosophy, Confucianism is nevertheless treated as a religion in a large body of literature. Confucius (about 551–446 B.C.) was more concerned with human relationships than with relationship to the Divine, though he acknowledged Ti-en (Providence, heaven) and gave a place to religion. Like Lao-tse he believed that people are born good, but unlike Lao-tse he thought that people could be kept good through education. He emphasized the Superior Man (who modeled the ideal life) and five basic relationships (ruler-subject, father-son, husband-wife, elder brother-younger brother, and friend-friend).

Devotion to the ancestors and filial piety were prominent in his teaching and practice. Confucius was devoted to the wisdom of the past, especially of the Golden Age of China. He compiled that wisdom and added some of his own in The Classics and The Four Books. Though Confucianism has no separate priesthood as such, it has persisted as a religion in China in temples in which Confucius is revered as the Superior Man and in elaborate rituals associated with nature worship, the emperors, and the ancestors. As a philosophy the teachings of Confucius have been the single most formative factor in the development of China and Chinese character down through history and until the present century.

Judaism

Historically Judaism finds its religious center in the one God, the Creator, the God of Abraham, Isaac, Jacob, Moses, David, and the prophets of the Old Testament. Following the destruction of the temple in Jerusalem (A.D. 70), Judaism underwent profound changes. Synagogues became central to Jewish life; rabbis chosen from among the people replaced the Levitical priesthood; and the study of the law and prayer were substituted for the sacrificial system.

Contemporary Judaism is divided into three distinct schools. Orthodox Judaism emphasizes the traditional teachings and practices. Reform Judaism is mainly an ethical system based on interpretations of the teachings and traditions. Conservative Judaism allows for various interpretations of the law but attempts to maintain the centrality of religion in Jewish life around the world. The majority of practicing Jews are Orthodox. In the new state of Israel, Orthodox Judaism and Reform Judaism oppose each other, but indifference to the religion is widespread. Adherents to the various types of Judaism number over eighteen million worldwide.

From a Christian point of view, Judaism is distinctive. Christ came not to destroy the law but to fulfill it (Matt 5:17), so Christianity is the fulfillment of Old Testament Judaism in a sense in which it is the fulfillment of no other religion. At the heart of Christian witness to Jewish people is the testimony that Jesus Christ is indeed their Messiah and the Savior of the world. Many Christians believe in a future for Israel and are persuaded that multitudes of Jews will yet believe on Him (Rom 11:25-27).

Islam

The latest of the major religions to be developed was founded by Muhammad (A.D. 570–631). Born in Mecca, Arabia, Muhammad rebelled against the polytheistic beliefs and practices that surrounded him. He was undoubtedly influenced by both Judaism and Christianity but in forms that were truncated and heretical. After a number of visions, Muhammad believed himself called to preach the religion of Allah (Arabic for God), the Creator, Ruler, and Judge of the universe. He was opposed in Mecca and fled to Medina in 622. This flight is called the Hegira and marks the beginning of the Islamic religion. By 630 Muhammad and his followers had conquered Arabia. Within a century Islam was in the ascendancy in North Africa, the Near East, and Spain.

Jews, Christians, and Muslims are considered to be "people of the Book." Allah is said to have sent down as many as 104 books, of which only four remain: the Pentateuch of Moses, the Psalms of David, the Injil (Evangel) of Jesus, and the Koran. The Koran supersedes the others and is held to be the only holy book that exists in uncorrupted form, being a replica of the Mother of the Book, which is in heaven. Dictated to Muhammad by Gabriel in a series of visions, it is said to be uncreated and eternal.

The *kalima,* or Muslim creed, is that "there is no God but Allah (Arabic for God), and Muhammad is His prophet." Allah is omnipotent and sovereign. His will is arbitrary and absolute. Angels are His messengers; Gabriel, as the revealer of Allah's truth, is the most important of four archangels. Shaitan or Iblis is a fallen angel who is served by evil beings. Twenty-eight prophets are named in the Koran including Adam, Abraham, Moses,

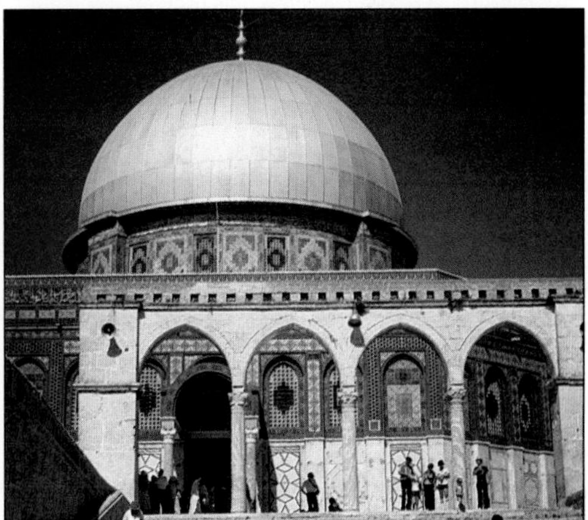

The Dome of the Rock—a Muslim mosque built over the site of the ancient Jewish temple in the city of Jerusalem.

An ancient carving of the Persian god Ahura Mazda (god of light in Zoroastrianism) standing inside the winged ring, official emblem of the Persian Empire.

Jesus, and Muhammad. Muslims trace themselves to Abraham but through Ishmael. Jesus is the only prophet who is not "named in sin." Muslims deny that He died on the cross. Muhammad is the final prophet. Men are to believe Allah's message in the Koran and obey the "Five Pillars." Their hope must be that on the final day of judgment they will be counted worthy of a heaven depicted as a place of sensuous delights.

The Five Pillars which are obligatory for all Muslims include: (1) recitation of the *kalima*, (2) prayer five times daily, (3) fasting, especially during Ramadan, which occurs during the ninth month on the lunar calendar, (4) almsgiving, and (5) a pilgrimage to Mecca once during a lifetime (required of all who are able).

There are many sects in Islam. The Sunnis are most numerous. They constitute orthodox Islam, subscribing to the Sunna or customs and "usage" of the prophet as recorded by Muhammad's companions and contained in the Hadith. The Shi'as, or Imamiyyas, reject the first three successors to Muhammad and follow Muhammad's cousin and son-in-law, Ali, and his successors. The last of Ali's successors disappeared in A.D. 940 and is supposed to reappear as the Mahdi, or restorer of Islam. Shi'as are in the majority in Iran, where Shi'a is the state religion. Mirza Ghulam Ahmad (1839–1908) claimed to be the Imam-Mahdi. His followers are known as Ahmadiyyas. From early on some Muslims—the Sufis—have been mystics seeking for truth by means of inward enlightenment.

Still evidencing the aggressiveness of Muhammad, who advanced his religion by means of the *jihad,* or holy war, Islam remains as a militant and growing religion. There are approximately 935 million Muslims in the world today, and some predict that there may be as many as 1,200,000,000 by the year 2000.

Other Religions

Certain other religions, though very significant, are more circumscribed geographically or of less importance internationally. The majority of the Japanese adhere to at least the basics of Shintoism (along with Confucianism and Buddhism), although a small minority are active members of one or another of the Shinto sects. Shintoism is a national religion based on the notion that both the people and the land have a divine origin and destiny. The emperor is held to be the direct descendant of Amaterasu Omikami, the Sun Goddess.

The religion founded by Zoroaster (Zarathustra, about 660–583 B.C.) in ancient Persia, has approximately 200,000 followers largely in India and Iran. Zoroastrianism is dualistic, positing a constant battle between Ahura Mazda (or Ormazd), the god of light, and Angra Mainyu (or Ahriman), the bad spirit.

Nanak (1469–1538) attempted to reconcile Hinduism and Islam. Sikhism, the religion he founded, uses both Hindu and Muslim names for the one God also referred to as Sat Nam ("True Name"). But Guru Nanak has been elevated to the level of deity and even as an incarnation of Brahma. Sikhism has as many as 18 million followers primarily in India.

Contemporary Christian Missions

The missionary nature of the church gives rise to fundamental questions having to do with the need of non-Christian peoples to hear and believe the Gospel, the encounter with those of other cultures and faiths, the progress of the missionary enterprise, and the present status of Christianity.

Universalism and Limitarianism

Universalism of the kind that asserts that God is the Creator (and in that sense, the Father) of all humankind and that in Christ He has provided a way of salvation for all is biblical and accepted by all Christians. But problems arise when it is asserted that all people ultimately *will be saved* irrespective of whether or not they hear and believe the gospel of Christ. This kind of universalism finds numerous advocates within the church. As appealing as it is, it not only tends to undercut Christian missions but also is challenged by many Bible passages.

Universalism: Sources and Types

The ancient Logos philosophy of Justin Martyr and Clement of Alexandria held that the Logos (the Word, Reason, or Christ) and therefore salvation is operative in all religions. Recently, and probably influenced by both Eastern monism and Western naturalism, people have said that conversion is unnecessary because as the various religions evolve they lead people to the same goal.

The type of universalism that likely has had the greatest impact on the church, however, does indeed hold to the uniqueness of the gospel and attempts to ground itself more firmly in Scripture. It insists that Christ is the unique Savior and that there is no salvation outside of Him. But it goes on to assert that in one way or another—and sooner or later—all will participate in the salvation Christ has provided. It draws biblical support from such phrases as "that the world might be saved" (John 3:17) and "God was in Christ reconciling the world unto himself" (2 Cor 5:19).

Karl Barth concludes that all people are reprobate and also are elect in Christ—have died in Him, were raised in Him, and live in Him. Though Barth is not always consistent at this point, it logically follows that all people are saved or will be saved. The most significant division in the world, then, is not between the saved and the unsaved but between those who realize they are saved and those who do not. Barth concludes that the missionary task is to *inform* the people of the nations that they *are* accepted in Christ.

Limitarianism is the doctrine that some men and women are saved and some are lost now and that this division will also mark their eternal state. In the final judgment those who have not repented of their sin and availed themselves of God's gracious offer of forgiveness in Christ will suffer a final separation from God. This understanding is in accord with the overwhelming testimony of Scripture including descriptions of the final judgment in Matthew 25 and Revelation 20. Significantly, some of the most dire warnings of Christ Himself have to do with the plight of the lost (Matt 9:44-48; 10:28).

Orthodox Christianity has always held to some form of limitarianism. Disagreement has come at the point of whether salvation can be obtained without specifically hearing and believing the gospel. Building on Peter's words to Cornelius ("I now see how true it is that God has no favorites, but that in every nation the man who is Godfearing and does what is right is acceptable to him," Acts 10:34-35, NEB), Norman Anderson conjectures that those who are truly sincere and show mercy will eventually find it in Christ even though they may not hear the gospel in this life (*The World's Religions*). Anderson does not reckon with the significance of Peter's own account of God's insistence that he go to Cornelius's household and the angel's word to Cornelius: "Send to Joppa for Simon who is called Peter. He will bring you a message through which you and all your household will be saved" (Acts 11:13-14, NEB). The New Testament emphasizes that whoever calls upon the Lord will be saved but that before one can call, one must hear; before one can hear, someone must preach; and before someone can preach, someone must be sent.

Kenneth S. Kantzer cautions us lest we go beyond Scripture in conjecturing what God will do with those who do not hear the gospel. He says: "No one questions what God could do. In mysterious matters of the human soul, however, we can only be guided by his Word of revelation. And that divine Word seems to tie what the Bible means by salvation very tightly to the preaching of the Gospel" (*Evangelism on the Cutting Edge*).

WORLD A: THE UNREACHED WORLD

World A is made up of all people who have never heard about the saving power of Jesus Christ because they have not had access to the gospel. It is the unreached world.

Who are these unreached? Consider the following illustration. Imagine you live in a world of four people. You have plenty of food, but the other three people are starving. You see two of them going down a road and, recognizing their plight, you tell them where they can find a storehouse filled with good things to eat. The other person is on a different path. In fact, without knowing it, he is walking away from both you and the storehouse that contains the only nourishment capable of saving him.

The other person, in terms of spiritual salvation, is World A. In real life, he represents approximately 1.2 billion people—one-fourth of humanity—people groups in which one out of every two individuals has neither heard nor has had the opportunity to hear the gospel of Jesus Christ. Researchers estimate that 85 percent of these unreached individuals in our world live in the large green band shown on the map below extending through North Africa and Central Asia. He will perish, not because he has rejected Christ, but because he has no understanding of what Christ has offered. He has not been reached with any communication about the Christian hope of salvation.

The following statistics represent the urgency of the global Christian mission endeavor:

Christians spend 99.9% of Christian income on themselves, 0.09% on World B, also referred to as the evangelized non-Christian world, and 0.01% on World A, the unevangelized world.

The same percentage breakdown (99.9, 0.09, 0.01) is applicable when considering money provided specifically for "Christian" purposes.

Approximately 99% of all Christian literature is consumed by World C; approximately 0.1% is produced for World A.

Only 1% of all Scripture distribution occurs in World A; 62% of Scripture distribution occurs in World C.

Approximately 3,000 foreign missionaries target populations in World A; nearly 260,000 foreign missionaries are sent out to other countries considered to be in World C.

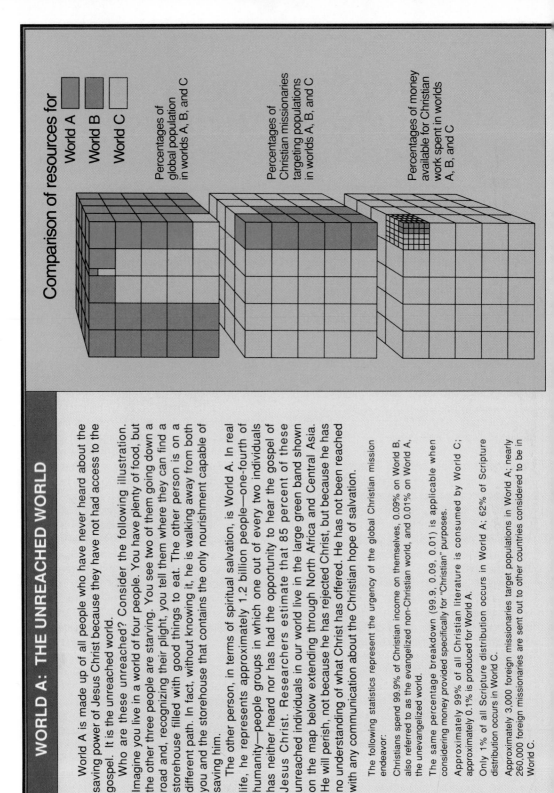

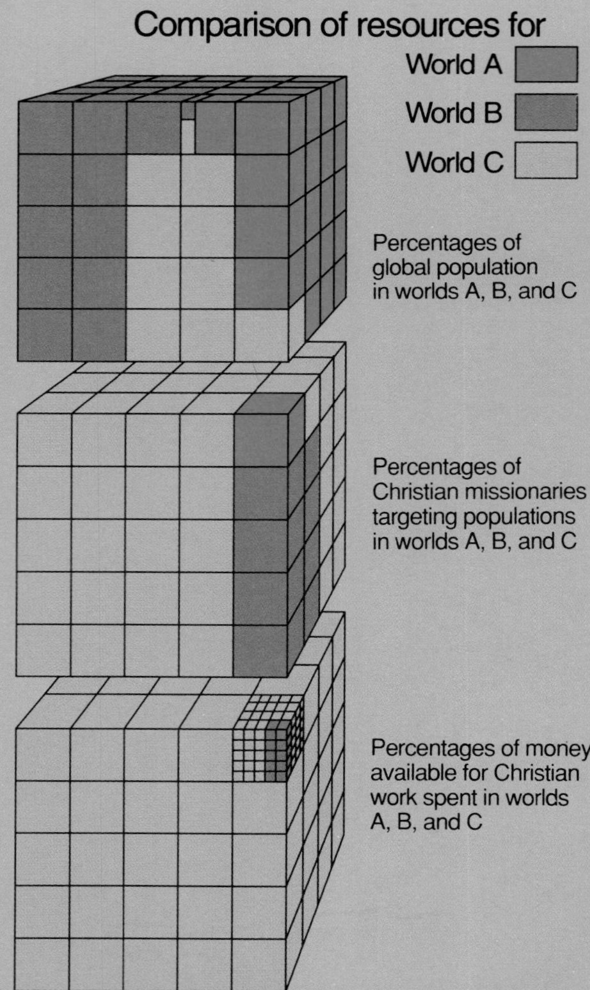

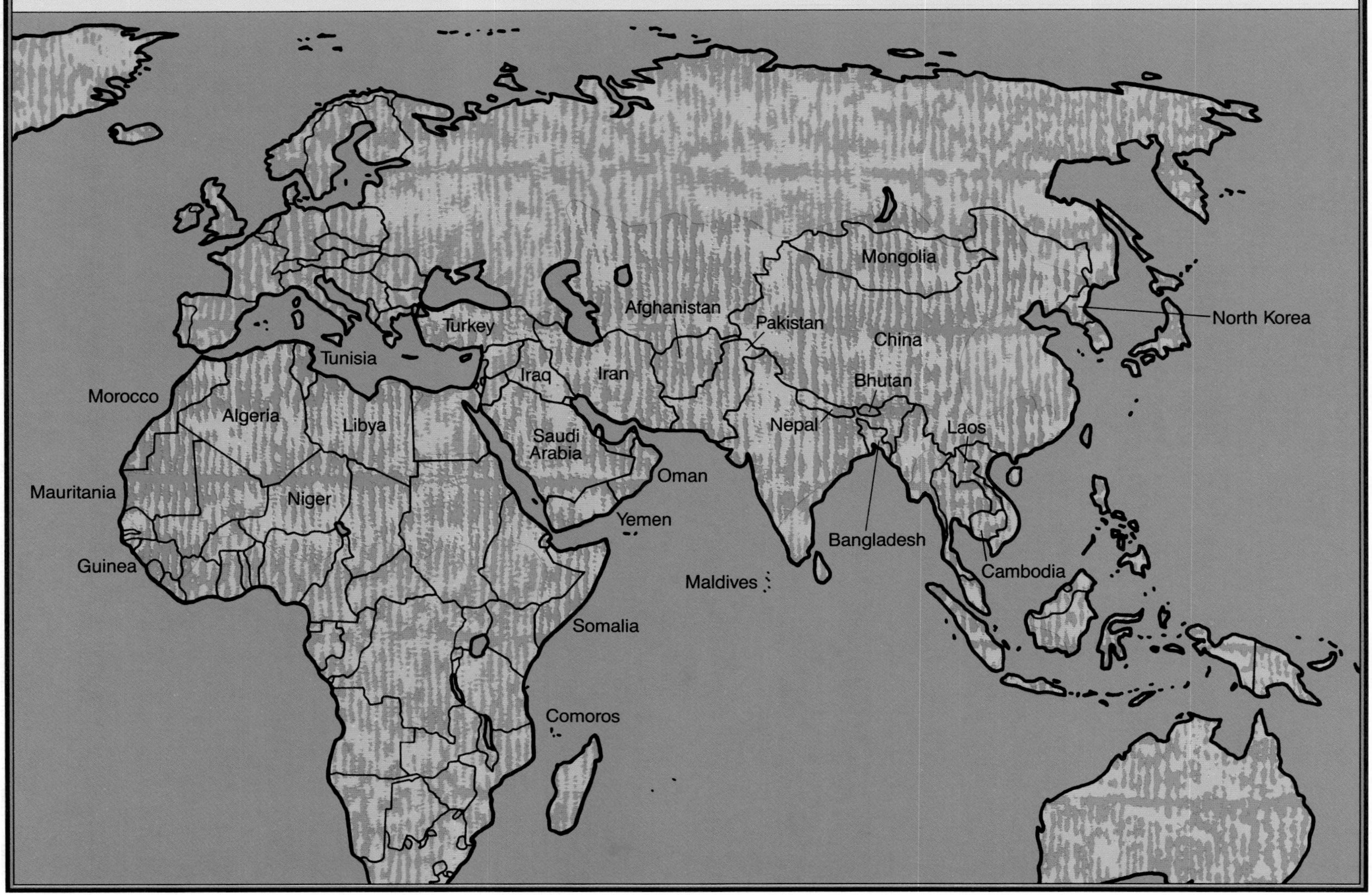

North Korea
Mongolia
Afghanistan
Pakistan
China
Turkey
Tunisia
Iraq
Iran
Bhutan
Morocco
Algeria
Libya
Nepal
Laos
Saudi Arabia
Oman
Mauritania
Niger
Yemen
Bangladesh
Guinea
Cambodia
Maldives
Somalia
Comoros

The Christian Approach to People of Other Religions and Cultures

Throughout the era of modern missions—and, indeed, at times previous to it—much attention has been given to appropriate and effective ways in which to communicate the gospel and establish viable churches throughout the world. Historically, some of the most noteworthy attempts at making the missionary message relevant were those put forth by Raymond Lull among Muslims in the seventh century, by Jesuits in Asia in the sixteenth century, and by William Carey and his "Serampore Trio" colleagues in India as the eighteenth century gave way to the nineteenth. Later in the nineteenth century, Henry Venn of England and Rufus Anderson of the United States collaborated on an approach that came to dominate Protestant missions for almost one hundred years. At its heart was the notion of raising up *indigenous* churches on the mission fields—churches that would be self-supporting, self-governing, and self-propagating.

The twentieth century has witnessed a rethinking of indigenous church missionary strategy on four grounds. First, suborthodox understandings such as some of those reviewed above have led many to question whether mission should be described in terms of preaching the gospel and establishing churches at all. Second, some have insisted that, in view of the fact that churches have now been established on every continent and in most nations, missions should now be seen in terms of interchurch aid or should give way to churches themselves that can be centers of divine activity in the world. Third, many have questioned whether or not the indigenous concept went far enough. They point out that many non-Western churches that became self-supporting, self-governing, and even self-propagating were nevertheless very Western in such things as organization, worship style, and architecture—in a word, "foreign" to their own culture. Recently, therefore, the key word that has come to describe a more appropriate way to approach other cultures and religions is the word *contextualization*.

The contextualization concept goes considerably beyond the old indigenization concept. Unfortunately, it is variously defined and described and therefore confronts us once again with certain critical alternatives.

Contextualization. Theorists have always insisted upon the importance of context to communication. "Contextualization," however, is a new word. It made its public debut in the publication *Ministry in Context: The Third Mandate Programme of the Theological Education Fund (1970–77)*. The TEF (now the Programme of Theological Education) was launched by the International Missionary Council (now the Division of World Mission and Evangelism of the World Council of Churches) in 1957-58. Over the years the TEF was given three mandates, the so-called "advance," "rethink," and "reform" mandates.

Contextualization as a word and plan of action was adopted in the early 1970s as a part of the reform mandate. To its originators it involved a new point of departure and a new approach to theologizing and theological education: namely, *praxis* or involvement in the struggle for justice within the existential situations in which people around the world find themselves today. For them it had socioeconomic objectives in view, not just spiritual ones. But it soon became an "in word" in Christian theology and missiology and therefore came to be used in a variety of ways, often without attention to changed meanings. Fundamentally, it has to do with the age-old problem of making the Christian message meaningful, relevant, and effective in the cultural contexts of our contemporary world. But many users take exception to the TEF definition.

The Contextualization Continuum. Four profoundly different and universally recognized theological orientations—Orthodoxy, Neo-Orthodoxy, Liberalism, and Neo-Liberalism—yield very different approaches to contextualization.

1. Biblical orthodoxy takes the historic position that the Bible is an authentic disclosure of the nature and will of God. For those who hold to this view, to contextualize means to make the unchanging content of the biblical gospel meaningful to people in their various cultures and existential situations (Bruce Nicholls). This can be termed *apostolic* contextualization because it bases its message squarely on the written Word of God in a manner reminiscent of the early apostles. Its method is *didactic*, that is, teaching truth to the people of the nations as the Great Commission requires, adapting the message so as to make it understandable in terms of their worldview, thought patterns, and language.

2. Neo-Orthodoxy holds that the human authorship entails imperfections in the Bible, and it therefore employs the methods of higher criticism in biblical interpretation and doctrinal formulation. This position yields a kind of contextualization that puts great emphasis on the work of the Spirit and the skill of the contextualizer in making the written Word heard as the Word of God, in making it become the Word of God to the hearer. It can be termed *prophetic* contextualization because it emphasizes receiving the Word of the Lord in the existential situation. Its method is more *dialectical*—discovering God's Word in the ebb and flow and the give and take of specific cultural situations.

3. Classical Liberalism tends to view all strivings after truth as legitimate and no one statement of truth as having final validity. In doing contextualization, therefore, it approaches the various cultures and religions of the world as already in possession of truth that is somehow complementary to its own (partial) truth. This can be thought of as *syncretistic* contextualization because, though it may point to Christ and the Christian faith as the most complete or highest single expression of truth, it attempts to "blend" the various religious teachings and cultural expressions. Its method is *dialogical.* It dialogues with people of other faiths with a view to pursuing truth with them—that is, pursuing truth that will be more complete than the truth brought to the dialogue by the representatives of any one faith, including the Christian faith.

4. Neo-Liberalism takes the Bible more seriously than does classical liberalism. Nevertheless, human reason is the final arbiter as to what will be accepted as true. The Bible and historic creeds may not be the starting point for doing theology, though they will furnish significant points of reference. Like neoorthodox contextualization, it advocates *prophetic* contextualization through the *dialectical* method. But it puts more stress on the "spirit of the contextualizer" in this process than neoorthodox contextualizers do. And its dialectic is often informed by Marxism. A key concept here is *praxis,* which means that one must go into the give-and-take struggle of the "marketplace" in order to ascertain message and means.

All messages—including the biblical message—must come in culturally determined linguistic and other forms because this is all we can understand. But the more one distances oneself from the complete authority of Scripture, the more tentative and tenuous becomes the resultant contextualization.

Contextualization and "Power Encounter." The encounter with those of other religions and cultures is now conceived of as entailing both a "truth encounter" and a "power encounter." The distinction can be somewhat misleading if the former is thought of as solely a mental exercise in which reason is primary and the latter becomes a spiritual power struggle in which "signs and wonders" are all that counts. Actually, both are aspects of a cosmic battle between God and Satan and their respective kingdoms as the Scriptures make clear. Though the formulation and presentation of the gospel in culturally meaningful terms is a task that deserves our best effort, it has become apparent that God's representatives must go forth in dependence upon prayer and the power of the Spirit, who alone can convince people of sin, righteousness, and judgment (John 16:8-10) and overcome the Evil One in any situation.

The Present Status of Christianity, World Religions, and World Evangelization

In the late nineteenth and early twentieth centuries, many mission leaders felt that false religions would gradually weaken or even die due to the impact of Christianity and Western culture. That this has not occurred is now apparent to all. Not only have the historic religions survived in the twentieth century, but also they have grown and made significant inroads into the Western world. In addition, the number of new religionists and nonreligionists has increased significantly.

Again, if one thinks in terms of the percentage of world population that purports to be Christian, even the most optimistic projections indicate that that percentage will drop somewhat from the approximately 34 percent of the year 1900. Some non-Christian religions (especially Islam) are growing rapidly. However, there is another side to the picture—and one that is especially encouraging to the Christians.

First, in the twentieth century Christianity has become the world's first universal religion in the sense that it has

The faces of the unreached people of Brazil who are waiting to hear the message of God's love for them.

representatives in every part of the world and in most every nation. The number of Christians (estimated and broadly defined) worldwide is 1,759 million distributed as follows: over 400 million in Europe, 400 million in Latin America, almost 300 million in Africa, over 230 million in North America, over 200 million in Asia, and over 20 million in Oceania. Nevertheless, the progress of Christianity in the modern era is arresting.

Second, though the vast majority of professing Christians were located in the Western world at the beginning of the century, this situation has changed dramatically. Today, the churches of North America and Western and Eastern Europe are more or less static or even shrinking, but the churches of the non-Western world are growing to a degree that more than offsets any losses in the Western world. The church in sub-Saharan Africa alone has registered a gain of over 5,000,000 per year over the last decade. Since 1950 and under a Communist regime the church in China has grown from several million to 40,000,000 or more. Protestant Christianity has made significant gains in Central and South America. And the largest churches in the world are now to be found in Korea, one of them alone numbering over 750,000 members.

Third, the churches of the non-Western world have become increasingly involved in cross-cultural missions over the last two decades until it is now calculated that well over 20,000 (figures go as high as 36,000) missionaries have been sent out by Third World churches to date. At the present rate of increase, the number of Third World missionaries would equal the number of North American Protestant missionaries (67,200) sometime in the middle 1990s.

Fourth, if we define "evangelized" as those people who have had an *understandable* hearing of the gospel, the percentage of the world's population that is evangelized has climbed from slightly over 50 percent in 1900 to about 75 percent today. This means that world evangelization would be possible even before the end of the century if the church were to make an all-out effort.

All of this adds up to the fact that, despite obvious weaknesses, the Christian missionary enterprise has been eminently successful—far beyond the awareness of most of its detractors and even many of its supporters. At the same time, some analysis is required in order to better understand the current situation and future prospects.

The Churches and Their Missions in the Post-World War II Era

The progress of the various segments of the church and their missions has been varied. The Orthodox churches have made but a limited contribution to the worldwide expansion of Christianity over recent years due to internal factors, Muslim power, and Communist pressures. Nevertheless, they have grown somewhat so as to number somewhat over 175,000,000.

From a missionary viewpoint far and away the single most significant event of the postwar era in the Roman Catholic Church was Vatican II, held in Rome from 1962 to 1965. In effect, Vatican II redefined the Catholic mission. It recognized other Christian bodies as ecclesiastical assemblies with whom Catholics could associate. It redirected mission away from "schismatics and heretics" and toward nonbelievers around the world. The ambiguity of some of the Vatican II statements, however, had the effects of lessening the mission concern of many (there has been a gradual decline in missions personnel from Europe and America since 1965); of obscuring the way in which Catholicism views non-Christian religions; and of allowing space for a political interpretation of mission such as is evident in Liberation Theology. Despite the fact that the Catholic Church is undergoing profound change and appears more vulnerable than previously, some overall growth (to over 925,000,000 members worldwide) is reported.

Generally speaking, Protestant churches and their missions have experienced growth since World War II. Protestantism has increased to reach a present 311,000,000. And if one were to include the 135,000,000 members of the so-called nonwhite indigenous churches of the Third World (largely Protestant), the number would be far greater.

Growth has not been uniform within the various segments of Protestantism, however, and missionary involvement also has varied greatly. In Europe both attendance and mission involvement in the state churches have been in decline in recent years. The same is true in most of the mainline denominations in the United States. Wider ecumenical cooperation signaled by the formation of the World Council of Churches in Amsterdam in 1948 and by the incorporation of the International Missionary Council (which grew out of the World Missionary Conference held in Edinburgh in 1910) into the WCC as its Division of World Mission and Evangelism has not been a deterrent to this trend.

Conservative Evangelicals and Pentecostals, on the other hand, have experienced rather steady growth, especially in North America. By 1960 the number of missionary personnel in the agencies affiliated with the Division of Overseas Ministries of the National Council of Churches of Christ (USA) was exceeded by the number of nonconciliar Protestant missionaries—a trend that has

A family in Papua New Guinea reads Bibles brought to them by missionaries.

continued until the present time. Two significant features of nonconciliar mission growth have been the rapid increase in the number of short-term missionaries and the growth of newer and parachurch missions. Some 42 percent of 67,200 North American Protestant missionaries are short-termers. Over 100 new missions have been organized each decade since 1950. And though the Interdenominational Foreign Mission Association and the Evangelical Foreign Missions Association (affiliated with the National Association of Evangelicals) have shown growth, with a very few exceptions, such as the Southern Baptists, far and away the greatest growth has been among parachurch missions such as Youth with a Mission, Operation Mobilization, and Wycliffe Bible Translators, which are unaffiliated with any such group.

The growth of the Charismatic movement in both Catholic and Protestant communions has been a significant feature of recent years. Until very recently, however, the movement has not made a significant contribution to missionary vision and outreach.

Things to Look For

Recent trends in the church and its missions (including those indicated above) alert Christians to possible future developments.

First, the growth of Third World churches and their missions will make it incumbent upon Western leaders to give greater consideration to a true partnership in church and mission endeavors.

Second, changes in all branches of Christendom will increasingly require that all Christians who would be faithful to Scripture and the historic creeds of the church rethink the basis of true faith, of interchurch and intermission cooperation, and of world mission.

Third, the expanding penetration of non-Christian religions and ideas into the Western world will force true Christians to reaffirm the implications of the uniqueness of Christ and the Christian faith in the face of religious relativism and inclusivism.

Fourth, a justifiable and growing concern for the alleviation of injustice, poverty, and suffering make it more difficult for Christians who take the Great Commission seriously to sustain a priority for the preaching of the gospel and the development of New Testament churches worldwide.

Fifth, antagonism on the part of foreign governments

toward missionary endeavors that aim at the conversion of non-Christians to Christ will mean that Christians will have to think of alternative ways in which to reach a needy world for Christ.

When looking ahead, Christians are exhorted to be alert and ready for Christ's second coming (Matt 14:42). In His Olivet Discourse (Matt 24–25; Luke 21), Christ prophesied of dire events both in the church and in the world. But none of those events will prevent either world evangelization or His glorious return (Matt 24:14,30).

The Gospel Message

Did you ever read something you did not understand? If we understood everything we read in the Bible, there would be no reason to buy Bible handbooks, Bible dictionaries, and other study helps. A long time ago there was a man from Ethiopia who stopped his chariot beside the road he traveled to read a portion of the Bible. He was reading in the OT Book of Isaiah, but he could not understand what he read. God sent Philip to help. Philip asked him, "Do you understand what you are reading?" (Acts 8:30).

"How can I," the man replied, "unless someone explains it to me?" Philip climbed into the chariot and explained to the man the meaning of what he read. He explained the good news about Jesus to him, and the man believed in Christ that day and was baptized. The Ethiopian man had no trouble reading the words of the Bible, but he could not understand its meaning for his life until Philip helped him.

The Bible has a message for each of us. Although its words are simple, its meaning for our lives is profound. God speaks to us through the words of Scripture to tell us important truths that can change our lives.

The Bible tells us that God has a plan for every person. He created us to live in relationship with Him. He desires to give us eternal life so we can live fulfilled lives on earth and forever in heaven.

God wants us to have eternal life, but the Bible says we have sinned. Sin is anything we do or fail to to that separates us from God and causes us to break our relationship with Him. Without the Lord in our lives, we are helpless to overcome the damage sin causes. We cannot overcome our sins by being religious, moral, or good. We do not have the power within ourselves to get away from the effects of our sins.

The Bible says that God is holy, which means He is without any sin and does not allow sin near Him. He is also perfect and just. His nature is such that He does not tolerate sin but punishes it. God loves us and wants us to have eternal life, but our sins prevent this. He loves us, but He must punish sin. The Bible says the punishment for our sins is death. When we could not do anything for ourselves, God chose to send Jesus to take the punishment for our sins by dying for us.

Jesus is God who came to earth as a man to die for us. He died willingly for us and took the pain and punishment for us. His death satisfied God's judgment for our sins and showed His love for us at the same time. Because Jesus is God, He can do for us what only God can do. Because He is a human being, He could take our sins on Himself and die for us.

The Bible says Jesus came to life again to offer us forgiveness of our sins and eternal life. According to Scripture, we have to turn from our sins, trust Christ completely to do what the Scripture says He did, and follow Him in complete faith and obedience.

The following Scriptures will help you receive the gift of eternal life through Jesus Christ if you have never trusted Him.

1. Romans 3:23 tells us we are all sinners: **All have sinned and fall short of the glory of God.**

2. Romans 6:23 tells us sin brings death to us, but Christ brings us eternal life as God's gift: **The wages of sin is death, but the gift of God is eternal life in Jesus Christ our Lord.**

3. Romans 8:1 tells us people who trust in Christ are forgiven and not condemned by God: **Therefore, there is now no condemnation for those who are in Christ Jesus.**

4. Romans 10:9 tells us we are released from our sins when we admit our sins to God and place our complete trust in Christ: **If you confess with your mouth, "Jesus is Lord," and believe in your heart that God raised him from the dead, you will be saved.**

Romans 10:13 tells us: **Everyone who calls on the name of the Lord will be saved.** If you have called on His name, you have been forgiven of your sins and given eternal life. □

ART CREDITS

The publishers express deep gratitude to the following persons and institutions for the use of art materials in this book.

PHOTOGRAPHS AND ARTIFACTS

Abernathy, Morris, Fort Worth, TX. Pp. 844; 845.

Arnold, Nancy, Nashville, TN. Pp. 1 (modern Jerusalem with the Gate Beautiful in view); 533; 620.

The Baptist Sunday School Board, E. C. Dargan Research Library, Fon H. Scofield, Jr., Collection, Nashville, TN. Cover photo; and pp. 86; 113; 221; 554; 566; 580; 645.

***Biblical Illustrator*, Nashville, TN.** David Rogers: pp. 210 (The Louvre, Paris); 304 (The Louvre, Paris); 348; 646; 648; 650; 705; 711; 713; 715. Ken Touchton: pp. 116; 119; 582; 591, left (Israel Museum, Jerusalem); 592; 719; 731; 859.

©Billy Graham Evangelistic Association. Pp. 96; 857.

Brisco, Thomas V., Fort Worth, TX. Pp. 33 (the Treasury building at the rock city of Petra); 77, bottom; 109 (Mt. Sinai area of Sinai peninsula); 314; 338; 524; 548; 567; 574; 611; 685.

Ellis, C. Randolph, Malvern, AR. Pp. 36; 76; 271; 295; 296; 429, bottom; 601; 714; 717.

Holman Pictorial Collection of Biblical Antiquities, Holman Bible Publishers, Nashville, TN. Allon, A.: pp. 316; 372; 405; 470, top. British Museum, London: pp. 35; 43; 80; 81; 82; 262; 284; 286; 317; 321; 347; 363, right; 371; 386; 393; 403; 415; 428; 440; 441; 466; 472; 475, top and bottom; 486; 540; 689; 799, left; 804. Chester Beatty Collection of Papyri: pp. 576; 588; 682. N. de G. Davies and A. H. Gardiner, *Ancient Egyptian Paintings*: pp. 343; 362. Hebrew University, Jerusalem: pp. 48 (Archaeological Department); 105 (The Ben-Zvi Institute); 692 (and Hebrew Museum, Rome); 799, right. Hittite Museum, Ankara: pp. 268; 350, bottom. Kluger, Z.: pp. 412; 470, bottom; 480. The Louvre, Paris: pp. 242; 259; 310; 336, top; 349; 354; 359; 388; 398; 437; 446; 505; 766. Metropolitan Museum of Art, New York: pp. 320; 370; 413; 451; 457. Museum Haaretz, Tel Aviv: pp. 319; 358. Museum of Fine Arts, Boston: pp. 47; 684. Museum of the Ancient Orient, Istanbul: pp. 52; 265, bottom. National Museum, Damascus: pp. 790; 797. National Museum, Naples: pp. 506-7; 511; 570; 623; 759; 798. Ny-Carlsberg Glyptothek, Copenhagen: pp. 263; 508. The Orient Press Photo Company: pp. 85; 578; 595; 755; 792. Oriental Institute, Chicago: pp. 40, left; 417; 433. Pennsylvania University Museum, Philadelphia: pp. 350, top; 439, right. Rockefeller Museum, Jerusalem: pp. 40, right; 336, bottom; 346; 367; 382; 583. Rothenberg, B.: pp. 397; 613. Vatican Museum, Rome: pp. 690; 741. Volk, A.: pp. 342; 474. Other photographs and artifacts: pp. 34 (Ashmolean Museum, Oxford); 39 (L. Woolley, *Ur Excavations, V*); 42 (A. Lhote-Hassia, *Les Chefs-d'oeuvre de la Peinture Egyptienne*); 57 (R. A. Parker, *The Calendars of Ancient Egypt*); 106 (Shrine of the Book, Jerusalem); 252 (Nautical Museum, Haifa); 266 (Rijksmuseum v. Oudenheden, Leiden); 270 (Calah, Iraq); 272 (Clark Collection, Y.M.C.A., Jerusalem); 303 (Cincinnati Art Museum, Cincinnati); 326 (Tomb of Menna, Sheikh Abd-el-Qurnah); 327 (The Bezalel National Museum, Jerusalem, A. Bernheim photographer); 329 (P. C. Gau, *Antiquitiés de la Nubie*); 334 (National Museum, Aleppo); 337 (Tomb of Kenamon, Thebes); 339 (Mrs. L. Even-Ari); 341 (H. Frankfort, *Cylinder Seals*); 344; 355 (Luxor, Egypt); 356 (Musée Municipal de l'Eveché, Limoges); 363, left (Bibliothéque Nationale, Paris); 373 (C. R. Lepsius, *Denkmäler aus Ägypten und Äthiopien*); 383 (Baltimore Museum of Art); 396 (Thebes, Egypt); 401; 414 (A. Mekhitarian, *Egyptian painting* [Skira]); 416 (Eva Avi-Yonah); 419 (E. Gjerstad et al., *The Swedish Cyprus Expedition III*); 439, left (Egyptian Museum, Cairo); 490 (M. Burrows et al. eds., *The Dead Sea Scrolls of St. Mark's Monastery*); 493 (Behistun, Persia); 534 (E. L. Sukenik, *Otsar ha-Megillot ha-Genozot*); 546; 550 (National Museum of the Villa Giulia, Rome); 609 (John Rylands Library, Manchester); 656, top; 678 (Landesmuseum, Trier); 687 (E. Nash, Rome); 718 (Kunsthistorisches Museum, Vienna); 737 (Municipal Museum of Antiquities, Haifa); 756 (O. Bender, *Rom*); 760 (National Museum delle Terme, Rome); 761 (Crypt of St. Peter's, Rome); 780 (Vatican Library, Rome); 787 (San Apollinaire in Classe, Ravenna); 801 (Beth Shan, Israel); 802 (Archaeological Museum, Venice); 886 (Fogg Art Gallery, Harvard University, Boston).

Langston, Scott, Fort Worth, TX. Pp. 87 (the ancient Acropolis in Athens, Greece); 143; 232; 265, top; 514; 544; 578; 695; 699.

Southwestern Baptist Theological Seminary, A. Webb Roberts Library, Fort Worth, TX. P. 74.

Smith, Marsha A. Ellis, Nashville, TN. Pp. 67; 79; 84; 115; 513; 571; 805 (Zambia, Africa); 850; 884; 885.

Stephens, Bill, Nashville, TN. Pp. 289 (British Museum, London); 618.

Tolar, William B., Fort Worth, TX. Pp. 37; 73; 77, top; 149; 183 (National Iraq Museum, Baghdad, Iraq, and The Louvre, Paris); 199; 201; 226; 285; 429, bottom; 476; 547; 626; 651, top and bottom; 652; 653; 658, top and bottom; 659; 661; 664; 697; 700; 721; 726; 728; 734; 788.

Veneman, Jim, Nashville, TN. Pp. 846; 855; 891; 893.

PAINTINGS AND ILLUSTRATIONS

©Baptist Sunday School Board (The Sunday School Board of the Southern Baptist Convention). Nashville, TN. Violet Oakley: p. 100; Ralph Pallen Coleman: pp. 701; 744.

Blashfield, Edwin H. P. 820.

©Broadman Press, Nashville, TN. Ben Stahl: pp. 32; 205; 450; 479; 543; 763.

©Convention Press, Nashville, TN. Bill Myers: p. 10.

©Dover Pictorial Archives. Gustave Doré: pp. 124; 133; 134; 138; 185; 196; 207; 215; 217; 222; 244; 248; 311; 379; 422; 430; 432; 445; 454; 455; 463; 473; 484; 510; 531; 598; 599; 643; 778; 796; 807; 821; 826; 831; 836; 840. T. Philippoteaux: pp. 656, bottom; 671. Other paintings: pp. 161, top (Andreas Müller); 575; 748 (H. M. Snyder).

©Dynamic Graphics, Inc. P. 161, bottom.

©The Foreign Mission Board of the Southern Baptist Convention, Richmond, VA. Jack Woodson: p. 879.

The Historical Commission of the Southern Baptist Convention, Nashville, TN. Pp. 94; 870 (from portrait by Hondius).

Latta, Bill, Nashville, TN. Pp. 172; 202; 238-39; 250; 523; 557; 602-3; 647.

©Philadelphia Museum of Art, The W. P. Wilstach Collection. Henry Ossawa Tanner: p. 589.

©Superstock. Carl Heinrich Bloch: pp. 563; 579; 591, right; 627; 629. James Tissot: pp. 273; 323; 408; 452; 465; 467; 471; 477; 483; 487; 489; 491; 494; 499; 502; 757; 771; 812. Other paintings: pp. 16 (Antonello de Messina); 24 (Hugo Vogel); 98 (Jusepe Ribera); 866 (Andrea di Bonaiuti); 869 (Paul Friedrich Thumann).

MAPS

©Holman Bible Publishers, Nashville, TN. Pp. 130; 169; 198; 204; 228; 230; 236; 239; 253; 294; 302; 389; 409; 509; 537; 649; 655; 657; 663; 669; 791.

©The Foreign Mission Board of the Southern Baptist Convention, Richmond, VA. P. 889.

CHARTS

©Holman Bible Publishers, Nashville, TN. Pp. 3; 9; 13; 15; 17; 21; 30; 44-45; 54-55; 58-65; 69; 71; 93; 103; 126; 127; 139; 145; 147; 154; 159; 171; 173; 178; 190; 192; 212; 214; 240; 275; 282; 283; 290; 298; 309; 330-31; 332-33; 377; 384-85; 512; 520-21; 527; 539; 549; 552-53; 555; 561; 581; 586; 593; 597; 607; 612; 615; 616; 665; 666; 672; 674-75; 694; 793-95; 808-9; 881; 888-89.

©The Foreign Mission Board of the Southern Baptist Convention, Richmond, VA. Pp. 881; 888-89.

For further information regarding art materials in this book, contact Holman Bible Publishers, 127 Ninth Avenue North, Nashville, Tennessee, 37234.